Learning and Memory

From Brain to Behavior

Mark A. Gluck

Rutgers University – Newark

Eduardo Mercado

University at Buffalo, The State University of New York

Catherine E. Myers

Rutgers University – Newark

Worth Publishers ■ New York

Publisher: Catherine Woods
Acquisitions Editor: Charles Linsmeier
Executive Marketing Manager: Katherine Nurre
Development Editors: Mimi Melek, Moira Lerner, and Elsa Peterson
Assistant Editor: Justin Kruger
Project Editor: Kerry O'Shaughnessy
Media & Supplements Editor: Christine Ondreicka
Photo Editor: Bianca Moscatelli
Photo Researcher: Julie Tesser
Art Director, Cover Designer: Babs Reingold
Interior Designer: Lissi Sigillo
Layout Designer: Lee Mahler
Associate Managing Editor: Tracey Kuehn
Illustration Coordinator: Susan Timmins
Illustrations: Matthew Holt, Christy Krames
Production Manager: Sarah Segal
Composition: TSI Graphics
Printing and Binding: RR Donnelley

Chapter Opening Credits: Chapter 1: William Wegman, xxiii; Chapter 2: age
footstock/Superstock, 42; Chapter 3: O.S.F./Animals Animals – Earth Sciences, 82; Chapter 4:
Steve Bloom Images/Alamy, 124; Chapter 5: Bernard Castelein/naturepl.com, 168; Chapter 6:
Reinhard Dirscherl/Alamy, 204; Chapter 7: Tony Evans/naturepl.com, 242; Chapter 8:
The National Trust Photolibrary/Alamy, 292; Chapter 9: Digital Archive Japan/Punchstock, 336;
Chapter 10: T.J. RICH/naturepl.com, 380; Chapter 11: 2007 John Hyde/AlaskaStock.com, 420;
Chapter 12: David Bagley/Alamy, 462; Chapter 13: A. Morris/VIREO, 500

Library of Congress Control Number: 2007930951
ISBN-13: 978-0-7167-8654-2
ISBN-10: 0-7167-8654-0

Printed in the United States of America

Third printing

Worth Publishers
41 Madison Avenue
New York, NY 10010
www.worthpublishers.com

To the memories, lost and cherished, of Rose Stern Heffer Schonthal.
M. A. G.

To my wife, Itzel.
E. M. III

To my mother, Jean, and all the strong women who continue to inspire me.
C. E. M.

ABOUT THE AUTHORS

Mark A. Gluck is Professor of Neuroscience at Rutgers University–Newark, co-director of the Memory Disorders Project at Rutgers–Newark, and publisher of the project's public health newsletter, *Memory Loss and the Brain*. His research focuses on computational and experimental studies of the neural bases of learning and memory and the consequences of memory loss due to aging, trauma, and disease. He is co-author of *Gateway to Memory: An Introduction to Neural Network Modeling of the Hippocampus and Learning* (MIT Press, 2001) and co-editor of three other books: *Neuroscience and Connectionist Theory* (Lawrence Erlbaum Associates, 1990), *Model Systems and the Neurobiology of Associative Learning: A Festschrift for Richard F. Thompson* (Lawrence Erlbaum Associates, 2001), and *Memory and Mind: A Festschrift for Gordon H. Bower* (Taylor & Francis, 2007). In 1996, he was awarded an NSF Presidential Early Career Award for Scientists and Engineers by President Bill Clinton. That same year, he received the American Psychological Association (APA) Distinguished Scientific Award for Early Career Contribution to Psychology.

Eduardo Mercado is Assistant Professor of Psychology at University at Buffalo, The State University of New York. His research focuses on how different brain systems interact to develop representations of experienced events, and how these representations change over time. Dr. Mercado uses techniques from experimental psychology, computational neuroscience, electrical engineering, and behavioral neuroscience to explore questions about auditory learning and memory in rodents, cetaceans, and humans.

Catherine E. Myers is a Research Professor of Psychology at Rutgers University–Newark, co-director of the Memory Disorders Project at Rutgers–Newark, and Editor-in-Chief of the project's public health newsletter, *Memory Loss and the Brain*. Her research includes both computational neuroscience and experimental psychology, and focuses on human memory, specifically on memory impairments following damage to the hippocampus and associated brain structures. She is co-author of *Gateway to Memory: An Introduction to Neural Network Modeling of the Hippocampus and Learning* (MIT Press, 2001) and author of *Delay Learning in Artificial Neural Networks* (Chapman and Hall, 1992).

BRIEF CONTENTS

CONTENTS

205 CHAPTER 6 Non-Associative Learning: Learning about Repeated Events

PREFACE

The field of learning and memory has undergone enormous changes over the last decade, primarily as a result of new developments in neuroscience. As we have gained a greater understanding of the neurobiological bases of behavior, the boundary between the biological approach and the psychological approach to the study of learning and memory has begun to disappear.

A related consequence of this fusion of brain research and psychology is that it no longer makes sense to study animal learning and human memory as separate disciplines. After several decades during which animal and human learning were described by independent paradigms, the discovery of basic biological mechanisms common to all species has launched a unified approach to animal and human behavioral studies.

Recent advances in neuroscience as applied to learning and memory have also produced dramatic changes in clinical practices over the last decade. Neurologists, psychiatrists, clinical psychologists, and rehabilitation specialists are now able to use neuroscience in the diagnosis and treatment of the clinical disorders of learning and memory. Alzheimer's disease, autism, schizophrenia, Parkinson's disease, Huntington's disease, dyslexia, ADHD, and stroke are just a few of the disorders for which new treatment options have been developed as a result of basic behavioral and cognitive neuroscience studies of learning and memory.

With these developments in mind, we set ourselves the task of writing a comprehensive, accessible, and engaging introduction to learning and memory that provides an introduction to a field in transition. *Learning and Memory: From Brain to Behavior* presents a new curriculum that integrates coverage of human memory and animal learning and includes three key components of the field: behavioral processes, brain systems, and clinical perspectives.

Neuroscience Focus

Neuroscience has altered the landscape for behavioral research, shifting priorities and changing our ideas about the brain mechanisms of behavior. To that end, *Learning and Memory: From Brain to Behavior* integrates neuroscience research into each chapter, emphasizing how new findings from neuroscience have allowed psychologists to consider the functional and physiological mechanisms that underlie the behavioral processes of learning and memory. Chapter 2: The Neuroscience of Learning and Memory offers an accessible introduction to neuroscience for students unfamiliar with the basics.

Clinical Focus

Learning and Memory: From Brain to Behavior examines new research in learning and memory and traces how these findings have spurred the development of new diagnoses and treatments for a variety of neurological and psychiatric disorders. Each core content chapter (chapters 3–13) includes a section that shows how behavioral processes and brain substrates apply to clinical psychology. These "Clinical Perspectives" sections are one way in which the book emphasizes the influence of learning and memory research in the real world.

Research Focus

Throughout the pages of *Learning and Memory: From Brain to Behavior*, we introduce new breakthroughs, which will spark student interest and imagination, and discuss how material from each chapter applies to daily life. Two types of boxes support this focus on cutting edge research and real life applications:

- *Unsolved Mysteries* boxes explore compelling research conundrums to capture student interest and imagination. These include topics such as:
  - Why can't experts verbalize what they do?
  - Is working memory the key to intelligence?
  - Why did the cerebral cortex evolve?
  - Diagnosing and preventing Alzheimer's disease
- *Learning and Memory in Everyday Life* boxes in each chapter illustrate the practical implications of research, especially those that are relevant and interesting to undergraduate students. These include topics such as:
  - Top ten tips for a better memory
  - Are video games good for the brain?
  - Can we reduce memory overload?
  - Discrimination and stereotypes in generalizing about other people

Student Focus

- **No Prerequisites** We understand that students may come to this course from different backgrounds, even different disciplines, so we do not assume any level of familiarity with basic psychology or neuroscience concepts. The first two chapters of the text offer a complete overview of the field of the psychology of learning and memory and the neuroscience foundations of behavior. Later chapters explain all new concepts clearly with emphasis on real-life examples and teaching-oriented illustrations.

- **Memory First** In contrast to many older books, we cover memory topics before learning. The philosophy here is to start off with the big picture, giving students a broad overview of memory systems and brain regions, before getting into the fine details of neuronal processes and cellular interactions. We believe this ordering makes the material more accessible to students, and also prepares them to understand why the lower-level information matters. However, the chapters stand on their own to allow alternate organizations, if desired.

- **Engaging Narrative** We present learning and memory concepts using a lively, clear, and example-rich narrative. We have tried to present our vision of an exciting field in transition as a colorful dialogue—a conversation between authors and readers.

- **Full-Color Art Program** The first full-color book for the course, *Learning and Memory: From Brain to Behavior* uses original anatomical art, state-of-the-art brain scans, and color-coded figures to help students visualize the processes involved in learning and memory. Photos offer a link to the real world, as well as a look back in time; cartoons offer occasional comical commentary (and often additional insights) alongside the main narrative.

- **Real-World Implications** In addition to the section on clinical perspectives, we have included many concrete everyday life examples of learning and memory that help students grasp the implications of what they're studying and the relevance of learning and memory in their own lives.

Purposeful Pedagogy

- **Test Your Knowledge** features give students the opportunity to check their comprehension and retention of more challenging topics. Suggested answers are provided at the end of the chapter.

- **Interim Summaries** follow the behavioral processes and brain substrates sections, to help students review major concepts presented in the previous section.

- **Concept Checks** at the end of each chapter ask critical thinking questions that require an understanding and synthesis of the key material in the chapter. These features ask students to apply the knowledge they've gained to a real-life situation. Suggested answers are provided at the end of the book.

- **Key Points,** presented as bulleted summaries at the end of each chapter, review core material.

- **Key Terms** with page references appear at the end of each chapter; these allow students to review new terminology presented in the chapter. All key terms with their definitions are included in an end-of-text glossary.

- **Further Reading** sections at the end of each chapter offer accessible resources for students who wish to delve more deeply into the material.

Media/Supplements

Book Companion Site at www.worthpublishers.com/gluck

The companion site serves students as a virtual study guide, 24 hours a day, 7 days a week. The password-protected instructor's section offers a variety of assessment, presentation, and course management resources.

Book Specific Lecture & Art PowerPoint Slides

Mary Waterstreet, *St. Ambrose University*

To ease your transition to *Learning and Memory*, a prepared set of lecture and art slides, in easy-to-adopt PowerPoint format, are available to download from the instructor's side of the Book Companion Site.

Instructor's Resource Manual and Test Bank

(Mark Krause, *University of Southern Oregon*,
and Wendy Braje, *SUNY-Plattsburgh*)

The Instructor's Resource Manual includes extensive chapter-by-chapter suggestions for in-class presentations, projects and assignments, as well as tips for integrating multimedia into your course. It also provides more comprehensive material on animal learning for instructors who allocate more of their courses to the classic studies of animal learning. The Test Bank features approximately 75 multiple-choice questions per chapter as well as an assortment of short-answer and essay questions. Also included in the Test Bank are the chapter-specific Web quizzes (10-15 questions each) that appear on the Book Companion Site.

Diploma Computerized Test Bank (Available in Windows and Macintosh on one CD-ROM)

The CD-ROM allows instructors to add an unlimited number of questions, edit questions, format a test, scramble questions, and include pictures, equations, or multimedia links. With the accompanying gradebook, instructors can record students' grades throughout a course, sort student records and view detailed analyses of test items, curve tests, generate reports, add weights to grades, and more. This CD-ROM is the access point for Diploma Online Testing. Blackboard and WebCT formatted versions of the Test Bank are also available within the Course Cartridge and ePack.

Acknowledgments

This book has benefited from the wisdom of expert reviewers and instructors from laboratories and classrooms around the country. From the earliest stages of the development process, we solicited feedback and advice from the leading voices in the field of learning and memory to ensure that the book expresses the most current and accurate understanding of the topics in each chapter. Over the course of this book's development, we have relied on these experts' criticism, corrections, encouragement, and thoughtful contributions. We thank them for lending us their insight, giving us their time, and above all for sharing in our commitment to creating a new textbook and a new curriculum that reflects a contemporary perspective on the field.

Michael Todd Allen
University of Northern Colorado

John Anderson
Carnegie Mellon University

Hal Arkes
Ohio State University

Amy Arnsten
Yale University

Ed Awh
University of Oregon

Deanna Barch
Washington University, St. Louis

Carol Barnes
University of Arizona

Mark Basham
Metropolitan State College of Denver

Mark Baxter
Oxford University

April Benasich
Rutgers University—Newark

Gordon Bower
Stanford University

György Buzsáki
Rutgers University-Newark

John Byrnes
University of Massachusetts

Larry Cahill
University of California, Irvine

Thomas Carew
University of California, Irvine

KinHo Chan
Hartwick College

Henry Chase
Cambridge University

Roshan Cools
Cambridge University

James Corter
Columbia University

Stephen Crowley
Indiana University

Clayton Curtis
New York University

Irene Daum
Ruhr University Bochum Germany

Nathaniel Daw
New York University

Mauricio Delgado
Rutgers University—Newark

Dennis Delprato
Eastern Michigan University

Mark D'Esposito
University of California, Berkeley

Michael Domjan
University of Texas, Austin

William Estes
Indiana University

Robert Ferguson
Buena Vista University

John Forgas
University of South Wales

Joaquin Fuster
University of California, Los Angeles

Sherry Ginn
Wingate University

Robert Goldstone
Indiana University

Robert Greene
Case Western Reserve University

Martin Guthrie
Rutgers University-Newark

Stephen Hanson
Rutgers University-Newark

Kent Harber
Rutgers University

Michael Hasselmo
Boston University

Robert Hawkins
Columbia University

Kurt Hoffman
Virginia Tech University

Steven Horowitz
Central Connecticut State University

James Hunsicker
Southwestern Oklahoma State University

Stephen Joy
Albertus Magnus College

Lee Jussim
Rutgers University-New Brunswick

Daniel Kahneman
Princeton University

E. James Kehoe
University of South Wales

Szabolcs Kéri
Semmelweis University, Hungary

Alan Kluger
New York University Medical School

Stephen Kosslyn
Harvard University

John Kruschke
Indiana University

Joseph LeDoux
New York University

Elizabeth Loftus
University of California, Irvine

Robert Lubow
Tel-Aviv University

Elliot Ludvig
University of Alberta

Gail Mauner
University at Buffalo, SUNY

James McClelland
Stanford University

James McGaugh
University of California, Irvine

Barbara Mellers
University of California, Berkeley

Earl Miller
MIT

George Miller
Princeton University

Mortimer Mishkin
National Institutes of Mental Health

John Moore
University of Massachusetts

Lynn Nadel
University of Arizona

Ken Norman
Princeton University

Robert Nosofsky
Indiana University

Laura O'Sullivan
Florida Gulf Coast University

Ken Paller
Northwestern University

Michael Petrides
McGill University

Elizabeth Phelps
New York University

Steven Pinker
Harvard University

Russell Poldrack
University of California, Los Angeles

Sarah Queller
Indiana University

Garbiel Radvansky
Notre Dame

Arthur Reber
Brooklyn College, Graduate Center CUNY

Trevor Robbins
University of Cambridge

Herbert Roitblat
OrcaTec

Carolyn Rovee-Collier
Rutgers University—New Brunswick

Jerry Rudy
University of Colorado

Linda Rueckert
Northeastern Illinois University

Richard Schiffrin
Indiana University

David Shanks
University College London

Sonya Sheffert
Central Michigan University

Art Shimamura
University of California, Berkeley

Daphna Shohamy
Columbia University

Shepard Siegel
McMaster University

Edward Smith
Columbia University

Paul Smolensky
Johns Hopkins University

Larry Squire
University of California, School of Medicine, San Diego

Joseph Steinmetz
Indiana University

Paula Tallal
Rutgers University-Newark

Herbert Terrace
Columbia University

Philip Tetlock
University of California, Berkeley

Frederic Theunissen
University of California, Berkeley

Richard Thompson
University of Southern California

Endel Tulving
University of Toronto

Barbara Tversky
Stanford University

Anthony Wagner
Stanford University, MIT

Jonathon Wallis
University of California, Berkeley

Daniel Weinberger
National Institutes of Health

Norman Weinberger
University of California, Irvine

J. W. Whitlow, Jr.
Rutgers University—Camden

Bonnie Wright
Gardner-Webb University

Thomas Zentall
University of Kentucky

All of our partners at Worth Publishers have been invaluable in realizing our highest hopes for this book. We came to Worth in large part because of Catherine Woods, our publisher, who is viewed by many as the preeminent publisher of psychology textbooks. Several of our colleagues who have written multiple textbooks for various publishers described her as the best publisher or editor they had ever worked with. As we discovered ourselves, Catherine has a well-deserved reputation for being a talented publisher who focuses her efforts on a few select books in which she believes deeply, and makes them the best they can possibly be. She has been a steady source of encouragement and leadership throughout this process.

Charles Linsmeier, Acquisitions Editor, is bar none, the best acquisitions editor with whom we have ever dealt. At each choice point in the book's development, Chuck always focused on making sure that every part of the content and production was as strong and compelling as possible. He cut no corners, and was always available for email and phone conversations, day or night (no small task when dealing with three independently-minded authors). His attention to every aspect of the project provided us with a trusted source of knowledge on the multitude of issues that arise as a book approaches publication. We consider ourselves lucky to have had his guidance on this project.

Development Editor Mimi Melek is a brilliant, insightful, and delightful editor who served, in many ways, as our shadow fourth author. She attacked the manuscript at every level from deep conceptual meanings to the gloss of the style of our prose. By stepping back and seeing the whole project in one broad view, she served as our continuity editor, keeping all the pieces connected and woven into a seamless whole. Even when we thought a passage was as good as could be, a pass by Mimi would usually show us how that text could be made clearer, tighter, and usually much shorter. Working with her has been an education for each of us in how to write better for a student audience. Development Editors Moira Lerner and Elsa Peterson came on board to edit the final chapters and art, and lived up to the impossible standards set by our experience with Mimi. We appreciate all their contributions to the final book.

Associate Managing Editor Tracey Kuehn managed the production of the textbook and worked tirelessly to bring the book to fruition and keep it on schedule. Production Manager Sarah Segal's skill in producing a beautiful book allowed us to see a final product as visually appealing as we had hoped. Assistant Editor Justin Kruger was efficient and helpful in every respect.

Babs Reingold, Art Director, is inspiring in her passionate commitment to artistic values. She stuck with us through many revisions and produced numerous alternatives to both the cover art and the internal design until we were all satisfied. Kevin Kall, Designer, and Lee Mahler, Layout Designer, united clarity with beauty in every chapter. Photo Editor Bianca Moscatelli and Photo Researcher Julie Tesser were relentless in tracking down and securing rights for all the various photos we wanted to illustrate key ideas and stories in the book.

Christine Ondreicka, Media and Supplements Editor, and Stacey Alexander, Production Manager, guided the development and creation of the supplements package, making life easier for so many instructors.

Katherine Nurre, Executive Marketing Manager, and Carlise Stembridge, Associate Director of Market Development, quickly understood why we believe so deeply in this book and each contributed their tireless efforts to be relentless and persuasive advocates of this first edition with our colleagues across the country.

To Our Readers

The original plans for this book began to be formulated back in 2000, when Eddie Mercado was a postdoctoral fellow in Mark Gluck's lab at Rutgers University-Newark, working with Mark and Catherine on experimental and computational studies of animal and human learning. Over the last seven years—and especially the last three since we signed with Worth Publishers—creating this book has been a major focus of our professional lives. We tremendously enjoyed working on the book, collaborating with each other, and interacting with many scientists in the field of learning and memory who joined us in ways, small and large, to bring the book to its final form. We have learned much about our own field through the process of organizing the material and presenting it to you. We hope this book is as enjoyable and educational for you to read as it was for us to write.

Learning and Memory

CHAPTER 1

The Psychology of Learning and Memory

AT AGE 46, CLIVE WEARING HAD IT all. He was a well-known, highly regarded symphony conductor; he was handsome, charming, and witty; and he was passionately in love with his wife, Deborah. Then his memory was stripped from him. Clive suffered from a rare condition in which the herpes simplex virus, which usually causes nothing more than cold sores, invaded his brain. The brain tissue swelled, crushing against the confines of his skull. Most patients with this condition die. Clive survived, but the virus cut a path of destruction through his brain.

When Clive awoke in the hospital, he had lost most of his past. He could recognize Deborah, but couldn't remember their wedding. He knew he had children, but couldn't remember their names or what they looked like. He could speak and understand words, but there were huge gaps in his knowledge. On one test, when shown a picture of a scarecrow, he replied: "A worshipping point for certain cultures." Asked to name famous musicians, he could produce four names: Mozart, Beethoven, Bach, and Haydn. Conspicuously absent from this list was the sixteenth-century composer Lassus: Clive had been the world expert on this composer (Wilson & Wearing, 1995).

But Clive Wearing hadn't just lost the past: he'd also lost the present. He was conscious of what happened to him for a few seconds, then the information melted away without forming even a short-term memory. During his stay in the hospital, he had no idea where he was or why he was surrounded by strangers. Whenever he caught sight of Deborah—even if she'd only left him for a quick trip to the bathroom—he'd run to her and kiss her, joyously, as if she'd been absent for years.

A few minutes later, he'd catch sight of her again and stage another passionate reunion. Clive now lived "in the moment," caught in an endless loop of just awakening.

His numerous journals are filled with pages in which he desperately tried to make sense of what he was experiencing: "7:09 a.m.: Awake. 7:34 a.m.: Actually finally awake. 7:44 a.m.: Really perfectly awake. . . . 10:08 a.m.: Now I am superlatively awake. First time aware for years. 10:13 a.m.: Now I am overwhelmingly awake. . . . 10:28 a.m.: Actually I am now first time awake for years. . . ." Each time he added a new entry, he might go back and scratch out the previous line, angry that a stranger had written misleading entries in his journal.

Yet even when Clive knew nothing else, he knew that he loved his wife. Emotional memory—love—survived when almost everything else was gone. And he could still play the piano and conduct an orchestra so competently that a nonmusician wouldn't suspect anything was wrong with Clive's mind. Those skill memories survived, along with more mundane skills, such as making coffee or playing card games. And although Clive was unable to consciously learn any new facts, he could acquire some new habits through repeated practice. After moving to a nursing home, he eventually learned the route from the dining room to his room and, when prompted to put on his coat for his daily walk past the local pond, he would ask if it was time to go feed the ducks (Wilson & Wearing, 1995). Clive's memory was more like an imperfectly erased blackboard than a blank slate.

Clive Wearing's case is tragic, but it makes two important points. The first underscores the incredible importance of learning and memory to our lives. Most of the time, we take for granted our memories of who we are and what we know, our abilities to learn and remember new information and ideas. When these are stripped away, life becomes a series of unrelated moments, isolated from past and future, like those fuzzy moments we all experience when we've just awakened and are unsure of where we are.

The second point is that speaking of memory as if it were a single cohesive process is misleading. In fact, there are many different kinds of memory and, as happened in Clive's case, some can be damaged while others are spared. Normally these different kinds of memory function together seamlessly, and we aren't aware of whether we've encoded information as a fact or a habit or a skill or an emotion. But this cohesion is in many ways an illusion. By confronting the limits of this illusion, we can begin to understand how memory works, both in healthy people and in individuals whose memory has broken down.

This book is about **learning,** the process by which changes in behavior arise as a result of experience interacting with the world, and **memory,** the record of our past experiences acquired through learning. The study of learning and memory began far back in human history and still continues today, as some of humanity's greatest minds have struggled with the question of how we learn and remember. We hope that, as you read this chapter, you'll see why the questions that fascinated early philosophers and psychologists long ago are still relevant today.

Many of these earlier researchers were social activists, who (for better or worse) tried to apply their insights to the real world in domains such as advertising, education, and warfare. Some of the insights may apply to your own experience, as ideas for improving your memory in your daily life and school. To whet your appetite, see "Learning and Memory in Everyday Life" on page 3.

▶ **Learning and Memory in Everyday Life**

Top Ten Tips for a Better Memory

1. *Pay attention.* Often when we "forget" something, it's not that we've lost the memory but that we didn't learn the thing properly in the first place. If you pay full attention to what you are trying to learn, you'll be more likely to remember it later.

2. *Create associations.* Associate what you're trying to learn with other information you already know. For example, while memorizing the periodic table for a chemistry class, it will be easier to remember that Ag = silver if you know that *argentum* is the Latin for "silver." It might also help if you knew that Argentina got its name from early European explorers who thought the region was rich in silver (in fact, the native populations had imported their silver from elsewhere).

3. *A picture is worth a thousand words.* Information such as names and dates is more memorable if you can link it to an image. The effort you expend generating an image strengthens the memory. For example, in an art history course, you might have to remember that Manet specialized in painting figures and his contemporary, Monet, is famous for paintings of haystacks and water lilies. Picture the human figures lined up acrobat-style to form a letter "A" for Manet, and the water lilies arranged in a daisy chain to form the letter "O" for Monet.

4. *Practice makes perfect.* There's a reason kindergarteners drill on their ABCs and elementary school children drill on their multiplication tables. Memories for facts are strengthened by repetition. The same principle

"*As I get older, I find I rely more and more on these sticky notes to remind me.*"

holds for memories for skills such as bike riding and juggling: they are improved by practice.

5. *Use your ears.* Instead of just reading information silently, read it aloud. You will encode the information aurally as well as visually. You can also try writing it out; the act of writing activates sensory systems and also forces you to think about the words you're copying.

6. *Reduce overload.* If you're having trouble remembering everything, use memory aids such as Post-It notes, calendars, or electronic schedulers to remember dates and obligations, freeing you to focus on remembering items in situations where written aids won't work—say, during an exam!

7. *Time-travel.* Remembering information for facts doesn't depend on remembering the exact time and place where you acquired it. Nevertheless, if you can't remember a fact, try to remember where you first heard it. If you can remember your high school history teacher lecturing on Napoleon, perhaps what she said about the causes of the Napoleonic Wars will also come to mind.

8. *Get some sleep.* Two-thirds of Americans don't get enough sleep and consequently are less able to concentrate during the day, which makes it harder for them to encode new memories and retrieve old ones (see Tip 1). Sleep is also important for helping the brain organize and store memories.

9. *Try a rhyme.* Do you have to remember a long string of random information? Create a poem (or better yet, a song) that includes the information. Remember the old standard: "'I' before 'E,' except after 'C,' or sounded as 'A,' as in 'neighbor' or 'weigh'"? This ditty uses rhythm and rhyme to make it easier to remember a rule of English spelling.

10. *Relax.* Sometimes trying hard to remember is less effective than turning your attention to something else; often, the missing information will pop into your awareness later. If you are stumped by one question on a test, skip the troublesome question and keep working; come back to it later, and perhaps the missing information won't be so hard to retrieve.

1.1 The Philosophy of Mind

Today, learning and memory researchers consider themselves scientists. They develop new theories and test those theories with carefully designed experiments, just like researchers in any other branch of science. But this wasn't always the case. In fact, for most of human history, the study of learning and memory was a branch of *philosophy,* the abstract study of principles that govern the universe, including human conduct. Philosophers gain insight not through scientific experiments but through a process of reasoned thought and logical argument. These insights may be no less important than those gained through modern science; some are so profound that we are still talking about them centuries later.

Aristotle and Associationism

Aristotle (384–322 BC), a Greek philosopher and teacher, was one of the earliest philosophers to write about memory. Like many wealthy young men of his day, Aristotle was educated in Athens, the preeminent intellectual center of the western world at that time. There, he studied under Plato (c. 427–347 BC), perhaps the greatest of the Greek philosophers. Years later, Aristotle himself became a mentor to many students, including a young prince later known as Alexander the Great, who conquered much of the Mediterranean world.

In some ways, Aristotle was the western world's first scientist. A keen observer of the natural world, he loved **data,** the facts and figures from which he could infer conclusions. He collected plants and animals from around the world and made careful notes about their structure and behavior. From such data, Aristotle attempted to formulate **theories,** sets of statements devised to explain a group of facts. His data-oriented approach to understanding the world was in marked contrast to that of his intellectual forebears, including Plato and Plato's teacher, Socrates, both of whom relied primarily on intuition and logic rather than natural observation. Aristotle accumulated data and came to conclusions about how the world worked based on those data.

One of Aristotle's key interests was memory. His view, called **associationism,** espoused the principle that memory depends on the formation of linkages ("associations") between pairs of events, sensations, and ideas, such that recalling or experiencing one member of the pair elicits a memory or anticipation of the other. Imagine someone reading a list of words and, for each word, asking you to say the first word that comes to mind. If he says "hot," you might say "cold"; if he says "chair," you might say "table"; and so on. The words "hot" and "cold" are linked or associated in most people's minds, as are "table" and "chair." How do these associations come about?

Aristotle argued that such linkages reflect three principles of association. The first principle is **contiguity,** or nearness in time and space: events experienced at the same time (temporal contiguity) or place (spatial contiguity) tend to be associated. The ideas of "chair" and "table" are linked because we often see chairs and tables together at the same time and in the same place. The second principle is *frequency:* the more often we experience events that are contiguous, the more strongly we associate them. Thus, the more often we see tables and chairs together, the stronger the table–chair link grows. The third principle is *similarity:* if two things are similar, the thought or sensation of one will tend to trigger a thought of the other. Chairs and tables are similar in that,

Aristotle (right) and his teacher, **Plato**

often, both are made of wood, both are found in kitchens, and both have a function associated with eating meals. This similarity strengthens the association between them. Together, Aristotle concluded, these three principles of association—contiguity, frequency, and similarity—are the basic ways in which humans organize sensations and ideas.

Although Aristotle's ideas have been refined in the ensuing two millennia, his work provided the foundation for modern theories of learning in both psychology and neuroscience. Aristotle's view was that knowledge emerges from experience. This idea identifies him with a philosophical school of thought known as **empiricism,** which holds that all the ideas we have are the result of experience. (The Greek word *empiricus* means "experience.") To Aristotle, the mind of a newborn child is like a blank slate, not yet written on.

In this regard, Aristotle departed sharply from his teacher, Plato, who believed staunchly in **nativism,** which holds that the bulk of our knowledge is inborn (or native), acquired during the past lifetimes of our eternal souls. In fact, Plato's most influential book, *The Republic*, describes an idealized society in which people's innate differences in skills, abilities, and talents form the basis for their fixed roles in life: some rule while others serve. The tension between empiricism and nativism has continued through the centuries, although today it is more often called the "nature versus nurture" debate: researchers argue about whether our "nature," including genes, or our "nurture," including upbringing and environment, has the greater influence on our learning and memory abilities. Table 1.1 shows some of the major philosophers and scientists who have contributed to this debate over the millennia, and which side of the debate they espoused.

Table 1.1

Nativism and Empiricism: The Role of Nature and Nurture in Learning and Memory

Nativism: Knowledge is inborn	Empiricism: Knowledge is acquired through experience
Plato (c. 427–347 BC) Most of our knowledge is inborn and acquired during past lifetimes of the soul.	**Aristotle (384–322 BC)** Memory depends on the formation of associations, for which there are three principles: contiguity, frequency, and similarity.
René Descartes (1596–1650) The mind and the body are distinct entities, governed by different laws. The body functions as a machine with innate and fixed responses to stimuli.	**John Locke (1632–1704)** A newborn's mind is a blank slate (a *tabula rasa*) that is written on by experience. Education and experience (learning) allow common people to transcend their class.
Gottfried Leibniz (1646–1716) Three-quarters of human knowledge is learned, but a quarter is inborn.	**William James (1842–1910)** Habits are built up from inborn reflexes through learning; memory is built up through networks of associations.
Charles Darwin (1809–1882) Natural selection: species evolve when they posses a trait that is inheritable, varies across individuals, and increases the chances of survival and reproduction.	**Ivan Pavlov (1849–1936)** In classical (Pavlovian) conditioning, animals learn through experience to predict future events.
Francis Galton (1822–1911) Humans' natural talents are hereditary.	**Edward Thorndike (1874–1949)** The law of effect (instrumental conditioning): an animal's behaviors increase or decrease depending on the consequences that follow the response.

Western philosophy and science have deep roots in the ideas and writings of the ancient Greeks. Greek philosophy and science continued to flourish under the Roman Empire, but by the fifth century AD the empire had collapsed and Europe plunged into the Dark Ages, overrun by successive waves of warring tribes who seemed to care little for philosophy or higher thought. (Meanwhile, in China, India, Persia, and the Arabian peninsula, flourishing civilizations achieved major advances in science, mathematics, medicine, and astronomy—but that's another story.)

It was not until the middle of the fifteenth century that European science flourished once again. This was the Renaissance, the era that brought forth the art of Leonardo da Vinci, the plays of William Shakespeare, and the astronomy of Nicolaus Copernicus and Galileo Galilei. This cultural and scientific revival set the stage for the emergence of new ideas about the philosophy of mind and memory.

Descartes and Dualism

René Descartes (1596–1650) grew up in France as the son of a provincial noble family. His family inheritance gave him the freedom to spend his life studying, thinking, and writing, most of which he did in bed (he hated to get up before noon). Although raised as a Roman Catholic and trained by the Jesuits, Descartes harbored deep concerns about the existence of everything, including God. Despairing of being able to know anything for certain, he concluded that the only evidence that he himself existed was his ability to think: "*Cogito ergo sum*," or, "I think, therefore I am" (Descartes, 1637).

Where does Descartes' *cogito*—his ability to think—come from? Descartes was a strict believer in **dualism,** the principle that the mind and body exist as separate entities, each with different characteristics, governed by its own laws (Descartes, 1662). The body, Descartes reasoned, functions like a self-regulating machine, much like the clockwork statues and fountains that were so fashionable during the Renaissance. A person strolling through the royal gardens of Saint-Germain-en-Laye, just outside Paris, would step on a hidden trigger, releasing water into pipes that caused a gargoyle to nod its head, a statue of the god Neptune to shake its trident, and the goddess Diana to modestly retreat. The body, Descartes reasoned, works through a similar system of hydraulics and switches. The process begins when a **stimulus,** a sensory event from the outside world, enters the system; for example, the image of a bird enters the eye as a visual stimulus. Like the trigger switch in the gardens, this stimulus causes fluids (Descartes called them "spirits") to flow through hollow tubes from the eyes to the brain, and then to be "reflected" back as an outgoing motor response, as illustrated by Descartes' sketch in Figure 1.1 (Descartes, 1662). Such a pathway from sensory stimulus to motor response is called a **reflex.**

Medical science has shown that Descartes got many of the details of reflexes wrong: not all reflexes are as fixed and innate as he believed, and there are no spirits that flow through the body in the hydraulic way he described. Nevertheless, Descartes was the first to show how the body might be understood through the same mechanical principles that underlie physical machinery.

In contrast to Aristotle, who was a staunch empiricist, Descartes, like Plato before him, was strongly in the nativist camp. Descartes had no interest in theories of learning. Although he acknowledged that people do derive some information from experience, he believed that much of what we know is innate.

René Descartes

Descartes spent the last years of his life coping with the demands that came from being one of Europe's foremost mathematicians and philosophers. He moved to Holland, living in remote homes around the countryside to avoid unwanted visitors who might interrupt his early morning writing and thinking. Late in his life, he took a position as tutor to Queen Christina of Sweden, who insisted they begin each day's lessons at 5 a.m., thoroughly disrupting Descartes' usual morning solitude in bed. Descartes survived this routine, and the harsh Swedish winter, for only 4 months before dying of pneumonia. With coffins in short supply, a local mortician chopped off Descartes' head so as to fit the rest of his body into an undersized coffin. His posthumous decapitation was an ignominious end for one of the leading minds of the Renaissance.

John Locke and Empiricism

By the late 1600s, England (along with the rest of Europe) had undergone the Reformation, a religious and political movement that weakened the political power of the Roman Catholic Church and placed new emphasis on individual rights and responsibilities. This was a period when science flourished. Famous scientists were the celebrities of their day; people attended lectures on philosophy and natural sciences the way they go to movies and rock concerts today. One especially renowned scientist, Isaac Newton, demonstrated that white light can be refracted into component colors by a prism lens and then recombined by another lens to produce white light again.

Inspired by Newton's work, John Locke (1632–1704) hoped to do for the mind what Newton had done for light: to show how it could be broken down into elements that, when combined, produced the whole of consciousness. Locke, like Descartes before him, borrowed methods from the physical sciences that would help him better understand the mind and the processes of learning and memory. This pattern of philosophy and psychology borrowing from other, more established and rigorous domains of science continues to this day, as summarized in Table 1.2.

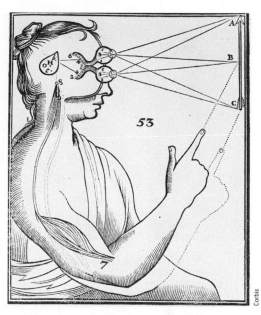

Figure 1.1 Descartes' reflex A mechanism for automatic reaction in response to external events, as illustrated in Descartes' *De Homine* (1662). The diagram shows the flow of information from the outside world, through the eyes, to the brain, and then through the muscles of the arm to create a physical response, moving the arm to point to an object in the external world.

Table 1.2

Borrowing from the Physical and Natural Sciences to Explain the Mind

Who . . .	Borrowed Ideas from . . .
René Descartes	Hydraulic engineering
John Locke	Physics (Newton), chemistry (Boyle)
Hermann Ebbinghaus	Laws of perception (Fechner and Weber)
Ivan Pavlov	Telephone exchanges
Edward Thorndike	Evolution by natural selection (Darwin)
Clark Hull	Theory of relativity (Einstein)
George Miller	Information theory (Shannon)
Herbert Simon	Computer science
David Rumelhart	Neuroscience and computer science

Northwind Picture Archives

John Locke

How do we get from elementary associations to the more complex ideas and concepts that make up our memories and knowledge? Again, Locke drew inspiration from the physical sciences, this time from his former Oxford medical instructor, Robert Boyle, who 30 years before had demonstrated that chemical compounds are composed of elementary parts (what we now know to be molecules and atoms). Locke reasoned that complex ideas are similarly formed from the combination of more elementary ideas that we passively acquire through our senses (Locke, 1690). For example, simple ideas such as "red" and "sweet" are acquired automatically by our senses of sight and taste, and more complex ideas such as "cherry" are acquired by combining these simpler components.

Perhaps Locke's most lasting idea is that all knowledge is derived from experience and experience alone. Borrowing Aristotle's analogy of a tablet on which nothing is yet written, Locke suggested that children arrive in the world as a blank slate or tablet (in Latin, a *tabula rasa*) just waiting to be written on.

Locke's view of the power of nature and experience to shape our capabilities through a lifetime of learning had great appeal to reformers of the eighteenth century who were challenging the aristocratic system of government, in which kings ruled by right of birth. Locke's ideas meant that a man's worth was not determined at birth. All men are born equal, he believed, with the same potential for knowledge, success, and leadership. Common people, through striving and learning, could transcend the limits and barriers of class. Therefore, Locke argued, access to a good education should be available to all children regardless of their class or family wealth (Locke, 1693). These ideas heavily influenced Thomas Jefferson as he drafted the Declaration of Independence, which in 1776 proclaimed the American colonies' independence from Great Britain and asserted that "all men are created equal," with the same innate rights to "life, liberty, and the pursuit of happiness"—words taken almost verbatim from Locke's writings.

Although Locke's writings were influential throughout European philosophical and scientific circles, he was not without his critics. One of Locke's contemporaries, German mathematician Gottfried Wilhelm Leibniz (1646–1716), conceded to Locke that three-quarters of knowledge might be acquired, but claimed that the other quarter is inborn and innate, including habits, predispositions, and potentials for success or failure (Leibniz, 1704). In many ways, Leibniz's more moderate position echoes that adopted by many modern researchers who believe that human ability is not due solely to nature (nativism) or solely to nurture (empiricism) alone, but is a combination of both: nature (as encoded in our genes) provides a background of native ability and predispositions that is modified by a lifetime of experience and learning (nurture).

William James and Association

Born to a wealthy and prominent New York family, William James (1842–1910) spent his early years traveling around the world, living in the finest luxury hotels, and meeting many of the great writers and philosophers of his time. After receiving his medical degree in 1869, James accepted a position as an instructor of physiology and anatomy at Harvard, where he offered an introductory course on psychology. It was the first course on psychology ever given at Harvard, or at any college in America. James's views on psychology were largely the result of his own introspections and observations. He once joked that the first psychology lecture he ever heard was his own.

James's introductory psychology course soon became one of the most popular courses at Harvard, and he signed a contract with a publisher, promising to deliver within 2 years a book based on his acclaimed lectures. In the end, it took him 12 years to finish the book. James's two-volume *Principles of Psychology* (1890) was an immediate scientific, commercial, and popular success. Translated into many languages, it was for decades the standard psychology text around the world.

James was especially interested in how we learn habits. He enjoyed telling the story of a practical joker who, seeing a recently discharged army veteran walking down the street carrying a load of groceries, shouted: "Attention!" The former soldier instantly and instinctively brought his hands to his side and stood ramrod straight as his mutton and potatoes rolled into the gutter. The soldier's response to this command was so deeply ingrained as a reflex that, even after he had left the army, it was all but impossible to suppress. James believed that most habits were similarly formed by our experiences, especially early in life. He proposed that a central goal of psychology should be to understand the principles that govern the formation and maintenance of habits, including how and why old habits may block or facilitate the formation of new habits (James, 1890).

William James

Like Aristotle, James believed in associationism. The act of remembering an event, such as a dinner party, he wrote, would involve multiple connections between the components of the evening. These might include memories for the taste of the food, the feel of his stiff dinner jacket, and the smell of the perfume of the lady seated next to him (Figure 1.2). Activation of the memory for the dinner party, with all of its components, could in turn activate the memory for a second event that shared some related elements—such as a date to go dancing with the same lady on the next night. This second event was composed of its

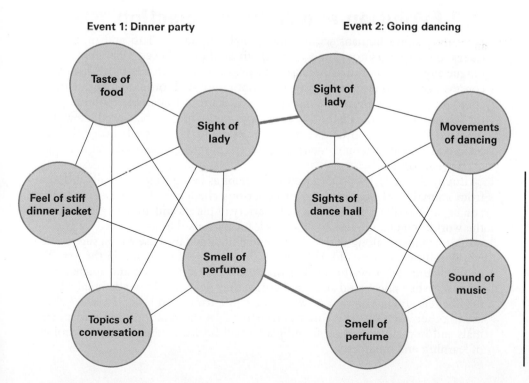

Event 1: Dinner party

Event 2: Going dancing

Figure 1.2 William James's memory model Memory of an event, such as a dinner party, has multiple components, such as the taste of the food, the topics of conversation, and the smell of perfume, all linked together. Another event, such as going dancing with a lady from the dinner party, also has component parts linked together. An association between the two events in turn consists of multiple connections between the underlying components.

own parts: the sights of the dance hall, the movements of dancing, the smell of his partner's perfume, and so on. The association between the two events (dinner party and dancing) was a linkage between common or related components (the sight of the lady and the smell of her perfume).

This model, or simplified description, of memory was one of James's many seminal contributions to psychology. James took his model literally, believing that the associations it described would eventually be mapped directly onto physical connections in the brain (James, 1890). With this idea, James was far ahead of his time; linking brain processes to learned behaviors didn't attract much interest or progress for many decades. Today, most modern theories of memory draw on James's idea of learning as a process of forming associations between the elements of an experience.

Interim Summary

Early philosophers of mind wrestled with many key issues that are still central to modern studies of learning and memory. Aristotle was an associationist, who believed that the effect of experiences can be understood as associations formed between sensations or ideas. He described three key principles of associative learning: contiguity (in space and time), frequency, and similarity. A later associationist, William James, proposed an early and influential memory model built on the principles of associationism.

John Locke, like Aristotle and James, was an empiricist; he believed that we are all born equal, as blank slates, to be shaped by our experiences. In the other camp, René Descartes was a nativist, arguing that we are shaped by our inherited nature. He showed how the body could be understood as working like a machine through mechanical (especially hydraulic) principles; as a dualist, he believed that the mind was a separate entity from the body. Modern researchers are less likely to be strict nativists or empiricists and are more likely to accept that both nature (genes) and nurture (experience) play a role in human learning and memory.

1.2 Evolution and Natural Selection

How unique are humans within the animal kingdom? Plato and other early Greek philosophers took one extreme view: they believed that humans are unique among living things because they posses an everlasting soul. Aristotle, in contrast, argued that humans exist in a continuum with other animals, with the ability to reason as their sole distinguishing feature. Renaissance philosophers tended to side with Plato, bolstered by the Church-sponsored view that mankind was created in God's image. For example, Descartes believed that humans and animals are fundamentally different, just as he believed that mind and body are separate.

But by the early 1800s, this view of humans as being fundamentally different from animals was beginning to meet serious challenge. European naturalists had begun to collect and study a wide variety of plants and animals from around the world. The geological study of rock formations that are shaped by eons of water movement, along with fossils found embedded in these rocks, suggested a world millions of years old. What naturalists and geologists saw in their studies contradicted the prevailing belief that the world was stable and unchanging. The facts they uncovered and the theories they developed upended many long-held beliefs about who we are, where we come from, and how similar we really are to other animals. These new perspectives on the relationship between animals and humans would profoundly affect all future studies of the psychology of learning and memory.

Erasmus Darwin and Early Proponents of Evolution

Erasmus Darwin (1731–1802) was the personal doctor to King George III of England, who presided over the loss of the American colonies. An eclectic man, Darwin published books on both botany and poetry, and studied how electrical current applied to the muscle of a dead animal could cause the muscle to contract and move as if it were alive. This finding inspired his English contemporary Mary Wollstonecraft Shelley (1797–1851) in writing her classic horror story, *Frankenstein.* But Erasmus Darwin is best remembered as a vocal proponent of **evolution,** the theory that species change over time, with new traits or characteristics passed from one generation to the next. With sufficient time, he argued, one species could evolve so far that it would constitute an entirely different species from its ancestor (E. Darwin, 1794).

Erasmus Darwin

By the late 1700s, a growing number of naturalists believed in evolution, but they were faced with two unresolved questions: How do various traits arise and how do they change? A giraffe's long neck, for example, is perfectly suited to allow the animal to reach and feed on leaves growing high up on trees. How did the giraffe's neck get that way? Jean-Baptiste Lamarck (1744–1829), a French naturalist and early evolutionary theorist, argued that the constant effort of straining for high branches lengthened a giraffe's neck. Such acquired traits, Lamarck inferred, might then be passed on to offspring through heredity (Lamarck, 1809). So the giraffe's offspring would have slightly longer necks as the result of their parents' stretching; if they stretched their necks in turn, their own offsprings' necks would be longer still. Eventually, after many generations, the result would be a hugely elongated neck, just as is seen in modern giraffes.

The Lamarckian view of the evolution and inheritance of traits is now known to be false. Lamarckian evolution would mean that, if a man trained for a marathon and developed strong leg muscles, his children would be born with strong leg muscles too; on the other hand, if he had become paralyzed in an accident, and his leg muscles had atrophied through disuse, his children would be born with atrophied legs too. Clearly, this is not how inheritance works. Some other mechanism must drive evolution.

Charles Darwin

Charles Darwin and the Theory of Natural Selection

Charles Darwin (1809–1882) was Erasmus Darwin's grandson. Charles's father was a prosperous doctor, and his mother hailed from the wealthy Wedgwood family of ceramic ware fame. Expected to become a doctor like his father, Darwin began his medical studies, but he soon dropped out, nauseated by watching patients undergoing surgical operations without anesthesia. Fortunately, his family's financial position meant that he didn't have to work for a living. Instead, what Darwin most enjoyed was spending afternoons walking through the English countryside, collecting and cataloging animals.

In 1831, at age 22, with no career direction other than his amateur interest in natural history, Charles Darwin accepted an offer to accompany the captain of H.M.S. *Beagle* on an expedition to chart the coast of South America. The *Beagle*'s voyage was scheduled to last for

HIP/Art Resource, NY

Figure 1.3 Finches of the Galápagos Islands Note the strong heavy beak of the bird at the upper left (good for cracking nuts) and the long narrow beak of the bird at the lower right (good for grabbing insects from cracks in bark).

2 years, but it stretched into 5. In South America, Darwin encountered an abundance of previously unknown species, many on the Galápagos Islands, an isolated archipelago off the coast of Ecuador. Of particular interest to Darwin were the many species of birds he observed, especially the finches—of which he identified at least 14 varieties, each on a different island (Figure 1.3). On one island that had plentiful nuts and seeds, the finches had strong, thick beaks that they used to crack open nuts. On another island, with few nuts but plenty of insects, the finches had long narrow beaks, perfect for grabbing insects from the crevices of tree bark. Each isolated island in the archipelago was populated by a different kind of finch, with a beak ideally suited to that island's distinct habitat. In his account of the trip, Darwin wrote that "one might really fancy that from an original paucity of birds in this archipelago, one species had been taken and modified for different ends" (C. Darwin, 1845). Charles Darwin, like his grandfather, was convinced that life on earth was evolving and was not immutably fixed.

Darwin's most important legacy was his theory of **natural selection,** which proposed a mechanism for how evolution occurs (C. Darwin, 1859). He proposed that species evolve when they possess a trait that meets three conditions (see Table 1.3). First, the trait must be inheritable, meaning it can be passed from parent to offspring. (Keep in mind that genes—the carriers of inherited traits—had not yet been discovered in Darwin's time.) Second, the trait must vary, having a range of forms among the individual members of the species. Third, the trait must make the individual more "fit," meaning that it must increase reproductive success—that is, increase the chance that the individual will survive, mate, and reproduce, passing on the trait to its offspring. This, in turn, will make the offspring more fit, increasing their chances of surviving and passing on the trait. Over time, natural selection (sometimes called "survival of the fittest") means that the trait will spread through the population. This, Darwin argued, was the underlying mechanism by which species evolve.

Remember Lamarck's giraffes? According to the principles of natural selection, giraffes' long necks didn't come about by stretching. Instead, there was some natural variation in neck size among giraffes. Those whose necks happened to be a bit longer were better able to reach food on high branches. In times of scarcity, long-necked individuals had a slight survival advantage over their shorter-necked comrades—and had a correspondingly better chance of living longer and producing more offspring, some of whom also had slightly longer necks. Among this next generation, some individuals happened to have necks that were longer still, and these giraffes in turn were more likely to survive

Table 1.3

Darwin's Three Criteria for Traits to Evolve through Natural Selection

Criterion	Giraffes	Finches
1. Inheritable trait	Neck length	Beak shape
2. Natural variability	Short to long	Thin or thick
3. Relevance to survival	Longer necks allow greater access to high branches of trees, and thus to leaves	Correct shape improves access to insects (thinner beak) or ability to crack nuts (thicker beak)

and breed. Thus, after many generations, most of the giraffes in the population were long necked. Long necks in giraffes thus evolved as "fit" individuals passed on their inherited traits to their offspring.

Darwin tinkered with his ideas for 20 years. Finally, in 1859, he published *On the Origin of Species by Means of Natural Selection, or the Preservation of Favoured Races in the Struggle for Life*, more commonly known by its abbreviated title, *The Origin of Species*. Darwin's book became a best-seller, was translated into many languages, and ignited a major public controversy that resulted in thousands of reviews, articles, and satires. Why the uproar? Darwin's view of natural selection upset many people's view that there is an important distinction between "man and beast." Theologians were alarmed because the idea that humans and apes evolved from a common ancestor seemed to challenge the biblical doctrine that people were created by the hand of God, in God's own image. *The Origin of Species* is among the most controversial scientific books ever written.

What are the implications of Darwin's work for the psychology of learning and memory? Darwin argued that behavioral traits could evolve through the same process of natural selection as do physical traits (C. Darwin, 1872). Today, the study of how behavior evolves through natural selection is known as **evolutionary psychology.** The basic premise of evolutionary psychology is that learning has enormous value for survival, allowing organisms to adapt to a changing and variable world. Organisms with more capacity for learning and memory are more fit—better able to survive and more likely to breed and pass their inherited capacities on to offspring. Notice that the *content* of what is learned is not passed on; learned knowledge is an acquired trait, which cannot be inherited. What can be inherited is the *capacity* or ability for learning and memory. (See "Unsolved Mysteries" on p. 14 for more on learning and evolution.)

Following publication of *The Origin of Species* in 1859, Darwin was the subject of many personal attacks, including caricatures as a half-man/half-ape, as in this illustration from *Hornet* magazine (March 22, 1871).

English School/Getty Images

Francis Galton: Variability of Nature

Francis Galton (1822–1911) was another grandson of Erasmus Darwin. A precocious child, Galton learned to read before he was 3 years old, wrote his first letter at 4, and spoke several languages by the time he was 5. After traveling for several years through African jungles and deserts, he returned to England, fascinated by the enormous variability he had seen in human characteristics. He began to measure everyone he could, comparing mental powers, auditory acuity, physical size, even fingerprints (and, in doing so, Galton invented the modern police method of fingerprinting).

Inspired by his cousin Charles Darwin's theory of natural selection and survival of the fittest, Galton grew especially fascinated by the fittest of humans. He proposed that "a man's natural abilities are derived by inheritance under exactly the same limitations as are the form and physical features of the physical world" (Galton, 1869, p. 1). Galton soundly rejected Locke's (and Aristotle's) view of the blank slate. It is a "fairy tale," he wrote, "that babies are all born pretty much alike" (p. 14). In no uncertain terms, Galton—who viewed himself as a genius—railed against the idea of natural equality.

As a by-product of his comparative studies of people's physical and mental abilities, Galton invented much of modern statistics and scientific methodology. He found that many attributes—such as height or blood pressure or scores on memory tests—show what he termed a *normal distribution:* out of a large sample of measurements, most will

Francis Galton

Bettmann/Corbis

▶ **Unsolved Mysteries**

Can Learning Influence Evolution?

Evolution operates on a time scale of millennia, changing the genetic makeup of an entire species. Learning operates over a very different time scale—an individual life—and it changes a single organism. Evolution clearly influences learning: as an organism's brain evolves, its capacity for learning will change. But researchers have long puzzled over the question of whether the relationship works in the other direction too: can learning influence evolution?

In the late nineteenth century, several scientists, including American philosopher and psychologist James Mark Baldwin (1861–1934), suggested that the capacity for behaviors could evolve if those behaviors were highly advantageous for survival (Baldwin, 1896). For example, suppose a particular monkey is born with a genetic mutation that allows it to learn a new trick, such as using a stick to knock fruit from a high branch. If food is scarce, this gives the monkey an advantage over its fellows who can't learn the stick trick. As a result, this monkey is more likely to survive and breed—and pass on its mutation to offspring. Generation by generation, the mutation for learning, because it increases reproductive success, will tend to spread through the population, until most monkeys have inherited the capability to learn the stick trick. Thus, Baldwin argued, it is the *capacity* for a particular type of learning— not the learning itself—that is inheritable and can influence evolution.

This idea (which came to be known as the *Baldwin effect*) found some support in the strange case of the bottle-opening titmice.

English milkmen used to deliver milk in bottles to the doorstep of customers' houses. Originally, in the 1900s, the bottles had no top, and local birds (such as robins and titmice) had easy access to the cream that rose to the top of the milk. After World War I, English dairies began to put aluminum foil caps on the bottles. In 1921, an observer reported that a few titmice near Southampton had learned how to peck through the foil caps to get at the cream inside. Over the next 20 years, the bottle-opening behavior spread to titmice throughout the region (Fisher & Hinde, 1949). By the end of the twentieth century, titmice were routinely opening foil-topped milk bottles throughout England and in several other European countries.

On the surface, this seems to be just what the Baldwin effect predicts. One lucky titmouse was born with a genetic mutation that enabled it to learn to peck at a milk bottle's foil top. This gave the bird access to a highly nutritious food source, increasing

Ronald Thompson, Frank Lane Picture Agency/Corbis

its odds of surviving and reproducing. This bird produced offspring with the same mutation who could also learn the trick. Over many generations, the gene spread throughout the population, until most titmice carried the gene and had the ability to learn to open milk bottles.

However, the Baldwin effect remains controversial (Weber & Depew, 2003). For one thing, critics note that there is another way to explain the spread of bottle-opening abilities in titmice. Titmice are born knowing how to peck, and are by nature attracted to shiny objects like the silvery foil of the bottle caps (Blackmore, 1999). Perhaps around 1921 a few innovative titmice, particularly ones who had previously gotten cream from uncapped bottles, randomly pecked at some bottle caps and learned that this resulted in access to the cream. Other birds watched these innovators and learned by observation to repeat the procedure themselves (Hinde & Fisher, 1951). In fact, in the lab, chickadees (a North American relative of the titmouse) that see another bird opening a cream container are likely to perform this behavior (Sherry & Galef, 1984, 1990). We don't have to presuppose any special genetic mutation at work here—just the normal ability of birds to learn by observing each other's actions.

Supporters of the Baldwin effect note that, just because we haven't yet found hard evidence that learning drives evolution (in titmice or any other species), this doesn't mean such examples aren't out there, waiting to be found. Perhaps the central contribution of Baldwin and his contemporaries is that they suggested one possible way in which learned modifications to behavior might eventually become genetically coded. And where there is one possible way for learning to influence evolution, there might be others which remain to be discovered.

cluster in some middle range, with relatively few at the extreme high and low ranges (Galton, 1899). One example is shown in Figure 1.4. Data on height were collected for a national sample of American men, from 1971 to 1974. For most of the men, height was between about 168-176 cm; relatively few had a height under 160 cm or over 190 cm. The sample approximates a normal distribution, shown in red in Figure 1.4. This is sometimes also called a *bell-shaped curve*, or simply a bell curve, because of its shape. Knowing that a variable, such as height or memory abilities, follows a normal distribution allows statisticians to make inferences about whether an individual falls within the expected "normal" range or represents an unusually high or low value.

Using his newly developed statistical techniques, Galton sought to assess the efficacy of prayer; in doing so, he established many basic statistical methods still used today. Galton started with a **hypothesis,** a tentative explanation for an observation, phenomenon, or scientific problem that can be tested by further investigation. He hypothesized that prayer would increase the health and lifespan of the persons being prayed for (Galton, 1872). Galton then proceeded to test this hypothesis by designing a **correlational study,** seeing whether two variables (being prayed for, and health and longevity) tended to vary together: as prayer increased, did health and longevity increase too?

He considered two groups: an **experimental group,** which received treatment based on the hypothesis, and a **control group,** which did not. In Galton's case, the experimental group consisted of people who, he assumed, were the most prayed-for members of society: the ruling monarchs. The control group consisted of nonroyals: aristocrats and common people. According to Galton's hypothesis, the highly prayed-for monarchs of English history should have lived longer and healthier lives than members of the control group. Galton calculated that the mean age of death of English sovereigns was about 64 years, whereas, on average, members of the aristocracy (other than the ruling monarchs) lived about 67 years, and common people lived even longer—70 years on average. Thus, Galton concluded, not only did prayer not increase longevity, but it seemed to have the opposite effect!

From the perspective of modern research methods, we can ask: was Galton's study really the best way to test his hypothesis? What if royalty died young because monarchs ate and drank too much, and were occasionally assassinated? The problem with Galton's correlational approach was that he was not able to control for the possibility of **confounds:** extraneous variables (such as diet and assassination) that

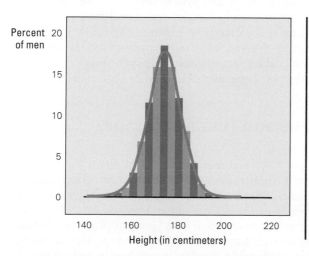

Figure 1.4 A bell curve The distribution of variables in the natural world often shows a bell-shaped curve called a normal distribution, with many values in the middle range and few extreme outliers. Here, for example, a plot of height data for 4,635 American men, collected between 1971 and 1974 shows that most values cluster in the middle range, around 168–176 cm, with relatively few extremely tall or extremely short outliers. The blue line shows the statistically expected distribution, and the height data mirror this distribution quite well. Adapted from Carl J. Schwarz.

happen to co-vary with the variable (prayer) being examined. Confounds can lead to erroneous assumptions about what is really causing an observed result.

Following his seminal contributions to the development of experimental and statistical methods in science, Galton's later years were largely consumed with applying natural selection to the betterment of mankind. Borrowing from the Greek word for "well-born," *eugenes*, Galton introduced the term **eugenics:** a program for encouraging marriage and procreation among the healthiest, strongest, and most intelligent members of society, while at the same time discouraging childbearing in the mentally or physically unfit (Galton, 1883). Galton's eugenics movement grew in popularity and respectability during the early 1900s, as people were excited by the prospect of applying Charles Darwin's ideas of natural selection to improve the human condition. Today, the eugenics movement is remembered mostly for the disreputable applications it spawned, including the forced sterilization of mentally ill individuals in California in the 1920s and the Nazis' mass murder of Jews, Gypsies, and others whom they deemed unfit to survive and breed. Despite his association with eugenics, Galton's most enduring legacies are his contributions to understanding the role of inheritability in behavioral traits and the development of novel statistical and experimental methods for psychology.

Interim Summary

Early proponents of evolution, including Erasmus Darwin and Jean-Baptiste Lamarck, believed that species evolve over time, although they did not know how or why evolution occurs. Charles Darwin's theory of natural selection proposed a mechanism for evolution: survival of the fittest. According to this theory, evolution occurs when one variation of a naturally occurring and inheritable trait gives an organism a survival advantage, making the organism more fit—more likely to survive and reproduce and pass this trait on to its offspring.

Francis Galton was an avid proponent of the inheritability of behavioral traits. He made fundamental contributions to experimental methods and statistics, including the process of testing hypotheses by comparing two groups: an experimental group (that is subject to the variable of interest) and a control group (that is not).

1.3 The Birth of Experimental Psychology

The scientists and philosophers covered so far observed the natural world and inferred general principles to explain what they saw. In the late 1800s, an important change took place. Instead of merely looking for correlations, scientists began to conduct **experiments,** specific tests to examine the validity of a hypothesis by actively manipulating the variables being investigated. In psychology, this new approach was called **experimental psychology,** in which psychological theories are tested by experimentation rather than merely by observation of natural occurrences.

Hermann Ebbinghaus and Human Memory Experiments

Hermann Ebbinghaus (1850–1909), a contemporary of William James, conducted the first rigorous experimental studies of human memory. After earning his Ph.D., Ebbinghaus lived an itinerant life, traveling, attending occasional seminars, and working for short periods as a teacher and private tutor. One day, browsing at a book stall, he came across a book by a German physicist, Gustav Fechner (1801–1887), that described the science of human perception. Fechner showed that there are highly predictable regularities in how people perceive variations in physical stimuli, such as changes in the brightness of a light or the weight of a ball. The book showed how a simple mathematical equation could describe the relationship between the physical world and the psychological world. Captivated by these ideas, Ebbinghaus believed that the psychology of memory could also become a rigorous natural science, defined by precise mathematical laws.

Unlike many of the scientists discussed in this chapter, Ebbinghaus was not a wealthy man. He had no family inheritance, no laboratory, no resources to pursue experimental studies, and no colleagues with whom he could discuss his scientific ideas. Unable to afford to pay anyone to participate in his research, he did his studies using himself as the only participant. Despite these limitations, his work laid the foundation for all future experimental studies of human memory; in fact, Ebbinghaus is often considered to be the father of modern memory research.

Ebbinghaus sought mathematical equations to explain how memories are acquired and how they fade. Early on, he realized that if he studied lists of real words, his data would be strongly affected by the fact that he was more familiar with some words than others. To avoid this problem, he used three-letter nonsense words, such as BAP, KEP, and DAK, which would be unfamiliar to him. Where did he get this idea? Some historians suggest it came from reading a recently published and highly popular book from England, Lewis Carroll's *Through the Looking Glass* (1872), the sequel to *Alice in Wonderland*, which included verses of rhyming nonsense words (Shakow, 1930).

Regardless of its genesis, Ebbinghaus's use of simple, unfamiliar nonsense words was a critical advance in the methodology for studying principles of human memory. In one of his experiments, Ebbinghaus read a list of 20 words out loud to himself, put away the list for a period of time, then tried to remember as many words as possible. Afterward, he checked which words he missed, reviewed the list, and tried again. He repeated this process until he could remember all 20 words from the original list. This experiment illustrates the four key stages of a memory experiment—learning, delay, test, relearning—that established the basic methodology for human memory experiments for years to follow.

Ebbinghaus was especially interested in **forgetting**: how memory deteriorates over time. He measured forgetting by examining how long it took him to relearn a previously learned list. If it initially took him 10 minutes to learn the list, and later took only 6 minutes to relearn the same list, Ebbinghaus recorded a "time savings" of 4 minutes, or 40% of the original learning time. By testing himself at various intervals after learning, Ebbinghaus was able to plot a **retention curve** (Figure 1.5), which shows the percentage savings in time for relearning the list, at various delays between the initial learning and relearning (Ebbinghaus, 1885/1913).

As you can see in Figure 1.5, there is a strong savings (nearly 100%) if the delay between learning and relearning is short. But as the delay grows longer, to about 100 hours (approximately 4 days), savings declines to 25%. The retention curve also illustrates that most forgetting occurs early on; if a memory can survive the first few hours after learning, there is little additional forgetting. Thus, Ebbinghaus showed a savings of 25% after 150 hours, and this dropped only to 20% after 750 hours. In other studies, Ebbinghaus showed that shorter lists were easier to remember than longer lists. He also demonstrated that increasing the amount of initial practice improved later recall.

Hermann Ebbinghaus

Figure 1.5 Ebbinghaus's retention curve These experimental data show the percentage savings in time for relearning a list of words as a function of the delay between learning and relearning. Ebbinghaus's early study demonstrated that retention drops quickly in the first few days (up to about 100 hours for the task shown here) and then tapers off more slowly with increasing delays. Adapted from Ebbinghaus, (1885/1913).

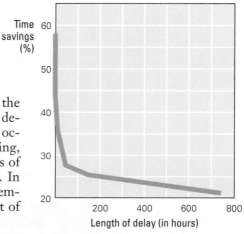

In contrast to Galton's correlational studies of prayer, which examined the effects of prayer as it naturally occurred among members of society, Ebbinghaus designed and conducted experiments to examine the validity of his hypotheses. Each of Ebbinghaus's experiments included a single **independent variable,** the factor carefully manipulated in the study, such as the length of the delay between learning and relearning; and a **dependent variable,** the observed factor whose change was being measured, usually memory retention. Through this design, Ebbinghaus was able to show how changes in the independent variable (delay length) determine changes in the dependent variable (memory retention).

The major limitation of Ebbinghaus's studies was that they were conducted with just one participant, Ebbinghaus himself. There are several reasons why such self-experimentation is problematic and would not meet modern scientific standards for research. First, what if Ebbinghaus's memory was different from most other people's? If so, the results of his experiments would tell us lots about Ebbinghaus but would not be applicable to other people. For this reason, modern research on memory usually involves testing a large number of people.

A second problem is that Ebbinghaus, as the participant, knew which variables were being manipulated. If, for example, he believed that longer lists were harder to learn, then this might subtly influence him to take longer to learn those lists. This problem is sometimes called **subject bias.** To avoid such problems, modern studies of memory employ a **blind design,** which means that the participant does not know the hypothesis being tested. There is also a corresponding problem of **experimenter bias,** which means that even a well-meaning experimenter might influence the outcome (for example, by implicitly encouraging the participant to respond in an expected manner). Experimenter bias can be avoided by use of a **double-blind design,** in which neither the participant nor the experimenter knows the hypothesis being tested. Common examples of double-blind studies are modern tests of experimental medications, in which patients receive either the test drug or a **placebo** (an inactive pill that looks just like the real drug). In a double-blind design, neither the patients nor the doctors know who is receiving which kind of pill; only the people analyzing the results (who never interact directly with the research participants) know which is which.

Despite all these limitations, Ebbinghaus led the way in the study of learning and memory through scientific experimentation. There are few studies of human memory conducted today that don't owe their methodology to the early and influential studies of Hermann Ebbinghaus.

Ivan Pavlov and Animal Learning

While Ebbinghaus was revolutionizing the study of human memory, the Russian physiologist Ivan Pavlov (1849–1936) was developing methods for studying animal learning that are still in widespread use today. As a young man, Pavlov trained to be a Russian Orthodox priest, like his father and grandfather. In addition to his religious readings, Pavlov read Darwin's recently published *Origin of Species*. Inspired by Darwin's accomplishments, Pavlov abandoned his plan to become a priest and enrolled in the school of natural sciences at the University of St. Petersburg. For the rest of his life, Pavlov would acknowledge the enormous impact of Darwin's writings on his own career and thinking.

Although remembered today for his seminal contributions to the psychology of learning, Pavlov's 1904 Nobel Prize in Physiology or Medicine was awarded for his research on the physiology of saliva and digestion in dogs. Like many advances in science, Pavlov's discovery of basic principles of animal learning was largely accidental. In the course of his studies of digestion, Pavlov noticed that his dogs often started salivating even before they received their daily meat rations—when they saw the bowl that usually contained their food, or when they heard the footsteps of the laboratory assistant who fed them (Pavlov, 1927). Initially, Pavlov viewed these effects as nuisances that interfered with his efforts to understand how the digestive system responds to food. Soon, however, Pavlov realized that he had stumbled on a way of studying how associations are formed in the brain of a dog.

Pavlov and his assistants began a systematic study of factors that influence how an animal learns. Each dog was restrained and had a surgical tube (not shown here) inserted into its mouth to collect saliva (Figure 1.6a). Pavlov could then measure salivation in response to various cues. In one study he began by first training a dog that a doorbell always preceded delivery of food; over many such paired doorbell–food trials, the dog developed a stronger and stronger salivation response to the sound of the doorbell. This form of learning, in which an animal learns that one stimulus (such as a doorbell) predicts an upcoming important event (such as delivery of food) is known today as **classical conditioning** (or Pavlovian conditioning), and it is so widely studied that we'll cover it in detail in Chapter 7. Modern studies of classical conditioning usually report the results as a **learning curve,** like that shown in Figure 1.6b, which plots the number of training trials (the independent variable, plotted on the horizontal axis) against the animal's response (the dependent variable, plotted on the vertical axis).

Pavlov's view of how an animal learns a new behavioral response was based on an analogy to a new technology that had recently been introduced in Russia: the telephone. As Pavlov explained it, he could call his lab from home via a direct private line, which was a fixed connection, much like the fixed connection between food and salivation in a dog's brain. Alternatively, he could call his lab by going through a switchboard operator, a new and modifiable connection, like that between a bell and salivation (Pavlov, 1927).

In other studies, Pavlov and his assistants showed that they could also *weaken* an animal's trained response to the bell. This was done by first pairing the bell with food, until the animal had learned to salivate to the bell, and then pairing the bell with the absence of food. Pavlov called this process **extinction:** the salivation to the bell gradually decreased as the animal learned that the bell no longer predicted food.

Figure 1.6 **Pavlov and learning experiments** (a) Pavlov (with white beard) and his assistants in the laboratory. A restrained dog has a surgical tube (not shown here) inserted into its mouth to collect and measure salivation in response to meat placed in front of it or to a cue such as a doorbell, which predicts delivery of the food. (b) A learning curve from a modern study of classical conditioning. The curve plots the number of training trials (the independent variable) against the animal's conditioned response (the dependent variable).

(b) Adapted from Allen et al., 2002.

(a)

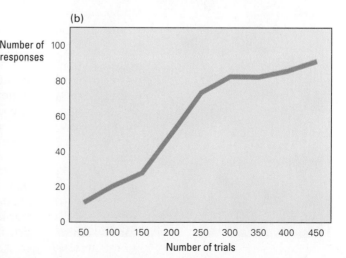

(b)

Number of responses

Number of trials

Pavlov also demonstrated that an animal will transfer what it has learned about one stimulus to similar stimuli. For example, he observed that once an animal learned to respond to a metronome ticking at 90 beats per minute, it also responded to similar sounds, such as a metronome ticking at 80 beats per minute or 100 beats per minute. However, the more dissimilar the new stimulus was to the original stimulus, the less intense was the dog's salivation response. These graded responses to stimuli of varying dissimilarity to the original training stimulus are an example of **generalization,** the ability to transfer past learning to novel events and problems. In Chapter 9 we'll discuss how generalization occurs in many different forms of learning and memory.

Ivan Pavlov lived through the Russian revolution of 1917, developing a deep animosity toward the new Communist regime (especially after it stole his Nobel Prize money). Nevertheless, when Pavlov died in 1936 he was given an elaborate funeral with full honors as a hero of the Soviet state.

Edward Thorndike: Law of Effect

Meanwhile, over in the United States, Edward Thorndike (1874–1949), a student of William James, was studying how animals learn relationships or connections between stimuli, responses, and behavior. Some of Thorndike's most influential studies involved how cats learn to escape from puzzle boxes—cages secured with complex locking (and unlocking) devices. This kind of training, in which organisms learn to make responses in order to obtain or avoid important consequences, is called **instrumental conditioning,** because the organism's behavior is instrumental in determining whether the consequences occur. This is in contrast, for example, to the learned response (salivation) of Pavlov's dogs, in which the dogs received their food reward regardless of whether they made the learned response. You'll read about instrumental conditioning in greater detail in Chapter 8.

In his studies, Thorndike observed that the probability of a particular behavioral response increased or decreased depending on the consequences that followed. He called this the **law of effect** (Thorndike, 1911). If a particular response led to a desirable consequence, such as access to food, then the probability of the animal making that response in the future *increased*. On the other hand, if the response led to an undesirable consequence (say, an electric

Edward Thorndike

Bettmann/Corbis

shock), then the probability of the animal making that response in the future *decreased*. Fascinated, Thorndike began to methodically investigate the factors that influence how an animal learns new behaviors to maximize its chances of obtaining desirable consequences and avoiding undesirable ones.

Like many psychologists of his era, Thorndike was strongly influenced by Charles Darwin's theory of natural selection. The basic idea of Thorndike's law of effect has much in common with Darwin's principle of survival of the fittest. In Darwin's theory of evolution, variability in traits was key: those animals who possess a trait that increases the likelihood of survival pass it on to future generations. Thorndike's law of effect applied the same principle to explain how behavioral traits evolve during an animal's lifetime. According to the law of effect, an animal has a range of behaviors; those behaviors that lead to positive consequences for the animal tend to persist; those that do not, tend to die out. Starting from this basic principle, Thorndike argued, the psychology of learning should center on the search for the rules describing how, when, and to what degree connections among stimuli and responses are increased or decreased through experience (Thorndike, 1932, 1949).

In 1917, Thorndike was the first psychologist elected to the prestigious U.S. National Academy of Sciences, and in the early 1920s he was often identified as one of the most influential scientists in the United States. He died in 1949, the last of the pioneers in experimental psychology of learning and memory. His work set the stage for the next major movement in learning research: the behaviorists of the mid-twentieth century.

Interim Summary

Starting in the late 1800s, the emergence of experimental psychology meant that the study of learning and memory, like other branches of psychology, began to be treated as a serious scientific endeavor, with experiments designed to test specific hypotheses. Many of the central figures in this movement were strongly influenced by Charles Darwin's recent work on evolution and natural selection.

Hermann Ebbinghaus conducted the first rigorous experimental studies of human memory. He introduced the technique of studying lists of short nonsense words, and collected data on how information is retained and forgotten. Ivan Pavlov discovered a basic method for training animals to associate a previously neutral stimulus, such as a bell, with a naturally significant stimulus, such as food.

Edward Thorndike showed that the probability of an animal making a behavioral response increases or decreases depending on the consequences that follow. He called this principle the law of effect. It was analogous to Darwin's idea of survival of the fittest: those responses that produce the most beneficial effects survive, while others die out.

Test Your Knowledge

Who's Who in the History of Learning and Memory?

Below is a (slightly tongue-in-cheek) review of the major researchers and ideas covered in the first two sections of this chapter. See if you can fill in the blanks with the names of the researchers.

1. Old _____ was a Greek
   Who thought about association.
   _____, the dualist, liked to speak
   Of mind-and-body separation.

2. To _____, a baby's mind was blank,
   As all empiricists have said.
   Nativists called him a crank,
   Believing knowledge is inbred.

3. _____'s models of the mind
   Had features linked together,
   Updating Greeks from ancient times
   And going them one better.

4. _____ _____ thought all beasts
   Evolved toward perfection.
   His grandson _____ proposed the
   means, Called natural selection.

5. _____ _____ now is known
   For championing eugenics
   But we should also note it down:
   He pioneered statistics.

6. _____ learned nonsense words;
   Dogs learned to drool for _____.
   _____ studied food rewards
   (And coined "effect, the law of").

LIB

1.4 The Reign of Behaviorism

Building on the work of Pavlov and Thorndike, an American approach to learning emerged in the 1920s that was called **behaviorism.** It argued that psychology should restrict itself to the study of observable behaviors (such as lever presses, salivation, and other measurable physical actions) and avoid reference to unobservable, and often ill-defined, internal mental events (such as consciousness, intent, and thought). Proponents of this approach, who were called *behaviorists*, wanted to distance themselves from philosophers and psychologists who pondered the inner workings of the mind through personal introspection and anecdotal observation. Behaviorists wanted psychology to be taken seriously as a rigorous branch of natural science, no less than biology or chemistry.

John Watson and Behaviorism

Brash, ambitious, and self-made, John Watson (1878–1958) is considered the founder of behaviorism. Born in Greenville, South Carolina, he was the son of a ne'er-do-well father who abandoned the family when Watson was 13 years old. Although a poor student in school, Watson wrangled a personal interview with the president of a local college and pleaded for a chance to show he was capable of college-level work. The president agreed to give Watson a chance, and the gamble paid off. Watson not only finished college but went on to graduate school, where he conducted research on how rats learn. In these studies, Watson placed a rat at the entrance to a maze and rewarded it with food if it found its way through the corridors to the exit.

Initially, a naive (i.e., untrained) rat might spend half an hour wandering randomly through the maze until it reached the exit. After 30 training trials, however, the rat could traverse the maze in less than 10 seconds. To find out what drove the rat's performance, Watson systematically eliminated various possibilities. First, he trained rats to run through the maze under normal conditions. Then, he surgically blinded the rats, or rendered them deaf, or removed their whiskers (which rats use like fingertips to feel their way). None of these treatments impaired the rats' performance. Thinking the rats might be using olfactory cues to find their way, Watson boiled the mazes to eliminate all odors. The rats still found their way through. Only when the maze was rotated or when the corridors were made shorter or longer did the rats show a significant loss in their ability to navigate the maze. From these studies, Watson argued that the rats had learned an automatic set of motor habits for moving through the maze and that these motor habits were largely independent of any external sensory cues (Watson, 1907).

Watson's experiments were widely admired by his scientific colleagues. Unfortunately, the reception in the popular press was not so kind. The media described Watson as a cruel torturer of animals and he was threatened with criminal prosecution (Dewsbury, 1990). When the anti-vivisectionist (pro–animal rights) *Journal of Zoophily* reported, incorrectly, that Watson planned to do similar studies on humans, this led to an even greater outcry. Watson's department chair defended him by pointing out that the surgeries were all done under antiseptic conditions, with the animal anesthetized and with a minimum of pain.

John Watson

The tension between animal rights' activists and psychological researchers continues to this day. In contrast to Watson's era, when there were few constraints on animal research, studies today are strictly controlled by the government and professional organizations to ensure that all experimental animals are handled as humanely as possible. Before any experiment can be conducted, the researchers must seek approval from their institution's ethics board, a committee composed of scientists and lay members of the community, and describe the measures that will be taken to minimize the animals' pain or suffering. Researchers conducting studies on humans are subject to additional ethical scrutiny to ensure protection of participants' rights, privacy, and safety. Only if the ethics board approves the procedures can the research begin. In Watson's day, though, such ethical considerations were left largely to the discretion of the researcher.

Despite the public outcry about his sensory-deprivation studies, Watson continued to work on further studies of rat learning. By 1913, taking advantage of his new position as editor of the prestigious journal *Psychological Review*, Watson presented his behaviorist manifesto. According to Watson, psychology should be viewed as a "purely objective experimental branch of natural science. Its theoretical goal is the prediction and control of behavior" (Watson, 1913). An important component of Watson's behaviorist approach was the integration of studies of animal and human learning.

Watson was a strong empiricist, sharing Locke's belief in the overwhelming influence of experience (nurture) versus heredity (nature) in determining our behaviors and capabilities. In a rousing affirmation of Aristotle's principle of the blank slate, Watson wrote: "Give me a dozen healthy infants, well-formed, and my own specified world to bring them up in, and I'll guarantee to take any one at random and train him to become any type of specialist I might select—doctor, lawyer, artist, merchant, chief, and yes even beggarman and thief, regardless of the talents, penchants, tendencies, abilities, vocations, and race of his ancestors" (Watson, 1924, p. 82). In the years following World War I, many people hoped for a new dawn of equal opportunity and freedom from class-based constraints on social progress. Watson's bold claims had a strong appeal for scientists and the wider public. By the early 1920s, behaviorism had become the predominant approach to the psychology of learning, especially in the United States.

Watson's career as an academic researcher came to a sudden end when he became involved in a relationship with his research assistant, Rosalie Rayner. Given Watson's fame as a scientist, his status as a married man, and Rayner's socially prominent family, the affair received intense media scrutiny. In the end, the scandal grew so great that the Johns Hopkins University gave Watson a choice between ending his affair or resigning his position at the university. Watson chose to stay with Rayner, and he resigned from Johns Hopkins.

Unable to find another position in academia, Watson started a new career in advertising, where he applied the same strict scientific principles to marketing research as to his earlier experiments. For example, he conducted "taste tests" in which smokers recorded their reactions to different cigarettes without knowing which brands they were smoking (Watson, 1922). Watson also championed advertising methods such as demographic surveys of consumer preferences, free samples in exchange for filling out questionnaires, and testimonials from celebrities to promote products. Advertising paid off in more than professional pride; by 1930, Watson was earning more than 10 times the salary he'd earned as an academic at Johns Hopkins. He died in 1958, not long after the American Psychological Association honored him with a gold medal for lifetime contributions to the field of psychology.

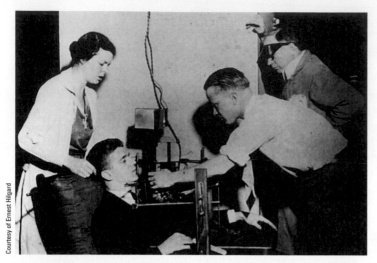

Clark Hull (standing with visor) and his young graduate student **Ernest Hilgard** (seated) in a study of Pavlovian conditioning at Yale University in the 1920s. Hull trained Hilgard to blink in anticiparion of a slap to the face. Despite this early experience, Hilgard went on to a long and productive career in learning research.

Clark Hull and Mathematical Models of Learning

Born on a farm near Akron, Ohio, Clark Hull (1884–1952) devoted his career to developing mathematical equations to describe the relationships among the factors that influence learning. Hull's early life was marked by life-threatening illness. He survived an attack of typhoid fever but sustained lasting brain damage, which caused memory difficulties that plagued him for the rest of his life. He also survived a bout of polio that left him paralyzed in one leg and dependent on crutches to walk. These disabilities, however, didn't stop Hull from making a lasting contribution to psychology.

In Hull's day, the new doctrine of behaviorism claimed that all behavior could be understood as a simple mapping from stimuli to responses. When Pavlov's dogs heard the doorbell, they salivated (doorbell → salivation); when Watson's rats entered the maze, they made a series of motor-habit responses (maze entry → turn left, turn right, and so on). Such learning is often called *stimulus-response learning*, abbreviated as *S-R learning*, to emphasize the centrality of this mapping. Of course, the behaviorists acknowledged that the real world is complicated and that other factors might affect the response. For example, Pavlov's dogs might salivate to the doorbell only if they are hungry. Still, the behaviorists believed that, if you could specify all the existing factors, you ought to be able to predict exactly whether and when a stimulus would provoke an animal to make a response.

Hull set himself the goal of developing a comprehensive mathematical model of animal learning that would predict exactly what an animal will learn in any given situation. Much as Einstein had recently shown that a single equation, $E = mc^2$, could explain the complex relationship between energy (E), mass (m), and the speed of light (c), Hull hoped to find a similarly powerful equation to relate all the key factors contributing to a learning experience. The variables that Hull entered into his equations included the number of learning trials, the frequency of reward, the spacing between trials, the intensity of the stimulus cues, the ani-mal's motivation for reward, and the incentive value (desirability) of the reward (Hull, 1943). Hull conducted an intensive program of research on learning in animals and humans, seeking to test and refine his mathematical models. One measure of a model's value is its ability to serve as a heuristic for stimulating experimental research; in this regard, Hull's model was a great success. By the 1940s, Hull's work was cited in 70% of all scientific papers on learning published in the major journals (Spence, 1952).

Although Hull's equations were influential in their time, their specifics are no longer considered relevant today. In part, Hull's models have been abandoned because modern psychologists have despaired of ever being able to reduce all the factors governing learning into a single equation, as Hull hoped to do. Nevertheless, Hull's

"Oh, if only it were so simple."

many students and followers (often called neo-Hullians) worked toward a smaller goal: to develop mathematical equations to describe basic kinds or components of learning. (You'll read in Chapter 7 about one of the most enduring: the Rescorla-Wagner rule, which describes some of the factors governing classical conditioning, like the learning in Pavlov's dogs.) Neo-Hullian researchers showed that learning indeed follows reliable, predictable patterns, and pointed the way toward an understanding of how the same basic patterns govern learning in humans as in other animals.

B. F. Skinner: Radical Behaviorism

Burrhus Frederic Skinner (1904–1990), born in rural Pennsylvania, became the most famous—and perhaps most infamous—behaviorist of the twentieth century. Although his original goal was to be a writer, Skinner instead went to graduate school in psychology. He placed himself squarely in the behaviorist camp, believing that psychologists should limit themselves to the study of observable behaviors and not try to speculate about what might be going on in the mind of an animal while it learns.

Skinner's research focused on extending and refining the techniques Thorndike had developed to study how animals learn new responses. He developed an automated learning apparatus that was widely adopted by other researchers, who dubbed it the "Skinner box" (you'll read more about this and Skinner's other innovations in Chapter 8). He also made many important contributions to our understanding of how animals learn the relationship between responses and consequences. One of the most important happened quite by accident.

In the early 1940s, Skinner was in his laboratory on a Friday afternoon, setting up some rat studies in which he taught rats to perform a response in order to obtain food pellets. He realized he didn't have enough food pellets to get him through all the experiments planned for that weekend. Rather than cancel the experiments or go out and get more rat food, Skinner decided to save pellets by providing food only after the rats made two or three correct responses in a row. This led Skinner to one of his greatest discoveries: when trained with an intermittent program of reinforcements, rats learn to respond as quickly and as frequently as when they are rewarded on every trial—in fact, sometimes even better. Skinner and his students began a massive new program of research on how learning is affected by the reliability with which an organism's responses result in consequences (such as obtaining a food pellet). We will return to discuss this research in greater detail in Chapter 8.

As World War II loomed, Skinner began "Project Pigeon" to explore the application of behaviorist methods to training pigeons for use as missile guidance systems. The control system for the missile involved a lens at the front of the missile that projected an image of the ground below to a screen inside. There, Skinner put three pigeons, in little harnesses, each bird trained to recognize the target and peck at it. As long as at least two of the three pigeons pecked at the center of the screen, the missile would fly straight. However, if two or all three pigeons pecked off-center, this would cause the missile to change course. Skinner hoped the military would use his system for anti-submarine warfare. However, despite the encouraging initial results, the military did not adopt the Skinner pigeon system, because of another, top-secret project unknown to Skinner—radar guidance. Thus, Skinner's pigeons never saw service in World War II (B. F. Skinner, 1959).

Around the same time, Skinner's daughter Deborah was born. Rather than bundle her in layers of warm clothing for the winter, Skinner built Deborah a

Deborah Skinner in her heated crib, with her mother looking on.

heated crib that allowed her to play and sleep wearing only a diaper. The *Ladies Home Journal* ran a profile of the famous scientist, focusing on his childrearing experiences; the article reported that little Deborah was happy and healthy, and showed a picture of the girl frolicking in her heated crib (B. F. Skinner, 1945). The story was picked up by various news services, which ran the photo along with the article. Then, as now, the media didn't always get their facts quite right, and a series of negative stories appeared on Skinner, many of which confused the heated crib with the Skinner boxes used to train animals in the lab. As recently as 2004, a book asserted that Skinner had wired Deborah's crib to automatically provide food and shocks to his daughter, just like pigeons in the lab (Slater, 2004). An adult Deborah angrily rebutted the claims in a newspaper article entitled "I Was Not a Lab Rat" (D. Skinner, 2004).

Today, B. F. Skinner's name is far better known than Watson's or Thorndike's, because his influence extended beyond the laboratory. Fulfilling his early ambition of becoming a writer, Skinner wrote several popular books, including *Walden Two* (1948), which described a highly regulated utopian society in which socially desirable behaviors would be maintained through the same kind of training regimens Skinner applied to his pigeons and rats. Although the book had disappointing initial sales, its reputation and readership grew in the following decades and it became a best-seller in the late 1960s and early 1970s, especially on university campuses, where it appealed to students' growing interest in alternative lifestyles and communal living.

By the middle of the twentieth century, Skinner was the most famous psychologist in the world, partly due to his controversial best-seller *Beyond Freedom and Dignity* (1971). In this book, Skinner advocated an extreme form of behaviorism, often called **radical behaviorism,** in which he asserted that consciousness and free will are illusions. Humans, like all other animals, he argued, function by blindly producing pre-programmed (learned) responses to environmental stimuli. Appearing at the end of the 1960s, a decade in which many people had broken free from societal control, the book attracted a great deal of attention, not all of it positive.

Skinner continued promoting radical behaviorism right up until the night of his death in 1990, which he spent working on a talk for an upcoming convention. The talk was to be titled "Can Psychology Be a Science of the Mind?" (His answer, of course, was a resounding no!) But by that time, mainstream psychology had moved past the strict confines of behaviorism to focus on the very mental events that Skinner and his fellow behaviorists had fought so hard to discredit.

Edward Tolman: Cognitive Maps

Edward Tolman (1886–1959) was born into a well-educated upper-class New England family. Tolman attended the Massachusetts Institute of Technology (MIT), where he studied chemistry. During his senior year he read William James's *Principles of Psychology*, and was so inspired that he abandoned his plans for a career in chemistry and instead pursued a graduate degree in psychology.

Tolman began building a series of rat mazes for the study of learning, much as Thorndike and Watson had done before him. In contrast to Watson, who had argued for a purely mechanical approach to describing rat learning as the formation of connections between stimuli and responses, Tolman was convinced that his rats were learning something more. He believed that they had goals and intentions such as finding the exit and seeking food. Rats, he argued, are intrinsically motivated to learn the general layout of mazes, forming what he called a **cognitive map,** an internal psychological representation of the spatial layout of the external world (Tolman, 1948). "Behavior reeks of purpose" was Tolman's well-known and oft-repeated maxim (Tolman, 1932).

In one series of studies, Tolman showed that cognitive maps are key for understanding how rats can apply what they have learned in novel situations. Rats, he showed, are able to find food in mazes by using alternative routes if their preferred route is blocked, as shown in Figure 1.7 (Tolman, 1948). They can also find their way to the goal if they are started from a novel position in the maze, rather than the usual start box. None of this could be explained by the learning of simple stimulus–response connections.

Tolman even showed that rats can learn cognitive maps in the absence of any explicit reward (such as food). He allowed some rats to freely explore a maze (like the one in Figure 1.7), with no food in it, for several days. Later, when he placed these rats in the maze with a food reward at one point ("goal box"), the rats learned to find the food much faster than rats not previously exposed to the maze. This, Tolman argued, showed that on the initial days, the rats were learning a cognitive map that they could exploit later. He called this **latent learning,** meaning learning that takes place even when there is no specific training to obtain or avoid a specific consequence such as food or shock (Tolman, 1932). Tolman argued that such latent learning is a natural part of our everyday life. The idea of latent learning challenged a strict behaviorist assumption that all learning reflects stimulus–response associations.

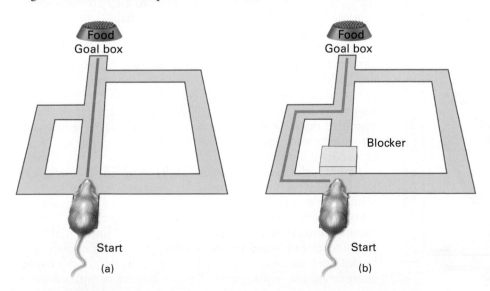

Figure 1.7 Cognitive maps in rats Tolman believed that rats form cognitive maps, internal representations of the layout of the world. (a) In one experiment, rats placed in a maze (at Start) learned to run directly to a box (Goal) where food was provided; the green line shows the rat's route. (b) If the preferred route was blocked, rats could easily find an effective alternative route (red line); this indicates that they had information about the spatial layout of the maze.

At a time when Clark Hull and other theorists were seeking to discover the rules of learning, Tolman formulated the very modern idea that there are, in fact, many different forms of learning. By emphasizing the importance of internal representations of the environment, and utilizing concepts such as purpose and intent that are not directly observable, only inferable, Tolman broke away from the stricter confines of behaviorist dogma, all the while satisfying the behaviorists' high standards of experimental control and methodological rigor. For this reason, Tolman is often referred to as a *neo-behaviorist*. His influential theoretical and experimental research—though at odds with many of his contemporary behaviorists—laid the foundation for cognitive studies of animal and human learning.

Interim Summary

Behaviorists argue that psychologists should study only observable events and should not attempt to speculate about what's going on inside an organism. Behaviorism doesn't deny that internal mental processes exist, just that they are unnecessary and inappropriate subjects for scientific study of behavior. John Watson, the father of behaviorism, proposed that psychology should be a purely experimental branch of natural science whose goal is the prediction and control of behavior in both animals and humans. Clark Hull developed comprehensive mathematical theories of animal and human learning, which could be rigorously tested in experimental studies. B. F. Skinner conducted detailed studies of the factors that control behavior, while at the same time taking the behaviorists' message to the broader public through widely read and controversial books.

Edward Tolman, a neo-behaviorist, combined the scientific rigor of the behaviorist methodology with consideration of internal mental events such as goals and cognitive maps of the environment. Although few modern psychologists are strict behaviorists, the behaviorists' emphasis on experimental data and the search for lawful and replicable regularities in behavior continues to influence all forms of psychology, including the cognitive studies of human learning and memory.

THE FAR SIDE® BY GARY LARSON

"Stimulus, response! Stimulus, response! Don't you ever *think?*"

1.5 The Cognitive Approach

The behaviorist approach to learning had great appeal. It was rigorous, it was precise, and it lent itself to mathematical specification. By avoiding the vague and unverifiable introspections of the early philosophers, it seemed to ensure that psychology would rise in the twentieth century to become a serious branch of science, alongside chemistry and physics. However, by the mid-1950s, it was becoming increasingly apparent that behaviorism could not, ultimately, deliver a full account of human behavior. As you've just read, it failed to account for Tolman's cognitive maps. It also failed to explain language, perception, reasoning, and memory: the fundamental components of higher-level human cognition.

Skinner, the radical behaviorist, had argued that language and language acquisition could be explained with behaviorist principles: as a (complex) series of stimulus–response associations (B. F. Skinner, 1957). To counter these claims, linguist Noam Chomsky wrote what may be the most influential book review ever published in the sciences: a critique of Skinner's book, demonstrating how and why behaviorist principles alone could not explain how children acquire complex aspects of language such as grammar and syntax (Chomsky, 1959). By the early 1960s, many psychologists interested in human cognition began to turn away from behaviorism, with its focus on animal research and the idea that all learning could be reduced to a series of stimulus–response associations. The stage was set for the rise of **cognitive psychology,** a new subfield of psychology that focused on human abilities such as thinking, language, and reasoning—the abilities not easily explained by a strictly behaviorist approach.

W. K. Estes and Mathematical Psychology

William K. Estes's long and productive career encompassed the science of learning and memory from behaviorism to cognitive science, with seminal contributions to both. Estes, born in 1919, began his graduate studies under the tutelage of Skinner during the early 1940s. The United States had not yet entered World War II. The Germans were using a new technology—rockets—to bomb England. As Londoners heard the whine of the rocket engines approaching, they stopped whatever they were doing—eating, walking, or talking—and waited for the explosions. After the rockets dropped elsewhere and people realized they were safe, they resumed their daily activities.

Intrigued by these stories from London, Estes and Skinner developed a new conditioning paradigm for rats that was similar, in some respects, to what Londoners were experiencing. This paradigm, called the **conditioned emotional response,** was a new technique for studying learned fear (Estes & Skinner, 1941). Estes and Skinner placed hungry rats in a cage that delivered food pellets whenever the rats pressed a lever. The cage also had a metal grid floor wired to deliver a mild shock to the rats' feet. Normally, the hungry rats busily pressed the lever to obtain food; but if the experimenters trained the rats to learn that a tone predicted an upcoming shock, the rats would freeze when they heard the tone, interrupting their lever presses and waiting for the shock. Measuring this freezing behavior allowed Estes to quantify trial-by-trial changes in the learned response. Within a few years, this conditioned emotional response paradigm became one of the most widely used techniques for studying animal conditioning, and it is still in use today. (In Chapter 10, you'll read that learning about emotions, such as fear, has become a broad subfield of learning and memory research.)

As soon as he completed his Ph.D., Estes was called into military service. He was stationed in the Philippines as the commandant of a prisoner-of-war camp, a not very demanding job that gave him lots of free time to read the mathematics books sent from home by his wife. When the war ended, Estes returned to the United States and to the study of psychology. Much to Skinner's dismay, Estes soon began to stray from his mentor's strict behaviorism. He began to use mathematics to describe mental events that could only be inferred indirectly from behavioral data, an approach quite unacceptable to behaviorists. Years later, in his autobiography, Skinner bemoaned the loss of Estes as a once-promising behaviorist, speculating that Estes's preoccupation with mathematical models of unobservable mental events was a war-related injury, resulting perhaps from too much time in the hot Pacific sun (Skinner, 1979).

Estes built on Hull's mathematical modeling approach to develop new methods for interpreting a wide variety of learning behaviors (Estes, 1950). Most learning theorists of that era, including Hull, assumed that learning should be viewed as the development of associations between a stimulus and a response. For example, suppose that a pigeon is trained to peck whenever it sees a yellow light, in order to obtain a bit of food. Hull assumed that this training caused the formation of a direct

W.K. Estes

Courtesy of William Estes

link between the stimulus and the response, so that later presentations of the yellow light evoked the peck-for-food response (Figure 1.8a).

Estes, however, suggested that what seems to be a single stimulus, such as a yellow light, is really a collection of many different possible elements of yellowness, only a random subset of which are noticed (or "sampled," in Estes's terminology) on any given training trial (Figure 1.8b). Only those elements sampled on the current trial are associated with the food. On a different trial, a different subset is sampled (Figure 1.8c), and those elements are now associated with the food. Over time, after many such random samples, most elements become associated with the correct response. At this point, any presentation of the light activates a random sample of elements, most of which are already linked with the response.

Estes called his idea *stimulus sampling theory*. A key principle is that random variation ("sampling") is essential for learning, much as it is essential for the adaptation of species in Charles Darwin's theory of evolution through natural selection (Estes, 1950). Estes's approach gave a much better account than other theories (such as Hull's) of the randomness seen in both animal and human learning, and it helped to explain why even highly trained individuals don't always make the same response perfectly every time: on any given trial, it's always possible that (through sheer randomness) a subset of elements will be activated that are not yet linked to the response. In Chapter 9 you'll see how Estes's stimulus sampling theory also explains how animals generalize their learning from one stimulus (e.g., a yellow light) to other, physically similar stimuli (e.g., an orange light), as Pavlov had demonstrated back in the 1920s.

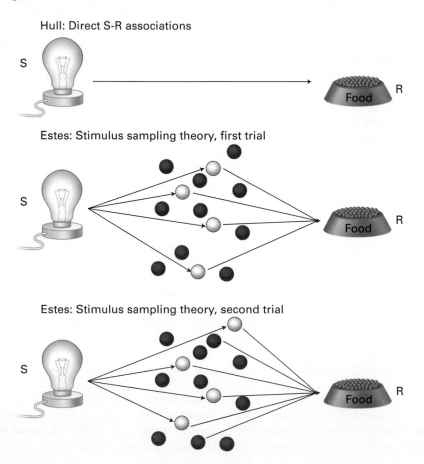

Figure 1.8 Stimulus–response models How does a stimulus (S) become associated with a response (R)? (a) Hull assumed that a direct link was formed between a stimulus (such as a yellow light) and a learned response (such as, in pigeons, pecking for food). (b) Estes proposed an intervening stage, in which a stimulus activates a random sample of elements encoding "yellow"; the activated elements are then associated with the response. (c) On a different trial, a different random subset is activated and associated with the response. Over time, with many such random samples, most elements become associated with the response. At this point, presentation of the light activates a random sample of elements, most of which are already linked with the response.

Estes's work marked the resurgence of mathematical methods in psychology, reviving the spirit of Hull's earlier efforts. Estes and his colleagues established a new subdiscipline of psychology, **mathematical psychology,** which uses mathematical equations to describe the laws of learning and memory. From his early work in animal conditioning, through his founding role in mathematical psychology, to his more recent contributions to cognitive psychology, Estes has continued to be a vigorous proponent of mathematical models to inform our understanding of learning and memory.

Gordon Bower: Learning by Insight

Gordon Bower was born in 1932 in Scio, Ohio, a small town struggling to survive the Great Depression. Inspired by the movie *The Lou Gehrig Story,* Bower resolved at the age of 8 to become a professional baseball player. After playing varsity baseball in college, he had two career choices: professional baseball or graduate school in psychology. Although tempted by the former, Bower figured he had a better chance of long-term success in psychology than in baseball. In graduate school at Yale, Bower got caught up in the heady excitement of mathematical psychology, as he learned how Estes and other mathematical psychologists were striving to describe behavior with mathematical equations.

The dominant psychological learning theories of the time assumed that human learning, like animal learning, proceeded gradually through incremental changes either in association strengths (the Hull approach) or in the statistical probability of a correct response (the Estes approach), both of which predicted gradual transitions in learning performance. In contrast, Bower proposed a new "one-step" model of human learning. For example, suppose you are asked to guess the name of someone you don't know. In the beginning, you have no idea, but you try some names at random until, by good fortune, you guess correctly. From that point on, you know the correct answer. Unlike the smooth, incremental learning curves seen in classical conditioning, you go from ignorance to knowledge in a single trial. Similarly, if you've ever solved a difficult puzzle or word game, you may have experienced an "aha" moment of insight: Initially, you don't know the answer; then, all of a sudden, you do know it.

Although behaviorists had largely avoided talking about learning by insight, Bower thought it could be explained by a simple mathematical model (Bower, 1961; Bower & Trabasso, 1968). Suppose a person is assigned some task, such as figuring out the sequence in which to press four buttons to open a combination lock. In the beginning, he has no knowledge of the correct answer, but on each trial he will probably try out a different sequence. Odds are that it will take a few trials before he happens to try the correct order. But once he does, and he opens the lock— aha!—he knows the answer. Thereafter, he will press the correct sequence on all subsequent trials. Unlike the smooth learning curve shown in Figure 1.6b, this person's learning curve would look like the one in Figure 1.9a (on page 32): a long period of 0% correct responding, which transitions all at once into a period of 100% correct responding.

The problem, however, is that most psychologists report *average* learning curves for a group of people, summarizing the data from many participants in the same experiment. Bower's

Gordon Bower (seated) and his graduate advisor, **Neal Miller,** conduct a rat learning experiment at Yale University in the 1950s

Figure 1.9 Bower's learning by insight If individuals are assigned a task and have no knowledge of the correct answer, they start off by guessing, stumble across the correct answer, and from then on respond correctly. (a) One participant might guess incorrectly on each of the first 11 trials (making 0% correct responses), but on trial 12 he makes the correct response. Thereafter, he continues to give the correct response (100% correct from Trial 13 onward). Other participants might make their first correct response on a different trial, but all show the same basic pattern of an early period of incorrect responding followed by a sharp shift to uniformly correct responding. (b) If individual performances like that in (a) are averaged across many individuals, the result may be a smooth learning curve—even though no single participant showed such incremental learning.

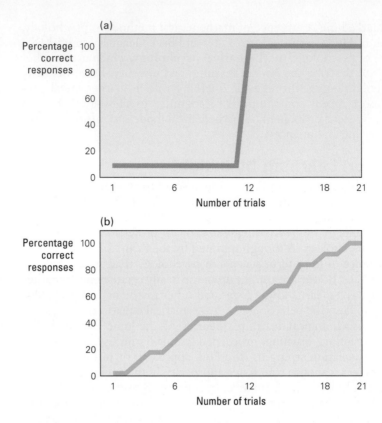

important insight was that, if every participant solves the task in one insightful moment, the trial on which this occurs will vary from one person to another. One participant might learn on the 5th trial, another might get lucky and guess the correct answer on the 1st or 2nd trial, and someone else might not guess the correct answer until the 15th trial. If a large number of participants are tested, the data will show that almost no one responds correctly on the 1st or 2nd trial; a few respond correctly on the 3rd or 4th trial; a few more respond correctly on the trials after that; and so on, until, by the end of the experiment, almost everyone is giving the correct response. If we graph the percentage of subjects who give the correct response on each trial of the combination-lock task, the result will look very much like a standard learning curve that moves incrementally from 0% to 100% across the experiment (Figure 1.10b), even though no *individual* participant ever showed incremental learning! By studying such phenomena, Bower showed that, to understand learning, it is necessary to consider individual performance, not just averages across a large group of participants.

Bower's influence on the field of memory research stems not only from his own research but also from his role as a prolific educator and mentor to young psychologists, many of whom went on to play major roles in the growing field of cognitive psychology.

George Miller and Information Theory

Estes and Bower were not the only ones becoming disillusioned with the strict confines of the behaviorist approach. Other psychologists began to seek answers to questions that were not so easily resolved by simply assuming an incrementally learned association between stimulus and response. One of these was George Miller, born in 1920, who grew up in Charleston, West Virginia, another child of the Depression era.

During World War II, many of Harvard's faculty worked on problems for the military. As a graduate student at Harvard, Miller was given the task of designing a jamming signal to disrupt German radio communications. This wartime research on communications led Miller to study other questions in speech perception, such as how context affects communication. For example, if a man floundering in the sea shouts, "Help, I'm drowning!" you might understand the message easily, even if the speech is garbled or indistinct—given the context, it's obvious what the man is trying to communicate. On the other hand, if you meet the same man on the street, with no prior expectation of what he might be trying to communicate, his speech would need to be much clearer for you to understand the message: is he greeting you, asking for directions, telling you your shoelaces are untied, or soliciting money?

While puzzling over this, Miller read a paper that described *information theory*, a mathematical theory of communication that provides a precise measure of how much information is contained in a message, based not only on the message itself but also on the listener's prior knowledge (Shannon, 1948). For example, if a friend tells you that Chris, a student in his psychology class, is male, how much information is in the message? That depends on what you already know. If you already know that all the students in his class are male, then the message contains no new information. If, however, you know that the class is co-ed, information theory would say that your friend's message contains 1 *bit* of information, where a bit is a "binary digit," 1 or 0, that can represent two alternative states (such as 1 = female, 0 = male). If you ask your friend about Chris's gender, all he has to do is reply "1" (female) or "0" (male)—a message composed of a single bit of information is all the answer you need.

Miller's goal was to adapt information theory to psychology. Specifically, could information theory help us understand how people make judgments about the magnitude of various stimuli. How bright is it? How loud? How high in pitch? Miller discovered that people's capacity to make judgments across a range was limited to about seven alternative values (this is why many rating scales ask you to rate your opinions on a scale of 1 to 7).

At the same time, Miller was pursuing a seemingly unrelated project to measure the capacity of people's short-term memory for digits: he would read aloud strings of numbers and ask people to repeat the numbers from memory. Most people, Miller found, could accurately repeat strings of up to 5-9 numbers, but almost no one could remember strings of 10 or more digits. The average memory capacity for numbers (sometimes called a *digit span*) seemed to be about 7 digits, plus or minus 2.

Noting that a capacity of seven appeared in both projects—magnitude rating and digit span—Miller used this seemingly superficial connection as the humorous title of a paper that summarized both projects: "The Magical Number Seven, Plus or Minus Two" (Miller, 1956). The paper became one of the most influential and oft-cited papers in cognitive psychology, and spurred later research that showed similar limits on the capacity of

George Miller

Jon Roemer

human memory for other kinds of information: the "magic number seven" applied not just to digits but to words, pictures, and even complex ideas. Miller's central message was that the human mind is limited in capacity, that information theory provides a way to measure this capacity, and that these limits apply throughout a diverse range of human capabilities.

Herbert Simon and Symbol-Manipulation Models

Herbert Simon (1916–2001) won the 1978 Nobel Prize in Economic Science for his work on why people sometimes choose the first thing available instead of waiting for a later but better option. But psychologists and computer scientists remember him as one of the fathers of **artificial intelligence (AI),** the study of how to build computers that can perform behaviors that seem to require human intelligence. Today, it's common to think of computer memory as a useful metaphor for human memory. This insight is largely due to the work of Simon and his colleagues, who developed a new computational approach to the psychology of memory and cognition.

Born in Milwaukee, Wisconsin, Herbert Simon was the son of immigrants from Germany. After earning his Ph.D., he took a few teaching positions before landing at the newly established industrial administration school at the Carnegie Institute of Technology (now Carnegie-Mellon University). There, Simon was granted access to a new type of machine, the computer. At the time, most people viewed the computer as just a tool for fast numerical calculations; Simon and his colleague Alan Newell quickly realized that the computer could be applied to understanding human intelligence.

In contrast to theories of human learning and memory (such as those of James, Hull, and Estes) that were based on associations, Simon and Newell argued that cognition could be understood by describing how the mind manipulates **symbols,** internal representations of concepts, qualities, ideas, and other things found in the outside world (Newell & Simon, 1976). For example, in their model of human memory, symbols might represent different animals, people, and objects. A small portion of such a memory is shown in Figure 1.10. At first glance, this may look similar to earlier associationist models, like those of William James (compare with Figure 1.2). The key difference is that Simon's models allow for a wide range of differently labeled

Herbert Simon

Bettmann/Corbis

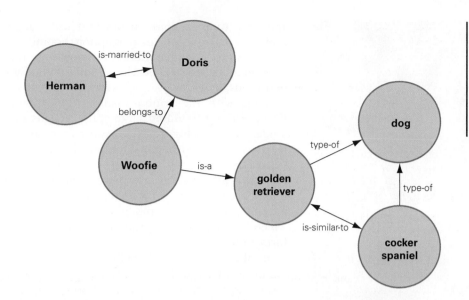

Figure 1.10 A symbol-manipulation model of memory
Symbols, shown here as circles, represent different animals, objects, and people. Associations between symbols are encoded as labeled lines that specify certain relationships, such as "is-a," "is-similar-to," and "belongs-to."

associations such as "is-a," "is-married-to," and "belongs-to" that link symbols to each other. The system shown in Figure 1.10 can store specific relationships, such as "Herman is married to Doris," and "Woofie belongs to Doris" and "Cocker spaniel is a type of dog and is similar to a golden retriever." Simon and Newell also provided rules and procedures for how to manipulate, search, and update these symbols and associations. Models of learning and memory that store and manipulate symbols and labeled links are called **symbol-manipulation models.**

Using their symbol-manipulation models, Simon and Newell argued that the human mind operates much like a computer, encoding, storing, and retrieving information (Newell, Shaw, & Simon, 1958). Their work in the 1960s formed the core of a new revolution in cognitive psychology in which computers were used to study thinking, reasoning, and memory. Other researchers picked up the thread, including Gordon Bower and his graduate student John Anderson, who produced a computer simulation of how people use memory to organize and access new knowledge (Anderson & Bower, 1973).

Simon acknowledged that his work on so-called thinking machines made many people uncomfortable. "The definition of man's uniqueness has always formed the kernel of his cosmological and ethical systems," he wrote. "With Copernicus and Galileo, [mankind] ceased to be the species located at the center of the universe, attended by the sun and stars. With Darwin, he ceased to be the species created and specially endowed by God with soul and reason. . . . As we begin to produce mechanisms that think and learn, he has ceased to be the species uniquely capable of complex, intelligent manipulation of his environment" (Simon, 1977). Discomfort or not, there was no stopping the revolution. Newell and Simon's computer models, and those that followed, have forever changed the way we think about minds and machines.

David Rumelhart and Connectionist Models

David Rumelhart, born in 1942 in rural South Dakota, was the first of his family to graduate from college. As a graduate student working under Estes, Rumelhart developed a firm grounding in both psychology and mathematics. He began to

David Rumelhart

Courtesy of Don Rumelhart

apply the tools of mathematics to a wide range of problems in cognition and perception, hoping to improve on the cognitive models of knowledge representation championed by Simon and others. By the mid 1970s, however, Rumelhart was becoming disillusioned with the symbol-manipulation approach. For one thing, building large-scale versions of the model shown in Figure 1.10 required the programmer to know in advance all the possible kinds of labeled links that could exist, and then to laboriously enter this information into the computer. This was fine (if a bit daunting) for a computer program, but not so satisfying as a model of the human mind, which doesn't have a programmer to supply such information.

By the late 1970s, Rumelhart and his colleague James McClelland shared a growing belief that cognition did not function like a symbol-manipulation system but was best understood as networks of uniform and unlabeled connections between simple processing units called *nodes*. Borrowing a term from Thorndike (who had thought much the same), Rumelhart and McClelland called such networks **connectionist models** (Rumelhart & McClelland, 1986).

In connectionist models, ideas and concepts in the external world are not represented as distinct and discrete symbols (such as "golden retriever" and "dog" in Figure 1.10), but rather as patterns of activity over populations of many nodes. In a connectionist model, a golden retriever might be represented by a pattern of activation across a set of nodes (the yellow circles in Figure 1.11a). A cocker spaniel might be represented by a different pattern of nodes (blue circles in Figure 1.11b). Such a representation is known as a **distributed representation,** because the information is distributed across the many different nodes, similar to what Estes had proposed in his stimulus sampling theory. Remember that in Newell and Simon's symbolic model of memory, the node for "cocker spaniel" needed a link to the node for "golden retriever" with the label "similar-to." In contrast, in a connectionist model, there are no labeled connections: the similarity of spaniels to retrievers emerges naturally because they activate common elements—the "dog" elements coded as yellow-and-blue circles in Figure 1.11c.

As you'll read in the next chapter, connectionist models were inspired, in part, by ideas about how the brain is organized. Part of the promise of connectionist models was that they would fulfill William James's hope for a psychology that links brain and behavior. In this way, connectionist models laid the groundwork for a more complete integration of neuroscience with psychology, which is the topic of the rest of the book.

After many productive years helping psychologists understand the computational power of networks of brain connections, David Rumelhart's own brain networks began to fail him. In 1998, at the age of 56, he was diagnosed with Pick's disease, an illness (similar to Alzheimer's disease) that causes degeneration of the brain. He is now cared for by his brother in Ann Arbor, Michigan, but is no longer able to speak or recognize old friends and colleagues. Like Clive Wearing, David Rumelhart has lost the vital memories that define who he is.

(a) "Golden retriever"

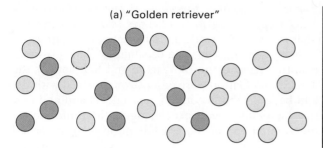

(b) "Cocker spaniel"

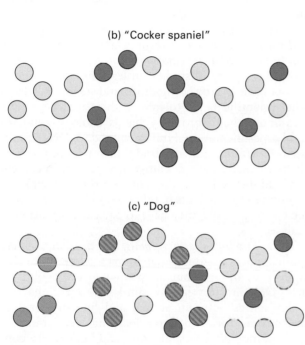

(c) "Dog"

Figure 1.11 Distributed representations (a) The representation of "golden retriever" activates one subset of nodes, shown in yellow. (b) "Cocker spaniel" activates a different subset, shown in blue. (c) The similarity between them—both are dogs—emerges naturally as a function of the overlap between representations, shown by the yellow-and-blue nodes.

CONCLUSION

As you read through the history of the psychology of learning and memory, from the perspectives of Aristotle to David Rumelhart, you probably noticed four themes interwoven throughout the narrative.

How do we learn to link two sensations or ideas in our mind? Aristotle identified the basic principles for association more than 2,000 years ago: contiguity, frequency, and similarity. Pavlov showed how we can study and measure learning about associations that exist in the world. Thorndike showed how reward and punishment govern which associations we learn to make. Both Hull and Skinner built upon the work of Thorndike, with Hull focusing on mathematical models to explain the factors that influence learning, and Skinner expanding the experimental analyses of reward and punishment and applying his research to society. Today, most psychologists take for granted the idea that memory involves learning associations to link ideas or concepts, although there are still arguments about exactly how these associations are formed and how they are used.

To what extent are our behaviors and abilities determined by our biological inheritance (nature) versus their being shaped by our life experiences (nurture)? Aristotle and Locke firmly believed that we enter the world as blank slates, with our experiences the sole factor influencing our behavior and capabilities. This position, empiricism, carried over into the behaviorism of Watson and Skinner. At the other extreme, Descartes, Locke, and Galton were more strongly allied with the nature (or nativist) camp and believed that we inherit our talents and abilities. Today, most researchers take the middle road: acknowledging the profound influence of genes (nature) on learning and memory, while noting that inherited abilities form a background against which a lifetime of experience (nurture) modifies the basic blueprint.

Can the psychological study of the mind be a rigorous scientific endeavor, held to the same standards as the physical sciences? If so, might there be universal principles of learning and memory that can be expressed as fundamental laws described by mathematical equations? Throughout the history of studies on learning and memory, philosophers and psychologists have borrowed methods and metaphors from physics, chemistry, and other scientific fields to inform their understanding. Galton and Ebbinghaus were among the first to show that psychology could, indeed, be the subject of careful experimentation. Hull attempted to devise mathematical equations to describe learning, and the tradition was continued by Estes and others working in mathematical and cognitive approaches. In current research, most psychologists hold themselves to the same rigorous principles of experimental methodology followed by scientists in other disciplines; if psychologists want their work to be taken seriously, they have to pay close attention to experimental design and analysis.

What do we, as humans, share in common with animals, and in what ways are we different? Most early philosophers assumed that humans were quite distinct from and innately superior to animals, but the proponents of evolution, such as Erasmus and Charles Darwin, showed how similar we are. Behaviorists also emphasized the similarities between animal and human learning, through the study of mechanisms for associative learning that could be demonstrated in several species, including rats, pigeons, and humans. In contrast, the early cognitive psychologists chose to focus on computer-based models of language and abstract reasoning—cognitive behaviors that are not easily studied in nonhuman animals. More recent efforts to reconcile the associationist theories of animal learning and the higher capabilities of human cognition are seen in the connectionist models of Rumelhart, McClelland, and their intellectual descendents. Today, many researchers think of cognition as a continuum, with some animals (e.g., rats and pigeons) perhaps possessing only limited capability for abstract reasoning, but others (e.g., dolphins and chimpanzees) capable of a degree of communication, reasoning, and symbol use that approaches that of humans.

And . . . what next? In the past few decades there has been a revolution in the field of learning and memory. As you will see in the next chapter, our growing ability to measure and manipulate brain function has fundamentally altered how we look at learning and memory. One consequence of this recent progress has been a fusion of neuroscience and psychology into the integrated study of learning and memory in animals and humans. Despite these recent changes, most current research in the field of learning and memory can be understood as building on the challenges, issues, and questions that have been evolving in philosophy and psychology over the centuries.

Key Points

- Learning is the process by which changes in behavior arise from experience through interaction with the world; memory is the record of past experiences acquired through learning. Neither learning nor memory is a single cohesive process; there are many kinds of memory and many ways to learn.

- Associationists believe that memory depends on associations, or links, between events, sensations, and ideas. An early associationist, Aristotle, argued that three key principles govern associations: contiguity (temporal and spatial), frequency, and similarity.

- William James took the idea of associationism further, suggesting that the act of remembering an event involves learning associations between the components that make up that event; activation of one component could then activate others, filling in the memory. The association between two events involves a linkage between common or related components.

- Empiricists believe that creatures are born as "blank slates" and that all knowledge comes from experience; nativists believe that the bulk of knowledge is inborn. Aristotle, John Locke, and John Watson were all empiricists; prominent nativists include Plato, René Descartes, and Francis Galton. The debate between these positions continues today, in the "nature versus nurture" debate, although many researchers now believe that nature (genes) provides a background that is modified by experience.

- Descartes was a dualist, believing that the mind and body are separate. He viewed the body as a machine that could be understood through mechanical principles, and described a reflex pathway from sensory stimulus to brain and back to motor response.

- Locke, a strong believer in empiricism, argued that all humans are born with equal potential for knowledge and success, and so all should have equal access to education and opportunity.

- The theory of evolution states that species change over time, with new traits or characteristics passed from one generation to the next. Charles Darwin proposed that natural selection ("survival of the fittest") is a mechanism for evolution and that evolution occurs when a trait has three properties: inheritability, natural variation, and relevance to survival or reproductive success.

- Galton believed that all our natural abilities are inherited, and he developed much of modern statistics and experimental methodology in his efforts to prove this.

- Hermann Ebbinghaus, best remembered for his studies on memorizing nonsense syllables, developed basic experimental techniques for the study of human memory and forgetting that are still used today.

- Ivan Pavlov developed a technique, called classical (or Pavlovian) conditioning, for studying how animals learn that an (initially) neutral stimulus (a bell) can predict an upcoming significant event (food or shock).

- Edward Thorndike used puzzle boxes to study how animal behavior is modified by consequences, such as reward or punishment. His law of effect states that the probability of a particular behavioral response increases or decreases depending on the consequences it elicits.

- Behaviorists sought to distance themselves from the introspective methods of philosophers and psychologists who pondered the inner workings of their own minds, and instead argued that psychology should be the study of observable behaviors.

- John Watson, an early behaviorist, conducted systematic sensory-deprivation studies to determine how rats learn to navigate through mazes.

- B. F. Skinner promoted radical behaviorism, arguing that consciousness and free will are illusions and that even "higher" cognitive functions such as human language can be explained as a series of learned stimulus–response associations. He also developed many tools and procedures for studying learning that are still in use today.

- Edward Tolman began to break away from strict behaviorism by studying how animals use goals and intentions; he believed that rats could form cognitive maps of their environment and that some learning (called latent learning) could occur even in the absence of explicit training or observable responses.

- Frustrated with the limits of strict behaviorism, a new wave of cognitive psychologists set out to study higher mental processes, such as consciousness and language, that were not easily explained by a strict behaviorist approach.

- Gordon Bower noted that all learning is not simple, smooth, and incremental, but can involve all-or-none moments of sudden insight.

- George Miller applied mathematical models of communication and information to the study of learning and memory. His work on the "magic number seven" demonstrated limits on both absolute judgments and short-term memory capacity.

- Mathematical psychology uses mathematical equations to describe laws of learning and memory. Clark Hull attempted to devise one complex equation to describe all the variables that interact during learning. His followers worked toward smaller goals of developing equations to describe basic kinds or components of learning. W. K. Estes used a mathematical psychology approach to describe how the randomness of perception affects memory and generalization.

- Herbert Simon and Alan Newell used the new technology of computers as a metaphor for the brain and also as a tool for implementing models of how the mind learns about and manipulates symbols.

- David Rumelhart and colleagues focused on connectionist models of memory and cognition. These are networks of simple processing units in which information is represented as a pattern of activity across many nodes.

Key Terms

artificial intelligence (AI), p. 34
associationism p. 4
behaviorism p. 22
blind design p. 18
classical conditioning p. 19
cognitive map p. 27
cognitive psychology p. 29
conditioned emotional response p. 29
confound p. 15
connectionist models p. 36
contiguity p. 4
control group p. 15

correlational study p. 15
data p. 4
dependent variable p. 18
distributed representation p. 36
double-blind design p. 18
dualism p. 6
empiricism p. 5
eugenics p. 16
evolution p. 11
evolutionary psychology p. 13
experiment p. 16
experimental group p. 15
experimental psychology p. 16

experimenter bias p. 18
extinction p. 19
forgetting p. 17
generalization p. 20
hypothesis p. 15
independent variable p. 18
instrumental conditioning p. 20
latent learning p. 27
law of effect p. 20
learning curve p. 19
learning p. 2
mathematical psychology p. 31
memory p. 2

nativism p. 5
natural selection p. 12
placebo p. 18
radical behaviorism p. 26
reflex p. 6
retention curve p. 17
stimulus p. 6
subject bias p. 18
symbol p. 34
symbol-manipulation models p. 35
theory p. 4

Concept Check

1. If John Watson were to conduct his studies with rats in mazes today, his methods of sensory deprivation would be reviewed by an ethics board. How might he have designed his experiments differently so as to minimize the animals' pain or suffering?

2. Several studies have shown a correlation between schizophrenia and smoking: people with schizophrenia are more likely than people without schizophrenia to smoke. Does this prove that schizophrenia causes smoking? Explain your answer.

3. Several studies have shown what seems to be a genetic influence on some kinds of memory ability: parents with high memory ability are likely to have children who also have high memory ability. How would an empiricist account for such findings?

4. As a child growing up near Manchester, England, Adrian always noticed a large number of hedgehogs dead on the roadside, having been hit by cars. Thirty years later, there seems to be far less roadkill, despite many more cars on the road. Adrian thinks this is evidence of natural selection: in the past 30 years, hedgehogs have evolved to be smart enough to stay off the roads. Is this possible? Could there be another explanation?

5. The 10 tips for better memory in "Learning and Memory in Everyday Life" on page 3 include several that spring directly from principles espoused by associationists (Aristotle, James, and others). Identify which ones and explain your choices.

6. Symbol-manipulation models capture something essential about the way we relate and use concepts. Connectionist models, on the other hand, don't require as many preconceived notions about the meaning of nodes and links. Which is a better model of the brain, and why?

Answers to Test Your Knowledge

Who's Who in the History of Learning and Memory?
1. Aristotle; Descartes
2. Locke
3. James
4. Erasmus Darwin; Charles (Darwin)
5. Francis Galton
6. Ebbinghaus; Pavlov; Thorndike

Further Reading

Dawkins, R. (1986). *The blind watchmaker*. New York: Norton. • A general introduction to Darwin's principles of natural selection and evolution. Dawkins's goal is "to persuade the reader, not just that the Darwinian world-view happens to be true, but that it is the only known theory that could, in principle, solve the mystery of our existence."

Hothersall, D. (2004). *History of psychology* (4th ed.). New York: McGraw-Hill. • A broad overview of the major historical figures in psychology and their contributions to the field, from the ancient Greeks to modern researchers.

Pinker, S. (2002). *The blank slate: The modern denial of human nature*. New York: Viking. • An accessible introduction to the role of nature and nurture in behavior, by the author of several popular books on the mind, brain, and evolution, including *The Language Instinct*. Pinker argues that an infant's mind is not a blank slate and that human beings have an inherited universal language structure and constraints on brain function.

Wearing, D. (2005). *Forever today: A memoir of love and amnesia*. London: Doubleday UK. • Clive Wearing's wife tells his story and her own. Although Clive's memory has improved somewhat in the two decades since his illness, he remains "out of time," living in an endless loop of just awakening. The only constants in his life remain his music and his love for his wife.

CHAPTER 2

The Neuroscience of Learning and Memory

IMAGINE YOU'RE A DOCTOR WORKING the night shift in an emergency room. Most of the patients come in with broken bones or severe colds, but one young woman is wheeled in unconscious, accompanied by her distraught mother. The nurse takes a case history and learns that the young woman, Jennifer, suffered accidental carbon monoxide (CO) poisoning from a faulty gas heater in the family home. Jennifer's mother found her unconscious in the basement, could not rouse her, and phoned 911. The ambulance team started Jennifer on oxygen. Now you give instructions to rush her to an oxygen chamber in the hospital.

The next patient to arrive is Sean, a 65-year-old man who experienced a terrible headache during the afternoon and then began complaining of numbness in his arms and legs. Thinking he was having a heart attack, his wife brought him to the hospital. But Sean isn't having a heart attack; he's having a stroke—a disruption of blood flow to the brain. You order an MRI (magnetic resonance imaging) scan for Sean to determine the location and extent of his damage, after which surgeons will try to repair the damaged blood vessels in his brain.

Both Sean and Jennifer survive the night, but their problems are not over. The next day, Jennifer is sluggish and confused, speaking gibberish and unable to understand anything that's said to her. Sean, on the other hand, is alert and can hold an intelligent conversation, but his movements are uncoordinated and he's unable to walk without assistance because he can't keep his balance.

Both of these patients are lucky to be alive, but they have sustained damage to their brains. Their different symptoms reflect the fact that different brain areas are affected. Jennifer's damage probably involves areas of the brain that store memories of how to generate and understand language; Sean's damage is probably affecting areas important for storing or retrieving memories of coordinated movement patterns.

The story of how we know about these parts of the brain, and what might be done to help Jennifer and Sean, is the story of brain research. While there's still a long way to go in understanding how the brain works, we know more than ever before about the brain's structure, its functions, and the ways in which it is modified during learning. New technologies allow researchers to look at healthy human brains as they form and retrieve memories, while new techniques for animal research allow them to measure and manipulate how the brain changes during learning.

2.1 A Quick Tour of the Brain

When Ancient Egyptians mummified a body, they first removed the important organs, preserving them in special airtight jars. Most important was the heart, which was thought to contain a person's essence. The brain they discarded, thinking it to be of little importance. (Paradoxically, Egyptian physicians wrote the first text on the behavioral effects of brain damage.) Many centuries later, Aristotle, one of the most empirically oriented philosophers in history, thought the brain served primarily to cool the blood. Today, there is still a debate about what defines the essence of a person, but researchers in the field of **neuroscience**—the study of the brain and the rest of the nervous system—overwhelmingly believe that the brain is the seat of learning and memory. There is no one particular experiment that confirms this hypothesis conclusively, but many observations over several centuries have convinced scientists that brain activity controls behavior and, by extension, controls the changes in behavior associated with learning and memory.

You'd think that scientists interested in learning and memory would focus their efforts on understanding how the brain enables these functions. But, as you read in the last chapter, most early studies of learning and memory focused on behavior, rather than on brain function. This is not because learning and memory researchers were oblivious to the role of the brain. Ivan Pavlov designed all of his behavioral experiments to answer questions about how the brain works. John Watson, the originator of behaviorism, started out studying how developmental changes in neural structures correlate with developmental changes in learning abilities. B. F. Skinner, considered by some to be the patron saint of learning research, began his career as a physiologist. Why, then, did researchers place so much emphasis on behavior rather than on brain function?

The simple answer is complexity. Brains are among the most complex structures in nature, and even as recently as 50 years ago, the complexity of the neural functions required for something as seemingly simple as a rat learning to run through a maze seemed to lie beyond the reaches of science. As new technology becomes available, however, study of the complexities of brain function becomes more manageable. Already, aspects of brain function that were inaccessible 50 years ago are being measured daily in laboratories and medical institutions around the world. These new technologies have dramatically increased the number of studies exploring neural mechanisms of learning and memory.

The Brain and the Nervous System

When most of us think about our learning and memory abilities—or any kind of ability—we usually think of the brain as running the show. And, certainly, the brain is critical. But it doesn't function alone.

Think of a submarine commander, navigating a vessel underwater from San Diego to Hawaii. At each step of the way, the commander receives crucial information about the outside world, including satellite tracking data to help locate the submarine's current position on a map, and sonar to help identify other objects in the water nearby. The commander also receives information about the inner workings of the submarine: gauges report on fuel level, oxygen reserves, and so on. Based on all this input, the commander issues commands: if there is an object in the water ahead, divert course to go around it; if oxygen is low, prepare to surface before the crew suffocates; and so on. Without the input of information, the commander couldn't make any useful decisions. At the same time, without output systems—steering and ballast and motors—none of the decisions could be executed. Successful operation of a submarine requires input systems to provide information about the outside world and internal conditions, a commander to integrate this information and decide how to act, and output systems to execute these commands.

Similarly, the brain is just one—albeit very important—component of a larger system called the **nervous system.** The nervous system consists of tissues that are specialized for distributing and processing information. These include cells called **neurons** that collect incoming information from the sensory systems (such as sight, taste, smell, touch, and sound) and from the rest of the body (information on conditions such as hunger and sleepiness), process this information, and respond to it by coordinating body responses (such as muscle movement and activity of internal organs). So, for example, you read in the last chapter how Pavlov's dogs learned to salivate whenever they heard a bell that signaled food was coming. Sound inputs entered a dog's ears, and from there, neurons carried the sound information to its brain, which processed the information and then generated a response by stimulating the salivary glands to produce saliva. Similarly, when you see a friend's face, visual information travels from your eyes through your nervous system to your brain and back out to the muscles of your face, which cause you to smile in greeting. The brain is the commander of the nervous system, but it can't operate without its inputs and outputs.

In vertebrates, the nervous system can be divided into two parts: the central nervous system and the peripheral nervous system. As its name suggests, the **central nervous system (CNS)** is where the bulk of the learning and memory action takes place: the CNS is composed of the brain and the spinal cord (Figure 2.1). The **peripheral nervous system (PNS)** consists of nerve fibers that carry information from sensory receptors (for example, visual receptors in the eye or touch receptors in the skin) into the CNS, and then carry instructions from the CNS back out to the muscles and organs. Most of these connections pass

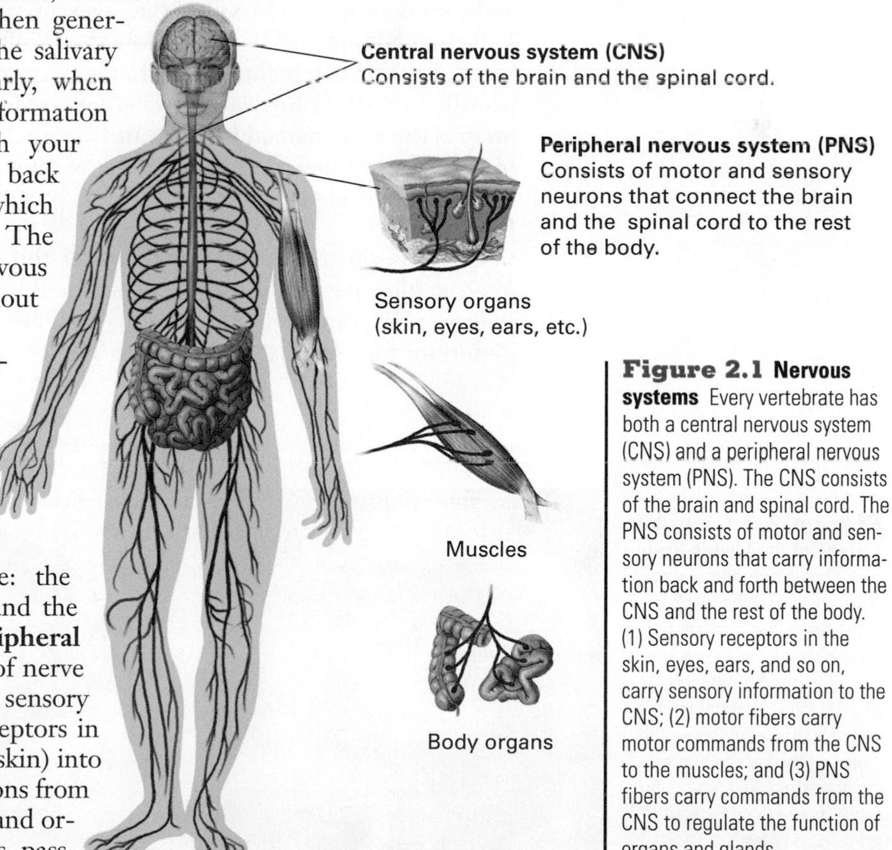

Central nervous system (CNS)
Consists of the brain and the spinal cord.

Peripheral nervous system (PNS)
Consists of motor and sensory neurons that connect the brain and the spinal cord to the rest of the body.

Sensory organs
(skin, eyes, ears, etc.)

Muscles

Body organs

Figure 2.1 Nervous systems Every vertebrate has both a central nervous system (CNS) and a peripheral nervous system (PNS). The CNS consists of the brain and spinal cord. The PNS consists of motor and sensory neurons that carry information back and forth between the CNS and the rest of the body. (1) Sensory receptors in the skin, eyes, ears, and so on, carry sensory information to the CNS; (2) motor fibers carry motor commands from the CNS to the muscles; and (3) PNS fibers carry commands from the CNS to regulate the function of organs and glands.

through the spinal cord, but a few—such as those of the light receptors in your eyes and the muscle fibers controlling how you move your eyes—travel directly to the brain without first stopping off in the spinal cord.

Although all vertebrates possess a CNS and PNS, there are big differences among the nervous systems of different species. Let's start with the vertebrate you're probably most familiar with: the human.

The Human Brain

The **cerebral cortex,** the tissue covering the top and sides of the brain in most vertebrates, is by far the largest structure of the human brain (Figure 2.2a). The word "cortex" is Latin for "bark" or "rind." If the cortex were spread out flat, it would be about the size of the front page of a newspaper, but only about 2 millimeters thick. To fit inside the skull, the cerebral cortex is extensively folded, much like a piece of paper crumpled into a ball. In humans, as in all vertebrates, the brain consists of two sides, or *hemispheres*, that are roughly mirror images of one another, so brain scientists talk about cortex in the "left hemisphere" or the "right hemisphere." In each hemisphere, the cortex is divided further into the **frontal lobe** at the front of the head, the **parietal lobe** at the top of the head, the **temporal lobe** at the side of the head, and the **occipital lobe** at the back of the head (Figure 2.2b). If you have trouble memorizing these four terms, remember: "*F*rontal is *F*ront, *P*arietal is at the *P*eak, *T*emporal is behind the *T*emples, and *O*ccipital lobe is *O*utermost."

Your cerebral cortex is responsible for a wide variety of perceptual and cognitive processes. The frontal lobes help you to plan and perform actions, the occipital lobes allow you to see and recognize the world, the parietal lobes enable you to feel the differences between silk and sandpaper, and the temporal lobes make it possible for you to hear and to remember what you've done.

Sitting behind and slightly below the cerebral cortex is the **cerebellum** (Figure 2.2b). The cerebellum contributes to coordinated movement and is thus especially important for learning that involves physical action. At the base of the brain is the aptly named **brainstem** (Figure 2.2b). The brainstem is a collection of structures connecting the brain to the spinal cord and also playing key roles in regulating automatic functions such as breathing and regulation of body temperature.

Other brain structures, buried under the cerebral cortex, are not visible in photographs like that in Figure 2.2a. You'll learn about many of these *subcortical* structures later in the book; for now, we'll just introduce a few that are especially important for learning and memory (Figure 2.3).

(a)

(b)

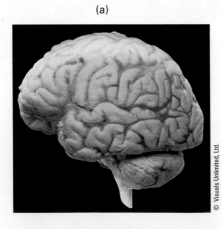
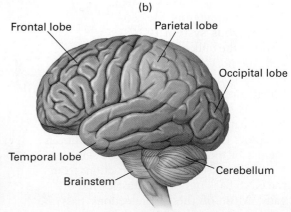

Figure 2.2 The visible surface of the human brain (a) A photograph of the human brain. (b) In each hemisphere of the brain, the cerebral cortex is divided into four principal areas: the frontal lobe, parietal lobe, occipital lobe, and temporal lobe. Below the cortex sit the cerebellum and the brainstem. The brainstem connects the brain to the spinal cord below.

Frontal lobe

Parietal lobe

Occipital lobe

Temporal lobe

Cerebellum

Brainstem

© Visuals Unlimited, Ltd.

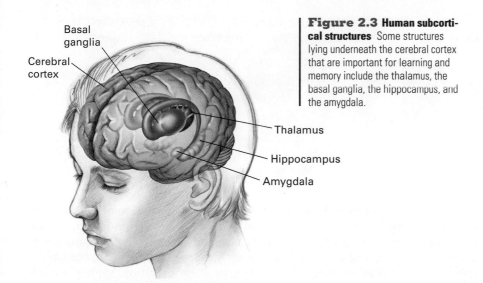

Basal ganglia

Cerebral cortex

Thalamus

Hippocampus

Amygdala

Figure 2.3 Human subcortical structures Some structures lying underneath the cerebral cortex that are important for learning and memory include the thalamus, the basal ganglia, the hippocampus, and the amygdala.

First, near the center of the brain lies the *thalamus*, a structure that receives sensory information (sights, sounds, touch, and so forth) from the peripheral nervous system and relays this information into the brain. You can think of the thalamus as a gateway through which almost all sensory information enters the brain. Sitting near the thalamus are the *basal ganglia*, a group of structures that are important for planning and producing skilled movements such as throwing a football or touching your nose. The *hippocampus* lies a little further away, inside the temporal lobes; it is important for learning new information about facts (say, the capital of France) or remembering autobiographical events (what you did last summer). Because you have two temporal lobes—one in each hemisphere of the brain—you also have one hippocampus on each side of the brain. Sitting at the tip of each hippocampus is a group of cells called the *amygdala*; this little brain region is important in adding emotional content to memories. If you remember the happiest—or saddest—day of your life, it is probably because your amygdala was particularly active at the time, adding emotional strength to those memories.

Scientists are only beginning to understand in any detail what these brain areas do and how they relate to learning and memory, but it is becoming increasingly clear that it's a mistake to think of the brain as a single organ, like a liver or a kidney. Instead, the brain is a collection of "experts," each making its own specialized contribution to what we do and what we think.

Comparative Brain Anatomy

In spite of the wide differences in nervous systems from species to species, much of what is known about the neural bases of learning and memory comes from studies of animals other than humans. Many aspects of a rat brain, a monkey brain, or even an insect brain are similar enough to a human brain to have made this possible. The study of similarities and differences among organisms' brains is called *comparative brain anatomy*. Comparative anatomical studies provide a foundation for understanding how brain structure and function relate to learning and memory abilities.

The brains of vertebrate species are similar in that all have a cerebral cortex, a cerebellum, and a brainstem; all vertebrate brains are also similarly organized into two hemispheres. Figure 2.4 shows the brains of some representative vertebrate species. In general, bigger animals have bigger brains. It might seem that

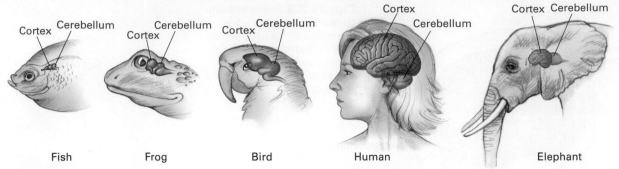

Fish   Frog   Bird   Human   Elephant

Figure 2.4 Comparative anatomy of the brains of several vertebrate species All vertebrate brains have two hemispheres; all have a recognizable cortex, cerebellum, and brainstem. But species differ in the relative volumes of these brain areas. In mammals (such as the human) and in birds, the cortex is much larger than the cerebellum; in fish and in amphibians (such as the frog), the cortex and cerebellum are more similar in size.

bigger brains go hand-in-hand with increased intelligence; human brains are bigger than frog brains, and humans seem to be ahead of frogs intellectually. But elephant brains are larger than human brains, and elephants, while quite clever in their own right, probably aren't significantly more intelligent than humans (at least they don't read and write, build cities, or study calculus). So, just as birds with larger wings are not necessarily better at flying than smaller birds, animals with larger brains are not necessarily smarter than other animals. In general, scientists don't yet fully understand the relationship between brain size and functional capacity.

Aside from overall brain volume, different species have different proportions of cerebral cortex. In humans, the cerebral cortex takes up a much larger percentage of total brain volume than it does in, say, frogs. Whereas the large human cortex has to be folded up to fit inside the human skull, the frog cortex can fit quite comfortably in its skull, without wrinkles. The relative size of the human cortex is intriguing because the cerebral cortex is associated with functions such as language and complex thought—the very things that seem to distinguish human cognition from cognition in other animals. And in fact, other species with relatively large cortex—including chimpanzees, dolphins, and, yes, elephants—are often those that we associate with the most ability for abstract thought, problem solving, and other "higher" cognitive functions.

Even within a species, different individuals have different brain sizes and layouts. For example, men's brains are on average significantly larger than women's brains. Again, this seems to reflect body size: men are not on average smarter than women, but they are on average bigger. On the other hand, the volume of the hippocampus is, on average, larger in women than men. This doesn't mean that women are better at learning new information, but it may imply a slight difference in how male and female brains process new information. (You'll read more on possible gender differences in learning and memory in Chapter 12.)

Learning without a Brain

Only vertebrates have both a CNS and a PNS. Some invertebrates—the octopus and the bee, for example—have a recognizable brain, but these brains are organized very differently from vertebrate brains. The octopus keeps much of its "brain" distributed around its body, particularly inside its rubbery legs. Yet the octopus is a remarkably smart animal: it can learn to find its way through a maze, it can learn to open a jar to get at the food inside, and there is even some evidence of observational learning, in which an octopus can learn from watching another octopus's behavior. In one such study, some octopuses (chosen to be "demonstrators") were trained that, when presented with a white ball and a red ball, they should reach out and grab the white ball. Untrained octopuses (chosen to be "observers") were then allowed to watch the demonstrators at work in a neighboring aquarium. Later, when the observers were shown the two balls, they promptly grabbed the white one—just as they had seen the demonstrators doing (Fiorito, Agnisola, d'Addio, Valanzano, & Calamandrei, 1998). Such learning by observation was once believed to be exclusive to "higher" animals such as humans, dolphins, and chimpanzees. But we now know that an octopus, with a decentralized brain, can do it too.

Other invertebrates, such as worms and jellyfish, have no recognizable brains at all. These animals have neurons that are remarkably similar to vertebrate neurons. But the neurons are few in number, and they're not organized into any central structure like a brain. For example, microscopic worms known as nematodes (which include the species that infects pigs, and the humans who eat them, causing trichinosis) have 302 individual neurons, compared with a few hundred million in the octopus and about 100 billion in the human. Nematode neurons are organized into a "nerve net" that is similar to a vertebrate PNS, but with no central processing area that resembles a CNS. Yet these little organisms can be surprisingly sophisticated learners; nematodes can learn to approach tastes or odors that predict food, and to avoid tastes and odors that predict the absence of food (Rankin, 2004). Not bad for a creature without a brain.

The octopus is an invertebrate, with a brain very different from that of mammals and other vertebrates; yet the octopus is a sophisticated learner.

Studies of invertebrates have been particularly rewarding because invertebrate nervous systems are fairly simple. For example, because a nematode has such a small number of neurons, it's possible to map out the entire set of connections in its nervous system in a way not possible for a human brain or even a rat brain. Many of the important insights into human brains and human learning came from studying how invertebrates learn and remember.

Observing Brain Structure and Function

Remember Jennifer and Sean, in the opening story of this chapter, who arrived at the emergency room suffering from brain damage? Jennifer suffered accidental poisoning from exposure to carbon monoxide leaking from a faulty heating unit. Carbon monoxide poisons a person by decreasing the ability of red blood cells to bind to oxygen, so less oxygen is carried throughout the body. The brain is the body's largest user of oxygen and thus is especially vulnerable when blood oxygen content drops. Sean suffered a stroke, a blocking or breaking of a blood vessel in his brain that caused reduced blood flow, starving the brain regions that normally depend on that blood vessel to supply their oxygen and nutrients.

Jennifer's and Sean's cases represent just two of the many ways in which humans can experience brain damage. Other causes of brain damage include head injuries and surgical removal of brain tissue (such as might be required to remove a tumor). Brain injury can also occur from malnutrition, from sensory deprivation, from chemotherapy and radiation therapy, from diseases such as Alzheimer's disease and Parkinson's disease—the list goes on and on. In each case, the first step in diagnosing the effects of brain damage on learning and memory abilities is to determine exactly where in the brain the damage lies.

The Dark Ages of Brain Science

Locating a specific site of brain damage is not as easy as finding a broken bone. Throughout most of human history, the only ways that physicians could detect brain damage were to look through holes in the patient's skull or to remove the patient's brain from the skull (either after the patient was dead or with the expectation that the patient would die in the process). These two techniques may seem crude, but they were critical to the development of neuroscience. For example, a

Greek physician named Galen (129–c. 199 AD), who served as a surgeon to Roman gladiators, observed that certain head injuries impaired gladiators' mental abilities. Galen used this evidence to turn the tide against Aristotle's influential claim that the heart was the seat of the intellect. Galen's views about brain function, gained from witnessing men with bashed-in skulls, greatly affected all subsequent studies of learning and cognition.

In the late 1800s, the French physician Paul Broca (1824–1880) studied a patient named Monsieur Leborgne, who was able to read and write normally but, when asked to speak, could say only the word "tan." When Leborgne died, Broca inspected the man's brain and discovered that part of the left frontal lobe was missing. From this observation, Broca concluded that the left frontal lobe contains a specialized region that is the center of speech production (Broca, 1986 [1865]). Broca's work gave birth to an entire field of research focused on associating deficits in mental and physical abilities with damage to specific brain regions.

Around the same time, Franz Joseph Gall (1758–1828), a German anatomist and physiologist, was also pioneering the idea that different areas of the cortex are responsible for different capabilities. Even among healthy people, he reasoned, individuals have different talents that should be reflected in the underlying shape of the brain: people with a special skill for learning language must have a larger-than-average part of the brain associated with speech; people prone to violence or aggressive behavior must have an overgrown "aggressiveness" area in the brain. Gall assumed that these differences in brain areas would be reflected in the shape of the skull, and so by identifying bumps in a person's skull, one could deduce which areas of the brain were enlarged—and, thus, what abilities and personality traits that person would display. Gall and his colleagues pursued a systematic study, called **phrenology,** in which they carefully measured the size and shape of many individuals' skulls and compared those measurements to the individuals' personalities and abilities (Gall & Spurzheim, 1810). The result was maps of the skull, showing the presumed function of the brain area underlying each portion of the skull—functions such as language skill, aggressiveness, friendliness, decision making, and so on.

Phrenology captured the public imagination. The field was quickly taken over by quacks, who found various ways of making the idea pay. Victorian firms often hired phrenologists to examine job applicants, in much the same way that personality tests are used by some companies today. The ruling classes also liked the phrenologists' idea that bumps on the skull could be used to prove the innate inferiority, and thus justify the institutionalized mistreatment, of criminals and other social undesirables.

There was just one problem. Phrenology's fundamental premise—that the shape of the skull reflects the shape of the brain underneath—was simply wrong. Bumps on the skull do not imply bulges in the underlying brain. Part of the problem with Gall's work was that he had no way to examine the brain of a living person. Measuring bumps on the skull was the closest he could get. And even Broca, who directly examined human brains, was limited to studying the brains of patients who had already died. It would be nearly 200 years before technology advanced to the point where scientists could see inside the skull of a healthy, living person.

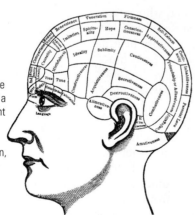

Phrenology maps attributed various aspects of cognition and personality to different regions of the brain. Enlargement of a brain area was thought to represent an enhancement of the corresponding function, detectable as a bump on the skull.

© Charles Walker/Topfoto/The Image Works

NAMES, NUMBERS AND LOCATION OF THE MENTAL ORGANS.

1. AMATIVENESS.—Connubial love, affection.
A. CONJUGAL LOVE.—Union for life, pairing instinct.
2. PARENTAL LOVE.—Care of offspring, and all young.
3. FRIENDSHIP.—Sociability, union of friends.
4. INHABITIVE.—Love of home and country.
5. CONTINUITY.—Application, consecutiveness.
E. VITATIVENESS.—Clinging to life, tenacity, endurance.
6. COMBATIVENESS.—Defence, courage, criticism.
7. DESTRUCTIVENESS.—Executiveness, push, propelling power.
8. ALIMENTIVENESS.—Appetite for food, etc.
9. ACQUISITIVENESS.—Frugality, economy, to get.
10. SECRETIVENESS.—Self-control, policy, reticence.
11. CAUTIOUSNESS.—Guardedness, care-taking, safety.
12. APPROBATIVENESS.—Love of applause and display.
13. SELF-ESTEEM.—Self-respect, dignity, authority.
14. FIRMNESS.—Stability, perseverance, steadfastness.
15. CONSCIENTIOUSNESS.—Sense of right, justice.
16. HOPE.—Expectation, anticipation, perfect trust.
17. SPIRITUALITY.—Intuition, presence, faith.
18. VENERATION.—Worship, adoration, deference.
19. BENEVOLENCE.—Sympathy, kindness, mercy.
20. CONSTRUCTIVENESS.—Ingenuity, invention, tools.
21. IDEALITY.—Taste, love of beauty, poetry and art.
B. SUBLIMITY.—Love of the grand, vast, magnificent.
22. IMITATION.—Copying, aptitude for mimicry.
23. MIRTH.—Fun, wit, ridicule, facetiousness.
24. INDIVIDUALITY.—Observation, curiosity to see.
25. FORM.—Memory of shape, looks, persons, things.
26. SIZE.—Measurement of quantity by the eye.
27. WEIGHT.—Control of motion, balancing.
28. COLOR.—Discernment, and love of colors, hues, tints.
29. ORDER.—Method, system, going by rule, arrangement.
30. CALCULATION.—Mental arithmetic, numbers.
31. LOCALITY.—Memory of place, position, travels.
32. EVENTUALITY.—Memory of facts, events, history.
33. TIME.—Telling when, time of day, dates, punctuality.
34. TUNE.—Love of music, sense of harmony, singing.
35. LANGUAGE.—Expression by words, signs or acts.
36. CAUSALITY.—Planning, thinking, philosophy.
37. COMPARISON.—Analysis, inferring, illustration.
C. HUMAN NATURE.—Sagacity, perception of motives.
D. SUAVITY.—Pleasantness, blandness, politeness.

Structural Neuroimaging: Looking inside the Living Brain

Today, several techniques are available that allow physicians to see a living person's brain without causing damage or malfunction. These modern techniques for creating pictures of anatomical structures within the brain are called **structural neuroimaging,** brain imaging, or "brain scanning." The brain scans produced by these methods can show the size and shape of brain areas, and they can also show **lesions,** areas of damage caused by injury or illness.

One method of brain imaging is **computed tomography (CT).** CT scans are created from multiple x-ray images. If you've ever passed through airport security and seen an x-ray of your luggage, you've seen how an x-ray can show the internal structure of the object being scanned. The trouble is that everything appears shadowy and flattened into two dimensions. An x-ray may show a comb and a toothbrush lying on top of each other in the suitcase, but it's impossible to tell which item is on top and which is on the bottom. Similarly, when doctors x-ray the body, the resulting image can show the presence of an abnormality, such as a broken bone or a tumor, but not the depth at which this abnormality lies.

CT provides a way around this problem by taking multiple x-rays at multiple angles, using a computer to integrate the various signals to generate images that look like "slices" or cross-sections through the body. Doctors can then look at multiple slices to pinpoint the exact location of internal anatomical structures in three-dimensional space. A CT scan can show the location of an abnormality such as a tumor with much better accuracy than a single x-ray. Unfortunately, the soft tissues that make up the brain show up much less clearly on CT scans than do bones and tumors. So, although the advent of CT opened new vistas in brain science, the technique is in waning use by brain researchers.

Today, the use of CT for structural brain imaging has largely been supplanted by **magnetic resonance imaging (MRI),** a technique that uses changes in magnetic fields to generate images of internal structure. MRI employs an extremely powerful magnet. Usually, the magnet is shaped like a giant tube, and the patient lies on a pallet that slides into the tube. The magnet aligns the magnetic properties of a small fraction of the atoms within the patient's brain (or whatever part of the body is under study). Next, radio waves are broadcast that disturb the atoms, causing them to generate tiny electrical currents. When the radio waves are stopped, the atoms return to their stable, aligned state. Different brain regions require different amounts of time to return to their stable state, depending on the density of atoms in the region. A computer collects all the signals emitted and, as with CT, uses them to generate images that look like slices of the brain. For example, a slice taken vertically through the middle of the brain results in a cross-section showing the cerebral cortex, cerebellum, and brainstem, as well as the patient's facial structures (Figure 2.5a). A horizontal slice taken at the level of the eyeballs would show a different cross-section (Figure 2.5b).

Figure 2.5 MRI images (a) This "slice," taken near the center of the head, shows a cross-section through the cortex and cerebellum, with the brainstem and upper portion of the spinal cord visible, as well as the nose and mouth cavities. (b) A horizontal slice taken at the level of the eyeballs (visible at the top of the image) contains little cortex (since the slice is so low) but captures the low-hanging cerebellum.

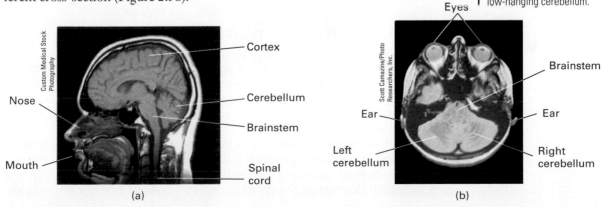

(a)   (b)

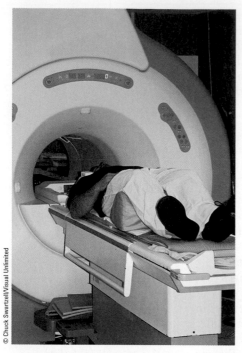

In magnetic resonance imaging (MRI) of the head, the patient lies with his head in a tube that contains a powerful magnet and a source of radio waves. Using data obtained from this machine, a computer measures the density of atoms at various locations in the brain and constructs a high-resolution image showing the brain's interior structures.

© Chuck Swartzel/Visual Unlimited

Brain lesions show up as blotches on an MRI image, indicating areas where brain tissue has been damaged or destroyed. In the case of Sean in our introductory story, MRI revealed damage to his right cerebellum, (a healthy cerebellum is visible in Figure 2.5b). As you'll read in Chapter 4, the cerebellum is important for coordinating movement, which is why Sean has trouble walking and balancing. Jennifer's MRI would look different. Her cerebellum would be fine, but there might be signs of damage in the left hemisphere of her cerebral cortex, especially in the left temporal lobe. This part of the brain is important for language and for new memory formation; you'll read more about this later in the book when we discuss fact and event memory and language learning.

For Sean and Jennifer, structural brain imaging reveals obvious brain damage, but not all brain damage is easily visible in structural images. Sometimes, areas of the brain don't work properly even though an MRI scan doesn't reveal any obvious abnormality. Furthermore, although structural imaging techniques such as CT and MRI are powerful research tools that have greatly increased our understanding of the brain, they all share a fundamental limitation: knowing the anatomical characteristics of a brain structure doesn't necessarily tell us much about what that structure actually does in normal operation. For this, we have to turn from brain to behavior.

Interim Summary

Vertebrates have both a central nervous system (that is, a brain and spinal cord) and a peripheral nervous system (connections to muscles and sensory receptors). All vertebrate brains have several key components, including the cerebral cortex, the cerebellum, and the brainstem. However, vertebrate species have different overall brain size and different relative sizes of various brain regions. Although "higher" animals such as humans and other primates have larger brains than "lower" animals such as rats and birds, brain size alone doesn't reliably predict differences in learning and memory abilities. Invertebrates can also accomplish feats of learning and memory, even though some (e.g., the octopus or bee) have brains very unlike vertebrate brains, while others (e.g., the nematode) have no recognizable brain at all.

Structural brain imaging techniques (such as CT and MRI) provide images of the physical structure of a living brain. CT is based on multiple x-rays; MRI is based on changes in magnetic fields. Both techniques involve computer reconstruction of signals to generate images that look like cross-sections (slices) through the brain.

2.2 From Brain to Behavior

Today, phrenology is dismissed as a pseudo-science, much like astrology—that is, a field of study that has no basis in scientific fact. However, while acknowledging phrenology's errors and its abuse, we must also acknowledge that Gall was fundamentally correct in his assumption that brain function could be localized. He was wrong only in the method he used to assign functions to specific parts of the brain.

Modern brain scientists assume that brains are composed of multiple systems that specialize in collecting, processing, and storing particular kinds of information. But there is no one-to-one relationship, as phrenologists supposed, with each individual function or ability performed in a dedicated corner of the brain.

Instead, one brain area may play a role in many functions, and one function may rely on contributions from many brain areas.

What makes each of these brain regions perform a particular function? Major factors determining what a brain region does are the kind of input it receives and the kind of output it produces.

Information Pathways in the Central Nervous System

In Chapter 1, we defined learning as a change in behavior that occurs as a result of experience. Thus, when Pavlov's dogs began to salivate whenever they heard the bell that signaled food, this change in behavior—salivation—represented learning about the relationship between bell and food. But even before Pavlov began using the dogs in his experiments, they would salivate when they saw food. This salivation is not learned; it is a reflexive behavior that dogs (and other mammals) are born with; it helps the digestive system get ready to process incoming food.

A **reflex** is an involuntary and automatic response "hardwired" into an organism; in other words, it is present in all normal members of a given species and does not have to be learned. Just like Pavlov's dogs, humans have a salivation reflex in response to the sight and smell of food. This is only one of several reflexes that babies are born with: newborns suck when they encounter a nipple (sucking reflex), hold their breath when submerged underwater (the diving reflex), and grasp a finger so tightly that they can support their own weight (the palmar grasp reflex). Adults have reflexes too, such as the knee-jerk reflex when the doctor hits your knee with a rubber mallet, and an eyeblink reflex when someone blows air at your eye.

How do reflexes work? Recall from Chapter 1 that Descartes explained reflexes as hydraulic movements caused by spirits flowing from the brain into the muscles. For many years, scientists accepted this explanation, assuming that there must be some kind of fluid carrying instructions from the brain to the muscles. It wasn't until the early twentieth century that researchers discovered this is not the case and that the brain isn't in absolute control of the muscles at all.

Behavior without the Brain: Spinal Reflexes

In the early 1800s, Scottish surgeon Charles Bell (1774–1842) and French physiologist François Magendie (1783–1855) were busily studying the nature of nerve fibers passing into and out of the spinal cord. The two men were bitter rivals, with Bell's supporters claiming that their man published his ideas first and that Magendie later stole them. Bell worked out most of his theories by reason and logic, in the tradition of philosophers like Locke and Descartes. Magendie, in contrast, was constantly experimenting with animals to see what would happen. In fact, Magendie became notorious for performing live dissections on animals during his public lectures. In one lecture, Magendie took an awake greyhound and nailed its paws and ears to the table. After dissecting many nerves in the dog's face, Magendie left the dog for the night so that he could continue the dissection the next day. Public outrage over such incidents helped give birth to the animal rights movement.

These gruesome experiments enabled Magendie to identify two specific types of nerve fibers: one set carrying sensory information from the PNS into the spinal cord, and a second set carrying motor signals back from the spinal cord to the muscles (Magendie, 1822). If a pinprick or other painful stimulus was applied to a dog's leg, the leg would jerk reflexively (just as you'd pull your leg away if someone pricked you). If the sensory fibers were cut, the dog's sensation

With the palmar grasp reflex, this infant's grasp can support her full weight.

Johns Hopkins Medical Institution

of pain disappeared, but the dog could still move its leg normally. On the other hand, if the motor fibers were cut, the animal could still feel pain, but not make the reflexive leg movement. Magendie's work confirmed (or instigated) Bell's idea that sensory and motor fibers are separated in the spinal cord (Bell, 1811).

The rivalry between Bell and Magendie was not resolved in their lifetime, but the finding that the spinal cord has two parallel nerve systems, one devoted to sensing and the other to responding, is now called the *Bell-Magendie law of neural specialization*, to acknowledge both men's contributions. The law is important historically because it represents the first step toward understanding the physiological mechanisms of learning.

Following up on this work, English physiologist Charles Sherrington (1857–1952) conducted many studies on dogs whose spinal cord had been surgically cut. When the spinal cord is severed below the brainstem, it no longer receives any signals from the brain. Yet such surgically altered dogs could still show many basic reflexes, such as jerking their leg away from a painful stimulus. Because the brain could not be contributing to these reflexes, the reflexes had to be generated by the spinal cord alone. In fact, we now know that sensory inputs traveling into the spinal cord can activate motor fibers traveling out of the spinal cord, without waiting for brain involvement. If you've ever stuck your hand into dangerously hot or cold water and jerked it away almost before realizing what you've done, or watched your knee jerk in response to the doctor's rubber mallet, then you've experienced a reflex mediated by your spinal cord without needing any help from your brain.

Sherrington concluded that such simple "spinal reflexes" could be combined into complex sequences of movements and that they were the basis of all behavior (Sherrington, 1906). Sherrington's description of reflexes differed from that of Descartes in that spinal reflexes did not depend on the brain and did not involve the pumping of spirits or fluids into the muscles. Sherrington received a Nobel Prize in 1932 for his work in this area, and he is now considered to be one of the founding fathers of neuroscience. Sherrington's ideas provided the groundwork and motivation for Pavlov's early investigations of learning in dogs (Pavlov, 1927) and have continued to influence learning and memory researchers ever since.

If the spinal cord controls reflexes, and complex actions are simply combinations of these reflexes, then where does the brain come in? Sensory fibers enter the spinal cord and connect to motor fibers there, but some fibers also travel up to the brain. The brain processes these inputs and produces its own outputs, which can travel back down the spinal cord and out to the muscles. In effect, the parallel sensory and motor pathways traveling up and down the spinal cord to and from the brain are similar to the parallel sensory and motor pathways that Magendie identified traveling into and out of the spinal cord. The Bell-Magendie law of neural specialization thus applies not just to the spine but to the entire central nervous system.

Incoming Stimuli: Sensory Pathways into the Brain

Let's now consider those sensory pathways that send branches up to the brain. As noted earlier in the chapter, most sensory information enters the brain through the thalamus. The thalamus in turn distributes these inputs to cortical regions specialized for processing particular sensory stimuli, such as the primary auditory cortex (A1), the primary somatosensory cortex (S1), and the primary visual cortex (V1). A1 is located in the temporal lobe, S1 in the parietal lobe, and V1 in the occipital lobe (Figure 2.6). Such areas, collectively called *primary sensory cortices*, are the first stage of cortical processing for each type of sensory information.

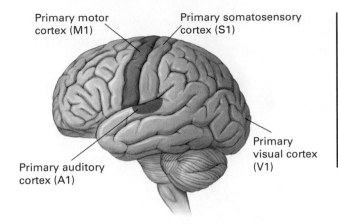

Primary motor cortex (M1)

Primary somatosensory cortex (S1)

Primary visual cortex (V1)

Primary auditory cortex (A1)

Figure 2.6 Cerebral cortical regions for processing inputs and outputs Specific regions of cerebral cortex are specialized for processing light (primary visual cortex, or V1), sound (primary auditory cortex, or A1), and sensation produced by physical movement (primary somatosensory cortex, or S1). Other regions are specialized for generating coordinated movements (primary motor cortex, or M1).

Each primary sensory cortex can then transmit outputs to surrounding cortical regions for further, more advanced, processing. For example, the primary visual cortex may start the processing of stimuli from the eye by extracting general features—say, lines and shading—from a visual scene; later stages of cortical processing elaborate by detecting motion or shape in the scene and, finally, by responding to features of individual objects and their meaning.

Damage that inactivates specific brain regions can "erase" particular perceptual experiences. For example, some people lose the ability to see because of damage to their eyes, but people with damage to V1 can also become blind, even though their eyes are in perfect working order. The latter phenomenon is called *cortical blindness*. Similarly, damage to A1 can cause cortical deafness, and damage to S1 can cause people to lose feeling in parts of their body.

Outgoing Responses: Motor Control

Just as various brain regions are specialized for processing sensory inputs, other brain regions are specialized for processing outputs to control movements. In particular, activity in the primary motor cortex (M1) generates coordinated movements. M1 is located in the frontal lobe, adjacent to S1 in the parietal lobe (Figure 2.6), and it sends output to the brainstem, which in turn sends instructions down the spine to activate motor fibers that control the muscles.

How does M1 generate actions? M1 gets much of its input from the frontal lobes. The frontal lobes provide information about high-level plans based on the present situation, past experience, and future goals. (Should you pick up that hot coffee cup? Should you try to catch that ball with one hand or two?) Other important inputs come from the basal ganglia and cerebellum, which help to translate this high-level plan into a concrete set of movements. Based on all these inputs, M1 sends its outputs to the brainstem. Other motor areas—including the cerebellum, basal ganglia, frontal cortex, and the brainstem itself—also produce their own outputs, all of which converge on the spinal cord and travel from there to the muscles. Complex motor movements—such as picking up a hot coffee cup without spilling the liquid or burning your hand, or picking up an egg without crushing it, or dancing without stepping on your partner's toes—require exquisitely choreographed interactions between all of these brain structures and the muscles they command.

Let's consider one of these actions: you see a cup of coffee and pick it up (Figure 2.7). First, visual input from your eyes travels to your visual cortex (including V1), which helps you identify the cup and locate it in space. Your frontal cortex constructs the plans needed to reach it: the proper plan of attack

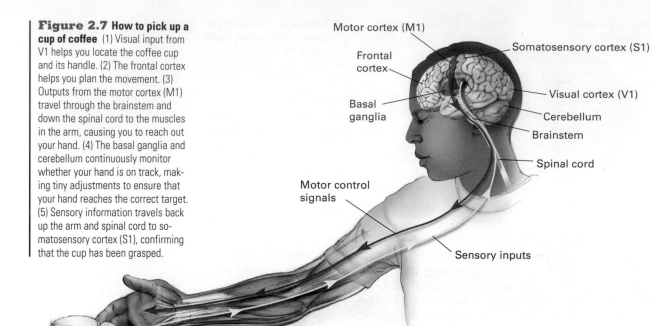

Figure 2.7 How to pick up a cup of coffee (1) Visual input from V1 helps you locate the coffee cup and its handle. (2) The frontal cortex helps you plan the movement. (3) Outputs from the motor cortex (M1) travel through the brainstem and down the spinal cord to the muscles in the arm, causing you to reach out your hand. (4) The basal ganglia and cerebellum continuously monitor whether your hand is on track, making tiny adjustments to ensure that your hand reaches the correct target. (5) Sensory information travels back up the arm and spinal cord to somatosensory cortex (S1), confirming that the cup has been grasped.

is to pick up the cup by the handle (so you won't burn your hand on the hot sides) and to keep it level (so you won't spill the coffee). Areas near the border between frontal cortex and M1 help plan a specific sequence of movements to accomplish this goal, which M1 then directs by means of outputs through the brainstem, down the spinal cord, and out to the muscles of the arm and fingers. As you reach for the cup, your basal ganglia and cerebellum continually monitor the movement, making tiny adjustments as necessary so that your hand travels accurately through space until your fingers can close around the handle. You also have to exert just the right amount of pressure: enough to lift the cup against gravity, but not so much that you yank the cup off the table and spill the liquid, or even break the handle. As you pick up the cup, sensory information from touch, heat, and pressure receptors in your fingers travels back up your arms, through the spinal cord, and to the somatosensory cortex (S1), reporting that you've grasped the cup.

All that, just to pick up a cup—and it doesn't even include taking your first sip! Infants of many vertebrate species, including humans, are born fairly clumsy and spend a large part of their infancy and childhood learning motor programs that let them walk or fly or swim gracefully, reach accurately, move the throat and tongue muscles needed to produce sounds, and so on. This relatively long period spent learning coordinated motor control reflects both the complexity of the operation and the many brain structures that have to learn to interact with one another and with the outside world.

Observing Brain Systems in Action

It's relatively easy to figure out the general function of brain structures such as V1, which receives visual input directly from the eyes (some of it bypassing even the spinal cord), or M1, which sends motor outputs directly to the muscles (some of it, such as that to the muscles that move the eyes, again bypassing the spinal cord). But what about all those other brain areas that don't connect so obviously to external inputs and outputs? In short, what about all those cortical areas that aren't labeled in Figure 2.6? How can we figure out what they do?

Modern neuroscience has several techniques, which range from observing the results of brain damage in humans and other animals to observing blood flow and electrical activity in the brain as it goes about its business.

Clues from Human Neuropsychology

Imagine that a Martian scientist comes to Earth and is confronted with an automobile, a method of transportation unknown on Mars, powered by an energy source also unknown to Martians. Since the Martian speaks no Earth languages and can't simply ask a mechanic for an explanation, how might he go about figuring out how the car works? One way would be to look under the hood and examine the many components there. But studying the car's "anatomy" would only get him so far; to really understand the car, he'd have to take it for a test drive and see how it behaved normally. Then, he could try disconnecting wires, one at a time, and noting how the car behaved (or, rather, misbehaved) in each case. He could try removing or disabling pieces of the motor, again noting the results. If he removed the axle, he'd learn that the motor would work but couldn't transfer energy to make the wheels turn. If he removed the radiator, he'd learn that the car would run but would quickly overheat. In the end, by understanding the function of each of the components under the hood, the Martian could probably develop a pretty good idea of how the car worked.

Neuroscientists trying to understand the brain are confronted with a similar puzzle: trying to figure out how the brain works without help from a design manual. One of the earliest ways to understand brain function was to take an approach something like the Martian's: examine a brain with one or more pieces removed, and see how the remaining system behaved (or misbehaved). While no one would disassemble a human the way a Martian might disassemble a car, nature has provided us with cases in which humans, through accident, injury, or disease, have damage to one or more brain areas.

Neuropsychology is the branch of psychology that deals with the relation between brain function and behavior, usually by examining the functioning of patients with specific types of brain damage. These patients volunteer their time and effort by participating in experiments that test their learning and memory abilities as well as other kinds of cognitive function—language, attention, intelligence, and so on. The results of this testing can potentially be used to guide a patient's rehabilitation. But they also serve a research purpose. By examining the pattern of impaired and spared abilities in a group of patients who have experienced damage to a similar region of the brain, researchers hope to build a better picture of that brain region's normal function—just like the Martian could try to understand what a radiator does by watching what happens to a car that doesn't have one.

Knowing the sites of patients', such as Sean's and Jennifer's, brain damage and observing their behavioral problems gives clues about what those parts of the brain might be doing in a normal, healthy human. It was studies in patients like these that provided the first insights into the role of the cerebellum in motor control and of the temporal lobes in memory and language.

Experimental Brain Lesions

At the same time that neuropsychologists are studying the relationships between brain and behavior in humans, animal researchers conduct parallel research, removing or deactivating specific brain regions to create animal "models" of the human patients. Modern experimental brain surgery is a far cry from the days of Magendie; nowadays, ethics boards and legal guidelines ensure that test animals are treated with respect, that anesthetic and other techniques are used to minimize pain and suffering, and that the value of the information to be gained justifies the cost in animal life.

Often the strongest justification for animal research is that experimental brain lesions in animals allow a precision that is usually not possible in human studies. Human brain damage is always caused by accident, injury, or illness; as a result, every patient's damage—and disability—is slightly different. By contrast, in animal models, researchers can remove or disable specific brain regions with great precision, making it much easier to compare results across individual animals. When the experimental results from human patients and animal models converge, this gives the clearest possible picture of how the brain works normally and how it functions after damage.

Some of the most famous experimental brain lesion studies were conducted by Karl Lashley (1890–1958), an American psychologist who was looking for the location of the **engram,** a physical change in the brain that forms the basis of a memory. Lashley would train a group of rats to navigate through a maze, and then he'd systematically lesion a small area (say, 10%) of the cortex in each rat. He reasoned that, once he'd found the lesion that erased the animal's memories of how to run the maze, he would have located the site of the engram (Lashley, 1929).

Alas, the results were not quite so straightforward. No matter what small part of the cortex Lashley lesioned, the rats kept performing the task. Bigger lesions caused increasing disruptions in performance, but no one cortical area seemed to be more important than any other. Hence, Lashley couldn't find the engram. Finally, in mock despair, he confessed that he might be forced to conclude that learning "simply is not possible" (Lashley, 1929).

Eventually, Lashley settled on a different explanation. He endorsed the **theory of equipotentiality,** which states that memories are not stored in one area of the brain; rather, the brain operates as a whole to store memories. Although Lashley is often credited with formulating this theory, it was actually first proposed in the 1800s as an alternative to phrenology (Flourens, 1824). An analogy for this idea might be a rich investor who spreads his assets over a great many investments. If any one investment fails, his net worth won't change much; if a large number of investments fail, he can still rebuild his net worth by savvy use of what's left, although it may take him some time. In effect, his wealth is a function of all of his many investments. Similarly, in the theory of equipotentiality, memories are spread over many cortical areas; damage to one or two of these areas won't completely destroy the memory, and—with additional training and time—surviving cortical areas may be able to compensate for what's been lost.

Lashley's work, and his endorsement of the theory of equipotentiality, were milestones in brain science, because researchers could no longer think in terms of the compartmentalized structure-function mapping that phrenologists had proposed. But, like the phrenologists before him, Lashley was only partly right. The phrenologists were on the right track when they proposed that different brain areas have different specialties; the specialization just wasn't as extreme as they thought. Lashley was also on the right track when he proposed that engrams aren't localized to tiny areas of the cortex, but we now know that the cortex isn't quite as undifferentiated as he came to believe. The truth is somewhere in the middle.

Possibly, Lashley's main problem was the task he chose for assessing memory. Learning a path through a maze is an extremely complex problem, and an animal learning this task probably relies on all the available sources of information: visual cues, odor cues, textural cues, spatial cues, and so on. If Lashley lesioned a small area of the cortex that specialized in, say, visual processing, then the animal would lose this source of input—but the other sources of input would remain. These might suffice to allow the animal to continue to navigate through a familiar maze, just as you could probably find your way around your home if the lights were turned off. Only when lesions were large enough to abolish most or all of the animal's sources of input would they disrupt the task irreparably.

Another problem for Lashley was the primitive technology available at the time of his research. In those days, the only way to produce a brain lesion was to open the animal's skull and cut out a portion of the brain by hand. Researchers today are able to produce lesions that are far more precise. For example, experimenters can inject toxins that kill specific types of neurons in well-defined areas, without damaging nearby neurons or fibers. Through such methods, scientists have at last begun to uncover evidence of engrams. Interestingly, the engrams identified so far are located not in the cortex, where Lashley (and the phrenologists) focused their efforts, but in subcortical structures such as the cerebellum (Thompson, 2005). We describe how the cerebellum contributes to learning and memory in our discussion of skill memory and of classical conditioning in later chapters.

Useful as brain lesion experiments are, they are limited in what they can reveal. Suppose a researcher lesions part of a rat's cortex and then finds, as Lashley did, that the rat can still learn to run a maze. Would that prove that this cortical area is not involved in maze learning? Not necessarily; the rat may be learning the maze, but in a different way. This would be analogous to your being able to find your way around a house with the lights out, even though you use visual input when it's available. Data from lesion studies are strongest when supplemented by data from other techniques that provide evidence of whether a brain region "normally" participates in a given behavior.

Functional Neuroimaging: Watching the Brain in Action

Whereas structural neuroimaging allows researchers to look at the *structure* of a living human brain, **functional neuroimaging** allows them to look at the *activity* or function of a living brain. When a brain structure becomes active, it requires more oxygen. Within 4–6 seconds, blood flow (with its cargo of oxygen) increases to that region. On the other hand, when a brain structure becomes less active, it requires less oxygen, and blood flow decreases. By tracking local changes in blood flow, researchers can determine which brain regions are active or inactive.

One such technology, called **positron emission tomography (PET),** measures brain activity by detecting radiation from the emission of subatomic particles called positrons. During PET, a small amount of a radioactive chemical is injected into the individual's bloodstream. Molecules of this chemical gradually accumulate in different regions of the brain, the degree of accumulation depending on the activity and oxygen demands of those regions. As the radioactive chemical breaks down within the brain, it releases positively charged particles (positrons) that trigger the release of gamma rays, which can be detected by a PET scanner. A PET scanner looks very much like an MRI scanner, but it contains gamma-ray detectors rather than a magnet. As with MRI, a computer collects all the signals and constructs a detailed map of the brain, showing where the gamma rays originated (Figure 2.8a). More gamma rays coming from a particular brain region means that more of the radioactive chemical has accumulated in that region, which in turn means that more blood has flowed in that region.

Figure 2.8 Creating a difference image with functional neuroimaging (PET) A PET scanner is used to generate an image of blood flow during a task (a), such as viewing pictures or reading words projected on the inside of the PET scanner. The resulting image is compared against a baseline image (b), taken while the participant is not performing the task. A point-by-point comparison of the two images produces a difference image (c), color coded to show areas where blood flow significantly increased (or decreased) in the task condition compared with the baseline condition. The white lines in (c) are a drawing of a standard brain, showing the same cross-section as the PET image, to help the viewer understand which brain regions correspond to the colored areas.

(a) Activity during task — (b) Activity at baseline = (c) Difference image

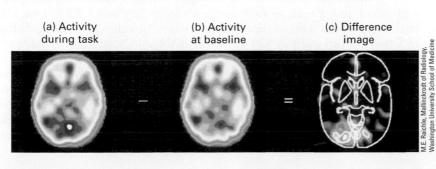

M.E. Raichle, Mallinckrodt of Radiology, Washington University School of Medicine

But this is only the first step. The next step is to ask how blood flow in a particular brain region *changes* depending on what the person is doing or thinking about. To see such changes in blood flow, researchers first scan the brain while the person is relaxed—not doing anything. The resulting image is called a *baseline* image. Even though the person isn't performing any task, some areas of the brain are still active (as in Figure 2.8b). Next, the researchers scan the brain again while the person is performing a task, such as looking at pictures or reading a story. (The pictures or words are projected on the inside ceiling of the scanner, so that the person can see them while lying on his or her back.) During the task, some areas of the brain that weren't active at baseline should become more active (as in Figure 2.8a). Others might decrease in activity. For each point (or pixel) in the image, researchers then subtract the activity from that identical point in the baseline image. The result, called a **difference image,** shows how activity at each point in the image has increased or decreased in the task condition compared with the baseline condition (Figure 2.8c). Usually, the difference image is color coded, with white, red, or yellow indicating areas where blood flow *increased* most during the task relative to the baseline. Uncolored areas indicate regions where no significant change took place.

Difference images (like the one shown in Figure 2.8c) may be responsible for the oft-cited statistic that we humans use only 10% of our brain. The implication, of course, is that we would all be a lot smarter if we got the other 90% going. But as Figure 2.8b shows, there is activity throughout the brain at all times, even at "baseline" when we're not doing anything in particular. The real secret of brain function seems to be that different brain areas can increase or decrease their activity depending on what we're doing at the moment. For example, the difference image in Figure 2.8c shows the parts of the brain that become significantly more active when a person is viewing pictures, confirming the current understanding that areas of the cerebral cortex in the occipital lobe are important for visual processing.

PET is only one functional neuroimaging method. Another technology makes use of the same MRI machine used for structural imaging. Researchers can take an MRI at baseline and a second MRI while the person is performing a task. Oxygenated blood produces slightly different electrical signals than deoxygenated blood, and so there are fluctuations in the signal received from areas of the brain that become more (or less) active during the task. Researchers can compare these images and construct a difference image based on the MRIs, just as they do for the PET images. The resulting images look very similar to PET scans, with color-coded areas representing brain regions that are significantly more or less active during the task than during the baseline condition. This technique for observing activity-related changes in the brain by finding small alterations in MRI images is called **functional MRI (fMRI),** because it can provide a snapshot of how the brain is functioning.

Because both PET and fMRI measure local changes in blood flow, they generally produce similar results. For example, Joseph Devlin and colleagues asked a group of young men to view words while undergoing a PET scan. On each trial, the men saw a list of three words (such as "dolphin, seal, walrus") followed by a fourth word (such as "OTTER" or "BANANA"), and had to judge whether the fourth word belonged to the same category as the first three. The brain activations during this category judgment were compared against brain activations during a comparison task in which the men saw three groups of letters (such as "aaaaaaaa, aaa, aaaaa") and then had to decide whether the fourth group (such as "AAAAA" or "SSSSS") was the same or different. This comparison task involved many of the same features as the category task, but only in the category task did the men have to think about the *meaning* of the words. The researchers then subtracted the PET images of the comparison task from those of the category task to produce difference images that showed which brain areas were particularly active when the men were thinking about word meanings (Figure 2.9). Several brain areas appeared to be involved, including areas in the left frontal lobe, the left temporal lobe, and the right cerebellum (Devlin et al., 2002).

The researchers then repeated the experiment with a new group of participants, but this time they used fMRI to investigate brain activity. Difference images based on the fMRI showed brain activation in some of the same areas as in the PET study, including areas in the left frontal lobe. But there were differences: the PET study had shown strong activation in the left temporal lobe and the right cerebellum; fMRI activation in these areas was much less evident (see "Unsolved Mysteries" on p. 62. This study is an example in which PET picked up more areas of activation than were detected by fMRI.

On the other hand, fMRI has its advantages. It typically has better spatial resolution than PET: whereas points on a PET image can be localized to within about 5 millimeters, points on an fMRI can be localized to within about 1–2 millimeters. There are also methodological and economic considerations: fMRI doesn't require injecting radioactive materials into the person under study, as PET does, and while PET requires an expensive machine, fMRI can usually be done by adapting the existing MRI scanners found in most major hospitals. In short, both functional imaging techniques have advantages and disadvantages.

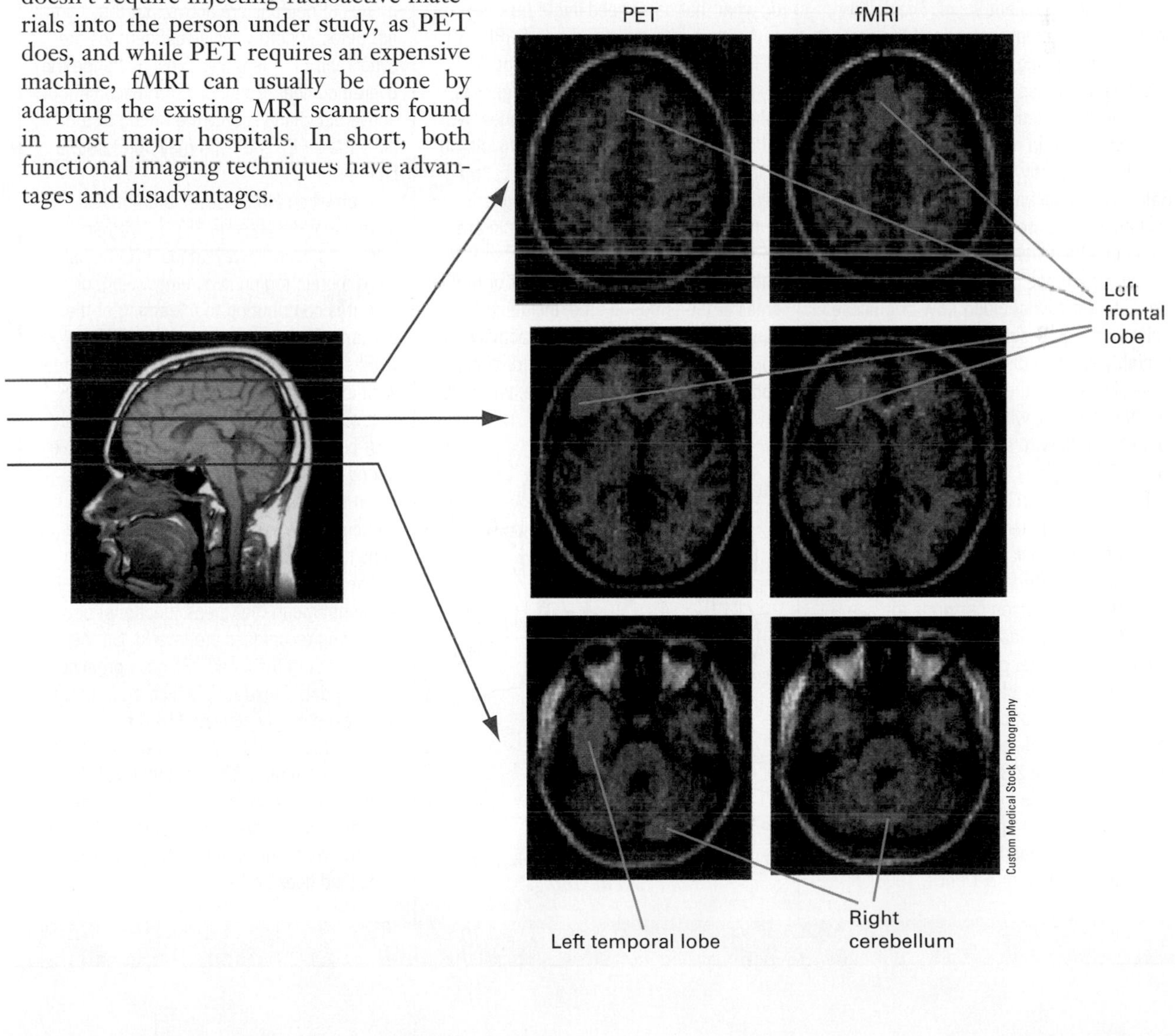

Figure 2.9 Brain activation during category judgment: comparing PET and fMRI Researchers constructed difference images of brain activation in people making category judgments, compared with a baseline task that did not require category judgments. Representative difference images are shown, corresponding to horizontal slices at three levels in the brain. Both PET and fMRI revealed activity in several brain areas, including the left frontal lobe and the right cerebellum. But the two types of images also differed: PET revealed activity in the left temporal lobe that did not appear on fMRI; and fMRI revealed activity in the left cerebellum that was not visible on PET. Adapted from Devlin et al., 2002.

PET   fMRI

Left frontal lobe

Left temporal lobe

Right cerebellum

Custom Medical Stock Photography

► **Unsolved Mysteries**

What Do Functional Neuroimaging Techniques Really Measure?

Functional imaging methods, such as fMRI and PET, are responsible for many of the most exciting findings in neuroscience in recent years. They allow researchers to create images of the brain in action, highlighting areas that are especially active during a particular task. But what does this brain activity really mean?

As you learn in this chapter, fMRI and PET do not directly measure neural activity. Rather, these techniques measure metabolic changes that are believed to correlate with neural activity. fMRI signals (typically) reflect local blood oxygenation, and PET signals reflect local blood flow or glucose utilization. The assumption is that neurons in highly active brain areas use extra fuel—increasing their oxygen consumption (visible on fMRI), which in turn requires extra blood flow to supply the oxygen (visible on PET).

But the story isn't always so clear. A difference image generated by PET as a person performs a task doesn't always look identical to a difference image produced by fMRI while the person performs the same task (Xiong, Rao, Gao, Woldorff, & Fox, 1998). For example, presenting a visual stimulus increases blood flow to the vision-processing areas of cortex in the occipital lobe by about 29%, producing a strong PET signal (see Figure 2.8). The same stimulation only increases oxygen consumption by about 9%, however, producing a much weaker fMRI signal (Fox & Raichle, 1986; Fox, Raichle, Mintun, & Dence, 1988). If

both PET and fMRI are indirect measures of brain activity, why would they produce different results?

One answer is that brain cells don't require vastly more oxygen when they are highly active than when they are less active. When a brain region is hard at work, there's a huge increase in blood flow to the area (resulting in a strong PET signal), but only a fraction of the available oxygen in that blood is absorbed by the neurons (resulting in a less dramatic fMRI signal). This implies that the large increases in blood flow must fulfill some need other than just supplying oxygen to hungry neurons (Fox et al., 1988). It's not clear, however, what that other need might be.

Another difference between fMRI and PET may reflect some limitations of fMRI. Remember that fMRI (like MRI in general) relies on detecting magnetic changes. Not all parts of the brain are equally visible on fMRI, because of differences in local magnetic fields (sometimes called magnetic artifacts). For example, when people are asked to learn new information, both fMRI and PET show activity in the inner or medial areas of the temporal lobe, including the hippocampus. But on fMRI, the activity appears mostly in the posterior (or back) half of the medial temporal lobe, while PET

"We've given you a brain scan and we can't find anything."

shows activity mostly in the anterior (or front) half of the medial temporal lobe (Schacter et al., 1999). Part of the reason for this difference is that activity in the anterior half of the medial temporal lobe is very difficult to see on fMRI, due to magnetic artifacts. So, fMRI may not be able to detect changes there, even though PET can.

There may also be conditions under which both PET and fMRI miss the brain activity altogether (Poldrack, 2000). For example, the brain encodes information not just in terms of *which* neurons are active but also in terms of *when* they become active. PET and fMRI can detect large changes in how strongly or how often groups of neurons are active, but they cannot detect whether individual neurons are synchronized. If learning doesn't change the overall number of neurons that become active but changes only the timing of that activation, PET and fMRI may not detect a change.

Even when we do observe an overall increase or decrease in PET or fMRI activations, this is not always enough to reveal what a brain region is actually doing, or how it is contributing to a learning or memory task. Additionally, even if the PET or fMRI signal seems to be strongly correlated with learning, it is important to remember that *correlation does not imply causation*. Just because a brain region appears active during a task, that does not necessarily mean the brain region is needed for that particular task—only that the region happens to be receiving extra blood.

The limitations of fMRI and PET, however, do not mean that these functional neuroimaging techniques are invalid. On the contrary, both fMRI and PET have produced exciting data illustrating which brain areas are most strongly activated by different kinds of tasks and how this brain activity changes with time. The limitations of these imaging techniques simply mean that neuroscientists have to be careful in evaluating exactly what a given neuroimaging result does (and does not) show.

Although functional neuroimaging is a powerful tool for observing the brain in action, keep in mind that PET and fMRI are only indirect measures of brain activity; they measure blood flow (or blood oxygenation) in a brain region, rather than directly measuring the activity of brain cells. Also, both techniques are comparatively slow: fMRI allows images to be taken every few seconds, while PET images can be taken only every few minutes. Changes in the brain occur much more rapidly than that. To track changes in real time, other techniques are needed.

Electroencephalography: Charting Brain Waves

Electroencephalography (EEG) is a technique for measuring electrical activity in the brain. (The Greek word *enkephalos* means "brain," and so "electro-encephalo-graphy" means drawing or graphing the electrical activity of the brain.) In EEG, researchers place recording electrodes on a person's scalp. These electrodes, the same type used in electrocardiograms (EKGs, or ECGs), simply record changes in electrical activity. When electrodes are placed on a person's chest, they measure electrical activity resulting from heart contractions. When the electrodes are placed on the scalp, they measure the combined tiny electrical charges of large numbers of neurons in the brain, especially those near the location on the skull where the electrodes are placed. The resulting picture is called an *electroencephalogram* (also abbreviated EEG) or, more informally, a "brain wave."

Just as blood is always flowing through the brain, so electrical activity is always occurring in the brain, reflecting the activity of neurons. But the exact pattern of activation changes depending on what the brain is doing. For example, when a tone sounds, sensory receptors in the ear become active, and signals travel to primary auditory cortex (area A1), affecting electrical activity there. But detecting this particular electrical change by EEG is difficult, because lots of other neurons in other brain areas not involved in hearing are also active—those responding to visual stimuli, for instance, or those activated as you wiggle your fingers and think about what you want to have for lunch.

To detect an electrical change associated with hearing a single tone, or with detecting another particular stimulus, researchers often present the same stimulus repeatedly and average the EEGs produced throughout those repetitions in a given individual. The principle is that activity in other brain areas will come and go, but only the neurons responding to the specific sensory stimulus will be consistently activated each time the stimulus is repeated—and so only their activity patterns will survive the averaging process. EEGs averaged across many repetitions of the same event are called **event-related potentials (ERPs).**

Just as functional neuroimaging shows how the brain changes while performing a task, so ERP monitoring can be used to show different brain states. For example, a recent study showed how EEG signals change while people are learning to discriminate two very similar sounds (Tremblay & Kraus, 2002). ERPs were recorded while participants listened to repetitions of two syllables that sounded roughly like "ba" and "mba." These sounds are so similar that most native English speakers can't tell the difference. The thin line in Figure 2.10b shows the resulting ERP, recorded by an electrode located at the crown (center top) of the scalp. The ERP shows three characteristic components that are correlated with stimulus presentation: an initial positive change (called the P1) occurring about 50 milliseconds after stimulus onset; a steep negative change (the N1) occurring about 100 milliseconds after stimulus onset; and a slight positive rebound (the P2) occurring about 200 milliseconds after stimulus onset. By about 300 milliseconds after stimulus onset, the waveform settles back down to its baseline amplitude. You should note that although these increases may look dramatic, they typically entail a change of about 1–2 microvolts, or one-millionth of a volt; by comparison, a standard wall outlet in North America carries 110 volts.

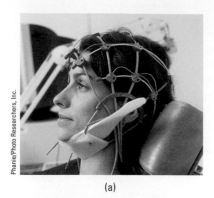

(a)

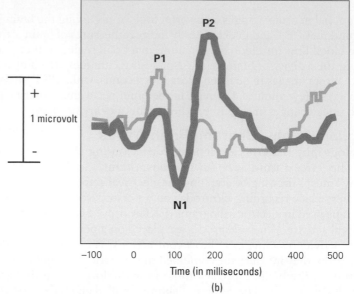

Time (in milliseconds)

(b)

Figure 2.10 Use of electroencephalography to demonstrate learning-related changes (a) To obtain an electroencephalogram (EEG), researchers place electrodes on the participant's scalp. Computers then track changes in the electrical activity detected by the electrodes. Event-related potentials (ERPs) are EEG signals averaged over several repetitions of a stimulus. (b) ERPs can change as a result of learning. Initially, participants heard repetitions of "ba" and "mba," two syllables that native English speakers don't normally discriminate. The ERP from an electrode near the crown of the scalp (thin line), generated by these sounds, showed certain standard components, including an immediate increase soon after stimulus presentation (the P1 wave), followed by a large decrease (the N1) and a subsequent large increase (the P2). After several days of training to discriminate "ba" and "mba," the participants were hooked up to the EEG again. Now the ERP was markedly different (thick line). Most notable was a sharp decrease in P1 and a sharp increase in P2. Possibly, the increase in P2 reflects increased attention to subtle acoustic cues. (b) Adapted from Tremblay and Kraus, 2002.

After participants received several days of training to distinguish "ba" from "mba," the ERPs changed, as illustrated by the thick line in Figure 2.10b. Most notably, the P1 wave decreased sharply, while the P2 wave increased to several times its original size. What these changes mean in terms of brain activity is not completely clear, but one possibility is that P1 may reflect initial attention to a stimulus, and it therefore decreases as the stimulus becomes more familiar through repetition over several days. A training-related increase in P2, on the other hand, may reflect heightened sensitivity to subtle differences in the acoustic cues, subtle differences that the participants could not easily hear before training (Tremblay & Kraus, 2002).

As you might surmise from this discussion, there are still many unanswered questions about how ERPs, and EEGs in general, relate to learning and memory. However, given the similarities between ERPs produced by different individuals, it is fairly easy to see abnormalities in the waveform, even if we don't yet know exactly what those abnormalities represent. Compared with functional imaging (fMRI and PET), EEG is a simple and cheap way to monitor changes in brain activity during learning and memory tasks. It does not require a large and expensive scanner or injection of a radioactive substance into the bloodstream. In addition, EEG can provide more precise information than fMRI or PET about rapid changes in the brain: whereas fMRI and PET are based on blood flow, which lags a few hundred milliseconds behind neural activity, EEG is almost instantaneous.

Yet what EEG gains in temporal precision it sacrifices in spatial precision. Whereas fMRI and PET can localize activation to within a few millimeters, EEG signals show activity over a wide swath of brain area. In a promising new approach, functional neuroimaging and EEG are used together to generate a picture that shows not only precisely when (EEG) but also precisely where (fMRI) neural activity occurs.

Interim Summary

In humans and other vertebrates, most sensory information travels from sensory receptors to the spinal cord, and motor responses travel from the spinal cord to the muscles and organs. Even if the spinal cord is detached from the brain, sensory inputs traveling to the spinal cord can activate motor fibers traveling out of the spinal cord, causing motor reflexes. Some early researchers believed that all complex behavior is built up from combinations of such spinal reflexes. Sensory information also travels up the spinal cord to the brain, where there are cortical regions specialized to process sensory inputs and motor outputs. Projections from these motor areas travel back down the spinal cord and out to the fibers that control muscles and organs.

Currently, several techniques are available to map behavior onto brain structures. One method is to examine impairments that arise when a brain structure is damaged or disabled. This can be done by testing human patients with brain damage who participate in neuropsychological studies, or by testing animals in which experimenters have generated precise lesions. Functional brain imaging techniques (such as PET and fMRI) provide a way to visualize the brain in action without causing lasting harm. PET detects patterns of blood flow to different brain areas; fMRI detects regional differences in oxygen levels in the blood. In principle, both of these functional imaging techniques can show which brain areas are more active during a particular task. Another method for observing the brain in action is electroencephalography, which measures electrical signals representing a summation of tiny electrical currents produced by many active neurons. EEG has more temporal precision than PET or fMRI, but less spatial precision.

2.3 Learning and Synaptic Plasticity

So far, you've read about some basics of brain anatomy and the general roles of the major brain regions in producing behavior. Now it's time to get down to specifics: what, exactly, goes on in these brain regions to allow learning and memory?

Neurons, as noted earlier in the chapter, are cells that are specialized to process information. Neurons are the building blocks of the nervous system; the human nervous system has about 100 billion of them. They include the sensory receptors (such as those in the eyes, ears, and tongue that respond to visual, auditory, and taste stimuli), and the "motor fibers" that carry commands from the spinal cord to the muscles. But, in vertebrates, the vast majority of neurons are centralized in the brain. These neurons are capable of changing their function and modifying the way they process information. These changes are the basis of learning in the brain.

The Neuron

The prototypical neuron has three main components: (1) **dendrites,** input areas that receive signals from other neurons; (2) the **cell body,** or **soma,** which integrates signals from the dendrites; and (3) one or more **axons,** which transmit information to other neurons (Figure 2.11). For the most part, information flows in one direction, from dendrites to axons.

It is reasonable to talk about a "prototypical neuron," but in reality neurons come in a wide array of shapes and sizes. For example, *pyramidal cells* are neurons with pyramid-shaped cell bodies; *stellate cells* have star-shaped cell bodies. Some neurons have a single main axon, some have two, and some have many. Neurons known as *interneurons*, which connect two neurons, have short axons or no axons at all. The neurons that carry signals from the spinal cord to the feet have axons that stretch a meter or more in humans. The various shapes and sizes of different kinds of neurons undoubtedly contribute to their function. But, in many cases, neuroscientists do not know the specific advantages that a particular shape or size provides.

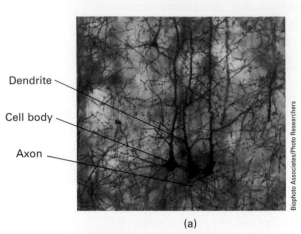

(a)

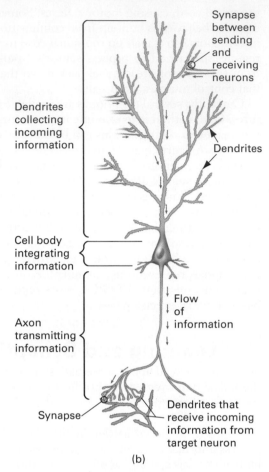

(b)

Figure 2.11 Neurons, the cells specialized to process information (a) This photograph of brain tissue was taken with a powerful microscope after staining the tissue to make neurons evident. Several neurons are visible, with pyramid-shaped cell bodies and extensive networks of interconnecting branches. (b) Most neurons have three main components: dendrites specialized for collecting information, a cell body (soma) that integrates this information, and one or more axons that transmit information to other neurons. Information flows mainly in one direction, from dendrites to axon(s).

Neurons are not the only kind of cell in the brain; they are far outnumbered by **glia,** cells that provide functional and structural support to neurons. *Astrocytes* are glia that line the outer surface of blood vessels in the brain and may help in the transfer of oxygen and nutrients from the blood to neurons. *Oligodendrocytes* wrap the axons of nearby neurons in *myelin,* a fatty substance that insulates electrical signals transmitted by neurons, speeding information transmission down the axon. Glia are as important as neurons for normal brain (and overall central nervous system) function. For example, multiple sclerosis is a disease in which the myelin coating of axons degenerates; this interferes with the ability of neurons to transmit information, leading to jerky muscle movements and impaired coordination, as well as problems with vision and speech. Even so, most neuroscientists who study the neural bases of learning and memory focus their efforts on understanding neurons: how they transmit information, and how they change to reflect learning.

The Synapse: Where Neurons Connect

Generally, neurons that communicate with each other do not actually touch. Rather, there is a narrow gap of about 20 nanometers (1 nanometer [nm] is one-billionth of a meter), called a **synapse,** across which the neurons pass chemical messages (Figure 2.12a). Most synapses are formed between the axon of the **presynaptic** (or sending) neuron and a dendrite of the **postsynaptic** (or receiving) neuron; but synapses can also be formed between an axon and a cell body, between an axon and another axon, and even between dendrites.

Synaptic transmission, the sending of a message across a synapse, begins with the presynaptic neuron, which contains molecules called **neurotransmitters,** chemical substances that can cross a synapse to carry a message to the postsynaptic neuron. Neurotransmitter molecules are kept conveniently on hand at the end of the presynaptic axon, in packets known as vesicles. When the presynaptic neuron sends a message, it allows one or more vesicles to burst, spilling neurotransmitter molecules into the synapse (Figure 2.12b). So far, nine neurotransmitters have been the focus of most research: *acetylcholine, dopamine, norepinephrine, epinephrine, serotonin, histamine, glutamate, glycine,* and *gamma-aminobutyric acid (GABA).* In addition, there are about 100 other chemicals in the brain that can serve as neurotransmitters, and researchers are discovering new ones every year.

Once the chemical signal has been released into the synapse by the presynaptic neuron, the next step is for the postsynaptic neuron to pick it up. **Receptors** are molecules on the surface of the postsynaptic neuron that are specialized to bind particular kinds of neurotransmitters. Neurotransmitter molecules fit into these receptors like keys in a lock, activating them. The effect of a particular neurotransmitter depends on what its corresponding receptors do when activated. Some receptors open a channel for electrically charged molecules to flow into or out of the cell, thus changing the charge characteristics in a small area of the neuron. Similar electrical changes occur simultaneously in other locations on the neuron, as other receptors on other dendrites become active. The neuron's cell body integrates this cocktail of electrical signals; if the total electrical charge exceeds a threshold, the neuron "fires," propagating an electrical charge down its axon. This is an all-or-nothing event: either the neuron fires or it doesn't; there is no in-between stage. When the electrical charge reaches the end of the axon, it causes the release of neurotransmitter molecules, passing the message along to the next neuron.

Usually, a given neuron produces and releases only one kind of neurotransmitter. But that neuron may be able to receive and interpret messages from many different presynaptic neurons, each releasing a different kind of neurotransmitter. As long as the postsynaptic neuron has receptors coded to a particular neurotransmitter, it will be able to receive the message.

After a neuron fires, there is a brief period, called a *refractory period,* during which it can't fire again, no matter how much input it receives. Once this refractory period has passed, the neuron is again open for business. If the neuron is still receiving a lot of input from its neighbors, it may fire again and again in rapid succession. If the inputs are less frequent or less strong, some time may pass before the neuron fires again.

Figure 2.12 Information flow across a synapse (a) This photo, taken through an electron microscope, shows the end of an axon of a presynaptic neuron with a tiny gap, or synapse, between a presynaptic neuron and the dendrite of another, postsynaptic neuron. Vesicles filled with molecules of neurotransmitter, ready for release into the synapse, are visible as circular packets inside the presynaptic neurons. (b) Information exchange across a synapse starts when (1) the presynaptic (sending) neuron becomes active, allowing vesicles to burst and release neurotransmitter molecules into the synapse. (2) Some of these molecules find their way across the synapse and dock at receptors on the surface of the postsynaptic (receiving) neuron. The summed effects of activation at multiple receptors on the postsynaptic neuron may result in that neuron becoming active, passing the message along to other neurons. Leftover molecules of neurotransmitter in the synapse are either (3) broken down (a process called inactivation) or (4) reabsorbed into the presynaptic neuron (a process called reuptake). After the neurotransmitter molecules are cleared out of the synapse, synaptic transmission is terminated and the synapse is ready for future messages.

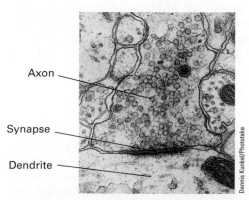

Axon

Synapse

Dendrite

Dennis Kunkel/Phototake

(a)

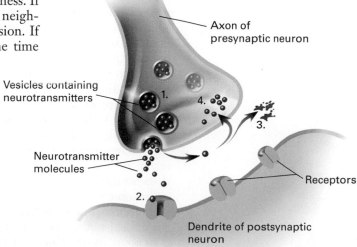

Axon of presynaptic neuron

Vesicles containing neurotransmitters

Neurotransmitter molecules

Receptors

Dendrite of postsynaptic neuron

(b)

In the meantime, neurotransmitter molecules have to be cleared out of the synapse, so that the synapse can receive future messages. Neurotransmitter molecules can be broken down into their constituent parts, in a process called *inactivation*, or they can be reabsorbed into the presynaptic neuron and recycled for use in future messages, a process called *reuptake*. When this cleanup is complete, the synapse and receptors are ready to receive new transmissions.

Neuromodulators: Adjusting the Message

Synaptic transmission is not the only way in which neurotransmitters affect brain activity. Several areas in the brainstem contain neurons that send axons widely throughout the brain; when they fire, these neurons release neurotransmitters called **neuromodulators** that can affect activity in entire brain areas, rather than just at a single synapse. Neuromodulators alter, or modulate, how neurons exchange messages, although they themselves are not part of the message. For example, acetylcholine often functions as a neuromodulator, and one of its effects is to temporarily alter the number of receptors that have to be active before a postsynaptic neuron can fire. If you think of synaptic transmission as a message, then acetylcholine levels help determine whether the message is heard as a whisper or a shout.

Many human diseases seem to involve a global decline in neuromodulators. Examples include Alzheimer's disease, which involves a reduction in acetylcholine (Francis, Palmer, Snape, & Wilcock, 1999), and Parkinson's disease, which involves a reduction in dopamine (Evans & Lees, 2004). Many of the drugs used to treat these diseases are designed to increase neuromodulators to more normal levels.

Measuring and Manipulating Neural Activity

In the brain, information is conveyed not only by *which* neurons fire but also by *how often* they fire. Both functional neuroimaging and EEG can reveal activity in large areas of the brain, but they don't reveal much about which individual neurons are firing, or how often. To gather this information, researchers have to record neuronal activity deep in the brain. **Neurophysiology** is the study of the activity and function of neurons.

Recording from Neurons

The main technique scientists use to measure firing patterns in individual neurons is **single-cell recording** (the single cell in this case is a neuron). To collect single-cell recordings, researchers implant microelectrodes into an animal's brain, either temporarily or permanently. These electrodes are similar in function to EEG electrodes, but they are shaped like extremely thin needles that can penetrate brain tissue with a minimum of damage. The electrode is inserted until the tip is very close to, or sometimes even inside, a single neuron. Since neurons are so tiny, placing the recording electrode takes a lot of skill. One placement technique is to transmit signals from the electrode to audio speakers, so that individual spikes can be heard as clicks. When the researcher begins to hear an interesting pattern of clicking, she knows the electrode is near an interesting neuron—in much the same way a beachcomber knows, when his metal detector starts clicking, that some coins are buried in the sand nearby.

In some cases, researchers anesthetize an animal and surgically implant one or more recording electrodes in the brain area they wish to study. Then, when the animal wakes, the researchers can record from the neuron(s) as the animal goes about its daily business. (Most animals don't seem to be much bothered by, or even aware of, the wires connected to their heads.) Such experiments allow researchers to determine what role a given neuron might play in the animal's behavior. Alternatively, if the researcher is interested in looking more closely at how individual neurons interact, it is possible to remove pieces (or "slices") of a brain, keep the neurons alive in a bath of nutrients, and record neural activity from the slices.

Single-cell recordings have provided some of the most dramatic evidence to date of how neuronal firing relates to behavior. For example, Apostolos Georgopoulos and colleagues recorded spike patterns from the motor cortex of a monkey while the monkey moved a joystick in different directions (Georgopoulos, Taira, & Lukashin, 1993). Some neurons fired most strongly when the monkey pushed the lever in a particular direction (Figure 2.13). For example, Figure 2.13b shows recordings from one such neuron as the monkey moved the lever toward different compass points. Each vertical line in the recording represents one "spike," or firing event. When the monkey moved its arm toward the point labeled 6 in Figure 2.13a, the neuron initially let off a sharp burst of spikes, then fell silent. When the monkey moved its arm to a slightly different position, point 7, the neuron let off a more sustained burst of activity, continuing to spike for the duration of the movement. But when the monkey moved its arm directly away from its body, toward point 1, the neuron really went into action: spiking as fast and frequently as it could. By contrast, when the monkey moved its arm in the opposite direction, toward its body (point 5), the neuron fell almost silent. Thus, this neuron's behavior is correlated with arm movements, and neuroscientists would say it is specialized, or "tuned," to fire maximally during movements in a particular direction: away from the body. Georgopoulos and colleagues found that other neurons in the motor cortex were tuned to fire during movements in other directions. Given what we know about the motor cortex from functional imaging and lesion studies, it is reasonable to assume that these neurons may be playing a direct role in issuing the commands that cause the monkey's arm to move.

To record neural activity from animals as they perform tasks, researchers surgically implant one or more electrodes into the desired brain areas. Held in place by a "head stage" attached to the animal's head (a rat is shown here), the electrodes detect neural activity as the animal moves freely; wires transmit this information to a computer, which records and analyzes the signals.

ALY SONG/Reuters/Corbis

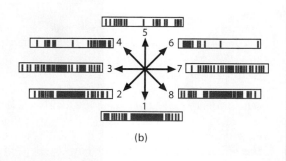

Electrode implanted in motor cortex

(a)

(b)

Figure 2.13 Recording from single neurons in a monkey's motor cortex (a) Researchers implanted recording electrodes into the motor cortex of a monkey, which was then trained to move a joystick in different directions. (b) One recorded neuron showed spiking behavior (illustrated as vertical lines) when the monkey moved its arm in various directions. This neuron showed strongest firing when the monkey moved its arm away from the body (position 1) and weakest firing when the monkey moved its arm toward the body (position 5). Thus, this neuron is tuned to fire during movements away from the monkey's body. (b) Adapted from Georgopoulos et al., 1993.

Stimulating Neurons into Activity

In addition to using recording electrodes to observe neuronal behavior, researchers can try to evoke neuronal activity by using electrodes to deliver tiny amounts of electrical stimulation. As you read above, when neurons fire, an electrical charge sweeps down the axon, triggering the release of neurotransmitter molecules into the synapse. A stimulating electrode can provide this electrical charge, causing spiking activity to happen where and when the researcher is ready to observe and record it.

Electrical stimulation of neurons was used as early as the 1800s, to prove that neuronal activity in the motor cortex produces motor behavior. Pavlov, for instance, was able to produce a wide range of movement patterns in an anesthetized dog by electrically stimulating its motor cortex (Pavlov, 1927). Similar techniques can be used in primates to map which parts of the motor cortex are responsible for generating movements in particular body parts (Figure 2.14a). For example, electrical stimulation delivered to certain neurons in M1 in the right hemisphere, near the top of the brain, cause a monkey's lips to twitch. A little farther down, and an arm might twitch. Still lower, and movement occurs in the legs. By painstakingly testing the effects of stimulating each point in M1, scientists can draw a map—called a *homunculus* (or "little man")—on the surface of M1, showing which part of the body each region of M1 controls. The homunculus for M1 in humans has been worked out with the assistance of patients who were candidates for brain surgery (for example, to remove a tumor). Before removing any brain tissue, neurosurgeons do preliminary testing, which often involves cutting away a piece of the skull to expose the brain underneath and then carefully stimulating different areas. The idea is to determine whether the brain tissue can be cut away without leaving the patient in even worse shape than before. To remove a tumor, for example, it may be reasonable to risk damaging the part of M1 that controls movements in one leg; but risk to other parts—say, the areas that control the tongue and allow swallowing and speaking—may call for extra caution.

Looking at the homunculus of Figure 2.14a, you'll notice that some body areas (the lips and hands, for example) seem grossly enlarged, while others (the arms and legs) seem shrunken. In other

Figure 2.14 The homunculus corresponding to human motor cortex (a) By electrically stimulating each point of motor cortex (M1) and recording the evoked movements, researchers can map out the regions of the body controlled by each area of M1. If the homunculus so produced (here, for a male) is assembled into a model of a person (b), with the size of each body part determined by the relative amount of cortex devoted to it, the result is a figure with enlarged lips and hands—areas where human motor control is particularly sensitive.

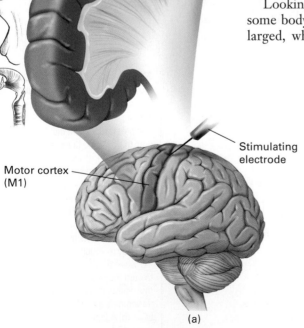

Motor cortex
(M1)

Stimulating
electrode

(a)

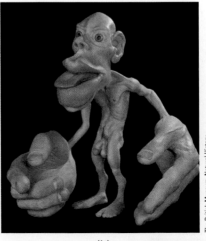

The British Museum, Natural History

(b)

words, the physical size of a body area doesn't directly correspond to its size in the cortical map. In fact, if the homunculus were assembled into a figurine, it would look something like Figure 2.14b. The distortions aren't random. The parts of the body that are exaggerated on the homunculus, because disproportional amounts of surface area are devoted to them in the cortical map, are precisely those parts in which humans have the highest degree of fine motor control: fingers that are able to type, knit, and play the piano; lips and tongue that move through the complicated contortions of speech; and facial muscles that display emotion. Other areas of the body that are physically larger, like the arms and legs, have proportionately less fine motor control, and so proportionately less area of motor cortex is devoted to them.

It's also worth noting that the motor homunculus of Figure 2.14 is an average representation (of a male, in this case). The homunculus of an actual individual would differ somewhat from this representation, reflecting the areas of the body over which that individual has more or less fine motor control. In an extreme example of this principle, people who have devoted time and practice to a particular motor skill—say, concert pianists or tap dancers—often have larger representations of the corresponding body parts on their motor homunculus. It seems that extensive practice of motor skills changes the homunculus, allocating more space in M1 to those body parts for which extra motor control is needed. We'll discuss this topic in greater detail later, in the chapters on skill memory and perceptual learning.

Neural stimulation studies in a variety of species have greatly increased our understanding of how neuronal activity is translated into behavior. Although such studies are rarely done in humans, the relatively new method of *transcranial magnetic stimulation (TMS)* allows researchers to stimulate parts of the brain by placing a magnet on the skull. TMS activates entire brain areas rather than individual neurons, but it has the advantage that it requires no surgery and causes no lasting harm. Data from TMS studies may be most useful when considered in combination with results from studies of neural stimulation in animals and functional neuroimaging in humans, to help build the most complete picture possible of which parts of the brain give rise to which kinds of behavior. We describe this technique in greater detail in the chapter on skill memories.

Manipulating Neuronal Function with Drugs

Besides electrical and magnetic stimulation, a third method for manipulating neural activity is by the use of drugs. **Drugs** are chemical substances that alter the biochemical functioning of the body; drugs that work on the brain generally do so by altering synaptic transmission. For example, drugs can affect any of the processes depicted in Figure 2.12b. In each case, the effects of the drug on behavior depend on which neurotransmitters are involved and whether their ability to carry messages across the synapse is enhanced or impaired. We can summarize drug effects on processes 1 through 4 in Figure 2.12b as follows:

1. Drugs can increase or decrease the ability of the presynaptic neuron to produce or release neurotransmitter. For example, amphetamines alter the function of neurons that produce the neurotransmitter dopamine, causing the cells to release greater than normal quantities of dopamine. This means that postsynaptic neurons receive stronger and more frequent messages than normal. Because the dopamine system is involved in how the brain processes reward, this can lead to feelings of pleasurable anticipation or excitement. (More about this in the chapter on instrumental conditioning.)

2. Drugs can increase or decrease the ability of postsynaptic receptors to receive the chemical message. For example, heroin and morphine are chemically very similar to a class of naturally occurring neurotransmitters called opioid peptides. When heroin or morphine is released into the brain, molecules of the drug can fit into the receptors normally activated by the opioid peptides. In effect, the drugs "fool" the postsynaptic neuron into thinking a message has been received. The opioid peptides seem to be important in how the brain processes and signals pleasure, most likely explaining why drugs that mimic opioid peptides often cause intense feelings of pleasure. (More about this, also, in the chapter on instrumental conditioning.)

3. and **4.** Drugs can alter the mechanisms for clearing neurotransmitter molecules out of the synapse. Some antidepressant medications (the selective serotonin reuptake inhibitors, or SSRIs) work by reducing the rate at which serotonin is cleared from synapses. Thus, each time a presynaptic neuron releases serotonin molecules into the synapse, they remain in the synapse longer, increasing their chance of eliciting a reaction in the postsynaptic cell.

This list is just the beginning of the ways in which drugs can affect brain function. A drug can have more than one effect, and it can affect more than one neurotransmitter system. Some of the most commonly used drugs, including alcohol and nicotine, have been intensively studied, so we know their effects on behavior. But they seem to have incredibly varied and complex effects on neurons and synaptic transmission, and the precise mechanisms by which these drugs affect brain activity are not yet entirely clear.

Few pharmaceutical drugs have been developed specifically to affect learning and memory abilities. More commonly, a drug's positive or negative effects on these abilities are side effects. For example, general anesthesia administered to ease the pain of childbirth can "erase" a mother's memory of her baby being born. General anesthesia effectively turns off parts of the CNS that respond to pain by stopping those neurons from firing; it is not known exactly how. The main goal of using general anesthesia during nonsurgical births is to relax the mother by alleviating pain. A side effect, however, is that memories several hours before and after the anesthetic is administered are lost.

Researchers may not always have a clear idea of why specific drugs enhance or hinder learning, but drugs can change neural activity and can therefore alter behavior. In this way, drugs are like learning: learning also produces changes in neural activity and behavior. (See "Learning and Memory in Everyday Life" on p. 73 for an interesting look at the possibilities of memory-enhancing drugs.) The difference is that learning does not require chemicals or electrical currents to be introduced into the brain from outside. Rather, a person's observations and actions produce activity in the brain that can change the way it functions in the future. The following section describes some of the ways in which such experiences lead to physical changes in neurons.

Synaptic Plasticity

Learning can lead to numerous physical changes in a neuron. The most easily observed changes involve alterations in the cell's shape or size, but there can also be changes in supporting structures such as the glia or the circulatory system. All of these physical changes can affect how neurons communicate and how brain systems function. Nevertheless, memory researchers have focused almost exclusively on understanding **synaptic plasticity,** the ability of synapses to change as a result of experience.

▶ **Learning and Memory in Everyday Life**

Can a Pill Improve Your Memory?

If you've ever studied for a difficult exam, you've probably wished for a pill that could make your brain function like a copy machine. Instead of reading, reviewing, and rehearsing, you could swallow the pill, read the material once, and have it encoded in your brain forever (or at least until the exam is over). Sounds like science fiction, right?

In fact, several companies, including some pharmaceutical giants and smaller biotech companies, are looking for a drug to improve memory in healthy people. Some possible candidates are currently being tested on laboratory rats, and a few are even being tested in small groups of human volunteers. It remains to be seen which of these new drugs will be safe and effective. A drug might work well in the laboratory but have little effect on everyday life outside the lab. Other drugs might have a significant impact on memory but cause unacceptable side effects. Still others might have benefits for people with memory impairments but be of little use to individuals with normal memory abilities.

If drugs do become available to boost memory in otherwise healthy people, this will raise a host of ethical questions. For example, if drugs can make a person "smarter," will parents feel compelled to give their children drugs to help them excel in school? Will adults feel similarly compelled to pop pills to compete in the workplace? And, given that some existing drugs cost $6 to $20 for a single dose,

would the rich get smarter while the poor fall behind?

Until the new generation of memory-boosting drugs becomes available, researchers are examining whether existing drugs, already approved for the treatment of other illnesses, might provide a memory boost in normal, healthy people. For example, in the treatment of Alzheimer's disease, several drugs—including donepezil (Aricept)—increase brain levels of the neurotransmitter acetylcholine, which is abnormally low in people with Alzheimer's. These drugs can produce modest, temporary memory improvements in many of these patients, raising the possibility that they might also improve memory in healthy (or mildly impaired) adults (Whitehead et al., 2004). However, there is little evidence so far to suggest that these drugs can boost memory in otherwise healthy people (Beglinger et al., 2004). One reason is that healthy brains already have appropriate levels of acetylcholine. Adding extra neurotransmitter to an already replete brain may have no benefit (or might even cause impairments).

Another approach is based on the fact that attention and concentration increase the chance that new information will be successfully stored and retained in memory. So, drugs that improve attention might also improve memory. Such attention-boosting drugs include modafinil (Provigil), which is used to treat sleep disorders, and methylphenidate (Ritalin), used to treat attention deficit hyperactivity disorder (ADHD). Many college students already pop Ritalin in an effort to boost studying or exam performance. Caffeine (in coffee, soda, or tablet form) also provides a temporary boost in attention.

But it's not clear that boosting attention beyond normal levels is necessarily

good for memory. Normally, attention works by helping us process (and encode) important information at the expense of less important information. An overall increase in attention may just mean that all incoming information gets encoded and important information fails to receive the priority it deserves. The jury is still out on whether these drugs improve memory in healthy humans (Mehta et al., 2000; Turner et al., 2003).

Purveyors of a vast array of dietary supplements, including ginkgo biloba and phosphatidylserine (commonly abbreviated PS), also claim that these products work as memory enhancers. Dietary supplements, just like Ritalin and Aricept, are technically drugs, insofar as they are chemical substances that can alter brain chemistry. But because their manufacturers market them as "supplements" rather than "medicines," the products are not subject to the same strict government regulatory oversight as most other drugs. Despite huge sales of these dietary supplements, most researchers agree that there is currently little, if any, convincing evidence that they improve memory in healthy adults (Gold, Cahill, & Wenk, 2003; Jorissen et al., 2001). In addition, some supplements can have dangerous side effects; ginkgo biloba, for example, may interact dangerously with certain kinds of anticoagulant medications (including aspirin), increasing the risk of stroke.

The bottom line is that, so far, no pill can substitute for the hard work of learning. Instead of spending money on "brain-boosting" drugs of questionable efficacy and safety, healthy people are best advised to do their learning the old-fashioned way: by taking the time to study the material.

The idea that connections between neurons change during learning was first popularized by Santiago Ramón y Cajal (1852–1934), a famous Spanish physiologist and anatomist. At about this time, the Italian anatomist Camillo Golgi had developed a new technique, called the Golgi stain: a small piece of brain tissue is treated with a solution of silver chromate, and a small percentage of neurons in the tissue sample (apparently at random) take up this stain. This new process allowed the production of stunning pictures (like the one in Figure 2.11a) that show neuronal structure in exquisite detail. Neurons are so densely packed in brain tissue that if they all took up the stain, the picture would be solid black!

Using Golgi's technique, Cajal was able to study neurons in fine detail, revealing that they are individual cells, most with the same basic structure of dendrites, cell body, and axon. Based on these studies, Cajal concluded that neurons don't actually touch, but instead communicate by means of specialized junctions called synapses—a theory that was later proven largely correct (partly by the advent of electron microscopes, which allowed the construction of hugely magnified images such as that in Figure 2.12a). Cajal further speculated that learning involves changes in synapses, strengthening or weakening the ability of messages to cross from one neuron to another (Ramón y Cajal, 1990 [1894]).

But how does the brain know which connections to weaken or strengthen? One of neuroscience's most enduring insights came from Donald Hebb, a Canadian neuroscientist who studied under Karl Lashley and had read the works of Sherrington and Pavlov. Hebb's basic idea was that "neurons that fire together, wire together." More formally, if two neurons—say, neuron A and neuron B—often fire at nearly the same time, then the synapse between them should be strengthened, "wiring" the two neurons together. This would increase the probability that whenever neuron A became active in future, it would cause neuron B to become active too (Hebb, 1949).

According to Hebb, neurons could change synaptic connections automatically, as a function of their mutual activity. We now know that Hebb was on the right track. But it was several more decades before technology advanced to the point where a graduate student became the first person to observe experience-related changes in neuronal activity.

Long-Term Potentiation

In the late 1960s, Terje Lømo was pursuing his doctorate in the lab of Per Andersen at the University of Oslo in Norway. Part of Lømo's research consisted of finding two neurons that shared a synapse, then inserting a stimulating electrode into the presynaptic neuron A and a recording electrode into the postsynaptic neuron B (Figure 2.15a). Lømo then stimulated neuron A and recorded the response in neuron B. Normally, a certain amount of stimulation produced a certain level of response: a single weak stimulation in A would produce a low response in B, and a strong burst of high-frequency stimulation in A (say, 100 stimulations in a second) would produce a robust response in B. But to Lømo's surprise, the high-frequency stimulation of neuron A also caused a lasting change in neuron B, so that B would over-respond to subsequent weak stimulation from A (Figure 2.15b). This change could last for hours (Bliss & Gardner-Medwin, 1973; Bliss & Lømo, 1973; Lømo, 1966).

By way of analogy, imagine you have a brother who constantly torments you with his snide comments. Most of the time, you don't react. But one day he says something that's really over the top, and you respond with some strong language of your own. A few minutes later, before you've had a chance to calm down, he makes another little snide comment. Ordinarily, you might not have bothered to

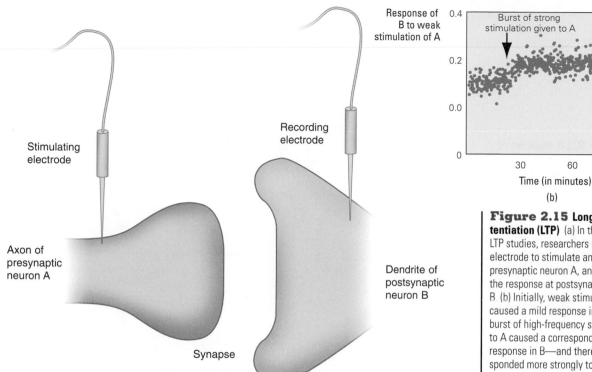

(a)

(b)

Figure 2.15 Long-term potentiation (LTP) (a) In the original LTP studies, researchers used one electrode to stimulate an axon of presynaptic neuron A, and recorded the response at postsynaptic neuron B. (b) Initially, weak stimulation of A caused a mild response in B. But a burst of high-frequency stimulation to A caused a correspondingly strong response in B—and thereafter, B responded more strongly to weak stimulation of A than it had previously. In other words, the high-frequency stimulation increased, or "potentiated," B's response to subsequent stimuli. Such potentiation can last for hours or longer and may reflect changes in neuronal connections as a result of experience.

respond. But this time you haven't yet cooled down from the earlier explosion, so you snap back again. Your prior anger has *potentiated* your response to a weak stimulus that normally wouldn't have evoked such a strong reaction.

In just the same way, a strong stimulation can potentiate a neuron, making it more likely to respond to any subsequent stimulus. This effect, in which synaptic transmission becomes more effective as a result of recent activity, came to be called **long-term potentiation (LTP).** The reports by Lømo and his coworkers were the first demonstrations that neurons could actually change their activity as a function of experience and that these changes could last for hours or days (Bliss & Gardner-Medwin, 1973; Bliss & Lømo, 1973). Since that time, LTP has become one of the most intensively studied phenomena in neuroscience. Although the first LTP experiments were done using neurons in the hippocampus of a rabbit, later studies showed that LTP occurs in many brain regions and many other species (Shors & Matzel, 1997) and that electrical stimulation of the presynaptic neuron is not required. As long as the presynaptic neuron and the postsynaptic neuron are active at the same time, LTP can occur.

Some forms of LTP affect only the synapse between the two coactive neurons; other synapses on the same postsynaptic neuron (that were not active at the same time) are not changed (Figure 2.16). This type of LTP, called *associative LTP*, provides a way in which specific synapses can change as a result of conjoint activation (McNaughton, Douglas, & Goddard, 1978). In other words, neurons that fire together, wire together—just as Hebb had predicted several decades previously. When shown these results, Donald Hebb is said to have appeared pleased but not surprised: for Hebb, it had simply been a question of when, not whether, he would be proven correct (McNaughton & Barnes, 1990). Other forms of LTP have also been hypothesized.

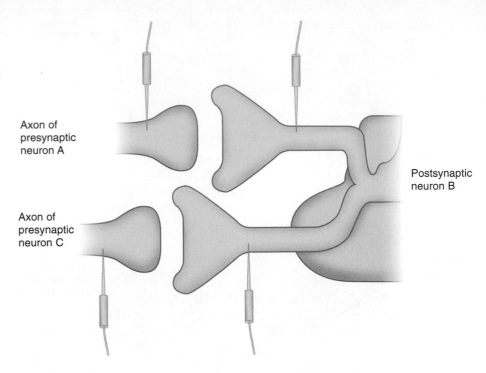

Figure 2.16 Associative long-term potentiation If neuron A and neuron B are conjointly active, the synapse between them is potentiated, so that subsequent activation of presynaptic neuron A is more likely to cause a response in postsynaptic neuron B. But this does not affect the degree to which activation of other neurons, such as presynaptic neuron C, will cause a response in B. Just as Hebb proposed, only neurons that fire together will wire together.

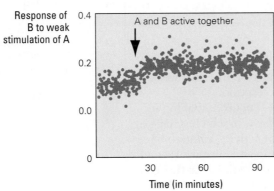

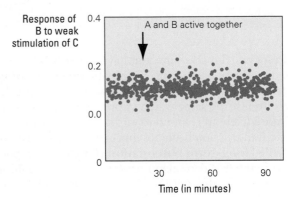

How Is LTP Implemented in a Neuron?

Despite intensive study of LTP in the decades since Lømo and others published the initial reports, many questions remain about what actually goes on inside a neuron during LTP. There may be (at least) three separate components.

First, postsynaptic receptors may change to become more responsive to subsequent inputs. This would mean that when neuron A fires again, releasing neurotransmitter into the synapse (see Figure 2.15a), neuron B will have a heightened sensitivity to that neurotransmitter, producing the enhanced responding seen in Figure 2.15b.

A second component of LTP may change the presynaptic neuron. This idea is still controversial, as it isn't clear how signals could travel backward across the synapse. But perhaps some kind of chemical—a *retrograde messenger*—could be released by the postsynaptic neuron, diffuse across the synapse to the presynaptic neuron, and increase the amount of neurotransmitter it releases in the future.

This process would also mean that future firing in neuron A would lead to a heightened response in neuron B, just as shown in Figure 2.15b.

These presynaptic and postsynaptic changes might occur within a few minutes and last several hours. Most researchers currently believe there is a third component of LTP that takes place over several hours and can last a lifetime. This would involve structural changes to the postsynaptic neuron, perhaps a strengthening of existing synapses, or even the building of new ones. As yet, though, the details remain largely murky.

What Is the Relationship of LTP to Learning?

In all the excitement about LTP, one important fact is often overlooked: in the original experiments, LTP was not associated with any learning or memory process. No change was observed in the animals' behavior as a result of the experimental manipulation of their neurons. In fact, surprisingly, a recent review of LTP experiments revealed that of the more than 1,000 research articles with "LTP" in the title, fewer than 80 contained any behavioral manipulation related to learning or memory (Shors & Matzel, 1997). And just a subset of these few articles reported evidence consistent with the idea that LTP is involved in memory formation. So far, the best evidence linking LTP to memory comes from studies showing that: (1) drugs that block LTP can impair an animal's ability to learn, and (2) rats that have been genetically bred to have enhanced LTP often show better learning than normal rats. But a significant minority of researchers remain unconvinced that a link from LTP to learning and memory has been definitively proved.

Long-Term Depression

As exciting as LTP was to researchers looking for a possible mechanism for learning, there was one immediate problem. LTP provides a way to strengthen neuronal connections, but this alone isn't much use. If you think of the activity patterns of a neuron as being like an audio signal, then LTP corresponds to pumping up the volume of particular input patterns. But imagine an orchestra conductor who can only make the musicians play louder. Every symphony would end in cacophony! There has to be a way to turn individual sounds down, as well as up. Similarly, LTP is only effective as a way to increase the strength of useful synapses if there is an opponent process that can decrease the strength of unneeded synapses.

Fortunately, soon after Lømo and others' original reports, such an opponent process was discovered (Dunwiddie & Lynch, 1978). **Long-term depression (LTD)** occurs when synaptic transmission becomes less effective as a result of recent activity. One way this can happen is if the presynaptic neuron is repeatedly active but the postsynaptic neuron does not respond. Neurons that fire together wire together, but neurons that don't fire together become disengaged. The presynaptic neuron will become even less effective at evoking a response from its neighbor. This is believed to reflect a weakening in the synapse. As with the synaptic changes in LTP, the weakening could occur in various ways: there may be a decrease in the responsiveness of postsynaptic receptors, a decrease in presynaptic neurotransmitter release, or long-term structural changes in the neurons and synapses.

But, as with LTP, many of the details of LTD remain to be worked out. There is even an odd form of LTD in some parts of the brain, including the cerebellum, in which conjoint activation of the presynaptic and postsynaptic neurons can *weaken*—instead of strengthen—the synapse between them. There's still a long way to go in understanding these processes and the exact relationship between them, and in understanding how an organism's behavior changes as a result of learning.

Test Your Knowledge

Mechanisms of Synaptic Plasticity

Synaptic plasticity is one of the most researched phenomena in the field of neuro-science, yet in many ways it remains poorly understood. Identify which of the following statements accurately describe what is known about synaptic plasticity.

1. Memories cannot be formed unless LTP occurs.
2. Synaptic change can be produced through electrical stimulation.
3. Synaptic plasticity is most easily observed by monitoring changes in the concentration of neurotransmitters.
4. Whenever firing patterns change in a neural circuit, synaptic change has occurred somewhere in the circuit.
5. Synaptic plasticity can weaken or strengthen connections between neurons.
6. Synaptic plasticity can be measured in humans with fMRI.
7. Learning experiences can produce changes in any synapse.
8. LTP is observed only in animals that have recently been learning.

CONCLUSION

We've covered a lot of ground in this chapter. We started with the basic geography of the brain, moved on to some key principles of how the various brain regions process different kinds of information and give rise to different kinds of behavior, and ended with a closer look at how neurons transmit messages and change as a result of experience.

If you get the feeling that, for all this information, there is still a frustrating number of unresolved questions about learning and memory, you're absolutely correct. But this is also a time when technology and research are providing brain scientists with an unprecedented selection of techniques: functional imaging and EEG methods that allow visualization of brain activity, electron microscopes that make visible synapses and neurotransmitter-containing vesicles, and systems capable of recording single-cell activity from dozens of neurons simultaneously. These tools, now in fairly routine use, didn't even exist a few decades ago. When you look at the situation this way, it's amazing how much has been learned in such a short time.

Knowledge for its own sake is always worthwhile, but we're also living in an age when some of this knowledge can be put to practical use to improve the human condition. With that in mind, let's return to the two patients, Jennifer and Sean, introduced at the beginning of the chapter.

Once they arrived at the hospital, both Jennifer and Sean benefited from the availability of modern technology such as MRI, and from medical staff specialized in the study of the nervous system and its relation to behavior. This staff included the neurologists who performed brain surgery to repair the blood vessels in Sean's brain and the neuropsychologists who examined Sean and Jennifer after their initial treatment to document what cognitive problems they might have.

Now the two patients will begin a long program of rehabilitation, as they slowly learn to compensate for what's been damaged. In Jennifer's case, this may mean laboriously relearning to speak and use words. In Sean's case, it may mean weeks or months of physical therapy, relearning the skills of walking and keeping his balance when standing. To a certain extent, the rehabilitation techniques will be based on the therapists' practical knowledge of what methods have been helpful for similar patients in the past. But a good therapist is also aware of emerging knowledge of how brain systems function and interact, the kind of training regimens that are most likely to promote growth of new neuronal connections, and perhaps new medications that can encourage such growth. In short, the more neuroscientists learn about the brain and about neurons, the more knowledge will be available to the medical community working to help people like Jennifer and Sean.

So how do Jennifer's and Sean's stories end? Both patients still have some hard work ahead of them. Both have sustained brain damage that is beyond the ability of modern medicine to simply "fix" by transplant or medication. (The study of the brain and neural function may bring us closer to such miracle cures, but those days are not yet here.) Maybe Jennifer and Sean will eventually learn to function—speak and walk—almost as well as before their emergencies. And maybe not. In the meantime, the best hope for such patients may lie in ongoing research into how the brain creates, stores, and uses memories.

Key Points

- The brain and spinal cord comprise the vertebrate central nervous system. The brain controls behavior through connections with the peripheral nervous system, consisting of sensory neurons coming from sensory receptors and motor neurons going to body muscles. Most of these connections pass through the spinal cord.

- The vertebrate brain is organized into the cerebral cortex (including frontal lobes, temporal lobes, parietal lobes, and occipital lobes), cerebellum, and brainstem. Different parts of the cerebral cortex are specialized to process particular kinds of sensory information and to generate motor outputs.

- Learning can occur in animals with very simple nervous systems, including animals without a recognizable brain. Studying such "simpler" nervous systems has given researchers insights into how vertebrate and even human brains work.

- Phrenology was an early attempt to understand brain function by relating a person's mental abilities and personality to the size and shape of the skull. Other early studies of brain anatomy relied mainly on examining healthy and abnormal brains after death.

- Modern structural brain imaging techniques (including MRI and CT) provide ways to look at the physical structure of living brains, without causing harm. Brain lesions or abnormalities may be visible on the images.

- Reflexes are hardwired (unlearned) responses to stimuli. Sherrington and other early neuroscientists believed that all complex learning was built up from combinations of simple spinal reflexes.

- Bell proposed and Magendie demonstrated parallel fiber systems carrying sensory information into the spinal cord and commands from the spinal cord back out to the muscles and organs.

- In the brain, sensory information is initially processed in cortical regions specialized for processing particular sensory stimuli, such as primary auditory cortex (A1) for sounds, primary visual cortex (V1) for sights, and primary somatosensory cortex (S1) for touch stimuli. Each of these areas can transmit signals to other brain areas for further processing.

- Primary motor cortex (M1) produces outputs that guide coordinated movements. The area of the portion of motor cortex devoted to a given body part reflects the (innate or learned) degree of motor control for that body part.

- Accidental brain lesions in humans have revealed much about how the brain functions. Intentional brain lesions in animal models have similarly provided insights into the neurobiology of learning and memory. Lashley's experimental brain lesion studies led him to conclude that the engram, or physical trace of a memory in the brain, is not stored in any one place but rather is a function of the brain as a whole. More modern studies, however, have uncovered some localized evidence of engrams, particularly in subcortical structures (e.g., the cerebellum).

- Functional neuroimaging methods (such as fMRI and PET) allow researchers to track brain activity indirectly by measuring increases and decreases in blood flow to different brain regions as the brain performs a task. A difference image is created by subtracting an image of the brain at rest from an image of the brain at work, to identify those areas that are significantly more (or less) active during a specific behavior.

- Electroencephalography is a way of detecting electrical activity, or "brain waves," by means of electrodes placed on a person's scalp. These brain waves represent the summed electrical charges of many neurons near the recording site. Event-related potentials are EEG recordings averaged across many repeated stimulations or events, to allow enhanced detection of electrical signals.

- Neurons usually have extensions called dendrites, specialized to collect signals (input) from other neurons, and an axon, specialized to transmit messages (output) to other neurons. Most communication takes place across tiny gaps, or synapses: the presynaptic, or sending, neuron releases a neurotransmitter into the synapse; this chemical message crosses the synapse to activate receptors on the postsynaptic, or receiving, neuron.

- Single-cell recordings allow researchers to monitor and record from single neurons as they become active (or "fire"). Researchers can also use implanted electrodes to deliver electrical charges that stimulate a neuron into activity, so that the behavior it evokes can be observed.

- Drugs are chemicals that alter the biochemical functioning of the body. Drugs that affect the brain generally affect neural activity by increasing or decreasing the transfer of information between subsets of neurons.

- Learning requires physical changes in neural circuits. Neurons can physically change in many ways, and many of these changes can affect their firing behavior. The most prominent and easily observable changes involve changes in neurons' shape, size, and number of connections to other neurons.

- The ability of synapses to change with experience is called synaptic plasticity. Strengthening or weakening the connections between neurons can influence how they fire.

- Long-term potentiation occurs when synaptic transmission becomes more effective as a result of experience. One form of LTP is described by Hebb's rule that "neurons that fire together, wire together." Specifically, synapses are strengthened as a result of conjoint activity of the presynaptic and postsynaptic neurons.

- An opponent process to LTP, called long-term depression, occurs when synaptic transmission becomes less effective with experience, thereby weakening connections between neurons.

Key Terms

axon, p. 65
brainstem, p. 46
cell body, p. 65
central nervous system (CNS), p. 45
cerebellum, p. 46
cerebral cortex, p. 46
computed tomography (CT), p. 51
dendrite, p. 65
difference image, p. 60
drug, p. 71
electroencephalography (EEG), p. 63

engram, p. 58
event-related potential (ERP), p. 63
frontal lobe, p. 46
functional magnetic resonance imaging (fMRI), p. 60
functional neuroimaging, p. 59
glia, p. 66
lesion, p. 51
long-term potentiation (LTP), p. 75
long-term depression (LTD), p. 77

magnetic resonance imaging (MRI), p. 51
nervous system, p. 45
neuromodulator, p. 68
neuron, p. 45
neurophysiology, p. 68
neuropsychology, p. 57
neuroscience, p. 44
neurotransmitter, p. 67
occipital lobe, p. 46
parietal lobe, p. 46
peripheral nervous system (PNS), p. 45
phrenology, p. 50

positron emission tomography (PET), p. 59
postsynaptic, p. 66
presynaptic, p. 66
receptor, p. 67
reflex, p. 53
single-cell recording, p. 68
soma, p. 65
structural neuroimaging, p. 51
synapse, p. 66
synaptic plasticity, p. 72
temporal lobe, p. 46
theory of equipotentiality, p. 58

Concept Check

1. In addition to learning to salivate whenever they heard a bell, some of Pavlov's dogs learned to salivate whenever Pavlov walked into the room. Why might this have occurred, and what region(s) of a dog's cortex might have changed as a result of this learning?

2. Neuroimages of different individuals performing the same task often differ greatly in the brain regions shown to be activated. Does this mean that all of these individuals' brains function differently? If not, why not?

3. Drugs or genetic manipulations that block LTP in the hippocampus impair learning in some tasks but facilitate learning in other tasks. Similarly, some researchers have correlated LTP-like effects with

learning in a variety of tasks, whereas others have observed learning in the absence of these LTP effects. What does this tell us about the relationship between LTP and learning?

4. Brain damage caused by carbon monoxide poisoning (such as Jennifer experienced) can result in many deficits, including color blindness, an inability to recognize objects, an inability to detect movement, and severe impairments in language and memory.

How can a neuropsychologist determine what part(s) of the brain might have been damaged?

5. Lashley's findings from lesion experiments in rats suggest that the brain can function when only part of the cerebral cortex is available. Additionally, invertebrates have been learning successfully for millions of years with less than 1% of the total neurons mammals have. What does this information imply about the role of the cerebral cortex in learning and memory?

Answers to Test Your Knowledge

Mechanisms of Synaptic Plasticity

1. False. It is not yet known exactly which types of memory formation require LTP, but some kinds of learning can occur even when LTP is blocked.

2. True. This is what happened in the original LTP studies: the researchers stimulated one neuron and observed LTP in the postsynaptic neuron, indicating that the synapse had been strengthened.

3. False. The best ways to observe synaptic plasticity are to look for physical changes in synapses or for changes in firing patterns as a result of the learning experience.

4. False. A neuron changes its firing pattern when its inputs change, whether or not any synaptic change takes place.

5. True.

6. False. fMRI does not measure neural activity and cannot detect synapses; it measures changes in blood flow, which is an indirect measure of neural activity.

7. False. It is not yet known which synapses in most neural circuits are affected by learning.

8. False. LTP has only occasionally been observed in animals that are learning. It is commonly measured independent of any observable behavior.

Further Reading

Campbell, R., & Conway, M. (Eds.). (1995). *Broken memories: a case study in memory impairment*. Cambridge, MA: Blackwell. • A collection of chapters, by various contributors, on different kinds of memory problems. This is a good resource if your main interest is the neuropsychology of memory. The book contains descriptions of individuals who have sustained brain damage that decreased their memory abilities.

Gazzaniga, S. (2000). *The new cognitive neurosciences*. Cambridge, MA: MIT Press. • Everything you ever wanted to know about brain imaging studies in humans but were afraid to ask. This comprehensive text contains insights from the greats of the field, and only weighs about 10 kilograms. The author discusses memory, attention, thinking, perception, decision making, imagery, problem solving, language, and more.

Gordon, B. (1995). *Memory: remembering and forgetting in everyday life*. New York: Mastermedia. • A readable description of

how drugs, age, and gender affect memory. This book provides everyday examples of how these different variables are involved in learning.

Kandel, E. R. (2006). *In search of memory: the emergence of a new science of mind*. New York: W. W. Norton. • An autobiography of Eric Kandel, who received a Nobel Prize for his work exploring the neural bases of learning and memory in the sea snail.

Kandel, E. R., Schwartz, J. H., & Jessell, T. M. (2000). *Principles of neural science*. New York: McGraw Hill. • The bible of neuroscience. The book discusses neurons, axons, dendrites, synapses, neurotransmitters, and basic tenets of neuroscience.

Squire, L. R., & Kandel, E. R. (2000). *Memory: from mind to molecules*. New York: Freeman. • Descriptions of several memory processes and the cellular and molecular mechanisms that are currently thought to underlie them.

CHAPTER 3

Episodic and Semantic Memory

Memory for Facts and Events

I N THE 2000 MOVIE *MEMENTO*, LEONARD Shelby attempts to track down the man who raped and murdered his wife. The dramatic twist is that, while trying to save his wife, Leonard suffers a brain injury that leaves him unable to form new memories for autobiographical events. He can remember all the details of his life up until the night of the attack, but he can't recall anything that has happened to him since then. His immediate memory is unaffected: as long as he is carrying on a conversation or thinking intently about a piece of information, he can remember what he is doing. But as soon as he turns his attention to something else, the prior memories fade. In one scene, a hotel employee swindles Leonard, who can't remember that he's already paid for a room; in another scene, Leonard learns a nasty truth about a character who claims to be helping him, only to forget the vital information a few minutes later.

Leonard struggles to piece together the clues leading to the identity of his wife's murderer. He makes notes to himself on scraps of paper, or has them tattooed on his body, so that in a few minutes, when the memories have faded, he can use the written cues to remind himself of what he's learned so far.

Such **amnesia,** or memory loss, has formed the plot of countless movies, television shows, and stories. Sometimes, as in *Memento*, the hero is unable to form new memories. More often, the hero loses past memories. For example, in the 2002 film *The Bourne Identity*, Jason Bourne awakes on a fishing boat with no memory of his own name, his past, or his identity as a CIA assassin. In the 1990 sci-fi classic *Total Recall*, Douglas Quaid experiences the opposite problem: false memories are *added* to his brain—making him "remember" a past that never actually happened. Unlike Leonard Shelby, who can't learn anything new, Bourne and Quaid can acquire new information: for them, it's the past that has been lost or changed.

Amnesia is a real medical condition—although it is much rarer in real life than its prevalence in the movies suggests. It is such an attractive and enduring plot device precisely because it taps into our instinctive feeling that our memories—the facts we know and the autobiographical events we remember—define our very identity.

3.1 Behavioral Processes

Think back to the day of your high school graduation. Where was the ceremony held? Who sat near you? What were you wearing? Did the class valedictorian speak? Did the school band perform? What were your feelings—pride, excitement, or perhaps impatience for the ceremony to end so you could celebrate with your friends?

These details of your graduation constitute what University of Toronto psychologist Endel Tulving called an **episodic memory:** a memory for a specific autobiographical event (Tulving, 1972, 1983, 2002). An episodic memory includes information about the spatial and temporal context: where and when the event occurred.

Highly related to episodic memories are **semantic memories,** memories for facts or general knowledge about the world. Unlike episodic memory, semantic memory is not tagged in time and space. For example, if asked to name the first president of the United States, you can state the answer. But you may not remember exactly where or when you first learned this information. Whereas episodic memory is information we "remember," semantic memory is information we "know" (Tulving, 1985).

Episodic (Event) Memories and Semantic (Fact) Memories

Episodic and semantic memories share two key features (Table 3.1). First, both episodic and semantic memories can be communicated flexibly, in different formats than the one in which they were originally acquired. When you remember an episodic memory—say, attending your graduation—you recall various details, including the spatial and temporal location, and you can describe these details to others, even if you've never tried putting them into words before.

Table 3.1

Comparing and Contrasting Episodic and Semantic Memory

Episodic Memory	Semantic Memory
Autobiographical: "I remember"	Factual: "I know"
Can be communicated flexibly—in a format other than that in which it was acquired	Can be communicated flexibly—in a format other than that in which it was acquired
Consciously accessible (you know that you know)	Consciously accessible (you know that you know)
Tagged with spatial and temporal context	Not necessarily tagged with a context
Learned in a single exposure	Can be learned in a single exposure, but can also be strengthened by repetition

Similarly, if someone were to show you a photo of the graduation taken from a different vantage point (perhaps taken from the stage rather than from where you and your classmates were seated), you would probably be able to recognize the scene, even though you had never seen it in quite this way.

Semantic memory can also be communicated flexibly. If someone asks you how to get from your home to class, you can answer by giving verbal directions or by drawing a map, even though you may never have attempted to put the information into these formats before. Similarly, after studying a list of historical facts, you can generally communicate that knowledge on an exam, whether the format is true/false, multiple choice, or essay questions.

This flexibility may sound trivial, but many memories are hard to communicate in ways other than how they were originally learned. For example, in the next chapter you'll read about skill memories, such as memory for motor skills like tying our shoes. You can probably tie a shoe easily; but suppose someone asked you for a short description of how to do it. Odds are you'd find it very difficult—you might even have to go through the hand movements to remind yourself what comes next. Motor skill memories are generally not easy to communicate flexibly in the same way as semantic and episodic memories are.

The second key commonality between episodic and semantic memories is that both are generally accessible to conscious recall. When someone asks you about a specific episodic memory, you know whether you remember it or not. Similarly, when someone asks you about a specific semantic memory, you generally know whether you know the answer. If asked about the first U.S. president, you know that you know the answer; even if the name temporarily slips your mind, you know that sooner or later you'll remember it. Many other kinds of learning are not normally consciously accessible. Again, a good example is skill learning. People with amnesia (who can't acquire new episodic memories) can often learn new skills such as solving puzzles or reading mirror-reversed text. But when asked about these new skills, they may deny that they know how to do these things, because they have no conscious memories of acquiring these skills.

Because of these similarities between semantic and episodic memory, some researchers use the term **declarative memory** as a broader term that includes both semantic and episodic memory (Anderson, 1976; Cohen & Squire, 1980; Squire, Knowlton, & Musen, 1993). Other researchers prefer the term **explicit memory** (Graf & Schacter, 1985; Schacter, 1987). These terms reflect the fact that episodic and semantic information is consciously accessible or "explicit" (you know that you know), and it is usually easy to verbalize or "declare" your knowledge. This property of declarative memory contrasts with all the other kinds of memory—sometimes grouped under the heading **nondeclarative memory** or **implicit memory**—which are not always consciously accessible or easy to verbalize (Squire & Knowlton, 1995).

Differences between Episodic and Semantic Memory

Despite their similarities, episodic and semantic memory have several contrasting properties (Table 3.1). First, episodic memories must have autobiographical content (they must have happened to you) and you must remember when and where the events occurred. Semantic memories need not have this autobiographical content, and you need not necessarily remember when or how you learned the information.

Second, by definition, episodic memory is acquired in a single exposure: the event itself. In principle, semantic memories can be acquired in a single exposure too, particularly if the information is sufficiently interesting or important. For example, it might take you several exposures to memorize the Latin word for "arc" or "arch"—*fornix*—unless you are also told that, in ancient Rome, prostitutes used

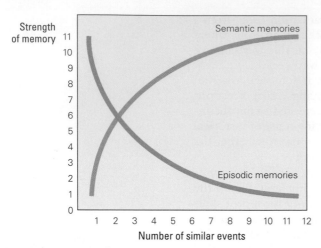

Figure 3.1 Episodic and semantic memory In general, semantic memory is strengthened by repetition, but episodic memory may be weakened by repeated exposure to similar events.

to ply their trade under such arches, which is where we get the word "fornicate." Such extra information, which relates the vocabulary item to other information you know, may help you remember the word after only a single exposure.

But ordinary semantic information generally needs a few additional exposures before being fully acquired. So, for example, you may have to study a Latin vocabulary list several times before you have all the items memorized. In general, repeated exposures strengthen semantic memory (Linton, 1982); by contrast, repeated exposure to very similar events may weaken episodic memory for any one event (Figure 3.1). If you park your car in the same large parking lot every day, you may confuse the episodic memories of all the prior, highly similar parking events, making it hard to remember exactly where you parked the car today. This is one reason why any large parking lot contains a number of people walking around aimlessly with panicked expressions on their faces.

Which Comes First, Episodic or Semantic Memory?

The exact relationship between episodic and semantic memory is unclear. One possibility, espoused by Tulving and others, is that episodic memory grows out of semantic memory (Tulving, 2002). According to this view, an organism has to have a certain amount of semantic information before episodic memories can be formed based on that framework. If you don't know what a graduation is, you can hardly have an episodic memory for any specific graduation—even your own.

An alternative possibility is that semantic memory is information we have encountered repeatedly, often enough that the actual learning episodes are blurred and only the semantic "fact" content remains. For example, if you remember the very first time you learned about George Washington, then you have an episodic memory for that event—perhaps a history lesson. But if you have heard about George Washington in many different classes and have also read about him in books and seen television depictions, then you have accumulated a general store of knowledge about the first U.S. president, whether or not you remember the individual episodes.

Can Nonhumans Have Episodic Memory?

The easiest way to assess semantic memory in humans is by question-and-answer. If an experimenter asks you the name of the first U.S. president and you reply "George Washington," then the experimenter can safely conclude that you have a semantic memory of that fact. Things get a little more problematic with animals; we can't ask a rat to name the president. Nevertheless, many nonhuman animals can express knowledge about the world in a way that seems to suggest they have general semantic memories of where food is located or how to avoid an electric shock.

Episodic memory is harder to assess in animals. In fact, Tulving has explicitly argued that animals cannot maintain episodic memories, at least not in the way that humans do (Tulving, 2002; see also Roberts, 2002). For Tulving and many others, episodic memory requires "mental time travel" to re-experience the event in memory. This requires a conscious sense of self, as well as a subjective sense of time passing. With the possible exception of the findings in large-brained mammals such as dolphins and gorillas, most research has failed to document either self-awareness or a sense of time in animals. However, other researchers argue that there is mounting evidence that animals can form memories for specific events, including information about the spatial and temporal context in which those events occurred (Clayton, Yu, & Dickinson, 2001; Schwartz & Evans, 2001).

For example, gorillas seem to remember specific autobiographical events, and they can communicate this information flexibly to human testers. One gorilla, King, was taught to "name" various fruits and humans by using cards with drawings that represented the fruits and humans (Schwartz, Colon, Sanchez, Rodriguez, & Evans, 2002). This general knowledge about how to use the cards qualifies as semantic memory. Researchers then attempted to assess whether King could remember distinct autobiographical episodes. During the day, King received pieces of fruit from his human handlers. Twenty-four hours later, when asked (via the cards) who gave him fruit the day before, King could produce the correct cards to name the fruit and the human. Because King had eaten several fruits and interacted with other humans during the course of the day, his performance seems to demonstrate that he has episodic memory for the events of the prior day—remembering not just that he ate fruit, but the specific type of fruit, who gave it to him, and approximately when this happened. And he could communicate this behavior to the experimenters, using abstract symbols on cards. This behavior seems to satisfy most of the criteria for an episodic memory (Schwartz & Evans, 2001). Other large-brained animals such as dolphins may also be able to remember specific past events, including objects, locations, and environmental cues (Mercado, Murray, Uyeyama, Pack, & Herman, 1998).

Birds may also be able to remember specific events and how long ago they happened. Scrub jays, for example, bury extra food in caches, so they can retrieve it later. These birds accurately remember their cache locations and will return there later, even if an experimenter has secretly removed the food in the meantime, proving that the birds aren't just sniffing out the buried food.

In addition to remembering cache locations, scrub jays may form episodic memories of what they stored when. Nicola Clayton and her colleagues allowed scrub jays to cache two of the birds' favorite foods, worms and nuts, in sand-filled compartments of an ice-cube tray (Figure 3.2a). The birds were then allowed to recover food either 4 hours or 124 hours later. Normally, scrub jays prefer worms to nuts, and when tested after a 4-hour interval they generally choose to recover the worms (Figure 3.2b). But worms decay over a 124-hour interval, and nuts do not. And, indeed, when tested at a 124-hour interval, the birds typically preferred to recover the nuts (Clayton & Dickinson, 1999). These results suggest that scrub jays can remember not only where they have stored food, but what type of food was stored and how long ago (Clayton et al., 2001; Griffiths, Dickinson, & Clayton, 1999).

Figure 3.2 Episodic memory in birds (a) Scrub jays were allowed to cache worms and nuts in the compartments of sand-filled ice-cube trays. (b) Some time later, the birds were allowed to recover food from the trays. If the delay was 4 hours, the birds tended to recover buried worms (their favorite food). But if the delay was 124 hours, during which time the worms would have rotted, the birds tended to recover the nuts instead. This suggests that the birds remembered what they had buried where, and how long ago—an "episodic-like" memory. (a) Adapted from Griffiths et al., 1999; (b) adapted from Roberts, 2002.

(a)

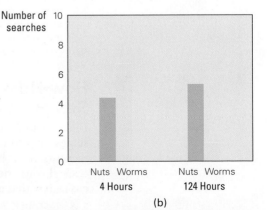

(b)

Even social insects, including bees and wasps, may form rudimentary episodic memories. In each beehive, some females serve as foragers, leaving the hive to hunt for food. When a forager bee locates a source of food, she returns to the hive and communicates this information to her sisters, so they can visit the food source too. She does this by "dancing" or "waggling," executing a complex set of movements that indicate both the direction and distance to the food source (Menzel & Muller, 1996). For this system to work, the forager bee has to learn the food location on a single trial, maintain this information long enough to get back to the hive, and then communicate the information to her sisters in a new format—by dancing. Again, this behavior seems to fit many of the criteria for episodic memory.

For the rest of this chapter, we'll adopt the convention of referring to "episodic" memories in nonhuman animals if those memories include information about the spatial and temporal context in which the episode occurred. Bear in mind, though, that these memories may be very different from human episodic memory. Indeed, some researchers believe that only humans can have the conscious recollection of autobiographical history that characterizes human episodic memories. If episodic memory requires the ability to perform "mental time-travel," to relive and review past experiences, then we currently have little evidence that nonhuman animals can do this.

Test Your Knowledge

Episodic versus Semantic Memory

Episodic memories are autobiographical memories, set in a particular time and spatial location; semantic memories are memories for fact or general knowledge about the world, independent of when and how this information was acquired. Sometimes, though, the line between the two is blurred. A single behavior can contain components of both semantic and episodic information. Read the following scenarios to check whether you understand the difference.

1. A college senior is helping a new student learn her way around campus. When the tour finishes, the newcomer asks where she can buy a cup of coffee. The senior thinks for a moment, then says that the coffee is better at a nearby Starbucks than at the student center. Is this an example of semantic or episodic memory?

2. The senior walks into his Latin vocabulary exam, later that day. The first phrase to be translated is *carpe diem*. This is an easy one; he knows the answer is "seize the day," even though he can't remember exactly where he first heard this expression. Is this student using semantic or episodic memory?

3. The second phrase to be translated is *ne tentes, aut perfice*. This is harder; the student can remember studying the phrase, and he even recalls that the phrase was printed in black ink on the lower left of a page in his textbook, but he can't recall the translation. Is the student using semantic or episodic memory?

How Humans Acquire and Use Episodic and Semantic Memories

Like all memories, episodic and semantic memories have three distinct life stages: first, the information must be encoded, or put into memory. Second, the memory must be retained, or kept in memory. Third, the memory must be retrieved when needed. Many factors affect each of these stages. Below, we'll discuss a few that apply to both episodic memory and semantic memory.

Memory Is Better for Information That Relates to Prior Knowledge

Earlier in the chapter, you read that the Latin word for "arc" or "arch" is *fornix*. To help make this information memorable, we presented the tidbit about Roman prostitutes. The idea is that knowing the link between *fornix* and "fornication" (a word you already know) will help you remember better than just trying to memorize an otherwise meaningless Latin word.

A basic principle of memory is that it is easier to remember information you can interpret in the context of things you already know. In a classic study, John Bransford and Marcia Johnson read the following paragraph to a group of people:

> If the balloons popped, the sound wouldn't be able to carry, since everything would be too far away from the correct floor. A closed window would also prevent the sound from carrying, since most buildings tend to be well-insulated. Since the whole operation depends on a steady flow of electricity, a break in the middle of the wire would also cause problems. Of course, the fellow could shout, but the human voice is not loud enough to carry that far. An additional problem is that a string could break on the instrument. Then there could be no accompaniment to the message. It is clear that the best situation would involve less distance. Then there would be fewer potential problems. With face-to-face contact, the least number of things could go wrong.

The first time you encounter this paragraph, it makes little sense. Unsurprisingly, Bransford and Johnson found that, on testing, most people recalled very little information from the paragraph—only about 20% of the ideas (Figure 3.3a) (Bransford & Johnson, 1972). However, a second group of people saw the sketch shown in Figure 3.3b before hearing the paragraph. The sketch shows a man serenading a woman at a high window. With this context, if you read the paragraph again, you will find that it makes more sense. Indeed, people who saw the picture first were able to recall twice as much information from the paragraph. Importantly, the effect of organization on memory is limited to encoding; people who heard the paragraph first, then saw the picture, did not recall the information any better than people who never saw the picture at all. Only people who knew the context ahead of time remembered the paragraph well.

This principle has clear implications for studying. In general, you will remember textbook material better if you take the time to scan a chapter first, to get a sense of the major points, before reading in detail. This is also the reason that many professors ask students to read the relevant chapter before coming to the lecture, so that the students' minds are prepared to encode and remember the information presented in the lecture.

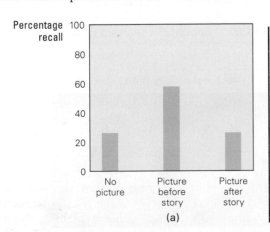

(a)

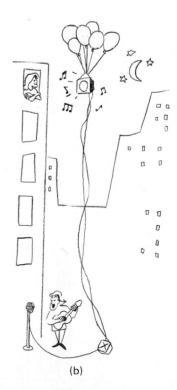

(b)

Figure 3.3 The effects of organization on memory An experimenter read aloud to participants a paragraph describing a scene. (a) Participants who heard the paragraph alone recalled few items; but participants who saw the picture in (b) and then heard the paragraph recalled more items. Participants who saw the picture only after hearing the paragraph performed no better than those who had never seen the picture. (a) Data from and (b) adapted from Bransford and Johnson, 1972.

On the other hand, sheer amount of exposure to information is not enough to guarantee memory. One telling example of this occurred when BBC Radio in the United Kingdom was planning to change its broadcast frequency. The BBC saturated the airwaves with announcements informing listeners about the new station call numbers. A survey of radio listeners who had heard the announcement at least 25 times a day for many weeks found that less than a quarter of these individuals had learned the new call numbers (Bekerian & Baddeley, 1980). Just hearing the information again and again wasn't enough to guarantee that listeners would remember. In short, it's *how* you study, not *how much* you study, that affects memory most.

Deeper Processing at Encoding Improves Recognition Later

So, how should you study to maximize memory? One answer is that the more deeply you analyze information, the more likely you are to encode the information in memory—and the more likely you are to remember it later (Craik & Lockhart, 1972; Craik & Tulving, 1975). This is known as **depth of processing.** If you think about the word *fornix* and its relationship to "fornication," you're processing the word more deeply than if you just tried to memorize the fact that *fornix* = "arch." Many experiments have shown that people remember words better if they're forced to think about the semantic content (meaning) of words rather than simply asked to memorize them without such efforts.

In one study, healthy young adults saw a list of adjectives. For some words, they were instructed to generate a mental image (for DIRTY they might imagine a garbage dump); for other words, they were asked to imagine pronouncing the word backward (for HAPPY they might say YIP-PAH). Presumably, the "image" condition required thinking deeply about the meaning of the word, but the "pronounce" condition required only superficial thinking about how the letters were arranged. Later, the participants were shown a list of words and asked to recognize those they had studied. And, just as you'd expect, Figure 3.4a shows that the deeply processed "image" words were better recognized than the superficially processed "pronounce" words (Davachi, Mitchell, & Wagner, 2003).

One criticism of the depth-of-processing idea is that it is vague. How, exactly, can we be sure whether individuals are processing information "deeply" or "superficially"? Just because an experimenter asks them to process words superficially, how can we know they are not thinking about the meaning of the word too? And, for that matter, how can we be sure that thinking about word meanings requires deeper processing than pronouncing words backward?

It is hard to answer these questions by using purely behavioral measures, but functional neuroimaging provides some clues. Lila Davachi and her colleagues used functional magnetic resonance imaging (fMRI) to look at brain activity during either the "image" condition or the "pronounce" condition (Davachi et al., 2003).

Figure 3.4 Depth of processing Young adults were shown a list of words and asked either to generate a mental image of a place described by the word (the "image" condition) or to imagine pronouncing the word backward (the "pronounce" condition). (a) Later, when shown a list of previously viewed words, the participants correctly recognized many more words from the "image" condition than from the "pronounce" condition. This suggests that deeper processing leads to better recognition later. (b) Researchers conducted fMRI scans during the "image" and "pronounce" conditions, and then subtracted activity levels to produce the difference images shown here. Several brain areas, shown in red, were significantly more active during the "image" condition than during the "pronounce" condition. (a) Data from and (b) adapted from Davachi et al., 2003.

(a) Recognition performance

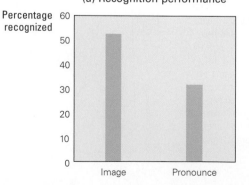

(b) Brain activity (fMRI)

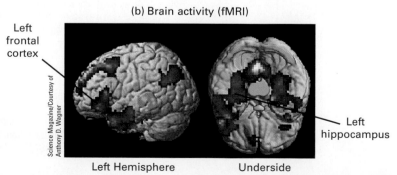

The two activity patterns were then subtracted to produce the difference images shown in Figure 3.4b. Overall, participants' brains were much more active during the "image" trials than during the "pronounce" trials. This suggests that the brain is indeed working harder during the "image" condition. Activity during the "image" condition was particularly high in the left frontal cortex, the left hippocampus, and nearby areas in the medial temporal lobe. Later in this chapter, we'll talk more about these brain areas and their roles in episodic and semantic memory; for now, though, note that the psychological concepts of deep versus superficial processing seem to correspond to physiological measures of how hard the brain is working.

The Forgetting Curve and Consolidation

As is probably obvious, you are more likely to remember things that happened recently than things that happened long ago. For example, you probably remember what you ate for breakfast today, and you might remember what you ate for breakfast 3 days ago, but you probably can't recall what you ate for breakfast on, say, July 16, 2003. However, if someone had asked you on July 17, 2003, what you had eaten the morning before, you probably could have answered. Somehow, that information has trickled away during the interval. What governs how fast we forget?

As you'll remember from Chapter 1, Hermann Ebbinghaus conducted a series of studies that were the first attempt to quantify human learning and forgetting. Ebbinghaus memorized lists of nonsense words and then tested his own memory for these items. He concluded that most forgetting occurs in the first few hours or days after learning (Ebbinghaus, 1885 [1964]). Information that survives the critical first few days might last in memory indefinitely.

Ebbinghaus's basic findings have since been replicated in a variety of studies. For example, memory researcher Larry Squire developed a test in which people were queried about television shows that had aired for a single season from 1 to 15 years earlier (Squire, 1989). On average, people did quite well at this test of semantic memory. Most people could correctly recognize the names of more than 75% of TV shows that had aired in the prior year, although they recognized progressively fewer shows from earlier years (Figure 3.5a). Most forgetting occurred within the first decade, so people remembered almost as many TV shows from 15 years ago as from 10 years ago.

Figure 3.5a suggests that, if you can still remember a fact or event after a few months, then the odds are very good that you'll remember it permanently. One

Figure 3.5 Forgetting in humans (a) In healthy adults, recognition of the names of television shows that aired for a single season declines with time. (b) Depressed patients, before electroconvulsive shock therapy (ECT), show a forgetting curve (purple line) similar to that of the healthy adults. After these patients undergo ECT (red line), recent memories are temporarily disrupted, but older ones are not affected. (a) Adapted from Squire, 1989; (b) adapted from Squire et al., 1975.

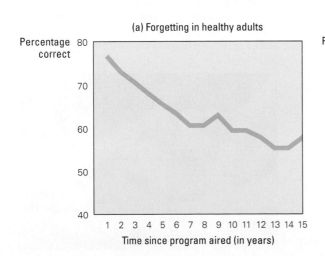

(a) Forgetting in healthy adults

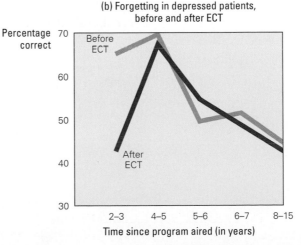

(b) Forgetting in depressed patients, before and after ECT

implication of this finding is that episodic and semantic memories have a **consolidation period,** a length of time during which new memories are vulnerable and easily lost (McGaugh, 2000; Ribot, 1882).

In an early demonstration of the consolidation period, Carl Duncan trained rats to make a response, and then gave the rats **electroconvulsive shock,** a brief pulse of electricity passed through the brain via electrodes on each side of the head. If the shock was given 20 seconds after training, the rats' memory was severely disrupted, suggesting that, at that point, the memory was still very vulnerable. However, if the shock was given an hour or more after training, there was little disruption. Intermediate delays produced intermediate levels of disruption (Duncan, 1949). This general pattern is consistent with the predictions of a consolidation period: older memories (in this case, memories from a few hours ago) are relatively stable and difficult to disrupt; more recent memories (in this case, memories from less than a minute ago) are very vulnerable to disruption.

No one is completely sure why electroconvulsive shock has the effects it does, but a useful analogy may be to think of a computer without a surge protector. If you are working on the computer when an electrical surge comes through the system, the computer may crash. When the computer reboots, any unsaved changes in the files you were working on may be lost, but older files—ones already saved to the hard drive when the surge occurred—may survive unscathed.

Electroconvulsive shock may sound dramatic, but it does not cause pain. The procedure is sometimes performed on humans to provide temporary relief from some kinds of mental illness, particularly severe depression (Cerletti & Bini, 1938; Coffey, 1993). Patients are given general anesthesia and a muscle relaxant beforehand, to prevent convulsions. The entire procedure (called *electroconvulsive therapy*, or *ECT*) takes about 30 minutes. No one knows exactly why ECT relieves depression, but patients often experience relief for weeks afterward (Glass, 2001; National Institutes of Health Consensus Conference, 1985).

By studying patients who are undergoing this therapy for medical reasons, researchers have been able to investigate the effects of electroconvulsive shock on human memory. For example, Larry Squire and his colleagues administered the TV-show test to patients with depression who were getting ready to undergo ECT (Squire, Slater, & Chace, 1975; Squire, Slater, & Miller, 1981). Before the therapy, the patients remembered recent shows (from 2–3 years earlier) very well, and older shows (from 8–15 years earlier) less well (Figure 3.5b). This is the same as the standard pattern observed in healthy adults. A week after therapy, the patients took the same test. Almost invariably, they had forgotten some of the information they'd reported earlier, especially memories for shows that had aired within the last few years; older memories (5+ years) were generally unaffected. A similar pattern was seen for autobiographical memories.

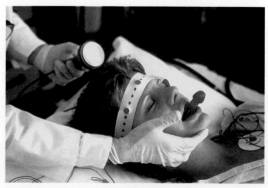

Electroconvulsive shock therapy is sometimes used to treat patients with severe depression.

Will McIntyre/Photo Researchers, Inc.

For most patients undergoing ECT, many of the missing memories return with time. Typically, only the memories for a short period before and after the ECT session are gone forever. For many patients, this limited memory loss is a minor irritation—and a small price to pay for relief from the debilitation of severe depression.

Transfer-Appropriate Processing

It isn't just individuals receiving ECT who experience temporary failure to retrieve items from memory. You've probably experienced the "tip-of-the-tongue" phenomenon, when you needed to access a word or a name from memory, an item that you were sure you knew but couldn't produce at the moment. In these cases, the information is not permanently lost, only temporarily inaccessible. You may recall the information later, often after you've turned your attention to something else.

Why can we retrieve stored memories at some times, yet at other times they elude us? One factor is the context. **Transfer-appropriate processing** refers to the principle that retrieval is more likely if the cues available at recall are similar to those that were available at encoding. For example, suppose you are shown a series of pictures of objects (a dog, a house, and so on). Then you take a recognition test, with some of the objects presented as pictures and some as words. Which objects do you think you'd remember best? Most people show better recognition if the format is the same at encoding and at testing: objects presented as words and tested as words, or presented as pictures and tested as pictures (Köhler, Moscovitch, Winocur, & McIntosh, 2000). Performance is worse when the encoding and testing formats differ.

Some researchers have argued that the depth-of-processing effect, whereby "deeper" processing leads to better memory than "superficial" processing, is really a transfer-appropriate processing effect in disguise. People who process a word "deeply," thinking about its meaning and visualizing it, may indeed be better at a standard visual recognition test (as you saw in Figure 3.4a). But people asked to merely rhyme a word—a "superficial" processing task that doesn't involve thinking about the word's semantic meaning—actually perform better if the later memory test involves rhyming recognition (Morris, Bransford, & Franks, 1977). In short, deep processing during encoding may help only if the test also requires deep processing. If the test instead involves the physical attributes or sounds of a word, superficial processing may be preferable!

Transfer-appropriate processing involves not only the physical appearance of the stimuli but also the physical context in which memory is stored and retrieved. Have you ever been at the gym or the supermarket and run into someone you know from school and been temporarily unable to recognize that person in the unusual context? You may even have struggled to chat for a while (without admitting you couldn't remember exactly who this person was) before something "clicked" and the memory fell into place. If you've ever had this type of experience, then you already know that context has a powerful effect on memory retrieval.

In a famous demonstration of this principle, researchers tested memory in members of a diving club (Godden & Baddeley, 1975). Some of the divers were asked to learn a list of 40 words while on dry land; the remainder learned the list underwater. The divers were then tested on their recall of the words. Divers who were tested in the same environment where they had studied the list (either on land or underwater) could remember more words than those who were trained in one environment and tested in the other. The same principles have been demonstrated—somewhat less dramatically—in a number of ways. For example, students who learn a list either standing up or sitting down will later recall a few more words if they are in the same position during testing (Godden &

Baddeley, 1975). A list learned while classical or jazz music plays will be remembered better if the same music plays during recall (Smith, 1985). In each case, then, recall is slightly better if the retrieval context is similar to the encoding context.

So, does this mean that studying in the same room where you will take a test will improve your performance? Not necessarily. A large study of 5,000 college students found no effect on performance when final exams were administered in the same room where the course had been taught or in a novel classroom (Saufley, Otaka, & Bavaresco, 1985). But there are other ways to use the principles of transfer-appropriate processing to your advantage. For example, suppose you can study for an exam either by taking online multiple-choice tests or by recruiting a friend to ask you open-ended questions from your class notes. If you know that the professor usually gives essay exams, which study method should you use? The best way to prepare for a test is by processing the material in a way that is similar to how you expect to be tested on it: making the study and recall format as similar as possible.

More Cues Mean Better Recall

Of course, several formats are available for testing recall. The first and most obvious is **free recall,** in which you are simply asked to generate the information from memory ("What is the Latin word for 'arch'?"). A second possibility is **cued recall,** in which you are given some kind of a prompt ("What is the Latin word for 'arch'?" F_____). A third possibility is **recognition,** in which you pick out the correct answer from a list of possible options ("Is the Latin word for 'arch': *fenestra, fornix,* or *fundus*?").

In general, free recall is harder than cued recall, which in turn is harder than recognition. This ranking directly reflects the number of cues available to jog the memory. In free recall, the experimenter provides no (or minimal) explicit cues; in cued recall, the experimenter provides at least some cues; and in recognition, the entire item is provided. In one study, when asked to recall the names of their high school classmates, recent graduates could, on average, produce about 50% of the names; individuals who had graduated several decades earlier could produce only about 20–30% of the names. But when shown a list of names and asked to recognize whether each person had been a classmate, recent graduates could get about 90% correct, and even long-ago graduates got about 85% correct (Bahrick, Bahrick, & Wittlinger, 1975).

Most people instinctively understand that free recall is harder than recognition. This is one reason why many students prefer to take exams with questions involving multiple choice (a recognition test) rather than essays (a free-recall test). Of course, professors know this too, and they usually compensate by designing multiple-choice questions to include alternative answers that can easily be mistaken for the correct response if a student hasn't studied the material closely. (Have you ever wished you were better at memorization? See "Learning and Memory in Everyday Life" on p. 95).

When Memory Fails

You've just seen some key factors that affect successful acquisition, retention, and recall of episodic and semantic memories. At each stage, various conditions (how the material is presented, whether you're underwater, etc.) can help or hinder the process. When you consider all the opportunities for failure, it is amazing how often our memories work properly. However, there are several common ways in which fact and event memory can malfunction. We'll consider three here: interference, source amnesia, and false memory.

▶ Learning and Memory in Everyday Life

Total Recall! The Truth about Extraordinary Memorizers

We have all heard stories about people who claim to have a *photographic memory,* meaning that they store "snapshots" in memory that they can later access and read like a book. However, there is no scientific evidence that photographic memory exists. The closest documented phenomenon is called *eidetic imagery,* the ability to store visual information vividly and faithfully, so that random details can be "read" out of the image later. The good news is that everyone possesses some degree of eidetic imagery. The bad news is that eidetic images typically fade after a few seconds and the information is lost.

Even if photographic memory does not exist, some people clearly have phenomenal memorization abilities. Probably the most famous expert memorizer was a Russian newspaper reporter named D. Shereshevskii (more commonly known as S.). Russian neuropsychologist Aleksandr Luria could read S. a list of 70 words, which S. then repeated from memory; 15 years later, Luria wrote: "S would sit with his eyes closed, pause, then comment: 'Yes, yes . . . This was a series you gave me once in your apartment. You were sitting at the table and I in the rocking chair . . . You were wearing a gray suit . . .' And with that he would reel off the series precisely as I had given it to him at the earlier session" (Luria, 1982 [1968], p. 384).

S. visualized stimuli mentally, in great detail, and these images helped him recall information later. But, Luria reports, S. paid a price. Because S. viewed everything in such extraordinary detail—and remembered all those details—he had little ability to categorize or generalize, little ability to understand poetry or metaphor, little ability even to recognize a voice on the telephone, because, he claimed, a person's voice changed over the course of a day.

Apparently, S.'s feats of memory came naturally to him. Other people have labored to learn memorization techniques called **mnemonics** (pronounced "nee-MON-ics"). You have used a simple mnemonic if you've ever memorized an acronym such as ROY G. BIV (the colors of the spectrum: red, orange, yellow, green, blue, indigo, violet) or a rhyme such as "Thirty days hath September . . ."

Expert memorizers like S. typically use more elaborate mnemonic strategies. One is the *peg-word* method. To start, you need to memorize a list of items or "pegs" to be associated with the numbers 1 to 10; usually each peg rhymes with the number. Thus, one is a bun, two is a shoe, three is a tree, and so on. To remember a list of three objects—say, monkey, guitar, table—you associate each object with a peg. Perhaps you'd visualize the monkey eating a bun, the guitar stuffed in a shoe, the table up in a tree, and so on. Later, to remember the items, you recall each peg in order and remember what word was associated with each peg.

A similar method, known as the *method of loci,* allows the learner to memorize a list of objects by visualizing a stroll through a familiar environment. For example, suppose you had to memorize a chronological list of U.S. presidents—Washington, Adams, Jefferson, and so on. You could imagine entering your house at the front door, where you would first visualize George Washington chopping down a cherry tree; turning into the living room, you would visualize John Adams, perhaps sharing a lager with his cousin Samuel (after whom the beer is named); next, in the kitchen, you'd visualize Thomas Jefferson at the table, working on a draft of the Declaration of Independence; and so on. Later, to retrieve the list, you could simply imagine strolling through the house and meeting each man in turn. The method of loci dates back at least to the ancient Greeks, who used it to help debaters remember the points of their arguments, in order.

Most world-class memory performers use mnemonics of one sort or another. A recent neuroimaging study of exceptional memorizers found no differences in brain anatomy between world-class memory performers and people with average memories (Maguire, Valentine, Wilding, & Kapur, 2003). The implication is that almost anyone could attain a "world-class memory" by mastering the right techniques, such as a mnemonic system (Ericsson, 2003). Unfortunately, there is no evidence that such world-class memory masters are any better than the rest of us at memory challenges in the real world, such as remembering where we parked the car or when someone's birthday is.

This sixteenth-century woodcut was used by monks to memorize speeches. Each idea in the speech was associated with an object on a chart (left), and the object was then mentally placed along a route through the abbey (right). While giving the speech, the monk mentally retraced the route, remembering each object and the associated idea in the correct order.

Interference

Remember the parking lot example, in which memories of prior days' parking locations interfere with your ability to recall where you parked the car today? This is an example of **interference:** when two memories overlap in content, the strength of either or both memories may be reduced.

Suppose you're participating in a memory experiment and the experimenter asks you to learn a list of word pairs—say, List 1 in Figure 3.6. You might practice this list, repeating it aloud, until you have it memorized. Then, after some delay, the experimenter provides the stems (e.g., DOG-_____) and asks you to fill in the appropriate associate (CHAIR) for each stem.

Now suppose the experimenter asks you to memorize a second list, List 2 in Figure 3.6. Note that some of the items (DOG, SHIRT) appear in both lists. As you attempt to learn the new pair DOG-WINDOW, the stem (DOG) will stimulate recall of the old associate (CHAIR). This may interfere with your learning of List 2, and when it comes time to test memory for List 2, you may mistakenly respond with the old associate (CHAIR) instead of the new one (WINDOW). This process, whereby old information can disrupt new learning, is called **proactive interference** (Anderson, 1981; Wickelgren, 1966).

The opposite process also occurs: suppose that, after heavy practice with List 2, you try to go back and recall List 1. Now, when the experimenter prompts DOG-_____, you might recall WINDOW from List 2, instead of CHAIR from List 1. This process, whereby new information can disrupt old learning, is called **retroactive interference.** One way to remember the difference between proactive interference and retroactive interference is that *PRoactive* interference means that *PReviously acquired* information is at fault; *REtroactive* interference means that *REcently acquired* information is at fault.

Proactive and retroactive interference occur in many real-life contexts. For example, if you have ever changed your telephone number, you probably went through a phase where, when someone asked for your number, you gave the old number by mistake. This is an example of *proactive* interference, as memory of the *previous* number interfered with your ability to retrieve memory for the new number. On the other hand, once you had successfully mastered the new telephone number, you might have had some trouble remembering the old one. This is an example of *retroactive* interference, as memory of the *recently* acquired number interfered with your ability to remember the old number.

Figure 3.6 Two kinds of interference Imagine you are asked to learn the word pairs in List 1, then the word pairs in List 2. If you are then asked to recall List 2, items from List 1 may interfere (proactive interference). Conversely, if you are asked to recall List 1, newer items from List 2 may interfere (retroactive interference).

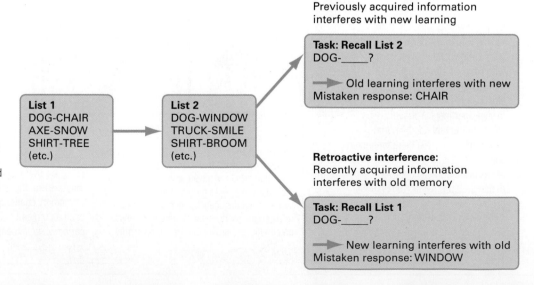

Proactive interference:
Previously acquired information interferes with new learning

Task: Recall List 2
DOG-____?

Old learning interferes with new
Mistaken response: CHAIR

List 1
DOG-CHAIR
AXE-SNOW
SHIRT-TREE
(etc.)

List 2
DOG-WINDOW
TRUCK-SMILE
SHIRT-BROOM
(etc.)

Retroactive interference:
Recently acquired information interferes with old memory

Task: Recall List 1
DOG-____?

New learning interferes with old
Mistaken response: WINDOW

Source Amnesia

Another kind of memory failure bears the impressive name "source amnesia." Normally, "amnesia" refers to catastrophic memory failures—as experienced by *Memento*'s Leonard Shelby, who can't form any new episodic memories, or *The Bourne Identity*'s Jason Bourne, who can't recall his own history. By contrast, "source amnesia" refers to a more subtle failure, one that we all experience from time to time.

In **source amnesia,** we remember a fact or event but attribute it to the wrong source (Schacter, 1984). For example, we may think we remember a childhood party, when what we really remember is a home movie of the event. Or we may dream about an experience and later remember the images and think the experience really happened. We may read some gossip in a trashy tabloid and, even though we know better than to take such reading material seriously, we may later remember the gossip but forget the source—and thus give the rumor more credence than it deserves.

Source amnesia crops up fairly often in real life and may be particularly pronounced as people get older. One famous example involves former U.S. president Ronald Reagan. During his campaigns, Reagan often told an inspiring story about a World War II gunner who was unable to eject after his plane was hit by enemy fire. The gunner's commander, who could have parachuted to safety, refused to abandon his injured comrade. "Never mind, son," he said, "We'll ride it down together." The commander was posthumously awarded the Congressional Medal of Honor for his bravery.

Only later did anyone wonder how the heroic words had been recorded, given that both commander and gunner had perished in the crash. Journalists began to dig deeper and found no recorded Medal of Honor winner who fit the profile of Reagan's hero. In fact, the touching scene was the fictional climax of a 1944 movie, *Wing and a Prayer*. Apparently, Reagan remembered the story but had forgotten its source.

A special kind of source amnesia is **cryptomnesia,** in which a person mistakenly thinks that his current thoughts are novel or original (Schacter, 1987). Cryptomnesia can lead to inadvertent plagiarism: a student reads a sentence in a textbook and remembers it; later, when the sentence pops to mind, it "feels" new and gets included in a term paper. The student may honestly think this is an original idea—but if the instructor has read the same textbook, accusations of plagiarism will follow.

Cryptomnesia has been studied scientifically, using a puzzle that is similar to the game Boggle (Marsh & Bower, 1993). Each puzzle is a set of 16 letters, and

DOONESBURY

Why might Zonker think he was at Woodstock?

the task is to form words with those letters. In the experiment, research participants played against a computer, with human and computer taking turns to generate words. Later, the participants were asked to write down all the words they had generated (but not the words generated by the computer). Participants remembered many of the words they had generated—but about 10% of the words they wrote down had, in fact, been generated by the computer.

The simplest explanation of cryptomnesia is that it is a special case of source amnesia: in the Boggle-like study, people could remember the words but not where those words had come from. They mistakenly thought they had generated all the words they remembered.

One famous example of cryptomnesia occurred in the early 1970s, when ex-Beatle George Harrison released the hit single "My Sweet Lord" and was sued for copyright infringement, because the tune was so similar to an earlier song, the Chiffons' "He's So Fine." Harrison argued that "My Sweet Lord" was his own creation and denied any plagiarism, although he admitted to having heard the Chiffons' song. A judge decided that Harrison had indeed been influenced by his memories of the earlier song, although the judge was convinced that Harrison's plagiarism was unintentional. Apparently, the ex-Beatle had suffered cryptomnesia: remembering the melody and mistakenly thinking he had composed it himself.

False Memory

Source amnesia and cryptomnesia involve good memories gone bad. Even Reagan's story about the heroic World War II commander was a perfectly valid memory—the only error was in forgetting that it was a scene from a movie, not from real life. **False memories** are memories of events that never actually happened.

Elizabeth Loftus and her colleagues have presented several dramatic examples of purposefully "implanting" false memories in ordinary people. For example, in one study the researchers invented several fictitious events, such as getting lost in a shopping mall, and then told research participants that these events had happened to them as children (Loftus & Pickrell, 1995). Family members (who had agreed to collaborate) also spoke about the events as if they had really happened. Sure enough, a few days later, about 25% of the participants seemed to believe the events were real—and even "remembered" additional details that had not been present in the original story.

In another study, Kimberley Wade and her colleagues pasted childhood photos of their adult research participants into a photograph of a hot-air balloon ride. Figure 3.7 shows how one such photo was constructed. The researchers showed participants the doctored photos and asked them to describe everything they could remember about the fictitious ride. After three such sessions, about half the people in the study claimed to remember having taken such a ride—even though none had ever been in a hot-air balloon (Wade, Garry, Read, & Lindsay, 2002).

False memories tend to occur when people are prompted to imagine missing details; later, they may mistakenly remember those details as the truth—a process similar to cryptomnesia and other forms of source amnesia. The more people imagine an event, the more likely they are to subsequently believe it really happened (Garry, Manning, Loftus, & Sherman, 1996; Goff & Roediger, 1998).

Even without going to such lengths as faking family photos or convincing family members to collaborate, researchers can elicit false memories in the laboratory by asking people to learn lists of words organized around a particular theme (Deese, 1959; Roediger & McDermott, 1995). For example, given the theme

BEHAVIORAL PROCESSES | **99**

Figure 3.7 Creating false memories in the laboratory To create false memories in healthy adults, researchers pasted childhood pictures (left) of their adult participants into a photograph of a hot-air balloon ride (right). When prompted to recall the details of the trip, about half the participants claimed they could remember the episode—even though none had ever been in a hot-air balloon. Reprinted with permission from Wade et al., 2002.

"sweet," the list might contain words such as CANDY, SUGAR, HONEY, and TASTE (but not the word SWEET itself); for the theme "sleep," the list might contain BED, REST, TIRED, and DREAM (but not SLEEP). Figure 3.8 shows data from one such study. In general, people correctly recognize the studied words and correctly reject (fail to recognize) novel, unrelated words (e.g., DOG, HOUSE, or TOMATO). But people also often claim to recognize the theme words (e.g., SWEET and SLEEP), even though these words weren't on the lists. Apparently, while learning the lists, people encode the semantic meaning of the words—the theme—and this leads them to believe they have actually seen the theme words (Cabeza, Rao, Wagner, Mayer, & Schacter, 2001).

If false memory occurs in the real world at anything like the rate observed in the lab, it could be a very commonplace, widespread phenomenon. This can be a matter of public concern if it affects eyewitness testimony in a criminal case. For example, if an eyewitness is shown a picture of a suspect in the case, the witness's memory of that picture may become confused with the actual memory of the crime, leading the witness to "recognize" the suspect as the actual perpetrator even though he is innocent. A case in point occurred when a woman who had been raped identified psychologist Donald Thompson, as her attacker (Thompson, 1988). Fortunately for Thompson he had an iron-clad alibi: he was appearing on live TV at the time the rape occurred. Apparently, the woman had been watching TV just before the assault and mistakenly attributed her memory of Thompson's face to the event of the rape.

Elizabeth Loftus and other false-memory researchers have been vocal in warning that eyewitness memory is more prone to error than most people realize.

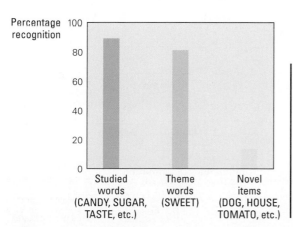

Figure 3.8 False memory for studied words People were first asked to learn lists of words organized around an unseen theme (such as "sweet"). Later, participants were generally accurate at recognizing the studied words and at rejecting (failing to recognize) novel, unrelated words. But they would also claim to recognize the unstudied theme words. Data from Cabeza et al., 2001.

These researchers argue that the types of procedures that induce false memory in the lab (such as showing witnesses the picture of a suspect, or asking them to imagine missing details of the witnessed event) must be scrupulously avoided in the justice system, to minimize convictions based on false memory (Loftus, 1996, 2003; Radelet, 2002). And such convictions may be all too frequent. One study reviewed 62 cases in which people were convicted of crimes and later exonerated based on DNA evidence (Neufield & Dwyer, 2000). In more than 80% of these cases, the crucial evidence leading to conviction was eyewitness testimony, where witnesses had mistakenly identified people later proven to be innocent.

Models of Semantic Memory

Since episodic and semantic memory play such an important role in our lives, it is not surprising that many researchers have attempted to model how we organize, store, and retrieve such memories. Much of this research has focused on semantic knowledge. For example, consider the question "Do dogs breathe air?" You probably think you know the answer—but how could you? You have not seen every dog that ever lived, and although you have seen many dogs that do breathe air, perhaps there are some dogs that live happily underwater or in outer space.

The fact is that dogs do breathe air, and you know this not only based on your own experiences with dogs but also based on the semantic knowledge that dogs are one example of the category "mammals" and that all mammals breathe air. Semantic information is organized in a way that lets us search and retrieve information by knowing the relationship between different items (such as "dogs" and "mammals" and "breathing").

M. Ross Quillian, one of the pioneers of artificial intelligence, was among the first to suggest that semantic memory is organized in networks, like the one shown in Figure 3.9 (Collins & Loftus, 1975; Collins & Quillian, 1969; Quillian, 1967). Each object or concept is represented as a node (shown as boxes in Figure 3.9), and each node can be associated or linked with one or more features. For example, the node "bird" is linked to the feature "has wings," encoding the fact that birds have wings. Nodes can be arranged hierarchically, so that "bird" is a member of a larger (superordinate) class of objects, "animal," with lower (subordinate) categories such as "canary" and "ostrich" encoding specific kinds of bird. This kind of network is called a **hierarchical semantic network.**

Features (such as "barks" or "breathes air") are listed only once, at the highest relevant node; a feature then automatically applies to all the nodes below it. If you are asked, "Do dogs bark?" all you have to do is enter the network at the node for "dog" and look for a link to "barks." If you are asked, "Do dogs breathe

Figure 3.9 A hierarchical semantic network The node representing "dog" is an instance of a higher category, "mammal," and inherits features from that higher category, such as "has fur" and "bears live young." "Dog" also has its own features, such as "barks," that generalize down to lower categories, such as "Chihuahua" and "Dalmation." Atypical exemplars, such as the sea-dwelling dolphin or the flightless ostrich, have features that override the features inherited from higher categories. Learning occurs as a process of adding new nodes, links, and facts to the semantic network.

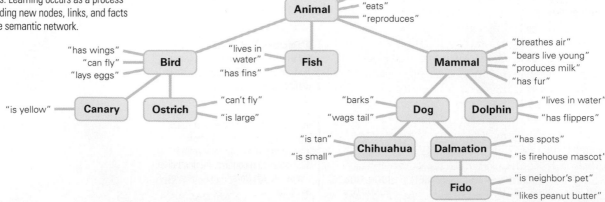

air?" you have to do a little more work: enter at "dog," traverse up a category to "mammal," and then find the link to "breathes air." The hierarchical semantic network model predicts that the time it takes a person to answer a question about a particular node relates to the distance between that node and the answer. In general, this is exactly what happens: people are faster to answer the question "Do dogs bark?" than "Do dogs breathe air?" or "Can dogs reproduce?" (Anderson, 1976; Collins & Loftus, 1975; McClelland & Rumelhart, 1981; McNamara, 1992).

Hierarchical semantic networks can also incorporate information about atypical exemplars. For example, according to the "bird" node in Figure 3.9, all birds have wings and can fly. Yet consider the ostrich: it can't fly, has only vestigial wings, and looks very unlike our normal concept of a bird. The hierarchical semantic network model handles these atypical cases by adding special notes at the level of the atypical node. In Figure 3.9, the presence of such a note ("can't fly" on the "ostrich" node) overrides a more general rule at a higher node ("can fly" on the "bird" node).

Some levels of the hierarchy are easier to access than others. For example, people can usually answer questions about dogs faster than they can answer questions about mammals (the superordinate category) or Chihuahuas (a subordinate category). Categories such as "dog" that are easier to access than their superordinate or subordinate neighbors are called *basic levels* (Mervis & Rosch, 1981). Basic levels are probably not innate but, rather, may gain their special psychological status through training: in real life, many of us have a lot of experience with dogs but less experience with a particular subtype, such as Chihuahuas—and, outside a biology class, few of us have occasion to think about the concept of mammals. Support for the idea that basic levels are learned, not innate, is the finding that basic levels can be altered by training: Chihuahua breeders may be so familiar with the breed that they find it easier to access information about their specialty than about dogs in general (Tanaka & Taylor, 1991).

In semantic networks, learning is a process of adding nodes and links to represent new information. Each time we learn a new fact, this semantic knowledge is incorporated into the network by adding new links and features. Each time we are presented with a new object, we can use the network to infer information about that object. For example, even before we meet Fido, the neighbor's new Dalmatian, we can infer certain facts about Fido based on our general knowledge: Fido probably has spots (because he's a Dalmatian), barks (because he's a dog), and breathes air (because he's a mammal). This ability to generalize saves us the time and effort of having to learn all these facts over again, each time we meet a new dog. On the other hand, information specific to Fido ("likes peanut butter") can be added to differentiate Fido from all other dogs and all other Dalmatians.

We can even use hierarchical semantic networks to store episodic information. If we tag the "Fido" node with information about the spatial and temporal context where we first met him, then, when we activate the "Fido" node, the episodic memory of our first meeting can be retrieved too.

Hierarchical semantic networks, like the one pictured in Figure 3.9, are not meant to represent connections between individual neurons in the brain. They are a metaphorical approach to understanding how information might be stored and associated in memory. In later elaborations, many researchers have attempted to incorporate more anatomical detail into computer models of memory, by devising separate network modules to represent different brain areas, or even by replacing abstract nodes and links with representations of real neurons (Alvarez & Squire, 1994; Gluck & Myers, 1993, 2001; Marr, 1971; O'Reilly & Rudy, 2000; Wilson & McNaughton, 1994). The next section delves more deeply into the brain regions that participate in episodic and semantic memory.

Interim Summary

Episodic memory is memory for specific autobiographical events that occurred in a unique spatial and temporal context. Semantic memory is memory for facts and general information about the world, which does not necessarily include information about where or when the memory was originally acquired. Episodic memory is information we remember; semantic memory is information we know. Both episodic and semantic memories can be flexibly communicated in ways other than that in which they were originally acquired, and both are available to conscious recollection. Researchers still debate whether nonhuman animals can have true episodic memories; some believe this faculty belongs to humans alone. Memory for new information is stronger (1) if it can be related to existing knowledge, (2) if encoding and retrieval conditions match, and (3) if more cues are available to prompt recall. Memory can also "fail" in many ways, including forgetting, interference, source amnesia, and creation of false memories. In hierarchical semantic networks, concepts are encoded as nodes, and relations between concepts are encoded as links between the nodes. Such semantic networks can help us understand how information is organized in memory, but they are not literal models of how neurons encode information in the brain.

3.2 Brain Substrates

In the movie *Memento*, Leonard Shelby loses his ability to form new memories as a result of damage to his hippocampus (and presumably also to nearby brain structures). The movie isn't far off base: the hippocampus and nearby brain structures are indeed critical for forming new episodic memories. Leonard's fund of semantic memory—his general knowledge about the world—is generally intact, and this is also consistent with brain studies showing that semantic memories are stored in the cerebral cortex (which was uninjured in Leonard). The frontal cortex and some subcortical areas also help determine what gets stored and when. It seems that both episodic and semantic memory depend on a wide variety of brain areas, each contributing to the process.

The Cerebral Cortex and Semantic Memory

In the 1930s, a Canadian neurosurgeon named Wilder Penfield was experimenting with human brains: removing pieces of the skull to expose the cerebral cortex, then stimulating different areas of cortex with an electrical probe to see how the person would respond (Penfield & Boldrey, 1937; Penfield & Rasmussen, 1950). Penfield wasn't a mad scientist; his patients were preparing for brain surgery to remove tumors or for other medical reasons. Penfield's techniques mapped the patient's cortex to help guide the surgeons. Similar techniques are still used today, although modern surgeons also use noninvasive techniques such as fMRI to map brain function (Achten et al., 1999).

Each of Penfield's patients was given local anesthesia to prevent pain from the incision, but was otherwise fully conscious. The brain itself contains no pain receptors, so Penfield's probes didn't hurt the patients.

When Penfield and his colleagues touched an electrode to areas in the parietal lobe, the patient might report feeling a localized numbness or tingling in the skin. When the electrode touched areas of cortex in the occipital lobe, the patient might report "seeing" a flashing light; when the electrode touched areas in the superior temporal lobe, the patient might report "hearing" a buzzing noise. These results are what you would expect, given that we now know that these areas of **sensory cortex** are involved in processing sensory information such as sight and sounds. Other cortical areas (e.g., those shown in pale pink in

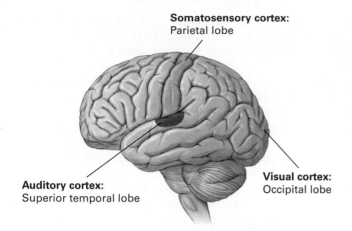

Somatosensory cortex:
Parietal lobe

Auditory cortex:
Superior temporal lobe

Visual cortex:
Occipital lobe

Figure 3.10 **Semantic memory and the cerebral cortex** Some areas of the cerebral cortex are specialized to process specific kinds of sensory information; these include areas in the parietal lobe (somatosensory cortex), the occipital lobe (visual cortex), and the superior temporal lobe (auditory cortex). Many of the remaining cortical areas are association areas that link information within and across modalities.

Figure 3.10) are called **association cortex,** meaning they are involved in associating information within and across modalities. Association cortex helps us link the word "dog" with the visual image of a dog and with semantic information about what dogs are like, as well as with linguistic information about how to pronounce and recognize the spoken word itself.

People with cortical damage can display **agnosia,** a relatively selective disruption of the ability to process a particular kind of information. ("Agnosia" is from the Greek for "not knowing.") For example, patients with *associative visual agnosia* have difficulty recognizing and naming objects, even though they can "see" the objects (and can usually copy them accurately). If such a patient is shown a pen or a cup, she may be unable to name it or say what it is used for—though she may recognize the object by feel if it is placed in her hand (Farah, 2003). In contrast, patients with *auditory agnosia for speech* can "hear" sounds and echo them, but they are unable to understand the meaning of spoken words—though they can often recognize written words (Bauer & McDonald, 2003). These patients may describe hearing their native language as if it were a foreign tongue—little more than a stream of unintelligible gibberish. Patients with *tactile agnosia* may be able to recognize an object by sight or description but not by feel if it is placed in their hands (Caselli, 2003). In each case, the agnosia results from the loss of semantic knowledge linking the perception of an object (through sight, sound, or touch) with its identity (or name or function).

On the basis of what you read in Chapter 2, you might expect that sensory agnosias are caused by damage to the corresponding areas of sensory cortex (see Figure 3.10). And to a first approximation you'd be right. Patients with associative visual agnosia often have damage to cortex in the inferior temporal lobe; those with auditory agnosia for speech often have damage to the cortex in the superior temporal lobe; and those with tactile agnosia often have damage to the cortex in the parietal lobe (Zeki, 1993).

But, sometimes, individual patients show agnosias that are frankly bizarre. For example, one man developed a peculiar kind of visual agnosia that left him unable to name living things and foods, though he could successfully name inanimate objects (Warrington & Shallice, 1984). Another man developed a form of auditory agnosia that left him able to use and comprehend nouns—but not verbs (McCarthy & Warrington, 1985). And a woman showed a selective deficit when asked questions about the physical attributes of animals ("What color is an elephant?"), although she could respond perfectly well about nonphysical attributes such as whether the animals are kept as pets or used as food (Hart & Gordon, 1992).

Such agnosias seem to suggest that specific categories of semantic knowledge are stored in unique places in the brain, so that a cortical lesion can destroy knowledge for a particular kind of object (foods, say, or verbs) but not closely related objects. Yet this is exactly the opposite of what Lashley concluded in his theory of equipotentiality (see Chapter 2). It also seems to go against common sense. Do we really have a specific brain module for knowledge about animal colors? And one for verbs? And one for foods? Where does this end?

Martha Farah and Jay McClelland have proposed a solution to this dilemma (Farah & McClelland, 1991). They suggest we don't need to assume that there are dozens of specialized modules, only a few. Our semantic networks, they propose, are organized by object properties including visual properties (color, texture, size), functional properties (uses, places found), and so on. A cortical lesion might damage one area of the network—say, visual properties—but leave other kinds of semantic information intact. What would happen in a person with such a lesion? She would have great difficulty answering questions about object appearance, but less difficulty answering questions about object function. And this is exactly the pattern in the woman who could not describe the color of an animal but could describe its "function"—whether it was kept as a pet or raised for food. Conversely, another patient might have damage to the "function" part of his language network (leaving him unable to understand abstract action verbs), but not to his "visual" areas (leaving him able to understand nouns by recalling the visual properties of the objects they represent).

This is a hypothetical account, but it may be a useful theoretical framework for studying how specific agnosias could arise. New studies, using functional neuroimaging to observe the brain in action during tasks of semantic memory, will help shed light on the existence of such localized semantic networks in the cortex of healthy humans. Meanwhile, further study of agnosia in patients with localized cortical damage may help us understand the microstructure of these networks.

The Medial Temporal Lobes and Memory Storage

The single most famous patient in the history of psychology is probably H.M. (known only by his initials to protect his privacy). By the age of 10, H.M. was having epileptic seizures, episodes in which the neurons in his brain fired wildly and uncontrollably. By age 16, the seizures became frequent and debilitating. Severe attacks, during which H.M. convulsed and lost consciousness, occurred weekly; minor attacks occurred up to 10 times a day. H.M. struggled to complete high school, finally graduating at age 21, but the seizures were so frequent and severe that he had difficulty holding a simple job. His doctors put him on a near-toxic diet of anticonvulsant drugs, but the seizures continued.

In 1953, in desperation, H.M. and his family agreed to his undergoing brain surgery. At the time, doctors knew that, in many epileptic patients, seizures started in either the left or right hemisphere, usually in the **medial temporal lobe,** the inner (or medial) surface of the temporal lobe. As shown in Figure 3.11, the medial temporal lobe includes the **hippocampus,** the *amygdala*, and several nearby cortical areas called the *entorhinal cortex*, *perirhinal cortex*, and *parahippocampal cortex*. Doctors had found that surgical removal of the medial temporal lobe from the hemisphere where the seizures originated often eliminated the source of the problem and cured the epilepsy in these patients. Because H.M.'s seizures were so severe, and because the precise origin could not be determined, the doctors decided to remove his medial temporal lobes bilaterally. Surgeons removed about 5 cm of tissue from each side of H.M.'s brain, including about two-thirds of the hippocampus, most of the amygdala, and some surrounding cortex (Corkin, Amaral, Gonzalez, Johnson, & Hyman, 1997).

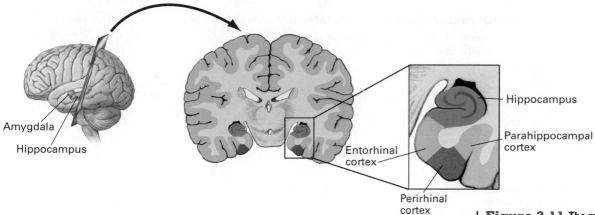

Entorhinal cortex

Perirhinal cortex

Hippocampus

Parahippocampal cortex

Amygdala

Hippocampus

Figure 3.11 The medial temporal lobe in humans The medial (inner) portion of the temporal lobes contains the hippocampus, the amygdala, and several nearby cortical areas, including the entorhinal cortex, perirhinal cortex, and parahippocampal cortex.

Medically, the operation was a success: H.M.'s seizures declined drastically in frequency and severity and could now be controlled with nontoxic levels of medication. But there was a terrible cost. H.M. developed **anterograde amnesia,** an inability to form new episodic and semantic memories (Scoville & Milner, 1957). He could no longer remember what he had eaten for breakfast or why he was in the hospital. He could spend all morning working intensively with a psychologist, take a break for lunch, and an hour later have no recognition of the psychologist (Haglund & Collett, 1996). Some time after the operation, H.M.'s uncle died. When H.M. found out, he experienced intense grief—then forgot. Again and again, he asked after the uncle and reacted with surprise and fresh grief (Milner, 1966). H.M. himself, now an old man, is painfully aware of his problems and described his life as constantly waking from a dream he can't remember (Milner, Corkin, & Teuber, 1968).

H.M.'s impairment after the operation affected only his memory. His personality was basically unchanged, and his IQ actually went up—probably because, without constant seizures, he could now concentrate on what he was doing. He could no longer follow the plot of a television show (ads would interrupt his memory of the story line), but he could still amuse himself solving difficult crossword puzzles. As long as H.M. paid attention to a task, he could perform well; as soon as he turned his attention to something else, the information vanished without a trace. The fictional character Leonard Shelby, in *Memento*, experiences the same problem and has to scribble notes to himself with each new plot twist, or he forgets the most recent clue to his wife's murder by the time the next scene rolls around.

As of this writing, H.M. is living in a nursing home in Connecticut, still gamely volunteering to participate in memory research, still unable to recognize Brenda Milner, the neuropsychologist who has tested him regularly for half a century. He has no real idea of how profoundly his story has influenced brain science, or how much he has taught us about human memory. "It's such a shame there's no way of rewarding him," Milner says. "He always says he just wants to help—you would like to pay him back somehow. But there's nothing he wants" (Clair, 2005).

The Hippocampal Region and Memory in Nonhuman Animals

Obviously, after H.M., no more surgeries were performed to remove the medial temporal lobes bilaterally in humans (although unilateral surgeries, which don't cause amnesia, are still sometimes performed for patients with intractable epilepsy). Unfortunately, bilateral medial temporal lobe damage does occur in humans as a result of various kinds of injury and disease. We know from studies of these patients that H.M.'s anterograde amnesia was caused by bilateral damage to the hippocampus and associated nearby cortical areas.

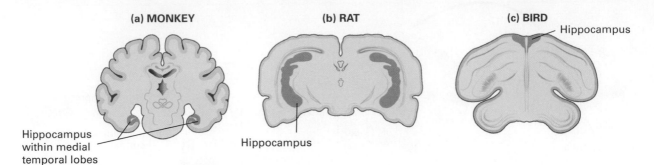

(a) MONKEY **(b) RAT** **(c) BIRD**

Hippocampus
within medial
temporal lobes

Hippocampus

Hippocampus

Figure 3.12 The hippocampal region in several types of animals Cross-sections through the brain of (a) a monkey, showing the hippocampus and medial temporal lobes; (b) a rat, showing the hippocampus; and (c) a bird (a finch), showing the hippocampal region (including the dorsomedial forebrain, which is believed to be the avian analog of the hippocampus).

Monkeys have medial temporal lobes that look roughly similar to those of humans (Figure 3.12a). Other mammals, such as rats and rabbits, have the same structures (hippocampus, entorhinal cortex, etc.), although the geographical layout and relative sizes may be different (Figure 3.12b). Birds and reptiles also have a brain structure that seems to serve the same function as the mammalian hippocampus (Figure 3.12c). Given the variation across species, it is sometimes useful to refer to the *hippocampal region*, defined as including the hippocampus and nearby cortical areas, which lie in the medial temporal lobes in primates.

Like H.M., animals with lesions of the hippocampal region have difficulty learning new information (Mishkin, 1978; Squire, 1992). These animals are especially impaired at learning that involves memory of unique events set in a particular scene—just like the episodic memory disruption in humans with anterograde amnesia (Gaffan & Hornak, 1997; Gaffan & Parker, 1996). For example, researchers often train rats in a *radial arm maze*: a maze with a central area from which several arms branch off like the spokes of a wheel (Figure 3.13a). The researchers place a piece of food at the end of each arm. The rat's task is to obtain all the food; this can be done most efficiently by entering each arm once (subsequent entries are worthless, because the food is already eaten).

To solve this task efficiently, entering each arm only once, the rat needs to remember where it's already been. Unfortunately, competing with this memory will be all the memories of occasions on previous days when the rat entered the maze arms and found food there. Proactive interference affects rats in a radial arm maze, just as it affects humans in a parking lot! The only way out of this dilemma is to remember the spatial and temporal context of visits—namely, whether a specific arm was visited yet *today*, as distinct from all other visits on all other days. In other words, the rat needs at least a rudimentary episodic memory, remembering not just what happened, but when.

Figure 3.13 Learning in the radial arm maze (a) A radial arm maze with eight arms radiating from a central area. On each trial, food is placed at the end of every arm; the rat is placed in the center and allowed to collect all the food it can. An "error" is counted if a rat reenters an arm it has already visited on this trial. (b) Rats with hippocampal lesions (HL) make many more errors than control, unlesioned rats, indicating that they have trouble remembering which arms they've already visited on this trial. (b) Data from Cassel et al., 1998.

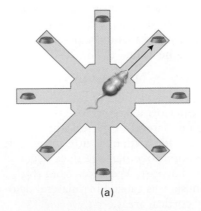

(a)

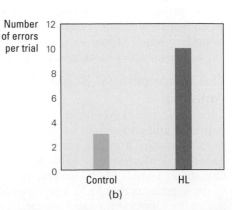

(b)

After several days of training, healthy rats learn to navigate the radial arm maze very efficiently: in other words, they collect all eight rewards and, in the process, they make very few errors of reentering previously visited arms (Figure 3.13b). In contrast, rats with hippocampal lesions make many more errors: they repeatedly reenter previously visited arms, apparently aware that there is food to be found but unable to remember which arms they've already visited on this particular day (Cassel et al., 1998; Jarrard, Okaichi, Steward, & Goldschmidt, 1984; Olton, 1983).

A similar pattern of disrupted memory for spatial and temporal context occurs in birds with hippocampal-region lesions. Remember the scrub jays, who can bury food in caches and then relocate the caches later? When the hippocampal region is lesioned, the birds lose the ability to locate their caches (Capaldi, Robinson, & Fahrback, 1999). They continue to store new food, but they quickly forget where they've put it; they search almost at random—almost like the lesioned rat running around the radial maze.

We see the same kind of disrupted spatial learning in humans with hippocampal damage. Patients like H.M. have a very difficult time learning new spatial information, such as the layout of a new home. To study spatial learning in the lab, researchers devised a virtual reality environment (based on the videogame Duke Nukem 3D), in which the user navigates through a series of rooms, meeting, interacting with, and receiving items from animated characters. Healthy people can usually master this task fairly easily, but in one study, an individual with amnesia (named Jon) had great trouble learning to navigate his way around the environment. Jon also had very poor memory for which characters he had met where and what they had given him (Spiers, Burgess, Hartley, Vargha-Khadem, & O'Keefe, 2001). This task is broadly similar to the kind of who-gave-what-when memory studied in the gorilla named King, discussed earlier in the chapter.

Hippocampal Function in the Healthy Brain

Damage to the hippocampal region could cause memory failure because this region is needed to *encode* information, to *retain* or consolidate it, to *retrieve* it when needed, or any combination of these factors. Determining which is very hard. But we can get some clues from functional neuroimaging studies of the hippocampus in action in healthy brains. For example, Anthony Wagner and his colleagues have used a *subsequent forgetting* paradigm, in which they show people a list of words and take fMRI images of the brain during this learning phase (Wagner et al., 1998). Next, the researchers present a recognition test for the previously viewed words; not surprisingly, people remember some of the words and forget others. The important new finding is that fMRI activity during learning differs for words that are later remembered and words that are later forgotten. Specifically, the difference image in Figure 3.14a shows that the left medial temporal lobe is more active during initial learning of words that are subsequently remembered than during learning of words that are subsequently forgotten. (There is a similar effect in the left frontal cortex, as shown in Figure 3.14b; we'll return to this later in the chapter.)

In effect, during the learning phase we can "see" the left medial temporal lobe working to store the new words; the greater the activity, the better the storage, and the more likely that the information will be retrieved later. If the to-be-remembered stimuli are pictures, the medial temporal lobe is again more active for pictures that will be remembered than for pictures that will be forgotten (Brewer, Zhao, Desmond, Glover, & Gabrieli, 1998). The major difference between picture and word storage is that pictures activate the medial temporal lobes bilaterally whereas words tend to activate only the left medial temporal lobe.

Figure 3.14 The "subsequent forgetting" paradigm Brain imaging (fMRI) records activity while participants learn a series of words. Difference images, constructed by subtracting activity during learning of to-be-forgotten words versus during learning of to-be-remembered words, show high activity in (a) the left medial temporal lobe and (b) the left frontal lobe. (a, b) Adapted from Wagner et al., 1998.

(a) Medial temporal lobe

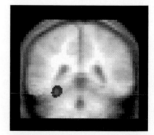

(b) Frontal lobe

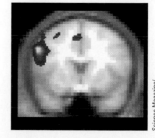

Science Magazine/
Courtesy of Anthony D. Wagner

These studies demonstrate that the medial temporal lobes are intimately involved in memory encoding. Pictures and words that are processed more elaborately in the medial temporal lobes (visible as increased temporal lobe activity on fMRI) are more likely to be encoded and remembered later. This is similar to the depth-of-processing phenomenon discussed earlier in the chapter, in which "imaging" a word produces better memory than merely "pronouncing" a word backward. And the hippocampus itself may play a crucial role in the what-happened-where aspect of episodic memory. When the experimenters asked people to remember not only the word but also where they'd heard it—during the "image" condition or the "pronounce" condition—the hippocampus was more active when both word and source were recalled than when the word was recalled without the source (Davachi et al., 2003). Apparently, the hippocampus helps bind together memory of objects (such as words) with the unique spatial and temporal context in which they were experienced. This seems to be true in rats and monkeys as well as humans (Eichenbaum, 2000; Gaffan & Parker, 1996; Honey, Watt, & Good, 1998).

This, in turn, suggests an application to false memory, in which people "remember" events that never actually occurred. In the false memory experiment described earlier, in which people studied a list of words related to an unseen theme word, fMRI during the recognition phase showed a striking pattern. Several brain areas were more active for familiar (learned) list words than for novel words, but the unseen theme words evoked high activity too (Cabeza et al., 2001). This could explain why people are prone to falsely recognize the theme words.

The hippocampus is one of the brain areas that is "fooled" into responding as strongly to the theme words as to the familiar words. But a small area in the medial temporal lobe shows a different pattern. A region of cortex just behind the hippocampus also responds more strongly to familiar words than to novel words, but it does not respond strongly to the theme words. In other words, the medial temporal lobe is apparently the only place in the brain that can correctly distinguish true episodic memories from false ones (Cabeza et al., 2001; Okado & Stark, 2003). If this kind of finding extends to false memories outside the lab, it may have real-world application, particularly in court cases where a witness claims to remember details of a crime and the defense charges that this is a false memory. Maybe someday the defense will be able to present an fMRI of a witness's brain as evidence that the witness may not have experienced the event the way she is recalling it now.

Hippocampal–Cortical Interaction in Memory Consolidation

In the late 1800s, French philosopher Theodore Ribot noticed that individuals with head injury often developed **retrograde amnesia,** loss of memories for events that occurred before the injury (Ribot, 1882). For example, in a modern context, a man who hit his head during a car accident might lose all memories of the accident itself, and might also have some disruption of memories from the minutes or hours before the accident, but he would have relatively little disruption of memories for events that occurred months or years earlier. This pattern of memory loss is called the **Ribot gradient** (Figure 3.15). It is similar to the effects of electroconvulsive shock, which also disrupts recently formed memories (see Figure 3.5b).

People with bilateral hippocampal damage generally show some retrograde amnesia, along with their anterograde amnesia. These patients don't forget their own identity—they can remember their name, their childhood, their high school graduation—but they often lose memories for events that happened before the brain damage, and this retrograde amnesia can affect information acquired decades earlier (Manns, Hopkins, & Squire, 2003). One such patient, known as

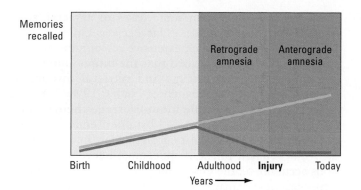

Figure 3.15 The Ribot gradient In a healthy person (green line), there is near-total recall for events that happened today and progressively less recall for events that happened weeks, months, and years ago—until the period just after birth, for which most of us have few if any memories. A person with bilateral hippocampal damage (red line) may suffer anterograde amnesia: loss of the ability to form new episodic and semantic memories since the injury. The individual may also have retrograde amnesia, or memory loss for prior events, and this is generally most severe for events that occurred days or weeks before the injury. If the brain damage extends beyond the hippocampus into nearby cortex, retrograde amnesia may be much more severe and may extend back for decades or longer.

E.P., suffered an attack of herpes simplex encephalitis in 1992 that left him with bilateral medial temporal lobe damage and dense anterograde amnesia, meaning that he could recall almost nothing that had happened to him since 1992. In addition, E.P. displayed retrograde amnesia. His memory for childhood events was excellent—as good as that of healthy controls of the same age. But when asked about events from adulthood, decades before his encephalitis, E.P. remembered less than did healthy controls (Reed & Squire, 1998; Stefanacci, Buffalo, Schmolck, & Squire, 2000).

You've already read about the consolidation period, during which new memories are especially vulnerable to disruption. E.P.'s case suggests that the consolidation period may last for decades, because for at least some decades-old events his memories were lost. So just how long is the consolidation period? How long before a new memory becomes independent of the medial temporal lobes and is "safely" stored in sensory and association cortex?

A great deal of debate rages around this question. One position, sometimes called **standard consolidation theory,** holds that the hippocampus and related medial temporal lobe structures are initially required for episodic memory storage and retrieval but their contribution diminishes over time until the cortex is capable of retrieving the memory without hippocampal help (Dudai, 2004; McGaugh, 2000; Squire, 1992). You can think of an episodic memory as consisting of many components (sight, sound, texture, context, etc.) that are stored in different areas of the cortex (Figure 3.16a). Initially, all of these components are linked together via the hippocampus into a single episodic memory (Figure 3.16b). Over time, through the process of consolidation, the components can form direct connections with each other and no longer need hippocampal mediation (Figure 3.16c).

Figure 3.16 Standard consolidation theory (a) An episodic memory consists of many components, such as sight, sound, texture, and other features, stored in sensory and association cortex. (b) Initially, the hippocampal region (turquoise) helps link these components into a single episodic memory. (c) Over time, the components become linked to each other and hippocampal involvement is no longer required.

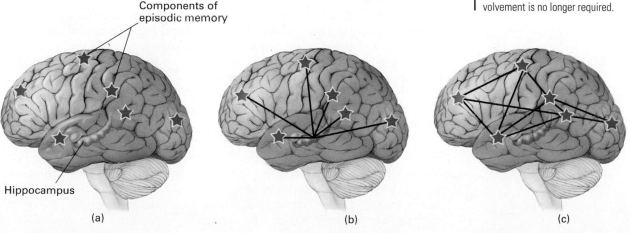

(a)　　　　　　　　　　(b)　　　　　　　　　　(c)

On the other hand, in some cases of amnesia, patients have retrograde memory loss that extends as far back as childhood (Nadel & Moscovitch, 1997). To account for such extensive retrograde amnesia, Morris Moscovitch and Lynn Nadel have argued that the hippocampus is not a temporary store but, rather, mediates storage and retrieval throughout the lifetime of an episodic memory (Moscovitch & Nadel, 1998; Nadel & Moscovitch, 2001). According to this **multiple memory trace theory,** episodic (and possibly semantic) memories are encoded by an ensemble of hippocampal and cortical neurons, and the cortical neurons never, in normal circumstances, become fully independent of the hippocampal neurons. Over time, as more connections accumulate, the ensemble grows, and memories may be partially spared if hippocampal damage occurs. This explains why patients with amnesia tend to lose newer memories more readily than older ones, and why semantic memory (which may have been encoded many times) is sometimes spared even when episodic memory (which may have been encoded only once) is lost. (See also "Unsolved Mysteries" on p. 111). In such a case, Nadel and Moscovitch point out, individuals might be able to rehearse a piece of autobiographical information so many times that it becomes a semantic memory (Nadel, Samsonovich, Ryan, & Moscovitch, 2000). But this is a far cry from how a healthy person recalls episodic memories. It would be equivalent to a healthy person "remembering" the day she was born because she's heard the family stories so often. She has semantic information about the event, and knows it happened to her, but that isn't quite the same thing as remembering the episode firsthand.

At this point, debate continues as to whether standard consolidation theory or multiple memory trace theory provides a better description of the hippocampal role in memory. Part of the confusion may reflect the fact that individual patients have widely different extents of brain damage. There is some evidence that the degree of retrograde amnesia in a particular patient reflects the size of the brain lesion. In other words, individuals with damage limited to the hippocampus may have retrograde amnesia that extends back a year or two, but individuals (like E.P.) with broader medial temporal damage may have retrograde amnesia that extends back for years, perhaps decades (Nadel et al., 2000; Reed & Squire, 1998). Retrograde amnesia may be greatest of all in individuals whose brain damage extends beyond the medial temporal lobe and into other areas of cerebral cortex (Bayley, Gold, Hopkins, & Squire, 2005).

The Role of the Frontal Cortex in Memory Storage and Retrieval

So far you've read that the temporal lobes are important sites for episodic and semantic memory storage and that the hippocampal region is critical for acquisition and consolidation of memories into long-term storage. Recall that Wagner's study found heightened medial temporal lobe activity during the encoding of subsequently remembered information (Figure 3.14a). As Figure 3.14b shows, the left frontal lobe was also more active during exposure to verbal information that was later remembered than during exposure to information that was later forgotten (Wagner et al., 1998).

The **frontal cortex,** those regions of cortex that lie within the frontal lobes, may help determine what we store (and therefore remember) and what we don't

► **Unsolved Mysteries**

Are There Different Brain Substrates for Episodic and Semantic Memory?

Beth was born without a heartbeat. The delivery team resuscitated her, but she continued to have seizures for the next few weeks. After that, her condition stabilized and she seemed to grow into a normal little girl. It wasn't until age 5, when Beth started school, that her family noticed she was amnesic. Beth has almost no memory for any autobiographical events. She cannot remember the day's activities, reliably report a telephone conversation, or follow the plot of a television program. When Beth was 14 years old, a structural MRI showed that her hippocampus was much smaller than normal on both sides; other parts of her brain—including the rest of her medial temporal lobes—looked normal (Gadian et al., 2000; Vargha-Khadem et al., 1997).

Given what we know about the hippocampus, Beth's episodic memory difficulties are not too surprising. What is surprising is that Beth progressed relatively successfully through a mainstream school, getting average grades, and even participating in extracurricular activities. She was competent in language and speech and could read and write nearly as well as her peers. She scored well on tests of vocabulary and intelligence. When asked a general knowledge question, Beth gave a reasonable answer—proving that she had as much semantic knowledge as any other girl of her age.

Because Beth's hippocampal damage occurred at birth, all of this semantic knowledge was, by definition, acquired after the onset of her amnesia. Farina Vargha-Khadem and other neuropsychologists working with Beth conclude that the hippocampus is necessary for the acquisition of new autobiographical or episodic information (of which Beth has none), but not for new semantic information (of which Beth has plenty).

Beth is not the only person who shows good semantic memory despite poor episodic memory. Another patient, K.C., became amnesic following a head injury at age 30, and lost the ability to acquire new episodic memory while retaining good semantic memory (Tulving, 1989). For example, K.C. can remember where he works and how to play chess, but he cannot recall a single specific event that occurred at work or a single specific chess game he played. Other patients show the same pattern. And even H.M. has acquired some semantic information about prominent individuals, such as Martin Luther King Jr. and Ronald Reagan, who both became famous after the onset of H.M.'s amnesia (O'Kane, Kensinger, & Corkin, 2004). In isolation, each of these cases is a curiosity; together they suggest that brain damage can sometimes devastate episodic memory but at least partially spare semantic memory.

Vargha-Khadem and her colleagues suggest that semantic learning depends on medial temporal areas, including the entorhinal cortex and perirhinal cortex, that were spared in Beth (Vargha-Khadem et al., 1997). This is why Beth could pass her high school classes. But the hippocampus is needed for the extra ability to record the autobiographical context in which those memories were formed (Tulving & Markowitsch, 1998). In effect, episodic memories are semantic memories that have context information added on, courtesy of the hippocampus. With no hippocampus, Beth can remember the information but not the context.

But other researchers, including Larry Squire and Stuart Zola, have argued just the opposite: that semantic memories depend on episodic memories (Squire & Zola, 1998). They suggest that semantic memories are built up through repetition and rehearsal of many individual episodes. In other words, if you hear a fact once and remember it, you have an episodic memory for the learning experience. If you hear the same fact many times in many different spatial and temporal contexts, the episodes may blur together until only the fact remains. If semantic memories are based on episodic memories, you would expect people with hippocampal damage to show impairments at learning new factual information, because they don't have their episodic memory to help. In fact, many patients with amnesia are impaired in learning new semantic information as well as episodic information (Manns et al., 2003). This is particularly true if the brain damage extends beyond the hippocampus and into the cortex.

The debate continues. At this point, it is still an open question whether the hippocampus is critical for semantic memory formation or only for episodic memory formation.

As for Beth, she's now a young woman. She can hold an intelligent conversation, but she can't handle a job or live independently. Even with a fund of semantic information at her disposal, her lack of episodic memory is devastating. Cases like Beth's remind us that general knowledge about the world is not enough without autobiographical memories to show us how to use that knowledge.

store (and therefore forget). A recent series of studies suggests that the prefrontal cortex suppresses hippocampal activity, inhibiting storage and retrieval of "unwanted" memories. Michael Anderson has studied a **directed forgetting** task, in which he trained people on a series of word pairs: ORDEAL-ROACH, STEAM-TRAIN, JAW-GUM, and so on (Anderson et al., 2004). Then he showed the participants the first word of some pairs. For some words (OR-DEAL), people were asked to *remember* the associate (ROACH). For others (STEAM), they were asked to try to *forget* the associate (TRAIN). Later, Anderson tested memory for all the pairs (Figure 3.17a). People were less able to remember the associates they'd tried to forget (STEAM-TRAIN) than those they'd practiced (ORDEAL-ROACH) or those they hadn't seen since original training (JAW-GUM).

What could underlie this difference? Anderson and colleagues collected fMRI data on the middle phase, during which participants were being asked to remember or forget the word associates. As Figure 3.17b shows, the hippocampus was more active during the remember trials than during the forget trials; this is not particularly surprising, given the role of the hippocampus in memory. More surprising is the finding that several areas in the prefrontal cortex were more active during the forget trials than during the remember trials. One possibility is that prefrontal activation "turns off" the hippocampus on forget trials, suppressing memory. And indeed, the greater the prefrontal activation in a given participant during a given trial, the more likely the participant was to forget the word on the final test.

These and similar experiments strongly suggest that the frontal lobes contribute to the acquisition of new episodic and semantic memories. In general, the frontal lobes play a role in such processes as attention, judgment, and cognitive control. All of these processes help determine what enters memory and how strongly it is stored. The frontal lobes may also help us bind contextual information with event memory, allowing us to form episodic memories that encode not only what happened but also where and when the episode took place (Schacter & Curran, 1995).

As a result, you might expect that people with frontal lobe damage would be especially prone to source amnesia—confusing where and when an event occurred. And this seems to be the case. Like Reagan and his tale of the heroic World War II commander, individuals with frontal lobe damage may be able to remember a story but not whether it occurred in their own past, or on television, or in their imagination (Kapur & Coughlan, 1980). As you read earlier, source amnesia is generally not as devastating as the all-out memory failure of anterograde amnesia or retrograde amnesia, but it can still be a serious problem if a person can't reliably tell the difference between a fictional story and a real-life experience.

Figure 3.17 Directed forgetting People learned a series of word pairs (e.g., ORDEAL-ROACH, STEAM-TRAIN, JAW-GUM). They were then shown some words (e.g., ORDEAL) and asked to remember the paired word (ROACH); for other words (e.g., STEAM) they were asked to forget the paired word (TRAIN). (a) When later tested on memory for all the word pairs, participants were indeed worse at remembering pairs they'd been asked to forget than pairs they'd been asked to remember or pairs they hadn't seen since the original training (e.g., JAW-GUM). (b) During the training phase, fMRI difference images showed the hippocampus to be *less* active (blue) while people were trying to forget than while they were trying to remember. Several prefrontal areas, however, were *more* active (yellow) while participants were trying to forget. (a) Data from and (b) adapted from Anderson et al., 2004.

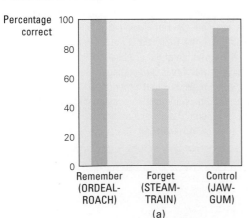
(a)

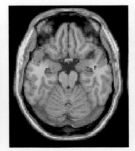
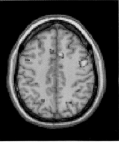

More active during "forget" than "remember"

More active during "remember" than "forget"

(b)

Subcortical Structures Involved in Episodic and Semantic Memory

Two other brain structures deserve special mention in the context of episodic and semantic memory: the diencephalon and the basal forebrain. The **diencephalon** is a group of structures including the mammillary bodies and the mediodorsal nucleus of the thalamus; the **basal forebrain** is a group of structures lying—as the name suggests—at the base of the forebrain. Figure 3.18 shows these brain regions. Parts of the diencephalon and basal forebrain connect to the hippocampus via an arch-like fiber bundle called (you guessed it) the fornix. Damage to the diencephalon, the basal forebrain, or the fornix can result in anterograde amnesia.

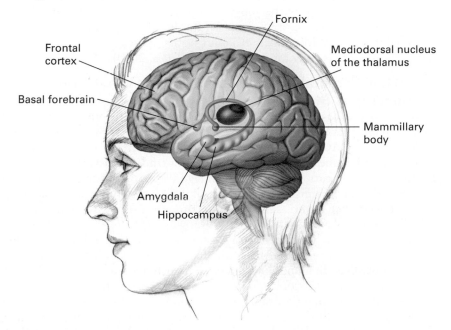

Frontal cortex
Basal forebrain
Fornix
Mediodorsal nucleus of the thalamus
Mammillary body
Amygdala
Hippocampus

Figure 3.18 The diencephalon and basal forebrain
The diencephalon (including the mediodorsal nucleus of the thalamus and the mammillary bodies) and the basal forebrain both connect to the hippocampus via a fiber bundle called the fornix. Damage to either the diencephalon or the basal forebrain can cause anterograde amnesia that resembles the effects of hippocampal damage.

The Diencephalon May Help Guide Consolidation

Over a century ago, doctors noted memory problems in individuals with **Korsakoff's disease,** a condition associated with a deficiency in thiamine (a B vitamin) that sometimes accompanies chronic alcohol abuse (Butters, 1985; Kopelman, 1995; Parsons & Nixon, 1993). Korsakoff's disease consistently damages the mammillary bodies and the mediodorsal nucleus of the thalamus, although other brain regions are damaged too. In many cases of Korsakoff's, patients develop the same kind of anterograde amnesia and time-graded retrograde amnesia observed in H.M. and other individuals with medial temporal lobe damage—even though patients with Korsakoff's have no direct damage to their medial temporal lobes. Rats given conjoint lesions to the mammillary bodies and mediodorsal nucleus of the thalamus also show memory impairments (Aggleton & Mishkin, 1983; Mair, Knoth, Rabehenuk, & Langlais, 1991).

It is still unclear why diencephalic damage causes amnesia; in fact, there is still considerable debate about whether the memory deficits in Korsakoff's disease are primarily due to mammillary damage, thalamic damage, or both. Because these brain areas are anatomically connected to both the cerebral cortex and the medial temporal lobes, one possibility is that these diencephalic structures are somehow responsible for the interaction between the frontal cortex and the hippocampus during memory storage and consolidation, and thus diencephalic damage disrupts this interaction.

When questioned about past events, many individuals with Korsakoff's will make up stories rather than admit memory loss, a phenomenon called *confabulation*. For example, asked what he did yesterday, a patient may say that he went into the office for a few hours, met an old friend for lunch, and then did some grocery shopping on the way home; the story may sound perfectly logical, except for the fact that he has been in the hospital for the past two weeks!

Individuals who confabulate are not lying. Rather, they seem to believe the stories they've made up and are often confused when confronted with proof that the stories are false. Some examples of confabulation seem to be no more than a kind of source amnesia. In the above example, the patient can't remember what he did yesterday, because of his amnesia. But he can retrieve a plausible answer from old memory. Without help from his frontal cortex, he may mistakenly believe this memory is recent instead of old (DeLuca, 2000).

The Basal Forebrain May Help Determine What the Hippocampus Stores

Damage to the basal forebrain is yet another cause of amnesia. The basal forebrain receives blood and oxygen from a small artery, the anterior communicating artery (ACoA). The ACoA is a common site of *aneurysm*, a type of stroke in which the artery wall balloons out under pressure and may even rupture. If this occurs, it may cause damage to the basal forebrain. Like people with Korsakoff's disease, survivors of an ACoA aneurysm rupture often have amnesia that is very similar to the amnesia caused by medial temporal lobe damage (DeLuca & Diamond, 1995).

Why should basal forebrain damage cause amnesia? Some basal forebrain nuclei send acetylcholine and GABA to the hippocampus, and these neurotransmitters affect plasticity in hippocampal neurons, which helps to determine how likely the hippocampus is to store information. One theory is that the hippocampus spends its time recalling previously stored information and transferring this information to long-term storage in the cortex *except* when something interesting is happening in the outside world, at which point the basal forebrain signals the hippocampus to turn its attention to processing and encoding incoming information (Buzsaki & Gage, 1989; Damasio, Graff-Radford, Eslinger, Damasio, & Kassell, 1985; Hasselmo, 1999; Myers, Ermita, Hasselmo, & Gluck, 1998). This could explain why a basal forebrain lesion leads to amnesia—although the hippocampus and medial temporal lobes are undamaged, they can't work effectively without instructions from the basal forebrain telling them when to store new information.

Like patients with Korsakoff's disease, patients who survive an ACoA aneurysm can also confabulate, providing detailed and fictitious stories when questioned about events they've forgotten. Confabulation appears when there is conjoint damage to the basal forebrain and the frontal cortex. The basal forebrain damage leaves patients unable to store new memories; when questioned about recent events, they can't remember but may retrieve a plausible answer—and the frontal cortex damage leaves them unable to determine whether it's old or new (DeLuca, 2000).

Many questions remain unanswered about diencephalic amnesia and basal forebrain amnesia and about their relation to medial temporal amnesia. But these different classes of amnesia provide compelling evidence that memory is a function of the whole brain. Many structures—including the hippocampus, cortex, diencephalon, and basal forebrain—must all be working well and working together for episodic and semantic memory to succeed.

Interim Summary

Semantic memories seem to be stored in the cortex; to some extent, specific kinds of semantic information are stored in the cortical areas that process that kind of information. The hippocampal region is important for new episodic and semantic memory storage; people with amnesia caused by bilateral hippocampal-region damage show anterograde amnesia (failure to encode new episodic and semantic memories); they may also show retrograde amnesia (disruption of old memories dating back some period before the damage). In healthy humans, functional neuroimaging shows that the hippocampal region is especially active during encoding of information that will be successfully remembered later. It remains an issue of debate whether episodic memories ever become fully independent of the hippocampus or whether the hippocampus always helps access memories stored in the cortex. Other areas involved in episodic and semantic memory include the frontal cortex (especially important for remembering source information), the diencephalon (which may mediate communication between the hippocampus and the cortex during information storage and consolidation), and the basal forebrain (which may help regulate hippocampal processing).

3.3 Clinical Perspectives

So far in this chapter you've read about several kinds of amnesia. In patients like H.M. and E.P., the amnesia is a permanent condition caused by brain damage. E.P.'s amnesia, for example, can be traced directly to medial temporal lobe damage dating to his bout with herpes encephalitis, and H.M.'s amnesia stems from his brain surgery. Once the medial temporal lobes are damaged or destroyed, the lost memories cannot be recovered.

In other cases, however, the memory dysfunction may not be permanent. You've already learned about one kind of "temporary amnesia" in patients who undergo electroconvulsive shock therapy. These patients typically experience anterograde amnesia for the events of the ECT session and retrograde amnesia for events that happened a short time before the session. But their memory machinery is not permanently damaged. After a few hours, their brains are again able to encode new memories and retrieve old ones. In this section we review three other kinds of temporary memory loss: transient global amnesia, functional amnesia, and childhood amnesia.

Transient Global Amnesia

As its name suggests, **transient global amnesia (TGA)** is a transient, or temporary, disruption of memory (Brand & Markowitsch, 2004; Kritchevsky, Squire, & Zouzounis, 1988; Markowitsch, 1983). Typically, TGA starts suddenly, persists for several hours, and then gradually dissipates over the course of a day or so. During the amnesic episode, the person shows severe anterograde amnesia and is unable to learn new autobiographical information. There is usually also some degree of retrograde amnesia—not a complete identity loss as in *The Bourne Identity*'s amnesic assassin, but patchy loss of autobiographical information for events that occurred within the preceding decade or so (Kritchevsky et al., 1988; Kritchevsky & Squire, 1989).

Transient global amnesia is difficult to study because the brain malfunction doesn't usually last long, but there are a few well-documented cases in the literature. One such case involves a 38-year-old man, S.G., who underwent brain surgery (Kapur, Millar, Abbott, & Carter, 1998). The surgery seemed to go smoothly, but there may have been some complication that temporarily reduced blood flow to his brain. When S.G. woke up, he knew his name but did not remember his occupation, the month, or how long he had been in the hospital.

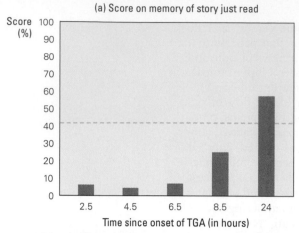

(a) Score on memory of story just read

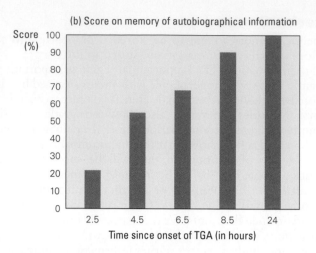

(b) Score on memory of autobiographical information

Figure 3.19 Transient global amnesia (TGA) (a) Patient S.G., 2.5 hours after the onset of amnesia, could remember almost nothing from a story he'd heard a few minutes ago. By 24 hours after onset, however, he could remember about as much of a just-read story as a healthy control ("normal" performance indicated by dotted line). (b) Similarly, 2.5 hours after the onset of his amnesia, S.G. showed severe retrograde amnesia for autobiographical information; his memories returned to normal 24 hours later. (a, b) Adapted from Kapur et al., 1998.

The onset of S.G.'s amnesia occurred around 12:30 p.m. Memory researchers rushed to the scene, and S.G. agreed to an extensive battery of testing. At about 3 p.m., S.G. showed profound anterograde amnesia: he could listen to a short story, but a few minutes later he would recall only a few words of it (Figure 3.19a). S.G. also showed retrograde amnesia. Given a questionnaire about jobs he had held, places he had lived, and other personal information, he could provide only a few answers (Figure 3.19b). (The correct answers were verified by S.G.'s fiancée.) His memory was similarly poor for recent public events, although it was better for events that had happened at least a few decades before.

Researchers continued to test S.G. every few hours through the afternoon and evening; gradually, his anterograde and retrograde amnesia lessened. By noon of the next day, 24 hours after the onset of amnesia, S.G.'s memory had returned to normal, except for a slight retrograde amnesia for events that had occurred shortly before the surgery. The TGA was over; S.G.'s brain seemed to be back in working order.

Why might TGA occur? Like S.G., many individuals with TGA probably experienced a temporary interruption of blood flow to the brain from a head injury, a hypoglycemic episode (low blood sugar), or a heart attack or stroke. As in ECT, the temporary disruption in neuronal activity might completely erase nonconsolidated memories of recent events but merely limit access to fully consolidated older memories. When the blood flow resumes, so does the brain function.

Certain drugs (including tranquilizers and alcohol) can also prompt TGA episodes, or "blackouts," in which memories for the duration of the blackout are not stored (Wixted, 2004). In other cases of TGA, patients have no obvious brain injury or history of drug abuse, although it is possible that something has occurred in their brain that is too subtle to be detected by modern medical techniques.

Functional Amnesia

So far in this chapter we've talked about amnesia in patients who sustain some kind of injury or disruption to the brain. By contrast, *The Bourne Identity*'s amnesic assassin suffers no particular brain injury, but nevertheless forgets his name, his profession, and what he's doing on a fishing boat.

Such memory loss without brain damage can happen in real life, although it is rarer than Hollywood might lead you to believe. **Functional amnesia** (sometimes also called *psychogenic amnesia*) refers to amnesia that seems to result from psychological causes rather than from any obvious physical causes, such as brain injury (Kritchevsky, Chang, & Squire, 2004; Schacter & Kihlstrom, 1989). Such cases are very rare, and the picture is complicated by the fact that some individuals who claim to have lost their memory later admit to faking amnesia in order to avoid dealing with a difficult situation such as a crime or a relationship problem. Some cases, however, do seem to involve genuine memory loss.

Daniel Schacter records one case involving a 21-year-old man, P.N., who was admitted to the hospital complaining about back pains (Schacter, Wang, Tulving, & Freedman, 1982). When questioned about his identity, P.N. could not remember his name or anything about his own past, except that he had once been given the nickname "Lumberjack." Schacter later concluded that P.N. had developed functional amnesia following the death of his grandfather, to whom P.N. had been close. P.N.'s extreme grief was the psychological trauma that triggered the memory loss.

In contrast to P.N.'s severe retrograde amnesia for autobiographical events, his semantic memories were intact. His language functions and knowledge about the world also seemed normal. P.N. also showed some anterograde amnesia; he had extreme difficulty remembering new information for more than a few minutes at a time. The functional amnesia persisted for about a week, until P.N. happened to watch a television show that included a funeral scene; as if by magic, lost memories came flooding back, and P.N. recalled his own identity and history. Only the memories of events that occurred during P.N.'s amnesia were permanently lost, presumably because his anterograde amnesia had prevented the memories from being successfully stored in the first place.

Not all cases of functional amnesia resolve so simply. Mark Kritchevsky and his colleagues studied 10 individuals with functional amnesia; all were unable to report their names or personal histories (Kritchevsky et al., 2004). One of these patients later admitted to feigning his amnesia (and Kritchevsky and colleagues suspect a second may have been feigning, too). But of the eight patients whose amnesia seemed genuine, only one fully recovered all the lost memories. And a few never recovered any memories at all, even 2 or more years after the onset of their amnesia. Currently, there is no way to predict when or whether a particular patient will recover his memory.

Given that patients with functional amnesia have no known brain damage, what could cause this syndrome? Functional imaging may provide some clues. In one positron emission tomography (PET) study, an individual with functional amnesia had decreased glucose metabolism in the medial temporal lobes and medial diencephalon; these abnormalities disappeared when the amnesia resolved (Markowitsch et al., 1998). This suggests that functional amnesia may result from a (possibly temporary) malfunction of the brain areas involved in memory storage and retrieval. If so, functional amnesia would not be qualitatively different from the kinds of amnesia experienced by patients with brain damage. The major difference would be that functional amnesia is brought on by a psychological trauma, rather than a physiological one.

Infantile Amnesia

Another kind of memory loss is **infantile amnesia,** forgetting of events that occurred during infancy. As adults, we cannot consciously remember autobiographical events that occurred before age 3 or 4 (Kihlstrom & Harackiewicz, 1982; Waldvogel, 1982 [1948]; Weigle & Bauer, 2000). Occasionally, someone claims to remember autobiographical episodes from infancy, but these are probably semantic memories: after repeatedly looking at the photos and hearing the stories of your first birthday, you might have detailed semantic information about the party, but this is not the same thing as an actual episodic memory of experiencing the event firsthand. Unlike many other kinds of amnesia discussed in this chapter, infantile amnesia is a normal part of human life. Fortunately, we outgrow it. By the age of 5 or 6, most of us are reliably forming new episodic memories that can last a lifetime.

Why does infantile amnesia occur? Does something special occur around age 3 or 4 that suddenly supports the acquisition and retention of episodic memory? Again, the answer is unclear, but a number of factors may be involved (Eacott, 1999). Parts of the hippocampus and frontal cortex are immature at birth and continue to develop during the first few years of life (Durston et al., 2001; Serres, 2001). Because these brain areas are critical for encoding and recall of episodic memories, it could be that we are simply not biologically equipped to store episodic memories until these brain areas are mature.

Another age-related change occurs between 16 and 24 months of age, when children begin to show evidence of a "cognitive self." One test of whether a child has a sense of self is whether she can recognize herself in the mirror. If a researcher surreptitiously marks a child's face with rouge, and then the child sees herself in the mirror and touches the marked spot, we may conclude that she recognizes the image as her own ("Hey, that's me—and what's that red dot doing on my nose?"). Chimps and dolphins show the same kind of mirror-recognition behavior, which is often taken as evidence that these animals, too, have a sense of themselves as individuals (de Waal, Dindo, Freeman, & Hall, 2005). In contrast, many species of fish, on seeing themselves in a mirror, respond by trying to attack the fish staring back at them, suggesting they can't recognize their own reflection ("Hey, who's that intruder in my territory?").

Infants younger than 16 months don't show mirror-recognition behavior, but children older than 24 months do (Lewis & Brooks-Gunn, 1979). This implies that 2-year-olds, but not 1-year-olds, have a sense of themselves as individuals. This cognitive milestone is probably a prerequisite for forming autobiographical memories (Howe & Courage, 1993). You can't remember that a particular event happened to you unless you have a sense of yourself and how you exist in time (Fivush & Nelson, 2004).

Yet another possible explanation of infantile amnesia is that infants, who have not yet acquired language, cannot encode and store episodic memories in a manner that the adult brain can retrieve. Memory researcher Elizabeth Loftus has suggested that an adult brain trying to access an infant memory is comparable to a computer trying to read a document formatted by an earlier version of the operating system: the information may be there, but it doesn't make any sense when interpreted by the modern operating system (Loftus & Kaufman, 1992).

All of these factors—a fully developed hippocampus and frontal cortex, a cognitive sense of self, and a mastery of language—may have to be in place before we can form episodic memories that we can access for the rest of our lives.

Test Your Knowledge

Don't Forget Your Amnesias

"Amnesia" is a general term that refers to memory loss. Each kind of amnesia refers to a specific way in which memory can be disrupted. For each type of amnesia listed below, can you remember what kind of information is lost or disrupted, as well as what kinds of brain damage might cause each?

1. Anterograde amnesia
2. Functional amnesia
3. Infantile amnesia
4. Retrograde amnesia
5. Source amnesia
6. Transient global amnesia

CONCLUSION

At the beginning of this chapter we introduced three fictional characters: Leonard Shelby (*Memento*), Jason Bourne (*The Bourne Identity*), and Douglas Quaid (*Total Recall*). Knowing what you now know about memory and amnesia, you should be able to go back and assess the plausibility of each of these characters—as well as amnesia portrayals in other movies, TV shows, and books.

Let's start with Leonard Shelby. According to the movie, Leonard suffers damage to his hippocampus that leaves his identity intact but prevents him from holding on to any new episodic memory for more than a few minutes at a time. His predicament is not so different from the anterograde amnesia faced by patients such as H.M. and E.P.—although, ironically, Leonard himself denies that he has amnesia, preferring the term "short-term memory loss." (He's wrong: he does have amnesia, and his short-term memory is fine!) *Memento* also notes that Leonard can learn some new information by encoding it as habit or skill, and this is also accurate: H.M. and E.P. have impaired episodic memory, but they are quite proficient at learning new habits and skills. One feature of real-world individuals with medial temporal lobe damage is that they also have retrograde amnesia—loss of at least some (and often quite a lot) of their memories from before the brain damage. Leonard Shelby, on the other hand, believes he can remember events right up to the moment of his wife's death (although there are hints at the end of the movie that all may not be exactly as he thinks he remembers).

The Bourne Identity presents a very different scenario; hero Jason Bourne does not have anterograde amnesia. Instead, Bourne suffers a complete loss of identity. This resembles the real-world (though rare) phenomenon of functional amnesia. Bourne maintains his semantic memory about the world, as well as his professional skills. This profile is relatively similar to that of patient P.N., whose functional amnesia stripped him of personal history, though his knowledge about the world seemed to be normal. Functional amnesia is caused by psychological trauma rather than physical brain damage. Indeed, Bourne spends much of the movie trying to solve the mystery of what brought on his amnesia, as well as trying to recover his lost identity. In this sense, *The Bourne Identity* and other "lost identity" stories share many features with real-world cases of functional amnesia. These stories mainly depart from reality in their resolution: many a soap-opera heroine has lost her memory following a blow to the head, and a second blow is all that's needed to bring the memories flooding back. In the real world, head injuries (and similar plot devices) don't cure functional amnesia. Some patients recover spontaneously, but others recover slowly or not at all.

Our third protagonist, Douglas Quaid of *Total Recall*, experiences false memories. Tired of his workaday life, he pays to have memories of an expensive trip to Mars implanted in his brain. The company providing the service promises that the false memories will be every bit as realistic and enjoyable as true memories, at a fraction of the time and cost it would take to vacation on another planet. The vacation packages are obviously science fiction, but the premise of false memories is real: researchers can implant false memories, using techniques much simpler than those that *Total Recall*'s villains employ. And, once implanted, false memories can indeed feel as real and rich as true memories—so real that research participants will often argue when researchers attempt to explain the hoax. False memories lead to an exciting adventure in *Total Recall*, the movie, but they can lead to serious real-world problems, too, as when eyewitnesses confuse memories of a crime scene with pictures of a suspect aired on the nightly news.

In all of these movies, the drama springs from a universal sense that our episodic and semantic memories—the facts we know and the events we've experienced—make us who we are. It is easy to empathize with a character whose autobiographical memories have been stripped away, because we can imagine the devastating impact. Many fewer movies have been made in which the hero suddenly loses other kinds of memory; Arnold Schwarzenegger, who portrays Quaid in *Total Recall*, probably turned down the script in which evil villains *took away his memory of how to tie his shoes*.

But we all experience occasional failures of episodic and semantic memory. Some failures, such as forgetting what we ate for breakfast on July 16, 2003, or blanking on the name of someone we meet unexpectedly at the gym, are just a normal part of everyday life. Some of us have experienced an episode of TGA following a sports injury, or have fallen prey to cryptomnesia while writing a term paper, or even suffer from source amnesia for a childhood event that we don't really remember but have often seen in home movies or heard retold many times at family get-togethers. Most of the time, our memory is effortless, long lasting, and largely accurate—but at the same time, it may fail more often than we normally suspect. Understanding these memory processes may help us increase the successes and reduce the failures, while giving us—like Jason Bourne and his fellows—a better appreciation of the episodic and semantic memories we do have.

Key Points

- Episodic memory is memory for autobiographical events we "remember." Semantic memory is general fact information we "know." Both are generally accessible to conscious recall and can be communicated flexibly.

- There are key differences between episodic and semantic memory. Episodic memory is always acquired in a single exposure, but semantic memory may be strengthened by repeated exposure. Episodic memory always includes information about spatial and temporal context; semantic memory need not include this information. Some researchers believe that only adult humans, with a sense of self and the ability to perform "mental time-travel" to relive past events, are capable of true episodic memory.

- Several factors affect whether episodic and semantic memories are successfully encoded and retrieved. Factors include whether the information can be related to preexisting knowledge, how it is processed (e.g., deeply or shallowly), the degree to which encoding and recall conditions match, and how many cues are available to prompt recall.

- Most simple forgetting occurs early after the event; the Ribot gradient suggests that, if older memories survive a consolidation period, they tend to be "safe" from subsequent forgetting. Memories can also be lost or distorted through processes such as interference, source amnesia, cryptomnesia, and false memory.

- Hierarchical semantic networks are one model for how information is encoded as links (relationships) between nodes (concepts or objects).

- The cerebral cortex is a site of storage for semantic memories. People with different kinds of cortical damage may show disruptions in various semantic abilities, reflected in difficulties remembering the purpose or meaning of words, objects, or faces.

- Many cortical areas fall prey to the false-memory effect—activity is similar for false items and familiar ones—but a region in the medial temporal lobes may signal whether the memory is true or false.

- The hippocampal region is particularly active during encoding of material that will be remembered later. Humans and other animals with damage to the hippocampal region typically show severe anterograde amnesia, or failure to acquire new event memories, as well as retrograde amnesia, or loss of memory for events that occurred before the injury.

- It remains unclear whether episodic memories ever become fully independent of the hippocampus, or whether the hippocampus always helps access memories stored in the cerebral cortex.

- The frontal cortex may help bind together memory of events with information about the spatial and temporal context in which the events occurred. Individuals with damage to the frontal cortex are prone to source amnesia.

- The diencephalon and basal forebrain also play key, but poorly understood, roles in memory. Damage to

either area can result in anterograde amnesia that is similar to the memory loss in patients with medial temporal lobe damage.

- Transient global amnesia may reflect a temporary brain disruption during which the medial temporal lobes are unable to carry out their normal role in encoding new information.

- Functional amnesia may also be temporary; it may be caused by psychological trauma rather than by any discernable brain injury.

- Infantile amnesia is the general lack of episodic memories from the first few years of life, possibly due to immaturity of brain structures, lack of a cognitive sense of self, or absence of language skills.

Key Terms

agnosia, p. 103
amnesia, p. 83
anterograde amnesia, p. 105
association cortex, p. 103
basal forebrain, p. 113
consolidation period, p. 92
cryptomnesia, p. 97
cued recall, p. 94
declarative memory, p. 85
depth of processing, p. 90
diencephalon, p. 113
directed forgetting, p. 112

electroconvulsive shock, p. 92
episodic memory, p. 84
explicit memory, p. 85
false memories, p. 98
free recall, p. 94
frontal cortex, p. 110
functional amnesia, p. 116
hierarchical semantic network, p. 100
hippocampus, p. 104
implicit memory, p. 85

infantile amnesia, p. 117
interference, p. 96
Korsakoff's disease, p. 113
medial temporal lobe, p. 104
mnemonics, p. 95
multiple memory trace theory, p. 110
nondeclarative memory, p. 85
proactive interference, p. 96
recognition, p. 94
retroactive interference, p. 96

retrograde amnesia, p. 108
Ribot gradient, p. 108
semantic memories, p. 84
sensory cortex, p. 102
source amnesia, p. 97
standard consolidation theory, p. 109
transfer-appropriate processing, p. 93
transient global amnesia (TGA), p. 115

Concept Check

1. Suppose you join a club with six members, and you want to remember each member's name for the next meeting. What are three ways, based on the principles in this chapter, that you can improve the probability of remembering the names?

2. A semantic memory is a memory for a fact without memory of the spatial and temporal context in which that fact was learned. How does this differ from source amnesia?

3. Failures of episodic and semantic memory can be annoying, but they serve a purpose. Why might it be desirable for an organism to be able to forget some information?

4. In healthy adult humans, fMRI shows that the hippocampus is active even for retrieval of very old autobiographical information (Ryan, 2001). Does this prove that autobiographical memories always remain at least partially dependent on the hippocampus?

5. An Italian glassblower had a cyst removed from his brain (Semenza, Sartori, & D'Andrea, 2003). After the surgery, he experienced a type of agnosia involving a selective deficit in retrieving people's names when shown their faces. Given pictures of famous people (including the pope), he had great difficulty retrieving the names. But he could easily retrieve the

names of master glassblowers when shown pictures of their most typical products. Using the idea of a hierarchical semantic network, suggest why this patient might have trouble retrieving names from pictures of faces, but not from vases.

6. Suppose you are working in an emergency room when a man comes in who claims to have forgotten his entire identity. What questions would you ask the friend who drove him to the hospital? What kinds of tests might you conduct to help find out what's going on?

Answers to Test Your Knowledge

Episodic versus Semantic Memory

1. It depends. Knowing that coffee is better at Starbucks than at the student center is an example of general knowledge about the world, so it counts as semantic memory. (Knowing how to get to Starbucks from the present location counts as semantic memory too.) But why does the college senior think that the coffee is better at Starbucks? If he can remember a specific episode in which he went to the student center and had terrible coffee, and if this is why he believes Starbucks is superior, then that is an episodic memory.

2. The student remembers the meaning of *carpe diem* using semantic memory, and he has no episodic memory of acquiring this information.

3. Here, the student does have an episodic memory, tagged in space and time, of studying the phrase *ne tentes, aut perfice*, but no semantic memory for what the phrase means in English (roughly, "either succeed, or don't bother trying").

Don't Forget Your Amnesias

1. *What is lost or disrupted:* the ability to form new episodic and semantic memories. *Common causes:*

damage to the medial temporal lobes (or the diencephalon or basal forebrain).

2. *What is lost or disrupted:* all personal (episodic and semantic) memories. *Common causes:* strong psychological trauma but no obvious physiological injury.

3. *What is lost or disrupted:* episodic memories for events in early childhood. *Common causes:* possibly, immaturity of the brain areas that encode episodic memories, lack of a cognitive sense of self, and/or absence of language skills.

4. *What is lost or disrupted:* the ability to retrieve existing episodic memories. *Common causes:* broad damage to the medial temporal lobes and beyond.

5. *What is lost or disrupted:* the context describing where or when an episodic memory was acquired. *Common causes:* possibly, damage to the frontal cortex; also can occur intermittently in healthy people.

6. *What is lost or disrupted:* anterograde (and possibly retrograde) memory, usually for a day or less. *Common causes:* head injury, hypoglycemic episode, or brief interruption of blood flow to the brain.

Further Reading

Borges, J. L. (2000). Funes, his memory. In J. Lethem (Ed.), *The Vintage book of amnesia: An anthology of writing on the subject of memory loss* (pp. 119–126). New York: Vintage Crime. (Reprinted from Borges, J. L., *Collected fictions* [A. Hurley, Trans.], 1998, New York: Penguin Putnam) • A fictional account of a young man with a "perfect memory" who can recall every detail of every experience, leaving his mind a garbage heap incapable of abstract thought.

Griffiths, D., Dickinson, A., & Clayton, N. (1999). Episodic memory: What can animals remember about their past? *Trends in Cognitive Sciences*, 3, 74–80. • The authors argue that many animals can and do form something very similar to human episodic memories.

Loftus, E. (2003). Our changeable memories: Legal and practical implications. *Nature Reviews Neuroscience*, 4, 231–234. • A review of how false memories can be constructed in the lab, along with a review of several cases in which "eyewitness" testimony wrongly convicted suspects who were later exonerated, and the testimony proved to be based on false memories.

Luria, A. (1982). The mind of a mnemonist (L. Solotaroff, Trans.). In U. Neisser (Ed.), *Memory observed: Remembering in natural contexts* (pp. 382–389). San Francisco: Freeman. (Reprinted from *The mind of a mnemonist*, by A. Luria, 1968, New York: Basic Books) • Portions of a classic report on a famous mnemonist and his life.

Schacter, D. (2001). *The seven sins of memory: How the mind forgets and remembers*. New York: Houghton-Mifflin. • A well-written book that covers the many ways in which memory can fail—and why these "failures" are not always a bad thing!

Among the many film depictions of anterograde amnesia are *Memento* (2000, Sony Pictures), a psychological thriller featuring a protagonist (played by Guy Pearce) who is unable to form new episodic or semantic memories; and *50 First Dates* (2004, Sony Pictures), a comic take on the same dilemma, as a man (Adam Sandler) pursues a woman (Drew Barrymore) who cannot remember their previous dates. Pixar's *Finding Nemo* (2003) also features an animated fish (voiced by Ellen DeGeneres) who suffers from anterograde amnesia.

Psychogenic amnesia is an even more common movie plot. *The Bourne Identity* (2002, Universal Studios) follows a character (played by Matt Damon) who has forgotten his identity and past but retains his unique job skills. *Spellbound* (1945, Anchor Bay Entertainment) was director Alfred Hitchcock's contribution to the amnesia genre, with Ingrid Bergman playing a psychiatrist trying to help her patient (Gregory Peck) recover his lost memories. Ingrid Bergman later won an Oscar for her portrayal in *Anastasia* (1956, 20th Century Fox) of an amnesic woman who may be the lost heir to the Russian throne. (In the 1997 animated version [20th Century Fox], Anastasia [voiced by Meg Ryan] suffers from infantile amnesia rather than psychogenic amnesia.)

Exploring the concept of false memories, *Total Recall* (1990, Lion's Gate), starring Arnold Schwarzenegger, considers a future where people can pay to have memories of exotic vacations implanted in their minds. In the classic film *The Manchurian Candidate* (1962, Metro-Goldwyn-Mayer, starring Frank Sinatra; remade in 2004 by Universal Studios, starring Denzel Washington), an evil corporation uses brainwashing and hypnotism to implant false memories. The opposite procedure is imagined in *Eternal Sunshine of the Spotless Mind* (2004, Universal Studios), starring Jim Carrey and Kate Winslet, in which people can pay to erase unwanted or painful memories.

CHAPTER 4

Skill Memory

Learning by Doing

"When starting a kiss, the rule of thumb is to start slow. This just makes sense, and it lets everyone get used to the dynamics of that particular kiss. A slow start is a good introduction . . . and sometimes the kiss should just stay slow. Jumping into rapid tongue maneuvers can scare your partner, and is rude to boot. Athletes always warm up before moving onto serious play . . . why should kissing be any different?"

(Hays, Allen, & Hanish, 2005)

DO YOU REMEMBER YOUR FIRST KISS? For some, it is a magical memory. For others, that kiss was a somewhat awkward experience in which a single thought kept recurring: "Am I doing this right?" Kissing is simple enough in concept. Take your lips and press them against someone else's lips. What could be easier? After just a few experiences with bad kissers, however, it becomes clear that this apparently simple ability is not one that humans are born with. By the same token, a single encounter with an especially good kisser is enough to make you appreciate that kissing requires some skill.

The success of a first kiss may depend in part on the setting and the partner, but most young people are savvy enough to know that they need to practice if they want their first real kiss to be a good one. Practice might consist of kissing one's own hand or arm, a pillow, or a stuffed animal. The hope is that these practice sessions will give you an edge when a real opportunity comes along. Practicing by kissing your hand or arm is a good strategy, because that way you get feedback about what your lips feel like. Attending a Kissing 101 class might also help, but you will not become an adept kisser by memorizing lists of rules about how to kiss. To become an expert, you need to kiss (a lot), you need to get feedback about your kissing, and, most important, your brain has to store memories of your kissing successes and failures.

This chapter describes how repeated experiences incrementally enhance the performance of a skill by gradually modifying memories of how the skill can best be executed. As you will discover, repeated experiences not only can change how a person performs a skill, such as kissing; they also can change the structure of the brain circuits that are used to perform that skill. Skill memories are formed and processed by several brain regions, including the basal ganglia, the cerebral cortex, and the cerebellum. People with damage in one or more of these brain regions have trouble learning new skills, as well as performing skills already learned.

4.1 Behavioral Processes

The previous chapter dealt with memories for events and facts—in other words, information a person remembers and knows. Skill memory, in contrast, consists of what a person knows how to do. By reading this sentence you are exercising a skill that you learned a long time ago. Reading may seem so effortless now that you can hardly recall the challenge of learning to read. When you turn a page, highlight a sentence, type or write notes, or think about what you'll need to do to remember the contents of this chapter, you are accessing memories of several different skills.

Qualities of Skill Memories

A **skill** is an ability that you can improve over time through practice. Skill memories are similar in many respects to memories for events (also called episodic memories) and facts (semantic memories), but they also possess some unique qualities (Table 4.1). Like memories for facts, skill memories are long-lasting and improved by repeated experiences. Unlike memories for events and facts, however, skill memories can't always be verbalized; moreover, skill memories may be acquired and retrieved without conscious awareness. As you'll recall from Chapter 3, psychologists sometimes classify skill memories as nondeclarative memories, because these memories are not easily put into words.

All memories for events and facts depend on skill memories, because the abilities to speak, write, and gesture to convey information are learned abilities that improve over time with practice. In contrast, skill memories do not necessarily depend on verbalizable memories, although memories for events and facts can play an important role in acquiring skills. Given the dependence of memories for events and facts on skill memories, perhaps it would be fairer to describe declarative memories as "non-skill" memories, rather than calling skill memories "nondeclarative."

Table 4.1

Comparison of Memories for Skills, Events, and Facts	
Skill Memory	**Memory for Events and Facts**
1. Is difficult to convey to others	1. Can be communicated flexibly
2. May be acquired without awareness	2. Has content that is consciously accessible
3. Requires several repetitions	3. Can be acquired in a single exposure

Memories can be classified in many ways, but often don't fit neatly into the conventional classification schemes. Contemporary researchers generally classify skill memories into two basic types: perceptual-motor skills and cognitive skills (Gabrieli, 1998; K. M. Newell, 1991; Rosenbaum, Carlson, & Gilmore, 2001; van Lehn, 1996; Voss & Wiley, 1995).

Perceptual-Motor Skills

The kinds of skills you are probably most aware of are those that athletes demonstrate when they compete. More mundane skills include opening and closing doors, driving a car, dancing, drinking out of a glass, and snapping your fingers. These are all examples of **perceptual-motor skills:** learned movement patterns guided by sensory inputs.

Consider dancing. An important part of dancing is being able to move your body in certain established patterns. This requires significant voluntary control of your movements. If you can't control where your arms go, you'll end up being more of a spectacle than a dance sensation. Dancing is more than just repeatedly moving your feet and arms in a pattern, however; you also have to move to the beat (that is, respond to auditory inputs). In addition, some well-established dances, such as the Hokey Pokey or the Macarena, require specific movements to be performed at specific points in a song. The goal in learning these kinds of dances is to perform a consistent sequence of movements in a prescribed way. Professional ballet dancers, too, learn precisely choreographed dance sequences. Psychologists classify skills such as ballet dancing, which consist of performing predefined movements, as **closed skills.** Other kinds of dancing, such as salsa or swing dancing, also involve particular movement patterns, but dancers may vary the way they combine these movements when they dance, at least in social dance settings. Such dances depend to some extent on the dancers' predicting (or directing) their partner's next move. Researchers classify skills that require participants to respond based on predictions about the changing demands of the environment as **open skills.**

These classifications apply to a wide range of perceptual-motor skills. For example, athletes who are gymnasts or divers are perfecting closed skills, whereas athletes who participate in coordinated team sports such as soccer or hockey depend heavily on open skills. Dogs can learn to catch a Frisbee (an open skill), and they can also learn to play dead (a closed skill). Catching a Frisbee is an open skill because many environmental variables—such as quality and distance of the throw, wind speed, and terrain characteristics—determine which movements the dog must make to perform the skill successfully. Most perceptual-motor skills contain aspects of both closed skills and open skills, and so it is better to think of any particular skill as lying somewhere along a continuum from open to closed (Magill, 1993).

Most research on perceptual-motor skills focuses on much less complex skills than those needed to dance or play soccer. Skills studied in the laboratory might consist of pressing buttons quickly or tracking the position of a moving object (Doyon, Penhune, & Ungerleider, 2003). It's not that knowing how a person learns to dance is uninteresting to psychologists. Rather, research psychologists want to keep things as simple as possible so they can control the relevant variables more precisely. This gives them a better chance of understanding how experience affects an individual's ability to perform a particular skill. For example, it is much easier to assess quantitatively whether someone's tracking abilities are improving than to measure improvements in their dancing abilities.

Cognitive Skills

What are some other activities that improve with practice? How about playing cards, budgeting your money, taking standardized tests, and managing your time? These are all examples of **cognitive skills,** which require you to use your brain to solve problems or apply strategies, rather than to simply move your body based on what you perceive (J. R. Anderson, Fincham, & Douglass, 1997; Singley & Anderson, 1989). Researchers often conduct experiments on cognitive skills that participants can learn relatively quickly, such as those used to solve simple puzzles like the Tower of Hanoi (Figure 4.1). In this puzzle, the objective is to move different-sized disks from one peg to another, one disk at a time (we discuss this task in greater detail in Chapter 5). The puzzle would be trivially easy, except that one of the rules is that you cannot put a larger disk on top of a smaller one. The numbered sequence in Figure 4.1 shows one solution to the puzzle. Normally, people get better at this puzzle with practice. This is not because they are getting better at moving the disks from one peg to another (a perceptual-motor skill), but because they are learning new strategies for moving the disks so that they end up in the desired position (J. R. Anderson, 1982).

Psychologists usually associate cognitive skills with the ability to reason and solve problems. Descartes proposed that the ability to reason is what distinguishes humans from other animals. Descartes would probably have been willing to accept that dogs can store memories for perceptual-motor skills such as how to catch a Frisbee, but he would have considered it impossible for a dog or any other nonhuman animal to learn a cognitive skill. Following Descartes' lead, many psychologists assume that only humans can reason. Certainly, this is one reason that most of what we currently know about cognitive skills comes from studies of humans.

Nevertheless, humans are not the only animals with cognitive skills. To give an example, it was once thought that only humans used tools and that this particular problem-solving ability played a key role in the evolution of the human mind. In the past two decades, however, psychologists and animal behavior researchers have described tool use in many animals (Beck, 1980; Hart, 2001; Hunt, Corballis, & Gray, 2001; Krutzen et al., 2005; Whiten et al., 1999). Researchers have observed chimpanzees in the wild that learn how to use stones to crack nuts (Whiten & Boesch, 2001). In the lab, experimenters have taught primates and

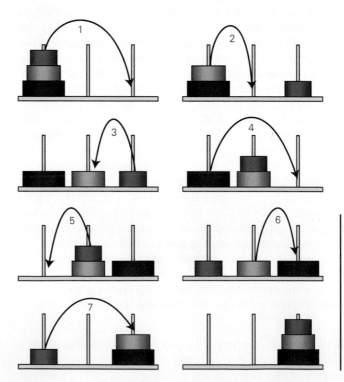

Figure 4.1 The Tower of Hanoi puzzle The objective of this task is to move all the disks from the leftmost peg to the rightmost peg, one disk at a time, without placing a larger disk on a smaller disk. The numbered sequence shows one way of doing this. The ability to solve such puzzles is a cognitive skill.

Lars Bedjer

Figure 4.2 Dolphins using tools? Some dolphins in Australia have taken to carrying around sponges when they are foraging. Researchers suspect that the dolphins use the sponges as tools to protect themselves against injuries from sea urchins and other spiny sea creatures as they probe the seafloor for food.

other animals to use various tools. There is also recent evidence that, in the wild, animals can teach themselves to use tools—for example, dolphins have learned to use a sponge while foraging (Krutzen et al., 2005), as shown in Figure 4.2.

Tool use is an ability that typically involves both perceptual-motor and cognitive skills. Movement patterns required to use a tool improve with practice, and the recognition that a particular tool (or strategy) can be useful in solving various problems also improves with practice. Some animals can use tools more flexibly and imaginatively than others. By comparing different animals' abilities to learn perceptual-motor and cognitive skills, and by exploring which neural systems they use when forming and retrieving memories of different skills, scientists are beginning to gain a clearer understanding of the brain systems underlying skill memories.

Historically, philosophers and psychologists have distinguished perceptual-motor skills from cognitive skills. However, recent evidence suggests there are many more similarities in how humans learn and remember both types of skills than was previously thought (Rosenbaum, Carlson, & Gilmore, 2001). As you read this chapter, consider what, if anything, makes memories of perceptual-motor skills different from memories of cognitive skills. Is it how they are learned, how they are remembered, how they are forgotten, or something else? Perhaps the differences lie not in how a person forms and recalls these memories but where in the brain the memories are formed and recalled. We will return to these questions about how and where memories for skills are processed later, in the Brain Substrates section.

Test Your Knowledge

Open and Closed Skills

Psychologists classify skills in many ways. One conventional scheme for classifying perceptual-motor skills is the extent to which skills are open or closed. Open skills involve movements that are modified based on predictions about environmental demands, and closed skills depend on performing predefined movements that, ideally, never vary. Where would you place each of the following perceptual-motor skills along the continuum of skills: toward the open or closed end?

1. A sea lion balancing a ball
2. A girl swimming
3. A young man kissing
4. A bear catching fish
5. A fish catching insects
6. A boy playing a piano
7. A young woman throwing darts

Now that you know how researchers classify different kinds of skills, let's consider the question of what allows some people to excel at a particular skill. You won't be surprised to hear that practice is an important factor. We'll examine how different kinds of practice affect performance and retention of skill memories, and why people who are great at one skill are not necessarily as good at other, similar skills. We'll also describe a classic psychological model of skill learning.

Expertise and Talent

You might be able to dance as well as an all-star basketball player, a virtuoso pianist, or a Nobel Prize–winning scientist, but they clearly have mastered other skills at a level that would be difficult for you to match. Different individuals start with different skill levels, and the extent to which practice can improve their performance levels also varies from one person to the next. People who seem to master a skill with little effort (the way Mozart mastered anything related to music) are often described as having a **talent** or "gift" for that skill, and people who perform a skill better than most are considered to be **experts.** The people who start off performing a skill well are often those who end up becoming experts, but someone who initially has little ability to perform a skill may, with practice, become better at that skill than someone who seemed destined to become a star. So, if your significant other is currently lacking in the kissing department, don't lose hope! Additional practice may yet unleash his or her full potential.

What role does talent play in achieving expertise in cognitive or perceptual-motor skills? Even child prodigies are not born able to perform the skills that make them famous. Like everyone else, they learn to perform these skills. Mozart's father, a professional musician, trained Mozart extensively from a young age. So it's difficult to determine whether Mozart's musical abilities were a result of heredity or of his father's teaching abilities.

Psychologists have attempted to gauge the role of genetics in talent by conducting studies with twins—some identical (sharing 100% of their genes) and some fraternal (sharing, like other siblings, 50% of their genes)—who were raised in different homes. Other twin studies look at the differences between twins reared together.

In one large study of twins reared apart, researchers at the University of Minnesota trained participants to perform a skill in which they had to keep the end of a pointed stick, called a stylus, above a target drawn on the edge of a rotating disk, as shown in Figure 4.3a (Fox, Hershberger, & Bouchard, 1996). Researchers frequently use this task, known as the **rotary pursuit task,** to study perceptual-motor skill learning. The task requires precise hand–eye coordination, much like the coordination used by potters to shape a clay pot on a pottery wheel. When individuals first attempt the rotary pursuit task, they generally show some ability to keep the stylus over the target, but often have to adjust the speed and trajectory of their arm movements to do so. With additional practice, most individuals rapidly improve their accuracy, increasing the amount of time they can keep the stylus tip over the target (Figure 4.3b).

The researchers found that when they trained twins to perform the rotary pursuit task, identical twins' abilities to keep the stylus on the target became more similar as training progressed, whereas fraternal twins' abilities became more dissimilar. That

IT REQUIRED INNATE SKILL AND INTENSE CONCENTRATION TO KEEP THE FLAME DIRECTED PRECISELY OVER THE COLLECTION OF JOHN DENVER ALBUMS.

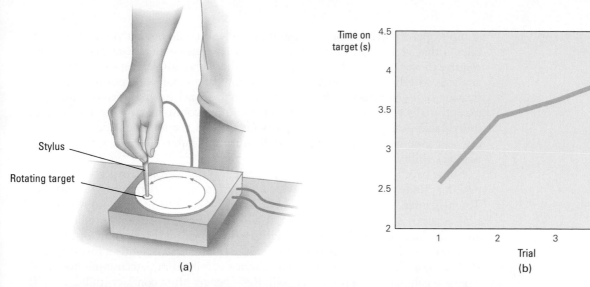

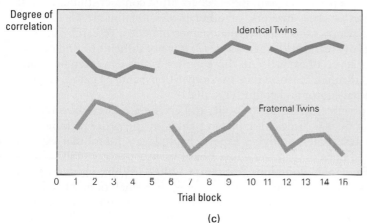

Figure 4.3 **Effects of practice on performance of the rotary pursuit task** (a) In the rotary pursuit task, a person gradually learns to keep a stylus above a particular point on a rotating disk. (b) With repeated trials, individuals become better able to keep the stylus over the target. (c) In studies of how twins perform on this task, correlations between the performances of identical twins increased slightly as training progressed, indicating that, after training, the accuracy at tracking a rotating target is similar for each twin. In contrast, correlations between the performances of fraternal twins decreased with training, indicating that their capacity to track the rotating target becomes less similar with practice. These findings suggest that practice decreases the effects of previous experiences on motor performance and increases the effects of genetic influences. (b, c) Adapted from Fox et al., 1996.

is, during training, the performance of one twin became more correlated with the performance of the second twin only when the two twins shared 100% of their genes (Figure 4.3c). Put another way, if you were to view videos of the participants' hands, after training, as they attempted to keep the stylus above the rotating target, you would judge the movements of identical twins' hands to be the most similar. If you saw a pair of identical twins performing this task side by side after training, their movements might remind you of synchronized swimming. In the case of fraternal twins, however, you would probably judge their movements after training to be very dissimilar. For example, one twin might keep the stylus over the target continuously, while the other twin increased her speed every few seconds to catch up with the target.

One interpretation of these data is that, during the experiment, practice decreases the effects of participants' prior experiences on the accuracy of their tracking movements and increases the effects of genetic influences. Identical twins have identical genes, so when practice increases the role of their genes in behavior, their behavior becomes closer to identical. Because fraternal twins have different genes, increasing the role of their genes in behavior makes their behavior more different. Researchers have tested for such effects only in tasks, such as the rotary pursuit task, that require individuals to learn simple perceptual-motor skills. It is possible, however, that practice has similar effects on more complex perceptual-motor and cognitive skills. It could be that you have hidden talents that you're unaware of because you have never practiced the skills that require those talents, or have not practiced them enough. Perhaps future genetic analyses will discover biological correlates of specific talents, permitting identification of individuals who have an inherited propensity to perform certain skills exceptionally well. Currently, however, the most common way of evaluating an individual's potential to excel at a particular skill is the nonscientific one of asking someone with expertise in the skill to make a subjective assessment of that person's ability.

Some psychologists argue that innate talent plays no role in expertise and that practice alone determines who will become an expert (Ericsson, Krampe, & Tesch-Romer, 1993; Ericsson & Lehman, 1996). Until more is known about how practice affects skill memories, it will be difficult to reliably predict either an individual's maximum level of skill performance or the amount of practice someone needs to reach peak performance. In any case, scientists investigating skill memory in experts suggest that practice is critical in determining how well a person can perform a particular skill. Researchers often conduct studies of skill memories in athletes or chess masters, or other professional game players, for several reasons: (1) people who learn to play games outside a research lab provide good examples of "real world" memories; (2) it is not difficult to find people with widely varying levels of expertise in these games, which can often be quantitatively measured through performance in competitions; and (3) games require a variety of perceptual-motor and cognitive skills.

A person must practice thousands of hours to become a master chess player, learning more than 50,000 "rules" for playing chess in the process (Simon & Gilmartin, 1973). Researchers studying expert chess players found that experts and less experienced players scan the game board (a visual-motor skill) differently (Charness, Reingold, Pomplun, & Stampe, 2001). When chess masters look at chess pieces, their eyes move rapidly to focus on a small number of locations on the board, whereas amateur chess players typically scan larger numbers of locations and do so more slowly. When experts stop moving their eyes, they are more likely than non-experts to focus on empty squares or on strategically relevant chess pieces. Similarly, inexperienced soccer players tend to watch the ball and the player who is passing it, whereas expert players focus more on the movements of players who do not have the ball (Williams, Davids, Burwitz, & Williams, 1992).

Humans may need to practice many hours to become experts at chess, but practice is not a universally necessary prerequisite for expert chess performance.

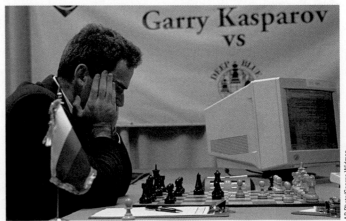

Kasparov falls to Deep Blue. Computers can now perform many tasks as well as, or better than, experts.

Computer programmers have designed software that can compete with the best chess players. For example, Deep Blue, a chess-playing computer designed by IBM, defeated world champion Garry Kasparov in 1997. Computers access large databases of stored information to replicate some of the abilities of human experts. If a skill is an ability that improves with practice, chess-playing computers can be considered experts without skills, unless they are programmed to improve their performance based on past experiences. Although humans also make use of large amounts of information in performing certain skills, the way their brains store and access information differs greatly from the way computers do this. For example, if one computer can be programmed to perform a particular task, the same ability is usually easy to replicate in another computer. If only humans could acquire abilities so easily! For better or for worse, information can't yet be copied from one brain to another. If you want to become an expert at a particular skill, you'll probably have to do it the old-fashioned way: practice, practice, practice.

Practice

In *The Karate Kid*, a classic movie from the 1980s, a teenage boy asks a karate master to give him a crash course in martial arts. The master reluctantly agrees and begins by making the student wax his collection of cars, sand his wood-floored yard, and paint his large fence. When setting each task, the master demonstrates the exact movements he wants the student to use. The student does as he is told, and later discovers that the movements he has been laboriously repeating are the karate movements he needs to know to defend himself. Because he has repeated these movements hundreds of times while doing his chores, he is able to reproduce them rapidly and effortlessly. He has learned the skills of karate without even knowing it!

Hollywood's portrayal of the relationship between practice and skill memories in this movie is similar to several early psychological theories. The basic idea is that the more times you perform a skill, the faster or better you'll be able to perform it in the future. Is this how practice works? Or is there more to practice than just repetition? To address this issue, Edward Thorndike conducted experiments in which he repeatedly asked blindfolded individuals to draw a line exactly 3 inches long (Thorndike, 1927). Half of the participants were told when their line was within one-eighth of an inch of the target length, and the other half were not given any feedback about their lines. Both groups drew the same number of lines during the experiment, but only the participants who received feedback improved in accuracy as the experiment progressed. This simple study suggests that waxing cars and sanding floors may not be the most effective way to learn karate moves. Feedback about performance, what researchers in the field usually call **knowledge of results,** is critical to the effectiveness of practice (Butki & Hoffman, 2003; Ferrari, 1999; Liu & Wrisberg, 1997; A. P. Turner & Martinek, 1999; Weeks & Kordus, 1998).

Acquiring Skills

The earliest detailed studies of how practice affects performance were conducted by military researchers who were interested in the high-speed, high-precision performance of perceptual-motor skills such as tracking and reacting to targets (these studies are reviewed by Holding, 1981). One of the basic findings from this early research was that, with extended practice, the amount of time required to perform a skill decreases at a diminishing rate. For example, Figure 4.4a shows that as participants practiced a reading task, the amount of time spent reading each page decreased (A. Newell & Rosenbaum, 1981). Initially, there was a large decrease in the time required to read a page, but after this initial improvement, the decreases in reading time gradually got smaller. Figure 4.3b

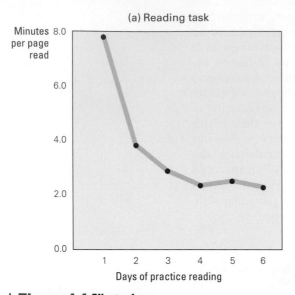

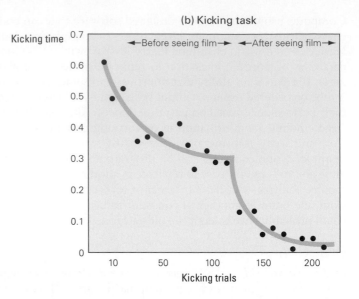

Figure 4.4 Effects of practice and feedback on skill performance (a) As training on a reading task progressed, improvements in reading speed became smaller. (b) In a kicking task, new sources of feedback can lead to a new burst of rapid improvement. In this case, after his initial rate of improvement had begun to slow, the participant was shown a film of optimum kicking. The film helped him improve the speed of his own kicking. (a) Adapted from Singley and Anderson, 1989; (b) adapted from Hatze, 1976.

shows a similar pattern in individuals learning the rotary pursuit task—the initial gain in performance is the largest. This "law of diminishing returns," also known as the **power law of learning,** holds for a wide range of cognitive and perceptual-motor skills, both in humans and in other species.

When you first learned to use a computer keyboard, you had to search for keys, and the number of words you could type per minute was probably low. After your first year of using a keyboard, you probably had doubled or tripled the number of words you could type per minute. If your typing speed doubled after every year of practice, you would be typing incredibly fast by now! The power law of learning, however, predicts that this does not happen. According to the power law, each additional year of practice after the first produces smaller increases in typing speed; learning occurs quickly at first, but then gets slower.

It may seem obvious that as you become more proficient at a skill, there is less room for improvement. What is surprising about the power law of learning is that the rate at which practice loses its ability to improve performance is usually predetermined, regardless of the skill being practiced or the type of animal learning the skill. In many cases, psychologists can use a simple mathematical function (called a power function) to describe how rapidly individuals will acquire a skill; the number of additional practice trials necessary to improve a skill increases dramatically as the number of completed practice trials increases.

The power law of learning provides a useful description of how practice generally affects performance. It is possible to overcome this law, however, and enhance the effects of practice. For example, in one experiment, researchers asked a participant to kick a target as rapidly as possible. With feedback about his kicking speed, the rate at which he was able to decrease the time required to kick the target was predicted by the power law of learning (Hatze, 1976). When the man stopped improving, the researchers showed him a film comparing his movements with movements known to minimize kicking time. After seeing the film, the man improved his kicking time considerably (Figure 4.4b). This is an example of *observational learning,* a topic we discuss in detail in Chapter 11. The participant observing the film forms memories of the observed performance techniques that he later uses to improve his own performance. These memories act as a powerful form of feedback about how successfully he is performing the learned skill relative to what is physically possible.

All feedback is not equally helpful, and the kinds of feedback provided can strongly determine how practice affects performance. The secret to improvement is to discover what kinds of feedback will maximize the benefits of practicing a particular skill. Experiments show that frequent feedback in simple perceptual-motor tasks leads to good performance in the short term but mediocre performance in the long term, whereas infrequent feedback leads to mediocre performance in the short term but better performance in the long term (Schmidt & Wulf, 1997; Schmidt, Young, Swinnen, & Shapiro, 1989). For the most part, however, instructors, coaches, and their students discover through trial and error what types of feedback work best in each situation. For example, dance instructors have discovered that the visual feedback provided by mirrors enhances the effects of practicing dance movements, and most dance studios now have mirrors on the walls. Can you think of any similar advances that college professors have made in the last century in providing feedback to improve students' cognitive skills? An example might be online tutorials that provide immediate feedback; some research suggests that these can produce faster learning and greater achievement levels than classroom instruction (J. R. Anderson, Corbett, Koedinger, & Pelletier, 1995).

Feedback is critical to the acquisition of skill memories because it affects how individuals perform the skills during practice. Certain forms of information that precede practice, such as instructional videos, can have similar effects. Skill memories do not depend only on the way skills are practiced, however. They also depend on how effort is apportioned during practice. Concentrated, continuous practice, or **massed practice,** generally produces better performance in the short term, but **spaced practice,** spread out over several sessions, leads to better retention in the long run.

Consider the following classic experiment. Four groups of post office workers were trained to use a keyboard to control a letter-sorting machine. One group trained for 1 hour a day, once a day, for 3 months. The other three groups trained either 2 or 4 hours a day for 1 month (Baddeley & Longman, 1978). Contrary to what you might guess, the group that trained for only 1 hour a day (spaced practice) required fewer total hours of training than any other group to become proficient at using the keyboard (Figure 4.5). The downside was that this group had to be trained over a longer period—3 months instead of 1. Although researchers have conducted many studies to determine what kind of practice schedule leads to better learning and performance, there is still no consensus about an optimal schedule for any given individual attempting to learn any given skill.

Researchers observe similar kinds of effects when participants practice with a very limited set of materials and skills, called **constant practice,** versus a more varied set, called **variable practice.** Constant practice consists of repeatedly

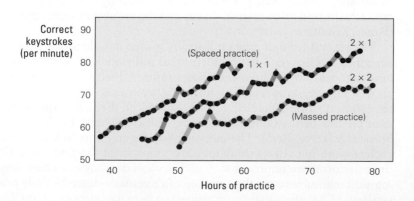

Figure 4.5 Benefits of spaced practice versus massed practice The performance of post office workers using a keyboard to control a letter-sorting machine improved at different rates depending on their training schedules. Workers who practiced for 1 hour a day (1 × 1) for 3 months (spaced practice) improved their performance at a faster rate than workers who practiced for 2 hours a day (2 × 1) or for two sessions of 2 hours each a day (2 × 2; massed practice). Although the first group (1 × 1) learned the task in fewer total hours, the training took longer (3 months). Adapted from Baddeley and Longman, 1978.

practicing the same skill—for example, repeatedly attempting to throw a dart at the bull's-eye of a dartboard under fixed lighting conditions, or attempting to master a single trick shot in pool. Variable practice consists of practicing a skill in a wider variety of conditions, such as attempting to hit each number sequentially on a dartboard under various levels of lighting, or trying to improve one's performance at interviews by applying for a diverse range of jobs. Several studies have shown that variable practice leads to better performance in later tests. In one such study, individuals tracked targets that were moving along various paths. People who used variable practice to learn this task performed better, both in training sessions and in later tests, than individuals who trained with constant practice (Wulf & Schmidt, 1997). Variable practice is not always more effective than constant practice, however (van Rossum, 1990); researchers have not discovered how to reliably predict when variable practice will lead to better learning and performance. Researchers and coaches alike continue to vigorously debate which schedules and which types of practice are most effective.

Implicit Learning

Typically, when you acquire a skill, it is because you have made an effort to learn the skill over time. In some cases, however, individuals can learn to perform certain skills without ever being aware that learning has occurred. Learning of this sort, called **implicit learning,** probably happens to you more often than you think. Given that, by definition, implicit learning is learning that you are not aware of, you'd be hard pressed to estimate how many skills you've acquired in this way. For all you know, you're implicitly learning right now!

Implicit skill learning comes in at least two forms (Knowlton et al., 1996; Pohl, McDowd, Filion, Richards, & Stiers, 2001; Willingham, 1999; Wulf & Schmidt, 1997). In one type, individuals perform some task, such as washing windows, and incidentally learn an underlying skill that facilitates their performance: maybe they learn that circular rubbing movements shine the window brighter and faster than random rubbing. The learners may or may not realize that they have discovered a faster, better manner of execution.

A task that psychologists commonly use to study implicit skill learning of this kind is the **serial reaction time task,** in which participants learn to press one of four keys as soon as a computer indicates which key to press. The computer presents the instructional cues in long sequences that are unpredictably ordered (the so-called random condition) or occur in a fixed sequence of about 12 cues (the implicit learning condition). For example, if we designate the four keys from right to left as A through D, then the fixed sequence might be ABADBC-DACBDC. Participants eventually begin to get a feel for the repeating patterns and anticipate which key to press next, as reflected by faster reaction times for implicitly learned sequences relative to random sequences (Figure 4.6). When researchers interviewed participants after training, however, the participants typically showed no awareness that any of the sequences were repeating patterns (Exner, Koschack, & Irle, 2002).

The second form of implicit learning is seen in individuals with amnesia. We described in Chapter 3 the problems that individuals with anterograde amnesia have with learning and remembering events and facts. However, such individuals can acquire skills relatively normally from one session to the next, even if they show no awareness that they have practiced the skill in the past or have ever seen the task before (Cohen, Poldrack, & Eichenbaum, 1997; Seger, 1994; Sun, Slusarz, & Terry, 2005). The individuals make an effort to learn the skill during each session, but always think they are trying it for the first time. The fact that their performance improves with each session demonstrates that they are forming skill memories even though they can't verbally describe their prior practice sessions. H.M., the patient with amnesia whom we introduced in Chapter 3, was

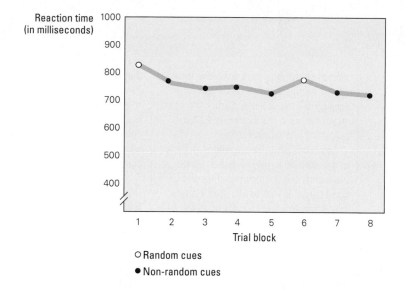

Figure 4.6 Serial reaction time task in the study of implicit learning In a serial reaction time task, participants learn to press keys as rapidly as possible in response to cues provided on a computer screen. Participants' reaction times are slower when the sequences of instructional cues vary randomly (trial blocks 1 and 6) than when the sequences are fixed (blocks 2–5, 7, and 8). Quicker reaction times for the fixed sequences indicate that the participants implicitly learn to anticipate which key they need to press next, even though they cannot report what the sequence is. Adapted from Exner et al., 2002.

able to learn new perceptual-motor skills, but he did not know that he had learned them (Corkin, 2002; Gabrieli, Corkin, Mickel, & Growdon, 1993; Tranel, Damasio, Damasio, & Brandt, 1994).

The ability of people with amnesia to learn complex skills without being aware that they have learned them suggests that the neural systems underlying memories for skills are different from the systems involved in storing and recalling memories for events and facts. This form of implicit learning in amnesia differs from implicit learning in people with no memory impairment in that the individual with amnesia may be explicitly taught how to perform the skill that is being "implicitly" learned. Nevertheless, because the individual shows no evidence of recalling these training sessions, the learning is typically considered implicit. For example, if you learn to sing a song by practicing it, psychologists would not say you are implicitly learning the song (because you are explicitly encoding and recalling the song and are aware that your ability to sing the song is improving over time). However, neuropsychologists would describe this type of learning in patients with amnesia as implicit learning, because the patients are not aware that they are improving at singing a particular song, nor do they remember learning the song. The fact that individuals with amnesia can learn skills implicitly but cannot recall recent events has often been cited as evidence that skill memories are fundamentally different from memories for facts and events.

As mentioned earlier, people often have difficulty verbalizing what they have learned after acquiring a perceptual-motor skill, which seems to suggest that perceptual-motor skills are more likely than cognitive skills to be learned implicitly. But people can also acquire many features of cognitive skills by implicit learning. No one becomes a chess master simply by reading the rules of chess and listening to other players explaining why they made particular moves. Mathematical whizzes do not become experts by simply hearing about mathematical axioms (Lewis, 1981). Development of both of these skills requires practice during which certain improvements are learned implicitly. In the case of acquiring cognitive skills, it is difficult to assess which abilities are improving independent of awareness, because the changes in thinking produced by practice are not easy to observe. (See "Unsolved Mysteries" on p. 138 on the ability or inability to verbalize learned skills.) Moreover, the learner is often unaware of these changes and therefore cannot report them. Consequently, there is currently no way to assess whether implicit learning is more likely to occur during the learning of perceptual-motor skills than the learning of cognitive skills.

Why Can't Experts Verbalize What They Do?

Noted philosopher Henri Bergson described skill memory as "a memory profoundly different . . . always bent upon action, seated in the present and looking only to the future. . . . In truth it no longer represents our past to us, it acts it; and if it still deserves the name of memory, it is not because it conserves bygone images, but because it prolongs their useful effect into the present moment" (quoted in Squire & Kandel, 2000). Many psychologists believe that skill memories are fundamentally different from memories for events and facts, precisely because memories for events and facts typically involve conscious recollection and description of the past, whereas skill memories do not. But do such differences really indicate two qualitatively different types of memory?

We can learn something about this from split-brain patients. As a last resort to prevent debilitating seizures, these patients have undergone a surgical procedure in which the neurosurgeon cuts the corpus callosum, which connects the two cerebral hemispheres. The hemispheres themselves remain intact, but they lose many of the connections that normally allow information exchange between them. Experiments with split-brain patients have produced some amazing findings (Gazzaniga, 1998). We now know that the left hemisphere can provide verbal reports of current and past experiences, but the right hemisphere cannot. The right hemisphere does, however, retain the ability to initiate perceptual-motor skills. Does this mean that the left hemisphere has declarative memories while the right hemisphere has only skill memories and other nondeclarative memories? If so, this is a very odd situation, because the hemispheres contain the same structures; each has its own intact hippocampus and cerebral cortex.

Now consider someone who is an expert at a certain skill—say, an expert dancer. All her friends see her dancing and wish they could dance as well as she does. Can the expert simply tell her friends what she does to make her movements so graceful, so that they can do it too? Usually, this is not possible. If it were, you would be signing up for online dance classes. There are two likely reasons for why experts can't verbalize what they do that makes their performance superior. Either they cannot consciously access the information that allows them to dance so well, or they do have access to this information, but the constraints of language prevent them from transforming this information into words.

In the first scenario, the expert resembles the split-brain patient. Her brain holds the information necessary to move her body rhythmically and beautifully, but the specific brain regions that provide her with conscious experiences cannot access this information. The second possibility, that language is insufficient for describing complex perceptual-motor skills, can be assessed by studying communication between experts. Many experts develop special ways of communicating that allow them to describe particular skills in such a way that other experts (but only other experts) can precisely replicate these skills. Musical notation, for example, allows musicians to recreate complex sequences of sounds that they have never experienced before. Written music does not, however, transmit to a non-musician an ability to play the piano. Similarly, complex mathematical equations (which are facts that can be recalled) do not enable a non-mathematician who reads them to later generate those same equations. Perhaps it is as difficult for an expert mathematician to verbalize complex mathematical facts in a way that non-mathematicians can understand as it is for an expert dancer to verbalize complex skills in ways that would enable a non-expert dancer to perform those skills.

From this perspective, the reason the expert dancer cannot tell her friends what to do is that she doesn't have the words to describe what she does. Perhaps dancers have not developed these words because dancing is simpler to show than to tell. If the expert dancer had friends who were also expert dancers, she probably would be able to convey the dance moves that are her particular specialty simply by demonstrating them.

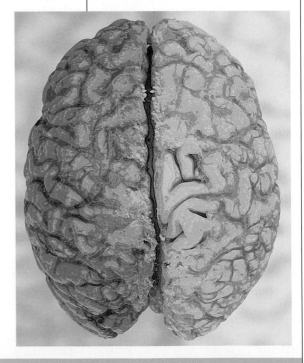

Retention and Forgetting

Like memories for facts and events, the memorability of a skill—how well the skill is performed on a later occasion—depends on the complexity of the skill, how well the skill memory was encoded in the first place, how often it has subsequently been recalled, and the conditions in which recall is attempted (Arthur, Bennett, Stanush, & McNelly, 1998). The common wisdom that once you learn to ride a bicycle, you never forget how to do so, is not accurate. Although skill memories can last a lifetime, they do deteriorate with non-use. Generally, retention of perceptual-motor skills is better than retention of cognitive skills, but unless you actively maintain your bike-riding skills, the skill memories you created when you first learned to ride will gradually deteriorate.

Researchers have studied the forgetting of events and facts much more than they have studied the forgetting of skills. Perhaps this is because if someone loses the ability to do something, it is hard to judge whether he has forgotten how to do it, or forgotten that he knows how to do it, or lost the physical control or mechanisms necessary to perform what he recalls. Loss of motor control does not imply that a skill memory is forgotten. To the outside observer, however, it may be impossible to distinguish whether someone knows how to perform a skill but has impaired movement abilities or has never learned to perform the skill. In fact, the only way to distinguish between these two possibilities is by observing differences in neural activity during the performance or nonperformance of a skill.

Psychologists call loss of a skill through non-use **skill decay.** Most of the data collected so far indicate that skill decay follows patterns similar to those seen in the forgetting of memories for events and facts. Motor deficits and injuries can clearly affect skill decay, because they are likely to lead to non-use of learned skills.

In some ways, forgetting a skill is like learning it in reverse. Not performing the skill is almost the opposite of practice: if you don't use it, you lose it. Most forgetting occurs soon after the last performance of the skill; as time goes by, less and less forgetting occurs. Thus, forgetting curves are similar to learning curves. Forgetting occurs quickly at first, then gets slower.

Does the passage of time simply cause a skill to be "unlearned"? It often may seem this way, but forgetting can also result when new memories interfere with the recollection of old memories. As time passes, you perform more new skills, creating more memories that potentially interfere with the recollection of earlier skill memories. (Recall from Chapter 3 that interference and decay are also involved in the forgetting of memories for events and facts.) Much of this interference can occur without any awareness on the part of the person attempting to recall a skill. For example, you might have difficulty recalling some of the dances you learned when you were younger, but easily recall dance steps you learned recently. Rather than thinking this recent learning is hampering your ability to perform the old dances, you'd probably assume that you can't remember an older dance simply because it has been so long since you last did it. However, there is no subjective way for you to distinguish whether your forgetting results from the passage of time or from interference.

Recently, researchers observed that interference of skill memories can occur even within a single day. Students trained to perform a finger-tapping task, similar to the serial reaction time task discussed above, demonstrated more rapid and accurate pressing times after a period of sleep (Walker, Brakefield, Hobson, & Stickgold, 2003; Walker, Brakefield, Morgan, Hobson, & Stickgold, 2002; Walker, Brakefield, Seidman, et al., 2003). However, if students learned to press keys in two different sequences on the same day, sleep-dependent enhancement of their performance was seen only for the *second* sequence learned. If participants learned the second sequence one day after the first sequence, sleep enhanced the performance of both sequences. Interestingly, if on the second day the students reviewed the first day's sequence immediately before learning the new sequence, then on the third day sleep enhanced their accuracy on only the second sequence. Thus, not only can practicing two skills on the same day interfere with retention of memories for the first skill, but reviewing a recently learned skill before beginning to practice a new one can interfere with subsequent recall of the skill that was reviewed! These findings highlight the intimate relationship between skill acquisition and skill recall, and the fragile nature of newly acquired skill memories. Note, however, that athletes and musicians commonly practice multiple skills in parallel with no evidence of interference, and variable practice generally leads to better long-term performance than constant practice. Thus, skills more complex than learning a sequence may be less susceptible to interference effects.

Research has also shown that a major determinant of whether a person will recall a particular skill is the similarity between the retrieval conditions and the conditions she experienced while learning the skill. In many situations, of course, the conditions under which a skill must be recalled are *not* the same as the training conditions. In this case, trained performance must "transfer" to the novel conditions.

Transfer of Training

Skills are often highly constrained in terms of how they can be applied (Goodwin, Eckerson, & Voll, 2001; Goodwin & Meeuwsen, 1995; Ma, Trombly, & Robinson-Podolski, 1999). You may have mastered the culinary skills needed to make great Italian food, but this will not make you a great sushi chef. In some cases, skill memories are so specific that the introduction of additional informative cues can disrupt performance. For example, after individuals were trained to touch a target with a stylus without visual feedback about their arm movements, their performance was *worse* when researchers allowed them to see their arm moving as they carried out the task (Proteau, Marteniuk, & Levesque, 1992). Most people normally use visual feedback when learning to aim at a target, so it is surprising that providing such information can interfere with the recall of skill memories.

In other cases, skills seem to be easily transferable to novel situations. For example, you learned to write with your right or left hand, and you may even have practiced with each hand, but have you ever written with your mouth or feet? If you try, you'll discover that you can write semi-legible text using these and other body parts. You are able to transfer what you have learned about writing with one hand to other body parts, despite large differences in the specific movements you must perform to do so. In sports, teams spend much of their time practicing in scrimmages, with the hope that these experiences will transfer positively to similar situations in real games. If skills learned in scrimmage did not transfer to real games, it is unlikely that so many coaches in so many different sports would train their teams in this way.

Will practicing cricket on the beach help this woman improve her stroke in tennis or her swing in softball?

Paul Jones /Getty Images

The restricted applicability of some learned skills to specific situations is known as **transfer specificity.** This phenomenon led Thorndike to propose that the transfer of learned abilities to novel situations depends on the number of elements in the new situation that are identical to those in the situation in which the skills were encoded (Thorndike & Woodworth, 1901). Thorndike's proposal, called the **identical elements theory,** provides one possible account of why transfer specificity occurs. It predicts that a tennis player who trained on hard courts might suffer a bit if a game were moved to clay courts, and would do progressively worse as the game was changed from tennis to badminton or table tennis. Conceptually, transfer specificity is closely related to transfer-appropriate processing, described in Chapter 3. The main differences between the two stem from whether the memories being recalled are memories of skills or memories of facts.

When you apply existing skill memories to the performance of novel skills, you are generalizing based on past experience. Generalization of learning is a topic that psychologists have studied extensively (you will learn more about this in Chapter 9). Nevertheless, we do not yet know how one skill generalizes to another, or what factors limit how well a learned ability can be generalized. Even if Thorndike's identical elements theory is on the right track, it doesn't tell us what the "elements" of skill memories are or how to assess the similarities and differences between those elements.

When you perform a skill that you have learned in the past, you are generalizing from a past experience to the present. From this perspective, every performance of a skill involves transfer of training. For example, each time you open a door you are making use of memories you acquired by opening doors in the past. Practice improves performance and recall, and thus increases the stability and reliability of skill memories over time. How might elements of skill memories be made stable? Current theoretical models of skill acquisition suggest that an individual stabilizes skill memories by converting them from memories for events and facts into memories for predefined sequences of actions called motor programs (J. R. Anderson, 1982), as discussed below.

Models of Skill Memory

In the previous chapter, we described how psychologists have modeled memories for facts using semantic networks, with facts represented as nodes within the network, and connections between different facts represented as links between nodes. This type of model is useful for describing how facts are organized in memory. Scientists studying skill memories have developed similar models, but most models of skill memory focus on how individuals learn skills over time rather than how they organize what they have learned.

Motor Programs and Rules

When you practice a skill, you probably do so because you want to become better at performing that skill. To most people, "becoming better" means that their performance becomes more controlled and effortless. Say the skill you are practicing is juggling. The goal is to keep the objects moving in the air, and in and out of your hands. Ideally, you'd probably like to be able to juggle while casually talking to a friend. In this case, your friend would know you are an expert juggler because you don't need to pay attention to what you are doing. The skill has become automatic. Some might even say that your juggling actions have become reflexive. Reflexes, however, are inborn, involuntary responses to stimuli, distinct from highly learned responses. Sequences of movements that an organism can perform automatically (with minimal attention) are called **motor programs.** Unlike reflexes, motor programs can be either inborn or learned. Releasing an arrow from a bow is not an inborn reflex, but for the expert archer it has become as automatic and precise as a reflex. More complex action sequences such as juggling can also become motor programs. One way to determine whether a skill has become a motor program is to remove the stimulus during the action sequence and observe the results. For example, if someone grabs one of the balls in midair as you are juggling, does your arm still "catch and throw" the nonexistent ball? If so, it suggests that your juggling skill has become a motor program.

Classifying highly learned perceptual-motor skills as motor programs is straightforward, but what about highly learned cognitive skills? Might they also, with extended practice, become motor programs? The surprising answer is yes. Think back to when you learned the multiplication tables. This probably required some practice, but now if someone asks you, "What is two times three?" you will respond promptly: "Six." You no longer need to think about quantities at all. You perceive the spoken words, and your brain automatically generates the motor sequence to produce the appropriate spoken word in response. Similarly, in the laboratory, once a person has solved the Tower of Hanoi problem many times, she has learned that particular movement sequences always lead to the solution. Eventually, practicing enables her to perform these motor sequences rapidly, without thinking about which disk goes where. In both cases, a cognitive skill has become a motor program.

The learning of new skills often begins with a set of instructions. You give your great aunt a new microwave oven, and later discover that she refuses to set the time on the display. Why? Because she doesn't know how to do it. The manufacturer of the oven predicted that your great aunt might not possess this skill, and so it provided written rules—a list of steps to take to display the correct time. In a perfect world, your great aunt would read the manual and acquire the skills necessary to set the time on the microwave oven. More likely, though, the rules are ambiguous and open to interpretation, making her first attempts at setting the time awkward and possibly unsuccessful; but, with your encouragement, she finally does manage it. However, at a later date, when she wants to reset the time, she may recollect that the manual was little help in providing rules she could understand, and she may prefer trying to recall the steps from memory. Because she will depend on her memories for events and facts to perform the skill, you could say that her skill memories are her memories of the rules. In other words, skill memories can be memories for events and facts!

Following a recipe in a cookbook provides another example of how memories for facts can serve as skill memories. A recipe teaches you the facts you need to know to prepare a certain dish: what ingredients you need, in what proportions, and how to combine them. However, after some practice—with baking cookies, for example—you no longer need to depend as heavily on the written "rules."

How can skill memories lead to reflex-like automatic movements, but also consist of remembered events and facts? A classic model proposed by Paul Fitts in 1964 suggests that this is possible because practice transforms rules into motor programs.

Stages of Acquisition

Fitts proposed that skill learning includes an initial period when an individual must exert some effort to encode a skill, acquiring information through observation, instruction, trial and error, or some combination of these methods (Fitts, 1964). This period is followed by stages in which performance of the skill becomes more "automatic" or habitual. Fitts called the first stage the **cognitive stage,** to emphasize the active thinking required to encode the skill. When your great aunt is setting the time on the microwave based on instructions or memories of the steps that were previously successful, she is in the cognitive stage of skill acquisition. During this stage, she bases her performance on what she knows, as well as on her ability to control her movements and thoughts so as to accomplish specific goals. Humans are likely to depend on memories of verbalizable facts or rules at this stage, but this is not what happens in other animals. A monkey can learn to change the time on a microwave oven, if motivated to do so, but the goals and strategies the monkey employs to learn this skill are very different from the goals and strategies available to your great aunt. Researchers do not yet know the degree to which memories for facts or events are important for skill acquisition in nonhumans or preverbal children as compared with adult humans.

Fitts called the second stage in his model of skill acquisition the **associative stage.** During this stage, learners begin using stereotyped actions when performing the skill and rely less on actively recalled memories of rules. The first few times you play a video game, for example, you may need to keep reminding yourself about the combinations of joystick movements and button presses necessary to produce certain outcomes. Eventually, you no longer need to think about these combinations. When you decide that you want a particular action to occur on the screen, your hands do what is necessary to make it happen. How do they do this? Your brain has encoded specific combinations and is recalling them as directed. What began as a process of understanding and following verbalizable rules has become a process of remembering previously performed actions.

Of course, mastering the skills needed to play a video game requires far more than simply memorizing hand movements. You must be able to produce very rapid sequences of precisely timed combinations to achieve specific outcomes. To reach high levels of performance, your movement patterns must become rapid and effortless. In Fitts's model, this level of skill is represented by the third stage, the **autonomous stage**—the stage at which the skill or subcomponents of the skill have become motor programs. At this stage it may be impossible to verbalize in any detail the specific movements being performed, and performance may have become much less dependent on verbalizable memories for events and facts. If you can juggle while having a casual conversation, you have reached the autonomous stage. You can perform the skill without paying much attention to what you're doing, and if someone unexpectedly snatches a ball, your arms will continue to move as if the missing ball were still there.

In the autonomous stage, the actions of a monkey trained to set the time on a microwave oven might be almost identical to the actions performed by your great aunt when she is setting the time. The monkey and your great aunt may have learned this skill through different strategies, but their end performance is very similar. Is your great aunt's motor program substantially different from the monkey's? The observable skills look the same, but the memories underlying the skills may be very different. Comparing neural activity in your great aunt and in the monkey would be one way to determine whether they are accessing information similarly while performing the same learned skill.

Fitts's model of skill acquisition (summarized in Table 4.2) provides a useful framework for relating skill performance to practice. Although psychologists

Table 4.2

Fitts's Three-Stage Model of Skill Learning

Stage	Characteristics	Example
1. Cognitive stage	Performance is based on verbalizable rules	Using written instructions to set up a tent
2. Associative stage	Actions become stereotyped	Setting up a tent in a fixed sequence, without instructions
3. Autonomous stage	Movements seem automatic	Setting up a tent while carrying on a discussion about politics

have developed this model extensively over the past 40 years, many recent versions retain the same basic progression of stages. The "three stages" are, of course, abstractions. There is generally no single performance that can be identified as the last performance belonging to, say, stage one. Additionally, like semantic network models, the three-stage model of skill learning is primarily descriptive. It won't help you predict how much practice you need to convert your skill memories to motor programs or give you pointers about how and when you should practice. The model does suggest, however, that learned abilities may rely on different kinds of memory as practice progresses. Different kinds of memory may in turn require different kinds of neural processing, or activation of different brain regions. By examining the neural activity associated with skill acquisition, scientists have explored the idea that skill memories take different forms as learning progresses.

Interim Summary

When you learn a skill, you form memories that allow you to take advantage of your past experiences. Two major kinds of skills are perceptual-motor skills and cognitive skills. You are born with certain talents and can use and enhance them by developing appropriate skills. With extensive practice you may even become an expert. It is unlikely that you will become an expert at every skill you practice, but you can retain many skills in memory for extended periods of time. How long after learning skills you can retrieve the skill memories depends on how well you learned the skills, how often you've recalled them, and how complex the skills are.

4.2 Brain Substrates

What neural systems do humans and other animals need in order to acquire memories of perceptual-motor and cognitive skills? Is there something special about the human brain that allows us to acquire skill memories more effectively than other animals? Or do humans use the same brain systems as other animals to learn skills, but use them in slightly different ways? How might one judge whether the skill memories that underlie a dolphin's ability to use a sponge differ from those of a window washer?

Neuroscientists have used neuroimaging and neurophysiological recording techniques to identify brain systems involved in the formation and recall of skill memories. These techniques allow researchers to monitor brain activity in humans and other animals during the performance of skills. Researchers have also compared brain activity in experts and amateurs, as well as in individuals before and after they have learned a particular skill. Neuropsychological studies of skill learning by patients with brain damage are also an important source of information. Through these kinds of research, neuroscientists hope to associate stages of skill acquisition with changes in brain activity.

All movements and postures require coordinated muscle activity. As you saw in Chapter 2, a major function of the nervous system is to initiate and control muscle activity. The spinal cord and brainstem play a critical role in skill performance by controlling and coordinating movements. Brain regions dedicated to sensation and perception, including the sensory cortices, are also involved, processing information that contributes to skill learning. Remember the experiment described earlier in this chapter in which researchers instructed the participant to kick a target as quickly as possible? He improved at the task by processing visual feedback about how effectively he was coordinating the muscles in his leg.

The importance of the peripheral nervous system and spinal cord to humans' performance of perceptual-motor skills is illustrated by the total paralysis that results when the spinal cord becomes disconnected from the brain. A well-known case is that of the actor Christopher Reeve, who suffered a spinal cord injury after falling from a horse. This injury caused him to lose the ability to feel and move his limbs, as well as the ability to breathe on his own.

Christopher Reeve also serves as an example of the possible effects of practice on the nervous system. Several years after his accident, Reeve regained some sensation in parts of his body, as well as the ability to move his wrist and one of his fingers. Some researchers believe that new rehabilitation techniques, in which a person's muscles are electrically stimulated to generate movements simulating bicycle pedaling, caused this recovery of function (J. W. McDonald et al., 2002). In other words, practicing movements may help the brain and spinal cord replace or repair lost or damaged connections.

In this section we describe how practicing skills can change neural circuits in less extreme circumstances. Although you can form skill memories in ways other than practice (such as studying videos of expert athletes or expert kissers), neuroscientists have focused much of their effort on understanding the incremental effects of practice on brain activity during skill learning.

Sensory processing and motor control by circuits in the spinal cord are clearly necessary for learning and performing skills. However, the core elements of skill learning seem to depend in particular on three other areas of the brain: the basal ganglia, the cerebral cortex, and the cerebellum (Figure 4.7).

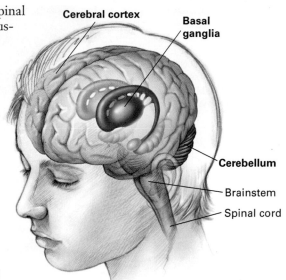

Figure 4.7 Brain regions that contribute to skill learning Skill-memory systems in the brain involve the basal ganglia, cerebral cortex, and cerebellum. These three regions modulate the control of movements by circuits in the brainstem and spinal cord.

The Basal Ganglia and Skill Learning

"Basal ganglia" is one of the few terms for a brain structure that literally describe the region (or in this case regions) to which they refer. The **basal ganglia** are ganglia (clusters of neurons) located at the base of the forebrain (the most prominent part of the human brain). As you'll recall from Chapter 2, the basal ganglia are positioned close to the hippocampus. Like the hippocampus, the basal ganglia receive large numbers of inputs from cortical neurons. In fact, most cortical areas send inputs to the basal ganglia. These inputs provide the basal ganglia with information about what is happening in the world—in particular, about the sensory stimuli the person is experiencing. Unlike the hippocampus, the basal ganglia send output signals mainly to the thalamus (affecting interactions between neurons in the thalamus and motor cortex) and to the brainstem (influencing signals sent to the spinal cord). By modulating these motor control circuits, the basal ganglia play a role in initiating and maintaining movement.

The basal ganglia are particularly important for controlling the velocity, direction, and amplitude of movements, as well as for preparing to move (Desmurget, Grafton, Vindras, Grea, & Turner, 2003; Graybiel, 1995; R. S. Turner, Grafton, Votaw, Delong, & Hoffman, 1998). For example, suppose you are performing the rotary pursuit task. You need to move your arm in a circle at a velocity that matches that of the rotating target. In this task, your basal ganglia will use information from your visual system about the movements of the target, the stylus, and your arm, as well as information from your somatosensory system about the position of your arm, to control the direction and velocity of your arm movements. Similarly, if you dive into a pool to retrieve a coin, your basal ganglia will help you avoid colliding with the bottom of the pool.

Once a highly skilled boxer, Muhammad Ali experienced rapid deterioration in his perceptual-motor skills due to Parkinson's disease, which disabled his basal ganglia. Some doctors believe his Parkinson's disease was caused by boxing, and call this form of the disease "pugilistic Parkinson's syndrome."

Reuters/ CORBIS

Given all the interconnections between the basal ganglia and motor systems, it's not surprising that disruption of activity in the basal ganglia impairs skill learning. Such disruption does not, however, seem to affect the formation and recall of memories for events and facts. Consider the case of Muhammad Ali. Ali was one of the most agile and skilled boxers of his era, but his career was ended by a gradual loss of motor control and coordination. Doctors identified these deficits as resulting from Parkinson's disease, a disorder that disables basal ganglia circuits (we discuss this disease in more detail later in the chapter). Over time, the loss of basal ganglia function resulting from Parkinson's disease affects even the most basic of skills, such as walking. Whereas H.M.'s hippocampal damage (described in Chapter 3) prevents him from reporting on his past experiences, Muhammad Ali's basal ganglia dysfunction prevents him from making use of skill memories and learning new skills; it has not affected his memory for facts or events.

Many researchers suspect that processing in the basal ganglia is a key step in forming skill memories, although the specific processes whereby sensory inputs lead to motor outputs are currently unknown (Barnes, Kubota, Hu, Jin, & Graybiel, 2005; Graybiel, 2005). Most researchers agree, however, that practicing a skill can change how basal ganglia circuits participate in the performance of that skill, and that synaptic plasticity is a basic neural mechanism enabling such changes (Conn, Battaglia, Marino, & Nicoletti, 2005; Graybiel, 2004). We describe here the experimental results that show the importance of the basal ganglia not only for performing skills but also for forming and accessing skill memories.

Learning Deficits after Lesions

Much of what is known about the role of basal ganglia in skill learning comes from studies of rats learning to navigate mazes, such as the radial maze shown in Figure 4.8a. In the standard radial maze task, rats learn to search the arms in the maze for food, without repeating visits to the arms they have already searched. This task simulates some features of natural foraging, because food does not magically reappear at locations where a rat has just eaten. However, the entrances to the arms of the maze are all very similar, so unless the rat remembers specifically which arms it has visited, it is likely to go to the same arm more than once. In early sessions, this is just what rats do. They often go to the same arm multiple times, and consequently waste a lot of time running back and forth along arms that contain no food. With practice, the rats learn that they can get more food for their effort by keeping track of where they have been, and they make fewer repeat visits to the same arm. Food acts as a kind of feedback in the radial maze task, in that correct performance leads to food. (This is a particularly important class of feedback that is of great interest to learning researchers, as you'll learn in Chapter 8.)

To learn to navigate the radial maze efficiently, rats must remember certain aspects of past events. Not surprisingly, rats with hippocampal damage have major problems with this task (Figure 4.8b). Even after many sessions, they continue to visit arms they have visited before. In contrast, rats with basal ganglia damage learn this task as easily as rats with no brain damage. This shows that basal ganglia damage does not disrupt rats' memories for events, nor does it prevent them from performing the skills necessary to find food in a radial maze.

Researchers can modify the radial maze task slightly, to make it less dependent on memories of past events. If instead of putting food in all the arms, the experimenter places food only in arms that are illuminated, rats quickly learn to avoid the non-illuminated arms (Figure 4.8c). Rats with hippocampal damage can also learn this version of the task, because they only need to associate light with food, which does not require keeping track of arms they've visited. Surprisingly, rats with basal ganglia damage have difficulty learning this "simpler" version of the task. They continue to search non-illuminated arms even though they never find food in those arms (Packard, Hirsh, & White, 1989). Basal ganglia damage seems to prevent rats from learning the simple perceptual-motor skill of avoiding dark arms and entering illuminated arms.

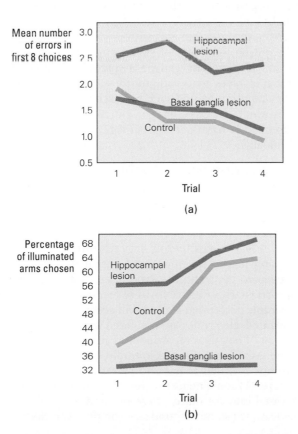

(a)

(b)

Figure 4.8 Effect of brain damage on rat's learning in a radial maze (a) The radial maze is often used in studies of perceptual-motor skill learning by rats. (b) When placed in a maze with food at the end of each arm, intact control rats learn, over repeated trials, to avoid revisiting arms they have already visited. Rats with basal ganglia damage can also learn this, but rats with a dysfunctional hippocampus cannot. (c) Intact rats can also learn to enter only the illuminated arms in a radial maze. Rats with hippocampal damage can also learn this, but rats with basal ganglia damage cannot. This result shows that basal ganglia damage can disrupt perceptual-motor skill learning. (b, c) Adapted from Packard et al., 1989.

Rats may show similar learning deficits in another task: the Morris water maze. In the standard version of this maze, experimenters fill a circular tank with murky water. They then place rats in the tank, and the rats must swim around until they discover a platform hidden just beneath the water surface. Once a rat finds the platform, it no longer has to swim, and the trial is over. Researchers measure the time it takes a rat to find the platform, and use this as a measure of learning. Intact rats gradually learn the location of the hidden platform after repeated trials in the tank. Rats with hippocampal damage have severe difficulties learning this standard task, but have no problem learning the task if the platform is visible above the surface of the water. Rats with basal ganglia damage can learn the location of the platform whether it is visible or not. This seems to suggest that basal ganglia damage does not affect a rat's ability to learn this task.

Tests of transfer of training, however, tell a different story. If experimenters move a visible platform in the Morris water maze to a new location during testing, rats with hippocampal damage (or no damage) swim directly to the platform to escape the water. Rats with basal ganglia damage, however, swim to where the platform used to be, and only afterward do they find the platform in its new location (R. J. McDonald & White, 1994). One interpretation of this finding is that rats with basal ganglia damage have difficulty learning to swim toward a platform to escape the water (even when the platform is clearly visible), and instead learn to swim to a particular location in the tank to escape. This study illustrates how two animals may seem to be performing a skill in the same way, but their skill memories and their ability to use them in novel situations are not necessarily equivalent. Your great aunt and a trained monkey may be using very different motor programs to set the time on a microwave oven, even though their actions might look the same.

The findings from these experiments with rats illustrate the effects of damage to the basal ganglia on the formation of skill memories. Such studies have led researchers to conclude that the basal ganglia are particularly important in perceptual-motor learning that involves generating motor responses based on environmental cues. The basic assumption behind such research is that there is nothing unique about the way in which the basal ganglia function in rats learning to navigate mazes, and consequently basal ganglia damage should disrupt skill learning in similar ways in humans.

Neural Activity during Perceptual-Motor Skill Learning

Measures of neural activity in the basal ganglia during learning provide further clues about the role of the basal ganglia in the formation of skill memories. Experimenters can train rats to turn right or left in a T-shaped maze, by using a sound cue that the rats hear just before reaching the intersection where they must turn (Figure 4.9). For example, an experimenter releases a rat in the maze, and then a computer plays a specific sound, instructing the rat to make a right turn. If the rat turns to the right, the experimenter gives the rat food (as noted earlier, this is a particularly effective form of feedback). With practice, rats learn to perform this simple perceptual-motor skill accurately. In a recent experiment, researchers implanted electrodes in the basal ganglia of rats before training them in the T-maze. They then recorded how neurons in the basal ganglia fired as rats learned the task (Jog, Kubota, Connolly, Hillegaart, & Graybiel, 1999).

These recordings revealed four basic patterns of neural activity when rats were in the T-maze: (1) some neurons fired most at the start of a trial, when the rat was first released into the maze; (2) some fired most when the instructional sound was broadcast; (3) some responded strongly when the rat turned right or

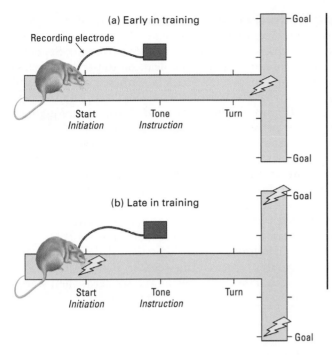

Figure 4.9 Changes in basal ganglia firing patterns during skill learning (a) Researchers implanted electrodes in rats' basal ganglia, then trained the rats to turn right or left in a T-maze after hearing a tone instruction. Early in training, 50% of basal ganglia neurons fired strongly (indicated by the lightning bolt) when the rats chose which direction to turn. (b) As training progressed, basal ganglia neurons began to fire mainly at the beginning and end of the rats' movements through the maze; finally, more than 90% of neurons fired almost exclusively when rats were at these positions. Adapted from Jog et al., 1999.

left; and (4) some fired at the end of a trial, when the rat received food. During the early stages of learning, about half of the recorded basal ganglia neurons showed one of these four patterns of activity. Most of these neurons fired only when a rat turned right or left in the maze (Figure 4.9a). The remaining neurons fired in ways that were not clearly related to the rats' movements or experiences in the maze. As the rats' performance improved with practice, the percentage of neurons that showed task-related activity patterns increased to about 90%, with most neurons firing strongly at the beginning and at the end of the task rather than during turning (Figure 4.9b). These measurements show that neural activity in the basal ganglia changes during the learning of a perceptual-motor skill, suggesting that encoding or control of skills by the basal ganglia changes as learning progresses.

The increased neural activity seen in the beginning and end states during the maze task suggests that the basal ganglia develop a motor plan that the rat's brain initiates at the beginning of each trial. The motor plan then directs the rat's movements until the trial ends (Graybiel, 1997, 1998). This hypothetical process is consistent with Fitts's model of skill learning, in which automatically engaged motor programs gradually replace active control of movements (Fitts, 1964). Someone learning to juggle might show similar changes in basal ganglia activity—that is, if we could record signals from her neurons, which currently is not possible. In a novice juggler, basal ganglia neurons might fire most strongly when the balls are in the air (when an action must be chosen based on visual information). In an expert juggler, basal ganglia neurons might fire most strongly when she is catching and tossing the balls.

Earlier in the chapter we raised the question of whether cognitive skills might involve some of the same brain regions and neural mechanisms as perceptual-motor skills. The data presented above show that the basal ganglia do indeed contribute to learning of perceptual-motor skills. Do the basal ganglia also contribute to cognitive skill learning?

Brain Activity during Cognitive Skill Learning

Neuroimaging studies of the human brain reveal that the basal ganglia are active when participants learn cognitive skills (Poldrack, Prabhakaran, Seger, & Gabrieli, 1999). In these experiments, participants learned to perform a classification task in which a computer presented them with sets of cards and then instructed them to guess what the weather would be, based on the patterns displayed on the cards (Figure 4.10a). Each card showed a unique pattern of colored shapes. Some patterns appeared when rain was likely, and others appeared when the weather was likely to be sunny. As each card was presented onscreen, participants predicted either good or bad (sunny or rainy) weather by pressing one of two keys. The computer determined the actual weather outcome based on the patterns on the cards. Participants had to learn through trial and error which patterns predicted which kind of weather. The task mimics real-world weather prediction, in that no combination of "patterns" (that is, of cloud cover, temperature, wind, and so on) is 100% predictive of the weather that will follow; meteorologists must develop a wide range of cognitive skills to accurately forecast the weather. For participants in the study, the task may have seemed more like reading Tarot cards than learning a cognitive skill, but they usually improved with practice.

Figure 4.10 Neuroimaging during learning of the weather prediction task (a) In the weather prediction task, a participant, lying with his head in the MRI scanner, is shown a set of cards onscreen that he must use to judge what weather conditions are likely to occur. Different patterns correspond to different predictions about whether it will rain; for example, the pattern of squares on the leftmost card shown here predicts a 60% chance of rain. The participant is not given this information but must figure out through trial and error which patterns indicate a high chance of rain. (b) fMRI images show increased activity in the basal ganglia as a participant learns the weather prediction task. Activation during weather prediction was analyzed relative to baseline activity in a perceptual-motor control condition. Regions of significantly increased activity are shown in red through yellow, and regions of reduced activity in blue through white. During the weather prediction task, difference images show activation (orange) in the basal ganglia and deactivation (blue) in the hippocampal region. (b) Adapted from Poldrack et al., 2001.

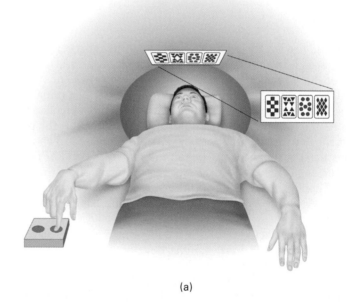

(a)

Brain activity at different horizontal depths

Hippocampal region

Basal ganglia

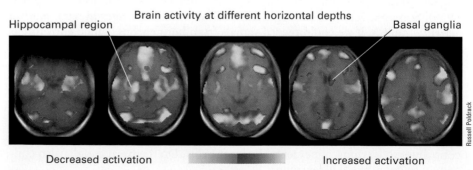

Decreased activation

Increased activation

(b)

Russell Poldrack

Although each card was associated with the likelihood that a particular kind of weather would occur, there was no simple rule that participants could use to make accurate predictions. Instead, to improve at the task, participants gradually had to learn which cards *tended* to predict certain types of weather. Brain imaging data showed increased activity in the basal ganglia as individuals learned to make these judgments (Figure 4.10b). This and similar imaging studies suggest that the basal ganglia contribute to both cognitive and perceptual-motor skill learning. But how?

Despite considerable evidence that the basal ganglia enable skill learning, their specific function in this learning is still under debate. For example, since the basal ganglia are involved in the control and planning of movements, perhaps damage to the basal ganglia leads to changes in performance that impair learning processes in other brain regions: if you can't control how your arms are moving, you will have difficulty learning how to juggle. In short, changes in skill learning caused by lesions to the basal ganglia, as seen in rats learning the radial maze task, do not definitively prove that this region is critical for encoding or retrieving skill memories. Similarly, learning-dependent changes in the activity of basal ganglia neurons, as seen in rats learning to follow instructions in a T-maze, could reflect changes in the information coming from the sensory cortex rather than changes generated in the basal ganglia.

Are basal ganglia neurons doing most of whatever is required to form memories of skills, or are other brain regions such as the cortex and cerebellum doing the bulk of the encoding and retrieval? Could it be that the basal ganglia contribute as much to skill-memory formation as do other brain regions, but the basal ganglia are specialized for specific aspects of the learning process? We need to take a closer look at different cortical regions during and after practice sessions to shed some light on these issues. (See "Learning and Memory in Everyday Life" on p. 152 for some insight into how video-game playing develops perceptual-motor skills and cognitive skills alike.)

Cortical Representations of Skills

How important is the cerebral cortex for the learning and performance of skills? Given that most animals don't have a cerebral cortex, and that animals born with a cortex can make many movements after surgical removal of all their cortical neurons, you might conclude that the cortex isn't very important for skill learning. In fact, mammals are the only animals that make extensive use of cortical circuits for any purpose, so whatever the role of the cerebral cortex in skill memory, it probably plays this role most extensively in mammals. Coincidentally (or not), mammals are highly trainable compared with most other species.

Neural circuits in the cerebral cortex that are active when you run, jump, or sing change over time in ways that enhance the activities you perform most often, as well as the activities you find most rewarding. From this perspective, skill memories are the neural outcomes of repeated performances. A simple analogy is the way your body shape changes in response to a bodybuilding regimen. Just as increasing the strength and flexibility of your muscles can affect how well you jump, changes in networks of cortical neurons can also influence your jumping ability.

Cortical Expansion

If cortical networks are like brain "muscles," you'd expect the practice of different skills to affect different regions of cerebral cortex, just as different physical exercises affect different muscle groups. This seems to be true. Regions of the cerebral cortex involved in performing a particular skill expand in area with practice, while regions that are less relevant to the skill show fewer changes.

Are Video Games Good for the Brain?

Since the advent of television, many humans have been spending more and more of their daily lives staring at the glow of a rectangular screen. Video games have transformed this passive viewing into an interactive process, and today's video games are as complex as any sport, card game, or board game. By now, most games invented before the video-game era have been made into video games, often with artificially intelligent computer programs serving as competitors. Video games are quickly replacing other recreational activities as the preferred pastime of children around the world. Many parents are concerned that this new pastime is turning children's brains into mush and that the skills acquired by playing such games are worthless. What is actually going on? Do the skills learned during video-game playing transfer positively to other situations, or do they limit how a person's brain functions in the real world?

Video games have many advantages over traditional games. They offer a wide variety of game-playing options; they take up minimal space and require essentially no maintenance; they build expertise without requiring instruction from an expert; they present minimal risk of injury; and they can be played in any weather at any time of day or night. On the other hand, video games are blamed for provoking teen violence, contributing to a general lack of physical fitness and to the obesity epidemic, reducing literacy, decreasing opportunities for face-to-face interactions with family members and peers, and occupying children's minds with useless information (see C. A. Anderson & Bushman, 2001, for a review of the scientific literature on this topic).

However, the question of whether video games are good or bad for your brain has seldom been addressed scientifically. Less physical activity would seem to be correlated with fewer head injuries, which is good news for the brain. But poor health resulting from lack of physical activity is probably bad for the brain. A reduction in the variety of video game players' other activities (fewer social interactions, less reading) might be expected to lead to a less-fit brain. But the opportunities that video games offer for problem solving against high-level competition (such as chess programs or games that allow players from around the world to compete) might increase brain fitness. After all, proficiency at playing video games requires the development of perceptual-motor skills and cognitive skills alike. At the moment, all of these possibilities are speculative, and so it is inaccurate to label video games as either "good" or "bad" for brains. Nonetheless, a few recent experiments have identified situations in which playing certain types of video games can help improve the brain's capacity to perform complex skills.

Most parents worry less about computerized flight simulators and computerized solitaire than they do about video games that involve blowing up everything in sight, including simulated humans—especially given recent school shootings and other widely reported acts of violence committed by adolescents. Ironically, violent action games are the only games, so far, that researchers have found to improve brain function.

A recent series of experiments found that college students who played high-action video games such as *Grand Theft Auto 3, Crazy Taxi, Counter-Strike,* and *Spider-Man* at least 1 hour a day, at least 4 days a week, for at least 6 months, had increased visual attention abilities compared with students who did not play video games (Green & Bavelier, 2003). The benefits of playing fast-action games included increased visual capacity and enhanced spatial attention, with an increased ability to visually apprehend and count sets of visual stimuli. Enhancements in visual abilities carried over to standard attention tasks that in many ways are dissimilar from the commercial video games. These results suggest that the effects of systematic practice with fast-action video games are transferable to a wide variety of other visual-motor activities, such as catching airborne popcorn in your mouth.

Perhaps people with above-average attention capacities are more likely to play high-action video games, accounting for the effects described above. To test this possibility, experimenters measured the effects of 10 hours of action video-game playing (1 hour a day) on the attention capacities of people who generally do not play video games. With this group as well, the researchers found that practice with fast-action video games enhanced the ability to attend to visual stimuli. Interestingly, a control group that spent the same amount of time playing a non-action video game, *Tetris,* showed no enhancement in attention capacity. Apparently, rapidly blowing up images on an illuminated display screen is better for enhancing visual attention than trying to make falling blocks fit together on a similar display.

Based on the limited evidence available so far, it seems that video games are to the brain what food is to the body. But, just as what you eat does not determine what you look like and has only a limited effect on how healthy you are, so playing video games will not entirely determine how your brain functions or what all your mental capacities are.

Russell Poldrack

Destroying other cars and mowing down pedestrians in the *Crazy Taxi 2* game (above) can improve your visual-motor processing skills, but stacking falling blocks in the *Tetris* game does not.

Neuroimaging techniques such as fMRI reveal this expansion by showing increased blood flow to particular regions. As one example, brain imaging studies of professional violinists showed that representations in the somatosensory cortex of the hand used to control note sequences (by pressing individual strings with different fingers) are larger than in non-violinists (Elbert, Pantev, Wienbruch, Rockstroh, & Taub, 1995). Interestingly, the cortical maps of violinists' bow hands (the fingers of which always move together) showed no such elaborations: the changes are specific to the hand that moves the fingers separately.

Measures of blood flow reveal larger areas of cortical activation after extensive practice, which implies that experience is affecting cortical circuits. These measures do not reveal what physical changes occur, however. Recent studies using structural MRI techniques indicate that practice can change the amount of cortical gray matter (where the cell bodies of neurons are found). For example, after about 3 months of training, people who learned to juggle three balls continuously for at least 1 minute showed a 3% increase in gray matter in areas of the visual cortex that respond to motion (Draganski et al., 2004). No comparable structural changes were observed in the motor cortex, basal ganglia, or cerebellum. It is not known whether expansion of gray matter reflects changes in the number or size of synapses, changes in the number of glia (the cells providing functional and structural support to neurons), or changes in the number of cortical neurons.

Electrophysiological studies also show that practice can expand cortical representations. In one such study, researchers trained monkeys to perform a tactile discrimination task (Recanzone, Merzenich, Jenkins, Grajski, & Dinse, 1992). The task required the monkey to release a handgrip whenever it felt a stimulus on its fingertip that differed from a standard stimulus. During each trial, the monkey initially felt a surface vibrating at a fixed speed on one of its fingers, for about half a second. This initial tactile stimulus, always the same, provided a standard for comparison. The initial stimulus was followed by a half-second interval of no stimulation, and then a series of one to four additional vibrating stimuli, each vibrating either at the same rate as the standard or faster. The monkey was given fruit juice if it released the handgrip when vibrations were faster than the standard. This task is similar to the T-maze task described earlier, in which researchers recorded the activity of basal ganglia neurons in a rat as it learned to turn right or left in response to acoustic cues. Both the T-maze and the tactile discrimination task require the animal to perform one of two responses (in one task, turn right or turn left; in the other, grip or release) based on specific cues provided to a single sensory modality (sound in one task, touch in the other).

When a monkey learned to respond to a vibrating stimulus that predicted the delivery of juice, the area of the somatosensory cortex that processed the cue increased. As a result, monkeys that learned the tactile discrimination task had enlarged cortical representations for the finger they used to inspect tactile stimuli.

Studies such as these show that perceptual-motor skill learning is often associated with the expansion of the regions of the sensory cortex involved in performing the skill. Similarly, practicing a perceptual-motor skill can also cause regions of the motor cortex to expand. For example, electrical stimulation of the motor cortex in monkeys trained to retrieve a small object showed that the area of the cortex that controlled movements of the fingers expanded (Nudo, Milliken, Jenkins, & Merzenich, 1996). In monkeys that learned to turn a key with their forearm, cortical representation of the forearm expanded. Researchers don't know how many different cortical regions are modified during learning of a particular skill, but the current assumption is that any cortical networks that contribute to performance of the skill are likely to be modified as training improves (or degrades) performance. Researchers also have yet to determine exactly how cortical expansion occurs and what it consists of, but most neuroscientists believe that the expansion reflects the strengthening and weakening of connections within the cortex resulting from synaptic plasticity.

Are Skill Memories Stored in the Cortex?

Many experiments have shown that cortical networks are affected by practice, but this tells us only that the two phenomena are correlated, not that changes in the cerebral cortex improve performance. Such studies also do not establish that skill memories are stored in cortical networks. As you saw earlier, changes in neural activity in the basal ganglia also take place during skill learning. The cerebral cortex clearly influences skill learning and performance, but knowing this is not the same as knowing what cortical circuits do during skill learning.

One way to get closer to understanding cortical function is to measure cortical activity during training. Much of what is known about skill learning relates to how different practice regimens lead to differences in the rate of skill improvement and in the rate of forgetting. If it were possible to show that changes in the cortex parallel behavioral changes, or that improvements in performance can be predicted from cortical changes, we could be more certain that skill levels and cortical activity are closely related. Initial investigations in this direction suggest that the behavioral stages of skill acquisition are indeed paralleled by changes in cortical activity.

Data from brain imaging studies show that when people begin learning a motor skill that requires sequential finger movements, the portion of the motor cortex activated during performance of the task increases rapidly during the first training session and more gradually in later sessions. Avi Karni and colleagues required participants to touch each of their fingers to their thumb in a fixed sequence as rapidly and accurately as possible (Karni et al., 1998). In parallel with the changes seen in the motor cortex, participants' performance of the task improved rapidly in early sessions and more gradually in later sessions (Figure 4.11a), consistent

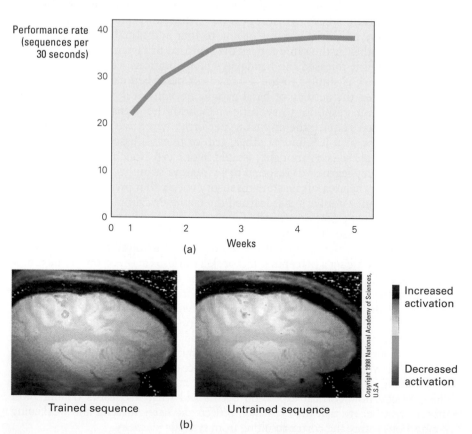

Figure 4.11 Changes in skill performance and associated motor cortex during training (a) Participants who trained to perform a sequence of finger movements gradually increased the rate and accuracy with which they could perform this skill. The plot shows average scores for the group of participants. (b) After the training, fMRI scans revealed that the area of motor cortex activated as participants performed the practiced sequence expanded (left panel) relative to the region activated as they performed an untrained sequence of identical finger movements (right panel). Adapted from Karni et al., 1998.

Copyright 1998 National Academy of Sciences, U.S.A

with the power law of learning. Imaging data collected over 6 weeks of training suggested that additional practice resulted in additional, more gradual increases in the representation of learned movements in the motor cortex.

Overall, the region of motor cortex activated during performance of the practiced sequence expanded relative to the area activated by different, untrained sequences of identical finger movements (Figure 4.11b). Karni and colleagues hypothesized that the period of "fast learning" involves processes that select and establish the optimal plans for performing a particular task, whereas the subsequent slower stages of learning reflect long-term structural changes of basic motor control circuits in the cortex. Recent data from studies of perceptual-motor skill learning in rats are consistent with this interpretation. Rats trained in a reaching task showed significant differences in their motor map only after practicing the task for at least 10 days (Kleim et al., 2004). This finding suggests that structural changes in the cortex reflect the enhancement of skill memories during later stages of training.

Circuits in the cerebral cortex are activated by many sensory and motor events, so it is not surprising that these brain regions contribute to skill learning. However, until researchers look at interactions between the cerebral cortex and the basal ganglia while individuals are learning a wide variety of perceptual-motor and cognitive skills, assessing the respective roles of the cortex and basal ganglia in forming and recalling skill memories will remain a difficult task.

The Cerebellum and Timing

What about skill learning in animals such as birds and fish that don't have much cortex? Researchers can train pigeons to perform a wide range of perceptual-motor skills, and fish can rapidly learn to navigate mazes. Animals without much cortex must rely on evolutionarily older parts of the brain to learn skills. One region that seems to be particularly important in this process is the cerebellum.

The cerebellum is probably one of the most basic neural systems involved in encoding and retrieving skill memories. Even animals as lowly as fish and frogs, which may seem to have little potential for skill learning, have a cerebellum. Although you aren't likely to see a fish or a frog performing in a circus, this doesn't mean these animals cannot learn perceptual-motor skills; for example, with practice, fish can learn to press little levers for food. You are more likely to have seen parrots riding tricycles or heard them producing intelligible sentences. Birds, too, have a cerebellum, which may facilitate their ability to learn such tricks. In fact, most animals that have a spine also have a cerebellum. Yet there are relatively few studies of cerebellar function in nonmammals. Consequently, much less is known about how the cerebellum contributes to skill-memory formation in animals with little cortex than is known about cerebellar function in mammals that make extensive use of cortex.

Most of the inputs to the cerebellum are from the spinal cord, sensory systems, or cerebral cortex, and most of the output signals from the cerebellum go to the spinal cord or to motor systems in the cerebral cortex. Experiments conducted in the early 1800s showed that cerebellar lesions impair the performance of motor sequences. People with cerebellar damage, for example, have difficulty writing or playing a musical instrument. (Chapter 7 provides further details on how cerebellar damage affects human performance.) Collectively, these anatomical and neuropsychological data indicate that the cerebellum contributes to the performance of perceptual-motor skills in mammals. Because the structure of the cerebellum is organized similarly across different species, it is presumed to serve similar functions in both mammals and nonmammals (Lalonde & Botez, 1990).

Other evidence suggests that, in addition to facilitating the performance of skills, the cerebellum is involved in forming memories for skills. For example, early brain imaging studies of systems involved in motor learning showed that there is a sudden increase in cerebellar activity when humans begin learning to perform sequences of finger movements (Friston, Frith, Passingham, Liddle, & Frackowiak, 1992). Similarly, rats that learn complex motor skills to navigate an obstacle course (for example, balancing on tightropes and see-saws) develop predictable physiological changes in cerebellar neural circuitry, such as increased numbers of synapses (Kleim et al., 1997).

Cerebellar changes in acrobatic rats seem to depend on skill learning rather than on activity levels, because rats that run in an exercise wheel for the same amount of time do not show such changes. More generally, animals such as birds and dolphins that routinely perform three-dimensional acrobatic skills—flying between branches; rapidly jumping or diving while spinning—typically have a larger cerebellum than animals that do not learn such skills. The cerebellum is especially important for learning movement sequences that require precise timing, such as acrobatics, dancing, or competitive team sports. A person with cerebellar damage might be able to learn new dance moves but would probably have trouble learning to synchronize those moves to musical rhythms.

The cerebellum is also important for tasks that involve aiming at or tracking a target. A task that psychologists commonly use to assess such abilities is **mirror tracing**. In this task, individuals learn to trace drawings by looking at their hand, and the figure to be traced, in a mirror (Figure 4.12a); meanwhile, the hand and the figure are hidden from their view. It's hard to draw well under these conditions, but if the cerebellum is working properly, the participant will gradually improve at this task. In contrast, a person with cerebellar damage would find learning this task difficult. For example, Robert Laforce and Julien Doyon found that patients with cerebellar damage were much slower at performing a mirror tracing task than individuals in a control group, even after several sessions of training, as shown in figure 4.12b (Laforce & Doyon, 2001).

It is interesting to note in Figure 4.12b that the *rate* of learning for patients with cerebellar damage was comparable to that of the control group. This seems to suggest that the learning process in the patients with cerebellar damage was similar to that of the control group, and that the patients simply performed more poorly. However, subsequent transfer tests in which both groups traced more complex figures revealed that the individuals in the control group

Figure 4.12 The mirror tracing task (a) In this task, participants learn to trace a figure using only a mirror reflection of their hand and the figure for guidance. (b) Cerebellar lesions disrupt learning and performance of the mirror tracing task. Note, however, that the *rate* of learning is the same for both control and cerebellar lesion groups. (b) Adapted from Laforce and Doyon, 2001.

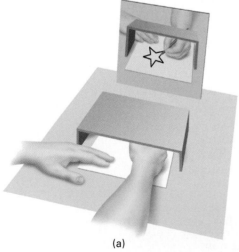

(a)

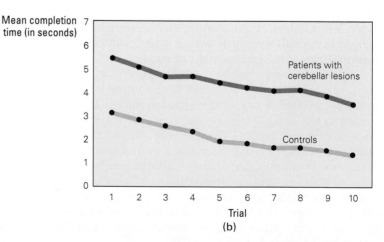

(b)

benefited more from their training experiences than did the individuals with cerebellar damage. Thus, although both groups were learning at a similar rate, they were not learning the mirror tracing skill in the same way.

A simple way to show that disrupted cerebellar activity diminishes the ability to learn and perform perceptual-motor skills such as those used in the mirror tracing task is to temporarily disable a person's cerebellum with an alcoholic drink, then require the person to learn such a task. The cerebellum is one of the first brain regions affected by alcohol, which is why police officers often use tasks that involve tracking (walking along a stripe in the road, or touching finger to nose) as tests for drunkenness.

So far, we have discussed how the cerebellum contributes to perceptual-motor skill learning. Recent brain imaging studies show that activity in the cerebellum also changes when individuals learn certain cognitive skills, such as **mirror reading.** In the mirror reading task, individuals learn to read mirror-reversed text. Researchers found that cerebellar changes that occur during learning of the mirror reading task are *lateralized*—that is, are different in each hemisphere (Figure 4.13), with the left cerebellum showing decreased activity and the right cerebellum showing increased activity with training (Poldrack & Gabrieli, 2001). Are you assuming that both sides of your brain are doing the same thing while you're reading this chapter? Think again. How such hemisphere-specific differences in cerebellar processing contribute to skill learning or performance is not yet known.

Keep in mind that almost all cognitive skills require the performance of some perceptually guided movements, such as eye movements. Remember learning earlier in this chapter how chess masters move their eyes to scan a chessboard more efficiently than less experienced players? Similar perceptual-motor skills may also be important for tasks such as mirror reading. So, it is

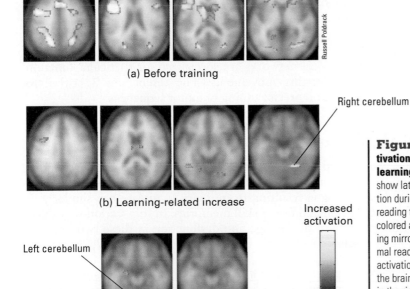

(a) Before training

Russell Poldrack

(b) Learning-related increase

Right cerebellum

Left cerebellum

(c) Learning-related decrease

Increased activation

Decreased activation

Figure 4.13 Cerebellar activation during cognitive skill learning fMRI imaging studies show lateralized cerebellar activation during the learning of a mirror reading task. (a) Before training, the colored areas are regions active during mirror reading but not during normal reading. The four images show activation at different depths within the brain. After training, (b) activity in the right cerebellum increased and (c) activity in the left cerebellum decreased. Adapted from Poldrack and Gabrieli, 2001.

possible that changes in cerebellar activity during the learning of cognitive skills might partially reflect the learning of motor sequences required for performing the cognitive activity.

In summary, then, the cerebellum, cerebral cortex, and basal ganglia are each critical, in different ways, to skill learning. If you're having trouble learning a skill, which part of your brain should you blame? Currently, there is no cut-and-dried division of labor between these three brain regions. How critical each region is for encoding or performing any given skill probably depends on the particular skill and your level of expertise. Nevertheless, the cerebellum seems most critical for timing; the cerebral cortex, most critical for controlling complex action sequences; and the basal ganglia, most critical for linking sensory events to responses. Knowing this, which brain region do you think would be most critical for learning to run downstairs? The answer is probably all three, at some point in the learning process. Early on, the cerebellum, visual cortex, and motor cortex may work together to coordinate the timing and sequencing of leg movements. After extensive practice, the basal ganglia may begin to initiate and control more automatic sequences of leg movements. How these three brain regions work together during the acquisition and retention of skill memories is a question that researchers are still attempting to answer.

One feature that all three systems have in common is that skill learning is associated with gradual changes in the firing of neurons in these areas during performance of the skill. This finding means that practice can change the structure of neural circuits to make the control and coordination of movements (or thoughts, in the case of cognitive skills) more accurate and efficient. The most likely mechanism for such changes is synaptic plasticity. Understanding how and when the brain is able to adjust specific synapses within and between the cerebellum, basal ganglia, and cortex will clarify how humans and other animals learn skills.

Interim Summary

Three brain regions involved in the formation and recall of skill memories are the basal ganglia, the cerebral cortex, and the cerebellum. The basal ganglia direct interactions between sensory and motor systems during the learning process, and different cortical networks are specialized for particular functions in controlling and coordinating movements. The cerebellum is critical for learning skills that depend on precise timing of motor sequences.

4.3 Clinical Perspectives

In Chapter 3 you learned how damage to the hippocampus and surrounding brain regions can disrupt memories for events and facts. Damage to the cerebral cortex and basal ganglia resulting from injury or disease can similarly interfere with the formation and use of skill memories. In this section we explore the types of deficits caused by damage and dysfunction in these two brain regions. (We defer discussion of cerebellar disorders to Chapter 7, on classical conditioning.)

The disorders reviewed here have a major impact on society, affecting millions of individuals. Experiments conducted with groups of patients with these disorders provide unique opportunities for understanding how the neural systems involved in skill learning can be disrupted. Unlike the various types of amnesia, in which memory loss can be measured with standard tests, disorders that affect skill learning are difficult to distinguish from disorders that impair skill performance. Nevertheless, clinical studies of patients with skill deficits provide clues about the neural systems responsible for skill learning—information that would be difficult or impossible to obtain through experiments with unimpaired individuals.

Apraxia

Damage to the cerebral hemispheres, especially the parietal lobe of the left hemisphere (Figure 4.14), can lead to problems in the coordination of purposeful, skilled movements. This kind of deficit is called **apraxia.** The most common causes of apraxia are sharp blows to the head (a typical outcome of motorcycle accidents) and interruption of blood supply to neurons (as occurs during a stroke). Tests for apraxia generally require asking patients to perform or mimic specific gestures. A patient with apraxia can usually voluntarily perform the individual steps that make up the movement or gesture requested by the experimenter, but most such patients cannot combine these steps in appropriately sequenced and coordinated patterns when instructed to do so.

The position and extent of cerebral cortical damage determines what abilities are affected. For example, in patients with left parietal lesions, the greatest impairment is in the ability to imitate actions, whereas in patients with lesions in more frontal areas, the greatest loss is in the ability to pantomime actions that involve the use of both hands (Halsband et al., 2001). Sometimes patients are unable to perform a skill with one hand and yet can perform it quite easily with the other. These patients understand what the neuropsychologist is instructing them to do, but they are unable to comply.

Early case studies describing patients with apraxia, such as this description by Pick in 1904, give some sense of the severe problems associated with this disorder:

> The patient is requested to light a candle in its holder. He takes the match, holds it with both hands without doing anything further with it. When asked again, he takes the match upside down in his hand and tries to bore it into the candle. . . . A box of matches is put in his hand. He takes a match out and brushes his beard with it, and does the same thing when given a burning match. Even though he burns himself doing this, he continues. (quoted in Brown, 1988)

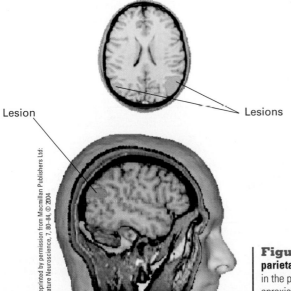

Lesion

Lesions

Reprinted by permission from Macmillan Publishers Ltd: Nature Neuroscience, 7, 80–84, © 2004

Figure 4.14 Cortical lesions in the parietal lobes Regions in blue show lesions in the parietal lobe that are associated with apraxia. Adapted from Sirigu et al., 2004.

Cortical damage clearly causes deficits in skill performance. For example, researchers have found that apraxia can affect individuals' abilities to perform both perceptual-motor skills and cognitive skills (Leiguarda & Marsden, 2000; Zadikoff & Lang, 2005). What is less clear is how the cortical damage might be affecting the memories of skills that are lost or the ability to form new memories. One hypothesis for why individuals with apraxia have difficulty performing skills is that they cannot flexibly access memories of how to perform those actions (Rothi, Ochipa, & Heilman, 1991). For example, patients with apraxia who were unable to pantomime gestures such as flipping a coin also had difficulty identifying when an actor in a film performed a specific gesture, such as opening a door (Heilman, Rothi, & Valenstein, 1982). This inability to recognize actions suggests that these patients have not simply lost the ability to generate certain actions, but instead can no longer access memories of those actions.

Studies of skill learning in patients with apraxia suggest that cortical damage interferes with the control and execution of skills more than with the learning and recalling of skills. For example, with practice, such patients can improve at performing skills, and their rate of improvement is comparable to that of unimpaired individuals. The highest level of performance they can reach, however, may be lower than the levels at which unimpaired individuals can perform with no training (Jacobs et al., 1999). How well someone with apraxia can learn a particular task seems to depend on both the nature of the person's deficits and the nature of the task. It remains unclear whether learning in individuals with apraxia occurs through the same neural processes as in unimpaired individuals. Patients with apraxia might make do with a subset of these processes, or they might use alternative mechanisms, such as adopting different strategies during practice sessions.

One way to investigate the conditions leading to apraxia is to create temporary states of apraxia in healthy individuals by inactivating cortical circuits, and then examine the effect on skill learning and recall. This strategy has recently

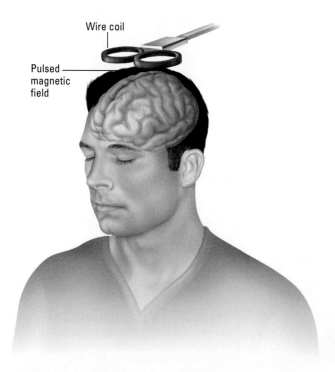

Wire coil

Pulsed magnetic field

Figure 4.15 Using TMS to modulate cortical activity A volunteer undergoing transcranial magnetic stimulation. This technique enables researchers to disrupt cortical activity to temporarily simulate conditions such as apraxia.

been made possible by **transcranial magnetic stimulation,** (Figure 4.15), a procedure in which a brief magnetic pulse (or series of pulses) applied to the scalp produces small electrical currents in the brain that interfere with normal patterns of activity over an area of about 1 square centimeter. The disruption lasts for just a few tens of milliseconds, but if timed properly, it can impair skill learning and performance. Researchers can disrupt activity in different cortical regions simply by changing the position of the stimulating device. Transcranial magnetic stimulation is a powerful way of studying how cortical deficits affect the formation and recall of skill memories; however, its use is currently limited, because the stimulation has caused seizures in some participants and the physiological effects of repeatedly disrupting cortical function are unknown.

Currently, the main technique for helping patients with apraxia overcome their deficits is behavioral training that involves extensive repetitive practice. Knowing how different variables such as feedback, pacing, and variety of practice can influence learning (as described above in the Behavioral Processes section) is important for developing appropriate behavioral therapies. Future advances in understanding the cortical networks underlying skill memory will probably suggest important ways of enhancing existing treatments for people with apraxia and developing new therapies.

Huntington's Disease

Huntington's disease is an inherited disorder that causes gradual damage to neurons throughout the brain, especially in the basal ganglia and cerebral cortex. The disease leads to a range of psychological problems (including mood disorders, hypersexuality, depression, and psychosis) and a gradual loss of motor abilities over a period of about 15 years. Facial twitching usually signals the onset of the disease. As Huntington's progresses, other parts of the body begin to shake, until eventually this shaking interferes with normal movement.

Patients with Huntington's disease show a number of memory deficits, some affecting skill memory. Such patients can learn new perceptual-motor and cognitive skills (with performance depending on how far the disease has progressed), but they generally learn more slowly than healthy individuals (Willingham & Koroshetz, 1993). People with Huntington's have particular difficulty learning tasks that require planning and sequencing actions, and they cannot perform the mirror reading or weather prediction tasks (described above) as well as healthy individuals (Knowlton et al., 1996). For example, Barbara Knowlton and colleagues found that an experimental group of 13 patients with Huntington's disease who performed the weather prediction task showed no signs of learning over 150 trials, whereas a control group of 12 healthy persons rapidly improved at the task (Figure 4.16). Recall that experimental studies with animals show that lesions of the basal ganglia can greatly impair skill learning. The basal ganglia damage in patients with Huntington's may explain why they find the weather prediction task so difficult to learn. However, they can learn some other cognitive skills that require similar abilities, such as the Tower of Hanoi task (Butters, Wolfe, Martone, Granholm, & Cermak, 1985).

Individuals with Huntington's typically show large deficits in perceptual-motor skill learning that seem to be related to problems with retrieval and decreased storage capacity. They have difficulty learning the serial reaction time task, the rotary pursuit task, and most other skills that require aiming at or tracking a target. However, it is difficult to determine to what extent deficits in learning of perceptual-motor skills are a direct result of cortical or basal ganglia damage, as opposed to being a side effect of patients' inability to move normally.

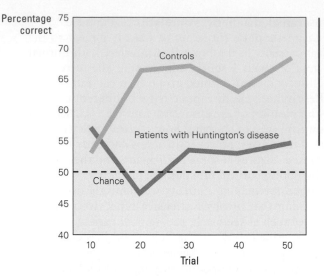

Figure 4.16 Impaired skill learning in people with Huntington's disease The graph shows data on accuracy in performing the weather prediction task. People with Huntington's had problems learning this task compared with the control group, which consisted of healthy elderly individuals. Adapted from Knowlton et al., 1996.

Imagine trying to learn to throw darts with someone randomly pushing your arm. You would probably have problems improving your throw under those conditions—not because you've lost the ability to store and recall memories of past attempts, but because you don't have control of your movements. It's also not easy to know how the combination of abnormal psychological states and damaged neural systems might affect learning in persons with Huntington's.

Scientists have made great progress in using genetic markers to diagnose Huntington's disease, but prevention and treatment of symptoms are still rudimentary. Using knowledge about the genetic abnormalities found in people with Huntington's, researchers have produced mice and fruit flies with similar genetic abnormalities. Experiments with these genetically engineered animals may provide critical new information about how Huntington's disease affects skill-memory systems and how the deficits caused by this disorder might be overcome. For example, recent experiments with Huntington's disease mice have revealed severe deficits in perceptual-motor skill learning and in the changes in cortical circuits that should occur during learning (Mazarakis et al., 2005). Synaptic plasticity mechanisms such as long-term potentiation and long-term depression (see Chapter 2) are also abnormal in these mice (Murphy et al., 2000). Thus, learning and memory deficits in patients with Huntington's may reflect not only basal ganglia damage but also more fundamental deficits in the ability to modify synapses based on experience.

Parkinson's Disease

Parkinson's disease is another nervous system disease involving disruptions in the normal functions of the basal ganglia and progressive deterioration of motor control. Unlike Huntington's disease, however, Parkinson's does not seem, in most cases, to be the result of heritable genetic abnormalities, or to involve large-scale neuronal death in either the cerebral cortex or the basal ganglia. The main brain damage associated with Parkinson's disease is a reduction in the number of neurons in the brainstem that modulate activity in the basal ganglia and cerebral cortex. These brainstem neurons normally determine the levels of dopamine in the basal ganglia, and when these neurons are gone, dopamine levels are greatly reduced. (We'll give more details on the contribution of dopamine neurons to learning in Chapter 8.)

Patients with Parkinson's disease show increasing muscular rigidity and muscle tremors, and are generally impaired at initiating movements. Symptoms of the disease usually do not appear until after the age of 50, but can arise much earlier (for example, the actor Michael J. Fox was diagnosed with Parkinson's when he was in his thirties).

Not surprisingly, people with Parkinson's have many of the same skill-learning impairments as people with Huntington's. Both diseases make it harder to learn certain perceptual-motor tasks, such as the serial reaction time task and tracking tasks (including the rotary pursuit task). On the other hand, individuals with Parkinson's can learn some skills, such as mirror reading, that cause problems for those with Huntington's (Koenig, Thomas-Anterion, & Laurent, 1999). This suggests that although both diseases affect processing in the basal ganglia and cerebral cortex, the damage each causes leads to different but overlapping deficits in skill-memory systems.

Currently, the main treatments for Parkinson's disease are drug therapies for counteracting the reduced levels of dopamine and surgical procedures aimed at counteracting the disruption caused by lack of dopamine in the basal ganglia. One recently developed surgical technique, **deep brain stimulation,** seems to hint at a way of curing Parkinson's disease, but scientists do not yet know exactly why it works. It involves delivering an electrical current through one or more electrodes implanted deep in the patient's brain. Neurosurgeons place the end of the electrodes near neurons that are part of the basal ganglia–cortical loop (for example, in the thalamus or basal ganglia), as shown in Figure 4.17. When electrical current from an implanted stimulator passes through these electrodes, many of the motor symptoms associated with Parkinson's disease, such as

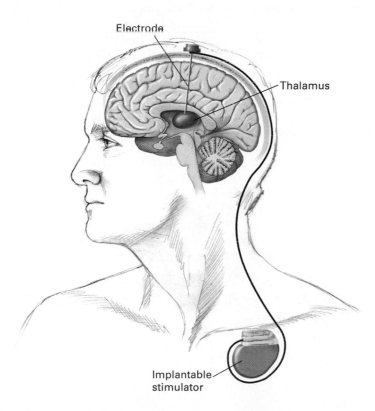

Electrode

Thalamus

Implantable stimulator

Figure 4.17 Deep brain stimulation for treatment of Parkinson's disease To perform deep brain stimulation, neurosurgeons position the tip of an electrode in a brain location (such as the thalamus) that, on stimulation, will maximally interfere with electrical transmission in the basal ganglia–cortical loop. An implantable stimulator passes current through this electrode to temporarily relieve symptoms of Parkinson's disease.

tremors, disappear within seconds, although they eventually return. One theory of how this technique works is that without proper levels of dopamine, interactions between neurons in the cerebral cortex and the basal ganglia become locked into fixed patterns (Dowsey-Limousin & Pollak, 2001). This creates a situation similar to the endless back and forth of young children arguing (Child 1: "No, you be quiet!" Child 2: "No, you be quiet!" Child 1: "No, you . . ."—ad infinitum) and disrupts the control of movements. Stimulation from the electrode is thought to quiet both brain regions, allowing normal brain activity to resume. Deep brain stimulation is still in the early stages of development, but it illustrates how increased knowledge of the brain systems underlying skill memories can help doctors treat these systems when the systems go awry.

CONCLUSION

Kissing requires both perceptual-motor and cognitive skills, acquired and improved through observation and practice. Differentiating the cognitive aspects from the perceptual-motor ones can be difficult, as this chapter shows. Cognitive skills often depend on perceptual-motor skills (and vice versa), and may even become transformed into perceptual-motor skills over time.

Certainly, one cognitive aspect of kissing is the use of social skills to motivate someone to want to kiss you or be kissed by you. Once you solve this problem—which in some cases may be as strategically challenging as a chess game—you face the perceptual-motor challenge of coordinating your own kissing movements with those of your partner, based on what you perceive of your partner's maneuvers. Your skills at this point will depend on how much and how often you have practiced, as well as on the types of feedback you have received from past partners. Perhaps you are in the cognitive stage of learning to kiss, still thinking carefully about each move you make; or perhaps in the associative stage, feeling comfortable with your performance but knowing there is room for improvement. Possibly you are at the autonomous stage of skill acquisition, having become an expert—your kissing depends on various motor programs that you perform without thinking. If you are an experienced kisser, the skill memories you rely on are dependent on the coordination of several brain regions, including the basal ganglia, the cerebral cortex, and the cerebellum.

In short, there is more to kissing than simply recalling and executing a fixed series of movements. Kissing is an open skill in which the recent actions and reactions of your partner provide important feedback that you can use to guide your own actions. Keeping track of what has happened in the recent past is thus a key component of skillful kissing. The ability to maintain and flexibly use memories of the recent past depends on different brain regions from those we have focused on thus far in our discussion of skill learning and performance. You will learn more about these kinds of memories and their neural substrates in the next chapter, on working memory.

Key Points

- A skill is an ability that an individual can improve over time through practice. Skills that depend on performing predefined movements that, ideally, never vary are called closed skills. Open skills are those that require performing movements in response to predictions about ongoing changes in circumstances.

- Practice can decrease the effects of previous experience on motor performance and increase the effects of genetic influences. Feedback about performance, or knowledge of results, is critical to the effectiveness of practice.

- The power law of learning states that with extended practice, the amount of time required to complete a task decreases at a diminishing rate. This "law of diminishing returns" holds for a wide range of cognitive and perceptual-motor skills.

- Massed practice, or concentrated, continuous practice, generally produces better performance in the short term, but practice that is spaced out over several sessions leads to better skill retention in the long run. Similarly, constant practice, which means repetition of the skill under fixed conditions, does not improve performance as much as variable practice, practicing the skill in varying contexts.

- Implicit learning, which is the learning of skills without an awareness of learning, is often tested with the serial reaction time task. Implicit learning is also studied in patients with amnesia.

- Thorndike's identical elements theory proposes that the degree to which learned abilities are transferred to novel situations depends on the number of elements that are identical between the learning context and the novel situation. When an individual no longer uses a learned skill, it is lost in a process called skill decay.

- Changes in skill memories produced by extended practice may occur in stages: the cognitive stage, when the skill is encoded through active thinking; the associative stage, when the skill is performed using stereotyped actions; and the autonomous stage, when the skill has become a motor program.

- Skill learning depends on three brain areas: the basal ganglia, the cerebral cortex, and the cerebellum. Output signals from the basal ganglia are sent mainly to the thalamus (affecting interactions between thalamic and cortical neurons) and to the brainstem (influencing signals sent to the spinal cord).

- Studies of how rats with basal ganglia damage learn to navigate mazes suggest that the basal ganglia are critical for learning to generate motor responses based on environmental cues.

- Neural response patterns in the basal ganglia change during the learning of a perceptual-motor skill, suggesting that representations of that skill are dynamically modified as learning proceeds. The basal ganglia are also activated when people learn cognitive skills such as the weather prediction task.

- Regions of the somatosensory cortex and motor cortex needed to perform a particular skill expand with practice, but regions that are less relevant show fewer, if any, changes.

- An intact cerebellum is necessary for performing many perceptual-motor skills. The cerebellum is especially critical for learning movement sequences that require precise timing, such as dancing, and tasks that involve aiming at or tracking a target.

- Whereas the cerebellum is critical for timing, the cerebral cortex is mainly involved in controlling complex actions, and the basal ganglia link sensory events to responses.

- Apraxia results from damage to cortical regions, most commonly from a head injury or stroke. Patients with apraxia have difficulty producing purposeful movements.

- Skill learning by patients with apraxia suggests that the damage interferes with control and execution of skills more than with the learning and recall of skills. Transcranial magnetic stimulation allows researchers to simulate apraxia in healthy volunteers and study the effects of cortical disruption on skill memory.

- Huntington's disease is an inherited disorder that causes gradual damage to neurons throughout the brain, but especially in the basal ganglia and the cerebral cortex. Patients with Huntington's typically show large deficits in perceptual-motor skill learning that seem to be related to problems with retrieval and decreased storage capacity. Scientists have made progress identifying Huntington's through genetic markers, but prevention and treatment of deficits are still in the early stages of research.

- Parkinson's disease involves both disruptions in the normal functioning of the basal ganglia and progressive deterioration of motor control. Patients with Parkinson's show increasing degrees of muscle tremors and rigidity. Deep brain stimulation, which delivers an electrical current to the basal ganglia–cortical loop, may offer treatment possibilities.

Key Terms

apraxia, p. 159
associative stage, p. 143
autonomous stage, p. 143
basal ganglia, p. 145
closed skill, p. 127
cognitive skill, p. 127
cognitive stage, p. 142
constant practice, p. 135
deep brain stimulation, p. 163

expert, p. 130
Huntington's disease, p. 161
identical elements theory,
    p. 141
implicit learning, p. 136
knowledge of results, p. 133
massed practice, p. 135
mirror reading, p. 157
mirror tracing, p. 156

motor programs, p. 141
open skill, p. 127
Parkinson's disease, p. 162
perceptual-motor skill, p. 127
power law of learning, p. 134
rotary pursuit task, p. 130
serial reaction time task, p. 136
skill, p. 126
skill decay, p. 139

spaced practice, p. 135
talent, p. 130
transcranial magnetic stimula-
    tion, p. 161
transfer specificity, p. 141
variable practice, p. 135

Concept Check

1. A teenage girl wants to improve her kissing skills but doesn't want to practice with lots of different boys because of the possible harm to her reputation. What are some strategies she might try for learning these skills?

2. A graduate student who believes his pet tarantula is exceptionally bright wants to prove to the world that spiders can reason and solve problems. How might he convince others that he is correct?

3. Some researchers believe that the right kinds and amounts of practice can make anyone an expert. What sort of experimental evidence might convince these researchers that there is such a thing as talent?

4. According to Fitts's model of skill learning, individuals must go through an initial cognitive stage before they can master a skill. Does this imply that for a fish to learn to press a lever, it must first think about what is required to perform the task?

5. Neuroscience research has shown that regions the in somatosensory cortex and motor cortex expand in parallel with learning of perceptual-motor skills. Does this mean that practicing a skill causes regions of cortex not involved in performing that skill to shrink?

6. Patients with Huntington's or Parkinson's disease are often also diagnosed as having apraxia. Why might this be?

Answers to Test Your Knowledge

Mechanisms of Synaptic Plasticity
Open and Closed Skills

1. Open: balancing requires continuous feedback.

2. Closed: swimming movements are predefined, and inputs are stable.

3. Open, if skilled: kissing requires continuous feedback.

4. Open: fishing requires accurate prediction of changing inputs.

5. Depends on the fish and the insect. Closed, if the insect falls into the water; open, if the insect lives underwater.

6. Depends on the type of music. Closed, if classical; open, if jazz.

7. Closed: dart-throwing movements are predefined, and inputs are stable.

Further Reading

Anderson, J. (Ed.). (1981). *Cognitive skills and their acquisition.* Hillsdale, NJ: Lawrence Erlbaum. • A collection of papers on how cognitive skills develop over long periods of practice, the power law, algebraic skills, automaticity, and problem-solving skills. These papers represent some of the best work in the study of cognitive skills and provide a good historical review of progress up to the 1980s.

Doyon, J., Penhune, V., & Ungerleider, L.G. (2003). Distinct contribution of the cortico-striatal and cortico-cerebellar systems to motor skill learning. *Neuropsychologia, 41,* 252–262. • A review paper that focuses on neuroimaging studies in healthy humans, documenting the functional neuroanatomy and neural plasticity associated with the encoding, storage, and recall of skill memories. The authors review evidence that the cerebellum and basal ganglia contribute differently to learning of different perceptual-motor skills.

Halbert, C. (2003). *The ultimate boxer: understanding the sport and skills of boxing.* Brentwood, TN: Impact Seminars • A practical guide to the skills involved in boxing, including practice techniques for improving both the cognitive and perceptual-motor aspects of the sport.

Rose, D. (1996). *A multilevel approach to the study of motor control and learning.* San Francisco: Benjamin Cummings. • This book includes chapters on motor control, action planning, and sensory processing during action, and on how these processes influence learning. The author also discusses strategies for maximizing the efficacy of practice sessions.

Wichmann, T. (1998). A neuropsychological theory of motor skill learning. *Psychological Review, 105,* 558–584. • This review article uses evidence from patients with impairments in motor skill learning to support a theory of skill learning that takes into account mental practice, the representation of motor skills, and the interaction of conscious and unconscious processes.

CHAPTER 5

Working Memory and Executive Control

T IS TUESDAY AT 9:10 a.m., AND ROBERTA must rush if she is going to make it across campus in time for her 9:30 a.m. French class and still have time to do several errands along the way. She has only 20 minutes to get cash from the bank machine, sign up for the afternoon yoga class, and drop off her biology homework, which is due by 10 a.m. Before heading out the door, Roberta grabs the various things she will need for the rest of the day, including her yoga mat and her organic chemistry textbook (for last-minute cramming for this afternoon's quiz). The sign-up sheet for the yoga class is in the student center, which is near the biology building and close to where her French class is being held. It is quicker, she figures, to go to the bank machine first, as that requires just a short detour from her dorm room. Punching in her four-digit PIN number, she gets some quick cash from the ATM and then heads to the student center, signs up for yoga, and then starts to walk to French class when, *zut alors!*, she realizes she forgot one of her errands. She doubles back quickly to the biology department, drops off her homework there, and then heads on to French class.

As she walks toward the French building, Roberta remembers that today's class has been moved from the usual classroom on the third floor to the large auditorium in the basement where they will have a guest speaker. She is so used to running up the stairs every Tuesday and Thursday that she has to struggle to remember that today she needs to bypass those stairs and take the elevator to the basement instead.

Slipping into the back of the auditorium, Roberta listens with half an ear to the speaker. Some of the material he is presenting is new, but when he covers topics that are familiar from her own past reading, she switches her attention to her organic chemistry textbook,

Behavioral Processes
Transient Memories
Working Memory
The Central Executive
Unsolved Mysteries - Is Working Memory the Key to Intelligence?

Brain Substrates
Behavioral Consequences of Frontal-Lobe Damage
Frontal Brain Activity during Working-Memory Tasks
Mapping Baddeley's Model onto PFC Anatomy
Prefrontal Control of Long-Term Declarative Memory
Test Your Knowledge - Functional Neuroanatomy of the Prefrontal Cortex

Clinical Perspectives
Schizophrenia
Attention-Deficit/Hyperactivity Disorder
Learning and Memory in Everyday Life - Improving Your Working Memory

lying discretely in her lap, so she can study for this afternoon's exam. It isn't the perfect situation for studying chemistry or for learning about French literature, but by switching back and forth between them, she manages to keep up with both tasks at once.

A day in the life of a college student is taxing, indeed. To keep track of all her activities and commitments, and deal efficiently with emergencies and last-minute changes, Roberta needs something like a mental blackboard. In fact, that is a good description of her working memory, the active and temporary representation of information that is maintained for the short term in Roberta's mind to help her think and allow her to decide what to do next. As she attends to her various responsibilities during the day, Roberta's ability to control the flow of information in and out of her working memory is critical to the multi-tasking and planning she has to do to thrive during her sophomore year of college. This manipulation of working memory to facilitate setting goals, planning, task switching, stimulus selection, response inhibition, and ultimately the achievement of goals is called executive control.

5.1 Behavioral Processes

Chapter 3 discussed long-term memories that may last for hours, days, or even years. In contrast, the memories we focus on in this chapter are transient—existing briefly for seconds or minutes at most. These temporary memories are crucial for performing many high-level cognitive functions, such as planning, organization, and task management.

Transient Memories

Transient memories are short lasting and temporary, sometimes persisting for only a few seconds. We will discuss here two types of transient memory—sensory memory and short-term memory—which represent the first two stages through which information from the world enters our consciousness, and potentially becomes part of our long-term memories.

Sensory Memory

Sensory memories are brief, transient sensations of what you have just perceived when you have seen, heard, or tasted something. Considerable research has been devoted to understanding how sensory memories are held in the mind so that they are accessible for further processing. Take a quick look at the table of letters in Figure 5.1; just glance at it for a second, no more. Now, without looking back at the figure, try to remember as many of the letters as you can. You probably only recalled four or five letters, or about 30–40% of the total array.

Based on this exercise, you might imagine that four or five items are the limit of your **visual sensory memory,** the temporary storage for information perceived by your visual system. Perhaps, however, you felt as if your eyes saw more than four or five letters, but you just couldn't recall more of them. In a seminal 1960 paper, George Sperling conducted a study confirming that you probably did, very briefly, register more than just the few items you were able to recall. Sperling presented people with a 3-by-4 visual array much like that shown in Figure 5.1. He then played one of three tones after the array was removed. A high tone indicated that participants were to report the first row of letters, a medium tone corresponded to the middle row, and a low tone corresponded to the bottom row.

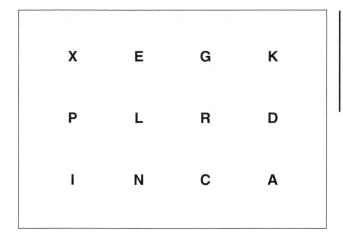

Figure 5.1. The Sperling task These three rows of four letters each are similar to the array George Sperling used in his studies of visual sensory memory (Sperling, 1960). How many of the letters did you remember after glancing at them for a second?

When this partial-report procedure was used, participants were able to report about 75% of the letters. Note that this is about double the number of letters recalled when people are simply asked to report as many letters as they can after the array is removed. What accounts for this doubled recall in Sperling's partial-report procedure? Sperling interpreted it as meaning that people have a visual memory that persists for a very short time—less than a second—but includes *all* the items recently seen.

This rapidly decaying visual sensory memory was called **iconic memory** by Ulric Neisser, who argued that it is critical for recognizing and processing briefly presented information (Neisser, 1967). If there is iconic memory for visual information, you might imagine that there would also be iconic memory for other sensory modalities, such as touch, smell, and hearing. Indeed, there have been studies showing similar phenomena with auditory memory (Moray, Bates, & Barnett, 1965). Most likely there is a sensory memory for each modality, which lasts very briefly and encodes incoming sensory stimuli in a raw form that can then be processed and stored.

Each of these sensory memories, including the visual iconic memory, can be thought of as an information *buffer*, a temporary storage system for information that may subsequently undergo additional processing. We will now discuss how these sensory memories are used, manipulated, and stored.

Short-Term Memory

Consider the common experience of looking up a phone number and then repeating it over and over to yourself as you prepare to press the buttons on the phone. The phone number has already been recognized and registered by sensory memory, but now it is the job of your **short-term memory** to maintain this information temporarily through active rehearsal. Your ability to hold onto this information is limited in several ways. First, your memory is limited in capacity; a 10-digit phone number is a lot to keep in mind, and even more so if you also have to remember a 4-digit extension. In Chapter 1 you read about the classic studies of George Miller, who in the early 1950s suggested that the capacity of short-term memory is about 7 items, a number he described as "The Magic Number 7" because it recurred so frequently in studies of memory capacity (Miller, 1956). Actually, Miller argued that there are a range of short-term memory capacities centered on 5 items but ranging from about 5 to 9 in most people (with the lower limits being more common).

Short-term memory is also limited to what you can pay attention to. If you get distracted by something else, you are likely to forget all or some of the

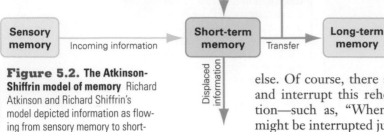

Figure 5.2. The Atkinson-Shiffrin model of memory Richard Atkinson and Richard Shiffrin's model depicted information as flowing from sensory memory to short-term memory (STM) to long-term memory (LTM).

phone number as you walk across the room to the phone: that's why you rehearse it over and over in your head. By continuing to rehearse the number, you could potentially remember it indefinitely, as long as you do nothing else. Of course, there are plenty of things that could distract you and interrupt this rehearsal. If your roommate asks you a question—such as, "When is the chemistry final?"—your rehearsal might be interrupted just long enough for you to forget some or all of the phone number. If you do forget it, you have to go back to the Internet phone book and look up the number again.

For many years, psychologists described the brain as having three distinct memory stores: iconic (sensory) memory, short-term memory (STM), and long-term memory (LTM). This view was detailed in an influential model by Richard Atkinson and Richard Shiffrin, diagrammed in Figure 5.2 (Atkinson & Shiffrin, 1968).

Their model of the interaction between short-term memory and long-term memory proposed that incoming information arrives in short-term memory after initially passing through a sensory-based iconic memory store. Short-term memory is a halfway station of sorts, where new information stops for a while before moving on to long-term memory storage. The main idea portrayed in this model is that information in short-term memory must be maintained by active rehearsal but can be displaced by new information or distractions (like a question from your roommate).

Transferring Information from Short-Term Memory to Long-Term Memory

According to Atkinson and Shiffrin's model, repeated rehearsal loops are required to maintain information in short-term memory (see Figure 5.2). Sufficient maintenance leads automatically (through some unspecified mechanism) to the transfer of the information from short-term memory to long-term memory.

But rehearsal doesn't ensure long-term storage. How many times have you rehearsed a phone number or a name, only to have it slip away as soon as you were distracted? Remember that chemistry exam that Roberta was cramming for during French class? For her long-term understanding and mastery of chemistry, which of the following two methods do you think would work better? She could either memorize the key chemistry terms and their definitions through rote repetition, or she could work on the Test Your Chemical Knowledge exercises at the end of the chapter. A series of studies by Fergus Craik and Endel Tulving illustrated the importance of **depth of processing,** the level of activity devoted to processing new information. The more actively you go about processing new information, by applying it in meaningful ways, the more likely you are to remember it. In contrast, passive rehearsal through repetition has very little effect on whether or not information is later recalled from long-term memory (Craik & Watkins, 1973). Thus, while passive rehearsal is good for keeping information in short-term memory, Craik and Tulving argued that it is not sufficient for transferring the information along to long-term memory.

"These drugs will affect your short-term memory, so you better pay me now."

Paul Taylor/CartoonResource.com

In one study that illustrated the depth-of-processing effect, Craik and Tulving gave people a series of words and asked them to make one of three judgments for each: a *shallow*-level judgment, as to whether the word was printed in upper- or lowercase letters; an *intermediate*- level judgment, about whether or not the word rhymed with another word; and a *deep*-level judgment, as to whether the word fit logically into a particular sentence (Craik & Tulving, 1975). As shown in Figure 5.3, there was a direct relationship between the depth of processing and the proportion of words that were recalled. This means that while rote memorization of chemistry words might be useful for short-term recall and performance on an upcoming exam, Roberta's ability to master chemistry for the long term would be better served by doing the homework exercises in the textbook.

As a concept, depth of processing was important because it lead to many testable predictions (as in the study that produced Figure 5.3) and because it refuted the prevailing view in the field, illustrated by the Atkinson and Shiffrin model of Figure 5.2, which had suggested that passive rehearsal alone was sufficient to transfer information from short-term memory into long-term memory. What still remains a mystery, however, is *why* deep processing enhances storage more than rote rehearsal does. One possible reason is that deep processing creates a richer web of connections among stored memories, which facilitates later retrieval.

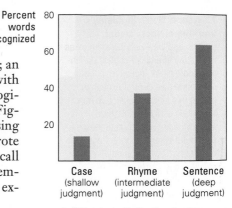

Figure 5.3. Depth of processing A study by Craik and Tulving measured participants' recollection of words (by recognition) as a function of the type of initial processing the words had been given (Craik & Tulving, 1975). Shallow judgments (of upper- or lowercase) produced the poorest recognition, intermediate judgments (of rhyme) produced moderate recall, and deep judgments (of sentence logic) produced the highest rate of recognition.

Working Memory

Craik and Tulving's studies demonstrated that maintenance of information through passive rehearsal is *not* enough to cause the information to be transferred from short-term to long-term memory. Nevertheless, rehearsal is an important part of how we keep information active and accessible within short-term memory. As you walk across the room from your computer—where you found the Internet phone listing—to the phone, you rehearse the number to keep from forgetting it. Your goal isn't necessarily to store the phone number in your long-term memory (although that might be useful for future reference); rather, your immediate aim is to remember the number just long enough to make the call correctly.

Short-term memory used in this way serves as a buffer, or temporary holding station, for maintaining information for a brief period before it is manipulated or otherwise utilized to affect behavior. When short-term memory is maintained and manipulated in this fashion, it is referred to as our **working memory.** The maintenance and manipulation of working memory is described as the **executive control** of working memory.

Baddeley's Working-Memory Model

Alan Baddeley, an English psychologist, proposed what is currently the most influential model of working memory, illustrated in Figure 5.4 (Baddeley & Hitch, 1974). Baddeley's model includes two independent short-term memory buffers, the visuo-spatial sketchpad and the phonological loop. The **visuo-spatial sketchpad** holds visual and spatial images for manipulation. The **phonological loop** does the same for auditory memories, maintaining them by means of internal (subvocal) speech rehearsal (much like a "loop" of recording tape that goes around and around, playing the same song over and over). A key feature of Baddeley's theory is that visuo-spatial information and verbal-phonological information are stored separately in working memory.

A third component of Baddeley's model is the **central executive,** which monitors and manipulates both of these working-memory buffers, providing

Figure 5.4. Baddeley's working-memory model This model describes working memory consisting of a visuo-spatial sketch pad and a phonological loop, both controlled by a central executive. Baddeley's model makes two important kinds of distinction. First, it distinguishes between two processes: manipulation and maintenance. Second, its two buffers are material-specific: one stores verbal material and the other stores object and location material.

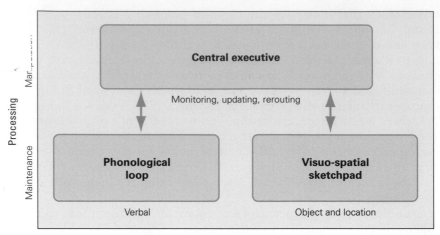

executive control of working memory. The central executive's manipulations include adding to and deleting from the items in the buffers, selecting among the items in order to guide behavior, retrieving information from long-term memory, and transferring information from the visuo-spatial sketchpad and phonological loop to long-term memory.

Figure 5.4 calls attention to two important distinctions in Baddeley's model. First, it distinguishes between two general *processes* of working memory: manipulation (which depends on the central executive) and maintenance (which requires only rehearsal of information in the two memory buffers). Second, it identifies the memory buffers as being *material-specific*: one stores verbal material and the other stores object and location material. We will discuss next the two memory buffers, the phonological loop and the visuo-spatial sketchpad.

The Phonological Loop

Read the following seven numbers: 5 6 2 8 1 7 3. Now look away for 5 seconds and then repeat the list out loud. How did you solve the problem of remembering the numbers in this digit-span test? Most likely, you rehearsed them silently in your mind during the interval. In fact, if you didn't rehearse the numbers, you probably would have been unable to remember them. Without rehearsal, people can hold only about 2 seconds' worth of information in their phonological memory. Because of this time limit, people with slow rates of speech but normal intelligence do worse on short-term verbal memory tasks than people of normal intelligence who speak at a normal rate (Raine et al., 1991). (A person's internal speech proceeds at about the same rate as the person's speech spoken aloud.) This internal, unspoken speech used during rehearsal is key to the phonological loop and verbal working memory.

In fact, if this internal rehearsal is disrupted or eliminated, phonological storage cannot occur. For instance, if you were to say out loud, "good morning, good morning…" during the delay period while you were trying to remember the list of numbers in the digit-span test, your ability to internally rehearse would be greatly disrupted, impairing your performance on the task.

Additional evidence concerning internal rehearsal in short-term memory comes from studies where people are asked to remember lists of words. For example, which list do you think would be easier to remember?

bat, hit, top, cat, door

university, expedition, conversation, destination, auditorium

Most people would say the first is easier. As the length of the words increases, the number of words you can remember declines; this is known as the **word-length effect.** Short, one-syllable words like "bat" and "hit" are easier to rehearse in working memory than longer, multisyllable words like "university" and "auditorium." Longer words take longer to rehearse (Baddeley, Thomson, & Buchanan, 1975). Based on studies of phonological memory span, Baddeley and colleagues estimated that the average person's phonological loop can retain approximately 2 seconds' worth of speech.

The Visuo-Spatial Sketchpad

Baddeley's model of working memory also includes a visuo-spatial sketchpad (see Figure 5.4) which is a mental workspace for storing and manipulating visual and spatial information. Here's an example of it in use: without writing anything down, picture a 4-by-4 grid (16 squares) in your mind and imagine a "1" in the square that is the second column of the second row. Then put a 2 to the right of that. Then in the square above the 2, put a 3, and to the right of that put a 4. Below the 4, put a 5 and below that, a 6, and then to the left of that, a 7. Now, what number is just above the 7? To correctly answer this question ("2") you had to use your visuo-spatial sketchpad.

Just as the phonological loop has a 2 second time limit, the visuo-spatial sketchpad also has a limited capacity. The two capacities, however, are independent—filling up one does not much affect the capacity of the other. Dual-task experiments, in which subjects are asked to perform a primary task using one buffer (for example, to maintain information in the visuo-spatial sketchpad) while simultaneously carrying out a secondary task using the other (such as retaining an auditory list of words in the phonological loop), provide evidence for the independence of these two memory buffers.

For example, Lee Brooks used a dual-task paradigm in which people were shown a block-capital letter "F" and were then asked to visualize this letter (from memory) and imagine an asterisk traveling around the edge of it (Figure 5.5a; Brooks, 1968). When the imaginary asterisk reaches a corner, it turns left or right to continue following the outline of the letter F. At each such turning point, the people were asked to indicate whether or not the asterisk was at an extreme point on the F (for example, the point at the F's upper right), rather than at some intermediate point (such as one of the inner corners). The crucial manipulation was that the participants were divided into three groups, and each group was assigned a different way of signaling. The *vocal group* signaled their answer to each question with a verbal "yes" or "no," the *tapping group* signaled with one tap for yes and two taps for no, and the *pointing group* pointed to a visual array of "Y"s and

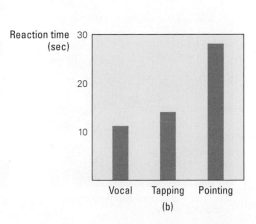

(a)

(b)

Figure 5.5. A dual-task experiment (a) Participants were asked to imagine an asterisk traveling along the periphery of a letter "F." Whenever the asterisk was turning a corner, they were to signal whether it was turning at an extreme corner rather than at some intermediate corner. (b) Reaction times varied depending on whether subjects signaled vocally (fastest times), by tapping (intermediate times), or by pointing (slowest times). Adapted from Brooks, 1968.

"N"s on a screen. Of the three groups, the pointing group performed most slowly, suggesting that the visuo-spatial demands of pointing interfered with the visuo-spatial memory task (Figure 5.5b).

Because visual memory can be easily studied in a wide range of species, it has become the sensory memory of choice for many carefully controlled laboratory experiments on working memory in animals. For example, in an early study of spatial working memory, Carlyle Jacobsen trained monkeys on a delayed spatial-response task (Jacobsen, 1936). Each monkey watched food being placed in either the left or the right of two bins. Next, an opaque screen came down and blocked the monkey's view of the bins for several seconds or minutes. When the screen was removed, the bins now had covers hiding the food. To be marked correct, the monkey first had to remember in which bin the food had been stored and then displace the cover of just that bin to retrieve the reward.

The **delayed nonmatch-to-sample** task is another test of visual memory. Each trial involves remembering some novel object. Figure 5.6a shows Pygmalion, a rhesus monkey in Mortimer Mishkin's laboratory at the National Institute of Mental Health, being shown a novel "sample" object, a blue ring, under which he finds a food reward, such as a peanut or a banana pellet. Next, an opaque black screen obscures Pygmalion's view (Figure 5.6b) for a delay period which may range from seconds to minutes, depending on the experiment design. During this delay period, the experimenters introduce a new object, a red disk. When the screen is raised, Pygmalion sees both objects, one on the right and the other on the left. As shown in Figure 5.6c, Pygmalion has learned that a reward will now be found under the red disk because this is the novel object, a "nonmatch" to the sample object he saw previously. Training on this delayed nonmatch-to-sample task continues for several trials, each of which involves two objects not used in previous trials. Thus, the next trial might involve a yellow box as the sample and a green disk as the novel object. Over many such trials, the correct answer is sometimes on the left and sometimes on the right, so that spatial location will not be a useful cue.

Because each trial uses a new set of objects, the monkeys must learn to remember which unique sample they saw previously and hold this memory in their visuo-spatial memory buffer until presented with the choice of that previous sample and the novel object.

Figure 5.6. Delayed nonmatch-to-sample task (a) A monkey is shown a sample object, a blue ring, and finds a reward under it. (b) During the delay period, an opaque black screen blocks the monkey's view of any test objects. (c) The monkey is shown two objects, the blue ring from before (the sample) and a new object, a red disk. The food reward is hidden under the new object, the nonmatch to the original sample. The monkey chooses the nonmatch.

A. Monkey moves sample object for reward.

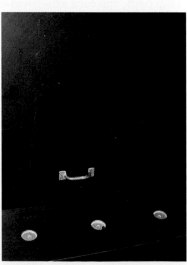

B. Screen obscures monkey's view during delay.

C. Monkey chooses novel nonmatch object.

Courtesy of David Yu, Mortimer Mishkin, and Janita Turchi, Laboratory of Neuropsychology, NIMH/NIH/DHHS

The Central Executive

Most of the tasks described in the preceding section require the person or animal simply to maintain some word, digit, object, sound, or location in working memory during a delay period. But there is much more to working memory than just the maintenance of phonological or visuo-spatial memories: there is the far more complex and involved process of *manipulating* working memory.

We saw earlier, for example, that Roberta has to keep several of her day's goals in mind: get cash, prepare for yoga, study for chemistry, and listen to a French lecture. Balancing these multiple goals often requires her to switch her thoughts back and forth between them as the situation requires: while studying for her chemistry exam during French class she jumps back and forth between the two topics, reading a bit of chemistry, then listening to some of the French lecture. Her working memory is constantly being updated and reorganized to accomplish different and competing tasks. New tasks are constantly added, as when Roberta's boyfriend text-messages her to find out where she wants to go for dinner. All of these functions require the executive-control functions of her working memory's central executive.

Of the three components of Baddeley's model, the central executive is the most important, the most complex, and the least well understood. What is common to all the functions of the central executive is that they involve the *manipulation* of information in short-term memory, including adding or removing items, reordering items, and using working memory to guide other behaviors. Through this manipulation of information held in short-term memory, the central executive goes beyond simple rehearsal to become, in effect, the *working* component of working memory. Researchers have found evidence of executive control in many cognitive functions, including, but not limited to, (1) controlled updating of short-term memory buffers, (2) setting goals and planning, (3) task switching, and (4) stimulus selection and response inhibition. We will discuss each of these in the next section.

Controlled Updating of Short-Term Memory Buffers

The central executive for working memory functions much like a manager at a large corporation who is responsible for assigning specific people to certain jobs at particular times. On Monday, he might tell Mike to work the front desk and Stephanie to work on the sales floor. Come Tuesday, however, he might fire Mike, promote Stephanie to the front desk, and then hire Kristy to work on the sales floor. In an analogous fashion, the central executive for working memory updates working memory by receiving and evaluating sensory information, moving items into and retrieving them from long-term memory, and deciding which memories are needed for which tasks.

To study the controlled updating of working memory, researchers often use what is called a 2-back test. In a 2-back test, a participant is read a seemingly random list of items, usually numbers. A certain item—let's say the number 7—is designated as the "target." Whenever the target number 7 is read, the participant is to respond with the number that was read *two numbers previously* (hence the name 2-back). Sound tough? Try it. If the numbers read aloud are 4 8 3 7 8 2 5 6 7 8 0 2 4 6 7 3 9…, what would the correct responses be? (Answer: "8" after the first 7, "5" after the second 7, and "4" after the third 7.)

To succeed at this task, the participant must constantly keep track of the last two numbers that were read: the 1-back and 2-back numbers. As each new number is read, a new 1-back number must be stored, and the old 1-back number must be shifted to the 2-back slot, replacing the previous 2-back number in working memory. In addition, each number must be checked as it is read, to see if it is the target number. If it *is* the target number, the participant has to respond with the 2-back number; if it isn't the target number, the participant says nothing. Not easy!

Performing the 2-back task requires active maintenance of many kinds of items in working memory. First are the target number and the rules for performing the task, both of which stay constant throughout the experiment. Second, the last two numbers that were read must always be remembered in case the next number is the target number. These two items change in identity, priority, or both, with each new number that is read, and must be regularly updated in working memory.

What might happen to your performance on this type of task if you were asked to repeat the 3-back or 4-back number instead of the 2-back number? Although the 2-back task is the most commonly used variation, this class of tasks is generally called *N*-back because *N* can be any number. The larger *N* is, the greater the challenge. The *N*-back task taps into many aspects of the central executive's manipulation of working memory, including online storage of recent information, selective attention, remembering task demands, and updating and reorganizing stored items. For this reason, it is considered an excellent tool for assessing the central executive. We will discuss several experimental studies of the *N*-back task in the Brain Substrates section.

A more common situation faced by your own central executive is the need to keep track of the various everyday tasks you need to perform: What have you done already? What remains to be accomplished? For example, if you have lost your eyeglasses *somewhere* in your home, you might search every room for them. While it may not matter which rooms you search first, you do want to keep track of the rooms so as not to waste time searching where you have already been. Self-ordered tasks that ask people to keep track of their previous responses (analogous to keeping track of the rooms they already searched) are another tool that can be used to assess the central executive's manipulation of working memory.

Michael Petrides and a colleague at McGill University in Canada used self-ordered memory tasks in studying the behavioral and neural bases of working memory. In the human version of their task, people were shown a stack of cards, each containing eight items, as in Figure 5.7a (Petrides & Milner, 1982; Petrides, 2000). (In some versions the items are abstract designs or words rather than rep-

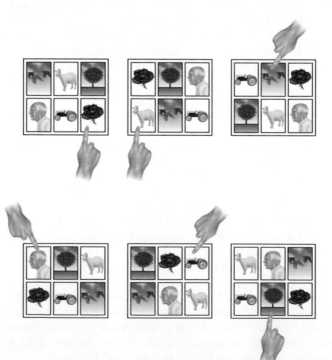

Figure 5.7. Petrides' self-ordered memory task for humans Sample cards from a self-ordered search task for humans (Petrides & Milner, 1982). Participants are presented with a stack of cards, each containing all the items in the target set but in different random order. The task: the participant must point to a different item on each card without repeating any of the items. Adapted from Petrides, 2000.

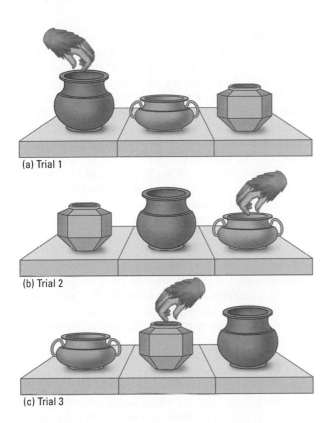

(a) Trial 1

(b) Trial 2

(c) Trial 3

Figure 5.8. Petrides' self-ordered memory task for monkeys In a monkey version of the self-ordered memory task, (a) the monkey sees three distinct containers and selects a reward from one of them. (b), (c) Their order is shuffled on each trial, and the monkey must remember which containers have had rewards removed so that on subsequent trials the monkey does not pick a previously chosen (and hence empty) container.

resentational line drawings of different objects.) Each card contained the same eight items, but the order of their placement on each card was different. Thus, the drawing of a tractor that appears third from the top of the first column in Figure 5.7a appears second from the top of the second column in part b.

In trial 1, a participant is shown the first card and is asked to choose one of the eight items on it (as in Figure 5.7a). This card is then flipped over. Next, in trial 2, the participant is shown the second card (with the same eight items in a different order) and is asked to choose any of the seven items that have not yet been selected (as in Figure 5.7b). This second card is then flipped over. Then the participant is shown the third card and must pick any of the six remaining items that were not chosen on the previous two cards. This self-ordered task continues until the participant has pointed to eight different items without repeating any.

This task is appealing to researchers who want to understand working memory in both human and nonhuman primates because it can also be studied in monkeys, as shown in Figure 5.8 (Petrides & Milner, 1982). On the first trial, a monkey sees a row of three nonmatching containers, each of which contains a reward, and selects the reward from one of them. Following this step, an opaque screen is placed between the monkey and the containers for 10 seconds, and the containers are shuffled so that on the second trial the monkey sees the same containers in a new order. Now the monkey must choose one of the other containers in order to get a reward. Like the human self-ordered task described above, this task requires the monkey to remember the items chosen previously. On the third trial, the monkey has to choose again, with only one remaining container still baited with a reward. Because this kind of working-memory task can be performed by both monkeys and humans, it is useful for comparative studies of the neural substrates of working memory, as will be described later in the Brain Substrates section.

Setting Goals and Planning

As Roberta prepared for the school day ahead of her, she had to be aware of her immediate goals (getting to French class on time in the morning) as well as her goals for later that afternoon (taking yoga). To make sure she could take a yoga class in the afternoon, she had to (1) search through her closet to find her yoga mat and (2) stop by the student center to sign up for the yoga class. Only then would she go to French class (where she intends to also work on her organic chemistry). Roberta's busy schedule requires her to keep track of many goals at once and to juggle them in her mind as the day passes, noting which tasks have been accomplished and which are left to be done, and of those left to be done, which should be done next. Keeping track of goals, planning how to achieve them, and determining priorities all draw heavily on the central executive of working memory.

The French mathematician Edouard Lucas invented a game back in 1883 that requires many of these same planning and goal-setting abilities. The game is based on an ancient legend about a temple in India, where the puzzle was used to develop mental discipline in young priests. A stack of 64 gold disks, each slightly smaller than the one beneath, were all stacked on a large pole. The young priests' assignment was to transfer all 64 disks from the first pole to a second and, finally, to a third pole, by moving 1 disk at a time and only placing smaller disks on top of larger disks. According to the legend, if any priest ever solved the problem, the temple would crumble into dust, and the world would vanish. Perhaps one reason the world still exists today, thousands of years later, is that even if a very smart and quick priest were to move 1 disk per second, solving this task with 64 disks would take him 580 billion years.

Lucas called his simplified three-disk version, which was marketed as a board game, the Tower of Hanoi. You were briefly introduced to it in Chapter 4. At the game's start, the three disks are placed on the left-most of three pegs, arranged by increasing size from bottom to top, as was shown in Figure 4.1 (see p. 128): a small red disk on top of a medium black disk on top of a large white disk. In order to move the disks properly and solve the puzzle, it helps to establish sub-goals, such as getting the large white disk over to the right-most peg, a maneuver that takes four moves.

Solving the Tower of Hanoi requires a great deal of manipulation of working memory because you must remember at least three things at all times: (1) what subgoals have been accomplished, (2) what subgoals remain, and (3) what is the next subgoal to be addressed. After each move, some of these will be updated and changed, while others will stay the same. This kind of goal-directed controlled updating of short-term memory is exactly the kind of task that places a heavy load on your central executive. It is hard enough to do with the real disks and pegs. Do you care to try doing it in your head?

Task Switching

In French class, Roberta listens with half an ear to her professor. When the material in the lecture is familiar, she switches her attention to her organic chemistry reading. This kind of task switching requires the manipulation of working memory, because Roberta must pay attention to the task she is doing at a given moment while at the same time monitoring external cues for information that may signal the need to switch to another task.

A commonly used procedure for studying task-shifting in the laboratory is the Wisconsin Card Sort Test, in which people are shown cards with graphics that differ in three characteristics, or dimensions: color, shape, and number. One sample card might have three red circles, while another card might have one yellow triangle. Initially, people learn to sort the cards by one of these dimensions: for example, all the blue cards might go on one pile, all the yellow cards on another, and so forth, as illustrated in Figure 5.9a.

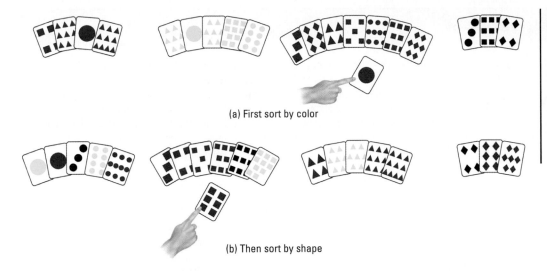

(a) First sort by color

(b) Then sort by shape

Later, after the person has learned this sorting rule, the task changes without warning, and she must learn a new rule for sorting based on one of the other dimensions. For example, if the original rule was to sort by color, now the rule might switch to sorting by shape, with a pile for circles, a pile for squares, and so on, as shown Figure 5.9b. This task taps into people's working memory and executive control because it requires not only learning a rule and keeping it in mind while they sort, but also learning to change the rule and keep track of the new one without confusing it with the old.

Stimulus Selection and Response Inhibition

While visiting Los Angeles, California, from his home in England, Trevor walks to an intersection and prepares to cross the street. He automatically begins turning his head toward the right to check for oncoming cars but quickly reminds himself that he is in the United States and oncoming cars will come from the left, not the right. In this situation, information about his current context has inhibited Trevor's ingrained, reflexive response and redirected his attention. Trevor's well-functioning central executive allows him to inhibit a habitual response that he has developed and shift his attention to an alternative, context-specific rule ("look left when crossing streets in the United States") that he must remember—perhaps by repeated rehearsal when walking through Los Angeles—as long as he remains in the United States.

A test known as the Stroop task can assess stimulus selection and response inhibition behavior analogous to Trevor's adapting to a new traffic pattern. The Stroop task consists of a series of names of colors, each printed in a color that is *different* from the color being named (Figure 5.10). The word "green" might be printed in red ink, the word "blue" in green ink, the word "red" in black ink, and so forth. The task is to look at each word in turn and say the color it is printed in, ignoring what the word happens to say.

Because people usually respond automatically to a written word by reading it, the Stroop task is very difficult to perform smoothly. Try it and you will see how hard it is to overcome the almost irresistible urge to read what the words say. To perform the task rapidly, you must inhibit your automatic impulse to read the words and instead keep a context-specific goal in your working memory to remind you of the task at hand: to attend to the ink color alone, much as Trevor must keep in mind the rule "look left for cars" when he is crossing the road in the United States. Thus, the Stroop task requires inhibiting currently inappropriate reflexive responses, while attending to the task-specific aspects of a stimulus on the basis of a goal in working memory—all key aspects of executive function.

Green
Blue
Black
Red
Orange
Purple
White
Yellow

▶ **Unsolved Mysteries**

Is Working Memory the Key to Intelligence?

Intelligence, defined as the capacity for learning, reasoning, and understanding, is a familiar enough term, but the concept itself is often poorly understood. Intelligent people are frequently described as "quick." But is intelligence the same as mental processing speed? Are people who are more intelligent than others just faster at solving problems than other people? A growing body of research suggests that intelligence has less to do with brain speed, and more to do with executive control of working memory.

Assessing students' working memory using a delayed recall task, Meredyth Daneman and Patricia Carpenter found a strong correlation between working-memory scores and verbal SAT tests of reading comprehension, widely accepted as an approximate indication of intelligence (Daneman & Carpenter, 1980). In a subsequent study, they found that students with low working-memory scores were especially prone to misunderstand complex reading comprehension tasks that involve carrying the context of one sentence over to another (Daneman & Carpenter, 1983).

However, the relationship between working memory and intelligence does not depend only on verbal intelligence. Carpenter and her colleagues used puzzles based on a standard nonverbal test of intelligence that uses a two-

dimensional visual analogy problem in which the participant is directed to select the design that completes the pattern. An illustrative example is shown here, depicting a 3-by-3 array of geometric figures with one in the lower right-hand corner missing. Participants must pick which of the six alternatives at the bottom best fits the pattern. What is the pattern? Note that each figure varies on two dimensions: the color (black, grey, or white) and the number of triangles (1, 2, or 3). Moreover, no row or column has two

Block patterns

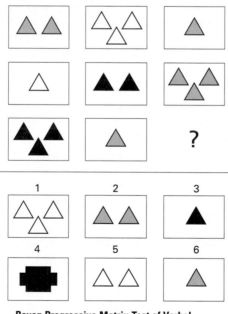

1   2   3

4   5   6

Raven Progressive Matrix Test of Verbal Intelligence Subjects are shown a three-by-three array of eight geometric figures and a space, in the lower right-hand corner, where the ninth figure belongs. They must pick which of the six alternatives shown at the bottom best fits the pattern. (The correct answer is #5.)

figures with the same number of triangles or the same color. To complete this pattern, the figure in the lower right would have to be white (there is no white figure in the third row or third column) and contain two triangles (there is no figure with two triangles in the third row or third column). Thus, the correct answer is #5, two white triangles.

An enormous range of difficulty can be introduced into this kind of task simply by increasing the complexity of the patterns or the number of components. Because these tasks require no language or factual knowledge, they are often considered to be "culture fair," meaning not prone to cultural or educational bias. Carpenter and colleagues showed that the relative difficulty of these geometric puzzle-type intelligence tests correlated positively with the number of rules each puzzle involved. It appears that being able to juggle many rules in one's head is correlated with scoring high on nonverbal tests of intelligence.

Functional brain imaging confirms the role of working memory and of the prefrontal cortex in solving such intelligence tests. John Gabrieli and colleagues have shown that the same prefrontal areas that are activated by working-memory tasks (see the Brain Substrates section) are also activated by geometric puzzles much like those used on intelligence tests (Gabrieli et al., 1997).

These kinds of evidence suggest that general intelligence, as detected by intelligence tests, is not just a matter of thinking or responding quickly. It appears to be associated with a strong working memory, including executive control and manipulation of a larger number of multiple rules, concepts, goals, and ideas.

In the Brain Substrates section, we discuss recent data from neuroscience suggesting how both the material-specific and process-specific dichotomies in Baddeley's model of working memory have guided research on the brain mechanisms of working memory and executive control.

Interim Summary

Transient memories are temporary representations of information that was either just perceived or just retrieved from long-term memory storage. They include both sensory memories, which are brief transient sensations of what you have just perceived when you see, hear, or taste something, and short-term memories, which can be maintained by active rehearsal and are easily displaced by new information or distractions. Rehearsal helps maintain short-term memories, but you are more likely to encode that information permanently as long-term memory if you actively process it in a deep and meaningful way.

Alan Baddeley characterized working memory as consisting of two independent short-term memory buffers—the visuo-spatial sketchpad, which holds visual and spatial images, and the phonological loop, an auditory memory that uses internal speech rehearsal—along with a central executive. The central executive is responsible for manipulating memories in the two buffers by, for example, adding and deleting items, selecting items to guide behavior, and retrieving information from and storing it in long-term memory. These functions of the central executive are needed for a wide range of mental activities, including (1) controlled updating of short-term memory buffers, (2) setting goals and planning, (3) task switching, and (4) stimulus selection and response inhibition.

Baddeley's model of working memory is described in terms of two dichotomies. First, the model distinguishes between two principal processes performed by working memory: the manipulation of information (by the central executive) and the maintenance of information by the two rehearsal buffers. Second, it distinguishes between the kinds of short-term memories stored in each buffer: the phonological loop holds verbal-phonological information, and the visuo-spatial sketchpad holds object and location information.

5.2 Brain Substrates

Studies of animals and humans implicate the frontal lobes—especially the **prefrontal cortex (PFC),** the most anterior (farthest forward) section of the frontal lobes—as being critical for working memory and executive control. In humans, the frontal lobes encompass approximately a third of the cerebral cortex (Goldman-Rakic, 1987). Cats and many other mammals, on the other hand, get by with frontal lobes that occupy less than 4% of their cerebral cortex. Figure 5.11 compares the relative sizes of the prefrontal cortex in several mammalian species.

Since the prefrontal cortex occupies a markedly larger proportion of the cerebral cortex in humans than in other mammals, many people have suggested that it is what makes us human. Could the frontal lobes be the brain's CEO, in charge of working memory and other cognitive functions? Does Baddeley's model, in which a central executive manipulates short-term and long-term memories in separate visuo-spatial and phonological-verbal rehearsal buffers, correspond to how the frontal lobes are organized? This section on brain substrates looks at how these psychological concepts and analogies have guided our research into the functional neuroanatomy of the frontal lobes.

The earliest insights into the role of the prefrontal cortex in working memory and executive control came from observing the behaviors of people with frontal-

Figure 5.11. Comparative frontal-lobe anatomy These drawings show the relative sizes of the prefrontal cortex in different mammals. Adapted from Fuster, 1995.

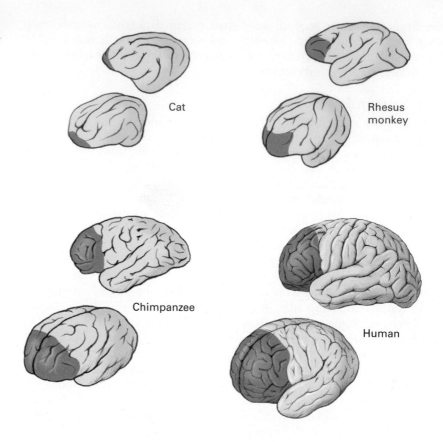

lobe damage. After reviewing data from such observations, and from later studies of nonhuman primates and other animals, we will discuss studies of brain activity in the frontal lobes during working-memory tasks.

It is important to remember, as you read these descriptions, that working memory is used not only to keep track of recent events but also to access memories of facts and events, both during encoding of new memories and during retrieval of old ones, as we will describe at the end of the Brain Substrates section.

Behavioral Consequences of Frontal-Lobe Damage

Elliot, a successful and happily married accountant, had always been viewed by others as reliable and responsible. Then, in his late thirties, he developed a large tumor in his frontal lobes. Surgeons were able to remove the tumor and save his life. However, the operation severely damaged his frontal lobes (Eslinger & Damasio, 1985; Damasio, 1994; Miller & Wallis, 2003). Neuropsychological tests performed after the operation indicated that all of his basic mental functions were intact. He showed normal language and memory abilities and scored well on general intelligence tests. However, Elliot's behavior and personality were radically altered. Soon after the surgery, he divorced his wife, remarried and divorced again, lost touch with most of his friends and family, got involved in corrupt business deals, and was soon bankrupt. The formerly responsible and cautious Elliot became impulsive and easily swayed by momentary whims, retaining little of his previous ability to organize and plan.

Elliot was behaving as we might expect in the absence of an executive-control system. He was no longer guided by long-term goals or task-specific constraints. For this reason, patients like Elliot are described as having a **dysexecutive**

syndrome, a disrupted ability to think and plan (Duncan et al., 1996). As you will read below, patients with frontal-lobe damage like Elliot's routinely exhibit deficits in both executive function and working memory, despite normal long-term memory and skill-learning abilities. Such patients are at the mercy of their reflexive stimulus–response reactions.

Dysexecutive Syndrome and Working-Memory Deficits in Patients with Frontal-Lobe Damage

In addition to tumors and surgery, frontal lobes can be damaged by strokes or blunt trauma to the front of the head—or, as often happens, from a rapid deceleration (as in a car crash) in which the frontal lobes compress against the front of the skull. People with damage to the frontal lobes show deficits on all of the working-memory and executive-control tasks described in Section 5.1. For example, they have great difficulty updating working memory in the *N*-back task, as well as performing self-ordered tasks that require frequent updating to recollect items that have been previously chosen (Petrides, 2000). Patients with frontal-lobe damage are also often impaired at tasks which tap short-term memory span, including digit-span tasks, where they may fail to recall even a short series of numbers (Janowsky et al., 1989). Other studies of these patients have shown similar impairments in short-term memory for colors, shapes, and object locations (Baldo & Shimamura, 2000; Ptito et al., 1995).

A loss of ability to plan and to organize is a noted characteristic of frontal-lobe damage. You may recall Wilder Penfield, the famous neurosurgeon from the mid-twentieth century, whose work on brain mapping was reviewed in Chapter 3. One case described by Penfield was his own sister, who had had a large tumor removed from her frontal regions. She had been an accomplished cook, but after the surgery she lost all ability to organize her cooking; she would move haphazardly from dish to dish, leaving some uncooked while others burned (Miller & Wallis, 2003). As you might expect, patients with frontal-lobe damage show deficits in neuropsychological tests such as the Tower of Hanoi, which assess planning abilities, and require maintaining and linking multiple subgoals to achieve some final desired goal. On this task, patients like Penfield's sister move the disks around aimlessly, without a clear plan for how to get the disks from the first peg to the last.

The ability to shift appropriately from one task to another is a central feature of executive control. Thus, the task-switching test procedures described in Section 5.1 provide a means of assessing frontal-lobe function. John Duncan had participants monitor two streams of simultaneously presented stimuli, a series of letters on the left and a stream of digits on the right (Duncan et al., 1996). At the beginning of the experiment, the participant was to read aloud the letters on the left. Later, when a signal cue was sounded, the person was supposed to switch to the other stream and begin reporting the digits. Later still, the signal would sound again as a sign that the participant should switch back to the letters. Although patients with frontal lesions had no trouble complying with the first part of the experiment, they had great difficulty switching between the left and right streams on cue.

The Wisconsin Card Sort Test (see Figure 5.9) is frequently used for assessment of frontal-lobe function. Frontal-lobe patients have no problem learning an initial sorting rule, such as color. Later, however, when the person must learn a new rule for sorting—say, by shape—frontal-lobe patients are severely impaired at making the transition. They show **perseveration,** which means they fail to learn a new rule but instead persist in using an old rule, despite repeated feedback indicating that the old rule is no longer correct. Many similar task-shifting tests are particularly difficult for patients with frontal-lobe damage

(Delis, Squire, Bihrle, & Massman, 1992; Owen et al., 1993). These severe deficits in set-shifting suggest that purposeful shifts in processing may be especially demanding of executive-control processes mediated by the frontal lobes.

Functional Neuroanatomy of the Prefrontal Cortex

Carlyle Jacobsen conducted animal studies in the early 1930s that implicated the frontal cortex in working memory (Jacobsen, 1936). Specifically, he looked at the effects of lesions in different parts of the frontal lobes on delayed spatial-response learning in monkeys. In these studies, monkeys were permitted to observe food being placed either in a location on the left or on the right of a surface outside their cages. After a delay during which the monkeys were not able to see the food, the monkeys were required to point to where the food had been placed. Jacobsen demonstrated that only monkeys with prefrontal lesions were impaired at responding correctly, exhibiting a selective and delay-dependent deficit in delayed spatial-response tasks. Based on these results, he argued that an animal's frontal lobes are critical for maintaining an internal representation of information in working memory over a delay prior to making some response.

One limitation of this early work is that Jacobsen's surgical techniques were relatively crude by modern standards: he removed a rather large portion of the prefrontal cortex. More recent research has shown that different subregions of the prefrontal cortex participate in different aspects of working-memory function.

For example, the primate prefrontal cortex can be divided into three main regions: the *orbital prefrontal cortex*, the *medial prefrontal cortex*, and the *lateral prefrontal cortex*. Figure 5.12 shows a side (lateral) view of human and monkey brains, with the locations of the two lateral components of the prefrontal cortex most relevant to this chapter: the **dorsolateral prefrontal cortex** (often abbreviated as DLPFC) in green lying on the top and the *ventrolateral prefrontal cortex* in purple, lying just below it. In these images, the orbital frontal cortex is not visible because it lies ventral (below) the regions shown, and the medial prefrontal cortex is also not visible because it is inside the regions shown, tucked away above and behind the orbital region. The orbital and medial prefrontal cortexes are both implicated in many memory functions, but they are less involved in working memory than are the lateral regions of the prefrontal cortex.

Recordings of brain activity in humans and monkeys have interesting things to say about the roles of these subregions in working memory, as we will discuss next.

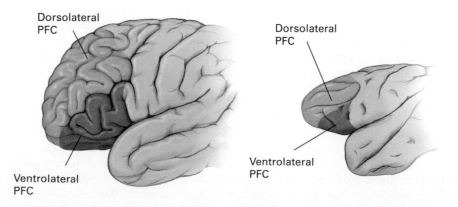

Figure 5.12. Primate frontal lobes These drawings show subdivisions of the frontal lobes in the (a) human and (b) Macaque monkey, identifying the dorsolateral prefrontal cortex (DLPFC) in green and the ventrolateral prefrontal cortex (VLPFC) in purple. Note that the very tip of the DLPFC is sometimes also referred to as the frontal polar cortex.

Dorsolateral PFC

Dorsolateral PFC

Ventrolateral PFC

Ventrolateral PFC

Frontal Brain Activity during Working-Memory Tasks

Guided by lesion studies suggesting that the prefrontal cortex plays a role in working memory, Joaquin Fuster and colleagues, in the early 1970s, were the first to record prefrontal-cortex neural activity during a working-memory task (Fuster & Alexander, 1971; Kubota & Niki, 1971). In this delayed-response task, similar to the one used in the Jacobsen studies described above, rhesus Macaque monkeys were required to remember either where they had seen a target object or what object they had previously seen. Fuster found that many prefrontal-cortex neurons fired only during a delay period when the animals were required to maintain information about a spatial location of a particular object. This suggested that the prefrontal cortex was "holding in mind" information needed to make a later response. Fuster hypothesized that the neural activity in the prefrontal cortex acted as a temporal bridge between stimulus cues and a contingent response, linking events across time. If so, the activity would be a key component of sensory-motor behaviors that span delays (Fuster, 2001, 2003).

Instead of requiring an animal to reach out and pick an object, point to a location, or swim to a speaker, some experiments simply track the animal's gaze. Eye-tracking technology offers well-controlled methods for testing spatial and object working memory in animals. Patricia Goldman-Rakic of Yale University Medical School, one of the pioneers in working-memory research, used this technology in a series of highly influential studies of primate working memory.

In her studies, Goldman-Rakic trained monkeys to fixate on a central spot on a display as shown in Figure 5.13 (a, fixation). The monkeys maintained their fixation on the central spot while a square cue was presented at one of eight locations around the edge of the display (b, cue). After the cue was removed, the monkeys waited during a delay period of several seconds (c, delay) and then moved their gaze to the cue's former location (d, response). Moving the gaze to the correct location resulted in a reward. An alternative version of this task required monkeys to remember a visual pattern and move their gaze to wherever it appeared next (Wilson, Scalaidhe, & Goldman-Rakic, 1993). Monkeys were able to learn both types of tasks. These studies allowed Goldman-Rakic to make some important inferences about how working memory is organized in the brain.

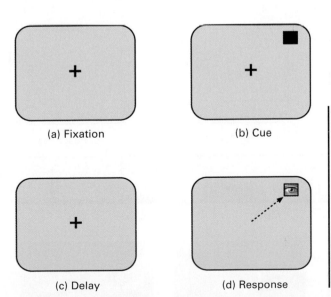

(a) Fixation   (b) Cue

(c) Delay   (d) Response

Figure 5.13. Goldman-Rakic's eyegaze response test of spatial memory in monkeys (a) Monkeys begin the task by fixating at a central point and keeping their focus on that central spot when (b) a cue appears on the periphery. (c) After the cue is removed, there is a delay of several seconds before the central spot disappears. (d) After this, the monkeys are rewarded if they shift their gaze to the place on the screen where the cue had previously appeared.

In electrophysiological recordings of these tasks, Goldman-Rakic and colleagues found that some of the neurons in the dorsolateral prefrontal cortex fired only while the animal was remembering the stimulus location (Funahashi, Bruce, & Goldman-Rakic, 1989). As shown in the electrical recordings in Figure 5.14, certain neurons in the prefrontal cortex fire during presentation of the cue itself (left column), others fire during the response required to earn the reward (right column), and still others fire only during the delay period (center column).

Most interesting of all, these "delay" neurons were individually tuned to different directional movements. For example, one neuron might code for a movement to the right, while another neuron might code for a downward movement, and so on. Figure 5.15 shows the strong response of a particular neuron when the cue was located at the bottom center of the screen, that is, at 270 degrees (bottom center graph), compared to the inhibition of its electrical activity when the cue was in the opposite location, namely, at 90 degrees, and only moderate activity at other positions.

The strong firing seen in Figure 5.15 during the delay for the trial (when the cue was at 270 degrees) could represent one of two things: it could be a memory for where the cue had appeared or it could be an anticipatory coding for the later movement of the eyegaze to that location. To distinguish between these alternatives, the researchers conducted an experiment in which the monkeys were trained to move their eyes to the location opposite to the cue. In that study, about 80% of the delay cells seemed to encode where the target had been (regardless of the eye-gaze response), while the other 20% seemed to encode the intended movement. These results suggest that the neurons of the dorsolateral prefrontal cortex that fire during the delay are encoding a combination of sensory- and movement-response information.

The monkeys did quite well at this delayed-response task, but they never performed it with 100% accuracy. Occasionally, they would make an error and move their eyes to the wrong position. Was it just a motor mistake, or was the prefrontal cortex itself confused as to the correct answer? The researchers found the latter to be true: the electrophysiological recordings predicted when a monkey was going to make an error, because the "wrong" neurons fired in the dorsolateral prefrontal cortex.

Figure 5.14. The spatial delayed-response eye-gaze task (a) The monkey fixates on a central spot on the screen while a cue flashes in the upper right corner. (b) During a delay period, the cue disappears and the monkey remains fixated on the central point. (c) Finally, when the central spot turns off, the monkey looks where the cue previously appeared. (For clarity, the monkey is shown in mirror image so that the monkey is looking, in the figure, in the direction of the stimulus shown above). As shown in the electrophysiological recordings, certain neurons in the prefrontal cortex fire when the cue is shown (a), others fire during the final response (c), while others fire only during the delay period (b). Data from Funahashi, Bruce, & Goldman-Rakic, 1989.

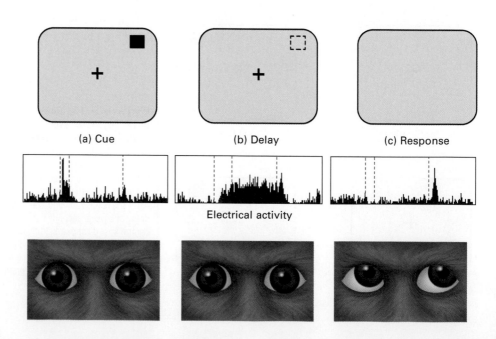

(a) Cue   (b) Delay   (c) Response

Electrical activity

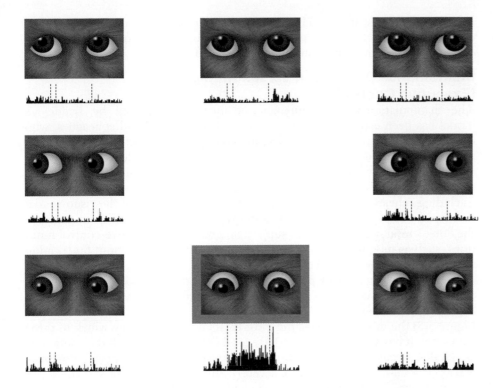

Figure 5.15. Response of one prefrontal-cortex neuron during the eye-gaze delayed-response task Electrophysiological activity of the neuron during the cue, delay, and response periods of the task when the cue was presented at different locations. Note the strong response when the cue was at the bottom location (indicated by the blue outline), compared to the inhibited activity when the cue was presented at the top, center location. From Funahashi et al., 1989. (For clarity, the monkey is shown in mirror image so that the monkey is looking, in the figure, in the same direction as the stimulus being shown to it.)

It is important to note that sustained neuronal activity during the delay period is not limited to the dorsolateral prefrontal cortex. Similar sustained activity can also be seen in the relevant primary and secondary sensory and motor regions in the temporal and parietal lobes of the brain. These regions are reciprocally connected to the prefrontal cortex.

If the sensory and motor cortexes can sustain activity to encode working memory, why should the prefrontal cortex be necessary for working memory to function? Earl Miller proposes that the key "cognitive" contribution of the prefrontal cortex to working memory is the ability of the prefrontal cortex to sustain activity despite distractions (Miller, 2000). To test his hypothesis, Miller and colleagues trained monkeys to maintain the visual memory of an object throughout a delay period filled with visually distracting events (Miller, Erikson, & Desimone, 1996). They found that activity in the posterior visual cortical areas was easily disrupted by the distracters. In contrast, the corresponding dorsolateral prefrontal-cortex activity remained robust despite distractions. The ability of the prefrontal cortex to provide focused control over working memory is consistent with lesion data which demonstrate that one salient consequence of prefrontal-cortex damage, both in humans and in monkeys, is a high degree of distractibility.

Mapping Baddeley's Model onto PFC Anatomy

The lesion studies and recording studies demonstrating that the frontal lobes play a key role in working memory leave two questions unanswered: (1) how are the frontal lobes organized, and (2) how does working memory actually work? More specifically, are there different regions in the brain for executive processes (memory manipulation) and rehearsal processes (memory maintenance), as suggested by Baddeley's model? That is, does the *functional* distinction between manipulation and rehearsal proposed by Baddeley correspond to an actual *anatomical* distinction between distinguishable brain regions? Also, are there anatomical distinctions between the two material-specific rehearsal stores, namely, the visuo-spatial sketchpad and the phonological loop? These questions concerning organization and function, to which we now turn our attention, have dominated research in the neurobiology of working memory.

Maintenance (Rehearsal) versus Manipulation (Executive Control)

The manipulation-versus-maintenance distinction suggested by Baddeley's model has been explored extensively by Michael Petrides and colleagues, who have concluded that the dorsal and ventral regions of the prefrontal cortex perform qualitatively different processes (Owen, Evans, & Petrides, 1996; Petrides, 1994, 1996). Their findings, summarized in Figure 5.16, indicate that the ventrolateral prefrontal cortex supports the encoding and retrieval of information (including rehearsal for maintenance), performing the roles of the visuo-spatial sketchpad and phonological rehearsal loops proposed by Baddeley. In contrast, the dorsolateral prefrontal cortex supports higher-order executive-control functions, such as monitoring and manipulating of stored information, functioning much like Baddeley's central executive.

To test this mapping of processes to brain regions as portrayed in Figure 5.16, Petrides and colleagues developed the self-ordered delayed-response tasks described in Section 5.1. You'll recall that in the monkey version of this task (see Figure 5.8) the monkey obtains the most treats by remembering which of three containers it has already chosen. A 10 second delay, during which the containers are hidden, occurs between each opportunity to choose. Monkeys with dorsolateral prefrontal-cortex lesions were severely impaired at this task and could not determine which containers had already been emptied and which still contained a reward, even though there was no spatial component involved (that is, the containers were not moved during the delays). In contrast, these same monkeys with dorsolateral prefrontal-cortex lesions were able to maintain object memories at varying delays and showed no problems solving basic delayed-recognition tasks (Petrides & Milner, 1982). In another study, Petrides (1995) showed that

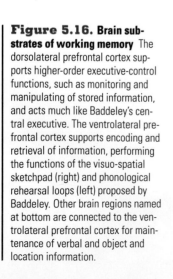

Figure 5.16. Brain substrates of working memory The dorsolateral prefrontal cortex supports higher-order executive-control functions, such as monitoring and manipulating of stored information, and acts much like Baddeley's central executive. The ventrolateral prefrontal cortex supports encoding and retrieval of information, performing the functions of the visuo-spatial sketchpad (right) and phonological rehearsal loops (left) proposed by Baddeley. Other brain regions named at bottom are connected to the ventrolateral prefrontal cortex for maintenance of verbal and object and location information.

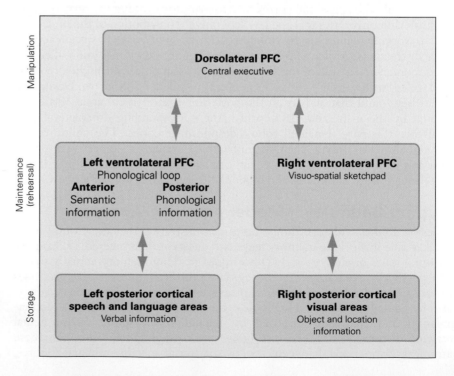

increasing the number of items to be monitored in these tasks exacerbated the impairments due to mid-dorsolateral prefrontal-cortex lesions, whereas simply extending the delay time did not. Again, this implicates the dorsolateral prefrontal cortex in monitoring but not in the maintenance of information in working memory.

These studies, along with many similar ones, suggest that DLPFC lesions produce severe deficits in temporal ordering, which requires active manipulation of working memory, much like the deficits seen in patients with frontal-lobe damage. In contrast, basic mnemonic judgments about recently seen objects, which require only maintenance of information during a delay, are not affected by DLPFC lesions. These maintenance functions are instead thought to be controlled by loops between the ventrolateral prefrontal cortex and posterior regions of the brain, such as the posterior cortical speech and language areas (for verbal information) and the posterior cortical visual areas (for object and location information), as shown in Figure 5.16.

In studies of humans performing self-ordered tasks, Petrides and colleagues used functional brain imaging to further explore the distinction between manipulation and maintenance (Petrides et al., 1993a, 1993b). They found that when the items to be remembered were abstract designs, these self-ordered tasks produced significant activity in the dorsolateral prefrontal cortex, especially in the right hemisphere (Figure 5.17a). When the items to be remembered consisted of verbal material, however, the tasks produced strong activity in both the left and right sides of the dorsolateral prefrontal cortex (Figure 5.17b). From these results, the researchers concluded that while the right DLPFC has a dominant role in all monitoring processes, the left DLPFC is specialized for verbal materials.

Several recent studies have attempted to differentiate between the passive rehearsal of information in working memory and the more active process of updating information in working memory. Rehearsal supports working memory by reactivating or refreshing briefly stored representations, whereas the updating of information consists of adding information to or removing it from working memory. Imaging studies indicate that there is brain activity in the premotor cortex during rehearsal of visuo-spatial information (Awh & Jonides, 1998). Other fMRI studies suggest that the ventrolateral prefrontal cortex is activated by simple rehearsal, especially internal rehearsal (Awh et al., 1996). In contrast, the posterior parietal regions and the occipital area appear to be involved only in the temporary maintenance of spatial working memory, not in its rehearsal. Many other neuroimaging studies have also confirmed a general distinction between storage mechanisms in the posterior regions of the brain and rehearsal mechanisms in the anterior regions, including the prefrontal cortex, as schematized in Figure 5.16 (Smith & Jonides, 2004).

The Visuo-Spatial and Phonological-Verbal Buffers

As you learned in the Behavioral Processes section, Baddeley's model of working memory assumed the existence of two main memory buffers, one for visuo-spatial memory and the other for phonological-verbal memory. Studies of working memory in monkeys have, of course, been limited to studies of visuo-spatial memory, due to the lack of verbal language in these nonhuman primates. All studies of phonological and verbal working memory have thus relied on the use of human participants. In spite of such limitations, there is evidence to support the idea that these two forms of working memory are produced in different parts of the brain.

Behavioral studies, for example, have indicated that verbal working memory retains items in a phonological code based on the sounds of the words, and that these items are retained through a rehearsal process similar to internally rehearsed speech (Baddeley, 1986). Consistent with the general tendency for language to be left-lateralized in the brain, frontal-lobe patients with damage to the left side are most likely to show specialized deficits in verbal (as opposed to visuo-spatial) working memory (Shallice, 1988).

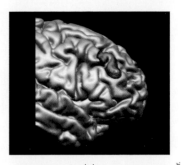

(a)

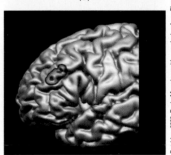

(b)

Petrides, 2000, Brain Mapping, with permission from Elsevier.

Figure 5.17. Brain imaging of self-ordered tasks (a) Imaging data from a self-ordered task in which subjects had to remember previous selections made from a set of abstract designs show predominantly right-hemisphere activity in the prefrontal cortex. (b) Imaging data from a self-ordered task in which the items to be remembered were a set of verbal stimuli produces both left- and right-hemisphere activity in the prefrontal cortex (although only left activity is shown here). Adapted from Petrides, 2000.

Edward Smith and John Jonides conducted what became an influential series of studies in the early 1990s using PET imaging to compare spatial working memory and object working memory. In a study of spatial working memory, they presented people with three dots arranged in random locations on a display screen (Figure 5.18a; Smith & Jonides, 1995). The dots disappeared for a delay period of 3 seconds, after which a single circle appeared somewhere on the screen. Then participants were asked to indicate whether the circle contained the location of one of the previously displayed dots.

This task clearly involves spatial memory, but it also involves an ability simply to encode spatial information. To disentangle these two processes, Smith and Jonides conducted a second control study that maintained identical encoding and responding requirements but did not employ working memory. In this control study, the same stimuli were presented, but they did not disappear during the delay period or when the probe circle appeared. Consequently, when the probe circle appeared, subjects could easily see whether or not it covered one of the dots (Figure 5.18b). This second control task required only perceptual processing, not working memory. By subtracting areas of brain activity seen in the

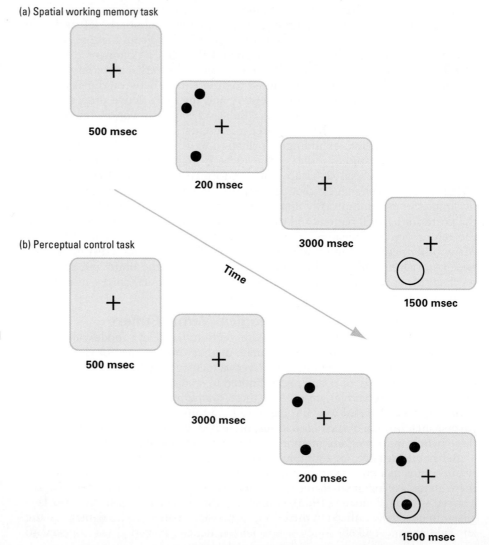

(a) Spatial working memory task

500 msec

200 msec

3000 msec

1500 msec

(b) Perceptual control task

Time

500 msec

3000 msec

200 msec

1500 msec

Figure 5.18. Spatial working-memory task (a) Experimental spatial working-memory task in which participants fixate on a central "+"; maintain fixation while three dots are displayed and after the dots disappear; and then must decide if a circle that appears on the screen covers a region where one of the dots had been located. (b) Control task that does not require spatial working memory. Participants fixate on a central "+" and maintain fixation when three dots and a circle appear on the screen. The participants are asked whether the circle surrounds one of the dots. Figure adapted from Smith & Jonides, 1995.

control task from activity areas in the experimental task, Smith and Jonides were able to identify which brain areas were activated specifically by the working-memory component of the experimental task illustrated in Figure 5.18. The subtraction analyses revealed considerable activity in many dorsal regions but only on the *right* side of the brain. This lateralization to the right side is consistent with the general tendency for the right brain in humans to be more involved with spatial and perceptual processing.

As suggested above, the correspondence between the monkey electrophysiology and lesion studies and human functional neuroimaging is only approximate. Although both of these areas of research indicate that spatial processing takes place in more dorsal regions of the brain, the human studies reveal activity in brain regions that are both more dorsal and more ventral than those in the monkey. Moreover, only the human studies show right-brain lateralization. This is consistent with a general tendency over many different paradigms for the human brain to show more lateralization of function than do the brains of other primates (Kolb & Wishaw, 1996).

More recently, James Haxby and colleagues compared spatial and object memory using one set of stimuli with two alternative sets of instructions (Courtney, Ungerleider, Keil & Haxby, 1997). In both the spatial and object versions of the task, participants were first shown three target faces, presented sequentially in three different positions. Then they were shown a target face in one of several possible positions. In the spatial version of the task, participants were asked, "Is the location of the target face identical to the location of any of the previous faces?" In the object version, they were asked, "Is the target face identical to the identity of any of the previous faces?"

The brain activity recorded during this study showed that the spatial-location task activated a region in the right hemisphere of the premotor cortex, while the object-identity task activated the right dorsolateral prefrontal cortex. This means that spatial working memory and object working memory are localized differently. (In addition, the specific areas implicated in the human brain were different from those implicated in studies of monkeys, and there was significant lateralization in humans that was not seen in monkeys.) This finding that spatial processing is regionally separate from object processing in human working-memory tasks has been replicated many times and appears to be a consistent property of visuo-spatial working memory in humans (Smith & Jonides, 1999).

Prefrontal Control of Long-Term Declarative Memory

In the beginning of this chapter, we defined short-term memory as an active, temporary representation of information that either was just perceived or was just retrieved from long-term memory. Most of this chapter has focused on the former class of information—information that was recently experienced. We will next briefly discuss how working memory (and hence, short-term memory) interacts with long-term memory, focusing especially on long-term memories of previously stored episodes or facts.

Let's start with an example of retrieving an episodic memory. What was the last movie you saw? To answer this question, you may have to perform a number of mental operations. For example, you might search your memory by calling to mind every movie that you know to be currently playing, noting which ones you have seen and then trying to recall which of them you saw most recently. Alternatively, you could search your memory by thinking back over your recent activities in reverse chronological order. Knowing that you go out to movies on the weekends, you might first think back to last weekend. Did you see a movie?

If not, think back to the previous weekend. However you choose to set about answering this question, the process of searching your memory requires considerable strategic manipulation and control of memory processes, as well as maintaining, throughout this search, an awareness of your ultimate goal: the name of the last movie you saw. This is exactly the kind of task that uses the prefrontal cortex in multiple capacities. Patients with prefrontal-cortex damage exhibit significant deficits in retrieval of long-term memories (Shimamura, Jurica, Mangels, Gershberg, & Knight, 1995; Mangels, Gershberg, Shimamura, & Knight, 1996).

Neuroimaging has been used to locate this kind of controlled search of long-term memory more precisely within the prefrontal cortex. Recall that Petrides and colleagues argued that the ventrolateral prefrontal cortex supports passive rehearsal and maintenance functions, while the dorsolateral prefrontal cortex supports higher-order executive-control functions, such as monitoring and manipulation of stored information. Thus, the kinds of executive control and manipulation of memory needed for retrieval of specific episodic memories, such as the last movie you saw, should be subserved by the dorsolateral prefrontal cortex. In fact, this is exactly what functional neuroimaging has shown: the dorsolateral prefrontal cortex is activated during people's attempts to remember past events (Nyberg, Kabeza, & Tulving, 1996; Wagner, Desmond, Glover, & Gabrieli, 1998).

Have you ever met someone at a party who seems familiar and yet you can't remember how you know her? (Is she an elementary-school classmate or did you meet on that summer trip to Israel?) You just can't recall, but you do know you met before. On the other hand, very often you will see a person and not only realize that she is familiar but immediately remember how and where you met. According to a study by Anthony Wagner, Daniel Schacter, and colleagues, you probably used your dorsolateral prefrontal cortex in the latter situation, in which you recollected the source of your memory, but not in the former situation, in which you knew that the person was familiar but could not remember why (Dobbins, Foley, Schacter, & Wagner, 2002). In their study, people were shown various words and asked one of two questions: "Is it abstract or concrete?" or "Is it pleasant or unpleasant?" Later, they were shown the words again and were asked either if they remembered seeing the word during the first part of the experiment (that is, did they recall whether the word was considered at all) or if they remembered which task the word appeared in (did they recall judging it on the concrete/abstract dimension or on the pleasant/unpleasant dimension). As shown in Figure 5.19, the dorsolateral prefrontal cortex was more active when people were asked to recall the source of the word (that is, which task it was used in) than when they were asked whether or not the word had appeared at all (regardless of task).

Figure 5.19. Dorsolateral prefrontal activity during recollection of source Comparing trials in which participants were asked to recall the source of a word versus trials where they were only asked if the word were familiar, fMRI studies show that multiple left prefrontal, as well as lateral and medial parietal, regions were more active during source recollection than on mere familiarity judgments. (a) The view from the front of the brain; (b) the brain's left side. Data from Dobbins et al., 2002.

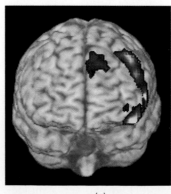

(a)   (b)

Dobbins, I.G., Foley, H., Schacter, D.L., & Wagner, A.D. (2002). Executive control during episodic retrieval: Multiple prefrontal processes subserve source memory. Neuron, 35, 989–996, with permission from Elsevier.

Of course, long-term memories can only be retrieved after having been encoded and stored. This encoding and storing of new information can be either incidental or intentional. When information is stored *incidentally*, it is learned as an accidental byproduct of some other task. For example, if asked when the pot on the stove began boiling, you might recall that the pot was copper colored, even if you were not asked to remember that information. The alternative, in which information is stored *intentionally*, means it is learned as the result of an explicit goal of remembering that particular fact or event for later retrieval. Much of your studying for exams is an effort to intentionally store new information to be recalled later, whereas recalling that the professor was wearing a hideous red plaid shirt during the lecture is more likely to be a result of incidental storage.

It is during encoding—when a recent episode or fact held in working memory is being processed for long-term memory—that we see the most evidence for prefrontal-cortex involvement. If, as Petrides argued, the ventrolateral prefrontal cortex supports passive rehearsal and maintenance functions, then we might expect to see more ventrolateral prefrontal-cortex activity during intentional encoding, in contrast to the dorsolateral prefrontal-cortex activity seen in retrieval.

Functional imaging studies using fMRI and PET have indeed reliably shown that intentional encoding of new memories activates the ventrolateral prefrontal cortex. Because most of these studies used meaningful stimuli, such as images of nameable real-word objects, the *left* ventrolateral prefrontal cortex is primarily activated, consistent with the general tendency of the left prefrontal cortex to be specialized for verbal processing (Nyberg et al., 1996).

The functional role of the left ventrolateral prefrontal cortex during encoding of new semantic information can be further subdivided into the contributions of its anterior (front) and posterior (back) regions, as illustrated in Figure 5.16. Anterior regions are activated during tasks that involve semantic processing (Thompson-Schill et al., 1997), while posterior regions are activated during phonological processing (Buckner, Rachle, Miezin, & Petersen, 1996). Thus, remembering the name of a wealthy new acquaintance, "Bill," by noting that he probably has lots of bills in his wallet (a *semantic* elaboration of a meaning of the word "bill") would likely involve processing by your *anterior* ventrolateral prefrontal cortex. In contrast, rehearsing a complex foreign-sounding name over and over likely involves *phonological* processing in the *posterior* ventrolateral prefrontal cortex.

Further support for this anterior–posterior differentiation comes from a study by Russell Poldrack, Anthony Wagner, and colleagues, who compared brain activity of people making either a semantic analysis of words ("Is it abstract or concrete?") or a phonological analysis ("How many syllables does it contain?"). Although the posterior region of the left ventrolateral prefrontal cortex was activated during both tasks—reflecting a common phonological component—only the semantic task resulted in activation of the anterior left ventrolateral prefrontal cortex (Poldrack et al., 1999). In contrast, Wagner and colleagues subsequently demonstrated that nonsemantic tasks that involved only phonological processing activated the posterior, but not the anterior, regions of the left ventrolateral prefrontal cortex (Wagner, Koutstaal, Maril, Schachter, & Buckner, 2000). Refer to Figure 5.16 for a schematic map to review which type of working memory tasks involve which brain regions.

Overall, there are numerous parallels between the role of the prefrontal cortex (and the precise location of its activity) in working memory and its role in episodic memory. The control processes and rehearsal mechanisms implicated in working memory appear to also play crucial roles in the encoding and retrieval of long-term memories for episodic and semantic information (Wagner, 2002).

Interim Summary

Studies with both animals and humans implicate the frontal lobes of the brain—especially the prefrontal cortex (PFC), the most anterior section of the frontal lobes—as critical for working memory and executive control.

The primate prefrontal cortex can be divided into three main regions: the orbital prefrontal cortex, the medial prefrontal cortex, and the lateral prefrontal cortex. The lateral prefrontal cortex, located along the sides of the frontal lobes, is further subdivided into a lower region, the ventrolateral prefrontal cortex, and an upper region, the dorsolateral prefrontal cortex (often referred to as the DLPFC). These two lateral regions are the primary regions involved in working memory and executive control.

Joaquin Fuster recorded neurons in the dorsolateral prefrontal cortex and showed that the region is needed for an animal to maintain an internal representation in its working memory during a delay, prior to making some response. Patricia Goldman-Rakic showed that for visual memory tasks, neurons in the dorsolateral prefrontal cortex maintain the memory of different directional movements during a delay. Earl Miller has argued that the contribution of the prefrontal cortex to working memory stems from the PFC's ability to resist distractions.

Michael Petrides and colleagues showed that the dorsal and ventral prefrontal cortices have different functions: the ventrolateral prefrontal cortex supports encoding and retrieval of information (including rehearsal for maintenance), performing as the visuo-spatial sketchpad and phonological rehearsal loops proposed by Baddeley. In contrast, Petrides argues that the dorsolateral prefrontal cortex supports higher-order executive-control functions such as monitoring and manipulating of stored information, thus doing the job of Baddeley's central executive.

The two short-term memory buffers—the verbal-phonological loop and the visuo-spatial sketchpad—appear to be lateralized in the human prefrontal cortex. Neuroimaging studies show that the *left* prefrontal cortex (both dorsolateral and ventrolateral) is essential for verbal working memory. This is consistent with the general tendency for language to reside in the left side of the brain. Clinical studies of frontal-lobe patients with left-side damage support this theory of lateralization, because these patients show deficits specifically in verbal (as opposed to visuo-spatial) working memory. The *right* hemisphere of the prefrontal cortex is more strongly associated with visuo-spatial processing. James Haxby and colleagues showed through functional imaging studies that an object (identity) task activated the right dorsolateral prefrontal cortex.

Test Your Knowledge

Functional Neuroanatomy of the Prefrontal Cortex

For each of the following four activities, identify the region in the prefrontal cortex whose activity is most critical:

1. Deciding who should sit where around a dinner table set for eight, to avoid seating ex-spouses and feuding ex-business partners next to each other.

2. Rehearsing the toast you will make at your brother's wedding.

3. Learning the difference between the functions of the distributor, ignition coil, and carburetor while you fix your car.

4. Remembering how to pronounce the name of the French exchange student you just met.

5. Remembering where you parked and deciding which way to walk to your parking spot as you exit the department store at the mall.

Working memory interacts with long-term memory, especially long-term declarative memories for previous episodes or facts. Anthony Wagner and colleagues have shown that the dorsolateral prefrontal cortex is activated during people's attempts to remember past events, as well as during encoding of new information. During encoding of new verbal information, the *anterior* prefrontal cortex is activated for tasks that involve *semantic* processing, while the *posterior* prefrontal cortex is activated for *phonological* processing.

5.3 Clinical Perspectives

Research on the role of the prefrontal cortex in working memory and executive control has provided clues for improving the diagnosis and treatment of several common neurological and psychiatric disorders. Two of the most common disorders involving dysfunctional prefrontal circuits are schizophrenia and attention-deficit/hyperactivity disorder (ADHD).

Schizophrenia

Schizophrenia is a psychiatric disorder characterized primarily by hallucinations and delusions. Patients see and hear things that are not really happening (such as the devil talking to them) and these experiences lead them to hold bizarre and often paranoid beliefs (for example, that they are the target of a big government conspiracy). However, people suffering from schizophrenia also display disturbances in cognition and memory, especially in working memory and executive control. Impairments in working memory in schizophrenia become apparent only when the patient must keep a large number of items in mind during a delay, a function associated with the dorsolateral prefrontal cortex. This finding is consistent with a wide range of other data suggesting that the dorsolateral prefrontal cortex is dysfunctional in schizophrenia. In contrast, functions attributed to the ventrolateral prefrontal cortex seem relatively unimpaired in patients with schizophrenia. For example, people with schizophrenia have close to normal performance on phonological or visuo-spatial memory tasks (Barch, Csernansky, Conturo, Snyder, & Ollinger, 2002) and on memory tasks involving only minimal delays or few items (Park & Holzman, 1992). However, patients with schizophrenia are impaired at visuo-spatial working-memory tasks only when these tasks involve the manipulation or updating of information in working memory (Park & Holzman, 1992). Similar executive-control deficits are also seen in close relatives of schizophrenic patients (Park, Holzman, & Goldman-Rakic, 1992).

Neuroimaging provides further insights into prefrontal-cortex dysfunction in schizophrenia. Daniel Weinberger and colleagues presented the first neuroimaging evidence for dorsolateral prefrontal-cortex dysfunction in schizophrenia by measuring blood flow in different cerebral regions (Weinberger, Berman, & Zec, 1986). They found that when patients with schizophrenia attempted to solve the Wisconsin Card Sort Test (see Figure 5.9), a task that depends on working memory and executive control, their dorsolateral prefrontal cortex showed no evidence of increased blood flow. Thus, in Figure 5.20, the healthy controls but not the schizophrenic patients show elevated frontal-lobe activation during card sorting ("WCS") as compared to a control task that involved only counting ("Number"). Moreover, there was a correlation among the schizophrenia subjects between the amount of blood flow in this region and performance: the greater the blood flow in the dorsolateral prefrontal cortex, the better the patients performed on the Wisconsin Card Sort Test.

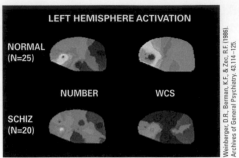

Figure 5.20. Cerebral blood flow during the Wisconsin Card Sort Test Healthy controls, but not the schizophrenic patients, show elevated frontal-lobe activation (shown as more yellow and red areas) during the Wisconsin Card Sort ("WCS") as compared to a control task ("Number"). From Weinberger et al., 1986.

More recent studies provide further evidence for an executive-control deficit in schizophrenia, localized within the dorsolateral prefrontal cortex. For example, researchers found that schizophrenia correlates with depressed dorsolateral prefrontal-cortex activity during the N-back task, which as you learned in Section 5.1 is a standard test of working memory. Ventral and posterior prefrontal-cortex activity, however, is normal, suggesting that passive rehearsal mechanisms, associated with these areas, are unaffected by schizophrenia (Barch et al., 2002). Such neuroimaging results are consistent with postmortem studies of schizophrenic patients that reveal neural pathologies in the dorsolateral prefrontal cortex but not in more ventral regions.

What is wrong with the dorsolateral prefrontal cortex in schizophrenia patients? One view is that the deficits in working memory and executive control found in schizophrenia may be linked to deficiencies in cortical dopamine processing. Most pharmacological treatments for schizophrenia work by altering the transmission of **dopamine,** a neuromodulator that alters neuron-to-neuron communication. Recent PET imaging studies using radiotracer chemicals sensitive to dopamine concluded that patients with schizophrenia had more of a certain kind of dopamine receptor, called D1 receptors, in the dorsolateral prefrontal cortex, than did healthy controls (Abi-Dargham et al., 2002). The researchers hypothesized that the increased number of these receptors might reflect the brain's attempt to compensate for dopamine dysfunction; in other words, a lack of sufficient dopamine release in the PFC might lead the PFC to try (unsuccessfully) to compensate by adding more receptors. Most strikingly, patients with the *highest* number of D1 dopamine receptors in their prefrontal cortex exhibited the *worst* performance on the N-back assessment of working memory. This provides compelling evidence for a link between dopamine regulation of dorsolateral prefrontal-cortex function and working memory.

Genetic research into the causes of schizophrenia includes a search for genes that convey a heightened susceptibility for the disease. For example, Daniel Weinberger and colleagues have shown that mutation in the COMT gene affects dopamine metabolism in the frontal lobes (Egan et al., 2001). Even in healthy, normal individuals, the status of the COMT genes was seen to predict 4% of the variance in performance on the Wisconsin Card Sort Test. As shown in Figure 5.21, having 0, 1, or 2 copies of the bad COMT gene predicted the number of perseverative errors a person would make on the Wisconsin Card Sort Test. Note that even healthy individuals with two copies of the bad gene showed worse performance on this task than individuals without the mutation. This was true both for siblings of schizophrenic patients (who are more likely to have the bad mutation) and for healthy controls drawn from the general population. This finding suggests that a mutation in one kind of gene causes only a small change in cognitive performance but that a combination of mutations in many different genes could push a person past a tipping point into a high-risk category for schizophrenia.

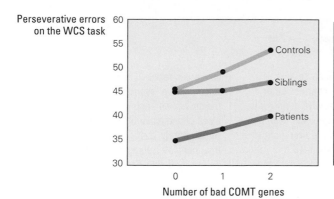

Figure 5.21. Effect of a gene mutation on frontal-lobe function The number of copies of a bad COMT gene correlates with the relative number of perseverative errors on the Wisconsin Card Sort Test in schizophrenic patients, their siblings, and healthy normal controls. Adapted from Egan et al., 2001.

Weinberger and colleagues also used the 2-back task, with its heavy dependence on working memory and executive control, to do brain-imaging studies of the effects of the COMT gene. They looked at the brains of healthy individuals with 0, 1, or 2 copies of the bad COMT gene to see which brain regions showed activity during the 2-back task. The region that was most highly correlated with this gene was the prefrontal cortex. The more copies of the bad COMT gene (and hence the worse the dopamine functioning), the less prefrontal-cortex activity was seen during the 2-back task. This suggests that having 1 or 2 copies of the bad gene (as is most common in those with schizophrenia) impairs activation of the prefrontal cortex during working-memory and executive-function tasks. These studies provide evidence that genetic mutations affecting dopamine activity in the prefrontal cortex are related to the emergence of cognitive deficits seen in schizophrenia.

Recent findings such as these concerning the genetic bases of prefrontal-cortex abnormalities in schizophrenia may soon lead to advances in treatment options. Perhaps in the near future, treatments for schizophrenia will be tailored to an individual patient's unique genetic composition, a leap forward from current approaches that prescribe a uniform treatment regimen based on broad generalizations about the disease.

Attention-Deficit/Hyperactivity Disorder

Attention-deficit/hyperactivity disorder (ADHD) is one of the most commonly diagnosed psychiatric problems in children, with estimates of 2–5% of children being affected. Children and adults with this disorder have great difficulty with executive-control processes such as planning, organizing their time, keeping attention focused on a task, and inhibiting responses to distracting stimuli. Most researchers and clinicians believe that ADHD involves dysfunction in the prefrontal cortex and its cortical and subcortical connections (Solanto, Arnsten, & Castellanos, 2000), including the cerebellum and the basal ganglia. Structural neuroimaging of children with ADHD shows that they have a smaller right prefrontal-cortex region, the region associated with spatial attention and working memory.

Behavioral research suggests that working memory in particular is impaired in patients with ADHD. In one recent study, adults with ADHD showed deficits in mental calculations that required use of working memory (Schweitzer et al., 2000). As with schizophrenia, current medications for ADHD act by altering dopamine function in the cortex. The most common treatments for ADHD, such as Ritalin (also known as methylphenidate), are stimulants that either increase dopamine release or block its reuptake at synapses. Unfortunately, the effects of these medications are temporary, and the behavioral problems reappear after 3 or 4 hours. To design more effective pharmacological or behavioral treatments, researchers must learn more about the effects of ADHD on the prefrontal cortex.

► **Learning and Memory in Everyday Life**

Improving Your Working Memory

Because working memory and executive control are fundamental to our higher cognitive abilities, it is natural to ask: what can I do to improve mine? A key finding from research on working memory is that our visuo-spatial and verbal working memories are independent, each with a limited capacity. You can probably keep only about 3 to 5 items in either store at any one time, which makes remembering a 10-digit phone number a bit tricky. One possible solution when you need to remember a long list of items is to make the independence of visuo-spatial and verbal memory stores work for you rather than against you. For example, if you need to remember several words at once, such as people's names, consider converting some of these words into pictures so that both memory buffers can share the daunting task.

Various tricks can be used to reduce the memory load of keeping in mind someone's phone number. For example, if you are familiar with the city where the person lives, you can probably encode the area code for the phone number as one chunk. Thus, if your aunt lives in Albany,

New York, where the area code is 518, you only have to remember her other 7 digits, since you can always deduce the area code. This technique was even easier 50 years ago, when the first 2 digits of a phone number corresponded to 2 letters in the name of the telephone exchange. For example, in New York City the MO in MO6-1078 stood for "Monument," so people calling that number had only to remember 5 digits, a piece of cake compared to today!

The biggest drain on our working memory comes from multitasking, or attempting to accomplish several goals at once. How often do you talk on the phone, listen to music, and surf the Internet all at the same time? You can bet that your dorsolateral PFC is working overtime when you do. Of more concern is multitasking during

dangerous tasks, like driving in traffic. Have you ever seen someone try to read the newspaper, apply nail polish, or talk on a cell phone while behind the wheel? Unfortunately, traffic accidents often result from people's attempts to multitask while driving their cars. For this reason, many states have banned cell-phone use while driving, especially using handheld phones.

An overloaded working memory impairs "metacognition," the ability to accurately monitor and evaluate our cognitive functioning. You may think your driving is just fine, or that you can absorb the main ideas in your professor's lecture while you work on other projects (like Roberta, who studies chemistry during French), but research has shown that you are probably not operating at as high a level as you think. Focusing on one task at a time greatly improves the ability to use working memory effectively. In contrast, high levels of stress reduce the working-memory span and the ability to concentrate and focus executive control. Some research has suggested that stress elevates dopamine levels in the prefrontal cortex, impairing its ability to efficiently monitor and update information.

Why tax your working memory if you don't need to? Maybe it is time to shut off that cell phone, put away the Ritalin, grab a pad of paper (think of it as a third working-memory buffer), and start writing things down.

Like schizophrenia, ADHD is a heritable psychiatric disorder (which therefore tends to run in families), and scientists are hot on the trail of the genetic bases for this heritability. Recent research has identified some of the genes believed to be linked to ADHD. Like the genes associated with schizophrenia, these ADHD genes in some way regulate the function of dopamine in the brain. Future research will hopefully identify these genes more clearly and discover how they relate to the behavioral problems of ADHD, providing us with clues for developing more effective treatments.

CONCLUSION

Let's return for the last time to Roberta, to see what insights we may have gained into her cognitive and other brain processes throughout the day. Early that morning, a Monday, as Roberta thinks over her class schedule, her dorsolateral prefrontal cortex sorts through her list of courses, selectively attending to the classes she has on Monday. This attention helps her plan and organize for that particular day, triggering her memory to recall a list of items she will need to bring along with her. As she considers them, the various objects are briefly represented in her ventrolateral prefrontal cortex. As she arranges them in her backpack, the order and location of each activate the spatial working-memory capabilities of her dorsolateral prefrontal cortex.

As she stops at the bank to get some cash, Roberta uses her DLPFC to retrieve her PIN number from long-term memory, and then rehearses it through her phonological loop, activating her ventrolateral PFC. With cash in hand she dashes to class and would have gone straight there had not her DLPFC been maintaining a reminder that she has to switch from her normal routine and route to make a side trip to the biology department to drop off her homework.

Finally she arrives at French class. While she listens to the lecture, she also discretely reads bits and pieces of organic chemistry; her DLPFC alerts her whenever it notices that the professor is discussing something especially new or important, at which times she tries to pay more attention to the lecture. What really grabs her attention, however, is his announcement of a surprise vocabulary quiz. Had Roberta not been playing guitar and singing at the local pub until 2 a.m. last night (her once-a-week gig), she might have had the time to study French verbs. This would have kept her left ventrolateral prefrontal cortex quite busy, with the anterior portion helping her distinguish the various tenses (semantic information), and the posterior portion capturing the subtle differences in pronunciation (phonological information). Unfortunately, she didn't do any such studying (although she had certainly been exercising her ventrolateral PFC recalling song lyrics). During the pop quiz, Roberta realizes she has far less knowledge in her long-term memory to draw upon than she needs. Her DLPFC desperately tries to find the answers to the pop quiz questions in her long-term memory but, alas, she never learned the material in the first place.

All in all, a busy morning for Roberta and her prefrontal cortex.

Key Points

- Sensory memories are brief, transient sensations produced when you see, hear, feel, or taste something.

- Short-term memory can be used as a buffer for maintaining information temporarily over short delays so that it can be manipulated to guide and control behavior.

- Baddeley's model of working memory includes two independent buffers: the visuo-spatial sketchpad, which holds visual and spatial images, and the phonological loop, a temporary storage for auditory memory, that uses internal speech rehearsal. Baddeley's model also includes a central executive system, responsible for manipulating the two memory buffers by adding and deleting items, selecting items to guide behavior, retrieving information from and storing information in long-term memory, and so on.

- Baddeley's model of working memory suggests a process-specific dissociation between the manipulation of information in short-term memory by the central executive and the maintenance of information by the two rehearsal buffers. In addition, Baddeley argued for a material-specific dissociation between the maintenance of verbal-phonological information and visuo-spatial information.

- Studies both of animals and humans implicate the frontal lobes of the brain—especially the prefrontal cortex (PFC), the most anterior section of the frontal lobes—as critical for working-memory and executive-control processes.

- The severe deficits found in task-switching tests in association with certain lesions suggest that purposeful shifts in processing may be especially demanding on executive-control processes mediated by the frontal lobes.

- Electrophysiological studies in animals by Joaquin Fuster and Patricia Goldman-Rakic suggested that the PFC is critical for maintaining an internal representation in working memory over a delay, prior to making some response.

- The primate PFC can be divided into three main regions: the orbital PFC, the medial PFC, and the lateral PFC. The lateral PFC, located along the sides of the frontal lobes, is further subdivided into a lower region, the ventrolateral PFC, and an upper region, the dorsolateral PFC (DLPFC).

- Earl Miller has argued that a key to understanding the "cognitive" contribution of the PFC to working memory is the PFC's ability to sustain activity despite distractions.

- Michael Petrides and colleagues have suggested that the process-specific functional dichotomy proposed by Baddeley is to be found in the organization of the PFC. The ventrolateral PFC supports encoding and retrieval of information (including rehearsal for maintenance), akin to the visuo-spatial sketchpad and phonological-rehearsal loops proposed by Baddeley. The dorsolateral PFC supports higher order executive-control functions such as monitoring and manipulating of stored information, akin to Baddeley's central executive.

- Many neuroimaging studies have also confirmed a general distinction between storage and rehearsal, with storage mechanisms being located in the posterior regions of the brain and rehearsal mechanisms being located in the anterior regions, including the PFC.

- Consistent with the general tendency for language to be left-lateralized in the human brain, frontal-lobe patients with left-side damage are most likely to show specialized deficits in verbal (as opposed to visuo-spatial) working memory.

- Working memory interacts with long-term memory, especially with long-term declarative memories for episodes or facts. Several studies have shown that the dorsolateral PFC is activated during people's attempts to remember past events.

- The functional role of the left ventrolateral PFC during encoding of new semantic information can be further dissected: the anterior regions are activated during tasks that involve semantic processing, while posterior regions are activated during phonological processing.

- Working-memory impairments in schizophrenia become apparent during attempts to maintain a large number of items over a temporal delay, requiring functions associated with the dorsolateral PFC. In contrast, functions attributed to the ventrolateral PFC seem relatively unimpaired; thus performance on phonological or visuo-spatial memory tasks, and on memory tasks involving only minimal delays or few items, appears normal.

- Schizophrenia patients who have the highest number of D1 dopamine receptors in their PFC relative to controls exhibit the worst performance on the *N*-back assessment of working memory, providing compelling evidence for a link between dopamine regulation of dorsolateral PFC function and working memory.

- Adults with ADHD show deficits in mental calculations that require use of working memory.
- Neuroimaging of children with ADHD indicates that they have a smaller right PFC region, the region associated with spatial attention and working memory.

Key Terms

central executive, p. 173
delayed nonmatch-to-sample task, p. 176
depth of processing, p. 172
dopamine, p. 198

dorsolateral prefrontal cortex, p. 186
dysexecutive syndrome, p. 184
executive control, p. 173
iconic memory, p. 171

perseveration, p. 185
phonological loop, p. 173
prefrontal cortex (PFC), p. 183
sensory memories, p. 170
short-term memory, p. 171

transient memories, p. 170
visual sensory memory, p. 170
visuo-spatial sketchpad, p. 173
word-length effect, p. 175
working memory, p. 173

Concept Check

1. Juan chats with a pretty girl at a party. She tells him her phone number is (617) 666–1812, extension 2001, but he has no way to write it down. How can Juan remember the 14 numbers of her phone number until he can find a pencil and paper?

2. Describe two aspects of executive control that are used in both driving a car and in talking on a cell phone.

3. If you viewed the human brain from behind and a little to the left, which areas of the frontal lobes would be visible? Which would be obscured or hidden?

4. If you could see an image of someone's frontal lobes while they were rehearsing a list of words, would you see more activity on the left side or the right side? What if they were rehearsing visual images?

5. Tanya is trying to concentrate during a neuroanatomy lecture, because she really wants to get into medical school, but she keeps noticing Peter's adorable dimples. Which part of her brain is showing sustained attention to the neuroanatomy images and which part is being distracted by Peter's dimples?

6. In an episode of the old TV show *Seinfeld*, Jerry is trying to remember the name of a woman he met, but all he can recall is that her name is similar to the word for a part of a woman's anatomy. As Jerry struggles to recall her name, is he more likely to be activating his anterior or his posterior left ventrolateral prefrontal cortex?

7. Would a person with ADHD be more likely to take up bird watching or duck hunting?

Answers to Test Your Knowledge

1. Monitoring and manipulating information requires the dorsolateral PFC.

2. Verbal rehearsal requires the left ventrolateral PFC.

3. Semantic encoding is done by the anterior left ventrolateral PFC.

4. Phonological encoding is a specialty of the posterior left ventrolateral PFC.

5. Visuo-spatial rehearsal requires the right ventrolateral PFC.

Further Reading

Goldberg, E. (2002). *The executive brain: frontal lobes and the civilized brain.* • Oxford, England: Oxford University Press. An academic and personal view of the frontal lobes by a noted neuropsychologist.

Nasar, S. (2001). *A beautiful mind.* • New York: Simon & Schuster. A biography of the Nobel Laureate John Nash and his descent into and recovery from schizophrenia.

CHAPTER 6

Non-Associative Learning

Learning about Repeated Events

JEFFREY'S GRANDMOTHER WAS FED UP. It was two o'clock in the morning, and once again her grandson was banging around in the basement. She couldn't remember how many times she had told him to stop making such a racket. It had taken her a couple of years to get used to the neighbor's dogs barking all night. They almost never woke her up now. But Jeffrey's noisiness was another matter altogether. Every time he started up with the sawing, the bumping, and the yelling it seemed worse than the last time. Eventually, she forced Jeffrey to move out of the house. Only later would she learn what the noises meant: Jeffrey had been murdering young men, having sex with their dead bodies, and then chopping them into pieces.

At first Jeffrey Dahmer was annoyed at being kicked out, but he soon got used to the convenience of having his own apartment. He took to cruising around the Pink Flamingo and other bars that were popular among young gay men, his potential victims. Dahmer had learned to recognize which of the customers were most likely to take his bait and follow him home. He couldn't say what it was about them that let him know they were susceptible, but by now he was confident that he could discriminate the "maybes" from the "probably-nots."

During this same period, reports began to appear in the news media of young men going missing from the neighborhood. But disappearances and murders were all too common in Milwaukee, and for most people this was just more of the same. When one of Dahmer's victims—a 14-year-old Laotian who spoke no English—escaped to run naked through the streets, police picked him up and returned him to Dahmer's apartment. Dahmer convinced them that the boy was his adult homosexual lover and that they were just having a lover's tiff. The police noticed a terrible stench in the apartment, but noxious smells weren't uncommon in this part of the city. The officers left, and the boy was not seen alive again. It wasn't until another victim escaped and flagged down a squad car that police returned to Dahmer's apartment. This time, they noticed some photos of dismembered bodies in the bedroom. That got the officers' attention, and when they investigated further, they found a human head in the refrigerator. The public, initially blasé about the news of one more captured murderer, paid considerably more attention when they learned that Dahmer was not only killing his victims but also raping and eating the dead bodies. The Jeffrey Dahmer case quickly became the biggest news story of its day.

When someone experiences repeated events, the brain creates memories of the experiences. Sometimes these memories lead a person to ignore future repetitions of the events. Dahmer's grandmother was used to being bothered by the neighbor's dogs; the police were used to smelly apartments; the public was used to news reports of murder. None of these occurrences elicited much of a reaction until new and more alarming aspects of the situation came to light.

Such loss of responding to originally noticeable stimuli as a result of repeated exposure is called *habituation*, and it's one of the most basic and widespread forms of learning. All organisms ever tested—even those without a brain, such as protozoa—show habituation. Habituation is just one example of how merely experiencing an event, over and over, causes a person to learn about that event (in habituation the person learns to disregard the event). Repeated exposure leads to certain other forms of learning, too, such as what Jeffrey Dahmer learned about choosing suitable victims. This chapter focuses on how memories for repeated events are acquired and expressed.

6.1 Behavioral Processes

The subject of this chapter is **non-associative learning:** learning that involves only one relatively isolated stimulus at a time. In comparison, **associative learning** involves learning to associate one stimulus with another or to associate a stimulus with a new response. Because it doesn't involve learning new associations, non-associative learning is often considered to be the simplest form of learning. Non-associative learning may be simple in concept, but it is far from trivial and it pervades daily human life.

Learning about Repeated Stimuli

Suppose a man who was born and raised in Jamaica has never seen snow. If he moves to Utah, he will probably be excited and fascinated by his first snowfall. But a man of the same age who has grown up near Utah's ski resorts will react to the same snowfall very differently. For him, snow is recognizable, common, nothing to write home about—except, perhaps, for the inconvenience it causes on his commute to work.

Everything is novel the first time it happens to you. Even the most ordinary events only become familiar after repeated exposure. Through repeated exposure, you may learn not to respond to a particular event, even if—like the Jamaican in the snow—you originally responded with great excitement. This kind of learning, **habituation,** is formally defined as a decrease in the strength or occurrence of a behavior after repeated exposure to the stimulus that produces the behavior.

The Process of Habituation

You've experienced habituation if you've ever moved to a new home. Probably, the first night or two, you had trouble getting to sleep because of the strange noises outside your window (whether wailing police sirens or chirping crickets). But after a few nights, you probably habituated to the noises and slept until morning.

In the laboratory, researchers examine simpler examples of habituation that they can describe in terms of a single easily controlled stimulus and a single easily measurable response. One such response is the **acoustic startle reflex,** which is a defensive response to a loud, unexpected noise. When a rat in an experimental chamber is startled by a loud noise, it jumps, much like you might jump if someone sneaked up behind you and yelled in your ear. If the same noise is presented over and over again, every minute or so, the rat's startle response declines (Figure 6.1a); if the process goes on long enough, the rat may cease to startle altogether. At this point, the rat has habituated to the loud noise.

Another common way to study habituation uses the **orienting response,** an organism's innate reaction to a novel stimulus. For example, if a checkerboard pattern (or any other unfamiliar visual stimulus) is presented to an infant, the infant's orienting response is to turn her head and look at it for a few seconds before shifting her gaze elsewhere. If the checkerboard is removed for 10 seconds and then redisplayed, the infant will respond again—but for a shorter time than on the first presentation (Figure 6.1b). The duration of staring, called *fixation time*, decreases with repeated presentations of the stimulus, in a manner very much like the habituation of rats' startle response (Malcuit, Bastien, & Pomerleau, 1996).

Normally, habituation is advantageous for an organism. By habituating to familiar stimuli, the organism avoids wasting time and energy on an elaborate response to every familiar event. But habituation carries risks. A deer that becomes habituated to the sound of gunshots is a deer whose head may end up as a trophy mounted in a hunter's cabin. A poker player who habituates to the excitement of winning a small pot may start to play for larger and larger stakes, putting his finances at risk. The dangers of habituation are immortalized in the story of the boy who cried wolf. In this folk tale, the boy plays practical jokes on his neighbors, calling them to come save him from an imaginary wolf; eventually the villagers learn there is no reason to respond when he calls. Later, when a real wolf attacks, the villagers have habituated to the boy's cries, and no one comes to save him.

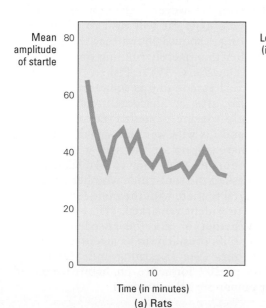

(a) Rats

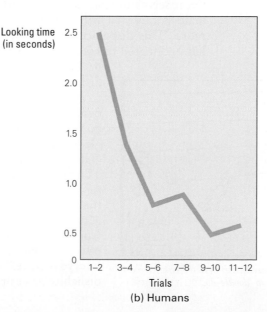

(b) Humans

Figure 6.1
Habituation (a) The acoustic startle response in rats declines with repeated presentation of a loud auditory stimulus. (b) The time infants spend looking at a visual stimulus declines with repeated presentation of the stimulus. (a) Adapted from Davis, 1980; (b) adapted from Malcuit et al., 1996.

Factors Influencing Rate and Duration of Habituation How rapidly a response habituates and how long the decrease in responding is observed are influenced by several factors: how startling the stimulus is, the number of times it is experienced, and the length of time between exposures. The relationship between the number and spacing of exposures and the strength of responses parallels the effects of practice on the performance of perceptual-motor skills, which you read about in Chapter 4. As an animal's exposure to a stimulus increases, its responsiveness gradually decreases. A group of animals given sessions of multiple closely spaced (that is, massed) exposures to stimuli with short intervals between sessions typically shows faster habituation than a group given sessions of more widely spaced exposures with longer intervals between sessions (Rankin & Broster, 1992; Thompson & Spencer, 1966). But if these two groups of animals are retested after a relatively long break, those in the spaced-exposure group show better memory of the stimulus, and respond less, than those in the massed-exposure group (Gatchel, 1975; Pedreira, Romano, Tomsic, Lozada, & Maldonado, 1998). Recall from Chapter 4 that the same effects were observed for skill learning after massed and spaced practice.

The effects of habituation may last for a few minutes or several hours, and under some circumstances may last a day or more, but they do not last forever. If a rat has habituated to a loud noise, and then there is a short delay of an hour or so, the rat is likely to startle anew when the noise is played again. The reappearance or increase in strength of a habituated response after a short period of no stimulus presentation is called **spontaneous recovery.**

Dishabituation An important feature of habituation is that it does not generalize freely to other stimuli; in other words, it is stimulus-specific. A baby that has habituated to one visual stimulus (say, a donut shape) will show a strong orienting response to a new visual stimulus (say, a cross shape). This renewal of response when a new stimulus is presented is called **dishabituation.** Dishabituation provides a useful way to demonstrate that the absence of responding to a repeated stimulus is indeed habituation and not some other factor—such as the baby falling asleep during testing.

Nonhuman animals show dishabituation, too. In the laboratory, a male rat will mate with an unfamiliar female many times over a period of a few hours, but it seems to reach a point of exhaustion. However, if the now-familiar female is replaced with a new female, the male rat will rush to mate some more. This dishabituation of the mating response shows that the male rat has habituated to his first partner, rather than merely running out of energy or interest in sex (Dewsbury, 1981; Fisher, 1962). The dishabituation of sexual responding is sometimes referred to as the *Coolidge effect,* after an anecdote involving President Coolidge. While touring a poultry farm, the story goes, the president and his wife were informed that a single rooster could mate dozens of times in a single day. "Ha," said Mrs. Coolidge. "Tell that to Mr. Coolidge." The president then asked the tour guide whether the rooster was always required to mate with the same female. Told that it was not, the president remarked, "Ha—tell that to Mrs. Coolidge." Whether or not the anecdote is true, Coolidge is the only U.S. president to have a psychological effect named after him. (See "Learning and Memory in Everyday Life" on p. 209 for more on habituation and dishabituation of human sexual response.)

"Sometimes I get so bored with myself I can barely make it to 'doodle-do.'"

> ## ▶ Learning and Memory in Everyday Life

Sex on the Beach

Advertisements for travel to exotic locales with long, sandy beaches often show happy couples falling in love all over again, rediscovering the romance that may have drained out of their everyday existence back home. Can two people really reignite their old flame simply by taking it to a new location? The answer may be yes—and the reason may be dishabituation.

In this chapter, you're reading about dishabituation of sexual responding in rats. It turns out to be significantly harder to study such phenomena in humans. You can't just lock a man and a woman in a room together and monitor how many times they have sex. So instead, most human studies have focused on the ability of sexually explicit photos and recordings to elicit sexual arousal in male undergraduate volunteers. Researchers gauge this ability using instruments that monitor objective measures of sexual arousal such as penis diameter (the technical term is "penile tumescence"). Increases in penis diameter reflect increased arousal. Such studies have shown that if the same arousing stimuli are presented repeatedly, sexual habituation is observed in the human male, just as in rats and monkeys (Koukounas & Over, 2001; Plaud, Gaither, Henderson, & Devitt, 1997). To rule out the possibility that the reduction in arousal reflects simple fatigue, researchers present a novel stimulus and demonstrate dishabituation of sexual arousal to the new stimulus.

Relatively few studies of habituation of sexual arousal have been conducted in women. One problem is that women usually do not become as aroused as their male counterparts when viewing sexually explicit photos. Obviously, it is hard for researchers to measure decreases in an arousal response if they can't reliably elicit arousal to begin with. But in studies that have

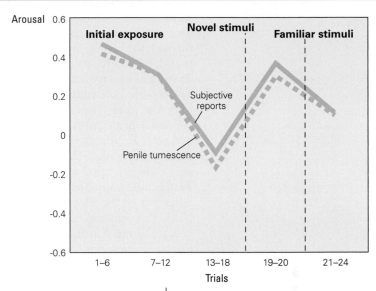

Sexual habituation and dishabituation. Participants in the study (in this case males) initially habituated to sexually explicit materials, but could be dishabituated by the introduction of novel material. Adapted from Koukounas and Over, 2001.

managed to solve this problem, it seems that female undergraduates do not habituate to sexual arousal as strongly as do male undergraduates (Laan & Everaerd, 1995; Youn, 2006). Might there be a gender difference in human sexual habituation? If so, is this difference specific to sexual arousal, or are females simply less likely to habituate in general? Not enough is known to answer these questions as yet, but certainly they are questions worth pursuing.

Another interesting aspect of sexual habituation is that it seems to happen without conscious awareness. For example, male students in a sexual habituation experiment often show habituation within a single session, responding less and less to the same sexually explicit photo as the session goes on—but they also habituate across sessions, responding less and less each day of a multi-day experiment (Plaud et al., 1997). Under these circumstances, participants often report that they were aware that their arousal was decreasing within a single session, but they seem to be unaware that their arousal also decreased across sessions, although penile measurements clearly show that it did. Such continuous but imperceptible decreases in arousal might be a factor in promiscuity and infidelity, which not only threaten

stable relationships but may contribute to the spread of sexually transmitted diseases (Plaud et al, 1997).

So, how can someone in a long-term relationship deal with the hidden scourge of sexual habituation? One strategy is to institute a prolonged period of abstinence, in the hope that this will lead to a spontaneous recovery of interest. In fact, couples who go through an extended separation (such as a long business trip by one partner) often find each other much more attractive when they are reunited. Another strategy is to use novel stimuli to bring about dishabituation—for example, staging romantic interludes in new locations, dressing up in costumes, or trying a different technique of lovemaking. Anything that introduces unfamiliar stimuli may help combat habituation. So the next time you're feeling bored with an old relationship, a trip to Tahiti might be just what the doctor ordered!

The Process of Sensitization

In the summer of 2005, as Hurricane Katrina bore down on the U.S. Gulf Coast, authorities warned the citizens of New Orleans to evacuate before the storm struck. Some people left, but thousands of residents were unable to evacuate or chose not to leave their homes. Katrina hit, the storm surge broke through the levees, and much of New Orleans was flooded. In the days that followed, the world saw graphic TV images of people stranded on rooftops, bodies floating down city streets, and refugees living in appalling conditions at the city's overcrowded convention center.

A few weeks later, Hurricane Rita entered the Caribbean. This time, Texas seemed a principal target, and authorities ordered Houston and Galveston to evacuate. Residents who might otherwise have opted to ride out the storm in their homes took to the roads instead; those who might have been unable to evacuate were provided with transportation. The result was incredible traffic jams. Traffic was so intense that some people took 15 hours or more to drive 80 or 90 miles out of the Houston area; some cars idled so long in bumper-to-bumper traffic that they ran out of gas before getting more than a few miles from home.

Part of the reason for the huge response to the Texas evacuation order was the recent memory of Katrina. Under other circumstances, the threat from Rita might have gone largely unheeded. But in the wake of Katrina, evacuation orders took on new significance. This is an example of **sensitization,** in which a startling stimulus (such as the TV coverage of Katrina) leads to a strong response to a later stimulus (such as the Texas evacuation orders) that might otherwise have evoked a weaker response. In this way, sensitization is the opposite of habituation, in which repetitions of a stimulus lead to decreases in responding.

Whereas habituation can attenuate a rat's acoustic startle reflex, sensitization can heighten it (Figure 6.2). As described above, when rats are subjected to a loud noise over and over again, their startle response habituates. But if some of the rats are given an electric shock, and then the loud noise is played again, their startle response will be much greater than in rats not receiving a shock (Davis, 1989). In other words, the strong electric shock sensitizes the rats, increasing their startle response to a subsequent loud noise stimulus. Such sensitization is usually short-lived, however. It may persist for 10 or 15 minutes after the shock, but beyond that, the startle response drops back to normal levels.

Humans also show sensitization of their startle reflexes. This is most easily shown using the **skin conductance response (SCR)** (also known as the galvanic skin response, or GSR), a change in the skin's electrical conductivity associated with emotions such as anxiety, fear, or surprise. These fluctuations in electrical conductance are recorded by electrodes similar to those used for an electroencephalograph (EEG). Lie detector tests usually involve measuring a person's SCR, because the emotions evoked by attempts at deception can alter the SCR. (Unfortunately, other emotions—such as nervousness or excitement—can also alter the SCR, which is why lie detector tests are not perfectly reliable indicators of truthfulness.)

Exposure to an unexpected loud noise (say, an explosion or a yell) causes a pronounced startle response in humans, accompanied by a sharp SCR. A neutral musical tone may cause a mild startle response, which is reflected as a small SCR. If the loud noise is played before presenting the tone, the participant's SCRs to the tone are stronger than they would be without the loud noise (Lang, Davis, & Ohman, 2000). The loud noise sensitizes the startle response to the tone, just as electric shock sensitizes the startle response in rats.

Figure 6.2 Sensitization of the rat acoustic startle reflex When a startle-provoking noise is presented again and again, the rat's startle reflex habituates (minutes 1 through 20). If a foot shock is then administered, the amplitude of the startle reflex to a subsequent noise is greater in the shocked rats than in the unshocked rats. Adapted from Davis, 1989.

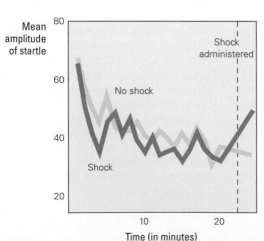

Like habituation, sensitization is seen in a wide range of species, including bullfrogs, sea slugs, and humans (Bee, 2001; Eisenstein, Eisenstein, & Bonheim, 1991; Marcus, Nolen, Rankin, & Carew, 1988). However, fewer exposures are necessary to produce sensitization than to produce habituation, and the resulting memories can last much longer—for days or weeks (Borszcz, Cranney, & Leaton, 1989; Davis, 1972). Moreover, whereas habituation is stimulus-specific, sensitization is not. For example, an animal's startle response may habituate to one loud tone, if that tone is repeated over and over; but if a different loud noise is presented, the startle response reappears in full force—habituation doesn't transfer to the new noise. By contrast, exposure to a sensitizing stimulus (such as an electric shock) can amplify the startle response to any stimulus that comes later: tone, loud noise, or anything else.

Priming

Sensitization increases an organism's probability (or frequency) of responding to a stimulus. Prior exposure to a stimulus can also improve the organism's ability to recognize that stimulus (or related stimuli) later; this effect is called **priming**. For example, priming in humans is often studied using a **word-stem completion task,** in which a person is given a list of word stems (MOT__, SUP__, and such) and asked to fill in the blank with the first word that comes to mind. On average, people are likely to fill in the blanks to form common English words (MOTEL or MOTOR, SUPPOSE or SUPPER). But if people were previously exposed to a list of words containing those stems (MOTH, SUPREME, and so on), then they are much more likely to fill in the blanks to form the words from that list (Graf, Squire, & Mandler, 1984). Interestingly, individuals with anterograde amnesia (such as those you read about in Chapter 3) also show word-stem priming—even though they have no conscious recollection of having studied the words (Graf et al., 1984). This suggests that priming does not depend on explicit recall abilities.

Nonhuman animals show priming too. For example, blue jays like to eat moths, and moths have evolved coloration patterns that help them blend into the background where they settle (Figure 6.3a). Therefore, blue jays have to be very good at detecting subtle differences of pattern that distinguish a tasty meal from a patch of tree bark. Researchers studied this detection ability by training blue jays to look at pictures on a screen and to peck at the screen to signal "there's a moth here" and to peck at a key to signal "no moth" (Figure 6.3b). The birds did very well, but they were quicker and more accurate at detecting a particular species of moth if they had recently detected other members of that species, as shown in Figure 6.3c (Bond & Kamil, 1999). In other words, recent observations of one kind of moth *primed* the jays' abilities to recognize it later.

Figure 6.3 Priming in blue jays (a) Virtual moths on a gray background are more detectable than the same moths on speckled backgrounds. Higher numbers indicate more cryptic backgrounds. (b) Blue jays learn to peck on screens when they detect a virtual moth, and to peck on a green key when they detect no moths. (c) When a moth is similar to a recently detected moth (that is, the dissimilarity is low), blue jays are better able to detect the moth, suggesting that prior exposure facilitates recognition. In other words, priming has occurred. Adapted from Bond and Kamil, 1999.

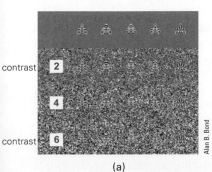

contrast 2

contrast 6

Alan B. Bond

(a)

Alan B. Bond

(b)

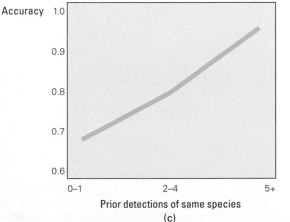

Accuracy

Prior detections of same species

(c)

Perceptual Learning

Habituation, sensitization, and priming are forms of learning in which repeated exposure to stimuli leads to an increase or decrease in responding to (or recognizing) those stimuli. But repeated exposure doesn't just change how a human or other animal responds to stimuli. Sometimes, it can change how the animal perceives those stimuli. For example, Jeffrey Dahmer learned to recognize individuals who would be likely to go home with him and could be murdered without too much difficulty. **Perceptual learning** is learning in which experience with a set of stimuli makes those stimuli easier to distinguish. Perceptual learning is conceptually similar to priming in that prior experience improves recognition. It differs in that priming generally improves the speed with which familiar or recently observed stimuli are recognized, whereas perceptual learning leads to an increased ability to make fine distinctions between highly similar stimuli.

For example, commercial poultry farmers like to sort male from female chicks as soon after hatching as possible, to save the cost of feeding male chicks (males don't lay eggs and they produce lower-quality meat than females). By 5 or 6 weeks, it's easy to tell the sex of a chick based on feather patterns. But highly trained individuals, called chicken-sexers, can distinguish whether a day-old chick is male or female just by glancing at the chick's rear end. Accomplished chicken-sexers can make this distinction with high accuracy at a viewing rate of one chick per half-second, even though the male and female chicks look identical to the untrained eye (Biederman & Shiffrar, 1987). Some chicken-sexers can't even verbalize the subtle cues they use to make the distinction; they have seen so many examples of male and female chicks that they "just know which is which." Medical diagnosticians have a similar talent. All rashes may look alike to an inexperienced medical student, but an experienced dermatologist can glance at a rash and tell immediately, and with high accuracy, whether a patient has contact dermatitis, ringworm, or some other condition.

Mere Exposure Learning

Sometimes, perceptual learning happens through mere exposure to the stimuli in question. For example, Eleanor Gibson and colleagues exposed one group of rats to large triangular and circular shapes mounted on the walls of their home cages for about a month (E. Gibson & Walk, 1956). The researchers then trained this group and a control group of rats to approach one of the shapes but not the other. Rats familiar with the shapes learned to discriminate between them faster than rats that had not seen the shapes before. During the initial exposure phase, nothing had been done to teach the rats in the experimental group about the shapes; *mere exposure* to the shapes seemed to facilitate later learning about those shapes. Because the original learning in such experiments happens without explicit prompting, through mere exposure to the stimuli, it is sometimes called **mere exposure learning.** A related term is **latent learning,** meaning that the original learning is undetected (latent) until explicitly demonstrated at a later time.

People show mere exposure learning, too. In one study, volunteers were trained to discriminate between complex line drawings—the scribbles seen in Figure 6.4—then were shown cards, each containing a scribble, and were told that some cards would be identical to previously viewed scribbles. Their task was to tell the experimenter whether they'd seen each particular scribble before. The experimenter gave no feedback—no indication of whether a participant's familiarity judgment was correct or not. Unbeknownst to the participants, there was only one scribble (the "target scribble" in Figure 6.4) that recurred from time to time. Initially, participants were pretty accurate at identifying repetitions of the target scribble, as well as correctly identifying as unfamiliar the novel

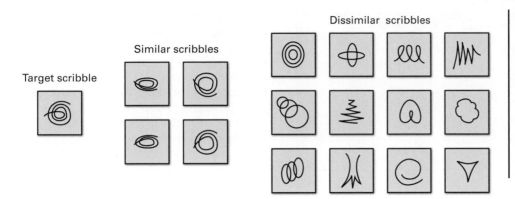

Figure 6.4 Mere exposure learning in humans A person repeatedly views a particular scribble (target), then tries to identify the scribble on a card mixed into a deck of cards with other scribbles, varying in similarity to the target scribble. Her ability to identify the target scribble gradually improves, even without feedback about performance. Adapted from J. J. Gibson and Gibson, 1955.

scribbles that were very unlike the target ("dissimilar scribbles"). Early in training, however, participants also made many mistakes by incorrectly "recognizing" scribbles that were similar to the target scribble. But with more and more exposure to scribbles, the participants could differentiate the target from very similar but novel stimuli (J. J. Gibson & Gibson, 1955). This is an example of perceptual learning through mere exposure to scribbles.

Discrimination Training

Of course, not all perceptual learning happens through mere exposure. Chicken-sexers don't just wander randomly through a poultry factory until they can spot males and females; they are intensively trained. Similarly, medical diagnosticians don't just happen across their knowledge; they spend years studying and interning. Part of this training—for both doctors and chicken-sexers—is a process of seeing examples, trying to distinguish between them, and receiving feedback about accuracy. Feedback training can greatly facilitate perceptual learning.

When you look at a dog, you probably notice many different things about it. It's big, it's cute, it has two eyes, there is drool coming out of its mouth. What you might not notice is the dog's apparent pedigree, how its tail posture compares with that of other dogs of the same breed, the ratio of its leg length to head length, its dental structure, or its likely value. If you happen to be a professional judge for dog shows, however, you may notice these features at first glance. Dog-show judges have been repeatedly exposed to dogs over many years. Some of what they've learned comes from mere exposure: after seeing a few thousand cocker spaniels, you begin to get an idea of what the breed should look like. But any sensible and successful dog-show judge hasn't relied on mere exposure: she's also made active attempts to learn about good and poor examples of the breed. Both processes—mere exposure learning and discrimination training—make an experienced dog-show judge better than other people at discriminating between individual dogs of the same breed.

Studies in which research participants learn novel discriminations shed light on some of the ways experts learn their discrimination skills. For example, an untrained person wearing a blindfold can discern the number of toothpicks—either 1 or 2—that are touching the skin on his arm, as long as the points are sufficiently far apart (about 30 mm). If the points are closer together (say, only 5 mm), then he won't be able to discriminate the two pressure points, and he will think that a single toothpick is touching his arm. But the ability to discriminate can improve with training. An early study of this phenomenon found that with 4 weeks of training, blindfolded individuals could discriminate two pressure points as close together as 5 mm (Volkmann, 1858). In other words, the ability to perceive and discriminate tactile stimuli can improve with training.

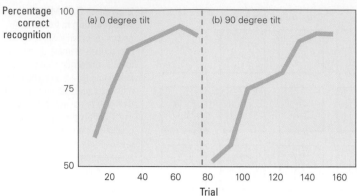

Figure 6.5 Learning specificity in humans People are first trained to distinguish patterns tilted at a particular angle (0 degrees) from patterns tilted at other angles. Next, they are trained on a task that is identical except for the tilt angle: now they are asked to recognize patterns with a 90 degree tilt. At the start of this new task, their performance is the same as at the start of the first task (50% correct, or "chance")—showing no benefits from their prior perceptual learning with a different stimulus. Adapted from Fiorentini and Berardi, 1981.

Experts at any kind of discrimination, including dog-show judges, acquire perceptual learning through training in the same fashion—by practicing with many examples and receiving feedback about the accuracy of their classifications. But what happens if the dog-show judge is asked to judge the prize pigs at the county fair? Is she likely to prove as eagle-eyed an expert on pigs as she is on dogs? The answer is generally no. In most cases, perceptual learning shows a high degree of **learning specificity,** which means that learning about one group of stimuli doesn't transfer automatically to another group of stimuli.

For example, people can be trained to distinguish a visual pattern tilted at a particular angle (say, 0 degrees) from other patterns tilted at different angles (Fiorentini & Berardi, 1981). Performance gradually improves until the correct choice is made about 90% of the time (Figure 6.5). If the same people are now tested on their ability to detect patterns tilted at a 90 degree angle, the earlier learning doesn't automatically transfer to the new task. In fact, the participants start the new task back at the "chance" level (50% correct, the rate of correct responses they'd be making if they were answering randomly) and have to learn the new discrimination, just as they had to learn the earlier one. In other words, the earlier perceptual learning had high specificity and did not transfer to novel stimuli.

The specificity of perceptual learning is determined partly by the difficulty of the discrimination task being learned. More difficult tasks lead to greater specificity, at least in humans (Ahissar & Hochstein, 1997). As you might imagine, discrimination tasks are more difficult when the target stimulus is very similar to the background in which it is hidden. As a result, learning specificity is high if the target stimulus and context are highly similar (Wagner, 1981). Remember the earlier example of the blue jays and the camouflaged moths (Figure 6.3)? Presumably, the better camouflaged the moths, the tougher the discrimination task, and the more unlikely it is that learning to recognize one species of moth against one background will transfer to the ability to recognize other moths against other backgrounds.

Spatial Learning

Many kinds of *spatial learning*—the acquisition of information about one's surroundings—take the form of perceptual learning; some even take the form of mere exposure learning. For example, when you were young, your parents may have driven you to school, or perhaps you took a bus. You probably were driven along the same roads hundreds of times over the course of several years. Eventually, perhaps, the day came when you walked (or drove) to school by yourself, and you probably knew the route by heart and found your way easily. How could you navigate successfully the very first time you tried? During all those prior trips, you were learning about the spatial arrangement of your neighborhood, as well as landmarks such as streets and buildings, without being aware you were learning. This was mere exposure learning, or latent learning—until the day you first exhibited this learning by navigating to school on your own.

Spatial learning is seen throughout the animal kingdom. One of the earliest demonstrations of spatial learning through mere exposure in rats was by Edward Tolman (Tolman & Honzik, 1930). He placed rats in a complex maze and trained them to make their way to a particular location in the maze—the food

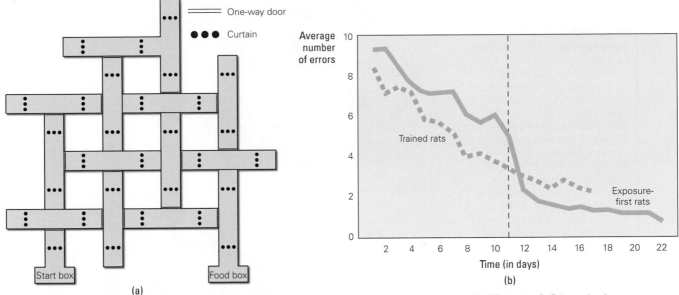

(a)

(b)

Figure 6.6 Learning by exploration in rats (a) Tolman placed rats in a complex maze with a food box. (b) Some rats (the trained rats) received a food reward each time they entered the box. These rats learned to run to the food box, making fewer and fewer errors (wrong turns) as the days went by. Other rats (the exposure-first rats) were simply placed in the maze and allowed to explore, with no food reward. On the eleventh day, these rats started receiving food when they entered the food box. The exposure-first rats quickly learned to run to the box for food, making fewer errors than the rats that had been trained on the task. Adapted from Tolman and Honzik, 1930.

box—to be rewarded with a bit of food (Figure 6.6a). These trained rats learned to run to the food box with fewer and fewer errors (wrong turns) as the days went by (Figure 6.6b). But rats in a second group were merely placed in the maze for the first 10 days and allowed to explore. If they stumbled into the food box, they received no food and were simply removed from the maze. On the eleventh day, these rats started getting food every time they entered the food box. As Figure 6.6b shows, these exposure-first rats also learned to run to the food box to get their food—and they learned so well that their performance quickly surpassed that of the rats who'd been training on this task all along! Tolman and Honzik concluded that both groups of rats had learned about the location of the food box. One group had learned by explicit training and the other by mere exposure—during their exploration of the maze environment. The latent learning made it easy for the exploring rats to later learn to run to a specific location in the maze.

What were the rats learning? Perhaps they were merely learning a sequence of turns: turn right from the start box, then left, and so on. Such learning does occur, but it isn't enough to account for everything the rats learned, because a rat could be placed in a new start position and still find its way to the goal. Rats, and other animals, also seem to navigate by landmarks. For example, a rat in a laboratory maze may use visual cues, such as the sight of a window or a wall decoration visible over the edges of the maze. As long as these cues are in sight, the rat may be able to navigate from any starting point in the maze. But if the cues are switched (or the maze is rotated inside the room), the rat may get temporarily confused (we describe an experiment on this later in the chapter).

Animals in the wild also seem to learn to navigate based on landmarks. In a classic study, Niko Tinbergen studied wasps' ability to locate their home nest. Certain species of wasps and bees engage in orientation flights before leaving their hives or burrows to look for food; during these orientation flights, they circle around their home base. Tinbergen and William Kruyt laid a circle of pinecones around a wasp burrow while the wasps were inside (Tinbergen & Kruyt, 1972 [1938]). The experimenters left the pinecone circle intact for several orientation flights—long enough for the wasps to get used to this landmark (Figure 6.7a). Then, while a wasp was away on a foraging trip, the experimenters moved the circle of pinecones away from the burrow (Figure 6.7b). When the

Figure 6.7 Use of land-marks by wasps (a) Tinbergen and Kruyt placed pinecones around a wasps' burrow (an underground nest) to provide visual information about the burrow's location. When leaving home, wasps take orienta-tion flights, during which they seem to note local landmarks (such as the pinecones) that will help them find their way home later. (b) When the circle of pinecones was moved to flat ground near the nest, the return-ing wasps searched for the burrow inside the circle of pinecones. Adapted from Tinbergen and Kruyt, 1972 (1938).

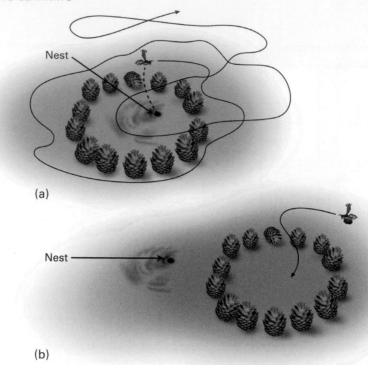

wasp returned, it repeatedly searched for its burrow within the ring of pinecones. Tinbergen and Kruyt concluded that when wasps leave home to for-age, they use the orientation flight to collect visual information about landmarks that will later help them locate the burrow. If these landmarks are repositioned while the wasp is away, the wasp will search for the burrow based on the land-marks, revealing that it has learned about the spatial relationship between the burrow and surrounding landmarks. Just like Tolman's rats, the wasps learn about the spatial properties of their environments through observation; much of this learning is latent and does not become evident until a subsequent test chal-lenges the animal to display what it has learned.

Test Your Knowledge

Perceptual Learning versus Habituation

Both habituation and perceptual learning can result from repeated exposures to stim-uli. Although the experiences that lead to these phenomena can be similar, the kinds of responses that provide evidence of these two forms of learning are notably different. For each photograph, (a) through (c), identify what kind or kinds of learning might have led to the scene depicted and how your hypothesis might be tested.

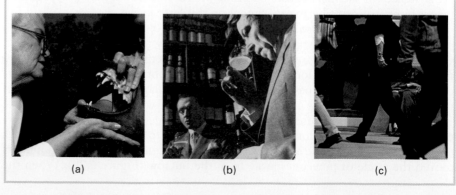

Models of Non-Associative Learning

As you have seen, habituation, sensitization, and perceptual learning are all forms of non-associative learning—meaning that they do not necessarily involve learning to associate one stimulus with another. The only change observed in non-associative learning is the way an organism responds to or perceives a particular stimulus. This is why non-associative learning is often considered to be simpler (or more basic) than associative learning. Even so, psychologists still disagree about what processes underlie non-associative learning. Here we examine a few of the most prominent models that have been proposed to describe those processes.

Dual Process Theory

The first theory of non-associative learning attempts to explain habituation. Apparently, habituation starts with a stimulus S that originally evokes a hardwired muscle reflex M, and repeated exposure to the stimulus simply weakens or inhibits the connection between S and M (Figure 6.8a). As you read earlier in the chapter, sensitization is in some ways the opposite of habituation: exposure to a strong stimulus (say, a tail shock T) temporarily increases the connection between S and M, meaning that stimulus S evokes a stronger reflex response than it would have evoked without T. **Dual process theory** suggests that habituation and sensitization are independent of each other but operate in parallel. Specifically, a stimulus S evokes some activity in intermediate nodes (for example, nodes 1 and 2 in Figure 6.8a) and eventually leads to activation of a motor reflex M. Repeated presentations of S can result in habituation, weakening the links between intermediate nodes and thus reducing the strength or likelihood of activity at M. In sensitization, by contrast, the strength or likelihood of activity at M is temporarily strengthened by exposure to an arousing stimulus T.

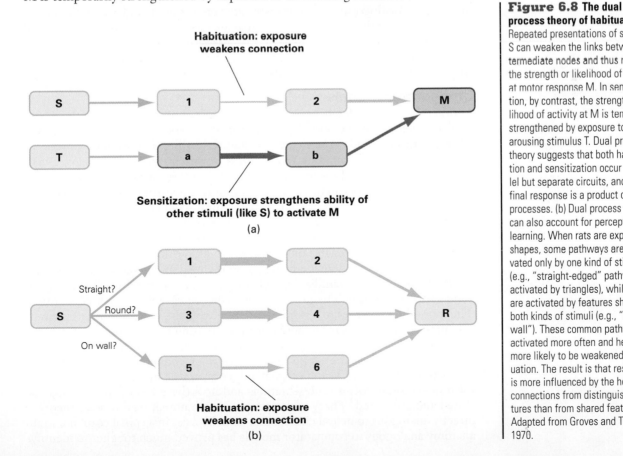

Habituation: exposure weakens connection

Sensitization: exposure strengthens ability of other stimuli (like S) to activate M

(a)

Habituation: exposure weakens connection

(b)

Figure 6.8 The dual process theory of habituation (a) Repeated presentations of stimulus S can weaken the links between intermediate nodes and thus reduce the strength or likelihood of activity at motor response M. In sensitization, by contrast, the strength or likelihood of activity at M is temporarily strengthened by exposure to an arousing stimulus T. Dual process theory suggests that both habituation and sensitization occur in parallel but separate circuits, and the final response is a product of both processes. (b) Dual process theory can also account for perceptual learning. When rats are exposed to shapes, some pathways are activated only by one kind of stimulus (e.g., "straight-edged" pathways are activated by triangles), while others are activated by features shared by both kinds of stimuli (e.g., "on the wall"). These common pathways are activated more often and hence are more likely to be weakened by habituation. The result is that response R is more influenced by the heavier connections from distinguishing features than from shared features. (a) Adapted from Groves and Thompson, 1970.

In dual process theory, the response to a stimulus observed after repeated exposures to that stimulus reflects the combined effects of habituation and sensitization (Groves & Thompson, 1970). The actual outcome—the strength of the response to S on a given presentation—depends on such things as how often S has been repeated and how intense and recent was the sensitizing event. This dual process theory of habituation was developed to account for habituation as observed in the spinal cords of cats (Thompson & Spencer, 1966). In fact, the schematic of nodes and connections shown in Figure 6.8a is similar to the actual anatomical organization of neural circuits in the cat spinal cord, which has one pathway going directly from stimulus to response and a second pathway that can modulate this stimulus–response chain.

Dual process theory can also explain perceptual learning. Consider again the experiment in which rats lived in a cage with triangles and circles on the walls (E. Gibson & Walk, 1956). The triangles and circles share some features: both are constructed of the same material, both occur on the walls (but never, for example, on the floor of the cage), and so on. They also differ in some features: for example, the triangles have straight sides and the circles have round sides. Figure 6.8b schematizes this situation. When the rat views a stimulus S that is triangular and on the wall, two pathways are activated—from 1 to 2 to response R, and from 5 to 6 to response R. Likewise, when the rat views a stimulus S that is circular and on the wall, two pathways are activated—from 3 to 4 to R and from 5 to 6 to R. Notice that the pathway corresponding to the shared feature is activated every time the rat views any shape, but the pathways corresponding to the distinguishing features are activated only when the rat views a certain shape. Since the pathway corresponding to the shared feature is activated most often, the effects of habituation on this pathway are larger. The end result is that the response R depends more on the distinguishing features (straight versus round) and less on the shared feature (being on the wall). In other words, the rats will have learned a perceptual discrimination between straight-edged triangles and round-edged circles. This discrimination, in turn, makes it easier for the rats to learn to respond to one shape but not the other—just as Gibson and Walk observed.

Comparator Models

Another explanation for habituation is provide by **comparator models.** These models assume that the underlying mechanism is not a change in the pathway between stimulus and response (as schematized in Figure 6.8) but a process of learning about the stimulus and the context in which it occurs (Sokolov, 1963). Each presentation of the stimulus results in a pattern of neural activity in the brain—a neural representation of that stimulus. Each time the brain detects a stimulus, it forms a representation of that stimulus and compares that representation with its memory (that is, existing representations) of previously experienced stimuli. If there is no match, then a response is triggered, such as an orienting response, allowing the organism to study this new stimulus further. On the other hand, if there is a match, then the response is suppressed. In other words, responding to familiar stimuli decreases, or habituates. According to comparator models, habituation is really a special case of perceptual learning. The more the exposures to a stimulus are repeated, the more familiar is the representation and the less need there is for an orienting response.

In some ways, comparator models are simpler than the dual process theory as shown in Figure 6.8: there's no need to consider connections or pathways or competing processes. On the other hand, comparator models have to account for how the brain forms representations and how these representations may be stored and compared. That's not so simple. As we noted, dual process theory is directly analogous to neural circuits that actually exist in a spinal cord, but brain anatomy analogous to comparator models has proved much tougher to identify.

Differentiation Theory

A third account of non-associative learning is **differentiation theory,** which suggests that stimulus representations are formed rapidly and vaguely but develop specificity over time by incorporating more and more details as the stimulus is repeated (E. Gibson, 1991). In other words, the brain is limited in how much information it can collect in a single exposure to a novel stimulus. A stimulus may have many features, but the brain's perceptual representations can only absorb information about one subset of these features at a time. Repeated exposures give the brain the opportunity to collect more information about a stimulus, and the mental representations become more refined as the amount of information stored about the stimulus increases. More complete representations allow more accurate discriminatory judgments between, as well as more accurate recognition of, stimuli. For example, the very first time you see a drawing of a complex carbohydrate molecule in chemistry class, you might only absorb the fact that it has a bunch of lines and letters; the next time, you might notice that some of the lines and letters are arranged in hexagonal shapes; the next time, you might notice relationships in the way the hydrogen and oxygen atoms are linked; and so on. By the time you complete your graduate degree in organic chemistry, you'll be so familiar with the fine details that you can easily distinguish one complex carbohydrate from another at a glance by zeroing in on the regions of the molecule that help you make that distinction.

There is still no consensus on which theory—dual process theory, comparator models, or differentiation theory—most accurately describes the processes that occur during habituation and perceptual learning. In fact, the different approaches may not be mutually exclusive. Each might explain some features of non-associative learning. Brain studies are helping to shed some light on the neuronal processes underlying non-associative learning, and such studies may help us understand how these forms of learning take place in the brain.

Interim Summary

Non-associative learning is an umbrella term for learning about repeated events without necessarily associating those events with other stimuli or responses. In habituation, repeated exposure to a stimulus that originally evoked a reflexive response leads to decreased responding to that stimulus. In sensitization, exposure to a strong stimulus (such as a loud noise or an electric shock) increases responding to other stimuli that follow. The dual process theory suggests that habituation and sensitization are independent but parallel processes and that the strength or probability of responding is a result of both processes. Priming is a process whereby prior exposure to a stimulus facilitates later recognition of (or responding to) that stimulus.

In perceptual learning, prior experience with a set of stimuli makes it easier to distinguish fine differences among those stimuli. Some perceptual learning happens through mere exposure, as an organism explores and observes its world; such learning is sometimes also called latent learning, since there is no behavioral demonstration of the learning until later, when the organism is called to act on what it has learned. Perceptual learning can also happen through discrimination training, in which an individual is exposed to stimuli along with explicit information about the class to which each stimulus belongs. Many kinds of spatial learning involve perceptual learning. This learning is latent until the organism uses the information by navigating to a destination.

6.2 Brain Substrates

Dogs and cats are natural antagonists, as any dog or cat owner knows. Some of the earliest brain studies on habituation, using dogs and cats as subjects, seemed to bear out the view that these animals are fundamentally antithetical. Ivan Pavlov, for example, found that when a dog's cortex was removed, the dog no longer habituated to auditory stimuli: the dog would instead continue to show orienting responses to the sounds, even after many exposures (Pavlov, 1927). Such findings led researchers to suggest that the cortex was critical for habituation and that it actively suppressed reflexive orienting responses to stimuli perceived as familiar (Sokolov, 1963).

The data from cats, however, seemed completely contradictory. Cats that had their brain disconnected from their spinal cord, called *spinal cats*, still habituated to tactile stimulation (Thompson & Spencer, 1966). This seemed to prove that the spinal cord by itself contained all the neural machinery necessary for habituation; the cortex—and indeed the rest of the brain—wasn't needed. The cat data were consistent with the finding that many other organisms known to habituate, including roaches, protozoa, and numerous other invertebrates, don't have a cortex.

How to reconcile the dog data and the cat data? For one thing, dogs' and cats' brains are organized somewhat differently; for another, the animals in these early studies were learning about different kinds of stimuli. Whether the cortex is involved in habituation depends on the features of those stimuli, where they are normally processed, and where memories of the stimuli are stored. That's a lot of information to understand before researchers can predict whether the cortex is involved, even in such a "simple," non-associative behavior as habituation. One way to simplify this problem is to start not with mammals such as cats and dogs, but with smaller-brained animals such as marine-dwelling invertebrates.

Invertebrate Model Systems

Much work on the neural substrates of habituation has been conducted on a group of marine invertebrates called *Aplysia*, the sea slugs, such as the species *Aplysia californica* shown in Figure 6.9. Like many marine animals, *Aplysia* breathes through gills, which extend out from the abdomen, and a structure called the siphon works like a tube to blow aerated water over the gills to assist respiration. The gills are delicate and easily damaged, so when danger threatens, the sea slug tends to retract them under the safety of its outer covering, the mantle. This is called a gill-withdrawal reflex (or gill-withdrawal response).

One reason for studying *Aplysia* is that it has a relatively simple nervous system—only about 20,000 neurons, compared with the tens of billions in a cat or human—and some of the neurons are very big; a few are large enough to be seen with the naked eye. Best of all, the pattern of neurons in *Aplysia* seems to be "hardwired" across a given species, meaning that researchers can often identify a particular neuron in one sea slug (say, motor neuron L7G) and find the same neuron in the same place in another member of the species. This type of nervous

Siphon
Mantle
Tail
Head

David Wrobel/Visuals Unlimited

Figure 6.9 *Aplysia californica,* **the sea slug** This marine invertebrate, a shell-less mollusk, has a relatively simple nervous system, useful for studying the neural bases of learning. If the siphon is touched lightly, both siphon and gill are protectively withdrawn (the gill-withdrawal reflex). With repeated light touches, the gill-withdrawal reflex habituates. Adapted from Squire and Kandel, 2000.

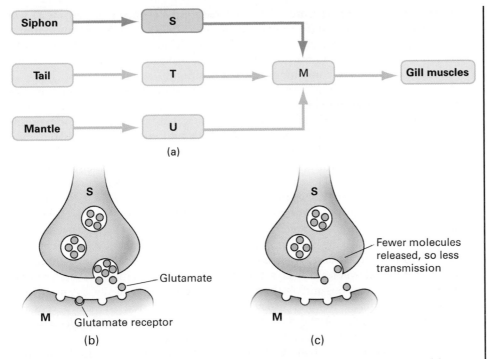

(a)

(b)

(c)

Glutamate

Glutamate receptor

Fewer molecules released, so less transmission

Figure 6.10 Neural circuits in *Aplysia*'s gill-withdrawal reflex (a) Some sensory neurons, such as neuron S, respond to a touch on the siphon; others, such as neurons T and U, respond to touch on the tail and upper mantle. All three types of sensory neuron converge on motor neurons such as M, which produces output that can contract the gill muscles. (b) When sensory neuron S fires, it releases the neurotransmitter glutamate into the synapse between S and M. The glutamate molecules (shown in yellow) may dock at specialized glutamate receptors on neuron M. If a sufficient number of receptors are activated by glutamate, neuron M will fire, causing the muscles to retract the gill. (c) If neuron S is activated repeatedly, it gradually releases less glutamate each time, decreasing the response in M. This synaptic depression is the mechanism underlying habituation of the gill-withdrawal response in *Aplysia*.

system makes things much easier for a neuroscientist trying to understand how the brain encodes new memories.

Neuroscientists have documented each of the neurons involved in *Aplysia*'s gill-withdrawal reflex. The siphon contains 24 sensory neurons that are directly connected to 6 motor neurons that innervate the gill. Figure 6.10a shows a simplified scheme of this system of neurons, consisting of three sensory neurons S, T, and U, and one motor neuron M. When the siphon is touched, sensory neuron M fires, releasing a neurotransmitter, *glutamate*, into the synapse (Figure 6.10b). Molecules of glutamate diffuse across the synapse to activate receptors in motor neuron M. If enough receptors are activated, neuron M generates an action potential that causes the muscles to retract the gill for a few seconds. This is a built-in sensory–motor reflex path in *Aplysia californica*, and all members of the species have the same neurons in the same layout within this pathway.

As simple as *Aplysia* is, it is still capable of adapting its behavior in response to experience. *Aplysia* exhibits habituation, sensitization, and several other forms of learning, just as rats and humans do. In *Aplysia*, however, scientists can actually watch the nervous system in action as these learning processes occur.

Habituation in Sea Slugs

Although an initial touch on the sea slug's siphon will activate the gill-withdrawal response, if the light touch is repeated, the gill-withdrawal reflex gradually weakens, or habituates. The degree of habituation is proportional to the intensity of the stimulus and the repetition rate, but if a sufficiently light touch is delivered every minute, the withdrawal reflex habituates after 10 or 12 touches, and this habituation can last for 10–15 minutes after the last touch (Pinsker, Kupfermann, Castellucci, & Kandel, 1970).

In the simple nervous system of *Aplysia*, we can see exactly what is causing this habituation. Refer back to the schematic diagram in Figure 6.10a. Recall that touching the siphon excites sensory neuron S, which releases the neurotransmitter glutamate, which in turn excites motor neuron M, which drives the withdrawal response (Figure 6.10b). With repeated stimulation, however, neuron S releases less glutamate (Figure 6.10c), decreasing the chance that neuron M will be excited enough to fire (Castellucci & Kandel, 1974). The reduction in glutamate release is evident even after a single touch stimulus, and lasts for up to 10 minutes. This decrease in transmitter release is associated with a decrease in the number of glutamate-containing vesicles positioned at release sites. Thus, in *Aplysia*, habituation can be explained as a form of **synaptic depression,** a reduction in synaptic transmission.

An important feature of habituation in *Aplysia* is that it is **homosynaptic,** meaning that it involves only those synapses that were activated during the habituating event: changes in neuron S will not affect other sensory neurons, such as T or U in Figure 6.10a. In other words, a light touch to the tail or upper mantle still elicits the defensive gill withdrawal, even though a touch to the siphon is ignored. Even the responsiveness of the motor neuron M is not changed; in this case, habituation in the short term affects only how much neurotransmitter neuron S releases. Habituation can often last much longer than 10 minutes, especially when exposures are spaced over several days (Cohen, Kaplan, Kandel, & Hawkins, 1997). How is *Aplysia* storing information about past exposures for such a long time? When a sea slug is habituated over several days, the actual number of connections between the affected sensory neurons and motor neurons decreases. Specifically, the number of presynaptic terminals in the sensory neurons of habituated animals is reduced. Synaptic transmission in *Aplysia* can thus be depressed not only by decreases in neurotransmitter release but also by the elimination of synapses.

Do the mechanisms of habituation in *Aplysia* tell us anything about habituation in larger-brained animals? It is currently impossible to trace the entire neuronal circuit of habituation through the billions of neurons in a mammalian brain, in the way this can be done for the much smaller number of neurons in *Aplysia*. However, neuroscientists have good reason to believe that the mechanisms of habituation documented in *Aplysia* occur in other species too. In fact, repeated stimulation of sensory neurons in other species, including crayfish and cats, also causes a reduction in neurotransmitter release. This suggests that at least some of the biological mechanisms of habituation are constant across species.

Sensitization in Sea Slugs

What about sensitization, which, in contrast to habituation, causes increased responding to stimuli? *Aplysia* also provides a way to study the neural processes involved in this kind of learning. Suppose, instead of a light touch to the siphon, the researcher applies a more unpleasant stimulus: a mild electric shock to the tail that causes a large, sustained gill-withdrawal response. This tail shock sensitizes subsequent responding, so that a weak touch to the siphon now produces a strengthened gill withdrawal.

To understand how this occurs, let's take the simplified circuit diagram from Figure 6.10a and add one more level of neural detail, as shown in Figure 6.11a. The tail shock activates sensory neuron T, which activates motor neuron M, causing the gill-withdrawal response. But neuron T also activates modulatory interneurons, such as I_N. An *interneuron*, as its name suggests, is a neuron that neither directly receives sensory inputs nor produces motor outputs, but instead carries a message between two other neurons. A *modulatory interneuron* is an interneuron that alters the strength of the message being transmitted. You'll recall from Chapter 2 that *neuromodulators* are neurotransmitters that can affect activity in entire brain areas, rather than just at a single synapse. In *Aplysia*, interneuron I_N connects neuron T to both S and U, communicating with them by releasing a neuromodulator such as *serotonin*. Serotonin increases the number of glutamate vesicles available to release glutamate from neuron S each time it fires. In effect, the interneuron does not tell S whether to fire; instead, it tells S, "When you do fire, fire strongly."

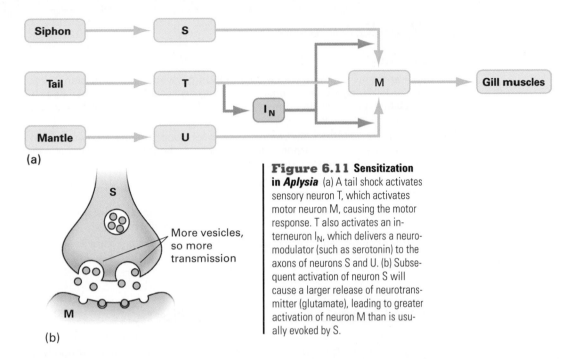

Figure 6.11 Sensitization in *Aplysia* (a) A tail shock activates sensory neuron T, which activates motor neuron M, causing the motor response. T also activates an interneuron I$_N$, which delivers a neuromodulator (such as serotonin) to the axons of neurons S and U. (b) Subsequent activation of neuron S will cause a larger release of neurotransmitter (glutamate), leading to greater activation of neuron M than is usually evoked by S.

Suppose *Aplysia* now experiences a mild touch to the siphon. Before the tail shock, this mild touch would have caused neuron S to release neurotransmitter from a small number of vesicles, leading to a weak gill withdrawal (as in Figure 6.10b). But now, this mild touch causes neuron S to release neurotransmitter from a larger number of vesicles (Figure 6.11b), so that M is more likely to fire, leading to a stronger gill-withdrawal response (Brunelli, Castellucci, & Kandel, 1976; Castellucci & Kandel, 1976). In effect, the prior tail shock at T has put the slug on alert, making it sensitive to a subsequent light touch.

The key to sensitization is that it is **heterosynaptic,** meaning that it involves changes across several synapses, including synapses that were not activated by the sensitizing event. Because of this feature, a tail shock increases responses to any future stimulus. For example, if the experimenter touched the upper mantle (activating sensory neuron U) instead of the siphon (neuron S), the same overreaction would occur.

In effect, the tail shock has increased the sea slug's level of arousal, making it more likely to respond to any other stimulus that follows. As with habituation, the degree of sensitization depends on the strength of the initial stimulus: a single mild shock can produce sensitization that lasts for minutes; four or five shocks together can produce sensitization that lasts two or more days (Marcus et al., 1988; Squire & Kandel, 2000).

In the sea slug, habituation decreases synaptic transmission, and sensitization increases synaptic transmission—just as predicted by dual process theory. In fact, the dual process theory of habituation does a good job of explaining non-associative learning in *Aplysia*. The multiple pathways in Figure 6.11a (which represent actual neural circuits in *Aplysia*) should remind you somewhat of Figure 6.8a (which represents pathways predicted by the dual process model). Dual process theory would therefore seem to provide a solid account of habituation and sensitization in the nervous system of the sea slug. It seems reasonable that similar processes would apply in other animals, too, such as in the spinal circuits of the cat. If so, what role does the rest of the brain play in non-associative learning? And why did cortical lesions affect non-associative learning in Pavlov's dogs?

Test Your Knowledge

Synaptic Mechanisms of Learning in *Aplysia*

Habituation and sensitization have different effects on synaptic transmission in sea slugs. For the following situations observed in *Aplysia,* see whether you can deduce whether habituation or sensitization has occurred and what is happening in the stimulus–response pathway.

1. Observations reveal that only one synapse, where once there were two, is now connecting a neuron that responds to stimulation of the tail to a neuron that contributes to the gill-withdrawal response.

2. Measurements of glutamate released around a motor neuron show that levels of glutamate are increasing over time.

3. Anatomical analyses of neural circuits reveal a larger number of synapses associated with the gill-withdrawal reflex circuit than are normally seen.

4. Recordings of motor neuron activity indicate that the neurons are generating fewer action potentials.

Perceptual Learning and Cortical Plasticity

A mammal without a cortex, but with its spinal cord intact, might be able to habituate to a repeated tactile stimulus. But could such a decorticate mammal learn to be a dog-show judge or a chicken-sexer? Would it be able to distinguish the feel of two toothpicks placed 5 mm apart on the skin? Almost certainly not. As described in Chapter 2, one of the most important jobs of the cerebral cortex is to process information about stimuli, and this includes learning to distinguish the features of those stimuli.

You learned in Chapter 4 that practice affects the response properties of cortical networks. When someone is acquiring a new skill, the regions of the cerebral cortex that play a role in that skill expand with practice, whereas other, less relevant brain regions show fewer changes. This effect has been observed in human violinists and in monkeys and various other species.

Similarly, areas of the cortex that process stimuli show changes resulting from repeated exposure to (that is, practice with) those stimuli. *Sensory cortices* are areas of the cerebral cortex that process visual stimuli, auditory stimuli, somatosensory (touch) stimuli, and so on (see Chapter 2). Within these sensory cortices, different neurons respond to different properties of a stimulus. The range of properties to which a given neuron responds is its **receptive field.** For example, Figure 6.12 shows the receptive field for one neuron in the auditory cortex of a guinea pig. This neuron responds most strongly to auditory stimuli of about 900 hertz (Hz), this neuron's "best frequency"; but it also responds to stimuli in the range of about 700 Hz to about 3000 Hz, this neuron's receptive field. Usually, the strength of responding drops off as stimuli become increasingly different from the preferred stimulus. However, as Figure 6.12 shows, response strength doesn't necessarily drop off at the same rate on either side of the best frequency. Scientists aren't yet sure how such asymmetries in receptive fields relate to the functions of cortical neurons.

Visual, auditory, and somatosensory cortices are organized into *topographic maps.* (The areas of cortex that process olfactory and taste stimuli may be topographically organized too, but we don't yet understand them well enough to know.) In topographic organization, neighboring neurons have overlapping receptive fields, so they respond to stimuli with similar features.

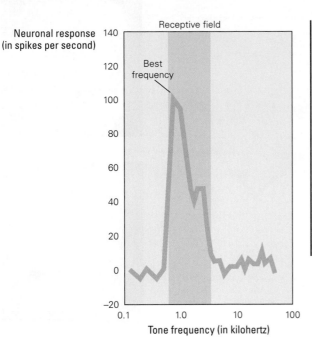

Figure 6.12 Receptive field of a neuron in the auditory cortex of a guinea pig Receptive fields are identified by measuring the amount of neural activity produced in response to different stimuli—in this case, to sounds ranging in frequency from 0.1 to 100 kilohertz (kHz). Like many cortical neurons, this neuron responds maximally to a particular input (this neuron's "best frequency"), but it also responds to a range of similar inputs (this neuron's receptive field). The strength of responding decreases as the stimuli depart farther from the best frequency. Adapted from Weinberger, 2004.

For example, if you could make an orderly examination across the surface of the auditory cortex, you would find that successive neurons respond to gradually increasing sound frequencies. One neuron might preferentially respond to sounds in the range 800–900 Hz (meaning that its receptive field includes those frequencies); a little to one side, you'd find neurons that respond to sounds of a slightly lower frequency, and a little to the other side, you'd find neurons responding to sounds of a slightly higher frequency. If you sat at a piano and played the keys one at a time from left to right up the keyboard, the activity in your auditory cortex would likewise gradually flow from one end to the other.

A neuron's receptive field can change as a result of repeated exposure to stimuli. Such changes can affect the topographic map as a whole. Changes in cortical organization as a result of experience are called **cortical plasticity.** Pavlov and Sokolov and other researchers in the late 1800s suggested the possibility of cortical plasticity, but not until the end of the twentieth century did the idea gain general acceptance.

Cortical Changes after Mere Exposure

As noted earlier in the chapter, through training, individuals can greatly increase their ability to discriminate between the feeling of two toothpick points pressing their skin and a single toothpick point pressing their skin. What do you think would happen if people were not trained but were merely exposed to repeated touches of one and two toothpick points on their fingertips? One possibility would be habituation to the repeated stimulus. Another possibility would be perceptual learning: improved discrimination of toothpick-point stimuli due to mere exposure to this type of stimulation.

Figure 6.13a shows what actually happens. Initially, people are able to discriminate between one and two simultaneous touches on the tip of their index fingers, as long as these touches are at least 1.1 mm apart. People then receive 2 hours of mere exposure consisting of repeated simultaneous stimulation of

Figure 6.13 Cortical reorganization in humans after mere exposure to finger stimulation (a) Before exposure, participants could distinguish two separate touch points on their index finger (IF), as long as the points were at least 1.1 mm apart. After 2 hours of passive exposure to simultaneous stimulation of closely spaced points on the right index finger, discrimination improved, so that touches only 0.9 mm apart were distinguishable. Discrimination with the unstimulated left index finger was unchanged. One day later, with no intervening stimulation, discrimination on the right index finger was back to normal. (b) fMRI showing cortical activation patterns evoked in somatosensory cortex by tactile stimulation of the right index finger before exposure. (c) After 2 hours of stimulation to the right index finger, regions of activation in both hemispheres have changed such that activation in the left hemisphere has increased relative to that in the right hemisphere.

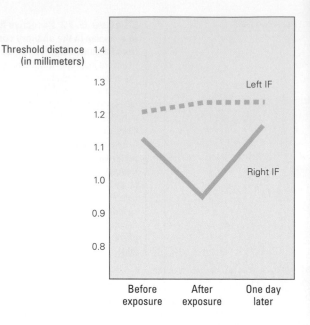

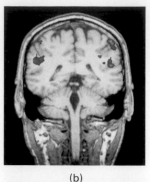

(b)

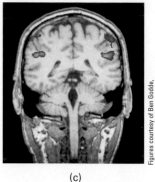

(c)

Figures courtesy of Ben Godde, Jacobs Center for Lifelong Learning, Jacobs University Bremen, Germany

(a)

two closely spaced points (0.25–3 mm apart) on the tip of their right index finger. After this exposure, the ability to discriminate touches on the right index finger improves: now, only a distance of about 0.9 mm is required to feel the two simultaneous touches as separate (Dinse, Ragert, Pleger, Schwenkreis, & Tegenthoff, 2003). (Perception of touches on the left index finger, which receives no stimulation, is unchanged.) The improvement in discrimination is only temporary, however; 24 hours later, with no intervening stimulation, the discrimination thresholds are back to normal (Godde, Ehrhardt, & Braun, 2003; Godde, Stauffenberg, Spengler, & Dinse, 2000; Hodzic, Veit, Karim, Erb, & Godde, 2004; Pilz, Veit, Braun, & Godde, 2004). In other words, humans show perceptual learning of fine tactile discriminations (if only temporarily) through mere exposure. What's going on in the brain when this happens?

One way to find out is by functional neuroimaging (fMRI). Before any training, touching the right index finger resulted in the neuronal activity of the somatosensory cortex shown in Figure 6.13b. Figure 6.13c shows activation by touches to the right index finger made after it was stimulated for 3 hours. The stimulated finger now activates a greater area of the somatosensory cortex than the unstimulated finger (Hodzic et al., 2004). Thus, mere exposure to the touch stimuli has resulted in cortical reorganization, reflecting perceptual learning.

A similar experiment used magnetoencephalographic (MEG) recording, which is similar to EEG recording in that it reflects neural activity rather than blood flow in the brain (as in fMRI); the main difference is that MEG measures small changes in magnetic fields rather than electrical fields. The MEG study showed that the degree of change in cortical responses to tactile stimulation was directly proportional to improvements in discrimination abilities; greater changes in cortical activity predicted better performance (Godde et al., 2003). Currently, the sophisticated devices required for MEG recording are only available at a small number of facilities.

Cortical Changes after Training

Given that perceptual learning after mere exposure is associated with cortical changes, does discrimination training correspond to similar changes in the cortex? Unfortunately, the answer isn't clear. Some studies find that activity in sensory cortex decreases as performance improves (Schiltz, Bodart, Michel, & Crommelinck, 2001), while others find that cortical activity increases with improvements in discrimination abilities (Schwartz, Maquet, & Frith, 2002). In view of the seemingly contradictory findings, interpreting what the cortex is doing is not easy!

One reason for some of these apparent contradictions is that, at least in the cortex, bigger may not always be better. Learning may change not only the overall area of cortical activity but also the condition of individual cortical neurons. For example, if a monkey is shown a random object, a certain number of neurons in its visual cortex respond strongly to one or more features of the object; another random object will evoke strong activity in a different (possibly overlapping) set of cortical neurons. If the monkey is then trained to discriminate among a group of such objects, the patterns of neural responding change. There may be an increase in the total number of cortical neurons that respond strongly to each object (Eyding, Schweigart, & Eysel, 2002; Logothetis, Pauls, & Poggio, 1995), but there may also be a decrease in the number of cortical neurons that respond weakly to each object. As a result, although the total number of active neurons may decrease, the remaining active neurons will be more sharply tuned to recognize and respond to the objects they've been trained to distinguish.

Many neuroscientists now believe that all forms of perceptual learning in mammals depend on cortical plasticity (Dinse & Merzenich, 2002). This view ties in closely with the comparator models of perceptual learning described earlier. Comparator models assume that experience generates changes in the cortex, and cortical plasticity—fine-tuning of neuronal responses to repeated stimuli—provides a mechanism for these changes. Moreover, an understanding of cortical involvement in perceptual learning may lead to such real-world applications as treatments for people with certain kinds of blindness and deafness (we'll have more to say about this in Section 6.3).

Plasticity during Development

If perceptual learning changes how the cortex responds to stimuli, what happens if stimulation is cut off, such as when a person loses her sight soon after birth? Given that cortical maps expand with repeated stimulation and shrink with disuse, you might expect the brain areas activated by visual stimuli in a blind person to be much smaller than those activated by the same stimuli in a sighted person. This seems to be the case. Neuroimaging studies show that the areas of the sensory cortex that normally respond to visual stimuli in sighted people will, in blind people, respond to sounds and tactile stimulation. For example, visual cortical activity increases in blind individuals during Braille reading and other tactile tasks, but decreases in sighted individuals performing these same tasks (Sadato et al., 1998).

This phenomenon has recently been studied experimentally in opossums (Kahn & Krubitzer, 2002). Researchers blinded half of the animals at birth and then, when the animals reached adulthood, exposed both the blinded and sighted opossums to visual, auditory, and somatosensory inputs and recorded the resulting patterns of cortical activation. In sighted opossums, different cortical areas responded to visual, auditory, and somatosensory inputs; in addition, some areas were **multimodal,** meaning that neurons in those areas responded to inputs from more than one sensory modality—for example, visual *and* auditory stimuli (Figure 6.14a). But a different pattern appeared in blinded opossums.

Figure 6.14 Cortical reorganization in opossums Researchers blinded half of a group of opossums at birth and allowed the others to develop normally. (a) At adulthood, a sighted opossum showed areas of cortical activity in response to visual, auditory, and somatosensory stimuli. Some areas were multimodal visual cortex, meaning that some neurons responded to stimuli from more than one modality: vision + audition, or vision + somatosensory stimuli. Black dots indicate placement of the electrodes used to record neuronal activity. (b) A blinded opossum showed overall shrinkage of areas that normally process visual information and, within those areas, some neurons now responded to auditory or somatosensory stimuli. Purple dots denote recording sites that responded only to touch; green dots, sites responding only to sound; and half-purple/half-green dots, sites responding to both touch and sound. Area X is a cortical region with unique anatomical and physiological features seen only in the blinded opossums. Adapted from Kahn and Krubitzer, 2002.

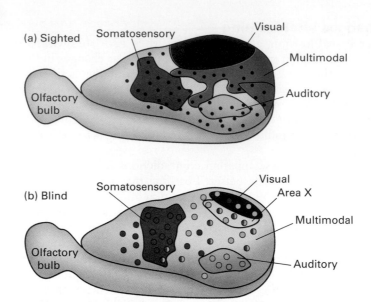

The cortical areas normally responding to visual stimuli had shrunk, and *within* those areas, some neurons now responded to auditory or somatosensory stimuli (Figure 6.14b). In addition, the auditory and somatosensory areas of the cortex had increased beyond normal size. And most striking of all, the blinded opossums had developed a new area, dubbed Area X, that didn't exist in sighted opossums' brains. Area X had unique anatomical and physiological characteristics; moreover, it was a multimodal area, with neurons responding to combinations of auditory and somatosensory stimuli.

Clearly, developmental experiences can have a huge effect on how cortical neurons respond to stimuli, influencing both the perception of sensory events and the development of responses to perceived events. In the case of blinded opossums, the absence of a sensory modality radically changes the sensory experiences to which cortical neurons are exposed during development, and the brain changes accordingly. In all animals, not just those that have been blinded (or similarly injured) at birth, experience modifies cortical maps. Your own cortical maps changed drastically during your infancy, and they will continue to change throughout your life, although you won't perceive that this is happening. (For more on what we don't know about cerebral cortex, see "Unsolved Mysteries" on p. 229.)

Hebbian Learning

You have now seen some of the evidence that neurons in the cortex change with experience, but what is the mechanism of this change? Several ideas have been proposed, but the most influential was suggested by psychologist Donald Hebb. In one of the most often-quoted passages in neuroscience, Hebb wrote: "When an axon of cell A is near enough to excite a cell B and repeatedly or persistently takes part in firing it, some growth process or metabolic change takes place such that A's efficiency, as one of the cells firing B, is increased" (Hebb, 1949). A shorthand version that neuroscientists often use is: *neurons that fire together, wire together.* One form of synaptic plasticity that seems to follow this rule is long-term potentiation (LTP), which, as you'll recall from Chapter 2, is thought to underlie many changes that occur in the brain. Learning that involves strengthening connections between cells that work together (typically neurons) is called **Hebbian learning.**

▶ Unsolved Mysteries

Why Did Cerebral Cortex Evolve?

Comparator models of habituation and perceptual learning propose that the cerebral cortex provides the brain with the capacity to store detailed memories of previously experienced events, especially those that are experienced repeatedly. The cortex is often viewed as the apex of evolution, the organ that gave rise to thought and the subsequent development of human societies and cultures. Did cortex evolve because detailed memories of recurrent events provide a survival advantage?

In considering how and why the cortex evolved, we must remember that even single-celled organisms (such as protozoa), which have no nervous system, can exhibit quite complex behavior. Much of this behavior serves to provide the cells with food, safety, and a chance to reproduce. Some multicellular organisms have a nervous system and some don't, but they all contain cells specialized to perform different tasks (if they didn't, they would be classified as a colony of single-celled organisms). The simplest multicellular organisms with a nervous system have sensory neurons and motor neurons with most of the structural and physiological features seen in cortical neurons. These cells enhance the organisms' ability to feed, flee, and reproduce. In short, the cortex did not evolve to provide the brain with new and better neurons. Instead, it seems likely that the cortex evolved to give the brain the ability to reorganize the interactions between existing neurons.

Current scientific debate about how and why the cortex evolved centers on which parts of the existing structures of more primitive brains expanded or split off into what we now call cortex (Northcutt & Kaas, 1995). Simple brain areas recognizable as cortex first appeared in vertebrates, in a group of early reptiles (therapsids) that lived 250 million years ago. Presumably these changes provided reptiles with abilities that their ancestors lacked, but it is unknown what those abilities were.

Subsequent vertebrate evolution included many changes in cortical structure, such as increases in the number of cortical units and specialization in how neurons are layered within the cortex. Mammals, in particular, have a very large cortex compared with the rest of their brain. More cortex means more neurons as well as more connections between those neurons. The large number of neurons in mammalian cortex has thus led many researchers to conclude that the cortex developed to increase neuronal interactivity, and that somehow such interactions are critical to performing complex memory-dependent operations such as thinking.

Scientists are unsure, however, why cortical networks might be better suited for this purpose than other networks of neurons. For example, octopus brains are relatively large—containing more than 150 million neurons—but contain no cortex; yet these animals have learning and memory abilities that are comparable to those of mammals (Mather, 1995). Apparently, cortex isn't a requirement for detailed memories that drive complex behaviors. On the other hand, octopus memories may be very different from human memories. Perhaps the organization of neurons in cortex makes it possible for mammals to store certain kinds of memories in ways that octopuses cannot.

Until the functions of the cortex are better understood, it will be difficult to say what drove (and continues to drive) the evolution of the cerebral cortex. If memories of repeatedly experienced events are stored in cortex, as suggested by comparator models, then perhaps identifying how these memories differ from those stored by animals without cortex will provide new clues to the advantages of cortically based memories.

Figure 6.15 shows a simple example of Hebbian learning. Eight hypothetical cortical neurons are shown, each with weak connections to the surrounding neurons (Figure 6.15a). Now let's assume that some sensory stimulus evokes activation in a subset of these neurons (solid circles in Figure 6.15a). As those neurons become active, they produce outputs that propagate along their connections with other neurons. According to Hebb's rule—neurons that fire together, wire together—the connections between coactive neurons are strengthened as a result. Repeated coactivity of the same subset of neurons, in response to the same stimulus, has a cumulative effect, resulting in the strong connections (heavy lines) shown in Figure 6.15b. Thus, repeated exposure to a stimulus can strengthen connections within a distinctive subset of cortical neurons, and this subset can then provide an increasingly reliable basis for identifying the stimulus that is activating them. Hebbian learning provides a possible neural mechanism for the representational processes proposed in differentiation

Figure 6.15 A simple model of Hebbian learning Circles correspond to cortical neurons, and lines denote connections between them. (a) Stimulus inputs activate a subset of the units (solid circles). (b) Connections between coactive neurons are strengthened (heavy lines). (c) After connections between coactive neurons have been established, an incomplete version of a familiar stimulus may activate just some of the neurons (solid circles) in the subset that represents the stimulus. Activation flows along the strengthened connections and ultimately retrieves the complete stimulus, resulting in the representation shown in (b).

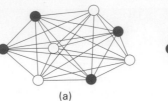
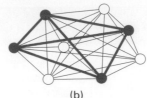
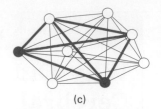

(a)   (b)   (c)

theory, as well as suggesting a possible explanation for how cortical networks can implement habituation and perceptual learning. Changing the connections between neurons creates a pattern that makes a repeated stimulus more likely to be recognized and distinguished from other stimuli.

Hebbian learning can also explain how repeated exposures facilitate recognition (the priming effect). Suppose that, once connections have been established between cortical neurons, the organism encounters an incomplete version of a familiar stimulus (Figure 6.15c). Only some of the subset of neurons that represents that familiar stimulus are activated at first (solid circles in Figure 6.15c), but the connections already established through repeated experiences will propagate outputs that complete the familiar pattern, reconstructing Figure 6.15b. This kind of pattern completion may correspond to retrieval in the word-stem completion task described above. Priming might then be explained as a temporary strengthening of existing connections between cortical neurons. Similarly, recognition of distorted versions of a familiar stimulus, such as might occur when a blue jay perceives a camouflaged moth, could also be facilitated by stored patterns encoded as connections between cortical neurons that were previously simultaneously active when moths were perceived.

The Hippocampus and Spatial Learning

You read earlier that at least some kinds of spatial learning reflect perceptual learning. One example is the latent learning that occurs as an organism explores its environment. Studies with rats offered the first hints about how spatial information is processed in the brain. Rats with damage to their hippocampal regions are impaired at learning a wide range of spatial tasks, such as visiting each arm in a radial maze without repetition (see Chapter 3). Humans with medial temporal amnesia are often impaired at learning how to find their way around a new neighborhood or how to play a video game that requires navigating through a virtual town. But knowing that the hippocampus is often involved in spatial learning is a far cry from understanding exactly how the hippocampus contributes to navigation.

As a first step toward understanding this process, English neuroscientist John O'Keefe implanted electrodes in rats' hippocampal regions to record neuronal activity under various conditions (O'Keefe & Dostrovsky, 1971). When the rats were placed in an environment and allowed to explore freely, the investigators made a surprising discovery. Some hippocampal neurons seemed to fire only when a rat wandered into particular locations, and other hippocampal neurons fired only when the rat was in other particular locations. O'Keefe coined the term **place cells** to refer to neurons with such spatially sensitive firing patterns. Each of these neurons had a certain preferred location to which it responded with maximal activity, and this location was termed the **place field** for that neuron. The response of these cells was so reliable that a blindfolded researcher could tell when a rat entered a particular region of the maze, just by hearing the corresponding place cell begin to fire. O'Keefe suggested that place cells might form the basis for spatial learning and navigation.

How might place cells help with the task of spatial navigation? If a certain neuron fires only when an individual is in a particular place, then that neuron can serve as an identifier for that place (much like road signs at street corners, or mile markers along the highway). When the neuron fires, the brain "knows" that the body is in a particular location. If you had enough place cells to code for every possible location you've ever visited—or ever might visit—you could work out where you are just by noting which place cell is firing.

Of course, that would require an impossibly large number of place cells. Such a method, in which cells are kept on reserve to encode locations that you haven't yet visited, would be extremely wasteful. Instead, it would be smarter to create place cells as you need them. In other words, place fields should form during learning, as an animal experiences an unfamiliar environment. This turns out to be the case.

Identifying Places

An explanation of how place cells work must begin with a discussion of what, exactly, defines a place. Put another way, what determines whether a place cell will respond? Part of what leads a place cell to respond seems to be the animal's inner sense of its location in space: a rat's place cells often continue to respond in an orderly fashion even when the rat is running through a maze with the lights out. But place cell responses also depend heavily on visual input. For example, suppose a rat is allowed to explore a maze like the one shown in Figure 6.16a. This maze has three identical arms (labeled 1, 2, and 3 in the figure) differentiated by one salient visual cue: a card placed outside the maze between arms 2 and 3. After the initial exploration, various place cells in the rat's hippocampus will have place fields corresponding to parts of this maze. One cell, for example, has the place field shown in Figure 6.16b (darker areas indicate maximal firing; lighter areas, lesser firing). In other words, this place cell responds preferentially when the rat is in the southwest corner of the maze (as oriented in Figure 6.16a), at the outer edge of arm 2, on the side nearest the card (Lenck-Santini, Save, & Poucet, 2001).

Now suppose the experimenter takes the rat out of the maze and rotates the maze and card 120 degrees clockwise (Figure 6.16c). What do you think will happen when the rat is put back in the maze? Will the place cell continue to fire

Figure 6.16 Effects of distant visual landmarks on place fields in rats Upper images show the rat's environment: a three-armed maze and a visual cue (a card, location marked in purple). Lower images show how a representative place cell fires in this environment: dark areas are regions that evoke heavy firing; lighter areas, regions that evoke lesser firing. (a, b) When the maze is in its initial position, this place cell fires maximally when the rat is in arm 2, at the southwest corner of the maze. (c, d) When the maze and cue card are rotated 120 degrees clockwise, the place field is determined by visual cues; maximal firing still occurs in arm 2, even though arm 2 is now in the northwest corner of the environment. (e, f) If the maze is rotated another 120 degrees, but the card is returned to its original location, the place cell again fires when the rat is in the southwest corner, even though this is now arm 3. In other words, place cell firing seems to depend on the rat's estimation of its location based on visual landmarks, in this case the purple card. Adapted from Lenck-Santini et al., 2001.

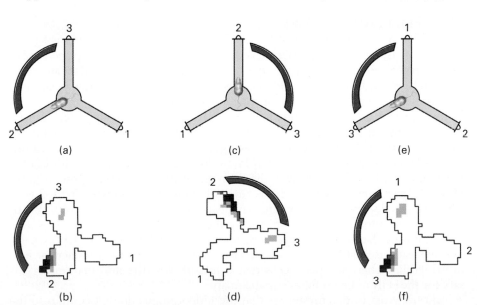

(a)   (c)   (e)

(b)   (d)   (f)

when the rat is in the southwest corner of the maze? Or will it fire when the rat is in arm 2, even though that is now the northwest corner of the maze? The answer is shown in Figure 6.16d: the place cell's preferred location rotates along with the maze. In this particular case, since the three arms all look, smell, and feel pretty similar, the rat is probably using the visual cue as a landmark. If the maze is rotated again, another 120 degrees clockwise, but the card is returned to its original place (Figure 6.16e), then the place cell will again fire in the southwest corner of the maze, even though this is now arm 3 (Figure 6.16f). These findings illustrate the importance of visual landmarks (such as the card) in determining whether a hippocampal place cell will fire. In addition to landmarks, some place cells in rats seem to be sensitive to other variables, such as the speed or direction in which a rat is moving.

Some place cells have place fields that are stable for months: if the rat is returned to the maze in Figure 6.16 after a long absence, the same place cell may still fire when the rat is in the same location as before. Research also shows that when place fields are unstable, spatial navigation is disrupted. The stability of place fields and their selectivity in terms of particular visual scenes are consistent with the idea that place cells provide the basis for a "cognitive map" that rats use to navigate through the world. But how, exactly, do place cells decide which place fields to encode?

One factor affecting the creation of place fields is experience. When rats repeatedly experience an environment, their place cells become increasingly selective about locations within those environments. In other words, the cells' place fields shrink (Lever, Wills, Cacucci, Burgess, & O'Keefe, 2002). Imagine the size of the dark place field in Figure 6.16 (b, d, and f) getting smaller and smaller, providing an increasingly precise and reliable report of where in the maze the rat is. This place-field shrinkage seems to correlate with rats' spatial navigation abilities in a maze; experiments in which rats' place-field shrinkage is disrupted (for example, by blocking inputs from the thalamus) show that the rats' spatial learning abilities decline (Cooper & Mizumori, 2001; Mizumori, Miya, & Ward, 1994; Rotenberg, Abel, Hawkins, Kandel, & Muller, 2000). The findings presented above suggest that spatial memory is correlated with the stability and selectivity of place cells' firing (Rosenzweig, Redish, McNaughton, & Barnes, 2003).

Place Fields Are Not Maps

Place cells in the hippocampus do not seem to be organized in topographic maps. That is, neighboring place cells do not encode neighboring place fields. In fact, place cells in the hippocampus don't seem to be organized in any way that can be related to physical relationships between real-world spatial positions. This presents a serious difficulty for the hippocampus.

Imagine that you have a street map and that you cut it into small rectangles, each about the size of a playing card, and then shuffle the "cards." Now suppose that, as you travel about, each card glows green whenever you enter the region depicted on that card, so you instantly know your immediate location (for example, you could look at the card to discover the name of the street you are on). However, just knowing which card is currently glowing green wouldn't tell you which streets depicted on other cards are nearby or far away, or how to get from one street to another. This is effectively the problem the hippocampus must solve if it uses place cells to guide navigation. Individual place cells identify particular locations, just like the cards described above, but so far, no scientist has identified links between place cells that would provide the information necessary for the cells to be useful as a spatial map.

Another twist to this mystery is that the hippocampus doesn't contain sufficient numbers of neurons to assign a place cell to every place you will encounter during your lifetime. Instead, the brain requires the same place cell to respond to locations in many different environments. For example, the place cell shown in Figure 6.16b has a place field in the southwest corner of the (unrotated) three-arm maze, but it might also have a place field in the northeast corner of the rat's home cage. Put the rat on a large circular tabletop, and the neuron might have a place field somewhere on that table, too. As mentioned above, some place cells fire in response to nonspatial cues such as movements and odors.

Take out the imaginary deck of cards again. Now imagine that some cards show the names of 10 different streets, others show the names of perfumes, and others name particular dance steps. Just as individual place cells respond to multiple locations, and even to things that are not locations, the cards in your deck now identify multiple streets, as well as stimuli that are not even streets. You probably wouldn't want to plan a road trip using this deck of cards as a navigational aid. Similarly, many researchers are beginning to question whether rats really rely on hippocampal place cells to decide what they need to do to reach a particular location. Perhaps there is a piece of the spatial navigation puzzle that researchers have yet to locate and understand.

Interim Summary

Much research on the neural substrates of non-associative learning has been conducted on invertebrates, such as *Aplysia*, that have relatively small nervous systems. In *Aplysia*, habituation involves a weakening of synaptic connections between glutamate-releasing sensory neurons and motor neurons; sensitization involves serotonin release that temporarily modulates these connections so that sensory stimuli become more likely to activate motor neurons. This mechanism seems consistent with the dual process model of habituation and sensitization, and is also consistent with what is known about sensory-motor circuits in the spinal cord of mammals such as the cat.

Perceptual learning seems to depend on the cerebral cortex in mammals. Cortical plasticity is often associated with changes in discrimination abilities, suggesting that cortical plasticity underlies perceptual learning. These cortical changes may involve changing the extent of the area that responds to a certain kind of stimulus and/or making the receptive fields of individual neurons more or less sensitive to stimulus features. Such changes in cortical fields are visible both after mere exposure to repeated stimuli and after explicit training of new discriminations. Experimental animals that are blinded just after birth show significant changes in the sensory cortex, with surviving sensory modalities (such as vision and touch) often taking over cortical areas that normally process visual input. Hebbian learning, the principle that *neurons that fire together, wire together*, suggests one possible mechanism of cortical change. Such changes may underlie the representational processes proposed in differentiation theory as well as the phenomenon of priming.

Place cells in the rat hippocampus respond strongly when a rat is in a particular spatial location. They seem to form (that is, to encode a place field) during latent learning as the rat explores its environment, and they depend heavily on visual input, including landmarks, for recognizing their place field when exposed to it again. Place cells also depend on experience, with place fields becoming more sharply defined (and thus representing a more precise location) as experiences with a given environment are repeated. Place cells seem to play a role in spatial learning, but because they are not topographically organized and because each cell may signal more than one location or other stimuli, how such a system could be useful in spatial navigation is as yet unknown.

6.3 Clinical Perspectives

Although you are not consciously aware of it, perceptual learning influences every experience you have. From your ability to understand speech to your ability to find your way to school or work, every sensation and perception is influenced by the memories you've acquired through repeatedly experiencing similar stimuli. As noted earlier in this chapter, much of perceptual learning involves cortical networks. These can be damaged through brain injury, and the result can be a fundamental change in how stimuli are perceived and processed.

Landmark Agnosia

As a child, you may have had the experience of being lost in a large store or shopping mall. Even as an adult you may become disoriented at times—for example, when driving in an area with which you are unfamiliar. Imagine if you were always so disoriented. This is the situation faced by people with **landmark agnosia.** In Chapter 3 we defined agnosia as a relatively selective disruption of the ability to process a particular kind of information. People with landmark agnosia have lost the ability to identify their location or find their way in relation to once-familiar buildings and landscapes (Aguirre & D'Esposito, 1999). Some individuals with this disorder become disoriented in novel places only, but others lose their way even in familiar places (Takahashi & Kawamura, 2002). Landmark agnosia is generally caused by loss of brain tissue, often from a stroke. Given what you read in Section 6.2, where do you think these lesions are typically located?

One possibility might be the hippocampus. People with hippocampal damage often have trouble with spatial learning (see Chapter 3). But such damage generally causes anterograde amnesia—a failure to form new episodic and semantic memories. Most patients with landmark agnosia don't have anterograde amnesia. They can recall recent experiences, and they can even draw pictures of the area where they live. Therefore, hippocampal damage doesn't seem to be the reason for landmark agnosia.

Figure 6.17 shows the location of brain lesions in two representative patients with landmark agnosia. Both lesions are in the medial temporal lobe of the left hemisphere, but they are not in the hippocampus itself. Instead, the lesions are in the **parahippocampal region,** the cortical areas that lie near the hippocampus inside the medial temporal lobe. Some patients with landmark agnosia (including patient 1 in Figure 6.17) have a lesion that is limited to the parahippocampal region; other patients (patient 2 in Figure 6.17) have lesions that include the

Figure 6.17 Lesions leading to landmark agnosia Shaded regions indicate the locations of cortical lesions caused by stroke. In patient 1 the lesion is limited to the parahippocampal region. Patient 2's lesion includes the parahippocampal region and extends back into areas of visual cortex. Adapted from Takahashi and Kawamura, 2002.

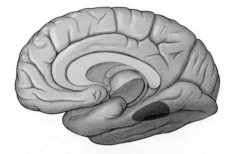

Patient 1

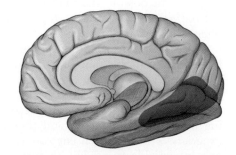

Patient 2

parahippocampal region but also extend to other nearby cortical areas (Aguirre, Detre, Alsop, & D'Esposito, 1996; Habib & Sirigu, 1987).

The parahippocampal region receives a large number of inputs from other sensory processing areas of the cortex. After every other part of the cortex processes its sensory inputs, that information is passed on to the parahippocampal region and is integrated there. The parahippocampal region in turn serves as a major source of inputs to the hippocampus. Therefore, although lesions such as those shown in Figure 6.17 don't directly damage the hippocampus, they probably disrupt hippocampal processing. By way of analogy, your cell phone may be in perfect working order, but if the network is down and the phone isn't receiving a signal, you won't be able to make calls. Similarly, a hippocampus may be in perfect working order, but if it isn't receiving visual inputs about places and landmarks, it's not going to be able to form place cells to represent those places and landmarks. And, if spatial learning and navigation do depend on place cells, then disrupting formation of these cells will severely disrupt spatial learning and navigation.

The parahippocampal region also has strong bidirectional connections with several areas of visual cortex. This is not surprising, given that visual inputs are critical for landmark recognition. Thus, damage to the parahippocampal region can disrupt normal processing in visual cortical regions as well as in the hippocampus. Because of all this interconnectivity, it is difficult to pinpoint one specific area devoted to landmark identification.

Landmark agnosia is only one example of the many ways in which damage to cortical networks can alter perception. For example, patients with landmark agnosia (such as patient 2 in Figure 6.17) whose lesions extend beyond the parahippocampal region and into the visual cortex also have direct disruptions in visual function. Such patients often have additional visual impairments, such as *prosopagnosia*, an inability to recognize faces, as a result of their more extensive cortical damage (Takahashi, Kawamura, Hirayama, Shiota, & Isono, 1995). Different kinds of agnosia damage the ability to learn about other kinds of visual, auditory, or tactile stimuli. Each of these agnosias, often caused by stroke, represents damage in a different part of the cortical network, resulting in the loss of a specific kind of perceptual processing.

Rehabilitation after Stroke

The specific deficits that result from damage to cortical networks can extend beyond the recognition deficits that are characteristic of agnosia. Damage caused by strokes can change the sensorimotor landscape to such an extent that the brain learns to ignore parts of itself. Immediately after a stroke, a patient often experiences large losses in perceptual function. For example, a patient may lose all sensation in one of his arms. Subsequently, although nothing may be wrong with the motor control of that arm, the patient may begin to ignore the desensitized arm and make greater use of the arm he can still feel. Over time, he may stop trying to use the desensitized arm altogether, a phenomenon called **learned non-use.**

Monkeys show similar patterns of learned non-use when they lose function. For example, if somatosensory information from a monkey's right arm is blocked so that it cannot feel the arm, the monkey will stop using it, relying instead on the functioning left arm. If the left arm is restrained, however, the monkey may go back to using the desensitized right arm, even if it has not used that arm for several years. After the monkey has become accustomed to using the right arm again, release of the left arm from its restraint typically leads to the monkey's using both arms again, showing that it can overcome the learned non-use of the desensitized arm (Knapp, Taub, & Berman, 1963).

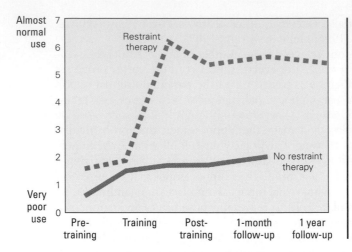

Figure 6.18 Overcoming learned non-use Patients with cortical lesions affecting one limb (e.g., an arm) often start using the unaffected limb in preference—a learned non-use of the affected limb. The graph shows results for two groups of patients who initially (pre-training) had very little use of one arm. One group underwent restraint therapy, which forced patients to use the affected arm for daily activities. These patients showed dramatic improvements in function of the injured arm, compared with control patients not receiving restraint therapy. Adapted from Taub, Uswatte, and Elbert, 2002.

Similar techniques are sometimes used in therapy for human stroke patients. For example, a patient who has lost the use of his left arm might consent to have his (working) right arm immobilized in a sling, so that he is forced to try to use his left arm for eating, dressing, and other daily activities. As Figure 6.18 shows, patients receiving this kind of restraint therapy often recover much more function in their affected arm than patients who are simply told to try to use their affected arm as often as possible (Taub, Uswatte, & Elbert, 2002).

The idea behind restraint therapy is simply to force the patient to use the affected arm as often as possible. This produces a wealth of sensory input to the brain, leading to cortical plasticity and thus new patterns of coactivation in cortical networks. This is similar to the cortical remapping seen in the opossums of Figure 6.14. Remember that the opossums had been blinded, so cortical areas normally devoted to visual processing were instead devoted to other functions, such as processing sounds and odors. In patients with stroke, just the opposite might happen: because the part of the cortex devoted to processing sensory stimuli is damaged, nearby undamaged cortical areas might take up some of the work that the damaged area once performed.

Not all cortical damage can be repaired by restraint therapy. The mechanisms that limit the extent to which cortex in an older adult can change to accommodate the loss of cortical tissue are not fully understood, and so clinicians don't yet know how best to promote cortical changes in older patients. Still, the general technique of altering the sensory environment to facilitate cortical changes shows great promise. New breakthroughs in technology and in our understanding of cortical plasticity may one day make it possible for stroke patients to recover fully from their injuries.

Man–Machine Interfaces

If damaged cortical networks can be changed to help an individual recover function after an injury, might it be possible to change undamaged cortex to provide functionality that was never present, for example in individuals who are blind or deaf? This is possible, and has in fact already been accomplished with sensory prostheses. **Sensory prostheses** are mechanical devices that contain sensory detectors able to interface with the brain areas that normally process such sensory information. The prostheses are designed to provide individuals with sensory-processing capabilities that they would not otherwise have.

To date, the most extensively developed sensory technology is the **cochlear implant** (Figure 6.19). This device electrically stimulates auditory nerves to produce hearing sensations in profoundly deaf individuals, primarily to assist them in processing speech. Multiple electrodes implanted in the cochlea modify responses in the auditory nerve in ways that roughly simulate the neural activity normally produced by an auditory stimulus. This technology is most effective in young children and in adults who have only recently lost their hearing. Conventional hearing aids amplify external sounds, but cochlear implants recreate the effects of sounds within the brain, generating "virtual sounds" from information about electronically detected and processed sounds in the environment. The virtual sounds generated by cochlear implants are quite different from normal speech, so people using the implants must be trained to discriminate between the new sounds and understand what they hear, an example of perceptual learning. Like most practice-based learning, speech perception by individuals with cochlear implants shows initial rapid improvement in the early months of use, followed by more gradual improvement over years (Clarke, 2002).

It is likely that changes in speech processing abilities after installation of a cochlear implant are mediated by cortical plasticity, but this has yet to be demonstrated experimentally. Many areas of cortex may be modified based on signals provided by the implant, because cochlear implants provide the brain with access not only to new auditory information but also to all of the abilities that this information provides (such as the ability to engage in spoken conversations). Researchers have found that cochlear implants in deaf cats lead to massive reorganization of the auditory cortex (Klinke, Kral, Heid, Tillein, & Hartmann, 1999). The auditory cortex of these cats is organized differently from that of deaf cats without implants, and from that of hearing cats, suggesting that the cortical organization in cats with cochlear implants is formed by the virtual sounds these cats hear. It is not yet known whether other cortical regions are also organized differently in cats with cochlear implants compared with cats with normal hearing.

As cochlear implant technology continues to improve, scientists are researching ways to provide retinal implants for blind people. Most current sensory prostheses are designed to replace lost abilities, but in principle, it should also be

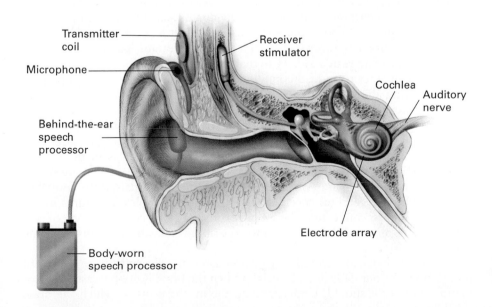

Transmitter coil

Receiver stimulator

Microphone

Behind-the-ear speech processor

Cochlea

Auditory nerve

Electrode array

Body-worn speech processor

Figure 6.19 Cochlear implant Cochlear implants use electricity to stimulate neurons in the auditory system, thereby creating virtual speech sounds in the brain. Adapted from Clarke, 2002.

Sensory prosthesis of the future? Blind *Enterprise* crewman Jordi LaForge (of *Star Trek: The Next Generation*) wears a visor with a neural interface that stimulates his visual cortex, allowing him to "see" better than his sighted crewmates.

Paramount/The Kobal Collection

possible to use such devices to enhance existing capabilities. We still don't know how well cortical networks would be able to handle inputs from sensors detecting stimuli such as infrared light or ultrasonic sounds that humans are normally unable to perceive. Given how easily deaf people have learned to process novel inputs from cochlear implants, however, it seems likely that the human brain could accommodate a wide range of machine-provided inputs. So sign up now for your bionic sense organs!

CONCLUSION

In many ways, habituation, perceptual learning, and the other phenomena classified as non-associative learning represent the simplest forms of learning. Even the most primitive animals show habituation; simple neural circuits are all that is required. Moreover, neither perceptual learning nor habituation demands any obvious effort from the learner, although in the case of perceptual learning, practice can be beneficial. The brain has evolved to collect information about what's new in the world, and to recognize the familiar.

In other respects, however, perceptual learning and habituation are highly complex. The neural mechanism mediating these forms of learning can involve almost any combination of brain regions interacting in any number of ways. A good example is the use of landmarks in spatial navigation. Complex combinations of stimuli including both visual patterns and specific movement patterns determine how place cells respond. Removing specific cortical regions such as the parahippocampal region can disrupt the processing of landmarks but leave intact the abilities to create maps and recognize visual scenes. Spatial learning can happen independent of observable responses, which means it is difficult for an observer to determine what another individual is learning about any particular set of landmarks. Who would guess that as you sit in a car staring out of the window, your brain is recording the locations of certain landmarks and that you'll be able to find your way back to that location later? Who would guess that removing a small portion of the inputs into your hippocampus would prevent you from being able to do this?

Non-associative learning can have various kinds of consequences. Repeated experiences can slow down the ability to learn (in the case of habituation) or speed it up (in the case of priming and perceptual learning), or can affect the organism's responses to other, seemingly unrelated stimuli (as in the case of sensitization). How is it that repeated exposures to stimuli can generate such a wide range of learning? Part of the answer, at least in mammals, is the contribution made by the cerebral cortex, one of the most complex structures in the brain. Changes in connections between cortical neurons constitute one of several powerful mechanisms that seem to contribute to both perceptual learning and habituation.

Changes in behavior stemming from non-associative learning have important implications for our daily lives, especially when the brain is not processing information the way it should. Understanding the mechanisms by which the brain learns from repeated experiences can help clinicians interpret the effects of cortical damage and take steps to alleviate sensory deficits. The ability of the brain to adapt in the ways described in this chapter may be the key to overcoming many mental deficits for which there are currently no cures. Thus, although habituation and perceptual learning can sometimes lead to negative outcomes (as described in the chapter-opening vignette about Jeffrey Dahmer), these processes also point to ways of rehabilitating patients and expanding people's perceptual abilities.

Key Points

- Habituation involves a decrease in the strength or frequency of a behavior after repeated exposure to the stimulus that produces the behavior. If the stimulus is presented again after a delay, the behavior may reappear at its original level, a process called spontaneous recovery. A behavior decreased through habituation can also be renewed (dishabituated) by a novel stimulus. Habituation is stimulus-specific.

- Whereas habituation decreases the response to a repeated stimulus, sensitization can increase the response to a stimulus. In sensitization, exposure to a threatening or highly attractive stimulus causes a heightened response to any stimuli that follow. Sensitization is not stimulus-specific.

- Priming is a phenomenon in which prior exposure to a stimulus improves the organism's ability to recognize that stimulus later.

- In perceptual learning, experience with a set of stimuli improves the organism's ability to distinguish those stimuli. In mere exposure learning, simply being exposed to the stimuli results in perceptual learning. (A related term is latent learning: learning that takes place without corresponding changes in performance.) Perceptual learning can also occur through discrimination training, in which an organism explicitly learns to distinguish stimuli through feedback about the class to which each stimulus belongs.

- Many kinds of spatial learning take the form of perceptual learning. Often, this is latent learning about the environment that results from mere exposure as the organism explores its world.

- Comparator models suggest that habituation is a special case of perceptual learning, whereas dual process theory proposes that changes in behavioral response after repeated exposures to a stimulus reflect the combined effects of habituation and sensitization, with habituation decreasing responses and

sensitization increasing responses. Differentiation theory explains perceptual learning as resulting from new details being added to existing stimulus representations.

- In marine invertebrates such as *Aplysia*, habituation can be explained as a form of synaptic depression (any change that reduces synaptic transmission) in circuits that link a stimulus (sensory neuron) to a particular reflexive response (motor neuron), as proposed by dual process theory. Habituation in *Aplysia* is homosynaptic, meaning that changes in one sensory neuron do not affect other sensory neurons. In contrast, sensitization in *Aplysia* is heterosynaptic and reflects increases in synaptic transmission.

- The capacity of cortical networks to adapt to internal or environmental changes is called cortical plasticity. During perceptual learning, cortical changes occur that parallel improvements in discrimination abilities. These changes include refinement of the receptive fields of neurons that respond to sensory inputs, which can lead to widespread changes in the cortical map. In extreme cases, such as when a form of sensory input is absent from birth, the cortical map may reorganize so that active inputs take over the areas normally devoted to processing the missing inputs.

- One mechanism for cortical plasticity is Hebbian learning, based on the principle that neurons that fire together, wire together. In other words, repeated exposure can strengthen associations within particular subsets of cortical neurons, and these subsets can then provide an increasingly reliable basis for discriminating the stimuli that activate them.

- Place cells are neurons in the hippocampus that become most active when an animal is at a particular location (the place field for that neuron). However, it is not clear how the information from different place cells is linked together to form a useful spatial map to guide navigation through an environment.

- Place fields change with learning, and if place cells are disrupted, spatial navigation is disrupted. As an environment becomes more familiar, the corresponding place cells become more selective, responding to increasingly precise locations in that environment.

- People with landmark agnosia have lost the ability to identify familiar buildings and landscapes. This condition often results from damage to the parahippocampal region of the cortex.

- Immediately after a stroke, many patients experience large losses in perceptual and motor function. The patients may suffer from learned non-use, which occurs when a functional limb takes over the role of a limb that still has motor function but has lost sen- sation. Learned non-use can be overcome by restraint therapy, forcing the individual to use the desensitized limb. Recovery of function in stroke patients is thought to result from cortical plasticity.

- Sensory prostheses, electronic devices that interface directly with neurons or sensory receptors, are designed to provide individuals with sensory processing capabilities they would not otherwise have. The most extensively developed sensory prosthesis is the cochlear implant, which is used to treat profound deafness. Training with a cochlear implant leads to perceptual learning that improves the user's ability to discriminate simulated speech sounds.

Key Terms

acoustic startle reflex, p. 207	habituation, p. 206	multimodal, p. 227	sensitization, p. 210
Aplysia, p. 220	Hebbian learning, p. 228	non-associative learning, p. 206	sensory prosthesis, p. 236
associative learning, p. 206	heterosynaptic, p. 223	orienting response, p. 207	skin conductance response (SCR), p. 210
cochlear implant, p. 237	homosynaptic, p. 222	parahippocampal region, p. 234	spontaneous recovery, p. 208
comparator model, p. 218	landmark agnosia, p. 234	perceptual learning, p. 212	synaptic depression, p. 222
cortical plasticity, p. 225	latent learning, p. 212	place cell, p. 230	word-stem completion task, p. 211
differentiation theory, p. 218	learned non-use, p. 235	place field, p. 230	
dishabituation, p. 208	learning specificity, p. 214	priming, p. 211	
dual process theory, p. 217	mere exposure learning, p. 212	receptive field, p. 224	

Concept Check

1. A weightlifter repeatedly lifts a barbell. After several repetitions, he begins lifting it more slowly, until eventually he stops. Is this habituation?

2. A common example of sensitization is the experience of walking down a dark alleyway at night. The setting may produce feelings of nervousness, which lead to heightened arousal: you'll jump if you hear a noise behind you. Can you think of any situations in which people are intentionally sensitized?

3. After reading this chapter, you'll have learned at least some of the material presented here. If you read the chapter again, you may learn even more. Is this non-associative learning?

4. You may have been surprised that the introduction to this chapter discussed cannibalism by a sexually deviant murderer. Why was this surprising?

5. When structural MRIs of London taxi drivers were compared with those of control participants who did not drive taxis, researchers discovered that the average size of the hippocampus in the taxi drivers was larger than in the controls and was correlated with the number of years they had been driving a taxi (Maguire et al., 2000). Why might that be?

Answers to Test Your Knowledge

Perceptual Learning versus Habituation

(a) The woman has learned to perceptually discriminate a dog's quality based on its teeth or other features of its mouth. The dog has habituated to strangers sticking their hands and face near its mouth. You could test the hypothesis of perceptual learning by comparing the woman's ability to discriminate dogs' teeth with the ability of a non-expert.

(b) The men have learned to perceive differences among wines based on odors. They've habituated to wearing coats and ties. You could test the hypothesis of perceptual learning by comparing the men's ability to interpret wine odors they've previously experienced with their ability to interpret odors they haven't experienced before.

(c) The homeless man has habituated to being ignored by the general public, and the pedestrians have habituated to seeing destitute people on the street. You could test this hypothesis by asking a famous actress to sit and talk with the homeless man; this would probably dishabituate both the man and the pedestrians.

Synaptic Mechanisms of Learning in *Aplysia*

1. The reduction in synaptic connections indicates habituation; less glutamate is being released in the stimulus–response pathway.

2. The increase in glutamate release indicates sensitization; stimulus–response pathways are more likely to become active.

3. The increased number of connections suggests sensitization; the increase in connections should increase the amount of glutamate released in stimulus–response pathways.

4. The number of action potentials generated generally reflects the amount of glutamate released; if this number is reduced, glutamate release is probably reduced, suggesting habituation.

Further Reading

Geary, J. (2002). *The body electric: an anatomy of the new bionic senses.* New Brunswick, NJ: Rutgers University Press. • A book for nonscientists who are interested in sensory prostheses; it includes chapters reviewing recent technologies designed to enhance, repair, or replicate the senses of touch, hearing, sight, smell, and taste.

Hall, G. (1991). *Perceptual and associative learning.* Oxford: Clarendon Press. • A scientific monograph that attempts to relate models of perceptual learning to more traditional models of conditioning (many of which we discuss in later chapters). It includes chapters on habituation and perceptual learning, reviewing key empirical studies and theoretical proposals.

Peeke, H. V. S., & Petrinovich, L. (Eds.). (1984). *Habituation, sensitization, and behavior.* Orlando. FL: Academic Press. • An edited collection of chapters written by scientists with expertise in habituation research. The chapters include reviews of the earlier research on habituation, including work with *Aplysia*, rats, and humans; details of comparator models and dual process theory; and unique discussions of the evolutionary role of habituation in nature.

CHAPTER 7

Classical Conditioning

Learning to Predict Important Events

WHAT DO THE FOLLOWING FOUR people have in common? Nathalie, a former cigarette smoker, who always feels the urge to light up a cigarette after sex; Garfield, who got the flu after his first taste of oysters and hasn't been able to stand them since; Mimi, who worked in the World Trade Center on 9/11 and feels her heart racing with anxiety every time she returns to lower Manhattan; and Sharon, who broke up with her ex-boyfriend years ago but still finds the sound of his voice arousing. The answer is Ivan Pavlov—or to be more precise, Ivan Pavlov's principle of classical conditioning. Nathalie, Garfield, Mimi, and Sharon have all had their behaviors altered by Pavlovian conditioning.

Most people, even if they never took a psychology course, are vaguely aware of the story of Ivan Pavlov and how he trained, or "conditioned," his dogs to salivate to cues like bells or tones that predicted the impending delivery of food. Chapter 1 introduced you to Pavlov and his training method (see Figure 1.7a). There is, however, much more to classical conditioning than dogs and saliva (Pavlov, 1927). This chapter will show you why an understanding of classical "Pavlovian" conditioning (despite its apparent simplicity) is indispensable for building a behavioral and biological explanation of learning and memory. Moreover, classical conditioning is one of the few forms of learning for which the brain substrates have

Behavioral Processes

Basic Concepts of Classical Conditioning

Error Correction and the Modulation of US Processing

From Conditioning to Category Learning

Modulation of CS Processing

Further Facets of Conditioning

Brain Substrates

Mammalian Conditioning of Motor Reflexes

Unsolved Mysteries - Riding the Brain's Waves into Memory

Invertebrates and the Cellular Basis of Learning

Clinical Perspectives

Learning and Memory in Everyday Life - Kicking the Habit

John Chase

been worked out in precise detail, for every step from the initial sensory input to the commands that drive the resulting motor responses. For these reasons, classical conditioning is avidly studied by psychologists, neuroscientists, and clinical neuropsychologists. Pavlov's accidental discovery of conditioning almost a hundred years ago has led to a broad range of scientific, educational, and medical research, far beyond what he could have anticipated.

7.1 Behavioral Processes

Classical Pavlovian conditioning is a way of learning about one's environment. A child who has learned that a jingle heard in the distance predicts the imminent arrival of an ice cream truck can exploit this awareness by asking her mother for money so she is ready at the curb when the truck approaches. This is an example of learning to anticipate a positive event and preparing to take maximal advantage of it. Being able to anticipate negative events is also useful. If a homeowner is surprised by a sudden rainstorm, he must run around the house closing windows to keep the rain from getting in. Had he learned to pay attention to the weather report, he would have been able to close the windows before the rain began and prevented his carpets and walls from getting soaked.

This section begins by introducing and defining the basic concepts and terminology of classical conditioning, and then explores the results of further research into this mechanism of learning. It describes an elegant and simple model of conditioning, developed in the early 1970s, that helps explain a wide range of conditioning phenomena; discusses how conditioning principles derived from studies of animal learning relate to more complex cognitive phenomena observed in human learning; explores alternative views of what happens during conditioning, especially with regard to the role of attention in learning; and finally, examines the role of timing and the importance of ecological constraints on what is or is not learned through classical conditioning.

Basic Concepts of Classical Conditioning

The first requirement of classical conditioning is an **unconditioned stimulus (US),** meaning a stimulus that naturally evokes some response, called the **unconditioned response (UR).** Pavlov actually referred to these in Russian as the "unconditional" stimulus and response because these reflexive responses occurred unconditionally, that is, without any training or conditioning. However, the terms were mistranslated into English almost a hundred years ago, and ever since psychologists have been using the term "unconditioned" rather than "unconditional."

In Figure 7.1, the unconditioned stimulus is food, and the unconditioned response is salivation. In the other examples described above, the ice cream and the rain are USs, while running toward the ice cream truck and closing the windows are URs.

If the US is repeatedly and reliably preceded by a neutral stimulus, such as the bell Pavlov used (Figure 7.1a), that neutral stimulus can become a **conditioned stimulus,** or **CS,** that evokes an anticipatory response, called the **conditioned response,** or **CR,** following repeated trials of CS–US pairing (Figure 7.1b). For Pavlov's dogs, the CR was salivation that anticipated the arrival of food. In the ice cream and rain examples, the CR would be running toward the curb with money after hearing the ice cream truck's song (the CS), and closing the windows of the

(a)

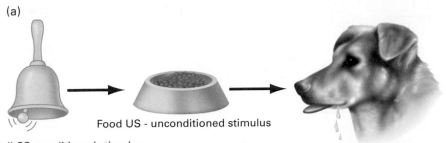

Bell CS: conditioned stimulus

Food US - unconditioned stimulus

Salivation UR - unconditioned response

(b)

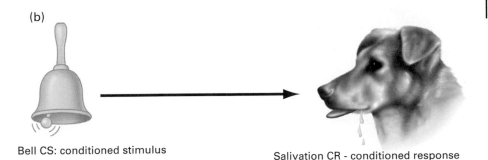

Bell CS: conditioned stimulus

Salivation CR - conditioned response

Time

Figure 7.1 Diagram of Pavlov's experiment and terminology Learning starts with an unconditioned stimulus (US), in this case, food, that naturally evokes an unconditioned response (UR), in this case, salivation. (a) If the US is preceded by a neutral stimulus, such as a bell (the conditioned stimulus, CS), this bell can be become conditioned to the US. (b) Following multiple pairings of the CS and the US, the CS comes to evoke a conditioned response (CR), salivation, in anticipation of the expected presentation of the food US.

house after hearing the weather report. In all three examples, a learned association between a CS and subsequently presented US leads to the generation of a CR that follows the CS but precedes the US.

Varieties of Conditioning

"Birds do it, bees do it, even educated fleas do it," wrote Cole Porter for the 1928 Broadway show *Paris*. Porter was, of course, referring to falling in love, but he could just as well have been writing about classical conditioning. All animals, including people, exhibit conditioning, even insects like fleas and flies. In fact, studies of classical conditioning of the fruit fly (*Drosophila*) have been enormously important for understanding the genetics of learning (we'll see an example of such a study later in this chapter).

Figure 7.2 illustrates the behavioral paradigm used in studies of fly conditioning (Dudai et al., 1976). First the flies are placed in a container that contains one odor, designated odor 1 (Figure 7.2a), and nothing happens. Then the flies are exposed to another odor, odor 2, and in the presence of that odor, they are given a mild but aversive shock (the US). Later, the flies are placed in the middle of a container that has odor 1 at one end and odor 2 at the other end (Figure 7.2b). As the flies explore the container, they avoid the side where they smell odor 2 (which has been associated with shock) and gravitate toward the side where they smell odor 1 (which was not paired with shock). Because the US is an unpleasant, or negative, event (such as a shock), this kind of conditioning is called **aversive conditioning.** When, in contrast, the US is a positive event (such as food delivery), the conditioning is called **appetitive conditioning.**

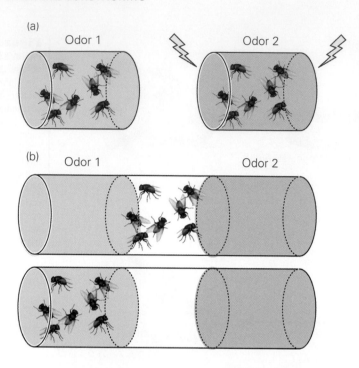

Figure 7.2 Odor conditioning in flies (a) Flies are sequentially placed in two different containers, first in one with odor 1 in which they are not shocked and then in another with odor 2 in which they are shocked. (b) Later, they are placed in the middle of a container that has odor 1 at one end and odor 2 at the other end. The flies move toward odor 1, which was not associated with shock, indicating that they have learned the odor 2→shock association from their previous training.

Sharon, one of the four people described at the chapter's beginning, was conditioned to the sound of her ex-boyfriend's voice by its past association to sex with him. Sex is among the most powerful of appetitive USs. Michael Domjan and colleagues have adapted Sharon's situation to the laboratory using male domesticated Japanese quail, who will copulate readily with a sexually receptive female (Figure 7.3). When an arbitrary stimulus, such as a light CS, is paired repeatedly with access to a sexually receptive female (the US), the male quail exhibits a CR of approaching and remaining near the light (Domjan et al., 1986).

So far we have introduced four different experimental preparations for studying classical conditioning, summarized here in Table 7.1. Two of these are aversive conditioning preparations: the fly shock preparation described above (Figure 7.2), and the conditioned emotional response preparation presented in Chapter 1, in which rats freeze when they hear a tone that predicts a floor shock (Estes & Skinner, 1941). The other two are appetitive conditioning preparations: Pavlov's original study with dogs and food, and the example with quails and sex, described above.

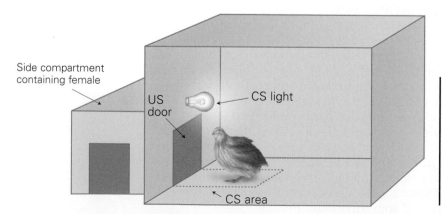

Figure 7.3 Sexual conditioning in male Japanese quail In an experiment developed by Michael Domjan and colleagues, the male domesticated Japanese quail is conditioned to approach and remain near a light (the CS) that is associated with access through a door to a sexually receptive female (the US).

Table 7.1

Widely Used Classical Conditioning Preparations

Preparation	Appetitive or aversive	Unconditioned stimulus (US)	Unconditioned response (UR)	Conditioned stimulus (CS)	Conditioned response (CR)
Fly shock conditioning	Aversive	Shock	Attempt to escape	Odor	Attempt to escape
Quail sex conditioning	Appetitive	Sexually available female	Approach, mounting, and copulation	Light	Approach
Dog salivation	Appetitive	Food	Salivation	Doorbell	Salivation
Conditioned emotional response	Aversive	Shock	Freezing	Tone	Freezing
Eyeblink conditioning	Aversive	Airpuff	Blink	Tone	Blink

In each of these four cases, we can ask: why does the animal exhibit the conditioned response? In all cases, the conditioned response can be understood as an anticipatory response that prepares the animal for the expected US, in much the same way that a child prepares for the arrival of an anticipated ice cream truck or a homeowner prepares for a predicted rainstorm. By moving away from the odor associated with shock, the fly hopes to avoid being shocked. By salivating in anticipation of food, the dog is better prepared to digest the food. By freezing in anticipation of a shock, the rat becomes more alert and watchful, and also avoids having ongoing motor behaviors (such as eating) disrupted by the shock. By moving toward the light, the quail prepares to mount and copulate with the female.

Another form of aversive conditioning—one that includes an anticipatory defensive response much like that of a homeowner shutting windows in advance of a rain storm—is **eyeblink conditioning,** perhaps the most thoroughly studied form of classical conditioning in mammals (Gormezano, Kehoe, & Marshall, 1983). In one common eyeblink-conditioning procedure, the animal is given a mild airpuff to one eye (see Table 7.1). This is not painful, but it does cause a reflexive eyeblink (if you don't believe this, ask a friend to blow lightly in your eye). An animal must sit still for its eyeblinks to be measured accurately; for this reason, rabbits are often used in eyeblink conditioning experiments (Figure 7.4a), being naturally quite good at sitting still for long periods of time. Moreover, they normally blink very little except when something occurs to bother their eyes.

In eyeblink conditioning, the airpuff is the US and the reflexive blink is the UR, as shown in Figure 7.4b. If this airpuff US is repeatedly preceded by a neutral stimulus, such as a tone, then the animal learns that the tone predicts the airpuff US and that it is a warning signal to get ready. Eventually, the animal will blink as a response to the tone. At this point, the tone has become a CS, and the anticipatory eyeblink is the CR, as shown in Figure 7.4c.

To the uninformed observer, the learned conditioned response, the eyeblink CR, is identical to the automatic unconditioned response, the eyeblink UR. However, psychologists know that the learned CR takes place during the warning period provided by the CS (analogous to a weather report predicting rain) in advance of the US and UR, adaptively protecting the eye from the onset of the airpuff. The same is true for Pavlov's original salivation study, in which the

(a)

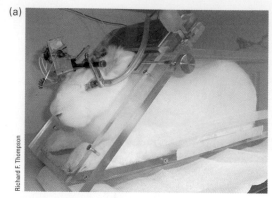

Richard F. Thompson

(b)

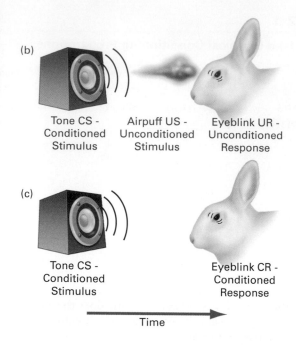

Tone CS - Conditioned Stimulus   Airpuff US - Unconditioned Stimulus   Eyeblink UR - Unconditioned Response

(c)

Tone CS - Conditioned Stimulus   Eyeblink CR - Conditioned Response

Time

Figure 7.4 Eyeblink conditioning (a) The tube at the upper right delivers the airpuff US to the rabbit in the restraining acrylic glass case; a photobeam measures the CR and UR. (b) Diagram of tone CS, airpuff US, and eyeblink UR in a naïve rabbit in an eyeblink conditioning experiment. (c) Diagram of tone CS and blink CR in a well-trained rabbit in an eyeblink conditioning experiment.

learned CR, salivation, is the same as the dog's natural unconditioned response to food, but it takes place *before* the food is presented, at the sound of the doorbell which predicts the food.

The eyeblink reflex has been used for studying human conditioning as well, as early as the 1920s, when researchers used a face slap as the US (as seen in the photo on p. 24, which shows Clark Hull of Yale University doing face-slap conditioning of a graduate student in the 1920s). For practical as well as ethical reasons, researchers no longer use the face slap as a US in human eyeblink conditioning. Instead, they use an airpuff and electromyography (EMG) detectors of electrical activity of muscles, as shown in Figure 7.5, produced by an apparatus that is similar to the one used with rabbits (Figure 7.4a). What is most important about eyeblink conditioning is that in most cases it appears similar across species, and thus results found in one species can reasonably be expected to apply to others.

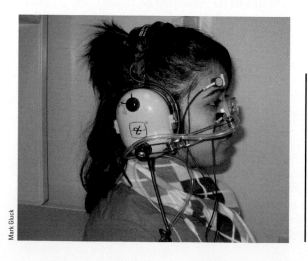

Mark Gluck

Figure 7.5 Contemporary human eyeblink preparation The CS is delivered as tones through the headphones. The US is a puff of air delivered through the rubber tube, as in the rabbit preparation (Figure 7.4). The eyeblink CR is recorded by EMG electrodes placed above and below the eye. Compare this to the earlier "face-slap" version of eyeblink conditioning used by Clark Hull and his students which was shown in Chapter 1.

Test Your Knowledge

Key Components of Pavlovian Conditioning

A classical "Pavlovian" conditioning experiment has four key components:

- US (unconditioned stimulus): A biologically significant stimulus that elicits a natural reflexive response.
- UR (unconditioned response): The natural reflex elicited by the US.
- CS (conditioned stimulus): A cue that was previously neutral but that through training ("conditioning") becomes associated with a US.
- CR (conditioned response): A learned response to a CS that has been paired with a US.

Got them all straight? Think you can tell the US, UR, CS, and CR apart? If so, test yourself by identifying each of them in the real-world situations described below:

1. Advertisements for a new sports car show a sexy model draped over the car's hood.
2. Mark loves pizza. When he was a boy, his parents frequently had it delivered to their home. Because the pizzas often arrived only lukewarm, his parents would put the pizza, still inside the box, into the oven to heat up. This caused the box to give off a smell of burning cardboard. Now, years later, whenever Mark smells cardboard burning, he gets hungry for pizza.
3. When Marge and her sisters were toddlers, their mother frequently used their nap time to vacuum. Now, when Marge and her sisters hear vacuum cleaners, they feel sleepy.

Learning a New Association

Figure 7.6a shows an eyeblink CR becoming stronger over several days of training in a rabbit eyeblink-conditioning study. The graphs show the extent to which the rabbit's eyelid lowers at different times during the trial; the higher the curve, the farther the eyelid has shut. Note that on day 1, the only response is the eyeblink UR that occurs *after* the onset of the airpuff US. However, with training, an eyeblink CR emerges. By day 3, in Figure 7.6a, there is movement of the eyelid before the US arrives. This anticipatory blink in response to the CS is the beginning of a CR. With further training, by about day 5, a strong anticipatory eyeblink CR occurs, timed so that the eyelid is safely closed before the airpuff US occurs.

In both rabbits and humans, eyeblink conditioning is a gradual process, occurring over many trials. Figure 7.6b and c show the trial-by-trial changes in the percentage of human participants and rabbits giving conditioned eyeblink responses in a study of tone–airpuff conditioning in both species. In both humans and rabbits, the percentage rises over time until most trials elicit an appropriately timed predictive eyeblink CR.

Extinguishing an Old Association

What do you think would happen if Garfield (from the chapter opening) ate oysters again and found not only that he enjoyed them but that afterward he did not get sick? Might he begin to lose his fear of eating oysters? If each successive time he ate oysters, he felt fine afterward, you might expect that his past aversion to eating oysters would disappear. Similarly, what about Sharon, who still finds her old boyfriend's voice so arousing? If she continued to see him socially, and he treated her badly or was no longer as attractive as he used to be, you might imagine that the sound of his voice would ultimately cease to have the

Figure 7.6 Acquisition of eyeblink conditioning
(a) Development of a conditioned response as measured at the beginning of day 1, day 3, and day 5 of training using a standard tone–airpuff trial sequence. On day 1, only a UR to the eyepuff is observed, but by day 3 an anticipatory eyeblink starts to emerge. By day 5, this anticipatory CR is strong and occurs reliably before the airpuff US. (b) A learning curve showing the percent of rabbits giving CRs across blocks of training trials. (c) Analogous learning curve for human eyeblink conditioning. While the curves are qualitatively similar in rabbits and humans, they reflect different training regimes, as the rabbits are usually trained in blocks of one-hour trial sessions on successive days, while humans are trained in a single hour-long session. (a) courtesy of R. F. Thompson; (b) from Allen, Chelius, & Gluck, 2002; (c) from Allen et al., 2002.

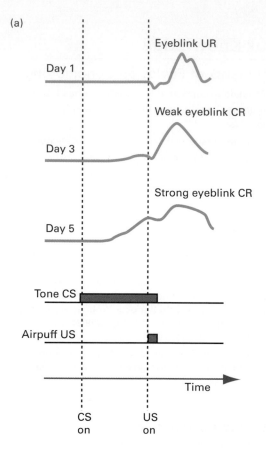

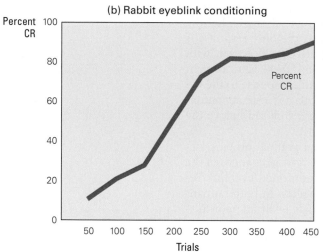

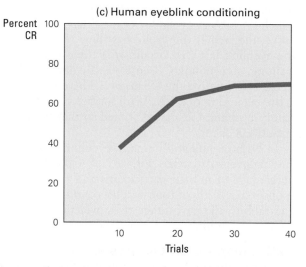

aphrodisiac properties that it once had. In both cases, a previously acquired association would have diminished through repeated presentation of the CS in the absence of the US, a process known as **extinction** that was first described in the early studies of Pavlov, as noted in Chapter 1.

Once it is acquired, eyeblink conditioning can undergo extinction if the former CS (tone) is presented repeatedly without an airpuff. Eventually, the rabbit (or person) that was formerly conditioned to blink to the tone begins to learn that the world has changed and the tone no longer predicts the US. Figure 7.7

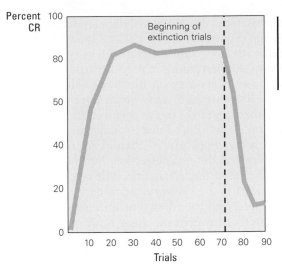

Percent CR

Figure 7.7 Acquisition and extinction of eyeblink conditioning Percent of rabbits exhibiting conditioned eyeblinks during 70 trials of acquisition and 20 trials of extinction. Adapted from data in Moore & Gormezano, 1961.

shows what happens if, after 70 trials of eyeblink-conditioning acquisition training, rabbits are given 20 trials of tone-alone extinction trials (Moore & Gormezano, 1961).

It is tempting to think of the extinction in Figure 7.7 as simply the unraveling of acquisition. However, in recent years a consensus has been building that supports the idea that extinction is not just unlearning but rather reflects a combination of unlearning and the learning of a new, opposing response to the CS. Specifically, it appears that during extinction the CS acquires a second "don't respond" meaning that competes with the originally acquired "do respond" association. This suggests that even though the animal (or person) is no longer responding to the CS at the end of extinction training (as seen in Figure 7.7), the learned response is not gone, just unexpressed. Evidence for this view of extinction comes from studies that show that the original learned response can reappear if the animal is moved to another context (such as another room or testing chamber) or if a long time passes before the animal is retested with a presentation of the CS. The return of a CR after such a delay is an example of spontaneous recovery (which you previously encountered in Chapter 6 in our discussion of habituation): the tendency for a previously learned association to reappear after a period of extinction. This suggests that the association was dormant following extinction training, but not lost.

Later in this chapter, in the box "Kicking the Habit," you will see a real-world example of spontaneous recovery in a drug addict who, although "in recovery" from the addiction (that is, no longer taking drugs), reexperiences the old cravings as strongly as ever in certain situations and slips back into the drug-taking habit she thought was gone. Ironically, the word "recovery" in learning research means the return of a learned habit, such as a conditioned response, whereas drug-abuse literature uses the word "recovery" to refer to the period during which an addict stays drug free. Be careful not to confuse these meanings!

Conditioned Compensatory Responses

If you had a pool in your backyard and were expecting heavy rains for several days, you might worry about the pool overflowing and damaging your lawn and house. Given the weather forecast, it might be prudent to partially drain your pool, lowering the level a few inches before the rain arrives. In this situation, your preparatory response compensates for your expectation of rising water levels by preemptively lowering the water level.

A similar, but *conditioned*, compensatory response was demonstrated by two of Pavlov's colleagues over 60 years ago (Subkov & Zilov, 1937). These researchers injected dogs on several occasions with adrenaline (also known as epinephrine), a chemical normally produced by the adrenal glands in response to stress or anxiety. The usual effect of adrenaline is an increase in heart rate. However, the dogs' heart rate increased less and less with each subsequent injection. Such a decrease in reaction to a drug so that larger doses are required to achieve the original effect is known as **tolerance.** What caused this tolerance to develop?

To explore this question, the researchers placed their dogs on injection stands, where the dogs normally received the drug injection, but they administered a neutral inert substance rather than the adrenaline. The researchers observed that this caused the dogs' heart rate to *decrease*. Apparently, the various cues (the stand, the injection) that predicted the adrenaline injection triggered a conditioned compensatory response that lowered the dogs' heart rate in anticipation of the adrenaline's causing an increase in heart rate. Such automatic compensatory responses occur primarily in body systems that have a mechanism for **homeostasis,** the tendency of the body (including the brain) to gravitate toward a state of equilibrium or balance.

Much like the homeowner who acts to prevent the pool from overflowing during a storm, the dogs in these studies unconsciously used advance information about the forthcoming adrenaline injection to compensate for the drug's effect. The learned anticipatory decrease in heart rate combined with the increase produced by the drug resulted in a lower total increase in heart rate than was experienced on the first (unexpected) administration of adrenaline. Since the dogs physiologically expected to receive adrenaline after seeing cues such as the stand or the syringe, their bodies compensated by lowering their heart rates to achieve a constant heart rate.

Human tolerance to drugs such as alcohol, cocaine, or ecstasy develops in the same way. As the addict's body adjusts to the drug effects, larger and larger doses are required to produce the same "high" experienced when the addict first took the drug. Later in this chapter you will see how this Pavlovian analysis of learned tolerance can help us better understand important aspects of drug abuse, addiction, and recovery.

What Cues Can Be CSs or USs?

The USs in a conditioning experiment are by definition events that are biologically significant, either because they are inherently positive (such as food or sex) or because they are inherently negative (such as shock or an airpuff to the eye). In contrast, a CS can be any cue in the environment, even a US. Thus, an airpuff to the eye, which is a US in the eyeblink conditioning paradigm, can serve as the CS in another experiment where, for example, an animal might learn that an airpuff predicts food delivery (the new US). Thus, stimulus cues are not inherently CSs or USs; rather, those terms define the roles the cues play in a particular learning situation.

Remember the description of Nathalie at the beginning of this chapter? She is a former smoker who gets an urge for a cigarette after sex. In Nathalie's case, sex is the CS that has become associated with cigarette smoking, the US. After a person gets into the regular habit of having a cigarette after sex, the craving for and expectation of cigarettes becomes the CR. (You'll read more about addiction and conditioning later on in this chapter.) In contrast, for Sharon, who becomes aroused at the sound of her ex-boyfriend's voice, his voice is now the CS and her sexual arousal is her CR. Thus, for Nathalie sex can be a CS that predicts cigarette smoking, while for Sharon it is the US that previously followed hearing her boyfriend's voice. It all depends on the individual's unique experiences.

Error Correction and the Modulation of US Processing

Chapter 1 introduced Aristotle's argument that contiguity—closeness in time and space—is necessary for a new association to be learned. For most of the first half of the twentieth century, psychologists believed that contiguity was both necessary and sufficient: so long as a potential CS and a US occur with little separation in time and space, animals and people were expected to form an association between them (Hull, 1943). But would it really make sense for animals or people to learn associations between all the simultaneously occurring stimuli that they perceive? Would it even be possible?

Kamin's Blocking Effect

Imagine you are a struggling stock investor whose livelihood depends on correctly predicting whether the stock market will go up or down the next day. One morning Doris, an eager new stock analyst, walks into your office and says that if you hire her, she will tell you each day which way the next day's market will go. You agree, and during her first week of work, you are amazed to see that she is 100% accurate, correctly predicting each day whether the market will rise or fall. The next week, Herman comes to visit and offers you his services as a stock analyst to predict the market's movements. Would you hire him? Probably not, because he is redundant if you already have Doris; that is, Herman offers no value beyond what you are already getting from Doris. You might say that Doris's early success at predicting the stock market has blocked you from valuing Herman's similar, but redundant, ability to do the same. As you will see next, conditioning studies have shown that humans and other animals are similarly sensitive to the informational value of cues in determining which associations they do or do not learn.

In the late 1960s, several psychological studies showed that pairing a potential CS and a US is not sufficient for conditioning to occur. Rather, for a potential CS to become associated with a US, the CS must provide valuable new information that helps an animal predict the future. Moreover, even if a given cue does predict a US, it may not become associated with that US if its usefulness has been preempted (blocked) by a co-occurring cue that has a longer history of predicting the US, much as Doris's predictive value blocked the hiring of Herman.

In a classic study by Leon Kamin, rats were first trained that a light predicts a shock and later trained that a compound stimulus of a light and tone also predicts the shock (Kamin, 1969). Kamin found that with this training, the rat will learn very little about the tone because the tone does not improve the rat's ability to predict the shock. This phenomenon is now known as **blocking;** it demonstrates that classical conditioning occurs only when a cue is both a useful and a nonredundant predictor of the future.

Kamin's 1969 blocking study is worth describing in detail because of its influence on subsequent theories of learning. In this study, one group of rats (the control group) was trained with a compound cue consisting of a light and a tone; this cue was reliably followed by a shock (see Table 7.2, control group, phase 2). The light and tone constituted a compound CS that the rats learned to associate with the shock US. Later, these rats would give a medium strong CR to either the tone alone or the light alone, though not as strong a response as to both the light and tone together.

Consider, however, the behavior of Kamin's second group of rats, identified as the experimental, or pre-trained, group in Table 7.2. These rats first received pre-training in which the light by itself predicted a shock (phase 1). From this training,

Table 7.2

The Blocking Paradigm

Group	Phase 1	Phase 2	Phase 3 (test)
Control group	Rat sits in chamber; no training	Tone CS combined with light CS —shock US	Tone CS → medium CR Light CS → medium CR
Experimental "pre-trained" group	Light CS —shock US	Tone CS combined with light CS —shock US	Tone CS → little or no CR *(learning is "blocked")* Light CS → big CR

they learned an association between the light CS and the shock US. Next (phase 2), they were given training that paired the light-and-tone compound cue and the shock, just like the control group animals had received. However, unlike the control rats, rats in the pre-trained group were already responding strongly to the light CS when they began the phase 2 compound training. For these rats, the additional presence of the tone provided no new information for predicting the US.

Phase 3 was a testing phase. When the pre-trained rats were tested with the light alone, they continued to exhibit a strong CR to the light, much as they had at the end of phase 1. However, in phase 3, if they were tested with the tone alone, they would give almost no response at all. This suggests that they learned almost nothing about the relationship between the tone and the US, despite the compound training received in phase 2, in which the tone was repeatedly followed by the US (Kamin, 1969). In contrast, rats in the control group, which did not receive phase 1 pre-training, exhibited significant (albeit medium strength) CRs to both the light and the tone in phase 3. Thus, the blocking phenomenon, exhibited by the pre-trained rats, can be summarized as follows: prior training of the light→shock association during phase 1 blocks learning of the tone→shock association during compound (light + tone) training in phase 2.

The blocking paradigm demonstrates that contiguity between a cue and a US is not enough to elicit a CR. In order for a stimulus to become associated with a US, it must impart reliable, useful, and nonredundant information (Kamin, 1969; Rescorla, 1968; Wagner, 1969). Apparently, "simple" Pavlovian conditioning is not as simple as psychologists once thought! In fact, you will now see that rats (and other animals, including humans) appear to be very sophisticated statisticians.

The Rescorla–Wagner Model and Error-Correction Learning

In the early 1970s, two psychologists at Yale, Robert Rescorla and Allan Wagner, were independently developing learning models to explain how blocking might occur. Although the two researchers worked at the same university, they didn't realize that they were using the same approach to solve the same problem until they happened to take a train together to a conference and began chatting about their research. To their surprise, they realized that they had each come up with the same idea, and so they decided to join forces.

Rescorla and Wagner's key idea was that the amount of change that occurs in the association between a CS and a US depends on a **prediction error,** the difference between whether the animal *expects* the US and whether the US actually occurs (Rescorla & Wagner, 1972). Rescorla and Wagner argued that there are three key situations to consider in interpreting a prediction error, as summarized in Table 7.3. If either no CS or a novel CS is presented followed by a US,

Table 7.3

Prediction, Surprise, and Learning in the Rescorla–Wagner Model

Situation	Error	Model Predicts
CS predicts nothing . . . Unexpected US occurs	Positive	Increase in association
CS predicts US . . . Predicted US occurs	Zero	No learning
CS predicts US . . . No US occurs	Negative	Decrease in association

the US will be unexpected; this is considered a positive prediction error. The Rescorla–Wagner theory expects that the CS→US association should increase proportionally to the degree that the US is surprising (the larger the error, the greater the learning). If, however, a well-trained CS is followed by the expected US, there is no error in prediction (the US was fully predicted by prior presentation of the CS), and thus no learning is expected. Finally, if the CS predicts a US and the US does not occur, the prediction error is considered negative, and Rescorla and Wagner expect it to be accompanied by a decrease in the CS→US association.

The real beauty and elegance of Rescorla and Wagner's approach was that it showed how this process of learning by error-correction could be described with a simple mathematical model that made only three assumptions:

Assumption 1: Each CS has an association weight that describes the strength of association between that cue and the US. In the blocking experiment we just saw, there would be two weights, formalized as V_{Light} and V_{Tone} for the light and tone, respectively. Think of these weights as numbers on a scale from 0 to 100 that indicate how strongly the CS predicts the US. A weight of 100 means that whenever the CS appears, the US will follow 100% of the time. If the weight is 90, then when the CS appears there is a 90% chance the US will follow (and a 10% chance it will not), and so on. Before any training takes place, all association weights are 0, meaning that when a potential CS first appears, there is no expectation that any US will follow. These association weights change through learning, as the animal learns which stimuli predict the US, and therefore which should have strong weights.

Assumption 2: An animal's expectation of the US is described by the sum of the weights of all the cues that are presented during a trial. In phase 1 pre-training in the blocking experiment (see Table 7.2), when only the light is presented, the expectation of the US is V_{Light}. However, in the phase 2 compound training, when both the light and the tone are presented, the expectation of the US is the sum of the weights of both those cues: $V_{\text{Light}} + V_{\text{Tone}}$.

Assumption 3: On each trial, learning is proportional to the difference between the outcome the animal expects (the expectation calculated for the US) and what actually occurs (calculated as described below). This difference is called the prediction error because it measures how much the animal's prediction differed from what really happened. A US that is totally unexpected precipitates a lot of learning while a US that is only partially expected results in less learning.

Putting all of this together, the Rescorla–Wagner model says the learning that takes place in a conditioning experiment can be predicted for each training trial by computing the prediction error, defined as:

Prediction error = Actual US − Expected US   **[Equation 1]**

The *actual US* is defined as 100 if the US occurs and 0 if it does not. The *expected US* is the sum of the weights of all the cues presented on that trial. Thus, in the compound training phase of the blocking experiment, expected US would be equal to $V_{Light} + V_{Tone}$.

Having defined prediction error with Equation 1, we use the next equation in the model to compute ΔV_{Cue}, Delta V_{Cue}, the amount that each cue weight will change on a trial due to learning. The cue in the blocking study would be either the tone or the light. Remember that V_{Cue} is a number between 0 and 100 that specifies how strongly a particular cue predicts the US. If ΔV_{Cue} for a trial is greater than 0, then V_{Cue} goes up; if ΔV_{Cue} is less than 0, then V_{Cue} goes down. According to the Rescorla–Wagner model, ΔV_{Cue} is calculated as:

$\Delta V_{Cue} = \beta$ (Prediction error)   **[Equation 2]**

This equation says that the change in V_{Cue} on a trial is equal to a small constant β, called the "learning rate," multiplied by the prediction error. Later we will discuss some of the implications of different learning rates.

To see all of this in action, suppose an animal is trained over many trials that a light CS predicts a shock US, just like in phase 1 of the blocking study. Initially, V_{Light} is 0, meaning that the animal has no expectation of a shock US when it sees the light:

Expected US = V_{Light} = 0

and

Prediction error = Actual US − Expected US = 100 − 0 = 100

To compute how this trial has changed the cue weight for light, we need to know the learning rate, β, which can range from 0 to 1. Small values of β imply that the animal learns very slowly, which means that changes in the weights will occur gradually over many trials. Large values of β imply that learning takes place very quickly, so there are big jumps in the weights from one trial to another. In practical applications of the Rescorla–Wagner model, this learning-rate parameter is often derived by determining which value of β fits best with the learning curves observed in laboratory experiments. Different animals in different learning situations may have different βs. However, part of the power of the Rescorla–Wagner model is that many of its most important predictions are independent of the actual β that is derived. For the purposes of illustrating how the model works, we will assume here that learning rate β is 0.2, which means that on each trial, the weights will change by 20% of the prediction error. Thus, on the first trial of a light→US training procedure:

$\Delta V_{Light} = \beta$ (Prediction error) = 0.2 × 100 = 20

That means V_{Light} changes from 0 to 20. On the next trial, when the light appears again, the animal will now have a modest expectation of the US:

Expected US = V_{Light} = 20

Not perfect, but better than before! Figure 7.8a plots the changes in V_{Light} over many trials. As you can see from Figure 7.8b, they are the same as the changes in expected US, because there is only one cue, and therefore only one weight used to calculate the expected US. The graphs show the values increasing gradually until after 20 trials they equal 98.5 (just less than a 100% prediction of shock). At this point, because the expected US is almost 100 and the actual US is 100 (the US is always present on these light→US trials), the prediction error will be

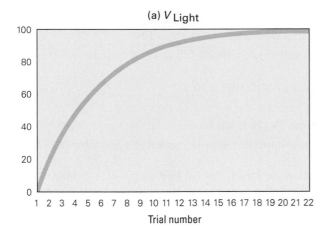

(a) V_{Light}

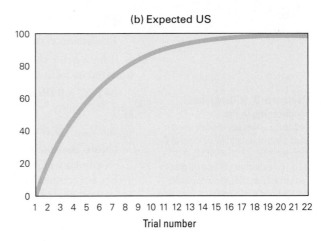

(b) Expected US

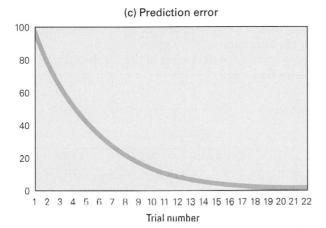

(c) Prediction error

Figure 7.8 Acquisition of CS–US association in the Rescorla–Wagner model (a) Trial-by-trial plot of V_{Light}. (b) Trial-by-trial plot of the expected US. (c) Plot of the prediction error over the same trials. The learning rate is .20. Note that because there is only one cue, the light, the expected US is the same as the cue weight, V_{Light}. As these values rise toward 100, the prediction error declines toward zero.

reduced after 20 trials to nearly 0, as shown in Figure 7.8c; this outcome indicates that the animal has learned the task.

Rescorla and Wagner argued that this is the principle by which rabbits (and people and other animals) learn incrementally, trial by trial, to adjust their associations between a CS and a US. The Rescorla–Wagner model (consisting of equations 1 and 2) is called an **error-correction rule,** because over many trials of learning, it reduces, or corrects, the likelihood of prediction errors.

Compound Conditioning

At the beginning of this chapter Garfield got the flu after eating oysters and thus developed an aversion to the taste of oysters. But what if he had eaten more than just oysters that night? What if he also had apple pie at that meal? Would he associate the oysters or the apple pie or perhaps both with having a gastrointestinal illness? As noted earlier, a key assumption of the Rescorla–Wagner model is that when multiple CS cues are present, the expected US is the sum of the weights of all cues presented in that trial. Consider, for example, the control group of animals in phase 2 of a blocking experiment (Table 7.2). Because these animals have never previously been exposed to the US, we can assume:

$V_{Light} = V_{Tone} = 0$

At the beginning of the first trial of compound conditioning, the expectation of the US will be calculated as:

Expected US $= V_{Light} + V_{Tone} = 0$

and

Prediction error = 100 − (Expected US) = 100 − (0) = 100

Then, after the first trial, on which a shock US does occur, the weights are updated as follows:

$$\Delta V_{\text{Light}} = \beta \text{ (Prediction error)} = .20 \text{ (100)} = 20$$

and

$$\Delta V_{\text{Tone}} = \beta \text{ (Prediction error)} = .20 \text{ (100)} = 20$$

(Note that we continue to assume, for simplicity's sake, a learning rate, ß, of .20 for both weights.)

So far, compound conditioning looks exactly like single-cue conditioning. However, the patterns characteristic of single-cue conditioning and compound conditioning diverge starting with the second trial. Figure 7.9 shows the trial-by-trial changes in V_{Light}, V_{Tone}, the expected US, and the prediction error during this compound training. Note that there is one prediction error for each trial, based on all the cues presented (and the expectation that they create for a US). This prediction error is used to calculate the trial-by-trial changes in weight for both the light and the tone cues.

At the beginning of the second trial of presentation of the combined tone and light followed by a shock US, we find that:

$$V_{\text{Light}} = V_{\text{Tone}} = 20$$

Figure 7.9 Compound conditioning in the Rescorla–Wagner model Simulated plots of data from 20 trials of (a) changes in V_{Light}, (b) changes in V_{Tone}, (c) expected US, and (d) prediction error. Note that the weights for the light and tone change at the same rate, as they both rise toward 50, and thus the curves in parts a and b are identical. By trial 12 both have reached their maximum. The expected US, shown in part d, is the sum of these two values and therefore rises to a maximum value of 100 by trial 12. The prediction error in part d declines from 100 to 0, mirroring the rise of the expected US from 0 to 100. These simulations were calculated assuming a learning rate of .20.

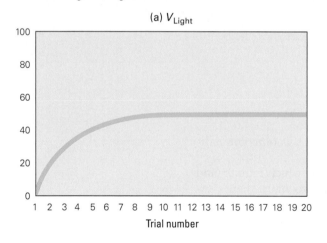

(a) V_{Light}

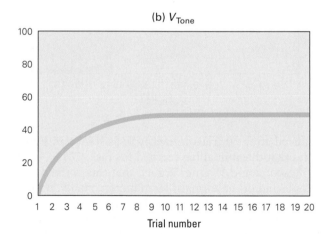

(b) V_{Tone}

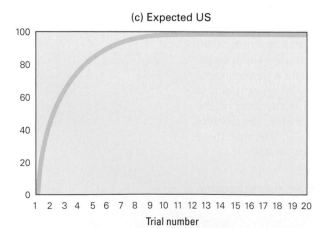

(c) Expected US

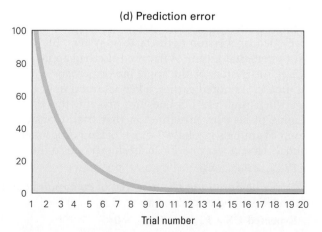

(d) Prediction error

and thus:

Expected US = $V_{\text{Light}} + V_{\text{Tone}}$ = 20 + 20 = 40

and:

Prediction error = 100 − (**Expected US**) = 100 − (4) = 60

After that second compound-conditioning trial, the weights are updated as follows:

ΔV_{Light} = β (**Prediction error**) = .20 (60) = 12

and:

ΔV_{Tone} = β (**Prediction error**)= .20 (60) = 12

Again, because there is a single prediction error on the trial, both weights are updated by the same amount, 12, leading to new weights at the end of trial 2 (and beginning of trial 3) of:

$\Delta V_{\text{Light}} = \Delta V_{\text{Tone}}$ = 20 + 12 = 32

Here again it is instructive to compare the learning that the model predicts after two trials for single-cue acquisition (Figure 7.8) and for compound conditioning (Figure 7.9). The difference is slight but significant: the weight under single-cue acquisition has risen to 36, whereas in compound conditioning the weights have only risen to 32. It appears as if the weights in compound conditioning are not rising as quickly as in single-cue conditioning. However, note that there are two weights in compound conditioning compared to only one weight in single-cue conditioning. The individual weights in compound conditioning are rising more slowly, but their sum, the expected US, is rising much more quickly.

By comparing Figures 7.8 and 7.9, you can see that in single-cue conditioning the expected US goes from 0 to 20 to 36 over the first three trials, while in compound conditioning the expected US progresses from 0 to 40 to 64. This suggests that having multiple (compound) cues should allow the expectation of the US to increase faster, even while the changes in the individual weights rise more slowly. Meanwhile, the cue weights in compound training never get as high as they do in single-cue training, because the two of them together must equal 100. The weights in compound conditioning with two cues eventually stabilize at 50, as shown in Figure 7.9a and b. This outcome can be compared to the weight of almost 100 that was realized after 20 trials of single-cue training in Figure 7.8a. Even with extended training consisting of 100, 200, or more such trials, the weights for the two cues in compound conditioning would still remain around 50. Why? Because of the way the prediction error is calculated. Assume that after many trials of compound training the weights are:

$V_{\text{Light}} = V_{\text{Tone}}$ = 50

and thus:

Expected US = $V_{\text{Light}} + V_{\text{Tone}}$ = 50 + 50 = 100

Then,

Prediction error = 100 − (**Expected US**) = 100 − (100) = 0

Regardless of how many more training trials are conducted, the weights will not change further, because:

ΔV_{Light} = β (**Prediction error**) = .20 (0) = 0

and:

ΔV_{Tone} = β (**Prediction error**) = .20 (0) = 0

From this we see that because the two weights of 50 add up to 100, the expected US equals 100 (the same as the actual US), and therefore no error is generated in these trials. As you saw before, without error, there is no learning, and no need for learning, in the Rescorla–Wagner model. When there are two cues predicting the US, each of them provides 50% of the prediction, making a total of 100%, which represents a perfectly accurate prediction of the US. If there were four cues, we would expect each of them to rise to a maximum value of 25 so that the total remains at 100.

What do you think would happen if, after this compound training with a tone and light, the experimenter presented just one of the cues—perhaps the light? We can see that:

Expected US = V_{Light} = 50

The expected US would be 50, because the weight of the light association is only 50. This means that if one of these cues is presented alone, following compound presentation with both, the CR (which reflects the expected value of the US) will be much lower in strength than it would be for the compound tone and light stimulus (Figure 7.9b).

The Rescorla–Wagner Model Explains Blocking

Now we can show how the Rescorla–Wagner model explains the blocking paradigm described in Table 7.2. Rats in the control condition get no training at all in phase 1, so the values of V_{Light}, V_{Tone}, and the expected US all remain 0 throughout this phase (Figure 7.10a, left). In phase 2, where the tone-and-light compound cue is paired with the US, we see that all three values follow the same patterns shown in Figure 7.9 for compound conditioning: the weights of both

(a) Control condition in blocking experiment

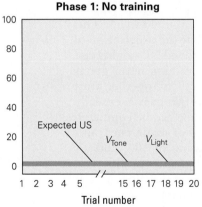
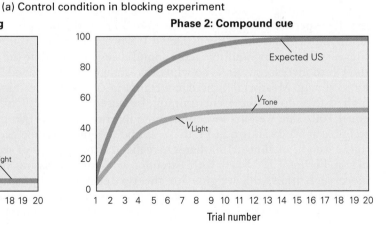

Figure 7.10
Simulation of the blocking paradigm by the Rescorla–Wagner model Graphs show V_{Tone}, V_{Light}, and expected US for (a) the control condition and (b) the pre-trained condition.

(b) Pre-trained condition in blocking experiment

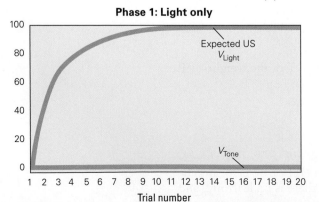
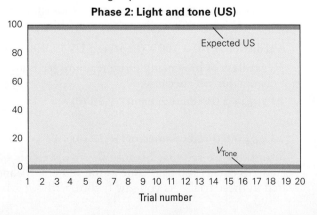

cues individually rise to 50 while the expected US (the sum of both weights) rises to 100, and then all stabilize at those values (Figure 7.10a, right). In a subsequent testing phase (phase 3 in Table 7.2), a medium-strong response is given to either the tone or the light if they are presented individually, because V_{Light} and V_{Tone} each equal 50 at the end of phase 2.

For rats in the "pre-trained" condition of the blocking paradigm described in Table 7.2, the values change as plotted in Figure 7.10b. In phase 1, the animals experience light→US conditioning. By the end of phase 1, V_{Light} is equal to about 100, so whenever the light is presented, the animal scores a perfect 100% in predicting that the US will follow. Because no tone is presented in phase 1, V_{Tone} remains 0 throughout that part of the experiment. In phase 2, the tone CS and light CS are presented together as a compound. With V_{Light} already equal to 100, prediction of the US is perfect, so the prediction error is 0. Therefore, by equation 1 above, there is no further change to any of the weights. V_{Tone} will be stuck at 0 and never change, no matter how many times the tone–light compound is paired with the shock. As a result, in phase 3, the testing phase, these rats will give a strong response to the light but little or no response to the tone, exactly as Kamin found in his classic study and as summarized in Table 7.2. This use of the Rescorla–Wagner rule to explain Kamin's blocking effect demonstrates the more general conclusion that for a potential CS to become associated with a US, the CS must provide valuable new information that helps an animal or person predict the future.

Influence of the Rescorla–Wagner Model

More than a quarter century after its publication, the Rescorla–Wagner model is generally acknowledged as the most influential formal model of learning. Its broad acceptance is due to its elegant simplicity and to the fact that it explains a wide range of previously puzzling empirical results. One hallmark of a successful model is that it reveals underlying connections between a series of observations that initially seemed unrelated or even contradictory.

The Rescorla–Wagner model also made surprising predictions about how animals would behave in new experimental procedures, and experimenters rushed to test these predictions. This is another feature of a successful model: it should allow scientists to make predictions that could not be made before. Ideally, modeling and empirical work should generate a cycle in which the model makes predictions that, when tested, provide new data. If the data match the predictions, the model is supported. If not, then the model must be revised. The revised model then generates new predictions, and the cycle continues.

Owing to its simplicity, the Rescorla–Wagner model cannot account for every kind of learning, and should not be expected to. However, many researchers have devoted themselves to showing how one or another addition to the model would allow it to explain a wider range of phenomena. With so many additions, the model may be in danger of losing some of its simplicity and appeal. Nevertheless, the Rescorla–Wagner model has been used as a starting point from which many subsequent models have been built, including the models of human learning discussed in the next section.

From Conditioning to Category Learning

Are concepts such as blocking, and conditioning models such as the Rescorla–Wagner model, limited in applicability to classical conditioning, or might they also provide insights into higher forms of human cognition and behavior, especially those that involve prediction or categorization? To what extent are the cognitive processes of human learning analogous to the more elementary learning mechanisms studied in animal conditioning experiments?

Although the fields of animal and human learning were originally closely intertwined, they became largely divorced from each other in the late 1960s and early 1970s. Animal learning at this time remained primarily concerned with elementary associative learning, while human learning studies focused more on memory abilities, characterized in terms of information processing and rule-based symbol manipulation, approaches borrowed from the emerging field of artificial intelligence. Ironically, this historical schism occurred just as animal learning theory was being reinvigorated by the new Rescorla–Wagner model in the early 1970s.

If animal conditioning and human learning do share common principles, we would expect to see evidence in human learning of conditioning phenomena such as Kamin's blocking effect. Early evidence for blocking in human learning comes from work by Gordon Bower and Tom Trabasso, who trained college students to categorize objects according to certain predefined rules (Bower & Trabasso, 1964). The students were presented with geometric figures varying in five dimensions: color, shape, number of internal lines, position of a dot, and position of a gap. Phase 1 of the experiment consisted of training the participants by asking them to guess whether each figure belonged to class A or class B; each time they were told whether they had guessed correctly or not. For example, some participants were trained that all circular shapes belong in class A while all triangular shapes belong in class B (and all other features are irrelevant), as illustrated by the two sample stimuli shown in Figure 7.11a. Given enough trials with different stimuli, participants would deduce the circle→A/triangle→B rule, much as the pre-trained rabbits learned the light→shock association in phase 1 of the blocking study (Table 7.2 on p. 254).

Once this lesson was mastered, the experimenter showed participants a slightly different set of figures: now, all figures that were circular and thus belonged to class A had a dot on top, while all figures that were triangular and thus belonged to class B had a dot on the bottom (Figure 7.11b). This addition of a redundant cue in phase 2 (position of the dot) parallels the addition of the light stimulus in phase 2 of the rat blocking study. Participants continued to perform well by using their old rule of sorting on the basis of shape; the question was whether they would also learn that the dot position by itself predicted class membership.

To test this, the experimenters used new figures, shown in Figure 7.11c. Given a figure with no dot, all participants continued to sort the circles into class A and the triangles into class B. However, when given a figure with a new shape (rectangle), none of the participants correctly sorted on the basis of dot position. Thus, these humans performed much like the pre-trained rats that displayed little or no response to the redundant light cue added in phase 2 of Kamin's experiment. In effect, prior learning that the shape predicted class membership appears to have *blocked* subsequent learning that the dot position also predicts class membership. More recent studies have verified that blocking is as pervasive in humans as it is in other animals (Kruschke, Kappenman, & Hetrick, 2005).

Figure 7.11 The blocking effect in humans (a) Examples of stimuli from phase 1 training, in which all circular shapes belong in class A and all triangular shapes belong in class B. (b) Examples of stimuli from phase 2. Participants are shown only circles and triangles, and the same circle→A/triangle→B rule still applies. However, now there is also a dot on the top of all class A items and a dot on the bottom of all class B items. (c) A final testing phase in which participants are given novel stimuli to see if they have learned that the dot-top→A/dot-bottom →B rule by itself can predict class membership. Adapted from Bower & Trabasso, 1964.

(a) Phase 1 training

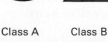

Class A   Class B

(b) Phase 2 training

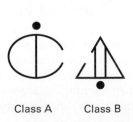

Class A   Class B

(c) Testing

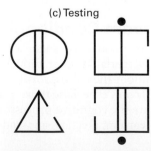

Cue–Outcome Contingency and Judgments of Causality

One area in which classical conditioning and cognitive studies of category learning have converged is the study of cues that are only partially valid predictors of category membership. Consider, for example, what would happen if Doris, the stock analyst you recently hired, was a good but not perfect stock predictor. Suppose her predictions are correct on 3 out of every 5 days. That rate is not bad, but you yourself may already be able to make accurate predictions about the stock market 3 out of 5 days just from reading the *Wall Street Journal*. In that case, you might decide that Doris doesn't provide you with any additionally useful information. If your ability to invest wisely is the same regardless of whether or not Doris is helping you, you probably wouldn't view her as a great asset to your business.

Rescorla showed a similar phenomenon in an animal conditioning experiment that provided additional support for the Rescorla–Wagner model (Rescorla, 1968). His experiment demonstrated that conditioning to a tone stimulus depends not only on the frequency of tone–US pairings but also on the frequency of the US in the absence of the tone. If the US occurs just as often without the tone as it does in the presence of the tone, then little or no conditioning will accrue to the tone. These results suggest that animals are sensitive to the *contingency* of, or degree of correlation between, the potential CS and the US. The Rescorla–Wagner model explains this effect by viewing the experimental chamber as a cue presented in combination with (compounded with) the experimentally manipulated tone. Thus, the experimental chamber can be thought of as the **context,** that is, the background stimuli that are relatively constant in all trials (rather than being manipulated by the experimentor), both when there is a US and when there is not; these stimuli include the sound, smell, and feel of the conditioning chamber. In the stock investor example, the context includes all the generally available information for investors, such as the stock analyses in the daily *Wall Street Journal;* the potential CSs are the extra tips occasionally provided by Doris.

In the Rescorla–Wagner model, the animal actually experiences the trials in which the tone occurs alone as trials in which a compound cue is present, a cue consisting of the tone CS in combination with the context. The Rescorla–Wagner model expects that the context will, in effect, compete with the tone for the credit of predicting the US. If the US occurs as frequently on context-alone trials as on context-and-tone trials, the context is a more reliable cue, and thus it wins the credit and hence the bulk of the associative weight. Therefore, according to the Rescorla–Wagner model, the degree to which the US is contingent on the CS depends on a competition between the CS and the co-occurring background context.

Similar sensitivity to cue–outcome contingencies has also been found in studies of human causal inference. These are studies of how people deduce cause and effect in their environment. In typical experiments, people might be asked to judge which risk factors (smoking, lack of exercise, weight gain) are more or less responsible for some observable outcome, such as heart disease. These studies have shown that increasing the frequency of the outcome in the absence of the risk factor (say, the frequency of lung cancer in the absence of smoking) decreases people's estimates of the causal influence on the outcome, in much the same way that the presence of the US in the context alone decreased conditioning to the potential CS as described above. What are the implications of this finding? For one thing, it suggests that if there is a spike in the frequency of a disease (like lung cancer) but no similar increase in a risk factor (like smoking), people will come to view smoking as less harmful than they did previously. In effect, if you're going to get lung cancer anyway, why not smoke?

A Neural Network Model of Probabilistic Category Learning

In the late 1980s, the expanding impact of computer simulations of neural network, or connectionist, models of human learning revived interest in relating human cognition to elementary associative learning. These models showed that many complex human abilities (including speech recognition, motor control, and category learning) emerge from configurations of elementary associations similar to those studied in conditioning paradigms.

One example is a simple neural network model developed by Mark Gluck and Gordon Bower to model how people learn to form categories (Gluck & Bower, 1988). In this study, college students were asked to learn how to diagnose patients suffering from one of two nasty-sounding diseases—midosis or burlosis. The students reviewed medical records of fictitious patients, who were each suffering from one or more of the following symptoms: bloody nose, stomach cramps, puffy eyes, discolored gums. During the study, each student reviewed several hundred medical charts, proposed a diagnosis for each patient, and then was told the correct diagnosis. The students initially had to guess, but with practice they were able to diagnose the fictitious patients quite accurately. The fact that the different symptoms were differentially diagnostic of the two diseases helped them guess. Bloody noses were very common in burlosis patients but rare in midosis, while discolored gums were common in midosis patients but rare in burlosis. The other two symptoms, stomach cramps and puffy eyes, were only moderately diagnostic of either disease.

This kind of learning can be modeled using the network in Figure 7.12a. The four symptoms are represented by four input nodes at the bottom of the network, and the two diseases correspond to the two output nodes at the top of the network. The weights of the arrows between the symptoms and the diseases are updated according to the learning rule from the Rescorla–Wagner model, much as if the symptoms were CSs and the diseases were alternate USs.

Learning and performance in the model works as follows: a patient with the symptoms "bloody nose" and "stomach cramp" is modeled by turning "on" the corresponding input nodes, as shown in Figure 7.12a. These act like two CSs present on the trial. In contrast to the classical conditioning paradigms described earlier, where there is one US (such as an airpuff), here there are two possible outcomes: the diseases burlosis and midosis. Thus, activating two symptoms (two input nodes) causes activity to travel up four weighted arrows, two to burlosis and two to midosis, as shown in Figure 7.12a. The arrows from these two symptoms to burlosis are much more heavily weighted than the ones to midosis, and thus the expected burlosis node is shaded a darker red because

Figure 7.12 Gluck and Bower's network model of category learning (a) The arrows from bloody nose and stomach cramp to burlosis and from puffy eyes and discolored gums to midosis are thick, indicating highly diagnostic relationships (that is, heavily weighted cues). The other cues are of only moderate diagnosticity. This figure shows a trial in which a patient presents with two symptoms, bloody nose and stomach cramp; thus, these two input nodes are active (dark red). The other two input nodes represent symptoms that are not present (puffy eyes and discolored gums), and these nodes are inactive (gray). Relative activation levels (dark red and light red) of the two "expected" category nodes are based only on the weight of the input flowing up the arrows from the active and present symptoms (bloody nose and stomach cramp). (b) Accuracy of the Rescorla–Wagner network model for predicting participants' diagnoses of 14 symptom patterns. Each pattern is represented by a green dot whose location is determined by the model's predictions (x-axis), and the actual proportion of "burlosis" responses for each pattern (y-axis). The fact that the 14 dots lie very close to the diagonal line indicates a very close fit of model to data. From Gluck & Bower, 1988.

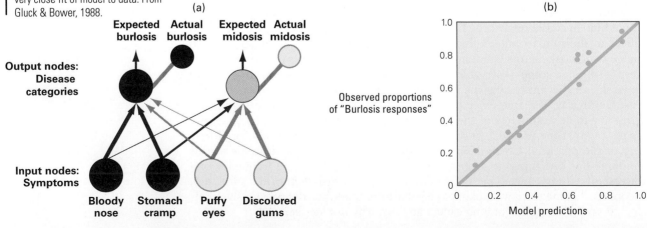

(a)

Expected burlosis   Actual burlosis   Expected midosis   Actual midosis

Output nodes: Disease categories

Input nodes: Symptoms

Bloody nose   Stomach cramp   Puffy eyes   Discolored gums

(b)

Observed proportions of "Burlosis responses"

Model predictions

the output activation for burlosis is calculated as the sum of all the weights projecting into the burlosis node from the cues that are present on that trial (that is, bloody nose and stomach cramps in Figure 7.12a). In contrast, the expected midosis node is only a light shade of red because the weights from the cues present on that trial to this node are much smaller, as indicated by the very thin red lines in Figure 7.12a. On this trial, burlosis is the correct label, indicated by the very dark actual burlosis node. Thus, the model is more likely to diagnose the patient as having the disease with the higher activation, namely, burlosis, which in fact is the correct diagnosis.

By analogy with the Rescorla–Wagner model, these output-node activations are equivalent to the network's *expectation* of one disease versus another. After a student guessed at a diagnosis and was told the correct answer, that answer was used by the student to modify the arrow weights so as to reduce future error, in accordance with the Rescorla–Wagner model's error-correction learning rule. The network model shown in Figure 7.12a incorporates nothing more than the learning principle of the Rescorla–Wagner conditioning model. Nevertheless, this "animal conditioning" model of human cognition accounts for variations in how the participants classified different patients. Let's see how the model does this.

With four possible symptoms, 16 possible patient charts can be constructed showing different combinations of present and absent symptoms. Gluck and Bower used only 14 of these possible charts, eliminating the variations in which there are no symptoms (all absent) or in which all four symptoms are present. After participants had completed several hundred training trials, Gluck and Bower asked themselves whether their model could predict the proportion of times that each of the 14 patterns was classified as burlosis and as midosis during the study. To generate the predictions, they looked at two output nodes, expected burlosis and expected midosis, for each of the 14 patterns. If, for a particular symptom pattern (such as "bloody nose and stomach cramp"), the output values were expected burlosis = 80 and expected midosis = 20, then the authors predicted that the subjects should classify this pattern as burlosis 80% of the time and as midosis 20% of the time. In this way, Gluck and Bower calculated a predicted proportion of "burlosis" responses for each of the 14 patterns based on their model and compared it to the actual proportion of students who responded "burlosis" to these patterns during the final 50 trials of the experiments.

The results of this analysis are shown in Figure 7.12b, where each of the 14 patterns is represented by a dot. The location of each dot corresponds, on the horizontal axis, to the model's predicted ratio of diagnoses (ranging from 0 to 1) and, on the vertical axis, to the actual experimental data. Thus, if the "bloody nose and stomach cramp" patient from Figure 7.12a, who has a predicted burlosis categorization proportion of 80%, is indeed categorized by the participants in this experiment as having burlosis in 80% of the trials, then the dot for "bloody nose and stomach cramp" would be found at the point (0.8,0.8) in this graph. Thus, the better the fit of the model, the more likely that each of the 14 patterns (dots) would lie on a straight line from (0,0) through (1,1). As you can see from Figure 7.12b, the fit is excellent.

Despite this and other successes of the Gluck and Bower model in predicting behavioral data, several limitations of the model became evident in further studies of human category learning. In particular, as a model of category learning, it fails to account for people's ability to actively focus their attention on one or another symptom feature, or to shift or refocus this attention during learning. As you will see in the next discussion, this limitation echoes many of the limitations found previously with the Rescorla–Wagner model, specifically its inability to account for some subtle aspects of stimulus attention in animal conditioning.

Modulation of CS Processing

What if, during Doris's first week on the job, your stock profits were no different from those before she came to work? You would probably view her as irrelevant and ineffective. However, suppose that in the second week, your profits did improve: would you credit Doris for this change? Maybe not at first, since you had already come to the conclusion that Doris doesn't provide you with any worthwhile stock information. This is exactly what happens in a study of cue pre-exposure in animal conditioning, as first described by Robert Lubow and Ulrich Moore (Lubow & Moore, 1959). Lubow and Moore's study was conducted using sheep and goats; however, for consistency with the rest of the chapter (and to facilitate comparison with other studies discussed in this chapter), we will describe their "latent inhibition" paradigm using rabbit eyeblink conditioning, which has reliably produced the same results.

Table 7.4

The Cue Pre-Exposure (Latent Inhibition) Paradigm

Group	Phase 1	Phase 2
Control group	Animal sits in chamber; no training	Tone CS —airpuff US
Experimental "pre-exposed" group	Tone CS	Tone CS —airpuff US

Latent inhibition studies use two groups of subjects; the first group, the control group, receives no pre-training, and the second group does receive pre-exposure training, as summarized in Table 7.4. Control animals simply sit in their chambers until they are ready for the critical phase 2, in which they are trained to associate a tone CS with an airpuff-in-the-eye US. In contrast, animals in the pre-exposed group are repeatedly exposed to a tone with no US in phase 1 before they undergo the same tone–airpuff training in phase 2 as the control animals do. Thus, the only difference between the two groups is that one group is pre-exposed to the tone in phase 1.

As illustrated in Figure 7.13, rabbits in the pre-exposed group learn much more slowly in phase 2 than those in the control group do to associate the tone with a puff of air in the eye (Shohamy, Allen, & Gluck, 2000). The same kind of slow learning following CS exposure is seen in a variety of species; for example, it is seen in human eyeblink conditioning as well (Lubow, 1973).

This phenomenon of impaired learning following cue pre-exposure is called **latent inhibition.** Its occurrence is problematic for the Rescorla–Wagner model: there is no surprise during the first phase of tone-alone exposure and therefore no error, so the Rescorla–Wagner model expects no learning to occur in phase 1. Thus, the Rescorla–Wagner model makes the incorrect prediction

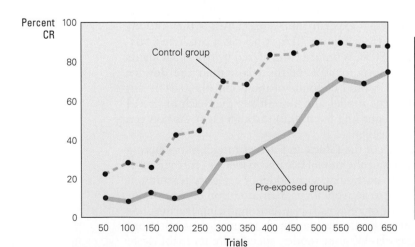

Figure 7.13 Latent inhibition in rabbit eyeblink conditioning This graph shows the percent of trials producing CRs in each block of 50 trials during the common phase 2 tone–airpuff training of the rabbits in the study. The rabbits in the control group (dotted line) learned rapidly. In contrast, the rabbits in the pre-exposed group (solid line), who had previously experienced 850 trials of tone-alone presentations in phase 1, learned much more slowly. Adapted from Shohamy, et al., 2000.

that the pre-exposed group should be no different from the control group at the start of phase 2, a prediction clearly disconfirmed by Lubow's studies, as well as by the data in Figure 7.13.

Latent inhibition, and similar paradigms that involve mere exposure to apparently neutral cues, suggests that there is more going on during conditioning than the error-driven learning characterized by the Rescorla–Wagner model. To account for latent inhibition and other phenomena beyond the scope of the Rescorla–Wagner model, several alternative theories of conditioning have been proposed, which are described below.

An Attentional Approach to Stimulus Selection

The Rescorla–Wagner model is often called a **US modulation theory** of learning because it argues that the manner in which the US is processed determines what stimuli become associated with that US. Thus, in the Rescorla–Wagner model, the ability of the US to promote learning is modulated by how unexpected the US is, given the potential CS that precedes it. An alternative class of learning theories focuses instead on the CSs, suggesting various mechanisms that modulate (either enhance or depress) the ability of potential CSs to enter into associations. For this reason, they are referred to as **CS modulation theories:** they propose that the way in which different potential CSs are processed determines which of them become associated with the US. One such theory, presented by Nicholas Mackintosh in the early 1970s, is based on the observation that people and animals have a limited capacity for processing incoming information (Mackintosh, 1975). This limited capacity means that paying attention to one stimulus diminishes our ability to attend to other stimuli. Thus, Mackintosh sought a way to understand how attention to CS cues might be modulated.

Remember the blocking analogy in which Doris was the first to establish herself as a reliable predictor of the stock market so that later, when Herman showed up, you gave him little credit for making equally successful predictions? The Rescorla–Wagner model argues that this outcome is due to the stock market (the US) already being well predicted by Doris (the first CS), so that no additional value (learning) accrues to Herman (a potential second CS). Mackintosh's view of blocking is quite different. He argues that you come to devote all your attention to Doris because she has a long history of predicting the stock market for you, and therefore you have no attention left to pay to Herman. The core idea of the Mackintosh theory is that a previously conditioned stimulus derives its salience from its past success as a predictor of important events (Mackintosh, 1975), and this happens at the expense of other co-occurring cues that don't get access to your limited pool of attention. In essence, Rescorla and Wagner's model lets Herman come in for an interview but doesn't consider him valuable for predicting the market, while Mackintosh's model never lets Herman in the door.

An Attentional Explanation of Latent Inhibition

Recall that the Rescorla–Wagner model cannot explain cue pre-exposure phenomena such as latent inhibition because, as a US modulation theory of learning, it only explains learning that takes place when a US is present or when previously trained cues predict the US. Thus, the Rescorla–Wagner model suggests incorrectly that no learning takes place when a neutral (previously untrained) cue is presented. In contrast, Mackintosh's theory predicts that the salience of a tone as a potential CS will decrease when the tone is presented without any US, because the tone develops a history of predicting nothing. According to Mackintosh, the animal treats these tone-alone trials as if they were the little boy who cried wolf. Eventually the tones (like the boy) are ignored because they don't reliably predict that anything bad or good is about to happen.

In addition to Mackintosh, several other learning theorists, most notably John Pearce and Geoffrey Hall, have proposed alternate models of how CS salience is modulated during training (Pearce & Hall, 1980). All of these theories share the basic underlying idea that the changes in weighting of the CS are due to modulations of the CS, not of the US.

While these CS modulation models have had many successes, especially in explaining behavioral phenomena that are not explained by the Rescorla–Wagner model, they have had less of an impact on the field of learning and memory, in part because they are more complex than the Rescorla–Wagner model, and because they don't explain as broad a range of behaviors. Moreover, as discussed earlier in this chapter, the Rescorla–Wagner model has been especially influential because it works on the same fundamental principle as the learning algorithms employed in the connectionist network models of human memory used by cognitive psychologists, including both the models of David Rumelhart and colleagues described in Chapter 1 (Rumelhart & McClelland, 1986) and the category learning model of Gluck and Bower (1988) discussed above.

Which view is correct, the CS modulation or the US modulation approach to conditioning? For many years the two camps were viewed as being in direct conflict, with each entrenched on a different side of the Atlantic Ocean: the US modulation view predominated in the United States (where Rescorla and Wagner worked), while the CS modulation view predominated in the United Kingdom (where Mackintosh, Pearce, and Hall worked). However, behavioral and biological studies of conditioning now suggest that *both* views are probably correct. That is, there are likely to be both CS modulation and US modulation mechanisms involved during learning. As you will see in section 7.2 (and later in Chapter 9), part of what has helped resolve this debate is new data from neuroscience that has helped identify differential neural substrates for these two types of learning processes. This is one more example of the many areas where new forms of data from neuroscience have informed and helped resolve long-standing questions in psychology.

Further Facets of Conditioning

Both the US modulation model of Rescorla and Wagner and the CS modulation model of Mackintosh have been influential in furthering our understanding of associative learning (Rescorla & Wagner, 1972; Mackintosh, 1975). They are powerful models precisely because they reduce the behavioral process of learning to its essential elements, so that we can see the underlying fundamental principles at work. However, as a result of such simplification, these models necessarily ignore many of the more subtle facets of conditioning, namely, the role of timing in conditioning and the importance of innate biases for associating different stimulus cues.

Timing

Both the Rescorla–Wagner and Mackintosh models treat classical conditioning as if it were always composed of a series of discrete trials that occur one after the other. Moreover, these **trial-level models** treat the entire trial as a single event, resulting in a single change in learning. In reality, conditioning is more complex, and a trial consists of many events that can vary in different ways from trial to trial. For example, these models don't describe the timing of the animal's response within a given trial: does the CR occur right after the CS begins, or is it delayed until just before the US occurs? This information is lost in a trial-level model that only describes the aggregate effect of a training trial in terms of an overall association strength. Thus, one cost of having a simple and powerful model is that it can't account for every detail of the animal's behavior.

One important aspect of many conditioning studies is the temporal relationship between the CS and the US. Figure 7.14a illustrates eyeblink conditioning using an approach known as **delay conditioning,** in which the tone CS continues ("delays") throughout the trial and only ends once the US has occurred (this is, in fact, how all of the animals were trained in the rabbit eyeblink conditioning studies reported so far in this chapter). In contrast, the **trace conditioning** procedure shown in Figure 7.14b uses a shorter CS that terminates some time before the onset of the US, requiring the animal to maintain a memory "trace" of the CS to associate with the subsequently arriving US. Although trial-level learning models treat these types of conditioning as if they were equivalent, many studies have shown that learning behaviors, and the neural substrates involved, can be quite different for trace and delay-training procedures.

Even within a simple delay-training procedure such as that shown in Figure 7.14a, variations in the **interstimulus interval (ISI),** the temporal gap between the onset of the CS and the onset of the US, can have significant effects. For eyeblink conditioning in the rabbit, the optimal ISI for fastest learning is about one-quarter of a second (250 msecs), as shown in Figure 7.14c. Shorter or longer intervals make learning more difficult for the animal and necessitate additional training trials. One of the remarkable aspects of eyeblink conditioning is that the timing of the CR corresponds exactly to the ISI (see Figure 7.6a), so that the eyelid is maximally closed at precisely the moment the onset of the US is expected, not before and not after. In the next section, you will see how the brain mechanisms for eyeblink conditioning, as well as for other motor reflexes, are similar to the brain mechanisms for many other finely timed functions, such as playing the piano or typing.

Researchers have begun to integrate both US modulation learning theories and CS modulation learning theories into unified learning theories that also accommodate some of the subtle temporal aspects of learning. One notable early example is the work of Allan Wagner, who proposed a model called SOP (Sometimes Opponent Process) that allows both for error-correction learning (US modulation) and for changes in the salience of CS cues (CS modulation), with these events occurring at different times through different processes (Wagner,

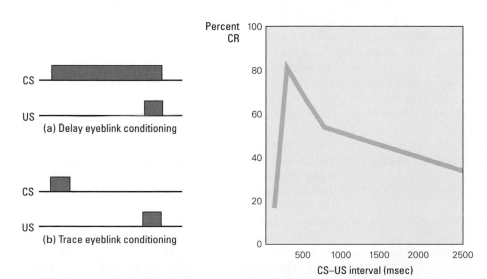

(a) Delay eyeblink conditioning

(b) Trace eyeblink conditioning

(c)

Figure 7.14 Delay and trace forms of eyeblink conditioning (a) In delay conditioning, the CS continues throughout the training trial and only terminates when the US terminates. (b) In trace conditioning, a short CS is followed by a gap before the US occurs. (c) The percentage of conditioned eyeblinks as a function of the length of the interval between the CS and the US. Adapted from McAllister, 1953.

1981). Other researchers, too, have argued that a full understanding of classical conditioning must involve closer attention to the subtle timing interactions that occur during and between trials (Gallistel & Gibbon, 2000). The need for a better understanding of the role of timing in learning is one of the challenges at the forefront of current learning research.

Associative Bias and Ecological Constraints

The formal learning models described above imply that any arbitrary cue (such as a tone or a light) can be associated with any outcome, be it a shock or food. But is that really true? Remember Garfield, who came down with the flu soon after eating oysters for dinner? The same evening that he ate the oysters, he also went out with his date to see a film starring the actor Adam Sandler. Later that night, he woke up with a terrible stomachache. Both the oysters and Adam Sandler were cues that preceded the illness. But whereas Garfield hasn't been able to eat oysters since that evening, he has not stopped going to see Adam Sandler films. What this suggests is that not all cues are equally likely to be associated with every outcome. Rather it appears that there is an associative bias whereby some cues (such as food) are more likely to be associated with some outcomes (such as illness).

This was strikingly demonstrated in a study of **conditioned taste aversion** by John Garcia and R. A. Koelling, in which rats learned to avoid specific tastes (Garcia & Koelling, 1966). Garcia and Koelling trained rats with compound stimuli consisting of an unfamiliar taste and an unfamiliar tone (a rat's version of Garfield watching an Adam Sandler movie while eating oysters). One group of rats was then injected with a poison that made them ill. A second group of rats was given an electric shock instead (see Table 7.5). Which cue would the rats in each group "blame" for their illness or shock, the taste or the tone stimulus? To see which cues were most readily associated with which outcomes, the experimenters subsequently tested the rats with each of the cues independently: on some test trials the rats were given food with the same novel taste but no tone, while on other test trials, the rats were presented with the tone but no food.

What the researchers found was that the rats in the poison group were far more likely to associate the taste stimulus with the poison than to associate the tone with the poison (much as Garfield would be more likely to blame oysters rather than Adam Sandler for his illness). In contrast, the rats in the shock group were more fearful in the presence of the tone stimulus than when they encountered the taste stimulus. Garcia and his colleagues concluded that taste is a more effective stimulus for learning to predict illness but that an audiovisual cue is more effective for learning to predict a shock. Clearly, rats, like people, have prior biases about what should predict what. Which isn't to say that you couldn't be trained to throw up at Adam Sandler movies, but it would be much harder (and require more training) than learning to avoid the taste of oysters.

Remember those quail that were trained to associate a light with sex? Although the quail were able to learn this association following many trials of training, Domjan and colleagues found that quail could be conditioned much faster and more robustly if the CS, rather than being an arbitrary cue like a light, is something that is naturally associated in the wild with available females, such as the sight of a female at a distance or the sight of a female's head when the rest of her body is hidden in the underbrush (Cusato & Domjan, 1998).

Why are both Garfield and Garcia's rats more likely to associate food, rather than other cues, with getting sick? The answer may have to do with the potential *causal* relationship between eating food and getting sick

Table 7.5

The Garcia-Koelling Taste-Aversion Study

Group	Phase 1	Phase 2
Poison group	Tone + taste → poison	Tone → ?
Shock group	Tone + taste → shock	Taste → ?

that is a very real part of the animal's natural environment. In contrast, there is unlikely to be a natural causal relationship between watching a movie (good or bad) or hearing a tone and getting sick. Perhaps a sensitivity to the likely causal relationships is what guides and biases associative learning in humans, quails, and other animals. The best predictors of future events are the causes of those events, or at least their detectable indices (Dickinson, 1980). Thus, it would make evolutionary sense for humans and other animals to be biased toward learning associations that correspond to causal relationships in the ecological niches in which the animals live and evolve.

Interim Summary

Studies of various classical conditioning paradigms show that learning involves more sophisticated processes than Pavlov and his successors initially expected. To produce effective conditioning, a CS must impart reliable and nonredundant information about the expected occurrence of the US. One explanation for this requirement is that cues compete with one another to predict the US, with the winner gaining associative strength. This principle is embodied in the Rescorla–Wagner model, which proposes that learning is driven by prediction error, the difference between the animal's expectation of the US and whether or not the US actually occurs. Thus, the Rescorla–Wagner model views classical conditioning as a process through which associations change on each training trial to minimize the likelihood that the animal is surprised in the future. The model has shown underlying order in a series of results that initially seemed unrelated or even contradictory.

The basic principle of the Rescorla–Wagner model holds true for humans doing complex category learning and prediction tasks. This suggests that some characteristics of classical conditioning are conserved across species, and that some complex human abilities can be understood as emerging from elementary processes at work in classical conditioning. While the Rescorla–Wagner model emphasizes that the processing of the reinforcing US can be modulated by surprise, models by Mackintosh and Pearce and Hall propose that other aspects of learning are determined by modulation of CS processing through attentionlike mechanisms. While these principles were originally thought to apply only to conditioning of elementary motor reflexes, more recent research shows that the associative learning principles seen in classical conditioning may also function in categorization, concept learning, and other forms of higher cognition in people.

These models of learning are powerful and have guided subsequent productive research, but they don't cover all the many facets of conditioning. For one thing, timing—both within trials and between trials—has a central role in learning, and more sophisticated models are needed to understand that role. For another, it is clear that not all associations are equally easy to form, and organisms have prior biases that determine which kinds of cues (such as food) are more likely than others to become associated with certain outcomes (such as being sick).

7.2 Brain Substrates

Pavlov was a physiologist. When he discovered associative learning in his dogs in the early 1900s, he was naturally interested in understanding the brain mechanisms responsible for it. He even conducted a few experiments examining how cortical lesions affect conditioning. However, at the beginning of the last century, the technology for observing the brain's inner workings was not highly developed. Only in recent years have scientists gained access to a wealth of knowledge and techniques that allow greatly detailed study of the neural circuits for conditioning. We review here two neural systems, one in mammals and the other in invertebrates, that illustrate how studies of the neural bases of conditioning have yielded insights into the circuits, cells, molecules, and genes that control the formation of new memories.

Mammalian Conditioning of Motor Reflexes

As you learned in Chapter 4, the **cerebellum** is located near the base of the brain (see Figure 4.10). It looks like a miniature brain itself, attached just below the rest of the brain. (The name "cerebellum" is Latin for "little brain.") In the early 1980s, Richard Thompson and his coworkers made a startling discovery: small lesions in the cerebellum of rabbits permanently prevented the acquisition of new classically conditioned eyeblink responses and abolished retention of previously learned responses (Thompson, 1986). The cerebellum has two main regions, as shown in Figure 7.15. Lying along its top surface is the *cerebellar cortex*, which contains certain large, drop-shaped, densely branching neurons called **Purkinje cells.** Beneath the cerebellar cortex lies the *cerebellar deep nuclei*, one of which is the **interpositus nucleus.**

There are two major input pathways to the cerebellum: the CS input pathway and the US input pathway. The CS input pathway is shown in dark blue in Figure 7.15. (Note that not all the cells in the cerebellum are shown here, only

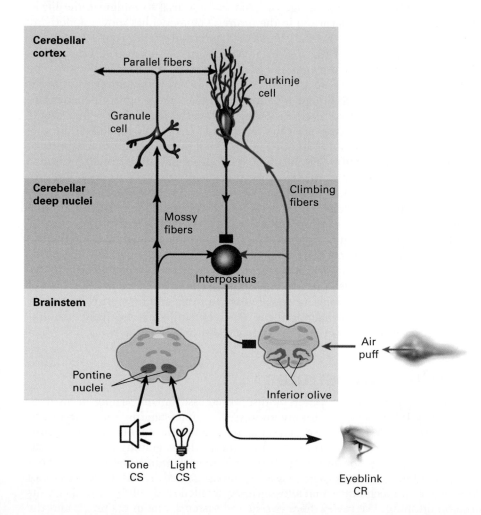

Figure 7.15 Cerebellar circuits for motor reflex conditioning in mammals A schematic diagram of the cerebellar circuits for conditioning. The CS input pathway is blue, the CR output pathway is red, and the US input pathway is green. Excitatory synapses are shown as arrows and inhibitory synapses terminate with a ■.

the cells and pathways critical for understanding the cerebellar circuits for motor-reflex conditioning.) CS pathways from elsewhere in the brain project first to an area in the brain stem called the pontine nuclei. The pontine nuclei have different subregions for each kind of sensory stimulation. Thus, a tone CS would travel to one area of the pontine nuclei, and a light CS to another. This CS information then travels up to the deep nuclei of the cerebellum along axon fibers called the mossy fibers, which branch in two directions. One branch makes contact with the interpositus nucleus in the deep nuclei region. The other branch projects up toward the cerebellar cortex (by way of the granule cells and other cells not shown), across the parallel fibers, connecting to the dendrites of the Purkinje cells.

The second sensory-input pathway, shown in green, is the US pathway. An airpuff US to the eye activates neurons in the **inferior olive** (an oval structure located in the lower part of the brain stem), which in turn activates the interpositus nucleus. In addition, a second pathway from the inferior olive projects up to the cerebellar cortex by means of the climbing fibers (see Figure 7.15). Each climbing fiber extends to and wraps around each Purkinje cell. The climbing fibers have a very strong excitatory effect on the Purkinje cells, indicated in Figure 7.15 by the large arrowhead at this synaptic junction.

Complementing these two converging input pathways is a single output pathway for the CR, shown in red, which starts from the Purkinje cells. The Purkinje cells project down from the cerebellar cortex into the deep nuclei, where they form an inhibitory synapse with the interpositus, shown as a dark square. The deep nuclei (including the interpositus) project the only output from the cerebellum. For eyeblink responses, activity in the interpositus nucleus projects (via several other intermediary cells) to the muscles in the eye to generate the eyeblink CR. You may notice that Figure 7.15 also includes an inhibitory pathway from the interpositus to the inferior olive, but we will postpone discussion of this pathway until later in the chapter. The unconditioned response (UR) pathway is not shown in Figure 7.15, because that is an innate response; it is not learned and does not originate in, or require, the cerebellum.

The most important thing to note about this circuit diagram is that there are two sites in the cerebellum where CS and US information converge and, thus, where information about the CS–US association might be stored: (1) the Purkinje cells in the cerebellar cortex and (2) the interpositus nucleus. These two sites of convergence are intimately interconnected through an output pathway: the Purkinje cells project down to the interpositus nucleus with strong inhibitory synapses, as shown in Figure 7.15.

Thompson and his colleagues have studied the cerebellum and motor-reflex conditioning for over 20 years. Their work provides an instructive example of how support for a theory can be strengthened by converging evidence from a variety of scientific methods, including electrophysiological recordings, brain stimulation, experimental lesions, temporary inactivation of brain structures, and genetically mutated animals.

Electrophysiological Recording in the Cerebellum

When an electrode is inserted into the interpositus nucleus (one of the two sites where CS and US information converge, and the final exit point of CR information from the cerebellum), the recordings of electrical activity there during conditioned eyeblink responses display a pattern that corresponds very closely to the pattern of the eyeblinks themselves, as seen in Figure 7.16a, taken from a rabbit after one day of tone CS–US training (McCormick & Thompson, 1984).

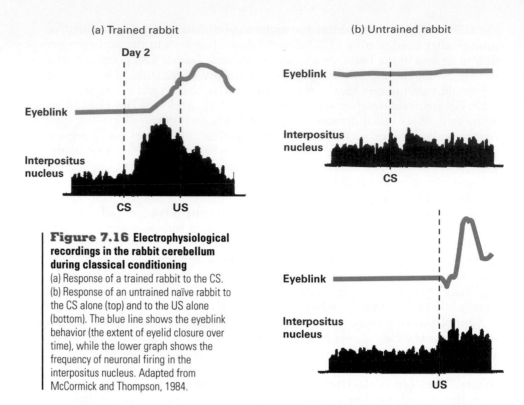

(a) Trained rabbit

Day 2

Eyeblink

Interpositus
nucleus

CS   US

(b) Untrained rabbit

Eyeblink

Interpositus
nucleus

CS

Eyeblink

Interpositus
nucleus

US

Figure 7.16 **Electrophysiological recordings in the rabbit cerebellum during classical conditioning** (a) Response of a trained rabbit to the CS. (b) Response of an untrained naïve rabbit to the CS alone (top) and to the US alone (bottom). The blue line shows the eyeblink behavior (the extent of eyelid closure over time), while the lower graph shows the frequency of neuronal firing in the interpositus nucleus. Adapted from McCormick and Thompson, 1984.

The main difference between the two patterns is that the neural activity occurs just a few milliseconds before the actual behavior. The upper blue line shows the eyeblink behavior (the extent of eyelid closure over time), while the lower graph shows the frequency of neuron firing in the interpositus nucleus, averaged over several rabbits and several trials.

Researchers can also record an unpaired-CS or a US-alone trial in a naïve rabbit. In both cases, where there is no CR, there is no activity in the interpositus nucleus, as seen in Figure 7.16b. The lack of substantial interpositus activity in the US-alone trial (despite a strong eyeblink UR), suggests that the cerebellum is only responsible for conditioned eyeblink CRs, and not for the unconditioned eyeblink URs that follow the US.

Thompson and colleagues also took recordings from a Purkinje cell in a well-trained rabbit, as seen in Figure 7.17, which shows the firing rates for a single Purkinje cell, with the time of the CS onset and the US indicated below. Purkinje cells spontaneously fire all the time, even when nothing is happening. However, in a well-trained animal, many of these cells *decrease* their firing in response to the tone CS, as shown in Figure 7.17. Why would the Purkinje cells turn off in response to a CS? Looking back at the diagram of cerebellar circuitry in Figure 7.15, note that Purkinje cells *inhibit* the interpositus nucleus, the major out-

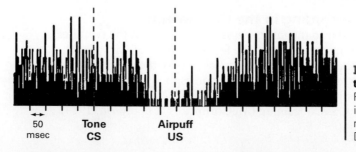

50
msec

Tone   Airpuff
CS   US

Figure 7.17 **Purkinje cell activity in a well-trained rabbit** The Purkinje cell's normal high rate of firing is shut off in response to the CS and resumes after the US has occurred. Data from R. F. Thompson.

put pathway driving the conditioned motor response. Shutting off the Purkinje cells removes inhibition from the interpositus, freeing the interpositus to fire (as shown in Figure 7.16a).

Brain Stimulation Substitutes for Behavioral Training

What if we knew exactly which pathways in your brain would change as a result of reading the words on this page? If so, we might be able to put electrodes in your brain and electrically stimulate those pathways in just the right pattern, at just the right time, to mimic the effect of reading this text. If that were possible, you wouldn't have to bother reading this book any further, or studying for the final exam. Instead you could stimulate a few neural pathways, create a little synaptic change, and then take the final exam and score an A+, even if you had never opened the textbook or sat through your professor's lectures! Science fantasy, right? Unfortunately it is, because we don't yet know exactly where or in what way complex learning like this is stored in the brain. However, for simpler forms of learning, like eyeblink conditioning, this scenario is not only possible, it's been done.

Through electrical brain stimulation of the CS and US pathways shown in Figure 7.15, an experimenter can create conditioned eyeblink responses in the rabbit that are indistinguishable from those arising from behavioral training. For example, direct stimulation of the inferior olive can be substituted for an airpuff US, as shown in Figure 7.18. Similar conditioning over 4 days of training is seen whether an airpuff US (dashed line) or a stimulation of the inferior olive (solid line) was used (Steinmetz, Lavond, & Thompson, 1989).

Recall that different parts of the pontine nuclei respond to different kinds of sensory input, such as auditory tones or visual signals, as illustrated in Figure 7.15. It is even possible to find a specific region in the pontine nuclei that responds to a *particular* tone. As a result, it is possible to condition rabbits merely by pairing electrical stimulation of the pontine nuclei (CS) with electrical stimulation of the inferior olive (US), that is, without presenting any external stimuli. After training with this type of brain stimulation, rabbits give precisely timed, reliable eyeblink responses the very first time they hear the tone corresponding to the pontine nuclear region that was stimulated, just as if they had been trained all along with tones and airpuffs (Steinmetz et al., 1989). Thus, rabbits that have had their inferior olives and pontine nuclei electrically stimulated "pass the eyeblink test" much as if they had gone through days of tone–airpuff training. Like the science fantasy alluded to earlier, stimulating the right pathways creates learning that seems indistinguishable from conditioning in a rabbit that has gone through the usual training with tones and airpuffs.

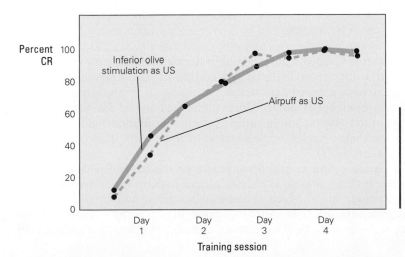

Figure 7.18 Substituting stimulation of the inferior olive for a US Similar conditioning over 4 days of training is seen whether an airpuff (dotted line) or a stimulation of the inferior olive (solid line) was used as the US. Adapted from Steinmetz et al., 1989.

Conditioning Is Impaired When the Cerebellum Is Damaged

Another experimental approach for investigating the neural bases of classical conditioning is to introduce brain lesions, that is, to selectively remove small areas of the brain. Recall that the interpositus nucleus (see Figure 7.15) projects the sole output pathway from the cerebellum that carries information about the CR. Thus, without the interpositus nucleus, you would expect that there could be no CR. This is exactly what Thompson and colleagues found: removing even 1 cubic millimeter of tissue from the interpositus nucleus completely and permanently abolishes all previously learned conditioned responses and prevents all future learning.

In contrast to lesions of the interpositus, which totally abolish learned responses, lesions of the cerebellar cortex (including the Purkinje cells) disrupt, but do not eliminate, conditioning. Animals with lesions of the cerebellar cortex show small, poorly timed conditioned responses (Perret et al., 1993). Recently, researchers have developed mutant mice with a genetic variation that causes selective degeneration of Purkinje cells. These mutant mice are slow at learning eyeblink conditioning, much like animals that have their cerebellar cortex physically removed (Chen et al., 1996). Together, these lesion and mutant studies provide strong converging evidence that the interpositus nucleus is involved in the formation and execution of the conditioned response, while the cerebellar cortex is involved in response timing.

Given the critical role of the cerebellum in motor-reflex conditioning, it is not surprising that patients with cerebellar damage display significant deficits in acquiring the eyeblink conditioning. Such patients are slower to learn the CR and show low overall frequency and abnormal timing of CRs (Daum et al., 1993). Interestingly, patients who have undergone surgery that spares the deep nuclei are able to acquire a little conditioning, while patients with more extensive cerebellar damage show no conditioning at all. It is important to note that cerebellar damage does not impair all forms of associative learning. For example, cerebellar patients perform within the normal range on learning verbal associations, such as matching names with faces, suggesting that other areas of the brain play a role in these more abstract tasks (Daum et al., 1993). There is also a clear lateralization of cerebellar involvement in eyeblink conditioning: damage to the left cerebellum interferes only with conditioning to the left eye, while damage to the right cerebellum interferes only with conditioning to the right eye; this is true in both rabbits and humans (Thompson & Krupa, 1994; Woodruff-Pak & Lemieux, 2001).

Another clinical syndrome that involves cerebellar damage (as well as many other brain abnormalities) is *autism*, a disorder that affects about 1 in every 1,000 births. Autism is characterized by severe impairments in a wide range of abilities, including impaired social and emotional skills as well as delayed language development. Although there is a high degree of variability in the brain regions affected in different individuals with autism, in many cases the cerebellar cortex appears to have reduced numbers of Purkinje cells (Ritvo et al., 1986). In addition, there are cerebellar abnormalities in the deep nuclei that vary depending on the age of the patient: young autistic patients show abnormally large cells in their deep cerebellar nuclei, while older autistic patients show reduced cell numbers (Baumann, 1991).

Given the data showing critical involvement of the cerebellar cortex in the timing of motor reflexes, how do you think autistic patients would perform in an eyeblink conditioning study? Much to everyone's surprise, autistic children actually learn to give eyeblink CRs to the CS *faster* than healthy normal children (Sears, Finn, & Steinmetz, 1994)! However, although the autistic children start generating CRs after only a few trials, their CRs are abnormally timed: the eye-blinks start too early and reach maximal closure too soon. This maladaptive timing of the conditioned response in children with autism is consistent with studies linking the cerebellar cortex to the control of timing in the conditioned response.

Genetics offers additional insights into human eyeblink conditioning. Irene Daum and colleagues have studied several groups of patients in whom chromosomal irregularities cause abnormalities and degeneration in either the cortical Purkinje cells or the deep nuclei (Daum et al., 1993). They found that patients with genetic abnormalities of the deep nuclei are severely impaired at acquiring the eyeblink CRs, while those with abnormalities in the Purkinje cells show more mixed results. These genetic studies provide additional evidence that the deep cerebellar nuclei are essential for learning the CR, while the Purkinje cells in the cerebellar cortex exert some modulating but nonessential influence on this learning.

Inhibitory Feedback Computes Error Correction

As described in Chapter 2, long-term potentiation (LTP) of a synapse occurs when simultaneous activity in two adjoining neurons leads to a strengthening of the connecting synapse. LTP is a mechanism for synaptic change that occurs whenever two adjoining neurons fire at the same time, and is thus much simpler than the error-correcting rule of the Rescorla–Wagner model, in which associative changes depend on many inputs (such as all the CSs present on a trial). Nevertheless, while the Rescorla–Wagner model of learning probably does not describe what takes place at the cellular level, error-correction mechanisms do appear to emerge from brain circuits.

If you recall the cerebellar network in Figure 7.15, there is an additional pathway within the cerebellum we have not yet discussed. This inhibitory feedback pathway projects from the interpositus nucleus to the inferior olive. In a well-trained animal, the production of a CR, with activation of the interpositus nucleus, will in turn inhibit the inferior olive from sending US information to the Purkinje cells in the cerebellar cortex (Sears & Steinmetz, 1991). This means that activity in the inferior olive will reflect the actual US minus (due to inhibition) the expected US, where the expected US is measured by the interpositus activity that drives the CR. Actual US–expected US: sound familiar? It should. This is the same difference (actual US–expected US) that the Rescorla–Wagner model uses to calculate the prediction error on a trial, which is then used to determine how much weight should accrue to the CS association.

If the inferior olive is where the brain codes the prediction error during conditioning, then we should be able to predict changes in the firing of the inferior olive based on the Rescorla–Wagner model (Gluck et al., 1990; 2001). Recall from Figure 7.6c that during CS–US acquisition training, the prediction error diminishes on each successive learning trial. Thus, we should expect to see inferior olive activity in response to the US diminish the more the US is predicted by the trained CS. Eventually, when the CR is well learned, there should be very little activity in the inferior olive (that is, when error in the Rescorla–Wagner model is close to zero). As predicted, this is exactly what Joseph Steinmetz and colleagues found: inferior olive activity starts off high early in training and then gradually diminishes as the conditioned response is acquired (Sears & Steinmetz, 1991).

This interpretation of how the cerebellar circuits compute the Rescorla–Wagner model's change in association weight implies that Kamin's blocking effect (the clearest experimental evidence for error-correction learning) should depend on the inhibitory pathway from the interpositus to the inferior olive. This prediction was confirmed in a study by Thompson and colleagues. The researchers first trained rabbits to give reliable eyeblink responses to a tone CS, and then injected a drug into the interpositus that temporarily disabled the inhibitory connection from the interpositus to the inferior olive. With this pathway disabled, they predicted, the inferior olive's activity would reflect the presence of the actual US and no longer the expected US.

The rabbits were then given phase 2 blocking training, in which a compound tone-and-light CS was paired with the US. The rabbits showed high inferior olive activity whenever the US was presented, whether or not a conditioned response was generated. As a result, in phase 3, the rabbits gave a strong response to the light CS. In other words, by disabling that one inhibitory pathway which is essential for the actual US–expected US computation, Thompson and colleagues were able to "*block* blocking" (Kim, Krupa, & Thompson, 1998). These and related results suggest that the cerebellar–inferior olive circuit plays a role in the execution of Rescorla and Wagner's error-correction rule.

The Hippocampus in CS Modulation

Error correction, as described by the Rescorla–Wagner model, is only one mechanism involved in classical conditioning. As described earlier, other mechanisms modulate the processing of CS cues, as suggested by the theories of Mackintosh and of Pearce and Hall. Here, we briefly discuss some of the brain systems that appear to govern these CS modulation mechanisms.

Recall from Chapter 3 that the hippocampus is critical for storing memories of new facts and events. The hippocampus does not, however, appear to be necessary for the acquisition of basic conditioned responses. For example, animals with hippocampal lesions and amnesic humans with broad hippocampal damage are able to learn a basic conditioned eyeblink response quite normally. Nevertheless, electrophysiological recording studies with animals show that the hippocampus is very active during conditioning, especially early in training. What role does the hippocampus play in conditioning? One way to obtain insights into the role of the hippocampus in learning is to look at more complex conditioning paradigms, such as latent inhibition (described in Table 7.4). As you learned in Section 7.1, latent inhibition is demonstrated when, prior to training, an organism is exposed to a cue unassociated with a US; later, during conditioning, the organism is then slow to learn that this CS does predict a US.

As you learned earlier, the Rescorla–Wagner model is *not* able to explain the phenomenon of latent inhibition. If the Rescorla–Wagner model's error-correction process cannot explain latent inhibition, and if the cerebellum implements the error-correction principle, then perhaps other brain regions involved in classical conditioning besides the cerebellum are responsible for latent inhibition. Might the hippocampus be such a region? If so, then looking at the animal learning theories that capture behavioral phenomena other than error-correction learning might provide us with some insight into what the hippocampus may do during classical conditioning.

The CS modulation theories of Mackintosh and of Pearce and Hall, discussed earlier in this chapter, suggest that to find the system responsible for latent inhibition and related phenomena, we should look for a system involved in determining the salience of sensory cues. If the hippocampal region, for example, is critical for CS modulation effects in classical conditioning, then an animal *without* a hippocampal region should *not* exhibit CS modulation effects such as latent inhibition. In fact, this is exactly what researchers have found: removing the hippocampal region eliminates the latent inhibition effect in classical conditioning of the rabbit eyeblink reflex (Solomon & Moore, 1975; Shohamy et al., 2000).

Riding the Brain's Waves into Memory

Several hundred yards off the coast of Malibu, a surfer waits patiently on his board. The waves swell, and he positions himself to catch a strong one. As his board rises and falls in the troughs and peaks, the surfer picks his wave, catches it at the peak, and then lets the momentum carry him across the water and all the way onto the beach. As new memories maneuver for entry into long-term storage in our brains, could it be that they, like this California surfer, must ride in on the peak of a brain memory wave?

A growing body of evidence suggests that oscillating waves of synchronized electrical activity in the hippocampus are necessary for the storage of new information. Neuroscientists believe that these waves, called theta waves, represent a "ready state" for learning. When the hippocampus is in a theta state, waves of synchronized neural firing travel back and forth across the hippocampus, about seven times a second (Buzsáki, 2002).

Early evidence for the role of theta waves in learning comes from studies done in the 1970s by Steven Berry and Richard Thompson (Berry & Thompson, 1978). By inserting recording electrodes into a rabbit's hippocampus, they were able to detect this rhythm and identify the theta state in the rabbit's hippocampus. Their study showed that rabbits exhibiting theta activity just prior to an eyeblink-conditioning experiment learned faster than rabbits that did not. In a more recent study, Berry and colleagues extended this finding by monitoring the rabbit's hippocampus throughout the experiment. The electrode was connected to a computer that generated the tone—airpuff trials, allowing each trial to be triggered by the presence of theta activity in the hippocampus (Seager et al., 2002). Rabbits exposed in this way learned much faster than a control group of rabbits whose trials were not triggered by theta

waves. They also learned faster than the rabbits not explicitly in a theta state when the tone CSs were presented.

Imagine how helpful it would be if your professor could monitor your hippocampal theta state, presenting you with new information only when a little green "ready to learn" light on your forehead turns on to indicate that you are in a receptive theta state. Perhaps you, like the theta-triggered rabbits, could learn twice as much in a day as you do now.

Exploration   Immobility

Two fundamentally different and antagonistic patterns characterize network states of the hippocampus. Rhythmic theta oscillations (7–9 Hz) are associated with exploration (left) and REM sleep, whereas irregular sharp waves are present during consummatory behaviors such as immobility (right), eating, drinking, and slow wave sleep. From Buzsáki, 1989.

Unfortunately, it is very difficult to detect the hippocampal theta rhythm noninvasively, from the scalp, because the hippocampus is buried deep inside the brain. However, electrodes are commonly inserted into the brains of patients with epilepsy as part of their treatment, to monitor the location and nature of their seizures, which usually originate in the hippocampus. Working with epileptic patients, Michael Kahana and his colleagues found direct evidence that theta activity in humans, much as in rabbits, is directly linked to learning new information (Kahana et al., 1999). When people are challenged to learn new information such as routes in a maze or lists of letters, researchers have recorded an increase in hippocampal theta activity. More recently, in a study reminiscent of the Berry and Thompson study a quarter century ago, Kahana and colleagues found that theta activity occurring during (or just after) the presentation of a word to be remembered increased the chance that participants would remember that word later on (Sederberg et al., 2003). This strengthens the evidence that theta rhythm plays a key role in the storage of new information in

both humans and other animals.

But why does the theta rhythm enhance learning? What role does it play in the mechanisms for memory storage? That is a major unsolved mystery in the neurobiology of learning and memory.

Gyorgy Buzsáki, a leading researcher in the study of the role of theta waves, argues that these waves play a crucial role in the communication between the hippocampus, where memories are first encoded and temporarily stored, and areas of cortex where memories are stored for the long term (Buzsáki, 2002). Theta waves, produced when animals are exploring and learning about their environment, represent the "input" phase of learning, during which external information is organized and stored in the hippocampus. When there is a break in this input stream, Buzsáki argues, the hippocampus shifts into a "broadcast" phase, in which irregular sharp waves of activity transmit a condensed version of the new information to cortical areas responsible for long-term storage (Buzsáki, 1989). By storing information during the breaks between periods of new exploration and input, the hippocampus readies itself to receive the next batch of new information. Buzsáki's work suggests that the hippocampus efficiently alternates between data-collection phases (theta) and data archiving (sharp waves). This theory still leaves us with the mystery of how the theta rhythms enable the hippocampus to store new information.

Despite considerable progress in unraveling the mysteries of the theta rhythm, many questions remain unanswered. For example, theta activity is known to predominate during REM sleep, as well as during active exploration and learning. If no new external sensory information arrives during sleep, why does the hippocampus exhibit theta waves? Buzsáki argues that sleep is a critical phase for learning, during which previously acquired information is consolidated into long-term memories elsewhere in the brain.

No doubt the coming years will bring many more new insights, and new theories, about how theta rhythm influences learning. But one thing is clear: To learn well, the brain's got to have rhythm!

Many other behavioral phenomena that cannot be explained by the Rescorla–Wagner model are also found to disappear in animals that have lesions to the hippocampal region. This suggests that the Rescorla–Wagner model may be better described as a model of the cerebellar contributions to motor-reflex conditioning in hippocampal-lesioned animals than as a model of conditioning in healthy, intact animals. Thus, the limitations of the Rescorla–Wagner model might now be reinterpreted as suggesting that the model isn't really dead, just "brain damaged." That is to say, the model applies best to the brain regions responsible for error-correction learning such as the cerebellum, but does not explain the additional contributions of the hippocampal region.

Invertebrates and the Cellular Basis of Learning

Chapter 6 introduced you to the sea snail *Aplysia* and studies by Eric Kandel and colleagues on the neural substrates of two forms of non-associative learning: habituation and sensitization. To briefly recap, habituation occurs when *Aplysia*'s siphon (see Figure 6.9 on p. 220) is repeatedly but lightly touched. Initially this results in a gill-withdrawal reflex, but each subsequent stimulation of the siphon elicits a progressively smaller response. The circuit for this learned response includes a sensory neuron (activated by touching the siphon) that makes an excitatory synapse with a motor neuron that controls the gill withdrawal (Figure 6.10 on p. 221). The neural mechanism for habituation is thought to be a progressive decrease in the number of neurotransmitter (in this case, glutamate) vesicles available in the sensory neuron's axon for each successive stimulation of the siphon. In contrast, sensitization is a global increase in responding to all or most stimuli following an unpleasant stimulus, such as an electric shock to *Aplysia*'s tail. The tail shock activates modulatory interneurons that release serotonin onto the axon terminals of all the sensory neurons that project to the gill-withdrawal motor neuron. Serotonin increases the number of glutamate vesicles released when the sensory neuron is stimulated. This results in the generalized (non-stimulus-specific) increase in gill withdrawal elicited by all future stimuli, including touches on either the siphon or the mantle. Table 7.6 summarizes the key differences between these two forms of non-associative learning.

Table 7.6

Varieties of Learning in *Aplysia*

Paradigm	Associative	Stimulus-specific	Mechanism(s)	Short- or long-term
Habituation	No	Yes	Decrease in glutamate	Short-term cellular process
Sensitization	No	No	Serotonin-induced increase in glutamate	Short-term cellular process
Classical conditioning	Yes	Yes	1. Presynaptic activity—dependent enhancement of glutamate release from sensory neuron	Short-term cellular process
			2. Postsynaptic change in receptors of motor neuron	
			3. A cascade of intracellular molecular events that activate genes in the neuron's nucleus, causing an increase in the number of sensory-motor synapses	Long-term structural change

(a)

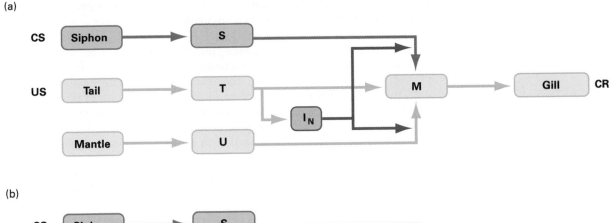

(b)

What do you think would happen if both kinds of stimuli—touching the siphon and shocking the tail—were repeatedly paired? Tom Carew, in collaboration with Kandel and other colleagues, showed that *Aplysia's* siphon-withdrawal reflex can be classically conditioned, as illustrated in Figure 7.19a. When touching the siphon (a potential CS) is repeatedly paired with shocking the tail (the US), an enhanced siphon withdrawal (CR) results in response to subsequent touches of the siphon (Carew, Hawkins, & Kandel, 1983). The enhanced siphon-withdrawal response to the siphon-touch CS following paired training is considerably greater than the generalized sensitization that occurs from presentation of the tail shock alone. Moreover, this classically conditioned siphon-withdrawal CR is also specific to the siphon and does not generalize to other stimuli, such as a touch on the mantle.

What happens inside the nervous system of *Aplysia* when these two stimuli are paired? Kandel and colleagues demonstrated that paired training produces an increase in the glutamate vesicles that are released in the siphon's synapse on the motor neuron, much like an exaggerated form of the mechanism for sensitization described in Chapter 6 (Hawkins et al., 1983). This implies that a cellular mechanism for classical conditioning can be understood as an elaboration of the same cellular mechanism used for sensitization. The pairing-specific enhancement of glutamate release in the sensory neuron synapse is called an **activity-dependent enhancement,** because it depends on prior activation of the sensory neuron.

Earlier in this chapter, we discussed how classical conditioning of the rabbit eyeblink response is sensitive to the order and timing of the tone CS and the air-puff US. The same holds true for conditioning of *Aplysia's* siphon withdrawal; conditioning occurs only if the siphon-touch CS is presented about half a second prior to the tail-shock US. If the US occurs much later (more than 2 seconds after the CS) or prior to the CS, nothing other than nonspecific

Figure 7.19 Classical conditioning in *Aplysia* (a) As with habituation and sensitization, classical conditioning in *Aplysia* results when three sensory pathways—the siphon (CS), the tail (US), and the mantle—converge on the gill-withdrawal motor neuron (the CR). The tail pathway includes a secondary pathway through an interneuron (I_N), and this releases serotonin onto the other sensory synapses when the tail is shocked. (b) Long-lasting forms of classical conditioning require the formation of new synapses between the sensory neurons of the siphon and the motor neuron. The new synapses are created through a molecular cascade set in motion by the serotonin released by the interneuron.

sensitization will occur. Thus, after sensory stimulation, whatever process occurs within the neuron that primes the neuron for an increase in glutamate release has a time course of about a half a second.

To summarize, Kandel and colleagues demonstrated that activation of *Aplysia's* sensory neuron has at least three consequences (see Table 7.6). First, it causes the motor neuron to fire, by the release of glutamate into the synapse. Second, it causes a short-term decrease in glutamate vesicles available for any subsequent stimulation of the sensory neuron, resulting in habituation. Third, it primes the synapse, through a series of intracellular events lasting about half a second, so that a subsequent presentation of serotonin (released following activation of an aversive tail shock) creates an increase in future glutamate release—resulting in a classically conditioned increase in gill withdrawal following pairing of the sensory stimulus (the CS) and the tail shock (the US).

This activity-dependent enhancement of the sensory neuron's release of glutamate onto the motor neuron is a presynaptic form of learning, because like the mechanism for sensitization discussed in Chapter 6, it involves a change in the sensory neuron. However, the story is actually more complicated. Later studies demonstrated that there is also a postsynaptic mechanism for conditioning that involves changes in neurotransmitter receptors on the motor neuron (Bao, Kandel, & Hawkins, 1998). Thus, the mechanisms for classical conditioning in *Aplysia* involve both presynaptic and postsynaptic changes in the circuits connecting the CS and the CR, as summarized in Table 7.6.

As discussed in Chapter 6, habituation and sensitization are relatively short-lived forms of learning, usually lasting only a few minutes (or a few hours at most). If, as suggested above, classical conditioning in *Aplysia* is built up from the synaptic plasticity mechanisms that mediate habituation and sensitization, shouldn't classical conditioning be similarly short-lived? In fact, behavioral studies of classical conditioning in *Aplysia*, rabbit eyeblink conditioning, and many other forms of conditioning clearly demonstrate that classically conditioned responses can be maintained for far longer—days, weeks, months, or more. This suggests that the short-term synaptic changes described above may be only one component of the neural mechanisms for classical conditioning in *Aplysia*, namely, those resulting in short-term, but not long-term, increases in responding to a CS.

One advantage of *Aplysia* as a model system for studying the intracellular molecular pathways of learning is that it is possible to identify key neurons (such as entire memory trace circuits), remove them from the animals, and keep those neurons functioning in a culture dish.

By isolating the key circuits for learning, and studying them outside the animal, Kandel and colleagues were able to explore the question: what long-term changes in *Aplysia* circuitry could account for long-lasting forms of classical conditioning? The search for the answer to this question took scientists back to the very origins of who we are—our genes—and has given rise to an important new field, the molecular genetics of memory (and also won Kandel the Nobel Prize for Physiology or Medicine in 2001). Genes are stretches of DNA molecules (deoxyribonucleic acid), found in the nucleus of every cell, that encode information needed to produce protein molecules. Most people are aware of the role that genes play in determining how our bodies and brains develop during gestation in the uterus. However, our genes don't stop working after birth; rather, they play a critical role throughout our lives, continuing to guide further growth and development of our brains, including the changes that result in long-lasting forms of memory. (Genes and the genetics of memory are discussed in Chapter 12.)

Using recent advances in molecular biology techniques, Kandel and colleagues were able to show that the serotonin released by *Aplysia's* interneurons following a tail-shock US does more than cause a short-term increase in the sensory neuron's release of glutamate; it also sets in motion a cascade of intracellular molecular events that set the stage for long-term structural changes in the neuron. Following multiple pairings of the CS and US, protein molecules in the sensory neuron's synapse travel back up the axon of the sensory neuron all the way to the cell body. There they switch on genes inside the nucleus of the neuron that in turn set in motion the growth of new synapses, as illustrated in Figure 7.19b.

Recent work by Kandel and others has identified two proteins, found inside neurons, that play critical regulatory roles in this synapse-creation process. The first protein, CREB-1, activates genes in the neuron's nucleus that initiate the growth of new synapses. The second protein, CREB-2, plays an opponent role, inhibiting the actions of CREB-1. The creation of new synapses during learning requires a cascade of processes inside the cell that activate CREB-1 and suppress CREB-2.

What do you think would happen if functioning of the CREB-1 protein was impaired? Kandel and colleagues demonstrated that if CREB-1 is rendered inactive by injecting molecules into the neuron that compete with CREB's ability to activate genes for new synapses, the circuits are rendered unable to show long-lasting forms of associative learning (Dash, Hochner, & Kandel, 1990). Most important, the inactivation of CREB-1 did not affect the short-lasting forms of learning that depend only on increased glutamate release. This study provided critical evidence for a dissociation between short-lasting forms of learning, which do not require the CREB-1 protein, and long-lasting forms, which do.

In a related study, Kandel and colleagues showed that removing the influence of the opponent protein, CREB-2, had the opposite effect: with the CREB-2 inactivated, long-lasting learning occurs rapidly at the sensory neurons, after even a single exposure to serotonin (Bartsch et al., 1995). The role of CREB molecules in modulating long-lasting forms of memory is not limited to *Aplysia*; increasing CREB-1 in fruit flies (*Drosophila*) allows them to learn much more rapidly than usual, while increasing their CREB-2 blocks the formation of long-term memories, such as those produced in the odor-conditioning task described earlier in this chapter (Yin et al., 1994). The CREB molecules also play a critical role in mammals' learning; studies in transgenic mice have shown that activity of CREB-1 in the hippocampus is critical to long-lasting, but not short-term, increases in neuron-to-neuron associations based on LTP (Bourtchuladze et al., 1994).

Studies of classical conditioning in *Aplysia* have demonstrated that anatomical changes in neural circuits, including the growth or deletion of synapses, are characteristic of long-lasting forms of memory. Short-term, labile forms of memory are, in contrast, limited to intracellular changes within existing anatomical pathways, including shifts in the location, size, or number of neurotransmitter vesicles, which alter synaptic transmission efficacy. Thus, the transition from short-term to long-term learning may be characterized as a shift from transmission-process-based changes within the neuron to structural changes within the neural circuits (Table 7.6).

Interim Summary

A variety of research techniques, including brain recording, brain stimulation, permanent and reversible inactivation of brain structures, and the study of genetically mutated animals, indicate that the essential memory trace for motor reflex conditioning in mammals lies in the cerebellum. There are two sites in the cerebellum where CS and US information converge and which are believed to be the locations for the stored memory of the CS–US association: (1) the Purkinje cells in the cerebellar cortex and (2) the interpositus deep nucleus. The interpositus nucleus is the only output pathway from the cerebellum and thus is the pathway for a conditioned response, such as an eyeblink CR.

While the Rescorla–Wagner model of learning probably does not represent the events taking place during conditioning at the cellular level, error-correction mechanisms do exist in brain circuits in the cerebellum. A feedback pathway that projects from the interpositus nucleus to inhibit the inferior olive suggests that the inferior olive could be computing the degree to which the airpuff US is surprising; thus, the inferior olive could be providing the information necessary to implement Rescorla and Wagner's principle of error-correction learning in the cerebellum. In general, the cerebellum appears to act as a predictive device for making anticipatory adjustments in timing-sensitive responses across a wide range of motor control behaviors.

Studies of the invertebrate sea snail *Aplysia* have provided us with a deeper appreciation for how non-associative and associative forms of learning may share common cellular processes. Moreover, they have shown that the transition from short-term to long-term learning may be characterized as a shift from transmission-process-based changes within the neuron to structural changes within the neural circuits. The latter are mediated by genes inside the nucleus of the neuron that control the growth of new synapses.

7.3 Clinical Perspectives

In this final section of the chapter we focus on several ways in which drug addiction and drug abuse are intimately linked to classical conditioning. The role of learning and memory in drug addiction is a fascinating topic that we consider from several viewpoints in this textbook. In Chapter 5 we discussed the role of the frontal lobes as the brain's executive controller, their importance in inhibiting inappropriate behaviors, and how this role is compromised in drug addicts. In Chapter 8, we will explore the neural mechanisms of reward that are impaired by most drugs of abuse. In the following discussion of clinical perspectives on classical conditioning, we will discuss how the behavioral and biological mechanisms of classical conditioning influence various aspects of drug addiction and abuse.

Imagine you are a detective called to the home of Colonel Mustard, who has been found face down in his living room beside a large picture window. According to the medical examiner, the Colonel has died from an overdose of morphine. Was it murder? Suicide? Or an accident? His daughter, Scarlet, tells you that she has been caring for her ailing father at home for the last month. As instructed by his doctor, she gave the Colonel four injections of morphine a day to relieve his pain. She swears that she gave him only his regular dose today, an amount he had tolerated well for the last month. You question Scarlet further and learn that her father stayed mostly in his dimly lit bedroom, which is where she administered each of his daily morphine doses. Today, however, the Colonel was feeling a little stronger and asked to be moved to the living room to enjoy the sunshine. It was there that she gave him his usual afternoon dose of morphine. Minutes later, Colonel Mustard's pupils began to constrict and his breath became shallow, common symptoms of opiate overdose; a few hours later he was dead. Did Scarlet murder her father, as the officer suspects, with an intentional overdose?

"Elementary," you proclaim, "Scarlet is innocent! The explanation should be apparent to anyone who understands the basic principles of classical conditioning." Recall the discussion, earlier in this chapter, of Subkov and Zilov's finding that dogs exhibited a conditioned compensatory response to environmental cues that predicted the injection of adrenaline. This response lowered the dogs' heart rate in anticipation of the drug's effect. Thus, the net effect of the anticipated adrenaline was less than when the adrenaline had initially (and unexpectedly) been administered to the dogs. Why did the same amount of morphine that Colonel Mustard tolerated yesterday kill him today? As an astute detective (and student of learning and memory), you immediately noticed the most important clue: the Colonel had changed the setting in which he took his regular dose. For the last month, he had been receiving his morphine in a dark bedroom, probably filled with medical paraphernalia. For Colonel Mustard, these environmental cues likely became conditioned predictors of the morphine's analgesic effects, causing a compensatory conditioned response in him to the drug's actual effect, much like occurred in Subkov and Zilov's dogs. When the Colonel moved into the brightly lit living room where no medical implements were to be seen, he changed context and lost the compensatory response that had been conditioned to the cues in his bedroom. Without this compensatory response, the net effect of his usual dose was far greater than he was used to and resulted in his death (for reports of similar real-life cases, see Siegel, 2001; Siegel & Ellsworth, 1986).

Colonel Mustard's experience is unfortunately not uncommon and applies to a wide range of drugs, including those that are frequently abused. In fact, victims of heroin overdose are rarely novice users (Siegel, 2001). Rather, they tend to be long-time heroin addicts who have developed a high degree of tolerance to the drug but make the mistake of taking their usual dose in an unusual setting. For example, you may recall reports of rock stars and others dying of heroin overdoses in hotel bathrooms, which perhaps were far different from the settings in which they were used to taking the drug. The situational cues that result in conditioned drug tolerance can be any sensory cues associated with drug use, including the feel of the needle and the method of injection. One long-time heroin addict is reported to have died of an overdose when, looking for an accessible blood vein, he injected himself in his penis for the first time (Winek, Wahaba, & Rozin, 1999).

An unusual taste to a drink can serve as a novel situational cue influencing the effects of alcohol on the brain. This was confirmed in a study that demonstrated that college students show greater cognitive and motor impairments when they consume a given amount of alcohol in an unusual drink (in this case, a blue, peppermint-flavored beverage) than when they have alcohol in a familiar drink, such as beer (Remington et al., 1977). Perhaps this is yet another reason why people get wilder at holiday parties when they are drinking alcohol in sweet and bubbly holiday punches.

Research has demonstrated conditioned tolerance in a wide variety of animal species. For example, Shepard Siegel and colleagues examined the effect of cues when heroin is administered to rats (Siegel et al., 1982). Siegel gave three groups of rats a fairly large (for their body weight) dose of heroin. The first group of rats had previously received a lower dose of heroin, administered in the same cage and room where they were later tested with the larger dose (the "same-tested" group in Figure 7.20). The second group of rats had

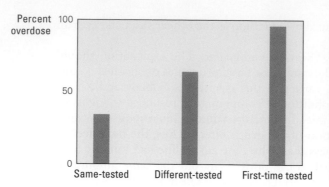

Figure 7.20 A study of drug tolerance Rats in the "first-time tested" group who received no prior heroin showed the highest percent of fatal overdose. Of those rats who had received a smaller prior dose, the ones tested in the same cage as previously ("same-tested") showed the lowest level of overdoses, while the ones tested in a different cage ("different-tested") showed an intermediate level of over-dosing. From Siegel et al., 1982.

also previously received the lower dose of heroin, but in a different cage and room (the "different-tested" group). Finally, the "first-time tested" group of rats received heroin for the first time in the test session.

As shown in Figure 7.20, Siegel and colleagues found that the large dose of heroin almost always (96% of the time) resulted in a fatal overdose in the "first-time tested" rats. In contrast, the "different-tested" group showed some evidence of tolerance; only 64% of these rats suffered a fatal overdose. But the "same-tested" rats, who were tested in the same environment in which they had previously been administered low doses of heroin, had a mortality rate of only 32%. Thus, these rats were protected from overdose by the conditioned tolerance that they learned during the administration of lower doses of heroin in the same setting.

If drug tolerance is a form of classical conditioning, you might expect that the same rules and principles would apply to it as to eyeblink and other forms of conditioning. This appears to be the case. Recall the paradigm of latent inhibition discussed earlier and shown in Table 7.4: pre-exposure to a CS delays subsequent learning of a CS–US association. If this latent inhibition effect applies to drug tolerance, then pre-exposing an animal to the cues that predict drug delivery should slow down development of learned tolerance to the drug. To test latent inhibition in the context of drug use, researchers have given animals an injection of an inert placebo to pre-expose them to the contextual cues (the sound and feel of getting an injection) of drug use. This pre-exposure does prove to slow down, by latent inhibition, the development of a cue–drug association where the cue is the CS and the drug is the US. In fact, this is exactly what Siegel and colleagues found in studies of morphine tolerance in rats (Siegel, 1983).

Such results provide compelling evidence for the applicability of Pavlovian analyses to learned drug tolerance. They suggest that drug tolerance and the loss of drug tolerance in novel drug-taking environments are mediated by basic processes of classical Pavlovian conditioning. Eventually, these and other studies, by deepening scientists' understanding of the role of classical conditioning in drug addiction, may provide new tools to help drug addicts kick their addiction. For example, perhaps further research on the extinction of conditioned responses will shed light on why addicts so often relapse when they are trying to kick their drug habit. You can read more about this mechanism right now, in "Learning and Memory in Everyday Life: Kicking the Habit."

▶ **Learning and Memory in Everyday Life**

Kicking the Habit

Kristin had been clean for 5 years, having kicked her alcohol and drug addictions through the combined support of her family, a rehabilitation ("rehab") clinic, and regular attendance at Narcotics Anonymous (NA) meetings. Then came an invitation to a twenty-first birthday party for Lucy, a former high school friend. Over at Lucy's house for the first time in years, Kristin found herself among the old crowd of friends with whom she used to get high. It didn't surprise her when one of the guests began passing around a joint. Soon someone took out a small mirror and a sharp penknife and began cutting lines of coke. Kristin was taken aback by the overwhelming urge she felt to take "just one smoke" and "just a little snort" after having abstained from both for 5 years. Sadly, that "one" smoke and "little" snort of cocaine fueled her craving for even more, and within a few hours Kristin was totally high, 5 years of abstinence and recovery a distant memory.

What happened to Kristin? Why did she relapse? The environmental cues that accompanied previous drug use can classically condition current and former users to expect to receive the drug. In other words, the environmental cues (people, places, and so on) act like CSs associated with the drug (the US). The intense craving an addict feels in response to these cues is the CR, which results from the body's conditioned compensatory response of lowering the levels of the brain chemicals enhanced by the drug in anticipation of the drug's arrival (we return to this phenomenon in Chapter 8). Like a rabbit that blinks to the same tone it was classically conditioned to years ago, Kristin responds to the cues that she was long ago conditioned to associate with drug use: the friends with whom she used to get high, the room where she used drugs, and the sight of the various kinds of paraphernalia connected with drug use. Like a rabbit to a tone, Kristin "blinked"—she responded to these drug-use CSs with an intense craving for drugs. Is it any wonder that recovery organizations like Narcotics Anonymous and Alcoholics Anonymous emphasize cutting all ties with companions and locations formerly associated with drug use?

Why did taking just one hit of cocaine enhance rather than satisfy Kristin's cravings for drugs? One view is that the sensory experiences associated with the drugs—their taste, smell, and initial effect on the body—also serve as conditionable cues. This hypothesis makes sense if you consider that the most reliable predictor of the future arrival of drugs is their initial presence in the body. Those first smokes and hits of cocaine set a vicious cycle in motion, leading to a stronger expectation of drugs and, therefore, an even stronger craving. The ability of a first dose to produce an enhanced craving is common to most, if not all, drugs. Alcoholics Anonymous recognized this in 1939 with its warning to alcoholics: "We are without defense against the first drink."

If we think of drug craving as a conditioned response, then we know from Section 7.1, "Behavioral Processes," that an extinction paradigm will eliminate (or at least reduce) the association between conditioned cues and conditioned response when the cues are repeatedly presented alone, and not paired with the prior US. In carefully controlled laboratory studies, rats who became addicted to alcohol showed significant recovery (and less relapse) through repeated nonreinforced exposure to experimentally manipulated cues that had previously been paired with administration of alcohol (Krank & Wall, 1990). In real life, however, it is very hard to both identify and extinguish all the cues that have become associated with drug use.

Even in a well-controlled laboratory, extinguishing a cue and keeping it extinguished turn out to be extremely difficult. Mark Bouton and colleagues, studying the extinction of conditioned responses in rats, demonstrated that manipulations such as changing the context, or just waiting a period of time, often result in the extinguished cues reacquiring their conditioned associative properties (Bouton, 2000). Is it any surprise, then, that efforts to adapt extinction methods to therapy for drug addiction have yielded only mixed results at best (Carroll, 1999; Siegel & Ramos, 2002)? The fact that the addict remains susceptible to the first drink or smoke suggests that to extinguish the drug associations we would have to include small doses of the drugs during cue-exposure therapy to better reproduce and extinguish the cravings. Clearly, such a procedure would have many practical and legal difficulties. Nevertheless, Bouton's work suggests four principles that can help guide anyone trying to extinguish a habit or association. They are:

1. Since extinction effects are highly context-sensitive, cue-exposure therapy should be conducted in as many different contexts as possible, including those that are part of the patient's everyday life. This will prevent the extinction of drug craving from becoming dependent on any one context (such as a drug rehab center).

2. The extinction training should be spread out over time rather than conducted all at once, because time serves as a powerful context. A 2-week stint in a rehab clinic may not be enough to make a long-term difference. Multiple therapy sessions at different times and in different contexts are more effective.

3. Whenever possible, the cue-exposure therapy should take place in the same contexts in which the original drug habits were acquired. Thus, it is better to go through the cue-exposure therapy at home rather than in a very unfamiliar setting, such as a drug rehabilitation center.

4. Since drug use itself is part of the context for further drug taking, extinction therapy can be more effective if it includes small amounts of drug use during cue exposure.

CONCLUSION

Classical conditioning is far more than just another behavioral process or tool for investigating brain systems: it is the mother of all memory systems. Evidence of classical "Pavlovian" conditioning surrounds us every day. Like the little girl who runs to the curb when she hears the music of an ice cream truck; like Nathalie, who feels compelled to light up a cigarette after sex; and like Garfield, who has sworn off oysters, everyone has been conditioned by cues in the environment to predict what might follow next.

In recent years, classical conditioning experiments have moved to the forefront of research into the physiological bases of learning because of the exquisite control they afford over what stimuli are presented as cues, and because of the highly refined behavioral analyses and models that have been developed as a result. Building on these analyses and models, biological research has shown how different forms of classical conditioning are mediated by different brain systems, leading to fundamental insights into the neurobiology of learning, and often providing us with tools that help us understand various clinical brain disorders.

Psychological studies of conditioning have resulted in elegant mathematical theories of learning, especially the error-correcting model of Rescorla and Wagner, which continue to influence and guide research into the neural bases of conditioning in a broad range of brain systems other than the cerebellum, including studies of the amygdala and fear conditioning (to be discussed in Chapter 10) and the role of dopamine in reward prediction (see Chapter 8). Links between conditioning and complex forms of cognition, such as category learning, help us see how mechanisms for learning studied in simple animal circuits can provide insights into the behavioral and neural bases of human cognition. In this way, the study of the neural bases of learning and memory illustrates the general biological principle that evolution does not work like an engineer, creating new specialized systems for each new function. Rather, evolution works more like a tinkerer, using preexisting components, in slightly modified form, to perform new functions. The behavioral and biological processes for classical conditioning are the basic building blocks, the biological alphabet, from which more complex forms of learning emerge in all species, including humans.

Key Points

- Classical conditioning involves learning about the predictive nature of stimuli in the environment, that is, what cues predict what desirable or undesirable events. If an unconditioned stimulus, US, is repeatedly and reliably preceded by a neutral stimulus, such as a bell, that neutral stimulus can become a conditioned stimulus, or CS, that evokes an anticipatory response, called the conditioned response, or CR. Conditioned responses are anticipatory responses that prepare an animal for the expected US.

- Eyeblink conditioning appears similar across species, and thus results found in one species can reasonably be expected to apply to others.

- Compensatory conditioned responses occur in body systems that are programmed for homeostasis, the tendency of various body functions (such as heart rate) to remain at a relatively constant level.

- The pairing of a potential CS with a US is not sufficient for conditioning to occur. Rather, for a CS to become associated with a US, it must provide valuable new information that helps an animal predict the future. Even if a given cue is predictive of a US, it may not become associated with that US if its usefulness has been preempted ("blocked") by a co-occurring cue that has a longer history of predicting the US.

- Rescorla and Wagner (1972) argue that learning should occur in proportion to the degree to which the US is unexpected the first time it is experienced. A key assumption in the Rescorla–Wagner model is that when there are multiple CS cues present, the expectation (or prediction) of the US is calculated as the sum of the weights of all of the cues present on that trial.

- Within its domain, the Rescorla–Wagner model combines explanatory power with mathematical simplicity. It takes an intuitively reasonable idea—namely, that classical conditioning is driven by a prediction error—pares away all but the most essential details, and explores nonobvious implications of this idea. The Rescorla–Wagner model is also a starting point from which many subsequent models have been built.

- Extinction is more than simply the loss of a learned association; rather, extinction also involves the learning of an opposing "don't respond" command that competes with, and masks, the original acquired CS–US association.

- In many ways, human learning is analogous to the more elementary learning processes studied in animal conditioning experiments. Some complex human abilities (including speech recognition, motor control, and category learning) can be understood as emerging from associative learning processes similar to those studied in conditioning paradigms.

- CS modulation theories of learning presume that a limited attentional capacity requires that attention to one stimulus decreases our ability to attend to other stimuli. In contrast, the Rescorla–Wagner model is a US modulation theory of learning, because associations are learned depending on how accurately the US is predicted based on all available information. Current behavioral and biological studies of conditioning now suggest that there are likely to be both CS modulation and US modulation mechanisms involved in learning.

- Trial-level models treat the entire conditioning trial as a single event resulting in a single change in learning. But in reality, conditioning is more complex, and a trial consists of many events, some of which are sensitive to the timing of the CS and US.

- Taste is more effective than an audiovisual stimulus for learning to predict illness, while an audiovisual cue is more effective for learning to predict a shock. One interpretation of this difference is the potential *causal* relationship between eating food and getting sick that is part of the animal's natural ecological environment.

- There are two sites in the cerebellum where CS and US information converge and which might potentially be locations for the storage of the CS–US association: (1) the Purkinje cells in the cerebellar cortex and (2) the interpositus nucleus. The interpositus nucleus is the only output pathway from the cerebellum; it is the route through which the learned response travels to the motor systems that control behavior, such as an eyeblink CR.

- Overall, it appears that the interpositus nucleus is involved in the formation and execution of the conditioned response, while the cerebellar cortex is involved in mediating response timing.

- The inferior olive may be computing the degree to which, say, the airpuff US is unexpected, providing the information necessary to implement Rescorla and Wagner's principle of error-correction learning in the cerebellum.

- The hippocampus is a structure underlying some of the CS modulation effects in conditioning. This is consistent with data showing that an animal *without* a hippocampus does *not* exhibit CS modulation effects such as latent inhibition. The amygdala plays a role in highly aversive and fear-inducing forms of conditioning.

- Kandel and colleagues demonstrated that activation of *Aplysia*'s sensory neuron primes the synapse, through a series of intracellular events lasting about half a second, so that a subsequent presentation of serotonin (released following activation of an aversive tail shock) creates an increase in future glutamate release, resulting in a classically conditioned increase

in gill-withdrawal following pairing of the sensory stimulus (the CS) and the tail shock (the US).

- After multiple pairings of the CS and US in *Aplysia*, protein molecules in the sensory neuron's synapse travel back up the axon of the sensory neuron all the way to the cell body. There they activate genes inside the nucleus of the neuron that in turn set in motion the growth of new synapses.

- Conditioning explains the development of drug tolerance and can lead to unexpected and sometimes fatal overdoses.

Key Terms

activity-dependent enhancement, p. 281
appetitive conditioning, p. 245
aversive conditioning, p. 245
blocking, p. 253
cerebellum, p. 272
classical Pavlovian conditioning, p. 244
conditioned response (CR), p. 244
conditioned stimulus (CS), p. 244
conditioned taste aversion, p. 270
context, p. 263
CS modulation theory, p. 267
delay conditioning, p. 269
error-correction rule, p. 257
extinction, p. 250
eyeblink conditioning, p. 247
homeostasis, p. 252
inferior olive, p. 273
interpositus nucleus, p. 272
interstimulus interval (ISI), p. 269
latent inhibition, p. 266
prediction error, p. 254
Purkinje cells, p. 272
tolerance, p. 252
trace conditioning, p. 269
trial-level model, p. 268
unconditioned response (UR), p. 244
unconditioned stimulus (US), p. 244
US modulation theory, p. 267

Concept Check

1. Following acquisition training with a tone predicting an airpuff, the Rescorla–Wagner model predicts that V_{Tone} will equal 100. What would happen, according to the model, if we then began extinction training, presenting the tone CS without administering an airpuff US? Assuming a learning rate of .20, compute the values of V_{Tone}, expected US, actual US, prediction error, and the change in V_{Tone} for the first five trials of extinction training.

2. Returning to our stock analysts Doris and Herman, consider what would happen if Doris showed up every day to work, but Herman only came in every now and then. On the days that Doris works alone, she does a great job of predicting the stock market. But on the days that Herman shows up, the pair of them do a lousy job. What would you think about Herman? You'd probably conclude that he is no great asset. In fact, worse than being a do-nothing, he seems to interfere with Doris's ability to perform. You might even say that Herman *inhibits* Doris's predictive value. The same situation occurs

in conditioning paradigms where a tone cue is always followed by the US, except when the tone appears as part of a compound tone-and-light stimulus. On these compound trials, no US occurs. What does the Rescorla–Wagner model predict will happen to the associations during this training?

3. The true test of a new theory is how well it predicts previously unobserved phenomena, especially when those phenomena are not obvious or are counterintuitive. A striking example of this kind of success occurred when Rescorla sought in the following way to test the limits of what the Rescorla–Wagner model could predict: in phase 1, he trained the animals with a tone followed by a US on half of the trials and a light followed by a US on the other half (Rescorla, 1976). Then in phase 2, he presented these two cues simultaneously, as a tone and light compound, and followed this compound cue with a US. Later, Rescorla tested the animals. What did the Rescorla–Wagner model predict for this study?

Answers to Test Your Knowledge

Reinforcement and Punishment

1. US: model; UR: sexual arousal (in middle-aged men who are the targeted customers); CS: the car; CR: arousal of pleasurable feelings at the thought and sight of the sports car.

2. US: hot pizza for dinner; UR: anticipation of dinner and salivation; CS: smell of cardboard burning; CR: hunger pangs and salivation.

3. US: children's nap time; UR: getting sleepy; CS: vacuum cleaner sound; CR: getting sleepy.

Further Reading

Gormezano, I., Kehoe, E. J., & Marshall, B.S. (1983). Twenty years of classical conditioning research with the rabbit. *Progress in Psychobiology and Physiological Psychology, 10*,197–275. • A comprehensive overview of the behavioral paradigm of eyeblink conditioning.

Kandel, E. (2006). *In search of memory.* New York: W. W. Norton. Kandel's life story, from his experience as a Jewish refugee fleeing Nazi Vienna in the late 1930s to his winning the Nobel Prize for Physiology or Medicine in 2000. It provides a very accessible overview of his research and research career.

Pearce, J. M., & Bouton, M. E. (2001). Theories of associative learning in animals. *Annual Review of Psychology, 52,* 111–139. • A review of all the major theories of associative learning including those of Rescorla and Wagner, Mackintosh, and Pearce and Hall, placing them in a modern context.

Thompson, R. F., & Krupa. D. J. (1994). Organization of memory traces in the mammalian brain. *Annual Review of Neuroscience, 17,* 519–549. • A comprehensive summary of the efforts by R. F. Thompson and colleagues to identify the cerebellar pathways for motor-reflex conditioning.

CHAPTER 8

Instrumental Conditioning

Learning the Consequences of Behavior

YOU PROBABLY DON'T REMEMBER being toilet trained, although you reap the benefits of this training every day. Most children are toilet trained during the toddler years. A few lucky children seem to grasp the idea almost intuitively; others are prone to wetting accidents during the early school years. But, for most children, the process occurs gradually, over a few days or weeks, as bladder control is mastered.

Consider toddler Annie. Her parents wait until after she has had a drink, when her bladder is full, and then put her on a toddler-sized potty seat and wait for nature to run its course. When Annie urinates in the potty, her parents provide verbal praise ("What a good girl you are, Annie!") or even a small toy. Gradually, the toddler learns that urination into the potty will result in reward, and she begins to run to the potty whenever she has the urge to urinate. At the same time, when she has a wetting accident, she is punished by verbal disapproval ("Mommy is very disappointed in you, Annie"). Gradually, Annie learns enough bladder control to recognize when urination is imminent, and to withhold the response long enough for a quick trip to the potty seat—thus obtaining the reward and avoiding punishment. Eventually, the behavior becomes automatic enough that Annie continues to use the potty seat, and then the toilet, even though she no longer receives an explicit reward for doing so.

This kind of learning is a classic example of **instrumental conditioning:** the process whereby organisms learn to make responses in order to obtain or avoid certain consequences. Instrumental conditioning is a form of associative learning, just like classical conditioning, which you read about in Chapter 7. But in classical conditioning, the consequence (the unconditioned stimulus, or US) arrives automatically, whether the organism makes a response or not. In instrumental conditioning, the consequence is a direct result of behavior. The learning is called "instrumental" because the organism's behavior is instrumental in producing the consequence.

Instrumental conditioning is a deceptively simple-sounding process, but it can be used to train fantastically complex behaviors, including waterskiing in squirrels and tap dancing in chickens, and—on a more serious note—to train sniffer dogs that monitor airports for drug smuggling or search rubble for survivors in a collapsed building. If you've ever been to the circus and seen bears dancing on their hind legs, elephants balancing on tiny stools, or a lion letting a trainer stick her head in its mouth, you've seen instrumental conditioning in action. In the days before computer animation, most television ads that featured animals singing, dancing, or otherwise pitching a product also depended on instrumental conditioning. A famous animal act from the 1950s, "Priscilla the Fastidious Pig," featured a pig who had learned a routine that involved turning on the radio, eating breakfast at a table, picking up dirty clothes and putting them in a hamper, running the vacuum cleaner, and—of course—picking out her favorite brand of pig chow (Breland & Breland, 1951). By the end of this chapter, you should have a pretty good idea of how to train your own pig to do the same.

8.1 Behavioral Processes

Humans have been using the principles of instrumental conditioning as long as there have been sheep to herd, horses to ride, and toddlers to toilet-train. But it wasn't until the end of the nineteenth century (about the same time that Ivan Pavlov was "discovering" classical conditioning) that Edward Thorndike first tried to systematically explore how animals learn new behaviors.

The "Discovery" of Instrumental Conditioning

In Chapter 1, you read about Edward Thorndike and his studies of how cats learned to escape from puzzle boxes, like the one shown in Figure 8.1a. The puzzle boxes were made from fruit crates, each with a door that could be opened on the inside through the correct sequence of pressing levers, pulling ropes, and stepping on pedals (Thorndike, 1898, 1911, 1932). The first time Thorndike put

Figure 8.1 Thorndike's studies of animal learning (a) A puzzle box. Thorndike studied how cats learned to escape from the box. (b) Data from one cat shows how it learned to escape efficiently after a few experiences. Data from Thorndike, 1911.

Yale University Library

(a)

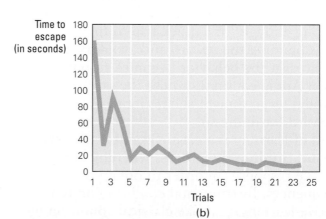

Time to escape (in seconds)

Trials

(b)

a cat in such a puzzle, the infuriated animal would hiss, claw at the walls, and generally try to fight its way free. Eventually, through some random sequence of responses, the cat happened to perform the movements needed to open the door. Thorndike recorded how long it took the animal to escape, then returned the cat to the box to try again. Cats are not stupid; after a few experiences in the box, the cat learned to escape efficiently. Figure 8.1b shows the data from one cat; after a dozen or so trials in the box, the cat was able to get out almost immediately.

Thorndike concluded that when an animal's response was followed by a satisfying consequence (such as escaping from a puzzle box or obtaining food), then the probability of that response increased. Alternatively, if a response was followed by an unsatisfying consequence (such as an electric shock), then the probability of that response occurring again decreased. Thorndike formalized this idea in his law of effect. As you read in Chapter 1, the law of effect states that the probability of a response (R) to a stimulus (S) is a function of the consequence (C) that has followed R in the past. In the case of a puzzle box, S is the box, R is the sequence of movements needed to open the door, and C is escape and food.

Stimulus S → Response R → Consequence C

Classical versus Instrumental Conditioning

A few years later, B. F. Skinner read Pavlov's work on classical conditioning and Thorndike's work on instrumental conditioning. Skinner concluded that these two types of learning were fundamentally different (Skinner, 1938). In classical conditioning, animals receive a consequence whether or not they have learned the conditioned response. In instrumental conditioning, by contrast, the consequence occurs only if the animal performs the response.

For example, in classical conditioning of the eyeblink response, a rabbit may hear a tone (conditioned stimulus, CS) that is reliably followed by an airpuff (US), and the rabbit may learn to make an eyeblink response (conditioned response, CR) to the tone. However, the airpuff follows the tone whether or not the response occurs—so this paradigm is classical conditioning. By contrast, in Thorndike's puzzle box experiments, a cat is placed in a crate (S) and must learn to make a series of responses (R) in order to escape and obtain food (C). If the responses are not made, the consequence doesn't happen. Therefore, this paradigm is instrumental conditioning. Whenever you have to determine whether a paradigm is instrumental or classical, focus on the consequence. If it occurs regardless of responding, then the paradigm is classical; if it is contingent on a response, then the paradigm is instrumental.

Differences aside, instrumental and classical conditioning share many characteristics, including a negatively accelerated learning curve (compare Figure 8.1b with Figure 7.7) and a tendency for learned responses to extinguish if no longer paired with a consequence. Researchers who want to investigate a particular learning phenomenon, such as extinction or latent inhibition, are generally free to use either classical or instrumental conditioning, depending on which is more convenient for them and what specific hypothesis they are testing.

Free-Operant Learning

In Chapter 1, you read about B. F. Skinner, the "radical behaviorist." Skinner was attracted to Thorndike's work, with its promise of animal responses that could be measured and evaluated without requiring speculation about the animal's mental states. But Skinner thought he could refine Thorndike's techniques. Thorndike's procedures involved **discrete trials,** meaning that the experimenter defined the beginning and end of each trial. For example, on one trial with the puzzle box, the experimenter would pick up the cat, put it in the box, shut the door, record how long it took the cat to escape, then pick up the cat and start over for the next trial. Similarly, when testing rats in a maze, the experimenter would put the rat at the start of the maze, record how long it took the rat to reach the goal, then pick up the rat and return it to the start for the next trial. Each trial is separate or discrete, and the experimenter decides when and how often to begin a new trial.

Skinner developed a different paradigm, in which the animal could be left in the apparatus and could respond as often (or as seldom) as it chose. He devised a cage—now commonly called a **Skinner box**—with a trough in one wall through which food could be delivered automatically (Figure 8.2a). The box also con-

(a)

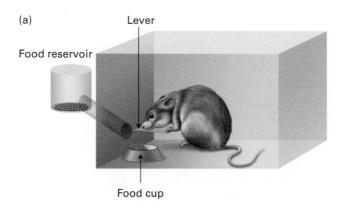

Figure 8.2 Operant conditioning (a) A Skinner box. A rat can press a lever to obtain food in the cup. (b) Hypothetical data illustrating learning by a rat in a Skinner box, shown as the mean response rate during a 26 minute experiment. During the first 13 minutes (acquisition phase), lever presses are reinforced by food delivery, so the rate of responding increases. During the last 13 minutes (extinction), lever presses are no longer reinforced by food delivery, so the rate of responding decreases. (c) A cumulative recorder. (d) Cumulative record version of the data in (b). The steep upward slope in the first half of the experiment reflects the increased rate of responding (acquisition); the flattened slope in the second half shows the rate of responding is petering out (extinction).

(b)

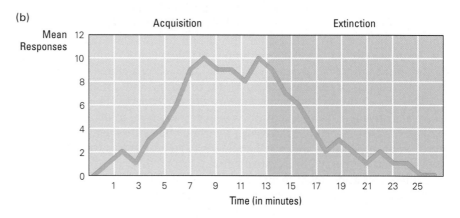

(c)

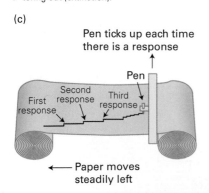

(d)

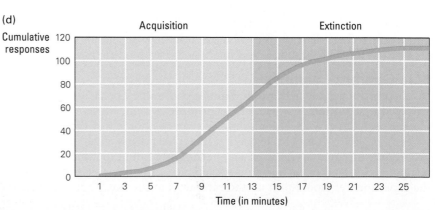

tained a mechanism, such as a lever or a pressure-sensitive disk, that controlled the delivery of food. When the animal pressed the lever or tapped the disk, food dropped into the trough. As the animal explored its cage, eventually it would accidentally depress the lever or disk and receive the food. Over time, as animals learned the relationship between response R (pressing the lever or disk) and consequence C (obtaining food), they would dramatically increase their rate of lever or disk pressing (Figure 8.2b).

Skinner called his system the **free-operant paradigm,** meaning that the animal could operate the apparatus freely, whenever it chose. In the decades that followed, Skinner's free-operant paradigm was so widely adopted that the term "operant conditioning" is often used more or less synonymously with "instrumental conditioning," the way "USA" and "America" are often used more or less synonymously, even though not all inhabitants of the Americas live in the United States. Such conventional usage is fine, as long as you don't forget that operant conditioning is only one subclass of instrumental conditioning: discrete-trial paradigms, such as Thorndike's puzzle boxes, are also a type of instrumental conditioning.

A free-operant experiment can be made a bit more elaborate by adding a stimulus S, such as a light on the cage wall, that signals whether response R will be reinforced: for example, pressing the lever while the light is on will trigger food delivery (consequence C), whereas lever presses while the light is off will not. As long as response R in the presence of S reliably produces consequence C, the mean response rate increases, as shown in minutes 1–13 of Figure 8.2b (acquisition). This process of providing consequences for a behavior that increase the probability of that behavior is called **reinforcement.** (The opposite process would occur if the consequence were, for example, an electric shock; formally, **punishment** is the process of providing consequences for a behavior that decrease the probability of that behavior.) The second half of the experiment shown in Figure 8.2b illustrates how a learned response R tends to extinguish if the reinforcement stops.

Skinner next invented a means of recording responses automatically. Back before the advent of modern computers, mechanical devices such as the one shown in Figure 8.2c recorded data on a long piece of paper rolling steadily underneath a pen. (Until fairly recently, such devices were also used for seismographs and lie detectors.) Skinner hooked up one of these devices to a Skinner box, so that the pen would move up slightly each time the animal responded. If the animal made no responses, the pen did not move, thus drawing a long straight line as the paper scrolled by. But whenever the animal made a response, the pen ticked up, and the resulting line sloped up more steeply as responses were made faster and faster (Figure 8.2d). The device shown in Figure 8.2c is called a **cumulative recorder,** because the height of the line at any given time represents the number of responses that have been made in the entire experiment (cumulatively) up to that time.

One modern example of a cumulative recorder is the odometer in a car. The odometer ticks off miles driven, and the ticks occur faster if you drive faster. When you park the car for the night, and then start it up the next morning, the odometer hasn't reset to zero during that pause in activity; instead, the new mileage is added right on top of the old, for a cumulative record.

Components of the Learned Association

Thorndike and Skinner formalized instrumental conditioning as consisting of three components: a stimulus (or set of stimuli) S, a response (or set of responses) R, and a consequence C. All three components are important parts of what is learned; in fact, instrumental conditioning can be thought of as a three-way association between S, R, and C (Rescorla, 1987). Let's consider each of these components separately, starting with the stimulus, S.

Stimuli

At a swim meet, swimmers line up at the edge of the pool before each race. At the sound of the starting whistle, they dive in as quickly as possible, to maximize their chances of getting a head start. But any swimmer who dives in too early (before the starting whistle) may be penalized or even disqualified. The consequences of diving into the pool vary, depending on whether the dive occurs before or after the whistle.

Discriminative stimuli are stimuli that signal whether a particular response will lead to a particular outcome. As you read in Chapter 7, a stimulus can be any object or event that the organism can detect. For the swimmers, the starting whistle is a discriminative stimulus signaling that dive responses will now result in a favorable consequence:

S (starting whistle) → R (dive) → C (head start in the race)

In a Skinner box, a light may be used as a discriminative stimulus: lever-press responses while the light is on result in the consequence of food delivery, and lever presses while the light is off do not:

S (light on) → R (press lever) → C (get food)

In the case of Annie, the toilet-training toddler, the potty seat is the discriminative stimulus: urination responses in the presence of the potty seat are reinforced with verbal praise, and urination responses in the absence of the potty seat are not:

S (potty seat) → R (urinate) → C (praise)

As the S-R-C notation suggests, the stimulus is the first part of the chain that triggers the response and leads to the consequence. Sometimes, the stimuli are so important that they seem to evoke learned responses automatically. In one striking example, well-trained rats in a familiar maze ran right through a pile of food on their way to the goal box (Stoltz & Lott, 1964). Apparently, the discriminative stimulus of the maze environment produced such a strong association with the familiar response (running) and consequence (food in goal box) that unexpected food encountered along the way couldn't disrupt the S-R-C association. This is sometimes called a *habit slip*. People exhibit habit slips all the time, particularly when drowsy or distracted. Perhaps you've started making a phone call and mistakenly dialed a familiar number (your best friend or your mother) instead of the one you intended to dial, or perhaps you've awoken bright and early one morning and started dressing for class, only to realize it's a weekend and you can stay in bed.

Habit slips aren't the only way in which organisms sometimes respond to discriminative stimuli by making seemingly irrational responses. In one study, pigeons in a Skinner box were first trained to peck at a lighted disk to obtain access to grain in a feeder. The box also contained a little food cup that was initially empty. But after the pecking response was well-learned, the cup was filled with grain, identical to the grain in the feeder. You might expect that the pigeons would now ignore the disk and instead gorge on the free grain. Instead, as Figure 8.3 shows, the pigeons continued to peck vigorously to obtain grain. Although they did sometimes eat from

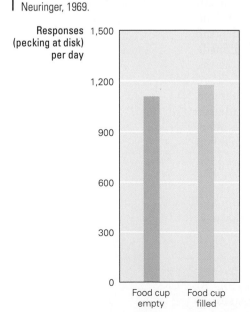

Figure 8.3 The Protestant ethic effect in pigeons Pigeons were first trained to peck at a lighted disk; pecks were reinforced with access to grain in a feeder. During training, there was also an empty food cup in the chamber. Later, the cup was filled with grain. Despite the presence of freely available food in the cup, pigeons continued to peck just as vigorously to obtain grain from the feeder. Adapted from Neuringer, 1969.

the cup, they got most of their food by pecking for it (Neuringer, 1969). Rats show a similar preference for obtaining food by working for it rather than by eating from a freely available source (Neuringer, 1969; Singh, 1970). This behavior has been nicknamed the *Protestant ethic effect*, because it echoes the religious precept that rewards should be earned and that hard workers are morally superior to freeloaders.

Children, too, show the Protestant ethic effect. In one study, children sat at one end of a large box with a lever that they could press to obtain marbles; they were instructed to obtain as many marbles as possible because the marbles could be exchanged for a toy later. After the children obtained five marbles this way, the experimenter seated them at the other end of the box, where marbles occasionally dropped into a tray without requiring any lever pressing. The children were then allowed to choose where to sit. Most of the children spent the majority of their time sitting in front of the lever and "working" for marbles rather than sitting at the other end of the box and simply collecting the marbles as they appeared (Singh, 1970). Just like habit slips, the Protestant ethic effect shows how strongly discriminative stimuli can evoke the associated responses, overruling other possible behaviors.

Responses

In instrumental conditioning, the organism learns to give a particular response to obtain (or avoid) a particular consequence. A response is defined not as a particular pattern of motor actions but by its effect on the environment. For example, a rat in a Skinner box may receive access to food when it presses a lever:

S (lever in box) → R (press lever) → C (get food)

The lever-press response is reinforced by food, whether the rat presses the lever with its left paw, its right paw, or even its nose—as long as the lever is sufficiently depressed to trigger the food delivery device. In another example, Karl Lashley trained rats to run through shallow water in a maze, making a correct series of turns to reach the goal; later, he raised the water level so that the animals had to swim. Even though swimming involved a new set of motor responses that the rats had never executed in this environment, the animals navigated the maze easily (Lashley, 1924). Similarly, Annie's parents may reinforce neatness in their older daughter, Becky, by providing an allowance if Becky cleans her room; the precise movements by which Becky accomplishes this are unimportant, as long as the clothes come off the floor and the toys are put away.

But how do Becky and the animals learn that their responses lead to consequences in the first place? As an extreme case, consider Priscilla the Fastidious Pig. If it took Thorndike's cats several hours to stumble across the response that opened a puzzle box door, one can only imagine how long it might have taken Priscilla to accidentally run a vacuum cleaner and discover that her trainers would reinforce this behavior.

As you may have guessed, researchers and animal trainers who want to elicit complex behaviors rarely rely on accidents. Instead, they use a process called **shaping,** in which successive approximations to the desired response are reinforced. For example, when a rat is first placed in a Skinner box, it may perform any of its natural behaviors: grooming, exploring, or just sitting quietly. The experimenter waits until the rat happens to wander near the food tray, and then drops in a piece of food. The rat eats the food, and starts to learn an association between the tray and food. After a few such trials, the rat starts spending all its time near the food tray. The experimenter now changes the rules so that being near the food tray isn't enough: now, the rat must also be near the lever before food is dropped. Soon, the rat learns to loiter in the vicinity of the lever. Once the rat has learned this, the rules change again: food is dropped only if the animal is actually touching the lever, then only if the animal is rearing up and touching the lever, then only if the animal is pressing down on the lever. Gradually, by a series of successive approximations, the desired response is learned: the rat presses the lever to obtain food.

If you think this sounds like a difficult and time-consuming process, you're right. Shaping requires a considerable amount of skill on the part of the experimenter, who must decide how fast to proceed, how hard to make each new stage, and even whether to back up a few steps if the animal is getting confused. The difficulties of shaping are one reason that people often pay professional animal trainers to housebreak puppies and to teach their pets to obey verbal commands like "sit" and "heel."

Priscilla's trainers used the same techniques to teach her to vacuum and perform her other tricks: initially, they reinforced approaches to the vacuum cleaner, then nearing and touching the vacuum, and so on. Fortunately, pigs are fairly intelligent and tractable animals, and (unsurprisingly) pigs are very motivated to obtain food, and so in the end Priscilla mastered the task.

Annie's parents use the same shaping procedure when first introducing the potty seat. When they think Annie might be about to urinate, they put her on the potty seat; if she does urinate while on the seat, they reinforce this behavior with praise. Gradually, through a series of progressive approximations, Annie learns to approach the potty and perform the response on her own.

The utility of shaping in humans is not limited to toilet training. Kindergarten teachers may use shaping to teach handwriting: reinforcing children (with food treats, gold stars, or verbal praise) first for scribbling with crayons, then for forming lines that approximate letters, then for drawing recognizable letters, and so on. Physical therapists use shaping to help patients recover the use of limbs, such as requiring the patient first to open and close the hands, then progressively working up to the fine motor control needed to grasp and use a spoon. Shaping has even been used to teach autistic children to speak, by first reinforcing any vocalizations, then reinforcing only vocalizations that sound like words, and eventually reinforcing actual word production (Lovaas, 1987).

A related technique is **chaining**, in which organisms are gradually trained to execute complicated sequences of discrete responses. Skinner once trained a rat to pull a string that released a marble, then to pick up the marble with its forepaws, carry it over to a tube, and drop the marble inside the tube (Skinner, 1938). Skinner couldn't have trained such a complex sequence of responses all at once. Chaining involves the organism's learning the links in the chain one at a time: first train the rat to pull the string, then train it to pull the string and pick up the marble, and so on. Sometimes, it is more effective to train the steps in reverse order, in a process called *backward chaining*: first train the rat to drop the marble in the tube, then train the rat to carry the marble to the tube and drop it in, and so on. At each stage, the rat must perform a progressively longer sequence of responses to gain its food.

Chaining is a useful technique for training humans, as well. Workers learning to manufacture items are often taught the process one step at a time (Walls, Zane, & Ellis, 1981), pilot trainees may master landing sequences by practicing progressively longer sequences on a flight simulator (Wight-

Twiggy is a squirrel who water-skis behind a miniature remote-controlled speedboat at a water park in Florida. How do you think she was trained to do this trick?

AP/Wide World Photos

man & Sistrunk, 1987), and budding pianists may learn keyboard techniques starting with one or two fingers, then one hand, and finally both hands (Ash & Holding, 1990).

Consequences

So far we've discussed consequences fairly loosely, but now let's get to a formal definition. A **reinforcer** is a consequence of behavior that leads to increased likelihood of that behavior in the future. Food, water, sleep, and sex are examples of **primary reinforcers,** meaning that organisms tend to repeat behaviors that result in access to these things. In fact, Clark Hull went so far as to propose **drive reduction theory,** which claims that organisms have innate drives to obtain primary reinforcers and that learning reflects the innate, biological need to reduce these drives (e.g., Hull, 1943, 1952). The motivation to obtain primary reinforcers was a key variable in Hull's equations with which, as you read in Chapter 1, he hoped to explain all learning.

One trouble with this approach is that all primary reinforcers are not created equal. Hungry animals will work to obtain food, but they will work even harder for food they like. For example, rats run a maze faster for bread and milk (which they find especially tasty) than for sunflower seeds, even though the seeds satiate hunger just as effectively (Simmons, 1924). Similarly, human infants will suck a nipple more vigorously for sweetened water than for plain water, even though both liquids reduce thirst equally (Kobre & Lipsitt, 1972).

In addition to primary reinforcers, learning can be driven by **secondary reinforcers,** which are reinforcers that initially have no intrinsic value, but that have been paired with primary reinforcers. The best example of a secondary reinforcer is money. Money itself has no biologically reinforcing properties, but it can be exchanged for any number of primary reinforcers, including food, shelter, and even sex (which is one reason why millionaires tend to attract potential mates much more easily than paupers do). People may work for food only so long as they are hungry, but they will work indefinitely for secondary reinforcers; as Donald Trump and Bill Gates demonstrate, you can never have too much money. For a student, grades can function as secondary reinforcers; good grades can (eventually) be exchanged for a degree, which in turn can be exchanged for a good job, which in turn can be exchanged for money, which in turn can be exchanged for primary reinforcers.

Secondary reinforcement is often used in prisons, psychiatric hospitals, and other institutions where the staff have to motivate inmates to behave well and to perform chores such as making beds or taking medications. Each desired behavior is reinforced with a token, and tokens can then be exchanged for privileges (say, access to the telephone or group activities). Such arrangements are called *token economies,* since the tokens function in the same way as money does in the outside world.

Animals, too, will work for secondary reinforcers. For example, trainers can use secondary reinforcement to teach dolphins to do tricks. The trainer first pairs a whistle sound with food reinforcement until the dolphin has learned an association between whistle and food; at this point, the whistle has become a secondary reinforcer, and the animal will work to obtain whistling (Pryor, Haag, & O'Reilly, 1969). As long as the whistle is sometimes followed by food, it will remain reinforcing. Horse trainers often use a similar technique, pairing a clicking noise with oats until the clicking alone can reinforce behavior (Skinner, 1951).

Although many things can function as reinforcers, the identity of the reinforcer does matter. The organism learns that response R to stimulus S results not just in any random consequence but in a particular consequence, C—and

African pouched rats have been trained to sniff out buried landmines in coastal Mozambique. As many as 100 million landmines were left over from the country's civil war, and they injure or kill an estimated 50 people daily. Rats, guided by little harnesses, scamper around the minefield without detonating the mines. When a rat smells explosive, it gives a decisive scratch with both forepaws, signaling to its handler that a landmine is nearby. The rats are trained by food reinforcement (pieces of banana) paired with a clicker. Eventually, the rats work for clicker reinforcement.

Reuters/Howard Burditt/Landov

the organism may react with surprise or anger if that consequence is switched. For example, in one study, a monkey had been trained to work to obtain pieces of banana. On one trial, the monkey was given a piece of lettuce instead; the monkey threw down the lettuce (which it would normally eat) and shrieked at the experimenter in annoyance (Tinklepaugh, 1928). This phenomenon, called *negative contrast*, reflects the fact that organisms who are switched from a preferred reinforcer to a less-preferred reinforcer will respond less strongly for it than if they had been given the less-preferred reinforcer all along.

Negative contrast can be observed in humans, too. As shown in Figure 8.4a, infants will normally suck a nipple providing either plain water or sweetened water, but the sweetened water elicits a higher rate of responding. Thus, sweetened water is a preferred reinforcer. Figure 8.4b shows what happens when infants are started on sweetened water for the first session, then switched to plain water in session 2: the sucking response plummets. When the infants are switched back to sweetened water in session 3, the sucking rate doubles—only to plummet again when plain water returns in session 4 (Kobre & Lipsitt, 1972). The infants who have been sucking sweetened water in sessions 1 and 3 will suck less plain water in sessions 2 and 4 that those (in Figure 8.4a) who received plain water all along. Similar negative contrast effects can be observed in children who go trick-or-treating expecting candy and instead get pennies (which they would usually appreciate), and in game-show contestants who hope to win the $1,000,000 grand prize and instead dejectedly settle for a consolation prize such as a new car or a trip to Hawaii.

Of course, reinforcers are not the only kind of consequence. There are also **punishers:** consequences of a behavior that leads to decreased likelihood of that behavior in future. Common punishers for animals include pain, loud noises, and exposure to predators (or even the scent of predators). Common punishers for humans involve monetary fines, social disapproval, and jail time. Whereas reinforcers increase behavior, punishers decrease it. A rat will learn to stop pressing a lever if it receives an electric shock for doing so; Becky will learn to stop teasing her younger sister, Annie, if teasing is always punished by parental scolding; and so on.

On the basis of a few early experiments, both Thorndike (1932) and Skinner (1938, 1953) concluded that punishment was not nearly as effective as reinforcement for controlling behavior. Modern researchers generally disagree, finding that punishment—if applied correctly—can be very effective indeed (see Staddon,

Figure 8.4 The negative contrast effect. A normally acceptable reinforcer elicits less responding if a preferred reinforcer is expected. (a) Human infants will suck somewhat more vigorously at a nipple that provides sucrose-sweetened water rather than plain water, even though both liquids reduce thirst equally, indicating that sweetened water is a preferred reinforcer. (b) But infants started on sweetened water in session 1 and then switched to plain water in session 2 will suck less vigorously. If the infants are switched back to sweetened water in session 3, the sucking rate increases again, only to plummet in session 4 when they again receive plain water. Data from Kobre and Lipsitt, 1972.

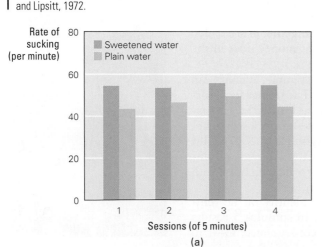

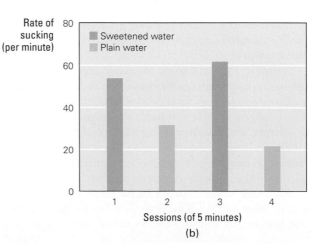

1995, for a review). The problem is that there are several factors that determine how effective the punishment will be. We describe three of these factors here.

First, *discriminative stimuli for punishment can encourage cheating*. Remember how discriminative stimuli can signal to an organism whether an instrumental response will be reinforced? Discriminative stimuli can also signal whether a response will be punished. For a speeding driver, the sight of a police car is a discriminative stimulus for punishment: speeding in the presence of this stimulus will probably be punished. But speeding in the absence of a police car will probably not be punished. In this case, punishment doesn't train the driver not to speed—it only teaches him to suppress speeding in the presence of the discriminative stimulus. When no police car is visible, speeding may resume. In effect, the driver has learned to cheat—speeding only when the discriminative stimulus for punishment is absent. Similarly, the dominant male in a group of chimpanzees may punish females for mating with any other males—but when his back is turned, the females often sneak off into the bushes with lower-ranking males. And rats, trained to eat no more than four pellets at a time, will happily eat all the food in sight if no human is watching (Davis, 1989).

Second, *concurrent reinforcement can undermine the punishment*. The effects of punishment can be counteracted if reinforcement occurs along with the punishment. Suppose a rat first learns to press a lever for food, and later learns that lever presses are punished by shock. Unless the rat has another way to obtain food, it is likely to keep pressing the lever to obtain food reinforcement, in spite of the punishing effects of shock. Similarly, a child who is reprimanded for talking in class will suppress this behavior much less if the behavior is simultaneously reinforced by approval from classmates. And although a speeding driver risks a hefty ticket, the effects of this punisher may be counteracted by the reinforcement provided by the fun of driving fast.

Third, *initial intensity matters*. Punishment is most effective if a strong punisher is used from the outset—from the initial exposure. For example, rats received a mild shock as they ran through a maze to the goal box (Brown, 1969). At the lowest intensities (1 or 2 volts), the shock had little effect on behavior. Gradually, across several days, shock intensity increased to 40 volts. Behavior was essentially unaffected, even though a naive rat, given a 40-volt shock, would have stopped running immediately. In a sense, the early weak shocks made the rats immune to the stronger ones. As a result, the effectiveness of the strong shock was completely undermined by starting weak and working up from there.

On the other hand, the principle of intense punishment for a first offense often conflicts with our sense of what is appropriate and fair. Instead, humans have a tendency to start with a mild punisher and work up to more intense punishments for repeated offenses. A child who misbehaves in class may first receive a warning, then a scolding, then detention, then expulsion. The expulsion, when it comes, may be much less effective at deterring future misbehavior because of the prior, milder punishments. Similarly, a speeding driver may not be deterred much by a $500 ticket if he is accustomed to paying lesser fines. In each case, the prior weaker punishers may undermine the effectiveness of the severe punisher, when it finally comes. (See "Learning and Memory in Everyday Life" on p. 304 for more discussion of the problems with punishment.)

Putting It All Together: Building the S-R-C Association

Now that you've read about stimulus, response, and consequence in some detail, it's time to think about the ways in which they can be arranged. An experimenter can vary several factors: the temporal spacing between S and R and

▶ **Learning and Memory in Everyday Life**

The Problem with Punishment

In the United States, 94% of parents of toddlers report that they use spanking or other forms of physical punishment to discourage unwanted behaviors (Kazdan & Benjet, 2003). There is no question that physical punishment is an effective technique for reducing the frequency of an unwanted response. Spanking is a form of punishment that even a very young child can understand. And, used correctly, a single light spanking can effectively modify behavior.

Physical punishment is controversial, however. Many people believe that hitting a child is never justifiable. Some studies have suggested that children who are spanked can develop emotional problems, including aggression and stress (Gershoff, 2002), although other studies have found that occasional mild spanking does not cause any lasting harm (Baumrind, 2002; Larzelere, 2000). This debate is quite heated. From time to time the news media report a case in which a parent who has spanked a child faces criminal prosecution for child abuse. In the United States, parents are generally prosecuted only for extreme, repeated hitting, but in Sweden, any corporal punishment of children, even by the parents, is prohibited by law (Durrant, 1999).

Punishment doesn't have to be painful to be effective. Scolding is a form of positive punishment that does not cause physical harm; negative punishments can include time-out, grounding, or withholding of allowance. Parents can rely on these forms of punishment to avoid spanking altogether. But there is still the problem that punishment is hard to apply effectively.

For example, you may know a child who persists in unruly behavior despite strict discipline—almost as if the punishment increased the likelihood of the response, instead of decreasing it. If so, the discipline is actually acting as a reinforcer, not a punisher. Let's take a hypothetical example. Shawn has two busy working parents, and he has to compete for their attention with his older siblings. When Shawn is well-behaved, his siblings tend to get most of the parental attention; but when Shawn breaks china, fights with his brothers, or causes trouble at school, the parental spotlight shines on him. Although they may think they are punishing Shawn, his parents are actually reinforcing his bad behavior by giving him attention when he misbehaves. Similarly, one study concluded that children may be "trained" to steal if each theft brings reinforcement in the form of social attention from school staff and parents (Luiselli & Pine, 1999). Another study found that psychiatric inpatients who engage in delusional speech often receive attention from their nurses; in effect, the attention is reinforcing the unwanted behavior (Ayllon & Haughton, 1964).

What's to be done? One approach is to punish unwanted behavior with a minimum of fuss, so that the offender gets less attention—and less reinforcement—for the bad behavior. At the same time, unwanted behaviors can be reduced by differential reinforcement of alternative behaviors. For example, when the psychiatric nurses were trained to ignore patients' delusional speech and to reward normal conversations with attention and candy, the rate of delusional speech dropped and the rate of normal speech increased (Ayllon & Haughton, 1964).

Similarly, Shawn's parents should try to discipline him with a minimum of fuss, so that he gets less attention—and less reinforcement—for his bad behavior. At the same time, they should try to give him positive reinforcement for good behavior. This means they have to commit the extra time and effort of paying attention to their youngest child, especially when he's good. The payoff may be a well-behaved child and a happier family, while avoiding many of the problems with punishment.

Physical punishment for children is controversial, and some (but not all) experts believe it can lead to aggressive behavior in punished children.

Myrleen Ferguson Cate/PhotoEdit

C, whether the consequence is added or subtracted following the response, and even the regularity (or schedule) with which the consequence follows the response.

Timing Affects Learning

In most of the instrumental conditioning examples presented so far, the consequence (reinforcer or punisher) has immediately followed the response. For example, as soon as the rat presses a lever, food drops into the Skinner box; as soon as a dolphin executes a trick, the trainer provides whistle reinforcement; as soon as Becky teases her sister, her parents scold her.

Normally, immediate consequences produce the best learning. This principle—that instrumental conditioning is faster if the R-C interval is short—is similar to the principle of temporal contiguity in classical conditioning, in which learning is fastest when the CS and US are closely related in time. If there is a significant delay between instrumental response and reinforcement, learning decreases. Figure 8.5 shows that rats learn a lever-pressing task quickly when the delay between response and food delivery is 0 seconds, but are slower to learn the association if the delay is 4 seconds; if the delay is 10 seconds, there seems to be little learning at all (Schlinger & Blakely, 1994).

Temporal contiguity of response and consequence also has an impact on the effectiveness of punishment. Punishers are most effective if there is no delay between response and consequence. A dog is more easily housebroken if punished for each accident on the rug immediately after it occurs; if the householder doesn't find the evidence until a few hours later, the dog will probably not associate the punishment with the earlier accident, and so the punishment will be much less effective. Human society often employs delayed punishment, however. Criminals may not come to trial—much less serve their sentence—until months or years after committing the crime. A middle school student who misbehaves in the morning and receives detention after school experiences a delay of several hours between response and consequence. Similarly, a parent who delays punishment ("Just wait till we get home!") is undermining the punishment's effectiveness. From a conditioning point of view, these delays weaken the effectiveness of the punishers, retarding learning.

Why does a delay weaken the effectiveness of reinforcers and punishers? One reason is that, when a consequence occurs, the learner may tend to associate it with recent behaviors. If there is no delay, then the odds are good that the most recent behavior was the response that caused the consequence. But if there is a long delay, it is more likely that other behaviors have crept in during the interval; now these are more likely to be associated with the consequence (reinforcer).

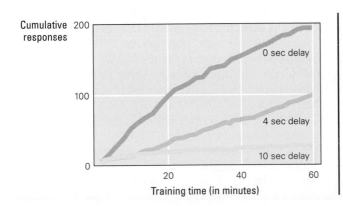

Figure 8.5 The delay between response and consequence affects speed of learning Rats were trained to lever-press, with food reinforcement delivered after an interval of 0, 4, or 10 seconds. During the first session, rats with the 0 second delay learned very quickly, rats with the 4 second delay learned more slowly, and rats with the 10 second delay hardly ever pressed the lever, as indicated by a nearly flat cumulative response curve. Adapted from Schlinger & Blakely, 1994.

A striking example of this principle is the phenomenon of superstition. In common usage, **superstitions** are responses that individuals make because they believe those responses lead to desired outcomes (or avert undesired outcomes). For example, a baseball player might wear a favorite shirt to his games because he believes it brings him good luck; a person might avoid walking under a ladder because she believes this brings bad luck.

Although Skinner stressed that we can't be sure what a lab animal "believes," he did condition animals to display what seemed to be superstitious behaviors. In a classic experiment, he presented food to pigeons every 15 seconds, without requiring any response (Skinner, 1948). All the pigeons had to do was stand there and wait for the food to drop into the box. But instead, the pigeons tended to develop complex behaviors, "rituals" that they performed in the intervals between food arrivals. One bird turned in clockwise circles, one pointed its head toward an upper corner of the cage, one pecked at the floor, and so on. The birds performed these rituals faithfully, almost as if they believed that these actions caused the food delivery. Such superstitious behavior echoes the Protestant ethic effect, in which animals prefer to work for their food rather than obtain it freely—even if, as in this case, they have to invent the work themselves.

Superstitious behaviors can be conditioned in humans, too. In a study involving college students, each student was left alone in a room with a table containing several levers and a counting device that periodically registered points (Ono, 1987). The student was told to earn as many points as possible. The counter operated randomly, independent of what the student was doing. But most of the students—who didn't know this—developed some form of superstitious behavior: pulling the lever, tapping the table, and so on. One student happened to be touching the table just as a point was recorded. She then started to touch things around the room, trying to "earn" another point. She had just climbed on the table and jumped off when the counter clicked again. Thinking she was on to something, she continued jumping, and another point happened to be delivered just as she had jumped up to touch the ceiling with her shoe in one hand. The student spent the next 25 minutes jumping to touch the ceiling, until she apparently gave out from fatigue!

Skinner interpreted superstitious behaviors as accidental contiguities between a response and a reinforcer. For example, one of Skinner's pigeons probably just happened to be turning in a clockwise circle the first time that food was delivered. The temporal contiguity between this circling response and the reinforcement increased the probability that the pigeon would make the same response again. Skinner went so far as to speculate that similar accidental contiguities might underlie the origin of human superstitions such as rain dances; sometimes, by chance, rain does follow a rain dance and so, although the dances do not actually cause the rain, the association between the dance response and the rain consequence is strengthened. Similar associations underlie the behavior of the baseball player who always wears a lucky shirt, because he happened to wear it once when he broke out of a batting slump.

Even people who think they know better are not immune to superstitious behavior. A common example is a person who catches a cold and, after a few days of suffering, goes to the doctor to demand antibiotics. Most colds are caused by viruses, and antibiotics are ineffective against viruses. Typically, a cold

B. F. Skinner suggested that some human superstitions may develop when a behavior is accidentally paired with arrival of a desired consequence. The reinforcement may lead to increased future performance of the behavior.

Phil Cole/Getty Images

lasts a week or two before the body's own immune system fights it off. But the person who has taken the antibiotics may nevertheless associate them with the cure. The next time he catches a cold, he'll return to the doctor to demand more antibiotics, just like the pigeon circling to obtain food.

The time lag between response and consequence is also an important factor in understanding **self-control,** an organism's willingness to forego a small immediate reward in favor of a larger future reward. For example, suppose a pigeon can choose to peck at one key for a small, immediate food reinforcement or at a second key for a larger food reinforcement that arrives 6 seconds later. Under these circumstances, pigeons almost always choose the small, immediate reinforcement—even though, overall, they obtain less food this way (Green, Fischer, Perlow, & Sherman, 1981).

The same trade-off occurs in humans: it is easy to convince a student to study if a test is coming up tomorrow; it is harder if the exam is not for 5 weeks—the delay between response (studying) and reinforcement (good grade) makes the reinforcement less effective in eliciting the response. Similarly, one reason a weight-loss diet is difficult to maintain is that, at each meal, the dieter has to choose between the immediate reward of a dessert and the delayed reward of weight loss.

The ability to wait for a delayed reinforcement differs across individuals and across the age span. When asked, "Would you rather receive $500 today or $1,000 in one year?" adults in their sixties are likely to choose the larger, delayed reward; college students are somewhat less likely to choose the delayed reward; and 12-year-olds almost never choose the delayed reward—preferring immediate gratification (Green, Fry, & Myerson, 1994).

One way of improving an individual's ability to wait for a reward is to use *precommitment,* in which the individual makes a choice that is difficult to change later. So, for example, a student may be more likely to study early in the semester if he joins a weekly study group—so there is peer pressure for him to attend the group and to study. A dieter may find be less likely to cheat on her diet if she first empties the kitchen of chips and ice cream—so that when the cravings hit, it is difficult to sneak some junk food. These precommitments do not make it impossible to get the immediate reward (the student can skip a study meeting, and the dieter can drive to the supermarket to buy ice cream), but they make it harder to get the immediate reward, and the individual is more likely to stick by an earlier decision to wait for the later, larger reward.

Consequences Can Be Added or Subtracted

So far in this chapter, you've seen paradigms in which a response results in presentation of a consequence:

Stimulus S $\rightarrow$ Response R $\rightarrow$ Consequence C

For example, toddler Annie will learn that, in the presence of the potty seat (S), urination (R) will result in the reinforcement of parental praise (C); in other contexts (S), urination (R) will result in the punishment of parental disapproval (C).

In both these examples, the consequence is "added" to Annie's environment. For that reason, these paradigms are technically called **positive reinforcement** and **positive punishment.** Note that here the word "positive" doesn't mean "good"; instead it means "added" in the mathematical sense (like a positive number). In positive reinforcement, the response causes the reinforcer to be "added" to the environment; in positive punishment, the response must be withheld, or else the punisher is "added" to the environment.

But there are also learning situations in which the consequence is taken away, or "subtracted," from the environment. For example, in **negative reinforcement,** something is subtracted from the environment, and this encourages (reinforces) behavior. Thus, if you have a headache, you can take aspirin to make the headache go away. In this case, the stimulus is the headache, the response is taking aspirin, and the consequence is that the headache goes away:

S (headache) → R (take aspirin) → C (no more headache)

The net result is that you are more likely to take aspirin again next time you have a headache, so this scenario is an example of reinforcement. The consequence, though, is not something added but something subtracted—the headache is taken away. Similarly, a rat can be placed in a chamber with an electrified floor grid from which it receives electric shocks. The rat can escape these shocks by climbing onto a wooden platform. In this case, the response is climbing, and the consequence is escape from shock—shock has been subtracted (negative) from the rat's immediate environment:

S (shock) → R (climb) → C (no more shock)

The net result is that the rat is more likely to climb the platform in the future. In other words, the climbing response has been reinforced. Because the consequence involves a subtraction (shock is taken away), this is an example of negative reinforcement.

Just as behavior can be reinforced by taking bad things away, so behavior can be punished by taking good things away. This kind of paradigm is called **negative punishment,** because something is subtracted (negative) from the environment, and this punishes the behavior. Again, as with negative reinforcement, the word "negative" does not mean "bad"; it means "subtraction" in a mathematical sense. For example, if Becky displays aggressive behavior toward other children during recess, the teacher may make Becky sit by herself while the other children play. In this case, the response is Becky's aggressive behavior, and the consequence is loss of playtime:

S (recess) → R (aggressive behavior) → C (loss of playtime)

The net effect is that Becky may be less likely to display aggressive behavior in the future. This kind of negative punishment is sometimes called a "time-out"; in other words, Becky is punished by time away from a normally reinforcing activity: play. Time-outs work only if the activity being restricted is something reinforcing: a time-out from an activity the child doesn't like may actually serve to reinforce, rather than reduce, the bad behavior that earned the time-out!

Negative punishment is widely applied in human society: teenagers may be grounded for staying out too late, drivers may have their licenses suspended for speeding, and health club members who don't pay their fees may be forbidden access to the gym until they pay up. In each case, an undesirable behavior is punished by revoking privileges, in the hope of decreasing the likelihood that such behavior will occur again in the future.

Table 8.1 summarizes the four types of training. Keep in mind that the terms "reinforcement" and "punishment" describe whether the response increases (reinforcement) or decreases (punishment) as a result of training. The terms "positive" and "negative" describe whether the consequence is added (positive) or taken away (negative). Negative punishment is sometimes called *omission training,* meaning that a response is stopped in order to prevent a positive consequence from being omitted or removed from the environment. Negative reinforcement is sometimes called *escape* (or *avoidance*) *training,* since the response is made to escape or avoid an aversive consequence. (We'll consider avoidance again in more detail in Chapter 10.)

Laboratory experiments often fit neatly into the grid shown in Table 8.1, but real life is more complicated. Sometimes it is difficult to determine whether an individual is learning based on reinforcement or punishment or both. For exam-

Table 8.1

Instrumental Conditioning Paradigms

	Response increases (reinforcement)	Response decreases (punishment)
Consequence is added (positive)	Positive reinforcement	Positive punishment
Consequence is removed (negative)	Negative reinforcement (escape/avoidance)	Negative punishment (omission)

ple, when students study for an exam, are they working to obtain a good grade (positive reinforcement) or to avoid flunking (negative reinforcement)? It could be either—or both. Similarly, a driver who exceeds the speed limit may risk a monetary fine (positive punishment) as well as the threat of having his license taken away (negative punishment)—and either or both considerations may motivate him to drive at a legal speed.

Test Your Knowledge

Reinforcement and Punishment

It's easy to confuse the ideas of negative reinforcement, positive punishment, and so on, since we often use the words "positive" and "negative" to mean "good" and "bad." Don't fall into this trap! In instrumental conditioning, "positive" and "negative" mean "added" and "subtracted"—without any judgment about whether this addition or subtraction is pleasant or unpleasant.

You can determine what kind of paradigm you're dealing with by asking yourself whether the consequence is added to (positive) or subtracted from (negative) the environment, and whether the response increases as a result of learning (reinforcement) or decreases as a result of learning (punishment). Try your hand at the following scenarios, and see if you can tell whether each is an example of positive reinforcement, negative reinforcement, positive punishment, or negative punishment. For each scenario, ask yourself: (a) Who does the learning? (b) What is the stimulus? (c) What is the response? (d) What is the consequence of making this response? (e) Is something added or taken away? (f) Does the response increase or decrease as a result of learning?

1. Lucy Smith is 2 years old. At the grocery store, Lucy sees candy and wants it. Her mother refuses, and Lucy starts to cry. The situation quickly escalates into a full-blown temper tantrum. Eventually, Lucy's mother relents and buys Lucy some candy. The next time they go shopping, Lucy sees the candy again and throws another tantrum. This time, she gets the candy quickly.

2. An interesting aspect of conditioning is that sometimes more than one person is doing the learning. Scenario 1 is presented from Lucy's point of view. But consider the same story from another point of view: Susan Smith takes her toddler on a shopping trip. The child sees candy, wants it, and throws a tantrum. Overtired and in a rush, Susan gives the child some candy, and the tantrum stops. On the next trip, as soon as the child starts to wail, Susan quickly gives her some candy, to stop the screaming.

3. Shevonne has a dog named Snoopy. Shevonne installs an electric fence system around the perimeter of her yard, and Snoopy wears a collar that makes a high-pitched noise whenever he gets too close to the boundary. The first time Snoopy strays out of bounds, the noise plays and distresses him. Soon, Snoopy learns to avoid the noise by staying inside the yard.

4. Miguel is a wide receiver on a professional football team. During a close game, an opposing player tackles him roughly, and Miguel starts a fistfight. Considering this behavior to be unacceptable, the coach revokes Miguel's playing privileges for a week. When allowed to rejoin the team, Miguel is tackled again. This time, he reacts by shouting at the opposing player and protesting to the referee—but stops short of starting another fistfight.

Schedules of Reinforcement

In addition to determining whether a response results in reinforcement or punishment being added or taken away, an experimenter can also determine the schedule with which these consequences are delivered. So far, almost all of the examples in this chapter have been ones in which the consequence reliably follows the response. For example, whenever the rat presses a lever, it gets food; whenever Annie uses the potty, she gets praise; and so on. These examples involve **continuous reinforcement,** meaning that each response is always followed by the consequence.

But researchers have also considered other kinds of arrangements, such as requiring a certain number of responses before the consequence occurs. For example, Becky has to clean her room 7 days in a row to obtain her weekly allowance (seven responses for one reinforcement), and a baseball player is allowed to swing and miss three times before he strikes out (three responses for one punishment). In laboratory terms, an experimenter can devise a schedule defining exactly when consequences are delivered. Although these schedules could be applied to either a reinforcer or a punisher, for simplicity they are usually just called **reinforcement schedules.** We'll consider four basic alternatives to the continuous reinforcement schedule.

First and simplest is the **fixed-ratio (FR) schedule,** in which some fixed number of responses must be made before a reinforcer is delivered. For example, if a rat must press a lever five times to obtain one pellet, the ratio of responses to reinforcers is 5:1; this is often called an FR 5 schedule. Using this same notation, continuous reinforcement can also be expressed as an FR 1 schedule: every response results in one reinforcement. Ratios can gradually be increased, starting with an FR 1 schedule, working up through an FR 5 schedule, to an FR 50 schedule, and so on. In fact, animals can be trained to make several hundred responses for each reinforcement on an FR schedule.

Rats on an FR schedule show a consistent pattern of fast responding leading up to the reinforcement, followed by a few seconds with no responding (called the **postreinforcement pause**). Figure 8.6a shows the hypothetical behavior of a rat trained to respond on an FR 5 schedule: steady response rates leading up to each reinforcement, followed by a brief pause, before another round of responding for a new reinforcement.

During the postreinforcement pause, it seems almost as if the animal is pausing to take a breath before its next bout of responding. And in fact, the length of

What kind of learning is going on here?

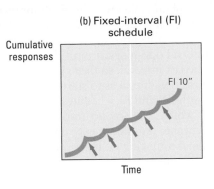

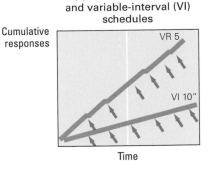

Figure 8.6 Reinforcement schedules In each figure, data show cumulative responding by a hypothetical rat; orange arrows indicate food delivery (reinforcement). (a) An FR 5 schedule (reinforcement after every fifth response) produces steady responding, with a short postreinforcement pause (flat line) following each food delivery. (b) An FI 10" schedule (reinforcement for the first response after a 10 second interval) produces a characteristic scallop-shaped curve. After each postreinforcement pause, the response rate gradually increases until the next reinforcement arrives. (c) A VR 5 schedule (reinforcement after every fifth response, on average) produces fast and steady responding, with little or no postreinforcement pause—because the next response could produce another reinforcement. A VI 10" schedule (reinforcement for the first response after a 10 second interval, on average) also produces steady responding, with no postreinforcement pause, as the rat keeps checking to see whether a new reinforcement is available yet.

the postreinforcement pause is related to the number of upcoming responses: thus, the postreinforcement pause when an animal is on an FR 50 schedule is longer than when the animal is on an FR 5 schedule. In effect, the rat is behaving like a human teenager who does a short chore (say, taking out the trash) the first time his mother asks, but procrastinates for hours before starting in on a really time-consuming chore (mowing the lawn).

Examples of fixed-ratio schedules in human life include factory workers who get paid a flat fee for every 100 pieces they turn out, and migrant farm workers who get paid a fixed amount for every bushel of apples picked. In fact, such workers tend to show behavior similar to that of rats on an FR schedule—steady bursts of responding followed by postreinforcement pauses: the workers complete a batch, take a few minutes for a coffee break, and then start in again. A similar phenomenon occurs in readers: they may complete a chapter or a fixed number of pages before putting the book aside. Authors try to combat this "postreinforcement pause" by ending each chapter with an exciting moment, so that readers will keep turning pages to see what happens next.

In contrast to a fixed-ratio schedule, where the reinforcement comes after a fixed number of responses, a **fixed-interval (FI) schedule** reinforces the first response after a fixed amount of time. For example, on an FI 50" schedule (where 50" = 50 seconds), the ideal solution would be for the rat to wait exactly 50 seconds after each reinforcement, then respond once to obtain the next reinforcement. Earlier responses (before the 50 seconds have elapsed) are wasted effort. However, real data don't conform to this ideal situation. Figure 8.6b shows how an animal on an FI schedule actually behaves: after each reinforcement, there is a period of few or no responses, but the rate of responding gradually increases as the end of the interval nears. Presumably, animals (including humans) cannot judge time intervals perfectly, so they estimate as best they can how much time has passed and err a little on the side of wishful thinking, by responding too soon.

An example of fixed-interval schedules outside the laboratory is baking a cake without a timer. You know from the recipe that the cake needs to bake for 30 minutes. Because you don't have a timer, you have to estimate when the cake's done—you don't want it to burn. There is little point in checking after the first 5 or 10 minutes, but it might be worth checking after you estimate 20 or 25 minutes have passed. And as it gets closer and closer to 30 minutes, you might check more and more frequently, not wanting to leave the cake in past the deadline. In this example, the response is checking on the cake, the reinforcement is taking out a perfectly baked cake, and only the response that occurs immediately after the end of the baking interval is reinforced—the rest are "wasted" responses.

The important thing to remember about FI schedules is that the reinforcement does not simply appear after the fixed interval; the reinforcement merely becomes obtainable after the fixed interval—the organism must still respond in order to get that reinforcement. Once the interval has elapsed, the reinforcement remains available until the response is made to get it—there is no time limit. The next interval doesn't start until the response is made to obtain the reinforcement from the last interval, so there is a built-in incentive to get each reinforcement as quickly as possible so as to start the clock ticking toward the next reinforcement.

In both FR and FI schedules, the postreinforcement pause represents a period during which little or no responding occurs. In many cases, what the experimenter wants is a nice steady rate of responding, without long periods in which the animal is making no measurable response. Fortunately, there are ways around this problem.

One approach is to use a **variable-ratio (VR) schedule.** Whereas an FR 5 schedule produces reinforcement after every fifth response, a VR 5 schedule produces reinforcement after every 5 responses, *on average.* Thus, the responder never knows exactly when a reinforcement is coming. As a result, there is a nice stable rate of responding even immediately after a reinforcement is delivered, because the very next response just might result in another reinforcement (Figure 8.6c).

A real-life example of a variable-ratio schedule is gambling. You might know that, on average, the slot machine pays off on every tenth game (in a very generous casino), but you don't know exactly which games will pay off. Even if you have just won a game, the very next game might be a winner too, so there is a strong incentive to keep playing.

Just as a fixed-ratio (FR) schedule can be modified into a variable-ratio (VR) schedule, so a fixed-interval (FI) schedule can be modified into a **variable-interval (VI) schedule.** Whereas an FI schedule reinforces the first response after a particular interval (e.g., 50 seconds), a VI schedule reinforces the first response after an interval that averages a particular length of time. So, for example, a VI 50" schedule reinforces the first response after an interval that is 50 seconds *on average*—but the actual interval might be longer or shorter on any particular trial.

In the VI schedule, as in the VR schedule, the responder never knows exactly when the next reinforcement is coming: a response a few seconds after the previous reinforcement just might be reinforced too. The rate of rats responding on a VI schedule is usually slow and steady, as the rats check periodically to see whether reinforcement is available (Figure 8.6c). Notice that the pattern of responding on a VI schedule looks very similar to the pattern of responding on a VR schedule (Figure 8.6c): both schedules produce stable response curves without long periods of inactivity.

An example of a VI schedule in real life might be checking email. Suppose that, on average, you receive 15 emails a day from friends, but you can never be sure exactly when the emails will arrive. You want to read these messages promptly—but you don't want to waste your whole day sitting in front of the computer just in case a new message arrives. By periodically checking your email at a steady rate, say once an hour or so, you will minimize the time an unread email sits in your inbox, while you are free to pursue other behaviors in the meantime.

All of these schedules—continuous, FR, FI, VR, VI—can be applied to punishment as well as reinforcement. For example, a rat may receive a shock every time it presses a lever (continuous schedule of punishment), or every fifth time (FR 5), or every 60 seconds on average (VI 60"), and so on. As with reinforcement, the more regular the punishment, the faster the learning. If a child is punished by verbal reprimand every time he talks in class (continuous schedule), he will learn to suppress this behavior more quickly than if the weary teacher reprimands him only on every fifth infraction or so (a VR 5 schedule), meaning that the child gets away with this behavior on about 80% of trials. (See "Unsolved Mysteries" on p. 313.)

Instinctive Drift

Keller and Marion Breland, the folks who trained Priscilla the Fastidious Pig, were former students of B. F. Skinner. They set up a small business to train animals, using the instrumental conditioning techniques they had studied with Skinner. The animals were exhibited at county fairs or on TV, to advertise products such as farm chow (Breland & Breland, 1951). Priscilla was one of the Brelands' more famous successes. But there were failures, too.

For one exhibit, the Brelands wanted to train a pig to use a piggy bank: the pig would pick up a coin, carry it over to the bank, and drop it inside (Breland & Breland, 1961). The task was fairly simple compared with Priscilla's exploits. The Brelands used shaping: initially, the pig got a food reinforcement for approaching a coin, then for picking up the coin, then for picking it up and depositing it in the bank. The pig learned the trick fairly quickly; it would run for the coin, pick it up, run to the bank, and deposit it. But over the next few weeks, the behavior became slower and slower. The pig would run over for a coin, but on the way back, instead of depositing the coin in the piggy bank, the pig would drop the coin and begin pushing it around with its snout, then pick up the coin again, drop it again, nose it again, and so on. Sometimes the pig spent up to 10 minutes playing with the coin instead of depositing it.

Thinking they simply had a perverse animal on their hands, the Brelands tried several other pigs—and the same misbehavior developed spontaneously in each animal. The Brelands even tried to train a raccoon to

do the trick. Like the pigs, the raccoon quickly learned to deposit coins to obtain food. But again, spontaneous behaviors crept in: instead of dropping the coin in the bank, the raccoon would slide the coin halfway into the bank, then pull it back out, clutching the coin to its chest and rubbing it. This seemed to violate the fundamental principles of instrumental conditioning: behaviors associated with a reinforcer should increase in frequency, while behaviors that are not reinforced should decrease in frequency. These animals' misbehaviors actually prevented or delayed reinforcement, and yet the misbehaviors increased, instead of decreasing, as training continued.

Rooting in pigs and washing in raccoons are normal, instinctive behaviors that may be triggered by association with food.

What was going wrong? The Brelands suggested that the problematic behaviors might not be random. In the wild, raccoons dip their food in water and then rub it between their paws as if washing it. This instinctive "washing" behavior is very much like what the Brelands' raccoon was doing with the coins, suggesting that instinct was interfering with learning. Similarly, pigs in the wild find food by rooting through the undergrowth with their snouts; this instinctive "nosing" resembles the trained pigs' misbehavior. The Brelands suggested that food reinforcements were triggering instinctive species-specific feeding behaviors that overruled learned responses; they called this phenomenon *instinctive drift.*

For example, perhaps pigs have a hardwired link in their brain between food-related stimuli and species-specific responses such as food-searching and rooting behaviors. When the Brelands trained their pig to approach a coin to obtain food, the coin became a stimulus associated with food. Later, the sight of the coin would trigger the learned response— but also the innate species-specific response of nosing. The innate response overruled the learned response (Timberlake, 1983, 1984).

This could account for why the Brelands' pigs and raccoons might first learn, and then lose, a trained behavior. But it begs the question of where in the brain these hardwired responses might be stored, and why the hardwired responses can't be overruled through learning. In short, decades after the Brelands first documented instinctive drift, researchers have yet to provide a completely compelling explanation for the phenomenon, much less instructions for how to combat it (see also Domjan, 1983; Domjan & Galef, 1983). And, as far as we know, the Brelands never did manage to teach a pig to use a piggy bank.

Choice Behavior

In addition to the four kinds of schedule discussed above (FR, VR, FI, VI), there are also *concurrent schedules*, in which the organism can make any of several possible responses, each with its own consequence. This allows us to examine how organisms choose to divide their time and efforts among different options. For example, suppose a pigeon is in a chamber with two keys, key A and key B. Pecking on key A is reinforced on a VI 2' schedule (2' = 2 minutes), and pecking on key B is reinforced on a VI 1' schedule. In other words, the pigeon can obtain food by pecking on A at 2 minute intervals or by pecking on B at 1 minute intervals. What should the pigeon do?

Looking at the problem logically, within a 2 minute interval, the pigeon can get two food pellets for pecking on B but only one for pecking on A. So, you might think that the pigeon should concentrate on key B and ignore key A. On the other hand, if the experiment goes on for longer than a few minutes, there is a food pellet just waiting to be delivered as soon as the pigeon pecks at A—and this pellet will never be obtained if the pigeon totally ignores A. Therefore, the optimal behavior is some strategy that allows the pigeon to maximize the amount of food it can get from both keys, probably by spending the most effort on B but occasionally switching over to A, just to check. In fact, this is more or less what animals do. This behavior is analogous to channel surfing in humans: confronted with several possible television programs, one solution is to watch the preferred program but switch over to other choices during the commercials, just in case something interesting is going on.

Variable-Interval Schedules and the Matching Law

Let's stick with the pigeon given a choice between key A on a VI 2' schedule and key B on a VI 1' schedule. Can we be more precise about exactly how the pigeon will allocate its time? One way to determine the pigeon's strategy is simply to let the pigeon peck away for a few minutes, according to its own preference, and then calculate the proportion of time spent on key A versus key B. In fact, given this dilemma, a pigeon will spend about 33% of its time pecking on A and about 67% of its time pecking on B—or about twice the time on B as on A (Herrnstein, 1961). Note that this ratio is identical to the relative rate of reinforcement on the two keys, since B is reinforced twice as often as A. Thus, the pigeon's rate of responding to A versus B roughly matches the rate of reinforcement on A versus B. This is known as the **matching law of choice behavior** (Herrnstein, 1961):

$$\frac{\text{Rate of pecking on A}}{\text{Rate of pecking on B}} = \frac{\text{Rate of VI reinforcement on A}}{\text{Rate of VI reinforcement on B}}$$

The matching law of choice behavior states that an organism's relative rate of responding will (approximately) match the relative rate of reinforcement. Figure 8.7 shows data from one pigeon, tested on a range of possible reinforcement schedules (Herrnstein, 1961). The horizontal axis shows the relative rate of reinforcement on A. If the relative rate of reinforcement on A is 20%, then the relative rate of reinforcement on B is 80%, and B is reinforced four times as often as A; if the relative rate of reinforcement on A is 50%, then the relative rate of reinforcement on B is also 50%; and so on. The matching law predicts that the rate of pecking on A should be approximately equal to the relative rate of reinforcement on A; this behavior would result in the yellow line in Figure 8.7. The pigeon's actual behavior (green line) is quite similar: the rate of pecking on A is approximately equal to the rate of reinforcement on A, for a whole range of possible VI schedules.

Of course, even within a lab experiment, a rat or pigeon has more options than pressing one of two levers: it will spend some of its time eating the food it earns, and it can even take a break and spend some of its time grooming, exploring, or sitting quietly. Nevertheless, as Figure 8.7 illustrates, if the animal is sufficiently motivated (through hunger) to spend most of its time trying to obtain food, then the matching law is a fairly good description of how the animal will allot its time and effort among the responses that result in food.

Behavioral Economics and the Bliss Point

The problem of a pigeon confronted with two keys is the simplest possible example of a choice situation. Outside the laboratory, choices are even more complicated. A college student has to divide her allotted studying time among different classes according to how that studying is likely to pay off best, and she has to divide her total time among studying, sleeping, eating, socializing, and so forth. Farmers have to decide how to distribute their acreage among stable crops that will survive rough weather and higher-risk, higher-payoff specialty crops, in order to maximize expected profit. A dieter who is allowed a fixed number of calories per day must decide whether to eat several low-calorie meals or splurge on a single bowl of ice cream (and then survive on water and lettuce for the rest of the day).

Behavioral economics is the study of how organisms "spend" their time and effort among possible options, and it is parallel to economics, the study of how consumers spend their money. In economics, a worker who makes $1,000 a week after taxes can distribute this income on rent, food, new clothes, trips to the movies, savings, and so on. If she lives in a very expensive apartment, there is less money available for clothes and movies; if she rents a less expensive apartment, she has more money to spend on other things. How does she choose?

Economic theory predicts that each consumer will allocate resources in a way that maximizes her "subjective value" or "satisfaction." (In microeconomics, the word "utility" is used instead of "subjective value.") The allocation of resources that provides maximal subjective value is called the **bliss point** (Allison, 1983; Timberlake, 1980). We determine an individual's bliss point simply by recording what that individual chooses to do. For example, suppose Jamie, a college student, takes a part-time job delivering pizza and makes about $100 a week (after taxes). Assuming that Jamie has no other expenses, he can spend this money on his hobby of collecting DVDs (say, $10 apiece) or going out to dinner (say, $20 at the local restaurant). He can spend the full $100 on ten DVDs, or he can eat out five times—or any other combination that adds up to $100.

Figure 8.8a shows Jamie's possible options. So, given these options, what does Jamie actually do? Most weeks, he eats out twice and buys six DVDs. This point (shown in Figure 8.8a) is Jamie's bliss point—the distribution of expenditures that (apparently) results in maximum subjective value for this individual: he gets plenty of DVDs and gets to eat out frequently. Of course, both the curve and the bliss point can shift if economic conditions change: if the restaurant raises its prices ($50 for dinner), then Jamie may shift to one dinner out and five DVDs per week—resulting in the new bliss point shown in Figure 8.8b.

Animals seem to show similar patterns of compromise between existing options. For example, a pet gerbil in a cage can distribute its time among eating, drinking, sleeping, grooming, and running on the exercise wheel. The amount

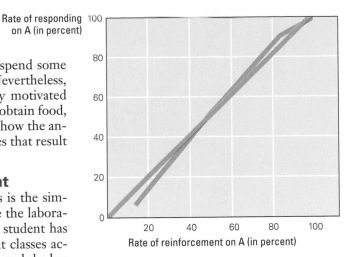

Rate of responding on A (in percent)

Rate of reinforcement on A (in percent)

Figure 8.7 Choice behavior
A pigeon is presented with two keys, A and B, with each key reinforced on a different variable-interval (VI) schedule. The matching law predicts that the rate of responding (pecking) on A versus B should approximately equal the relative rate of reinforcement on A versus B, for a whole range of possible reinforcement schedules (yellow line). The actual behavior of the pigeon (green line) closely approximates this prediction. Adapted from Herrnstein, 1961.

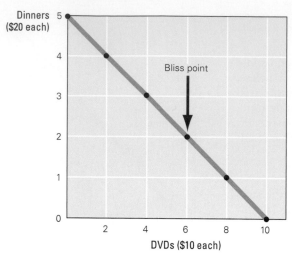

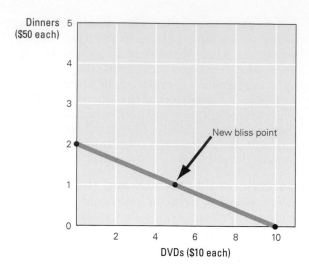

Figure 8.8 Behavioral economics (a) A student with $100 income per week may choose to distribute it between DVDs ($10 apiece) and eating out ($20 per meal); any point on the line will satisfy the budgetary criteria. The bliss point is the point at which this particular student gets maximum subjective value for his money. (b) The bliss point may shift as conditions change—for example, if the cost of eating out increases to $50.

of time it spends on each behavior defines the animal's bliss point. Looked at this way, a naive rat in a Skinner box will spend some amount of time grooming, exploring, sitting quietly—and a very small amount of time pressing the lever. However, after the rat learns that lever pressing results in food (and assuming that the animal is hungry), it will begin to spend more of its time on lever pressing (and eating) and proportionately less on other activities. From the behavioral economics perspective, then, instrumental conditioning is not so much training an organism to execute a novel behavior as causing the organism to shift its allocation of time and energy among existing behaviors.

The Premack Principle: Responses as Reinforcers

One final complication in the study of choice behavior: although organisms do spend a lot of time and effort on responses that result in reinforcers, they also spend a lot of time and effort on behavior that does not produce obvious reinforcement. For example, pet gerbils often run enthusiastically in an exercise wheel, dogs happily chase their own tails for minutes on end, and humans spend hours reading novels, watching television, and listening to music. In none of these cases does the behavior result in a primary reinforcer, such as food, or even an obvious secondary reinforcer, such as money. And yet organisms devote considerable time and resources to these behaviors, at the expense of doing other things such as eating and sleeping. So why do organisms do these things?

This question was explored by David Premack, a student of B. F. Skinner (Premack, 1959, 1961, 1962). Premack gave a group of rats free access to drinking water and a running wheel (Premack, 1959). He recorded their behavior across several minutes. Initially (at baseline), each rat spent some time drinking and some time running, but on average rats spent more time running than drinking: about 250 seconds running and only about 50 seconds drinking. Then, Premack restricted the rats' access to the wheel: they were allowed to run only after they had drunk a certain amount of water. The rats soon learned the contingency and started drinking water in order to gain access to the running wheel. Unsurprisingly, the total amount of running decreased, because the rats now had to work to obtain access to the wheel. But the total amount of drinking increased to more than 100 seconds, as the rats now performed this behavior more often in order to gain access to the wheel. In effect, the activity of running was acting as a reinforcer, and it was increasing the probability of an otherwise infrequent behavior, drinking:

S (running restricted) $\rightarrow$ R (drinking) $\rightarrow$ C (access to wheel)

Premack went on to show a similar pattern in human children (Premack, 1959). He put the children in a room that contained a pinball machine and a bowl of candy, and he recorded how much time each child spent playing pinball and eating candy. Some of the children spent more time playing pinball. Premack then restricted access to the pinball machine, allowing these children to play only after they had eaten some candy. Candy eating increased, showing that access to the preferred activity (pinball) could reinforce the less-preferred activity (candy eating). Conversely, children who preferred eating candy in the first place could be trained to play more pinball, by making access to the candy contingent on playing pinball.

Thus, in both rats and children, the opportunity to perform a highly frequent behavior can reinforce a less-frequent behavior. This idea came to be known as the **Premack principle.** Examples of the Premack principle abound in human life. For example, left to their own devices, most children will spend more time watching television than doing their homework. Thus, watching television is a preferred activity, and it can be used to reinforce the less-preferred activity of homework. The parent restricts television time, making it contingent on homework. As a consequence, the child spends more time doing homework than he would have done if television had not been restricted.

A later extension of the Premack principle, the **response deprivation hypothesis,** suggests that the critical variable is not which response is normally more frequent but merely which response has been restricted: by restricting the ability to execute almost any response, you can make the opportunity to perform that response reinforcing (Allison, 1993; Timberlake & Allison, 1974). For example, perhaps you have a chore, like cleaning your room or doing laundry, that you normally detest. But if access to this activity is restricted, it can become reinforcing. If you have been studying for several hours straight, the idea of "taking a break" to clean your room or do the laundry could begin to look downright attractive. If so, you've experienced the Premack principle at work.

Interim Summary

In instrumental conditioning, organisms learn to make responses in order to obtain or avoid consequences: Stimulus S $\rightarrow$ Response R $\rightarrow$ Consequence C. A consequence that an organism will work to obtain is called a reinforcer; a consequence that an organism will work to avoid is called a punisher. Instrumental conditioning is different from classical conditioning in that the consequence (reinforcement or punishment) occurs only if the organism makes the response. In classical conditioning, by contrast, the unconditioned stimulus (US) occurs whether or not the organism makes a conditioned response (CR).

Schedules of reinforcement define whether the consequence follows every response, or is available only after a fixed or variable number of responses, or is available only after a fixed or variable time interval. The four basic types of instrumental paradigm are positive reinforcement, negative reinforcement, positive punishment, and negative punishment. The words "positive" and "negative" denote whether the consequence is added or subtracted; "reinforcement" and "punishment" denote whether the response increases or decreases as a result of learning.

Behavioral economics is the study of the way in which organisms choose to allocate their time and energy among various behaviors. One rule that governs choices is the Premack principle, which states that the opportunity to perform a highly frequent behavior can reinforce performance of a less-frequent behavior. An extension of the Premack principle, the response deprivation hypothesis, states that any behavior can be reinforcing if the opportunity to perform that behavior is restricted.

8.2 Brain Substrates

You may have noticed by now that there are similarities between instrumental conditioning and skill learning. Priscilla, the pig who learned to eat breakfast at a table and run the vacuum cleaner, acquired a complex skill set. Similarly, Annie, the toilet-training toddler, acquired a skill—namely, bladder control. Instrumental conditioning is merely the way in which Priscilla's handlers and Annie's parents choose to train these skills. Even chess masters and concert pianists practice their skills over and over for the reinforcement of being able to win games and perform flawlessly in concert. For this reason, it should not be surprising that the parts of the brain that are involved in learning motor skills—including the basal ganglia and the motor cortex—play an important role in instrumental conditioning.

The Basal Ganglia and Instrumental Conditioning

Instrumental conditioning involves learning a three-way association between stimulus S, response R, and consequence C. In most cases, R is a voluntary motor response, such as lever pressing by a rat, key pecking by a pigeon, or vacuuming by a pig. Voluntary motor responses arise in the motor cortex, which produces outputs that travel to motor neurons to implement movement responses. The motor cortex receives its primary inputs from cortical areas that process sensory information, such as the visual cortex (V1) and the somatosensory cortex (S1), and also from the frontal cortex. Thus, when you see a book, this visual stimulus is registered by your visual cortex. If you decide to pick up the book, this "decision" is made in your frontal cortex, and signals from both the visual cortex and the frontal cortex travel to motor cortex, which integrates these signals and produces the appropriate instructions, resulting in your picking up the book.

Information from the sensory cortex to the motor cortex can also travel via an indirect route, through the basal ganglia (Figure 8.9). Remember from Chapter 4 that the basal ganglia are a group of structures lying beneath the cortex, including the dorsal striatum and the nearby and highly interconnected **nucleus accumbens.** The basal ganglia receive highly processed stimulus information from sensory cortical areas and project to the motor cortex, which produces a behavioral response. The basal ganglia may be where at least some S-R associations are stored, particularly those in which R is a learned movement.

The basal ganglia play a critical role in instrumental conditioning, particularly if discriminative stimuli are involved. Rats with

Figure 8.9 Basal ganglia The basal ganglia include the dorsal striatum and the nucleus accumbens. Stimulus information is processed in cortical areas such as the visual cortex (V1), somatosensory cortex (S1), and frontal cortex; voluntary responses are generated by the motor cortex (M1). During instrumental conditioning, the basal ganglia may help link associations between the sensory cortex and the motor cortex so that the stimuli can elicit the appropriate motor responses.

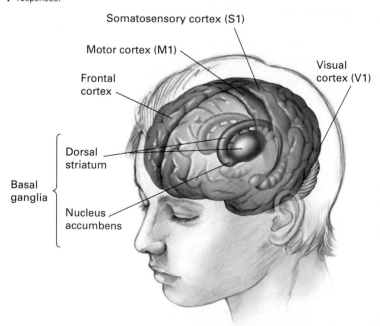

Somatosensory cortex (S1)

Motor cortex (M1)

Frontal cortex

Visual cortex (V1)

Dorsal striatum

Basal ganglia

Nucleus accumbens

lesions of the basal ganglia can learn a simple R-C association (e.g., lever-press to obtain food) as well as control rats. But if discriminative stimuli are added (e.g., lever-press, but only in the presence of a light), then the lesioned rats are markedly impaired (Featherstone & McDonald, 2004). In humans, too, individuals with damage to the basal ganglia due to Parkinson's disease or Huntington's disease show deficits in the ability to associate a stimulus with a correct response (Ashby & Waldron, 2000; Robbins, 1996). In short, the basal ganglia are necessary for learning stimulus–response associations based on feedback about reinforcement and punishment (McDonald & White, 1993).

Mechanisms of Reinforcement in the Brain

Assuming that at least some of the stimulus–response associations of instrumental conditioning are stored in the basal ganglia and in corticocortical connections, this is only part of the puzzle. Remember that instrumental conditioning involves learning a three-way association: Stimulus S → Response R → Consequence C. The basal ganglia can receive information about stimulus S from the sensory cortex, and they can produce output to the motor cortex that drives behavioral response R; but where does the information about consequence C fit in?

Consider the diagram in Figure 8.10. Suppose stimulus S, the sight of a lever, activates neurons in visual cortex, and information travels from there to excite neurons in the motor system (basal ganglia and motor cortex) that can drive behavioral response R, lever pressing. (Obviously, the sound, smell, taste, and texture of the stimulus could excite neurons in other regions of sensory cortex, and the principles would be the same.) Learning occurs if the links between the visual cortex neurons and the motor system neurons are altered (green arrow), changing the probability that future encounters with the same stimulus will evoke the same response. If this connection is strengthened, S is more likely to evoke R; if it is weakened, S is less likely to evoke R.

Let's suppose that response R is reinforced by food delivery. The taste of the food activates brainstem gustatory nuclei, which signal whether the food tastes "good." If it's good, these signals may activate a "reinforcement system" in the brain. It is the activation of this "reinforcement system" that provides the missing

Figure 8.10 Instrumental conditioning in the brain Stimulus S activates neurons in the sensory cortex (e.g., the sight of a lever activates the visual cortex); information travels from here to the motor system, including the basal ganglia and motor cortex; outputs can produce behavioral response R, such as pressing a lever. If the response is reinforced by consequence C, such as food, then eating the food activates the taste system, including gustatory nuclei in the brainstem. Outputs from this taste system, in conjunction with hunger (signaled by the hypothalamus), activate a hypothetical "reinforcement system." Outputs from the reinforcement system travel to the motor system, where they strengthen active associations from the visual cortex (and other areas of sensory cortex). The next time the stimulus is encountered, it is more likely to evoke the same response.

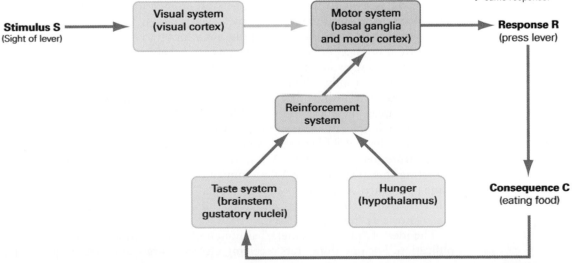

piece of the puzzle and allows strengthening of the S-R link by the usual principle that "neurons that fire together, wire together." Inputs carrying sensory information about the stimulus and reinforcement converge on neurons in the motor system; if the stimulus inputs are active at the same time as the reinforcement inputs, then the ability of the stimulus inputs to activate the motor system is strengthened.

There is still one more piece of the puzzle: motivation. In the case of this example, the consequence food is reinforcing only if the animal is hungry. Hunger and satiety signals may come from the lateral hypothalamus, and only when these signals converge with signals from the taste system will the reinforcement system be activated (Figure 8.10).

Other potential reinforcers, such as water or (for humans) money, will activate the reinforcement system only in the context of corresponding drives. Water will not activate the reinforcement system of an animal that is not thirsty, and money may similarly be of little interest to a man starving in the desert.

Electrical Brain Stimulation

The schematic shown in Figure 8.10 is, of course, highly simplified and could be elaborated in many ways, to include additional kinds of stimuli and additional kinds of reinforcers and punishers. But the basic concept seems to account for many aspects of instrumental conditioning. Yet it leaves open a fundamental question: What is this "reinforcement system," and where is it located in the brain?

In 1954, James Olds was experimenting with delivering electrical stimulation to the rat brain. He inserted an electrode into an area that we now believe to have been the lateral hypothalamus. Olds waited until the rat wandered into one corner of the experimental chamber, and then he applied a brief electrical current. To his surprise, the animal seemed to like it. In fact, after a few minutes of wandering around the chamber, the rat came back to the same corner, where Olds gave it a second stimulation. The rat caught on quickly, and began to hang around that corner of the chamber, apparently hoping for more electrical stimulation (Olds, 1955). Thus, electrical stimulation to this area of the brain seemed to directly activate the reinforcement system of Figure 8.10—eliminating the need for primary reinforcers such as food to strengthen stimulus-response associations.

Olds was intrigued, to say the least. He rigged a Skinner box so that the rats could press a lever to turn on the electrical stimulation. The rats were soon lever-pressing at a furious rate: as many as 700 times an hour (Olds, 1958). If allowed, rats would press the lever continuously for up to 48 hours, until they collapsed from physical exhaustion! Given a choice between electrical stimulation and food, the rats would literally starve themselves, preferring the stimulation (Routtenberg & Lindy, 1965).

Later studies identified that rats would work for electrical stimulation in several brain areas, including most notably the **ventral tegmental area (VTA),** a small region in the brainstem of rats, humans, and other mammals (Figure 8.11). The electrodes in Olds's original studies were probably stimulating hypothalamic neurons that project to the VTA, so that the electrical current was indirectly activating this area. Because VTA stimulation was such a powerful reinforcer, some researchers inferred that the rats "liked" the stimulation, and the VTA and other areas of the brain where electrical stimulation was effective became informally known as "pleasure centers."

The idea of "pleasure centers," although obviously attractive, is an oversimplification. For one thing, rats receiving electrical brain stimulation don't tend

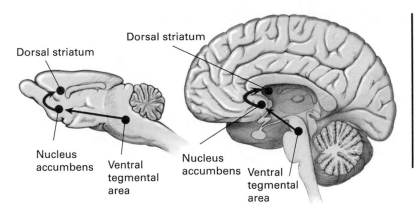

Figure 8.11 Dopamine pathways involved in processing reinforcement Animals lever-press vigorously if responses are reinforced by electrical brain stimulation to the ventral tegmental area, a brainstem region that projects dopamine to the nucleus accumbens, which in turn projects dopamine to the dorsal striatum. The basic pathways are similar in many mammals, including (a) rats and (b) humans.

to act as if they're enjoying it; they tend to become agitated and may bite the lever instead of simply pressing it, or even scratch the walls or show other behaviors such as eating, fighting, or shredding of nesting material. This is more like the behavior of an excited animal than one who is enjoying food. Skinner, of course, would note that we can't infer what an animal might be feeling just by watching its behaviors. Nevertheless, some researchers have suggested that electrical brain stimulation causes not pleasure but rather excitement or anticipation of reinforcement—much like the anticipation we experience when expecting a good meal or a big present (Flynn, 1972).

Some neurons in the VTA project to the nucleus accumbens, which is part of the basal ganglia; these neurons release the neurotransmitter dopamine. In turn, dopaminergic neurons in the nucleus accumbens project to motor areas in the dorsal striatum that can drive motor responses. Rats can learn to lever-press to self-administer direct electrical stimulation of either the VTA or the nucleus accumbens (Olds & Forbes, 1981; Routtenberg & Malsbury, 1969). Conversely, if rats are given drugs that block dopamine signals, these animals no longer work for electrical brain stimulation (Mora, Sanguinetti, Rolls, & Shaw, 1975). This suggests that dopamine is part of the brain's reinforcement system. Dopamine is also produced in brain areas outside the VTA, and it targets many brain regions in addition to the basal ganglia, but the VTA–nucleus accumbens pathway is a good place to start looking at the relationship between dopamine and reinforcement.

Dopamine and Reinforcement

Electrical brain stimulation of dopaminergic neurons in the VTA can provide reinforcement, but what about primary reinforcers such as food or sex—do they also involve the dopaminergic projections from the VTA to the nucleus accumbens?

Recent studies have shown that they do. In rats, dopamine release from the VTA to the nucleus accumbens is triggered by encounters with food, sex, drugs of abuse, and secondary reinforcers. In humans, PET and fMRI studies have shown that presentation of reinforcers such as juice, cocaine, money, humor, and even video games causes heightened activity in dopamine target sites such as the basal ganglia (Berridge & Robinson, 1998; Mobbs, Greicius, Abdel-Azim, Menon, & Reiss, 2003). Even in invertebrates, such as the sea slug *Aplysia*, dopamine is released in conjunction with positive reinforcement during instrumental conditioning (Brembs, 2003; Nargeot, Baxter, Patterson, & Byrne, 1999). In other words, reinforcers trigger dopamine release from the VTA to the nucleus accumbens,

Figure 8.12 Extinction mimicry After training to lever-press for food, healthy rats continue to respond vigorously as long as lever pressing is reinforced with food (control + reinforcement). If food is not delivered (control + no reinforcement), healthy rats gradually stop responding; this is the process of extinction. Rats given the dopamine blocker pimozide gradually stop responding too, even though they are still obtaining food when they lever-press (pimozide + reinforcement); this is extinction mimicry. Data from Wise et al., 1978.

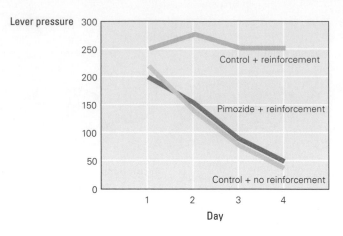

suggesting that the VTA and nucleus accumbens may form part of the reinforcement system shown in Figure 8.10.

Drugs that interfere with dopamine production or transmission reduce responding in a trained animal. For example, in one study, healthy rats were trained to press a lever to obtain food (Wise, Spindler, de Wit, & Gerberg, 1978). After learning this, the rats were split into three groups. For one control group, lever pressing was still reinforced by food; unsurprisingly, these rats kept responding to obtain food (Figure 8.12). For the second control group, lever presses were no longer reinforced; here, as you'd expect, responding gradually extinguished. Rats in the third group were given pimozide, a drug that blocks dopamine receptors, so that dopamine released in the brain cannot activate the neurons it normally targets. For these rats, lever presses were still reinforced, but responding started to extinguish anyway. In fact, responding by the rats receiving pimozide was indistinguishable from that by control rats no longer receiving reinforcement. This effect is called *extinction mimicry*, since the response in pimozide-treated rats seemed to be extinguishing too, even though the animals were still receiving food for their lever presses.

Why might extinction mimicry occur? Three important theories have been proposed to provide an answer.

The simplest explanation of Figure 8.12 might be that the rats given pimozide simply stopped liking the taste of food. The **anhedonia hypothesis,** originally proposed by Roy Wise, suggests that dopamine gives food its "goodness," or hedonic qualities; dopamine-blocking drugs take away the "goodness," reducing organisms' incentive to work for food (Wise, 1982, 2002). (The word "anhedonia" means "without pleasure.") In simplest terms, dopamine-blocking drugs such as pimozide block the link from the taste system to the reinforcement system shown in Figure 8.10.

The anhedonia hypothesis explains the extinction mimicry shown in Figure 8.12 in the following way. Before the pimozide was administered, the food tasted "good" and was worth more than 200 lever presses an hour. After the drug was administered, the food stopped tasting "good," and the rats gradually stopped bothering to work for it. Note that the drugged rats were still physically capable of pressing the lever; the pimozide did not prevent them from making the motor responses—it merely reduced their motivation to do so (Fouriezos & Wise, 1976; Gallistel, Boytim, Gomita, & Klebanoff, 1982).

The anhedonia hypothesis quickly gained widespread acceptance, and dopamine became known in the media as the "brain's pleasure chemical": just a little squirt, and you'll feel pleasure. However, more recent evidence suggests that dopamine does not directly manipulate hedonia. For example, Parkinson's disease damages dopamine-producing neurons in the basal ganglia, causing reduced levels of dopamine in the brain. The anhedonia hypothesis predicts that patients with Parkinson's disease should therefore have reduced hedonia: good things should taste less good, and so on. But when Parkinson's patients are asked to rate the perceived pleasantness of sweet and salty tastes, their ratings are the same as those of healthy people. Apparently, people with Parkinson's suffer no loss of ability to "like" pleasurable stimuli (Travers et al., 1993).

Researchers can also infer degree of liking in nonhuman animals, by watching the animals' reaction to various tastes. When a sweet substance is placed in a rat's mouth, the animal shows a recognizable cluster of responses that include rhythmic movements of the mouth and protrusion of the tongue. This is sometimes called the hedonic or "yum" reaction. A bitter taste elicits a different cluster: gapes, shakes of the head, and wiping of the face with paws (the aversive or "ugh" reaction). By watching the rat's reaction, researchers can try to infer whether the animal likes or dislikes the taste of the food. Similar "yum" and "ugh" reactions can be seen in monkeys and in human infants as early as the day of birth, suggesting the response patterns are hardwired into the brains of mammals (Berridge & Robinson, 1998).

Rats given injections of a drug (called 6–OHDA) that destroys dopaminergic neurons in the basal ganglia exhibit hedonic and aversive responses that are just as strong as or stronger than those of control rats (Berridge & Robinson, 1998). This suggests that rats with damaged dopamine systems continue to "like" and "dislike" food just as much as control rats do. Apparently, reduced hedonic value is not enough to explain how dopaminergic drugs disrupt learning. What, then, could explain the data in Figure 8.12? Some researchers have suggested that the role of dopamine in instrumental conditioning has less to do with how much you "like" a hedonic stimulus and more to do with how much you "want" it—how motivated you are to work for it. The **incentive salience hypothesis** states that dopamine helps provide organisms with the motivation to work for reinforcement. This means that the incentive salience of food and other reinforcers—their ability to attract attention and motivate work—is reduced in dopamine-depleted animals (Berridge, 1996; Berridge & Robinson, 1998). Given a choice between competing alternatives, normal animals will tend to choose a preferred reinforcer, even at the cost of a little extra work. Without dopamine, animals are still perfectly willing to eat a preferred food if it is placed in front of them, but they are unwilling to work hard to earn it (Salamone et al., 2002). Under this hypothesis, the pimozide-drugged rats (Figure 8.12) still "liked" the food they earned, they were just increasingly unmotivated to work for it by lever pressing.

In effect, rats with dopamine depletion become lazy. A good example of this is seen in experiments where rats can choose to work for food. For example, most healthy rats prefer sugar pellets to rat chow, and they will work for the pellets by lever pressing, even if chow is freely available (Figure 8.13). Rats with disruption of dopamine in the nucleus accumbens also prefer sugar to rat chow, if both are freely available. But if they have to work for the sugar pellets, they mostly settle for the free chow rather than bother with lever pressing for the pellets (Salamone, Arizzi, Sandoval, Cervone, & Aberman, 2002; see also Koch, Schmid, & Schnitzler, 2000; Salamone, et al., 1991). You can think of this as an inversion of the Protestant ethic effect: animals with normal dopamine levels prefer to work to obtain their food; animals with reduced dopamine prefer not to work, even if this results in inferior food.

Figure 8.13 Dopamine and the Protestant ethic effect
Dopamine depletion makes rats less willing to work for a preferred reinforcer. If rat chow is freely available, but sugar pellets have to be "earned" by pressing a lever, healthy rats will spend most of their time working for sugar pellets and eating relatively little free chow. Rats with dopamine disruption (DA) are much less willing than healthy rats to work for the sugar pellets, and instead settle for eating the freely available chow. Adapted from Salamone et al., 2002.

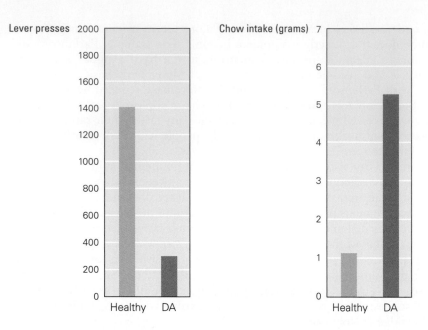

Dopamine seems to affect incentive salience in humans, too. So, for example, the drug amphetamine can produce pleasurable feelings in humans; these pleasurable feelings are not altered if the human is also given the dopamine-blocker pimozide (Brauer & de Wit, 1996, 1997). But pimozide does suppress cravings for the amphetamine high. In other words, interfering with the dopamine system reduces "wanting" but not "liking" of amphetamine.

Increasing brain dopamine levels, on the other hand, can increase craving. For example, human volunteers can be trained to perform an operant task for cocaine reinforcement; when the volunteers are given the drug pergolide, which increases brain dopamine levels, they report an increased craving for cocaine, but no increase in the self-reported "high" from cocaine (Haney, Foltin, & Fischman, 1998). Thus, stimulating the dopamine system increases "wanting" but not "liking" of cocaine.

One novel prediction of the incentive salience hypothesis is that dopamine release should be highest when "wanting" is strongest—just before reinforcement is delivered; and it should drop off when "wanting" is weakest—just after a reinforcement is delivered. In fact, this seems to be the case. In rats trained to lever-press for sucrose, dopamine levels in the VTA are highest just before the sucrose is delivered, and then drop off when the sucrose is actually in the mouth—even though, presumably, pleasure is highest at this point (Kosobud, Harris, & Chapin, 1994). Note that the anhedonia hypothesis would have predicted exactly the opposite result: that dopamine release would be highest at the point where the hedonic stimulus is actually delivered.

The same pattern was seen in rats trained to press a lever to self-administer a shot of heroin. Generally, the rats pressed the lever every 20 minutes or so. Meanwhile, researchers recorded dopamine levels in the nucleus accumbens. Dopamine levels rose as the time of expected heroin administration neared and dropped off sharply thereafter, only to rise slowly until the next administration (Kiyatkin, 2002). Again, this pattern is consistent with the predictions of the incentive salience hypothesis, but not with the anhedonia hypothesis.

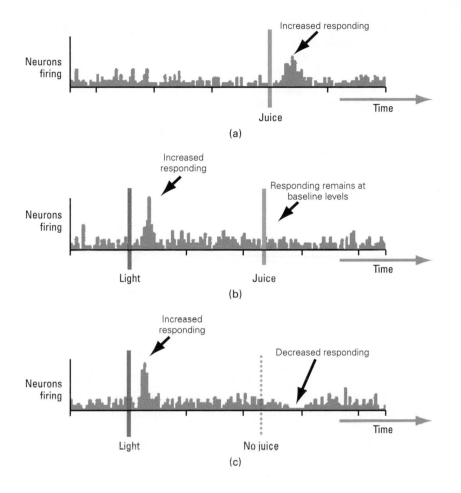

Figure 8.14 Dopamine levels and reward prediction
(a) In untrained monkeys, an unexpected treat of juice causes a brief increase in the firing rate of dopaminergic neurons. (b) If juice is signaled by a light, dopaminergic neurons fire in response to the light but not in response to the juice itself. In effect, the dopaminergic neurons signal that reinforcement is predicted to arrive soon. (c) If juice is predicted by the light but then fails to arrive, the dopaminergic neurons show an increase of firing in response to the light, followed by decreased firing at the time the juice was expected to arrive. Adapted from Schultz, 2002.

A third hypothesis about dopamine function is the **reward prediction hypothesis,** which posits that dopamine is involved in predicting future reward (Hollerman & Schultz, 1998; Schultz & Dickinson, 2000). The key data supporting this hypothesis come from studies recording the firing rate of dopaminergic neurons in the ventral tegmental area of monkeys (Schultz, 1998). These dopamine neurons usually show a steady, low rate of responding, but if a drop of juice is delivered to the monkey's mouth, the dopaminergic neurons exhibit a brief burst of activity (Figure 8.14a). In effect, they are signaling that an unexpected reinforcement has arrived.

The monkey is then trained to press a lever when a light comes on to obtain the juice:

S (light) → R (press lever) → C (juice)

Before the monkey was trained, the dopaminergic neurons didn't respond much to the light, but they did respond strongly to the juice (as shown in Figure 8.14a). But after training, the pattern changed: the dopamine neurons responded to the light but not to the juice itself (Figure 8.14b). Thus, the dopamine response can be modified by learning. In effect, dopaminergic neurons signal that reinforcement is predicted soon, but they don't respond to the reinforcement itself if that reinforcement has already been predicted. If the light comes on but the juice fails to materialize, the dopaminergic neurons decrease their firing rate (Figure 8.14c). In effect, the dopaminergic neurons are now signaling that the predicted reinforcement has been omitted (Schultz, 1998). Similar effects appear in humans: the dorsal striatum (a target of dopamine from the VTA) shows increased activity on fMRI when juice is expected, and decreased activity if a predicted juice reinforcement fails to materialize (O'Doherty, Dayan, Friston, Critchlet, & Dolan, 2003).

In summary, the dopaminergic neurons don't simply respond to reinforcement; instead, they seem to be signaling information about whether reinforcement is predicted (Figure 8.15b), or arrives as a surprise (Figure 8.15a), or is predicted and then omitted (Figure 8.15c).

The reward prediction hypothesis and incentive salience hypothesis are similar in spirit: the first focuses on "prediction" or "expectation" of reinforcement, the second on "wanting" of reinforcement. In many cases, it seems reasonable that the two processes are related. At this point, it remains an open question as to which of these two theories is a better description of how the dopamine system operates during reinforcement learning or whether they describe different subsets of the many dopamine pathways in the brain.

Currently, most research on the role of dopamine in instrumental conditioning has focused on the interaction between dopamine release and primary reinforcers, such as food, juice, or sex. It was originally thought that dopamine's role was limited to these reinforcement situations. But now there is emerging evidence that dopaminergic neurons also respond to secondary reinforcers, such as money (Knutson, Fong, Adams, Varner, & Hommer, 2001), and even to punishers, such as shock (Berridge & Robinson, 1998). It is not yet clear, though, whether the role of dopamine in learning about punishers is the same as its role in learning about reinforcers, or whether different brain systems and mechanisms are involved.

There is also the open question of exactly how dopamine works to strengthen stimulus–response associations during learning. Dopamine does generally encourage synaptic plasticity, and so it may be that the presence of dopamine at the time other neurons are firing simply increases the chance of associations being formed between those neurons. However, the effects of dopamine on neurons are notoriously variable and complicated, and a great deal remains to be understood about this neurotransmitter and its role in learning.

Opioids and Hedonic Value

If, as the above studies suggest, dopamine is involved in "wanting" reinforcement, what brain systems might be involved in evaluating how much an organism "likes" reinforcement? In other words, what signals the hedonic value of a stimulus?

Probably the best-studied candidate is the opioid system. Opiate receptors in the brain were discovered quite by accident, as researchers tried to figure out how heroin and morphine work. Heroin and morphine belong to a class of drugs called *opiates*, which bind to a special class of neuronal receptors, the *opiate receptors*. Rather than assume that the brain evolved special receptors to respond to the plant products heroin and morphine, researchers suspected there might be naturally occurring brain chemicals that also activate the opiate receptors. They found a class of brain chemicals, called the **endogenous opioids**, that are naturally occurring neurotransmitter-like substances (peptides) with many of the same effects as opiate drugs. (The word "endogenous" means "originating on the inside"; "opioid" means "opiate-like.") Endogenous opioids are distributed through the central nervous system, and when released into the body they have a wide range of effects, including lessening the normal perception of pain and producing feelings of euphoria.

The first endogenous opioids were identified as recently as the 1970s, and there is still a great deal we don't know. But many researchers believe that endogenous opioids may mediate hedonic value—the "liking" part of reinforcement. Viewed this way, the reason that heroin and morphine are so intensely pleasurable is that they happen to activate the same brain receptors as the endogenous opioids.

For example, opiate drugs can increase the hedonic impact (tastiness) of food in humans and animals. Morphine makes sweet food taste sweeter and bitter food taste less bitter (Rideout & Parker, 1996; see also Berridge, 1996). It can also make pain feel less painful; morphine is used medically for patients who are enduring extreme, long-term pain—for whom the benefits of relieving suffering outweigh the risks of morphine addiction. These patients usually report that they still feel the pain, but it doesn't trouble them as much as it did before.

How do endogenous opioids and dopamine interact? The answer is not yet clear. One possibility is that some endogenous opioids may modulate dopamine release. For example, dopaminergic neurons in the VTA have opiate receptors on their dendrites that, when activated, could affect the neurons' normal tendency to release dopamine. In this way, the endogenous opioids would signal "liking," which in turn would affect the VTA's ability to signal information about "wanting." Some drugs, including heroin, may manipulate both "liking" and "wanting": activating the endogenous opioid system to produce a pleasurable high and activating the dopamine system to produce a craving for more of the drug and the high.

Interim Summary

Stimulus–response associations may be stored in direct corticocortical connections or indirectly via the basal ganglia. Some reinforcers may activate neurons in the ventral tegmental area, which project dopamine to the basal ganglia and elsewhere. Interrupting this pathway, by lesions or drugs, disrupts instrumental conditioning.

Dopamine plays a key role in signaling reinforcement during instrumental conditioning, but the specifics of this role remain a matter of debate. The anhedonia hypothesis suggests that, in the brain, dopamine signals reinforcement—how much an organism "likes" a reinforcement and thus how motivated an organism will be to work for that reinforcement. The incentive salience hypothesis suggests that dopamine modulates "wanting" rather than "liking," determining how hard an organism is willing to work for a reinforcement. The reward prediction hypothesis suggests that dopamine signals when reinforcement is expected, rather than signaling when it is experienced.

Other neurotransmitters that play a key role in instrumental conditioning are the endogenous opioids, which are mimicked by many highly addictive drugs. Endogenous opioids may signal the hedonic value ("goodness") of reinforcers and punishers such as food and pain.

8.3 Clinical Perspectives

The brain's reinforcement system ensures that animals are hardwired to seek and obtain the things they need for survival (food, water, sleep, etc.) and to avoid those things that threaten survival (pain, sickness, predators, etc.). The pleasure that we feel when we eat fatty food ensures that we are sufficiently motivated to repeat the experience. The human brain evolved millennia ago, when our ancestors had to forage for food and could never be sure when they'd find their next meal. Fat could be stored in the body and used for energy later, when food was scarce. Under these conditions, seeking out fatty foods was a good strategy for survival. In twenty-first-century America, food is comparatively easy to obtain, but our biological drives remain and many of us—still driven to obtain the taste of fatty foods—have become dangerously overweight. This is one way in which the brain's powerful reinforcement system can go awry.

Drugs represent another way in which the reinforcement system can malfunction (or, rather, function only too well). You read in chapter 7 how classical conditioning can contribute to drug addiction. Yet another piece of the puzzle is instrumental conditioning: learned responding to obtain a particular kind of reinforcement. Insights from instrumental conditioning theory may help us to understand this component of addiction and to develop more effective treatments.

Drug Addiction

We all know people who are "addicted" to their morning cup of coffee, their afternoon chocolate bar, or even their favorite television show. Such people experience intense cravings for the addictive substance between uses and may experience withdrawal symptoms if the addictive substance is taken away. Someone who is addicted to her morning coffee may show signs of withdrawal (crankiness, sleepiness, headaches, difficulty paying attention) if she goes without. However, in most cases, such everyday addictions are not serious enough to interfere with our lives or our health.

Medically, **pathological addiction** is defined as a strong habit (or compulsion) that is maintained despite harmful consequences (Berke, 2003; Leshner, 1999; McLellan, Lewis, O'Brien, & Kleber, 2000). The difference between pathological addiction and simple habit is largely one of degree. A coffee drinker may be sleepy or cranky until she gets her morning caffeine, and she may have trouble kicking the habit, but this would not usually be considered a pathological addiction unless she drank enough coffee to cause harmful medical consequences or to interfere with her normal life (for example, if she failed to pay the rent because she's spending all her income at Starbucks).

By contrast, a person is diagnosed as pathologically addicted to cocaine if he is unable to quit, shows withdrawal symptoms between highs, and is obsessed with obtaining his next hit of the drug, to the point where he starts neglecting other aspects of his life—such as his family and his job—because nothing else is as important to him as cocaine. Alcohol can drive pathological addiction in the same way: an alcoholic may be unable to give up drinking, even though it has cost him his job and his family. A rat that starves itself because it won't stop lever pressing for electrical brain stimulation could also be considered pathologically addicted to the stimulation.

Remember the college student Jamie who had to choose how to allocate his resources between eating out and buying DVDs (see Figure 8.8)? We can think of a person with addiction as having a similar choice to allocate resources (time, money, effort) among all possible behaviors—and increasingly choosing the addictive substance at the expense of all other options.

Many individuals with pathological addictions want to quit, and they try very hard to overcome their addictions. Unfortunately, there are several processes working against them. Addiction may involve not only seeking the "high" but also avoiding the adverse effects of withdrawal from the drug. In a sense, the "high" provides a positive reinforcement to keep taking the drug, and the avoid-

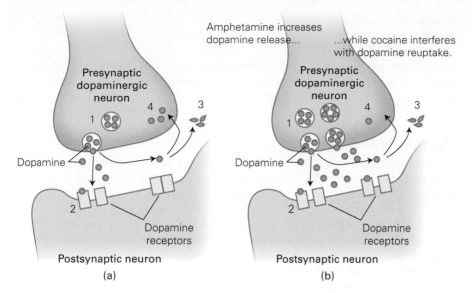

Amphetamine increases dopamine release...

...while cocaine interferes with dopamine reuptake.

Figure 8.15 The effects of amphetamine and cocaine on dopaminergic neurons (a) A presynaptic dopamine-producing neuron releases dopamine into the synapse (1). These molecules activate dopamine receptors on the postsynaptic neuron (2). Any unused molecules are either broken down (3) or taken back into the presynaptic neuron through the process of reuptake (4). (b) Amphetamine works by causing dopaminergic neurons to make and release more dopamine (1). Cocaine works by blocking the reuptake of unused dopamine molecules (4). Both drugs thus increase the amount of dopamine in the synapse, increasing the chance that dopamine molecules will activate receptors on the postsynaptic neuron (2).

ance of withdrawal symptoms provides a negative reinforcement—and both processes combine to reinforce the drug-taking responses.

Many highly addictive drugs are opiates, meaning that they target opiate receptors in the nucleus accumbens and VTA, as well as other brain areas. As you already know, heroin and morphine are two examples of opiate drugs. Other commonly abused drugs, including amphetamines and cocaine, work by increasing brain dopamine levels. Recall from Chapter 2 that neurons communicate when the presynaptic neuron releases molecules of a neurotransmitter into the synapse, and these neurotransmitter molecules activate receptors on the postsynaptic neuron (Figure 8.15a). Amphetamine causes dopaminergic neurons to release higher levels of dopamine. Cocaine works by blocking dopamine reuptake, so dopamine remains in the synapse longer before being broken down and reabsorbed. In both cases, the end effect of the drug is to increase the amount of dopamine available to activate the postsynaptic neuron (Figure 8.15b). Both amphetamine and cocaine can be used as reinforcers. Animals will lever-press vigorously for injections of amphetamine into the nucleus accumbens, which is full of dopamine-producing neurons. Cocaine is most effective as a reinforcer when injected into frontal cortex or other areas where dopamine-producing neurons terminate (Bardo, 1998).

One interesting thing about cocaine and amphetamine is that, although "liking" seems to be critical in the early stages of drug use, people with long-term addictions often report that they no longer gain an appreciable high from the drug, but crave it anyway—as if their "wanting" system has disconnected from their "liking" system and has run amok. In fact, individuals who have taken a dose of cocaine or amphetamine don't typically report feeling happy or pleasured—they feel aroused or excited. These facts fit nicely with the incentive salience hypothesis of reinforcement, which proposes that dopamine is involved in "wanting" but not necessarily in "liking."

In summary, drug addiction results from several factors, including positive reinforcement (the pleasurable high), negative reinforcement (avoiding withdrawal), malfunction of the dopaminergic "wanting" system in the nucleus accumbens (the craving), and physiological changes in the synapse, requiring ever-larger doses of drug to get the same effect (Di Chiara, 2000). Of course, the relative role of each of these factors varies unpredictably across individuals, as a function of genetics, personality, and experience. Some people become strongly addicted to drugs after a single use, some become addicted over time, and a very few individuals can use drugs over a long period without developing pathological addictions. As yet there is no way to predict what will happen to a particular individual who starts using a particular drug, or how difficult it will be for that individual to kick the habit.

Behavioral Addiction

Most researchers think that heroin and cocaine work because they contain chemicals that interact with the brain's reinforcement system; drug addiction occurs when an individual pursues the drug relentlessly, driven by both a craving for the high and a desire to avoid painful withdrawal. For some people, behaviors such as skydiving or winning at gambling can provide highs that are just as reinforcing as drugs—and just as addicting. **Behavioral addictions** are addictions to behaviors, rather than drugs, that produce reinforcements or highs, as well as cravings and withdrawal symptoms when the behavior is prevented.

Perhaps the most widely accepted example of a behavioral addiction is compulsive gambling. Many people gamble occasionally, buying a weekly lottery ticket, playing online poker once in a while, or going on occasional weekend trips to Las Vegas or Atlantic City. These people pay their money, have their fun, and then walk away. But other people get hooked: they start to gamble more and more often, risking progressively larger sums of money, until nothing is as important as the chance to gamble. Up to about 1.6% of the general population may suffer from compulsive gambling in their lifetime, and the problem may be even more widespread in particular groups, such as African Americans and college students (Potenza, Kosten, & Rounsaville, 2001).

Skinner suggested that one reason gambling is so seductive is that it is often reinforced on a VR schedule: you can never be sure when the next big payoff will come, which makes it easy to talk yourself into playing just one more time, then just one more time . . . (Skinner, 1953). Each big win provides a powerful reinforcement of the gambling behavior, and this more than compensates for the small losses experienced between wins.

Gambling is not the only behavior that can affect the brain's reinforcement system and become addictive. Other behavioral addictions include compulsive eating, sex addiction, kleptomania, compulsive shopping—the list goes on and on. In each of these cases, the addicted person experiences a high, followed by craving for another high, and withdrawal symptoms if the behavior is prevented.

For some, gambling is an occasional, harmless pastime. For others, it can develop into a pathological addiction.

Everynight Images/Alamy

It increasingly seems that these behavioral addictions may reflect dysfunction in the same brain substrates affected by drug addictions. Modern research using fMRI has documented that gambling activates the nucleus accumbens (Breiter, Aharon, Kahneman, Dale, & Shizgal, 2001), and this pattern of brain activation is very similar to the pattern seen in people with cocaine addiction who receive an infusion of the drug (Breiter et al., 1997). These results suggest there is a general reinforcement system in the brain, like the one illustrated in Figure 8.10, and that this reinforcement system is activated in a similar way for different categories of reinforcers, including primary reinforcers (food), secondary reinforcers (money), behaviors (gambling), and drugs (cocaine) (Breiter et al., 2001). If so, a better understanding of the biochemical and behavioral principles underlying drug addiction may also help in the treatment of individuals suffering from behavioral addictions.

Treatments

Until fairly recently, addiction was generally considered to be a character flaw: all a person had to do was display enough willpower to stay away from the addictive substance (whether a crack pipe, a gambling table, or a pack of cigarettes). However, given that these addictions all cause intense cravings, not to mention the often excruciating physical pain of withdrawal, it is perhaps not surprising that many people with addictions can't manage to kick their habits without outside help.

Currently, in the United States, the vast majority of treatment for addiction includes cognitive therapy, often centered around self-help sessions with a support group (such as Alcoholics Anonymous and its many spin-off organizations—Gamblers Anonymous, Narcotics Anonymous, Overeaters Anonymous, and so on). Medical treatment may also help. For example, naltrexone is a drug that blocks opiate receptors, presumably decreasing the ability of heroin to bind to those receptors and cause a hedonic reaction. In some studies, people with heroin addiction who had undergone detoxification were able to stay off heroin longer if they received continuing treatment that included naltrexone (Kirchmayer et al., 2002; Rawson & Tennant, 1984). Some preliminary evidence also suggests that compulsive gamblers may experience reductions in gambling urges following naltrexone treatment (Kim, 2001). These studies generally take place over a short period (typically a few weeks or months), and it is not yet clear whether naltrexone's effects will hold over the long term or if patients relapse once treatment is discontinued.

The behavioral principles of instrumental conditioning suggest some other therapies to help fight addiction. These behavioral therapies can be useful for people who have bad habits (such as nail biting or cigarette smoking) as well as for people with pathological addictions (compulsive gambling or heroin use). Consider addiction as a strong S-R-C association, with some set of environmental stimuli (S) that triggers the addictive behavior (R), resulting in the reinforcing consequence (C) of a high and/or a reduced craving. When we look at it this way, the challenge is to break or reduce the strength of the conditioned association. Perhaps the most obvious approach is simple *extinction:* if response R stops producing consequence C, the frequency of R should decline. This is one way of interpreting the effectiveness of medical therapies for addiction: once the brain's reinforcement system is blocked, subsequent heroin (or gambling) doesn't produce the strong consequence that it used to, so the response (drug taking or gambling) should decline.

Another conditioning-inspired method for combating addictions and habits is *distancing:* avoiding the stimuli that trigger the unwanted response. For example, a cigarette smoker who gets the urge to light up whenever she visits a bar, or hangs out with friends who are heavy smokers, should try to avoid those situations. If the S is never present, the R may never be triggered.

A third method is *reinforcement of alternate behaviors*. If the smoker makes it through a whole week without a cigarette, she can reinforce her own behavior: treating herself to a favorite food or activity. Friends can also provide reinforcement, if they praise the nonsmoking behavior (one aspect of Alcoholics Anonymous is the social reinforcement provided by the group for each week the alcoholic stays sober). Some programs for heroin addicts reinforce abstinence with actual monetary vouchers, providing yet another form of reinforcement for the alternative behavior of not using the drug (Preston, Umbricht, & Epstein, 2000). Positive reinforcement of alternative behaviors can also be viewed as negative punishment of the unwanted behavior: if the smoker does give in and light a cigarette, she punishes herself by removing access to the ice cream or trip to the movies she had promised herself.

A final conditioning-inspired technique is *delayed reinforcement:* whenever the smoker gets the urge to light up, she can impose a fixed delay (e.g., an hour) before giving in to it. Recall that increasing the delay between response and consequence weakens learning of the R-C association (Figure 8.5). Imposing long delays between cravings and cigarettes may similarly weaken the association and will also, by default, reduce the total number of cigarettes smoked per day.

These and other behavioral approaches can be used in combination, increasing the chances of success. But even with all these behavioral therapies, addicted cigarette smokers (and nail biters and alcoholics and drug users and gamblers) can still have a very hard time kicking their habits. Currently, the most successful approach often combines cognitive therapy (including counseling and support groups) with behavioral therapy based on conditioning principles—and medication for the most extreme cases (Legg & Gotestam, 1991).

CONCLUSION

Remember Priscilla the Fastidious Pig? Her trainers taught her to turn on the radio, eat breakfast at a table, put away dirty clothes, and run a vacuum cleaner. They did this using the basic principles of instrumental conditioning: they started by shaping one element of the routine, reinforcing the response with a bit of food each time the animal approximated a desired behavior, and then chaining the various elements of the routine together. The same general principles applied to Annie the toilet-training toddler: her parents shaped the desired response (urination on the potty), reinforcing this behavior by verbal praise and punishing alternate responses with scolding.

Instrumental conditioning is a powerful form of learning that can be applied to adult humans as well as infants and pets. You can even use it on yourself, if you want to break a habit or reinforce good study habits. And the applications have been implicitly appreciated at least since the time of the ancient Greeks; in Aristophanes' play *Lysistrata*, the women of Athens agree to withhold sexual favors from their men until the men call off a frivolous war with Sparta—a clear example of negative punishment.

"Oh, not bad. The light comes on, I press a bar, they write me a check. How about you?"

S-R-C associations may be stored in corticocortical connections (and indirectly via connections with basal ganglia). The brain also seems to have a general-purpose reinforcement system—including the VTA dopaminergic system—that helps strengthen the S-R connection. Many kinds of addiction, including drug addictions and behavioral addictions, may result when chemicals or behaviors alter this reinforcement system; behavioral therapy for addiction is a clear application of instrumental conditioning procedures to help improve people's lives. Instrumental conditioning also forms the basis for behavioral economics, the study of how individuals allocate their time and energy among different available responses.

The bottom line: instrumental conditioning isn't just for circus animals. People use many instrumental conditioning techniques in daily life without even realizing it. By understanding the underlying principles, you can use them much more effectively.

Key Points

- Instrumental conditioning involves learning a three-way association (S → R → C) between discriminative stimulus S, response R, and consequence C, which may be a reinforcer or a punisher. In instrumental conditioning, consequence C occurs only if response R is made; by contrast, in classical conditioning, the consequence (US) occurs automatically after the stimulus (CS).

- Four basic classes of instrumental conditioning are positive reinforcement, negative reinforcement, positive punishment, and negative punishment. "Negative" and "positive" denote whether the consequence is subtracted or added; "reinforcement" and "punishment" denote whether the response increases or decreases as a result of learning.

- Operant conditioning is a subclass of instrumental conditioning in which the organism may respond at its own rate. Complex responses may be trained by shaping (reinforcement of progressive approximations) and chaining (training a sequence of responses, one step at a time).

- Drive reduction theory states that learning is driven by an organism's need or drive to obtain primary reinforcers such as food and sex. However, organisms will also work to obtain secondary reinforcers such as money or social approval. Even responses can be reinforcing; the Premack principle states that the opportunity to perform a preferred behavior can be used to reinforce a less-preferred behavior.

- Behavioral economics describes how organisms allocate time and resources among available options. The matching law of choice behavior states that the rate of responding to each alternative approximately equals the rate of reinforcement available for each alternative.

- In the brain, instrumental S-R-C associations may be stored in corticocortical connections and via the basal ganglia.

- The brain's reinforcement system may include release of dopamine from the ventral tegmental area to the basal ganglia. Drugs that interfere with the dopamine system disrupt instrumental conditioning.

- There are several hypotheses on the interaction of dopamine and reinforcement. The anhedonia hypothesis suggests that dopamine gives reinforcers their "goodness." The incentive salience hypothesis suggests that dopamine modulates "wanting" rather than "liking"—that is, modulates how hard an organism is willing to work for a reinforcement. The reward prediction hypothesis suggests that dopamine signals whether reinforcement is expected.

- Whereas dopamine may be involved in "wanting," the endogenous opioids may be involved in "liking." Drugs that affect brain opiate receptors affect the hedonic ("goodness") value of primary reinforcers and punishers such as food and pain.

- Addictive drugs (heroin, caffeine, etc.) may hijack the brain's reinforcement system. There may be psychological as well as physiological addiction. Behavioral addictions may reflect the same brain processes as drug addictions. Treatment for people with addictions may include cognitive therapy, medication, and behavioral therapy, including principles learned from instrumental conditioning.

Key Terms

anhedonia hypothesis, p. 322
behavioral addiction, p. 330
behavioral economics, p. 315
bliss point, p. 315
chaining, p. 300
continuous reinforcement, p. 310
cumulative recorder, p. 297
discrete trial, p. 295
discriminative stimuli, p. 298
drive reduction theory, p. 301
endogenous opioids, p. 326

fixed-interval (FI) schedule, p. 311
fixed-ratio (FR) schedule, p. 310
free-operant paradigm, p. 297
incentive salience hypothesis, p. 323
instrumental conditioning, p. 293
matching law of choice behavior, p. 314
negative punishment, p. 308
negative reinforcement, p. 307
nucleus accumbens, p. 318

pathological addiction, p. 328
positive punishment, p. 307
positive reinforcement, p. 307
postreinforcement pause, p. 310
Premack principle, p. 317
primary reinforcer, p. 301
punisher, p. 302
punishment, p. 297
reinforcement, p. 297
reinforcement schedule, p. 310
reinforcer, p. 301
response deprivation hypothesis, p. 317

reward prediction hypothesis, p. 325
secondary reinforcer, p. 301
self-control, p. 307
shaping, p. 299
Skinner box, p. 296
superstition, p. 306
variable-interval (VI) schedule, p. 312
variable-ratio (VR) schedule, p. 312
ventral tegmental area (VTA), p. 320

Concept Check

1. A new kindergarten teacher wants to train her pupils to put away toys after playtime. Suggest three conditioning techniques she could use to train this behavior.

2. An employer wants to start testing her employees for drugs. According to the principles of conditioning, what would be the best way to schedule these drug tests (assuming the employer wants to use the threat of tests to encourage employees to avoid drug use)?

3. Some researchers believe that organisms are biased to engage in behaviors that allow them to "control" their environment. How could this idea explain superstitious behavior? How could it explain the Protestant ethic effect?

4. According to the reward prediction hypothesis, dopamine is involved in predicting future reward, and dopaminergic neurons fire most strongly in response to an unpredicted reward. Why might humor activate dopaminergic neurons?

5. Imagine that the police raid a house party and find the crowd taking an unfamiliar kind of drug. The users are sitting in front of a TV enthusiastically munching on stale bread and laughing hysterically at an old sitcom. Even without submitting samples of the drug to a laboratory, what might we hypothesize about the mechanisms by which this drug works?

Answers to Test Your Knowledge

Reinforcement and Punishment?

1. (a) Lucy; (b) S is seeing candy (or going shopping with mother); (c) R is tantrum; (d) C is obtaining candy; (e) candy is added—so this is "positive"; (f) response increases—so this is a reinforcement paradigm. *Conclusion:* Lucy learns to throw tantrums to obtain candy. This is positive reinforcement.

2. (a) Susan; (b) S is her child's tantrum; (c) R is giving candy; (d) C is the tantrum stops (or is avoided altogether); (e) the tantrum is taken away—so this is "negative"; (f) response increases—so this is a reinforcement paradigm. *Conclusion:* Susan learns to give her child candy

to stop (or avoid) tantrums. This is negative reinforcement.

3. (a) Snoopy; (b) S is being in the yard; (c) R is crossing the boundary; (d) C is the noise; (e) the noise is added—so this is "positive"; (f) response decreases—so this is a punishment paradigm. *Conclusion:* Snoopy learns to stay inside the yard. This is positive punishment.

4. (a) Miguel; (b) S is a rough tackle; (c) R is starting a fistfight; (d) C is playing privileges taken away; (e) playing privileges are taken away—so this is "negative"; (f) response decreases—so this is a punishment paradigm. *Conclusion:* Miguel learns not to fight. This is negative punishment.

Further Reading

Bjork, D. (1983). *B. F. Skinner: a life.* New York: Basic Books. • A personal view of B. F. Skinner, inventor of the Skinner box and "father" of behaviorism, who almost single-handedly launched the field of operant conditioning. One of the most interesting facets of Skinner's work is the idea that the principles of instrumental conditioning could help us understand—and control—"higher" cognitive behaviors in humans.

Breland, K., & Breland, M. (1961). The misbehavior of organisms. *American Psychologist, 16,* 681–684. • The Brelands' famous, easy-to-read paper that describes the phenomenon of instinctive drift in their trained animals.

Dostoyevsky, F. (2003). *The gambler* (C. Garnett, Trans.). New York: Modern Library. • A short novel narrated in the first person by a young man who is addicted to gambling. This is a moving description of the despair of behavioral addiction, based on Dostoyevsky's own experience as a compulsive gambler (an addiction he eventually overcame).

Kazdan, A., & Benjet, C. (2003). Spanking children: evidence and issues. *Current Directions in Psychological Science, 12,* 99–103. • A broad review of the two sides of the spanking debate, with particular note of the many unanswered questions that remain.

Potenza, M., Kosten, T., & Rounsaville, B. (2001). Pathological gambling. *JAMA, Journal of the American Medical Association, 286,* 141–144. • A short review of pathological gambling from a physician's point of view, with a focus on how to identify and treat individuals with gambling addictions.

Staddon, J. (1995). On responsibility and punishment. *Atlantic Monthly, 275,* 88–94. • A thought-provoking essay on why punishment works and how this relates to the legal concept of personal responsibility for one's actions: Does a person's "guilt" just reflect the degree to which punishment may prevent further recurrences of his crime?

CHAPTER 9

Generalization, Discrimination, and the Representation of Similarity

I T HAS BEEN ALMOST A FULL DAY SINCE his last meal, and Uggh, a Neanderthal living 100,000 years ago, is very hungry. Seeing an unfamiliar round, yellow fruit hanging from a tree, Uggh plucks it from the branch. He takes a few bites, discards the rest, and wanders on in search of other things to eat. Soon he feels ill. The next day, Uggh comes upon a similar-looking fruit in another part of the forest. Its shape and size are like yesterday's fruit, but its color is orange, not yellow. If yesterday's yellow fruit made Uggh sick, will the orange fruit do the same? If so, Uggh should certainly avoid it. But Uggh is hungry, and food is scarce; if the orange fruit (in contrast to the yellow one) is safe to eat, he'd hate to pass up a meal. Uggh faces what philosophers and psychologists have long understood to be a fundamental challenge for learning: how and when to generalize. **Generalization** is the transfer of past learning to new situations and problems.

If, after eating the poisonous yellow fruit, Uggh assumes that all fruits and berries hanging from trees are poisonous, he might find himself without enough food to survive the winter. On the other hand, if he assumes that only fruits that look exactly like the one that made him sick are poisonous, he may suffer over and over again from eating other poisonous fruits. Uggh is faced with the core issue of generalization: the need to find an appropriate balance between *specificity*—deciding how narrowly a rule applies (for example, deciding that only yellow, round fruits make you sick)—and *generality*, deciding how broadly a rule applies (for example, deciding that all fruits make you sick).

To survive, Uggh needs to learn quickly from his past experiences and use them to predict in advance which fruits are good for eating and which are not. He not only has to recognize the similarities between different fruits and treat some of them the same (generalization), but he also has to discriminate correctly between good fruits and bad fruits. **Discrimination** is recognition of differences between stimuli.

When you recognize that a problem on your calculus exam is similar to one on a previous homework assignment, when you rent an unfamiliar car for the weekend and are able to drive it based on your past experience with other cars, and when you reach for a tangerine because it reminds you of oranges (and you know you love oranges), you are generalizing. Life rarely, if ever, replays exactly the same events, with exactly the same objects and/or circumstances that you have experienced before. To adapt—to survive and prosper—you need to apply what you have learned in the past to novel situations that may be similar, but not identical, to what you have previously experienced. Understanding similarity, what it means, and how it is represented in the brain, is an essential part of the challenge of understanding generalization and discrimination.

This chapter considers the behavioral and biological principles of generalization and discrimination, and how they allow us to apply past learning to novel future situations. Our ability to function in a complex world and deal with novel challenges depends on our ability to form categories, recognize similarities between events or objects, make generalizations, and discriminate between members of different categories.

9.1 Behavioral Processes

Two scenarios are possible given Uggh's dilemma of whether or not to eat the round, orange fruit. Either the two similar-looking fruits have the same consequence—and the orange fruit will also make him sick—or the two similar-looking fruits will lead to different consequences, and the orange fruit, unlike the yellow one, will not make him sick. This section discusses the behavioral processes of learning that occur when similar stimuli predict similar consequences (such as when both the yellow and the orange fruit makes Uggh sick). Then we consider what happens when similar stimuli predict different consequences (as when the yellow fruit is poisonous but the orange fruit is not). Note that there are also other circumstances to consider: What if Uggh found that a completely different looking fruit also made him sick? We end the section by discussing the learning that takes place when dissimilar stimuli predict the same consequence.

When Similar Stimuli Predict Similar Consequences

In a study similar in structure to the problem of Uggh and his fruit, Harry Guttman and Norman Kalish trained pigeons to peck at a yellow light for food reinforcement (Guttman & Kalish, 1956). They then tested what the pigeons had learned. In each of a succession of test trials, the pigeons were shown a single colored light that might be green, yellow, orange, or the in-between colors yellow-green or yellow-orange. The investigators measured how often the pigeons pecked at each color, and they were thus able to measure how the similarity of the color to the yellow training stimulus affected the amount of pecking. Because the sensation of color results from physically different wavelengths of light—for example, yellow light has a wavelength of 580 nanometers (nm)—researchers can compare colors in terms of wavelengths. In this case, the colors ranged along a physical continuum from green (520 nm) to orange (620 nm).

Figure 9.1 shows how the pigeons responded. Not surprisingly, the pigeons pecked most at the stimulus on which they were trained: the yellow light, with its wavelenth of 580 nm. However, the pigeons also responded to lights of other colors. Lights most similar to yellow (as measured by wavelength) produced the next highest levels of responding. As the colors grew increasingly different from the original training stimulus (yellow), responding decreased rapidly.

The curve shown in Figure 9.1 is a **generalization gradient,** a curve showing how changes in the physical properties of stimuli (plotted on the horizontal axis) correspond to changes in responding (plotted on the vertical axis). The curve is called a "gradient" because it generally shows that an animal's response changes gradually depending on the degree of similarity between a test stimulus and the original training stimulus. From looking at a generalization gradient, we can deduce to what degree animals (including people) expect similar outcomes for stimuli that vary in some physical property, such as light wavelength. Thus, a generalization gradient is often taken to be a measure of the animal's or person's perception of similarity, such that if two stimuli are perceived as being highly similar there will be significant generalization between them.

Generalization gradients have been studied for stimuli that vary in height, angle, size, or tone frequency. In all cases, the generalization gradients show a peak, or point of maximal responding, corresponding to the original stimulus on which the animal was trained. This responding drops off rapidly as the test stimuli become less and less similar to the training stimulus.

Generalization gradients have been plotted for classical Pavlovian conditioning (such as the rabbit eyeblink conditioning preparation described in Chapter 7) and for instrumental conditioning (such as training pigeons to peck keys for food, described above). In fact, generalization is seen in all the forms of learning and memory presented in this book. Even the fact and event memories discussed in Chapter 3 can be the bases for generalizations. For example, when you learned in Chapter 1 that Descartes and Darwin were both born to wealthy families you might have tentatively generalized from those facts to infer that many early philosophers and scientists were from well-to-do families, a generalization

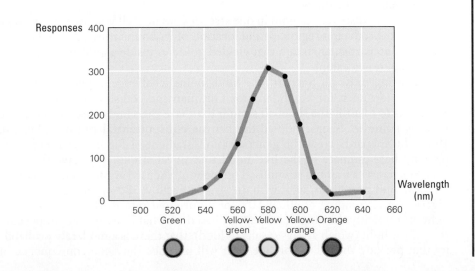

Figure 9.1 Stimulus-generalization gradients in pigeons Pigeons were trained to peck at a yellow light, which has a wavelength of about 580 nm. When the pigeons were tested with other colors of light, their response rates decreased as the colors (wavelengths) departed farther from the trained color. Thus, a 560-nm light (yellow-green) still produced a strong response, but a 520-nm light (green) produced little or no responding. Similarly, a 600-nm light (yellow-orange) produced more responding than a 620-nm light (orange), which produced little. The shape of this generalization gradient, showing how responses fall off with increasing deviation from the trained stimulus, is characteristic of generalization in a wide range of tasks and species. Adapted from Guttman & Kalish, 1956, pp. 79–88.

that is mostly true, although there were some exceptions (Ebbinghaus was one). Many facts that you know are actually generalizations of episodic memories. If you recall that the ice cream truck came around at 4 p.m. yesterday, and at the same time the day before and the day before that, you might generalize from these event memories to form a semantic memory that says the ice cream truck comes every day at 4 p.m. The skill memories you learned about in Chapter 4, such as driving an automobile or juggling, are also common sources of generalized behaviors. If you have learned the specific skills needed to drive a Toyota, you can apply that knowledge to driving a Ford, even though the layout of a Ford's interior is slightly different. If you learn to juggle three balls, this will help you acquire the skill of juggling four balls. Any time we learn, we can generalize that learning to future novel situations.

The generalization gradient shown in Figure 9.1 represents typical behavior for many different stimuli and generalization paradigms. The fundamental characteristic of these generalization gradients is that they decline exponentially from the peak, meaning that responding decreases rapidly the more the stimuli differ from the trained stimulus. Roger Shepard, an influential American cognitive psychologist, described the exponentially declining generalization gradient as one of the most constant basic laws of psychology (Shepard, 1987).

Generalization as a Search for Similar Consequences

Why should a pigeon that has been trained to peck at a yellow light respond to an orange light at all? Could the pigeon be making a mistake—confusing the orange light and the yellow light, or failing to tell them apart? Probably not. Pigeons can easily be trained to discriminate yellow from orange, as you will see in a later discussion. One explanation for generalized responding is that pigeons (and all animals, including humans) are savvy estimators of the probability of future events.

Imagine you are prospecting for gold and you find a mountain stream that yields bountiful quantities of ore. After you've taken all the gold from that one stream, you wonder where you might find more. At your most optimistic, you imagine that you have stumbled onto a fabulous mother lode, and that all the streams in the entire valley are filled with gold (your fortune is made). At your most pessimistic, you realize that there may only be gold in this one particular stream (you have earned barely enough to pay for your prospecting trip). Alternatively, the truth lies between these two extremes, and there is gold in just a few more streams in the valley.

Your initial discovery of gold in one stream does not tell you the size or shape of the gold-producing region, or the location of its boundaries. All you know is that this one particular stream that yielded gold lies inside a gold-producing region of unknown extent.

According to Roger Shepard, the fundamental challenge of generalization—for the gold miner, for Uggh, and for Guttman and Kalish's light-pecking pigeons—is to identify the set of all stimuli that have the same consequence as the training stimulus. Shepard called this set the **consequential region** (Shepard, 1987). In Shepard's view, the generalization gradient in Figure 9.1 reflects the pigeon's best estimate of the likelihood that novel stimuli will have the same consequence as a training stimulus. The pigeon, Shepard argues, is not *confusing* a yellow-orange 600-nm light with the original yellow 580-nm light; rather, the pigeon, by responding at about 50% of its original rate to the yellow-orange light, is implicitly showing that it *expects*, based on what it learned about pecking the yellow light (which always results in food), that there is a moderate probability that pecking the yellow-orange light will produce the same consequence of food delivery. The shape of generalization gradients, Shepard argued, suggests that animals (including people) consistently expect that the chance that two stimuli will have the same consequence drops off sharply as the stimuli become more distinct. This implies that we can view generalization gradients as representing an attempt to predict, based on past experience, how likely it is that the consequences of one stimulus will also be connected with other similar stimuli.

The Challenge of Incorporating Similarity into Learning Models

Chapter 7 described formal models of classical conditioning, such as the Rescorla–Wagner model: simple associative networks that link stimuli (lights and tones) to outcomes (airpuffs or shocks). In the studies that led to these models, the cues were highly distinct, with little perceptual similarity between different light stimuli or different tone stimuli. But what if the stimuli in a conditioning experiment were similar in type, differing only in their distribution along some continuum? In other words, what if the stimuli were two tones of similar frequency, or two lights of similar wavelength? The application of Rescorla and Wagner's associative learning model from Chapter 7 to Guttman and Kalish's pigeon experiment (which used similarly colored lights) provides a good illustration of how easily the Rescorla–Wagner model breaks down unless we incorporate a way of dealing with the physical similarity.

Recall from Chapter 7 that when learning involves multiple cues, the Rescorla–Wagner model can be visualized as a simple one-layer network with links from the various cues to the possible outcomes, as was illustrated in Figure 7.12 (Gluck & Bower, 1988a). In our earlier applications of this model to classical conditioning, you saw how a tone and a light were identified as two distinct stimuli, each with an associative weight connecting it to the conditioned response. To apply the same idea to Guttman and Kalish's pigeon paradigm, we'd need five input nodes, one for each of the five discrete colors that might be presented.

Figure 9.2a shows how one might model stimulus generalization using a simple network that has a single input node for each possible color of light (five are shown). This is called a **discrete-component representation**, meaning that each possible stimulus is represented by its own unique node (or "component") in the model. The network also contains a single output node for the response and has weights from the input nodes to the output node that are modifiable by learning, according to a learning algorithm such as the Rescorla–Wagner rule. Each of the input nodes in Figure 9.2a represents a different color of light (for example, green, yellow, orange, and so on). Depending on the pattern of inputs, activity may be evoked in the output node; strong activity in this output node

Figure 9.2 A model of stimulus generalization using discrete-component representations A first attempt to model stimulus generalization could have one input node for each possible color of light, making this a discrete-component representation. The model includes a single output node for the response and weights from each input node to the output node. These weights can be modified by learning. Active nodes and weights are shown in red. (a) The network is first trained to respond to a yellow light, which activates a particular "yellow" input node. At the end of training, the weight from the "yellow" input node to the output node is strong (illustrated by a thick red line). At this point, further presentation of the yellow light causes activation of 1 in the output node. (b) When a novel yellow-orange light is presented to the network, the yellow-orange light activates a different input node. This input node has never had its weight strengthened, and so it does not cause activation in the output node. Thus, the discrete-component network does not produce any response to the yellow-orange light, despite the similarity to the trained yellow light.

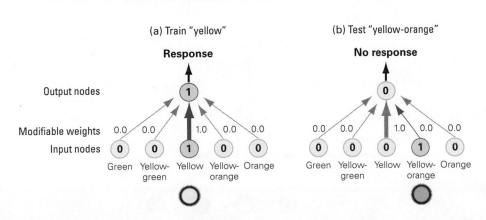

will cause the model to generate a response. Before training, the weights from all the input nodes to the output node are set to 0.0, meaning that there are no prior associations between any of the lights and the response. If the model is given repeated training in which the yellow light is presented followed by a reward, then the weight of the association connecting the yellow node to the response node will increase until it has a value of about 1.0. Figure 9.2a displays the weight from the yellow node as being thicker than the others, to represent this greater weight.

Figure 9.2b shows what happens when this model is now tested with presentation of a novel yellow-orange light. There is still a strong 1.0 weight from the yellow node to the output node (because of the previous training), but that weight is not active (because a pure yellow light is not presented during this new test trial). Instead, only the yellow-orange input node is active, and it causes no activity in the output node, because the weight from this input node is still 0.0. Thus, the model will produce no response to the yellow-orange light, even though that stimulus is very similar to the trained yellow light. In fact, this model will produce no response to any stimulus other than the original yellow training stimulus, and thus no generalization. The result would be a generalization gradient as shown in Figure 9.3: the model produces complete (100%) responding to the yellow test stimulus but no (0%) responding to any other color. This does not look at all like the more gently sloping generalization gradient obtained from Guttman and Kalish's pigeons, seen in Figure 9.1. Clearly the model in Figure 9.2 is wrong: it predicts a generalization gradient that is totally at odds with what Guttman and Kalish actually found.

This analysis suggests that the simple models based on the Rescorla–Wagner rule have a limited scope. They are useful for describing, understanding, and predicting how organisms learn about highly dissimilar stimuli, such as a tone and a light, but they don't work as well with stimuli that have some inherent similarity, such as lights of different colors. Do we throw out the old models when we run into a problem like this, and simply assume that the Rescorla–Wagner rule is wrong? Not necessarily. Instead, given the otherwise wide range of success of this learning algorithm, researchers have tried to extend it to account for generalization gradients. In this way, simple models can be considered to be preliminary steps towards a more complete understanding of learning and memory that builds, cumulatively, on past progress.

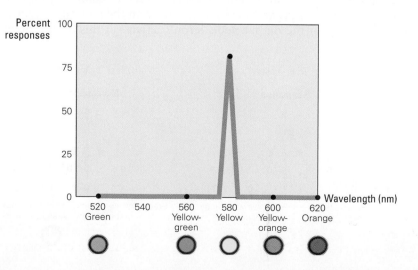

Figure 9.3 The generalization gradient produced by the discrete-component network of Figure 9.2 The discrete-component network gives no response to the yellow-orange light, despite the similarity in color to the previously trained yellow light. It only responds to the trained "yellow" stimulus. In other words, this simple network fails to show a smooth generalization gradient like that shown by the pigeons in Figure 9.1.

The Limitations of Discrete-Component Representations of Stimuli

The discrete-component model shown in Figure 9.2 uses the simplest possible scheme for representing stimuli: a discrete-component representation in which each distinct stimulus is represented by a single input node which is then connected, by a modifiable weight, to an output node. Discrete-component representations are applicable to situations in which the similarity among the features is small enough so that there is negligible transfer of response from one to another. This was the case in the experiments discussed previously in Chapter 7, which used one tone and one light. But discrete-component representations fail in cases where stimuli have a high degree of physical similarity, since they produce unrealistic generalization gradients like the one shown in Figure 9.3.

Before moving on, we should pause to consider the consequences of using different kinds of representations, whether in our models, in our mental activities, or in the actual physical workings of our brain. Let's compare some of the different kinds of representations we use in everyday life. The letters in these words on the page, for example, are representations of sounds, and the words themselves represent ideas and concepts. To represent Karen Tenner, a student at Brown University, the government may use her nine-digit social security number, 015–88–6999; the university uses her student ID number; her friends in her dorm refer to her by her nickname, "KT"; and the Department of Motor Vehicles identifies her by a sequence of letters and numbers on her driver's license, "MA 834702." Each of these representations was chosen to suit a particular need. When you call Karen on the phone, you wouldn't think to ask to speak with "015–88–6999." The government, however, must organize records for millions of people, and needs a unique way to represent Karen so as not to confuse her with other people who have the same name, which is why it uses her social security number. In other words, representations are context-specific. They allow us to highlight, communicate, and store for retrieval various aspects of the real-world referent. However, what is appropriate for use as a representation in one context may not be appropriate in others. Of particular importance to our discussions in this chapter is the fact that different representations in different contexts yield different patterns of similarity: Karen is most similar to Cary when their names are spoken aloud. However, to the government, Karen may be most similar to Hui-Ling, whose social security number, 016–88–6999, differs by only one digit from Karen's.

With these ideas in mind—and a deeper appreciation for how similarity and representations are intimately linked—we next explore how psychological theorists have grappled with the limitations of various representation schemes in learning models, and how their solutions changed modern approaches to understanding the interplay between similarity, representation, and generalization.

Shared Elements and Distributed Representations

Recall from Chapters 1 and 8 the work of Edward Thorndike, who developed the *law of effect*, which states that the probability of a response will increase or decrease depending on the consequences that follow. Thorndike was well aware, back in the 1920s, of the limitations of discrete-component representations of stimulus features. He proposed that stimulus generalization results from the elements shared by similar stimuli (Thorndike, 1923). For example, in Thorndike's view, yellow and yellow-orange are not two totally separate stimuli. Rather, he argued, they are each composed of many distinct elements, some shared and others not shared. As you read back in Chapter 1, similar ideas were embraced by W. K. Estes, in his *stimulus sampling theory*, and by David Rumelhart and colleagues, in

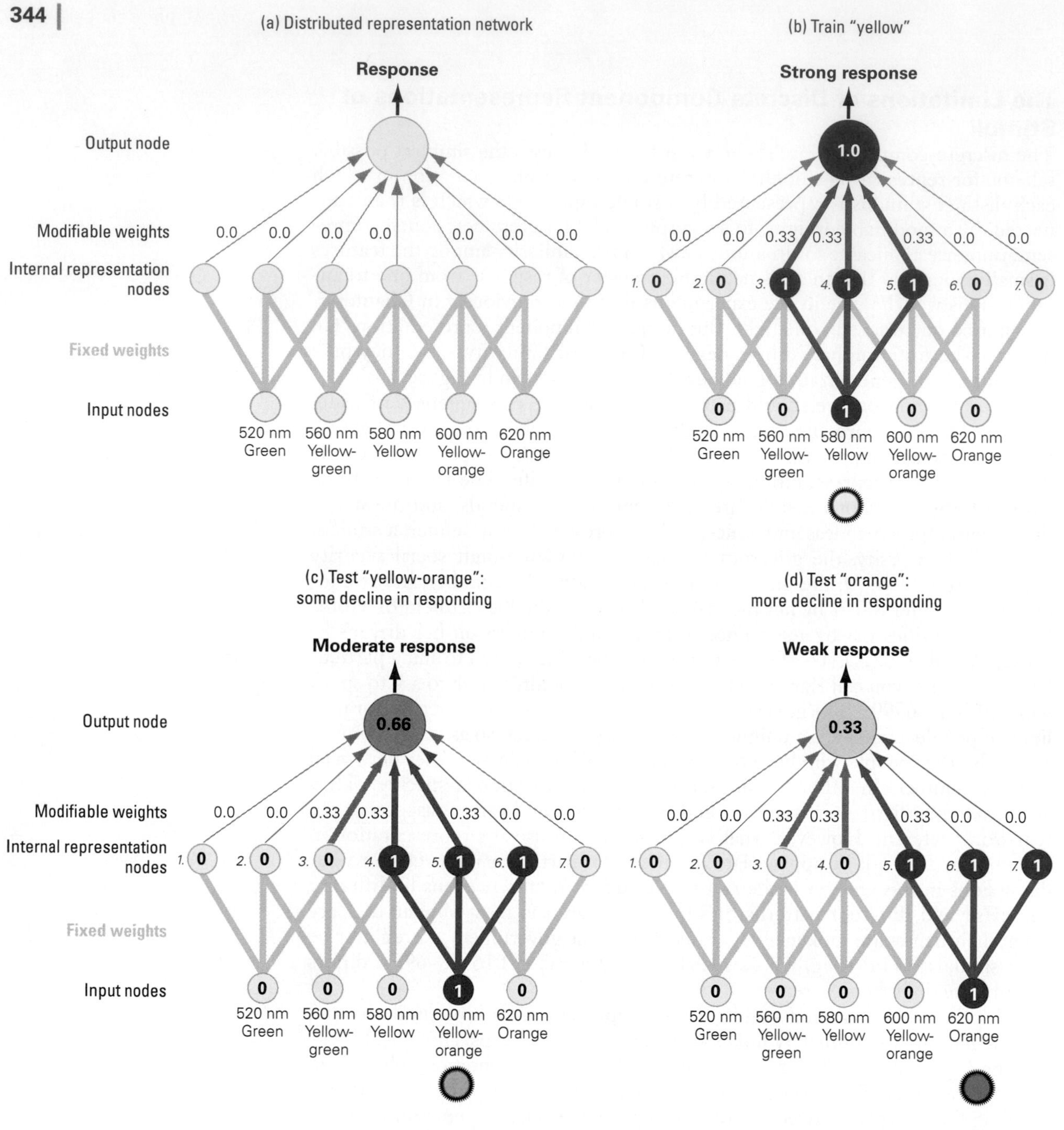

Figure 9.4 A network model using distributed representations. (a) Presentation of a colored light activates a unique node in the input layer of the network. Each input layer node is connected, via fixed (nonmodifiable) weights—shown in light blue—to several nodes in the *internal representation* layer. Nodes in the internal representation layer are then connected, via modifiable weights, shown in grey, to a single output node. (b) First, the network is trained to respond to yellow light. Presentation of the stimulus activates the corresponding input node, which activates three nodes in the internal representation layer, which connect to the output node. If the yellow light is repeatedly paired with a reward, weights from the active internal representation layer nodes (*3, 4,* and *5*) to the output node are strengthened. Eventually, the weights are strengthened enough that presentation of the yellow light evokes a response. (c) Next, the network is tested with a similar stimulus (a yellow-orange light). The response depends on the degree of overlap between the sets of internal representation nodes activated by yellow and by yellow-orange. Because yellow-orange and yellow share two overlapping internal representation nodes (*4* and *5*), some activation is produced at the output node. (d) An even more different color, orange, evokes even less overlap in the internal representation nodes, and evokes even less output.

their *connectionist models.* All these approaches embraced the basic idea of **distributed representations,** in which stimuli are represented by overlapping pools of nodes or stimulus elements. Similarity emerges naturally from the fact that two similar stimuli (such as yellow and orange lights, or golden retrievers and cocker spaniels) activate common elements. Thus, what is learned about one stimulus will tend to transfer or generalize to other stimuli that activate some of the same nodes.

Figure 9.4a shows how such distributed representations might be used in a network model that is only slightly more complicated than the model of Figure 9.2. This network has three layers of nodes and two layers of weights. In the network model in Figure 9.4a, each stimulus activates an *input node* that is connected, by a layer of fixed (nonmodifiable) weights to several nodes in an *internal representation* layer. These fixed weights, which do not change during learning, are drawn in light blue to help distinguish them from the modifiable weights, which are shown in gray. (Later, we'll consider more complicated models where the lower weights can be trained, but for now let's stick to this simpler case.) The internal representation nodes are then connected, via modifiable weights (in gray), which will change during learning, to a final *output* node. Thus, the presentation of a yellow light would activate the corresponding "yellow" node in the input layer, which in turn would activate three nodes at the internal representation layer (nodes *3, 4,* and *5*); but notice that two of these internal representation nodes (*3* and *4*) could also be activated by a yellow-green light, and nodes *4* and *5* could also activated by yellow-orange light. In this manner, yellow-green, yellow, and yellow-orange all activate overlapping sets of internal representation nodes.

The nodes in Figure 9.4a are laid out as a **topographic representation,** meaning that nodes responding to physically similar stimuli (such as yellow and yellow-orange light) are placed next to each other in the model. However, the physical layout itself is not what's important. What is important to a topographical representation is that the degree of overlap between the representations of two stimuli reflects their physical similarity. Thus, in Figure 9.4a, there is more overlap between the representations for yellow and yellow-orange than between those for yellow and orange. There is no overlap between the representations of very different colors, such as green and orange.

Now suppose that this network model is trained to respond to a yellow light, which activates the three internal representation nodes as shown in Figure 9.4b. Note that this network transforms a representation of yellow light on the input layer to a different representation in the middle layer. If we were to view the input layer as a string of 1s and 0s where 1 means a node is on (colored red in Figure 9.4b) and 0 means a node is off (colored gray in Figure 9.4b), then this network transforms the representation 00100 at the input layer to 0011100 at the middle layer. Both of these strings of numbers represent the yellow light, but in different ways at different places in the model (much the way Karen, in the earlier example, can be represented both by her social security number and by her familiar nickname, in different contexts and for different purposes).

Note that the representation of yellow at the input layer (00100) is a discrete-component representation, because each light has one and only one node that is activated (and no other colors activate this node). In contrast, the representation at the middle layer (0011100) is a distributed representation, because the yellow color's representation is distributed over three nodes (*3, 4,* and *5*).

If the yellow light is always followed by a reward, the network in Figure 9.4a should learn to generate an appropriate response. This learning will take place in the upper layer of modifiable weights that connect the internal representation layer to the output node.

One way of determining how much the active weights should be increased is to use the Rescorla–Wagner learning rule. As you read in Chapter 7, this rule states that weights should be changed proportional to the error on each trial (with error defined as the mismatch between the outcome that occurred and the outcome that was predicted). Following many trials of training in which yellow is paired with reward, the weights from the three active nodes would each come to equal .33, as shown in Figure 9.4b, illustrated by the thickened lines connecting internal representation layer nodes *3*, *4*, and *5* to the output node. Presentation of a yellow light now activates nodes *4*, *5*, and *6*, which in turn results in a net activation of 1.0 in the output node, the sum of these three weights. (Note that the weights from internal representation layer nodes that have never been activated or associated with reward remain at their initial value of 0.)

Compare the distributed network in Figure 9.4b, which was trained to respond to a yellow light, with the discrete-component network from Figure 9.2b, which was trained with the very same stimulus and outcome pairings. In the distributed network of Figure 9.4b, the learning is distributed over weights from three internal representation layer nodes, each with a trained weight of 0.33; in contrast, the discrete-component network in Figure 9.2 localizes this same respond-to-yellow rule into a single weight of 1.0 from one input node. Both network models give a response of 1.0 when the original yellow light is presented.

The difference between the distributed network of Figure 9.4 and the discrete-component network of Figure 9.2 becomes apparent only upon presentation of stimuli that are similar—but not identical—to the trained stimulus. The distributed network is able to generalize. This generalization behavior can be assessed by testing a yellow-orange light, as shown in Figure 9.4c. Here, yellow-orange activates an internal layer representation that has considerable overlap with the representation activated by the trained yellow light. Specifically, both nodes *4* and *5* are also activated by the yellow-orange light, and each of these internal representation layer nodes will contribute to partially activate the output node. As a result, a reasonably strong output node activation of 0.67 results, proportional to the two-thirds degree of overlap between the representations for yellow and yellow-orange light. If the same network were tested with orange light, there would be less overlap with the representation of yellow light, and a consequently weaker response of 0.33 (as shown in Figure 9.4d).

Figure 9.5 shows that when this model is used to generate responses to a series of novel lights, it produces a stimulus-generalization gradient that decreases

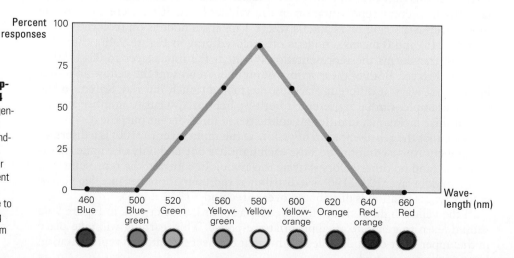

Figure 9.5 Stimulus-generalization gradient produced by the distributed representation model of Figure 9.4 The trained network in Figure 9.4 generates this stimulus-generalization gradient, which shows peak responding to the trained stimulus, yellow. Responding decreases smoothly for stimuli that are increasingly different from this trained stimulus. This smooth gradient is similar in shape to the ones seen in animals (including humans), such as that obtained from pigeons in Figure 9.1

smoothly for stimuli of increasing distance from the trained stimulus, which is similar to the pigeons' generalization gradient shown in Figure 9.1. This result contrasts markedly with the (lack of a) generalization gradient in Figure 9.3, which was produced using the network that had only discrete-component representation. Thus, even though the two models can learn the same initial task (respond to yellow light), they differ considerably in their generalization performance. This illustrates a very important point: to evaluate alternative models for learning mechanisms, it is often necessary to look not only at how well the models predict initial learning performance but also at how well they predict subsequent patterns of generalization behavior.

The generalization gradients in Figures 9.5 and 9.1 are not identical. The network model responds more strongly to orange light than the pigeons do. The exact width and shape of the generalization gradient produced by a model can be manipulated by varying the number and amount of overlap of nodes in the model. Nevertheless, the overall shape makes the important point: a model that uses distributed representations—what Thorndike and Estes called shared elements—yields generalization gradients that are more like those seen in animals and people than are the generalization gradients produced by a model that uses a discrete-component representation. Distributed-representation models capture a fundamental property of learning: humans and other organisms tend, all other things being equal, to treat similar events similarly and to expect similar stimuli to have similar consequences.

When Similar Stimuli Predict Different Consequences

Remember the Neanderthal, Uggh, introduced at the beginning of this chapter? Uggh generalizes about fruits in much the way Guttman and Kalish's pigeons generalized about lights: if a yellow fruit makes him sick, he will assume that a similar-colored fruit, such as an orange fruit, has a good chance of making him sick too. On the basis of this prediction, he may decide it isn't worth the risk of another horrible tummy ache to eat the orange fruit . . . *unless* he is really hungry and there are few other fruit-bearing plants in the region. If hunger motivates Uggh to take a chance on the orange fruit and he finds that he *doesn't* get nauseous, he now has new information: Yellow fruit makes him sick, but orange fruit does not. From this experience, Uggh has learned that it is important to *discriminate* between yellow and orange fruit: even though they have similar features, they lead to different outcomes when eaten.

William James, whom you read about in Chapter 1, described another example of discrimination between similar stimuli (James, 1890). When he was first exposed to red wines, James thought they all tasted the same. However, after many years, James began to realize that different varieties of red wine had quite distinct tastes, and he could easily distinguish examples of one class, such as claret, from examples of another, such as burgundy. Many American children learn similarly fine distinctions, discriminating the tastes of Pepsi and Coca-Cola, or discriminating the french fries at McDonald's from those at Burger King. Two objects or substances that initially seem very similar, or even indistinguishable, eventually come to be distinguishable through repeated exposures. Similarly, dog breeders may learn to distinguish subtle differences in related breeds, gem cutters may learn to distinguish diamonds of subtly different color or quality, and parents of identical twins learn to tell their children apart. What determines whether two stimuli are to be treated as similar (generalization) or different (discrimination)?

Discrimination Training and Learned Specificity

Herbert Jenkins, a Canadian psychologist, performed a classic study of discrimination learning that captures a situation similar to Uggh learning that yellow fruit—but not orange fruit—makes him sick. Jenkins's experiment used two groups of pigeons. One group received standard training in which a 1000-Hertz (Hz) tone signaled that pecking a key would result in food delivery (Jenkins & Harrison, 1962). Because the birds only received the food after pecking the key, the food reinforcement was contingent upon the birds' behavior. Recall from Chapter 8 that this instrumental conditioning can be described as:

S (1000 Hz tone) → R (key peck) → C (food)

The second group of pigeons received **discrimination training,** in which one of two different (but similar) stimuli was presented on each trial. As in standard training, a 1000–Hz tone signaled that the next key peck would result in food reinforcement. However, another, very similar tone of 950 Hz signaled that a key peck would *not* result in food reinforcement:

S(1000 Hz tone) → R (key peck) → C (food)

S(950 Hz tone) → R (key peck) → C (no food)

Following this training, both groups of pigeons were given test trials with new tones, ranging from very low (300 Hz) to very high (3500 Hz). The experimenters measured how frequently the birds pecked in response to each test tone. As shown in Figure 9.6, the group receiving standard training showed a generalization gradient similar to what Guttman and Kalish found for light stimuli (see Figure 9.1).

In contrast, the pigeons given discrimination training showed a very different pattern of generalization. Their generalization gradient was much steeper, centered right around the 1000-Hz tone and dropping off much more rapidly—so that they were not responding at all to the nearby 950-Hz tone, or anything else. The difference in shape of the two generalization gradients in Figure 9.6 shows that with discrimination training, the generalization gradient can change to reflect more specific (narrowly focused) responding to the reinforcing stimulus.

Studies in humans have provided additional evidence concerning the effects of discrimination training on generalization. In one study, participants were first trained to categorize squares into two groups based on either their size or brightness (Goldstone, 1994). Sixteen stimuli were provided in the form of squares that varied according to four levels of size (S1–S4) and four levels of brightness

Figure 9.6 Generalization gradients for tones of different frequencies One group of pigeons learned that a 1000-Hz tone signaled that key pecks would be reinforced ("standard training"); these birds showed a standard generalization gradient when tested with novel tones. A second group of pigeons learned that the 1000-Hz tone signaled that pecks would be rewarded, but that the (very similar sounding) 950-Hz tone signaled no reward ("discrimination training"); these birds showed a much steeper generalization gradient. Adapted from Jenkins and Harrison, 1962.

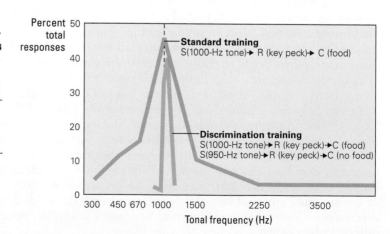

Why Are Some Feature Pairs Easier to Discriminate between Than Others?

When we look at an object that can be described by multiple features, why are some of the features easier to distinguish than others? Imagine you were shown drawings of several rectangles that vary in height. Inside each rectangle is a vertical line; some of the lines are located toward the left side of the rectangle, others toward the middle, and still others toward the right, as shown below. Thus, each figure can be described by two features: the height of the rectangle and the position of the internal line. Could you make a quick judgment about the height of the rectangle and ignore the line's position? Alternatively, consider a different set of stimuli: rectangles that vary in both height and width. Do you think you could easily tune out height and sort the rectangles by width, or vice versa?

You would probably find that it is not difficult to consider the rectangle's height separately from the position of an internal line. In contrast, you would find it harder to consider the rectangle's height separately from its width, because the width interacts with, or interferes with, our perception of height. Stimulus features that are easy to dissociate (such as the height of a rectangle and the position of an internal line) are called *separable* features. Features that tend to be processed more holistically and are harder to tease apart (such as the height and width of a rectangle) are called *integral* (Garner, 1974). Separability and integrality are properties of *pairs* of features, not of any individual features. Thus, the height of a rectangle combines in a separable fashion with internal line position but in an integral fashion with rectangle width (Garner, 1974).

The same phenomena occur in the perception and categorization of color. The color of an object can be defined by three features: hue (or wavelength; for example, 580 nm is perceived as yellow), brightness (how light or dark the stimulus is), and saturation (the intensity; you can think of this as relating to how long the stimulus has been steeped in dye of the appropriate color). Brightness and saturation are integral features: varying either of them leads to a change in the holistic perception of the color. In contrast, brightness and hue are separable: you can look at two stimuli of the same wavelength and perceive easily that one is brighter than the other.

Understanding how pairs of features interact during categorization is essential for understanding generalization and discrimination learning. With pairs of integral features, such as brightness and saturation, we tend to generalize holistically to past stimuli that are similar in both features. In contrast, with separable features, like brightness and hue, generalization may be driven by similarity in one or the other feature independently.

While it is possible to identify empirically which pairs of stimulus features tend to be separable and which integral, it is still a great unsolved mystery why they are this way. To solve the mystery of integrality and separability, researchers may have to delve more deeply into how various primary sensory cortices, such as A1, V1, and S1, process stimulus inputs and pass the information on to other brain regions, such as higher cortical areas and the hippocampus (Tijsseling & Gluck, 2002). Only then will we know if the integral-separable distinction is an inherent property of the brain or if it simply reflects the way we learn about stimuli over a lifetime of experience.

(a) Separable dimensions   (b) Integral dimensions

The two-dimensional filtering task (a) Stimuli varying by height and line position, two separable features. (b) Stimuli varying by height and width, two integral features.

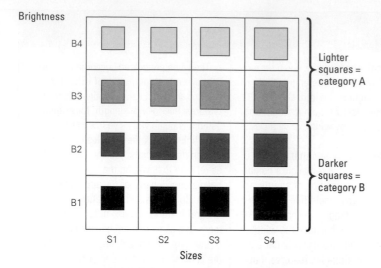

Figure 9.7 Stimuli for discrimination of squares on the basis of size or brightness Sixteen stimuli were constructed using squares that varied according to four levels of size and four levels of brightness. Some participants were trained that the eight brightest squares belonged to category A, and the eight darkest belonged to category B, as shown here. Other participants were trained to categorize the same squares based on size (small versus large) rather than brightness. Adapted from Goldstone, 1994.

(B1–B4). As shown in Figure 9.7, some participants were trained to categorize the squares according to brightness, with the brighter squares (in rows B3 and B4) belonging to Category A, and the darker squares (in rows B1 and B2) belonging to Category B. Other participants were trained to categorize based on size rather than brightness, with the larger squares (columns S3 and S4) belonging to one category and the smaller squares (columns S1 and S2) belonging to the other.

After this training, all participants were asked to judge the perceived similarities or differences between squares: "Are these two squares physically identical?" Of particular interest were the comparisons of squares that differed only on size, such as the square at B2–S2 versus the square at B2–S3, which are the same brightness (B2), or squares that differed only in brightness—such as square B2–S2 versus square B3–S2, which are the same size (S2). Participants who had been initially trained to make brightness discriminations, as illustrated in Figure 9.7, were far less likely to confuse squares that differed in brightness (for example, B2–S2 versus B3–S2) and more likely to confuse squares that differed in size (for example, B2–S2 versus B2–S3).

In contrast, participants who were initially trained in size discrimination showed the opposite pattern: they showed much more confusion of similar brightnesses and far less confusion of similar sizes. Thus, people who had been trained on one dimension (size or brightness) were subsequently more able to make fine distinctions between stimuli that differ along that dimension than between stimuli that differ along a different, untrained, dimension.

Negative Patterning: Differentiating Configurations from Their Individual Components

Two of the rules Uggh has learned while foraging for food are that most round fruits taste good and that most red fruits taste good. Given these two rules, what do you think he will expect of a round, red fruit? Super tasty! That is because Uggh naturally assumes that a combination of two positive cues, "round" and "red," will result in a positive outcome, possibly even extremely positive. Similarly, if a young girl believes that freckle-faced boys are usually bratty and that red-haired boys also tend to be bratty, she might expect a red-haired, freckle-faced boy to be really horribly bratty. All other things being equal, we tend to assume that combinations of cues will have consequences that parallel (or even combine) what we know about the individual cues.

But is this always the case? What if a certain combination of cues implies something totally different from what the individual cues mean? For example, suppose you're driving a car. While waiting at an intersection, you notice that the car in front of you has its *left* rear red taillight flashing, signalling that the car is about to turn left (Figure 9.8a). If its *right* rear red taillight were flashing, you would know that the driver intends to turn right (Figure 9.8b).

But what if both taillights were flashing, as in Figure 9.8c? Although one turn signal flashing indicates a turn, both taillights flashing does not indicate a combination of two turns (that the car is simultaneously going to turn left and right). Instead, twin flashing taillights signal a hazard; the car is proceeding slowly or is disabled. Although our tendency may be to assume that what is true of compo-

(a) (b) (c)

Figure 9.8 The challenge of interpreting combined cues (a) Left blinking light means left turn, (b) right blinking light means right turn, (c) both lights blinking means that the driver has turned on the hazard lights.

nent features presented individually is also true of their combination, clearly it is possible to override this tendency to generalize. As a result, drivers easily learn that the combination of both left and right lights flashing means something quite different from what is meant by either feature alone.

This kind of situation has been extensively studied with both animal and human learning tasks. Suppose, for example, that a rabbit is trained to expect that either a tone or a light, presented alone, predicts an airpuff US will be delivered to the eye—but that there will be *no* airpuff US if the tone and light appear together. To respond appropriately, the animal must learn to respond to the individual tone cue or light cue but to withhold responding to the compound tone-and-light cue. This task is known by two different names: psychologists call it **negative patterning,** because the response to the individual cues is positive while the response to the compound (i.e., the "pattern") is negative (no response). Logicians call this same problem the *exclusive-or* (or *XOR*) task because it requires learning to respond *exclusively* to either the tone *or* the light, but not to the combination of both together.

Because both the tone and the light cues are part of the tone-and-light compound, there is a natural tendency for the animal to generalize from the component cues to the compound cue, and vice versa. However, this natural tendency to generalize from component features to compounds doesn't serve here, because the components and the compound are associated with very different outcomes. Negative patterning is difficult to learn, because it requires suppressing the natural tendency to generalize about similar stimuli.

With training, the negative patterning task can be mastered by rats, rabbits, monkeys, and humans. Figure 9.9 shows an example of negative patterning in rabbit eyeblink conditioning (Kehoe, 1988). After only a few blocks of training,

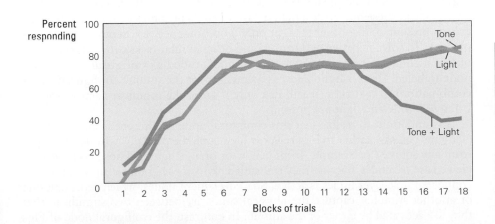

Percent responding

Figure 9.9 Negative patterning in rabbit eyeblink conditioning Negative patterning involves learning to respond to two cues (a tone and light) when presented separately but to withhold the response when the two cues are presented together. With extensive training, rabbits can be trained to produce eyeblinks to the tone or light separately and to withhold responding to the tone-and-light compound. Adapted from Kehoe, 1988, Figure 9.

Figure 9.10 Failure of a single-layer network with discrete-component representations to learn negative patterning Network models with discrete-component representations and a single layer of modifiable weights connecting the input nodes to an output node cannot learn negative patterning. (a) For the tone cue to correctly generate a strong response, the connection from that input to the output must be strongly weighted. (b) For the light cue to correctly generate a strong response, the connection from that input to the output must also be strongly weighted. (c) Consequently, when both tone and light cues are present, the network will incorrectly give a strong response—in fact, the network's response to the compound (tone plus light) will always be stronger than the response to either component cue alone.

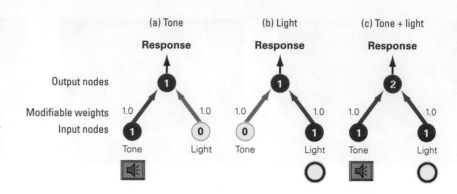

the animals learned to give strong responses either to the tone alone or to the light alone. But during this early phase of training, the rabbits make the mistake of generalizing, giving strong responses to the compound tone-and-light stimulus. Only with extensive further training do the rabbits begin to suppress responding to the tone-and-light compound while still responding strongly to the tone or the light when presented individually.

Can simple network learning models provide an explanation of how rabbits and other animals learn negative patterning? Figure 9.10 illustrates why single-layer network models using discrete-component representations cannot learn the negative-patterning problem. In order to produce correct responding to the tone alone, the weight from the input unit encoding tone must be strengthened to 1.0. (Figure 9.10a). In order to produce correct responding to the light alone, the weight from the input unit encoding light must also be strengthened to 1.0 (Figure 9.10b). But this means that if the tone and light are presented together, activation will flow through both those modifiable weighted connections and produce strong responding to the compound—stronger responding, in fact, than to either component alone (Figure 9.10c).

All the weights could be decreased, of course, to reduce the level of response to the compound in Figure 9.10c, but this would also incorrectly reduce responding to the individual components. It is a lose-lose situation. Changing the network to alter responding to the compound will alter responding to the component cues, and vice versa. In fact, there is no way to assign association weights in the network of Figure 9.10 that would make the network respond correctly to all three different types of training trials.

One way to resolve this dilemma is to use a three-layer network, as shown in Figure 9.11. This example network has three nodes in its internal representation layer. One of these nodes (designated "Tone only") becomes active whenever the tone is present, and another ("Light only") becomes active whenever the light is present. To solve negative patterning (and other similar tasks), the internal layer of this model also contains a new type of node, called a **configural node.** This node (labeled "Tone + light") acts as a detector for the unique configuration (or combination) of two cues. It will fire only if *all* of the inputs are active, that is, when *both* tone and light are present.

It is important to realize that this configural node is different from the shared elements you saw earlier in Figure 9.4, which could be partially activated by input from any source (for example, from yellow or orange lights). Those nodes can be viewed as "*or*" nodes, because they transmit activity if either one *or* the other of the connected first-layer nodes is active. Shared-element nodes, which represent one or another stimulus, capture the physical similarity between two stimuli, in that they are activated by either of the stimuli. In contrast, the configural node of Figure 9.11 captures the presence of one stimulus *and* another, allowing the network

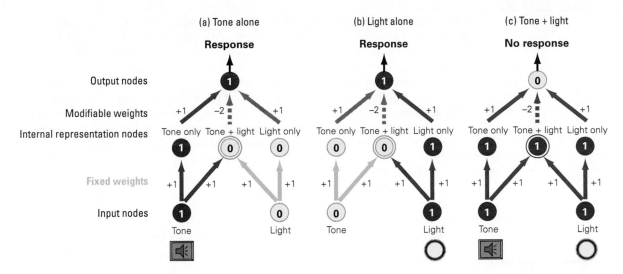

Figure 9.11 Solving negative patterning with a network model A multilayer network with configural nodes in the internal representation layer can solve the negative-patterning problem. One node in the internal representation layer (labeled "Tone only") becomes active whenever the tone is present, while another ("Light only") becomes active whenever the light is present. A third node ("Tone + light") becomes active when both tone and light are present, but not when either alone is present. This configural node is represented by a double circle around the node. (a) When the tone alone is present, the tone-only node becomes active and sends an excitatory signal (+1) to the output node, and the network generates a response. (b) When the light alone is present, the light-only node becomes active and sends an excitatory signal (+1) to the output node, and the network generates a response. (c) When both tone and light are present, the tone + light configural node is also activated. This node sends strong inhibitory signals to the output node (of –2), counteracting the excitatory (+1) signals from the tone-only and light-only nodes, so the net activation of the output node is 0, and the network generates no response. In this way, the network responds to the components but not the configuration of tone and light, thus solving the negative patterning task.

to learn about the unique implications of the cue compound. Configural nodes which require all their inputs to be on before they fire are indicated in Figure 9.11 by a double circle.

Figure 9.11 shows how such a network might look after it has been trained to solve the negative patterning problem. Figure 9.11a shows that when the tone (alone) is present, the tone-only node in the internal representation layer becomes active and in turn activates the output node. Similarly, in Figure 9.11b, the light by itself activates the light-only node, which subsequently activates the output node. However, when both tone and light are present (Figure 9.11c), all three internal representation layer nodes are activated. The tone-only and light-only internal nodes each have a weight of +1.0 to the output node so their activation together would tend to cause—contrary to the rules—an output activation of 2.0 (their sum). However, the connection of the tone-and-light compound node to the output node is given a *negative* weight of –2.0. Thus, when the configural node is activated, it cancels out the effect of the tone-only and light-only nodes, for a net output activation of (+1) + (+1) + (–2), or 0, as shown in Figure 9.11c. Thus, the network correctly responds to either cue alone, but (equally correctly) not to the compound, solving the negative patterning problem.

Negative patterning is just one example of a larger class of learning phenomena that involve configurations of stimuli and that cannot be explained using single-layer networks or networks whose internal nodes are "or" nodes only. To master configural learning tasks, an animal must be sensitive to the unique configurations (or combinations) of the stimulus cues, above and beyond what it knows about the individual stimulus components.

Configural Learning in Categorization

Configural learning is a critical component of human learning. It is especially important in **categorization learning,** the process by which humans learn to classify stimuli into categories. Chapter 7 reviewed work by Mark Gluck and Gordon Bower that utilized simple networks based on the Rescorla–Wagner model to capture some aspects of how people learn to categorize multidimensional stimuli (Gluck & Bower, 1988a). As you will recall, these studies showed that people acquire feature-category associations in much the same way that animals acquire CS-US associations in classical conditioning.

One of these studies tested people's ability to learn to diagnose fictitious medical patients. On each trial, participants were given the description of a patient who had particular symptoms. They were then asked to determine, based on that pattern of symptoms, whether the patient had a rare disease. Gluck and Bower's original model for this task (shown in Figure 7.12a) looked much like the associative network in Figure 9.2, with discrete-component representations for each input symptom, and one layer of modifiable associative weights connecting those inputs to an output node. However, just like the network in Figure 9.2, this category-learning model could only capture learning for tasks in which there were no important configural relationships among the cues. To ensure that their model could solve complex multicue tasks like negative-patterning, Gluck and Bower added configural nodes to their category-learning model (Gluck & Bower, 1988b; Gluck, Bower, & Hee, 1989).

As an example of how such a model could work, Figure 9.12a shows a network that can learn to diagnose hypothetical patients based on three symptoms: fever, ache, and soreness. Each symptom has its own input node, which is active whenever that symptom is present. This network also has one internal represen-

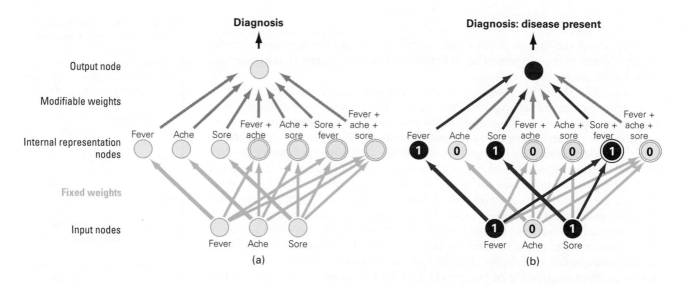

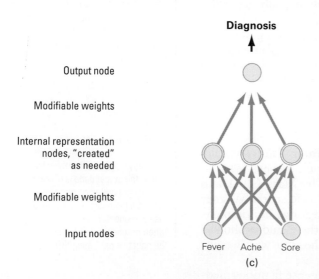

Figure 9.12 A configural-node model of category learning
(a) This multilayer network encodes a categorization problem in which a configuration of symptoms is used to diagnose the presence or absence of a disease. Diagnosis may be predicted by the occurrence of individual symptoms or by combinations of two or more symptoms. For simplicity, the numbers corresponding to weight strengths are omitted from this figure; instead, line thickness approximates the strength of the connections. Upper layer weights (shown in gray) are modifiable, but the lower layer weights (shown in blue) are fixed. A double-circle around a node indicates that it is a configural node that is activated if, and only if, all of the weights entering into the node are active themselves. (b) Here, the presence of both fever and soreness produces strong activation in the output node, resulting in a diagnosis that the disease is present. But fever or soreness presented alone (or in combination with the third symptom, ache) will not activate the output node, and thus predicts the absence of disease. This kind of multilayer network with configural nodes shows behaviors during learning that are similar to humans learning the same task. (c) An alternative approach to a network with large numbers of preexisting nodes in the internal representation layer (to capture every possible stimulus configuration) is a more flexible network that has a smaller number of nodes in the internal representation layer but that can "create" configural nodes as needed.

tation node for each individual symptom, as well as nodes that represent each possible combination of two or more symptoms. The output node is used to make a prediction of disease: when the output node is highly active, the diagnosis is that the disease is present; otherwise, the diagnosis is that the disease is absent. For instance, if a patient reports fever and soreness, the internal-layer nodes corresponding to these individual symptoms are activated, as are nodes corresponding to the configuration of fever and soreness combined, as shown in Figure 9.12b. This leads to strong activation of the output node, resulting in a diagnosis that the disease is present.

There is, however, a critical drawback to this configural representation. Note that the disease-diagnosis network of Figure 9.12b has one internal-layer node for each symptom and another for each possible combination of symptoms. When there are only three symptoms, the model need only keep track of the weights of eight nodes. If the problem included ten symptoms, however, more than a thousand internal-layer nodes would be required to encode every possible combination of symptoms. Unfortunately, problems in the real world contain numerous stimuli occurring alone or in combination. The number of nodes needed in a network to encode all possible combinations of all possible stimuli would be vast—too many for even a powerful computer to handle. And yet only a small fraction of these combinations will ever actually occur. This dilemma, called **combinatorial explosion,** reflects the rapid expansion of resources required to encode configurations as their number of component features increases.

An alternative to the configural-cue network model of Figure 9.12b would be a network like the one shown in Figure 9.12c. This alternative has a smaller number of nodes in the internal representation layer, but those nodes can be assigned the role of configural nodes when needed. The problem of how a network might designate new configural nodes on the fly puzzled researchers for many years. Then, in the mid 1980s, David Rumelhart and his colleagues, about whom you read in Chapter 1, developed sophisticated new learning algorithms to show how the problem might be solved (Rumelhart & McClelland, 1986). In this algorithm, the network has two layers of modifiable weights—one layer going from the input nodes to the internal nodes, and another layer going from the internal nodes to the output node. When experience shows a particular combination of stimuli (for example, fever + ache) to be useful for the purposes of solving a problem, changes in the values of the lower-layer weights can cause the network to change so that in the future a certain internal node will become active only when that particular combination of inputs is present. This advance in learning theory created an explosion of research in network models for learning, memory, and other aspects of cognition.

When Dissimilar Stimuli Predict the Same Consequence

Not all generalization is based on physical similarity; generalization can also occur when physical similarities between the stimuli are absent. For example, what if Uggh notices that there is always a five-pointed leaf next to blueberries? Although the blueberries and the five-pointed leaves share no significant physical similarities, they tend, in Uggh's experience, to co-occur on the same bushes. If Uggh loves the taste of blueberries, he may tend to try other fruits that occur on bushes with five-pointed leaves, even if the fruits aren't blue. Because blueberries and five-pointed leaves occur together frequently and the blueberries have been good food, Uggh transfers his interest in blueberries to the fruits on other bushes with five-pointed leaves. In this way, Uggh generalizes his conclusions about blueberries into conclusions about five-pointed leaves, not because of physical similarity between the two, but rather because these two stimuli co-occur frequently.

The idea that co-occurrence increases generalization goes back at least as far as William James (James, 1890). He argued that if all cold objects were wet and all wet objects were cold, the two characteristics would be viewed as a single concept; the presence of one (for example, wet) would infer the presence of the other (that is, cold). James concluded that organisms would tend to cluster, or treat equivalently, stimulus features that tend to co-occur. Much common wisdom is based upon examples of this kind of clustering, such as "where there's smoke, there's fire." And the same kind of clustering can be demonstrated in the learning laboratory, too.

Sensory Preconditioning: Similar Predictions for Co-occurring Stimuli

One of the more popular ways of drinking the Mexican liquor tequila is by mixing it with lemons. As a result, most people who drink tequila associate its taste with the taste of lemon juice. What do you think would happen if, at some later point, such a person drank a bottle of straight tequila (that is, without lemons or anything else) and it made him very sick afterwards? You might expect from what you have learned so far that he would develop an aversion to the taste of tequila. But what about the taste of lemons? They weren't present in the tequila when he got sick, but in the past he had so often paired the two that he might also start avoiding lemons, by association.

What has happened here? Psychologists would say that the tequila drinker had experienced a phenomenon called **sensory preconditioning,** in which prior presentation of two stimuli together, as a compound, results in a later tendency for any learning about one of these stimuli to generalize to the other stimulus.

In the laboratory, sensory preconditioning is usually tested in three phases, as summarized in Table 9.1. In phase 1, animals in the compound-exposure group (that is, the experimental group) are first exposed to a compound of two stimuli, such as a tone and a light presented simultaneously. In phase 2, the animals learn that one of the stimuli by itself (such as a light) predicts an important consequence (such as a blink-evoking airpuff), and they eventually give a blink response to the light. In phase 3, the animals are then exposed to the tone only. Most will show at least some response to the tone. In contrast, a second (control) group of animals are given exposure to the tone and light separately in phase 1. They are then given phase 2 training identical to the phase 2 training given the other group: they learn that the light by itself predicts the airpuff. But when tested with the tone alone in phase 3, these animals show little or no response (Thompson, 1972).

Table 9.1

Sensory Preconditioning

Group	Phase 1	Phase 2	Phase 3: Test
Compound exposure	Tone + light (together)	Light ⟶ Airpuff ⇒ Blink!	Tone ⇒ Blink!
Separate exposure (control group)	Tone, light (separately)	Light ⟶ Airpuff ⇒ Blink!	Tone ⇒ No blink

It seems that the compound exposure in Phase 1 establishes an association between the tone and light. In Phase 2, the light becomes associated with the airpuff, and this learning is indirectly transferred to the tone too, just as a bad experience with tequila can generalize to the lemons that were often paired with tequila in the past. This transfer can be interpreted as a *meaning-based generalization*, because the tone and light are assumed to have the same meaning (that is, they both predict the airpuff), even though they do not have any relevant physical similarity. A meaning-based generalization can be contrasted with a *similarity-based generalization*, which arises naturally between two stimuli that are physically similar (such as Uggh's yellow and orange fruit). Sensory preconditioning shows that co-occurrence of two stimuli is sufficient to produce meaning-based generalization from one stimulus to the other.

Acquired Equivalence: Novel Similar Predictions Based on Prior Similar Consequences

Another form of meaning-based generalization can occur when two stimuli share the same consequence, that is, they predict the same outcome. In this case, it is possible for generalization to occur between two very dissimilar stimuli, even if they never co-occur. Consider two girls, Mandy and Kamila, who look nothing alike but who share the same favorite breed of dog, golden retrievers. Later you learn that Mandy's favorite fish is a guppy. Given that Mandy and Kamila have similar taste in dogs, you might expect that Kamila will also like guppies.

Geoffrey Hall and colleagues have found a similar form of generalization in their studies with pigeons. In one study they trained pigeons to peck at a light that changed between six different colors, identified as A1, A2, B1, B2, X1, Y1. The researchers then trained the animals that four two-color sequences (A1–X1, A2–X1, B1–Y1, and B2–Y1) predicted arrival of a food reward (Table 9.2, left column).

In effect, the colors A1 and A2 were "equivalent" because they were both paired with X1. Likewise, colors B1 and B2 were equivalent in their pairing with Y1. Next, the pigeons learned that pecking to A1 alone resulted in food; in contrast, no food followed pecks to B1 alone (Table 9.2, middle column). In phase 3, the pigeons were tested for response to A2 and B2. The birds responded strongly to A2 but not to B2 (Table 9.2, right column), suggesting that the birds had learned equivalencies in phase 1 between A1 and A2, and between B1 and B2. After phase 1 training that A2 was "equivalent" to A1, and phase 2 training that responses to A1 resulted in food, the birds expected that responses to A2 would also result in food. Hall and colleagues called this behavior **acquired equivalence,** because prior training that two stimuli were equivalent increased the amount of generalization between them—even if those stimuli were superficially dissimilar.

Table 9.2

Acquired Equivalence

Phase 1 Training	Phase 2 Training	Phase 3: Test
A1 → X1 → food	A1 → food	A2: strong pecking response
A2 → X1 → food		
B1 → Y1 → food	B1 → no food	B2: no strong response
B2 → Y1 → food		

▶ **Learning and Memory in Everyday Life**

Stereotypes and Discrimination in Generalizing about Other People

Stereotypes have a long history of being associated with racism, prejudice, and other social evils. If stereotypes are associated with so many social wrongs, should we also assume that they are factually wrong? One dictionary defines a stereotype as "a generalization, usually exaggerated or oversimplified and often offensive, that is used to describe or distinguish a group" *(American Heritage New Dictionary of Cultural Literacy,* Third Edition, 2007). Other definitions in common use also emphasize that stereotypes are often biased, distorted, and simplistic. In contrast, many psychologists have adopted a more neutral definition of stereotypes that says they are widely held, often oversimplified beliefs about the personal attributes of people who belong to some category (Schneider, 2004; Ashmore & Del Boca, 1981). Under this definition, the question of whether or not a given stereotype is accurate or erroneous, positive or negative, or the cause (or the effect) of prejudice and bias, is left open to empirical investigation (Jussim et al., 2007).

Regardless of the exact definition, few would deny that stereotypes are often hostile and resistant to correction and have been used to justify many harmful forms of discrimination. Note that the word *discrimination* in the preceding sentence does not have the same meaning as in the rest of this chapter. In the context of neuroscience

and the study of learning, and as defined earlier in this chapter, *discrimination* is the ability to tell apart two or more stimuli and generate different responses to each. In everyday social contexts, however, *discrimination* means the differential treatment of individuals on the basis of the group to which they belong, whether that group is defined by race, ethnicity, income, gender, religion, age, or any of a host of other variables.

The line between offensive stereotypes and rational generalizations about other people is often a very thin one and a matter of heated debate, especially when individuals feel that they are being discriminated against as a result of a stereotypical generalization. What is frequently overlooked in these debates is that many generalizations about categories of people *can* be rational.

The formation of categories is a basic cognitive process through which we organize, describe, and understand the world around us. Such categories allow us, as well as other animals, to recognize statistical patterns that can help predict future events. For example, a rat will learn to freeze to a tone if the tone is frequently followed by a shock, especially if the shocks rarely occur otherwise (Rescorla, 1968). The rat has categorized tones as predictors of shocks because doing so provides it with valuable information that enables it to better anticipate, and prepare for, future shocks. In such a case, we could say that the rat has learned to generalize about the category of tones, creating a "stereotype" of tones as likely predictors of danger.

This ability of rats to be sensitive to the informational value of cues is a fundamental feature of associative learning found in all species. Humans are also sensitive to the informational value of cues for organizing and interpreting the world around us, using them as the basis for the formation of new categories (Gluck & Bower, 1988a;

Corter & Gluck, 1992). For example, if all the golden retrievers you have encountered in the past have curly hair and friendly personalities, then you are likely to generalize from those cues and predict that all golden retrievers you will meet in the future are likely to be curly-haired and friendly too. The same principles apply to how we form and maintain general ideas about different groups of people. Thus, if you meet several people from a particular racial group and all are good (or bad) students, you may generalize and predict that all people of that racial group whom you meet in future will also tend to be good (or bad) students.

Our sensitivity to the informational value of cues in the formation of generalizations suggests that, from the perspective of learning theory, we (like rats) are most likely to develop stereotypes when the perceivable cues (such as racial, ethnic, gender, or national identity) are statistically predictive of (or contingent on) other variables of great interest to us, such as income level, crime rate, or amount of education.

The trouble arises principally when people use generalizations, especially stereotypes, about a particular group of people to justify discrimination against individual people, denying the possibility that the generalization may not pertain to every individual in the group. In cognitive terms, it is neither prejudiced, nor irrational, to note actual differences in average characteristics of different groups; what is prejudicial, and irrational, is when a statistical generalization is applied over-rigidly or otherwise misused.

Many commonly held assumptions about specific groups of people do accurately reflect statistical realities (Jussim, 2005). There are, however, two common ways in which a statistically accurate generalization about other people can be misused.

The first is to assume that all members of a category must inflexibly conform

Andrew D. Bernstein/NBAE via Getty Images

Spud Webb, of the Atlanta Hawks, winning the 1986 Slam Dunk Championship

to the generalization. For example, consider the generalization that basketball players are tall. In fact, the overwhelming majority of players in the NBA are over 6'4" in height, and this is greater than the average height of adult males in America. Thus, the assumption is generally accurate and can be confirmed by simply examining the evidence. However, even though it is true that basketball players tend to be tall, there are exceptions, such as Spud Webb, who was only five feet seven inches tall yet played in the NBA in the late 1980s and won a national "Slam Dunk" championship. Though we may know this fact, it is not irrational for us to continue to believe that *most* NBA players are taller than the average American man (who stands about 5'9"). In truth, the typical

NBA player is very tall. However, it *is* irrational to believe that they *all* are. Similarly, it is a fact of life in the United States today that different racial groups in this country have statistically different crime rates, medical issues, educational achievements, and average incomes. But there are large numbers of individuals in every group who do not fit the statistical profile. It is irrational to continue to believe that all members of a racial group must conform to a preconceived idea of that group even after learning about individuals who do not.

The second way in which accurate generalizations are commonly misused is by faulty inverse reasoning. For example, consider the fact that almost 80% of the players in the NBA today are black (Thomas, 2002). Thus, it is an accurate generalization to expect that most professional basketball players are black. However, the *inverse* is not true: most black men are not professional (or even amateur) basketball players. Nevertheless, in a broad range of situations, people routinely misinterpret statistics in this way (Bar-Hillel, 1984). Education and expertise do not make a person immune to this kind of faulty inverse reasoning. For example, a woman with breast cancer truly does have a high probability of having a positive reading on her mammogram. But the inverse is not true: not every woman with a positive reading on her mammogram has a high probability of having breast cancer; this is because the test has a tendency to produce a high rate of false positives. However, by confusing these two relationships, physicians routinely assume that a woman who has a positive mammogram probably has breast cancer, and this mistake in logical inference on the part of the physician results in many women undergoing needless and painful biopsies and surgery (Eddy, 1982).

Thus, even a fundamentally accurate generalization can be used to draw inaccurate conclusions. And yet, accurate generalizations about people can also be put to beneficial use, as long as they are interpreted correctly as descriptors of the average characteristics of a large group. However, even in situations where it would seem rationally and morally justifiable to use statistical group differences to guide behavior, the decision to do so can be difficult. For example, sickle-cell anemia is a disease that appears primarily in individuals of African descent; so, is a physician who routinely tests his black patients—but not his white patients—for this disease acting responsibly, or is he discriminating based on race? If a pharmaceutical company develops a new treatment to protect against breast cancer, and tests it only on women because so few men get the disease, is the company acting reasonably, or is it discriminating based on sex? When states set minimum age limits for obtaining a driver's license, or for purchasing alcohol, or marrying without parental consent, are they acting in a way consistent with the general good, or are they discriminating based on age? What about states that require annual driving exams for senior citizens but not for younger drivers? The issues seem endless, the answers elusive, partly because so many of us have a vested interest in one side of the argument or the other.

Psychological theories and data from learning studies offer no easy solutions to the social problems caused by stereotyping and discrimination, and no clear ethical guidelines by which everyone can agree on what is or is not racism and prejudice. However, the psychological study of categorization, discrimination learning, and generalization does help us understand that generalizing about categories of people is a natural and often useful manifestation of the basic cognitive processes through which we seek to understand and predict the world around us.

In summary, although physical similarity is a frequent cause of generalization, generalization may also occur in other ways. Animals and people can learn to generalize between superficially dissimilar stimuli that have a history of co-occurring or of predicting the same consequence.

Test Your Knowledge

Discriminating between Generalization Paradigms

To be sure that you have learned to discriminate between the various behavioral paradigms of generalization, see if you can assign each of the following four paradigms to the real-world example that best exemplifies it in the numbered list below.

- Discrimination training
- Negative patterning
- Sensory preconditioning
- Acquired equivalence

1. Connie is quite impressed by men who, on a first date, bring her either candy or flowers. However, if a man shows up with both, she is turned off, feeling he is coming on too strong.

2. As a child, Samson learned that people who have deep voices also tend to have hair on their faces. When he later learned that men with beards are strong, he inferred that having a deep voice was also a sign of strength.

3. By playing snippets of music by Brahms, then Shubert, and then Brahms again, the conductor and musician Leonard Bernstein was able to teach an audience of children how to recognize the style of each.

4. In Caleb Carr's novel, *The Alienist,* a serial killer in nineteenth-century New York City has a childhood in which everyone he loves—his mother, father, and others—all beat him savagely. Later, as an adult, he comes to love various new people. But he experiences great difficulty in relationships because he always expects that violence and love will occur together, and becomes physically abusive to those he loves.

Interim Summary

Generalization is an indispensable learning tool that enables us to apply prior experience to new situations. However, using it requires finding an appropriate balance between specificity (knowing how narrowly a rule applies) and generality (knowing how broadly the rule applies). Generalization gradients show how strongly the consequences of one stimulus are expected to follow other similar stimuli. Through discrimination training, the generalization gradient can be modified to allow an organism to distinguish (and respond differently to) highly similar stimuli.

Different models of generalization represent stimuli in different ways. A discrete-component representation depicts each stimulus (or stimulus feature) as one node (or network component). Such representations only apply to situations in which the similarity between the stimuli is small enough that learning about one stimulus should not transfer appreciably to the others. Distributed representations, in which stimuli are represented by sets of nodes (that overlap when the stimuli share some of the same features or elements), provide a framework for modeling stimulus similarity and generalization. Although physical similarity is usually enough to produce generalization, generalization may also occur in other ways; for example, animals and people can learn to generalize between stimuli that have a history of co-occurrence (sensory preconditioning) or that predict the same consequence (acquired equivalence).

9.2 Brain Substrates

Saul Steinberg created a famous cover for *The New Yorker* magazine (Figure 9.13) caricaturing his view of a typical New York City dweller's mental map of the world. Within his depiction of New York City, Ninth and Tenth avenues are drawn in such fine detail that they take up half the map. The rest of the country, the area between New Jersey and California, is represented as a largely barren strip marked by a few scattered rocks and hills.

This painting satirizes the fact that many New Yorkers believe they are living in the most important place in the world. It also illustrates an important psychological principle. Fine distinctions that are meaningful to New Yorkers, such as the differences between fashionable street addresses, are emphasized and highly differentiated in their mental maps; that is, these places are physically pulled apart within this drawing. At the same time, distinctions that may be irrelevant to the typical New Yorker, such as the difference between Illinois and Indiana, are de-emphasized and compressed into less space on the map.

The idea that representations of important areas are elaborated with fine details and take up lots of space, while less important areas lack definition, may sound familiar to you. In Chapter 4 you read about cortical maps and how they expand and shrink during learning. The basic principle explored in those studies was that regions of the cerebral cortex that mediate a highly practiced skill can expand with practice, while regions that are less used may even shrink. The result could be a cortical map that is not so unlike Steinberg's caricature.

What does this have to do with generalization? As described by the models in Section 9.1, representations directly influence generalization behaviors. If the drawing in Figure 9.13 were, indeed, an accurate representation of a New Yorker's mental map of the world, what would this imply? Based on this representation, you might expect very little generalization by a New Yorker between different neighborhoods in New York, despite their proximity. A New Yorker can discriminate between real estate prices on Central Park West (expensive) and those on Columbus Avenue (much cheaper), even though these two streets are actually only a few hundred yards apart. In other words, a New Yorker is unlikely to generalize from one to the other and make the mistake of expecting that an apartment for sale on Central Park West would cost the same as an identical apartment one block over on Columbus Avenue (but if you find one that does, grab it!).

The preceding example might suggest that New Yorkers are pretty knowledgeable people (and, indeed, they like to think so). However, everything changes when they are tested on their knowledge of the Midwest. For a New Yorker with a mental map like Figure 9.13, all the Midwest states are functionally equivalent. If you tell this New Yorker that Kansas has lots of corn farms, he will probably assume the same must surely be true of Iowa and Illinois. In other words, a New Yorker who has identical (or very similar) mental representations of these

Figure 9.13 A stereotypical New Yorker's mental map Saul Steinberg's cover of *The New Yorker* caricatures a stereotypical New York City resident's mental map of the United States. Regions that are important to the New Yorker, such as Ninth and Tenth avenues, are exaggerated in the representation, while other regions, such as the entire Midwest, are disproportionately small. To some degree, we all have similar distortions in our own mental maps, exaggerating information that is important to us at the expense of information we categorize as less important.

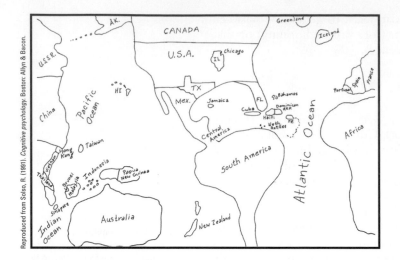

Figure 9.14 Representational distortion: The Midwest version A student from Chicago, when asked to sketch a map of the world, drew his home state disproportionately large and omitted most of the other states. He also drew North America larger than the other continents.

states will automatically generalize from one Midwestern state to another, and have great difficulty telling them apart.

Are New Yorkers unusual in having such a warped view of the world, with extreme generalization in some areas and extreme discrimination in others? To some extent, we all create similarly idiosyncratic worldviews, with uniquely distorted representations; distinctions important to us are enhanced, while less relevant ones are de-emphasized. For example, students asked to sketch a map of the world tend to draw their home region disproportionately large—and in the center of the map. Figure 9.14 is an actual map drawn by a student from Illinois, who overemphasized Illinois relative to the rest of the country, omitted most other states (including New York!), and enlarged North America relative to the other continents. Many American students have the same tendency. In contrast, European students tend to draw Eurocentric maps, while students from Australia are naturally more likely to place Australia and Asia in the center.

These kinds of representational distortions, although sometimes comic in their egocentricity, are actually very useful. A similar process allows a violinist to devote more of her cerebral cortex to the fine control of her left hand, which is involved in the demanding work of holding down different combinations of strings on the proper frets of the instrument, as compared to her right hand, which is only used for the less intricate movements of drawing the bow back and forth across the strings. With only a finite number of neurons available to control all our behaviors, it makes sense to allocate them efficiently according to which distinctions are, and are not, most needed.

The studies reviewed in the first part of this Brain Substrates section will relate the plasticity of the sensory cortices to behavioral properties of stimulus generalization and discrimination learning. The section concludes with a look at the special role of the hippocampal region in stimulus generalization.

Cortical Representations and Generalization

Chapter 6 discussed three main findings about perceptual learning and cortical plasticity. First, when perceptual learning occurs in humans, cortical changes accompany the enhanced discrimination abilities. Second, the selectivity of individual cortical neurons in responding to specific stimulus features can be modified through experience. Third, learning can change the spatial organization of neuronal networks in the sensory cortex. Each of these principles of perceptual learning and cortical plasticity has a bearing on the generalization and discrimination behaviors described in the Behavioral Processes section.

Cortical Representations of Sensory Stimuli

Let's begin our discussion of cortical representations by reviewing some basic features of cortical anatomy. Recall that the initial cortical processing of sensory information occurs in a region dedicated to the sensory modality in question: primary visual cortex (or V1) for vision, primary auditory cortex (or A1) for sounds, primary somatosensory cortex (S1) for touch, and so on. From these initial processing regions, sensory information progresses to higher sensory areas that further integrate the information, first within and then across sensory modalities. Many primary sensory cortical areas are organized topographically (as described in Chapter 6). This means that each region of the cortex responds preferentially to a particular type of stimulus, and neighboring cortical regions respond to similar stimuli. It is therefore possible to draw various "maps" on the cortical surface by studying the responses of different cortical regions.

For example, S1 is a thin strip of cortex running down each side of the human brain (Figure 9.15). By recording the activity of individual neurons in S1 in response to touches on various parts of the body, researchers learned that different neurons respond maximally when different places on the body are stimulated. Some neurons only respond to touch stimulation on a particular finger, some only to touch on a certain region of the face, and so on. If this procedure is followed for a large number of S1 neurons, it is possible to draw a "map" of the body on S1, with each body part lying over the cortical region that shows the greatest response when touched (Figure 9.15).

To some extent, adjacent areas of S1 contain neurons that respond to nearby areas of the body (albeit with some discontinuities: Figure 9.15 shows that the parts of S1 that respond to sensations on the fingers lie near those that respond to sensations on the forehead). Parts of the body that are especially sensitive to touch, such as fingers and lips, activate larger areas of S1. The result is a *homunculus*, a distorted neural representation of the human figure with exaggerated hands and lips but a greatly shrunken torso, as shown in Figure 9.15. (Recall one such homunculus and representations of skill learning from Chapter 4; see especially Figure 4.11). This figure of a human is distorted in

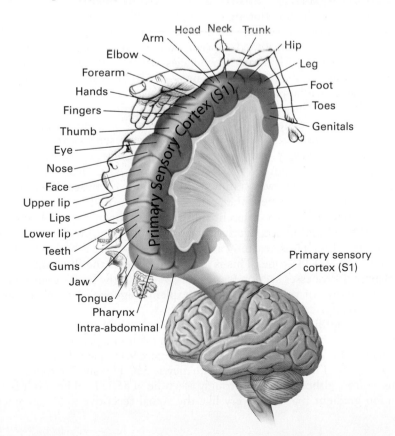

Figure 9.15 A topographic map of the primary sensory cortex (a) Different neurons on the surface of the primary sensory cortex, S1, respond to touch stimuli on different parts of the body. Neurons in each area respond most to input received from the body parts shown above them. (b) As a result, these areas form a distorted map of the body, often termed a homunculus. Nearby regions of cortex are responsible for secondary processing of the incoming sensory information. Adapted from Penfield & Rasmussen, 1950.

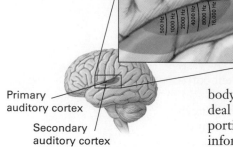

Primary
auditory cortex

Secondary
auditory cortex

Figure 9.16 A topographic map of the primary auditory cortex In the primary auditory cortex, neurons respond to auditory stimuli of different frequencies. Areas lying adjacent to each other respond to similar frequencies.

much the same way as *The New Yorker* cover in Figure 9.13: regions where fine discriminations are important (like sensations on the fingertips) are disproportionately large and detailed.

The primary sensory cortex in other animals shows similar organization, with the homunculus replaced by a distorted figure of the species in question, altered to reflect body areas important to that animal. For instance, primates receive a great deal of touch information through their fingers and lips, which are disproportionately elaborated in their cortical map. Rats receive a great deal of information from the displacement of their whiskers, meaning that a rat's whisker area is disproportionately represented on its cortical map.

The primary auditory cortex (A1) lies near the top of the temporal lobe in humans, and it too is organized as a topographic map, as shown in Figure 9.16. In A1, however, neurons respond to sound instead of touch stimulation. Areas of A1 that are adjacent to each other respond to similar frequencies. Each neuron in the auditory cortex responds most to one particular tone: this is called the neuron's *best frequency*, as was discussed in Chapter 6.

We know what these auditory maps look like because of studies that recorded how often a single neuron fires in response to tones of different frequencies. Figure 6.12 presented data collected from such an electrophysiology experiment with rats by Norman Weinberger. This information represents the **receptive field** for a neuron, meaning the range (or "field") of physical stimuli that activate it. The wider a neuron's receptive field is, the broader the range of physical stimuli that will activate the neuron.

Shared-Elements Models of Receptive Fields

How well does the functioning of receptive fields of neurons match the theories of generalization described in the section on behavioral processes? If the brain is organized to use distributed representations, then physically similar stimuli, such as two tones with similar frequencies, will activate common nodes, or neurons. In other words, two similar tones—of 550 Hz and 560 Hz, for example—should cause overlapping sets of neurons to fire.

Figure 9.17a shows how brain organization might resemble the distributed-component representation (or "shared elements") model from the Behavioral Processes section. A 550-Hz tone might activate sensory receptors in the ear that travel to primary auditory cortex (A1) and activate three nodes—labeled #2, #3, and #4 in Figure 9.17a. Activation from A1 neurons might then travel (through one or more way stations in the brain) to activate other neurons (possibly in the motor cortex) that can execute a learned behavioral response. A 560-Hz tone activates a different subset of A1 neurons—#3, #4, and #5 in Figure 9.17b. These subsets overlap, both activating neurons #3 and #4, as shown in Figure 9.17c. Thus, learning about the 550-Hz tone is highly likely to generalize to the 560-Hz tone. This is much the same as the illustration used in the Behavioral Processes section (see Figure 9.4) to show how a common-elements representation of yellow and orange explains pigeons' generalization between these two physically similar stimuli.

This simplified network may explain why cortical neurons display receptive fields. For each tone in a continuum, we can ask how a particular A1 neuron, such as neuron #3, will respond. The curve in Figure 9.18 (page 366) shows the results we'd expect. The neuron's best frequency is 550 Hz; similar tones also activate this neuron, although not as strongly as a tone of 550 Hz. The result is a generalization gradient that looks very like the actual receptive fields obtained during

Output node:
motor cortex neurons
that guide a behavioral
response

Internal representation nodes:
neurons in primary
auditory cortex (A1)

Input nodes:
sensory receptors in
the ear

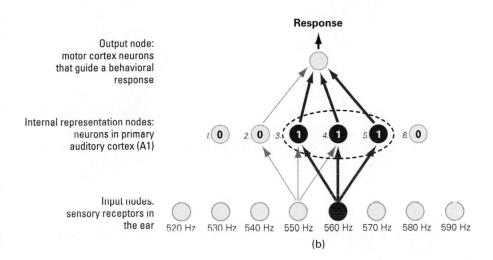

(a)

Output node:
motor cortex neurons
that guide a behavioral
response

Internal representation nodes:
neurons in primary
auditory cortex (A1)

Input nodes:
sensory receptors in
the ear

(b)

Output node:
motor cortex neurons
that guide a behavioral
response

Internal representation node:
neurons in primary
auditory cortex (A1)

Input node:
sensory receptors in
the ear

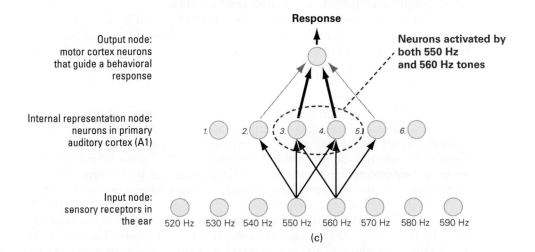

(c)

Figure 9.17 A shared-elements network model of generalization This network has a series of input nodes that each respond to one sound frequency, each of which activates a distributed representation in the nodes of the internal representation layer. (For simplicity, only a few of these lower-layer weights are shown here.) (a) A 550-Hz tone activates nodes *2, 3,* and *4* in the internal representation layer. (b) A very similar 560-Hz tone activates nodes *3, 4,* and *5.* (c) The overlap between these two distributed representations determines the degree to which learning about one tone will generalize to the other.

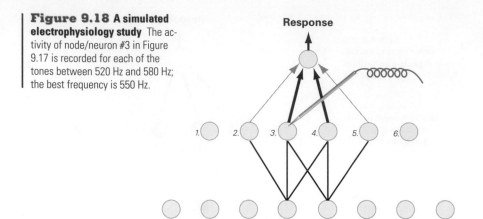

Figure 9.18 A simulated electrophysiology study The activity of node/neuron #3 in Figure 9.17 is recorded for each of the tones between 520 Hz and 580 Hz; the best frequency is 550 Hz.

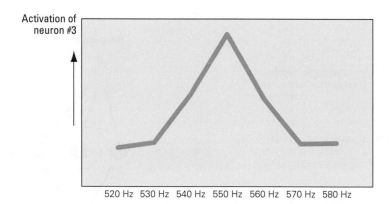

cortical mapping studies, like the one shown in Figure 6.12. Thus, distributed representations appear to be a good explanation of how sensory neurons encode stimulus information.

Topographic Organization and Generalization

The idea of topographic organization was a central part of Pavlov's theories of learning in the early 1920s, but it remained only a theoretical conjecture until nearly a half a century later. In the 1960s, Richard Thompson established a direct relationship between behavioral properties of auditory generalization and certain anatomical and physical properties of the auditory cortex (Thompson, 1962).

A common experimental finding was that cats trained to respond to a tone of a particular frequency would show a generalization gradient to tones of other frequencies, much like the sloping gradient seen in Figure 9.1. However, after Thompson removed the primary auditory cortex (A1) of some of the cats, they responded equivalently to all tones, even those separated by 5 octaves or more! This experiment demonstrated that A1 was necessary for the production of appropriate generalization gradients to auditory stimuli (Thompson, 1965). The indiscriminate behavior of the lesioned cats reflected massive overgeneralization resulting in a flat generalization gradient. As a control study, Thompson also tested other cats who had undergone removal of primary somatosensory cortex (area S1). These animals showed normal generalization behavior to tones, indicating that the auditory overgeneralization occurred specifically in animals with

A1 lesions. Similar overgeneralization of visual stimuli has been reported in monkeys with damage to V1, the primary visual cortex (Thompson, 1965).

These studies suggest that, although it is possible for an animal to learn to respond to stimuli while lacking the corresponding areas of sensory cortex, an intact sensory cortex is essential for normal generalization. Thus, without A1, animals can learn to respond to the presence of *a tone*, but cannot respond precisely to a *specific tone*. In other words, without the primary sensory cortex, animals overgeneralize, and have difficulty discriminating stimuli in the corresponding sensory modality. What the studies do not show is whether the receptive sets of neurons in the brain can be changed as a result of learning and experience. This question is addressed in more recent research.

Plasticity of Cortical Representations

If a particular part of the body receives frequent stimulation, the corresponding parts of the somatosensory map will grow and expand (at the expense of adjacent cortical areas, which compensate by contracting). Lack of stimulation or use can also cause changes in cortical representations, with disused cortical areas shrinking. For example, when a limb is amputated, the part of S1 representing the lost limb does not receive any more sensory input. Rather than allowing that region of cortex to remain idle, nearby areas of the homunculus may "spread" into the vacated space. As a result, those areas acquire increased cortical representation and consequent increased sensitivity to stimulation and touch.

Seminal studies on the neural bases of learning and cortical plasticity come from the work of Norman Weinberger and his colleagues. To examine the plasticity of representations in the primary auditory cortex, they recorded responses from individual neurons in guinea pigs before and after the animals learned about auditory cues (Weinberger, 1993). In one study, Weinberger and colleagues recorded from cortical neurons in A1 before and after the animals experienced presentations of a 2500–Hz tone paired with a shock. Through training, most neurons changed their best frequency to more closely resemble that of the 2500–Hz tone. One such neuron is shown in Figure 9.19. This neuron, which had originally responded most strongly to tones of about 1000 Hz now responded most strongly to tones of the trained frequency. If enough neurons were to show this type of change, the overall result could amount to cortical remapping that allows a larger area of A1 to respond to the trained frequency. These cortical changes occurred quickly, after as few as five pairings of the tone and shock.

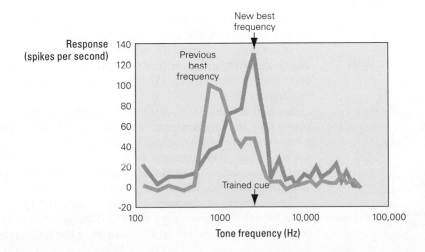

Figure 9.19 Plasticity of representation in the primary auditory cortex After training in which a 2500-Hz tone predicted a shock, the response of an A1 neuron changed from its previous best frequency (about 1000 Hz) to a best frequency nearer that of the trained stimulus. Adapted from Weinberger, 1977, figure 2.

In another study, Weinberger showed that if a tone is repeatedly presented alone (as in habituation, described in Chapter 4), then the opposite effect occurs: there is a decrease in neuronal responding to this frequency (Condon & Weinberger, 1991). Moreover, if the tone and shock are both presented but not paired (that is, if they are presented separately), then no significant changes are observed in the neurons' responses to tones (Bakin & Weinberger, 1990). This result indicates that the cortical plasticity is due to the tone-shock pairing. It implies that stimulus presentation alone doesn't drive cortical plasticity; the stimulus has to be meaningfully related to ensuing consequences, such as a shock.

If cortical change occurs when a stimulus is meaningfully related to—or in other words, is predictive of—a salient consequence (such as food or shock), how does information about that consequence reach the primary sensory cortex? After all, A1 is specialized to process information about sounds, but food is a gustatory (taste) stimulus and shocks are somatosensory, not auditory, stimuli. However, the findings in Figure 9.19 clearly indicate that pairing a tone with a shock *does* bring about a change in auditory cortex.

Weinberger has argued that A1 does not receive specific information about somatosensory or gustatory stimuli, but instead only receives information that some sort of salient event has occurred (Weinberger, 2004). This information is enough to instigate cortical remapping and expand the representation of the stimulus. The primary sensory cortices (A1, V1, S1, and so on) only determine which stimuli, within the corresponding modalities, deserve expanded representation and which do not.

How does the brain determine whether a stimulus merits cortical remapping, without necessarily specifying exactly why? It turns out that several brain regions may serve this function. Recall from Chapter 3 that the basal forebrain is a tiny structure important for learning and memory; damage to it can produce *anterograde amnesia*, or severe impairment in forming new fact and event memories. Many cortical mapping researchers have focused on a small group of neurons located in an area of the basal forebrain called the **nucleus basalis** (Figure 9.20). The nucleus basalis projects to all areas of the cortex and to the amygdala. When nucleus basalis neurons are activated, they release **acetylcholine** (**ACh**), a neurotransmitter that has many functions in the brain, including the promotion of neuronal plasticity. In summary, the nucleus basalis functions to enable cortical plasticity: when a CS is paired with a US, the nucleus basalis becomes active and delivers acetylcholine to the cortex, enabling cortical remapping to enlarge the representation of that CS (Weinberger, 2003).

Figure 9.20 The role of the nucleus basalis in cortical plasticity This medial view of the human brain shows the nucleus basalis within the basal forebrain. Neurons in the nucleus basalis transmit the neurotransmitter acetylcholine throughout the cerebral cortex.

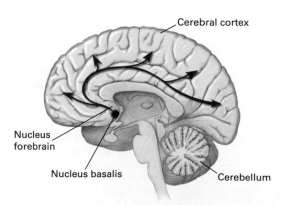

Cerebral cortex

Nucleus forebrain

Nucleus basalis

Cerebellum

But how does the nucleus basalis "know" when to become active? It receives the information through connections from areas such as the *amygdala*, which codes affective information like discomfort and pain (for example, from an electric shock) and pleasure (from food). (You'll read more about the amygdala in Chapter 10.)

Several studies have confirmed that the nucleus basalis can play a role in mediating cortical plasticity. Most important, if a tone is paired with nucleus basalis stimulation—rather than with a "real" consequence such as food or shock—cortical remapping occurs to enhance response to that tone (Bakin & Weinberger, 1996; Kilgard & Merzenich, 1998).

These findings are very exciting because of their implications for rehabilitation after cortical damage. It may eventually be possible to use judicious stimulation of the nucleus basalis to encourage cortical remapping in individuals who have lost the use of one of their cortical areas. Although that is still far in the future, Michael Merzenich and colleagues have shown that strategic application of behavioral training procedures that encourage cortical remapping can be used to remediate certain types of brain disorders in people, a topic to which we will return in the Clinical Perspectives section of this chapter.

Generalization and the Hippocampal Region

One region of the brain that plays a critical role in cortical functioning is the hippocampal region, which is often defined as including the hippocampus and other nearby cortical areas that lie in the medial temporal lobes in humans (see Figure 3.11 and the corresponding discussion in Chapter 3). We explore the role of this region in stimulus generalization next.

The Hippocampal Region

Sensory preconditioning is one form of generalization that is disrupted by lesions to the hippocampal region. Recall the three phases of the sensory preconditioning experiments summarized in Table 9.1. Animals in the compound exposure group are first exposed to a compound of two stimuli, such as a tone and a light, presented together. In phase 2, presentation of one of the stimuli by itself—say, the light—predicts a salient event, such as a blink-evoking airpuff; the animals learn to respond to the light with an eyeblink. Finally, in phase 3, the animals are tested with the tone. Normal animals, after this procedure, will give a significant eyeblink response to the tone in phase 3, indicating that they have generalized the training from the tone to the light, based on the prior co-occurrence of tone and light (Figure 9.21). By contrast, normal animals given separate exposure to the tone and light in phase 1 show little or no responding to the tone in phase 3.

The results are different, however, for animals with damage to their hippocampal region. Rabbits with surgically created lesions in the fornix (part of the hippocampal region) display no sensory preconditioning (Figure 9.21; Port & Patterson, 1984). That is, lesioned animals in the compound exposure group show no more transfer in phase 3 than animals in the separate exposure group. It seems that an intact and functioning hippocampal region is needed for generalizing between stimuli that have co-occurred in the past.

Similarly, Mark Good, Rob Honey, and colleagues have used a version of the acquired-equivalence paradigm described in Table 9.2 and found that rats with hippocampal-region damage (specifically lesions of the entorhinal cortex, which lies next to the hippocampus) show impaired acquired equivalence: they can learn the associations in phases 1 and 2, but show no generalization in phase 3. Again,

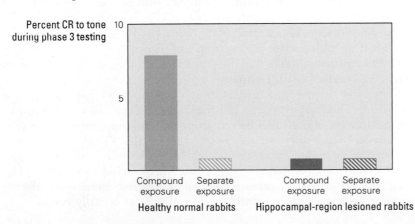

Percent CR to tone during phase 3 testing

Healthy normal rabbits — Compound exposure, Separate exposure

Hippocampal-region lesioned rabbits — Compound exposure, Separate exposure

Figure 9.21 The hippocampal region and sensory preconditioning In sensory preconditioning, animals in the "Compound exposure" group are given phase 1 exposure to a compound stimulus, such as a tone and light, followed by phase 2 training to respond to the light alone. In phase 3, animals are tested for their response to the untrained tone stimulus. Normal animals give at least some response to the tone. By contrast, animals in the "Separate exposure" group, who experienced the tone and light separately in phase 1, show little or no responding to the tone in phase 3. In rabbit eyeblink conditioning, hippocampal damage abolishes the sensory preconditioning effect, so that lesioned rabbits given compound exposure to tone and light in phase 1 show no more response to the tone in phase 3 than do rabbits given separate exposure. Drawn from data presented in Port & Patterson, 1984.

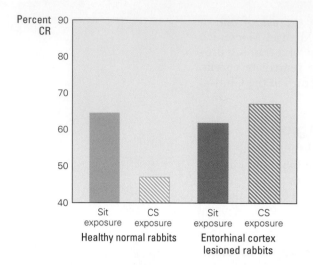

Figure 9.22 Latent inhibition in rabbit eyeblink conditioning Latent inhibition in rabbit eyeblink conditioning is eliminated by hippocampal-region damage, specifically a lesion of the entorhinal cortex. Control rabbits in the "Sit-exposure" condition (solid green bar) who did not receive any preexposure to the tones produced many more eyeblink CRs during subsequent tone-airpuff training than control rabbits who had been previously exposed to the tone (striped green bar). In contrast, animals with entorhinal cortex (EC) lesions (shown in red) showed no such effect. In fact, the rabbits with EC lesions in the "CS-exposure" group (red striped bar) learned better than control rabbits in the equivalent "CS-exposure" group (striped green bar). Brain damage actually helped these rabbits learn faster. Adapted from Shohamy, Allen, & Gluck, 2000.

the hippocampal region seems critical for producing a meaning-based generalization.

Other evidence supporting a key role for the hippocampal region in generalization comes from studies of latent inhibition, a classical conditioning paradigm (described in Chapters 6 and 7) in which learning a CS-US association is slower in animals given prior exposure to the CS (*CS Exposure* condition) compared to animals given equivalent prior exposure to the context alone (*Sit Exposure* condition). This is essentially a generalization task in which the CS-exposed animals are tricked into overgeneralizing from phase 1 (where the CS leads to no US) to phase 2 (where the CS now does predict a US).

One such finding is shown in Figure 9.22, from a study of rabbit eyeblink conditioning by Daphna Shohamy and colleagues (Shohamy, Allen, & Gluck, 2000), who demonstrated that latent inhibition in rabbit eyeblink conditioning is eliminated by hippocampal-region damage—specifically a lesion of the entorhinal cortex. One interpretation of latent inhibition is that the experimental procedure manipulates the relationship between the stimulus cue and the context during preexposure. According to this view, in the CS-exposed group, the CS is generalized to the context during phase 1 and therefore is harder to discriminate from the context in phase 2, when the animal has to learn to respond to the CS in the context, but not to the CS alone. Consistent with this idea, other studies have shown that latent inhibition is highly context sensitive and requires that the animal be exposed (phase 1) and trained (phase 2) in the same context (Lubow, 1989).

Modeling the Role of the Hippocampus in Adaptive Representations

Chapter 3 noted that the hippocampal region, which lies in the medial temporal lobes in humans, is critical for semantic and episodic memory. The data reviewed above suggest that the hippocampal region is also involved in even the most elementary forms of associative learning, including classical conditioning. This does not mean that the hippocampal region is *necessary* for learning a stimulus-response association. Instead, the hippocampal region appears to be critically involved in developing new representations. Mark Gluck and Catherine Myers proposed a theory and computational model in which the hippocampal region operates as an "information gateway" during associative learning (Gluck & Myers, 1993, 2001). In this theory, the hippocampal region selects what information is allowed to enter memory and how it is to be encoded by other brain regions. Specifically, Gluck and Myers proposed that the representation of redundant or unimportant information undergoes "shrinkage" or compression, while the representation of usefully predictive or otherwise meaningful information is "elaborated" or differentiated.

Remember Figure 9.13, caricaturing a typical New Yorker's mental map of the world? This image captures just the kind of compression (for example, of the entire Midwest into a small barren strip) and differentiation (for example, the exaggerated detail of Ninth and Tenth avenues) that Gluck and Myers propose are dependent on the hippocampal region. In their model, these representational changes are computed in the hippocampal region and then used by other brain regions, such as the cerebral cortex and the cerebellum, where the stimulus-response associations that control motor outputs are actually stored.

Gluck and Myers applied their model of the hippocampal region's role in conditioning to a broad range of experimental findings, including the studies of sensory preconditioning and latent inhibition summarized above. In both cases, they showed that the learning displayed by healthy normal animals was similar to how the model behaved when the representational compression and differentiation processes were turned on. In contrast, when these hippocampal-dependent changes in representation were turned off, the resulting "lesioned" model provided a good description of the altered learning seen in animals with lesions to their hippocampal region (Gluck & Myers, 2001).

Further support for Gluck and Myers's model of hippocampal-region function comes from functional brain imaging. The model predicts that the hippocampal region should be very active early in training, when subjects are learning about stimulus-stimulus regularities and developing new stimulus representations, but should be less active later in training when other brain regions (such as the cerebellum and cerebral cortex) are using these representations to perform the behavioral response. As predicted, a functional magnetic resonance imaging (fMRI) study of normal humans learning a probabilistic categorization task (similar to Gluck and Bower's study of medical diagnoses, described earlier) found that activity in the hippocampal region was high early in training and then tapered off as the task was learned (Poldrack et al., 2001).

Interim Summary

Plasticity in the organization of sensory cortices directly impacts behavioral properties of stimulus generalization and discrimination learning. While animals can learn to respond to auditory stimuli without the primary auditory cortex, an intact A1 is essential for normal auditory learning and generalization. Without A1, animals can learn to respond to the presence of a tone, but cannot respond precisely to a specific tone.

Cortical plasticity is driven by the correlation between stimuli and salient events. This implies that stimulus presentation alone doesn't drive cortical plasticity; instead, the stimulus has to be meaningfully related to ensuing consequences, such as shock or food. However, primary sensory cortices do not necessarily receive direct information about the nature of these salient consequences (because the salient consequence may be one that is detected by a different sensory system than the one that detects the predictive stimulus); they need only receive notification that some sort of salient consequence has occurred. Thus, the primary sensory cortices determine which stimuli deserve expanded representation and which do not.

The hippocampal region plays a key role in learning behaviors that depend on stimulus generalization, including the classical conditioning paradigms of sensory preconditioning and latent inhibition. Computational modeling suggests that one role of the hippocampal region is to bring about compression or differentiation of stimulus representations as appropriate.

9.3 Clinical Perspectives

The previous section discussed how the cerebral cortex and hippocampal region both play important roles in generalization. It will not surprise you, therefore, to learn that damage to the cerebral cortex or to the hippocampal region can have devastating consequences for learning and generalization, leaving an individual severely impaired at coping with the world, especially with novel situations. In this final section, we discuss two kinds of brain damage that lead to deficits in generalization: hippocampal-region atrophy in the elderly and language-learning impairments, such as dyslexia, in children.

Generalization Transfer and Hippocampal Atrophy in the Elderly

One reason for trying to understand generalization is that it may help us understand some of the cognitive deficits seen in **Alzheimer's disease,** a degenerative neurological illness in which the first signs of brain damage occur in the hippocampal region. (You'll read about Alzheimer's disease in much greater detail in Chapter 12.) Brain imaging studies of elderly patients have shown that several brain structures, including the hippocampus and entorhinal cortex, show pathology very early in the course of Alzheimer's disease (Golomb et al., 1993; Jack et al., 1998; Killiany et al., 2002). In fact, the physical damage to the brain may begin to appear even before individuals start showing the behavioral symptoms of the disease. Medically healthy elderly individuals with shrinkage, or *atrophy*, in the hippocampus or nearby entorhinal cortex visible from structural imaging of their brains are at heightened risk for cognitive decline and Alzheimer's disease in the next few years relative to same-aged individuals who do not show such atrophy in the hippocampal region (Apostolova et al., 2006; de Leon et al., 1993; Killiany et al., 2002). In fact, progressive hippocampal atrophy itself may represent an early, or prodromal, stage of Alzheimer's disease (Jack et al., 1999).

For example, Figure 9.23 shows two MRIs of human brains, taken in the horizontal plane (meaning the slices depicted here would parallel the floor if the individual were standing). In each image, an arrow points to the hippocampus on one side of the brain. Figure 9.23a shows a normal brain, while Figure 9.23b shows an individual whose hippocampus is considerably shrunken (de Leon et al., 1997). Statistically, the latter individual is at heightened risk for cognitive decline and development of Alzheimer's disease in the next few years, even though at the time the image was taken, he was showing no overt behavioral symptoms that would lead him to be diagnosed with Alzheimer's. Not every individual with hippocampal atrophy will develop Alzheimer's disease, but hippocampal atrophy may be one warning sign.

As discussed earlier, a large body of studies in humans and animals have documented a role for the hippocampal region in tasks such as acquired equivalence and sensory preconditioning that require the ability to generalize when familiar information is presented in a new arrangement or in a new context. These data suggest that individuals with damage to the hippocampal region may be selectively impaired at such generalization, experiencing subtle deficits that may appear well before the onset of clinical symptoms. If so, tests that tap into generalization abilities may have utility as screening tools for detecting individuals in the early stage of Alzheimer's disease—maybe even before other, more characteristic, symptoms appear.

Acquired equivalence might be one such task that is sensitive to hippocampal atrophy. Catherine Myers and colleagues tested this proposition using an experimental procedure in which participants saw cartoon faces and colored fish. On each trial, participants saw one of the faces and two of the fish, and were asked to learn which fish belonged with each person (Myers et al., 2003). In phase 1, for example, the participants might be asked to learn that one face (a brown-haired girl) should be paired with a blue fish; and that another face (a blond-haired woman) should also be paired with the blue fish (Figure 9.24, left). In other words, participants should gradually learn that these two faces are equivalent in the sense that they are to be paired with the same fish. In phase 2, participants learn some new

(a) Normal elderly brain

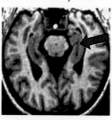

(b) Hippocampal atrophy in elderly brain

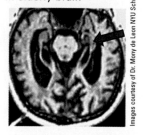

Images courtesy of Dr. Mony de Leon NYU School of Medicine

Figure 9.23 The hippocampus and Alzheimer's disease Two magnetic resonance images (MRIs) showing horizontal slices through the human brain. In each image, an arrow points to the hippocampus. (a) In this brain, the hippocampal volume appears normal for the person's age group. No hippocampal atrophy is apparent in either brain hemisphere. (b) This brain shows significant atrophy or shrinkage of both hippocampi. The atrophy indicates that the individual whose brain is shown in (b) is at much higher risk for cognitive decline than the individual in (a), and may even represent the earliest stages of Alzheimer's disease, when the brain pathology has not yet advanced to the point where behavioral symptoms begin to appear (Golomb et al., 1993). Images adapted from de Leon et al., 1993.

Phase 1: equivalence training   Phase 2: train new outcome   Phase 3: transfer

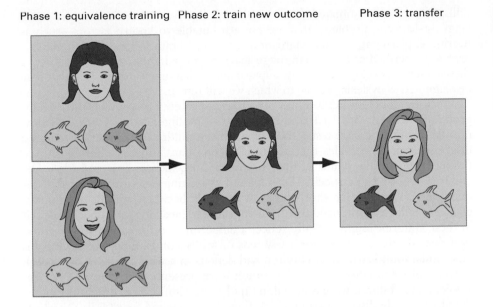

Figure 9.24 Human acquired equivalence study On each trial of this task, participants must choose which of two fish they think the woman will prefer. The figure shows a schematic diagram of the task's three phases. Adapted from Myers et al., 2003.

information: the brown-haired girl should also be paired with a red fish (Figure 9.24, center). Finally, phase 3 is a testing phase, in which participants are quizzed on all the pairings they've learned so far. Intermixed with this testing are some critical pairs that the participants have never seen before. For example, when presented with the blond-haired woman and a red and a yellow fish (Figure 9.24, right), which fish do the participants choose?

In fact, healthy adults reliably pair the blond-haired woman with the red fish, even though they've never specifically been trained to associate this pair before (Myers et al., 2003). In essence, subjects are showing acquired equivalence: if the two faces are equivalent (as trained in phase 1), and if one of those faces belongs with the red fish, then the other probably does too. But individuals with hippocampal atrophy, like the one shown in Figure 9.23b, perform very differently. They can do the learning in phases 1 and 2 as well as controls, but on the testing phase, confronted with new pairs, they perform as if they were guessing blindly. Just like the rabbits with hippocampal-region damage, these humans can learn simple stimulus-response pairings, but they do not exhibit acquired equivalence. Failure on acquired equivalence tasks and tests of other kinds of learning that depend on the hippocampal region may thus represent very early, subtle warning signs of hippocampal atrophy, and if so could be useful as very early detectors for diagnosing which elderly individuals are at highest risk for cognitive decline in the next few years.

Rehabilitation of Language-Learning-Impaired Children

In the Brain Substrates section we described studies by Michael Merzenich and colleagues of cortical remapping and reorganization in monkeys. In a follow-up study, Merzenich, in collaboration with Paula Tallal, an expert on language development in children, applied the principles of cortical remapping observed in monkeys to improve language skills in children.

Most children who are exposed to language throughout their infancy master the incredible complexities of speech generation and comprehension with seemingly little effort, but some children lag behind their peers in the development of these skills. Studies have estimated that 3 to 10% of all preschoolers have at least some language-learning problems that are not attributable to known factors—such as hearing impairment, mental retardation, or known brain lesion—and these children are described as having **language learning impairment (LLI)**. A subset of these children develop a cluster of impairments in language and reading that may be diagnosed as dyslexia, a topic to which we will return.

Work by Tallal and colleagues over the past twenty years identified a subgroup of children with LLI who have normal intelligence but score far below normal on oral language tests. Tallal tested these children on tasks that required discrimination of syllables that begin with consonant sounds differing only in the initial few milliseconds of their pronunciation, such as /ba/ and /da/. The children proved to be specifically impaired at making discriminations that require sensitivity to very short-duration intervals between stimuli or stimulus changes. Tallal hypothesized that what appeared to be a language-specific deficit in these children might actually reflect a deficit in discrimination for information that is only presented for a few tens of milliseconds. Consistent with this idea, Tallal found that these children had deficits in a wide range of nonspeech stimulus discriminations when the stimuli were presented very briefly. For example, if the children were touched in rapid succession on two different fingers, they had trouble discriminating which finger was touched first (Tallal, Stark, & Mellits, 1985; Johnston, Stark, Mellits, & Tallal, 1981). This means that in some cases LLI may not be primarily a linguistic impairment but rather a problem in rapid sensory processing, which has its most obvious expression in the critical discrimination tasks required for normal language.

The next step was to consider how these children with LLI might be helped. Given the extensive support for plasticity in the adult cortex (reviewed in the previous section), Tallal and Merzenich expected that the ability to make distinctions between stimuli could be modified by experience, specifically by intense practice with those stimuli (recall the Merzenich studies with monkeys). Practice in making fine distinctions concerning temporal differences might cause the cortex to remap so as to devote more neural resources to processing rapid successions of phonemic stimuli.

But what kind of training would encourage the cortex to remap so as to bring more resources to bear on the phonemic distinctions that are difficult for children with LLI? Douglas Lawrence, a leading learning researcher in the mid-twentieth century, had wrestled with a similar problem years ago when he sought to identify the conditions under which particular cues acquire greater distinctiveness over other cues during training. Lawrence found that rats given initial training in an easy black-versus-white discrimination were better able to acquire a more difficult discrimination between dark gray and light gray compared to rats who were trained all along on discriminating grays (Lawrence, 1952). Lawrence's easy-to-difficult transfer strategy is quite powerful, as it allows animals to learn to respond accurately to barely perceptible differences between stimuli.

Tallal and Merzenich built upon Lawrence's principle of easy-to-difficult transfer to develop a training program for remediating learning deficits in children who have difficulty making rapid temporal discriminations. Specifically, they created several computer exercises intended to drill children in acoustic recognition of rapidly presented sounds (Merzenich et al., 1996; Tallal et al., 1996). One exercise involved the presentation of two tones that could each be either high or low; the children were required to execute keyboard responses that depended on the order of tone presentation (Figure 9.25). Initially, the tones were relatively long and were separated by a brief but distinct interval, so that the children could perform the task with ease. As the drill progressed, the stimulus duration and intervals were gradually reduced.

In other computer-based exercises, the children were required to distinguish syllables that had been acoustically modified so that the difficult, rapidly changing aspects (such as those differentiating /ba/ from /da/) were artificially extended, for example, from 40 to 80 milliseconds. The syllables sounded distorted but were easy to discriminate, even for the children with LLI. Again, the distorted sounds were gradually speeded up until they were as rapid as in normal speech.

Scientific Learning Corporation

Figure 9.25 Remediating learning deficits by tasks based on Tallal and Merzenich's studies of dyslexia This girl is working on computer-based exercises that drill children in acoustic recognition of rapid sequences of sounds. Photo courtesy of Scientific Learning Corporation.

Experimental and control groups of children were drilled on these computer exercises several times a day for several weeks, and by the end of this training period, many of the children with LLI were able to perform the exercises with the same speed and accuracy as non-LLI children. Following this training, the children with LLI were given a test of their ability to process rapidly presented stimuli. Their performance was seen to have improved dramatically relative to pretraining levels, and this improvement was still evident in a test six weeks after training (Tallal et al., 1996). More important, after a summer of practice, many teachers and parents reported improved performance when the children returned to school in the fall.

More recently, Elise Temple, Paula Tallal, and John Gabrieli used functional brain imaging to show that the brains of children with dyslexia (a specific form of LLI) can be rewired by intensive remediation training to function more like the brains of normal readers (Temple et al., 2003). *Dyslexia*, sometimes called "word blindness," is defined as a specific difficulty in reading that is severe enough to interfere with academic functioning and cannot be accounted for by lack of educational opportunities, personal motivation, or problems perceiving sights or sounds.

The brains of children with dyslexia were scanned using functional magnetic resonance imaging (fMRI) before and after the children participated in the eight-week training program. A control group of children with normal reading abilities also had their brains scanned but did not participate in the training. At the beginning of the study, both the dyslexic children and the control group were asked to perform a simple rhyming task while the initial brain scans were made. Participants were shown two uppercase letters and told to push a button if the names of the two letters rhymed with each other. For example, "B" and "D" would rhyme, but "B" and "K" would not. During the rhyming exercise, control children showed activity in both the left frontal and temporal regions of the brain, as shown in Figure 9.26a. Both of these brain regions are important for processing language (as will be described in greater detail later, in Chapter 13). Children with dyslexia, however, struggled with the task and failed to activate the left temporal region, as shown in Figure 9.26b.

Figure 9.26 Brain plasticity in children with dyslexia Brain activity (fMRI) while rhyming letters differs between controls and dyslexics: Training *alters* functional activity such that it more closely resembles normal activity. (a) Brain images of children with no reading disability show strong left-brain activity in language processing regions, the frontal and temporo-parietal areas. (b) Brain images in children with dyslexia show frontal activity but a lack of activation in the temporo-parietal area. (c) Children with dyslexia display increased brain activity in both these language-processing areas after training, more closely resembling the normal activity seen in the control subjects in (b). Data from Temple et al., 2003.

(a) Controls

(b) Dyslexics pre-intervention

(c) Dyslexics post-intervention

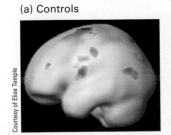
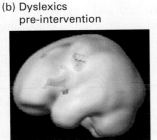
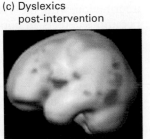

Courtesy of Elise Temple

Next, the children with dyslexia were trained using a program similar to the tone discrimination tasks described above, five days a week, as part of their regular school day. The program consisted of seven computer-based exercises that rewarded players when they answered questions correctly. For example, the computer might show a picture of a boy and a toy, and a voice from the computer would ask the player to point to the boy. A correct response requires the player to distinguish the very brief difference in the sound of the first consonant of "boy" versus "toy." Initially, the questions were asked with those key initial consonants presented in a slower, more exaggerated fashion than in normal speech, to help the children recognize the sounds inside the words. As the player progressed, the speed of the voice in the program slowly increased.

After the training, the children scored higher in language and reading tests. In addition, the brains of the children with dyslexia showed significant increases in activation of language-processing areas, behaving much more like the brains of good readers (Figure 9.26c). This suggests that children's brains are remarkably plastic and adaptive, and that language-intervention programs can alter the brain in helpful ways.

These studies of dyslexia and other forms of language learning impairment demonstrate that insights about cortical function drawn from animal research (specifically, the finding that intensive training with particular stimuli can result in cortical remapping to improve discrimination of those stimuli) can have clinical implications for humans with language learning impairments. Potentially, this idea could be applied to other domains of human learning impairment, as well.

CONCLUSION

Since we last met him, Uggh has been out in the forest for several days hunting for food. As he approaches a stream to get a drink of water, he sees a small brown animal blocking his path. It turns to Uggh and begins to growl. Uggh has never seen this sort of animal before. It looks something like the small brown animals he knows are good to eat, but its growling resembles that of the tigers that have killed two of Uggh's family group. Should Uggh attack or flee?

Uggh's visual cortex registered the visual information about the animal's brown fur, and his auditory cortex picked up the growling sound. Because brown animals are often associated with essential food, the brown-detecting regions of Uggh's visual cortex are highly sensitive and enlarged, the better to quickly detect and recognize them. On the other hand, his auditory cortex is highly attuned to the sound of growling, which has been paired several times in his past with the very aversive experience of seeing his relatives killed and eaten.

As his primary sensory cortices are processing the sights and sounds associated with this animal, Uggh's hippocampal region is combining this information with other information about the overall context in which this event is occurring: the bank of a river, at noon, on a winter's day. In the combination of this contextual information with the visual and auditory cues about the animal, Uggh's hippocampus detects an important pattern: the edible brown animals are frequently found near rivers such as this, while the growling dangerous animals have more often appeared in the mountains. Based on this configuration of local contextual information (the river) and the sight and sound of the animal, Uggh infers that this particular brown animal is more likely to be his dinner than vice versa. He stands his ground, hurls his spear, and brings down his prey, providing food for himself and his whole family group. Although Uggh has never seen this animal before, or even been in this part of the forest before, his power of learning from past experiences and generalizing them to novel situations has served him well.

You yourself will face a similar, if less life-threatening, decision the next time you encounter a buffet dinner. Is the lumpy brown concoction in front of you more similar to your mother's roasted potatoes, which you love, or to the mystery meat served in the school cafeteria, which you consider almost as objectionable as Uggh's tigers? Your ability to discriminate and generalize will govern your choice—and will also determine what you learn from the experience.

Key Points

- Generalization is the transfer of past learning to new situations and problems. It requires finding an appropriate balance between specificity (knowing how narrowly a rule applies) and generality (knowing how broadly the rule applies). Discrimination is the recognition of differences between stimuli and knowing which to prefer.

- Understanding similarity, what it means, and how it is represented in the brain, is an essential part of the challenge of understanding generalization and discrimination.

- A representation that assigns each stimulus (or stimulus feature) to its own node is called a discrete-component representation. Discrete-component representations are applicable to situations in which the similarity among the features is small enough so that there is negligible transfer of response from one to another. Distributed representations, in contrast, incorporate the idea of shared elements and allow the creation of psychological models in which concepts are represented as patterns of activity over populations of many nodes. These representations provide a way of modeling stimulus similarity and generalization.

- All other things being equal, we tend to assume that patterns formed from combinations of cues will have consequences that parallel (or even combine) what we know about the individual cues. However, some discriminations require sensitivity to the configurations, or combinations, of stimulus cues above and beyond what is known about the individual stimulus cues.

- Animals and people can learn to generalize between stimuli that have no physical similarity but that do have a history of co-occurrence or of predicting the same outcome.

- While it is possible for an animal without an auditory cortex to learn to respond to auditory stimuli, an intact auditory cortex is essential for normal auditory generalization. Without their auditory cortex, animals can learn to respond to the presence of *a tone*, but cannot respond precisely to a *specific tone*.

- Cortical plasticity is driven by the correlation between a stimulus and a salient event, such as the arrival of food or a shock. Stimulus presentation alone doesn't drive cortical plasticity; instead, the stimulus has to be meaningfully related to ensuing consequences. However, the primary sensory cortices do not receive information about *which* consequence occurred, only that some sort of salient event has occurred. Thus, the primary sensory cortices only determine which stimuli deserve expanded representation and which do not.

- When a stimulus is paired with a salient event (such as food or shock), the nucleus basalis becomes active and delivers acetylcholine to the cortex, enabling cortical remapping to enlarge the representation of that stimulus in the appropriate primary sensory cortex.

- The hippocampal region plays a key role in learning behaviors that depend on stimulus generalization, including the classical conditioning paradigms of sensory preconditioning and latent inhibition. Computational modeling suggests that this role is related to the hippocampal region's compression and differentiation of stimulus representations.

- Some forms of generalization depend on medial temporal lobe mediation. Elderly individuals with hippocampal region atrophy (a risk factor for subsequent development of Alzheimer's disease) can learn initial discriminations but fail to appropriately transfer this learning in later tests.

- Studies of dyslexia and other language impairments provide examples of how insights from animal research on cortical function can have clinical implications for humans with learning impairments.

Key Terms

acetylcholine (ACh), p. 368

acquired equivalence, p. 357

Alzheimer's disease, p. 372

categorization learning, p. 353

combinatorial explosion, p. 355

configural node, p. 352

consequential region, p. 340

discrimination, p. 338

discrimination training, p. 348

discrete-component representation, p. 341

distributed representation, p. 345

generalization, p. 337

generalization gradient, p. 339

language learning impairment (LLI), p. 374

negative patterning, p. 351

nucleus basalis, p. 368

receptive field, p. 364

sensory preconditioning, p. 356

topographic representation, p. 345

Concept Check

If you are competing in a tennis tournament, you might assume that your best strategy for preparing is to play tennis each day in the weeks before, rather than spending time playing squash or ping-pong or other similar games. But is this necessarily the case? Consider the following experiment conducted by Robert Rescorla in 1976: In phase 1, he trained rats to associate a yellow light (the CS) with a US (Rescorla, 1976). After all the rats were fully trained and giving reliable CRs to the yellow light, he divided the rats into two groups. Rats in the experimental group received a second phase of training with an orange light as the CS until they learned to give reliable CRs. The control rats, however, continued to be trained with the yellow-light CS. Finally, in a third test phase of the experiment, all animals were exposed to a yellow light as the possible CS. The experimental procedure up to this point can be summarized as shown below.

This leads us to the following question: In phase 3, do you think the rats in the experimental group gave a larger or smaller response to the yellow light compared to the rats in the control group? Why? And what does this suggest about the best way to prepare for that tennis tournament?

Hint: In keeping with the shared elements approach of Thorndike and Estes, designate X as a shared element common to both yellow lights and orange lights (capturing the similarity of these two cues), and designate Y and O as the elements unique to yellow and orange lights, respectively. Thus, the yellow light can be viewed as a compound cue YX, and the orange light can be viewed as a compound cue OX. Using this shared-elements representation for these two similar stimuli, apply the Rescorla–Wagner model to each of the three phases of the experiment and predict which group should give a stronger response to the yellow light in phase 3.

Group	Phase 1	Phase 2	Phase 3: Test
Experimental group	Yellow light → US	Orange light → US	Yellow light?
Control group	Yellow light → US	Yellow light → US	Yellow light?

Answers to Test Your Knowledge

Discriminating between Generalization Paradigms

1. Negative patterning.

2. Sensory preconditioning.

3. Discrimination training.

4. Acquired equivalence.

Further Reading

Pavlov, Ivan. *Conditioned reflexes*. Mineola, NY: Dover Publications, 2003, 448 pages. • An unabridged paperback version of Pavlov's classic 1927 book in which he provided a complete exposition of his experimental and theoretical treatment of learning and generalization.

Schauer, Frederick. *Profiles, probabilities, and stereotypes*. Cambridge, MA: Belknap Press, 2003, 384 pages. • A law professor looks at the timely question of whether we can justifiably generalize about members of a group on the basis of statistical tendencies of that group. It includes a review of issues relating to the concept and application of profiling based on racial and other generalizations.

Schneider, David. *The psychology of stereotyping*. New York: Guilford Press, 2004, 704 pages. • A comprehensive, balanced, and readable overview of current research on the formation of stereotypes, including many concrete everyday examples and personal anecdotes.

CHAPTER 10

Emotional Learning and Memory

WHERE WERE YOU ON THE morning of September 11, 2001? When and how did you learn of the terrorist attacks on New York City and Washington, DC? If you are like most Americans, that morning is etched into your memory in crisp detail, even if you lived far from the sites, and even if you did not know anyone who died in the attacks. You may remember hearing the news on TV or radio, or from a friend; you may remember what you were doing at that moment, what emotions you felt, and how you spent the rest of the day. You may even remember the weather (it was a glorious autumn day in New York) or the day of the week (a Tuesday).

But do you remember where you were on, say, the morning of September 10, 2001? Unless something significant happened to you on that day, the odds are that you have few, if any, memories about it, particularly in contrast to your vivid memories of September 11. The reason for this contrast is emotion: the events of September 11 aroused intense emotions, but for most of us, September 10 was just another ordinary day. The intense emotions of 9/11 helped burn the day's events into people's memories in vivid and long-lasting detail.

Why should emotions influence memory so strongly? For one thing, events that arouse strong emotions tend to be those that teach important life lessons. A rabbit that runs past a wolf in its lair and narrowly escapes being eaten needs to remember exactly where the encounter occurred, so it can avoid that place in the future. The emotional response of fear caused by the encounter with the wolf may help signal that something important is happening—something the rabbit needs to remember particularly well. In modern life,

Highly emotional events such as the 9/11 terrorist attacks can produce exceptionally strong and long-lasting memories.

Peter C. Brandt/Getty Images

few humans encounter wild wolves, but we do experience situations that cause intense fear, as well as other strong emotions such as joy, anger, shame, lust, and surprise. Memories laid down during times of such heightened emotion are more likely to be remembered longer, and in greater detail, than memories that are not connected with strong emotions.

This chapter explores the relationship between memory and emotion. Most of the time, this is a positive relationship, with emotion promoting faster learning and more enduring memory. But the darker side of emotion is that too much of it can *interfere* with memory, even to the point of causing or contributing to clinical disorders—depression, stress disorders, and phobias. One of the chief reasons for studying emotion is to understand this linkage—and to help those who suffer from emotions gone awry.

10.1 Behavioral Processes

Suppose a young man, Sammy, is walking home alone late at night and takes a shortcut through a dark alley. He is aware that he's not in the safest of neighborhoods, and he is feeling a little nervous. Suddenly he hears a noise behind him—possibly an attacker—and jumps out of his skin. His heart skips a beat, his hands grow clammy, and he grows pale. Breathing heavily, he turns to look behind him for the source of the threat. All of these responses are part of the emotional experience of fear. Some emotional responses—like the reaction to a loud noise in a dark alley—are innate, and others—like a sports fan's joy when his team wins an Olympic event—are learned through experience or cultural transmission.

What Is Emotion?

We all know an emotion when we feel one; yet emotion, like attention and consciousness, is one of those psychological concepts that are maddeningly difficult to define. In scientific terms, **emotion** is a cluster of three distinct but interrelated kinds of responses: physiological responses, overt behaviors, and conscious feelings. Physiological responses associated with emotion may include changes in heart rate, increased perspiration, increased respiration, and so on. Examples of overt (or observable) behaviors are facial expression, vocal tone, and posture. The conscious feelings associated with emotion are the subjective experiences of sadness, happiness, and so on. The function of emotion is to marshal the body's resources to respond to an important situation.

For Sammy, walking in the dark alley, the physiological responses include an increase in heart rate, an increase in perspiration (which makes his hands clammy), and a diversion of blood away from the capillaries in his face (making him look pale). The motor responses include jumping and looking around. The conscious feeling is the fear that accompanies his understanding that he is potentially in danger. This cluster of physiological, motor, and conscious reactions constitutes a fear response. Other emotions produce different combinations of physiology, behavior, and conscious feelings. For example, 6-year-old Caitlin, asked to eat broccoli, may experience a conscious feeling of disgust; her overt behaviors may include sticking out her tongue and poking at her food, and her physiological responses may include a decrease in heart rate.

Emotion researcher Paul Ekman suggests there is a small set of universal emotions, hardwired in humans from birth (Figure 10.1). This set includes happiness, sadness, anger, fear, disgust, and surprise (Ekman & Friesen, 1984). (Other researchers would enlarge the basic set slightly to include other emotions, such as interest and shame.) All humans, from all cultures, feel these emotions and can recognize the markers of these emotions in others. For example, Ekman and his colleague Wallace Friesen showed pictures like those in Figure 10.1 to people of an isolated tribe in New Guinea. Although these New Guineans lived in a culture very different from that of industrialized North America, they had no difficulty in recognizing the facial expressions of North American college students—and the New Guineans' facial expressions were equally understandable by North Americans (Ekman & Friesen, 1971).

This is not to say that all cultures treat emotion identically. Different cultures may teach their members different rules about the appropriate ways to display emotions in various social contexts. For example, traditional Japanese culture (which places a premium on respect and orderly behavior) encourages suppression of emotional display to a greater degree than American culture (which tends to value individualism more than social order). Thus, while watching a film containing unpleasant scenes, both American and Japanese students express similar overt behaviors (such as grimacing at the nastiest parts); but, if an authority figure such as an experimenter is present, the Japanese students tend to mask their negative expressions more than American students do (Ekman, 1992). Similarly, in many cultures around the world, men and women show similar physiological measures of emotion, but women are much more likely to express happiness and sadness overtly, perhaps because of cultural rules dictating that "real men don't cry" (Eisenberg & Lennon, 1983; Kring & Gordon, 1998). In short, emotion seems to be innate, but its outward expression may be modified by learning.

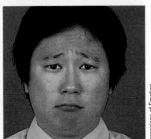
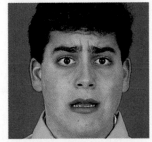
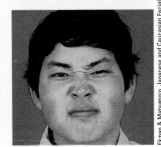

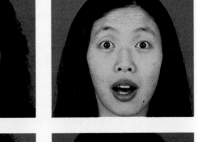

Ekman & Matsumoto, Japanese and Caucasian Facial Expressions of Emotion

Figure 10.1 Faces illustrating "universal" human emotions Humans everywhere, regardless of race and culture, seem to experience happiness, surprise, fear, sadness, anger, and disgust, and can recognize the expression of these emotions in others. From Matsumoto and Ekman, 1989.

Autonomic Arousal and the Fight-or-Flight Response

Facial expressions are a kind of overt behavior associated with emotion. But remember that overt behavior is only one component of emotion; emotions also cause physiological responses.

Imagine you are walking through the forest, and you come face to face with a bear. What happens? First, you probably freeze (an overt behavior). But physiological responses occur too. Your heartbeat speeds up, your respiration rate increases. Fine hairs on your arms and neck may stand on end, and your hands may sweat. Hormones flood your body, causing you to feel a "rush" of energy and excitement. Your body undergoes many other changes that are less noticeable to you: digestion halts, your pupils dilate, and extra blood is directed to your brain and legs, in case you have to run away.

Table 10.1

The Fight-or-Flight Response

Increases in:	Energy diverted to:	Energy diverted from:
• Respiration • Blood pressure and heart rate • Blood glucose level • Release of stress hormones	• Large muscles in legs and arms • Pain suppression • Reflexes • Perception and awareness (e.g., pupils dilate)	• Digestion • Reproduction • Immune system • Sensation (e.g., touch receptors in the skin)

This collection of bodily responses, called **arousal** or (more colorfully) the **fight-or-flight response,** is the body's way of preparing you to face a threat: either by fighting or by running away. Blood flow—with its cargo of glucose that provides energy—is diverted toward the body systems that are most likely to help you in this effort, including your brain, your lungs, and the muscles in your legs (Table 10.1). Other systems such as digestion and the immune system are temporarily deprived of energy. These latter systems are important for keeping you alive—but if you don't survive the immediate threat, it doesn't really matter whether you digested that last meal or fought off that cold.

These bodily changes are mediated by the **autonomic nervous system (ANS),** a collection of nerves and structures that control internal organs and glands. The word "autonomic" is related to "autonomous," meaning that these nerves can operate autonomously, without conscious control. When the brain senses a threat, the ANS sends a signal to the adrenal glands, which release **stress hormones,** including **epinephrine** (also called adrenaline) and **glucocorticoids** the chief of which is **cortisol** in humans. These stress hormones act throughout the body to turn the fight-or-flight response on and off.

Strong, pleasant emotions, such as happiness and surprise, can cause physiological arousal that is very similar to the components of the fight-or-flight response. Thus, a young man in the throes of sexual pleasure may experience the same kind of physiological symptoms (dilated pupils, increased heart rate and blood pressure, sweating, and so on) as one who is suddenly attacked by a masked gunman. As you will soon see, each component of the fight-or-flight response—heart rate, sweating, hormone level, and so on—is a physiological variable that can be measured by experimenters to document what the organism has learned.

Which Comes First, the Biological Response or the Conscious Feeling?

Think back to Sammy, walking through the dark alleyway late at night. He hears a noise behind him and he reacts with a full-blown fight-or-flight response. A fraction of a second later, he recognizes the noise as a friend calling his name. A wave of relief washes over him as he greets his friend and, after a few minutes, his heart rate slows down, his blood pressure returns to normal, and the rest of his body returns to its normal, nonaroused state. One of the interesting features of this scenario is the timing: Sammy jumps *before* he recognizes the sound as friendly (or threatening). This often seems to be the case; in many situations, our automatic emotional responses are a beat ahead of our conscious awareness.

In fact, as early as 1884, William James explicitly proposed that conscious feelings of emotion occur when the mind senses the physiological responses associated with fear or some other kind of arousal. According to this view, Sammy doesn't jump because he feels afraid; instead, he feels afraid because something made him jump. This idea, illustrated in Figure 10.2a, was also proposed by the Danish physiologist Carl Lange, and is often called the **James-Lange theory of emotion** (LaBar & LeDoux, 2003).

One prediction of the James-Lange theory is that researchers should be able to evoke a given emotion in a person by inducing the corresponding bodily responses. For example, experimenters can often produce moods in volunteers just by asking the volunteers to move various facial muscles (without specifying what mood they are trying to produce). For example, one instruction went as follows: "Pull your eyebrows down and together, raise your upper eyelids and tighten your lower eyelids, narrow your lips and press them together."

Can you tell what facial expression this is meant to simulate? How do you feel when you make this expression and hold it for a few seconds? In case you couldn't guess, these facial contortions were meant to simulate anger. Volunteers who made such a face generally showed physiological responses corresponding to the emotion of anger, including increased heart rate and blood pressure. Most of them also reported "feeling" a mild version of anger or annoyance (Ekman, 1992).

This process works for positive emotions, too. When volunteers were told to turn up the corners of their mouths and crinkle their eyes, they reported a mild overall increase in feelings of happiness (Ekman, 1992). Another way to "induce" happiness is by holding a pencil between your teeth without letting your lips touch the wood; the muscles involved are the same ones that are active during a natural smile, and after a few seconds, your biological responses should affect your conscious feelings and your mood should improve (Strack, Martin, & Stepper, 1988).

In short, there seems to be some truth behind the old notion of "put on a happy face"—the simple act of smiling can actually make you feel happier. These findings are consistent with the James-Lange theory that our conscious feelings of emotion depend on what our body is telling us: biological responses come first, conscious feelings second (see also Zajonc, 1980, 1984).

Figure 10.2 Theories of emotion (a) The James-Lange theory: bodily states evoke conscious feelings—"we are afraid because we run." (b) Modern emotional theory: emotional stimuli give rise to bodily responses, which, interpreted in a particular context, give rise to conscious feelings of emotion.

(a) James-Lange theory

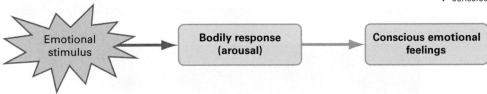

(b) Modern emotional theory

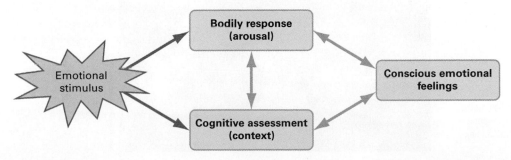

One difficulty with the James-Lange theory is that many emotion-provoking stimuli give rise to similar sets of biological responses. As mentioned earlier, fight (anger), flight (fear), and sexual pleasure all give rise to a similar cluster of physiological responses, including increases in heart rate, perspiration, and hormone release. How, then, does your conscious mind determine which emotion is being signaled by the increased heart rate and other biological responses?

To investigate this issue, researchers tried injecting volunteers with epinephrine, one of the stress hormones that help produce physiological arousal (increased heart rate, increased blood pressure, and so on). They then put individual volunteers in a room with a person who (unbeknownst to the volunteer) had been instructed to act joyful. The volunteers began to catch the mood of their companions. Other volunteers received the same kind of epinephrine injections but were paired with companions who were acting irritated. These volunteers began to act irritated themselves. In other words, epinephrine injections caused bodily arousal, which a volunteer's brain interpreted according to the context in which that individual had been placed (Schachter & Singer, 1962). This suggests that the same ambiguous bodily responses can occur in different emotions, and the label we apply to them depends on the situation we are in.

This idea may seem counterintuitive, but it helps explain the popularity of horror movies, where viewers expect to be made to scream in terror. Given that fear is a "negative" emotion, why would otherwise rational people stand in line and pay good money to experience it? Part of the answer is that the strong biological responses caused by a terrifying movie are not so different from the strong biological responses caused by intense joy or sexual pleasure. Viewers know they are relatively safe in the context of the movie theater, and this cognitive assessment allows them to interpret the strong arousal as pleasurable rather than threatening.

Most modern theories of emotion hold that emotions depend on the interaction of bodily responses, conscious feelings, and cognitive assessment of context (Figure 10.2b), with each able to affect the others (e.g., Damasio, 1999). On the one hand, as James proposed, the particular pattern of bodily responses we feel contributes to our conscious feelings of emotion; on the other hand, our cognitive awareness helps us to interpret that arousal in accordance with our current context. In sum, emotion is a complex phenomenon that includes a constant interplay of conscious feelings, cognitive assessments, and bodily responses.

These moviegoers seem to be enjoying the experience of biological responses normally associated with fear and excitement.

Ryan Mcvay/Getty Images

Do Animals Have Emotions?

Poachers shoot an elephant nicknamed Tina; the other elephants in her tribe try to revive her by propping her up and sticking grass in her mouth. When Tina dies despite their efforts, they sprinkle earth and branches over the body; Tina's daughter returns to the gravesite periodically thereafter and strokes the bones with her trunk (Moss, 1988, p. 73). A female chimpanzee gives birth; as the baby is delivered, the chimpanzee who is the mother's best friend shrieks and embraces nearby chimpanzees, then spends the next few days caring for mother and baby (de Waal, 1996, p. 19). A killer whale grows sick; his podmates flank him and protect him, helping him stay near the surface where he can breathe, even guiding him into shallow waters at the risk of beaching themselves, refusing to abandon him until he finally dies (Porter, 1977).

Can animals feel emotions? Can elephants feel sadness, monkeys feel empathy, and killer whales feel sympathy? Or are the animals described above simply acting on blind instinct, without any of the emotional overtones we would attribute to humans? Certainly these animals often *seem* to behave as if they feel emotions, but the fact is that we may never know if they experience subjective feelings in the same way humans do. But remember that subjective feelings are only one component of emotions. The other two components, biological responses and overt behaviors, are certainly apparent and can be studied in animals.

As early as the mid-nineteenth century, Charles Darwin noted that many species of animals react to arousing stimuli in similar ways (Darwin, 1965 [1872]). For example, when a gorilla is confronted with a frightening stimulus, its first reactions may include jumping and freezing. It may display **piloerection,** meaning that its body hair stands on end; this makes the animal look bigger and more threatening than it is. In extreme situations, the gorilla may defecate or urinate. These responses are remarkably similar to Sammy's reactions in the dark alley: when Sammy hears a suspicious noise, he may "jump out of his skin," then "freeze" while he assesses the situation. Tiny hairs on the back of Sammy's neck and arms may stand on end, and he may develop goose bumps, which Darwin suggested are the remnants of our hairy ancestors' piloerection response. In extreme circumstances, Sammy may even be terrified enough to lose bladder or sphincter control. All of these fear reactions in humans seem to have direct analogues in primates.

To a lesser degree, we can see the same reactions in other mammals. A startled rat shows changes in blood pressure, heart rate, and hormonal release that are

Photographs by Frans de Waal

Emotional displays in animals often have striking similarities to displays of human emotion. This is especially apparent in primates, our closest relatives in the animal kingdom. *Left.* Friendly bonobos display "play faces" that look similar to the expressions worn by humans interacting with their friends. *Right.* Primates often hoot with apparent joy in anticipation of food or when meeting companions they haven't seen for a while—a display that seems similar to human celebration.

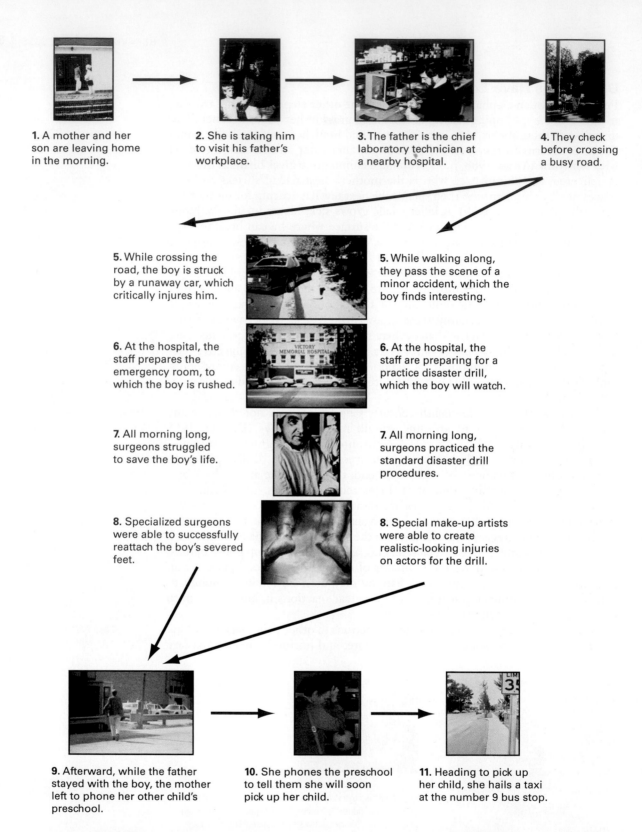

1. A mother and her son are leaving home in the morning.

2. She is taking him to visit his father's workplace.

3. The father is the chief laboratory technician at a nearby hospital.

4. They check before crossing a busy road.

5. While crossing the road, the boy is struck by a runaway car, which critically injures him.

5. While walking along, they pass the scene of a minor accident, which the boy finds interesting.

6. At the hospital, the staff prepares the emergency room, to which the boy is rushed.

6. At the hospital, the staff are preparing for a practice disaster drill, which the boy will watch.

7. All morning long, surgeons struggled to save the boy's life.

7. All morning long, surgeons practiced the standard disaster drill procedures.

8. Specialized surgeons were able to successfully reattach the boy's severed feet.

8. Special make-up artists were able to create realistic-looking injuries on actors for the drill.

9. Afterward, while the father stayed with the boy, the mother left to phone her other child's preschool.

10. She phones the preschool to tell them she will soon pick up her child.

11. Heading to pick up her child, she hails a taxi at the number 9 bus stop.

Figure 10.3 Pictures illustrating both an emotional and a neutral story In this experiment, all participants saw pictures 1–4 (as a slide show), with accompanying narration played on tape. Half of the participants then saw pictures 5–8 accompanied by narration of an "emotional" story (in red) describing a serious accident; the remaining participants saw the same pictures, but with narration that told a "neutral" story (in black) describing a disaster drill. Finally, as both groups of participants looked at pictures 9–11, both heard the same narration. Photos courtesy of Larry Cahill, based on an original design from Heuer and Reisberg, 1990.

broadly similar to the changes seen in cats, rabbits, monkeys, and humans. Even nonmammalian animals, such as fish and reptiles and birds, show some of these same responses. For example, many birds fluff their feathers when alarmed, and some fish spread their fins wide or puff up their bodies, which makes them look larger in a defensive adaptation analogous to piloerection in mammals. When these reactions appear, most researchers feel comfortable claiming that the animal is expressing a fear response, whether or not that animal has conscious feelings similar to a terrified human's.

Emotions Influence How Memories Are Stored and Retrieved

Now that we've defined emotions and their three components (conscious feelings, overt behaviors, and physiological responses), let's turn again to the morning of September 11, 2001. Most Americans felt strong emotional responses that day, ranging from sadness at the deaths, to anger at the terrorists, to fear that further attacks would follow. And most Americans report that they still have vivid, detailed memories of that day.

One reason why we usually have strong memories for episodes of intense emotion (fear and anger, but also happiness and surprise) is that these tend to be memories that we rehearse frequently, reviewing them mentally and talking about them with others (Heuer & Reisberg, 1992). So, for example, in the days following the 9/11 attacks, you may have discussed the situation with many people and watched intensive TV coverage—and each time, your memories for the original event were retrieved, rehearsed, and strengthened. This is one reason why most of us remember September 11 better than September 10. However, the effect of emotion goes beyond rehearsal; strong emotions can actually affect the probability that a memory is encoded in the first place.

Emotion and Encoding of Memories

The effect of emotional content on memory can be studied in the laboratory by "creating" emotional experiences and then testing for memories of those events. In a classic set of experiments, participants saw a series of slides, pictures that tell a highly emotional story about a boy who is involved in a traumatic accident and rushed to surgery (Cahill, Babinsky, Markowitsch, & McGaugh, 1995; Cahill & McGaugh, 1995; Heuer & Reisberg, 1990). These pictures, shown in Figure 10.3, can also be used to tell a much less exciting story in which a boy visits the hospital during a disaster drill, when hospital workers are practicing on volunteers made up to look like trauma victims. Both stories have the same beginning and end, and only the critical middle portion distinguishes the "emotional" story from the "neutral" one. Participants watched the series of slides while listening to a narration of either the emotional, accident story or the less exciting, disaster drill story.

Two weeks later, the participants were shown the pictures again and asked to recall the accompanying narrative. Those who had heard the accident story remembered the dramatic middle events very well; their memories for the comparatively unemotional beginning and end portions were somewhat worse (see Figure 10.4). In contrast, participants who had heard the less exciting story about a disaster drill recalled fewer events, particularly of the

Figure 10.4 The effect of emotion on story recall People who see a series of pictures accompanied by an emotional story (as shown in Figure 10.3) are later able to recall more details of the story's dramatic middle portion than people who see the same pictures accompanied by an emotionally neutral story. Adapted from Cahill and McGaugh, 1995.

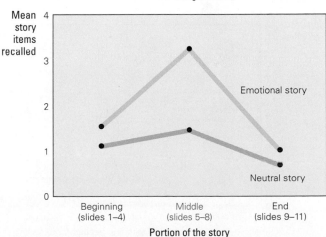

middle portion. Apparently, even though both groups of participants saw the same pictures, those for whom the story created an emotionally arousing context were better able to encode the details and remember them later (Cahill et al., 1995).

This phenomenon of emotional arousal increasing the strength of memory explains in part why television advertisers attempt to use arousing images in their commercials. If they can evoke emotion such as excitement, sexual interest, or humor, there is a better chance you will remember the commercial and, perhaps, buy the product later.

Emotion and Retrieval of Memories

Emotion doesn't only affect how memories are stored; it also affects how they are recalled. Recall from Chapter 3 the concept of *transfer-appropriate processing*, in which chances of recall are increased if the cues available at retrieval are similar to the cues available at testing. It is likewise easier to retrieve memories that match our current mood or emotional state; this effect is termed **mood-congruency of memory.** For example, in one study, students first listened to music and reported whether it made them feel happy or sad. They then saw a list of words (SHIP, STREET, etc.) and were asked to recall an autobiographical memory associated with each word. Students who had reported being in a happy mood tended to generate mostly positive memories, and relatively few neutral or negative memories, as shown in Figure 10.5 (Eich, Macaulay, & Ryan, 1994). Students in a sad mood recalled fewer positive and more negative memories. Few students in either mood generated neutral memories—consistent with the general principle that our strongest memories tend to be associated with strong emotions, whether those emotions are positive or negative.

Mood-congruent memory effects occur in real-life contexts too. For example, patients diagnosed with clinical depression are more likely to recall sad or unpleasant events than pleasant memories (Clark & Teasdale, 1982; Fogarty & Hemsley, 1983). This can lead to a vicious cycle in which the recollection of sad memories makes the patient feel even more depressed and hopeless.

Why might mood influence recall? A strong mood or emotion causes biological responses and subjective feelings, and these are stimuli that can enter into learned associations, just as contextual stimuli and other cues do. As you learned in Chapter 3, one of the factors influencing our ability to retrieve a memory is the number of cues available to guide retrieval. From this perspective, a strong mood or emotion is simply one kind of memory cue, and as the number of cues available at the time of recall increases, the more likely we are to successfully retrieve the original information.

Flashbulb Memories

You've just read how everyday emotions can strengthen memories. Extreme emotions can lead to memories of exceptional strength and durability. Such memories are called **flashbulb memories,** to reflect the idea that these memories are formed quickly, like "flash photographs" taken by the brain to preserve the incident forever in vivid detail, while other, less arousing, memories fade with time (R. Brown & Kulik, 1982 [1977]). Some of us have flashbulb memories for important personal events, like the death

Figure 10.5 Mood-congruency of memory People in a happy mood tend to recall more positive than negative or neutral autobiographical memories; people in a sad mood recall significantly fewer positive and more negative memories. Data from Eich et al., 1994.

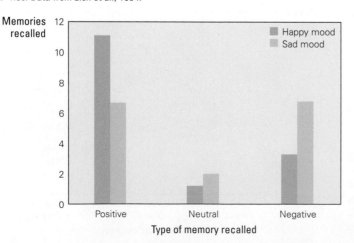

Memories recalled
Type of memory recalled

of a parent, a car accident, or a first kiss. We may remember these events in amazing detail, recollecting not just the place and time of day where, say, that first kiss occurred, but even things like the smell of the room, the sound of a clock ticking in the background, and the color and texture of the clothes we were wearing.

Every so often an event (usually a tragedy) occurs that causes an entire society to form flashbulb memories. September 11 is one example. Other examples include the assassination of public figures—President John F. Kennedy or Martin Luther King, Jr.—and disasters such as hurricanes, earthquakes, floods, or spaceship explosions (see Schmolck, Buffalo, & Squire, 2000). The assassination of President Kennedy is perhaps the most well-studied such event. Nearly 50 years later, many Americans still maintain vivid memories of when and how they heard that the president had been shot. For example, 10 years after the event, one man recalled:

> **"I was seated in a sixth-grade music class, and over the intercom I was told that the president had been shot. At first, everyone just looked at each other. Then the class started yelling, and the music teacher tried to calm everyone down. About ten minutes later I heard over the intercom that Kennedy had died and that everyone should return to their homeroom. I remember that when I got to my homeroom my teacher was crying and everyone was standing in a state of shock. They told us to go home."**
> **(R. Brown & Kulik, 1982 [1977], pp. 23–24)**

Other Americans recalled the moment in similar detail:

> **". . . I was having dinner in a French restaurant . . ."**

> **". . . talking to a woman friend on telephone . . ."**

> **"The weather was cloudy and gray . . ."**

> **". . . I was carrying a carton of Viceroy cigarettes which I dropped . . ."**
> **(R. Brown & Kulik, 1982 [1977], p. 30)**

We can expect that flashbulb memories for the events of 9/11 will turn out to be equally vivid and long-lasting. Take a few minutes and think back to the exact moment when you heard the news (or perhaps saw the Twin Towers fall, on television or in person). Where were you? Who were you with? What did you say and what did you hear other people say? What details can you remember about your emotional reaction, or what you were doing before you heard the news, or how you spent the rest of the day?

You probably remember a great deal, and you probably remember it vividly. But did it all really happen the way you remember? One of the most insidious features of flashbulb memories is that, despite being so vivid, they are often imperfect.

Can Flashbulb Memories Be Trusted?

Ulrich Neisser, one of the foremost memory researchers of the twentieth century, recounted a memory of his boyhood:

> **For many years I have remembered how I heard the news of the Japanese attack on Pearl Harbor, which occurred on [December 7, 1941] the day before my thirteenth birthday. I recall sitting in the living room of our house . . . listening to a baseball game on the radio. The game was interrupted by an announcement of the attack, and I rushed upstairs to tell my mother. This memory has been so clear for so long that I never confronted its inherent absurdity until last year: no one broadcasts baseball games in December! (Neisser, 1982, p. 45)**

THE FAR SIDE BY GARY LARSON

More facts of nature: All forest animals, to this very day, remember exactly where they were and what they were doing when they heard that Bambi's mother had been shot.

Some details of Neisser's flashbulb memory are obviously inconsistent with common sense, and so we (like he) can conclude that his memory is almost certainly wrong in some of its details. However, although baseball is not played in December, football is—and the New York Dodgers and Giants (two football teams with the same names as New York baseball teams of the day) were in fact playing on December 7, 1941, when the radio broadcast was interrupted with news of the Pearl Harbor bombing. Neisser's flashbulb memory was probably reasonably accurate—except for the minor detail that he misremembered the type of game he'd been listening to on the radio (Thompson & Cowan, 1986).

Unfortunately, it is not always so easy to determine whether the details of a flashbulb memory are correct or not. For example, when someone remembers dropping a carton of Viceroy cigarettes on hearing of the Kennedy assassination, how can we tell whether that detail is correct? In general, unless the detail is obviously inconsistent with known facts, we cannot be sure of its accuracy.

Several studies have attempted to address this issue by judging flashbulb memories immediately after the arousing event and again some time later. For example, on September 12, 2001, researchers Jennifer Talarico and David Rubin contacted 54 Duke University students and asked a series of open-ended questions about how the students had heard of the terrorist attacks (Talarico & Rubin, 2003). On average, students remembered about 12 details, such as where they heard the news, who was with them at the time, and so on. The researchers then contacted the same students again later. Talarico and Rubin found that the memories decayed over time, with students remembering fewer details as the weeks and months passed. Students contacted a week after the event might remember only about 10 of the details they'd previously reported, and students contacted 8 months after the event might remember only about 7. At the same time, inconsistent details crept into the reports. For example, on September 12, a student might have reported hearing the news from a friend; by May 2002, that same student might "remember" hearing the news on television.

A similar pattern of distortion over time has been demonstrated for memories of other notable events (e.g., Neisser & Harsch, 1993; Schmolck et al., 2000). In each case, people generally report being very confident of the accuracy of their flashbulb memories—even when those memories are different from what they themselves had previously reported about the event. The bottom line from all these studies is that flashbulb memories are long-lasting, vivid, and largely accurate—but they are not perfect photographic records of the event: they can be incomplete and can even contain inaccurate details.

Why should such errors creep into our memories? Many errors consist of forgetting where the news was first heard and misattributing it to television or radio (Greenberg, 2004). This is perhaps an understandable mistake, given our cultural tendency to become glued to the TV following a national tragedy; the repetition and visual impact of news coverage may swamp our memories of how we really heard the news. Another possibility is that memories of particularly important events are continuously pondered, rehearsed, and discussed. Each time, we are liable, quite unconsciously, to fill any little gaps in our memory with details that seem to fit the context. Later, we remember those inserted details as part of the original event. As you read in Chapter 3, this is one way that false memories can form. The result is that, although many remembered details may be quite correct, others—that seem equally vivid—may be entirely wrong. "Unsolved Mysteries" discusses more about how this process might underlie at least some cases of "recovered" memories of trauma and abuse.

▶ **Unsolved Mysteries**

Can People Forget, Then Recover, Traumatic Memories?

In 1992, a young woman named Beth was suffering from job-related stress. Beth's therapist suggested that the symptoms were similar to those shown by victims of childhood sexual abuse and that Beth herself might have been abused. The therapist taught Beth a kind of self-hypnosis so she could enter a dreamlike state in which buried memories could surface. The therapist also encouraged Beth to imagine past instances of abuse in detail.

Over the next few months, using these techniques, Beth began to "recover" terrible memories of being raped by her father over an 8-year period, starting when she was 7 years old. Twice, she said, he had impregnated her; the first time, he aborted her fetus using a coat hanger, and the second time he made her perform the abortion on herself.

Beth's father vehemently denied that he had raped his daughter. Finally, at the insistence of her family's attorney, Beth underwent a gynecological exam. The results revealed not only that Beth had never been pregnant, but that she was still a virgin. The abuse could not have happened as she recalled. Beth retracted her accusations. She also sued the therapist who had helped her "recover" her memories of childhood sexual abuse, and won a $1 million settlement.

Beth is not unique. Hundreds of people have "recovered" memories—of childhood sexual abuse, participation in bizarre satanic rituals, and even abduction by space aliens. Many of these people are sincerely convinced of (and horrified by) the events they remember. But in more than one case (like Beth's), information has subsequently surfaced to prove the recovered memories are false and the abuse never occurred (Loftus, 1997; Loftus & Ketcham, 1994). How could such mistakes happen?

There are really two questions here. Given that highly emotional events tend to form especially strong memories, could memories of a rape or a similarly traumatic episode ever be forgotten? And, if so, could the forgotten memory be recovered later?

It does seem possible that highly emotional information could, on occasion, be forgotten. Highly stressful events cause the release of stress hormones, particularly glucocorticoids, which in high enough doses can cause temporary malfunction of the hippocampus (see "Learning and Memory in Everyday Life" on p. 408). So, extreme stress could possibly disrupt the hippocampus, leading to incomplete memory formation for the traumatic event (LeDoux, 1990; Nadel & Jacobs, 1998). However, such a memory, having never been stored properly in the first place, could *not* be recalled in perfect detail later.

In fact, such incompletely formed memories would be particularly vulnerable to alteration. Researchers have shown that if people are encouraged to use their imagination to "fill in the gaps" of a partial memory, and if they rehearse this made-up information often enough, they may become sincerely convinced that the made-up memories are real. This is the phenomenon of *false memory*, which you read about in Chapter 3 (Loftus, 1997; Schacter & Curran, 1995). Recent studies suggest that individuals who report recovered memories of traumatic events may be particularly prone to exhibit false memory effects in the lab (Clancy, McNally, Schacter, Lenzenweger, & Pitman, 2002; Clancy, Schacter, McNally, & Pitman, 2000), and they may be similarly susceptible in real life.

Child abuse does occur, of course. There is no scientific reason to question the memories of people who have always remembered childhood abuse, or who have temporarily forgotten it and then remembered it on their own. But most memory researchers argue for extreme caution in evaluating memories recovered using techniques, such as guided imagery or hypnosis, that are prone to produce false memories in the lab (Kihlstrom, 1995; Loftus, 1997; Schacter, 1996).

Despite the agony Beth and her family suffered, their story had a somewhat happy ending. Beth's "recovered" memories were proven false, and she reconciled with her father. In most cases, there is no such simple resolution. If Beth had not still been a virgin at age 22, there would have been no clear way to determine whether she had been raped a decade previously. When both the accuser and accused believe they are telling the truth, how can we determine whether a memory is true or false? Advances in neuroscience may be helpful. In Chapter 3, you read about a study in which brain activity differed depending on whether an individual was retrieving a true memory or a false one (Cabeza, Rao, Wagner, Mayer, & Schacter, 2001). Perhaps a better understanding of the brain substrates of false memory will show us how to reliably document whether an accusation of abuse is a memory of actual events or a tragic mistake.

So, where were you when you heard about the 9/11 terrorist attacks? Whom were you with? It may be instructive to ask those people what they remember about the day and to see whether their memories match yours. Chances are, you will be right about many of the details—after all, strong emotions do encourage strong memories—but at least some of the details that you remember quite vividly, when you can check them against the facts, may turn out to be false memories.

Learning Emotional Responses: Focus on Fear

The preceding discussion focused on how emotions can influence storage and retrieval of memories. In most of the examples, the memory in question was an episodic memory of a single remarkable event. Strong emotions can help such memories form and endure (although, as in the case of flashbulb memories, the process is not always perfect).

Unfortunately, as you saw in Chapter 3, episodic memory is notoriously hard to study in animals, since animals cannot verbalize what they remember. Instead, most research on animal emotion has focused on the learning of physiological responses. In these studies, fear has been more intensely investigated than all the other emotions put together. One reason for this focus is that fear evokes similar biological responses in many species, so that insights gained in rats tend to generalize well to humans, and vice versa. A second reason is that fear responses are relatively easy to elicit. (Not everyone is made happy by the same kind of food or the same kind of music, but almost everyone—even a rat— reacts the same way at the prospect of receiving an electric shock.) So, while fear is not inherently more important than the other emotions, it is particularly amenable to study.

Conditioned Emotional Responses: Learning to Predict Danger

When a rat is given an unpleasant, surprising stimulus, such as an electric shock, it freezes; if nothing further happens, the rat soon goes back to whatever it was doing before. This freezing response is not learned; it is a rat's innate reaction to a threatening situation. As such, it qualifies as an unconditioned response (UR) elicited by a fear-evoking unconditioned stimulus (US). (See Chapter 7 if you need to review classical conditioning and the concepts of CS, US, CR, and UR.)

However, if the fear-evoking US is repeatedly preceded by a neutral conditioned stimulus (CS)—say, a tone or a light—the animal will learn the CS-US association and may then produce freezing conditioned responses (CRs) to the CS. The duration of freezing is an index of how well the animal has learned the CS–US association. At the same time, autonomic fear responses, such as increases in blood pressure and heart rate, occur too. *Conditioned emotional responses* (which were briefly introduced in Chapter 1) are behavioral and physiological CRs that occur in response to a CS that has been paired with an emotion-evoking US.

To begin a typical emotional conditioning experiment on a rat, researchers might play a 10 second tone CS, startling the animal enough that it responds mildly, with slightly raised blood pressure and brief freezing (see the "before pairing" condition in Figure 10.6a and b). Next, the CS is paired with a foot-shock US. Finally, the CS is again presented alone; now, the rat expects the foot-shock US and manifests this learning through conditioned emotional responses. One conditioned emotional response is physiological: a rise in blood pressure

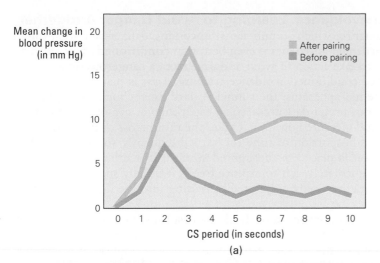

Mean change in blood pressure (in mm Hg)

CS period (in seconds)

(a)

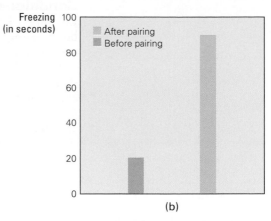

Freezing (in seconds)

(b)

Figure 10.6 Conditioned emotional responding in rats
Before pairing with a US, a tone CS evokes (a) a mild increase in blood pressure and (b) a brief period of freezing. This is an unlearned startle response. Next, the tone CS is paired with a foot-shock US. After pairing, the tone CS evokes (a) a strong increase in blood pressure and (b) extended freezing. These are conditioned emotional responses, indicating that the rat has learned a CS–US association. Adapted from LeDoux, 1993.

that peaks soon after CS onset and lasts for the duration of the CS period, that is, the 10 seconds during which the tone is played (Figure 10.6a, "after pairing"). Another conditioned emotional response is behavioral: freezing for about 90 seconds after the CS is presented (Figure 10.6b, "after pairing"). If the experimenters had chosen to measure other variables indicative of a fight-or-flight response—such as increased heart rate, stress hormone release, or defecation—the CS would probably have elicited many of these responses as well, as further proof of the conditioned emotional response. These learned fear responses are similar to the behaviors a rat would exhibit on being confronted with a natural fear stimulus, such as a cat (Fendt & Fanselow, 1999).

The same basic rules of conditioned emotional responding apply in other species too. For example, recall from Chapter 7 that the sea snail *Aplysia* can learn to withdraw its gill (a CR) in response to a fear-evoking CS, such as a light touch, that predicts a tail shock (US). Is the sea snail "feeling" fear in the same way as a rat huddling in a corner of its cage, or as a New Yorker trying to flee the scene of the terrorist attacks on 9/11? We can't be sure. All we can know is that *Aplysia's* overt behavior is a conditioned emotional response not so different from the overt behavior shown by a freezing rat or a fleeing human.

Conditioned freezing in rats may be seen after only a single CS–US pairing, and even the lowly *Aplysia* can learn a conditioned gill withdrawal in about four trials. Compare that with the eyeblink conditioning you read about in Chapter 7—which may require several hundred trials in rats and rabbits, and dozens of trials in humans—and the inescapable conclusion is that emotional learning is fast. It makes sense that emotional learning should be fast and efficient: presumably, in the wild, an animal doesn't have much opportunity for trial-and-error learning when trying to escape predators, since a single error can be fatal.

Another characteristic of conditioned emotional responses is that they are very long-lasting and hard to extinguish. It may take many extinction trials, in which the animal receives presentations of the CS alone with no US, before the animal stops giving a conditioned emotional response. Even then, extinction does not eliminate the learned response; it only reduces the chance that the CS will elicit it. For this reason, conditioned emotional responses are very easily reinstated after extinction: sometimes, placing the animal back in the experimental chamber where it experienced the US is enough to restore conditioned emotional responding (e.g., Bouton & Peck, 1989).

Conditioned Avoidance: Learning to Avoid Danger Altogether

Learning to recognize which stimuli signal upcoming danger is a good thing, but avoiding the danger altogether is even better. In **conditioned avoidance**, an organism learns to take action to avoid or escape from a dangerous situation.

In one kind of conditioned avoidance training, a rat is placed in a tunnel-shaped experimental apparatus; the tunnel is dark except for one brightly lit area. Normally, rats prefer dark areas, so an experimenter can place a rat in the lighted section and measure how long it takes the rat to cross over into the dark section, and what proportion of time the rat subsequently spends there. Initially, when the rat is placed in the lighted section, it may move to the dark section almost immediately; left to explore freely, it usually spends the bulk of its time in the dark area, only occasionally crossing into the lighted section to explore.

But suppose the rat is given a foot shock the first time it crosses into the dark section of the tunnel. What will the rat do the next time it is placed in the lighted section? First, the rat may remember its earlier unpleasant experience and freeze as soon as it is placed back in the experimental apparatus. This freezing is a classically conditioned response (CR) to the experimental context.

Second, the rat will probably delay before it crosses into the darkened section, and will probably not spend much total time there. This behavioral response of "avoiding" the place where it was previously shocked is an example of *instrumental conditioning*. Remember from Chapter 8 that instrumental conditioning involves a behavioral response R to a stimulus S leading to a consequence C:

Stimulus S → Response R → Consequence C

In this example, the stimulus S is the apparatus, the response R is entering the dark section, and the consequence C is getting a shock. The shock is a punisher, and by the laws of instrumental conditioning described in Chapter 8, the effect of punishment is to reduce the frequency of the response. Thus, the animal learns to decrease the response R (by delaying or avoiding entry to the dark area), thereby delaying or avoiding the unpleasant consequence.

Like conditioned emotional learning, avoidance learning can be fast and long-lasting. A rat that has received a single foot shock in the dark section of the apparatus may delay for several minutes before crossing back into that section, even if tested a day or more after the original learning experience.

Human analogues of conditioned avoidance abound. A victim of mugging may avoid the neighborhood where he was once robbed; a student may avoid taking classes in a subject that she's found difficult in the past; a husband and wife may avoid talking about a topic that has frequently led to heated arguments. In each of these cases, the frequency of a response decreases as a result of its pairing with an undesirable consequence, so these are all examples of negative punishment, just like the ones you read about in Chapter 8.

Learned Helplessness

Emotional learning and memory also provide interesting examples of the way classical conditioning and instrumental conditioning interact. Back in the 1960s, Martin Seligman and his colleagues studied an instrumental avoidance task involving a large box with a low wall that divided the box into two chambers (Overmier & Seligman, 1967; Seligman & Maier, 1967). They placed a dog in one chamber, called the "avoidance" chamber, where it received an electric shock. At first, dogs reacted to such a shock by running around the chamber; eventually, they learned that they could jump over the wall into the "safe" chamber to escape the shock. If the shock was always preceded by a warning signal, such as a tone, the dogs also learned to jump over the wall as soon as the tone sounded, thus avoiding the shock altogether. This is a straightforward example of instrumental conditioning based on negative reinforcement, which you read about in Chapter 8:

S (tone) → R (jump over wall) → C (escape or avoid shock)

Seligman and his colleagues wondered what would happen if, before a dog was first put in the avoidance chamber, the tone stimulus had already been paired with a shock in a classical fear-conditioning paradigm:

CS (tone) → US (shock)

If the dog had already learned the CS–US association and knew that the tone signaled shock, would the dog be able to transfer this learning to the instrumental paradigm? Might the dog jump over the wall the first time it heard the tone in the avoidance chamber, to avoid being shocked?

What the dogs actually did surprised everyone. The first time they heard the tone in the avoidance chamber, the dogs ran around for a few seconds—and then lay down in the corner and whined. Even after repeated trials in the chamber, these dogs never learned to jump over the wall and escape the shock. Intrigued, the experimenters tried to encourage the animals to escape: removing the barrier wall, baiting the safe chamber with food, even climbing into the safe chamber themselves and calling to the dogs to cross over. Nothing worked. The dogs continued to lie in the corner, miserably enduring the shock.

Seligman concluded that the prior exposure to an inescapable shock (during the classical conditioning phase) had taught the animals that they were helpless to escape *any* shock—even in the instrumental learning phase. Seligman named this phenomenon **learned helplessness,** meaning that exposure to an uncontrollable punisher teaches an expectation that responses are ineffectual, which in turn reduces the motivation to attempt new avoidance responses. Learned helplessness has since been demonstrated in a variety of species, from cockroaches (G. Brown & Stroup, 1988) to rats (Besson, Privat, Eschalier, & Fialip, 1999) to humans (Hiroto, 1974; Hiroto & Seligman, 1974).

Seligman suggested that learned helplessness may be an important component of human **depression,** a psychiatric condition that involves not only sadness but also a general loss of initiative and activity (Seligman, 1975). People suffering from depression spend a lot of time sitting around or sleeping, sometimes skipping work or school because they are unable to get up the energy to leave home. Sometimes depression seems to be triggered by external problems, but affected individuals are often unable to do anything to change the conditions that are making them feel depressed. Like Seligman's dogs, they seem to sit and endure their pain rather than explore ways to escape or avoid it. The idea that learned helplessness may at least partially underlie human depression is supported by the finding that antidepressant drugs, which alleviate depression in humans, can also eliminate learned helplessness in rats previously exposed to inescapable shock, as shown in Figure 10.7 (Besson et al., 1999).

If learned helplessness does play a role in human depression, then perhaps the same behavioral techniques that help animals overcome learned helplessness could also benefit depressed patients. For example, Seligman found that if he repeatedly took his helpless dogs and physically dragged them over the barrier into the safe chamber, they would eventually learn to escape on their own. Maybe patients with depression, if explicitly shown ways to escape (or change) their circumstances, could also eventually learn to make changes on their own. Of course, it is relatively easy to show a dog how to cross a barrier to escape a

Figure 10.7 Learned help-lessness in rats When placed in an experimental chamber, control rats (dark green line) quickly learn that a warning light signals an up-coming electric shock, and they will cross the chamber to a "safe" area to escape or avoid the shock. Rats given prior exposure to in-escapable shock (light green line) show learned helplessness: they do not learn to escape the shock, even with repeated training sessions. The antidepressant drug desipramine counteracts the learned helpless-ness effect, so that preexposed rats can learn the escape response (red line). Data from Besson et al., 1999.

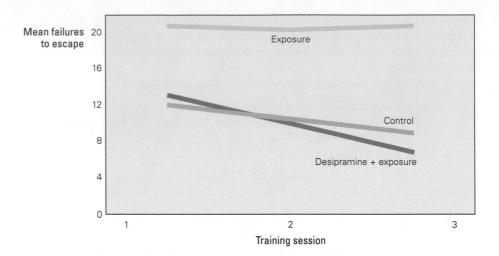

shock; the situations confronting a depressed human may be more complicated and harder to identify—much less learn to overcome by example.

Another possibility may be to prevent learned helplessness in the first place. If Seligman first trained his dogs to escape the shock, then exposed them to in-escapable shock, and then put them back in the avoidance chamber, the dogs continued to be able to escape the shock. Apparently, the earlier learning that they could escape shocks protected the dogs against learned helplessness when they were later exposed to inescapable shock. Perhaps some humans could be protected against depression in the same way: if humans are exposed early in life to adversities that they can overcome, perhaps this early training could protect them against learned helplessness when confronted with more difficult challenges later in life.

The same insight could apply to educational methods. Some children attrib-ute their academic failures to inescapable conditions: "I'm bad at math" or "I'm not as smart as the other children." Confronted with a new math problem, such a child might not bother to try—just like Seligman's helpless dogs. Maybe this attitude could be reversed or lessened by a training procedure that mixes hard problems with problems the child can solve, gradually teaching the child a way to "escape" from the cycle of failure by exposure to challenges that he can mas-ter (Dweck, 1975).

Interim Summary

Emotions have three components: physiological responses, overt behavioral re-sponses, and conscious feelings. Each component influences the others. The major emotions, such as happiness, fear, and anger, seem to be universal, al-though the overt display of these emotions may be influenced by culture. While we cannot be sure whether nonhuman animals have conscious emotional feel-ings, their physiological and behavioral responses to emotional stimuli are often very similar to those in humans.

Powerful emotions can increase the strength and duration of memory stor-age. Flashbulb memories are vivid and long-lasting, but they are not always completely accurate. Emotion can also affect retrieval: we are more likely to re-trieve memories that fit our current mood.

In addition, emotional responses can be learned. Emotional learning can in-volve classical conditioning, so that a CS (such as a tone) that has been paired with an emotion-evoking US (such as a electric shock) evokes a CR (a freezing response or an increased heartbeat). Emotional learning can also involve instrumental conditioning, so that a stimulus S (such as an experimental chamber) can evoke a motor response R (a reluctance to enter the chamber) to avoid a consequence C (foot shock). Sometimes, the same stimulus can evoke both classically conditioned and instrumentally conditioned emotional responses. Learned helplessness occurs when exposure to an inescapable punishment leads to reduced responding—and reduced attempts to escape future punishment.

10.2 Brain Substrates

From the earliest days of brain science, scientists have tried to understand how the brain gives rise to emotion. One of the most influential attempts to locate the brain substrates of emotion was made by Cornell University anatomist James Papez in 1937. (Papez is pronounced "papes," to rhyme with "grapes.") Papez reviewed literature showing that lesions to various parts of the brain caused different kinds of emotional impairments. For example, human patients with rabies, which causes damage to the hippocampus, can be overly aggressive, and patients with damage to the cingulate cortex often display apathy and depression. Therefore, Papez reasoned, the hippocampus and cingulate cortex must play major roles in emotions—along with other regions such as the thalamus, by which sensory information enters the brain, and the hypothalamus, which helps regulate the body's response to emotion. Papez proposed that these brain regions operate in a loop (later named the *Papez circuit*) that is the central processing pathway for emotion.

The Papez circuit is important historically because it represents one of the first systematic attempts to combine information about lesion studies with what was then known about anatomical structures. Remarkably, many of the pathways connecting the structures in the Papez circuit were not yet known to exist; Papez merely deduced they must be there. Almost all of them have since been discovered in the brain.

Despite his brilliant reasoning, Papez wasn't exactly right. Some of the structures he included—such as the hippocampus and hypothalamus—are indeed important for emotion, but they are not restricted to processing emotional information. On the other hand, Papez left out some structures, such as the amygdala, that we now know are critical for emotional learning. Nevertheless, the idea of grouping these structures together took hold, and the term **limbic system** is still used as a kind of anatomical shorthand for this area of the brain (shown in Figure 10.8), which includes the thalamus, hypothalamus, cingulate cortex, hippocampus, and amygdala (MacLean, 1949, 1952).

We now know that the limbic system is not a specialized "emotion circuit." Each emotion—happiness, sadness, disgust, fear, and anger—activates many different brain regions, including but not limited to structures of the limbic system (Phan, Wagner, Taylor, & Liberzon, 2002). For example, in addition to the structures of the limbic system, the frontal cortex also has a key role in emotion. And although many brain structures are activated by various emotions, no single brain region is activated by all the emotions. Thus, emotion seems to be a function of the brain as a whole, rather than arising from special circuits dedicated to individual emotions. All the same, some parts of the brain do seem to be more critically involved than others. First and foremost is the amygdala.

Figure 10.8 Key brain structures involved in processing emotion The structures of the limbic system, which have special roles in emotional learning, include the thalamus, hypothalamus, cingulate cortex, hippocampus, and amygdala. The frontal cortex also plays a key role in interpreting the context and monitoring the display of emotion.

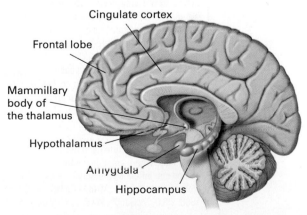

Cingulate cortex

Frontal lobe

Mammillary body of the thalamus

Hypothalamus

Amygdala

Hippocampus

The Amygdala: A Central Processing Station for Emotions

As shown in Figure 10.8, the **amygdala** is a small almond-shaped structure that lies at the anterior tip of the hippocampus; the word "amygdala" is Latin for "almond." (Note that just as the brain has one hippocampus in each hemisphere, it also has one amygdala in each hemisphere, at the tip of each hippocampus; but for convenience, most researcher refer to both amygdalae as "the amygdala," just as they talk about "the hippocampus.")

The amygdala is a collection of more than 10 separate subregions, or *nuclei*, all of which have somewhat different patterns of inputs and outputs. Figure 10.9 depicts some key nuclei and connections within the amygdala. The *lateral nucleus* is a primary entry point for sensory information into the amygdala; this sensory information comes directly from the thalamus, and also indirectly from the thalamus by way of the cortex. The *central nucleus* projects out of the amygdala to the autonomic nervous system, driving expression of physiological responses such as arousal and release of stress hormones, and to motor centers, driving expression of behavioral responses such as freezing and startle. The *basolateral nucleus* projects to the cortex, basal ganglia, and hippocampus, and provides a pathway by which emotion modulates memory storage and retrieval in those structures. The amygdala is critical both in learned emotional responses and in emotional modulation of memory storage and retrieval. In a natural situation, part of the response to fear is activation of the amygdala, which in turn distributes information to the rest of the body, initiating the fight-or-flight response.

The Amygdala and Learning of Emotional Responses

In the research lab, electrical stimulation of the amygdala can produce dramatic emotional displays. For example, stimulating the amygdala of a predator, such as a cat, can cause a species-typical defensive reaction, including lowering of the

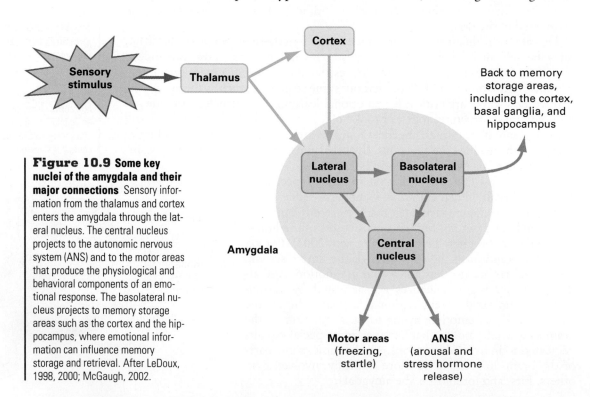

Figure 10.9 Some key nuclei of the amygdala and their major connections Sensory information from the thalamus and cortex enters the amygdala through the lateral nucleus. The central nucleus projects to the autonomic nervous system (ANS) and to the motor areas that produce the physiological and behavioral components of an emotional response. The basolateral nucleus projects to memory storage areas such as the cortex and the hippocampus, where emotional information can influence memory storage and retrieval. After LeDoux, 1998, 2000; McGaugh, 2002.

head, flattening of the ears, piloerection, and growling or hissing (Roldan, Alvarez-Pelaez, & Fernandez de Molina, 1974). In a prey animal, such as a rabbit, stimulation of the amygdala causes a different species-typical defensive reaction, including freezing and a lowered heart rate (Kapp, Gallagher, Underwood, McNall, & Whitehorn, 1981). Stimulating the amygdala in humans doesn't produce such dramatic results. Humans given amygdala stimulation may report subjective feelings of mild positive or negative emotion, but they are not likely to exhibit an all-out emotional response such as occurs in cats and rabbits (e.g., Bancaud, Brunet-Bourgin, Chauvel, & Halgren, 1994; Halgren, 1982).

Why might stimulation of the amygdala cause such a dramatic fear response in some animals but only mild feelings of foreboding in humans? According to modern emotional theory (see Figure 10.2b), our conscious emotional feelings depend not only on our biological responses but also on how we interpret the situation. In the relatively "safe" context of a lab environment, human participants receiving amygdala stimulation know they are in a controlled situation and that a full panic response is not warranted. On the other hand, in a truly menacing situation—such as a walk through a dark alley at night—outputs from the amygdala would initiate a biological fear response—a speeded heart rate, sweaty palms, and other components of the fight-or-flight response.

Given that the amygdala helps initiate the body's emotional responses, it is not too surprising that lesions of the amygdala disrupt the ability to learn, as well as display, new emotional responses. Bilateral damage limited to the amygdala is rare in humans (Markowitsch et al., 1994), although a few such cases have been identified and studied. These patients often show deficits in learning about fear-producing stimuli. For example, Chapter 6 introduced the *skin conductance response* (SCR), a tiny but measurable change in the electrical conductivity of the human skin that occurs when people feel arousal. In healthy people, the SCR can be affected by classical conditioning.

When healthy people hear a loud sound, such as a 100 decibel boat horn (the US), skin conductance increases sharply and then declines back to normal levels over a period of a few minutes. If the US is always preceded by a neutral stimulus, such as the appearance of a colored shape, healthy participants learn that the visual CS predicts the US, and they will produce an SCR to the CS alone (Figure 10.10a).

The SCR is mediated by outputs from the amygdala to the ANS that cause the skin conductance to change. As a result, conditioning of the SCR can be disrupted by damage to the amygdala. Figure 10.10b shows the responses of a patient with bilateral amygdala damage. Although the US evokes a strong SCR, the CS does not. The patient can exhibit arousal when startled, but cannot learn a conditioned emotional response (Bechara et al., 1995).

Similar deficits in learned fear responses are seen in animals with amygdala lesions. For example, let's return to the conditioned-emotion paradigm in rats. After three days of CS–US training, a normal rat, hearing the CS, will give an emotional

Figure 10.10 Conditioning of the human skin conductance response (SCR) (a) The US (a loud boat horn) produces a strong SCR in a healthy person (control). A colored shape (the CS) that has been paired with the US also produces a strong SCR. (SCR is measured in micro-siemens, a unit of conductance.) (b) A patient with bilateral amygdala damage responds to the US, but cannot learn an emotional response to the CS. Adapted from Bechara et al., 1995.

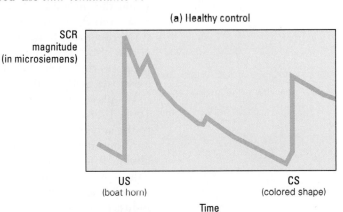

(a) Healthy control

SCR magnitude (in microsiemens)

US (boat horn) CS (colored shape)

Time

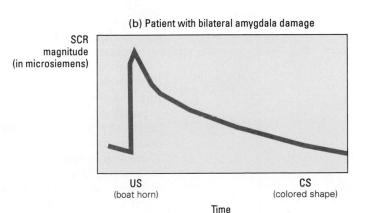

(b) Patient with bilateral amygdala damage

SCR magnitude (in microsiemens)

US (boat horn) CS (colored shape)

Time

response that can include physiological changes (such as increased blood pressure) and overt behavioral responses (such as freezing). Lesion of the amygdala abolishes this learned fear response, so there is no freezing to the CS alone. Likewise, healthy rabbits that have learned that a light CS predicts a shock US will respond to the CS with physiological responses such as decreased heart rate; damage to the amygdala abolishes this learned heart-rate response (Chachich & Powell, 1998).

These disruptions in emotional responding occur because amygdala lesions that damage the central nucleus disrupt the major output pathway to the ANS and to motor centers that drive the freezing response. (This pathway is shown in Figure 10.9.) However, lesion of the central nucleus might not affect whether the fear response is *learned*, but rather disrupt the ability to *express* this learned fear response. Some researchers believe that the CS–US association might be learned and stored in the lateral nucleus, with the central nucleus behaving more like a simple way station that signals other brain stations to turn on the fear responses (for further discussion, see Cahill, Weinberger, Roozendaal, & McGaugh, 1999; Fanselow & LeDoux, 1999; Maren, 1999; McGaugh & Cahill, 2003). Thus, animals with lesions of the central nucleus might still be able to learn about a fear-evoking CS; they would simply be unable to express this learning by freezing or by activating the ANS.

Two Pathways for Emotional Learning in the Amygdala

As you saw earlier, the amygdala receives sensory input from two separate pathways entering the lateral nucleus (Figure 10.9). The thalamus is the first site in the brain where most kinds of sensory input converge and are processed; for this reason, the thalamus is sometimes called the "sensory gateway to the brain." From the thalamus, stimulus information travels directly to the amygdala, and also up to the cortex. As you read in Chapter 6, the cortex processes sensory information more fully, discriminating fine details and so on. Information from the cortex also travels down to the amygdala. Emotion researcher Joseph LeDoux proposes that each of these pathways—the direct path from the thalamus to the amygdala, and the indirect path from the thalamus to the cortex to the amygdala—plays an important role in responding to fear-evoking stimuli (LeDoux, 1993, 1998). The direct path is faster—carrying information from the thalamus to the amygdala in about 12 milliseconds—but it also conveys less detail, just the bare outlines of stimulus information. The indirect pathway is slower—taking about 19 milliseconds for information from the thalamus to reach the amygdala—but the involvement of the cortex allows much finer discrimination of stimulus details. In LeDoux's terms, the direct path is "fast and rough" and the indirect path is "slow but accurate." The faster, direct path allows us to react quickly in a life-and-death situation, activating the fight-or-flight response; the slower, more accurate path then provides extra information, allowing us to terminate the fear response if the stimulus is not dangerous after all.

Here's a simple example of how this dual pathway might work. Suppose you're walking through the woods, worried about bears. A big, dark shape approaches through the foliage. This visual stimulus activates your thalamus, which shoots this information directly to the amygdala. The amygdala interprets this stimulus as possibly signaling danger, and activates an immediate fear response ("yikes!"), preparing you to fight or run away. A few milliseconds later, the signals from the thalamus reach your visual cortex, which processes the stimulus more fully and allows you to recognize the stimulus as nonthreatening: it's only a friend walking toward you. The cortex sends this information ("no danger here") down to the amygdala, shutting off the fear response. (It may take a few moments for stress hormone levels to decline enough so that your heart rate returns to normal and your goose bumps fade away.)

The cost of using the "fast and rough" pathway from thalamus to amygdala is that you have gotten yourself all worked up over nothing. On the other hand, the cost of overreacting to a harmless stimulus is much less, in general, than the cost of failing to respond to a truly dangerous stimulus (LeDoux, 1998, 2000). If the approaching shape really had been a bear, the cost of waiting for your cortex to make a definitive identification could have been the difference between escaping and being attacked. From an evolutionary perspective, mammals with a genetic predisposition to freeze or dart for cover when they see movement in the bush ("Was that rustling in the bushes caused by a predator or just the wind? Better to play it safe and survive another day . . .") are more likely to live long enough to produce offspring that share the same cautious instincts.

But having survived this initial brush with danger, the next challenge is to learn from it. Some of this learning probably takes place in the lateral nucleus of the amygdala, where neural connections change as a result of experiencing a neutral CS paired with a fear-evoking US. For example, in one study, researchers implanted recording electrodes into the lateral amygdala of rats so as to simultaneously monitor the activity of about 100 neurons (Rosenkranz & Grace, 2002). When the rats were presented with various odors—say, almond and anise—the neurons showed a low baseline level of response to each (Figure 10.11a). The researchers then trained the rats that one odor—say, almond—always preceded a tail-shock US. Not surprisingly, the rats quickly learned to freeze in anticipation of a shock whenever they encountered almond odor, although they showed no such fear response to the anise odor, which had not been paired with shock. Figure 10.11a shows that, after training, neurons in the lateral amygdala responded strongly to the almond odor that had been paired with the US. Meanwhile, neuron response to the unpaired, anise odor *decreased* a bit, probably due to habituation.

This is exactly the pattern you would expect to see if *long-term potentiation* (LTP) were occurring in the lateral amygdala. (To review LTP, see Chapter 2.) Assume that the almond odor activates sensory neurons in the rat's nose, and these in turn project (directly and by way of sensory cortex) to neurons in the lateral nucleus of the amygdala. Consider one such neuron (labeled N in Figure 10.11b). Initially, presentation of either odor causes little activity in N (the baseline condition in Figure 10.11a), but a shock stimulus strongly activates N. If the almond odor is paired with the shock, the almond odor arrives at N just as N is activated by shock input; and since "neurons that fire together, wire together," the synapse between them is strengthened (Figure 10.11c). The end result of

Figure 10.11 The lateral amygdala and conditioning (a) Baseline responding of lateral amygdala neurons of a rat is similar for two odors. If one of the odors (almond) is subsequently paired with a tail shock, the response to that odor increases strongly from the baseline value, while the response to the other (unpaired) odor, anise, declines. (b, c) A possible explanation for these data is long-term potentiation (LTP) in the lateral amygdala neurons, such as N, where odor and shock inputs converge. (b) Initially, shock causes a strong response in N, but neither odor alone causes such a response. (c) After shock is paired with almond odor, the pathway carrying almond-odor inputs to N is strengthened through LTP, but pathways carrying information about the unpaired anise odor are not. (a) Data from Rosenkranz and Grace, 2002.

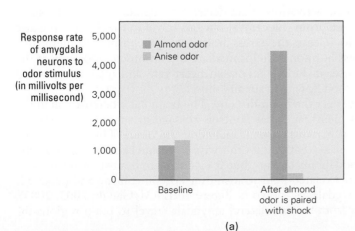

(a)

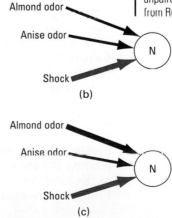

(b)

(c)

these events is that when the almond odor is presented again, it will cause more activity in the lateral amygdala (as shown in Figure 10.11a). No such strengthening occurs in pathways carrying information about anise, or other odors, because they have not been paired with shock.

Does this prove that the lateral amygdala is the site where conditioned emotional responses are stored? Unfortunately, this is not yet completely clear. Some researchers do believe that CS–US associations are stored in some subregions of the amygdala (e.g., LeDoux, 2000). Other researchers think the amygdala may merely guide storage in other brain areas such as the cortex (e.g., McGaugh, 2000; McIntyre, Power, Roozendaal, & McGaugh, 2003; Paré, 2002). However, these are not necessarily contradictory ideas (Fanselow & LeDoux, 1999, p. 229). Perhaps the amygdala specializes in learning the CS–US association and producing emotional CRs, but also modulates memory storage elsewhere that represents other aspects of the experience—such as the episodic memory of an emotional event. So, let's turn next to consider the ways in which emotion can modulate storage and recall of episodic memory.

Stress Hormones and the Emotional Modulation of Memory

Recall the experiment in which a slide show accompanied narration of either an emotionally arousing story or a neutral story (Figure 10.3). Healthy people remembered more details of the emotionally arousing story, particularly from the dramatic middle part, than of the neutral story. By contrast, a patient with amygdala damage recalled the beginning of the story about as well as did healthy controls, but showed no physiological arousal during the emotional middle section and no tendency, later, to recall that material better (Cahill et al., 1995). It wasn't that the patient couldn't remember the story, but that the memory of the emotional middle material didn't get an emotional "boost." This finding implies that the amygdala may provide a signal to strengthen the storage of emotional information in declarative memory.

Even in healthy brains, the degree of amygdala activation may reflect how effectively emotional information is processed and stored in memory. If healthy people are shown emotionally arousing short films while their brain activity is recorded using PET, those individuals with the highest level of amygdala activation during viewing tend to remember more details later than individuals with lower levels of amygdala activity (Cahill et al., 1996). Other studies have documented that the amygdala is activated while participants view pleasant pictures, and greater amygdala activity during encoding is correlated with better recognition later (Canli, Zhao, Brewer, Gabrieli, & Cahill, 2000; Hamann, Ely, Grafton, & Kilts, 1999).

How might amygdala activation affect declarative memory? One key aspect seems to be that outputs from the central nucleus travel to the ANS and cause the adrenal glands to release the stress hormone epinephrine. Epinephrine, along with other stress hormones, helps mediate the various components of the fight-or-flight response, including increased heart rate and dilation of blood vessels, to facilitate blood flow to brain and muscles.

Epinephrine can't affect the brain directly. The brain has a defense called the *blood–brain barrier,* a membrane that controls passage of substances from the blood into the central nervous system, including the brain. This protects the brain from many chemicals that might otherwise enter and harm it. Epinephrine cannot cross the blood–brain barrier, but it can activate brainstem nuclei that produce the chemically related neurotransmitter norepinephrine and project it to the basolateral amygdala, as shown in Figure 10.12 (McGaugh, 2002, 2003). From there, outputs from the basolateral amygdala travel to brain regions in-

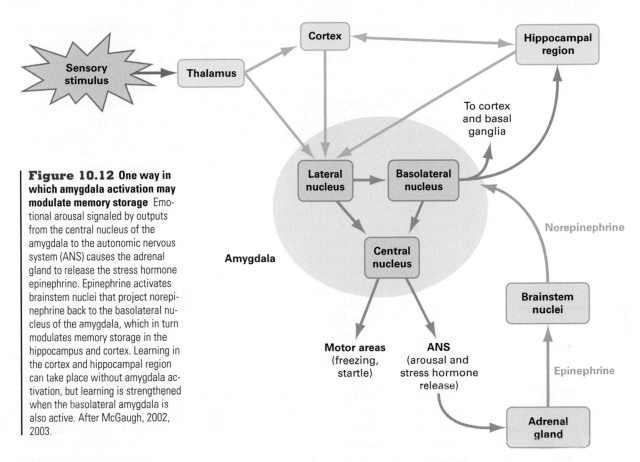

Figure 10.12 One way in which amygdala activation may modulate memory storage Emotional arousal signaled by outputs from the central nucleus of the amygdala to the autonomic nervous system (ANS) causes the adrenal gland to release the stress hormone epinephrine. Epinephrine activates brainstem nuclei that project norepinephrine back to the basolateral nucleus of the amygdala, which in turn modulates memory storage in the hippocampus and cortex. Learning in the cortex and hippocampal region can take place without amygdala activation, but learning is strengthened when the basolateral amygdala is also active. After McGaugh, 2002, 2003.

cluding the hippocampus and cortex. Emotional stimuli such as foot shocks do indeed cause increased levels of norepinephrine in the basolateral amygdala—and the precise amount of norepinephrine in an individual rat's amygdala is a good predictor of how well that rat will remember the learning experience (McIntyre, Hatfield, & McGaugh, 2000).

Just how might release of norepinephrine into the basolateral amygdala affect memory storage elsewhere? Let's assume that a rat (or human) experiences an emotional event that causes norepinephrine to activate the basolateral amygdala. The neurons of the basolateral amygdala tend to fire in rhythmic waves (Paré, 2003) and project out to the cortex, hippocampal region, and other memory storage sites, where they may cause similarly rhythmic activation in large groups of neurons. Such rhythmic activation of many neurons facilitates LTP between the coactive neurons (again, "neurons that fire together, wire together"). In this way, the basolateral amygdala may facilitate learning in the cortex and hippocampal region.

Just as basolateral activity can improve emotional memory, a disruption of the basolateral amygdala can impair emotional memory. Once again, let's consider the study in which Larry Cahill and colleagues showed participants a series of slides accompanied by an emotional story (Figure 10.3). In one variant, before starting the slides and story, Cahill gave some volunteers the drug propranolol, which blocks norepinephrine; the control group received an inactive placebo (Cahill, Prins, Weber, & McGaugh, 1994). Later, those people who'd received the placebo showed the normal pattern of remembering the emotionally charged middle portion best (just as shown in Figure 10.4). In contrast, people who had been given propranolol remembered the dramatic portion no better (and no worse) than the emotionally neutral beginning and end portions. In general, blocking stress hormones (by administering drugs that interfere with epinephrine, norepinephrine, or glucocorticoids) reduces the ability of emotions to enhance memory. On the other hand, increasing stress hormones (by injecting epinephrine, norepinephrine, or glucocorticoids) can improve memory for emotional material (Buchanan & Lovallo, 2001; Cahill & Alkire, 2003).

These results help explain why, on this same story-recall task, the patient with amygdala damage had poor memory for the emotional part of the story. Without input from the amygdala, the hippocampus and other memory storage areas may not be encouraged to form a strong memory of the emotionally arousing material, so the material is stored no more (or less) strongly than any other information.

Although the basolateral amygdala is important during new learning, the influence of the amygdala isn't limited to the initial learning experience. As you learned in Chapter 3, memories are not formed instantaneously but remain malleable throughout a *consolidation period*, during which time they are vulnerable to such interventions as electroconvulsive shock or head injury. Some researchers believe that whenever a memory is reactivated, it is similarly vulnerable all over again (e.g., Nader, 2003). This suggests one way in which *false memories* could be formed: the memory might initially be correct, but each time it is recalled, tiny details might be forgotten or altered and, over time, the memory becomes drastically different from its original form. The reactivation of a memory also provides a window of opportunity during which a fresh dose of stress hormones could strengthen the neural circuits encoding an emotional memory.

This kind of postlearning effect can be effectively demonstrated in rats, using a conditioned avoidance procedure. Control rats, after having received a shock in a dark chamber, will hesitate about 50–60 seconds before daring to enter the dark chamber again (Figure 10.13a). If the rats are given injections of epinephrine immediately (0 minutes) after the foot shock, this delay skyrockets, so that the rats now hesitate for more than 200 seconds before reentering the dark chamber (Figure 10.13b). As you saw in Figure 10.12, epinephrine stimulates norepineph-

Figure 10.13 Stress hormones increase memory If control rats are given a shock the first time they enter a dark chamber, they will delay an average of about a minute before reentering that chamber. Rats given an injection of epinephrine immediately (0 minutes) after the training session will delay much longer, indicating that the post-training epinephrine increased their memory for the episode. The effects are time-sensitive, so an injection given 120 minutes after training has no effect on behavior. Adapted from McGaugh, 2003; data from Gold and van Buskirk, 1975.

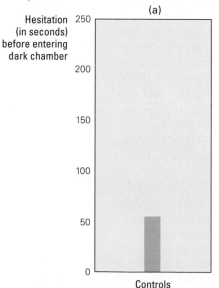

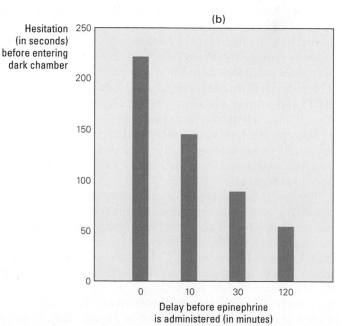

rine release to the basolateral amygdala, which in turn stimulates learning in the cortex and hippocampus—making the rats remember more strongly that the dark chamber is a dangerous place. The effects of epinephrine are greatest if injection occurs immediately after the foot shock, but epinephrine can still boost memory even 30 minutes after the training session (Gold & van Buskirk, 1975; see also Power, Thal, & McGaugh, 2002). By 120 minutes, though, the memory seems to have stabilized, and epinephrine injections have no effect.

Emotion researcher James McGaugh has suggested that there's an important reason why animals might have evolved so as to allow the emotional system to modulate memory after the fact. In many cases, the importance of a particular event might not be immediately apparent. If a pigeon drinks colored water that contains a nausea-inducing agent, the symptoms of sickness may not appear for some time—but once those symptoms do appear, it is very important for the sick pigeon to be able to encode a strong memory of the colored water. Similarly, a child who scribbles on the wall but isn't spanked until hours later, when Mother finds out, must be able to reach back in time and strongly associate the earlier action with the later consequence. In such cases, the ability of stress hormones to affect previously acquired memories allows the amygdala to tinker with the strength of the memory some time later, when the delayed consequences become apparent (McGaugh, 2003).

Encoding Emotional Contexts with the Hippocampus

In discussing how the amygdala might modulate learning about emotional events, we've already mentioned the hippocampal region, which is critical for new episodic (event) memory formation. The amygdala causes emotional arousal and the release of stress hormones, which can strengthen memory formation by the hippocampus (see "Learning and Memory in Everyday Life" on p. 408). The crisp detail in which you may remember the morning of 9/11 is probably due in large part to the action of stress hormones coursing through your body and increasing hippocampal-region storage on that emotional day. The memory was probably strengthened later, too, as you remembered and rehearsed the details.

But the hippocampal region is not limited to learning about facts and events. The hippocampal region also plays a role in some kinds of nondeclarative memory, especially those that require learning about context and other stimulus-stimulus relationships (see Chapter 9). Remember that simple association of a conditioned stimulus (CS) and unconditioned stimulus (US) is not dependent on the hippocampus. This is equally true of conditioned emotional learning. For example, consider the rat conditioning experiments described earlier in which a tone CS is associated with a fear-evoking shock US. Figure 10.14a shows that

Figure 10.14 Conditioned emotional learning (a) After experiencing a tone CS paired with a foot-shock US, control rats quickly learn to give a fear response (freezing) to the CS. Hippocampal lesions (HL) do not affect rats' ability to learn an emotional response to the CS, although amygdala lesions (AL) do. (b) Healthy humans (control group) exhibit a skin conductance response (SCR) to a CS that has been paired with a US (such as a loud boat horn). A patient with hippocampal damage (HL) also shows a conditioned SCR, but a patient with bilateral amygdala damage (AL) does not. (c) Healthy humans can report contextual information about the conditioning experiment; the patient with hippocampal damage cannot report this information—but the patient with bilateral amygdala damage can. This finding suggests a dissociation between conditioned emotional responding (which depends on the amygdala) and contextual or episodic learning (which depends on the hippocampus). (a) Adapted from Phillips and LeDoux, 1992; (b, c) adapted from Bechara et al., 1995.

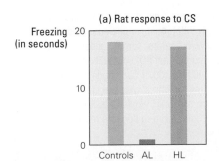

(a) Rat response to CS

Freezing (in seconds)

Controls AL HL

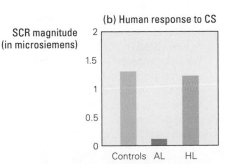

(b) Human response to CS

SCR magnitude (in microsiemens)

Controls AL HL

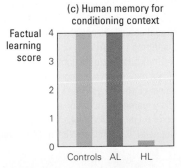

(c) Human memory for conditioning context

Factual learning score

Controls AL HL

► **Learning and Memory in Everyday Life**

A Little Stress Is a Good Thing

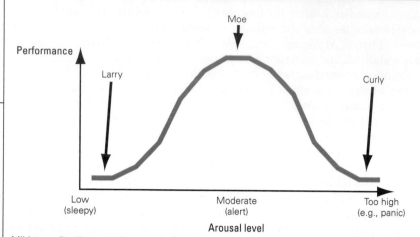

Mild stress (leading to moderate arousal) can improve memory encoding and recall, but high levels of stress and arousal can impair encoding and recall. Thus, of three students taking the SATs, Moe (who experiences moderate stress) may recall studied information better than Larry (who experiences little stress) or Curly (who is suffering a panic attack).

Three high school students, Larry, Moe, and Curly, are facing a stressful experience: taking their SATs. But the three students are reacting in different ways. Larry has already gained early acceptance to Princeton, so he is relatively relaxed as he takes the exam. Moe is more nervous; his grades are good but not great, and strong SAT scores could help him get into the college of his choice. Curly is downright panicked; his grades are lousy, and the only chance he has of going to a decent college is if he aces the SATs. On the (admittedly fictitious) assumption that all three students have equal knowledge going into the exam, who is likely to perform best?

As is probably obvious, Curly is at a disadvantage; he is so stressed out that he may well forget everything he ever knew as soon as he looks at the first question. It might be less obvious that Larry is also at a disadvantage: there is such a thing as being too relaxed. A little stress is good for memory, and this applies to recall (taking a test) as well as encoding (initial learning). Mild stress causes release of stress hormones, including epinephrine and glucocorticoids. The hippocampus has a particularly high concentration of glucocorticoid receptors (McEwen & Sapolsky, 1995), and low levels of stress hormones can facilitate LTP and encourage dendritic growth, improving memory formation and recall (McEwen, 1999; Shors & Dryver, 1994). Thus, Moe should actually benefit from his mild anxiety during the SATs.

Unfortunately, although low levels of stress can improve memory, chronic high levels of stress can impair recall of previously learned information (de Quervain, Roozendaal, & McGaugh, 1998; de Quervain, Roozendaal, Nitsch, McGaugh, & Hock, 2000). The inverted U-shaped relationship shown in the figure is sometimes called a *Yerkes-Dodson curve,* after two researchers who found that such a curve described the relationship between arousal and habit learning (Yerkes & Dodson, 1908). The relationship holds for stress and the hippocampus too. Although low levels of stress hormones facilitate hippocampal learning, higher levels may overexcite the hippocampus, interfering with learning and recall (Benjamin, McKeachie, Lin, & Holinger, 1981). Long-term exposure to high levels of stress can even cause neuronal death in the hippocampus (McEwen, 1997; Sapolsky, 1996). If this happens, the memory impairment will be permanent.

What triggers the transition from improved memory (at low levels of stress) to hippocampal damage (at high levels)? Put another way, how much stress is too much? Unfortunately, there is no easy answer: each individual seems to have a different breaking point (Kemeny, 2003). We all know people (think of stockbrokers and emergency-room nurses) who thrive under stressful conditions, while other people fall to pieces whenever they experience the least little setback. Each person should learn how much stress is too much at an individual level, and then try to stay within those bounds. If you are feeling regularly stressed, try making a list of the things that bother you and then look for ways of changing one or two of them. You can also try methods of reducing stress such as meditation, yoga, prayer, or exercise. These techniques provide a temporary escape from the ups and downs of daily life and, practiced daily, may have medical benefits. During times of stress, they may help get your hippocampus back into its normal operating range (Davidson et al., 2003).

As for Curly . . . the best thing he can do is try to calm himself during the test—perhaps by taking a few deep breaths and thinking positive thoughts (Naveh-Benjamin, 1991). Once his stress hormones drop back to normal levels, his hippocampus can again function normally. (This is one reason why, after the SATs are over, Curly will probably remember all those answers that he "forgot" under pressure during the test.) Of course, better planning would help too: if Curly hadn't let his grades get into such a sad state in the first place, the SATs wouldn't be so critical, and he could afford to be more relaxed during the test.

such CS–US learning is not disrupted by a hippocampal lesion, but it is devastated by an amygdala lesion (LeDoux, 1994).

During such classical fear conditioning, a normal rat learns not only about the CS and the US but also about the context in which the US is presented. Thus, after CS–US training in a particular chamber, the rat may show a conditioned emotional response as soon as it is placed back into that chamber—before any CS (or US) is presented. In fact, a healthy animal's response to the context may be almost as strong as its response to the CS! This contextual freezing response is greatly reduced in animals with hippocampal lesions. Amygdala lesions also abolish the contextual fear response, possibly because the lesion damages the output pathway from the central nucleus to the motor areas that produce the freezing response (Phillips & LeDoux, 1992).

A similar interplay occurs between hippocampus and amygdala in humans monitored for the skin conductance response. Earlier (see Figure 10.10) we described how healthy humans show an SCR to a US (a loud boat horn) as well as to a CS (a visual stimulus) that has been paired with the US. In these experiments, a patient with hippocampal damage showed the same conditioned response, but a patient with amygdala damage showed no SCR, as shown in Figure 10.14b (Bechara et al., 1995). This is exactly the same pattern as in rats.

After the SCR experiment was finished, experimenters asked participants what they remembered about the conditioning situation. Healthy individuals could report that the CS predicted that the US was coming (Figure 10.14c). The patient with hippocampal damage, who had learned the SCR, could not report any details of the conditioning experiment. This is consistent with the general expectation that a hippocampal lesion abolishes the ability to form new episodic memories but does not prevent simple classical conditioning. The patient with amygdala damage showed the opposite pattern: she could report the details of the conditioning experiment quite well—and she understood that the CS predicted the US—even though she did not generate an SCR to the CS. Thus, amygdala damage seems to spare hippocampal-dependent context learning but to disrupt fear conditioning. Emotional learning was spared—only the *expression* of an emotional response was disrupted.

How might contextual information, mediated by the hippocampal region, affect fear learning in the amygdala? The path from amygdala to hippocampal region is a two-way street (Figure 10.12). Signals from the basolateral amygdala travel to the hippocampal region. But signals from the hippocampal region containing information about the learning context also travel back to the lateral amygdala, where they can be incorporated into ongoing emotional processing. This is part of the reason why returning to the place (or context) where an emotional experience occurred is often enough to evoke arousal. For example, when individuals return to a place where they experienced intense sadness or fear, they are sometimes struck with a fresh wave of grief or terror. Similarly (and more happily), couples celebrating an anniversary sometimes choose the restaurant where they had their first date, because returning to the context where they once experienced strong feelings of romance can help evoke those same emotions again.

Feelings and the Frontal Lobes

Just as it interacts with the hippocampus during emotional learning and memory, the amygdala also interacts with the cortex. As you read in Chapter 5, the *frontal lobes* of the cortex are often considered the seat of executive function, where we do most of our planning and decision making. The frontal lobes are intimately involved in social behavior, and appropriate social behavior demands the ability to express emotion and to read it in others.

Patients with damage to the frontal lobes often exhibit fewer and less intense facial expressions (Kolb & Taylor, 1981) and are impaired in their ability to recognize negative facial expressions (such as fear and disgust) in others (e.g., Kolb & Taylor, 2000). These patients may show a general disruption of emotion and mood, which can be manifested as social withdrawal and loss of normal emotional display. (The old medical procedure of prefrontal lobotomy was a way of making chronically agitated people "calmer" by destroying parts of the frontal lobes so as to reduce emotional expression.) Other patients with frontal lesions experience the opposite extreme, that of heightened emotionality, and exhibit inappropriate social behavior (profanity, public masturbation, and so on) and rapid mood swings, including violent bouts of anger and aggression for no discernible reason. Apparently, the frontal lobes help people maintain a balance between too little emotion and too much.

The prefrontal cortex also plays a role in helping people "read" the expression of emotion in others. In a recent study, volunteers were shown pictures of fearful or neutral human faces (Figure 10.15a), while researchers measured skin conductance responses and observed brain activation with fMRI (Williams et al., 2001). By now, you should be completely unsurprised to hear that the fearful faces caused SCRs and amygdala activation, and that the neutral faces did not. The novel finding was that fearful faces caused more activity than neutral faces both in the amygdala and in the medial prefrontal cortex (Figure 10.15b). These data are consistent with the idea that the prefrontal cortex is active during emotional processing, helping to interpret the meaning of emotional stimuli, such as other people's facial displays of emotion.

Several researchers have further proposed that the frontal lobes, especially the medial prefrontal cortex, are specialized for processing emotional stimuli in a manner appropriate to the context in which the stimuli occur (e.g., Hornak et al., 2003; Kolb & Taylor, 1990; Rolls, 1999). For example, your emotional reaction to seeing a bear should be very different depending on whether you encounter the bear as you walk through the woods or through the zoo. If a friend tells you a funny joke, your reaction should be to laugh loudly if you are at a party—but not if you are sitting in a lecture. It seems to be the prefrontal cortex that exerts this control on our emotional reactions, modulating the degree to which amygdala outputs produce emotional responses in different contexts. Remember the study, described earlier in this chapter, that found Japanese students were more likely than American students to mask their emotional reactions in the presence of an authority figure? Most likely, the Japanese students felt the same emotional responses as the Americans but were successfully using their frontal cortex to inhibit facial expressions.

Figure 10.15 The prefrontal cortex and emotional processing (a) Volunteers were shown pictures of fearful and neutral faces while brain activity was recorded by fMRI. (b) Difference images show that the amygdala was more active during the viewing of fearful faces than the viewing of neutral faces—and so was the medial prefrontal cortex. This implies that the prefrontal cortex is active during emotional processing, helping individuals to interpret the emotional displays they see in others. Adapted from Williams et al., 2001.

(a) Fearful face   Neutral face

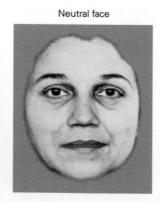

(b) Amygdala   Medial prefrontal cortex

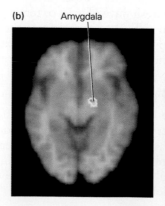
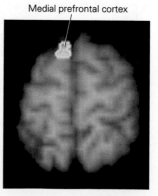

By looking at how the brain is wired, it's clearer why the frontal lobes have such an important role in learning about and processing emotion. The pathways schematized in Figure 10.12 show that stimulus information reaches the amygdala along both the fast-and-rough pathway direct from the thalamus and the slow-but-accurate indirect pathway through the cortex, as discussed earlier. When you see a big, dark shape approaching through the trees, it is the fast-and-rough direct pathway that signals "yikes!" and causes the amygdala to generate outputs that initiate the fight-or-flight response. If it isn't a bear, but merely an approaching friend, the visual cortex will figure this out and send instructions down to the amygdala to turn off the emotional response. But what if the big, dark shape really is a bear—and yet you are not really in danger, because you are viewing the bear in the zoo? Here, the amygdala will attempt to turn on the emotional response at the sight of the bear, but the medial prefrontal cortex will dampen this response. In effect, the medial prefrontal cortex tells the amygdala not to bother, because the bear *in this particular context* is no threat. Consistent with this idea, experiments show that stimulating the medial prefrontal cortex in rats "turns off" or inhibits the normal emotional response provoked by amygdala stimulation (al Maskati & Zbrozyna, 1989; Quirk, Likhtik, Pelletier, & Paré, 2003).

If this hypothesis on the role of the frontal lobes is correct, then frontal lobe lesions, particularly lesions of the critical medial prefrontal cortex, should interfere with the ability to learn to make an emotional response under some conditions but not others. In fact, this is the case. For example, you saw in Figure 10.6 that normal rats trained that a tone CS predicts a foot-shock US will generate various conditioned emotional responses to the CS. After a few sessions in which the CS appears without the US, these responses will extinguish. But rats with medial prefrontal lesions continue responding to the CS long after normal rats have learned to ignore it (LeDoux, 1998, p. 248). This failure to extinguish, called **perseveration,** seems to result from the failure to learn that an emotional response that was appropriate in a previous context is no longer appropriate in the current context. Similarly, humans with medial prefrontal damage are especially impaired in tasks that require suppressing a previously learned response—whether emotional or not. As you'll recall from Chapter 5, the Wisconsin Card Sort task, which requires sorting cards first by color, then by shape, and so on, is especially disrupted in patients with frontal lobe damage; such patients perseverate, clinging to the old sorting rules even though the old responses are no longer reinforced.

Test Your Knowledge

The Brain Substrates of Emotion

Emotional responses depend on a complex interplay between many brain areas, including the amygdala, hippocampus, and prefrontal cortex. Read the story below and identify some ways in which these brain areas could be contributing at each step identified by a number in parentheses.

> Jared is afraid of heights. However, on a visit to Washington, DC, his friends say he should go to the top of the Washington Monument for the best view of the city. On the elevator up, Jared feels the beginnings of a nervous reaction: his heart beats faster, his mouth feels dry, and his stomach tightens (1). He remembers when he was similarly terrified, standing on the high diving board at school (2).
>
> When he arrives at the observation area, Jared's first impulse is to flatten himself against the wall and stay as far away from the edge as possible. But having come this far, he takes a few deep breaths and walks up to the window and looks out over the city (3). In spite of everything, he is able to appreciate the beautiful view (4).

Interim Summary

Emotion depends on many brain areas, and each brain area may contribute to more than one emotion. Part of the body's response to strong emotion is to activate the amygdala; outputs from the central nucleus of the amygdala drive many components of the fight-or-flight response. Animals (including people) with amygdala damage show reduced emotionality and a reduced ability to learn conditioned emotional responses. The amygdala also modulates storage of emotional material elsewhere, by means of outputs from the basolateral nucleus projecting to the cortex and the hippocampal region. Memories can be formed in the cortex and hippocampus without amygdala input, but if the emotional system is triggered, then memory formation will be stronger. The hippocampal region can, in turn, influence emotional learning by providing information about the context in which the learning occurs. Animals and people with hippocampal damage can still learn an emotional response to a stimulus, but they will fail to learn about the context in which they encountered the stimulus. The frontal lobes seem to play an important role in humans' ability to display emotions appropriately and to read emotional expressions in others, and also in the ability to process emotional stimuli in a manner appropriate to the context in which they are experienced.

10.3 Clinical Perspectives

Much of the research covered in this chapter has focused on negative emotions—particularly fear—in part because negative emotions have a tremendous impact on our health and well-being. The stress associated with long-term unremitting fear and anger can lead to physiological problems such as high blood pressure and immune system suppression, which can increase susceptibility to colds and more serious infections. Negative emotions can also cause psychological problems such as **anxiety disorders**, a cluster of psychiatric conditions that includes panic disorders, phobias, posttraumatic stress disorder, and obsessive-compulsive disorders. Two of these in particular—phobias and posttraumatic stress disorder—may specifically involve a dysfunction of the normal fear response.

Phobias

A **phobia** is an excessive and irrational fear of an object, place, or situation. Examples of phobias include fear of closed spaces (claustrophobia), fear of open spaces (agoraphobia), fear of heights (altophobia), fear of public speaking (a form of social phobia), fear of snakes (ophidiophobia), and fear of spiders (arachnophobia). Each of these phobias centers on an object or situation in which a fear reaction might be justified. For example, it is appropriate to be alarmed by the sight of a snake, since snake venom can be deadly. Similarly, a healthy fear of heights may keep you from falling off cliffs. But when a fear has reached a point where it interferes with daily life, it is classified as a phobia. For example, if a person were so afraid of open spaces that she seldom left her house, or so afraid of dogs that she panicked whenever the neighbor's pet barked, these fears would be classified as phobias.

One theory about the formation of phobias is that they arise through classical conditioning. Early in the twentieth century, John Watson, the "father" of behaviorism, and his research assistant Rosalie Rayner claimed to have created a phobia in an 11-month-old boy known as Little Albert. Little Albert was not initially afraid of rats, but several times, while he was playing with a white laboratory rat, Watson and Rayner startled him with a loud noise (Watson & Rayner, 2000 [1920]). Eventually, Albert avoided the rat altogether; when it was put in front of

Michael Medford

Ophidiophobia, or fear of snakes, is a common phobia.

him, he cried and tried to crawl away. Little Albert had been conditioned to associate the rat (a CS) with a fear-provoking loud noise (the US). The learning even generalized to other white or furry objects: Albert began to react with fear to stimuli such as a rabbit and a Santa Claus beard.

Today, of course, ethical guidelines would preclude experiments like the one conducted on Little Albert. But the experiment did raise some interesting questions about classical conditioning and phobias. Maybe some other, naturally arising phobias also reflect classical conditioning; perhaps some people develop claustrophobia after a traumatic experience such as being locked in a closet, and others develop a fear of dogs after being threatened or even attacked by an out-of-control pet.

Notably, the stimulus in a phobia is almost always something that might have been legitimately threatening to our evolutionary ancestors. Ancient humans who were predisposed to react with fear and caution to the sight of a snake might have been more likely to survive and breed than people with a more cavalier attitude. The result may be that, even today, humans are *biologically predisposed* to fear some things, like snakes, but not others (for example, a predisposition to fear flowers would provide no evolutionary advantage). Perhaps, then, some items are especially apt to act as the CS in a fear-conditioning situation and thus are more likely to become the object of a phobia (Eysenck, 1979; Mineka & Sutton, 1992; Seligman, 1972).

On the other hand, not everyone who has a fear-evoking experience develops a phobia. One study reported that two-thirds of people with a phobia related to dogs can recall a dog-related trauma (such as being bitten), but so can the same percentage of people with no fear of dogs (DiNardo, Guzy, & Bak, 1988)! Conversely, some people have a terror of snakes despite never having come into contact with a living snake, and others are morbidly afraid of flying without ever having been in an airplane.

One possible explanation is that some phobias may be conditioned through social transmission. For example, a person can develop a fear of flying after seeing televised reports of an airplane crash, or a fear of snakes after seeing other people panic at the sight of snakes. Monkeys show socially transmitted fear, too. A monkey raised in the lab will not react with fear the first time it sees a snake. But if the lab-reared monkey is caged next to another monkey, and if that other monkey reacts with fear at the sight of a snake, the lab-reared monkey will begin to show the same fear response (Mineka & Cook, 1988). Possibly, the sight of a frightened neighbor is itself a fear-evoking US, and the object that evokes that fear becomes a CS in the observer monkey too. Again, biological predisposition matters. A monkey can be conditioned to fear a flower, if that flower is repeatedly paired with a shock, but a second monkey who observes this fear reaction will not fear the flower, no matter how many times it sees the first monkey demonstrate such a fear.

Given that at least some phobias seem to arise through conditioning, can phobias be extinguished in the same way as ordinary conditioned responses—by repeated exposure to the CS with no US? In many cases they can. In **systematic desensitization** therapy for phobias, successive approximations of the CS are presented while the patient learns to remain relaxed; eventually, even the CS itself does not elicit a fear response (Kazdin & Wilcoxon, 1976; Linden, 1981). For example, a person who is afraid of snakes may first be presented with some snake-shaped item (like a hose or rope), different enough from a real snake that no fear

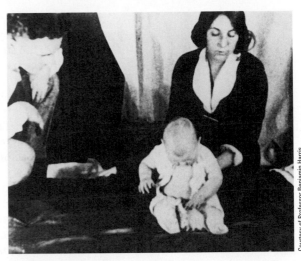

Courtesy of Professor Benjamin Harris

While Little Albert was playing with a pet rat, John Watson and Rosalie Rayner paired the rat with a loud, frightening noise. Albert developed a fear of the rat, and this fear generalized to other white or furry objects, such as a rabbit. Watson and Rayner (visible in the photo) claimed they had induced a phobia in Albert and that such classical conditioning could underlie the formation of real-world phobias.

reaction is evoked. In successive sessions, the patient is progressively exposed to, say, a toy rubber snake, then a photograph of a real snake, then a person holding a live snake; the steps are taken so gradually that they don't evoke a fear reaction. Eventually, the patient may be asked to touch a live snake, then to hold it himself. As you might imagine, systematic desensitization therapy can be a slow and painstaking process, but it is generally successful and long-lasting.

Sometimes, it is dangerous, inconvenient, or very expensive to expose the patient (and the therapist!) to the object of the phobia. For example, if the patient is afraid of flying over the ocean, systematic desensitization would require her to practice approaching an airport, then practice sitting on a grounded plane, then start taking short overland trips, and finally work up to longer transatlantic flights. This would be prohibitively expensive for most people. Instead, the therapist may recommend virtual reality therapy using computer-generated three-dimensional environments. The patient can "experience" sitting in an airplane seat, gradually getting used to the sights and sounds of an aircraft, and even take simulated flights, before spending the energy and money to board a real plane. Studies have suggested that virtual reality therapy, particularly in combination with other relaxation training and cognitive therapy, can be very effective in treating phobias (Emmelkamp et al., 2002; Muhlberger, Herrmann, Wiedeman, Ellgring, & Pauli, 2001).

Propranolol and other drugs that block or interfere with epinephrine can also help individuals who suffer from phobias. Because epinephrine is a critical mediator of the cascade of brain events involved in the fight-or-flight response (see Figure 10.12), blocking epinephrine helps suppress the body's biological response to fear-producing stimuli. Quieting the biological fear response can often help reduce the conscious feelings of fear. In fact, this is exactly what the James-Lange theory of emotion predicts.

Posttraumatic Stress Disorder

Following the terrorist attacks on the World Trade Center on September 11, 2001, thousands of counselors went to New York City to offer their services to survivors, families, and rescue workers. In addition to these volunteers, $23 million in federal funds was allocated to Project Liberty, a program that provided free counseling to New Yorkers.

The rationale for this convergence of mental health professionals and funding was the expectation that, in the wake of the attacks, many New Yorkers would develop **posttraumatic stress disorder (PTSD).** PTSD is a psychological syndrome that can develop after exposure to a horrific event (such as combat, rape, or natural disaster); the symptoms include reexperiencing the event (through intrusive recollections, flashbacks, or nightmares), avoidance of reminders of the trauma, and heightened anxiety (McNally, Bryant, & Ehlers, 2003). Such fear reactions are a perfectly normal human response to distressing events; but, for most people exposed to trauma, the fear reactions subside with time (Figure 10.16). For individuals with PTSD, the fear reactions may persist for months or years. One study estimated that about 10–20% of New Yorkers living within a few miles of the World Trade Center displayed fear symptoms 2 months after 9/11, but 6 months later, fewer than 2% still had PTSD symptoms related to the attacks (Galea et al., 2003). PTSD may be especially likely when the patient experiences intentional acts of personal violence; some studies estimate the rates to be as high as 30% for veterans of combat in Vietnam or Iraq, and as high as 50–80% for female rape victims.

Why might PTSD occur? One possible answer has to do with classical conditioning. By definition, PTSD involves exposure to a horrific stimulus, far outside the realm of ordinary life. This stimulus can function as a US, and it may be such a strong and effective US that any other stimuli that occurred along with it become strongly associated with that US. Thus, sights, sounds, and smells may all become conditioned stimuli. When any such CS is experienced again, it may evoke the memory of the US— which in turn provokes the emotional response. This is how PTSD differs from phobias: in phobias, a fear reaction is triggered by a particular stimulus (such as a snake); in PTSD, fear reactions can be triggered by a wide variety of stimuli reminiscent of the original trauma. For example, a war veteran with PTSD may show fear reactions to any loud noises reminiscent of gunfire, including the sounds of thunder or cars backfiring. For most people, reexperiencing these various stimuli without recurrence of the traumatic US should gradually lead to extinction of the fear response in the weeks and months after the trauma. Individuals with PTSD may simply fail to extinguish the normal fear response to stimuli associated with the traumatic event (Rothbaum & Davis, 2003).

Consistent with the idea that PTSD, like phobia, could reflect a failure of extinction, some of the most successful and widely used treatments for PTSD involve exposing the patient to cues that trigger his anxiety, but doing so in the absence of danger. The purpose is to encourage extinction of the abnormally strong fear response (Rothbaum & Davis, 2003). This so-called *extinction therapy* for PTSD may involve having the patient repeatedly imagine and describe the feared situations, under the guidance of a therapist. Virtual reality techniques also prove useful—for example, providing a "virtual Vietnam" in which a combat veteran can fly a simulated helicopter over a simulated jungle, undergoing repeated exposure to the fear-evoking stimuli within the safe context of a therapist's office. Under these conditions, many individuals experience gradual extinction of PTSD symptoms.

But the success of extinction therapy begs the question of why some individuals' fear responses fail to extinguish normally in the first place. Part of the answer may involve overactive stress hormones. As you read earlier, when a human being faces a threatening situation, the amygdala signals the ANS to release epinephrine and cortisol, which initiates the "fight-or-flight" response (see Figure 10.12). In most people, as the threat passes, the brain detects high levels of cortisol in the blood and responds by signaling the adrenal glands to stop producing stress hormones—a change that gradually brings the body back to normal. However, in patients with PTSD, cortisol rises only mildly in the aftermath of the trauma, which means that the fear response may persist for longer.

This suggests that we might be able to reduce the likelihood of an individual developing PTSD by administering drugs such as propranolol that interfere with epinephrine and thereby reduce the body's stress reactions. Some intriguing studies suggest that individuals who have experienced a traumatic episode, such as a car crash, and who then receive a series of propranolol injections may be somewhat less likely to develop PTSD than individuals who do not receive the injections (Pitman et al., 2002; Vaiva et al., 2003). These patients do not forget the traumatic episode, but they stop having such damaging emotional reactions to the memory. An important question is whether brain-altering treatments like this should routinely be prescribed for individuals who experience a traumatic

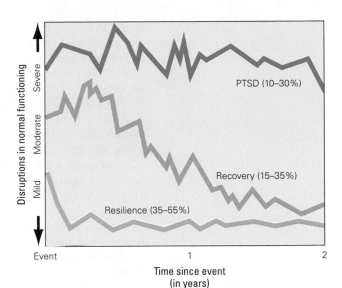

Figure 10.16 Patterns of psychological recovery after a traumatic event Immediately after a traumatic event, such as the death of a spouse or exposure to a terrorist attack, most people show a disruption in normal functioning due to fear reactions. As time passes, most people either bounce back quickly (a pattern described as "resilience") or show initial fear reactions that dissipate with time ("recovery"). But some individuals develop posttraumatic stress disorder (PTSD), which includes fear reactions that persist for months or years. Adapted from Bonanno, 2005.

event, to reduce the risk of PTSD. The question is a complicated one, given that the majority of people will never develop PTSD if simply left alone.

A better approach might be to give the preventive drugs only to those individuals who are most likely to develop PTSD. But, how can we identify such individuals in advance? Structural MRI suggests some answers. Individuals with PTSD typically have hippocampal volumes that are somewhat smaller than those of individuals who experienced similar trauma but did not develop PTSD (Smith, 2005). For example, one study used MRI to examine the brains of a group of combat veterans who had fought in Vietnam (Gilbertson et al., 2002). Those veterans who did develop PTSD typically had a somewhat smaller hippocampal volume than those veterans who did not develop PTSD (Figure 10.17a, c). One interpretation of these findings would be that PTSD might cause the hippocampus to shrink, since we know that chronic stress can damage the hippocampus (see also "Learning and Memory in Everyday Life" on p. 408). But another possibility is that the veterans who developed PTSD had a smaller hippocampus to start with—and that made them more vulnerable to PTSD.

The researchers found a clever way to determine the answer: each of the veterans included in the study shown in Figure 10.17 had a monozygotic (genetically identical) twin brother who had not fought in Vietnam and who had never developed PTSD. If the veterans who did develop PTSD (Figure 10.17a) experienced a reduction in hippocampal volume as a result of their trauma, then their unexposed brothers should have a normal hippocampal volume. But, if these veterans had a smaller hippocampal volume to start with, then their twins should also have smaller-than-average hippocampal volumes. In fact, the twins of the veterans with PTSD did have smaller-than-average hippocampal volumes too (Figure 10.17b). This suggests that PTSD doesn't *cause* hippocampal shrinkage; instead, it seems that some individuals (like those in Figure 10.17a, b) are born with a smaller-than-average hippocampal volume, and this may *predispose* them to develop PTSD later (Gilbertson et al., 2002). A smaller hippocampus might be slightly less efficient and, under conditions of extreme stress, less able to cope with the inputs it receives (McNally, 2003). If an individual leads a relatively quiet life (like the brothers who weren't sent to Vietnam, shown in Figure 10.17b), this may not be a problem; but if that same individual is exposed to horrific trauma

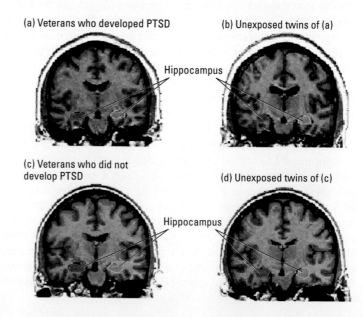

Figure 10.17 Hippocampal volume and PTSD Structural MRI images showing the hippocampus on each side (red and blue). (a) Combat veterans who developed PTSD typically had smaller-than-average hippocampal volume. (c) Combat veterans who did not develop PTSD had normal hippocampal volume. To test whether hippocampal volume reductions are a cause or an effect of PTSD, researchers examined the veterans' twin brothers who had not fought in Vietnam (and who did not have PTSD). (b) In fact, the twins of the veterans who developed PTSD had smaller-than-average hippocampal volumes too. This suggests that the veterans with PTSD (a) had smaller-than-average hippocampal volume before entering combat and that this may have predisposed them to develop this stress disorder. Adapted from Gilbertson et al., 2002.

(like the brothers who did serve in the war), there could be heightened risk for PTSD.

This kind of knowledge could be very useful in screening people for wartime service, as well as for jobs such as firefighting, disaster recovery, and foreign aid work, where traumatic situations are especially likely to occur. If we know in advance that some people's brains are more vulnerable to PTSD, it may be worth counseling them to consider another line of work—or at least preparing to provide extra care and counseling if trauma occurs.

EARNIE GRAFTON/Union-Tribune

Three to four months after return from combat in Iraq, up to 20% of U.S. soldiers meet the diagnostic criteria for PTSD (Hoge et al., 2004). Some are helped by therapy designed to encourage extinction of fear responses, such as virtual reality therapy providing the sights and sounds of a "Virtual Iraq" without the actual danger.

CONCLUSION

If you've ever tried to list the similarities between yourself and a rat, chances are that emotions did not top the list. Whatever a rat may (or may not) "feel" when it freezes in anticipation of a tail shock, it is probably very different from what Americans felt on the morning of September 11, 2001. Larger-brained animals, such as chimpanzees and whales, or even elephants and dogs, may "feel" some of the same emotions that humans do, but even that assertion is largely speculative.

What is certain, though, is that all these species do show emotional responses in the form of overt behaviors and physiological changes. Confronted with the prospect of an electric shock, a rat may freeze and defecate, a sea snail may retract its siphon, and a dog may whine and put its tail between its legs. Each animal is demonstrating a learned fear response, and these responses can be induced and measured by experimenters. The same goes for physiological variables, such as heart rate, respiration, and other components of the "fight-or-flight" response—many of which are shared by several species. Additionally, emotional learning depends on similar brain substrates in many species, especially mammals, including the amygdala, the hippocampus, and the frontal cortex. This commonality allows the use of insights gained in rats, and even *Aplysia*, to help elucidate the neural bases of human emotions.

The vast majority of research on emotions and learning has focused on a single emotion, fear. One reason is that the amygdala has long been recognized as a critical brain substrate for fear, whereas the brain substrates for happiness and other positive emotions are only now being discovered. And while we can reasonably assume that anticipating shock leads to fear in animals, because we can observe and measure fear responses, it has been less clear whether animals feel "happiness" and, if so, how we could induce and measure this emotion. Recently, though, researchers have found that rats will run a maze or press a lever for "tickle" reward (Burgdorf & Panksepp, 2001), and that rats engaging in play or tickle produce vocalizations that may be similar to human laughter (Panksepp & Burgdorf, 2003). We may be on the verge of developing animal models of joy that could soon lead to new insights into the biological bases of happiness and evolutionary antecedents of laughter.

Another reason for the historical emphasis on fear is its association with clinical syndromes such as phobias, PTSD, and other anxiety disorders, as well as depression and aggression. This link to real-world medicine drives many researchers to study fear, in the hope that their findings can help patients lead more tranquil lives. Indeed, as the propranolol PTSD studies show, we are on the verge of being able to manipulate the way emotion modulates our memory and our physiological responses. These studies suggest that we can dampen the emotional content of memories without erasing the episodic content. For patients whose lives have been devastated by trauma, there may be a moral responsibility to administer such treatment if it will help them recover.

But what do these findings mean for those who do not suffer from disabling emotional disorders? If off-the-shelf, emotion-modifying drugs were available, would people routinely want to lose the emotional content of their "negative" episodic memories? Would the result be happier lives for all, or a kind of gray existence in which nothing really matters because nothing causes lasting emotional scars? And, without lasting emotional scars, would humans lose some of the ability to learn from mistakes—the very reason emotions may have evolved in the first place?

Key Points

- Emotions consist of three distinct, but interrelated, processes: physiological responses (e.g., the "fight-or-flight" response), overt behaviors (e.g., smiling or freezing), and conscious feelings. While we cannot know if nonverbal animals "feel" emotions in the same way that humans do, many species react to emotional stimuli with similar constellations of physiological responses and overt behaviors.

- According to the James-Lange theory, conscious feelings of emotion occur when the mind senses the bodily responses associated with an emotion ("we feel afraid because we are running"). Modern researchers note that emotion is a complex phenomenon involving a constant interplay between cognitive assessments, conscious feelings, and bodily responses, with each able to influence the others.

- The major emotions seem to be constant across races and cultures, although the expression of emotion may be socially learned and may be modulated or suppressed by the frontal cortex.

- Emotional learning can be assessed by measuring the biological response to an emotional stimulus, including variables such as heart rate, skin conductance response, freezing responses, and conditioned avoid-

ance. There is no single brain system for emotion; rather, many brain regions participate.

- The fight-or-flight response is mediated by outputs from the central nucleus of the amygdala to the autonomic nervous system and temporarily diverts resources toward bodily systems needed to fight or run away. This cluster of responses is also called arousal. Stress hormones (e.g., epinephrine) help turn on arousal, and glucocorticoids may help dampen it once danger has passed.

- Emotional arousal increases the probability that memories will be stored and retained. Flashbulb memories are especially vivid, long-lasting memories of highly emotional events, but they are not always accurate in all details. Amygdala modulation of hippocampal and cortical storage may account for the strength of emotional memories.

- Stimulating the amygdala can initiate a fight-or-flight response. Lesions of the amygdala can lead to impairments in learned emotional responses.

- Anxiety disorders may reflect fear responses gone awry. Phobias are excessive fears that interfere with daily life. In posttraumatic stress disorder, a natural fear reaction does not subside with time.

Key Terms

amygdala, p. 400
anxiety disorders, p. 412
arousal, p. 384
autonomic nervous system (ANS), p. 384
conditioned avoidance, p. 396
cortisol, p. 384

depression, p. 397
emotion, p. 382
epinephrine, p. 384
fight-or-flight response, p. 384
flashbulb memory, p. 390
glucocorticoids, p. 384

James-Lange theory of emotion, p. 385
learned helplessness, p. 397
limbic system, p. 399
mood-congruency of memory, p. 390
perseveration, p. 411

phobia, p. 412
piloerection, p. 387
posttraumatic stress disorder (PTSD), p. 414
stress hormone, p. 384
systematic desensitization, p. 413

Concept Check

1. In earlier chapters, you read about habituation (decreased responding to a repeatedly presented stimulus). Do you think habituation is an example of emotional learning? Why or why not?

2. After losing a game by a lopsided score, professional football teams are statistically more likely to perform worse than usual in their next game, and this tendency is particularly pronounced if the upcoming opponent is considered hard to beat (Reisel & Kopelman, 1995). How might this phenomenon be explained in terms of the principles of emotional learning?

3. Decorticate animals (animals with their cortex surgically removed) often show "sham rage," overreacting to seemingly trivial stimuli as though they were being seriously threatened. Why might this happen?

4. Suppose you have a roommate who is terrified of spiders, to the point of being unable to take a shower if there is a spider in the bathtub unless you're there to kill the spider or remove it. Based on what you read in this chapter, speculate about why your roommate has this fear.

5. Continuing the above example, what might you suggest to help your roommate overcome this fear?

Answers to Test Your Knowledge

The Brain Substrates of Emotion

1. The elevator ride may be a CS that activates Jared's amygdala; outputs from the central nucleus travel to the ANS and turn on the fight-or-flight response.

2. Jared's current fear response acts as a contextual stimulus and helps the hippocampus and/or cortex trigger memories of earlier events that caused a fear response. If the diving incident was traumatic enough, Jared may even have a flashbulb memory for the event.

3. Rationally, Jared knows he won't fall off the Washington Monument. His prefrontal cortex, the site of higher decision making, helps to overrule the impulse to flee.

4. Appreciation of the beautiful view is itself an emotional response. If Jared is lucky, his amygdala will help process this emotional response and send signals to the prefrontal cortex and elsewhere. Maybe the next time he's at the top of a tall building, Jared will remember his pleasure at the view from the top of the Washington Monument, and this will help counteract some of his fear.

Further Reading

LeDoux, J. (1998). *The emotional brain: the mysterious underpinnings of emotional life*. New York: Touchstone. • This book provides an overview of LeDoux and colleagues' work elucidating how the brain learns to respond to emotion-evoking stimuli.

Loftus, E., & Ketcham, K. (1994). *The myth of repressed memory*. New York: St. Martin's Press. • Loftus is one of the foremost experts on false memory. This book reviews some real-life cases in which adult children claimed to recover memories of long-ago childhood abuse—often "aided" by therapists using suspect techniques.

McGaugh, J. (2003). *Memory and emotion*. New York: Columbia University Press. • McGaugh's work describes how emotion can influence memory and how memories are not fixed forever but can be manipulated long after the events they encode.

Sapolsky, R. (1998). *Why zebras don't get ulcers*. New York: Freeman. • Sapolsky weaves anecdote and humor through his presentation of a serious scientific theory: that humans are biologically unprepared to deal with the constant stress of modern life and therefore suffer a host of conditions that can damage the body and impair memory.

CHAPTER 11

Observational Learning

Watching, Listening, and Remembering

OLPHINS ARE THE ONLY ANIMALS other than humans that can imitate both the actions and the vocalizations of other animals upon request. Chimpanzees and orangutans can imitate other animals' actions when humans ask them, but they seem to be unable to imitate sounds. Parrots can imitate sounds, but they have only a limited ability to imitate novel sounds upon request. Most other animals show no ability to imitate actions or sounds when they are instructed to do so by humans. This could be because they don't know how to imitate, or don't have the right vocal control mechanisms, or have not been properly trained to imitate, or possibly because they don't understand human instructions.

Yes, you read that last paragraph correctly. Scientists can communicate with dolphins and apes, and these newly discovered communication channels have revealed unsuspected learning and memory abilities in those animals. One dolphin named Akeakamai (pronounced "uh KAY uh ka MY," Hawaiian for "lover of wisdom") learned to interpret hand signals asking her to imitate the actions of dolphins and humans. She learned to do this through one-on-one interactions with her human instructors. In particular, she learned to watch intently as a hairless ape in front of her gesticulated rapidly with its oddly shaped "flippers." When Akeakamai interpreted the gestures correctly, the instructor rewarded her with shouts of approval. Occasionally, such vocal accolades became infectious, and Akeakamai joined in the celebration with her own loud vocalizations. Akeakamai observed the actions of those around her and reacted based on her past training (interpreting gestures), her recent experiences (imitating actions or sounds), and her emotional state (responding to the excitement of a successful performance).

Observation can play a role in many forms of learning, including habituation, perceptual learning, classical conditioning, and instrumental conditioning. It is not always clear, however, what an animal or person is observing during learning. You can watch television to learn about exotic vacation destinations; listen to the radio to learn about an approaching storm; or read a book to learn about how your brain enables you to learn and remember. However, the fact that a radio is on within hearing range does not imply that anyone is listening to it. Observation entails active monitoring, not just the passive reception of external stimuli. Many people believe that humans learn much of what they know by interacting with others and observing how things work in the world, and that this makes human learning and memory different from that of all other animals. However, this view is often based on introspection rather than experimental evidence. This chapter describes what scientists have discovered about how humans and other animals learn through observation.

11.1 Behavioral Processes

Psychologists use the term **observational learning** to identify learning situations in which the learner actively monitors events and then chooses later actions based on those observations. The term **social learning** is often used as a synonym for observational learning, because the primary stimuli that lead to changes in behavior are often the actions of other individuals.

If you've ever found yourself in a situation where something seems to be expected of you but you aren't quite sure what that something is, you may have adopted the strategy of imitating what other people around you appear to be doing. Let's say you've taken a trip to Bourbon Street in New Orleans during Mardi Gras, and you see lots of people wearing and giving away necklaces made of colored plastic beads. Even though you might have no idea why they are doing this, if someone came up to you on the street and offered to put a bead necklace around your neck, you probably wouldn't resist. (If the same thing happened in your hometown grocery store, you probably would be a bit more nervous.) Having arrived on Bourbon Street without first gathering information about local customs, you need to rapidly assess the appropriate action to take in this novel context. You do so by observing other people in the vicinity. Of course, such on-the-spot learning by copying has its hazards. For example, a female who accepts beads on Bourbon Street during Mardi Gras is then expected to show the bead-giver her breasts. If you are not aware of this custom, your copying behavior could lead to surprising, unintended outcomes.

Learning by Copying

Unlike most other forms of learning, not all species can learn by reproducing observed actions. In fact, many psychologists believe that only humans learn extensively by copying actions. **Copying** consists of doing what one observes another doing. From an early age, children are encouraged to copy their parents' speech. Consider the case of Donna, your typical American child. Soon after Donna's birth, her mother began repeatedly encouraging her to speak, "Say Mama, MAA-MAA." When she got a little older, however, Donna had to be discouraged from repeating everything she overheard, including expletives and embarrassing facts about her relatives. Learning through copying is a form of observational learning. Much of the scientific interest in observational learning has focused on behavioral imitation (the copying of actions), despite the fact that behavioral imitation is rarely evident in most learning situations. As we will discuss next, some forms of observational learning that seem to involve imitation can be explained more simply as special cases of conditioning. Surprisingly, it is quite difficult to tell when imitation is occurring outside of a laboratory, and it's not much easier inside a lab!

Children may learn a great deal by imitating the actions and sounds of adults and other children. However, there is very little experimental data showing what it is that children learn through imitation, and most of that data was collected by a small number of researchers over 40 years ago. So, no one really knows the extent to which children learn through imitation compared to other kinds of learning such as instrumental or classical conditioning. Much of what we know has come from influential experimental studies of imitative learning conducted in the early 1960s by Albert Bandura. Bandura (b.1925) grew up in Canada before heading to the University of Iowa for graduate school. Soon after starting his academic career at Stanford University, he became interested in how parents' aggressive behavior impacted the actions of their children.

Bandura and his colleagues wanted to see whether preschool children would become more aggressive after observing aggressive adults (Bandura, Ross, & Ross, 1961). They had one group of children observe adults beating up a "Bobo doll" (an inflatable clown doll), while other groups of children (control groups) simply played in an empty room, or observed adults playing quietly with toys. Afterward, Bandura used a one-way mirror to spy on the children as they played in a room containing the Bobo doll (Figure 11.1). Children who had observed an adult pummeling the Bobo doll were more likely than children in the control groups to pound on the doll themselves, and most important, their attack styles were often similar to those used by the adults. Bandura and colleagues concluded that the children had learned new aggressive actions by observing the actions of an adult.

Studies like Bandura's Bobo doll experiment seem to suggest that children will copy aggressive acts they have observed. However, the children were tested in a context similar to the one in which they observed the aggression occurring, soon after they viewed the aggressive acts. It is unclear whether they would have

Figure 11.1
Scenes from a Bobo doll experiment After viewing an adult acting aggressively toward a Bobo doll, children imitated what they had seen (Bandura, Ross, & Ross, 1961). Children were not rewarded for their actions during their observation of the model or for their interactions with the Bobo doll. This means that the similarities between the children's actions and those of the adults were not the result of instrumental conditioning.

Bandura, A., Ross, D., & Ross, S. A. (1961) Transmission of aggression through imitation of aggressive models, *Journal of Abnormal and Social Psychology*, 63, 575–582.

behaved similarly if they had encountered a Bobo doll at their neighbor's house. Additionally, the children in Bandura's experiment who showed significant imitation of aggressive acts had first been provoked by being deprived of an attractive toy immediately before the test (Bandura, Ross, & Ross, 1961). Children who had viewed an aggressive model but who had not been provoked were actually less likely to behave aggressively during the test than children who did not observe any aggressive acts. This finding suggests that viewing aggressive acts can in some cases inhibit aggressive behavior rather than increase it.

One of the main findings from the Bobo doll experiments was that simply viewing an adult acting aggressively toward an inflatable toy strongly influenced the later behavior of children presented with that same toy, despite the fact that the children were neither reinforced nor punished for their behavior. The absence of reinforcement or punishment appears to exclude the possibility that they were learning through instrumental conditioning, which requires that the learners' actions be either reinforced or punished. Bandura's proposed that children observed the actions of the adult, formed ideas about what actions could be performed using the doll, and later used memories of those ideas to reproduce the adult's actions when presented with a similar situation (Bandura, 1969). Note that by this account, the learning occurred while the children were observing the adult, *not* when they were imitating the behavior. The children's imitative acts simply revealed what they had learned from watching someone demonstrate an action; Bandura called these demonstrations **modeling.**

Another finding of the Bobo doll study was that, among the children who observed adults behaving aggressively, imitative acts were most common in boys who observed an aggressive male model and least common in girls who observed an aggressive female model. This finding suggests that the likelihood of a person's imitating an action depends not just on the actions that were observed but also on the gender of the person performing the actions. Unfortunately, similar experiments have not been conducted in which children observe adults hugging and kissing the Bobo doll; that is, researchers have not yet assessed whether children also learn to copy adults' affectionate actions. Such an experiment might provide strong evidence of imitative learning (because Bobo dolls aren't designed for kissing, and they *are* designed to be hit), and might also increase the likelihood that girls would imitate the model.

Observational learning differs from classical and instrumental conditioning in that researchers cannot reliably predict what an organism will learn after observing the actions of others. One reason it is difficult to predict how observations will affect future behavior is that there is no way to detect what the organism perceives during its observations. This is because an organism can observe a wide variety of events without showing any changes in behavior. For example, if you watch your fellow students during a lecture, do you think you would be able to tell if one of them doesn't understand English, or if another is daydreaming about being on the beach? You can't tell from watching people stare at a professor what it is that they are observing or perceiving. Psychologists face a similar situation. Edward Thorndike found that cats did not imitate other cats that had learned to escape from a puzzle box (Thorndike, 1898). However, there is no way to know what Thorndike's observer cats were focusing on in these experiments. Perhaps the food outside the box or the identity of the cat trapped in the box were more interesting to them than the specific actions the cat inside the box was performing.

Another reason it is difficult to predict how observations will affect future behavior is that nothing compels an observer to copy any given model. Furthermore, even if the observer does copy a particular model, there is more than one way to copy. C. Lloyd Morgan (1852–1936) was a British psychologist famous for his "canon" (rule) that scientists should always explain an organism's behavior using the simplest possible mechanisms. He noted that copying could involve either replication of actions that have been observed or performance of novel actions that lead to the observed outcome of a modeler's actions (Morgan, 1896). For example, when Donna was still in elementary school, she happened to see her parents picking berries and putting them in a bucket. She then copied her parents' berry-picking technique, but put the berries in her pockets rather than in a bucket. The movements Donna made while picking berries replicated those of her parents. Copying that involves reproducing motor acts is called **true imitation.** The movements Donna performed to store the berries that had been picked, however, differed from those of her parents. But, Donna and her parents' actions produced a similar outcome—berries were collected in a container. Copying that replicates an outcome without replicating specific motor acts is called **emulation.** We'll discuss both kinds of copying and provide more examples of each, and examples of the use of Morgan's canon, in the following sections. We'll also describe a form of copying called *vocal learning* that has elements of both true imitation and emulation, after which we'll discuss some general theories of how copying facilitates learning.

True Imitation: Copying Actions

Scientists use the term "true imitation" because there are many situations in which, even though someone seems to be imitating others, the behavior can be explained more simply. According to Morgan's canon, psychologists should explain behavior in terms of the simplest psychological mechanisms possible. Morgan considered the "simplest" learning mechanisms to be those that were evident in organisms with the least complicated nervous systems; thus the simplest explanation often might be something other than what people might consider the "obvious" explanation. For example, seeing a chimpanzee put on lipstick in a commercial might convince many people that the chimpanzee is capable of imitating adults (since lipstick is generally applied and worn by adults and not by chimpanzees). In fact, seeing chimpanzees behave like humans has led to phrases like, "Monkey see, monkey do." Following Morgan's canon, however, a psychologist would point out that the chimpanzee could have been trained to use lipstick through instrumental conditioning. Slugs can be trained using instrumental conditioning (but not to imitate others), and so this explanation is "simpler" than the claim that the chimpanzee learned to use lipstick by imitating humans.

Morgan's canon may seem straightforward when used to explain a chimpanzee's behavior, but what about human behavior? Watching an 8-year-old child put on lipstick would probably convince most people that the child is capable of imitating adults. Although the natural assumption may be that the human child has copied the actions of an adult, scientists are not content with such assumptions. Young children put lots of things on their face without first seeing the action modelled by others. The fact that some children happen to choose something to put on their face that an adult might also choose could just be a coincidence. Or, the child may have been reinforced for putting on lipstick, just like the chimpanzee. Morgan's canon makes no distinction between children and chimps. In both cases, the simplest explanation is the preferred one unless additional evidence is provided that rules out this explanation.

Celebrity impersonators, like this Elvis tribute artist, replicate the actions of others precisely, often with astounding fidelity. Precise copying is the hallmark of true imitation, but similarities in behavior are not strong evidence of true imitation.

Masterfile

Psychologists might be more likely to concede that professional impersonators, who make a living copying the actions of others, are truly imitating the celebrities they resemble. Even in this case, however, it is not certain that true imitation is occurring; simpler learning mechanisms could potentially explain the behavior of the impersonator. For example, perhaps an individual's natural appearance and behavior were similar to that of a celebrity, attracting the positive attention and compliments of others who initially thought they had spotted that celebrity. Over time, such rewards could shape the behavior of the individual to be more similar to that of the celebrity, until eventually the individual uses these similarities to make money as an impersonator (further rewarding the behavior). This would be a case of simple instrumental conditioning rather than true imitation. So, even professional "imitators" may not be truly imitating!

Scientists often disagree about what behaviors really count as true imitation, and about which organisms possess the ability to imitate (Thorndike, 1898; Thorpe, 1963; Whiten, Horner, Litchfield, & Marshall-Pescini, 2004). So, how can researchers discover whether a person or animal can truly imitate? One technique that has been developed to demonstrate imitation abilities is called the **two-action test.** For this test, two animals are initially trained to perform different actions that lead to the same outcome. For instance, if the action is to press a lever for a reward, one animal might be trained to press the lever with its head, and the second animal might be trained to press the lever with its feet (two actions that achieve an identical outcome). Next, one group of naive animals is allowed to observe one of the trained animals, and a second group of naive animals is allowed to observe the other. If the naive animals learn to perform the operation in a way that matches the trained animal they observed, then their behavior is accepted as evidence of true imitation. Several species have been tested with this task, including birds (Akins & Zentall, 1998; Dawson & Foss, 1965), rodents (Heyes & Dawson, 1990), and primates (Whiten, Custance, Gomez, Texidor, & Bard, 1996), and most have shown some evidence that copying occurred. For example, quails that had recently observed a quail trained to press a lever by pecking it were more likely also to press the lever by pecking (Figure 11.2), whereas quails that had recently observed a quail trained to press a lever with its foot tended to press the lever with their foot (Akins & Zentall, 1996). This experiment demonstrates that quails have the capacity for true imitation (hereafter we use the term imitation to indicate true imitation).

The two-action test has enabled researchers to compare imitative capacities across species. For example, a recent experiment compared the imitative tendency of young children (ages 2–4) with that of juvenile chimpanzees (ages 4–5) (Whiten et al., 1996). In this study, children and chimpanzees were shown how to open a plastic box to obtain a food reward (Figure 11.3a). Half of the participants saw an adult human open the box by poking pins out of its latch before lifting the lid. The other half saw an adult human open the box by twisting and pulling the pins out of the latch. After observing their respective models, the participants were given a chance to open the box themselves.

Nothing about this task requires precise copying, because the box can be opened in many ways that are equally effective. Nevertheless, both children and chimpanzees usually copied the opening technique that they had observed (Figure 11.3b). Children were more likely than chimpanzees to copy the details of the observed actions, including details that were not essential to getting the box open. The researchers interpreted this finding as evidence that children are more likely to imitate actions than chimpanzees are. However,

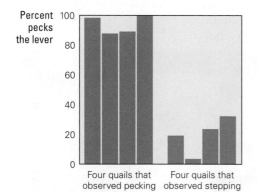

Percent pecks the lever

Figure 11.2 Two-action test of true imitation in quail
Observer quails were more likely to learn to peck a lever after they observed a trained quail peck the lever than after they observed a trained quail step on the lever. Quails' performance on the two-action test provides evidence that they can truly imitate. Adapted from Akins & Zentall, 1996.

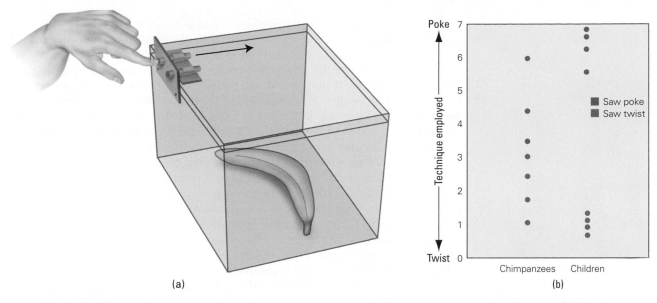

(a)

(b)

Figure 11.3 Two-action test of true imitation in children and chimpanzees (a) Children and chimpanzees observed an adult human use one of two techniques (poke or twist) to open a plastic box containing a reward. (b) Afterward, both children and chimpanzees were more likely to use the box-opening technique they had observed. This means that both chimps and children can truly imitate. Adapted from Whiten et al., 1996.

this is not a justifiable conclusion, because none of the participants was tested when the model was an adult chimpanzee rather than an adult human. In other words, children might be more likely (or better able) to imitate older humans, but might find it more difficult (or be less inclined) to imitate older chimpanzees. The identity of the model can affect the likelihood of imitation, as was shown in the Bobo doll study.

Humans can imitate a wide variety of actions and sounds. To assess whether any other animals can do this requires methods that are more flexible than the two-action test or the technique used by Bandura and colleagues. One approach involves teaching animals to imitate on command (often referred to as the "do-as-I-do" task). For example, researchers trained a chimpanzee to imitate a person's actions when the person gave the command "Do this!" (Hayes & Hayes, 1952). The researchers would perform an action, such as clapping hands, while telling the chimpanzee to "Do this!" and then would record whether or not the chimpanzee performed the same action. At first, the chimpanzee was unlikely to imitate the actions the first time they were demonstrated. However, after learning to "Do this!" for about 12 actions, the chimpanzee was able to replicate certain new actions the first time she was asked to do so. In a recent replication of this experiment, two other chimpanzees showed they could replicate 30 actions the first time they saw them, including actions such as hugging themselves and touching the back of their own head (Custance et al., 1995).

One reason psychologists have gone to such great lengths to define true imitation and to develop methods for revealing imitative abilities is because some researchers claim that imitative learning requires certain high-level cognitive processes that are unique to humans (Bandura, 1986; Piaget, 1962). For example, imitation by humans is often taken to imply some awareness on the observer's part that he or she is voluntarily copying actions. **Perspective taking,** or imagining oneself in the place of another, is another cognitive ability that some researchers have suggested is a prerequisite for learning through imitation. It is an ability that few species other than humans may possess. Perspective taking is thought to facilitate imitation, because it enables people (or animals) to imitate others without watching themselves doing so. For example, you can imitate someone's facial expressions without watching yourself make faces. How do you know that your face matches a face you are observing? Perhaps your ability to imagine an outside observer's perspective provides feedback that helps you to perform such a feat, but is this really what happens?

In order to evaluate the role of perspective taking in imitation, let us first recall Morgan's canon: if there is a simpler explanation, use it. Animals other than humans can imitate actions without visual feedback. Chimpanzees are as proficient at replicating gestures when they cannot see their own actions (for example, when they put their hand on their head) as they are when they can see their own actions (Custance et al., 1995). Dolphins too are highly proficient imitators (Herman, 2002), and given the placement of their eyes they are not likely to ever see themselves replicating actions. There is currently no way to determine whether or not dolphins and chimpanzees are imagining themselves in the place of another, so we must concede that their imitative abilities could potentially involve perspective taking. A simpler explanation, however, is that neither perspective taking nor visual feedback is necessary for imitation in dolphins, chimpanzees, or humans. This would mean that theories in which perspective taking and other higher-level cognitive processes are assumed to be necessary for imitation may be overestimating the complexity of the mechanisms underlying observational learning. In general, we do not yet know how high-level cognitive processes contribute to imitation.

Emulation: Copying Goals

Emulation was defined on page 425 as the attempt to replicate an observed outcome without reproducing the actions that the model used to achieve that outcome. Chimpanzees and adult humans often perform actions that replicate the outcome of another's actions, rather than copying the specific motor acts observed. For example, chimpanzees that saw people using a rake to collect food outside their cage were more likely to use a rake for this purpose than other chimpanzees, but they did not reliably copy the specific raking actions they observed (Nagell, Olguin, & Tomasello, 1993). A chimpanzee might hold the metal end of the rake and use the wooden end to knock the food closer to the cage. This type of copying has been distinguished from more exact copying, with some theorists claiming that when specific actions are not replicated, the copying does not qualify as true imitation (Tomasello, Davis-Dasilva, Carnak, & Bard, 1987; Wood, 1989). Of course, it is possible that by chance a chimpanzee might use the same actions as a demonstrator while attempting to achieve a particular observed outcome (especially if there are few actions that would work). Currently, there is no way to distinguish between this situation and true imitation, because behaviorally they are identical. Thus, psychologists use the term emulation only to describe instances in which observers use different actions to achieve the observed goal.

Most evidence of emulation in chimpanzees and adult humans comes from studies intended to show true imitation. For example, in the plastic-box study described on page 427, the human children were more likely to truly imitate the precise box-opening actions of the model (such as poking the pegs with an index finger), whereas the chimpanzees were more likely to emulate the behavior of the model while using their own methods for opening the plastic box (for example, pushing the pegs with their palms). One interpretation of this difference is that the chimpanzees learned some features of the task by observing the model's behavior but then chose actions different from the ones they had observed in order to perform the task. Matching the outcomes of a set of motor actions by performing somewhat different actions is one kind of emulation. Interestingly, when adult humans were tested on the plastic-box task, their matching behavior was more similar to that of the chimpanzees than to that of the children in that adults were more likely to emulate a model than to imitate the model (Horowitz, 2003).

Stimulus Matching: Copying Outcomes of Specific Actions

In some cases, emulation—copying the end results of a model's action—cannot be achieved unless certain specific actions are reproduced. Consider vocal imitation. When you imitate someone's speech, you never actually see most of the motor actions that produce that speech. You only observe (hear) the outcomes of those actions. Nevertheless, to reproduce the end results that you observed, you need to produce motor acts that match the ones the model used to produce the original speech.

When you are trying to imitate a sound that you hear, you compare the sounds you make with the sounds you originally heard. Copying of this type, in which stimuli are generated that can be directly compared with the originally observed stimuli, is called **stimulus matching.** When you imitate speech, you are in effect imitating a motor act that you have never directly observed. The only way you could directly compare how closely your actions match those of the speaker you are imitating would be by using an X-ray or other imaging machine to monitor your and your model's throat and mouth movements. However, the sounds you hear when you speak provide an indirect measure of your actions, and with this feedback you can greatly improve the match between your speech and what you originally heard. Because it is an indirect way of copying actions, stimulus matching is sometimes distinguished from true imitation. You should note that although stimulus matching can provide useful feedback, it requires that the observer/imitator first produce motor patterns appropriate for generating the sensory stimuli he or she wishes to imitate. You can only get feedback *after* you have performed an action. So, if your very first attempt to imitate a sound is nearly perfect, then clearly you did not learn the correct vocal actions through trial and error based on feedback.

One form of stimulus matching that researchers have studied extensively occurs in song learning by birds. Song learning, like the imitation of speech described in the preceding paragraph, is an example of **vocal learning,** which involves using memories of sounds to learn how to produce those sounds with one's own vocal organs. Song learning is the most extensively studied form of observational learning in any species (including humans). Bird songs typically consist of sounds lasting from one to 10 seconds that are separated by regular silent intervals. The timing, order, and qualities of individual sounds in the songs are all components that can be controlled by actions of the singer. Lots of animals sing, but usually the songs they sing are genetically predetermined rather than learned from experience.

How might scientists tell that birds or other animals learn songs through observation? One way is by isolating the animals at a very young age (possibly even prior to birth) so that they never hear another animal's voice. Singing insects, frogs, and monkeys that are isolated early in life will develop relatively normal singing behavior even if they never come into contact with another member of their species (Bradbury & Vehrencamp, 1998). In contrast, many songbirds never produce normal songs if they are isolated during certain stages of development (Hinde, 1969). Over time, a bird's song is gradually "shaped" by the songs of other birds in its environment. Like human speech, the songs that birds sing may show differences in dialect, or the locale-specific idiosyncrasies of a given language (Baptista & King, 1980; Marler, 1970; Thorpe, 1958). Just as your accent can reveal to others where you grew up and learned to speak, a bird's "accent" can

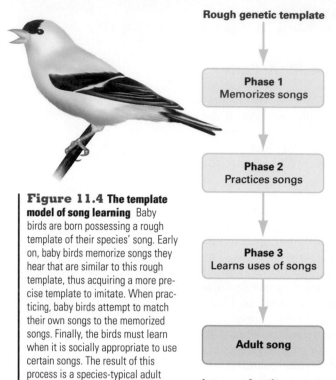

Rough genetic template

↓

Phase 1
Memorizes songs

↓

Phase 2
Practices songs

↓

Phase 3
Learns uses of songs

↓

Adult song

Figure 11.4 The template model of song learning Baby birds are born possessing a rough template of their species' song. Early on, baby birds memorize songs they hear that are similar to this rough template, thus acquiring a more precise template to imitate. When practicing, baby birds attempt to match their own songs to the memorized songs. Finally, the birds must learn when it is socially appropriate to use certain songs. The result of this process is a species-typical adult song.

reveal where the bird grew up and learned to sing. Baby birds raised by an adult of another species can sometimes even learn the foreigner's song (Immelman, 1969). This would be the equivalent of an infant being raised by chimpanzees and learning how to produce chimpanzee vocalizations (à la Tarzan).

Song learning seems to occur in three basic phases. To begin with, most songbirds seem to be born with a crude inherited "template" that biases their brain toward storing sounds that fit within this template. In the first phase of song learning, young birds memorize the songs they hear that best fit their template, and these memorized songs provide a model against which later performance is judged. The second phase ensues when the young bird begins attempting to sing songs. While the bird is singing, it hears itself singing, and can compare its own song to memories of songs it has heard in the past (a type of stimulus matching). With practice, the young bird increases the match between its own performance and the songs it remembers hearing. In the third stage of song learning, the bird learns when it is appropriate to sing. For example, a territorial songbird might sing primarily when it hears a song it has never heard before, or when it hears a familiar song sung by an unfamiliar bird. The behavior of a nearby female may influence a male songbird's singing through her reactions. These three phases of song learning are collectively called the **template model of song learning** (Figure 11.4).

Certain species-specific features of bird songs are genetically controlled, constraining what a learning bird is likely to copy. For example, young birds exposed to both the songs of their own species and the songs of other species will typically learn the song associated with their species (Marler, 1997). Similar constraints seem to operate in human infants as well. Infants are exposed to a wide range of sounds, possibly including the sounds of birds, dogs, and music, yet the sounds they learn to produce themselves are invariably the sounds produced by their own species—specifically, speech. This could be because sounds produced by members of the same species are inherently the easiest to replicate (because they were made using similar organs), or perhaps it is because neural templates within an animal's brain are genetically engineered to recognize species-specific sounds.

Some birds seem to be constrained to learn very stereotyped sound sequences. Other birds, such as parrots and mynah birds, can learn to reproduce a wide range of sounds that they experience. Mynah birds are able to reproduce speech that is virtually indistinguishable from human speech, despite the fact that if they never hear humans, they don't produce humanlike sounds. This means that genetics strongly determine the kinds of sounds that some animals (such as songbirds) can imitate, but provide other animals (humans and mynah birds) with more flexible vocal imitation abilities.

The fidelity with which some birds can replicate a spoken sentence is compelling evidence that some species flexibly learn to perform actions based on sounds they hear. Surprisingly, no mammals other than humans are able to imitate speech as well as birds can. In fact, most mammals, including our closest ape relatives, show no ability to imitate sounds or learn to produce vocalizations through experience. Dolphins are the only mammals that are known to be able to flexibly imitate sounds (Janik & Slater, 1997). Some dolphins, like Akeakamai, have been trained to imitate computer-generated sounds on command (Richards, Wolz, & Herman, 1984) and may also spontaneously imitate sounds (Reiss & McCowan, 1993). Sometimes when Akeakamai heard a sound that she could not easily reproduce, she would produce a transposed copy of the sound (Richards et al., 1984), much as a singer might transpose a song to a higher- or lower-pitch range to make it easier to sing.

No dolphin has learned to sing a song, but some of the larger whales do learn to sing songs by listening to other whales. Specifically, humpback whales learn to sing new songs throughout their lives by listening to other whales (Guinee, Chu, & Dorsey, 1983). They continuously change the properties of their songs (Payne & Payne, 1985) so that in any given year, whales are singing a song that no humpback whale has ever sung before (there are no "golden oldies" in the world of humpback whales). Researchers can tell that whales are learning their songs because when a whale introduces a new song into a particular region, many other whales will then begin to sing that song (Noad, Cato, Bryden, Jenner, & Jenner, 2000). This means the whales are copying the songs they hear other whales singing. No other mammals aside from humans show this ability. Thus, in mammals, learning through vocal imitation is a highly specialized ability rather than a general learning mechanism.

Parrots, dolphins, and humans are among the relatively few animals that have the ability to imitate sounds. Even fewer species appear to be able to imitate both sounds and actions. The ability to flexibly reproduce observed events appears to be rare in the animal kingdom. Does imitation represent a way of learning that is in some way superior to what is available to most animals? Or, is imitation just an ability that some species happened to evolve but that does not confer any specific learning advantages? As Bandura noted in the early 1960s, the act of observing others is what generally provides the information an organism needs in order to imitate or emulate—the learning happens during the observation, not when the observer is imitating. Nevertheless, researchers interested in understanding how humans learn have often argued that the ability to imitate is critical to learning. In an attempt to better understand how humans learn through observation, psychologists developed a framework specifically to explain human learning and behavior, called social learning theory.

Vocal imitators Parrots precisely copy sounds produced by other animals, despite being unable to directly observe the actions that generated those sounds.

Social Learning Theory

Social learning theory is a broad theory of human behavior that became prominent from the 1940s through the 1960s as an alternative or supplementary approach to more traditional behaviorist interpretations. A key feature of social learning theory is the idea that the kinds of reinforcements an individual has experienced in the past will determine how that individual will act in any given situation. Social learning theorists proposed that reinforcement determines personality traits (Rotter, 1954), and that observational learning is a special case of instrumental conditioning in which imitative acts are either directly or indirectly reinforced (Bandura, 1969; Miller & Dollard, 1941). According to Bandura, observers can gain information about whether a particular action will be rewarded or punished by observing the outcomes of a model's actions. If a person imitates actions that have been seen to lead to positive

Singing humpback whale Humpbacks are the only mammals other than humans that can learn to sing a song by hearing it—a unique case of learning through vocal imitation.

outcomes, those actions may lead to positive outcomes for the imitator. If they do, there is greater likelihood that the person will again copy such actions in the future (consistent with Thorndike's law of effect). For example, if Donna sees a child on TV being given ice cream after cleaning her room, it could inspire her to imitate the child's reward-producing behavior. Donna's parents are then likely to reinforce her for cleaning her room, which should increase the chances that Donna will clean her room again in the future, and also that she will continue to copy models that she sees getting reinforcers.

Social learning theory originally focused on instrumental conditioning and the successive approximation of target actions in response to reward and punishment (Miller & Dollard, 1941; Skinner, 1953). Modern social learning theory places less emphasis on conditioning and instead explains behavior in terms of more cognitive processes, such as thinking and evaluating possible future outcomes. A basic premise of contemporary social learning theory is that any behavior can be learned without direct reinforcement or punishment (Bandura, 1986). Expectations of reinforcers and punishments will influence the likelihood that a learned action will be performed, but the learning itself (the knowledge gained about an action and its outcome) is taken to be the result of observation rather than the result of conditioning. In other words, a relationship between an action and an outcome only needs to be observed, not performed, in order to be learned. Within this framework, an imitated action is simply a performance that reveals what has been learned. For example, Donna doesn't have to clean her room and be rewarded in order to learn that cleaning her room brings rewards, she only needs to be able to observe an appropriate model being rewarded for cleaning.

Bandura cited four basic processes to explain how people learn by copying. First, the presence of a model is thought to increase an observer's attention to the situation. The actions of others can be especially salient cues that act as a magnet for attention (Bandura, 1986). Second, memories for the observed situation must be stored in an accessible format, so that they can guide later actions. If the observer forgets how an action was performed, it will be difficult for that person to imitate the action. Third, the observer must have the ability to reproduce the action. You might remember quite well what it looks like when someone dunks a basketball, but unless you can jump quite high, you won't be able to imitate this action. Finally, the observer must have some motivation for reproducing the observed actions. You probably wouldn't burn your money just because you saw someone else doing it, even though it would be an easy action to perform.

In some cases, the status or identity of the model can provide the motivation for an observer to imitate an action. For example, individuals are more likely to imitate the actions of someone they admire. Similarity between a model and the observer increases the likelihood of copying, especially if the outcome is desirable. Donna would be more likely to beat up a Bobo doll if she sees a young girl her age doing it than if she sees an old woman attacking the doll, but not if she sees the girl spanked for her actions. In other cases, the desirability of the observed outcome in itself is enough to provide motivation for an imitative act. For example, you might be more likely to burn your money if you observe that other people who burn their money are invited to parties with celebrities.

Although much of the attention given historically to observational learning has been focused on organisms imitating the actions of others, there are a number of ways that humans and other animals can learn from observations that do not involve imitation or emulation. Experiments are critical for determining when observational learning involves true imitation, because many of these other phenomena look just like imitation to the casual observer.

▶ **Learning and Memory in Everyday Life**

What Can a Child Learn from a Teletubby?

Studies like Bandura's Bobo doll experiment have convinced many people that violence in movies, video games, television programs, and songs can have detrimental effects on children by causing them to imitate or emulate the violent behaviors they observe. By the same token, parents worry that their children's personalities and behaviors might be adversely affected by other undesirable things they see on television. Donna's parents were particularly concerned that she not be exposed to shows like *Teletubbies,* in which baby-faced creatures speak a nonsense language and sport televisions on their tummies, thereby enabling young kids to watch two TV screens simultaneously! Donna's parents weren't sure exactly what she might learn from watching this kind of show, but they were sure they didn't want their daughter to adopt the behaviors of a Teletubby, so they made sure she never had a chance to see the program at home.

What might Donna learn from watching *Teletubbies? Teletubbies* is one of the first shows to have been developed for viewing by children from 1 to 3 years old. The actors inside the Teletubby suits have been trained to act like infants or toddlers. The idea behind the show is that infants will be engaged by seeing the actions of other infantlike creatures, and therefore will be more likely to imitate them and learn from them. The educational goal of the program is to improve preschoolers' readiness for learning in schools. However, some parents and educators worry that the show overly

The Teletubby named Po Menace to children's development, or a model of positive social behavior?

promotes television watching by kids (because of the TVs in the characters' tummies). Others worry that the nonsense speech used by Teletubbies may disrupt language development, and that the bizarre environment where the Teletubbies roam may confuse young children. One religious leader has even warned parents not to let their babies watch the show because of his belief that it promotes a homosexual lifestyle. On the other hand, many parents ardently defend the show because the Teletubbies spend a good part of their time on the show hugging, sharing, and playing together without conflict. Pro-Teletubby parents reason that if watching violent shows can make a child more violent, then maybe watching peaceful, happy shows can make a child more peaceful and happy.

Social learning theory predicts that if Donna identifies with Teletubbies, then she is likely to imitate some of their actions. However, her ability to do so will depend on her ability to recognize those actions and to store memories of them. It is currently unclear what memories a 1- to 3-year-old child might be able to create from watching a video, or how long such memories will last. Recall from Chapter 3 that young children generally exhibit infantile amnesia—an inability to recall specific episodes. If Donna has no memories for observed acts, then those absent memories cannot guide her actions. In any case, imitated actions will obey Thorndike's law of effect just like any other actions. If Donna's actions become more Teletubby-like after she watches the show, her parents can counter them by reinforcing her non-Teletubby-like actions instead, and making sure she is not reinforced whenever she acts like a Teletubby.

Although we cannot as yet predict how Donna's exposure to *Teletubbies* or other shows will affect her behavior, we can expect that she will be more likely to copy models that she perceives as being similar to herself. If she identifies with a hugging Teletubby, she may copy its hugging behavior. If she identifies with an aggressive character on a show, she may copy its actions. For this reason, to a certain extent, Donna's behavioral history prior to watching a show is the best predictor of what the show might teach her.

Alternatives to Imitation

In imitating, an animal or person produces actions that match the actions of others. But, just because animals produce matching acts does not mean that one of the animals is imitating the other. Schooling fish, stampeding cattle, flocking birds, and cheering fans all perform acts that match those of their peers. Are they imitating one another? Seeing one organism's action followed by a similar action from another does not necessarily constitute evidence of imitation. Many conditions other than imitation can result in matching behavior. Below, we describe three phenomena that cause the reproduction of actions and thus resemble imitation, but which may be explained more simply: contagion, observational conditioning, and stimulus enhancement.

Contagion and Observational Conditioning

When you hear laughter, you too may feel the urge to laugh (which is why laugh tracks are a common feature of sitcoms). When you see someone yawn, you will be more likely to yawn. When one baby starts crying on a plane, then other babies who are there will likely join in. The inborn tendency to react emotionally to visual or acoustic stimuli that indicate an emotional response by other members of one's species is called **contagion** (Byrne, 1994). Contagion is a relatively common phenomenon that occurs when the observation of a response increases the likelihood that the observer will have a similar response. Typically, the kinds of motor acts that produce contagion are not actions that an animal or person has learned. Babies yawn and cry in utero. Actions that result from contagion usually match the observed actions, but *not* as a result of imitation; the matching reaction is instead an unconditioned response (UR).

Some cases of observational learning involve contagion, and they can appear very similar to those that involve imitation. For example, if in her youth Donna observed her mother panic after seeing a small spider run across the floor, she may now behave in the same way whenever she sees a spider. It seems like Donna is imitating her mother, right? Actually, this scenario can be explained more simply as a special case of classical conditioning—more specifically, as a type of fear conditioning (Shettleworth, 1998). For Donna, the conditioned stimulus (CS) is the spider. The unconditioned stimulus (US) is her mother's fear, which naturally causes a fear reaction (UR) in Donna as a result of contagion (Figure 11.5).

If the CS and US are paired often enough, Donna may come to exhibit a conditioned fear reaction (CR) to the spider alone. This is one way that *phobias* can develop (see Chapter 10 for a more detailed discussion of phobias).

We described a similar situation in Chapter 10 in which naive lab monkeys learned to fear snakes after watching wild monkeys react fearfully to them (Mineka & Cook, 1988). Instances such as these, in which an individual learns an emotional response after observing it in others, have been described as **observational conditioning** (Heyes, 1994). Observational conditioning need not always lead to panic. Observing individuals that respond fearlessly to "dangerous" situations can help a person to learn to overcome a fear of those situations. For instance, watching videotapes of sexual activity can reduce sexual anxiety and increase sexual activity in people with sexual dysfunctions (Nemetz, Craig, & Reith, 1978).

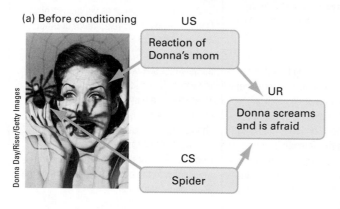

(a) Before conditioning

US — Reaction of Donna's mom

UR — Donna screams and is afraid

CS — Spider

(b) After conditioning

CS ⟶ CR

Spider · Donna screams

Figure 11.5 Classical conditioning through contagion
(a) As a child, Donna may have learned to fear spiders by observing her mother's responses to them.
(b) This learning process likely involves classical conditioning resulting from contagion rather than imitation.

Donna Day/Riser/Getty Images

Figure 11.6 Observational conditioning in blackbirds Black-birds can learn to attack harmless objects like bottles if they observe other blackbirds attacking that object—or are tricked into thinking that is what they are observing, as is shown here. Adapted from Shettleworth, 1998.

Some instances of observational conditioning are almost indistinguishable from situations that have been described as learning through imitation. In fact, behaviorists and early social learning theorists occasionally used this similarity to argue that all observational learning experiments involve nothing more than classical or instrumental conditioning. Consider the following example. In the wild, blackbirds learn to attack predators when they observe other blackbirds attacking those predators. Once a blackbird has learned from another bird that a particular object is worthy of attack, it will continue to attack this object on sight for quite a while. In lab studies of this phenomenon, one blackbird can "teach" a second bird to attack something as harmless as a plastic bottle (Curio, Ernst, & Vieth, 1978). Researchers get the birds to do this by showing the "model" bird a stuffed owl, a predator that blackbirds naturally attack. Meanwhile, the second bird observes the model's attacks. However, a clever optical illusion causes the second bird to think the model is attacking a bottle rather than an owl (Figure 11.6). Consequently, the second blackbird learns to attack bottles.

This might seem like a clear case of imitation: one bird sees another bird attacking a bottle and then does the same. In fact, this experiment is a lot like the Bobo doll experiment described above, which is considered to be a definitive demonstration of imitative learning by children. The key difference is that in the case of the blackbirds, attacking is a species-specific behavior that almost always occurs when a blackbird detects either a predator or an attacking blackbird. A simpler explanation of this example of observational learning is thus that the "model" is really an unconditioned stimulus, the initial attacks are an unconditioned response, and the bottle becomes a conditioned stimulus through classical conditioning.

Observational conditioning and contagion are two phenomena in which an observer seems to be imitating the actions of others but is not. A third phenomenon that bears a deceptive resemblance to imitation is when an observer's attention is drawn to stimuli by the actions of others, as you will now see.

Stimulus Enhancement

Information can be transferred to another individual simply by redirecting the individual's attention. This redirection can then lead to matching actions that

Getty Images/Imageworks

Pointing to produce stimulus enhancement Stimulus enhancement involves directing attention to a particular part of the environment; this can lead to matching actions that appear similar to imitation.

may be mistaken for imitation (Roberts, 1941; Thorpe, 1963). For example, you may have seen a group of people (typically younger people) collectively directing their attention to try and trick other people into looking up at the sky. The way this trick generally works is that the group will start looking up at the sky and pointing as if there were something interesting (or frightening) happening up there. Inevitably, a passerby will look up to where the group is looking, to see what all the excitement is about. The passerby then experiences confusion, because there is nothing to see.

Because the passerby replicates the head positions of the mischievous teenagers, one might think that the passerby is imitating the teenagers. In this case, however, the similarity in actions is a by-product of a similar focus of attention. Just because people watching a movie in a movie theater behave similarly does not mean that they are all imitating each other. Direction of one organism's attention toward specific objects, events, or locations within an environment as a result of another organism's action is called **stimulus enhancement** (Spence, 1937). Magicians and ventriloquists master techniques of stimulus enhancement to generate entertaining illusions. Animals often inadvertently draw attention to their actions, and when this provokes other animals to produce similar actions, it can lead to the illusion that the animals are imitating each other. For example, if one seagull dives toward a piece of food, other nearby seagulls will quickly follow suit.

In some cases it is obvious that the reason why people are behaving similarly is that they are focused on a similar event. In other cases, however, the contribution of stimulus enhancement is much harder to spot. About a century ago, it was discovered that blue tits (a kind of bird) in England were learning to puncture the tops of milk bottles that had been left outside homes by the local milkman to get the cream near the top of the bottle (Hinde & Fisher, 1951). This behavior was observed in only a few isolated areas, even though the birds and milk bottles were found throughout England. The geographically specific pattern of the behavior suggested that birds were learning to open milk bottles by observing the actions of other birds.

Initially, many viewed this phenomenon as clear evidence of behavioral imitation by birds in a natural setting. This interpretation is plausible: some birds may have been imitating other birds' bottle-opening actions (note, too, that at least a few birds would have had to learn the behavior on their own). However, it is also possible that the birds were simply paying more attention to the milk bottles because they observed other birds getting food from them. In that case, what the birds learned from their observations was not how to open a milk bottle but that milk bottle tops are of interest as a potential source of food. Once a bird has learned to pay attention to milk bottle tops, the chance that it would also learn through trial and error to puncture the tops would dramatically increase. Thus, blue tits in a particular region could learn through stimulus enhancement and instrumental conditioning to open milk bottles, and none of the birds would need to have ever watched another bird actually opening a milk bottle, or to have imitated such actions if they had seen them.

Stimulus enhancement can powerfully affect what an individual learns (Heyes, 1994). Essentially, the individual's focus is drawn to a subset of features of the environment (such as a front porch or the top of a milk bottle) that might provide more useful information than other features present. Humans have developed artificial means of directing an observer's attention, such as using spotlights in stage performances, and laser pointers in slide presentations. In general, stimulus enhancement increases the likelihood that an animal will be exposed to particular stimuli and their associated consequences. When such exposure is repeated, the opportunities for habituation, latent learning, classical conditioning, or instrumental conditioning are repeated as well. The kind of information that can be transmitted in this way is limited, however. The next section describes other, more flexible ways that organisms can learn from socially transmitted information.

Test Your Knowledge

What Is Imitation?

Much of what people describe as imitation may not be what scientists consider to be true imitation, and in fact might not even involve copying. Below are some scenarios that may seem to, and possibly do, involve imitation. Your job is to try to provide alternative explanations for what is happening.

1. You smile at your friend's baby. The baby smiles back. Is your friend's baby imitating you?

2. You discover that almost anything you do makes the baby smile (apparently, you are a talented clown). But when you stick out your tongue at the baby, the baby sticks out her tongue at you. Is she imitating you?

3. Donna sees her father make faces when he is eating asparagus, and his expression seems to indicate that he thinks asparagus is disgusting. Later in the week, Donna's grandmother serves asparagus and notices that Donna is making similar faces while eating. Is Donna imitating her father?

4. While watching *America's Funniest Home Videos,* you see a video of a cat jumping up to turn a doorknob so that it can open the door and go outside. Is the cat imitating people?

5. Donna has stumbled into one of the oldest conundrums of childhood. She tells her friend, "Stop repeating whatever I say!" Her friend replies, "Stop repeating whatever I say!" Donna counters, "I mean it, you better stop!" To which her friend replies, "I mean it, you better stop!" And so on. Is Donna's friend imitating her?

Social Transmission of Information

Imagine you are waiting to purchase a soda from a vending machine, and you notice that the person before you just lost money in the machine. On the basis of observing the person's misfortune, you might decide not to put your money into that particular machine. This is an example of **social transmission of information,** a process in which an observer learns something new through experiences with others. Social transmission of information is seen in all human cultures. It is historically evident in the development of spoken and written language, and more recently in the development of libraries, television, telephones, and the Internet. Through these various channels, information can be transmitted rapidly to vast numbers of individuals.

The many ways in which humans are able to transmit information enables them to learn more rapidly than all other animals in an almost unlimited range of contexts. Unfortunately, this phenomenon has seldom been studied in the laboratory, except in relation to skill learning. You may recall from Chapter 4, the experiment in which a person was asked to kick a target as rapidly as possible. His performance improved incrementally in keeping with the power law of

"That's not <u>my</u> political opinion. That's just stuff I hear on the radio."

learning: quickly at first and then more slowly. However, when he was shown a film of someone kicking the target in a more effective way, his performance improved dramatically. In this particular example, information about better ways to kick was socially transferred by means of a film. (The person in this experiment probably improved by imitating the model he visually observed, but because the experiment focused on skill learning rather than imitation, the exact mechanism of learning was not closely assessed.)

Because so much transfer of information between humans occurs in highly sophisticated ways, it is easy to overlook examples of socially transferred information in other species. However, the very complexity of social transmission of information in humans causes difficulty for researchers when they try to isolate the basic mechanisms involved. This is why the simpler forms of information transfer seen in animals are important for understanding the processes underlying this ability.

Learning through Social Conformity

If you've ever looked through your parents' or grandparents' photo albums, you've probably come across one or more pictures that made you wonder how they could have ever gotten it into their heads to wear clothes that were so ugly or uncomfortable. You may have even found a picture of the younger you wearing clothes and a hairstyle that you would be humiliated to be seen in today. In contrast, if you've seen photos of tigers taken in the 1920s, you would be hard pressed to tell them apart from photos of tigers that were taken yesterday. Why is it that humans do things to collectively change their appearance over time? Why do you even cut your hair or shave at all? A major reason you do any of these things is because you've learned to do them.

Here's how you know that learning, and not some other force of nature, is what is guiding your actions and preferences. If you go to a city in China or Africa that has a climate similar to the one you are used to and compare your hair, clothes, and speech to those of the native inhabitants, you will find that most of the inhabitants are more similar to each other in how they dress and speak than they are to you. This would not be the case if you yourself had lived in that city your whole life. If you were raised in the foreign city, you would probably dress and speak like everyone else there. Cultural differences in dress and language are easily apparent. What is not so apparent is how you learn to choose jeans over a kilt, or how you learn to say, "I would choose jeans over a kilt."

Studies of the social transmission of food preferences in rats may shed some light on such questions (Galef & Wigmore, 1983). Infant rats begin by preferring foods their mother has eaten, because they can taste those foods in her milk. However, rats naturally pay attention to the food consumption of other rats, and can learn to eat novel foods after observing that another rat has eaten them. In studies of this phenomenon, rats are typically housed together in pairs for a few days, during which they are fed rat chow (Figure 11.7a). One rat from each pair—chosen to be the "demonstrator" rat—is moved to another cage, *both* are deprived of food for one day, and *the demonstrator rat* is then fed cinnamon- or cocoa-flavored food (half of the demonstrator rats are given one flavor and half the other). The demonstrator rats are then returned to their original cages

(a)

1. Pairs of rats are fed rat chow.

2. The observer rat is removed to another cage: both rats are deprived of food.

3. The demonstrator is given a novel food (cinnamon!).

(b)

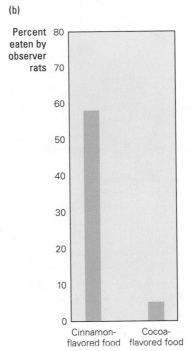

4. Briefly together again; the observer rat smells the novel food on the demonstrator rat's breath.

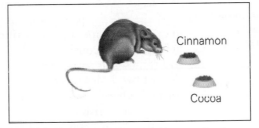

5. Later, the observer rat chooses the food that the demonstrator rat ate.

Figure 11.7 Social transmission of food preferences by rats (a) Two rats are initially housed together; then one of the rats (called the demonstrator rat) is moved to another cage, and both rats are deprived of food for a day. Next, the demonstrator rat is given a chance to eat a novel food (in this case, cinnamon-flavored food), after which it is returned to the original cage. Finally, the observer rat is exposed to two novel foods, one of which is the same food the demonstrator rat recently ate. (b) Observer rats are more likely to eat the food that they smelled on their cage mate's breath than another novel food. This means that information about food has been transmitted between the rats. Adapted from Shettleworth, 1998.

and allowed to interact with the "observer" rat for 15 minutes. On the subsequent day, the observer rat is given access to two food bowls, one containing cocoa-flavored food and the other cinnamon-flavored food. Observer rats typically eat more food of the flavor that they smelled on the demonstrator's breath (Figure 11.7b). This shows that the observer rats acquired information about foods from the demonstrator rat and later used this information to choose food.

Observer rats need to smell food in the context of another rat's breath to acquire a new food preference (Galef, 1996). Once a food becomes preferred, that preference may be transmitted to successive generations. Similarly, if certain foods are poisoned, observer rats can learn to avoid those foods by observing

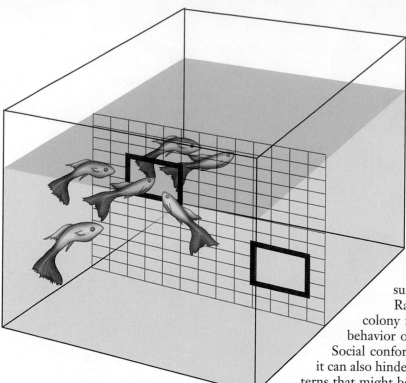

Figure 11.8 Social transmission of escape paths by guppies After demonstrator guppies were trained to escape from a net by swimming through a particular hole (with a second escape hole closed), observer guppies tended to use the same escape path as the demonstrator guppies when both holes were open. Adapted from Brown & Laland, 2002.

either the negative effects on or the aversion of demonstrators (Galef & Allen, 1995). This social transmission of acquired food aversions can be passed from one rat to the next for up to at least four generations, even though by that time no rat in the colony will have ever been negatively affected by the "bad" food. Several factors affect how easily food preferences or aversions are transmitted to others (Galef & Whiskin, 1997). For example, larger numbers of demonstrations and demonstrating rats increase the likelihood of transfer. Isolated (one-time) observations produce only a short-term effect, but repeated exposures lead to long-term retention.

Rats tend to follow what the majority of colony members do; this tendency to adopt the behavior of the group is called **social conformity**. Social conformity has many protective functions, but it can also hinder the development of novel behavior patterns that might be advantageous. In one experiment, guppies (a kind of fish) were trained to follow specific escape paths in order to escape from an artificial predator (Brown & Laland, 2002). The artificial predator consisted of a net being moved across a tank to trap the guppies, and the escape paths were holes at different positions in the net (Figure 11.8). One of two holes was closed during training, and demonstrator guppies quickly learned where the one open hole in the net was located. After training, the demonstrator fish continued to use only the escape path they had learned, even after the second hole was opened. When naive fish were introduced into this situation, with both holes open, they typically chose to escape through the hole that they observed the trained fish using. If the demonstrator guppies were then removed from the tank, the observer guppies continued to use the hole they had seen the demonstrator guppies using, even when the alternate path led to a quicker escape.

Social conformity allows rapid acquisition of information that is adaptive for a particular situation, but it can lead to traditions that may provide no general benefit. Interestingly, a reduction in the number of trained guppies (that is, a decrease in the number of demonstrators), increased the likelihood that new escape solutions would emerge (Brown & Laland, 2002). Apparently, even guppies can be affected by peer pressure.

Active Instruction and Culture

Rats are not the only animals that transmit information with their breath. Humans do too. Unlike rats, humans don't rely on the odor of their breath to transmit information, but rather use the sound of their breath: speech. Rats can learn to eat a novel food by smelling the food on another rat's breath. Is this comparable to the transmission of information from a professor to a college student? Not quite. Humans have the conscious intention of transmitting information, whereas rats appear to transmit the information involuntarily. In this way, at least, university professors differ from rats.

Evidence of active (intentional) instruction in animals other than humans is rare, and open to interpretation. Mother cats and orcas go hunting and bring back weakened prey on which the kittens and young whales can practice their hunting skills (Caro & Hauser, 1992; Guinet & Bouvier, 1995). Killer whales, which sometimes beach themselves temporarily to capture seals, have been seen pushing their young onto the beach, pushing them toward seals, and then helping the young whales return to the water. One researcher reports seeing chimpanzee mothers help their infants learn to crack nuts with stones (Boesch, 1991). The mothers made appropriately shaped rocks available, positioned the stone or nut to increase the probability of success, and changed their behavior depending on the infant's success. Perhaps the killer whales and chimpanzees were actively instructing their young to help them learn. However, it's difficult to verify that such teaching episodes actually lead to improvements in the youngsters' abilities. Their abilities may just improve naturally as the youngsters develop, independent of active instruction by adults. This is often true for human children and makes it difficult for researchers to determine the specific role that teaching plays in many human activities.

Orcas teaching young to hunt?
Killer whales temporarily beach themselves to capture seals. Adult whales push their young onto a beach toward seals and then help the young return to the water when they get stuck on the sand. This behavior may be an instance of active instruction of predatory strategies.

David McNew/Peter Arnold, Inc.

Effects of Violent Entertainment on Behavior

Eventually, Donna entered elementary school, and her parents (like most) began worrying about how much time she spent watching television. She didn't watch any more TV than the average child (about 24 hours per week), but this still seemed like a lot to Donna's parents. Their worries intensified when Donna reached adolescence and began copying what they considered to be the "bizarre" behaviors of her idols (such as wearing a nose ring). Like most parents, Donna's parents worry about what Donna will learn from observing and copying others.

Much public transfer of information in the United States occurs through the mass distribution of moving images and audio signals, in the form of television, movies, the Internet, and recorded music. Most of the content transmitted by these various media outlets is designed to entertain paying customers. Even news programs focus on the news stories that will attract the most viewers. Over the last few decades, however, there has been increasing concern that the entertaining images and words broadcast by the mass media are having negative effects on the population. In particular, numerous organizations have concluded that excessive depiction of violence in the mass media is a public health risk because it stimulates violent behavior (Anderson et al., 2003). The basic assumption driving this concern is "Monkey see, monkey do"—that people will imitate what they see.

Researchers have collected strong evidence of a general association between violent behavior and increased exposure to violent media (Anderson et al., 2003). For example, the amount of violent TV watched by children in elementary school is correlated with their aggressiveness as teenagers and with their criminal behavior as adults (Anderson et al., 2003). Similarly, statistics show the rate of homicides to have increased dramatically soon after television was intro-

Figure 11.9 Correlation between television and homicides in the United States The rate of homicides increased dramatically among whites in the United States soon after television was introduced, whereas no such increases were observed among whites in South Africa, where television was banned during the same time period. Adapted from Centerwall, 1992.

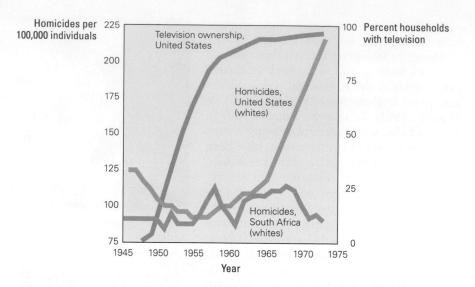

duced in the United States, whereas no such increases were observed in regions where television was banned during the same time period (Centerwall, 1992; see Figure 11.9). Given that such correlations exist, the main questions relevant to this discussion are (1) do violent media increase aggressive behavior, or do aggressive individuals find violent media more entertaining; and (2) does exposure to violent media lead to observational learning and the performance of imitative actions?

Most research addressing these questions has focused on the effects of viewing violent images. In the typical experiment, researchers randomly assign young participants to watch either a short violent film or a short nonviolent film. Later, the researchers observe the participants' behavior. Usually these observations are made a few minutes or days after viewing the film, in contexts where aggression might normally occur. Such experiments show that children exposed to the violent film are more likely to behave aggressively in play sessions immediately after viewing the film (Cornstock, 1980; Geen, 1990). For example, 7- to 9-year-old boys who scored high on measures of aggressiveness were more likely to physically assault other boys in a hockey game after watching a violent video (Josephson, 1987). As was seen in the Bobo doll experiment, aroused participants were more likely than nonaroused participants to behave aggressively after viewing the violent images. Researchers produced the arousal by some kind of provocation. Thus, college men who viewed a violent sex film were more willing to deliver electrical shocks to a woman who had previously provoked them than were men who viewed a violent film containing no sex (Donnerstein & Berkowitz, 1981).

Such short-term experiments generally do not prove that children have learned to be aggressive from watching the violent performances, because a general increase in arousal levels (brought on by watching violent behavior) might be what is leading to the children's increased aggressiveness, rather than anything specific they learned from watching the videos (Anderson et al., 2003). In addition, this research does not provide evidence that exposure to violence in movies and songs increases aggressive behavior any more than violence depicted in other sources of entertainment such as books, plays, and puppet shows. Last, researchers have seldom studied the possibility that exposure to violent television shows might be correlated with positive outcomes, such as an increased likelihood that a person will pursue a career as a medical professional, firefighter, soldier, or police officer. Many violent shows depict nonviolent heroes and violent villains, and nothing about watching a video compels children to choose the villains as their models.

Recently, interactive media such as video games and the Internet have become the subjects of similar research. Part of this interest stems from the fact that students who gunned down other students in recent school shootings were avid video game players (Anderson, 2004). Experiments designed to reveal the negative effects of violent video games compare aggressive behavior in children who have recently played a violent video game with aggressive behavior in children who recently played a nonviolent video game. As in studies of more passive media, children who played the violent video game generally were more likely to behave aggressively (Anderson, 2004; Irwin & Gross, 1995).

Such correlations do not prove that observing violence increases violent behavior. Another explanation could be that children who are predisposed to violence are also more likely to enjoy watching violence on television. This would mean that watching violent TV doesn't cause the violence but is merely another way in which the predisposition is manifested. Nevertheless, a report issued by the National Institute of Mental Health in the 1980s concluded that children who are repeatedly exposed to violent television may become less sensitive to the suffering of others, more fearful of the world around them, and more likely to behave in aggressive ways toward others (APA Online, 2004; http://www.psychologymatters.org/mediaviolence.html). Consequently, governmental agencies have introduced regulatory measures to reduce the possible negative effects of mass media on children, including requiring warnings to be displayed on CDs, placing ratings and age restrictions on movie viewing and video games, and requiring V-chips in new television sets to enable parents to restrict what their children watch.

Although researchers have proposed that observational learning involving imitation underlies the association between exposure to violent media and aggressive behavior (Anderson et al., 2003), most studies of exposure to violent media do not report instances of true imitation after exposure. Viewers of violent media might emulate what they observe, but researchers have not yet investigated that possibility. In general, it remains unclear what individuals learn from watching movies or listening to songs.

In addition to the mere presence or absence of violence in mass media, researchers and public officials have voiced concern about the total amount of violence being depicted. Their fear is that greater exposure to violent scenes leads to a higher incidence of aggressive behavior. This may be true, but there are no experiments showing that children who are repeatedly exposed either to the same violent movie or to multiple violent movies are more likely to behave more aggressively than children who have seen such a movie only once. Just as it is difficult to identify the effects of a single entertainment event on future behavior, it is also difficult to predict the effects of multiple exposures to depictions of violence. That being said, the general consensus is that massive amounts of viewing or listening to violence is more likely to do harm than good, whether or not observational learning plays a role.

In the next section, we'll review what is known about how different brain regions contribute to observational learning.

Interim Summary

Observational learning can involve copying of observed actions or copying of the goals and outcomes of observed actions. Observational learning is often described as a form of learning through imitation, but according to social learning theory the important learning actually occurs before any action is imitated.

Furthermore, it is seldom clear when learning involves true imitation (the copying of actions) versus other phenomena like emulation (copying that involves replicating outcomes). In fact, some situations that seem like imitation may be cases of observational conditioning or stimulus enhancement combined with instrumental conditioning, which involve no copying. Consequently, it is currently unclear whether true imitation plays any significant role in learning by humans or any other species of animal! Song learning by birds is the most extensively studied case of observational learning, and such learning does seem to involve both true imitation and emulation. The social transmission of information allows individuals to learn from others but does not necessarily involve imitation.

Observational learning includes aspects of many of the learning mechanisms we have discussed in previous chapters. For example, imitative learning depends on memories for facts, events, and skills. Because much of what is learned through observation is latent, observational learning is not as well understood as other forms of learning. What is clear, however, is that only a few species have the ability to flexibly imitate, and that this ability may confer unique opportunities for learning.

11.2 Brain Substrates

What enables some animals to learn through observation and to imitate while others cannot? Do the organisms that have these abilities possess special brain circuits that endow their owners with innate talents? Or do enhanced neural mechanisms of learning enable experience to modify "standard" brains in novel ways?

Differences in animals' abilities to imitate imply differences in the neural processes that underlie those abilities, but it is difficult to know how those differences depend on learning experiences. In the Behavioral Processes section, we discussed how observational learning often seems to depend both on memories for facts and events (such as memories of actions or sounds only experienced once) and skill memories (learning to do something novel from seeing another perform the action). So, you might expect that the neural substrates of observational learning would be similar to those described in the chapters on memories for facts, events, and skills. But the fact that only a few species seem to be capable of observational learning (especially learning based on imitation) suggests that something beyond these basic neural systems is needed for such learning. In the following discussion, we describe several cases of observational learning in mammals and birds that provide some clues about the kinds of neural processing that enable behavioral and vocal imitation, as well as the social transmission of information.

The basic problem faced by the brain of an imitating animal is how to map observed events onto the motor commands that are needed to generate those same events. In behavioral imitation, the model's observed actions are the events to be replicated. In vocal imitation, the outcomes of the model's actions (the produced sounds) are the events to be replicated. This is an oversimplification of the problem, because the motor patterns generated by the imitator never really recreate the observed event. Specifically, an imitator's actions never produce sensory patterns that are identical to those that were observed.

Consider the case of vocal imitation. Imitated sounds may "match" those produced by a model, but from the imitator's perspective they differ in many ways from the originally perceived sounds. First, no imitator has the control necessary to replicate most of the acoustic features present in the received sound. Unless you are a gifted mimic, you will repeat sentences in your own voice, rather than in the voice you heard. Second, no matter how closely you might reproduce the sounds, they will sound different to you, because you will hear your own voice modified by transmission through your head. Have you ever heard a recording of yourself? You were probably a little surprised at how your voice sounded. Scientists are just beginning to figure out how the brain enables learning through imitation, but cortical processing is thought to be a critical component. After all, dolphins and humans, two of the most proficient imitators, also have some of the most expansive cortices.

Before any action can be imitated, it must first be recognized. Although cortical circuits for recognizing visual patterns have been studied more extensively than any other region of cortex, relatively little is known about how cortical networks store memories of visual scenes involving dynamic actions performed by people. Two hypotheses have been proposed for how and where such memories are formed. The "visual hypothesis" proposes that memories for perceived acts are stored in visual cortical regions. Whereas the other hypothesis, referred to as the "direct-matching hypothesis," suggests that memories for actions are stored in cortical regions that map observed actions onto the motor representations of the acts (Buccino, Binkofski, & Riggio, 2004). In other words, observing an action automatically activates the same neural systems required to perform the act, and memories for the act are stored as part of this process.

These two hypotheses might both be right. Memories for perceived actions could be stored in multiple brain regions. However, in order to copy an observed action, the human or other animal must remember actions that were previously observed and use those memories to generate corresponding motor responses. The following sections will therefore focus on neurophysiological data relevant to the direct-matching hypothesis, which assumes that cortical networks link visual inputs to motor outputs.

Mirror Neurons in the Cortex

The fact that humans can imitate actions implies that the human brain can translate visual inputs into corresponding motor patterns. It wasn't until about twenty years ago, however, that researchers identified evidence of neural circuits performing such functions. Neurons that fire during both performance of an action and during visual observations of that same action were first identified in a monkey's cortex (di Pellegrino, Fadiga, Fogassi, Gallese, & Rizzolatti, 1992; Gallese, Fadiga, Fogassi, & Rizzolatti, 1996). Such neurons are called **mirror neurons** because they fire the same way when the monkey performs an action as they do when the monkey sees another monkey performing that action (Rizzolatti & Craighero, 2004). In other words, mirror neurons respond similarly to both of the events considered necessary for imitation.

There are several different "flavors" of mirror neurons. Mirror neurons that respond to actions involving the hands or the mouth are the most common (Ferrari, Gallese, Rizzolatti, & Fogassi, 2003). For example, the mirror neurons in area F5, shown in Figure 11.10, fire most strongly when a monkey either grasps, tears, or handles objects, or when the monkey observes those same actions. This means that the neurons behave the same way when a monkey sees tearing or is tearing something, and that when one monkey sees another monkey tearing a magazine, some of the same neurons become active that would be active if the observer were doing the tearing. Thus, mirror neurons provide a neural link between seeing an action and doing an action. A monkey could potentially use this link to imitate an observed action, since all the monkey would need to do is reactivate neural circuits that had recently been activated.

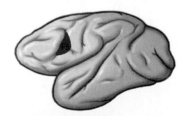

Figure 11.10 A mirror neuron area in a monkey cortex. The area shown in red (F5) is a region where mirror neurons have been identified in a monkey's cortex. Mirror neurons fire in the same way whether a monkey performs an action or observes another monkey performing that action and are therefore a possible mechanism for imitation and emulation.

Some mirror neurons seem to fire most strongly during observation of the outcome of an action rather than in response to observations of the action itself (Gallese, Fadiga, Fogassi, & Rizzolatti, 1996). This means that the neurons fire the same way when a monkey is seeing a particular outcome (which could be the result of various actions) as when the monkey is achieving that same outcome. Mirror neurons have also been found that fire most strongly in response to the acoustic outcomes of observed actions (for example, to the sounds produced by tearing paper), suggesting that other sensory modalities may also be mapped onto motor representations in cortex (Kohler et al., 2002). In addition, it suggests that vocal imitation too may depend on circuits that involve mirror neurons. For all these reasons, mirror neurons are considered to have a possible role in imitation and emulation, and in perceptual-motor skill learning and the interpretation of actions (Jeannerod, 1994; Rizzolatti & Arbib, 1998; Rizzolatti, Fogassi, & Gallese, 2002).

Researchers hypothesize that mirror neurons categorize observed events by linking them to the motor representations that are activated when an observer performs similar actions or tries to achieve a similar goal. Linking observed actions to the motor commands used to perform those actions is necessary for imitation (copying an action), and linking observed outcomes to representations of possible actions that might lead to that outcome is necessary for emulation (copying a goal). Unfortunately, no studies done to date have examined the role of mirror neurons in either imitation or emulation by monkeys, in part because monkeys are not great imitators. It turns out that in the real world, "Monkey see, monkey do," is a myth and almost never happens.

Neuroscientists have not directly observed mirror neurons in humans, because this would require doing invasive surgery to record directly from individual neurons. However, indirect measures of cortical activity, such as evoked potentials (Gastaut & Bert, 1954; Hari et al., 1998), transcranial magnetic stimulation (Gangitano, Mottaghy, & Pascual-Leone, 2001; Strafella & Paus, 2000), and cerebral blood flow (Rizzolatti et al., 1996), indicate that regions of the human cortex behave as if they contained mirror neurons. The basic procedure for such studies in humans generally involves an "observation-only" condition, an "imitation" condition, and an "instructed action" condition. For example, researchers might ask participants to (1) observe an image of someone moving a certain finger; (2) imitate someone moving a certain finger; or (3) move a certain finger in response to a specific command (Figure 11.11a). Neuroimaging experiments of this kind show overlap between cortical regions that are activated by the performance of an action and cortical regions that are activated by observing that action being performed (Figure 11.11b) (Rizzolatti & Craighero, 2004). The activity associated with mirror neuron regions is greater when an action is guided by observed actions (as occurs during imitation) than when it is guided by other cues, such as verbal instructions (Iacoboni et al., 1999). The areas of the human brain that become active during both the observation and performance of actions are located in cortical regions similar to those examined in monkeys (compare Figure 11.11b with Figure 11.10). This suggests that monkeys and humans may use similar circuits to match observations to actions.

Interestingly, cortical networks in the human brain respond to monkeys performing actions in much the same way that they respond to humans performing those actions (Buccino, Lui et al., 2004). Similar results have been seen in electrophysiological recordings from monkeys: a monkey's mirror neuron responds the same way when the monkey sees a human grabbing a stick as it does when the monkey observes another monkey grabbing a stick. This means that these neural circuits in both monkeys and humans are sensitive to relatively abstract

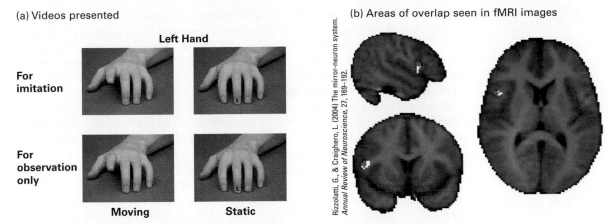

(a) Videos presented

Left Hand

For imitation

For observation only

Moving   Static

(b) Areas of overlap seen in fMRI images

Rizzolatti, G., & Craighero, L. (2004) The mirror-neuron system. *Annual Review of Neuroscience, 27,* 169–192.

Figure 11.11 Mirror neurons in a human cortex? (a) fMRI images are collected while participants merely observe videos of finger movements and also while the participants imitate the observed finger movements. (b) Comparison of those images to images collected while the participants merely observe a video of a static hand and also while they imitate the static hand enables researchers to identify cortical regions specialized for processing hand movements. The red and white areas indicate regions in cortex that become active when humans either watch or perform the finger movements. Adapted from Rizzolatti et al., 1996.

features of visual scenes (for example, movement of any sort of arm). This may explain why humans have little problem imitating the actions of other animals—actions observed in other species may be neurally mapped directly to corresponding motor patterns that humans can perform.

Researchers hypothesize that the mirror neuron system provides a basic mechanism for simple imitation (Rizzolatti et al., 1996). This idea is significant because in the past researchers assumed that imitation involved higher-level cognitive processes that would be difficult to trace to specific brain activity in humans and impossible to trace to specific brain activity in other animals. If mirror neurons are involved in imitation, then researchers would be able to directly examine the mechanisms of imitation in animal models.

It is not yet certain, however, that mirror neurons provide the neural processing necessary for imitation. Both monkeys and humans seem to possess cortical networks of mirror neurons, and yet only humans seem to be proficient at imitating actions. What might account for this difference? Recall that social learning theorists propose that memories of observed actions are necessary for learning through imitation. The fact that mirror neurons fire similarly both when the individual is observing motor acts and performing those motor acts reveals little about how and when memories of those experiences are stored. Perhaps proficient imitators like humans and dolphins are better at storing and accessing memories of experienced events than monkeys, which might make it easier for them to use information about actions gained from the activity of mirror neurons.

Researchers who study the neural mechanisms underlying observational learning have focused on circuits within the primate cortex. Primates are not the only animals that can learn from observations, however, and neural circuits in regions other than the cortex may also be involved. Consider the following example. Rats with cerebellar lesions are impaired at learning to find a hidden platform in a Morris water maze task. This should not surprise you given what you have learned in Chapter 4, on skill memories, about how the cerebellum contributes to skill learning, and about the swimming skills a rat needs to perform well in the water maze. Interestingly, if the rats are permitted to watch trained demonstrator rats perform the Morris water maze task for about 200 trials before undergoing lesioning, the lesioned observer will not be impaired at learning to find a platform in the Morris water maze!

Based on this finding, you might think that the rats were learning observationally, using some sort of visual-to-motor map, as in the human imitation experiments described on page 446. But wait! If the observer rats received a cerebellar lesion *before* being allowed to watch the demonstrator rats in the water maze, then they were just as impaired at learning the task as rats that had never seen any demonstrations (Leggio et al., 2000). Apparently, rats can learn the task by observing other rats, but not if their cerebellum is damaged. This discovery suggests that many of the systems involved in performing a skill may also be involved in learning that skill through observation. As you are about to see, this correspondence holds not only for the neural mechanisms mediating observational learning of actions by mammals, but also for the neural circuits mediating observational learning of songs by birds.

Song Learning in Bird Brains: Replicating Observed Events

Mechanisms like those involved in behavioral imitation may also play a role in other forms of observational learning, such as song learning by birds. Many birds that learn their songs do so by listening to other birds. Young songbirds in the wild use their memories of the songs produced by mature birds to guide their own song production (as described by the template model of song learning presented in the Behavioral Processes section). Birds can form memories of adult songs that last the rest of their lives. In this respect, song learning resembles some aspects of human culture (Rendell & Whitehead, 2001).

Many scientists are working to identify the neural circuits that birds use for learning and producing songs. Like behavioral imitation, song learning requires birds to map observed events, or memories of observed events, onto possible motor responses. Once a bird forms memories of what a "proper" song is like, it can improve its ability to produce songs by comparing its own song to its memories of other songs it has heard. Behavioral experiments show that in order to produce normal adult songs, birds must have heard the songs when they were young and must be able to hear themselves sing.

Several distinct regions of a bird's brain have been associated with song learning. Some regions provide the means for storing the memories of songs; others enable the bird to learn the perceptual-motor skills necessary to become an expert singer (Figure 11.12). Lesion studies and electrophysiological recordings have identified two main neural regions that birds use for producing songs: the high vocal center (HVC) and the robust nucleus of the archistriatum (RA). These two regions are specialized for controlling the production of different levels of song structure. Birds also possess a neural region called Area X that is thought to be analogous to the mammalian basal ganglia. Lesions to this area disrupt song learning. Area X receives inputs from the lateral magnocellular nucleus of the anterior neostriatum (LMAN). The LMAN is thought to function like the frontal cortex in mammals. Disrupting activity in this region when a songbird is first hearing other birds' songs impairs, but does not prevent, song learning (Basham, Nordeen, & Nordeen, 1996).

Figure 11.12 Neural circuits for song learning by birds
Circuits for producing songs are shown in purple, and circuits for storing skill memories used to produce songs are shown in red. The regions involved in song production include the high vocal center (HVC) and the robust nucleus of the archistriatum (RA). Area X and the lateral magnocellular nucleus of the anterior neostriatum (LMAN) are involved in forming memories. Note that these two circuits are interconnected such that memories can affect how songs are produced. Adapted from Brainard & Doupe, 2000.

Scientists are still debating about the specific brain region where birds store memories of heard songs, and about how birds compare their own songs to stored memories of songs. There is some evidence that simply exposing birds to songs makes neurons in their song-learning circuits respond more strongly to those songs. However, most of the changes that researchers have observed in the song-learning circuit occur when birds are practicing songs. This means that although observations of other birds can change how a listening bird's brain responds to those songs, the songs that the listener produces (and the associated auditory feedback) have a greater impact. In essence, songbirds learn more by doing than by observing, and the neural mechanisms underlying song learning reflect this asymmetry.

Neurons in the RA that fire strongly when a bird hears a song are also seen to become active just before the bird begins to sing. This means that the RA neurons fire similarly when the bird hears particular songs and when the bird sings those same songs. This statement should sound familiar to you, because it is very similar to the activity of mirror neurons, described above. Imitation invariably requires a circuit that maps sensory representations onto motor systems, so similar neural solutions to this problem may exist in different species. However, songbirds are predisposed to copy only a subset of the songs that they experience—specifically, those produced by members of their own species. Additionally, songs produced by birds that have never heard another bird singing do contain some features of normal songs, and naive birds respond more to songs of their own species than to songs of other species. These genetic predispositions suggest that vocal learning by songbirds is more constrained than behavioral imitation by mammals.

There is another difference between song learning and behavioral imitation that might be reflected in neural substrates. A bird learning to sing provides itself with auditory inputs that it can compare to remembered songs (a case of stimulus matching). In contrast, behavioral imitation often does not allow observed acts to be compared to visually observed events (the imitator may not be able to see the actions he or she is producing). These differences could mean that behavioral imitation relies on neural systems above and beyond those needed for vocal imitation—to imitate actions may require more "brain power" than to imitate sounds. On the other hand, more animals can imitate actions than appear to be able to imitate sounds, so perhaps the opposite is true: vocal learning may require neural specializations beyond those required for behavioral imitation. Clarifying the mechanisms underlying vocal learning by birds will make it easier to meaningfully compare the neural processes underlying both vocal and behavioral imitation.

▶ **Unsolved Mysteries**

Why Can't Most Mammals Imitate Sounds?

Children normally learn to talk by imitating speech produced by others around them. Young dolphins also imitate sounds in their surroundings, but it is not clear how many of the sounds that adult dolphins produce are learned, or what communicative functions particular dolphin sounds serve, and there is no evidence that dolphin vocalizations are grammatical or analogous to human words (Reiss & McCowan, 1993; Tayler & Saayman, 1973). Dolphins are not unique in the ocean in terms of their vocal imitation abilities. Several other marine mammal species appear to be capable of vocal imitation, including large whales, like the humpback whale. Even some seals and sea lions have shown signs of imitative abilities (Janik & Slater, 1997). Humans, however, are the only primate with the ability to speak, and possibly the only terrestrial mammal that learns to communicate by imitating sounds.

Why is it that most mammals appear to be unable to imitate sounds? One possibility might be that they simply haven't been given the chance to reveal their abilities. This does not appear to be the case for apes. Researchers in the twentieth century made great efforts to teach chimpanzees to speak. Catherine Hayes described the most successful effort of the time, in which a chimpanzee named Viki learned to garble "cup," "mama," and "papa." (Hayes, 1951). This achievement provides no evidence of vocal imitation abilities, because Viki was explicitly trained to produce these words through instrumental conditioning and physical molding of her lip positions. The researchers held the chimpanzee's mouth in certain positions so that when she exhaled she would produce sounds similar to human speech. After this initial practice, if she did move her lips as desired and exhale, she was rewarded. You have probably seen videos of dogs and cats that produce phrases such as "I love you," and "I want my mama." Many animals can be trained to produce speechlike sounds, but this is not imitation. Most mammals never imitate sounds.

Vocal imitation requires precise vocal control. So another possible explanation for why most mammalian species do not imitate sounds could be that only a few have the necessary vocal control. This seems plausible enough, but it leaves the interesting questions unanswered: What endows a select few mammals with the necessary control? Is a "vocal mimicry organ" required? Do humans have more control because they have more neurons, better neurons, specialized neurons, specialized muscles, a novel neural circuit, or something else? Why would only marine mammals and one primate species possess these unique control mechanisms?

Neuroscientists have only hints at answers to these questions because of the small pool of mammals capable of vocal imitation. Humans and marine mammals are not the most convenient subjects for neuroscience research, because it is unethical to invasively study their brain activity. Studies of vocally imitating birds can offer some comparative insights, but extrapolating from birds' brains to primate brains or marine mammal brains is problematic. Bats show some evidence of vocal learning abilities and might provide a useful model for future work, but so far no one has identified the mechanisms underlying bats' abilities (Janik & Slater, 1997). The fact that dolphins and humans both possess large cortices suggests cortical networks as a plausible neural substrate for vocal imitation mechanisms. Several other brain regions that are larger than normal in both humans and dolphins, such as the cerebellum, could also play a role.

Perhaps humans and dolphins have unique neural mechanisms that facilitate observational learning, auditory-to-motor transformations, or precise vocal control and thus allow them to imitate sounds when most other mammals can't, but there is another possibility. Unlike most mammals, humans and marine mammals have voluntary control over their respiratory systems—they can hold their breath for a desired amount of time and expel their breath when they choose. So, perhaps the key to vocal imitation is being able to control the release of air from the lungs, rather than possession of any unique observational learning capabilities! If so, then maybe all you need to do to enable your dog or cat to imitate your speech is perform surgery that would help Fido or Fluffy hold her breath. Good luck with that.

Although a human can imitate a howling dog, dogs and most other mammals show no ability to imitate any sounds. Dogs will howl when they hear other sounds that are similar to howls, such as an ambulance siren, but this is a case of contagion rather than imitation.

Photodisc/Getty Images

Hippocampal Encoding of Socially Transmitted Food Preferences

When rats learn a food preference from smelling the odor of the food on another rat's breath, they create memories of the experience that can influence their behavior for a lifetime. As little as ten minutes of exposure to a novel food odor on another rat's breath can create a memory that, with no repetition of exposure, influences eating behavior at least three months later (Clark, Broadbent, Zola, & Squire, 2002). You may recall from Chapter 3, on memories for facts and events, that when humans experience a unique event and are then able to remember it several months later, the memory is called an episodic memory. Do you think that rats might form episodic memories of experiences involving unique odors coming from another rat's mouth? Based on the studies of humans described in Chapter 3, you might expect that if a rat were forming memories for such events, then damage to the rat's hippocampus should disrupt its ability to learn about foods from interactions with other rats. Specifically, you might expect that hippocampal damage could disrupt the rat's old memories for past interactions (retrograde amnesia), or disrupt its ability to acquire new memories (anterograde amnesia).

This prediction has received some experimental support. Observer rats were exposed to a food odor on a demonstrator rat's breath and then were given hippocampal lesions 1, 10, or 30 days later. In each case, the lesions reduced the observer rats' preferences for the food, but the disruption was worst when the lesion was produced right after the observation period (Bunsey & Eichenbaum, 1995; Clark et al., 2002; Winocur, 1990). In other words, the rats appeared to show retrograde amnesia following hippocampal damage, and the amnesia was worse for newly acquired memories than for older ones. This effect is consistent with the human studies showing that hippocampal-region damage affected newer episodic memories more than older ones. Similar time-graded deficits have also been seen in mice that have dysfunctional hippocampal regions as the result of genetic alterations (Rampon & Tsien, 2000). In short, hippocampal damage disrupts the ability of animals to learn from social interactions in ways that parallel episodic memory deficits in humans suffering from amnesia.

In Chapter 3 we also described how lesions of the basal forebrain can lead to amnesia in human patients that is similar to the amnesia caused by hippocampal damage. Recall that this deficit resulted from the loss of neuromodulatory neurons in the basal forebrain that modulated activity in the hippocampus. It turns out that basal forebrain cholinergic neurons that modulate activity in a rat's hippocampus are similarly critical for social transmission of food preferences. If these neurons are damaged, the rats' memories of previously acquired food preferences will be drastically impaired, but their future ability to learn about novel foods from other rats will not be affected—a case of retrograde amnesia without anterograde amnesia (Berger-Sweeney, Stearns, Frick, Beard, & Baxter, 2000; Vale-Martinez, Baxter, & Eichenbaum, 2002).

Basal forebrain cholinergic neurons that modulate *cortical* activity are also involved in social transmission of rat's food preferences. If these neurons are destroyed, then rats become impaired at learning novel food preferences from demonstrator rats—a case of anterograde amnesia. In both cases, the specific memory deficits resulting from basal forebrain damage differ from the effects of hippocampal lesions. Just as in humans with amnesia, basal forebrain lesions in rats produce patterns of memory loss for socially transmitted information that are comparable to, but distinguishable from, those associated with hippocampal damage.

It would therefore appear that in rats, memory for socially transmitted information depends on the hippocampus and basal forebrain. This doesn't necessarily mean that food preferences are based on episodic memories in the same way as gossip that is passed from one person to the next, but it does mean that hippocampal processing is relevant to the mechanisms that enable both rats and humans to learn from socially transmitted information. Memories for facts and events are rarely described as resulting from observational learning—more often, these memories are described as resulting from an unspecified process of "storage" or "encoding"—but the similarities between memory loss in humans and impaired social transmission of information in rats suggest that researchers may be using different terminology to describe equivalent phenomena. If so, then all of the studies of human memory for facts and events discussed in this book can be viewed as studies of observational learning involving the social transmission of information. Similarly, all of the neural mechanisms underlying such memories can be viewed as brain substrates for observational learning.

Interim Summary

The animals with the best imitation abilities also possess the greatest amount of cortex. Mirror neurons within cortical networks respond most strongly when an animal performs an action or sees another animal perform that same action. These neurons may form an important part of the neural circuit that enables animals to imitate actions. The circuit likely includes noncortical regions as well, as exemplified by the extensive neural circuits that enable birds to learn to produce songs. Birds can learn to sing songs they have heard only a few times, and rats can learn to prefer a food that they have smelled on another rat's breath for only a few minutes. Such rapid storage of experienced events is reminiscent of hippocampal-dependent formation of episodic memories, and in fact, social transmission of food preferences is dependent on the hippocampus. Although researchers have only recently begun to explore the neural substrates of observational learning in nonhumans, it would appear that most (if not all) of the neuroscientific studies of memory for facts and events can be interpreted as studies of observational learning in humans.

11.3 Clinical Perspectives

For centuries, children who would today be diagnosed as having autism were grouped with the insane or mentally retarded. It was only in the last century that researchers began to identify autism (mentioned briefly in Chapter 7 but described in greater detail below) as a distinctive pattern of symptoms (Kanner, 1943). **Asperger's syndrome,** a condition marked by many of the same features as autism, was identified around the same time. In Asperger's syndrome, individuals have normal intellectual abilities but a reduced capacity for social skills. A major difference between Asperger's syndrome and autism is that individuals with Asperger's are more likely to speak fluently. In the old days, because autistic children often did not learn speech, they sometimes were misdiagnosed as being deaf! Studies of autism and Asperger's syndrome provide insight into how observational learning contributes to much of what humans learn throughout their lives, and into the neural systems that enable observational learning.

Imitation in Autistic Individuals

The patterns of behavior associated with autism were not widely known among the general public until the 1980s, when a major motion picture called *Rainman* appeared in theaters. In *Rainman*, Dustin Hoffman portrays an adult with a rare form of autism associated with amazing calculation and memorizing abilities. The autistic character in *Rainman*, while not prototypical, does behave in ways that are associated with autism. In particular, he has difficulties interacting socially, requires highly consistent routines, is susceptible to sensory overload, uses language abnormally when communicating with others, and repeatedly produces certain stereotyped movement patterns.

Autism is a complex disorder with many different symptoms. The most common symptoms are impaired social interactions, restricted behavior patterns, and delayed language development (Waterhouse, Fein, & Modahl, 1996). The typical time of onset is within three years after birth. (Like Asperger's syndrome, autism is classified as a developmental disorder, which means a disorder that appears at a certain stage of a person's development.) You may recall from Chapter 7 on classical conditioning that autism is often associated with cerebellar damage, and that children with autism often engage in repetitive and stereotyped actions. Additionally, autistic individuals may repeat words or phrases immediately after hearing them spoken, a phenomenon called **echolalia.** Echolalia requires vocal imitation abilities, which might seem to suggest that autistic individuals are good imitators. However, autistic children actually turn out to be worse at imitating than nonautistic children.

Some of the earliest evidence that autistic children are impaired at learning through observation came from the reports of mothers. For example, one mother reported that she was unable to teach her child to play the "patty-cake" game until she physically moved the child's arms in the correct patterns (Ritvo & Provence, 1953). The fact that the child did eventually learn to play this game correctly shows that the earlier learning deficit was not the result of impaired visual-motor coordination abilities. Instead, the autistic child's impaired social and language skills most probably prevented him from using the information that his mother was attempting to impart to him socially. (Remember, though, that the learning of both language skills and social skills depends on observational learning in the first place.) Another possible explanation for his difficulty, however, is that copying adults is less reinforcing for autistic individuals, and so they may be less motivated to do it, whatever their observational learning ability.

If autistic children suffer from impaired imitation abilities early on, perhaps this observational learning deficit is actually a source of other behavioral and social impairments typically seen in autistic children (Rogers & Pennington, 1991). Different studies have reported different levels of imitative deficits, however, so it remains unclear exactly which aspects of imitative abilities are affected by autism (Baron-Cohen et al., 1994; Beadle-Brown & Whiten, 2004). People with autism can recognize when they are being imitated, but they do not reliably imitate the actions of others (Smith & Bryson, 1994). Interestingly, imitations of meaningless gestures (like those used in the patty-cake game) and "nonsense" actions performed with a common object seem more likely to be impaired than meaningful actions (DeMeyer et al., 1972; Smith & Bryson, 1994; Williams, Whiten, & Singh, 2004). This finding suggests that different mechanisms are involved in imitating functional, as opposed to nonfunctional, actions.

Autistic individuals tend not to translate perspective; they recreate what they see rather than the action that produces what they see. In other words, they seem generally to have problems with perspective taking. When asked to imitate some-one whose palm is facing outward—such as a traffic cop ordering a driver to stop—an autistic boy might hold up his hand with his palm facing inward, so that his own palm faces him in the same way the cop's did. That they correctly copy the hand shape and arm motion shows that these children have the recognition and motor control processes necessary for imitation. Nevertheless, there is some-thing different about their perception of observed actions or their execution of actions that prevents then from precisely replicating the actions they observe.

When tested in the two-action task portrayed in Figure 11.3 on page 427 (the task with a plastic box containing a food reward), older autistic children imitated the model's actions normally, but younger autistic children did not (Smith & Bryson, 1998; Whiten & Brown, 1999). Older autistic individuals have fewer problems imitating, suggesting that the imitative deficits previously described reflect a neuro-developmental delay in autistic children rather than a missing or dysfunctional ability. Autistic children tested in a do-as-I-do task could imitate simple actions, like drinking, but had problems imitating sequences of actions (Beadle-Brown & Whiten, 2004). These studies suggest that autistic children have problems linking observed actions to actions that can be performed.

As mentioned earlier, spontaneous inappropriate copying of observed speech and actions is actually typical of autism; so why might autistic children have dif-ficulty imitating meaningless actions when explicitly instructed to do so? Neural abnormalities associated with autism provide some clues. Several areas in the brains of autistic individuals are anatomically abnormal, including the sensory cortex, prefrontal cortex, hippocampus, cerebellum, amygdala, and basal ganglia (Brambilla et al., 2003; Rogers & Pennington, 1991; Waterhouse, Fein, & Modahl, 1996). Structural MRI studies show the cerebellum, temporal lobes (including the hippocampus), amygdala, and corpus callosum of autistic individ-uals are often abnormal in size. In addition, functional MRI experiments show an overall decrease in activity-related circulation of blood within the temporal lobes, as well as abnormal patterns of cortical activation. Many of these differ-ences in brain structure and function seem to result from abnormal develop-ment early in life. Perhaps early changes in neural circuits (for example, connections between neurons) lead to differences in processing that negatively impact the development of neural function, leading to further maladaptive structural changes. One or more of these affected brain regions may contribute to the imitative abnormalities associated with autism.

Recently, researchers began exploring whether the mirror neuron system in the cortex might be contributing to the imitation deficits seen in autistic individuals and in those with Asperger's syndrome (Williams, Whiten, Suddendorf, & Per-rett, 2001). Neuroimaging studies show that circuits within and around the mirror neuron system in these individuals, and patterns of activation within these circuits, differ systematically from those in normal individuals (Nishitani, Avikainen, & Hari, 2004; Waiter et al., 2004). For example, Asperger's patients showed slower activation of cortical regions when asked to imitate facial expressions (Figure 11.13). In these studies, measures of cortical activity were recorded using a mag-netoencephalograph (MEG) while participants were imitating facial expressions. MEGs are similar to EEGs except that instead of recording changes in electrical activity in a person's brain over time, MEGs record changes in magnetic fields generated by the brain that are measured with highly sensitive magnetometers. Asperger's patients' imitations started later and took longer to complete than those of a control group. Measurements using MEG showed that when partici-pants were imitating the expressions (control participants and Asperger's patients alike), different cortical regions became active at different times, in the following sequence: (1) visual cortex; (2) auditory cortex; (3) frontal cortex; (4) Broca's area; and (5) motor cortex. Each of these regions was slower to become active in Asperger's patients, suggesting that in those patients the neural processes for imitating actions are impaired.

Mirror neurons vary in terms of how responsive they are to specific observed and performed actions (Rizzolatti et al., 2002). Some respond only to observed actions, whereas others respond to a wider range of stimuli. If some networks of mirror neurons in a person's brain were dysfunctional, the person could suffer deficits in particular imitative abilities, such as the ability to imitate nonfunctional actions (Williams et al., 2001). Because autistic individuals have difficulty imitating only certain actions, their deficit might be related to abnormal function in a subset of mirror neurons, rather than a general dysfunction of cortical neural circuits involved in imitation.

Mirror neurons have been the focus of recent research on autistic imitative deficits, but abnormal processing in other regions, such as the cerebellum and hippocampus, may also be contributing. Recall that hippocampal processing is known to be important in the social transmission of information among rats, and that cerebellar lesions impair the ability of rats to learn from observing the actions of other rats (Leggio et al., 1999). At the moment, it is not clear whether the deficit seen in autistic individuals is truly an imitative deficit or whether it might instead be a deficit in mechanisms underlying stimulus enhancement, emulation, reinforcement mechanisms, emotional processes, or generalization from past experience. Just as many nonimitative actions can look like imitation, many apparent deficits in imitative abilities may actually be deficits in mechanisms other than those directly involved in imitation. As our understanding of observational learning increases, so will our understanding of the role different brain regions play in autistic behavior.

Effects of Frontal Lobe Lesions on Imitation

One reason researchers suspect that deficits in cortical networks contribute to imitative deficits in autistic individuals is because patients with frontal lobe lesions are often unable to repeat actions they observe, despite having the motor control necessary to perform the movements. These patients can't even recreate an observed gesture using someone else as a model. For example, they can't position someone else's arms to match the positions of a mannequin's arms. Recall that mirror neurons, which link observed and performed actions, are found within the prefrontal cortex in monkeys. However, although researchers suspect that at least some circuits in the frontal lobe mediate imitation abilities, they do not yet know how damage to regions with mirror neurons affects these abilities.

As you learned in Chapter 5 on working memory, frontal lobe damage can radically alter a person's behavior and personality. Frontal lobe patients have profound deficits in both executive function and working memory, and have problems thinking and planning. Nevertheless, conditions associated with frontal lobe

(a)

(b)

Nishitani, N., Avikainen, S., & Hari, R. (2004). Abnormal imitation-related cortical activation sequences in Asperger's syndrome. *Annals of Neurology*, 55(4), 558–562.

Figure 11.13 Asperger's patients show slower responses when imitating facial expressions (a) Participants were asked to imitate facial expressions while measures of activity in their cortex were recorded using MEG. (b) Several different cortical regions became active more slowly in Asperger's patients, including visual cortex (black); auditory cortex (blue); parietal cortex (green); Broca's area (yellow); and motor cortex (red). Adapted from Nishitani, Avikainen, & Hari, 2004.

damage may go unnoticed for many years, particularly if the damage occurs at an early age. There are some children, for example, in whom the frontal lobes never develop (the children essentially are born with frontal lobe damage). One famous case, an individual referred to as J.P., was discovered to be missing 75% of his frontal lobes by a psychiatrist who examined him at the request of a lawyer defending him in a criminal case (Ackerly, 1964). J.P. was 19 years old. He was known to have behavioral problems from a young age, but otherwise did well in school and appeared to have normal conversational capabilities. His "willful" disregard of social norms had always been attributed to ineffective parenting. Brain damage had never been considered. In other words, deficits associated with frontal lobe damage can be subtle and difficult to recognize from behavior alone.

It was in attempting to identify such subtle indicators of brain damage that Alexander Luria discovered the tendency of patients with frontal lobe damage to produce unintended imitative responses (Luria, 1966). This tendency included echolalia, which you may recall is also common in individuals with autism. Luria examined unintentional imitative responses in his patients by having them perform an action at the same time that he performed a related but incompatible action. For example, Luria might show his fist immediately after asking a patient to hold up his palm. Often, seeing Luria make a fist would interfere with a frontal lobe patient's ability to show his palm. The patient would tend instead to involuntarily imitate Luria. Patients with reduced activity in the frontal lobes (such as occurs during major depressive episodes) also show this tendency to involuntarily imitate observed actions (Archibald, Mateer, & Kerns, 2001). Luria's finding suggests that activity in frontal lobe circuits normally inhibits such imitation.

The effects of frontal lobe damage and dysfunction on imitation provide support for the direct-matching hypothesis described in the Brain Substrates section. Recall that the direct-matching hypothesis assumes that observations of an action automatically activate the same neural systems as are required to perform those actions. This means that the same neural systems also become active when an action is voluntarily initiated. If external and internal stimuli activate the same systems, then perhaps some inhibitory mechanism (controlled by circuits in the frontal lobe) is necessary to prevent the external stimuli (the observations) from initiating the actions.

In a recent attempt to test this idea, Brass and colleagues measured the degree to which observations of finger movements by patients with brain damage interfered when the patients tried to move their fingers in response to commands (Brass, Derrfuss, Matthes-von Cramon, & von Cramon, 2003). Patients were asked to lift their index finger from a key when they saw the numeral 1 and to lift their middle finger when they saw the numeral 2 (Figure 11.14a). While they performed this task, they watched either a video image of a stationary hand,

Figure 11.14 Spontaneous imitation induced by frontal lobe damage Patients with lesions in the frontal cortex or posterior cortex, and control participants with no lesions, were asked to perform specific finger movements in response to numerals displayed on a screen, while ignoring the movements of a hand shown on the screen. (a) The finger movements shown on the screen were either consistent with the instructions or inconsistent with the instructions. (b) Patients with frontal lobe lesions were more likely (5% versus 2%) to make a mistake when the finger movement shown was inconsistent with the movement corresponding to the displayed numeral. Adapted from Brass, Derrfuss, Matthes-von Cramon, & von Cramon, 2003.

Brass, M., Derrfuss, J., Matthes-von Cramon, G., & von Cramon, D. Y. (2003). Imitative response tendencies in patients with frontal brain lesions. *Neuropsychology, 17*(2), 265–271.

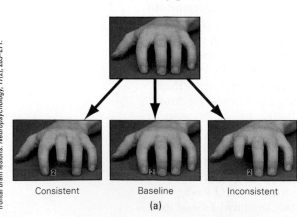

Consistent   Baseline   Inconsistent

(a)

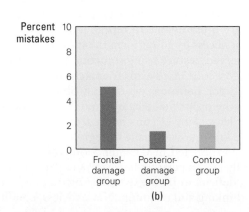

(b)

a video image of a hand producing finger movements consistent with the presented numeral, or a video of a hand producing movements inconsistent with the presented numeral. Frontal lobe patients (particularly those with lateral frontal damage) made more mistakes than patients with nonfrontal lesions when the movement on the video was inconsistent with the instruction (Figure 11.14b). This means that frontal lobe patients were less able to stop themselves from imitating observed movements.

Patients were also tested on other behavioral tasks that measure frontal deficits. The researchers found no correlation between patients' performance on a Stroop task (Chapter 5) and the degree of interference in the instructed-finger-lifting task (Brass et al., 2003). This suggests that the observed deficits were not simply a side effect of a more general dysfunction in executive-control processes but were specifically related to the initiating of actions in the finger-lifting task (Anderson, Damasio, Jones, & Tranel, 1991).

If circuits in the frontal lobe inhibit the initiation of imitative acts, this might explain how repeated exposure to violence in the mass media could increase aggressive behavior. Specifically, if desensitization is associated with reduced activity in the frontal lobes, then desensitization could decrease the inhibition of imitative actions, thereby increasing the likelihood that the desensitized viewer would imitate aggressive actions.

Not all frontal lobe patients display imitative deficits. There is some evidence that damage to certain frontal regions is more likely than damage in other frontal regions to produce this effect (Brass, Derrfuss, & von Cramon, 2005; De Renzi, Cavalleri, & Facchini, 1996; Lhermitte, 1983; Lhermitte, Pillon, & Serdaru, 1986). Some patients with frontal lobe damage may no longer have the circuits necessary to distinguish self-generated actions from externally triggered actions. This suggests an explanation for the connection between involuntary imitative acts and problems with perspective taking (Brass et al., 2003; Decety & Sommerville, 2003).

Another possible explanation for these behavioral deficits is that the imitative responses of frontal lobe patients are simply a special case of contagion. The fact that frontal lobe patients automatically replicate speech and arbitrary actions of examiners suggests, however, that conditioned responses rather than unconditioned responses are involved.

A last issue to consider is the question of why overactive imitation is correlated with deficits in the ability to imitate voluntarily. Note that both conditions suggest a loss of autonomy, specifically a lost ability to decide which observed acts to copy. The findings obtained from clinical populations may provide some insight into why so few animals can flexibly imitate observed actions. Perhaps in humans, cortical circuits in the frontal lobes provide key control mechanisms that enable external stimuli to activate the same neural systems that control the performance of self-initiated actions. At the same time, these cortical circuits provide a means for controlling when these stimuli (or memories of them) guide self-initiated actions. If so, it may be that voluntary control of imitation requires more frontal circuitry than most mammals possess.

CONCLUSION

Imitation, observational conditioning, stimulus enhancement, and social transmission of information are among the mechanisms that enable humans and certain other animals to learn through observation. When Donna's mother sees Donna sticking out her tongue at a neighbor's child, she is likely to conclude

moodboard/Corbis

College instructors rely on observational learning Professors lecture in the hope that students will learn through listening.

that Donna learned this gesture by imitating someone else. Sticking out your tongue at people to indicate you dislike them is probably not an innate response. It is a gesture whose only value lies in the message it conveys. Perhaps Donna did learn to stick out her tongue through imitation, as her mother suspects, but many other mechanisms could also account for her learning to do this that do not require copying. For example, Donna's older sister could have told her to go stick out her tongue at the neighbor. This kind of active instruction through social transmission of information seems to be limited to humans and is closely tied to language abilities. You're receiving socially transmitted information at this very moment. Active instruction with lectures and textbooks forms the basis for learning in almost all courses taught in universities and colleges.

Even if scientists had monitored all of Donna's experiences from birth, they might still be uncertain about how Donna learned to stick out her tongue at people. Ironically, observational learning may be impossible to understand through observations alone. Nevertheless, scientific observation and experimentation is of critical importance, especially for discovering the neural substrates underlying observational learning and for finding out when learning may involve imitation.

Learning theorists traditionally assume that learning results from the conditioning of passive reflexive reactions or from the reinforcement of responses. Is observational learning anything more than a combination of simpler learning processes? Research into how different cortical and subcortical brain regions mediate observational learning is already providing some insights into this issue. As you might expect, some learning processes, such as observational conditioning, can be explained as a special case of classical conditioning. Other abilities—as when humans, apes, and dolphins imitate actions on command—are more difficult to account for in terms of incremental-learning models and instead seem to require unique cortical-processing mechanisms.

Understanding what happens when observational-learning mechanisms go awry can also lead to new ideas about how neural circuits are involved. Correlating imitative deficits in autistic individuals with those of frontal lobe patients may provide clues about the relationship between automatic imitation and voluntary imitation. The fact that echolalia tends to co-occur with involuntary behavioral imitation and with an inability to imitate certain actions on command suggests that vocal and behavioral imitation may rely on overlapping neural systems. At the same time, many current psychological models of imitative learning assume that behavioral imitation requires processes that are fundamentally different from those involved in vocal imitation. Specifically, vocal imitation is assumed to depend on stimulus matching, whereas behavioral imitation is assumed to depend on higher-level cognitive processes like perspective taking.

Albert Bandura has suggested that observational learning is a process that permits the rapid, errorless acquisition of cognitive and perceptual-motor skills, and that humans who take full advantage of this process have "learned to learn." With luck, future behavioral and physiological studies of observational-learning processes will one day enable scientists to learn how it is that brains learn to learn.

Key Points

- Psychologists use the term "observational learning" to identify situations in which a learner actively monitors events and later chooses actions based on those observations.

- Observational learning differs from classical and instrumental conditioning in that there is no way to reliably predict what individuals exposed to the actions of others will learn.

- Copying that involves reproducing motor acts is called true imitation. Copying that involves replicating an outcome without replicating specific motor acts is called emulation.

- Seeing two organisms sequentially performing similar actions does not constitute evidence of imitation. True imitation can be demonstrated using a two-action test in which a single operation can be performed in at least two ways.

- Emulation involves using observation to acquire information about the environment and about consequences of events within that environment, so that outcomes can be replicated independently of the specific actions that a model may have used to achieve those outcomes.

- Seeing-based imitation and hearing-based imitation both involve the translation of sensory representations into the motor acts necessary to replicate the observed events.

- The ability to either imitate or emulate ultimately depends on the availability of memories for facts or events.

- Many bird species learn songs, but among mammals, only humans and a few species of whales show similar abilities.

- Social learning theorists describe imitative learning as a special case of instrumental conditioning in which the act of copying is either directly or indirectly reinforced. Similarity between a model and the observer increases the likelihood of copying, and copying is more likely to be attempted if the observed outcome is desirable.

- In contagion, the observation of a response reflexively evokes that same response. Stimulus enhancement increases the likelihood that an animal will be repeatedly exposed to particular stimuli and their associated consequences, thereby providing more opportunities for habituation, latent learning, classical conditioning, or instrumental conditioning.

- Before any action can be imitated, it must be recognized. Mirror neurons fire in the same way when the monkey performs an action as they do when the monkey sees another monkey performing that action.

- Neuroimaging studies of humans have correlated activation in cortical areas where mirror neurons are likely to be found with the performance or observation of particular actions.

- Many of the systems involved in performing a skill may also be involved in learning that skill through observation.

- Most of the changes in neural firing observed in the song-learning circuit occur when birds are practicing songs. Genetic predispositions suggest that vocal imitation by birds is more constrained than behavioral imitation by mammals.

- The memories that rats form based on socially transmitted information about foods depend on the hippocampus and basal forebrain.

- Autistic individuals may repeat words or phrases immediately after hearing them spoken. This phenomenon, called echolalia, requires vocal imitation abilities. However, autistic children actually seem less able to learn from imitation than children without autism.

- Like autistic individuals, patients with frontal lobe lesions tend to imitate observed actions automatically but have difficulty imitating actions when instructed to do so.

Key Terms

Asperger's syndrome, p. 452
contagion, p. 434
copying, p. 422
echolalia, p. 453
emulation, p. 425
mirror neurons, p. 445
modeling, p. 424
observational conditioning, p. 434
observational learning, p. 422
perspective taking, p. 427
social conformity, p. 440
social learning, p. 422
social learning theory, p. 431
social transmission of information, p. 437
stimulus enhancement, p. 436
stimulus matching, p. 429
template model of song learning, p. 430
true imitation, p. 425
two-action test, p. 426
vocal learning, p. 429

Concept Check

1. Some researchers have suggested that the only way you can be sure that you are observing imitation is if the actions or sounds being copied are so bizarre that there is no other plausible explanation for why they might occur (Thorpe, 1963). What are some other ways researchers can tell when an animal is truly imitating?

2. Descartes and some religious belief systems have championed the idea that, whereas humans learn through effort and insight, other animals learn only by accident. By describing examples of pets performing advanced intellectual feats (such as imitating the actions of their owners), Charles Darwin and his student George Romanes challenged this assumption and attempted to establish that a continuum of mental abilities exists across species (Darwin, 1883; Romanes, 1898). What do such examples tell us about imitation in humans and other animals?

3. Edward Thorndike (1898) defined imitation as learning to do an act from seeing it done, but visual observations are not the only way to get the information needed to imitate or emulate. What are some examples of imitative actions described in this chapter that would not count as imitation under Thorndike's definition?

4. In the wild, animals may gain an advantage from spending more time or effort investigating areas or objects where other members of the same species have been. Such behavior could increase the chances of finding food, mates, or a safe place to hide. What forms of observational learning might provide animals with these advantages?

5. Humans may learn to copy through experience, or they may be born with an ability to copy that depends on specialized mechanisms for matching visual perceptions to motor responses (Meltzoff, 1996; Piaget, 1955). In some instances, social learning through imitation may also require a child to consciously consider the perspective or social status of other individuals (Guillaume, 1971). For which of these types of learning have neural substrates been identified?

6. Albert Bandura argued that instrumental conditioning without imitation is an inefficient way of learning new actions, and that only humans learn by copying because learning from models requires abstracting rules and forming memories based on verbal codes and imagery (Bandura, 1986). Does this chapter provide examples that either support or refute these ideas?

Answers to Test Your Knowledge

What Is Imitation?

1. Perhaps the baby is imitating you. However, another possibility is that smiling faces are a reinforcing stimulus for the baby. Reinforced babies are more likely to smile, and thus the baby may be responding to you in the same way that she would if you had handed her a cookie (another reinforcing stimulus). No copying is required.

2. This could just be a case of contagion. If a few pigeons in a group start to fly, there is a good chance that you will see other pigeons start to fly, not because they are copying each other but as a reflexive response—the same as when schooling fish move in synchrony. To assess this possibility, you need to know more about what causes babies to stick out their tongues.

3. This could be a case of observational conditioning. Perhaps Donna has seen her father eating asparagus several times. Seeing her father express disgust might induce similar negative emotions in Donna.

The asparagus could become a conditioned stimulus that leads to a conditioned response of disgust. Alternatively, maybe this is the first time Donna has tried asparagus and she simply does not like it.

4. Darwin thought so. However, the cat might have been trained to perform these actions through shaping. (Remember the waterskiing squirrels in Chapter 8 on instrumental conditioning?) Alternatively, this could be a case of stimulus enhancement. Humans approaching the door always focus their actions on the doorknob, which might direct the cat's attention to the doorknob as well. Cats often hit the objects of their attention with their paws. A few instances of accidental door opening would likely increase the cat's tendency to swat at the doorknob. (Remember Thorndike's cats in the puzzle boxes?)

5. Yes. Donna's friend is replicating Donna's actions in a way that cannot be explained as anything other than imitation (unless they are both reading from scripts).

Further Reading

Bandura, A. (1986). *Social foundations of thought and action.* Englewood Cliffs, NJ: Prentice-Hall. • This book introduces social learning theory and challenges the proposal of learning theorists like B. F. Skinner that all learning can be accounted for as associative conditioning.

Kroodsma, D. (2005). *The singing life of birds: The art and science of listening to birdsong.* Boston: Houghton Mifflin. • An instructional book that, with its accompanying CD, describes the songs of 30 bird species, as well as how they are acquired, what makes them unique, what functions they serve, and how they have evolved. Read this if you want to know what scientists have really learned about imitation.

Romanes, G. J. (1982). *Animal intelligence.* Farnborough, Hants., England: Gregg International, Reprint Edition. • A summary of the original evidence collected to support Darwin's claim that the imitative abilities of animals show mental continuity across species. Contains humorous stories about animals smoking cigars and mauling their owners.

de Waal, F. (2002). *The ape and the sushi master: Cultural reflections of a primatologist.* • New York: Basic Books. An examination of imitative learning and active instruction in the lives both of nonhuman primates and apprentices to sushi chefs.

CHAPTER 12

Learning and Memory across the Lifespan

DENISE, A 20-YEAR-OLD COLLEGE junior, is entering the prime of her life. As a state champion on the basketball court, her body is at the peak of its physical strength and stamina. What she may be less aware of is that her brain is also at the peak of its abilities. Denise and other healthy young adults (from about 17 to 35 years of age) represent the gold standard of cognitive function, against which all other age groups are measured. Throughout this book, when you've read about "average" memory abilities in humans, the usual assumption has been that "average" means healthy young adult.

At Thanksgiving, Denise goes home to visit her family, and plays with her young nieces and nephews. The youngest, Kelly, is a 10-month-old busily soaking up information about the world. Kelly is just beginning to stand and start walking, to recognize and respond to spoken words, and to produce babbling sounds that will someday lead to fluent language.

At the other end of the lifespan are Denise's grandparents. Her grandmother, a wise, funny woman, is a walking library of family history and special recipes. But Denise's grandfather has gone downhill since last Thanksgiving. He repeats the same stories over and over again, and has trouble remembering Kelly's name. The family worries that this is not just normal old age but a sign of something more serious, such as Alzheimer's disease. The specter of this worry hangs over the family's holiday celebration.

In this chapter, we'll trace the development of learning and memory abilities across the lifespan, starting with infants like Kelly and culminating with elderly individuals like Denise's grandparents. You'll recognize many types

Behavioral Processes

The Developing Memory: Infancy through Adolescence

Learning and Memory in Everyday Life - Can Exposure to Classical Music Make Babies Smarter?

Sensitive Periods for Learning

The Aging Memory: Adulthood through Old Age

Test Your Knowledge - Learning and Memory in Old Age

Brain Substrates

The Genetic Basis of Learning and Memory

Neurons and Synapses in the Developing Brain

Gender Differences in Brain and Behavior

The Brain from Adulthood to Old Age

Clinical Perspectives

Down Syndrome

Alzheimer's Disease

A Connection between Down Syndrome and Alzheimer's Disease?

Unsolved Mysteries - Treating (and Preventing) Alzheimer's Disease of memory that were introduced in earlier chapters, but here we'll view them from the standpoint of how a person's memory changes over the lifespan and how this reflects underlying age-related changes in the brain. You'll also encounter topics that may be new to you, such as the ability of adult brains to grow new neurons, the effects of sex hormones on developing and mature memories, and the concept of sensitive periods—"windows of opportunity"—for specific kinds of learning, after which such learning may never again be so easy or effective.

12.1 Behavioral Processes

One reason to study learning and memory across the lifespan is to understand the different capabilities of children compared to young adults, and of young adults compared to older adults. Understanding the kinds of learning and memory that are comparatively strong or weak at each age can help us make the most of our potential at every stage of life and can also help educators to tailor teaching methods to different age groups.

As you read, though, be sure to keep in mind that we're talking about the *average* learning and memory abilities of groups at various ages. Within any age group, there is wide variation in the abilities of individuals. For one thing, certain kinds of memory can mature at different rates, so that there are always some youngsters who show a different pattern of development, acquiring new abilities faster or slower than their peers. Similarly, at the other end of the lifespan, certain kinds of learning and memory tend to decline, but some elderly individuals show relatively little decline—and others decline at an accelerated rate, due to injury or disease such as Alzheimer's disease.

With these thoughts in mind, let's begin at the beginning: with the learning and memory of individuals at the earliest stages of life.

The Developing Memory: Infancy through Adolescence

If you've spent any time with a young child, you've witnessed the immense surge of learning that takes place in the first few years of life. In those years, a child acquires abilities ranging from the motor skills needed to grasp and walk, to the ability to produce and understand language, to a fund of semantic knowledge about the world. Learning continues across the lifespan, of course, but its progress is especially dramatic in young children. More recently, it's become apparent that some learning occurs even before birth.

Some Learning Can Occur before Birth!

The human uterus is a surprisingly noisy place. A human fetus is exposed to the sounds of maternal speech and heartbeats, as well as noises from the outside world. By about 25 weeks **gestational age (GA),** or time since conception, a fetus's brain and sense organs are sufficiently developed for the fetus to start perceiving and learning about these sounds.

For example, remember from Chapter 6 that *habituation* is the phenomenon of reduced responding to a repeated stimulus. Habituation can be used to test fetal learning about sounds. Researchers can place a speaker against the mother's abdomen and play sounds that the fetus can hear. The first time a sound plays, fetuses of 34 to 36 weeks GA respond by moving (Figure 12.1). If the same sound is played several times, the fetuses gradually stop responding (Hepper & Shahidullah, 1992). When a different sound is played, the responses reappear—

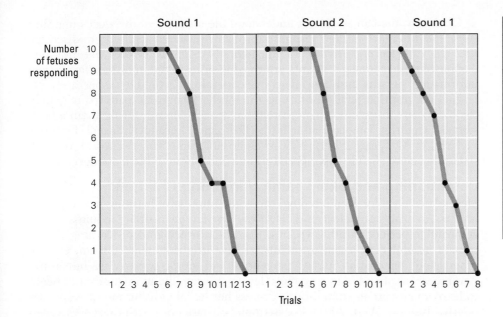

Figure 12.1 Habituation to sound in 10 human fetuses. When sound 1 is presented, all 10 human fetuses initially respond with movement; as the sound is repeated, the number of fetuses responding decreases. By trial 13, all have habituated. When a new stimulus (sound 2) is presented, all the fetuses again respond; this response also habituates over about a dozen trials. Finally, the original stimulus (sound 1) is presented again. The fetuses show spontaneous recovery of responding followed by fast habituation (only 8 trials). Adapted from Hepper & Shahidullah, 1992.

indicating that the loss of response to the first stimulus was due to habituation, not fatigue. Eventually, responses to the second stimulus habituate too. When the first sound is played again, the fetuses respond but habituate almost immediately, indicating that they "remember" having experienced that sound before. Fetal habituation can be observed in nonhuman species too, including rats (Smotherman & Robinson, 1992).

Such prenatal learning can persist after birth. Researchers Anthony De-Casper and Melanie Spence constructed a set of short stories with strong, simple rhyming patterns, such as excerpts from Dr. Seuss's *The Cat in the Hat* (De-Casper & Spence, 1986). The researchers then asked mothers in the last six weeks of pregnancy to read one of these stories aloud to their unborn babies, twice a day. Two or three days after birth, each newborn was placed in a crib with an artificial nipple positioned where the infant could suck at it. Under these conditions, infants usually suck in bursts: giving a series of brisk individual sucks, pausing a few seconds, and then giving another burst of sucks. For this experiment, the nipple was rigged so that each burst of sucking caused a tape recorder to turn on and play a story recorded in the mother's voice. But it wasn't always the same story. If a sucking burst followed a longer-than-average pause, then the familiar story played; but if a sucking burst followed a shorter-than-average pause, then an unfamiliar story played. Over a period of 20 minutes, the infants changed their sucking behavior, taking more long pauses between sucking bursts, which resulted in the familiar story being played more often. In short, the infants learned to respond in such a way as to produce the familiar story. This learning is an example of *instrumental conditioning*, which you read about in Chapter 8. Here, the familiar story served as a reinforcer, increasing the frequency of the target response:

S (artificial nipple) → R (long pause before sucking burst) → C (familiar story)

At the same time, the unfamiliar story served as a punisher, decreasing the frequency of the alternate response:

S (artificial nipple) → R (short pause before sucking burst) → C (unfamiliar story)

Obviously, the babies did not understand the meaning of the words in either story; the difference in their responses probably reflected an ability to discriminate the cadence and rhythm of the two stories. Still, studies like this one demonstrate that prenatal infants are capable of learning, and that the learned information persists and can affect behavior after birth. DeCasper and colleagues suggest that fetal exposure to the mother's language patterns may help the brain start to encode language-relevant speech sounds, giving them a head start on acquiring language after birth (DeCasper, Lecanuet, Busnel, Granier-Deferre, & Maugeais, 1994). Newborns do not come into the world as blank slates; they have already experienced stimuli and begun to learn about them.

Conditioning and Skill Learning in Young Children

Despite evidence for fetal learning, the really impressive learning machines are infants. An explosion in learning marks the first few years of life in humans, and comparable periods in other species. Just about every kind of learning that is present in adults is present in infants, at least in a rudimentary form. On the other hand, some of an infant's perceptual and motor systems are immature. Until these input and output systems develop more fully, an infant cannot begin to learn about certain stimuli or to express her learning using motor responses (Gerhardstein & West, 2003). For example, cats are born with their eyes sealed shut, so they obviously can't learn about visual stimuli that are presented to them in the first few hours of life. Human newborns may be able to recognize the sound of their mother's voice, but they can't express this learning verbally until they have mastered rudimentary speech.

Acquisition of complex *motor skills* comes gradually, as physical development produces improvements in muscle strength and perceptual-motor coordination. Newborn humans cannot even hold their heads up unsupported, but most babies can roll over by the time they're 5.5 months old; by 7 months, most can sit up; by a year, most have learned to stand alone or even walk. As coordination improves, babies develop the fine motor skills needed for accurate eye tracking, babbling, and reaching to pick up objects. Skill acquisition is not limited to motor skills either; between 1 and 2 years of age, children begin to master the rudiments of language, and complex grammar and reading are usually evident by 4–5 years.

Very young children can also show instrumental conditioning. You read about one example above, where infants learned sucking responses in order to turn on a familiar recording. In another instrumental conditioning procedure, researchers hang a mobile over an infant's crib, then tie one end of a ribbon to the baby's leg and the other end to the mobile. When the baby kicks her leg, the mobile moves:

S (crib with mobile) → R (kick) → C (mobile moves)

Just like a rat in a Skinner box, the baby makes her first response by chance. The resulting movement of the mobile, which babies find highly entertaining, reinforces this kicking response. Babies as young as 2 months of age quickly learn to kick vigorously to produce mobile movement (Rovee-Collier, 1993, 1997, 1999). The babies can maintain memory of this learned response for a few days with no reminders—or for up to 21 weeks, if they receive periodic reminders in which they see the mobile move when an out-of-sight experimenter pulls the ribbon (Hayne, 1996).

One of the most interesting features of this instrumental learning in babies is that it is context-dependent, just like the adult learning you read about in Chapter 9. For example, in one variant of the mobile experiment, learning takes place in a crib with a striped crib liner. If this liner is replaced with one having a different pattern, the babies gape passively at the mobile—but don't kick (Borovsky & Rovee-Collier, 1990). Apparently, the change in crib liners represents a new context in which the old rules might not continue to hold. Infants, just like adults, incorporate details of the context during ongoing learning.

Classical conditioning takes place in infants, too. In Chapter 7, you read about eyeblink classical conditioning, in which a human or rabbit learns that a tone or light (the conditioned stimulus, or CS) predicts an airpuff (the unconditioned stimulus, or US). In the *delay conditioning* paradigm, the CS and US overlap and co-terminate. With repeated CS-US pairings, the human or rabbit learns to respond to the CS by producing an eyeblink (the conditioned response, or CR) so that the eye is protected when the US arrives.

Infant humans can learn eyeblink CRs in the delay conditioning paradigm, and so can infant rats, although in both species the infants learn more slowly than adults do (Little, Lipsett, & Rovee-Collier, 1984; Ivkovich, Collins, Eckerman, Krasnegor, & Stanton, 1999; Ivkovich, Paczkowski, & Stanton, 2000). But the story is a bit different for the *trace conditioning* paradigm, where there is a gap between the end of the CS and the arrival of the US. Young adult humans can learn a trace CR about as quickly as they learn a delay CR, but 4-year-old children learn the trace CR much more slowly than the delay CR, and 2-month-old infants can't learn a trace CR at all (Herbert, Eckerman, & Stanton, 2003). In summary, the basic components of classical conditioning are available in very young individuals, but the process continues to develop as the organism matures, allowing the organism to learn more efficiently and under increasingly difficult conditions.

Instrumental learning in infants
The movement of the mobile reinforces kicks.

Development of Episodic and Semantic Memory

Much early learning takes the form of *observational learning.* For example, human infants and children learn many motor and cognitive skills by watching and imitating the actions of adults or older siblings. Juveniles of some primate species learn skills, such as cracking nuts, by watching and imitating what their elders do. Young humpback whales learn the route to breeding grounds by following their mothers on an initial migration, and adult killer whales appear to teach their offspring how to beach themselves intentionally in order to prey on seals lying on the sands (Rendell & Whitehead, 2001).

Often, such observational learning can occur after a single training session. A primary technique for assessing these memories in human infants is **elicited imitation,** in which infants are shown an action and tested for their ability to mimic this action later (Bauer, 1996). For example, researchers showed a group of 10-month-old children how to operate a toy puppet. Four months later, they presented the children with the same toy puppet. These children showed more interest and ability in operating the puppet than did a second group of same-aged children who had never seen the puppet used (Myers, Perris, & Speaker, 1994). The original children were brought back again as 5-year-olds; only two of these children could verbally recall the original event, but the group still showed more interest and ability in handling the puppet than another group of same-aged children who had never seen the puppet before. This difference suggests that the children had a memory of the earlier events, even if they couldn't verbalize it (Rovee-Collier, 1999).

Once children grow a little older and master language, it becomes much easier to investigate *episodic memory*. If you've ever asked a 3- or 4-year-old what she did on her last birthday, you know that such children can form and maintain episodic memories—sometimes for a year or more. But episodic memory in young children is still not up to adult standards. For example, Anna Drummey and Nora Newcombe provided children with a series of questions (such as, "What animal can't make any sounds?"). Some of these questions were presented by a human experimenter, and some were presented by a puppet. If the child didn't already know the answer, the answer was provided ("A giraffe."). If the child did know the answer, the experimenters tried a different question, until the child had been given 10 new facts: five by the human and five by the puppet. A week later, the children returned to the lab and were quizzed on those ten questions. Factual recall increased with age: 4-year-olds recalled about 23% of the answers they'd been given; 6-year-olds recalled about 32% of the answers;

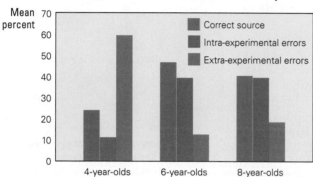

and 8-year-olds recalled about 50% of the answers (Drummey & Newcombe, 2002). In other words, the older children were better able to form and maintain new semantic memories than younger children.

The experimenters next tested whether the children had episodic memories: when a child correctly remembered a fact, the researchers asked the child where the fact had been learned. The oldest children (8-year-olds) could remember the source correctly on about 40% of trials (Figure 12.2). When the 8-year-olds did make a source error, it was usually an *intra-experimental error*, meaning that they correctly recalled having learned the fact during the experiment, but simply confused whether they'd heard it from the human or the puppet. Very seldom did the 8-year-olds make *extra-experimental errors*, meaning that they mistakenly recalled having learned the fact somewhere outside the experiment (for example, at school). In other words, if the older children had a semantic memory for the fact, they generally also had at least some episodic memory of the context in which they'd learned that fact (Drummey & Newcombe, 2002).

Six-year-old children performed very much like 8-year-olds. But the pattern was different in 4-year-old children. First of all, 4-year-olds remembered the correct source much less often than the older children. And, when the young children made a source error, they were especially prone to extra-experimental errors, meaning that they tended to misattribute their learning to some context outside the experiment. These results suggest that children as young as 4 can learn semantic information, but it is only by about age 6 or 8 that they can reliably remember not just the fact but also the episodic context in which that learning was acquired.

Figure 12.2 Episodic memory in children Children were taught 10 new facts, some presented by a human experimenter and some by a puppet, and then were quizzed on these facts one week later. For questions where the correct answer was recalled, researchers next asked where the fact had been learned. Six-year-olds and 8-year-olds could identify the correct source about half the time; when they made an error in identifying the source, the older children tended to make mostly intra-experimental errors, meaning that they correctly remembered learning the fact in the context of the experiment but simply confused whether they had heard it from the experimenter or the puppet. In contrast, the youngest children tended to make many extra-experimental errors, falsely "remembering" that they'd learned the facts somewhere outside the experiment (for example, at school). This suggests that children as young as 4 can learn some new semantic facts, but it is only after about age 6 or 8 that they can reliably remember the episodic context in which that new learning occurred. Data from Drummey & Newcombe, 2002.

Development of Working Memory

Working memory is an example of a memory system that reaches full potency relatively late in development. Recall from Chapter 5 that *working memory* is a short-term storage system where information can be held for active processing. For example, in humans, we often measure working memory capacity in terms of *digit span:* the number of digits that a person can hold in memory at once and repeat back correctly. English-speaking children aged 5–6 years have relatively short digit spans: on average, they can only remember and repeat three or four digits at a time. By age 9 or 10 years, children can usually remember five or six digits; by age 14 or 15, they can remember approximately seven digits—the same as adults (Engle & Marshall, 1983). Similar results are obtained if the items to be remembered are visual patterns rather than numbers: children's performance gradually increases with age to about age 11, at which point they can remember as many visual items as adults (Gathercole, 1998).

One reason why very young children can remember fewer numbers and pictures than adults is simply that the children have had less exposure to such things. Adults have had a lifetime of experience with numbers, words, and patterns, and this knowledge may give them an advantage at encoding those items into working memory. If we use material that the children are highly familiar with, their performance improves. In one clever study, adults and children were asked to remember the locations of chess pieces on a chess board. Ten-year-old chess experts could remember more pieces than non-chess-playing adults, even though the children's digit spans were lower (Chi, 1978). This suggests that the age-related improvement in working-memory capacity at least partially reflects exposure to and familiarity with the material to be remembered.

▶ Learning and Memory in Everyday Life

Can Exposure to Classical Music Make Babies Smarter?

Walk through any children's store and you're likely to find shelves of music, books, and videos representing an entire industry dedicated to the premise that a baby (or even a fetus) exposed to classical music will reap intellectual benefits. It all started in 1993, when physicist Gordon Shaw and developmental psychologist (and concert cellist) Francis Rauscher reported that college students who listened to 10 minutes of Mozart's Sonata for Two Pianos in D Major subsequently scored about 8 or 9 points better on an intelligence test than students who sat quietly during the same interval (Rauscher, Shaw, & Ky, 1993). The researchers concluded that hearing the music caused priming of neural pathways for spatial reasoning in the brain.

The media quickly picked up the story of the "Mozart effect." Entrepreneurs rushed to produce intelligence-enhancing music products for babies, and well-intentioned parents rushed to buy them. Pregnant mothers spent afternoons playing sonatas to their unborn children, often with speakers positioned directly over the belly for optimal effect. The states of Tennessee and Georgia began giving recordings of classical music to the parents of every newborn citizen, while Florida legislators proposed that all state-funded educational preschool programs play at least 30 minutes of classical music a day to children in their care. All this effort derived from public perception of the scientific evidence that music could make babies smarter.

But, in fact, scientific evidence for the Mozart effect is slim at best. Although some studies replicated the original findings (Rideout, Dougherty, & Wernert, 1998; Wilson & Brown, 1997), others did not (Bridgett & Cuevas, 2000; McKelvie & Low, 2002; Steele, Bass, & Crook, 1999; McCutcheon, 2000). Most researchers now conclude that the general claim of intellectual improvement following mere exposure to classical music is unwarranted (Chabris, 1999; Steele et al., 1999; Fudin & Lembessis, 2004). Even Rauscher and Shaw stress that their original paper only found an effect of classical music on very specific tasks involving abstract reasoning and mental imagery, such as imagining how a piece of paper will look when unfolded after several steps of folding and cutting (Rauscher & Shaw, 1998). And there is no evidence that this effect lasts more than 10–15 minutes.

The increased test scores that Rauscher and Shaw observed may be explained in part by the possibility that listening to complex music activates the same brain regions that are used in abstract spatial reasoning. The music may "prime" or prepare those brain regions so that they are more efficient on subsequent spatial reasoning tasks (Rauscher et al., 1993; Rauscher & Shaw, 1998). But such priming would not last more than a few minutes, and would not result in a long-term increase in intelligence or general memory ability.

Another possible explanation is that listening to music can produce changes in mood and arousal that might significantly affect performance on subsequent cognitive tasks (Chabris, 1999; Steele, 2003). In fact, cognitive improvement is most pronounced in studies where individuals listening to pleasant and arousing music are compared against individuals listening to sounds they find either relaxing or annoying. So, for example, British schoolchildren perform better after listening to pop music than to Mozart, but people who prefer new-age music show an enhancement after listening to Yanni (Chabris, 1999).

And what about those parents who want a quick way to make their children smarter? Spending large amounts of money on Mozart-for-babies products may not be the answer. At best, such exposure results in a small, temporary increase on a specific kind of spatial ability, and even that only occurs in individuals who enjoy classical music. On the other hand, no one has yet suggested that exposure to Mozart causes any actual harm to the babies, and if it fosters an early love of music, that may be a worthwhile benefit in and of itself.

Sensitive Periods for Learning

As you've just read, many kinds of learning are functional early in life but become more efficient as the organism matures. Sometimes, the opposite is true. In some species, certain kinds of learning are most effective early in life, during a specific time window known as a **sensitive period.**

For example, adult white-crowned sparrows have a repertoire of about seven different sounds that serve various functions, including territory defense and courtship. Six of these sounds are more or less the same in all white-crowned sparrows; but one—the male song—differs by geographical location. In effect, male sparrows from different regions have different "dialects," just as people in different regions may speak the same language but with different accents. Normally, a male white-crowned sparrow spends his first 10 days or so in the nest and then moves out, to live independently from, but close to, his parents. During the next few months, he will hear his father and other male neighbors singing, and eventually, he himself will begin to sing, using the same "dialect" as they do.

Male sparrows raised in isolation, with no opportunity to hear other adults, begin to sing too, but their songs are abnormal (Marler, 1970). This suggests that some of the song is innate—perhaps genetically hardwired—but that parts of it are learned through imitation of other adults in the area (Ball & Hulse, 1998). Males raised in isolation but allowed to hear tape recordings of male song can learn normally, as long as they hear the song during days 30–100 of their life (Marler, 1970). Earlier or later exposure is of no use. Apparently, these birds have a sensitive period during which they can learn their song; learning outside this time window is not possible.

Sensitive periods occur in mammals too. For example, David Hubel and Torsten Wiesel conducted a classic series of studies in which they sewed shut one eye of newborn cats or monkeys (Hubel & Wiesel, 1979, 1998). After several weeks, the eye was opened. The result? The animals were "blind" in that eye even though they had no physical damage to the visual system. For cats, the period from about 3 weeks to 60 days after birth is a sensitive period for the development of the visual system; for monkeys, the period may last for about the first 6 months of life. Similar effects are seen in human infants born with cataracts that block vision in one eye; if corrective surgery is performed within a few months of birth, vision will develop normally (Maurer & Lewis, 1999). But, if surgery is delayed for a few years, normal vision never develops (Vaegan, 1979).

Imprinting

Animals of many species, including birds, are especially likely to form an attachment to the first individual they see after birth. Konrad Lorenz named this phenomenon **imprinting** (Lorenz, 1935; Insel & Fernald, 2004). Normally, the first individual a baby bird sees is its mother or a sibling in the nest, and so the chick appropriately imprints on a member of its own species. But Lorenz found that if he removed a newly hatched goose chick from an incubator, the chick would imprint on him—and would follow him about as if he were its mother. If the gosling were later placed among a brood of goose chicks following a goose mother, it would ignore the members of its own species in preference for following its human "parent." Researchers have shown that chicks can be induced to imprint not only on individuals of the wrong species, but even on

Researcher Konrad Lorenz being followed by goslings that imprinted on him because he was the first moving object they saw after hatching. Thereafter, they responded to him as if he were their mother.

Thomas D. McAvoy/*Time* Magazine

rotating cylinders and stuffed chickens (Johnson, 1992). Imprinting has been demonstrated in a variety of other species, including turkeys, sheep, deer, and buffalo (Scott, 1958, 1962).

Some researchers use the term **critical period** to refer to a special kind of sensitive period that results in irreversible learning. The period for imprinting is a critical period, because once imprinting has happened, it cannot be undone, and its effects can last a lifetime. For example, a sheep that has been bottle-fed by humans for the first 10 days of life, and is then returned to its flock, never develops a natural bond with its mother. As an adult, this animal will care little for other sheep, preferring to be with people—and will itself be a poor mother, allowing its offspring to nurse but not taking any other motherly interest (Scott, 1962). Similarly, Konrad Lorenz's geese not only treated him like a parent but also, upon reaching maturity, courted him in preference to seeking mates from their own species! Apparently, creatures that mistakenly imprint on the wrong species learn that they should form social attachments with individuals from the same species as their assumed "mother" rather than with others of their own kind, and this learning persists throughout life.

Social Attachment Learning

Although primates don't appear to imprint, they do show evidence of a sensitive period for learning social attachment. In another classic series of studies, Harry Harlow reared rhesus monkeys in isolation from their mothers or any other monkeys (Harlow, 1958; Harlow & Harlow, 1962). Later, when these monkeys became adolescents, they were moved to group cages. There, they didn't interact socially the way normal monkeys do: they didn't mate or play with their fellows, and they always seemed to be socially retarded. Apparently, for rhesus monkeys, the first few months of life are a sensitive period for learning social interactions with others of their species.

There is evidence for a similar sensitive period in humans. We can see this evidence in tragic cases where infants are deprived of social interactions with a nurturing caregiver. During the 1970s, the ruling Ceausescu regime in Romania placed thousands of unwanted children into orphanages with appalling conditions. The children were given food and shelter, but little else. They had no toys and minimal personal interaction with caregivers, and they were bathed by being hosed down with cold water. When the Ceausescu regime fell, a group of these orphans were placed in adoptive care in the United Kingdom.

Sadly but unsurprisingly, these children were developmentally impaired. At the time of their entry into the United Kingdom, most scored in the mildly retarded range on a test of cognitive function. But after placement in adoptive homes, where they had access to medical care and loving families, many of these children showed amazing recovery of cognitive function, moving into the normal range for their age group in IQ. The single most important factor in predicting cognitive function at age four was the child's age at adoption (Rutter et al., 1998). Romanian infants who had been adopted before they were six months old now scored about as well as British four-year-olds who had also been adopted as infants (Figure 12.3, solid red line). In other words, these children appeared to be able to overcome the hardships

Figure 12.3 A sensitive period in humans A group of Romanian orphans, subjected to poor care in their early life, were later adopted in the United Kingdom. At the time of their adoption, these infants showed depressed cognitive scores. Tested again at four years of age, many showed spectacular improvements. Those Romanian orphans who had been adopted before six months of age (solid red line) now scored about normal for their age group (green line). But those Romanian orphans who had been 6 months or older at adoption continued to lag behind in cognitive function (dashed red line). Data from Rutter et al., 1998.

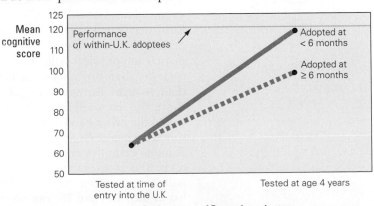

Performance of Romanian adoptees

of their infancy. Romanian infants who had been six months or older when adopted also showed improvement (Figure 12.3, dashed red line), but their scores still remained significantly below normal (Rutter et al., 1998; O'Connor et al., 2000). And there were mild social problems in these older adoptees too, including weakened attachment to the adoptive parents and wary or overexcited behavior around strangers (Rutter et al., 2004). Apparently, just like the infant monkeys, human infants deprived of social interaction and a stimulating environment during early childhood cannot easily catch up later.

The Aging Memory: Adulthood through Old Age

Learning and memory abilities develop through childhood and adolescence to a peak in young adulthood, but they often decline in old age. However, not every kind of memory declines at the same speed. Some kinds of learning may start to decline in humans as young as the mid-30s, but other kinds of learning tend to remain strong well into old age.

Working Memory Is Especially Vulnerable

Working memory, one of the last memory systems to fully mature in humans and other animals, is also one of the first to show deficits in the course of healthy aging. As you read on page 468, healthy young adults have a digit span that averages about seven digits; in elderly adults, the average drops to about six to six and a half digits. This small but significant drop could mean the difference between remembering or forgetting a seven-digit phone number. If the task is made more complicated, such as by presenting different digits simultaneously to each ear, reductions in digit span can be observed as early as age 30 or 40 (Barr, 1980).

Conditioning and Skill Learning Decline— But Well-learned Skills Survive

In general, conditioning also declines with age: older adults are less able than younger adults to adapt their behavior in response to reinforcement. For example, classical conditioning of the eyeblink response starts declining at about age 40 or 50 in humans. Older adults take about twice as long to learn an eyeblink response as younger ones do (Solomon, Pomerleau, Bennett, James, & Morse, 1989; Woodruff-Pak & Thompson, 1988). There are similar age-related declines in eyeblink conditioning in rabbits (Solomon & Groccia-Ellison, 1996), rats (Freeman & Nicholson, 2001), and cats (Harrison & Buchwald, 1983). Old age does not prevent learning, but it makes learning slower.

Skill learning also declines in old age. Recall that in Chapter 4 you read about the *rotary pursuit task*, which requires keeping a stylus positioned over a point on a disk that rotates rapidly. Middle-aged adults can learn this task about as well as young adults, but elderly adults (over age 60) show a precipitous drop-off in performance (Ruch, 1934). Real-world skill learning shows the same age-related decline. For example, one study found that elderly individuals can master the mental and physical skills needed to use computers, but their rate of acquisition is slower than in younger learners, and they make more errors during learning than younger learners do (Czaja, Hammond, Blascovich, & Swede, 1993). In short, you *can* teach an old dog new tricks, it just takes a while longer.

On the other hand, even though the learning of new associations and skills is slowed in healthy aging, older highly practiced skills tend to be maintained well. Famous examples are Spanish cellist Pablo Casals, who continued to conduct orchestras at an advanced age, and Jack Nicklaus, who continued to win major golf tournaments in his 40s and 50s—besting many younger players. Expert typists in their 60s and 70s can often execute their skill as quickly and accurately as typists in their 20s and 30s (Salthouse, 1984). Many expert chess and bridge players improve, rather than decline, with age, and airline pilots aged 40–60 actually have fewer accidents than younger pilots (Birren, 1964), all in support of the axiom that age and experience can often defeat youth and speed.

Episodic and Semantic Memory: Old Memories Fare Better than New Learning

As with other kinds of memory, older individuals may show a decline in the ability to form new episodic and semantic memories, but existing memories may survive well with age. Remember from Chapter 3 that semantic memory is normally strengthened by repeated exposure. By the time a person reaches old age, semantic information such as vocabulary and general knowledge about the world have all been encoded, retrieved, and re-encoded many times. Healthy elderly adults generally experience little or no drop-off in the ability to retain and retrieve such semantic memories (Light, 1991). Older individuals also tend to show only a modest drop-off in their ability to recall episodic memories from their distant past (Piolino, Desgranges, Benali, & Eustache, 2002).

On the other hand, although well-formed memories may survive, elderly adults are generally less effective at learning new information. For example, in a *paired associates* test, people study a list of word pairs; then, given the first word of each pair, they are asked to recall the second member of that pair. If, during study, the word pairs are presented at a rate of one pair every 1.5 seconds, elderly adults are much worse than young adults at later recall (Canestrari, 1963). This deficit appears to be due to encoding difficulties, rather than retrieval difficulties. If the presentation rate is slowed to one pair every 3 seconds, elderly adults' performance improves, presumably because they now have more time to encode the information. Elderly adults' performance improves too, if the studied items have some meaning (Graf, 1990). For example, in one study, college-age adults outperformed elderly adults on memorizing a list of names of current rock stars, but the elderly adults outperformed the students on memorizing a list with names of Big Band musicians who were popular with the earlier generation (Hanley-Dunn & McIntosh, 1984).

Test Your Knowledge

Learning and Memory in Old Age

Learning and memory abilities generally peak in young adulthood, and may decline thereafter. Some kinds of learning and memory may begin to decline in middle age, while others may remain relatively robust through healthy old age. See if you can identify the learning and memory processes involved in each of the tasks described below, and predict whether or not healthy older people should be able to perform them as well (or nearly as well) as when they were young adults:

1. Recalling one's wedding day
2. Remembering the items on this week's shopping list (without writing them down)
3. Remembering how to make coffee
4. Learning the name of a new friend
5. Learning how to program a new DVD player

Interim Summary

An individual's learning and memory abilities vary across the lifespan. Some simple learning, like habituation and recognition, can occur even before birth. The really impressive learning machines are infants, with most kinds of learning and memory ability present in at least a rudimentary form from a very early age, although they may become more efficient as the individual grows toward adulthood. Episodic memory and working memory are two kinds of memory that do not fully mature until relatively late, with working memory only reaching full adult capacity during adolescence. Learning and memory abilities generally decline in healthy aging. A rule of thumb is that old memories may survive well but new learning may be slowed in aging individuals.

12.2 Brain Substrates

Unsurprisingly, the age-related wax and wane of learning and memory abilities in an individual reflect underlying changes in the brain across the lifespan. In this section, you'll read about those changes.

Recall that in Chapter 1 you read about John Watson and the strict behaviorists, who believed that organisms come into the world as blank slates, and that learning and memory abilities, as well as all other cognitive abilities, are determined by experiences after birth. We now know that the strict behaviorists were wrong. Before an organism is born, at the moment of conception, some aspects of its learning and memory abilities are encoded in that organism's genetic structure, and guide its future development. Even the organism's gender can affect the brain, both before and after birth. After birth, learning continues to modify the brain throughout the lifetime, since every instance of new learning reflects some underlying change in the brain.

The Genetic Basis of Learning and Memory

DNA (or, more formally, *deoxyribonucleic acid*) is the material found within the nucleus of all cells that carries the instructions for making a living organism. A strand of DNA looks like a long twisted ladder, a shape famously described as a "double helix" (Figure 12.4a). The sides, or "backbones," of the ladder are long chains of sugar and phosphate molecules. Each "rung" of the ladder is called a **base pair,** because it is composed of a pair of smaller molecules called *bases.* There are four kinds of bases in DNA: adenine, thymine, cytosine, and guanine. When forming DNA base pairs, adenine (A) always pairs with thymine (T), and cytosine (C) always pairs with guanine (G). Because of this, the common practice for recording the sequence of base pairs along a strand of DNA is to report the bases that lie along one backbone, because you can always deduce what the other half of each base pair must be. For example, if one backbone carries the sequence GATCAG, then you know the other backbone must have the corresponding bases (CTAGTC) needed to complete the base pairs.

In humans and other mammals, DNA is organized into packages called **chromosomes.** Humans have 23 pairs of chromosomes, with one member of each pair inherited from the mother and one from the father (Figure 12.4b). Twenty-two of these pairs consist of two similar chromosomes. In females, the 23rd pair also has two similar chromosomes, called "X" chromosomes; in males, the 23rd pair has one "X" and one very different chromosome called the "Y" chromosome. Whether your 23rd pair of chromosomes is XX or XY determines whether you are genetically male or genetically female. The entire package of 23 chromosome pairs is duplicated in most of the cells in your body, so that your cells all carry the same genetic information. (Exceptions include egg and sperm cells, which each contain 23 unpaired chromosomes.)

Chromosomes can be subdivided into **genes.** A gene is a segment of a DNA strand that contains information for building a protein from amino acids. In

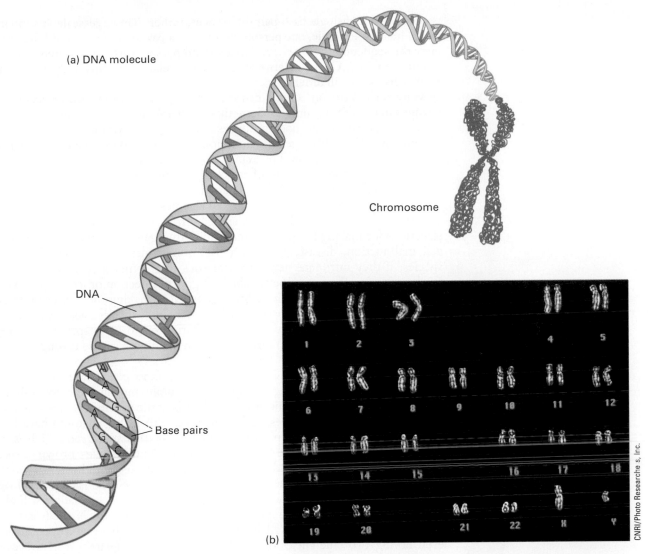

(a) DNA molecule

Chromosome

DNA

Base pairs

(b)

CNRI/Photo Researchers, Inc.

Figure 12.4 Genes and DNA (a) DNA is the genetic material found within the cells of all living things. A DNA molecule looks like a twisted ladder or a double helix. In mammals, DNA is organized into packages called chromosomes, which can be subdivided into functional areas called genes. Genes encode the blueprints for building and maintaining our body. (b) Most human cells have 23 pairs of chromosomes, with one member of each pair inherited from each parent. The set of chromosomes shown here has an XY combination as its 23rd pair, and so it belongs to a male.

total, humans probably have 20,000 to 25,000 genes (International Human Genome Sequencing Consortium, 2004). Genes are activated by events in their immediate environment. When a gene is activated, its structure is copied (or "transcribed") to produce a new molecule, *messenger RNA*, which is then used to produce a protein. For example, the *BDNF gene* on human chromosome 11 helps regulate production of brain-derived neurotrophic factor (BDNF), a protein that is vital for the health of neurons. A high level of neuronal activity may signal that more BDNF is needed, which activates the BDNF gene, which causes increased production of the protein, as required.

Genetic Variation among Individuals Affects Innate Learning Abilities

Unless you have an identical twin, no other human being has exactly the same DNA that you do. But if you compared a sample of your own DNA with a sample from any other human, you would find that on average the two samples would be 99.9% the same. The vast majority of genetic differences between people consist of single base-pair differences, rather than large-scale dissimilarities. Thus, for example, one person might have a part of a DNA strand that contains the sequence ...CAG..., and in a second person, this same stretch of DNA might contain ...CAA.... Between any two unrelated humans, only 1 in every 1,000 base pairs will differ.

Why such variation? Genes can vary as a result of **mutation,** or accidental changes in the DNA sequence. Sometimes, genetic mutations occur due to simple copying errors as the body produces new cells, each with its own copy of the genetic blueprint. Other genetic mutations occur due to outside causes such as radiation or viral infection. For example, HIV (the virus associated with AIDS) essentially replicates portions of its own genetic sequence and inserts these strands into the DNA of an infected patient.

Some genetic mutations are essentially harmless. For example, a change from ...CAG... to ...CAA... is harmless, since both sequences happen to encode instructions for making the same amino acid. Other genetic mutations can lead to cell malfunction, disease, and death. But some mutations are good for the species, if they introduce new characteristics that confer a survival advantage (such as making the carrier better able to fight off infection or less prone to develop cancer) or a reproductive advantage (such as making the carrier more attractive to members of the opposite sex). If an individual with a genetic mutation survives to reproduce, it may pass that mutation on to its offspring, who may pass it on to their offspring in turn, helping the mutation spread throughout the population.

As a result of mutations over many millennia, most genes have two or more **alleles,** or naturally occurring variants. For example, human eye color is determined by the amount of the melatonin in the iris of the eye: individuals with a lot of melatonin have brown eyes, and individuals with little melatonin have blue eyes. Melatonin production is partly controlled by the *bey-2 gene*, which is located on human chromosome 15. This gene comes in two alleles: brown (associated with high melatonin production) and blue (associated with lower melatonin production). A child who inherits two brown alleles (one from each parent) will have brown eyes. A child who inherits one brown and one blue allele will also have brown eyes, because the brown allele is *dominant* over the blue allele. Only a child who inherits two blue alleles of the bey-2 gene can have blue eyes. In fact, even having two blue alleles of bey-2 is not enough to guarantee blue eyes—other genetic factors have to be present too—but the point is that genetic variation among individuals can lead to variation in physical characteristics.

Genetic variations also influence brain function. This is a relatively new area of study, but researchers are beginning to understand some of the ways in which genes affect learning and memory. For example, remember that the BDNF gene regulates production of a protein that is vital for the health of neurons. Among other functions, the BDNF protein appears to affect learning and memory by enhancing *long-term potentiation*, or LTP (Lu & Gottschalk, 2000; Poo, 2001). The most common version of the BDNF gene is called the *Val allele*. However, about one-third of people inherit at least one copy of a different version, called the *Met allele*, which produces a slightly less effective version of BNDF protein. People carrying one or two copies of this Met allele are slightly worse at learning and memory tasks than people carrying two copies of the Val allele. Figure 12.5a shows performance on a test that requires participants to listen to short paragraphs and then repeat them from memory 20 minutes later. People with two copies of the common Val allele (Val/Val) perform better than those with two copies of the Met allele (Met/Met); people with one copy of each allele (Val/Met) are intermediate in performance (Egan et al., 2003).

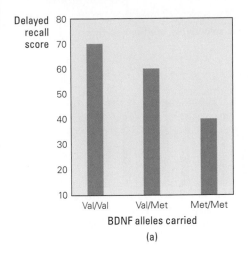

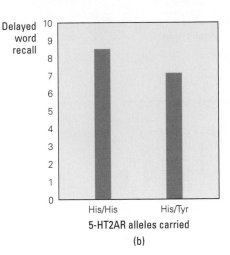

Figure 12.5 Genetic influences on learning and memory in humans (a) BDNF (brain-derived neurotrophic factor) is a protein needed for neuron health and function. People carrying two copies of the Met allele (Met/Met) of this gene show worse performance on a test of memory recall than people carrying two copies of the Val allele (Val/Val). People carrying one copy of each allele (Val/Met) perform at intermediate levels (Egan et al., 2003). (b) The 5-HT2AR gene contains the instructions for building a specific type of serotonin receptor in the brain. Most people carry two copies of the common His allele (His/His). Individuals carrying at least one copy of the Tyr allele of this gene (His/Tyr) are impaired at delayed word recall compared with people carrying His/His (de Quervain et al., 2003). (a) Data from Egan et al., 2003; (b) adapted from de Quervain et al., 2003.

Another gene, the *5-HT2AR gene* on human chromosome 13, encodes the instructions for building a particular kind of receptor for the neurotransmitter serotonin. The most common allele of this gene is the *His allele*; about 90% of people have two copies of the His allele, one inherited from each parent. The remaining 10% of people have one or more copies of a variant, called the *Tyr allele*, which results in construction of serotonin receptors that are a little less efficient than normal. This too has an effect on learning and memory: people with at least one copy of the Tyr allele are slightly worse on delayed word recall than people who have two copies of the His allele (Figure 12.5b; de Quervain et al., 2003).

We're only beginning to understand how and why these two genes affect learning and memory—and these are only two genes out of thousands that, together, determine people's innate learning and memory abilities. We are currently very far from understanding the functions of all our individual genes, much less understanding how combinations of genes interact with one another.

Selective Breeding and Twin Studies

Even without understanding the function of every possible allele of every gene, humans can manipulate genetics through selective breeding. Since ancient times, humans have bred animals to get particular characteristics: winning racehorses may be bred together to produce ever-faster racehorses, purebred dogs may be bred together to produce ever-better examples of the breed, and sheep can be bred together to produce thicker or finer wool. An early experiment considered whether animals could likewise be bred for learning ability (Tryon, 1940). Psychologist Robert Tryon trained a large group of rats in a complex maze; due to individual differences, some rats (which he called "maze-bright") learned quickly and others (which he called "maze-dull") learned slowly (Figure 12.6a). Tryon then selected the maze-bright rats and bred them together; he also bred together the maze-dull rats. He trained the resulting offspring in the maze. Again, some offspring from each group learned better than their peers, and some learned worse than average (Figure 12.6b).

Tryon repeated the process over and over, breeding together the best of the maze-bright offspring, and also breeding together the worst of the maze-dull offspring (Figure 12.6c). By the seventh generation of offspring, there was almost no overlap: those rats from the "maze-bright" line routinely outperformed those rats bred from the "maze-dull" line (Figure 12.6d). Later experiments

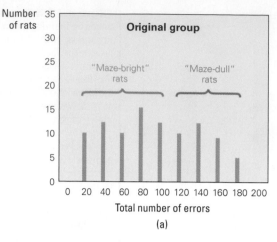

(a)

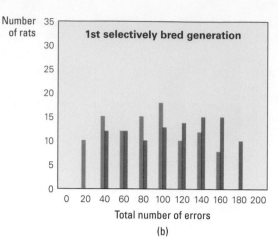

(b)

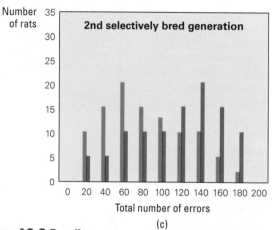

(c)

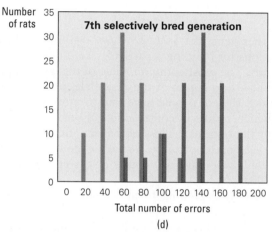

(d)

Figure 12.6 Breeding smart rats (a) Psychologist Robert Tryon took a group of rats and trained them in a maze; some rats ("maze-bright" rats) learned quickly, while others ("maze-dull" rats) learned more slowly. (b) Tryon then bred the "maze-bright" rats together and trained their offspring in the maze (blue bars); he also bred the "maze-dull" rats together and trained their offspring in the maze (purple bars). There was still considerable overlap between the two strains in terms of performance in the maze. (c) Tryon continued breeding the best of the "maze-bright" rats together and the worst of the "maze-dull" rats together and training the offspring of each line in the maze. (d) By the seventh generation of offspring, rats born into the "maze-bright" strain (blue bars) routinely outperformed rats from the "maze-dull" strain (purple bars) in maze learning. Data shown are hypothetical, based on Tryon, 1940.

have shown that many different species, including rats, mice, and fruit flies, can be bred for good (or poor) ability on a variety of learning tasks (Tully, 1996).

Presumably, "maze-bright" and "maze-dull" rats inherited a package of genes from their parents that contributed a variety of characteristics that, all together, resulted in good or poor performance in a maze. These genes might be modifying learning indirectly rather than directly. For example, "maze-bright" rats may be less emotional, or more prone to explore, or more active overall—and any of these characteristics could translate into better performance in a maze. In fact, learning ability, like all facets of intelligence, appears to be determined by multiple genes interacting, rather than by any single gene.

And what about inherited learning abilities in humans? Ethical concerns obviously prevent experiments in which pairs of "smart" or "dumb" people are made to breed with each other to see what kinds of offspring result. However, we can get some clues from twin studies. In these studies, researchers compare the mental abilities of identical twins (who have identical genetic makeup) and fraternal twins (who share 50% of their genes on average, just like any other siblings). Identical twins show more similarity than fraternal twins on several kinds of learning and memory measures, including tests of working memory (such as digit span) and memory for verbal and picture information (Finkel, Pedersen, & McGue, 1995; Swan et al., 1999). This suggests that genes play a strong role in determining our learning and memory abilities. Some studies of human twins suggest that over half of the variation in individuals' memory scores may be accounted for by differences in those individuals' genetic makeup (McClearn et al., 1997; Swan et al., 1999). However, this means that the rest of the variation must be accounted for by nongenetic factors, particularly environmental factors such as health, stress, living conditions, and social interactions. Genes set up the basic blueprint of an individual's learning and memory abilities, but the final outcome reflects an interaction of heredity and environment.

The Influence of Environment

Some of the earliest insights into the effects of environment on learning and memory came from memory researcher Donald Hebb; as you read in Chapter 2, Hebb postulated an important law of neural organization stating that "neurons that fire together, wire together." Hebb also studied rat behavior in his lab, and he sometimes took a few animals home for his children to play with. (Nowadays, researchers generally wouldn't be permitted to remove experimental animals from the testing facility, but in Hebb's day, the rules were more relaxed.) Hebb noted that the rats raised by his children as pets performed better on laboratory tasks than rats housed in cages in the lab (Hebb, 1947). Apparently, the pet rats led more interesting, complex lives, and this kept their learning and memory abilities finely honed.

Hebb's observation was later verified scientifically. Researchers housed one group of rats in an **enriched environment,** meaning an environment where there was plenty of sensory stimulation and opportunity to explore and learn. For the rats, this meant a large cage filled with toys to play with and other rats with whom to socialize. A second group of rats lived in standard laboratory housing, each rat isolated in a small chamber that contained nothing except a drinking spout and food cup. The results? The rats housed in the enriched environment showed better maze learning than the rats kept in standard laboratory housing (Rosenzweig, 1984; Renner & Rosenzweig, 1987).

And what about humans? There have recently been studies showing that preschool children placed in "high-quality" day care (with lots of toys, educational experiences, and teacher interaction) fare better in elementary school than children placed in day care where opportunities for learning are fewer (Peisner-Feinberg, Burchinal, & Clifford, 2001). At the other end of the lifespan, elderly individuals who lead highly social lives with plenty of exercise and challenging activities appear to maintain good cognitive function longer than individuals who are less active and more solitary (Rowe & Kahn, 1998; Craik, Byrd, & Swanson, 1987; Clarkson-Smith & Hartley, 1990). Just like the rats, people who have plenty of toys to play with and plenty of social interaction fare better than people who have fewer opportunities to engage their brain.

These behavioral improvements appear to reflect changes in brain morphology. Rats raised in an enriched environment have cortical neurons with more and longer dendrites than their experience-impoverished counterparts (Figure 12.7). The enriched rats' dendrites also have more synapses—meaning more connections with other neurons (Globus, Rosenzweig, Bennet, & Diamond, 1973; Greenough, West, & DeVoogd, 1978). These neuronal changes occur quickly: as little as 60 days of housing in an enriched environment can result in a 7–10% increase in brain weight of young rats and a 20% increase in the number of synapses in the visual cortex (Kolb & Whishaw, 1998). Similar changes are seen in the brains of monkeys and cats raised in enriched environments. And even the brains of fruit flies housed in large communal cages with visual and odor cues show neuronal changes, compared to flies housed alone in small plastic vials (Technau, 1984).

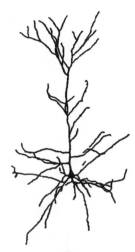

(a) Standard
laboratory housing

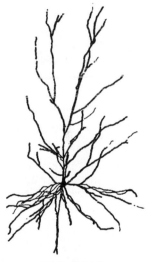

(b) Enriched
laboratory environment

Figure 12.7 Deprived environment vs. enriched environment Representation of neurons from the cortex of (a) a rat raised in standard laboratory housing and (b) a rat raised in an enriched laboratory environment. Neurons from rats raised in enriched environments typically have more and longer dendrites, and more synapses per dendrite, than their experience-impoverished counterparts.

There isn't yet definitive evidence that human brains undergo similar enlargement after environmental enrichment, but suggestive data come from a study of London taxi drivers. London is a sprawling city with hundreds of small, crooked streets. To receive an official license, London taxi drivers must study for up to three years and pass a grueling exam that requires them, for example, to indicate the shortest path between random London addresses. This means that licensed London taxi drivers are a group of people sharing an extensive fund of spatial knowledge.

Researcher Eleanor Maguire and her colleagues compared brain volumes in a group of London taxi drivers with those of age-matched Londoners who had not studied the geography of their city so extensively (Maguire et al., 2000). The only part of the brain that differed significantly between the groups was the hippocampus: among other things, the taxi drivers had slightly larger posterior hippocampal volumes than nontaxi drivers. Further, the size of the posterior hippocampus differed even among taxi drivers: those who had been driving for over a decade had a larger volume than those who had been driving for only a few years. One possible interpretation of these volume differences is that the intensive spatial learning in taxi drivers causes an increase in dendritic branching in hippocampal neurons—making those neurons take up more room, just like the rat neurons shown in Figure 12.7b. Of course, it's also possible that only individuals who have a large posterior hippocampus to start with are able to master the knowledge needed to obtain the license and to succeed as taxi drivers. In that case, genes rather than environment would be the key. To rule out this possibility, researchers would need to conduct studies in which they tested individuals both before and after starting the course of study, to see whether intensive study of geography could actually cause an increase in hippocampal volume.

Neurons and Synapses in the Developing Brain

As you read in the last section, our genetic inheritance lays down the blueprint for brain function, even before we're born. Acting on this basic plan, the developing brain produces neurons and synapses, as experience shapes our brains and our abilities. This process begins during gestation, and continues throughout childhood, with some brain areas taking until adolescence to reach full maturation.

Neurons Are Overproduced, Then Weeded Out

Before birth, the brain develops at an amazing rate; at certain points in human gestation, up to 250,000 new neurons are added *each minute* (Bornstein & Lamb, 1992). This process of neuronal birth is called **neurogenesis.** By about 25 weeks GA, the majority of the human fetus's neurons are in place. The lower brain centers responsible for such functions as breathing, digestion, and reflexes are almost fully developed at this point.

But the process of neurogenesis is not uniform throughout the brain. For example, Purkinje cells in the cerebellum are one class of neuron that form relatively early during gestation (Sidman & Rakic, 1973). This helps explain why classical eyeblink conditioning, which depends on the cerebellum, is already possible in very young infants. But the cerebellum continues to develop after birth too, which is probably why older children and adults can condition faster, and under more complicated circumstances, than infants can (Herbert, Eckerman, & Stanton, 2003).

Surprisingly, after a prenatal flurry of neurogenesis, the infant brain undergoes a period of reduction in the number of neurons. Normally, neurons derive compounds called *neurotrophic factors* that help them grow and thrive. BDNF, which you read about above, is one example of a neurotrophic factor, which neurons obtain from their neighbors. When a neuron is deprived of neurotrophic factor, genes become active that cause the neuron to die. Such natural cell death is called **apoptosis,** to distinguish it from the cell death caused by accident or disease. In a sense, apoptosis implements the brain's version of Darwinian natural selection: if many neurons are competing for a limited amount of neurotrophic factor, only some can survive. Those neurons that are densely connected to their neighbors, and thus probably play vital roles in brain function, are most likely to obtain BDNF and win the competition. Those neurons that have less contact with their neighbors—and thus probably contribute less to overall brain function—are more likely to die through apoptosis.

During development, apoptosis may cull as many as one-third of all the neurons produced prenatally. This may seem like a roundabout way to build a brain: creating billions of neurons and then destroying a large number of them soon after. But the process allows for a great deal of fine-tuning after birth. The brain starts off with plenty of resources, in the form of neurons, and experience determines which of those resources are critical, and which are not so necessary.

Of course, neurons are not the only brain cells; the adult brain contains more *glia* than neurons. Remember from Chapter 2 that some glial cells, the *oligodendrocytes,* generate *myelin sheaths* that improve signal transmission along axons. The birth of glial cells lags behind neurogenesis, so myelination of neurons in the human cortex doesn't start until after birth, and it continues throughout the first 18 years of life. Some brain areas, such as motor cortex and sensory cortex, are fully myelinated early; other areas, such as association cortex and frontal cortex, are myelinated later. Neurons can function before myelination is complete, but transmission will be slow and weak. This may also help explain why working memory and episodic memory, which depend on frontal and association cortex, are among the last types of learning and memory to fully mature.

Synapses Are Also Formed, Then Pruned

In the same way that the brain starts life with an oversupply of neurons, it also begins with a surplus of synapses. The creation of new synapses, called **synaptogenesis,** begins in the human brain as early as the fifth month GA. But after birth, synaptogenesis really gets going: with as many as 40,000 synapses being created *per second* in the infant macaque monkey! Again, synaptogenesis occurs at different rates in different brain areas. For example, in humans, the bulk of synaptogenesis in the visual cortex is completed by about 3 or 4 months of age, but in the prefrontal cortex high rates of synaptogenesis continue until about 6 years of age (Huttenlocher and Dabholkar, 1997).

After this peak in synaptogenesis, the number of synapses begins to decline as the brain begins to prune unnecessary or incorrect connections. Just like neurons, synapses are subjected to a kind of Darwinian natural selection. Those synapses that are frequently used (and, therefore, presumably important to the neuron's function) are strengthened; those that are seldom used (and, therefore, presumably less important) are weakened and may die away altogether. In humans, up to 42% of all synapses in the cortex may be pruned during childhood and adolescence (Bourgeois, 2001). Despite this pruning, there are still plenty of synapses to go around: the adult human brain, for example, has

"Young man, go to your room and stay there until your cerebral cortex matures."

Figure 12.8 Most synapses occur on dendritic spines (a) Left, a reconstruction of a neuron from the cerebral cortex of a monkey; right, a segment of one dendrite which is studded with spines, small protrusions where the majority of synapses with other neurons are formed. (b) Spines appear and disappear; over eight sequential days, this dendritic segment showed some spines that survived through the entire length of the experiment (yellow arrowhead), some that lasted a few days then disappeared (red arrowhead) and some that lasted less than a single day (blue arrowhead). (a) Adapted from Hof & Morrison, 2004; (b) adapted from Trachtenberg et al., 2002.

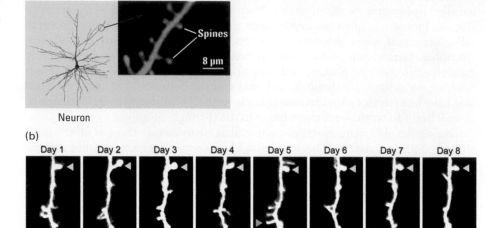

a staggering 10^{14} synapses. That's about 1,000 times as many synapses as there are stars in the Milky Way galaxy.

Synaptogenesis continues throughout life, although not at the same furious rate as during infancy. The vast majority of synapses on cortical neurons occur on **spines,** tiny protrusions from dendrites (Figure 12.8a; Ottersen & Helm, 2002). There may be about 100,000 spines per neuron. Throughout life, new spines periodically appear at random locations on the dendrite. If they are contacted by another neuron, synapses can be formed and strengthened; otherwise, the unneeded spines disappear to be replaced in due course by new spines elsewhere on the dendrite that may prove more useful (Figure 12.8b; Trachtenberg et al., 2002). Although individual spines come and go, the overall number of spines on a dendrite remains approximately constant; experience and learning determine which individual spines survive.

Sensitive Periods for Learning Reflect Sensitive Periods for Neuronal Wiring

Competition for resources may also underlie the phenomenon of sensitive periods. Sensitive periods in learning may reflect sensitive periods in neuronal development, when environmental inputs (such as visual stimulation) can easily alter brain organization by changing local cortical connectivity. For example, remember that infant cats and monkeys who have one eye sewn shut during a sensitive period (from 3 weeks to 3 months of age in the cat, and from birth to 6 months in the monkey) will be "blind" in that eye when it is opened (Hubel & Wiesel, 1977). Normally, visual stimulation activates sensory neurons in the retina of the eye that project (through several way stations) to neurons in the primary visual cortex (V1). During the first few weeks of life, this visual pathway is very active, and since "neurons that fire together, wire together," connections between neurons in this pathway are strengthened. But if one eye is deprived of sight, there is no activity along the pathway from that eye to V1. The inactive synapses will be weakened or eliminated. At the same time, synapses in the active pathway from the open eye will be strengthened. By the time the sight is restored, visual activity in the previously closed eye will no longer elicit much activity in V1, and this weak activity will not be able to compete for synapses with the strong pathways from the never-closed eye (Majewska & Sur, 2003).

Although sensitive periods restrict our later learning, they are actually beneficial to the developing brain. Early in life, the brain *should* be maximally open to new experiences, and be able to change accordingly. But, once its basic system is set up, the brain must not change dramatically with each new experience, or it would risk overwriting critical older information. Small, slow changes (such as the changes in cortical maps that occur with extensive practice of a new motor skill) are fine, but the basic organization must remain relatively consistent from day to day. Think of your brain as a canvas on which an artist's early broad strokes define the picture being painted; later, small details can be added or changed, but the basic organization of the picture is fixed.

Similarly, the older an organism becomes, the more information it has stored in its brain, and the less worthwhile is the encoding of new information, since this carries the risk of disrupting older memories that have been accumulated through a lifetime's experience. And this may be why, as you read earlier, older individuals are often slow to learn new information, but very good at retaining memories they acquired long ago.

The Promise of Stem Cells for Brain Repair

Of course, the cost of sensitive periods is that, if dramatic reorganization is actually required, older brains are less able to adjust than younger ones. This is seen most clearly in individuals with brain damage. When an adult suffers brain damage, there may be a loss of function that is never recovered. Young children, on the other hand, have a near-magical ability to recover from brain damage, as surviving brain areas reorganize to take over the functions of damaged tissue (see Stiles, 1998, 2000). The same pattern is seen in other mammalian species: infant monkeys with temporal lobe lesions have better recovery of function than adult monkeys (Bachevalier & Mishkin, 1994), and rats subjected to frontal cortex injury during postnatal days 7–12 show more complete recovery than rats injured in the same way after day 120 (Kolb, Gibb, & Gonzalez, 2001). One reason for this recovery may be that the young brain is still undergoing neurogenesis and synaptogenesis, so that new neurons and connections are readily available to take the place of the damaged ones.

The fact that young brains are highly plastic has led to recent interest in the possibility of using young brain tissue to repair injury to adult brain tissue. Fetal tissue, in particular, contains **stem cells,** cells that have the capacity to develop into a wide range of cell types, such as a skin cell, liver cell, or brain cell. Stem cells can also be isolated from adults (and children), although these *adult stem cells* are less adaptable than the *embryonic stem cells* isolated from fetal tissue.

In principle, stem cells could be implanted into injured brains, where they could grow into the specific kinds of neurons and glia needed to replace lost or damaged tissue. This would be particularly attractive for patients with disorders that destroy brain cells in a limited area. One example is Parkinson's disease, which destroys dopamine-producing cells in a small region of the basal ganglia, and causes motor symptoms such as tremors and rigidity. To date, a few attempts have been made to transplant stem cells into the brains of patients with Parkinson's disease, but the results so far have been rather disappointing. Some of the stem cells implanted into the basal ganglia do develop into dopamine-producing neurons (Figure 12.9). But only some patients receiving the transplants show any reduction in motor symptoms, and even these improvements may only be temporary (Trott et al., 2003; Freed et al., 2001).

Figure 12.9 A study of embryonic stem cell transplants into the brain of patients with Parkinson's disease. (a) A PET scan of a normal adult brain shows dopamine activity in the basal ganglia (red). (b) In Parkinson's disease, dopamine-producing cells in the basal ganglia die, resulting in reduction of dopamine there. (c) One year after transplant of embryonic stem cells, the brains of patients with Parkinson's disease show (as here) increased dopamine levels. However, in this study, only the youngest patients showed improvement in motor symptoms following the transplant, and even this improvement appeared to be temporary. Adapted from Freed et al., 2001.

(a) Healthy brain

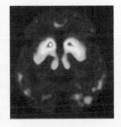

(b) Brain of Parkinson's patient

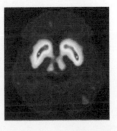

(c) Brain of Parkinson's patient after stem cell transplant

Part of the problem may be that the new neurons do not cure the underlying disease and therefore are gradually killed off, just as the original ones were.

Other studies have tried implanting human stem cells into rats that have been given brain lesions to mimic the brain damage in humans with Parkinson's disease. After transplants, the rats showed significant and long-lasting improvement of motor symptoms (Roy et al., 2006). But there was a darker side, too: in every rat examined, the stem cells appeared to be developing not only into new dopamine neurons, but also into tumors. No one yet knows exactly how to force stem cells to grow into the desired form, while avoiding risk of tumor growth. In short, although stem cells remain a promising and exciting direction for ongoing research, it may be some time before we discover how to use stem cells effectively and safely to repair human brains damaged through disease or injury.

Gender Differences in Brain and Behavior

So far, we've talked about the learning and memory differences between individuals of different age groups. But remember that there are wide variations among individuals within each of these age groups as well. One cause of these variations is gender. For example, young adult women often outperform same-aged men on tests of language and verbal memory, such as recalling a list or a story, and on some kinds of spatial learning, such as remembering the locations of objects (Barnfield, 1999). On the other hand, men generally outperform women on other kinds of spatial learning, such as learning the way around a maze (Astur, Ortiz, & Sutherland, 1998). In one study, men and women were asked to study a map of a fictitious town (Galea & Kimura, 1993). On average, men were quicker to learn a route within the town, but women were better at remembering the position of landmarks in the town.

What could cause such gender differences? One possible cause is cultural influences, such as sexual stereotypes in which boys are expected to excel at some kinds of learning, while girls are expected to excel at others. But this can't be the whole story. Nonhuman mammals show gender differences too, and these can't easily be attributed to sexual stereotyping. For example, in a radial arm maze, adult male rats are usually better than females at remembering which maze arms never contain any food, and adult female rats are usually better than males at remembering which arms have already been visited on the current day (Hyde, Sherman, & Denenberg, 2000; Bimonte, Hyde, Hoplight, & Denenberg, 2000). Given that male and female rats are unlikely to be subject to cultural stereotypes, a more likely cause for these gender differences in rats—and one which probably also contributes heavily to gender differences in humans—is sex hormones.

Effects of Sex Hormones on Brain Organization

Puberty, the process of physical change during which the body transitions to sexual maturity, occurs at different times in different species. In humans, puberty occurs during adolescence, which is the period from about 10–19 years of age; elephants reach sexual maturity at about 9–12 years of age, and rats reach sexual maturity by the time they're about 14 months old. In some species, puberty does not occur at a predetermined age. For example, a fully grown female prairie vole remains sexually immature until exposed to scent signals from a male outside her kin group; within 24 hours of this exposure, she will become sexually receptive, mate, and form an enduring pair bond with her chosen partner.

Starting in puberty, there is a dramatic increase in the release of sex hormones, primarily **estrogens** in mature females and **androgens,** particularly **testosterone,** in adult males. These sex hormones affect the adult brain in ways that can alter learning and memory abilities, as you'll read below. But sex hormones can exert an influence long before puberty. In mammals and birds, there is a surge in testosterone near birth. This surge occurs in both males and females, although it is greater in males. Testosterone levels decline during the first year of life in humans and then remain low in both genders until puberty (Overman, Bachevalier, Schuhmann, & Ryan, 1996). During that critical first year of life, testosterone strongly influences brain development. Curiously, in the brain, "male" hormones like testosterone are converted to estradiol (a form of the "female" hormone estrogen), and so it may be the high level of estradiol in young males that actually makes their brains develop differently than female brains (Cohen-Bendahan, van de Beck, & Berenbaum, 2005).

And develop differently they do. By adulthood, men's brains are about 100 grams heavier, and contain about 4 billion more neurons, than women's brains (Pakkenberg & Gundersen, 1997). Aside from this difference in overall volume, some brain areas are proportionately larger in one gender than in the other. Figure 12.10 shows some of these areas (Goldstein et al., 2001, 2002; Jacobs, Schall, & Schiebel, 1993). One is the lateral frontal cortex, which is important for working memory; this area is usually larger in women than in men, perhaps helping to explain why women often outperform men on working-memory tasks. Other areas that are usually larger in women are the hippocampus and some language areas (such as the area labeled "Supramarginal gyrus" in Figure 12.10). Again, this may help explain why women often outperform men on learning lists, which requires both hippocampal-dependent episodic memory and also language skill. Conversely, men are often better than women at navigating through space (Astur et al., 1998). Such spatial navigation may depend on brain areas that process visual and spatial information, and some of these areas tend to be larger in men than in women, such as the ones labeled "Angular gyrus" and "Visual cortex" in Figure 12.10. In sum, many of the gender differences in learning and memory may reflect the fact that male and female brains are simply wired differently.

Effects of Sex Hormones on Adult Behavior

Although male and female brains develop differently from an early age, many gender differences in performance don't emerge until after puberty. For example, in the task that involved remembering landmarks in a fictitious town, adult women outperformed adult men, but 8- to 13-year-old girls did no better than same-aged boys (Silverman & Eals, 1992). Similarly, gender differences in the radial arm maze task appear in sexually mature rats but not in immature ones (Kanit et al., 2000). Since these gender effects don't emerge until puberty, a likely explanation is that performance is affected by the level of circulating estrogen and testosterone in sexually mature adults.

How might circulating sex hormones affect memory? For one thing, estrogen reliably stimulates neuronal growth and synaptic plasticity (LTP) in rats (Woolley, Weiland, McEwen, & Schwartzkroin, 1997; Foy et al., 1999). These effects are particularly dramatic in the hippocampus, a brain structure that is very important for episodic learning, which might explain why females generally outperform males on list learning and landmark learning tasks that require learning about words or objects in particular contexts.

If estrogen promotes these types of memory, then women should do better on these tasks at times in their menstrual cycle when circulating estrogen levels are highest than at other points, when estrogen levels are lower. Unfortunately, such a clear pattern has not always been found. For example, although women

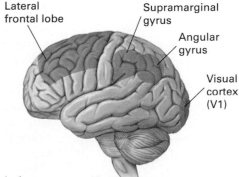

Figure 12.10 Gender differences in brain volume Several brain areas (red) are proportionately larger in women than in men, including the lateral frontal lobes, some language areas (such as the supramarginal gyrus), and the hippocampus (not shown). These brain areas are important for working memory and language processing tasks, at which women often outperform men. Other brain areas (blue) tend to be proportionately larger in men than women, including cortical regions important for visual and spatial processing (such as the angular gyrus and the primary visual cortex), which could help explain why men often outperform women on tests of spatial navigation. Adapted from Goldstein et al., 2002.

normally outperform men at learning word pairs, women tested at points in their menstrual cycle when estrogen is high don't outperform women tested when estrogen is low (Phillips & Sherwin, 1992). One reason for this confusing result may be that the fluctuations in women's estrogen levels at different points in the menstrual cycle are very small compared to the difference in estrogen levels between women and men.

Another way to evaluate the effects of estrogen on learning and memory is to compare learning in transsexuals before and after they have begun hormone therapy. In one study, male-to-female transsexuals on estrogen therapy scored higher on a paired-associate task than a similar group who had not yet started estrogen therapy (Miles, Green, Sanders, & Hines, 1998). Another study compared performance on a list-learning task. Control females recalled the most words; control males recalled the fewest; and male-to-female transsexuals on estrogen scored intermediately—better than control males, though not quite as well as control females (Cohen-Kettenis, van Goozen, Doorn, & Gooren, 1998).

Whereas estrogen may improve verbal learning, there is some evidence that testosterone can improve spatial learning. For example, adult male rats normally outperform females on learning to swim to an escape platform, hidden just below the surface in a pool filled with cloudy water. In one study, adult males given additional testosterone performed even better than ordinary males (Naghdi, Majlessi, & Bozorgmehr, 2005). But other studies have found that testosterone causes no improvement, or even impairs spatial memory (e.g., Goudsmit, Van de Poll, & Swaab, 1990). A further complication is the possibility that testosterone exerts its influence on the brain mainly by affecting estrogen levels: on the one hand, testosterone inhibits estrogen function; on the other hand, when testosterone levels are high, some testosterone may be converted to estrogen, actually increasing estrogen levels in the brain. Perhaps as researchers come to better understand the complicated relationship between estrogen and learning, this will also shed light on the relationship between testosterone and learning.

The Brain from Adulthood to Old Age

Gender differences aside, young adults generally perform better than older adults on various tasks, especially those that require working memory, episodic memory, and semantic memory, as you read in the Behavioral Processes section. Additionally, extreme old age brings impairments in conditioning and skill learning. These behavioral declines reflect changes in the brain that occur as we grow older.

Parts of the Aging Brain Lose Neurons and Synapses

Just as the brain grows in volume during development, so does it shrink in old age. This shrinkage begins in young adulthood and continues thereafter, so that by age 80, the average human brain has lost about 5% of its weight. Some of this loss may reflect the early stages of degenerative diseases like Alzheimer's. Some may reflect injury; a large-scale MRI study of 3600 "healthy" individuals aged 65–97 years found that over one-third had brain lesions consistent with small strokes, which had presumably gone unnoticed by the individuals themselves (Bryan et al., 1997). But even in healthy aging, where there is no known disease or injury, some brain shrinkage appears to occur.

What causes brains to shrink with age? In some areas of the mammalian brain, neurons die off during the course of normal aging. For example, you know that the prefrontal cortex is important for working memory. In a young adult monkey (11 years old) the prefrontal cortex contains numerous, densely packed neurons (Smith, Rapp, McKay, Roberts, & Tuszynski, 2004). In an older monkey (25 years old), the same area of prefrontal cortex shows nearly a third fewer neurons (Figure 12.11). This age-related loss of neurons in a brain area important for working memory is consistent with the fact that working memory generally declines with age. Moreover, the impairment shown by an individual aged monkey on working-memory tasks correlates with that individual's degree of neuron loss (Smith et al., 2004). Another brain region where neurons are lost with age is the cerebellum (Hall, Miller, & Corsellia, 1975; Woodruff-Pak & Sheffield, 1987). This cell loss is consistent with the finding that classical eyeblink conditioning, which depends on the cerebellum, declines with age (Woodruff-Pak, Logan, & Thompson, 1990).

There are also age-related decreases in the connectivity between existing neurons. Neurons in the cerebral cortex of aged monkeys tend to show fewer dendrites and less complex branching than neurons of young monkeys (Hof & Morrison, 2004). Such reductions in dendritic branching imply a reduction in the ability to receive signals from other neurons (Gallagher & Rapp, 1997). Neurons with fewer dendrites will also take up less space, which could be another reason why some cortical areas shrink with age.

On the other hand, some brain regions don't appear to lose appreciable numbers of neurons or synapses in old age. One such area is the hippocampus. Many early studies suggested that the mammalian hippocampus loses neurons during healthy aging (Coleman & Flood, 1987). However, newer studies using modern cell-counting methods find relatively little age-related loss of hippocampal neurons in humans (West, 1993), monkeys (Peters et al., 1996; Small, Chawla, Buonocore, Rapp, & Barnes, 2004), or rats (Rapp & Gallagher, 1996; Rasmussen, Schliemann, Sorensen, Zimmer, & West, 1996). In fact, many researchers now believe that significant reductions in the number of hippocampal neurons are warning signs of age-related disease, such as early Alzheimer's disease (Gallagher & Rapp, 1997). And it now appears that the aging hippocampus doesn't normally show a decrease in number of synapses either (Rosenzweig & Barnes, 2003). Yet, as you read in the Behavioral Processes section, age does cause decline in hippocampal-dependent episodic and semantic memory formation. If not loss of hippocampal neurons and synapses, what could cause this decline?

Synaptic Connections May Be Less Stable in Old Age

Carol Barnes and colleagues have suggested that the *total number* of hippocampal neurons and synapses doesn't decline appreciably with aging; what does change is the ability to *maintain changes in synapse strength* (Rosenzweig & Barnes, 2003; Barnes, Suster, Shen, & McNaughton, 1997). Remember that synapse strength is increased by *long-term potentiation* (LTP), the process whereby conjoint activity in two neurons strengthens the synaptic connection between them. This is one way that neurons encode new learning. If LTP occurs but then fades away, the new learning will be lost.

For example, Barnes and colleagues placed rats in a maze shaped like a squared-off 8 (Figure 12.12a). Figure 12.12b shows activity recorded from several neurons in the hippocampus of a young rat during its first session in this maze (Barnes, 1979). In this figure, each neuron is encoded as a different color, and each dot represents a location where the neuron fired. One neuron (coded

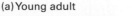

(a) Young adult (b) Aged

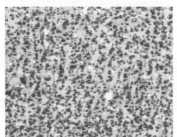
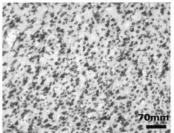

Figure 12.11 Neuron loss in the prefrontal cortex of aging monkeys (a) In young adult monkeys, neurons are densely packed. (b) Older monkeys show approximately 32% fewer neurons in the same brain area, and neuron loss in individual monkeys correlates with decline on working memory tasks. Adapted from Smith et al., 2004.

(a) 8-shaped maze

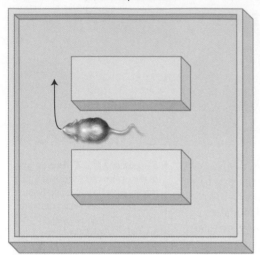

(b) Young rat, session 1

(c) Young rat, session 2

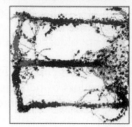

(d) Aged rat, session 1

(e) Aged rat, session 2

Figure 12.12 Hippocampal neurons encoding location in old and young rats. (a) A young rat was placed in an environment shaped like a squared-off 8. (b) While the rat explored, researchers noted when each of several hippocampal neurons fired. Each neuron was coded as a different color, and each dot of color means that the corresponding neuron fired when the rat was in that location. Thus, during the first session in the environment, one neuron (coded blue) fired when the rat was at the left end of the center arm; if the rat turned right, that neuron would stop firing and another (coded green) began to fire. (c) When the same rat was returned to the maze for another session, the pattern of place-dependent neuronal firing looked fairly similar to the previous day's pattern. (d) When an aged rat was placed in the maze, this rat's hippocampal neurons also fired when the rat was in specific spatial locations. (e) But when the rat was returned to the maze on another day, the firing pattern changed dramatically. This suggests that spatial learning from the first day does not persist in the aged rat. (b–e) adapted from Barnes et al., 1997.

as blue in Figure 12.12b) fired when the rat was near the western end of the center arm. If the rat turned the corner to the right, that neuron would stop firing, and another neuron (coded green in Figure 12.12b) would start firing. In this way, just by knowing which neuron was firing at a given moment, the experimenters (and presumably the rat) could deduce the rat's location in the maze.

When this same young rat was returned to the maze later, for a second session, the same hippocampal neurons tended to fire in the same spatial locations as before (Figure 12.12c). For example, the same neuron (coded blue) that had fired when the rat was in the left end of the center arm during session 1 also fired when the rat was in that location during session 2. This consistency of spatial encoding across sessions helps the rat form a reliable mental map of its environment. Obviously, the ability to learn and recognize the environment is a key part of learning and remembering how to navigate around that environment.

Figure 12.12d shows a similar mental map generated by the hippocampal neurons of an older rat on its first session in the 8-shaped maze. It looks a bit different from the session 1 map of the young rat, since each individual rat has its own way of encoding space. But when the older rat was returned to the maze for session 2 (Figure 12.12e), the neurons did not always fire in the same place as before. For example, the neuron (coded blue) that originally fired when the aged rat was in the middle of the maze now fired when the rat was in the top half of the left-hand arm. This differs from the results for the young rat, whose neurons tended to fire in the same places in both sessions. Apparently, both the young rat and the old rat learned about the environment during session 1, but the old rat lost this information much faster than the young rat. One reason this could happen is that LTP in the old rat's hippocampal neurons was unstable, and didn't last over the interval between session 1 and session 2. This instability of hippocampal LTP could contribute to age-related deficits in spatial learning, as well as in other kinds of learning and memory that depend on the hippocampus, such as episodic memory, which requires remembering the context in which an event occurred.

New Neurons for Old Brains? Adult Neurogenesis

The news isn't all bad. Yes, the aging brain may lose neurons and synapses, and LTP may become unstable. But the brain itself may contain some mechanisms to fight this decline, including the ability to grow new neurons. Once, it was thought that animals, particularly humans, were born with all the neurons they'd ever have. But we now know that neurogenesis occurs throughout life, although much less prolifically in the adult brain than in the developing brain.

Adult neurogenesis was first reliably observed in birds. Earlier, in this chapter you read how male white-crowned sparrows learn their song during a sensitive period early in life. In contrast, canaries are "lifelong" learners who can alter their song from year to year. Canary song is especially important during the spring, when males sing to defend their territory and attract mates. This seasonal variation in singing is mirrored in the canaries' brains: one brain area, called the *high vocal center*, or *HVC*, doubles in volume during the spring relative to its size in the fall (see Ball & Hulse, 1998). What could be causing this increase?

To investigate this seasonal variation, Fernando Nottebohm and his colleagues injected radioactive *thymidine* into adult canaries. Thymidine is a compound that is taken up by cells undergoing mitotic division, and so it can be used as a marker for newly born cells. The researchers found traces of thymidine in the birds' HVC, as well as in the forebrain (Goldman & Nottebohm, 1983), suggesting that new neurons were either being born in these brain areas in the adult bird or migrating there soon after being formed. Further, Nottebohm and his colleagues were able to demonstrate that these newly generated cells developed into functional neurons: making connections with existing neurons, and generally appearing anatomically and physiologically indistinguishable from older cells (Paton & Nottebohm, 1984; Burd & Nottebohm, 1985). Similar adult neurogenesis has since also been confirmed in fish, amphibians, and reptiles (Zupanc, 2001).

But what about mammals? In the 1990s, Elizabeth Gould and colleagues injected adult macaque monkeys with a synthetic form of thymidine called *BrdU* (short for bromodeoxyuridine). One to three weeks later, the researchers found areas in prefrontal, inferior temporal, and parietal cortices containing traces of BrdU, suggesting the presence of neurons that had been born in the last few weeks (Gould, Reeves, Graziano, & Gross, 1999). Around the same time, Swedish neuroscientist Peter Eriksson gave BrdU to human cancer patients, in an attempt to quantify the progress of their disease by tagging proliferating cancer cells (Eriksson et al., 1998). Unexpectedly, the BrdU labeled not only cancer cells but also neurons in the basal ganglia and in the hippocampus. Neurogenesis has also been observed in the hippocampus of adult rats (Kuhn, Dickinson-Anson, & Gage, 1996) and monkeys (Kornak & Rakic, 1999).

It would be nice to think that these new neurons can replace old ones that die off in the normal course of aging or even as a result of injury. But it is a long leap from the existing evidence to that conclusion. To date, neurogenesis in the adult primate brain has only been documented unambiguously in a few brain regions, including the hippocampus and the basal ganglia (Eriksson, 2003; Lie, Song, Colamarino, Ming, & Gage, 2004). A few studies have reported evidence of large-scale neurogenesis in the cerebral cortex of adult monkeys (Gould et al., 1999) and human children (Shankle et al., 1998), but other researchers have challenged the methodology of those studies (e.g., Korr & Schmitz, 1999; Nowakowski & Hayes, 2000; Rakic, 2002).

Worse, the vast majority of newly born neurons appear to die off within a few weeks after formation (Gould & Gross, 2000). In one study, researchers damaged the basal ganglia in rats and then watched for neurogenesis. The number of newly born neurons that survived longer than two weeks was less than one one-hundredth of the number of neurons that had died—meaning there probably

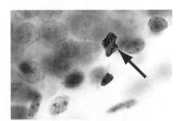

Neurogenesis in the brain of an adult monkey This radiograph shows a cell labeled with BrdU (arrow) in the dentate gyrus, a subregion of the hippocampus. The cell appears to be in anaphase, the phase of cell division in which chromosomes have begun to separate into two nuclei but the cell body itself is not yet divided in two. Adapted from Gould & Gross, 2000.

weren't enough new cells to make up for the function of the cells that had been damaged (Lie et al., 2004). And even those neurons that do survive may not become functional in the sense of forming viable connections with other neurons.

In sum, so far there's little evidence that adult neurogenesis in mammals is widespread enough—or that the new neurons last long enough—to serve as a general mechanism providing new brain power. The fact that adult mammals generally can't "regrow" cortical tissue following brain damage suggests that widespread replacement of dead neurons does not occur in mammalian brains (Eriksson, 2003). Neurogenesis in adult mammals may be limited to a few cells in a few brain regions (Kempermann, Wiskott, & Gage, 2004). Apparently, in most regions of the human brain, the benefits of new neurons are outweighed by the difficulties of integrating new neurons into old networks without disrupting existing memories.

Interim Summary

Genes strongly influence learning and memory abilities, although they do not fully account for all variation between individuals; environment also plays an important role. In the developing brain, neurons and synapses are first overproduced, then weeded out in a process similar to Darwinian natural selection: those that make functional connections (and presumably encode important information) survive, while others die off. Growth and pruning occur at different rates in different brain areas, perhaps helping to explain why some learning and memory abilities mature faster than others. Sensitive periods in learning reflect sensitive periods in neuronal development when specific kinds of environmental input can quickly and easily alter brain organization.

Gender differences in learning and memory may reflect the effects of sex hormones on the developing brain, and also on the activity of the adult brain. In the aging brain, some brain areas may lose appreciable numbers of neurons and synapses; changes due to neuronal plasticity (LTP) may also become less stable, meaning that new learning may not survive for long. Adult brains can grow new neurons, but many of these new neurons may die off before becoming functional.

12.3 Clinical Perspectives

Finally, let's consider two of the many ways in which learning and memory can be impaired at different points in the lifespan. Down syndrome strikes individuals at the beginning of their life, resulting in a lifelong impairment in learning ability and other aspects of intellectual function. At the other end of the lifespan, Alzheimer's disease strikes mainly elderly individuals, resulting in a gradual loss of memory and an intellectual decline. As different as these two syndromes may appear, it turns out that there is an intriguing genetic connection between them.

Down Syndrome

Mental retardation is defined as below-normal intellectual function that begins during early development (as opposed to loss of intellectual function that occurs later in life, for example, due to a head injury or stroke). **Down syndrome** is a congenital form of mental retardation that occurs in about 1 of 600 live births (Pennington, Moon, Edgin, Stedron, & Nadel, 2003). Children with Down syndrome show retarded development of speech and language. By adulthood, they usually score in the moderately-to-severely-retarded range on IQ tests (IQ = 25 − 55), although a few have IQs in the normal range (Pennington et al., 2003). Down syndrome occurs throughout the world and affects both genders equally. In addition to retarded intellectual development, individuals with Down syndrome have a characteristic facial appearance that includes slanted eyes and a flattened skull and nose.

Down syndrome was first described by English physician John Langton Down in the mid-1800s (Down, 1866), but its genetic basis wasn't discovered until a century later (LeJeune, Gautier, & Turpin, 1959). In Figure 12.4b (on page 475), you saw that healthy human beings carry 23 pairs of chromosomes in almost every cell of the body. In preparation for sexual reproduction, the pairs split, so that each sex cell (sperm or egg) contains one chromosome from each pair. When the egg and sperm join into an embryo, chromosomes from each parent combine to create a new set of 23 pairs. Down syndrome nearly always involves a genetic accident in which one parent's chromosome 21 fails to split properly. This means that the embryo has an extra copy of chromosome 21, a condition called **trisomy 21.** In 5 to 10% of cases, the genetic accident occurs in the father, but the bulk of cases originate with the mother, a risk that rises dramatically with maternal age. The likelihood of giving birth to a child with Down syndrome is approximately 1 in 2,000 for a 20-year-old mother, but 1 in 1,000 for a 30-year-old and 1 in 30 for a 45-year-old.

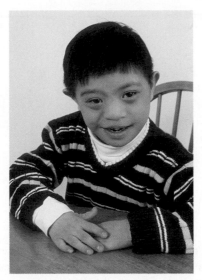

Children with Down syndrome
These children have a characteristic facial profile, including a flattened nose and folds of skin over the inner corner of the eyes. Down syndrome affects both genders equally and occurs throughout the world.

Brain Abnormalities and Memory Impairments

Chromosome 21 contains approximately 225 genes. At present, researchers don't know exactly which of those genes underlie the mental retardation in Down syndrome; currently, a half-dozen candidate genes have been identified, and any or all of these may contribute (see Crnic & Pennington, 2000). We do know that the brains of individuals with Down syndrome appear normal at birth, but as early as the first six months of life, their brains are visibly smaller than those of other same-aged children (Nadel, 2003).

There is some corresponding evidence that learning and memory may be normal (or nearly normal) very early in life for children with Down syndrome but decline later, as brain abnormalities emerge. For example, remember the conditioning procedure, described earlier in this chapter, in which infants kick their legs to obtain the reinforcement of a moving mobile? Three-month-old infants with Down syndrome can learn and remember this task as well as same-aged controls (Ohr & Fagan, 1991). But by 6 months, the infants with Down syndrome are impaired relative to controls (Ohr & Fagan, 1994).

By adolescence, several key brain areas are particularly small in individuals with Down syndrome; these include the hippocampus, frontal cortex, and cerebellum (Jernigan, Bellugi, Sowell, Doherty, & Hesselink, 1993). As a result, we might expect to see particular impairments in memory tasks that depend on these brain areas. To some extent, this seems to be the case. For example, one study considered a group of young adults with Down syndrome (mean age 21 years); on standard intelligence tests, these individuals were found to have an intelligence level slightly above that of 5-year-old children with normal mental abilities (Figure 12.13a; Vicari, Bellucci, & Carlesimo, 2000). But on a hippocampal-dependent task—recalling words from a studied list—the adults with Down syndrome performed significantly worse than the 5-year-olds (Figure 12.13b).

Figure 12.13 Impairments in Down syndrome may be particularly severe for hippocampal-dependent learning (a) A group of young adults (average age 21 years) with Down syndrome was given a series of intelligence tests and found to have an intelligence level comparable to that of 5-year-olds with normal mental abilities. (b) However, on hippocampal-dependent tests, such as recalling words from a studied list, the adults with Down syndrome performed much worse than the 5-year-olds. Data from Vicari, Bellucci, & Carlesimo, 2000).

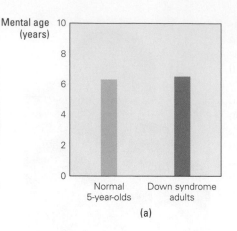

(a)

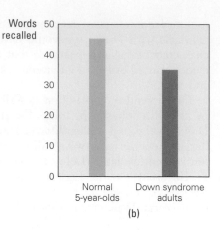

(b)

By the same token, children with Down syndrome are greatly impaired at recalling recent episodic events, such as what they had for breakfast or what time they went to bed last night (Pennington et al., 2003). In other words, although Down syndrome represents a general mental retardation, the impairments in Down syndrome are particularly profound for memory abilities that depend on the hippocampus (Nadel, 1999, 2003).

Animal Models of Down Syndrome

Since we know that trisomy 21 underlies Down syndrome, researchers have worked to develop animal models with the same genetic abnormality. In mice, for instance, a large region of chromosome 16 appears to serve the same functions as a region on human chromosome 21. Mice born with trisomy 16 (a third copy of their 16th chromosome) generally do not survive birth. (Down syndrome is also a common cause of miscarriage in humans.) So, researchers have bred mice with trisomy of only a segment of chromosome 16 (a condition called *segmental trisomy*). A widely studied example of these mouse strains is called the Ts65Dn mouse (Davisson et al., 1993).

Ts65Dn mice can be compared against littermates who share most of the same genes and environment, but who do not have the trisomy. Compared to the control littermates, Ts65Dn mice have irregularities in the hippocampus and cerebellum, just like humans with Down syndrome. The Ts65Dn mice also show memory deficits reminiscent of the memory deficits in humans with Down syndrome. For example, Ts65Dn mice show deficits on hippocampal-dependent tasks, such as remembering the goal location in a maze (Escorihuela et al., 1995).

One intriguing study has shown that being housed in an enriched environment improves spatial memory in Ts65Dn females (though they are never quite as good as littermate controls). But being housed in the enriched environment actually exacerbates the spatial memory impairment in Ts65Dn males (Martínez-Cué et al., 2002). This gender difference is curious, but the overall result is encouraging because it suggests that appropriately enriched postnatal experiences might help remediate the memory deficits associated with Down syndrome in humans.

Alzheimer's Disease

In 1901, German neuropathologist Alois Alzheimer examined a 51-year-old woman named Auguste Deter who could no longer remember her own last name or her husband's name. When Auguste died five years later, Alzheimer examined her brain and found curious abnormalities, including neurons that were bunched up like knotted ropes. Thinking Auguste was a unique case study, Alzheimer published a report on his findings (Alzheimer, 1907). The condition became known as **Alzheimer's disease,** a form of progressive cognitive decline due to accumulating brain pathology.

Initially, Alzheimer's report raised little interest; at a time when life expectancy was about 50 years, conditions that selectively affected older people appeared to be rare. Now we know that Alzheimer's disease is not rare at all. Recent U.S government figures estimate that 4.5 million Americans have Alzheimer's disease, including as many as 50% of people over age 85. The disease appears to have similar incidence throughout the world. Famous victims include boxing world champion Sugar Ray Robinson, film star Charlton Heston, and Ronald Reagan, who at age 89 no longer remembered having once been President of the United States.

Progressive Memory Loss and Cognitive Deterioration

For many patients, the earliest symptoms of Alzheimer's disease are episodic memory disruptions. Patients may fail to remember recent conversations or visitors, although other memory functions (including language and executive function) are more or less spared (Collie & Maruff, 2000). As the disease progresses, patients show marked declines in semantic memory, forgetting the names of acquaintances or their way around familiar locations like the local supermarket. Patients may ask the same question over and over again, forgetting not only the answer, but also the fact that they've asked the question before.

Among the memory processes that survive the longest in Alzheimer's patients are conditioning and skill memory. For example, many patients can execute well-learned skills (Rusted, Ratner, & Sheppard, 1995) and acquire new motor skills such as mirror tracing (Gabrieli, Corkin, Mickel, & Crowden, 1993) and rotary pursuit (Heindel, Salmon, Shults, Walicke, & Butters, 1989), even when they cannot remember verbal information for more than a few minutes. But by the late stages of the disease, memory fails completely, and other cognitive systems begin to fail too. Patients with late-stage Alzheimer's may display personality changes, disorientation, loss of judgment, confusion, loss of speech, and eventually an inability to perform daily activities like bathing, dressing, and eating. At this point, patients may require round-the-clock supervision and professional care.

Plaques and Tangles in the Brain

Technically, Alzheimer's disease is defined not by its behavioral symptoms, such as memory loss, but rather by the presence of two kinds of pathology in the brain: amyloid plaques and neurofibrillary tangles (Figure 12.14). **Amyloid plaques** are deposits of *beta-amyloid*, which is an abnormal by-product of a common protein (called amyloid precursor protein, or APP). In the brain of a patient with Alzheimer's disease, amyloid plaques accumulate and, for reasons that are not yet completely clear, these plaques are toxic to nearby neurons. One possible reason for this toxicity is that the body may recognize the plaques as foreign invaders and mount an immune system response that spirals out of control, damaging nearby neurons in its futile attempt to destroy the plaques (Davies, 2000).

The second hallmark of Alzheimer's disease in the brain is the presence of **neurofibrillary tangles,** the "knotted ropes" Alois Alzheimer described in his original report. Neurofibrillary tangles are the collapsed wreckage of proteins that normally function as scaffolding to hold a neuron in place and that help ferry nutrients around the cell (Figure 12.14b). Some researchers believe that the neurofibrillary tangles, rather than the amyloid plaques, hold the real key to understanding Alzheimer's disease (Johnson & Bailey, 2002).

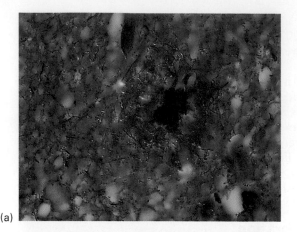

(a)

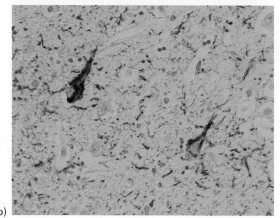

(b)

Figure 12.14 The hallmarks of Alzheimer's disease in the brain (a) An amyloid plaque (the dark spot in the center of the image), surrounded by a residue of degenerating cells. (b) Neurofibrillary tangles (seen as darkened areas) within neurons. (a) Cecil Fox/Science Source/Photo Researchers. (b) Adapted from Figure 3 of Hardy & Gwinn-Hardy, 1998.

As plaques and tangles accumulate in the brain, synapse loss and neuron death occur on a large scale. The damage is not uniform throughout: some brain areas are harder-hit than others. Amyloid plaques tend to be fairly evenly distributed throughout the cerebral cortex, with the hippocampus relatively spared. In contrast, neurofibrillary tangles accumulate first in the hippocampus and nearby areas. As a result, the hippocampus and nearby brain areas of patients with early Alzheimer's disease are smaller than normal, and this can be seen on structural MRI (de Leon, George, Stylopoulos, Smith, & Miller, 1989). In fact, such hippocampal shrinkage may provide an early-warning sign of Alzheimer's: elderly patients who show both hippocampal shrinkage and above-average forgetfulness are at statistically higher risk to develop Alzheimer's within the next few years than peers whose hippocampus appears normal (Convit et al., 2000; de Leon et al., 1993; Jack et al., 1999). This pattern of hippocampal damage with relative sparing of frontal lobes in early Alzheimer's is the opposite of "healthy" aging, which, as you read earlier, tends to involve shrinkage of the cerebral cortex with relatively little loss of neurons or synapses in the hippocampus (Braak & Braak, 1997; Price & Morris, 1999).

Since the hippocampus and nearby areas in the medial temporal lobe are critical for new memory formation, the fact that they are damaged early in the course of Alzheimer's is consistent with the fact that episodic and semantic memory impairments are among the earliest behavioral symptoms of Alzheimer's disease. Only later, as damage extends to the rest of the brain, do working memory, language skills, and judgment begin to decline too (Albert, 1996).

It's important to stress that a diagnosis of Alzheimer's disease is only verified if plaques and tangles are seen in the patient's brain. Currently, such verification is only made at autopsy, when a portion of the brain is removed and examined for these markers. For this reason, living patients with Alzheimer's symptoms can only be diagnosed as having "probable Alzheimer's," based on their behavioral symptoms as well as a range of other tests (possibly including MRI scans, PET scans, and tests of cerebrospinal fluid to check for unusually high levels of circulating beta amyloid). Even so, in as many as 10–20% of cases, the diagnosis of "probable Alzheimer's" turns out at autopsy to have been incorrect. There are literally dozens of other conditions that can mimic the cognitive decline of Alzheimer's—including vitamin B deficiency, hypothyroidism, and depression—some of which can be treated or even reversed. As a result, developing better diagnostic tests is an urgent part of the Alzheimer's research agenda. The other key task, of course, is to develop ways to treat, or even prevent, the disease (see Unsolved Mysteries: Treating [and Preventing] Alzheimer's Disease).

Genetic Basis of Alzheimer's Disease

To date, several genes have been implicated in Alzheimer's disease (see St George-Hyslop, 2000). Most progress has been made in understanding the genetic basis of a rare early-onset form of Alzheimer's. Early-onset Alzheimer's represents less than 1% of all cases of the disease, but it is especially heartbreaking because it can strike people as young as 35–50 years old. Mutations on three

▶ **Unsolved Mysteries**

Treating (and Preventing) Alzheimer's Disease

At the time of this writing, several drugs have been approved in the United States to treat mild Alzheimer's disease (AD). Most, including the widely-prescribed donepezil (brand name Aricept), are *cholinesterase inhibitors*. The neurotransmitter acetylcholine is depleted in the brains of patients with Alzheimer's; cholinesterase inhibitors work by inhibiting the normal breakdown of acetylcholine in the brain, so that the existing acetylcholine remains longer. These drugs help to treat the cognitive symptoms of Alzheimer's, like forgetfulness and anxiety, but they do not stop the accumulation of plaques and tangles; nor do they reverse existing neuronal damage. At some point, the disease progresses to the point where these drugs cease to be effective in remediating symptoms.

Another Alzheimer's drug, memantine (brand name Namenda), blocks glutamate receptors. Normally, glutamate is an important neurotransmitter for normal learning and memory. But, in Alzheimer's disease, neurons may overrespond to glutamate, leading to neuronal overactivity that can interfere with neuronal function and even cause neuronal death (Olney et al., 1997). It is hoped that, by blocking glutamate receptors, memantine may help protect neurons against this glutamate-mediated damage. Memantine has been shown to have some efficacy in slowing cognitive decline in patients with moderate-to-severe Alzheimer's (Reisberg et al., 2006). Many other drugs and treatments for Alzheimer's disease are under development, and by the time you read this, some may be on the market.

At the same time, there is great interest in understanding how to prevent people from developing Alzheimer's in the first place. Although many genes affect an individual's risk for developing Alzheimer's, environmental factors such as lifestyle and diet probably play an important role too.

For example, type-II diabetes greatly increases an individual's risk of developing Alzheimer's disease, possibly because the same enzyme that breaks down insulin also breaks down harmful beta-amyloid. In the early stages of diabetes, as the body becomes more resistant to insulin, more insulin is produced—and most of the enzyme might be occupied in breaking down the extra insulin, allowing beta-amyloid plaques to build up unchecked (Farris et al., 2003). As another example, individuals with high levels of LDL, or "bad" cholesterol, appear to be at increased risk for Alzheimer's, possibly because high levels of cholesterol may encourage the formation of beta-amyloid (Wollmer et al., 2003). A history of head injury, stroke, or high blood pressure also contributes to an individual's risk for Alzheimer's.

On the positive side, high levels of cognitive activity may help protect against Alzheimer's disease. There is accumulating evidence that older individuals who participate in stimulating pastimes—reading, playing chess or bridge, socializing—are less likely to experience cognitive decline than those who pursue less cognitively demanding pursuits such as watching television (Wilson & Bennett, 2003; Bennett et al., 2003). Individuals with high educational level and/or high occupational status are at lower risk of AD, and when such individuals do develop AD, they can often tolerate a greater degree of brain pathology before they begin to show clinical symptoms like forgetfulness (Scarmeas & Stern, 2004). In all these cases, the common theme is that mental activity protects against AD.

One possible interpretation of these findings is the idea of *cognitive reserve*. On average, cognitively-active individuals enter old age at a high level of cognitive function. If AD strikes, these individuals have further to decline before they would show sufficient loss of function to interfere with daily life (Stern et al., 1999; Scarmeas & Stern, 2004). A second, not exclusive, possibility is that cognitive activity actually combats AD. You read earlier in this chapter that environmental enrichment can lead to changes in the brains of adult animals, including growth of new neurons and connections. Similar changes in the brains of cognitively active people might help them compensate for the loss of neurons and connections that occur in early Alzheimer's (Wilson & Bennett, 2003).

So far, the studies linking cognitive activity with reduced Alzheimer's risk are *correlational studies*. As you read back in Chapter 1, just because two variables are correlated, we cannot simply conclude that one causes the other. It is indeed possible that mental exercise helps prevent Alzheimer's. But it is also possible that individuals in the earliest (presymptomatic) stages of Alzheimer's become less competent at mentally-challenging pursuits. In this case, cognitive inactivity is not a cause, but a symptom of the disease.

Further research will be needed before we understand how cognitive activity interacts with Alzheimer's risk—and before we can be sure that mental exercise truly protects against the disease. In the meantime, though, it is probably good advice to engage in activities that keep the mind active. A variety of pastimes that push you mentally might just help keep your brain fit—and even if they don't protect against Alzheimer's, they probably contribute to a more enjoyable and fulfilling life.

genes are associated with early-onset Alzheimer's: the APP gene on chromosome 21, the presenilin-1 (PS1) gene on chromosome 14, and the presenilin-2 (PS2) gene on chromosome 1. These genetic mutations are **autosomal dominant,** which means that a child who inherits just one of these mutated genes from either parent will inevitably develop Alzheimer's (unless she dies of something else first).

Another gene, APOE on chromosome 19, has been associated with the more common, late-onset form of Alzheimer's, which appears in individuals aged 60 or older. APOE comes in several alleles, three of which—called E2, E3, and E4—occur frequently in the general population. The E3 allele is the most common and is considered the "normal" allele. People carrying one copy of E3 and one copy of E4 (one allele inherited from each parent) are statistically at higher risk to develop Alzheimer's, and to develop it earlier in life, than people carrying two copies of E3. People carrying two copies of E4 are even more dramatically at risk. On the other hand, having one or two copies of the (rare) E2 allele reduces the risk of developing Alzheimer's.

At present, it's unclear why these alleles have such effects. Some studies suggest that E4 carriers have fewer dendritic spines in the hippocampus than E3 carriers do, but we don't know whether this is a cause or an effect of developing Alzheimer's disease (Teter & Finch, 2004). Another possibility is that the APOE gene may help control how the brain clears out beta-amyloid; some alleles (like E2) may perform this function well, but other alleles (like E4) may be less effective and allow plaques to build up, contributing to the brain pathology in Alzheimer's patients.

Another newly discovered gene, the GSTO1 or "Gusto" gene on chromosome 10, may also heighten the risk of late-onset Alzheimer's (Li et al., 2003). Gusto helps to regulate the brain's inflammatory response, mobilizing the immune system to fight off perceived invaders. You read above that one hypothesis of Alzheimer's disease proposes that the immune system regards amyloid plaques as foreign bodies, and attacks them, ferociously enough to damage nearby neurons. If so, an allele of Gusto that heightens the inflammatory system response wouldn't directly cause Alzheimer's disease, but it could increase the neuronal damage in individuals whose brains were already accumulating plaques.

Evidently, Alzheimer's disease is a multiple-gene disorder, meaning that many genes contribute. And these genes alone don't tell the whole story. Some individuals carrying two "good" copies of the APOE E2 allele still develop late-onset Alzheimer's, and some individuals carrying two "bad" copies of the APOE E4 allele never do. Possibly, there are additional genes whose role is waiting to be discovered (Pericak-Vance et al., 2000; Li et al., 2003). And probably, most of these genes only predispose a person to develop Alzheimer's, meaning that it takes additional environmental factors (such as exposure to toxins, poor vascular health, or brain inflammation) to actually trigger the disease. We still don't know.

A Connection between Down Syndrome and Alzheimer's Disease?

Did you notice a connection between the genes implicated in Down syndrome and Alzheimer's disease? Chromosome 21, the chromosome that is tripled in Down syndrome, also contains the APP gene, which is implicated in one form of Alzheimer's disease. This intriguing fact has led researchers to look for connections between Down syndrome and Alzheimer's. In fact, by about age 35 or 40, virtually all adults with Down syndrome develop plaques and tangles in their brains—just like Alzheimer's patients. And about half of adults with Down syndrome show memory decline and other symptoms similar to the cognitive impairments in Alzheimer's disease (Brugge et al., 1994; Cutler, Heston, Davies, Haxby, & Shapiro, 1985).

But the other half of adults with Down syndrome do not show age-related cognitive decline—even though they have the same brain pathology! As yet, it's not clear why this should be so. But the explanation might add to our understanding of both Alzheimer's disease and Down syndrome, and suggest some possible therapies to help prevent such brain pathology from causing memory decline.

CONCLUSION

At the beginning of this chapter, you met Denise, the quintessential "healthy young adult," at the peak of physical health and also of memory ability. Aside from appreciating her own memory abilities, how might Denise apply the lessons of this chapter next time she's home for the holidays?

First, let's think about Denise's young niece Kelly. At 10 months of age, many areas of Kelly's brain are still undergoing intensive neurogenesis, synaptogenesis, and myelination. Yet Kelly is already quite capable of habituation, conditioning, skill learning, and observational learning, and she can express this learning by action and imitation, if not yet by words. On the other hand, any episodic memories she forms now will probably not be accessible to her adult self. In addition, Kelly's frontal lobes are also not yet fully operational, which means she may have trouble juggling several pieces of information in memory at the same time. Kelly's environment is also affecting her brain development. Denise and the rest of the family can do Kelly a favor by trying to keep the child in surroundings, at home or in day care, where she is constantly stimulated and encouraged to explore and learn about the world around her.

Denise may also be able to apply learning and memory principles to her interactions with her grandparents. Although her grandmother seems to be handling old age well, Denise can expect there will be some deficiencies in the older woman's working memory and in her ability to form new episodic memories, and she can be understanding and supportive when her grandmother misplaces something or tells a favorite story for the tenth time. On the other hand, Denise should take advantage of her grandmother's fund of semantic and episodic knowledge while it's still available, perhaps encouraging the older woman to make a family cookbook or history to preserve these memories for future generations.

Denise's grandfather is a more difficult case. Instead of chalking his memory deficits up to old age, Denise should encourage the family to take him for a thorough neuropsychological exam, to determine whether his memory lapses reflect early Alzheimer's disease or whether they stem from some other condition that might be treatable. If the diagnosis is "probable Alzheimer's," then the sad fact is that Denise's family is in for a long struggle as they watch her grandfather slowly decline and become more dependent on a caregiver's assistance. Although there is currently no way to reverse or prevent the cognitive decline in Alzheimer's disease, the younger members of the family can hope that by the time they become grandparents themselves, better treatments will be available, increasing their chances of facing old age with their brains and memories intact.

Key Points

- Just about every kind of learning and memory observed in adults can also be observed in very young children. Some simple kinds of learning, such as habituation and recognition, can even be observed before birth. Other kinds of memory—particularly episodic memory and working memory—may be present at a very young age but do not fully mature until late childhood or adolescence.

- Development of learning and memory abilities at least partially reflects brain development. Temporal cortex and frontal cortex are among the last brain areas to fully mature, which may help explain why memory processes that depend on these areas are among the last to reach full adult potency.

- Sensitive periods (time windows early in life when certain kinds of learning advance most rapidly) may reflect times when external inputs can easily and profoundly alter brain connectivity; after a sensitive period, large-scale organization of the part of the brain in question may be fixed, and further learning (of the kind in question) may be limited to fine-tuning.

- Many kinds of learning and memory show some decline in healthy aging. Working memory is especially vulnerable, perhaps reflecting the fact that the frontal cortex shrinks in healthy aging. In many other memory domains—including skills, conditioning, episodic memory, and semantic memory—old, well-formed memories tend to survive well, but it may be harder to acquire new ones.

- The pattern of memory loss in healthy aging may reflect loss of neurons and synapses, as well as a decrease in the ability to maintain changes in synapse strength, meaning that newly encoded information may be lost.

- An individual's genes play a large role in determining learning and memory abilities, but enriched environment studies show that experiences can also have a profound impact on brain organization and on an individual's abilities.

- Before birth, the brain overproduces neurons and synapses; unnecessary neurons and synapses are then gradually eliminated.

- Sex hormones, like estrogen and testosterone, can influence performance leading to gender differences among adults in various kinds of learning and memory. But these sex hormones also influence the developing brain, leading to gender differences even in very young individuals.

- New neurons are produced throughout the lifespan; but particularly in humans, there is as yet little evidence that adult neurogenesis could provide large-scale replacement for damaged or aging neurons.

- Down syndrome is a condition in which babies are born with an extra copy of chromosome 21. Children with Down syndrome have cognitive impairments, including memory impairments; and certain brain areas, including the hippocampus, frontal cortex, and cerebellum, tend to be abnormally small.

- In Alzheimer's disease, plaques and tangles accumulate in the brain. Memory symptoms are prominent early in the disease, which is consistent with the finding that the hippocampus and nearby medial temporal areas suffer pathology early in the disease. Several genes have been identified that may contribute to an individual's risk for the common, late-onset form of the disease.

Key Terms

allele, p. 476
Alzheimer's disease, p. 493
amyloid plaques, p. 493
androgens, p. 484
apoptosis, p. 481
autosomal dominant, p. 496
base pair (of a DNA molecule), p. 474

chromosome, p. 474
critical period, p. 471
DNA, p. 474
Down syndrome, p. 490
elicited imitation, p. 467
enriched environment, p. 479
estrogen, p. 484

gene, p. 474
gestational age (GA) , p. 464
imprinting, p. 470
mutation, p. 476
neurofibrillary tangles, p. 493
neurogenesis, p. 480
sensitive period, p. 470

spines, p. 482
stem cells, p. 483
synaptogenesis, p. 481
testosterone, p. 484
trisomy 21, p. 491

Concept Check

1. Kelly is 10 months old and can already say a few words, such as "mama" and "juice." Kelly's older brother, Kyle, didn't speak until he was nearly 20 months old. What factors might have contributed to such a difference in healthy children?

2. A healthy 80-year-old businessman wants to continue working at his job, although he admits his memory isn't quite what it used to be. What are some habits he could develop that might help him play to his strengths and minimize memory lapses?

3. If one eye is blocked during an organism's sensitive period for vision, there may be no vision in that eye once the blindfold is removed. This sensitive period runs from three weeks to three months in cats, which are born blind, and from birth to a year or so in humans. Why might the sensitive period for visual development be different in different mammals?

4. Among tree lizards, some males are dominant and defend territories; others are nomadic foragers. Males given testosterone injections during the first 30 days of life are more likely to grow up to be dominant territory-holders, while similar injections have no effect on 60-day-old tree lizards or on adult nondominant males. Why might this be?

5. "Antagonistic pleiotropy" is a formal name for the idea that processes that are beneficial early in life (while an organism is still capable of reproducing) may have adverse consequences later in life. As long as the organism carrying a gene survives long enough to produce offspring, that gene can propagate through the population. How might this principle apply to the genes associated with Alzheimer's? Can you think of other examples from this chapter where processes that are beneficial early in life would be maladaptive if they continued into later life?

Answers to Test Your Knowledge

Learning and Memory in Old Age

1. This involves recalling an old episodic memory; recall of old, well-formed episodic memories tends *not* to decline much in healthy old age.

2. This involves working memory, and working memory *does* tend to decline with old age.

3. This involves performance of a well-learned skill, which tends *not* to decline with healthy aging.

4. This involves acquiring new semantic information, and acquisition of new semantic memories *does* tend to decline with old age.

5. This involves learning a new skill, and new skill learning *does* tend to decline with old age.

Further Reading

Brown, Bernard (1999). Optimizing expression of the common human genome for child development. *Current Directions in Psychological Science*, 8 (2): 37–41. • A general review of how genes and environmental factors interact during development, and ways in which we can modify environmental factors to "optimize" what's laid down in the genetic blueprint.

DeBaggio, Thomas (2003). *Losing my mind: An intimate look at life with Alzheimer's*. New York: Free Press. • A fascinating and sometimes harrowing memoir written by an ex-journalist who, at age 57, was diagnosed with early-onset Alzheimer's disease, and decided to keep a record of his thoughts and experiences.

Lorenz, Konrad (1952/2002). *King Solomon's ring: New light on animal ways*. New York: Routledge. Translated by Marjorie Kerr Wilson. • The "father of imprinting" shares his insights into animal behavior, based on personal experience in a home crowded with goslings, shrews, fish, dogs, and more.

McKhann, Guy, & Albert, Marilyn (2002). *Keep your brain alive*. New York: Wiley. • Two experts in the field of human aging provide information and suggestions for how to improve normal memory throughout the lifespan.

CHAPTER 13

Language Learning

Communication and Cognition

HELEN KELLER LOST HER SIGHT AND her hearing when she was only 19 months old. As a result, she showed no ability to speak or comprehend language as a young child. It was only after persistent demonstrations by a tutor named Anne Sullivan that Helen began to learn words in the form of manual gestures. Anne spelled out words by forming her hand into shapes, each associated with a different letter, and then pressing her hand into Helen's palm. Anne's hand spelling provided Helen with a model that Helen then replicated in Anne's palm. After years of practice, Helen Keller learned not only to understand gestural sentences but also to speak, read, and write. Ultimately, she wrote about a dozen books, traveled all over the world, and met twelve presidents!

Despite her handicaps, Helen Keller naturally developed the ability to run and play like other little girls. However, she did not spontaneously develop language skills. For that, she required instruction. Helen's brain had the capacity to learn and use language—in fact, as an adult she became a writer and lecturer—but Helen's language skills did not blossom until her teacher provided appropriate inputs. The inputs that taught language to Helen were different from those used by most children. Because she could not see or hear, she had to rely on the sense of touch, a sensory modality that is seldom associated with language learning.

Children learn to use language if appropriate inputs are provided, but their learning of language is not inevitable. Instead, human language learning is dependent on environmental conditions. Might this also be the case for other animals? Could other animals have a capacity for language learning that has not yet been discovered simply

Behavioral Processes
What Is Language?

Test Your Knowledge - Bird Song versus Human Language

Learning and Memory in Everyday Life - Teaching Babies Signs before Speech

Second Language Learning

Artificial Language Learning

Brain Substrates
Is There a Language Organ?

Unsolved Mysteries - Can Computers Master Human Language?

Cortical Coding of a Second Language

A Contemporary Model of Language Processing in the Brain

Clinical Perspectives
Sign Language

Language Learning in Isolation

Helen Keller as a child.

because they don't encounter appropriate environmental conditions? If other animals do not have this capacity, then what is it about human brains that enables us to learn language skills?

This chapter reviews what is known about how humans learn language and examines recent studies of similar capacities in other animals. The Behavioral Processes section considers such basic issues as (1) how people learn to recognize words and to use them to communicate information; (2) what makes learning additional languages different from learning a first language; and (3) what it is about language that is so difficult for other animals to learn. It also discusses some of the discoveries that researchers have made from observing how humans and other animals learn simpler "artificial" languages. (Note that this chapter focuses on language learning, not language performance. Consequently, much of what is known about the structure of language and about how adult humans use language is not included here.) In the Brain Substrates section, we identify regions of the brain that contribute to language processing and that change during language learning. The chapter also describes alternative communication systems that do not depend on the ability to speak or hear and that have revealed new clues about the nature of language learning.

13.1 Behavioral Processes

Like imitative learning (Chapter 11), language learning seems to be limited to a relatively small number of species, possibly only one. In fact, the ability to imitate may be a prerequisite for language learning, because early imitative abilities in children predict later language proficiency (Sigman & Ungerer, 1984; Stone, Ousley, & Littleford, 1997). For example, parents judge their children's early language skills based on how well the children mimic speech sounds that they have heard. Most words that children learn early on are acquired through observational learning. However, children also use words like "runned" and "mouses" that they probably have never heard in their environment, so language learning involves more than just copying. In fact, many of the sentences humans produce have never been produced before, suggesting that language skills are extremely flexible.

Language learning may be one of the most complex learning tasks faced by any species. Or, it may be one of the simplest. After all, if infants can do it, how hard could it be? Some theorists suggest that language is actually too complex to be learned by infants and that humans must therefore be genetically endowed with specialized language-processing mechanisms (Chomsky, 1965; Pinker, 1984). But, do infants really need specialized processors to learn language, or is a flexible ability to learn sufficient? If specialized language-processing centers are necessary, how specialized do they need to be? Might other animals have similar specializations? To begin to answer such questions, it is important to analyze the basic properties of language and consider different ways in which language might be learned.

What Is Language?

Language is a communication system for the social transmission of information. This system consists of words—stimuli that individually convey a meaning and consist of one or more morphemes, the smallest linguistic units of meaning. For example, the word "marbles" contains two morphemes: *marble* and *-s.* Words can be put together to make a sentence, a word or series of words that expresses a thought containing a subject and verb. The rules that dictate how words can be altered and combined to form sentences define, in part, the **grammar** of a language. For any organism to learn to use a language, it must be able to identify words, recognize the order of words, recognize abstract rules about word organization, and recognize categories of words. Understanding these language comprehension processes is fundamental to understanding how individuals learn language.

Language is often learned through speech perception, which requires that the learner recognize both sounds and sequences of sounds. Birds learning to communicate with sounds must also recognize sounds and sound sequences, and in fact, birds learning to sing progress through stages that are similar to those seen in children learning to speak (Brenowitz & Beecher, 2005; Doupe & Kuhl, 1999). These parallels suggest that at least some of the mechanisms underlying language learning are not unique to humans.

Identifying Words

Identifying spoken words is not as easy as you might think. Speech is essentially a continuous stream of sound; the task of recognizing where one word stops and another begins, called **word segmentation,** is not a trivial one. If you've ever listened to somebody speak a language that you didn't understand, then you probably know how difficult it can be to identify individual words. You can begin to get a sense of why it might be hard to segment words by examining Figure 13.1. This image is a graph made of someone saying "Where are the silences between words?" In graphs of this kind, silent intervals appear as flat lines. The graph of this sentence answers its own question: there are no silent intervals between most words. On the contrary, most of the lines indicating silence actually occur *within* words! So, even though it may seem to you that the words in normal speech are separated by silence, they usually are not.

One way that infants learn to identify words is by repeatedly hearing consistent patterns in the order of speech sounds (Saffran, Aslin, & Newport, 1996). For example, in English the syllable *hap-* precedes only a few other syllables, including *-py* (as in "happy"), and *-pen* (as in "happen"), to form a word. So, soon after an infant hears someone produce the syllable *hap-*, she will probably also hear the speaker produce one of these other predictable syllables. In contrast, there are many syllables that could follow the syllable *-py*, but only a few of these syllables combine with *-py* to form words (such as "peanut"). Over time, an infant that repeatedly hears phrases like "happy birthday," "happy baby," and "don't worry, be happy," will begin to recognize that *happy* is a word, but that *peebirth* and *peebay* are not (Saffran & Thiessen, 2003).

Both infants and adults are sensitive to such patterns, called **transitional probabilities,** the frequency with which one kind of syllable follows another. In one study, participants heard continuous sequences of syllables. Some of the syllables occurred repeatedly in combinations that created nonsense words. Afterward, researchers tested how well the participants recognized these nonsense

Figure 13.1 Continuity of sound within a spoken sentence The height of the vertical traces in this graph corresponds to the amplitude of the sounds being made. Silences produce flat horizontal traces. Note that the silences (highlighted by vertical lines) generally occur in the middle of a word rather than between words, proving that humans do not recognize words by detecting the silences between them.

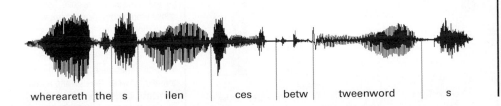

whereareth | the | s | ilen | ces | betw | tweenword | s

(a)

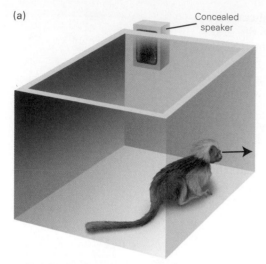

Concealed speaker

1. Playback initiated.

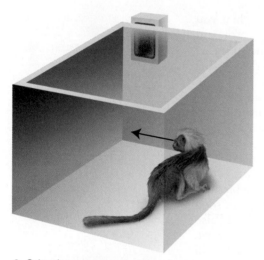

2. Orienting response begins.

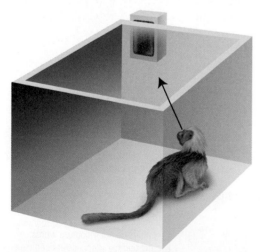

3. Orients back toward speaker.

words, in comparison with novel nonsense words that hadn't occurred in the sequences (Saffran et al., 1996). For example, if the listeners had repeatedly heard the syllable *–py* followed by *–po* (as in "peepo") within the stream of syllables, then this nonsense word would be more recognizable than the novel nonsense word "popee." Infants and adults rapidly learned to recognize combinations of speech sounds that had occurred frequently in a specific order, just by listening to the experimental sequences. This finding suggests that humans can learn to recognize spoken words without even trying. Infants and toddlers can learn words without knowing their meanings—indeed, without paying any attention to individual words.

The capacity to pick up on transitional probabilities in speech also helps humans learn other things besides language. For example, sounds within songs also occur in repeated sequences, and learning such sequences allows us to recognize musical tunes (Saffran, Johnson, Aslin, & Newport, 1999). Transitional probabilities are apparently recognized by other animals, too. For instance, monkeys can learn to recognize nonsense words simply by listening to recordings of speech (Hauser, Newport, & Aslin, 2001; Hauser, Weiss, & Marcus, 2002). In these experiments, cotton-top tamarins (a type of small monkey) heard the same recordings of speech as the human infants described above. One day later, the tamarins were placed inside individual sound-proof chambers (Figure 13.2a) containing a concealed speaker that broadcast both familiar nonsense words from the day before and novel nonsense words. Researchers monitored how often each tamarin looked toward the speaker as the words were played, and found that the tamarins were more likely to look toward the speaker after hearing a novel nonsense word (Figure 13.2b). You may recall from the chapter on habituation that organisms often produce an orienting response toward novel stimuli. The experiment therefore shows that the monkeys had learned to recognize the nonsense words of the first day. Given that monkeys do not learn language, it is unlikely that their ability to recognize words (as revealed in this experiment) is a specialized language-learning capacity (Hauser, Chomsky, & Fitch, 2002).

(b)

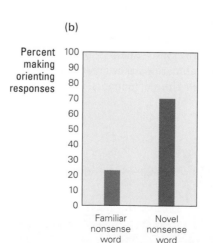

Percent making orienting responses

Figure 13.2 Nonsense-word recognition in cotton-top tamarins (a) Each tamarin was placed in a chamber in which sounds were broadcast over a concealed, computer-controlled speaker. This sequence shows a tamarin making an orienting response to the concealed speaker after a novel nonsense word is broadcast. Arrows show the direction the tamarin is facing. (b) The monkeys responded more to unfamiliar sound sequences, indicating that they could tell the difference between familiar and novel nonsense words. Adapted from Hauser, Newport, & Aslin, 2001.

Word segmentation and recognition might seem like simple processes, but audio engineers are still having difficulty developing speech-processing technologies that can reliably extract words from streams of speech. So, just because monkeys and infants can do it without even trying doesn't mean it's easy! Furthermore, as difficult as these processes are, language researchers suggest that sentence processing is far more difficult (Martin, 2003; McKoon & Ratcliff, 1998). There are a finite number of words in the vocabulary of any language, but an infinite variety of sentences can be created using those words. The average English-speaking college student in the United States has learned to recognize and understand about 100,000 words that can be combined in an infinite variety of sentences (Wingfield, 1993).

Although words are recognized based on their familiarity, sentences often contain unfamiliar sequences of words. To produce or comprehend a grammatically correct sentence, the speaker or listener must know the language's rules of word organization and must be able to extract meaning from words or combinations of words. The term **semantics** refers to the meaning or interpretation of words and sentences. For example, the spoken word "ball" may be interpreted as referring to a round object that bounces or to an event where people wear fancy clothes and dance, or as having various other definitions. Interpreting the word correctly, once it is recognized, requires semantic knowledge—knowing the possible meanings and deciding which one is intended in the particular context. For the purposes of language learning, a word is not considered to be fully identified unless its meaning is understood.

Stages of Language Learning

Language is learned in part through observation. It undoubtedly depends on innate capacities (as does all learning), but it does not develop independently of experience. The stages through which language develops in infants provide some insights into how it is learned. In particular, language learning appears to progress from an early stage in which infants recognize communication signals but do not produce them, to an intermediate stage in which infants produce the signals in a haphazard way, and then to a later stage in which infants produce signals that adults can interpret. These stages of language development are similar to the three phases of development in the template model of bird song learning that you read about in Chapter 11 (Doupe & Kuhl, 1999). Birds and humans both use complex sound sequences to communicate information.

In this section we will consider the development of these two communication systems, human language and bird song, in parallel. Surprisingly, more is known about how birds learn to sing than is known about how humans learn language. This is because it is extremely difficult, both technically and ethically, to conduct controlled experiments with infants and toddlers. The commonalities that have been found in the processes by which birds and humans learn to communicate can thus provide important clues about the underlying mechanisms of human language.

The first stage of learning that both baby songbirds and infants go through is a perceptual learning phase (Kuhl, 2004; Marler, 1970a). As we noted in the discussion of development in Chapter 12, there are specific times early in life, called *sensitive periods*, when certain kinds of learning are most effective. If baby songbirds do not hear adult birds singing during their sensitive period, they will never learn to sing normally (Marler, 1970b). Like bird song learning, human language learning also appears to have a sensitive period during which relevant sound sequences

Listening experiments have revealed that infants learn to recognize words long before they begin to speak.

Masterfile

are memorized and the capacity to discriminate experienced sounds improves. Specifically, infants improve at recognizing speech sounds, words, and phrases used in their native language. This sensitive period in humans ends by puberty (about age 12).

Evidence for a sensitive period for human language development comes from the famous and tragic case of Genie, a girl whose psychotic father kept her locked in an isolated room, chained to a potty chair, and who punished her if she made any noise (Curtiss, 1977). The California authorities found and rescued Genie in 1970, when she was 13 years old. Until that time, Genie had never been outside the room; she weighed only 59 pounds and could not straighten her arms or legs, nor control her bladder or bowels. She could not speak at all.

Over the next several years, physicians, psychologists, and social workers worked hard to undo the damage that had been done to Genie. Her health improved greatly, and her intelligence appeared to be in the low-normal range. But her language never developed beyond that of a 3- to 4-year-old. She learned to utter simple sentences ("want food"), but not much more. Apparently, Genie's lack of exposure to language during the first decade of life left her unable to acquire the complex grammar and vocabulary that characterizes normal adult speech (Curtiss, 1977). Similarly, her lack of social interactions during development greatly reduced her opportunities to observe how people use language.

Before infants and baby birds produce sequences of sounds like those used by adults, they both go through a second stage of learning during which they produce a wide variety of sounds, including sounds they have never heard (Kuhl & Meltzoff, 1982; Marler & Peters, 1982). In humans, this stage is called the **babbling stage;** the "babble" of baby songbirds is called **subsong.** Early babbling by deaf babies and by birds that have been deafened is similar in certain ways to babbling in hearing individuals (Marler & Sherman, 1983; Oller, Eilers, Bull, & Carney, 1985). However, babbling in deaf infants is noticeably delayed relative to that of hearing infants, and there are clear differences in the early sounds deaf infants make, suggesting that listening experiences affect sound production even at this early stage (Oller & Eilers, 1988).

During the final stage of song learning, young birds begin to produce songs comparable to the ones they heard as babies. Both singing birds and speaking humans need to be able to observe their own vocal output in order to reproduce what they hear and produce sequences of sounds that are familiar to adults. Songbirds deafened after the perceptual learning phase develop abnormal songs (Konishi, 1965; Nottebohm, 1968; Wilbrecht & Nottebohm, 2003). Similarly, deaf infants show abnormal production of early speech (Oller & Eilers, 1988). Even if speech or songs were memorized during earlier phases, an individual must practice while being able to hear oneself in order to learn to produce the sounds correctly (Konishi, 1965; Marler & Sherman, 1983). If children become deaf after the commencement of this stage but prior to puberty, speech production is not well maintained (Waldstein, 1990). Historically, the capacity to speak has been considered to be a critical aspect of language learning (which may be why the word "dumb" has come to mean, in different contexts, both "mute" and "stupid"). Today, however, the ability to speak is understood to be simply a perceptual-motor skill that builds upon previously learned language skills, meaning that individuals who never learn to speak may nevertheless be able to understand and use language quite fluently. For example, Helen Keller was writing books before she ever learned how to speak.

In summary, in both young birds and human infants, the perception and storage of sounds precedes the production of songs and speech, and for both species the development of these vocal communication systems is guided by auditory feedback. The early language skills of infants are much less sophisticated than those of adults, and may in fact be more similar to the communicative skills of songbirds and other animals.

When toddlers are about a 1½ years old, they begin using words in combinations to interact with other people and to describe the world around them. At first, their sentences are quite short and simple, like those you might see in a hurried text message. Nevertheless, from the very beginning toddlers produce sentences that seem sensible, saying things like "more juice" versus "juice more." Rules about how words should be ordered constitute the **syntax** of a language. Correct use and comprehension of syntactic structures within sentences is a cognitive skill—a mental ability that improves with practice (as discussed in Chapter 4, on skill memory). This cognitive ability depends on recognizing categories of words, such as nouns and verbs, and typical phrase structures. Learning to arrange words in certain orders may, in part, involve recognizing patterns in word sequences, just as recognizing words depends on learning patterns of syllables (Saffran & Wilson, 2003). At the same time, knowledge of syntax facilitates word identification by providing clues about what words are likely to occur in a given context. For example, if you are listening to someone speak, and they have just produced an adjective (for example, "rusty"), it is likely that the next word they produce will be a noun (for example, "knife") rather than a verb. In addition, because the phrase "rusty knife" is relatively common, it will be identified more easily than the phrase "rusty cupcake."

Rules about how sentences are used in conversations are the **pragmatics** of language. For example, a basic pragmatic rule is that statements should be intelligible by both speakers in a conversation. Another is that speakers should take turns rather than speaking simultaneously. When participants in a conversation break the rules, it can impede word identification. If three people are trying to talk to you at once, it will be very hard for you to identify the words each of

Test Your Knowledge

Bird Song versus Human Language

Although bird song learning shares some important similarities with human language learning, the two communication systems are very different in other respects. Identify which of the statements below accurately describe both bird song and spoken language.

1. Unique sound sequences are produced by individuals to convey specific meanings, and sounds produced in different orders have different meanings.

2. Individuals that grow up without the ability to hear will produce abnormal sound sequences.

3. Hearing sounds produced by others in the community is an important part of the learning process.

4. Individuals learn to use the sound sequences of other species if they grow up surrounded by individuals using those sounds.

5. Individuals memorize sound sequences that they hear in their environment before ever attempting to produce them.

6. Individuals seem to progress through a sensitive period during which learning is rapid; if learning does not occur in this sensitive period, it may never occur.

7. Early in development, individuals can produce many of the sounds they will need to use to communicate as adults, but they do not combine these sounds into coherent patterns or sequences that they can compare to adult sound sequences.

them is producing. Thus, politeness in conversation facilitates language processing. The syntactic and pragmatic features of conversational language suggest that learning the conventions of language, and to recognize the contexts in which certain rules apply, is an important aspect of learning to use language.

Learning Language through Observation

Do the stages of early language learning and birdsong learning sound like one of the other processes you've learned about in this textbook? In many ways, they are similar to the stages of learning proposed by social learning theory, which was presented in Chapter 11, on observational learning. In the earliest stage of language learning and song learning, the observer's attention is drawn to dynamic stimuli—in this case, sounds produced by other members of the observer's species. These early observations of sounds are then stored as memories that are used to guide later actions—the production of sounds that match those previously observed. These later actions occur when the observing bird or infant is motivated to reproduce the observed sounds.

Explicit reinforcement of observed sounds plays only a minor role in initial speech learning. This is especially true with regard to comprehension of language. Think about it. How exactly would you know if you were rewarding an infant's comprehension of speech? It is difficult to assess what an infant understands until she begins to speak, so you would be as likely to reward incorrectly processed language as you would be to reward correct interpretations.

Like the processes underlying observational learning, the mechanisms that enable humans to learn language remain unclear. Using language expertly requires perceptual-motor skills (such as those needed to produce fluent speech or gestures), cognitive skills (to construct meaningful word sequences), working memories of what has recently been said, and semantic memories about the meanings of specific words and the pragmatics of conversational engagement. Learning language seems to be an insurmountable task for most organisms, and yet humans can learn to use not only one language but several. The next section reviews what is known about how people learn to use multiple languages.

Second Language Learning

Understanding how individuals learn multiple languages is of great interest to both educators and scientists because of the difficulty people often have learning a second or third language. Intuitively, one might expect that learning a second language would be easier for an adult since adults already know what one language is all about and generally can learn things that infants cannot. It is thus something of a mystery why young children, given the chance, seem to easily acquire multiple languages, while literate adults may struggle to distinguish and produce the basic sounds and phrases of a foreign language.

Second language learning is acquisition of the ability to comprehend and produce a language in addition to one's first language. For teenagers and adults, learning a second language without some guidance or prolonged personal experience can be extremely difficult. For example, researchers spent centuries attempting to learn to understand Egyptian hieroglyphics but had little success until the Rosetta Stone was discovered (it contained a translation of Egyptian writing into Greek). Because unfamiliar languages are so difficult to decipher (and because it is relatively easy for a native speaker to detect a foreign accent in speech produced by someone who did not learn the language as a child), the U.S. Army recruited bilingual Navajo language speakers (called "code talkers") to transmit secret messages during wartime.

Historically, language learning has been treated as a single, monolithic process. B. F. Skinner, for example, attempted to explain language learning as a

▶ **Learning and Memory in Everyday Life**

Teaching Babies Signs before Speech

In the 2004 movie *Meet the Fokkers,* precocious Little Jack uses sign language to inform his grandfather that he'd like a snack, and then a nap, after which he'll probably need a diaper change. Just a Hollywood joke about overambitious parenting, right? Well, maybe not. Across America, parents are signing up for classes to learn how they can communicate with their infants using gestures. Based on parents' reports, children as young as 6–9 months can use gestures to communicate a desire for more food or for a bottle of milk (Acredolo & Goodwyn, 2002).

Anyone who's ever listened to a toddler whining or crying knows that from 10 to 24 months of age, children are highly motivated to communicate. Unfortunately, they may be months away from developing the fine motor coordination needed to voice the relevant words. But even though such infants haven't yet mastered spoken language, they can communicate by gestures. At about 10–12 months, children can reach toward an object to indicate that it is wanted, or hold an object upward to direct an adult's attention to it (Goodwyn, Acredolo, & Brown, 2000). A few months later, children master representational gestures, such as flapping their arms to represent "bird" or "flight," or spreading and unspreading the index and middle fingers to connote "scissors" or "cutting."

These gestures may appear well before the corresponding words do. In one study, infants acquired their first gesture at just under 12 months but their first spoken word at over 13 months (Goodwyn & Acredolo, 1993). The preponderance of gestures over spoken words persisted for a while, too: the children reached the "milestone" of a five-item vocabulary at about 13.5 months for gestures and 14.5 months for words.

A baby using sign language Amalia has learned to make a specific gesture to ask for more.

Eduardo Mercado

Many studies show a positive correlation between gesturing and verbal development: the more gestures children learn between 1 and 2 years of age, the larger are their verbal vocabularies at 2 and 3 years (Capone & McGregor, 2004; Goodwyn, Acredolo, & Brown, 2000). There is even some evidence that encouraging their use of gestures helps children learn to talk (Goodwyn, Acredolo, & Brown, 2000).

Why should communicating with gestures facilitate the development of verbal language? One possible reason is simply that infants learn verbal language more quickly if they are exposed to more vocalizations from their parents. A child who flaps his arms and points at a bird in a tree can elicit a parental response ("Yes! That's a birdie! There goes the birdie! Wave bye-bye!"). A child with 20 words and 20 gestures may be able to elicit such responses twice as often as a child with 20 words alone (Goodwyn, Acredolo, & Brown, 2000). And parents trained in communication with gestures may be especially responsive to their child's gestures.

A second possibility is that babies (like all creatures) learn best about the things they're interested in. A parent who labels a toy over and over is not going to have much success if the child is busily playing with something else. Communicating with gestures may allow the child to show the parent what the *child* is interested in, which then cues the parent to introduce language related to that interest (Goodwyn, Acredolo, & Brown, 2000).

A third possibility is that communicating with gestures provides a "scaffolding" for the development of verbal language (Goodwyn, Acredolo, & Brown, 2000). As in instrumental conditioning, the principle here is that the child learns an "easy" gesture that in turn provides insight into how useful communication can be. For example, a baby might learn that when she makes a certain gesture, her mother asks "More?" and then repeats a previous, desirable action (such as bouncing the baby or putting food on her plate). Over time the infant will become more likely to produce this gesture in contexts where the outcome will be rewarding (following Thorndike's Law of Effect). The infant's knowledge that her actions can produce desirable outcomes can, in turn, motivate the child to explore other ways to communicate, including spoken language.

For all these reasons, parents who help their children communicate with gestures may be encouraging language development. By the early school years, as speech blossoms, communication with gestures gradually dies out, until most children (like most adults) only use gestures to augment verbal language.

In the meantime, gestural language is a way for toddlers to communicate their needs when they do not have the ability to express themselves verbally. A child who can signal a need for food or a diaper change can get these needs met without crying. Goodwyn and her colleagues report an example in which a 14-month-old boy was able to use his "hot" gesture (blowing hard) to let his mother know when his bath water was too hot, while another toddler signaled "gentle" (petting the back of one hand) to complain that her parent was holding her legs too tightly during a diaper change (Goodwyn, Acredolo, & Brown, 2000). This isn't quite the sophistication of Hollywood's Little Jack, but it's still impressive for an infant who would otherwise be reduced to frustrated squalling to get her point across.

special case of instrumental conditioning that depended on social reinforcement and shaping, as described in Chapter 8, on instrumental conditioning (Skinner, 1957). A prominent linguist named Noam Chomsky argued strongly against this idea, describing language learning as an equally monolithic "filling-in-the-blanks" process in which the "blanks" are templates for syntactic structure and other basic features of language that are neurally predetermined (Chomsky, 1965). Interestingly, neither of these individuals ever conducted experimental studies of language learning by children. Instead, they based their arguments on logic and personal impressions. A major assumption underlying both of these ideas about language learning is that language is learned in a specific way. But, it's also possible that languages can be learned in multiple ways. For instance, adults learning a foreign language often make use of strategies that are unavailable to infants (such as formal coursework), and infants learning their first language may learn features of speech that are difficult, or even impossible for adults to master (such as how to produce native accents). Learning a second language can involve different mechanisms and different strategies depending on when, where, and how the second language is learned. It is not yet known why these factors make such a big difference, but studies of infants and apes are beginning to provide some clues.

Distinguishing Speech Sounds

Human languages typically contain about 25–40 speech sounds, but not all languages have the same sounds. Infants can distinguish and categorize speech sounds soon after birth. Other animals—including monkeys, birds, rats, and chinchillas—can discriminate and categorize speech sounds too (Kuhl & Miller, 1975; Kuhl & Padden, 1982; Toro, Trobalon, & Sebastian-Galles, 2005).

In general, children can learn a second language more easily, and approximate a native accent more precisely, than adults can (Newport, 1990). Adults who speak one language can distinguish the sounds differentiated in their own language but often cannot distinguish between pairs of similar sounds used in other languages. For example, /l/ and /r/ are differentiated in English but not in Japanese, so that although "ray" and "lay" are different words in English, monolingual Japanese adults often cannot distinguish them. On the other hand, monolingual English speakers can't hear the difference between two "p" sounds (a soft "p" and a sharp "p" with a burst of air) that are two separate speech sounds in the Thai language. In effect, /r/ and /l/ are part of the same sound category for Japanese speakers, while soft "p" and sharp "p" are part of the same sound category for English speakers.

Infants younger than 6–8 months old can distinguish all these sounds, even those that do not exist in their native language. Infants express this learning by turning their head appropriately to receive reinforcement after learning that only one of the sounds is accompanied by a reward, or by orienting when they perceive differences between speech sounds (Werker & Tees, 1984). Infants get better at distinguishing speech sounds from their native language as they age, but become less able to tell nonnative sounds apart (Kuhl, 2000; Kuhl et al., 1997). By about 11 months, babies can distinguish sounds from their own language only. This means that a 6-month-old "Japanese-speaking" baby will be able to distinguish /l/ and /r/, but an 11-month-old will not. Similarly, a 6-month-old "English-speaking" infant can distinguish Hindi syllables that sound alike to adult English speakers (see Figure 13.3), but this ability is lost by about 10–12 months (Werker & Tees, 1999).

Unlike infants, adults learning a second language can often generalize what they know of their native language to the new language. This background

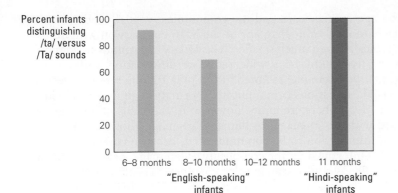

Percent infants distinguishing /ta/ versus /Ta/ sounds

"English-speaking" infants

"Hindi-speaking" infants

Figure 13.3 Decline in ability to distinguish nonnative language sounds At six months of age, "English-speaking" infants can easily distinguish sounds, like the Hindi /ta/ versus /Ta/, that are indistinguishable to monolingual English-speaking adults. By about 10–12 months of age, this ability is lost. Eleven-month-old "Hindi-speaking" infants can easily distinguish /ta/ from /Ta/. Adapted from Werker & Tees, 1984, 1999.

knowledge includes information about parts of speech, tenses, and the importance of word order. Such background knowledge facilitates the acquisition of vocabulary through memorization, and the understanding of grammatical structure, but it does not necessarily help an adult use a new language with proficiency. Like infants, adults can accelerate their learning of a second language through extensive listening experiences. This is one reason why six weeks of immersion in a foreign culture may facilitate second language learning more than several years of weekly language courses. For adults, learning a second language generally involves forming semantic memories as well as memories for perceptual-motor skills and cognitive skills that are needed to comprehend and produce novel sentences.

Animals Learning English

The role of observational learning in mastering multiple languages is highlighted by the abilities of a small number of animals that have learned to interpret English. Many pets have learned to respond appropriately to English commands such as "Stay!" and "Roll over!" This does not require the pet to learn English, however. To follow a trained command, the pet only needs to learn to associate a particular speech sound with some response. On the other hand, if you were able to tell your pet to do something that they had never done or seen done before, and they responded appropriately, this would be stronger evidence that your pet understands English, or at least some part of English.

Recent experimental studies revealed that a bonobo (a close relative of chimpanzees) named Kanzi learned to interpret the English words spoken by his caretakers (Savage-Rumbaugh et al., 1993). Kanzi was tested on his comprehension of English by being asked to perform novel actions with objects, and to point to objects that he heard named through headphones. Kanzi was not explicitly taught English, but he could follow novel instructions like "Put the pine cone in the freezer" and "Give the doggie some carrots." Kanzi's performance in these tests was comparable to that of a 2- or 3-year-old child (Savage-Rumbaugh et al., 1993). Kanzi also learned to associate new names with unfamiliar objects simply by watching humans use those names to describe the objects (Lyn & Savage-Rumbaugh, 2000).

A key aspect of Kanzi's learning of English words appears to be his early exposure to the use of language in social situations. It is worth noting, however, that several infant chimpanzees raised in similar situations failed to learn English. Thus, Kanzi's ability to learn to interpret human speech likely arose not only from his observations but also from the intrinsic abilities of his brain to encode and manipulate his memories of those observations.

Many nonhuman species learn and use communicative skills, but your own use of language is more flexible than any of them. In comparison with humans, other animals typically use a much smaller "vocabulary" of sounds to communicate. Animals can communicate a wide range of information without using sound or language. For example, as noted in Chapter 10, on emotional learning and memory, facial expressions communicate information about an individual's reaction to a situation. There are limits, however, to the kinds of messages that can be conveyed without language. In humans, language allows an almost unlimited range of information to be communicated, because languages are very complex systems. Unfortunately, the complexity of language makes it difficult to study experimentally. As you've seen in prior chapters, to deal with difficult topics of study, scientists develop simpler tasks containing a small number of the basic features found in the real world situation. In language studies, scientists have developed simpler artificial languages that possess some of the main features of real languages (words, syntax, and semantics). Artificial languages have allowed researchers to examine language learning in adults, children, and other animals.

Artificial Language Learning

Artificial languages consist of words (or symbols that function as words), along with rules for organizing them, and often alphabets for writing them, that exhibit one or more features of natural languages. These languages have extensive vocabularies, as well as rules of grammar and pronunciation, similar to a natural human language. As a result, the learning of artificial languages may involve mechanisms similar to those used to learn natural languages. Interestingly, not all artificial languages have been developed for scientific purposes. For example, Marc Okrand created the Klingon language to be used by an alien race in *Star Trek* movies, and as a hobby J.R.R. Tolkien developed the Elvish language used in his epic trilogy of novels, *The Lord of the Rings*. On a larger scale, Ludovic Zamenhof in the nineteenth century constructed a simplified international language called Esperanto, in the hope of promoting international understanding. Some estimates put the current number of speakers worldwide in the millions.

Artificial languages used as entertainment J. R. R. Tolkien developed this Elvish language as a hobby and used it in his literary epic *The Lord of the Rings*. Artificial languages such as this one consist of words (or symbols that function as words) and rules for organizing them that are comparable to those seen in natural languages.

In the laboratory, scientists use much simpler artificial languages. The words in these languages typically consist of initially meaningless images, sounds, or gestures. Each language has its own grammatical rules that dictate the order in which these words should occur. Psychologists use these languages to test hypotheses about how language is learned, identify constraints on what is learnable, and determine what features of language require specialized linguistic processing. (Braine, 1963; Epser, 1925; Reber, 1967).

Instructing Dolphins with Gestures

Artificial languages have been used to investigate the linguistic capacities of animals other than humans. For example, Akeakamai, the dolphin you were introduced to in Chapter 11, on observational learning, was one of the first dolphins to learn a simple artificial language based on gestural symbols, called a **gestural language** (Herman, Richards, & Wolz, 1984). Dynamic hand and arm movements served as symbols that Akeakamai learned to associate with objects, actions, and locations (see Figure 13.4). Akeakamai demonstrated her ability to understand sequences of symbols through the actions she performed. Specifically, she learned that sequences like *surfboard fetch* meant that she would be rewarded if she found a surfboard and brought it to the person making the gestures.

Researchers incorporated rules of syntax into the artificial language, so that when the same small set of gestures are produced in different orders, they convey different meanings. For example, *ball hoop fetch* meant that a hoop should be carried over to a ball, whereas *hoop ball fetch* meant that a ball should be carried over to a hoop. The sequence *left window right ball fetch* provided Akeakamai with precise instructions about which object should be moved to which location.

Using this simple artificial gestural language, Louis Herman and colleagues demonstrated that dolphins could learn both semantic information and syntactic rules. Akeakamai correctly interpreted new sequences consisting of familiar gestures, and even sequences that incorporated new words. Akeakamai did not learn the language from her parents. She learned this communicative system from human teachers who rewarded her with fish, vocal praise, and social interaction whenever she interpreted instructions correctly. Furthermore, like all artificial languages, the gestural language that Akeakamai learned included only a subset of the features of a natural language. For example, this gestural language did not include articles like "the," or past and future tenses.

Learning Syllabic Sequences

Researchers conducted artificial language experiments with Akeakamai to determine whether animals other than primates can learn to process both semantic and syntactic information within sentences. In contrast, artificial language studies with humans focus on identifying what infants can learn about language without explicit training. We noted above, for instance that infants naturally learn to extract words from sentences based on predictable sequences of syllables.

As with Akeakamai, researchers judge whether an infant has learned an artificial language by looking for behavioral evidence that the infant recognizes predictably ordered speech sounds. For example, the infant may show more surprise (indicated by an orienting response) when novel sequences of syllables are presented. Infants do not learn to produce the sound sequences within an artificial language (some are so young they can't speak at all), but their behavior reveals what they have learned. Unlike Akeakamai, however, the infants are not rewarded for their actions. Thus, the infants learn these sequences of syllables in a way that is more natural than the method used for teaching Akeakamai. Even so, what the infants actually learn from such artificial languages is different from natural language learning, because all the sequences are meaningless. The overall situation is similar to what it would be like for an infant attempting to learn language from observing its mother talking on the phone.

What exactly have artificial language learning studies revealed? For one thing, most researchers agree that artificial language experiments are useful for identifying basic mechanisms that individuals bring to bear when learning to process language. For example, studies with artificial languages show that infants can learn how words are grammatically ordered by listening to sequences of nonsense words organized using artificial grammars (Gomez & Gerken, 1999). Artificial grammars are a type of artificial language in which rules define the order of nonsense words. Even when infants were exposed to new sequences of nonsense words, they discriminated grammatical sequences from ungrammatical sequences, showing that they generalized the rules of the artificial

(a)

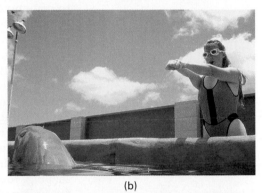

(b)

(c)

Figure 13.4 Gestures from Akeakamai's artificial language
A human trainer at tankside produces a specific sequence of arm movements to instruct a dolphin to perform particular actions involving specified objects and locations. The opaque goggles prevent the trainer from observing the dolphin's actions and inadvertently guiding the dolphin's responses. This particular sequence—in which the trainer signs (a) "pay attention," (b) "surfboard," and (c) "over"—instructs Akeakamai to "jump over the surfboard."

grammar to novel sequences (Gomez & Gerken, 1999; Marcus, Vijayan, Bandi Rao, & Vishton, 1999). Like Akeakamai, infants generalized from their experiences with grammatical sequences of familiar words to grammatical sequences of unfamiliar words. These studies demonstrate that both dolphins and infants can learn to recognize syntactic structures within series of gestures or sounds respectively.

Communicating with Apes

Artificial language experiments are also useful for determining what features of language might require specialized linguistic processing versus what features can be learned through more general learning mechanisms. For example, researchers have used artificial languages to study whether chimpanzees can learn to communicate with humans (and vice versa) using symbols. David Premack, whom you first met in Chapter 8, on instrumental conditioning, trained a chimpanzee named Sarah to use plastic objects that varied in shape and color as words (Premack, 1971, 1976). Like Akeakamai, Sarah was taught that different symbols corresponded to different actions, objects, and locations. For example, Sarah learned to place colored plastic tokens of different shapes on a magnetic board in sequences that conveyed instructions, such as *nose touch*. In addition, Sarah learned shapes that corresponded to qualities, such as color, and even shapes that referred to relationships between objects, such as *same*.

Initial attempts to teach Sarah to communicate with these symbols involved modeling their use, but eventually the prevalent teaching methods used were shaping, reward-based training, and active instruction. For example, a trainer might initially let Sarah take a piece of apple after the chimp had placed the *apple* token on the board. Once Sarah mastered this task, the trainer might subsequently require her to place both the *take* token and the *apple* token before allowing her to take the apple (this is an example of shaping). Sarah placed tokens in grammatically specified positions that served as a spatial syntax for the shape-based artificial language. Sarah was even able to use the symbols to answer questions about objects. Findings from these studies suggest that Sarah learned the rules of the artificial language and was able to use tokens to socially transmit information in a flexible way.

After the experiments with Sarah, several other chimpanzees were trained to use artificial languages based on visual symbols (Matsuzawa, 2003; Rumbaugh, 1977). These studies used complex visual patterns, called **lexigrams,** rather than simple shapes to represent words (see Figure 13.5). Researchers taught chimpanzees to point to lexigrams to solve problems, to make requests, and to communicate with each other (Rumbaugh & Washburn, 2003; Savage-Rumbaugh, 1986). Chimpanzees also learned to use lexigrams to categorize objects, photos, and other lexigrams. Two chimpanzees, Sherman and Austin, learned to use a *food* lexigram to classify edible items, each of which had its own individual lexigram (Savage-Rumbaugh, Rumbaugh, Smith, & Lawson, 1980). For example, Sherman could label apples with one lexigram and bananas with another, but could also label both with the *food* lexigram.

It is important to note that the fact that chimpanzees can learn to use symbols appropriately in these tasks does not mean the chimpanzees understand the symbols' meaning (Sebeok & Rosenthal, 1981; Seidenberg & Petitto, 1987; Terrace, Petitto, Sanders, & Bever, 1979). Nor does it mean the chimpanzees know that the humans observing them are interpreting their use of symbols as instructions and statements.

Artificial language training with chimpanzees has mainly consisted of active instruction and shaping with rewards to encourage performance. Recently, however, several bonobos, including Kanzi, learned to use an artificial language by observation (Savage-Rumbaugh & Lewin, 1994; Savage-Rumbaugh et al., 1993). Recall that Kanzi learned to comprehend simple English sentences from observing his caretakers. Similarly, Kanzi was the first bonobo to learn an artificial language by observing others, and he did it while he was still quite young by watching as researchers attempted to teach his mother to use lexigrams. Kanzi's mother never really learned the artificial language, despite being the focus of the teaching effort, whereas Kanzi rapidly learned it as a bystander. This difference in acquisition highlights the role that developmental stage, motivation, and social interactions can play in observational learning. Kanzi's model was his mother; what better model can a young chimpanzee have? Kanzi did not learn simply by imitating his mother, however, because his abilities surpassed his mother's. It seems more likely that he learned by emulating his mother's goals of interacting with humans using lexigrams.

These and other studies have helped to establish that specialized mechanisms are not necessary to learn certain features of natural language. For example, the experiments with apes and dolphins show that nonhumans can learn to use symbols that represent things in the world and can also learn that differently ordered sequences of symbols have different meanings. Experiments with infants show that they can learn to recognize structure within sentences independently of any semantic understanding. Similarly, artificial language studies with chimpanzees have shown that chimpanzees can learn to produce language-like sequences, although it is not known whether the chimps comprehend the meaning associated with those sequences.

Nevertheless, there are many researchers who are skeptical that any animals other than humans are truly able to learn language. They argue that artificial language learning is just that: artificial and contrived. It is certainly true that no animal other than humans naturally uses a communication system with all the features of human language, and it is true that no one has produced an animal with language skills comparable to those of an adult human. It is also true, however, that no Middle Eastern culture has developed a game with all the features of basketball and that no Asian country has ever produced a basketball team that would be competitive in the NBA. This does not imply either that Americans are born with a unique capacity to learn basketball skills or that people from the Middle East cannot become highly competitive basketball players. In a similar vein, it is a mistake to conclude that only humans can learn language, simply because no other animals to date have conversed with an adult human. Ultimately, it is impossible to say with certainty what skills a given organism cannot learn until we have a clear understanding of the learning mechanisms that make acquiring that skill possible.

Much has been made of the fact that no animals other than humans have proven to be able to learn to comprehend and flexibly use language as well as humans. In contrast, the fact that no scientist (or even team of scientists) has successfully learned to comprehend and flexibly use the reputedly "simpler" communication systems of any other species is often ignored. Apparently, learning another species' communication system is a much more difficult task than learning a second language. It remains a mystery whether this difficulty arises because our learning mechanisms are inadequate for dealing with the complexity of natural communication systems, or because of a lack of suitable or sufficient experiences for developing an appropriate understanding of the messages being

Language Research Center of Georgia State University

Figure 13.5 An artificial language using lexigrams Bonobos and chimpanzees have been trained to point to individual visual patterns on a board to request objects, identify locations, and perform other communication tasks.

communicated. Whether animals other than humans can learn certain aspects of language is relevant not only to understanding how humans acquire language but also for identifying the neural circuits that provide humans with this capacity.

Interim Summary

Language is a system for socially transmitting information, and language use is a skill that must be learned. Early on during language learning, perceptual learning processes enable infants to segment and recognize words. Recognition of predictable patterns in streams of speech facilitates this process. Word recognition precedes word production as well as word understanding. Human infants, bonobos, and possibly other animals can learn to recognize words and basic syntactic rules simply by repeatedly observing them being used.

Like any other skill, becoming an expert language user requires practice; observations alone are not sufficient. This is true for infants learning speech, baby birds learning songs, and college students taking foreign language courses. Language learning may be uniquely dependent on observational learning, but language use depends heavily on general mechanisms for encoding and retrieving short- and long-term memories for facts, events, associations, and skills.

Studies of individuals learning second languages or artificial languages can provide clues about the various ways that individuals learn a language. Comparative studies of language-trained animals suggest that many of the processes involved in human language learning can also occur in other animals.

ScienceCartoonsPlus.com

"Although humans make sounds with their mouths and occasionally look at each other, there is no solid evidence that they actually communicate with each other."

13.2 Brain Substrates

A person acquires the ability to use language over many years and thousands of hours of experience. This makes it very difficult for researchers to directly observe the neural processes associated with language learning. So far, most of what is known about the neural mechanisms underlying language learning has been inferred using two methods: (1) the analysis of language deficits in patients with brain lesions; and (2) the use of neuroimaging techniques to observe neural activity associated with language processing (that is, with the production and comprehension of a language that is already known).

Is There a Language Organ?

The functions that different neural regions may play in language processing are encapsulated in **Lichtheim's model of language processing** (Lichtheim, 1885). Ludwig Lichtheim (1845–1928) was a German physician who summarized past findings about how cortical lesions disrupted language production and comprehension using a simple diagram (Figure 13.6). This classic, early model posits the presence of three independent language processors: one produces speech, a second stores words and their associations, and a third uses conceptual information to guide the storage and production of sentences. Note that the model equates language with spoken language and thus does not account for language processing by deaf individuals. In Lichtheim's model, listeners understand speech by comparing perceived sounds ("auditory inputs") with memories of spoken words (in the "word store" processor). Recognized words then activate associated concepts (in the "conceptual information" processor). Similarly, speakers generate sentences (in the "speech production" processor) by accessing these same memories for words and concepts. This model is significant because it has guided many attempts to localize the places in the brain that serve these various functions.

Some linguists suggest that the neural regions that humans use to process language constitute a **language organ,** a hypothetical structure (or group of structures) in the body that is specialized for language. The basic idea here is that the human genetic plan includes instructions for building neural circuits that can learn, process, and generate language (Chomsky, 1965). Anatomically, human brains differ from those of other mammals mainly in that the human cerebral cortex is larger with more divisions. So if the human brain does contain a language organ, then this organ might logically be expected to reside somewhere in the cerebral cortex. In fact, parallels have been drawn between two of Lichtheim's hypothetical processors and two specific cortical regions. The speech production processor has been linked to a region of cortex known as Broca's area, and the word store has been linked to a region known as Wernicke's area. (You will see later, though, that these hypotheses were not entirely accurate.)

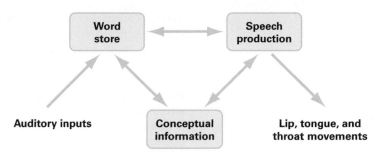

Figure 13.6 Lichtheim's classic model of language processing In this model, there are three major processes underlying language use. Heard sounds ("Auditory inputs") are compared with memories of words (in "Word store") to determine if they are speech, and recognized words activate associated concepts (in "Conceptual information"). These same memories of spoken words and concepts are also used to generate speech (in "Speech production"). All three processes can interact to influence how language is used and understood.

Broca's Area

The idea that language abilities depend heavily on the cerebral cortex is supported by numerous observations of patients suffering from **aphasia,** a group of problems of language production and comprehension caused by brain damage. Patients with aphasia provide evidence that the brain's two hemispheres play different roles in language processing in most individuals (see also Chapter 2, on the neuroscience of learning and memory). Some of the earliest evidence of an asymmetry in the hemispheres' contributions to language processing came in the late 1800s from a patient named Leborgne, who had lost the ability to produce sentences. After Leborgne's death, his physician Paul Broca found that part of Leborgne's left frontal lobe was damaged. The part of Leborgne's left frontal lobe that was damaged is now referred to as **Broca's area.**

Patients with damage to Broca's area often have trouble producing sentences. This symptom initially led researchers to associate Broca's area with the speech production processor in Lichtheim's model. However, patients with damage to this region of cortex actually show a wide range of symptoms. For example, they are often also impaired at comprehending certain features of speech. Moreover, patients with damage to Broca's area usually can produce comprehensible sentences; their sentences are just missing some syntactical features.

Neuroimaging studies show that when people produce syntactically correct speech, several other cortical regions are active in addition to Broca's area. For example, other frontal regions are consistently active when individuals are engaged in any of a wide range of language tasks (Demonet, Thierry, & Cardebat, 2005). Usually, the left hemisphere shows higher levels of cortical activation during language use, but the right hemisphere also shows cortical activation, especially during the processing of abstract words and when speech contains emotional content (Buchanan et al., 2000). This means that frontal cortical regions involved in generating language are also involved in language comprehension.

Damage to Broca's area clearly affects language use, but that does not mean this part of the cortex is specialized for processing language. For example, if damage to Broca's area were found to reduce a person's ability to maintain words in working memory, such damage would change the way the person constructed sentences, which might make the sentences appear abnormal, but the change might be due to a working-memory deficit, not to a specific language-processing deficit. Consistent with this idea, functional neuroimaging studies of language comprehension show that Broca's area becomes active during semantic working memory tasks, when no speech is being produced (Bookheimer, 2002). You may recall from Chapter 11, on observational learning, that this region also becomes active when individuals are imitating movements. So, although the link between Broca's area and speech production was initially pointed to as evidence of a language-specialized cortical region in humans, later research suggests that it is one of several brain regions that contribute to language production and comprehension.

Wernicke's Area

Around the same time as Broca's discovery, another physician, named Carl Wernicke, described two patients who had lost the ability to comprehend speech; moreover, although they spoke fluently in complex sentences, their sentences were meaningless. After both patients died, Wernicke examined their brains and discovered that they had damage to their left hemispheres, but the location of the damage was different from the one Broca had described. The new language-related area that Wernicke identified is now called **Wernicke's area.** Wernicke's observations suggested that at least two cortical regions (Broca's area and Wernicke's area) were involved in language processing.

Patients with damage to Wernicke's area often have problems comprehending language. Typically, they maintain fluent, though abnormal, speech production. For example, a person with damage to Wernicke's area might say, "You know that smoodle pinkered and that I want to get him round and take care of him like you want before," to explain that they need to take their dog for a walk (National Institutes of Health, 2007). This language comprehension deficit led early researchers to believe that Wernicke's area was the cortical region where auditory memories for words were stored (Wernicke, 1874). Consequently, this region was identified with the word storage processor in Lichtheim's model. Patients with Wernicke's aphasia may have problems comprehending sentences because they cannot identify parts of words or because they cannot access the meanings of words (Howard & Frankin, 1988). Neuroimaging data provide evidence that cortical networks in and around Wernicke's area are active when people comprehend speech (Demonet, Thierry, & Cardebat, 2005).

Early ideas about how Lichtheim's functional model could be mapped onto cortical regions specialized for language processing are summarized by the **Wernicke-Geschwind model** (Figure 13.7). In this model, Broca's area is thought to be responsible for speech production, Wernicke's area is considered responsible for word storage, and surrounding cortical regions are believed to provide the necessary conceptual information. Because both areas were found in the left hemisphere, the left hemisphere became identified with processing language. The discovery that the left hemisphere shows some specialization for speech production and comprehension changed the way that scientists thought about the neural substrates of language, because it proved that the two hemispheres were performing different functions, and suggested that specific language processes depended on localizable circuits in the cortex.

The Wernicke-Geschwind model supported many scientists' expectation that humans possess cortical processors specialized for language use that could be collectively thought of as a language organ. However, more recent work has called into question the idea that these regions are specialized for language processing.

Broca's area

Wernicke's area

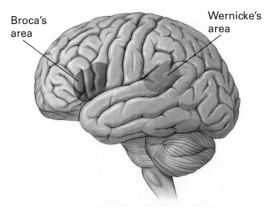

Figure 13.7 The Wernicke–Geschwind model
In this model, Broca's area is thought to be responsible for speech production, and Wernicke's area is held to be responsible for speech recognition. Surrounding areas are thought to provide the necessary conceptual information.

▶ **Unsolved Mysteries**

Can Computers Master Human Language?

Winter break is approaching, and you have decided to book reservations for travel through your favorite Internet site, which boasts a new "natural language" interface. The Web site software, recognizing your login, greets you:

Computer: Hello again! I hope you enjoyed the last trip you booked through us, which was your trip to Cancun.

You: Yes, it was great.

Computer: Where do you want to travel now?

You: Jamiaca.

Computer: Do you mean Jamaica?

You: Yes.

Computer: Will you be traveling alone?

You: No, I need two tickets.

Computer: OK. When do you want to travel?

You: Well, I want a full week. Winter break is the last week in December, but if I can get a cheaper fare by waiting until after Christmas, I could do that and then skip the first couple of days of class.

Computer: Sorry, I didn't understand. Please input your reply as a date in the format DD-MM-YYYY. When do you want to travel?

A human travel agent, by contrast, would have had no trouble understanding your response. Why can't we (yet) build a computer to do the same? Is it even possible to build a computer that really understands natural language?

Back in the 1960s, the creation of natural language interfaces seemed to be just around the corner. Computers of the 1960s and 1970s could answer questions posed in ordinary English on a range of topics, including baseball statistics, newspaper stories, and algebra problems (Schank, 1984, reviews many impressive early efforts). ELIZA, a famous program developed to simulate client-centered counseling sessions, interacted with human users so successfully that the latter often assumed they were communicating (via teletype) with another human being:

User: Men are all alike.

Eliza: In what way?

User: They're always bugging us about something or other.

Eliza: Can you think of a specific example?

User: Well, my boyfriend made me come here.

Eliza: Your boyfriend made you come here?

User: He says I'm depressed most of the time.

Eliza: I am sorry to hear that you are depressed.

But ELIZA and the like were specialized programs that "worked" only within a limited domain, by combining a small vocabulary, some basic grammatical rules, and a supply of cunning tricks. ELIZA's modern successors include some Web search engines (such as www.ask.com) and programs like the hypothetical travel agent above, that can recognize simple English queries as long as you stick to a small set of preprogrammed words and topics. Stray beyond their domains, and modern programs can't cope any better than the old ones could.

One school of thought holds that natural language is far too complicated to encode directly within a computer program (Dreyfus, 1998). Some of the researchers in this camp have instead tried programming computers to learn the syntax and seman-tics of natural language in the same way as humans do: by observing and exploring.

One classic attempt used a neural network—in this case, a computer program with two layers of processing: the first layer received input in the form of the sounds within a spoken verb; the second layer produced the speech sounds for the verb's past tense (Rumelhart & McClelland, 1986). Between the two layers were modifiable connections. On a learning trial, the network was presented with both the root form of a verb (like "come") and the correct past tense (like "came"). Connections between layers were gradually modified until, after many trials, the network produced the desired output for each input. After many training trials, the network not only produced the correct past tense for each trained verb but also had learned statistical regularities in verbs, such as the fact that, in English, the default rule for forming past tense is to add –ed. Given an unfamiliar verb (for example, "cratomize"), the network would apply the default rule—just as people do ("cratomized"). This early network system was very simple and has since been criticized as a model of human language learning, but it made the point that computer systems could learn grammar for themselves, without requiring a list of rules to be provided by a human programmer.

Clearly, it's a long way from software travel agents and neural networks to computers that can hold a meaningful conversation with a human. But, remember that humans need several years of intense experimentation and practice before mastering a natural language. Perhaps if software agents are given similar "lifetimes" of study, and if the hardware evolves in such a way as to better support language, the day will come when computers really can talk back to their masters. Or at least chat about cheap fares to Jamaica.

More important, none of the earlier studies addressed the question of whether these cortical regions were critical for learning language. They simply showed that damage to certain brain regions was associated with predictable deficits in the production and processing of speech. The following section summarizes what recent work has shown about how different brain regions contribute to language learning in adults.

Cortical Coding of a Second Language

Unlike many other skills such as learning a second musical instrument or a second sport, learning a second language can be more difficult than learning one's first language. This is especially true if the individual learning the second language is an adult. The difficulty associated with learning a second language as an adult suggests that learning a second language involves mechanisms different from those used to learn the first, depending on when, where, and how that second language is learned. One possible explanation might be that in adults, separate systems are used for processing each language. For example, one cortical region might be devoted to processing Spanish while another is specialized for processing English. Alternatively, perhaps overlapping neural circuits are used in bilingual processing in adults, with some brain regions being used for both languages and others only becoming active when one of the languages is being used.

Imagine that you learned English from your parents as a child and then learned French from your teachers in college as a young adult. If you could use an fMRI machine to see your own brain processing each of these languages, what do you think you would see? On the basis of classical models of language processing, you might expect to see that the part of your brain on the front left side (Broca's area) becomes active when you are generating either French or English, and that a different region in the back left side of your brain (Wernicke's area) becomes active when you are simply listening to either language. Do you think you would see any differences when you are processing French rather than English? Read on to find the answer.

Age-Dependent Reorganization

Bilingual patients with damage to either Broca's area or Wernicke's area may be impaired in only one of their languages (Paradis & Goldblum, 1989). This is consistent with the idea that separate cortical regions are used for different languages, since otherwise both languages should be equally affected. However, neuroimaging studies of bilingual individuals show similar patterns of activation in the cortex during processing of both languages (Chee, Tan, & Thiel, 1999; Illes et al., 1999). These findings are consistent with the idea that different languages are processed in the same general cortical regions. In the big picture, it seems that the parts of the cortex used to process different languages depend on the specific language-related task being performed as well as when the particular language was learned (Chee, Hon, Lee, & Soon, 2001; Marian, Spivey, & Hirsch, 2003).

In a recent neuroimaging study, Joy Hirsch and colleagues asked individuals who could speak both French and English to say sentences in their heads (Kim, Relkin, Lee, & Hirsch, 1997). The sentences described events that the participant had personally experienced in the recent past. The participants were told which language to use. fMRI images revealed that Wernicke's area became active during the task, and that there was little difference in the activity when participants performed the task in French as compared to English. In contrast, Broca's area became active in different ways when participants used different languages, but only in those participants who had learned to speak French as adults.

Of course, other language tasks might reveal different patterns of activation, in different cortical areas, that may or may not overlap with previously seen patterns. But, the results from this simple study illustrate that learning languages at different ages can affect which cortical regions are involved in language use. Cortical networks become less plastic as a person grows older, and this reduced plasticity can impact how learning affects cortical circuits. For example, the sensitive period for language learning in humans probably reflects a progressively decreasing capacity for cortical reorganization. Remember from the discussion earlier that infants younger than 6–8 months can distinguish the full set of sounds used in human languages, while after 11 months their ability to distinguish nonnative sounds declines. This decrease in infants' foreign-language perception happens just as the infants are beginning to master their native language. By the end of the sensitive period, the human language system is strongly wired, perhaps explaining why adults have a difficult time learning to distinguish sounds that are not found in their native language, and why adults have a hard time losing their accent when trying to produce speech sounds in a new language.

Activation Changes Associated with Language Learning

Neuroimaging of language use by adults reveals the final state of cortical processing reached after many years of language learning, but it doesn't show how the cortex and other brain regions change during the learning process. New studies that examined the brain activity of adults before and after learning Japanese show that increased experience with Japanese words changed how cortical regions responded when learners heard those words (Menning, Imaizumi, Zwitserlood, & Pantev, 2002). Participants improved their ability to distinguish words with practice, and as their performance improved, their neural responses got faster and faster. Changes in how their cortical networks processed language were seen after only 15 hours of training with the new language. (Keep in mind that several thousands of neurons would need to change before any differences would be seen in evoked responses.)

Similar changes in cortical networks have also been seen in college students learning French (McLaughlin, Osterhout, & Kim, 2004). Neurophysiological recordings of students studying French showed evidence of cortical changes after just 14 hours of instruction. Participants who showed no improvement in performance after instruction also showed no changes in language-related cortical activity. Changes in cortical activity after learning a second language have been seen in both Broca's and Wernicke's areas (Wang, Sereno, Jongman, & Hirsch, 2003). The most common changes are that the area of the cortex involved in performing the language task expands, and that additional cortical regions become involved.

Interestingly, you don't have to learn a second language to change the way your cortex processes language. Learning names for unfamiliar objects in your native language can also lead to cortical changes (Cornelissen et al., 2004). Humans learn new names for objects, events, and locations throughout their lives. By monitoring cortical activity with MEG recordings, researchers discovered that the acquisition of new words was associated with subtle changes in cortical activation (Cornelissen et al., 2004). During recording sessions, subjects named black-and-white outline drawings of real-world objects, some unfamiliar to them (ancient tools) and others familiar (modern-day tools), using labels provided by the experimenters. Participants practiced daily on the naming task until their accuracy exceeded 98%. Researchers collected MEG measurements before, during, and after training while the participants named the pictures. Eight to 14 distinct cortical areas became active during the naming task. Activity in

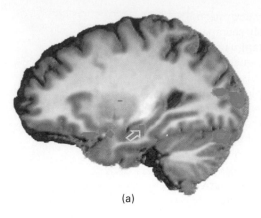
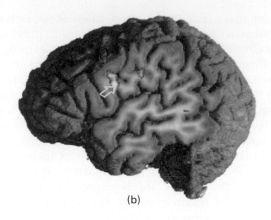

(a)　　　　　　　　　　　　　　　(b)

Figure 13.8 Cortical changes associated with learning an artificial grammar Two brain regions showed significant changes associated with learning. (a) Learning to detect words in the wrong position was associated with a decrease in activity, indicated by an arrow, in the left hippocampus; (b) learning a new grammatical rule was associated with an overall increase in activity, indicated by an arrow, in the left premotor cortex. These two findings indicate that different subtasks within language learning lead to changes in different neural regions. Neuroimages courtesy of Bertram Opitz.

only one or two of these areas was changed after learning, however. In four of the five individuals tested, the areas where activation changed after learning were located in the parietal lobe. This finding suggests that, like language processing, language learning may depend on cortical circuits in predictable regions of the cortex.

Another important finding of this study was that the same cortical regions that became active when participants named familiar objects were also activated when they were learning to name unfamiliar objects. In other words, no unique cortical areas devoted to learning new names were identified—the same areas used to generate familiar names were also used to learn new names.

Cortical changes are also observed during the learning of artificial languages. In one study, participants learned the rules associated with an artificial grammar. Then, researchers measured the participants' brain activity using fMRI while testing their ability to detect sequences that did not follow those rules (Opitz & Friederici, 2004). Half of the participants were presented with an ungrammatical sequence in which one of the nouns was in the wrong place (the WORD condition). The other half of the participants were presented with a new grammatical rule to learn (the RULE condition). In the WORD condition, learning of the detection task was associated with decreased activity in the left hippocampus. In the RULE condition, learning of the task was associated with increased activity in the left premotor cortex (near Broca's area; see Figure 13.8). These two findings indicate that different subtasks within language learning lead to changes in different neural regions (Opitz & Friederici, 2004). It is not yet clear why hippocampal processing would be modulated by changes in word position (the WORD condition). However, cortical changes associated with the RULE condition are consistent with the idea that circuits in and around Broca's area facilitate recognition of predictably ordered sequences.

Physical Changes Induced by Language Learning

Learning a second language can change cortical and subcortical activation patterns, but could language learning also affect the actual circuitry of the human brain? Recent structural MRI experiments show that second language learning is associated with increases in the density of grey matter (neurons and associated dendrites) in certain regions of cortex (as shown in Figure 13.9). The density of gray matter increases with the proficiency of second-language use, though this is less so the later the age at which the language was learned (Mechelli et al., 2004). Changes in cortical structure associated with second language learning were not observed in Broca's area, Wernicke's area, or in the auditory cortex. This does not mean that physical changes are not occurring in these regions as a result of

(a)

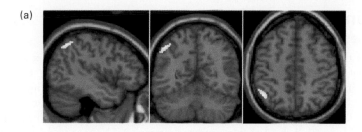

(b)

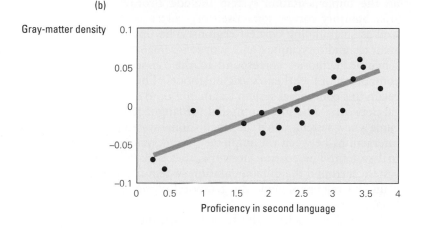

Figure 13.9 Increases in gray matter associated with learning a second language (a) The yellow areas show the cortical region with increased gray-matter density in bilinguals versus monolinguals. (b) Gray-matter density in those regions is positively correlated with second-language proficiency. (c) Gray-matter density is negatively correlated with the age at which the second language was learned. These correlations suggest that structural changes in cortical circuits associated with language learning are larger when learning occurs at a younger age, and when more is learned. From Mechelli et al., 2004.

(c)

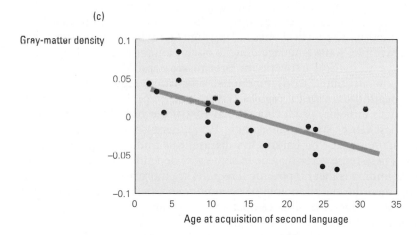

language learning, however. It simply means that any changes that are occurring in these regions are comparable in both monolingual and bilingual individuals. Recall from Chapter 4, on skill memory, that comparable physical changes in the cortex occur when a person learns to juggle. So, language learning is not special in this regard—many other kinds of skill learning can also lead to physical changes in the cortex.

Neuroscience studies make it increasingly clear that language learning generates extensive changes in neural processing throughout the brain. The rate at which neural circuits are able to change in response to language-related experiences may even be one of the constraints on how rapidly adult humans can learn language. If so, then perhaps the "language organ" which allows humans to learn languages in a way unique among animals actually consists of an enhanced capacity to reorganize neural circuits based on experience, rather than consisting of any language-specialized brain regions.

A Contemporary Model of Language Processing in the Brain

Studies that followed those of Broca and Wernicke show that a much broader range of cortical regions are involved in language processing than was envisioned in the Wernicke-Geschwind or Lichtheim models (Figure 13.10). In more recent models of language processing, the language production system and word store have been combined into what is now called the "implementation system." The cortical regions that make up the implementation system include Broca's area, Wernicke's area, auditory cortex, somatosensory cortex, and motor cortex, as well as surrounding cortical regions. The implementation system analyzes auditory inputs and activates semantic memories. These semantic memories correspond to the "conceptual information" component of Lichtheim's original model. The more recent models retain this conceptual system but map it onto a wide range of cortical networks. The modern models of language processing also include a new system, called the "mediational system," that coordinates interactions between the implementation system and the conceptual system. The cortical networks that make up the mediational system surround the implementation system like a belt. These surrounding regions include the temporal cortex as well as the prefrontal cortex.

(a)

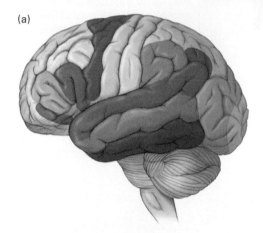

(b)

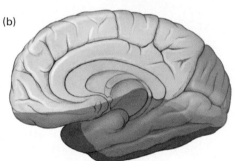

Figure 13.10 Cortical regions involved in language processing (a) Surface of left hemisphere of the human brain; (b) slice showing the right hemisphere of the human brain. Different images from fMRI studies show increased activation in each of the various colored regions during certain kinds of language use. Adapted from Demonet, Thierry, & Cardebat, 2005.

Researchers traditionally have focused on cortical networks in their attempts to localize language-related neural processing. But, there is increasing evidence that subcortical brain regions may be as important as cortical ones in language learning and processing. For example, some language deficits once thought to result from damage to cortical networks in Broca's area and Wernicke's area are now attributed to dysfunctional subcortical regions lying underneath those cortical regions (Dronkers, 1996). Parkinson's patients have difficulty producing regular past-tense verbs but not irregular past-tense verbs (Ullman et al., 1997). Because the basal ganglia are the major system affected by Parkinson's disease, this finding suggests that the production of past-tense verbs may be in some way dependent on the basal ganglia. Another finding is that hippocampal regions are more active during semantic encoding than during phonological encoding, and that changes in familiar word positions can increase hippocampal activity (Ullman, 2004). In addition, research has associated cerebellar damage with a wide range of deficits in language comprehension (Cook, Murdoch, Cahill, & Whelan, 2004). For example cerebellar damage impairs a person's ability to judge whether sentences are grammatical (Justus, 2004). In short, many subcortical regions are now thought to provide neural substrates for normal language use, weakening the argument that the evolution of specialized cortical structures was what enabled humans to learn and use language (Stowe, Paans, Wijers, & Zwarts, 2004).

In the contemporary models of language processing, the basal ganglia and cerebellum are associated with the implementation system, and the hippocampus is associated with the conceptual system. Unlike early models, which considered language processing to occur largely in localized cortical circuits, modern models suggest that language use involves broadly distributed networks of both cortical and subcortical neurons. Today, the general view is that the two hemispheres of the adult human brain often play different roles in language processing, that subcortical regions are as important to language processing as cortical regions, and that the cortical regions near the front of the brain play different roles from those toward the back.

At the same time, the fact that a particular region is involved in a language function does not imply that the region is specialized for language learning or processing. One way to assess whether cortical regions are specialized for language is to observe how active they are during nonlanguage tasks. For example, neuroimaging studies show that Broca's area also becomes active during music perception tasks (Maess, Koelsch, Gunter, & Friederici, 2001) (see Figure 13.11a). Patel and colleagues found that trained musicians showed nearly the same cortical activity in Broca's area when they listened to musical sequences as they did when they listened to sentences (Figure 13.11b) (Patel, Gibson, Ratner, Besson, & Holcomb, 1998). Even distinguishing between different tones can

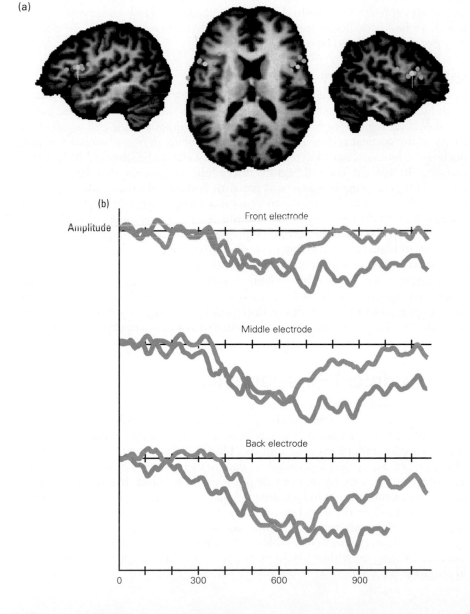

Figure 13.11 Overlapping activation of Broca's area by speech and music (a) MEG measures show selective activation of Broca's area during processing of musical features. Activation was localized to Broca's area and to the corresponding cortical region in the right hemisphere (indicated by yellow dots). (b) Event-related potentials seen during language processing (blue lines) are also seen when participants listen to music (purple lines). The traces show responses evoked by grammatical or musical incongruities at three electrodes located on the front, middle, and back of the scalp. Responses occurring up to 600 ms after stimulus onset are similar for both conditions. Adapted from Patel, 2003.

engage Broca's area (Muller, Kleinhans, & Courchesne, 2001). For example, when participants identified changes in the pitch of a tone versus simply detecting the onset of a noise, cortical networks in Broca's area were more active. These findings suggest that processing in Broca's area is not language-specific. Instead, it may involve a general mechanism for recognizing sequences of sounds or actions.

Many of the regions that have been identified as language centers within the brain are actually involved in various nonlinguistic functions in addition to language processing. Their varied functions suggest that, rather than being specialized for language processing, these different cortical regions are specialized for processing stimuli in particular ways. In other words, the brain may handle semantic and syntactic processing of words just as it handles any other stimuli that have predictable associations and sequential structure. Similarly, language learning probably does not require any specialized brain regions. Rather, many of the circuits involved in learning about other stimulus events, and in processing language, also appear to be involved in learning language. How humans are able to use these basic circuits to learn cognitive skills that other animals do not is a mystery that remains to be solved.

Interim Summary

Language processing relies on a complex network of cortical regions that in adult humans are asymmetrically distributed across the two hemispheres, as well as subcortical regions such as the basal ganglia, hippocampus, and cerebellum. Many of the cortical and subcortical systems involved in observational learning, declarative memory, and skill learning are likely also to be involved in language learning. In humans, cortical regions in the left hemisphere often become specialized for processing syntactic and semantic features of natural languages. You may use the same brain regions to process a second language that you use to process a first language, if you learned the second language during childhood. However, if you learned the second language as an adult, you may be using additional brain regions that you don't use when processing your native language.

Relatively little is known about the neural mechanisms of language learning. Most research has focused instead on language processing, particularly in patients with aphasias. Nevertheless, studies in the last decade have revealed that numerous regions of the brain are impacted by language-learning experiences, even after a relatively short period of practice with a new language or vocabulary.

13.3 Clinical Perspectives

Before the 1500s, people who were born deaf were barely treated as human. Ancient Greek philosophers equated speaking abilities with intelligence and education. They felt that individuals born without hearing could not use language, be educated, or even have ideas. Things did not get much better in the Middle Ages. Many deaf individuals ended up in asylums. Their problems were ascribed to possession by demons or punishment by God. Ironically, the same religious institutions that judged deaf people so harshly may have inadvertently helped them to join the world community. Monks who took vows of silence developed hand signals for communicating with each other without speaking. Such manual languages now enable deaf individuals to communicate as effectively as hearing individuals, helping them to avoid developmental disruptions in language learning.

Sign Language

You have probably seen sign-language experts on TV translating speech into sequences of gestures. If you do not know sign language, you probably found it difficult to identify anything resembling words or phrases in the movements of their hands. But there are many similarities between sign languages and spoken languages. Like spoken languages, there are many different sign languages. People can communicate using one sign language or more than one. Like spoken languages, sign languages possess semantics, syntax, and pragmatics. Sign-language gestures can be used in infinite combinations, just like words in spoken sentences. Sign languages also have some unique features. For example, the spatial position of a gesture relative to the signer's body can augment the meaning of a sign, as can the relative spatial positions of two sequential gestures. For example, the American Sign Language (ASL) gesture for "ask" (a single index finger pointing up) can mean "ask me," "ask you," "ask them," "ask often," "ask repeatedly," "ask everybody," or "ask them," depending on how the signer moves his or her gesturing hand relative to the body.

Spoken language requires the ability to hear one's own speech as well as the speech of others, and also the use of body parts capable of producing speech. But alternative communication systems like sign language open new channels of social interaction for a wide range of people who are impaired at processing speech. Sign language has been particularly useful socially, clinically, and in experimental studies. For example, Down syndrome (DS) children show delayed development of language skills. This may be due in part to certain neuromuscular deficits that impair the coordination of tongue and jaw movements and breathing. Also it may be due to frequent middle ear infections, which may impair the perception of speech sounds (Caselli et al., 1998). But children with DS may use gestural communication to compensate for their problems in speech production. Children with DS have been observed to produce a greater percentage of gestures than normally developing children, and these gestures are more sophisticated than would be expected given their levels of speech comprehension and production (Caselli et al., 1998).

Sign languages also provide new ways of communicating between species. The gestural language that Akeakamai and a small number of other dolphins have learned provides one example. Since the late 1960s, extensive efforts have been made to train apes to use sign languages, both to comprehend and to produce words. One of the first signing apes, named Washoe, learned about 170 different gestures (Gardner & Gardner, 1969). She often used these signs in combinations as part of ongoing activities, producing sequences such as *you me hide* or *you me go out hurry*. Chimpanzees and orangutans have learned to use signs to describe events they have observed and to request items. Clearly, signing apes can interact with humans and with other apes in ways that would not be feasible without the availability of these learned gestures. Furthermore, apes that have learned to use symbolic communication systems may actually think and problem solve in ways that are difficult or impossible to achieve without these systems (Boysen, Mukobi, & Berntson, 1999; Premack & Premack, 1984). For example, chimpanzees have great difficulty learning to select the smaller of two candy arrays to receive a larger reward, but when Arabic numerals are substituted for the candy arrays, they can easily learn the task (Boysen, Mukobi, & Berntson, 1999).

Autistic and deaf individuals that learn alternative communication systems may also be able to think and problem solve in new ways. For example, autistic children who learn sign languages sometimes show improvements in their use of natural speech. This suggests that learning about one mode of communication can transfer to other communication systems (Goldstein, 2002). These new findings highlight the benefits that a clearer understanding of the conditions that promote language learning can provide. Just a few hundred years ago, people with communication deficits (like Helen Keller and children with autism) were doomed to isolation. Now they have the opportunity to attend college and participate in society.

Language Learning in Isolation

In the Behavioral Processes section, you read about the sad case of Genie, the girl who was kept locked in a closet for most of her early life without being exposed to language. By the time Genie was found and released (at age 13), it was too late for her to develop all the complexities of human language. She learned simple words and phrases but never mastered complex grammar or extensive vocabulary.

Genie's case appears to support the idea of a sensitive period for language learning in humans: by age 13, it's too late to start from scratch. But we must be careful when drawing that conclusion: Genie was only one individual, and she was subjected to many other cruelties that made her development abnormal, aside from her lack of exposure to language. Perhaps it was these other factors (or even some congenital abnormality) that made Genie unable to acquire language.

Other evidence that there are key times during an infant's development when language learning can be disrupted comes from a broader population of otherwise healthy individuals who do not learn language at an early age. Deaf children born to speaking parents often receive limited exposure to language they can understand, if their parents do not use a conventional signed language such as ASL. Instead, these deaf children tend to develop idiosyncratic methods of communicating with gestures, a process called **homesigning.** Homesigners can develop extensive vocabularies including hundreds of words, noun–verb distinctions, and even syntactic markers to distinguish subjects and objects ("Jane likes Bill" versus "Bill likes Jane"). Sometimes an entire community learns a particular person's homesigns well enough to communicate with the person. Homesigners' linguistic accomplishments can be quite remarkable, but they generally fall well short of the complex syntax and morphology of conventional language (McDonald, 1997; Morford, 1996).

Normally, homesigners can later learn some ASL, but even after many years of exposure to ASL, they never quite reach the mastery of those who were exposed to ASL from early childhood. For example, one researcher tested the processing of verb morphology (for example, the use of "buy" versus "buys") in homesigners who learned ASL late (Newport, 1990). She found that mastery of the verb morphology was best in individuals who had been exposed to ASL before age 14. Homesigners who were first exposed to ASL after age 14 were significantly less accurate.

In another series of studies, ASL users were tested on their ability to perceive and repeat signed sentences (Mayberry, 1993; Mayberry & Fischer, 1989). Overall, late learners of ASL made many more errors than early learners of ASL, but the late learners' errors were also fundamentally different. The late learners of ASL made many production errors in which they used an incorrect sign that was physically similar to the correct sign. This suggests that the late learners were less able to quickly access the meaning of the signs they were shown, and retained only the surface features (the "image" of the sign).

It is important to note that the late learners' difficulties don't merely relate to the fact that they acquired a sign language late in life but also specifically to the fact that they had acquired no language in early childhood—they had missed their sensitive period. All the evidence currently available from late learners of a signed language points to the fact that early exposure to a conventional language (that is, before ages 9–13) is critical. It matters less whether this early language is spoken (as in late-deafened individuals) or gestural (as in early learners of ASL). What seems important is that the conventional language be rich in symbolic complexity and grammatical structure. Without such early exposure, a child's mastery of the complexities of human language may be forever impaired.

Lack of exposure does not always lead to language deficits, however. Both deaf children and hearing children generate sequences of speech and sequences of gestures beyond the ones they have experienced. This suggests that language learning is not simply a matter of registering external events and then re-creating them but that it involves a creative component as well. For example, groups of deaf children in Nicaragua have developed a sign language independently of spoken languages, and have passed this sign language from generation to generation. Once deaf children in Nicaragua developed this gestural language, the communication system took on a life of its own within the social group and surrounding community. These Nicaraguan children were active learners who explored possible channels of communication, rather than simply copying adults.

(a)

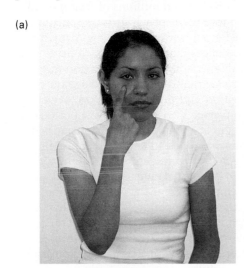 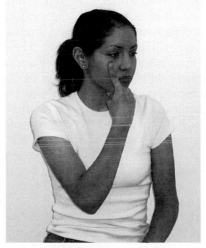

(b)

Senghas, A., & Coppola, M. (2001). Children creating language: How Nicaraguan sign language acquired a spatial grammar. *Psychological Science, 12*, 323–328.

Nicaraguan sign language Deaf children in Nicaragua developed a sign language without any instruction from adults. (a) The sign for "see." (b) The sign for "pay."

Specifically, they chose the gestures that would be used as words, and they developed the rules for using the gestures. Such examples show that acquisition of language is a creative process within which learners help to create the communicative signals that enable them to interact more effectively.

CONCLUSION

Imagine that you wake up one morning and discover that all the writing in your textbooks looks like gibberish, and that even your own speech sounds to you like a foreign language. (If this seems far-fetched, think back to the discussion in Chapter 2 of how brain damage resulting from carbon monoxide poisoning leads to comparable language deficits.) Without your language comprehension skills, you would have little if any hope of continuing in college, and your ability to function in society would be greatly impaired. In short, your life as you know it depends on your ability to use language.

Language learning is a prolonged, multistage process requiring a complex array of neural substrates. For most humans, language learning relies heavily on vocal learning, but the ability to hear and speak is not a prerequisite for language learning, as amply demonstrated by Helen Keller and millions of deaf individuals around the world. Language is much more than speech. It is a sophisticated communication system for the social transfer of information, taking many forms (including spoken, signed, and written sentences) and making use of many sensory modalities (auditory, visual, and somatosensory). To use this communication system successfully, humans must master numerous perceptual-motor and cognitive skills, including word segmentation and production, word selection, sentence processing, and the ability to converse. There are sensitive periods for language learning, so the process must begin at a young age, or language acquisition will become much more difficult or even impossible. Clearly, the ability to communicate through language is not a genetically predetermined ability.

Young human brains emerge prepared to learn language skills (and many other skills), but these skills do not develop "spontaneously" in the same way that crawling and walking do. Even in cases where children develop their own communications systems, such as with homesigning, learning depends on social interactions with others and is less sophisticated than language learning. Language skills are culturally dependent and rest heavily on observational learning mechanisms, such as the ability to imitate sounds.

Like humans, some other animals can learn artificial languages. Akeakamai the dolphin has learned an artificial language in which gestures have been assigned semantic meaning, and the ordering of the gestures follows syntactic rules. Kanzi the bonobo has learned to follow instructions provided in spoken English and through sequences of lexigrams. All three species share similar mammalian neural architectures, including a hefty amount of cortical tissue, so their ability to learn these communication systems may arise from similar neural processes. Of course, humans' language-learning skills are more extensive and flexible than those of other animals, but the reasons for this remain mysterious.

Language skills provide the foundation for much of human learning. Your memories for facts and events are influenced, and in some ways even defined, by how they can be verbalized. Your acquisition of new perceptual-motor skills and cognitive skills, such as cooking, sailing, skiing, or negotiating, is typically guided by spoken or written instructions and feedback. As a college student, your learning is shaped in great part by your ability to comprehend and respond appropriately to spoken and written sentences. The skills that you are being conditioned to perform as a student are largely language-dependent cognitive skills. For instance, many of the stimuli that you are expected to learn are descriptions. Even "critical thinking" skills that you acquire through practice are ultimately judged through your verbal responses to questions. Given the importance of language in human learning, much of what you have learned to date and what you can learn in the future is determined by the language skills you have acquired. In turn, your ability to learn language depends on a wide variety of basic mechanisms discussed throughout this book that many organisms share. Thus, your language skills are the consequence and the cause of the various memories you currently possess.

Key Points

- Language is a system for socially transmitting information.

- The requirements for learning to use a language include being able to identify words, recognize the order of words, recognize abstract rules about word organization, and recognize categories of words.

- Infants, adults, and tamarins rapidly learn to recognize frequent combinations of speech sounds produced in a specific order, even when not reinforced for doing so.

- Correct use and comprehension of syntactical structures within sentences is a cognitive skill.

- In both birds and humans, a period of perceiving sounds and storing them in memory precedes the ability to produce songs or speech, and the learning of that ability is guided by auditory feedback.

- Learning a second language can involve different mechanisms and strategies than were used to learn the first, depending on when, where, and how that second language is learned.

- For adults, learning a second language generally involves acquiring semantic memories as well as memories for the skills needed to comprehend and produce sentences.

- Artificial languages consist of sets of words (sometimes in the form of symbols) and rules for organizing them that exhibit one or more features of natural languages.

- Using a simple artificial gestural language, researchers demonstrated that dolphins could learn semantic information and syntactic rules.

- Artificial languages allow psychologists to test hypotheses about how language is learned, to identify constraints on what is learnable, and to determine what features of language require specialized linguistic processing.

- A chimpanzee named Sarah learned to answer novel questions using shapes, suggesting that she had learned to socially transmit information in a flexible way.

- A bonobo named Kanzi was the first nonhuman primate to learn an artificial language as well as basic English by observing others, and he did so by being present when researchers were attempting to teach his mother to use lexigrams.

- Aphasia, a group of language deficits caused by brain damage, shows that the two hemispheres of the brain play different roles in language processing.

- Patients with damage to Broca's area often have trouble producing sentences.

- Patients with damage to Wernicke's area often have problems comprehending language and produce fluent but meaningless speech.

- Processing in Broca's area is not language-specific. Instead, it may involve a general mechanism for recognizing sequences of sounds or actions.

- The cortical regions used to process different languages depend on the specific language-related task being performed, and on when the particular language was learned.

- Learning languages at different ages can lead to different changes in the neural substrates of language processing.

- The most common changes seen after language learning are that the area of cortex involved in the language task expands and that new cortical regions become involved.

- Even after only a few weeks of training in a second language, the adult human brain modifies how it processes the novel words.
- Different subtasks within language learning lead to changes in different neural regions.
- Second language learning is associated with increases in the density of gray matter (neurons and associated dendrites) in certain regions of the cortex.
- Subcortical brain regions may be as important in language processing as language-related cortical regions.
- Sign languages provide an alternative communication system for humans who cannot speak, and for certain other animals as well.

- Deaf individuals and children with developmental disorders may gain cognitive advantages from learning alternative communication systems.
- The reduced language abilities of late-learners of sign language suggest that early exposure to a conventional language before ages 9–13 is critical to language learning.
- Acquisition of language is a creative process within which learners help to create the communicative signals that enable them to interact more effectively.

Key Terms

aphasia, p. 517	homesigning, p. 528	pragmatics, p. 507	transitional probabilities, p. 503
artificial language, p. 512	language, p. 502	second language learning, p. 508	Wernicke–Geschwind model, p. 518
babbling stage, p. 506	language organ, p. 517	semantics, p. 505	Wernicke's area, p. 518
Broca's area, p. 517	lexigram, p. 514	subsong, p. 506	word segmentation, p. 503
gestural language, p. 512	Lichtheim's model of language processing, p. 516	syntax, p. 507	
grammar, p. 503			

Concept Check

1. Noam Chomsky once said, "Contrary to what people thought, language is not taught, not even learned. It's something that your mind grows in a particular environment, just the way your body grows in a particular environment." What evidence might have lead Chomsky to make this claim?

2. Initial attempts to teach apes or dolphins to understand and use natural spoken languages met with little success (Hayes & Hayes, 1952; Lilly, 1964). Do these failures reflect limitations in animals' abilities to use language, or limitations in their ability to use speech?

3. Infants seem to prefer a form of speech (sometimes called "motherese") characterized by exaggerated enunciation and inflections that change the features of speech sounds in ways that do not render words unrecognizable but that make them different from normal speech. Why might exposure to this abnormal speech enhance the learning of normal speech?

4. If many of the brain regions that we have discussed in previous chapters—such as the cerebellum, hippocampus, and basal ganglia—are involved in language use or language learning, then animal models

that have been used to study those regions may provide insights into the neural mechanisms underlying language learning. How might the neural circuits that enable birds to learn songs, monkeys to link observed actions to performed actions, and rats to socially transfer information about food preferences be involved in language learning?

5. You can memorize and produce a sentence in a foreign language without having a clue what the sentence means. Usually, however, you speak to express your thoughts. This requires constructing the sentence as well as producing the sentence. Which of these aspects of language production do you think might be performed by cortical neurons in Broca's area?

6. Although questions about language learning have motivated a great number of studies by philosophers, linguists, and psychologists, relatively little is known about the mechanisms that enable human brains to learn and use language. Why is this so?

7. In surgical settings, it is possible for physicians to validate neuroimaging data by electrically stimulating the cortex while individuals use language (Boat-

man, 2004). However, the effects of stimulation at a particular cortical location vary greatly between individuals, and stimulation sites that disrupt language production and comprehension are only weakly correlated with the positions identified by Broca and Wernicke. For this reason, neurosurgeons often map out the effects of stimulation in different cortical regions for each individual before performing surgery, so that they can better avoid damaging areas that are needed for language. What (if anything) does this imply about the genetic and neural bases of language abilities?

8. Because patients with left hemisphere damage are more likely to have language deficits, this hemisphere is often associated with language. However, children that do not have a left hemisphere can learn to use language quite well. What does this suggest about the role of hemispherical asymmetries in language learning?

Answers to Test Your Knowledge

Bird Song versus Human Language

All of the statements except 1 and 4 accurately describe both bird song and spoken language. Statement 1, that unique sound sequences produced by individuals convey specific meanings, and sounds produced in different orders have different meanings, is inaccurate because individual sounds within bird songs are not known to convey specific meanings. Statement 4, that individuals learn to use the sound sequences of other species if they grow up surrounded by individuals using those sounds, is inaccurate because humans grow up surrounded by the sounds of many species but do not learn to use them.

Further Reading

Anderson, S. R., & Lightfoot, D. W. (2002). *The language organ: Linguistics as cognitive physiology*. Cambridge, UK: Cambridge University Press. • A review of what is known about the development of language and how it relates to brain function.

Keller, H. (1970). *Helen Keller: The story of my life*. New York: Airmont Pub Co. • An autobiography describing how one person learned language without the benefit of vision or hearing.

Sebeok, T. A., & Rosenthal R. (1970). *The Clever Hans phenomenon: Communication with horses, whales, apes, and people*. New York: Annals of the New York Academy of Sciences. • A critique of studies reporting that animals other than humans can learn language.

acoustic startle reflex A defensive response (such as jumping or freezing) to a startling stimulus (such as a loud noise).

acquired equivalence A learning and generalization paradigm in which prior training in stimulus equivalence increases the amount of generalization between two stimuli, even if those stimuli are superficially dissimilar.

activity-dependent enhancement Paired training of CS and US that produces an increase in the glutamate vesicles released from sensory to motor neurons.

agnosia Disruption in the ability to process a particular kind of semantic information, such as difficulty recognizing objects (a form of visual agnosia) or understanding the meaning of spoken words (a form of auditory agnosia).

allele The naturally occurring variant in a gene.

Alzheimer's disease A form of progressive cognitive decline due to accumulating brain pathology (specifically, amyloid plaques and neurofibrillary tangles).

amnesia Memory loss, often due to brain damage or disease. See also *anterograde amnesia; functional amnesia; infantile amnesia; retrograde amnesia; source amnesia; transient global amnesia.*

amygdala A collection of brain nuclei lying at the anterior tip of each hippocampus and important for emotional learning and emotional memory.

amyloid plaques Deposits of clumped-together protein (beta-amyloid) that accumulate in the brain and are one of the hallmarks of Alzheimer's disease.

androgens The principal sex hormones present in adult males.

anhedonia hypothesis The theory that dopamine is important in giving reinforcers (e.g., food) their "goodness" or hedonic quality, and that disrupting dopamine reduces "goodness" or hedonia, therefore reducing an organism's motivation to work for reinforcement.

anterograde amnesia The inability to form new episodic and semantic memories, although older memories may be preserved largely intact.

anxiety disorders A cluster of psychiatric conditions that includes panic disorders, phobias, posttraumatic stress disorder (PTSD), and obsessive-compulsive disorders.

aphasia A condition in which brain damage causes problems with language production and comprehension.

Aplysia A marine invertebrate (sea slug) much studied by neuroscientists because of its simple and unvarying nervous system.

apoptosis Natural cell death, as distinct from cell death caused by injury or disease.

appetitive conditioning Conditioning in which the US is a positive event (such as food delivery).

apraxia A condition involving damage to the cerebral hemispheres and consequent difficulties in coordinating purposeful, skilled movements.

arousal A collection of bodily responses (including increased blood flow to muscles, increased respiration, and depressed digestion and immune function) that prepares the body to face a threat; also known as the fight-or-flight response.

artificial intelligence (AI) The study of how to build computers that can perform behaviors that seem to require human intelligence.

artificial language A set of words (or sometimes symbols) and a system of rules for organizing them that exhibits one or more features of natural languages.

Asperger's syndrome A developmental disorder in which individuals have normal intellectual abilities but a reduced capacity for social skills.

association cortex The areas of the cerebral cortex that are involved in associating information within and across sensory modalities.

associationism The principle that memory depends on the formation of linkages ("associations") between pairs of events, sensations, and ideas, such that recalling or experiencing one member of the pair elicits a memory or anticipation of the other.

associative learning Learning to associate one stimulus with another or to associate a stimulus with a new response.

associative stage The second stage in Fitts's model of skill learning; in this stage, learners begin using stereotyped actions when performing a skill and rely less on actively recalled memories of rules.

autonomic nervous system (ANS) A collection of nerves and structures that control internal organs and glands.

autonomous stage The third stage in Fitts's model of skill learning; in this stage, a skill or subcomponents of the skill become motor programs.

autosomal dominant A genetic allele that will be expressed (cause effects) if inherited from at least one parent (regardless of what allele is contributed by the other parent).

aversive conditioning Conditioning in which the US is a negative event (such as a shock or an airpuff to the eye).

axon The output extension of a neuron, specialized for transmitting information to other neurons or to muscles.

babbling stage The second stage of early language learning, during which infants produce a wide variety of sounds, including sounds they have never heard.

basal forebrain A group of brain structures near the base of the frontal lobe that may be important in modulating hippocampal function and therefore in regulating new memory formation.

basal ganglia A group of brain structures that includes the dorsal striatum and nucleus accumbens, and that are important in learning voluntary responses.

base pair (of a DNA strand) A pair of molecules (called bases) that join together to form one "rung" of a DNA double helix. Base pairs always consist of adenine (A) paired with thymine (T) or cytosine (C) paired with guanine (G).

behavioral addictions Behaviors, such as compulsive gambling, compulsive eating, and sex addiction, that produce reinforcements or highs and to which individuals can develop pathological addiction.

behavioral economics The study of how organisms "spend" their time and effort among possible behaviors.

behaviorism A school of thought that argues that psychology should restrict itself to the study of observable behaviors (such as lever presses, salivation, and other measurable actions) and not seek to infer unobservable mental processes.

blind design An experimental design in which the participants do not know the hypothesis being tested or whether they are part of the experimental group or the control group. See also *double-blind design*.

bliss point The allocation of resources in such a way as to maximize subjective value or satisfaction.

blocking A behavioral training paradigm in which a previously learned association between a cue (CS1) and the US prevents learning about a second cue (CS2) that is subsequently combined with the CS1 into a compound cue during (CS1 + CS2)US training.

brainstem A group of structures that connects the rest of the brain to the spinal cord and plays key roles in regulating automatic functions such as breathing and regulating body temperature.

Broca's area A region in the left frontal lobe where damage leads to language deficits, especially in speech production.

categorization learning The process by which humans learn to classify stimuli into categories.

cell body The central portion of the neuron that contains the nucleus and integrates signals from all the dendrites; also known as the soma.

central executive The component of Baddeley's model of working memory that monitors and manipulates the two working memory buffers.

central nervous system (CNS) The part of the vertebrate nervous system consisting of the brain and spinal cord.

cerebellum A brain region lying below the cerebral cortex in the back of the head. It is responsible for the regulation and coordination of complex voluntary muscular movement, including classical conditioning of motor-reflex responses.

cerebral cortex The brain tissue covering the top and sides of the brain in most vertebrates; involved in storage and processing of sensory inputs and motor outputs.

chaining A form of instrumental conditioning in which organisms are gradually trained to execute complicated sequences of discrete responses.

chromosome A package of DNA material; human cells contain 23 pairs of chromosomes, with one member of each pair inherited from the mother and one from the father.

classical conditioning A type of learning in which the organism learns to respond with a conditioned response (CR) to a previously neutral stimulus (the CS) that has been repeatedly presented along with an unconditioned stimulus (US); also called Pavlovian conditioning.

closed skill A skill that involves performing predefined movements that, ideally, never vary.

cochlear implant A sensory prosthesis that directly stimulates auditory

nerves to produce hearing sensations in deaf individuals.

cognitive map An internal psychological representation of the spatial layout of the external world.

cognitive psychology A subfield of psychology that focuses on human abilities—such as thinking, language, and reasoning—that are not easily explained by a strictly behaviorist approach.

cognitive skill A skill that requires problem solving or the application of strategies.

cognitive stage The first stage in Fitts's model of skill learning; in this stage, an individual must exert some effort to encode the skill on the basis of information gained through observation, instruction, and trial and error.

combinatorial explosion The rapid expansion of resources required to encode configurations as the number of component features increases.

comparator model of non-associative learning The theory that each time the brain detects a stimulus, it forms a representation of that stimulus to compare against existing representations of previously experienced stimuli; if there is no match, an orienting response is triggered.

computed tomography (CT) A method of structural neuroimaging based on multiple x-rays.

conditioned avoidance A conditioning paradigm in which an organism learns to take action in order to avoid or escape from a dangerous situation.

conditioned emotional response In classical conditioning, a behavioral response (such as freezing) or a physiological response (such as change in heart rate) that occurs in response to a conditioned stimulus (CS) that has been paired with an emotion-evoking unconditioned stimulus (US).

conditioned response (CR) The trained response to a conditioned stimulus (CS) in anticipation of the unconditioned stimulus (US) that it predicts.

conditioned stimulus (CS) A cue that is paired with an unconditioned stimulus (US) and comes to elicit a conditioned response (CR).

conditioned taste aversion A conditioning preparation in which a subject learns to avoid a taste that has been paired with an aversive outcome, usually nausea.

configural node A detector for a unique configuration of two cues, such as a certain tone and light.

confound An extraneous variable that happens to co-vary with the variable(s) being examined and could contribute to the observed results.

connectionist models Networks of uniform and unlabeled connections between simple processing units called nodes.

consequential region The set or range of stimuli that have the same consequence as the training stimulus.

consolidation period A length of time during which new episodic and semantic memories are vulnerable and easily lost or altered.

constant practice Practice involving a constrained set of materials and skills.

contagion An inborn tendency to react emotionally to visual or acoustic stimuli that indicate an emotional response by other members of one's species, typically in ways that replicate the observed response.

context The circumstances and environment in which an event occurs. These are the stimuli that are relatively constant on all trials rather than being manipulated by the experimenter.

contiguity Nearness in time (temporal contiguity) or space (spatial contiguity).

continuous reinforcement A reinforcement schedule in which every instance of the response is followed by the consequence.

control group In an experiment, the group of participants that does not get the experimental treatment; contrast *experimental group*.

copying The act of doing what one observes another organism doing.

correlational study A study that examines the degree to which two variables tend to vary together: as one

increases (or decreases), does the other increase (or decrease) too?

cortical plasticity Changes in cortical organization that occur as a result of experience.

cortisol The chief glucocorticoid in humans.

critical period A special kind of sensitive period that results in irreversible learning.

cryptomnesia A subclass of source amnesia in which a person mistakenly thinks that current thoughts are novel or original.

CS modulation theory Theories of conditioning holding that the stimulus that enters into an association is determined by a change in how the CS is processed.

cued recall A memory test that involves some kind of prompt or cue to aid recall.

cumulative recorder A device that records behavioral responses; the height of the line drawn represents the number of responses that have been made in the entire experiment (cumulatively) up to the present time.

data Facts and figures from which conclusions can be inferred.

declarative memory A category of memory that includes semantic memory and episodic memory, memories that can typically be verbalized or "declared."

deep brain stimulation A procedure that delivers an electrical current into a patient's brain through one or more implanted electrodes; used to alleviate tremors and other motor symptoms associated with Parkinson's disease.

delay conditioning A conditioning procedure in which there is no temporal gap between the end of the CS and the beginning of the US, and in which the CS co-terminates with the US.

delayed-non-match-to-sample task A test of visual memory in which a subject must indicate which of two novel objects is not the same as one that was just recently seen.

dendrite Extension of a neuron that is specialized to receive signals from other neurons.

dependent variable In an experiment, the factor whose change is measured as an effect of changes in the independent variable.

depression A psychiatric condition involving a general loss of initiative and activity, as well as feelings of inescapable sadness or apathy.

depth of processing The degree to which we analyze (or process) new information; in general, deeper processing of information leads to better remembering of that information.

diencephalon A group of brain structures, including the mammillary bodies and mediodorsal nucleus of the thalamus, that may help regulate communication between the hippocampus and the cortex.

difference image An image of differences in brain activity obtained by taking an fMRI or PET image of a person performing a particular task, then subtracting the image of the same individual at baseline (not performing a task).

differentiation theory of non-associative learning The theory that the brain develops representations of stimuli over time by incorporating additional details each time the stimulus is presented.

discrete trial paradigm An instrumental conditioning paradigm in which the experimenter defines the beginning and end of each trial.

discrete-component representation A representation in which each individual stimulus (or stimulus feature) corresponds to one element (node) in the model.

discrimination training Behavioral training in which one of a number of different (but similar) stimuli are presented on each trial, and only one of the stimuli is a correct choice.

discrimination Recognition that two stimuli are different, and knowing which to prefer.

discriminative stimuli In instrumental conditioning, stimuli that signal whether a particular response will lead to a particular outcome.

dishabituation A renewal of a response, previously habituated, that occurs when the organism is presented with a novel stimulus; compare *habituation*.

distributed representation A representation in which information is coded as a pattern of activation distributed across many different nodes.

DNA (deoxyribonucleic acid) The genetic material found within all living cells that contains the instructions for making an organism; it is shaped like a winding ladder, or "double helix."

dopamine A neuromodulator that alters neuron-to-neuron communication.

dorsolateral prefrontal cortex The left and right sides of the topmost part of the prefrontal cortex (PFC), often abbreviated DLPFC.

double-blind design An experimental design in which neither the participants nor the experimenters know the hypothesis or who is part of the experimental group versus the control group.

Down syndrome A congenital form of moderate-to-severe mental retardation due to trisomy 21.

drive reduction theory The theory that organisms have innate drives to obtain primary reinforcers and that learning is driven by the biological need to reduce these drives.

drug A chemical substance that alters the biochemical functioning of the body and/or brain.

dual process theory of non-associative learning The theory that habituation and sensitization are independent of each other but operate in parallel.

dualism The principle that the mind and body exist as separate entities.

dysexecutive syndrome A disrupted ability to think and plan.

echolalia The automatic repetition of words or phrases immediately after hearing them spoken.

electroconvulsive shock A brief pulse of electricity that is passed through the brain and can severely disrupt newly formed memories; electroconvulsive therapy is sometimes used to alleviate severe depression.

electroencephalography (EEG) A method for measuring electrical activity in the brain by means of electrodes placed on the scalp; the resulting image is an electroencephalogram (also EEG).

elicited imitation A technique for assessing memory in infants by observing their ability to mimic actions they have seen previously.

emotion A cluster of physiological responses, overt behaviors, and conscious feelings produced in response to an important situation.

empiricism A philosophical school of thought that holds that all the ideas we have are the result of experience; contrast *nativism*.

emulation Copying that involves replicating an outcome without replicating specific motor acts.

endogenous opioids Naturally occurring neurotransmitter-like substances that have many of the same effects as opiate drugs such as heroin and morphine; may help signal hedonic value, or "goodness," of reinforcers in the brain.

engram A physical change in the brain that forms the basis of a memory.

enriched environment An environment that provides sensory stimulation and opportunities to explore and learn; for a rat, this may mean housing in a large cage with many toys to play with and other rats to socialize with.

epinephrine A stress hormone (also known as adrenaline) that helps to mediate the fight-or-flight response.

episodic memory Memory for autobiographical events that occurred at a particular time and location.

error-correction rule A mathematical specification of the conditions for learning that holds that the degree to which an outcome is surprising modulates the amount of learning that takes place.

estrogens The principal sex hormones present in adult females.

eugenics A program for encouraging marriage and procreation for the healthiest, strongest, and most intelligent members of society, while discouraging childbearing for mentally or physically unfit people.

event-related potential (ERP) Electroencephalograms (EEGs) from a single individual averaged over multiple repetitions of an event (such as a repeated stimulus presentation).

evolution The theory that species change over time, with new traits or characteristics passed from one generation to the next; natural selection is one mechanism by which evolution occurs.

evolutionary psychology A branch of psychology that studies how behavior evolves through natural selection.

executive control The manipulation of working memory through the updating of stored information to facilitate goals, planning, task switching, stimulus selection, and response inhibition.

experiment A test made to examine the validity of a hypothesis, usually by actively manipulating the variable(s) being investigated and measuring the effect on a behavior.

experimental group In an experiment, the group of participants that gets some treatment or manipulation designed to test the experimental hypothesis; contrast *control group*.

experimental psychology A branch of psychology in which psychological theories are tested by experiment (e.g., a correlational study) rather than merely by observation of natural occurrences.

experimenter bias The degree to which an experimenter's prior knowledge or expectations can (consciously or unconsciously) influence the outcome of an experiment.

expert A person who performs a skill better than most.

explicit memory A category of memory that includes semantic memory and episodic memory; these memories tend to be "explicit": you know that you know the information.

extinction The process of reducing a learned response to a stimulus by ceasing to pair that stimulus with a reward or punishment.

eyeblink conditioning A classical conditioning procedure in which the US is an airpuff to the eye and the conditioned and unconditioned responses are eyeblinks.

false memory A memory of an event that never actually happened.

fight-or-flight response A collection of bodily responses (including increased blood flow to muscles, increased respiration, and depressed digestion and immune function) that prepares the body to face a threat; also known as arousal.

fixed-interval (FI) schedule In instrumental conditioning, a reinforcement schedule in which the first response after a fixed amount of time is reinforced; thus, FI 1 means the first response after 1 minute is reinforced.

fixed-ratio (FR) schedule In instrumental conditioning, a reinforcement schedule in which a specific number of responses are required before a reinforcer is delivered; for example, FR 5 means that reinforcement arrives after every fifth response.

flashbulb memory A memory of emotional events that seems especially vivid and long-lasting.

forgetting The loss or deterioration of memory over time.

free recall A memory test that involves simply generating the information from memory.

free-operant paradigm An instrumental conditioning paradigm in which the animal can operate the apparatus "freely," responding to obtain reinforcement (or avoid punishment) whenever it chooses.

frontal cortex An area of the cerebral cortex within the frontal lobes that may play a role in determining which memories are stored.

frontal lobe The part of the cerebral cortex lying at the front of the human brain; enables a person to plan and perform actions.

functional amnesia Amnesia that seems to result from psychological causes (such as psychological trauma) rather than physiological causes (such as brain injury).

functional magnetic resonance imaging (fMRI) A method of functional neuroimaging based on comparing an MRI of the brain during performance of a task with an MRI of the brain at rest.

functional neuroimaging Techniques (such as fMRI or PET) for observing the activity or function of a living brain.

gene A segment of a DNA strand that contains information for building a protein from amino acids; in essence, genes are the recipes for constructing and maintaining an organism.

generalization gradient A graph showing how physical changes in stimuli (plotted on the horizontal axis) correspond to changes in behavioral responses (plotted on the vertical axis).

generalization The transfer of past learning to novel events and problems.

gestational age (GA) Time since conception.

gestural language A simple artificial language in which arm and hand movements are used as words.

glia A type of cell that provides functional or structural support to neurons.

glucocorticoids A group of stress hormones (including cortisol in humans) that help to mediate the fight-or-flight response.

grammar The rules of a language that dictate how words can be altered and combined to form sentences.

habituation A decrease in the strength or occurrence of a behavior after repeated exposure to the stimulus that produces that behavior; compare *dishabituation*.

Hebbian learning The principle that learning involves strengthening the connections of coactive units; often

stated as, "Neurons that fire together, wire together."

heterosynaptic Occurring in several nearby synapses simultaneously.

hierarchical semantic network A model of semantic memory in which concepts are represented as nodes arranged hierarchically according to class membership; relationships between objects and concepts are encoded as connections or links between them and can be modified by learning.

hippocampus A brain structure in the medial temporal lobe that is important for new memory formation, especially of episodic and semantic memory.

homeostasis The tendency of the body (including the brain) to gravitate toward a state of equilibrium or balance.

homesigning A self-taught method of communicating with gestures, seen in deaf children.

homosynaptic Occurring in one synapse without affecting nearby synapses.

Huntington's disease An inherited disorder that causes gradual damage to neurons throughout the brain, especially in the basal ganglia and cerebral cortex; results in various psychological problems (e.g., mood disorders, hypersexuality, depression, and psychosis) and a gradual loss of motor abilities.

hypothesis A tentative explanation for an observation, phenomenon, or scientific problem that can be tested by further investigation.

iconic memory Rapidly decaying visual memories that last for less than a second but are critical for recognizing and processing briefly presented information.

identical elements theory Thorndike's proposal that learned abilities transfer to novel situations to an extent that depends on the number of elements in the new situation that are identical to those in the situation in which the skills were encoded.

implicit learning Learning that occurs without the learner's awareness of improvements in performance or, in the case of people with amnesia, awareness that practice has occurred.

implicit memory A category of memory (e.g., skill memory, conditioning, fear learning) that includes everything except explicit memory: you may not consciously realize that you know the information.

imprinting The tendency of a young animal to form an attachment to its mother (or the first motherlike object it sees) soon after birth.

incentive salience hypothesis The theory that dopamine helps provide organisms with the motivation to work for reinforcement.

independent variable The factor that is manipulated in an experiment, such as the factor that differentiates the control group and experimental group; contrast *dependent variable*.

infantile amnesia Normal forgetting in adulthood of events from infancy and early childhood.

inferior olive A nucleus of cells with connections to the thalamus, cerebellum, and spinal cord.

instrumental conditioning The process whereby organisms learn to make responses in order to obtain or avoid important consequences; compare *classical conditioning*.

interference Reduction in the strength of a memory due to overlap with the content of other memories.

interpositus nucleus One of the cerebellar deep nuclei.

interstimulus interval (ISI) The temporal gap between the onset of the CS and the onset of the US.

James-Lange theory of emotion The theory that conscious feelings of emotion occur when the mind senses bodily responses associated with that emotion.

knowledge of results Feedback about performance of a skill; critical to the effectiveness of practice.

Korsakoff's disease A condition of anterograde amnesia with some retrograde amnesia, caused by thiamine deficiency; often associated with chronic alcohol abuse.

landmark agnosia A form of agnosia in which patients lose the ability to identify and use landmarks for spatial navigation.

language A system for socially transmitting information, consisting of stimuli that communicate a meaning and that can be put together to make sentences.

language learning impairment (LLI) A description applied to children who have normal intelligence but score significantly below normal on oral language tests.

language organ A hypothetical structure (or group of structures) in the body that is specialized for learning, producing, or comprehending language.

latent inhibition A conditioning paradigm in which prior exposure to a CS retards later learning of the CS-US association during acquisition training.

latent learning Learning that is undetected (latent) until explicitly demonstrated at a later stage.

law of effect The observation, made by Thorndike, that the probability of a particular behavioral response increases or decreases depending on the consequences that have followed that response in the past.

learned helplessness The phenomenon that prior exposure to an inescapable punisher will reduce or impair later learning to escape from or avoid that punisher.

learned non-use A condition in which an individual gradually stops using a limb that has been affected by stroke or other brain injury and instead relies on the other, unaffected limb.

learning curve A graph showing learning performance (the dependent variable, usually plotted along the vertical axis) as a function of training

time (the independent variable, usually plotted along the horizontal axis).

learning specificity The degree to which learning about one set of stimuli transfers to another group of stimuli.

learning The process by which changes in behavior arise as a result of experiences interacting with the world.

lesion Damage caused by injury or illness.

lexigram A complex visual pattern used to represent a word.

Lichtheim's model of language processing A functional model in which three independent language processors are used to produce and comprehend language: one produces speech, a second stores words and their associations, and a third uses conceptual information to guide the storage and production of sentences.

limbic system A collection of brain structures important for memory and emotion, including the thalamus, hypothalamus, cingulate cortex, hippocampus, and amygdala.

long-term depression (LTD) A process in which synaptic transmission becomes less effective as a result of recent activity; with long-term potentiation, widely believed to represent a form of synaptic plasticity that could be the neural mechanism for learning.

long-term potentiation (LTP) A process in which synaptic transmission becomes more effective as a result of recent activity; with long-term depression, widely believed to represent a form of synaptic plasticity that could be the neural mechanism for learning.

magnetic resonance imaging (MRI) A method of structural neuroimaging based on recording changes in magnetic fields.

massed practice Concentrated, continuous practice of a skill.

matching law of choice behavior The principle that an organism, given a choice between multiple responses, will make one response at a rate proportional to how often that response is reinforced relative to the other choices.

mathematical psychology A subfield of psychology that uses mathematical equations to describe the laws of learning and memory.

medial temporal lobes Brain regions in each hemisphere that include the hippocampus, amygdala, and other areas important for memory.

memory The record of past experiences acquired through learning.

mere exposure learning Learning through mere exposure to stimuli, without any explicit prompting and without any outward responding.

mirror neurons Neurons that respond during performance of an action and during visual observations of that same action.

mirror reading An experimental task that requires individuals to read mirror-reversed text; used to test cognitive skill learning.

mirror tracing An experimental task that requires individuals to trace drawings by watching a mirror image of their hand and the figure to be traced, with the hand and figure concealed; used to test perceptual-motor skill learning.

mnemonic A strategy to aid in memorization.

modeling Demonstration of actions.

mood-congruency of memory The principle that it is easier to retrieve memories that match our current mood.

motor program A sequence of movements that an organism can perform automatically (with minimal attention).

multimodal Related to or responding to more than one sensory modality.

multiple memory trace theory The theory that episodic memories are encoded by an ensemble of hippocampal and cortical neurons and that both hippocampus and cortex are normally involved in storing and retrieving even very old memories.

mutation Accidental changes in the DNA sequence that may occur due to outside causes (such as radiation or viral infection) or are due to a copying error as the organism produces new cells.

nativism A philosophical school of thought that holds that the bulk of knowledge is inborn (or native); contrast *empiricism*.

natural selection A proposed mechanism for evolution, also known as "survival of the fittest," which holds that species evolve when there is some trait that varies naturally across individuals, is inheritable, and increases an individual's "fitness," or chance of survival and reproductive success.

negative patterning A behavioral paradigm in which the response to the individual cues should be positive while the response to the pattern is negative (no response).

negative punishment A type of instrumental conditioning in which the response causes a punisher to be taken away or "subtracted" from the environment; over time, the response becomes less frequent.

negative reinforcement A type of instrumental conditioning in which the response causes a reinforcer to be taken away or "subtracted" from the environment; over time, the response becomes more frequent.

nervous system An organism's system of tissues specialized for distributing and processing information.

neurofibrillary tangles Collapsed remains of the proteins that normally function as scaffolding to hold a neuron in place and that help transport nutrients around the cell; such tangles in the brain are one of the hallmarks of Alzheimer's disease.

neurogenesis Creation of new neurons in the brain.

neuromodulator A neurotransmitter that acts to modulate activity in a large number of neurons, rather than in a single synapse.

neuron A type of cell that is specialized for information processing.

neurophysiology The study of the activity and function of neurons.

neuropsychology The branch of psychology that deals with the relation between brain function and behavior.

neuroscience The study of the brain and the rest of the nervous system.

neurotransmitter One of several classes of molecule released by neurons to carry chemical messages to other neurons.

non-associative learning Learning that involves only one, relatively isolated stimulus at a time.

nondeclarative memory A category of memory that includes skill memory, conditioning, fear learning, and other memories that are difficult to verbalize or "declare"; contrast *declarative memory*.

norepinephrine A neurotransmitter chemically related to epinephrine and involved in mediating the fight-or-flight response in the brain.

nucleus accumbens A part of the basal ganglia that receives and releases dopamine and that may play an important role in learning about reinforcement.

nucleus basalis A small group of neurons located in the basal forebrain.

observational conditioning A process in which an individual learns an emotional response after observing similar responses in others.

observational learning A process in which the learner actively monitors events and then chooses later actions based on those observations.

occipital lobe The part of the cerebral cortex lying at the rear of the human brain; important for visual processing.

open skill A skill in which movements are made on the basis of predictions about changing demands of the environment.

orienting response An organism's innate reaction to a novel stimulus.

parahippocampal region Cortical areas of the brain that lie near the hippocampus inside the medial temporal lobe.

parietal lobe The part of the cerebral cortex lying at the top of the human brain; important for processing somatosensory (touch) information and motor outputs.

Parkinson's disease A disorder resulting from disruptions in the normal functioning of the basal ganglia and progressive deterioration of motor control and perceptual-motor skill learning.

pathological addiction A strong habit that is maintained despite known harmful consequences.

perceptual learning Learning in which experience with a set of stimuli makes it easier to distinguish those stimuli.

perceptual-motor skill Learned movement patterns guided by sensory inputs.

peripheral nervous system (PNS) The part of the nervous system that carries information from sensory receptors to the central nervous system and carries commands from the CNS to muscles.

perseveration A failure to learn a new response, especially as demonstrated by continued adherence to an old, no longer valid response rule.

perspective taking Imagining oneself in the place of another.

phobia An excessive and irrational fear of an object, place, or situation.

phonological loop An auditory memory maintained by internal (subvocal) speech rehearsal.

phrenology A field of study that attempted to determine mental abilities by measuring head shape and size.

piloerection An emotional response in mammals in which body hair stands on end, making the animal look bigger and more threatening than it is.

place cell A neuron that fires maximally when the organism enters a particular location within an environment.

place field The spatial location that evokes maximal activity in a place cell.

placebo An inactive substance, such as a sugar pill, that is administered to the control subjects in an experiment to compare against the effects of an active substance, such as a drug.

positive punishment A type of instrumental conditioning in which the response must be withheld, or else a punisher is "added" to the environment; over time, the response becomes less frequent.

positive reinforcement A type of instrumental conditioning in which the response causes a reinforcer to be "added" to the environment; over time, the response becomes more frequent.

positron emission tomography (PET) A method of functional neuroimaging based on injecting a radioactive chemical into the bloodstream and measuring its accumulation in active areas of the brain.

postreinforcement pause In instrumental conditioning with a fixed-ratio (FR) schedule of reinforcement, a brief pause following a period of fast responding leading to reinforcement.

postsynaptic On the receiving side of a synapse.

posttraumatic stress disorder (PTSD) An anxiety disorder that can develop after exposure to a traumatic event; symptoms can include intrusive recollections, flashbacks, nightmares, emotional numbing, heightened anxiety, and avoidance of reminders of the trauma.

power law of learning A law stating that the degree to which a practice trial improves performance diminishes after a certain point, so that additional trials are needed to further improve the skill; learning occurs quickly at first, then slows.

pragmatics Rules about how conversation is conducted in a language.

prediction error The difference between what was predicted and what actually occurred.

prefrontal cortex (PFC) The frontmost (anterior) part of the frontal lobe cortex, essential for working memory and executive control.

Premack principle The theory that the opportunity to perform a highly frequent behavior can reinforce a less-frequent behavior; later refined as the response deprivation hypothesis.

presynaptic On the sending side of a synapse.

primary reinforcers Stimuli (e.g., food, water, sex, and sleep) that are innately reinforcing, meaning that organisms will tend to repeat behaviors that result in access to these stimuli.

priming A phenomenon in which prior exposure to a stimulus can improve the ability to recognize that stimulus later.

proactive interference Disruption of new learning by previously stored information.

punisher A consequence of behavior that leads to a reduction of that behavior in future.

punishment In instrumental conditioning, the process of providing consequences for a behavior that decrease the probability of that behavior occurring again in the future.

Purkinje cell A large drop-shaped and densely branching neuron in the cerebellar cortex.

radical behaviorism An extreme form of behaviorism, championed by B. F. Skinner, holding that consciousness and free will are illusions and that even so-called higher cognitive functions (e.g., human language) are merely complex sets of stimulus-response associations.

receptive field The range (or "field") of physical stimuli that activate a single neuron.

receptor A specialized molecule, located on the surface of a neuron, to which one or more particular neurotransmitters can bind; when a neurotransmitter activates a receptor, effects may be initiated in the neuron.

recognition A memory test that involves picking out (or recognizing) a studied item from a list of possible options.

reflex An involuntary and automatic (unlearned) response; also, a pathway from sensory stimulus to motor response.

reinforcement In instrumental conditioning, the process of providing consequences for a behavior that increase the probability of that behavior occurring again in the future.

reinforcement schedule A schedule defining how often consequences are delivered in an instrumental conditioning paradigm. See also *continuous reinforcement; fixed-ratio (FR) schedule; fixed-interval (FI) schedule; variable-ratio (VR) schedule; variable-interval (VI) schedule.*

reinforcer A consequence of behavior that leads to increased likelihood of that behavior in the future.

response deprivation hypothesis A refinement of the Premack principle stating that the opportunity to perform any behavior can be reinforcing if access to that behavior is restricted.

retention curve A graph showing forgetting or relearning as a function of time since initial learning.

retroactive interference Disruption of old learning by recently acquired information.

retrograde amnesia The loss of episodic memories dating from before a brain injury or disruption; memory loss usually occurs in a time-graded manner, so more recent memories are devastated but very old ones may be spared.

reward prediction hypothesis The theory that dopamine is involved in predicting future reinforcement.

Ribot gradient A pattern of memory loss in which recently acquired memories are more prone to disruption than older memories.

rotary pursuit task An experimental task that requires individuals to keep the end of a pointed stick (stylus) above a fixed point on a rotating disk; used to study perceptual-motor skill learning.

second language learning Acquiring the capability to comprehend and produce any language after one's first language.

secondary reinforcers Stimuli that have no intrinsic value but that have been paired with primary reinforcers or that provide access to primary reinforcers.

self-control An organism's willingness to forgo a small immediate reinforcement in favor of a large future reinforcement.

semantic memory Memory for facts or general knowledge about the world.

semantics The meaning or interpretation of words and sentences.

sensitive period A time window, usually early in life, during which a certain kind of learning is most effective.

sensitization A phenomenon in which a salient stimulus (such as an electric shock) temporarily increases the strength of responses to other stimuli.

sensory cortex The areas of cerebral cortex involved in processing sensory information such as sight or sound.

sensory memory Brief, transient sensations of what has just been perceived when someone sees, hears, or tastes something.

sensory preconditioning Training in which presentation of two stimuli together as a compound results in a later tendency to generalize what is known about one of these stimuli to the other.

sensory prosthesis A mechanical device designed to supplement or substitute for a faulty sensory modality such as vision or hearing; the device's sensory detectors interface with brain areas that normally process those sensory inputs.

serial reaction time task An experimental task that requires individuals to press keys in specific sequences on the basis of cues provided by a computer; used to study implicit learning.

shaping A form of instrumental conditioning in which successive approximations to the desired response are reinforced.

short-term memory A temporary memory that is maintained through active rehearsal.

single-cell recording Use of an implanted electrode to detect electrical activity (spiking) in a single cell (such as neuron).

skill An ability that can improve over time through practice.

skill decay Loss of a skill because of non-use.

skin conductance response (SCR) A change in the skin's electrical conductivity associated with emotions such as anxiety, fear, or surprise; also known as the galvanic skin response (GSR).

Skinner box A conditioning chamber in which reinforcement or punishment is delivered automatically whenever an animal makes a response (such as pressing a lever); also called an operant chamber.

social conformity The tendency to adopt the behavior of the group.

social learning Learning from others; often used as a synonym for observational learning.

social learning theory A theory of human behavior prominent from the 1940s through the 1960s that proposed that the kinds of reinforcements an individual has experienced in the past will determine how that individual will act in any given situation.

social transmission of information A process seen in all human cultures in which an observer learns something new through experiences with others.

soma The central portion of the neuron that contains the nucleus and integrates signals from all the dendrites; also known as the cell body.

source amnesia Remembering a fact or event but misattributing the source or context in which this information was acquired.

spaced practice Practice of a skill that is spread out over several sessions.

spines Small protrusions on dendrites where synapses can be formed.

spontaneous recovery Reappearance (or increase in strength) of a previously habituated response after a short period of no stimulus presentation.

standard consolidation theory The theory that the hippocampus is initially required for episodic memory storage and retrieval but that, over time, its contribution diminishes until the cortex alone can store and retrieve old memories.

stem cells Undifferentiated cells (especially in fetal tissue) that have the ability to develop into particular cell types (for example, into neurons or glia).

stimulus A sensory event that provides information about the outside world.

stimulus enhancement A process in which observation of other individuals causes an organism's attention to be directed toward specific objects or events within an environment.

stimulus matching A type of imitation in which the observer generates stimuli that can be directly compared with the originally observed stimuli.

stimulus representation The form in which information about stimuli is encoded within a model or brain.

stress hormone A hormone that is released in response to signals from the autonomic nervous system (ANS) and helps mediate the fight-or-flight response; examples include epinephrine and the glucocorticoids.

structural neuroimaging Techniques (such as MRI and CT) for creating images of anatomical structures within the living brain.

subject bias The degree to which a participant's prior knowledge or expectations can influence the outcome of an experiment.

subsong The sounds baby songbirds produce when first learning to sing.

superstition Responses that individuals make because they mistakenly believe that those responses lead to desired outcomes.

symbol An internal representation of a concept, quality, idea, or other object.

symbol-manipulation models Models of learning and memory that store and manipulate symbols and the labeled links that connect them.

synapse A narrow gap between two neurons across which chemical messages can be transmitted.

synaptic depression A reduction in synaptic transmission; a possible neural mechanism underlying habituation.

synaptic plasticity The ability of synapses to change as a result of experience.

synaptogenesis Creation of new synapses.

syntax Rules about how words should be ordered within a language.

systematic desensitization A treatment for phobia, similar to extinction, in which the patient is exposed to successive approximations of the fear-evoking stimulus until the fear response is no longer produced to each stimulus.

talent A person's genetically endowed ability to perform a skill better than most.

template model of song learning A model of song learning having three basic phases: song memorization, song practice, and song utilization.

temporal lobe The part of the cerebral cortex lying at the sides of the human brain; important for language and auditory processing and for learning new facts and forming new memories of events.

testosterone The most important androgen and, hence, the principal male sex hormone.

theory A set of statements devised to explain a group of facts.

theory of equipotentiality The theory that memories are stored globally, by the brain as a whole, rather than in one particular brain area.

tolerance A decrease in reaction to a drug so that larger doses are required to achieve the same effect.

topographic representation A stimulus representation in which the physical closeness of the representations in the brain (or model) for two stimuli is a reflection of their physical proximity or similarity in the external world.

trace conditioning A conditioning procedure in which there is a temporal gap between the end of the CS and the beginning of the US.

transcranial magnetic stimulation A procedure applying a brief magnetic pulse or series of pulses to the scalp, thus modulating activity in cortical networks; used experimentally to temporarily disrupt cortical activity, enabling researchers to study the role of cortical circuits in skill learning and performance.

transfer specificity The restricted applicability of learned skills to specific situations.

transfer-appropriate processing The principle that memory retrieval is best when the cues available at testing are similar to those available at encoding.

transient global amnesia (TGA) A temporary disruption of memory, usually including both anterograde amnesia and retrograde amnesia.

transient memories Nonpermanent memories that last seconds or minutes, including both sensory memory and short-term memory.

transitional probabilities How often one kind of syllable follows another.

trial-level model A theory of learning in which all of the cues that occur during a trial and all of the changes that result are considered a single event.

trisomy 21 A genetic "accident" in which the organism has an extra (third) copy of chromosome 21, resulting in Down syndrome.

true imitation Copying that involves reproducing motor acts.

two-action test A technique developed to demonstrate imitation abilities that involves exposing naive animals to demonstrators trained to achieve the same goal using different actions.

unconditioned response (UR) The naturally occurring response to an unconditioned stimulus (US).

unconditioned stimulus (US) A cue that has some biological significance and in the absence of prior training naturally evokes a response.

US modulation theory Theories of conditioning that say the stimulus that enters into an association is determined by a change in how the US is processed.

variable practice Practice involving the performance of skills in a wide variety of contexts.

variable-interval (VI) schedule In instrumental conditioning, a reinforcement schedule in which the first response after a fixed amount of time, on average, is reinforced; thus, VI 12 means that the first response after 1 minute, on average, is reinforced.

variable-ratio (VR) schedule In instrumental conditioning, a reinforcement schedule in which a certain number of responses, on average, are required before a reinforcer is delivered; thus, VR 5 means that, on average, every fifth response is reinforced.

ventral tegmental area (VTA) A part of the brainstem that projects dopamine to the nucleus accumbens and that may play an important role in learning about reinforcement.

visual sensory memory The initial temporary storage for information perceived by the visual system.

visuo-spatial sketchpad The component of Baddeley's model of working memory that holds visual and spatial images for manipulation.

vocal learning Acquiring the ability to produce sounds using memories of those sounds.

Wernicke's area A cortical region in the left temporal lobe that when damaged produces language deficits, especially in relation to language comprehension.

Wernicke-Geschwind model A model of cortical function in which Broca's area is responsible for speech production, Wernicke's area is responsible for word storage, and surrounding cortical regions provide the conceptual information needed to produce and comprehend language.

word segmentation Recognizing where one word stops and another begins in a continuous stream of speech sounds.

word-length effect The tendency for a person to remember fewer words from a list as the length of the words increases.

word-stem completion task A task in which participants are asked to fill in the blanks in a list of word stems (e.g., MOT___) to produce the first word that comes to mind; in a priming experiment, participants are more likely to produce a particular word (e.g., MOTEL) if they have been exposed to that word previously.

working memory The active maintenance and manipulation of short-term memory.

Abi-Dargham, A., Mawlawi, O., Lombardo, I., Gil, R., Martinez, D., Huang, U., Hwang, D., Keiop, J., Kochan, L., VanHeertum, R., Gorman, J., & Laruelle, M. (2002). Prefrontal dopamine D1 receptors and working memory in schizophrenia. *Journal of Neuroscience, 22*(9), 3708–3719.

Achten, E., Jackson, G., Cameron, J., Abbott, D., Stella, D., & Fabinyi, G. (1999). Presurgical evaluation of the motor hand area with functional MR imaging in patients with tumors and dysplastic lesions. *Radiology, 210,* 529–538.

Ackerly, S. S. (1964). A case of paranatal bilateral frontal lobe defect observed for thirty years. In J. M. Warren & K. Akert (Eds.), *The frontal granular cortex and behavior* (pp. 192–218). New York: McGraw-Hill.

Acredolo, L., & Goodwyn, S. (1988). Symbolic gesturing in normal infants. *Child Development, 59*(2), 450–466.

Acredolo, L., & Goodwyn, S. (2002). *Baby signs.* Chicago: Contemporary Books.

Aggleton, J., & Mishkin, M. (1983). Visual recognition impairment following medial thalamic lesion in monkeys. *Neuropsychologia, 21,* 189–197.

Aguirre, G. K., & D'Esposito, M. (1999). Topographical disorientation: a synthesis and taxonomy. *Brain, 122,* 1613–1628.

Aguirre, G. K., Detre, J. A., Alsop, D. C., & D'Esposito, M. (1996). The parahippocampus subserves topographical learning in man. *Cerebral Cortex, 6,* 823–829.

Ahissar, M., & Hochstein, S. (1997). Task difficulty and the specificity of perceptual learning. *Nature, 387,* 401–406.

Akins, C. K., & Zentall, T. R. (1996). Imitative learning in male Japanese quail (Coturnix japonica) using the two-action method. *Journal of Comparative Psychology, 110*(3), 316–320.

Akins, C. K., & Zentall, T. R. (1998). Imitation in Japanese quail: the role of reinforcement of the demonstrator's response. *Psychonomic Bulletin & Review, 5,* 694–697.

al Maskati, H., & Zbrozyna, A. (1989). Cardiovascular and motor components of the defence reaction elicited in rats by electrical and chemical stimulation in amygdala. *Journal of the Autonomic Nervous System, 28,* 127–131.

Albert, M. (1996). Cognitive and neurobiological markers of early Alzheimer disease. *Proceedings of the National Academy of Sciences USA, 93,* 13547–13551.

Allen, M. T., Chelius, L., & Gluck, M. A. (2002). Selective entorhinal lesions and non-selective cortical-hippocampal region lesions, but not selective hippocampal lesions, disrupt learned irrelevance in rabbit eyeblink conditioning. *Cognitive Affective and Behavioral Neuroscience, 2,* 214–226.

Allen, M., Chelius, L., Masand, V., Gluck, M., Myers, C., & Schnirman, G. (2002). A comparison of latent inhibition and learned irrelevance pre-exposure effects in rabbit and human eyeblink conditioning. *Integrative Physiological and Behavioral Science, 37*(3), 188–214.

Allen, M. T., Myers, C., Schnirman, G., Chelius, L., Masand, V., & Gluck, M. (2002). A comparison of latent inhibition and learned irrelevance pre-exposure effects in rabbit and human eyeblink conditioning. *Integrative Physiological and Behavioral Science, 37,* 188–214.

Allison, J. (1983). *Behavioral economics.* New York: Praeger.

Allison, J. (1993). Response deprivation, reinforcement, and economics. *Journal of the Experimental Analysis of Behavior, 60,* 129–140.

Alvarez, P., & Squire, L. (1994). Memory consolidation and the medial temporal lobe: a simple network model. *Proceedings of the National Academy of Sciences USA, 91,* 7041–7045.

Alzheimer, A. (1907/1987). Über eine eigenartige Erkrangkung der Hirnrinde [About a peculiar disease of the cerebral cortex]. Translated by L. Jourvik H. Greenson. *Alzheimer's Disease and Associated Disorders, 1,* 3–8.

Anderson, C. A. (2004). An update on the effects of playing violent video games. *Journal of Adolescence, 27*(1), 113–122.

Anderson, C. A., Berkowitz, L., Donnerstein, E., Hucsmann, L. R., Johnson, J. D., Linz, D., Malamuth, N. M., & Wartella, E. (2003). The influence of media violence on youth. *Psychological Science in the Public Interest, 4,* 82–110.

Anderson, C. A., & Bushman, B. J. (2001). Effects of violent video games on aggressive behavior, aggressive cognition, aggressive affect, physiological arousal, and prosocial behavior: a meta-analytic review of the scientific literature. *Psychological Science, 12,* 353–359.

Anderson, J. R. (1976). *Language, memory and thought.* Mahwah, NJ: Lawrence Erlbaum.

Anderson, J. R. (Ed.). (1981a). *Cognitive skills and their acquisition.* Hillsdale, NJ: Lawrence Erlbaum.

Anderson, J. R. (1981b). Interference: the relationship between response latency and response accuracy. *Journal of Experimental Psychology: Human Learning and Memory, 7,* 311–325.

Anderson, J. R. (1982). Acquisition of cognitive skill. *Psychological Review, 89,* 369–406.

Anderson, J. R., & Bower, G. H. (1973). *Human associative memory.* New York: Halstead.

Anderson, J. R., Corbett, A. T., Koedinger, K. R., & Pelletier, R. (1995). Cognitive tutors: lessons learned. *Journal of the Learning Sciences, 4,* 167–207.

Anderson, J. R., Fincham, J. M., & Douglass, S. (1997). The role of examples and rules in the acquisition of a cognitive skill. *Journal of Experimental Psychology: Learning, Memory and Cognition, 23,* 932–945.

Anderson, M., Ochsner, K., Kuhl, B., Cooper, J., Robertson, E., Gabrieli, S., Glover, G., & Gabrieli, J. (2004). Neural systems underlying the suppression of unwanted memories. *Science, 303,* 232–235.

Anderson, S. R., & Lightfoot, D. W. (2002). *The language organ: linguistics as cognitive physiology.* Cambridge, England: Cambridge University Press.

Anderson, S. W., Damasio, H., Jones, R. D., & Tranel, D. (1991). Wisconsin Card Sorting Test performance as a measure of frontal lobe damage. *Journal of Clinical and Experimental Neuropsychology, 13*(6), 909–922.

APA Online. (2004). Violence in the media—Psychologists help protect children from harmful effects. Retrieved from http://www.psychologymatters.org/mediaviolence.html

Apostolova, L., Dutton, R., Dinov, I., Hayashi, K., Toga, A., Cummings, J., & Thompson, P. (2006). Conversion of mild cognitive impairment to Alzheimer disease predicted by hippocampal atrophy maps. *Archives of Neurology, 63,* 693–699.

Archibald, S. J., Mateer, C. A., & Kerns, K. A. (2001). Utilization behavior: clinical manifestations and neurological mechanisms. *Neuropsychology Review, 11*(3), 117–130.

Arthur, W., Bennett, W., Stanush, P. L., & McNelly, T. L. (1998). Factors that influence skill decay and retention: a quantitative review and analysis. *Human Performance, 11*(1), 57–101.

Ash, D., & Holding, D. H. (1990). Backward versus forward chaining in the acquisition of a keyboard skill. *Human Factors, 32,* 139–146.

Ashby, F., & Waldron, E. (2000). The neuropsychological bases of category learning. *Current Directions in Psychological Science, 9,* 10–14.

Ashmore, R. D., & Del Boca, F. K. (1981). Conceptual approaches to stereotypes and stereotyping. In D. L. Hamilton (Ed.), *Cognitive processes in stereotyping and intergroup behavior* (pp. 1–35). Hillsdale, NJ: Lawrence Erlbaum.

Astur, R., Ortiz, M., & Sutherland, R. (1998). A characterization of performance by men and women in a virtual Morris water task: a large and reliable sex difference. *Behavioural Brain Research, 93,* 185–190.

Atkinson, R. C., & Shiffrin, R. M. (1968). Human memory: a proposed system and its control processes. In K. W. Spence and J. T. Spence (Eds.), *The psychology of learning and motivation: advances in research and theory* (vol. 2, pp. 89–195). New York: Academic Press.

Awh, E., & Jonides, J. (1998). Spatial selective attention and spatial working memory. In R. Parasuraman (Ed.), *The attentive brain* (pp. 353–380). Cambridge, MA: MIT Press.

Awh, E., Jonides, J., Smith, E. E., Schumacher, E. H., Koeppe, R. A., & Katz, S. (1996). Dissociation of storage and rehearsal in verbal working memory: Evidence from PET. *Psychological Science, 7,* 25–31.

Ayllon, T., & Haughton, E. (1964). Modification of symptomatic verbal behavior of mental patients. *Behavior Research and Therapy, 2,* 87–97.

Bachevalier, J., & Mishkin, M. (1994). Effects of selective neonatal temporal lobe lesions on visual recognition memory in rhesus monkeys. *Journal of Neuroscience, 14,* 2128–2139.

Baddeley, A. D. (1986). *Working memory.* Oxford, England: Clarendon Press.

Baddeley, A. D., & Hitch G. (1974). Working memory. In G. A. Bower (Ed.), *Recent advances in learning and motivation* (vol. 8, pp. 47–90). New York: Academic Press.

Baddeley, A. D., & Longman, D. (1978). The influence of length and frequency of training session on the rate of learning to type. *Ergonomics, 21,* 627–635.

Baddeley, A. D., Thomson, N., & Buchanan, M. (1975). Word length and the structure of short-term memory. *Journal of Verbal Learning and Verbal Behavior, 14,* 575–589.

Bahrick, H., Bahrick, P., & Wittlinger, R. (1975). Fifty years of memory for names and faces: a cross-sectional approach. *Journal of Experimental Psychology: General, 104,* 54–75.

Bakin, J. S., & Weinberger, N. M. (1990). Classical conditioning induces CS-specific receptive field plasticity in the auditory cortex of the guinea pig. *Brain Research, 536,* 271–286.

Bakin, J. S., & Weinberger, N. M. (1996). Induction of a physiological memory in the cerebral cortex by stimulation of the nucleus basalis. *Proceedings of the National Academy of Sciences, 93,* 11219–11224.

Baldo, J. V., & Shimamura, A. P. (2000). Spatial and color working memory in patients with lateral prefrontal cortex lesions. *Psychobiology, 28,* 156–167.

Baldwin, J. (1896). A new factor in evolution. *American Naturalist, 30,* 441–451, 536–553.

Ball, G., & Hulse, S. (1998). Birdsong. *American Psychologist, 53,* 37–58.

Bancaud, J., Brunet-Bourgin, F., Chauvel, P., & Halgren, E. (1994). Anatomical origin of déjà vu and vivid "memories" in human temporal lobe epilepsy. *Brain, 117,* 71–90.

Bandura, A. (1969). *Principles of behavior modification.* New York: Holt, Reinhart, & Winston.

Bandura, A. (1986). *Social foundations of thought and action: A social cognitive theory.* Englewood Cliffs, NJ: Prentice-Hall.

Bandura, A., Ross, D., & Ross, S. A. (1961). Transmission of aggression through imitation of aggressive models. *Journal of Abnormal and Social Psychology, 63,* 575–582.

Bao, J. X., Kandel, E. R., & Hawkins, R. D. (1998). Involvement of presynaptic and postsynaptic mechanisms in a cellular analog of classical conditioning at *Aplysia* sensory-motor neuron synapses in isolated cell culture. *Journal of Neuroscience 18*(1), 458–466.

Baptista, L. F., & King, J. R. (1980). Geographical variation in song and song dialects of montane white-crowned sparrows. *Condor, 82,* 267–281.

Barch, D. M., Csernansky, J., Conturo, T., Snyder, A. Z., & Ollinger, J. (2002). Working and long-term memory deficits in schizophrenia: is there a common underlying prefrontal mechanism? *Journal of Abnormal Psychology, 111,* 478–494.

Bardo, M. (1998). Neuropharmacological mechanisms of drug reward: Beyond dopamine in the nucleus accumbens. *Critical Reviews in Neurobiology, 12,* 37–67.

Bar-Hillel, M. (1984). Representativeness and the fallacies of probability. *Acta Psychologica, 55,* 91–107.

Barnes, C. A. (1979). Memory deficits associated with senescence: a neurophysiological and behavioral study in the rat. *Journal of Comparative and Physiological Psychology, 93,* 74–104.

Barnes, C. A., Suster, M., Shen, J., & McNaughton, B. L. (1997). Multistability of cognitive maps in the hippocampus of old rats. *Nature, 388,* 272–275.

Barnes, T. D., Kubota, Y., Hu, D., Jin, D. Z., & Graybiel, A. M. (2005). Activity of striatal neurons reflects dynamic encoding and recoding of procedural memories. *Nature, 437,* 1158–1161.

Barnfield, A. (1999). Development of sex differences in spatial memory. *Perceptual and Motor Skills, 89,* 339–350.

Baron-Cohen, S., Ring, H., Moriarty, J., Schmitz, B., Costa, D., & Ell, P. (1994). Recognition of mental state terms: clinical findings in children with autism and a functional neuroimaging study of normal adults. *British Journal of Psychiatry, 165*(5), 640–649.

Barr, R. (1980). Some remarks on the time-course of aging. In L. Poon, J. Fozard, L. Cermak, D. Arenberg & L. Thompson (Eds.), *New directions in memory and aging* (pp. 143–149). Hillsdale, NJ: Lawrence Erlbaum.

Bartsch, D., Ghirardi, M., Skehel, P. A., Karl, K. A., Herder, S. P., Chen, M., Bailey, C. H., & Kandel, E. R. (1995). *Aplysia* CREB2 represses long-term facilitation: relief of repression converts transient facilitation into long-term functional and structural change. *Cell, 83,* 979–992.

Basham, M. E., Nordeen, E. J., & Nordeen, K. W. (1996). Blockade of NMDA receptors in the anterior forebrain impairs sensory acquisition in the zebra finch. *Neurobiology of Learning and Memory, 66,* 295–304.

Bauer, P. (1996). What do infants recall of their lives? Memory for specific events by one- to two-year-olds. *American Psychologist, 51,* 29–41.

Bauer, R., & McDonald, C. (2003). Auditory agnosia and amusia. In T. Feinberg & M. Farah (Eds.), *Behavioral neurology and neuropsychology* (2nd ed., pp. 257–270). New York: McGraw-Hill.

Baumann, M. L. (1991). Microscopic neuroanatomic abnormalities in autism. *Pediatrics, 87,* 791–796.

Baumrind, D. (2002). Ordinary physical punishment: is it harmful? Comment on Gershoff (2002). *Psychological Bulletin, 128,* 580–589.

Bayley, P., Gold, J., Hopkins, R., & Squire, L. (2005). The neuroanatomy of remote memory. *Neuron, 46,* 799–810.

Beadle-Brown, J. D., & Whiten, A. (2004). Elicited imitation in children and adults with autism: is there a deficit? *Journal of Intellectual & Developmental Disability, 292,* 147–163.

Bechara, A., Tranel, D., Damasio, H., Adolphs, R., Rockland, C., & Damasio, A. (1995). Double dissociation of conditioning and declarative knowledge relative to the amygdala and hippocampus in humans. *Science, 269,* 1115–1118.

Beck, B. (1980). *Animal tool behavior: the use and manufacture of tools by animals.* New York: Garland STPM Press.

Bee, M. A. (2001). Habituation and sensitization of aggression in bullfrogs (*Rana catesbeiana*): testing the dual-process theory of habituation. *Journal of Comparative Psychology, 115,* 307–316.

Beglinger, L. J., Gaydos, B. L., Kareken, D. A., Tangphao-Daniels, O., Siemers, E. R., & Mohs, R. C. (2004). Neuropsychological test performance in healthy volunteers before and after donepezil administration. *Journal of Psychopharmacology, 18,* 102–108.

Bekerian, D., & Baddeley, A. (1980). Saturation advertising and the repetition effect. *Journal of Verbal Learning and Verbal Behavior, 19,* 17–25.

Bell, C. (1811). *An idea of a new anatomy of the brain.* London: Strahan and Preston.

Benjamin, M., McKeachie, W., Lin, Y.-G., & Holinger, D. (1981). Test anxiety: deficits in information processing. *Journal of Educational Psychology, 73,* 816–824.

Bennett, D., Wilson, R., Schneider, J., Evans, D., Mendes de Leon, C., Arnold, S., Barnes, L. & Bienias, J. (2003). Education modifies the relation of AD pathology to level of cognitive function in older persons. *Neurology, 60,* 1909–1915.

Berger-Sweeney, J., Stearns, N. A., Frick, K. M., Beard, B., & Baxter, M. G. (2000). Cholinergic basal forebrain is critical for social transmission of food preferences. *Hippocampus, 10*(6), 729–738.

Berke, J. (2003). Learning and memory mechanisms involved in compulsive drug use and relapse. In J. Wang (Eds.), *Methods in molecular medicine: Vol. 79. Drugs of abuse: neurological reviews and protocols* (pp. 75–101). Totowa, NJ: Humana Press.

Berridge, K. (1996). Food reward: brain substrates of wanting and liking. *Neuroscience and Biobehavioral Reviews, 20,* 1–25.

Berridge, K., & Robinson, T. (1998). What is the role of dopamine in reward: hedonic impact, reward learning, or incentive salience? *Brain Research Reviews, 28,* 309–369.

Berry, S. D., & Thompson, R. F. (1978). Neuronal plasticity in the limbic system during classical conditioning of the rabbit nictitating membrane response. I. The hippocampus. *Brain Research, 145,* 323–346.

Besson, A., Privat, A., Eschalier, A., & Fialip, J. (1999). Dopaminergic and opioidergic mediations of tricyclic antidepressants in the learned helplessness paradigm. *Pharmacology, Biochemistry and Behavior, 64,* 541–548.

Biederman, I., & Shiffrar, M. (1987). Sexing day-old chicks: a case study and expert systems analysis of a difficult perceptual learning task. *Journal of Experimental Psychology: Learning, Memory, and Cognition, 13,* 640–645.

Bimonte, H., Hyde, L., Hoplight, B., & Denenberg, V. (2000). In two species, females exhibit superior working memory and inferior reference memory on the water radial-arm maze. *Physiology and Behavior, 70,* 311–317.

Birren, J. (1964). *The psychology of aging.* Englewood Cliffs, NJ: Prentice Hall.

Bjork, D. (1983). *B. F. Skinner: a life.* New York, Basic Books.

Blackmore, S. (1999). *The meme machine.* Oxford, England: Oxford University Press.

Bliss, T. V., & Gardner-Medwin, A. (1973) Long-lasting potentiation of synaptic transmission in the dentate area of the unanaesthetized rabbit following stimulation of the perforant path. *Journal of Physiology (London), 232,* 357–371.

Bliss, T. V., & Lømo, T. (1973). Long-lasting potentiation of synaptic transmission in the dentate area of the anaesthetized rabbit following stimulation of the perforant path. *Journal of Physiology, 232,* 331–356.

Boatman, D. (2004). Cortical bases of speech perception: evidence from functional lesions. *Cognition, 92,* 47–65.

Boesch, C. (1991). Teaching among wild chimpanzees. *Animal Behaviour, 41,* 530–532.

Bonanno, G. (2005). Resilience in the face of potential trauma. *Current Directions in Psychological Science, 14,* 135–138.

Bond, A. B., & Kamil, A. C. (1999). Searching image in blue jays: facilitation and interference in sequential priming. *Animal Learning and Behavior, 27,* 461–471.

Bookheimer, S. (2002). Functional MRI of language: new approaches to understanding the cortical organization of semantic processing. *Annual Review of Neuroscience, 25,* 151–188.

Borges, J. L. (2000). Funes, his memory. In J. Lethem (Ed.), *The Vintage book of amnesia: an anthology of writing on the subject of memory loss* (pp 119–126). New York: Vintage Crime. (Reprinted from Borges, J. L., *Collected fictions* [A. Hurley, Trans.], 1998, New York: Penguin Putnam)

Bornstein, M., & Lamb, M. (1992). *Development in infancy* (3rd ed.). New York: McGraw-Hill.

Borovsky, D., & Rovee-Collier, C. (1990). Contextual constraints on memory retrieval at six months. *Child Development, 61,* 1569–1583.

Borszcz, G., Cranney, J., & Leaton, R. (1989). Influence of long-term sensitization of the acoustic startle response in rats: central gray lesions, preexposure, and extinction. *Journal of Experimental Psychology: Animal Behavior Processes, 15,* 54–64.

Bourgeois, J.-P. (2001). Synaptogenesis in the neocortex of the newborn: the ultimate frontier for individuation? In C. Nelson & M. Luciana (Eds.), *Handbook of developmental cognitive neuroscience.* Cambridge, MA: MIT Press.

Bourtchuladze, R., Frenguelli, B., Blendy, J., Cioffi, D., Schutz, G., & Silva, A. J. (1994). Deficient long-term memory in mice with a targeted mutation of the CAMP-responsive element-binding protein. *Cell, 79,* 59–68.

Bouton, M. E. (2000). A learning theory perspective on lapse, relapse, and the maintenance of behavioral change. *Health Psychology, 19*(1), 57–63.

Bouton, M. E., & Peck, C. A. (1989). Context effects on conditioning, extinction and reinstatement in an appetitive conditioning paradigm. *Animal Learning and Behavior, 17,* 188–198.

Bower, G. H. (1961). Application of a model to paired-associate learning. *Psychometrika, 26,* 255–280.

Bower, G. H., & Trabasso, T. R. (1964). Concept identification. In R. C. Atkinson (Ed.), *Studies in Mathematical Psychology* (pp. 32–93). Stanford, CA: Stanford University Press.

Bower, G. H., & Trabasso, T. (1968). *Attention in learning: theory and research.* New York: John Wiley and Sons.

Boysen, S. T., Mukobi, K. L., & Berntson, G. G. (1999). Overcoming response bias using symbolic representations of number by chimpanzees (*Pan troglodytes*). *Animal Learning and Behavior, 27,* 229–235.

Braak, H., & Braak, E. (1997). Frequency of stages of Alzheimer-related lesions in different age categories. *Neurobiology of Aging, 18,* 351–357.

Bradbury, J. W., & Vehrencamp, S. L. (1998). *Principles of animal communication.* Sunderland, MA: Sinauer.

Brainard, M. S., & Doupe, A. J. (2000). Auditory feedback in learning and maintenance of vocal behavior. *Nature Reviews Neuroscience, 1,* 31–40.

Braine, M. D. S. (1963). On learning the grammatical order of words. *Psychological Review, 70,* 323–348.

Brambilla, P., Hardan, A., di Nemi, S. U., Perez, J., Soares, J. C., & Barale, F. (2003). Brain anatomy and development in autism: review of structural MRI studies. *Brain Research Bulletin, 61*(6), 557–569.

Brand, M., & Markowitsch, H. (2004). Amnesia: neuroanatomic and clinical issues. In T. Feinberg & M. Farah (Eds.), *Behavioral neurology and neuropsychology* (2nd ed., pp. 431–443). New York: McGraw-Hill.

Bransford, J., & Johnson, M. (1972). Contextual prerequisites for understanding: some investigations of comprehension and recall. *Journal of Verbal Learning and Verbal Behavior, 11,* 717–726.

Brass, M., Derrfuss, J., & von Cramon, D. Y. (2005). The inhibition of imitative and overlearned responses: a functional double dissociation. *Neuropsychologia, 43*(1), 89–98.

Brass, M., Derrfuss, J., Matthes-von Cramon, G., & von Cramon, D. Y. (2003). Imitative response tendencies in patients with frontal brain lesions. *Neuropsychology, 17*(2), 265–271.

Brauer, L., & de Wit, H. (1996). Subjective responses to D-amphetamine alone and after pimozide pretreatment in normal, healthy volunteers. *Biological Psychiatry, 39,* 26–32.

Brauer, L., & de Wit, H. (1997). High dose pimozide does not block amphetamine-induced euphoria in normal volunteers. *Pharmacology, Biochemistry, and Behavior, 56,* 265–272.

Breiter, H., Aharon, I., Kahneman, D., Dale, A., & Shizgal, P. (2001). Functional imaging of neural responses to expectancy and experience of monetary gains and losses. *Neuron, 30,* 619–639.

Breiter, H., Gollub, R., Weisskoff, R., Kennedy, D., Makris, N., Berke, J., Goodman, J., Kantor, H., Gastfriend, D., Riordan, J., Mathew, R., Rosen, B., & Hymen, S. (1997). Acute effects of cocaine on human brain activity and emotion. *Neuron, 19,* 591–611.

Breland, K., & Breland, M. (1951). A field of applied animal psychology. *American Psychologist, 6,* 202–204.

Breland, K., & Breland, M. (1961). The misbehavior of organisms. *American Psychologist, 16,* 681–684.

Brembs, B. (2003). Operant reward learning in *Aplysia*. *Current Directions in Psychological Science, 12,* 218–221.

Brenowitz, E. A., & Beecher, M. D. (2005). Song learning in birds: diversity and plasticity, opportunities and challenges. *Trends in Neuroscience, 28*(3), 127–132.

Brewer, J. B., Zhao, Z., Desmond, J. E., Glover, G. H., & Gabrieli, J. D. E. (1998). Making memories: brain activity that predicts whether visual experiences will be remembered or forgotten. *Science, 281,* 1185–1187.

Bridgett, D., & Cuevas, J. (2000). Effects of listening to Mozart and Bach on the performance of a mathematical test. *Perceptual and Motor Skills, 90,* 1171–1175.

Broca, P. (1986). Sur le siège de la faculté du langage articulé. In Berker, E., Berker, A., & Smith, A. (Trans.), Translation of Broca's 1865 report: localization of speech in the third left frontal convolution. *Archives of Neurology, 43,* 1065–1072. (Original work published 1865)

Brooks, L. (1968). Spatial and verbal components of the act of recall. *Canadian Journal of Psychology, 22,* 349–368.

Brown, B. (1999). Optimizing expression of the common human genome for child development. *Current Directions in Psychological Science, 8*(2), 37–41.

Brown, C., & Laland, K. N. (2002). Social learning of a novel avoidance task in the guppy: conformity and social release. *Animal Behaviour, 64,* 41–47.

Brown, G., & Stroup, K. (1988). Learned helplessness in the cockroach (*Periplaneta americana*). *Behavioral and Neural Biology, 50,* 246–250.

Brown, J. S. (1969). Factors affecting self-punitive locomotive behaviors. In B. Campbell & R. Church (Eds.), *Punishment and aversive behavior* (pp. 467–514). New York: Appleton-Century-Crofts.

Brown, J. W. (Ed.). (1988). *Agnosia and apraxia: selected papers of Liepmann, Lange, and Pötzl.* Hillsdale, NJ: Lawrence Erlbaum.

Brown, R., & Kulik, J. (1982). Flashbulb memories. In U. Neisser (Ed.), *Memory observed: remembering in natural contexts* (pp. 23–40). San Francisco: Freeman. (Reprinted from *Cognition, 5,* 73–99, 1977)

Brugge, K., Nichols, S., Salmon, D., Hill, L., Delis, D., Aaron, L., & Trauner, D. (1994). Cognitive impairments in adults with Down's syndrome: similarities to early cognitive changes in Alzheimer's disease. *Neurology, 44,* 232–238.

Brunelli, M., Castellucci, V., & Kandel, E. R. (1976). Synaptic facilitation and behavioral sensitization in *Aplysia*: possible role of serotonin and cyclic AMP. *Science, 194,* 1178–1181.

Bryan, R., Wells, S., Miller, T., Elster, A., Jungreis, C., Poirier, V., Lind, B., & Manolio, T. (1997). Infarctlike lesions in the brain: prevalence and anatomic characteristics at MR imaging of the elderly-Data from the Cardiovascular Health Study. *Radiology, 202,* 47–54.

Buccino, G., Binkofski, F., & Riggio, L. (2004). The mirror neuron system and action recognition. *Brain and Language, 89*(?), 370–376.

Buccino, G., Lui, F., Canessa, N., Patteri, I., Lagravinese, G., Benuzzi, F., Porro, C. A., & Rizzolatti, G. (2004). Neural circuits involved in the recognition of actions performed by nonconspecifics: an FMRI study. *Journal of Cognitive Neuroscience, 16*(1), 114–126.

Buchanan, T. W., Lutz, K., Mirzazade, S., Specht, K., Shah, N. J., Zilles, K., & Jancke, L. (2000). Recognition of emotional prosody and verbal components of spoken language: an fMRI study. *Brain Research: Cognitive Brain Research, 9*(3), 227–238.

Buchanan, T. W., & Lovallo, W. (2001). Enhanced memory for emotional material following stress-level cortisol treatment in humans. *Psychoneuroendocrinology, 26,* 307–317.

Buckner, R. L., Raichle, M. E., Miezin, F. M., & Petersen, S. E. (1996). Functional anatomic studies of memory retrieval for auditory words and visual pictures. *Journal of Neuroscience, 16,* 6219–6235.

Bunsey, M., & Eichenbaum, H. (1995). Selective damage to the hippocampal region blocks long-term retention of a natural and nonspatial stimulus-stimulus association. *Hippocampus, 5*(6), 546–556.

Burd, G., & Nottebohm, F. (1985). Ultrastructural characterization of synaptic terminals formed on newly generated neurons in a song control nucleus of the adult canary forebrain. *Journal of Comparative Neurology, 240*, 143–152.

Burgdorf, J., & Panksepp, J. (2001). Tickling induces reward in adolescent rats. *Physiology and Behavior, 72*, 167–173.

Butki, B. D., & Hoffman, S. J. (2003). Effects of reducing frequency of intrinsic knowledge of results on the learning of a motor skill. *Perceptual and Motor Skills, 97*, 569–580.

Butters, N. (1985). Alcoholic Korsakoff's syndrome: some unresolved issues concerning etiology, neuropathology and cognitive deficits. *Journal of Clinical and Experimental Neuropsychology, 7*, 272–273.

Butters, N., Wolfe, J., Martone, M., Granholm, E., & Cermak, L. (1985). Memory disorders associated with Huntington's disease: verbal recall, verbal recognition, and procedural memory. *Neuropsychologia, 23*, 729–743.

Buzsáki, G. (1989). Two-stage model of memory trace formation: a role for "noisy" brain states. *Neuroscience, 31*, 551–557.

Buzsáki, G. (2002). Theta oscillations in the hippocampus. *Neuron, 33*, 324–340.

Buzsáki, G., & Gage, F. (1989). Absence of long-term potentiation in the subcortically deafferented dentate gyrus. *Brain Research, 484*, 94–101.

Byrne, R. W. (1994). The evolution of intelligence. In P. Slater & T. R. Halliday (Eds.), *Behavior and evolution* (pp. 223–264). London: Cambridge University Press.

Cabeza, R., Rao, S., Wagner, A. D., Mayer, A., & Schacter, D. L. (2001). Can medial temporal lobe regions distinguish true from false? An event-related functional MRI study of veridical and illusory recognition memory. *Proceedings of the National Academy of Sciences USA, 98*, 4805–4810.

Cahill, L., & Alkire, M. (2003). Epinephrine enhancement of human memory consolidation: interaction with arousal at encoding. *Neurobiology of Learning and Memory, 79*, 194–198.

Cahill, L., Babinsky, R., Markowitsch, H., & McGaugh, J. (1995). The amygdala and emotional memory. *Nature, 377*, 295–296.

Cahill, L., Haier, R., Fallon, J., Alkire, M., Tang, C., Keator, D., Wu, J., & McGaugh, J. (1996). Amygdala activity at encoding correlated with long-term, free recall of emotional information. *Proceedings of the National Academy of Sciences USA, 93*, 8016–8021.

Cahill, L., & McGaugh, J. (1995). A novel demonstration of enhanced memory associated with emotional arousal. *Consciousness and Cognition, 4*, 410–421.

Cahill, L., Prins, B., Weber, M., & McGaugh, J. (1994). Beta-adrenergic activation and memory for emotional events. *Nature, 371*, 702–704.

Cahill, L., Weinberger, N. M., Roozendaal, B., & McGaugh, J. (1999). Is the amygdala a locus of "conditioned fear"? Some questions and caveats. *Neuron, 23*, 227–228.

Campbell, R., & Conway, M. (Eds.). (1995). *Broken memories: a case study in memory impairment.* Cambridge, MA: Blackwell.

Canestrari, R., Jr. (1963). Paced and self-paced learning in young and elderly adults. *Journal of Gerontology, 18*, 165–168.

Canli, T., Zhao, Z., Brewer, J., Gabrieli, J., & Cahill, L. (2000). Event-related activation in the human amygdala associates with later memory for individual emotional experience. *Journal of Neuroscience, 20*, RC99(1–5).

Capaldi, E., Robinson, G., & Fahrback, S. (1999). Neuroethology of spatial learning: the birds and the bees. *Annual Review of Psychology, 50*, 651–682.

Capone, N. C., & McGregor, K. K. (2004). Gesture development: a review for clinical and research practices. *Journal of Speech and Language Hearing Research, 47(1)*, 173–186.

Carew, T. J., Hawkins, R. D., & Kandel, E. R. (1983). Differential classical conditioning of a defensive gill-withdrawal reflex in *Aplysia californica. Science, 219*, 397–400.

Caro, T. M., & Hauser, M. D. (1992). Is there teaching in nonhuman animals? *Quarterly Review of Biology, 67*, 151–174.

Carroll, K. M. (1999). Behavioral and cognitive behavioral treatments. In B. McCrady & E. S. Epstein (Eds.), *Addictions: a comprehensive guidebook* (pp. 250–267). New York: Oxford University Press.

Carroll, L. (1872). Through the Looking-Glass. London: Macmillan.

Caselli, M. C., Vicari, S., Longobardi, E., Lami, L., Pizzoli, C., & Stella, G. (1998). Gestures and words in early development of children with Down syndrome. *Journal of Speech and Language Hearing Research, 41(5)*, 1125–1135.

Caselli, R. (2003). Tactile agnosia and disorders of tactile perception. In T. Feinberg & M. Farah (Eds.), *Behavioral neurology and neuropsychology* (2nd ed., pp. 271–283). New York: McGraw-Hill.

Cassel, J., Cassel, S., Galani, R., Kelche, C., Will, B., & Jarrard, L. (1998). Fimbria-fornix vs. selective hippocampal lesions in rats: effects on locomotor activity and spatial learning and memory. *Neurobiology of Learning and Memory, 69*, 22–45.

Castellucci, V. F., & Kandel, E. R. (1974). A quantal analysis of the synaptic depression underlying habituation of the gill-withdrawal reflex in *Aplysia. Proceedings of the National Academy of Sciences USA, 71*, 5004–5008.

Castellucci, V. F., & Kandel, E. R. (1976). Presynaptic facilitation as a mechanism for behavioral sensitization in *Aplysia. Science, 194*, 1176–1178.

Centerwall, B. S. (1992). Television and violence: the scale of the problem and where to go from here. *Journal of the American Medical Association, 22*, 3059–3063.

Cerletti, U., & Bini, L. (1938). Electric shock treatment. *Bolletino ed atti della Accademia medica di Roma, 64*, 36.

Chabris, C. (1999). Prelude or requiem for the Mozart effect? *Nature, 400*, 826–827.

Chachich, M., & Powell, D. (1998). Both medial prefrontal and amygdala central nucleus lesions abolish heart rate classical conditioning, but only prefrontal lesions impair reversal of eyeblink differential conditioning. *Neuroscience Letters, 257*, 151–154.

Charness, N., Reingold, E. M., Pomplun, M., & Stampe, D. M. (2001). The perceptual aspect of skilled performance in chess: evidence from eye movements. *Memory and Cognition, 29*, 1146–1152.

Chee, M. W., Hon, N., Lee, H. L., & Soon, C. S. (2001). Relative language proficiency modulates BOLD signal change when bilinguals perform semantic judgments. Blood oxygen level dependent. *Neuroimage, 13*(6 Pt 1), 1155–1163.

Chee, M. W., Tan, E. W., & Thiel, T. (1999). Mandarin and English single word processing studied with functional magnetic resonance imaging. *Journal of Neuroscience, 19*(8), 3050–3056.

Chen, L., Bao, S., Lockard, J. M., Kim, J. K., & Thompson, R. F. (1996). Impaired classical eyeblink conditioning in cerebellar-lesioned and Purkinje cell degeneration (pcd) mutant mice. *Journal of Neuroscience, 16*, 2829–2838.

Chi, M. (1978). Knowledge structures and memory development. In R. Siegler (Ed.), *Children's thinking: what develops?* Hillsdale, NJ: Lawrence Erlbaum.

Chomsky, N. (1959). A review of B. F. Skinner's *Verbal behavior. Language 35*, 26–58.

Chomsky, N. (1965). *Aspects of the theory of syntax.* Cambridge, MA: MIT Press.

Clair, E. (2005, April 2). Scientists probed secrets of the brain. *Toronto Star*, p. A24.

Clancy, S., McNally, R., Schacter, D. L., Lenzenweger, M., & Pitman, R. (2002). Memory distortion in people reporting abduction by aliens. *Journal of Abnormal Psychology, 111*, 455–461.

Clancy, S., Schacter, D. L., McNally, R., & Pitman, R. (2000). False recognition in women reporting recovered memories of sexual abuse. *Psychological Science, 11*, 26–31.

Clark, D., & Teasdale, J. (1982). Diurnal variation in clinical depression and accessibility of positive and negative experiences. *Journal of Abnormal Psychology, 91*, 87–95.

Clark, R. E., Broadbent, N. J., Zola, S. M., & Squire, L. R. (2002). Anterograde amnesia and temporally graded retrograde amnesia for a nonspatial memory task after lesions of hippocampus and subiculum. *Journal of Neuroscience, 22*(11), 4663–4669.

Clarke, G. (2002). Learning to understand speech with the cochlear implant. In M. Fahle & T. Poggio (Eds.), *Perceptual learning* (pp. 147–160). Cambridge, MA: MIT Press.

Clarkson-Smith, L., & Hartley, A. (1990). The game of bridge as an exercise in working memory. *The Journals of Gerontology: Psychological Science, 45*, P233–P238.

Clayton, N., & Dickinson, A. (1999). Scrub jays (*Aphelocoma coerulescens*) remember the relative time of caching as well as the location and content of their caches. *Journal of Comparative Psychology, 113*, 403–416.

Clayton, N., Yu, K., & Dickinson, A. (2001). Scrub jays (*Aphelocoma coerulescens*) form integrated memories of the multiple features of caching episodes. *Journal of Experimental Psychology: Animal Behavior Processes, 27*, 17–29.

Coffey, C. (Ed.). (1993). *Clinical science of electroconvulsive therapy.* Washington, DC: American Psychiatric Press.

Cohen, N. J., Poldrack, R. A., & Eichenbaum, H. (1997). Memory for items and memory for relations in the procedural/declarative memory framework. *Memory, 5*, 131–178.

Cohen, N. J., & Squire, L. (1980). Preserved learning and retention of pattern-analyzing skill in amnesia: dissociation of knowing how and knowing that. *Science, 210*, 207–210.

Cohen, T. E., Kaplan, S. W., Kandel, E. R., & Hawkins, R. D. (1997). A simplified preparation for relating cellular events to behavior: mechanisms contributing to habituation, dishabituation, and sensitization of the *Aplysia* gill-withdrawal reflex. *Journal of Neuroscience, 17*, 2886–2899.

Cohen-Bendahan, C., van de Beek, C., & Berenbaum, S. (2005). Prenatal sex hormone effects on child and adult sex-typed behavior. *Neuroscience and Biobehavioral Reviews, 29*, 353–384.

Cohen-Kettenis, P., van Goozen, S., Doorn, C., & Gooren, L. (1998). Cognitive ability and cerebral lateralisation in transsexuals. *Psychoneuroendocrinology, 23*, 631–641.

Coleman, P., & Flood, D. (1987). Neuron numbers and dendritic extent in normal aging and Alzheimer's disease. *Neurobiology of Aging, 8*, 521–545.

Collie, A., & Maruff, P. (2000). The neuropsychology of preclinical Alzheimer's disease and mild cognitive impairment. *Neuroscience and Biobehavioral Reviews, 24*, 365–374.

Collins, A., & Loftus, E. (1975). A spreading activation theory of semantic processing. *Psychological Review, 82*, 407–428.

Collins, A., & Quillian, M. (1969). Retrieval time from semantic memory. *Journal of Verbal Learning and Verbal Behavior, 8*, 240–247.

Condon, C. D., & Weinberger, N. M. (1991). Habituation produces frequency-specific plasticity of receptive fields in the auditory cortex. *Behavioral Neuroscience, 105*(3), 416–430.

Conn, P., Battaglia, G., Marino, M., & Nicoletti, F. (2005). Metabotropic glutamate receptors in the basal ganglia motor circuit. *Nature Reviews Neuroscience, 6*, 787–798.

Convit, A., de Asis, J., de Leon, M., Tarshish, C., De Santi, S., & Rusinek, H. (2000). Atrophy of the medial occipitotemporal, inferior, and middle temporal gyri in non-demented elderly predict decline to Alzheimer's Disease. *Neurobiology of Aging, 21,* 19–26.

Cook, M., Murdoch, B., Cahill, L., & Whelan, B. M. (2004). Higher-level language deficits resulting from left primary cerebellar lesions. *Aphasiology, 18,* 771–784.

Cooper, B. G., & Mizumori, S. J. (2001). Temporary inactivation of the retrosplenial cortex causes a transient reorganization of spatial coding in the hippocampus. *Journal of Neuroscience, 21,* 3986–4001.

Corkin, S. (2002). What's new with the amnesic patient H.M.? *Nature Reviews Neuroscience, 3,* 153–160.

Corkin, S., Amaral, D., Gonzalez, A., Johnson, K., & Hyman, B. (1997). H.M.'s medial temporal lobe lesion: findings from magnetic resonance imaging. *Journal of Neuroscience, 17,* 3964–3979.

Cornelissen, K., Laine, M., Renvall, K., Saarinen, T., Martin, N., & Salmelin, R. (2004). Learning new names for new objects: cortical effects as measured by magnetoencephalography. *Brain and Language, 89*(3), 617–622.

Cornstock, G. (1980). New emphases in research on the effects of television and film violence. In E. L. Palmer & A. Dorr (Eds.), *Children and the faces of television: teaching, violence, selling* (pp. 129–148). New York: Academic Press.

Corter, J. E., & Gluck, M. A. (1992). Explaining basic categories: feature predictability and information. *Psychological Bulletin, 111*(2), 291–303.

Courtney, S. M., Ungerleider, L. G., Keil, K., & Haxby, J. V. (1997). Transient and sustained activity in a distributed neural system for human working memory. *Nature, 386,* 608–611.

Craik, F. I. M., Byrd, M., & Swanson, J. (1987). Patterns of memory loss in three elderly samples. *Psychology and Aging, 2,* 79–86.

Craik, F. I. M., & Lockhart, R. (1972). Levels of processing: a framework for memory research. *Journal of Verbal Learning and Verbal Behavior, 11,* 671–684.

Craik, F. I. M., & Tulving, E. (1975). Depth of processing and the retention of words in episodic memory. *Journal of Experimental Psychology: General, 104,* 268–294.

Craik, F. I. M., & Watkins, M. J. (1973). The role of rehearsal in short-term memory. *Journal of Verbal Learning and Verbal Behavior, 12,* 599–607.

Crnic, L., & Pennington, B. F. (2000). Down syndrome: neuropsychology and animal models. In C. Rovee-Collier, L. Lipsitt, & H. Hayne (Eds.), *Progress in infancy research,* volume I (pp. 69–111). Mahwah, NJ: Lawrence Erlbaum.

Curio, E., Ernst, U., & Vieth, W. (1978). The adaptive significance of avian mobbing. *Zeitschrift fur Tierpsychologie, 48,* 184–202.

Curtiss, S. (Ed.). (1977). Genie: psycholinguistic study of a modern-day "wild child." London: Academic Press.

Cusato, B., & Domjan, M. (1998). Special efficacy of sexual conditioned stimuli that include species typical cues: test with a CS pre-exposure design. *Learning and Motivation, 29,* 152–167.

Custance, D. M., Whiten, A., & Bard, K. A. (1995). Can young chimpanzees imitate arbitrary actions? Hayes and Hayes revisited. *Behaviour, 132,* 839–858.

Cutler, N., Heston, L., Davies, P., Haxby, J. V., & Schapiro, M. (1985). Alzheimer's disease and Down's syndrome: new insights. *Annals of Internal Medicine, 103,* 566–578.

Czaja, S., Hammond, K., Blascovich, J., & Swede, H. (1993). Age-related differences in learning to use a text editing system. *Behavior and Information Technology, 8,* 309–319.

Damasio, A. (1994). Descartes' error: emotion, reason, and the human brain. New York: Putnam.

Damasio, A. (1999). *The feeling of what happens: body and emotion in the making of consciousness.* New York: Harcourt Brace.

Damasio, A., Graff-Radford, N., Eslinger, P. J., Damasio, H., & Kassell, N. (1985). Amnesia following basal forebrain lesions. *Archives of Neurology, 42,* 263–271.

Daneman, M., & Carpenter, P. A. (1980). Individual differences in working memory and reading. *Journal of Verbal Learning and Verbal Behavior, 12,* 450–466.

Daneman, M., & Carpenter, P. A. (1983). Individual differences in integrating information between and within sentences. *Journal of Experimental Psychology: Learning, Memory, and Cognition, 9,* 561–584.

Darwin, C. (1845). *Journal of researches into the natural history and geology of the countries visited during the voyage of H.M.S. Beagle round the world: under the command of Capt. Fitz Roy.* London: John Murray.

Darwin, C. (1859). *On the origin of species by means of natural selection, or the preservation of favoured races in the struggle for life.* London: John Murray.

Darwin, C. (1883). *The descent of man and selection in relation to sex.* New York: Appleton-Century-Crofts.

Darwin, C. (1965). *The expression of the emotions in man and animals.* Chicago: Chicago University Press. (Originally published 1872)

Darwin, E. (1794). *Zoönomia, Vol. I; or, the organic laws of life.* London.

Dash, P. K., Hochner, B., & Kandel, E. R. (1990). Injection of cAMP-responsive element into the nucleus of *Aplysia* sensory neuron blocks long-term facilitation. *Nature, 345,* 718–721.

Daum, I., Schugens, M. M., Ackermann, H., Lutzenberger, W., Dichgans, J., & Birbaumer, N. (1993). *Behavioral Neuroscience, 107*(5), 748–756.

Davachi, L., Mitchell, J., & Wagner, A. D. (2003). Multiple routes to memory: distinct medial temporal lobe processes build item and source memories. *Proceedings of the National Academy of Sciences USA, 100*, 2157–2162.

Davidson, R., Kabat-Zinn, J., Schumacher, J., Rosenkranz, M., Muller, D., Santorelli, S., Urbanowski, F., Harrington, A., Bonus, K., & Sheridan, J. (2003). Alterations in brain and immune function produced by mindfulness meditation. *Psychosomatic Medicine, 65*, 564–570.

Davies, P. (2000). A very incomplete comprehensive theory of Alzheimer's disease. *Annals of the New York Academy of Sciences, 924*, 8–16.

Davis, H. (1989). Theoretical note on the moral development of rats (*Rattus norvegicus*). *Journal of Comparative Psychology, 103*, 88–90.

Davis, M. (1972). Differential retention of sensitization and habituation of the startle response in the rat. *Journal of Comparative and Physiological Psychology, 78*, 260–267.

Davis, M. (1980). Habituation and sensitization of a startle-like response elicited by electrical stimulation at different points in the acoustic startle circuit. In E. Grastyan & P. Molnar (Eds.), *Advances in physiological science: Vol. 16. Sensory functions* (pp. 67–78). Elmsford, NY: Pergamon Press.

Davis, M. (1989). Sensitization of the acoustic startle reflex by footshock. *Behavioral Neuroscience, 103*, 495–503.

Davisson, M., Schmidt, C., Reeves, R., Irving, N., Akeson, E., Harris, B., & Bronson, R. (1993). Segmental trisomy as a model for Down syndrome. In C. Epstein (Ed.), *Phenotypic mapping of Down syndrome and other aneuploid conditions* (pp. 117–133). New York: Wiley-Liss.

Dawkins, R. (1986). *The blind watchmaker*. New York: W. W. Norton.

Dawson, B. V., & Foss, B. M. (1965). Observational learning in budgerigars. *Animal Behaviour, 13*, 470–474.

de Leon, M., George, A., Golomb, J., Tarshish, C., Convit, A., Kluger, A., de Santi, S., McRae, T., Ferris, S., Reisberg, B., Ince, C., Rusinek, H., Bobinski, M., Quinn, B., Miller, D., & Wisniewski, H. (1997). Frequency of hippocampal formation atrophy in normal aging and Alzheimer's disease. *Neurobiology of Aging, 18*(1), 1–11.

de Leon, M., George, A., Stylopoulos, L., Smith, G., & Miller, D. (1989). Early marker for Alzheimer's disease: the atrophic hippocampus. *The Lancet, 2*, 672–673.

de Leon, M., Golomb, J., George, A., Convit, A., Tarshish, C., McRae, T., De Santi, S., Smith, G., Ferris, S., Noz, M., & Rusinek, H. (1993). The radiologic prediction of Alzheimer disease: the atrophic hippocampal formation. *American Journal of Neuroradiology, 14*, 897–906.

de Quervain, D., Henke, K., Aerni, A., Coluccia, D., Wollmer, M., Hock, C., Nitsch, R. & Papassotiropoulos, A. (2003). A functional genetic variation of the 5-HT2a receptor affects human memory. *Nature Neuroscience, 6*, 1141–1142.

de Quervain, D., Roozendaal, B., & McGaugh, J. (1998). Stress and glucocorticoids impair retrieval of long-term spatial memory. *Nature, 394*, 787–790.

de Quervain, D., Roozendaal, B., Nitsch, R., McGaugh, J., & Hock, C. (2000). Acute cortisone administration impairs retrieval of long-term declarative memory in humans. *Nature Neuroscience, 3*, 313–314.

De Renzi, E., Cavalleri, F., & Facchini, S. (1996). Imitation and utilisation behaviour. *Journal of Neurology and Neurosurgical Psychiatry, 61*(4), 396–400.

de Waal, F. (1996). *Good natured: the origins of right and wrong in humans and other animals*. Cambridge, MA: Harvard University Press.

de Waal, F. (2001). *The ape and the sushi Master: cultural reflections of a primatologist*. New York: Basic Books.

de Waal, F., Dindo, M., Freeman, C., & Hall, M. (2005). The monkey in the mirror: hardly a stranger. *Proceedings of the National Academy of Sciences USA, 102*, 11140–11147.

DeBaggio, T. (2003). *Losing my mind: an intimate look at life with Alzheimer's*. New York: Free Press.

DeCasper, A., Lecanuet, J.-P., Busnel, M.-C., Granier-Deferre, C., & Maugeais, R. (1994). Fetal reactions to recurrent maternal speech. *Infant Behavior and Development, 17*, 159–164.

DeCasper, A., & Spence, M. (1986). Prenatal maternal speech influences newborns' perception of speech sounds. *Infant Behavior and Development, 9*, 133–150.

Decety, J., & Sommerville, J. A. (2003). Shared representations between self and other: a social cognitive neuroscience view. *Trends in Cognitive Science, 7*(12), 527–533.

Deese, J. (1959). On the prediction of occurrence of particular verbal intrusions in immediate recall. *Journal of Experimental Psychology, 58*, 17–22.

Delis, D. C., Squire, L. R., Bihrle, A., & Massman, P. (1992). Componential analysis of problem-solving ability: performance of patients with frontal lobe damage and amnesic patients with frontal lobe damage and amnesic patients on a new sorting test. *Neuropsychologia, 30*(8), 683–697.

DeLuca, J. (2000). A cognitive neuroscience perspective on confabulation. *Neuro-Psychoanalysis, 2*, 119–132.

DeLuca, J., & Diamond, B. (1995). Aneurysm of the anterior communicating artery: a review of neuroanatomical and neurophysiological sequelae. *Journal of Clinical and Experimental Neuropsychology, 17*, 100–121.

DeMeyer, M. K., Alpern, G. D., Barton, S., DeMyer, W. E., Churchill, D. W., Hingtgen, J. N., Bryson, C. Q., Pontius, W., & Kimberlin, C. (1972). Imitation in autistic, early schizophrenic, and non-psychotic subnormal children. *Journal of Autism and Childhood Schizophrenia, 2*(3), 264–287.

Demonet, J. F., Thierry, G., & Cardebat, D. (2005). Renewal of the neurophysiology of language: functional neuroimaging. *Physiological Reviews, 85*(1), 49–95.

Descartes, R. (1637). *Discours de la méthode pour bien conduire sa raison, et chercher la verité dans les sciences* [Discourse on the method of rightly conducting the reason in the search for truth in the sciences].

Descartes, R. (1662). *De homine.* Leyden. (in Latin)

Desmurget, M., Grafton, S. T., Vindras, P., Grea, H., & Turner, R. S. (2003). Basal ganglia network mediates the control of movement amplitude. *Experimental Brain Research, 153,* 197–209.

Devlin, J., Russell, R., Davis, M., Price, C., Moss, H., Fadili, M., & Tyler, L. (2002). Is there an anatomical basis for category-specificity? Semantic memory studies in PET and fMRI. *Neuropsychologia, 40,* 54–75.

Dewsbury, D. A. (1981). Effects of novelty on copulatory behavior: the Coolidge effect and related phenomena. *Psychological Bulletin, 89,* 464–482.

Dewsbury, D. A. (1990). Early interactions between animal psychologists and animal activists and the founding of the APA Committee on Precautions in Animal Experimentation. *American Psychologist, 45,* 315–327.

Di Chiara, G. (2000). Nucleus accumbens shell and core dopamine: differential role in behavior and addiction. *Behavioural Brain Research, 137,* 75–114.

di Pellegrino, G., Fadiga, L., Fogassi, L., Gallese, V., & Rizzolatti, G. (1992). Understanding motor events: a neurophysiological study. *Experimental Brain Research, 91*(1), 176–180.

Dickinson, A. (1980). *Contemporary animal learning theory.* Cambridge, England: Cambridge University Press.

DiNardo, P., Guzy, L., & Bak, R. (1988). Anxiety response patterns and etiological factors in dog-fearful and non-fearful subjects. *Behaviour Research and Therapy, 26,* 245–252.

Dinse, H. R., & Merzenich, M. M. (2002). Adaptation of inputs in the somatosensory system. In M. Fahle & T. Poggio (Eds.), *Perceptual learning* (pp. 19–42). Cambridge, MA: MIT Press.

Dinse, H. R., Ragert, P., Pleger, B., Schwenkreis, P., & Tegenthoff, M. (2003). Pharmacological modulation of perceptual learning and associated cortical reorganization. *Science, 301,* 91–94.

Dobbins, I. G., Foley, H., Schacter, D. L., & Wagner, A. D. (2002). Executive control during episodic retrieval: multiple prefrontal processes subserve source memory. *Neuron, 35*(5), 989–996.

Domjan, M. (1983). Biological constraints on instrumental and classical conditioning. In G. Bower (Ed.), *The psychology of learning and motivation* (pp. 216–217). New York: Academic Press.

Domjan, M., & Galef, B. G., Jr. (1983). Biological constraints on instrumental and classical conditioning: retrospect and prospect. *Animal Learning and Behavior, 11,* 151–161.

Domjan, M., Lyons, R., North, N. C., & Bruell, J. (1986). Sexual Pavlovian conditioned approach behavior in male Japanese quail (*Coturnix coturnix japonica*). *Journal of Comparative Psychology, 100,* 413–421.

Donnerstein, E., & Berkowitz, L. (1981). Victim reactions in aggressive erotic films as a factor in violence against women. *Journal of Personality and Social Psychology, 41*(4), 710–724.

Dostoyevsky, F. (2003). *The gambler* (C. Garnett, Trans.). New York: Modern Library.

Doupe, A. J., & Kuhl, P. K. (1999). Birdsong and human speech: common themes and mechanisms. *Annual Review of Neuroscience, 22,* 567–631.

Down, J. (1866). Observations on ethnic classification of idiots. *Mental Science, 13,* 121–128.

Dowsey-Limousin, P., & Pollak, P. (2001). Deep brain stimulation in the treatment of Parkinson's disease: a review and update. *Clinical Neuroscience Research, 1,* 521–526.

Doyon, J., Penhune, V., & Ungerleider, L. G. (2003). Distinct contribution of the cortico-striatal and cortico-cerebellar systems to motor skill learning. *Neuropsychologia, 41,* 252–262.

Draganski, B., Gaser, C., Busch, V., Schuierer, G., Bogdahn, U., & May, A. (2004). Neuroplasticity: changes in grey matter induced by training. *Nature, 427,* 311–312.

Dreyfus, H. (1998). Why we do not have to worry about speaking the language of the computer. *Information Technology and People, 11*(4), 281–289.

Dronkers, N. F. (1996). A new brain region for coordinating speech articulation. *Nature, 384*(6605), 159–161.

Drummey, A., & Newcombe, N. (2002). Developmental changes in source memory. *Developmental Science, 5,* 502–513.

Dudai, Y. (2004). The neurobiology of consolidations, or, How stable is the engram? *Annual Review of Psychology, 55,* 51–86.

Dudai, Y., Jan, Y. N., Byers, D., Quinn, W. G., & Benzer, S. (1976). Dunce, a mutant of *Drosophila* deficient in learning. *Proceedings of the National Academy of Science USA, 73*(5), 1684–1688.

Duncan, C. (1949). The retroactive effect of electroshock on learning. *Journal of Comparative and Physiological Psychology, 42,* 32–44.

Duncan, J., Emslie, H., Williams, P., Johnson, R., & Freer, C. (1996). Intelligence and the frontal lobe: the organization of goal-directed behavior. *Cognitive Psychology, 30,* 25–303.

Dunwiddie, T., & Lynch, G. (1978). Long-term potentiation and depression of synaptic responses in the rat hippocampus: localization and frequency dependency. *Journal of Physiology, 276,* 353–367.

Durrant, J. (1999). Evaluating the success of Sweden's corporal punishment ban. *Child Abuse and Neglect, 23*, 435–448.

Durston, S., Hulshoff, E., Hilleke, E., Casey, B., Giedd, J., Buitelaar, J., & van Engeland, H. (2001). Anatomical MRI of the developing human brain: what have we learned? *Journal of the American Academy of Child and Adolescent Psychiatry, 40*, 1012–1020.

Dweck, C. (1975). The role of expectations and attributions in the alleviation of learned helplessness. *Journal of Personality and Social Psychology, 31*, 674–685.

Eacott, M. (1999). Memory for the events of early childhood. *Current Directions in Psychological Science, 8*, 46–49.

Ebbinghaus, H. (1964). *Memory: a contribution to experimental psychology* (H. Ruger & C. Bussenius, Trans.) New York: Dover. (Original work published 1885)

Eddy, D. M. (1982). Probabilistic reasoning in clinical medicine: problems and opportunities. In D. Kahneman, P. Slovic, & A. Tversky (Eds.), *Judgement under uncertainty: heuristics and biases* (pp. 249–267). Cambridge, England: Cambridge University Press.

Egan, M. F., Goldberg, T. E., Kolachana, B. S., Callicot, J. H., Mazzanti, C. M., Straub, R. E., Goldman, D., & Weinberger, D. (2001). Effect of COMT Val 108/158 Met genotype on frontal lobe function and risk for schizophrenia. *Proceedings of the National Academy of Sciences, 98*, 6917–6922.

Egan, M. F., Kojima, M., Callicott, J., Goldberg, T., Kolachana, B., Bertolino, A., Zaitsev, F., Gold, B., Goldman, D., Dean, M., Lu, B., & Weinberger, D. (2003). The BDNF val66met polymorphism affects activity-dependent secretion of BDNF and human memory and hippocampal function. *Cell, 112*, 257–269.

Eich, E., Macaulay, D., & Ryan, L. (1994). Mood dependent memory for events of the personal past. *Journal of Experimental Psychology: General, 123*, 201–215.

Eichenbaum, H. (2000). A cortical-hippocampal system for declarative memory. *Nature Reviews Neuroscience, 1*, 41–50.

Eisenberg, N., & Lennon, R. (1983). Sex differences in empathy and related capacities. *Psychological Bulletin, 94*, 100–131.

Eisenstein, E. M., Eisenstein, D., & Bonheim, P. (1991). Initial habituation or sensitization of the GSR depends on magnitude of first response. *Physiology and Behavior, 49*, 211–215.

Ekman, P. (1992). Facial expressions of emotion: new findings, new questions. *Psychological Science, 3*, 34–38.

Ekman, P., & Friesen, W. (1971). Constants across cultures in the face and emotion. *Journal of Personality and Social Psychology, 17*, 124–129.

Ekman, P., & Friesen, W. (1984). *Unmasking the face.* Palo Alto, CA: Consulting Psychology Press.

Elbert, T., Pantev, C., Wienbruch, C., Rockstroh, B., & Taub, E. (1995). Increased cortical representation of the fingers of the left hand in string players. *Science, 270*, 305–307.

Emmelkamp, P., Krijn, M., Hulsbosch, A., de Vries, S., Schuemie, M., & van der Mast, C. (2002). Virtual reality treatment versus exposure in vivo: a comparative evaluation in acrophobia. *Behavior Research and Therapy, 40*, 509–516.

Engle, R., & Marshall, K. (1983). Do developmental changes in digit span result from acquisition strategies? *Journal of Experimental Child Psychology, 36*, 429–436.

Epser, E. A. (1925). A technique for the experimental investigation of associative interference in artificial linguistic material. *Language Monographs, 1*.

Ericsson, K. A. (2003). Exceptional memorizers: made, not born. *Trends in Cognitive Sciences, 7*, 233–235.

Ericsson, K. A., Krampe, R., & Tesch-Romer, C. (1993). The role of deliberate practice in the acquisition of expert performance. *Psychological Review, 100*, 363–406.

Ericsson, K. A., & Lehman, A. (1996). Expert and exceptional performance: evidence of maximal adaptation to task constraints. *Annual Review of Psychology, 47*, 273–305.

Eriksson, P. (2003). Neurogenesis and its implications for regeneration in the adult brain. *Journal of Rehabilitation Medicine, 41* (Supplement), 17–19.

Eriksson, P., Perfilieva, F., Björk-Eriksson, T., Alborn, A., Nordberg, C., Peterson, D., & Gage, F. (1998). Neurogenesis in the adult human hippocampus. *Nature Medicine, 4*, 1313–1317.

Escorihuela, R., Fernandez-Teruel, A., Vallina, I., Baamonde, C., Lumbreras, M., Dierssen, M., Tobena, A., & Florez, J. (1995). A behavioral assessment of Ts65Dn mice: a putative Down syndrome model. *Neuroscience Letters, 199*, 143–146.

Eslinger, P. J., & Damasio, A. R. (1985). Severe disturbance of higher cognition after bilateral frontal lobe ablation: patient EVR. *Neurology, 35*(12), 1731–1741.

Estes, W. K. (1950). Toward a statistical theory of learning. *Psychological Review, 57*, 94–107.

Estes, W. K., & Skinner, B. F. (1941). Some quantitative properties of anxiety. *Journal of Experimental Psychology, 29*, 390–400.

Evans, A. H., & Lees, A. J. (2004). Dopamine dysregulation syndrome in Parkinson's disease. *Current Opinion in Neurology, 17*, 393–398.

Exner, C., Koschack, J., & Irle, E. (2002). The differential role of premotor frontal cortex and basal ganglia in motor sequence learning: evidence from focal basal ganglia lesions. *Learning and Memory, 9*, 376–386.

Eyding, D., Schweigart, G., & Eysel, U. T. (2002). Spatio-temporal plasticity of cortical receptive fields in response to repetitive visual stimulation in the adult cat. *Neuroscience, 112*, 195–215.

Eysenck, M. (1979). Anxiety, learning, and memory: a reconceptualization. *Journal of Research in Personality, 13*, 363–385.

Fanselow, M., & LeDoux, J. (1999). Why we think plasticity underlying Pavlovian conditioning occurs in the basolateral amygdala. *Neuron, 23*, 229–232.

Farah, M. (2003). Visual perception and visual imagery. In T. Feinberg & M. Farah (Eds.), *Behavioral neurology and neuropsychology* (2nd ed., pp. 227–232). New York: McGraw-Hill.

Farah, M., & McClelland, J. (1991). A computational model of semantic memory impairment: modality specificity and emergent category specificity. *Journal of Experimental Psychology: General, 120*, 339–357.

Farris, W., Mansourian, S., Chang, Y., Lindsley, L., Eckman, E., Frosch, M., Eckman, C., Tanzi, R., Selkoe, D., & Guenette, S. (2003). Insulin-degrading enzyme regulates the levels of insulin, amyloid beta-protein, and the beta-amyloid precursor protein intracellular domain in vivo. *Proceedings of the National Academy of Sciences USA, 100*, 4162–4167.

Featherstone, R., & McDonald, R. (2004). Dorsal striatum and stimulus-response learning: lesions of the dorsolateral, but not dorsomedial, striatum impair acquisition of a simple discrimination task. *Behavioural Brain Research, 150*, 15–23.

Fendt, M., & Fanselow, M. (1999). The neuroanatomical and neurochemical basis of conditioned fear. *Neuroscience and Biobehavioral Reviews, 23*, 743–760.

Ferrari, M. (1999). Influence of expertise on the intentional transfer of motor skill. *Journal of Motor Behavior, 31*, 79–85.

Ferrari, P. F., Gallese, V., Rizzolatti, G., & Fogassi, L. (2003). Mirror neurons responding to the observation of ingestive and communicative mouth actions in the monkey ventral premotor cortex. *European Journal of Neuroscience, 17*(8), 1703–1714.

Finkel, D., Pedersen, N., & McGue, M. (1995). Genetic influences on memory performance in adulthood: comparison of Minnesota and Swedish twin data. *Psychology and Aging, 10*, 437–446.

Fiorentini, A., & Berardi, N. (1981). Learning in grating waveform discrimination: specificity for orientation and spatial frequency. *Vision Research, 21*, 1149–1158.

Fiorito, G., Agnisola, C., d'Addio, M., Valanzano, A., & Calamandrei, G. (1998). Scopolamine impairs memory recall in *Octopus vulgaris*. *Neuroscience Letters, 253*, 87–90.

Fisher, A. E. (1962). Effects of stimulus variation on sexual satiation in the male rat. *Journal of Comparative and Physiological Psychology, 55*, 614–620.

Fisher, J., & Hinde, R. (1949). The opening of milk bottles by birds. *British Birds, 42*, 347–357.

Fitts, P. (1964). Perceptual-motor skill learning. In A. Melton (Ed.), *Categories of human learning* (pp. 243–285). New York: Academic Press.

Fivush, R., & Nelson, K. (2004). Culture and language in the emergence of autobiographical memory. *Psychological Science, 15*, 573–577.

Flourens, P. (1824). Investigations of the properties and the functions of the various parts which compose the cerebral mass. In *Some papers on the cerebral cortex* (Trans. G. von Bonin, pp. 3–21). Springfield, IL: Charles C Thomas.

Flynn, J. (1972). Patterning mechanisms, patterned reflexes, and attack behaviour in cats. In J. Cole & D. Jensen (Eds.), *Nebraska symposium on motivation* (pp. 125–153). Lincoln: University of Nebraska Press.

Fogarty, S., & Hemsley, D. (1983). Depression and the accessibility of memories: a longitudinal study. *British Journal of Psychiatry, 142*, 232–237.

Fouriezos, G., & Wise, R. (1976). Pimozide-induced extinction of intracranial self-stimulation: response patterns rule out motor or performance deficits. *Brain Research, 103*, 377–380.

Fox, P. T., & Raichle, M. E. (1986). Focal physiological uncoupling of cerebral blood flow and oxidative metabolism during somatosensory stimulation in human subjects. *Proceedings of the National Academy of Sciences USA, 83*, 1140–1144.

Fox, P. T., Raichle, M. E., Mintun, M. A., & Dence, C. (1988). Nonoxidative glucose consumption during focal physiologic neural activity. *Science, 241*, 462–464.

Fox, P. W., Hershberger, S. L., & Bouchard, T. J., Jr. (1996). Genetic and environmental contributions to the acquisition of a motor skill. *Nature, 384*, 356–358.

Foy, M., Xu, J., Xie, X., Brinton, R., Thompson, R. & Berger, T. (1999). 17ß-estradiol enhances NMDA receptor-mediated EPSPs and long-term potentiation. *Journal of Neurophysiology, 81*, 925–929.

Francis, P., Palmer, A., Snape, M., & Wilcock, G. (1999). The cholinergic hypothesis of Alzheimer's disease: a review of progress. *Journal of Neurology, Neurosurgery, and Psychiatry, 66*, 137–147.

Freed, C., Greene, P., Breeze, R., Tsai, W., DuMouchel, W., Kao, R., Dillon, S., Winfield, H., Culver, S., Trojanowski, J., Eidelberg, D. & Fahn, S. (2001). Transplantation of embryonic dopamine neurons for severe Parkinson's disesase. *New England Journal of Medicine, 344*, 710–719.

Freeman, J., & Nicholson, D. (2001). Ontogenetic changes in the neural mechanisms of eyeblink conditioning. *Integrative Physiological and Behavioral Science, 36*, 15–35.

Friston, K. J., Frith, C. D., Passingham, R. E., Liddle, P. F., & Frackowiak, R. S. J. (1992). Motor practice and neurophysiological adaptation in the cerebellum: a positron emission tomography study. *Proceedings of the Royal Society London, 244*, 241–246.

Fudin, R., & Lembessis, E. (2004). The Mozart effect: questions about the seminal findings of Rauscher, Shaw & colleagues. *Perceptual and Motor Skills, 98,* 389–405.

Funahashi, S., Bruce, C. J., & Goldman-Rakic, P. S. (1989). Mnemonic coding of visual space in the monkey's dorsolateral prefrontal cortex. *Journal of Neurophysiology, 61,* 331–349.

Fuster, J. M. (1995). *Memory in the cerebral cortex.* Cambridge, MA: MIT Press.

Fuster, J. M. (2001). The prefrontal cortex—an update: time is of the essence. *Neuron, 30,* 319–333.

Fuster, J. M. (2003). Functional neuroanatomy of executive process. In P. Holligar (Ed.), *Oxford handbook of clinical neuropsychology* (pp. 753–765). Oxford, England: Oxford University Press.

Fuster, J. M., & Alexander, G. E. (1971). Neuron activity related to short-term memory. *Science, 173*(997), 652–654.

Gabrieli, J. D. (1998). Cognitive neuroscience of human memory. *Annual Review of Psychology, 49,* 87–115.

Gabrieli, J. D., Corkin, S., Mickel, S. F., & Growdon, J. H. (1993). Intact acquisition and long-term retention of mirror-tracing skill in Alzheimer's disease and in global amnesia. *Behavioral Neuroscience, 107,* 899–910.

Gadian, D., Aicardi, J., Watkins, K., Porter, D., Mishkin, M., & Vargha-Khadem, F. (2000). Developmental amnesia associated with early hypoxic-ischaemic injury. *Brain, 123,* 499–507.

Gaffan, D., & Hornak, J. (1997). Amnesia and neglect: beyond the Delay-Brion system and the Hebb synapse. *Philosophical Transactions of the Royal Society of London Series B, 352,* 1481–1488.

Gaffan, D., & Parker, A. (1996). Interaction of perirhinal cortex with the fornix-fimbria: memory for objects and "object-in-place" memory. *Journal of Neuroscience, 16,* 5864–5869.

Galea, A., & Kimura, D. (1993). Sex differences in route-learning. *Personality and Individual Differences, 14,* 53–65.

Galea, S., Vlahov, D., Resnick, H., Ahern, J., Susser, E., Gold, J., Bucuvalas, M., & Kilpatrick, D. (2003). Trends of probable post-traumatic stress disorder in New York City after the September 11 terrorist attacks. *American Journal of Epidemiology, 158,* 514–524.

Galef, B. G., Jr. (1996). Social enhancement of food preferences in Norway rats: a brief review. In C. M. Heyes & B. G. Galef, Jr. (Eds.), *Social learning in animals: the roots of culture* (pp. 49–64). New York: Academic Press.

Galef, B. G., Jr., & Allen, C. (1995). A new model system for studying behavioral traditions in animals. *Animal Behaviour, 50,* 705–717.

Galef, B. G., Jr., & Whiskin, E. E. (1997). Effects of social and asocial learning on longevity of food-preference traditions. *Animal Behaviour, 53*(6), 1313–1322.

Galef, B. G., Jr., & Wigmore, S. W. (1983). Transfer of information concerning distant foods: a laboratory investigation of the 'Information-centre' hypothesis. *Animal Behaviour, 31,* 748–758.

Gall, F., & Spurzheim, J. (1810). *Anatomie et physiologie du système nerveux en général, et du cerveau en particulier, avec des observations sur la possibilité de reconnaître plusieurs dispositions intellectuelles et morales de l'homme et des animaux, par la configuration de leur têtes.* Paris: F. Schoell.

Gallagher, M., & Rapp, P. (1997). The use of animal models to study the effects of aging on cognition. *Annual Review of Psychology, 48,* 339–370.

Gallese, V., Fadiga, L., Fogassi, L., & Rizzolatti, G. (1996). Action recognition in the premotor cortex. *Brain, 119* (Pt 2), 593–609.

Gallistel, C. R., Boytim, M., Gomita, Y., & Klebanoff, L. (1982). Does pimozide block the reinforcing effect of brain stimulation? *Pharmacology, Biochemistry, and Behavior, 17,* 769–781.

Gallistel, C. R., & Gibbon, J. (2000). Time, rate, and conditioning. *Psychological Review 107*(2), 289–344.

Galton, F. (1869). *Hereditary genius.* London: Macmillan.

Galton, F. (1872). Statistical inquiries into the efficacy of prayer. *Fortnightly Review, 12,* 125–135

Galton, F. (1883). *Inquiries into human faculty and its development.* London: Macmillan.

Galton, F. (1899). The median estimate. *Report of the British Association for the Advancement of Science, 69,* 638–640.

Gangitano, M., Mottaghy, F. M., & Pascual-Leone, A. (2001). Phase-specific modulation of cortical motor output during movement observation. *Neuroreport, 12*(7), 1489–1492.

Garcia, J., & Koelling, R. A. (1966). Relation of cue to consequence in avoidance learning. *Psychonomic Science, 4,* 123–124.

Gardner, R. A., & Gardner, B. T. (1969). Teaching sign language to a chimpanzee. *Science, 165*(894), 664–672.

Garner, W. R. (1974). *The processing of information and structure.* Hillsdale, NJ: Lawrence Erlbaum.

Garry, M., Manning, C., Loftus, E., & Sherman, S. (1996). Imagination inflation: imagining a childhood event inflates confidence it occurred. *Psychonomic Bulletin and Review, 3,* 208–214.

Gastaut, H. J., & Bert, J. (1954). EEG changes during cinematographic presentation: moving picture activation of the EEG. *Electroencephalography and Clinical Neurophysiology, 6,* 433–444.

Gatchel, R. (1975). Effect of interstimulus interval length on short- and long-term habituation of autonomic components of the orienting response. *Physiological Psychology, 3,* 133–136.

Gathercole, S. (1998). The development of memory. *Journal of Child Psychology & Psychiatry, 39,* 3–27.

Gazzaniga, M. S. (1998). The split brain revisited. *Scientific American, 279*(1), 50–55.

Gazzaniga, M. S. (2000). *The new cognitive neurosciences.* Cambridge, MA: MIT Press.

Geary, J. (2002). *The body electric: an anatomy of the new bionic senses.* New Brunswick, NJ: Rutgers University Press.

Geen, R. G. (1990). *Human aggression.* Pacific Grove, CA: Brooks/Cole.

Georgopoulos, A. P., Taira, M., & Lukashin, A. (1993). Cognitive neurophysiology of the motor cortex. *Science, 260,* 47–52.

Gerhardstein, P., & West, R. (2003). The relation between perceptual input and infant memory. In H. Hayne & J. Fagen (Eds.), *Progress in infancy research,* vol. 3 (pp. 121–158). Mahwah, NJ: Lawrence Erlbaum.

Gershoff, E. (2002). Child abuse and neglect and the brain: a review. *Journal of Child Psychiatry and Allied Disciplines, 41,* 97–116.

Gibson, E. (1991). *An odyssey in learning and perception.* Cambridge, MA: MIT Press.

Gibson, E., & Walk, R. (1956). The effect of prolonged exposure to visual patterns on learning to discriminate them. *Journal of Comparative and Physiological Psychology, 49,* 239–242.

Gibson, J. J., & Gibson, E. J. (1955). Perceptual learning: differentiation or enrichment. *Psychological Review, 62,* 32–41.

Gilbertson, M., Shenton, M., Ciszewski, A., Kasai, K., Lasko, N., Orr, S., & Pitman, R. (2002). Smaller hippocampal volume predicts pathologic vulnerability to psychological trauma. *Nature Neuroscience, 5,* 1242–1247.

Glass, R. (2001). Electroconvulsive therapy: time to bring it out of the shadows. *Journal of the American Medical Association, 285,* 1346–1348.

Globus, A., Rosenzweig, R., Bennet, E., & Diamond, M. (1973). Effects of differential experience on dendritic spine counts in rat cerebral cortex. *Journal of Comparative and Physiological Psychology, 82,* 175–181.

Gluck, M. A., Allen, M. T., Myers, C. E., & Thompson, R. F. (2001). Cerebellar substrates for error-correction in motor conditioning. *Neurobiology of Learning and Memory, 76,* 314–341.

Gluck, M. A., & Bower, G. H. (1988a). From conditioning to category learning: an adaptive network model. *Journal of Experimental Psychology: General, 117*(3), 227–247.

Gluck, M. A., & Bower, G. H. (1988b). Evaluating an adaptive network model of human learning. *Journal of Memory and Language, 27,* 166–195.

Gluck, M. A., Bower, G. H., & Hee, M. (1989). A configural-cue network model of animal and human associative learning. In *11th Annual Conference of Cognitive Science Society* (pp. 323–332). Ann Arbor, MI.

Gluck, M. A., & Myers, C. E. (1993). Hippocampal mediation of stimulus representation: a computational theory. *Hippocampus, 3,* 491–516.

Gluck, M. A., & Myers, C. E. (2001). *Gateway to memory: an introduction to neural network modeling of the hippocampus and learning.* Cambridge, MA: MIT Press.

Gluck, M. A., Reifsnider, E. S., & Thompson, R. F. (1990). Adaptive signal processing and the cerebellum: models of classical conditioning and VOR adaptation. In M. A. Gluck and D. E. Rumelhart (Eds.), *Neuroscience and connectionist theory* (pp. 131–185). Hillsdale, NJ: Lawrence Erlbaum.

Godde, B., Ehrhardt, J., & Braun, C. (2003). Behavioral significance of input-dependent plasticity of human somatosensory cortex. *Neuroreport, 14,* 543–546.

Godde, B., Stauffenberg, B., Spengler, F., & Dinse, H. R. (2000). Tactile coactivation-induced changes in spatial discrimination performance. *Journal of Neuroscience, 20,* 1597–1604.

Godden, D., & Baddeley, A. (1975). Context-dependent memory in two natural environments: on land and under water. *British Journal of Psychology, 66,* 325–331.

Goff, L., & Roediger, H. (1998). Imagination inflation for action events: repeated imaginings lead to illusory recollections. *Memory and Cognition, 26,* 20–33.

Gold, P. E., Cahill, L., & Wenk, G. L. (2003). The lowdown on *Ginkgo biloba. Scientific American, 288*(4), 86–91.

Gold, P. E., & van Buskirk, R. (1975). Facilitation of time-dependent memory processes with posttrial epinephrine injections. *Behavioral Biology, 13,* 145–153.

Goldberg, E. (2002). *The executive brain: frontal lobes and the civilized brain.* Oxford, England: Oxford University Press.

Goldman, S., & Nottebohm, F. (1983). Neuronal production, migration, and differentiation in a vocal control nucleus of the adult female canary brain. *Proceedings of the National Academy of Sciences USA, 80,* 2390–2394.

Goldman-Rakic, P. S. (1987). Circuitry of primate prefrontal cortex and regulation of behavior by representational memory. In F. Plum (Ed.), *Handbook of physiology: the nervous system* (pp. 373–417). Bethesda, MD: American Physiological Society.

Goldstein, H. (2002). Communication intervention for children with autism: a review of treatment efficacy. *Journal of Autism and Developmental Disorders, 32*(5), 373–396.

Goldstein, J., Seidman, L., Horton, N., Makris, N., Kennedy, D., Caviness, V., Faraone, S. & Tsuang, M. (2001). Normal sexual dimorphism of the adult human brain assessed by in vivo magnetic resonance imaging. *Cerebral Cortex, 11,* 490–497.

Goldstein, J., Seidman, L., O'Brien, L., Horton, N., Kennedy, D., Makris, N., Caviness, V., Faraone, S. & Tsuang, M. (2002). Impact of normal sexual dimorphisms on sex differences in structural brain abnormalities in schizophrenia assessed by magnetic resonance imaging. *Archives of General Psychiatry, 59*, 154–164.

Goldstone, R. L. (1994). Influences of categorization on perceptual discrimination. *Journal of Experimental Psychology: General, 123*, 178–200.

Golomb, J., de Leon, M., Kluger, A., George, A., Tarshish, C., & Ferris, S. (1993). Hippocampal atrophy in normal aging: an association with recent memory impairment. *Archives of Neurology, 50*(9), 967–973.

Gomez, R. L., & Gerken, L. (1999). Artificial grammar learning by 1-year-olds leads to specific and abstract knowledge. *Cognition, 70*(2), 109–135.

Gomez, R. L., & Gerken, L. (2000). Infant artificial language learning and language acquisition. *Trends in Cognitive Science, 4*(5), 178–186.

Goodwin, J. E., Eckerson, J. M., & Voll, C. A., Jr. (2001). Testing specificity and guidance hypotheses by manipulating relative frequency of KR scheduling in motor skill acquisition. *Perceptual and Motor Skills, 93*, 819–824.

Goodwin, J. E., & Meeuwsen, H. J. (1995). Using bandwidth knowledge of results to alter relative frequencies during motor skill acquisition. *Research Quarterly for Exercise and Sports, 66*, 99–104.

Goodwyn, S. W., & Acredolo, L. P. (1993). Symbolic gesture versus word: is there a modality advantage for onset of symbol use? *Child Development, 64*(3), 688–701.

Goodwyn, S. W., Acredolo, L. P., & Brown, C. (2000). Impact of symbolic gesturing on early language development. *Journal of Nonverbal Behavior, 24*, 81–103.

Gordon, B. (1995). *Memory: remembering and forgetting in everyday life.* New York: Mastermedia.

Gormezano, I., Kehoe, E. J., & Marshall, B. S. (1983). Twenty years of classical conditioning research with the rabbit. *Progress in Psychobiology and Physiological Psychology, 10*, 197–275.

Goudsmit, E., Van de Poll, N., & Swaab, D. (1990). Testosterone fails to reverse a spatial memory decline in aged rats and impairs retention in young and middle-aged animals. *Behavioral and Neural Biology, 53*, 6–20.

Gould, E., & Gross, C. (2000). New neurons: extraordinary evidence or extraordinary conclusion?—Authors' response. *Science, 288*, 771a.

Gould, E., Reeves, A., Graziano, M., & Gross, C. (1999). Neurogenesis in the neocortex of adult primates. *Science, 286*, 548–552.

Graf, P. (1990). Life-span changes in implicit and explicit memory. *Bulletin of the Psychonomic Society, 28*, 353–358.

Graf, P., & Schacter, D. L. (1985). Implicit and explicit memory for new associations in normal subjects and amnesic patients. *Journal of Experimental Psychology: Learning, Memory, and Cognition, 11*, 501–518.

Graf, P., Squire, L. R., & Mandler, G. (1984). The information that amnesic patients do not forget. *Journal of Experimental Psychology: Learning, Memory, and Cognition, 10*, 164–178.

Graybiel, A. M. (1995). Building action repertoires: memory and learning functions of the basal ganglia. *Current Opinion in Neurobiology, 5*, 733–741.

Graybiel, A. M. (1997). The basal ganglia and cognitive pattern generators. *Schizophrenia Bulletin, 23*, 459–469.

Graybiel, A. M. (1998). The basal ganglia and chunking of action repertoires. *Neurobiology of Learning and Memory, 70*, 119–136.

Graybiel, A. M. (2004). Network-level neuroplasticity in cortico-basal ganglia pathways. *Parkinsonism and Related Disorders, 10*, 293–296.

Graybiel, A. M. (2005). The basal ganglia: learning new tricks and loving it. *Current Opinion in Neurobiology, 15*, 638–644.

Green, C. S., & Bavelier, D. (2003). Action video game modifies visual selective attention. *Nature, 423*, 534–537.

Green, L., Fischer, E., Perlow, S., & Sherman, L. (1981). Preference reversal and self control: choice as a function of reward amount and delay. *Behavior Analysis Letters, 1*, 43–51.

Green, L., Fry, A., & Myerson, J. (1994). Discounting of delayed rewards: a life-span comparison. *Psychological Science, 5*, 33–36.

Greenberg, D. (2004). President Bush's false "flashbulb" memory of 9/11/01. *Applied Cognitive Psychology, 18*, 363–370.

Greenough, W., West, R., & DeVoogd, T. (1978). Subsynaptic plat perforations: changes with age and experience in the rat. *Science, 202*, 1096–1098.

Griffiths, D., Dickinson, A., & Clayton, N. (1999). Episodic memory: what can animals remember about their past? *Trends in Cognitive Sciences, 3*, 74–80.

Groves, P. M., & Thompson, R. F. (1970). Habituation: a dual-process theory. *Psychological Review, 77*, 419–450.

Guillaume, P. (1971). *Imitation in children.* Chicago: University of Chicago Press.

Guinee, L. N., Chu, K., & Dorsey, E. M. (1983). Changes over time in the songs of known individual humpback whales (*Megaptera novaeangliae*). In R. Payne (Ed.), *Communication and behavior of whales.* Boulder, CO: Westview Press.

Guinet, C., & Bouvier, J. (1995). Development of intentional stranding hunting techniques in killer whale (*Orcinus orca*) calves at Crozet archipelago. *Canadian Journal of Zoology, 73*, 27–33.

Guttman, N., & Kalish, H. (1956). Discriminability and stimulus generalization. *Journal of Experimental Psychology, 51,* 79–88.

Habib, M., & Sirigu, A. (1987). Pure topographical disorientation: a definition and anatomical basis. *Cortex, 23,* 73–85.

Haglund, K., & Collett, C. (1996). Landmarks interviews. *Journal of NIH Research, 8,* 42–51.

Halbert, C. (2003). *The ultimate boxer: understanding the sport and skills of boxing.* Brentwood, TN: Impact Seminars.

Halgren, E. (1982). Mental phenomena induced by stimulation in the limbic system. *Human Neurobiology, 1,* 251–260.

Hall, G. (1991). *Perceptual and associative learning.* Oxford, England: Clarendon Press.

Hall, T., Miller, K., & Corsellia, J. (1975). Variations in the human Purkinje cell population according to age and sex. *Neuropathology and Applied Neurobiology, 1,* 267–292.

Halsband, U., Schmitt, J., Weyers, M., Binkofski, F., Grutzner, G., & Freund, H. J. (2001). Recognition and imitation of pantomimed motor acts after unilateral parietal and premotor lesions: a perspective on apraxia. *Neuropsychologia, 39,* 200–216.

Hamann, S. B., Ely, T. D., Grafton, S. T., & Kilts, C. D. (1999). Amygdala activity related to enhanced memory for pleasant and aversive stimuli. *Nature Neuroscience, 2,* 289–293.

Haney, M., Foltin, R., & Fischman, M. (1998). Effects of pergolide on intravenous cocaine self-administration in men and women. *Psychopharmacology, 137,* 15–24.

Hanley-Dunn, P., & McIntosh, J. (1984). Meaningfulness and recall of names by young and old adults. *Journal of Gerontology, 39,* 583–585.

Hardy, J., & Gwinn-Hardy, K. (1998). Classification of primary degenerative disease. *Science, 282,* 1075–1079.

Hari, R., Forss, N., Avikainen, S., Kirveskari, E., Salenius, S., & Rizzolatti, G. (1998). Activation of human primary motor cortex during action observation: a neuromagnetic study. *Proceedings of the National Academy of Sciences, 95*(25), 15061–15065.

Harlow, H. (1958). The nature of love. *American Psychologist, 13,* 673–685.

Harlow, H., & Harlow, M. (1962). Social deprivation in monkeys. *Scientific American, 207,* 136–146.

Harrison, J., & Buchwald, J. (1983). Eyeblink conditioning deficits in the old cat. *Neurobiology of Aging, 4,* 45–51.

Hart, B. (2001). Cognitive behaviour in Asian elephants: use and modification of branches for fly switching. *Animal Behaviour, 62,* 839–847.

Hart, J., & Gordon, B. (1992). Neural subsystems for object knowledge. *Nature, 359,* 60–64.

Hasselmo, M. (1999). Neuromodulation: acetylcholine and memory consolidation. *Trends in Cognitive Sciences, 3,* 351–359.

Hatze, H. (1976). Biomechanical aspects of a successful motion optimization. In P. V. Komi (Ed.), *Biomechanics V-B* (pp. 5–12). Baltimore: University Park Press.

Hauser, M. D., Chomsky, N., & Fitch, W. T. (2002). The faculty of language: what is it, who has it, and how did it evolve? *Science, 298*(5598), 1569–1579.

Hauser, M. D., Newport, E. L., & Aslin, R. N. (2001). Segmentation of the speech stream in a non-human primate: statistical learning in cotton-top tamarins. *Cognition, 78*(3), B53–64.

Hauser, M. D., Weiss, D., & Marcus, G. (2002). Rule learning by cotton-top tamarins. *Cognition, 86*(1), B15–22.

Hawkins, R. D., Abrams, T. W., Carew, T. J., & Kandel, E. R. (1983). A cellular mechanism of classical conditioning in *Aplysia*: activity-dependent amplification of presynaptic facilitation. *Science, 219,* 400–405.

Hayes, C. (1951). *The ape in our house.* New York: Harper & Bros.

Hayes, K. J., & Hayes, C. (1952). Imitation in a home-reared chimpanzee. *Journal of Comparative and Physiological Psychology, 45,* 450–459.

Hayne, H. (1996). Categorization in infancy. In C. Rovee-Collier & L. Lipsitt (Eds.), *Advances in infancy research,* vol. 10 (pp. 79–120). Norwood, NJ: Ablex Publishing Corporation.

Hays, M., Allen, C., & Hanish, J. (2005). Kissing 101. Retrieved January 2007 from www.virtualkiss.com/kissingschool

Hebb, D. (1947). The effects of early experience on problem solving at maturity. *American Psychologist, 2,* 737–745.

Hebb, D. (1949). *The organization of behavior.* New York: Wiley.

Heilman, K. M., Rothi, L. J., & Valenstein, E. (1982). Two forms of ideomotor apraxia. *Neurology, 32,* 342–346.

Heindel, W., Salmon, D., Shults, C., Walicke, P., & Butters, N. (1989). Neuropsychological evidence for multiple implicit memory systems: a comparison of Alzheimer's, Huntington's and Parkinson's disease patients. *Journal of Neuroscience, 9,* 582–587.

Hepper, P., & Shahidullah, S. (1992). Habituation in normal and Down's syndrome fetuses. *Quarterly Journal of Experimental Psychology B, 44,* 305–317.

Herbert, J., Eckerman, C., & Stanton, M. (2003). The ontogeny of human learning in delay, long-delay, and trace eyeblink conditioning. *Behavioral Neuroscience, 117,* 1196–1210.

Herman, L. M., Richards, D. G., & Wolz, J. P. (1984). Comprehension of sentences by bottlenosed dolphins. *Cognition, 16*(2), 129–219.

Herrnstein, R. (1961). Relative and absolute strength of a response as a function of frequency of reinforcement. *Journal of the Experimental Analysis of Behavior, 4*, 267–272.

Heuer, F., & Reisberg, D. (1990). Vivid memories of emotional events: the accuracy of remembered minutiae. *Memory and Cognition, 18*, 496–506.

Heuer, F., & Reisberg, D. (1992). Emotion, arousal, and memory for detail. In S.-A. Christianson (Ed.), *The handbook of emotion and memory* (pp. 151–180). Hillsdale, NJ: Lawrence Erlbaum.

Heyes, C. M. (1994). Social learning in animals: categories and mechanisms. *Biological Reviews of the Cambridge Philosophical Society, 69*(2), 207–231.

Heyes, C. M., & Dawson, G. R. (1990). A demonstration of observational learning in rats using a bidirectional control. *Quarterly Journal of Experimental Psychology B, 42*(1), 59–71.

Hinde, R. A. (1969). *Bird vocalizations*. Cambridge, England: Cambridge University Press.

Hinde, R. A., & Fisher, J. (1951). Further observations on the opening of milk bottles by birds. *British Birds, 44*, 392–396.

Hiroto, D. (1974). Locus of control and learned helplessness. *Journal of Experimental Psychology, 102*, 187–193.

Hiroto, D., & Seligman, M. (1974). Generality of learned helplessness in man. *Journal of Personality and Social Psychology, 31*, 311–327.

Hodzic, A., Veit, R., Karim, A. A., Erb, M., & Godde, B. (2004). Improvement and decline in tactile discrimination behavior after cortical plasticity induced by passive tactile coactivation. *Journal of Neuroscience, 24*, 442–446.

Hof, P., & Morrison, J. (2004). The aging brain: morpho-molecular senescence of cortical circuits. *Trends in Neurosciences, 27*, 607–613.

Hoge, C., Castro, C., Messer, S., McGurk, D., Cotting, D., & Koffman, R. (2004). Combat duty in Iraq and Afghanistan, mental health problems, and barriers to care. *New England Journal of Medicine, 351*, 13–22.

Holding, D. H. (Ed.). (1981). *Human skills*. Chichester: John Wiley.

Hollerman, J., & Schultz, W. (1998). Dopamine neurons report an error in the temporal prediction of reward during learning. *Nature Neuroscience, 1*, 304–309.

Honey, R., Watt, A., & Good, M. (1998). Hippocampal lesions disrupt an associative mismatch process. *Journal of Neuroscience, 18*, 2226–2230.

Hornak, J., Bramham, J., Rolls, E., Morris, R., O'Doherty, J., Bullock, P., & Polkey, C. (2003). Changes in emotion after circumscribed surgical lesions of the orbitofrontal and cingulate cortices. *Brain, 126*, 1691–1712.

Horowitz, A. C. (2003). Do humans ape? Or do apes human? Imitation and intention in humans (Homo sapiens) and other animals. *Journal of Comparative Psychology, 117*(3),

325–336.

Hothersall, D. (2004). *History of psychology* (4th ed.). New York: McGraw-Hill.

Howard, D., & Frankin, S. (1988). Missing the meaning: a cognitive neuropsychological study of processing of words by an aphasic patient. Cambridge, MA: MIT Press.

Howe, M., & Courage, M. (1993). On resolving the enigma of childhood amnesia. *Psychological Bulletin, 113*, 305–326.

Hubel, D., & Wiesel, T. (1977). The Ferrier Lecture: functional architecture of macaque monkey visual cortex. *Proceedings of the Royal Academy of London B, 198*, 1–59.

Hubel, D., & Wiesel, T. (1979). Brain mechanisms of vision. *Scientific American, 241*, 150–162.

Hubel, D., & Wiesel, T. (1998). Early exploration of the visual cortex. *Neuron, 20*, 401–412.

Hull, C. L. (1943). *Principles of behavior*. Englewood Cliffs, NJ: Prentice Hall.

Hull, C. L. (1952). *A behavior system: an introduction to behavior theory concerning the individual organism*. New Haven, CT: Yale University Press.

Hunt, G. R., Corballis, M. C., & Gray, R. D. (2001). Animal behaviour: laterality in tool manufacture by crows. *Nature, 414*, 707.

Huttenlocher, P., & Dabholkar, A. (1997). Regional differences in synaptogenesis in human cortex. *Journal of Comparative Neurology, 387*, 167–178.

Hyde, L., Sherman, G., & Denenberg, V. (2000). Non-spatial water radial-arm maze learning in mice. *Brain Research, 863*, 151–159.

Iacoboni, M., Woods, R. P., Brass, M., Bekkering, H., Mazziotta, J. C., & Rizzolatti, G. (1999). Cortical mechanisms of human imitation. *Science, 286*(5449), 2526–2528.

Illes, J., Francis, W. S., Desmond, J. E., Gabrieli, J. D., Glover, G. H., Poldrack, R., Lee, C. J., & Wagner, A. D. (1999). Convergent cortical representation of semantic processing in bilinguals. *Brain Language, 70*(3), 347–363.

Immelman, K. (1969). Song development in the zebra finch and other estrildid finches. In R. A. Hinde (Ed.), *Bird vocalizations* (pp. 61–74). London: Cambridge University Press.

Insel, T., & Fernald, R. (2004). How the brain processes social information: searching for the social brain. *Annual Review of Neuroscience, 27*, 697–722.

International Human Genome Sequencing Consortium. (2004). Finishing the euchromatic sequence of the human genome. *Nature, 431*, 931–945.

Irwin, A. R., & Gross, A. M. (1995). Cognitive tempo, violent video games, and aggressive behavior in young boys. *Journal of Family Violence, 10*, 337–350.

Ivkovich, D., Collins, K., Eckerman, C., Krasnegor, N., & Stanton, M. (1999). Classical delay eyeblink conditioning in 4- and 5-month-old human infants. *Psychological Science, 10,* 4–8.

Ivkovich, D., Paczkowski, C., & Stanton, M. (2000). Ontogeny of delay versus trace conditioning in the rat. *Developmental Psychobiology, 36,* 148–160.

Jack, C. R., Jr., Petersen, R. C., Xu, Y., O'Brien, P. C., Smith, G. E., & Ivnik, R. J. (1998). Rate of medial temporal atrophy in typical aging and Alzheimer's disease. *Neurology, 51,* 993–999.

Jack, C. R., Jr., Petersen, R., Xu, Y., O'Brien, P., Smith, G. E., Ivnik, R. J., Boeve, B. F., Waring, S. C., Tangalos, E. G., Kokmen, E. (1999). Prediction of AD with MRI-based hippocampal volume in mild cognitive impairment. *Neurology, 52*(7), 1397–1403.

Jacobs, B., Schall, M., & Schiebel, A. (1993). A quantitative dendritic analysis of Wernicke's area. II. Gender, hemispheric, and environmental factors. *Journal of Comparative Neurology, 237,* 97–111.

Jacobs, D. H., Adair, J. C., Williamson, D. J. G., Na, D. L., Gold, M., Foundas, A. L., Shuren, J. E., Cibula, J. E., & Heilman, K. M. (1999). Apraxia and motor-skill acquisition in Alzheimer's disease are dissociable. *Neuropsychologia, 37,* 875–880.

Jacobsen, C. F. (1936). Studies of cerebral function in primates. I. The functions of the frontal association areas in monkeys. *Comparative Psychological Monographs, 13,* 1–60.

James, W. (1884). What is an emotion? *Mind, 9,* 188–205.

James, W. (1890). *The principles of psychology.* New York: Henry Holt.

Janik, V., & Slater, P. (1997). Vocal learning in mammals. *Advances in the Study of Behavior, 26,* 59–99.

Janowsky, J. S., Shimamura, A. P., Kritchevsky, M., & Squire, L. R. (1989). Cognitive impairment following frontal lobe damage and its relevance to human amnesia. *Behavioral Neuroscience, 103,* 548–560.

Jarrard, L., Okaichi, H., Steward, O., & Goldschmidt, R. (1984). On the role of hippocampal connections in the performance of place and cue tasks: comparisons with damage to hippocampus. *Behavioral Neuroscience, 98,* 946–954.

Jeannerod, M. (1994). The representing brain: neural correlates of motor intention and imagery. *Behavioral and Brain Sciences, 17,* 187–245.

Jenkins, H. M., & Harrison, R. H. (1962). Generalization gradients of inhibition following auditory discrimination training. *Journal of the Experimental Analysis of Behavior, 5,* 435–441.

Jernigan, T., Bellugi, U., Sowell, E., Doherty, S., & Hesselink, J. (1993). Cerebral morphological distinctions between Williams and Down syndrome. *Archives of Neurology, 50,* 186–191.

Jog, M. S., Kubota, Y., Connolly, C. I., Hillegaart, V., & Graybiel, A. M. (1999). Building neural representations of habits. *Science, 286,* 1745–1749.

Johnson, G., & Bailey, C. (2002). Tau, where are we now? *Journal of Alzheimer's Disease, 4,* 375–398.

Johnson, M. (1992). Imprinting and the development of face recognition: from chick to man. *Current Directions in Psychological Science, 1,* 52–55.

Johnston, R. B., Stark, R., Mellits, D., & Tallal, P. (1981). Neurological status of language impaired and normal children. *Annals of Neurology, 10,* 159–163.

Jorissen, B. L., Brouns, F., Van Boxtel, M. P., Ponds, R. W., Verhey, F. R., Jolles, J., & Riedel, W. J. (2001). The influence of soy-derived phosphatidylserine on cognition in age-associated memory impairment. *Nutritional Neuroscience, 4,* 121–134.

Josephson, W. L. (1987). Television violence and children's aggression: testing the priming, social script, and disinhibition predictions. *Journal of Personality and Social Psychology, 53*(5), 882–890.

Jussim, L. (2005). Accuracy in social perception: criticisms, controversies, criteria, components, and cognitive processes. *Advances in Experimental Social Psychology, 37,* 1–93.

Jussim, L., Cain, T. R., Crawford, J. T., Harber, K., & Cohen, F. (2007). The unbearable accuracy of stereotypes. In T. Nelson (Ed.), *The handbook of prejudice, stereotyping, and discrimination.* Hillsdale, NJ: Lawrence Erlbaum.

Justus, T. (2004). The cerebellum and English grammatical morphology: evidence from production, comprehension, and grammaticality judgments. *Journal of Cognitive Neuroscience, 16*(7), 1115–1130.

Kahana, M. J., Sekuler, R., Caplan, J. B., Kirschen, M., & Madsen, J. R. (1999). Human theta oscillations exhibit task dependence during virtual maze. *Journal of Neuroscience, 399,* 781–784.

Kahn, D. M., & Krubitzer, L. (2002). Massive cross-modal cortical plasticity and the emergence of a new cortical area in developmentally blind mammals. *Proceedings of the National Academy of Sciences USA, 99,* 11429–11434.

Kamin, L. (1969). Predictability, surprise, attention and conditioning. In B. Campbell and R. Church, *Punishment and aversive behavior* (pp. 279–296). New York: Appleton-Century-Crofts.

Kandel, E. R. (2006). *In search of memory: the emergence of a new science of mind.* New York: W. W. Norton.

Kandel, E. R., Schwartz, J. H., & Jessell, T. M. (2000). *Principles of neural science.* New York: McGraw Hill.

Kanit, L., Taskiran, D., Yilmaz, O., Balkan, B., Demiroeren, S., Furedy, J., & Poeguen, S. (2000). Sexually dimorphic cognitive style in rats emerges after puberty. *Brain Research Bulletin, 52,* 243–248.

Kanner, L. (1943). Autistic disturbances of affective contact. *Nervous Child, 2,* 217–250.

Kapp, B., Gallagher, M., Underwood, M., McNall, C., & Whitehorn, D. (1981). Cardiovascular responses elicited by electrical stimulation of the amygdala central nucleus in the rabbit. *Brain Research, 234,* 251–262.

Kapur, N., & Coughlan, A. (1980). Confabulation and frontal lobe dysfunction. *Journal of Neurology, Neurosurgery, and Psychiatry, 43,* 461–463.

Kapur, N., Millar, J., Abbott, P., & Carter, M. (1998). Recovery of function processes in human amnesia: evidence from transient global amnesia. *Neuropsychologia, 36,* 99–107.

Karni, A., Meyer, G., Rey-Hipolito, C., Jezzard, P., Adams, M. M., Turner, R., & Ungerleider, L. G. (1998). The acquisition of skilled motor performance: fast and slow experience-driven changes in primary motor cortex. *Proceedings of the National Academy of Sciences USA, 95,* 861–868.

Kazdan, A., & Benjet, C. (2003). Spanking children: evidence and issues. *Current Directions in Psychological Science, 12,* 99–103.

Kazdin, A., & Wilcoxon, L. (1976). Systematic desensitization and nonspecific treatment effects: a methodological evaluation. *Psychological Bulletin, 83,* 729–758.

Kehoe, E. J. (1988). A layered network model of associative learning. *Psychological Review, 95*(4), 411–433.

Keller, H. (1970). *Helen Keller: the story of my life.* New York: Airmont.

Kemeny, M. (2003). The psychobiology of stress. *Current Directions in Psychological Science, 12,* 124–129.

Kempermann, G., Wiskott, L., & Gage, F. (2004). Functional significance of adult neurogenesis. *Current Opinion in Neurobiology, 14,* 186–191.

Kihlstrom, J. (1995). The trauma-memory argument. *Consciousness and Cognition, 4,* 63–67.

Kihlstrom, J., & Harackiewicz, J. (1982). The earliest recollection: a new survey. *Journal of Personality, 50,* 134–148.

Kilgard, M., & Merzenich, M. M. (1998). Cortical map reorganization enabled by nucleus basalis activity. *Science, 279,* 1714–1718.

Killiany, R., Hyman, B., Gomez-Isla, T., Moss, M., Kikinis, R., Jolesz, F., Tanzi, R., Jones, K., & Albert, M. (2002). MRI measures of entorhinal cortex vs. hippocampus in preclinical AD. *Neurology, 58,* 1188–1196.

Kim, J. J., Krupa, D. J., & Thompson, R. F. (1998). Inhibitory cerebello-olivary projections and blocking effect in classical conditioning. *Science, 279,* 570–573.

Kim, K. H., Relkin, N. R., Lee, K. M., & Hirsch, J. (1997). Distinct cortical areas associated with native and second languages. *Nature, 388*(6638), 171–174.

Kim, S. (2001). Double-blind naltrexone and placebo comparison study in the treatment of pathological gambling. *Biological Psychiatry, 49,* 914–921.

Kirchmayer, U., Davoli, M., Verster, A., Amato, L., Ferri, A., & Perucci, C. (2002). A systematic review on the efficacy of naltrexone maintenance treatment in preventing relapse in opioid addicts after detoxification. *Addiction, 97,* 1241–1249.

Kiyatkin, E. (2002). Dopamine in the nucleus accumbens: cellular actions, drug- and behavior-associated fluctuations, and a possible role in an organism's adaptive activity. *Behavioural Brain Research, 137,* 27–46.

Kleim, J. A., Hogg, T. M., VandenBerg, P. M., Cooper, N. R., Bruneau, R., & Remple, M. (2004). Cortical synaptogenesis and motor map reorganization occur during late, but not early, phase of motor skill learning. *Journal of Neuroscience, 24,* 628–633.

Kleim, J. A., Swain, R. A., Czerlanis, C. M., Kelly, J. L., Pipitone, M. A., & Greenough, W. T. (1997). Learning-dependent dendritic hypertrophy of cerebellar stellate cells: plasticity of local circuit neurons. *Neurobiology of Learning and Memory, 67,* 29–33.

Klinke, R., Kral, A., Heid, S., Tillein, J., & Hartmann, R. (1999). Recruitment of the auditory cortex in congenitally deaf cats by long-term cochlear electrostimulation. *Science, 285,* 1729–1733.

Knapp, H. D., Taub, E., & Berman, A. J. (1963). Movements in monkeys with deafferented forelimbs. *Experimental Neurology, 7,* 305–315.

Knowlton, B. J., Squire, L. R., Paulsen, J. S., Swerdlow, N. R., Swenson, M., & Butters, N. (1996). Dissociations within nondeclarative memory in Huntington's disease. *Neuropsychology, 10,* 538–548.

Knutson, B., Fong, G., Adams, C., Varner, J., & Hommer, D. (2001). Dissociation of reward anticipation and outcome with event-related fMRI. *Neuroreport, 21,* 3683–3687.

Kobre, K., & Lipsitt, L. (1972). A negative contrast effect in newborns. *Journal of Experimental Child Psychology, 14,* 81–91.

Koch, M., Schmid, A., & Schnitzler, H.-U. (2000). Role of nucleus accumbens dopamine D1 and D2 receptors in instrumental and Pavlovian conditioning. *Psychopharmacology, 152,* 67–73.

Koenig, O., Thomas-Anterion, C., & Laurent, B. (1999). Procedural learning in Parkinson's disease: intact and impaired cognitive components. *Neuropsychologia, 37,* 1103–1109.

Kohler, E., Keysers, C., Umilta, M. A., Fogassi, L., Gallese, V., & Rizzolatti, G. (2002). Hearing sounds, understanding actions: action representation in mirror neurons. *Science, 297*(5582), 846–848.

Köhler, S., Moscovitch, M., Winocur, G., & McIntosh, A. (2000). Episodic encoding and recognition of pictures and words: role of the human medial temporal lobes. *Acta Psychologica, 105,* 159–179.

Kolb, B., Gibb, R., & Gonzalez, C. (2001). Cortical injury and neural plasticity during brain development. In C. Shaw & J. McEachern (Eds.), *Toward a theory of neuroplasticity* (pp. 223–243). Philadelphia: Taylor & Francis.

Kolb, B., & Taylor, L. (1981). Affective behavior in patients with localized cortical excisions: role of lesion site and side. *Science, 214*, 89–91.

Kolb, B., & Taylor, L. (1990). Neocortical substrates of emotional behavior. In N. Stein, B. Leventhal, & T. Trabasso (Eds.), *Psychological and biological approaches to emotion* (pp. 115–144). Hillsdale, NJ: Lawrence Erlbaum.

Kolb, B., & Taylor, L. (2000). Facial expression, emotion, and hemispheric organization. In R. Lane & L. Nadel (Eds.), *Cognitive neuroscience of emotion* (pp. 62–83). New York: Oxford University Press.

Kolb, B., & Whishaw, I. (1996). *Fundamentals of human neuropsychology* (4th ed.). New York: W. H. Freeman.

Kolb, B., & Whishaw, I. (1998). Brain plasticity and behavior. *Annual Review of Psychology, 49*, 43–64.

Kolb, B., & Whishaw, I. (2006). *An introduction to brain and behavior.* New York: Worth Publishers.

Konishi, M. (1965). The role of auditory feedback in the control of vocalization in the white-crowned sparrow. *Zeitschrift fur Tierpsychologie, 22*, 770–783.

Kopelman, M. (1995). The Korsakoff syndrome. *British Journal of Psychiatry, 166*, 154–173.

Kornak, D., & Rakic, P. (1999). Continuation of neurogenesis in the hippocampus of the adult macaque monkey. *Proceedings of the National Academy of Sciences USA, 96*, 5768–5773.

Korr, H., & Schmitz, C. (1999). Facts and fictions regarding post-natal neurogenesis in the developing human cerebral cortex. *Journal of Theoretical Biology, 200*, 291–297.

Kosobud, A., Harris, G., & Chapin, J. (1994). Behavioral associations of neuronal activity in the ventral tegmental area of the rat. *Journal of Neuroscience, 14*, 7117–7129.

Koukounas, E., & Over, R. (2001). Habituation of male sexual arousal: effects of attentional focus. *Biological Psychology, 58*, 49–64.

Krank, M. D., & Wall, A. M. (1990). Cue exposure during a period of abstinence reduces the resumption of operant behavior for oral ethanol reinforcement. *Behavioral Neuroscience, 104*, 725–733.

Kring, A., & Gordon, A. (1998). Sex differences in emotion: expression, experience, and physiology. *Journal of Personality and Social Psychology, 74*, 686–803.

Kritchevsky, M., Chang, L., & Squire, L. (2004). Functional amnesia: clinical description and neuropsychological profile of 10 cases. *Learning and Memory, 11*, 213–226.

Kritchevsky, M., & Squire, L. (1989). Transient global amnesia: evidence for extensive, temporally graded retrograde amnesia. *Neurology, 39*, 213–218.

Kritchevsky, M., Squire, L., & Zouzounis, J. (1988). Transient global amnesia: characterization of anterograde and retrograde amnesia. *Neurology, 38*, 213–219.

Kroodsma, D. (2005). The singing life of birds: the art and science of listening to birdsong. Boston: Houghton Mifflin.

Kruschke, J. K., Kappenman, E. S., & Hetrick, W. P. (2005). Eye gaze and individual differences consistent with learned attention in associative blocking and highlighting. *Journal of Experimental Psychology: Learning, Memory, & Cognition, 31*(5), 830–845.

Krutzen, M., Mann, J., Heithaus, M. R., Connor, R. C., Bejder, L., & Sherwin, W. B. (2005). Cultural transmission of tool use in bottlenose dolphins. *Proceedings of the National Academy of Sciences USA, 102*, 8939–8943.

Kubota, K., & Nikin, H. (1971). Prefrontal cortical unit activity and delayed alternation performance in monkeys. *Journal of Neurophysiology, 34*(3), 337–347.

Kuhl, P. K. (2000). A new view of language acquisition. *Proceedings of the National Academy of Sciences USA, 97*(22), 11850–11857.

Kuhl, P. K. (2004). Early language acquisition: cracking the speech code. *Nature Reviews Neuroscience, 5*(11), 831–843.

Kuhl, P. K., Andruski, J. E., Chistovich, I. A., Chistovich, L. A., Kozhevnikova, E. V., Ryskina, V. L., Stolyarova, E. I., Sundberg, U., & Lacerda, F. (1997). Cross-language analysis of phonetic units in language addressed to infants. *Science, 277*(5326), 684–686.

Kuhl, P. K., & Meltzoff, A. N. (1982). The bimodal perception of speech in infancy. *Science, 218*(4577), 1138–1141.

Kuhl, P. K., & Miller, J. D. (1975). Speech perception by the chinchilla: voiced-voiceless distinction in alveolar plosive consonants. *Science, 190*(4209), 69–72.

Kuhl, P. K., & Padden, D. M. (1982). Enhanced discriminability at the phonetic boundaries for the voicing feature in macaques. *Perception and Psychophysics, 32*(6), 542–550.

Kuhn, H., Dickinson-Anson, H., & Gage, F. (1996). Neurogenesis in the dentate gyrus of the adult rat: age-related decrease of neurongal progenitor proliferation. *Journal of Neuroscience, 16*, 2027–2033.

Laan, E., & Everaerd, W. (1995). Habituation of female sexual arousal to slides and film. *Archives of Sexual Behavior, 24*, 517–541.

LaBar, K., & LeDoux, J. (2003). Emotion and the brain: an overview. In T. Feinberg & M. Farah (Eds.), *Behavioral neurology and neuropsychology* (2nd ed., pp. 711–724). New York: McGraw-Hill.

Laforce, R., Jr., & Doyon, J. (2001). Distinct contribution of the striatum and cerebellum to motor learning. *Brain and Cognition, 45*, 189–211.

Lalonde, R., & Botez, M. (1990). The cerebellum and learning processes in animals. *Brain Research Reviews, 15*, 325–332.

Lamarck, J. (1809). *Philosophie zoologique.* Paris.

Lang, P. J., Davis, M., & Ohman, A. (2000). Fear and anxiety: animal models and human cognitive psychophysiology. *Journal of Affective Disorders, 61,* 137–159.

Larzelere, R. (2000). Child outcomes of nonabusive and customary physical punishment by parents: an updated literature review. *Clinical Child and Family Psychology Review, 3,* 199–221.

Lashley, K. S. (1924). Studies of the cerebral function in learning: V. The retention of motor habits after destruction of the so-called motor areas in primates. *Archives of Neurology and Psychiatry, 12,* 249–276.

Lashley, K. S. (1929). *Brain mechanisms and intelligence: a quantitative study of injuries to the brain.* Chicago: University of Chicago Press.

Lawrence, D. H. (1952). The transfer of a discrimination along a continuum. *Journal of Comparative and Physiological Psychology, 45,* 511–516.

LeDoux, J. (1993). Emotional memory systems in the brain. *Behavioural Brain Research, 58,* 69–79.

LeDoux, J. (1994). Emotion, memory and the brain. *Scientific American, 270*(6), 32–39.

LeDoux, J. (1998). *The emotional brain: the mysterious underpinnings of emotional life.* New York: Touchstone.

LeDoux, J. (2000). Emotion circuits in the brain. *Annual Review of Neuroscience, 23,* 155–184.

Legg, E., & Gotestam, K. (1991). The nature and treatment of excessive gambling. *Acta Psychiatrica Scandinavica, 84,* 113–120.

Leggio, M. G., Molinari, M., Neri, P., Graziano, A., Mandolesi, L., & Petrosini, L. (2000). Representation of actions in rats: the role of cerebellum in learning spatial performances by observation. *Proceedings of the National Academy of Sciences, 97*(5), 2320–2325.

Leggio, M. G., Neri, P., Graziano, A., Mandolesi, L., Molinari, M., & Petrosini, L. (1999). Cerebellar contribution to spatial event processing: characterization of procedural learning. *Experimental Brain Research, 127*(1), 1–11.

Leibniz, G. W. (1704). *Nouveaux essais sur l'entendement humain* [New essays on human understanding].

Leiguarda, R. C., & Marsden, C. D. (2000). Limb apraxias: higher-order disorders of sensorimotor integration. *Brain, 123*(Pt. 5), 860–879.

LeJeune, J., Gautier, M., & Turpin, R. (1959). Etudes des chromosomes somatiques de neuf enfants mongoliens. *Comptes Renus de l'Academic les Sciences, 48,* 1721.

Lenck-Santini, P. P., Save, E., & Poucet, B. (2001). Evidence for a relationship between place-cell spatial firing and spatial memory performance. *Hippocampus, 11,* 377–390.

Leshner, A. (1999). Science-based views of drug addiction and its treatment. *Journal of the American Medical Association, 282,* 1314–1316.

Lever, C., Wills, T., Cacucci, F., Burgess, N., & O'Keefe, J. (2002). Long-term plasticity in hippocampal place-cell representation of environmental geometry. *Nature, 416,* 90–94.

Lewis, C. (1981). Skill in algebra. In J. R. Anderson (Ed.), *Cognitive skill learning* (pp. 85–110). Hillsdale, NJ: Lawrence Erlbaum.

Lewis, M., & Brooks-Gunn, J. (1979). *Social cognition and the acquisition of self.* New York: Plenum.

Lhermitte, F. (1983). 'Utilization behaviour' and its relation to lesions of the frontal lobes. *Brain, 106*(Pt 2), 237–255.

Lhermitte, F., Pillon, B., & Serdaru, M. (1986). Human autonomy and the frontal lobes. Part I: Imitation and utilization behavior: a neuropsychological study of 75 patients. *Annals of Neurology, 19*(4), 326–334.

Li, Y.-J., Oliveira, S., Xu, P., Martin, E., Stenger, J., Scherzer, C., Hauser, M., Scott, W., Small, G., Nance, M., Watts, R., Hubble, J., Koller, W., Pahwa, R., Stern, M., Hiner, B., Jankovic, J., Goetz, C., Mastaglia, F., Middleton, L., Roses, A., Saunders, A., Schmechel, D., Gullans, S., Haines, J., Gilbert, J., Vancel, J., Pericak-Vance, M. (2003). Glutathione S-transferase omega-1 modifies age-at-onset of Alzheimer disease and Parkinson disease. *Human Molecular Genetics, 12,* 3259–3267.

Lichtheim, L. (1885). On aphasia. *Brain, 7,* 433–484.

Lie, C., Song, H., Colamarino, S., Ming, G.-l., & Gage, F. (2004). Neurogenesis in the adult brain: new strategies for central nervous system diseases. *Annual Review of Pharmacology and Toxicology, 44,* 399–421.

Light, L. (1991). Memory and aging: four hypotheses in search of data. *Annual Review of Psychology, 42,* 333–376.

Lilly, J. C. (1964). Vocal mimicry in tursiops: ability to match numbers and durations of human vocal bursts. *Science, 147,* 300–301.

Linden, W. (1981). Exposure treatments for focal phobias. *Archives of General Psychiatry, 38,* 769–775.

Linton, M. (1982). Transformations of memory in everyday life. In U. Neisser (Ed.), *Memory observed: remembering in natural contexts* (pp. 77–91). San Francisco: Freeman.

Little, A., Lipsitt, L., & Rovee-Collier, C. (1984). Classical conditioning and retention of the infant's eyelid response: effects of age and interstimulus interval. *Journal of Experimental Child Psychology, 37,* 512–524.

Liu, J., & Wrisberg, C. A. (1997). The effect of knowledge of results delay and the subjective estimation of movement form on the acquisition and retention of a motor skill. *Research Quarterly for Exercise and Sports, 68,* 145–151.

Locke, J. (1690). *An essay concerning human understanding.* London: T. Basset.

Locke, J. (1693). *Some thoughts concerning education.* London: Churchill.

Loftus, E. (1996). *Eyewitness testimony*. Cambridge, MA: Harvard University Press.

Loftus, E. (1997). Creating false memories. *Scientific American, 277*(3), 70–75.

Loftus, E. (2003). Our changeable memories: legal and practical implications. *Nature Reviews Neuroscience, 4,* 231–234.

Loftus, E., & Kaufman, L. (1992). Why do traumatic experiences sometimes produce good memory (flashbulbs) and sometimes no memory (repression)? In E. Winograd & U. Neisser (Eds.), *Affect and accuracy in recall: studies of "flashbulb" memories* (pp. 109–115). New York: Cambridge University Press.

Loftus, E., & Ketcham, K. (1994). *The myth of repressed memory*. New York: St. Martin's Press.

Loftus, E., & Pickrell, J. (1995). The formation of false memories. *Psychiatric Annals, 25,* 720–725.

Logothetis, N. K., Pauls, J., & Poggio, T. (1995). Shape representation in the inferior temporal cortex of monkeys. *Current Biology, 5,* 552–563.

Lømo, T. (1966). Frequency potentiation of excitatory synaptic activity in the dentate area of the hippocampal formation [abstract]. *Acta Physiologica Scandinavica, 68,* 128.

Lorenz, K. (1935). Der Kumpan in der Umwelt des Vogels ("Companions as factors in the bird's environment"). *Journal of Ornithology, 83,* 137–215.

Lorenz, K. (1952/2002). *King Solomon's ring: new light on animal ways*. New York: Routledge.

Lovaas, O. (1987). Behavioral treatment and normal educational and intellectual functioning in young autistic children. *Journal of Consulting and Clinical Psychology, 55,* 3–9.

Lu, B., & Gottschalk, W. (2000). Modulation of hippocampal synaptic transmission and plasticity by neurotrophins. *Progress in Brain Research, 128,* 231–241.

Lubow, R. E. (1973). Latent inhibition. *Psychological Bulletin, 79,* 398–407.

Lubow, R. E. (1989). *Latent inhibition and conditioned attention theory*. Cambridge, England: Cambridge University Press.

Lubow, R. E., & Moore, A. U. (1959). Latent inhibition: the effect of nonreinforced preexposure to the conditioned stimulus. *Journal of Comparative and Physiological Psychology, 52,* 415–419.

Luiselli, J., & Pine, J. (1999). Social control of childhood stealing in a public school: a case study. *Journal of Behavior Therapy and Experimental Psychiatry, 30,* 231–239.

Luria, A. R. (1982). The mind of a mnemonist (L. Solotaroff, Trans.). In U. Neisser (Ed.), *Memory observed: remembering in natural contexts* (pp. 382–389). San Francisco: Freeman. (Reprinted from *The mind of a mnemonist*, by A. Luria, 1968, New York: Basic Books)

Luria, A. R. (1966). *Higher cortical functions in man*. New York: Basic Books.

Lyn, H., & Savage-Rumbaugh, E. S. (2000). Observational word learning in two bonobos (Pan paniscus): ostensive and non-ostensive contexts. *Language and Communication, 20,* 255–273.

Ma, H. I., Trombly, C. A., & Robinson-Podolski, C. (1999). The effect of context on skill acquisition and transfer. *American Journal of Occupational Therapy, 53,* 138–144.

Mackintosh, N. J. (1975). A theory of attention: variations in the associability of stimuli with reinforcement. *Psychological Review, 82*(4), 276–298.

MacLean, P. (1949). Psychosomatic disease and the "visceral brain": recent developments bearing on the Papez theory of emotion. *Psychosomatic Medicine, 11,* 338–353.

MacLean, P. (1952). Some psychiatric implications of physiological studies on frontotemporal portion of limbic system (visceral brain). *Electroencephalography and Clinical Neurophysiology, 4,* 407–418.

Maess, B., Koelsch, S., Gunter, T. C., & Friederici, A. D. (2001). Musical syntax is processed in Broca's area: an MEG study. *Nature Neuroscience, 4*(5), 540–545.

Magendie, F. (1822). Expériences sur les fonctions des racines des nerfs rachidiens. *Journal de physiologie expérimentale et de pathologie, 2,* 366–371.

Magill, R. (1993). *Motor learning: concepts and applications*. Dubuque, IA: William C. Brown.

Maguire, E. A., Gadian, D. G., Johnsrude, I. S., Good, C. D., Ashburner, J., Frackowiak, R. S., & Frith, C. D. (2000). Navigation-related structural change in the hippocampi of taxi drivers. *Proceedings of the National Academy of Science USA, 97,* 4398–4403.

Maguire, E. A., Valentine, E., Wilding, J., & Kapur, N. (2003). Routes to remembering: the brains behind superior memory. *Nature Neuroscience, 6,* 90–94.

Mair, R., Knoth, R., Rabehenuk, S., & Langlais, P. (1991). Impairment of olfactory, auditory, and spatial serial reversal learning in rats recovered from pyrithiamine induced thiamine deficiency. *Behavioral Neuroscience, 105,* 360–374.

Majewska, A., & Sur, M. (2003). Motility of dendritic spines in visual cortex *in vivo*: changes during the critical period and effects of visual deprivation. *Proceedings of the National Academy of Sciences USA, 100,* 16024–16029.

Malcuit, G., Bastien, C., & Pomerleau, A. (1996). Habituation of the orienting response to stimuli of different functional values in 4-month-old infants. *Journal of Experimental Child Psychology, 62,* 272–291.

Mangels, J. A., Gershberg, F. B., Shimamura, A. P., & Knight, R. T. (1996). Impaired retrieval from remote memory in patients with frontal lobe lesions. *Neuropsychology, 10,* 32–41.

Manns, J., Hopkins, R., & Squire, L. (2003). Semantic memory and the human hippocampus. *Neuron, 38,* 127–133.

Marcus, E. A., Nolen, T. G., Rankin, C. H., & Carew, T. J. (1988). Behavioral dissociation of dishabituation, sensitization, and inhibition in *Aplysia. Science, 241,* 210–213.

Marcus, G. F., Vijayan, S., Bandi Rao, S., & Vishton, P. M. (1999). Rule learning by seven-month-old infants. *Science, 283*(5398), 77–80.

Maren, S. (1999). Long-term potentiation in the amygdala: a mechanism for emotional learning and memory. *Trends in Neurosciences, 22,* 561–567.

Marian, V., Spivey, M., & Hirsch, J. (2003). Shared and separate systems in bilingual language processing: converging evidence from eyetracking and brain imaging. *Brain and Language, 86*(1), 70–82.

Markowitsch, H. (1983). Transient global amnesia. *Neuroscience and Biobehavioral Reviews, 7,* 35–43.

Markowitsch, H., Calabrese, P., Wurker, M., Durwen, H., Kessler, J., Babinsky, R., Brechtelsbauer, D., Heuser, L., & Gehlen, W. (1994). The amygdala's contribution to memory: a study on two patients with Urbach-Wiethe disease. *Neuroreport, 5,* 1349–1352.

Markowitsch, H., Kessler, J., Van der Ven, C., Weber-Luxenburger, G., Albers, M., & Heiss, W. (1998). Psychic trauma causing grossly reduced brain metabolism and cognitive deterioration. *Neuropsychologia, 36,* 77–82.

Marler, P. (1970a). Birdsong and speech development: could there be parallels? *American Scientist, 58*(6), 669–673.

Marler, P. (1970b). A comparative approach to vocal learning: song development in white-crowned sparrows. *Journal of Comparative and Physiological Psychology, 71,* 1–25.

Marler, P. (1997). Three models of song learning: evidence from behavior. *Journal of Neurobiology, 33*(5), 501–516.

Marler, P., & Peters, S. (1982). Developmental overproduction and selective attrition: new processes in the epigenesis of birdsong. *Developmental Psychobiology, 15*(4), 369–378.

Marler, P., & Sherman, V. (1983). Song structure without auditory feedback: emendations of the auditory template hypothesis. *Journal of Neuroscience, 3*(3), 517–531.

Marr, D. (1971). Simple memory: a theory for archicortex. *Philosophical Transactions of the Royal Society of London Series B, 262,* 23–81.

Marsh, R., & Bower, G. H. (1993). Eliciting cryptomnesia: unconscious plagiarism in a puzzle task. *Journal of Experimental Psychology: Learning, 19,* 673–688.

Martin, R. C. (2003). Language processing: functional organization and neuroanatomical basis. *Annual Review of Psychology, 54,* 55–89.

Martínez-Cué, C., Baamonde, C., Lumbreras, M., Paz, J., Davisson, M., Schmidt, C., Diersson, M., & Flórez, J. (2002). Differential effects of environmental enrichment on behavior and learning of male and female Ts65Dn mice, a model for Down syndrome. *Behavioural Brain Research, 134,* 185–200.

Mather, J. A. (1995). Cognition in cephalopods. *Advances in the Study of Behavior, 24,* 317–353.

Matsumoto, D., & Ekman, P. (1989). American-Japanese cultural differences in intensity ratings of facial expressions of emotion. *Motivation and Emotion, 13,* 143–157.

Matsuzawa, T. (2003). The Ai project: historical and ecological contexts. *Animal Cognition, 6,* 199–211.

Maurer, D., & Lewis, T. (1999). Rapid improvement in the acuity of infants after visual input. *Science, 286,* 108–110.

Mayberry, R. I. (1993). First-language acquisition after childhood differs from second-language acquisition: the case of American Sign Language. *Journal of Speech and Language Hearing Research, 36*(6), 1258–1270.

Mayberry, R. I., & Fischer, S. D. (1989). Looking through phonological shape to lexical meaning: the bottleneck of non-native sign language processing. *Memory and Cognition, 17*(6), 740–754.

Mazarakis, N. K., Cybulska-Klosowicz, A., Grote, H., Pang, T., Van Dellen, A., Kossut, M., Blakemore, C., & Hannan, A. J. (2005). Deficits in experience-dependent cortical plasticity and sensory-discrimination learning in presymptomatic Huntington's disease mice. *Journal of Neuroscience, 25,* 3059–3066.

McAllister, W. R. (1953). Eyelid conditioning as a function of the CS-US interval. *Journal of Experimental Psychology, 45*(6), 417–422.

McCarthy, R., & Warrington, E. (1985). Category specificity in an agrammatic patient: the relative impairment of verb retrieval and comprehension. *Neuropsychologia, 23,* 709–727.

McClearn, G., Johansson, B., Berg, S., Pedersen, N., Ahern, F., Petrill, S., & Plomin, R. (1997). Substantial genetic influence on cognitive abilities in twins 80 or more years old. *Science, 276,* 1560–1563.

McClelland, J., & Rumelhart, D. (1981). An interactive activation model of context effects in letter perception: I. An account of basic findings. *Psychological Review, 88,* 375–407.

McCormick, D. A., & Thompson, R. F. (1984). Neuronal responses of the rabbit cerebellum during acquisition and performance of a classically conditioned nictitating membrane-eyelid response. *Journal of Neuroscience, 4*(11), 2811–2822.

McCutcheon, L. (2000). Another failure to generalize the Mozart effect. *Psychological Reports, 87,* 325–330.

McDonald, J. L. (1997). Language acquisition: the acquisition of linguistic structure in normal and special populations. *Annual Review of Psychology, 48,* 215–241.

McDonald, J. W., Becker, D., Sadowsky, C. L., Jane, J. A., Sr., Conturo, T. E., & Schultz, L. M. (2002). Late recovery following spinal cord injury: case report and review of the literature. *Journal of Neurosurgery, 97*(2 Suppl.), 252–265.

McDonald, R. J., & White, N. M. (1993). A triple dissociation of memory systems: hippocampus, amygdala and dorsal striatum. *Behavioral Neuroscience, 107,* 3–22.

McDonald, R. J., & White, N. M. (1994). Parallel information processing in the water maze: evidence for independent memory systems involving dorsal striatum and hippocampus. *Behavioral and Neural Biology, 61,* 260–270.

McEwen, B. (1997). Possible mechanism for atrophy of the human hippocampus. *Molecular Psychiatry, 2,* 255–262.

McEwen, B. (1999). Stress and hippocampal plasticity. *Annual Review of Neuroscience, 22,* 105–122.

McEwen, B., & Sapolsky, R. (1995). Stress and cognitive function. *Current Opinion in Neurobiology, 5,* 205–216.

McGaugh, J. (2000). Memory—A century of consolidation. *Science, 287,* 248–251.

McGaugh, J. (2002). Memory consolidation and the amygdala: a systems perspective. *Trends in Neurosciences, 25,* 456–461.

McGaugh, J. (2003). *Memory and emotion: the making of lasting memories.* New York: Columbia University Press.

McGaugh, J., & Cahill, L. (2003). Emotion and memory: central and peripheral contributions. In R. Davidson, K. Scherer, & H. Goldsmith (Eds.), *Handbook of affective sciences* (pp. 93–116). New York: Oxford University Press.

McIntyre, C., Hatfield, T., & McGaugh, J. (2000). Amygdala norepinephrine levels after training predict inhibitory avoidance retention performance in rats. *European Journal of Neuroscience, 16,* 1223–1226.

McIntyre, C., Power, A., Roozendaal, B., & McGaugh, J. (2003). Role of the basolateral amygdala in memory consolidation. *Annals of the New York Academy of Sciences, 985,* 273–293.

McKelvie, P., & Low, J. (2002). Listening to Mozart does not improve children's spatial ability: final curtains for the Mozart effect. *British Journal of Developmental Psychology, 20,* 241–258.

McKhann, G., & Albert, M. (2002). *Keep your brain alive.* New York: Wiley.

McKoon, G., & Ratcliff, R. (1998). Memory-based language processing: psycholinguistic research in the 1990s. *Annual Review of Psychology, 49,* 25–42.

McLaughlin, J., Osterhout, L., & Kim, A. (2004). Neural correlates of second-language word learning: minimal instruction produces rapid change. *Nature Neuroscience, 7(7),* 703–704.

McLellan, A., Lewis, D., O'Brien, C., & Kleber, H. (2000). Drug dependence, a chronic medical illness: implications for treatment, insurance, and outcomes evaluation. *Journal of the American Medical Association, 284,* 1689–1695.

McNally, R. (2003). Progress and controversy in the study of posttraumatic stress disorder. *Annual Review of Psychology, 54,* 229–252.

McNally, R., Bryant, R., & Ehlers, A. (2003). Does early psychological intervention promote recovery from posttraumatic stress? *Psychological Science in the Public Interest, 4,* 45–79.

McNamara, T. (1992). Priming and constraints it places on theories of memory and retrieval. *Psychological Review, 99,* 650–662.

McNaughton, B. L., & Barnes, C. (1990). From cooperative synaptic enhancement to associative memory: bridging the abyss. *Seminars in the Neurosciences, 2,* 403–416.

McNaughton, B. L., Douglas, R., & Goddard, G. (1978). Synaptic enhancement in fascia dentata: cooperativity among coactive afferents. *Brain Research, 157,* 277–293.

Mechelli, A., Crinion, J. T., Noppeney, U., O'Doherty, J., Ashburner, J., Frackowiak, R. S., & Price, C. J. (2004). Neurolinguistics: structural plasticity in the bilingual brain. *Nature, 431(7010),* 757.

Mehta, M. A., Owen, A. M., Sahakian, B. J., Mavaddat, N., Pickard, J. D., & Robbins, T. W. (2000). Methylphenidate enhances working memory by modulating discrete frontal and parietal lobe regions in the human brain. *Journal of Neuroscience, 20,* RC65.

Meltzoff, A. N. (1996). The human infant as imitative generalist: a 20-year progress report on infant imitation with implications for comparative psychology. In C. M. Heyes & B. G. Galef (Eds.), *Social learning in animals: the roots of culture* (pp. 347–370). San Diego, CA: Academic Press.

Menning, H., Imaizumi, S., Zwitserlood, P., & Pantev, C. (2002). Plasticity of the human auditory cortex induced by discrimination learning of non-native, mora-timed contrasts of the Japanese language. *Learning and Memory, 9(5),* 253–267.

Menzel, R., & Muller, U. (1996). Learning and memory in honeybees: from behavior to neural substrates. *Annual Review of Neuroscience, 19,* 379–404.

Mercado, E., Murray, S., Uyeyama, R., Pack, A., & Herman, L. (1998). Memory for recent actions in the bottlenosed dolphin (*Tursiops truncates*): repetition of arbitrary behaviors using an abstract rule. *Animal Learning and Behavior, 26,* 210–218.

Mervis, C., & Rosch, E. (1981). Categorization of natural objects. *Annual Review of Psychology, 32,* 89–115.

Merzenich, M. M., Jenkins, W., Johnston, P., Schreiner, C., Miller, S. L., & Tallal, P. (1996). Temporal processing deficits of language-learning impaired children ameliorated by training. *Science, 271,* 77–81.

Miles, C., Green, R., Sanders, G., & Hines, M. (1998). Estrogen and memory in a transsexual population. *Hormones and Behavior, 34,* 199–208.

Miller, E. K. (2000). The prefrontal cortex and cognitive control. *Nature Reviews Neuroscience, 1,* 59–65.

Miller, E. K., Erickson, C. A., & Desimone, R. (1996). Neural mechanisms of visual working memory in prefrontal cortex of the macaque. *Journal of Neuroscience, 16,* 5154–5167.

Miller, E. K., & Wallis, J. D. (2003). The prefrontal cortex and executive brain functions. In L. R. Squire, F. E. Bloom, J. L. Roberts, M. J. Zigmond, S. K. McConnell, & N. C. Spitzer (Eds.), *Fundamental neuroscience* (2nd ed., pp. 1353–1376). New York: Academic Press.

Miller, G. A. (1956). The magical number seven, plus or minus two: some limits on our capacity for processing information. *Psychological Review, 63,* 81–97.

Miller, N. E., & Dollard, J. (1941). *Social learning and imitation.* New Haven, CT: Yale University Press.

Milner, B. (1966). Amnesia following operation on the temporal lobes. In C. Whitty & O. Zangwill (Eds.), *Amnesia* (pp. 109–133). New York: Appleton-Century-Crofts.

Milner, B., Corkin, S., & Teuber, J. (1968). Further analysis of the hippocampal amnesic syndrome: a 14-year follow-up study of HM. *Neuropsychologia, 6,* 215–234.

Mineka, S., & Cook, M. (1988). Social learning and the acquisition of snake fear in monkeys. In T. R. Zentall & B. G. Galef (Eds.), *Social learning: psychological and biological perspectives* (pp. 51–73). Hillsdale, NJ: Lawrence Erlbaum.

Mineka, S., & Sutton, S. (1992). Cognitive biases and the emotional disorders. *Psychological Science, 3,* 65–69.

Mishkin, M. (1978). Memory in monkeys severely disrupted by combined but not by separate removal of amygdala and hippocampus. *Nature, 273,* 297–299.

Mizumori, S. J., Miya, D. Y., & Ward, K. E. (1994). Reversible inactivation of the lateral dorsal thalamus disrupts hippocampal place representation and impairs spatial learning. *Brain Research, 644,* 168–174.

Mobbs, D., Greicius, M., Abdel-Azim, E., Menon, V., & Reiss, A. (2003). Humor modulates the mesolimbic reward centers. *Neuron, 40,* 1041–1048.

Moore, J. W., & Gormezano, I. (1961). Yoked comparisons of instrumental and classical eyelid conditioning. *Journal of Experimental Psychology, 62,* 552–559.

Mora, F., Sanguinetti, A., Rolls, E., & Shaw, S. (1975). Differential effects of self-stimulation and motor behavior produced by microintracranial injections of a dopamine-receptor blocking agent. *Neuroscience Letters, 1,* 179–184.

Moray, N., Bates, A., & Barnett, T. (1965). Experiments on the four-eared man. *Journal of the Acoustical Society of America, 38*(2), 196–201.

Morford, J. P. (1996). Insights to language from the study of gesture: a review of research on the gestural communication of non-signing deaf people. *Language and Communication, 16,* 1–23.

Morgan, C. L. (1896). *Habit and instinct.* London: Edward Arnold.

Morris, C., Bransford, J., & Franks, J. (1977). Levels of processing versus transfer appropriate processing. *Journal of Verbal Learning and Verbal Behavior, 16,* 519–533.

Moscovitch, M., & Nadel, L. (1998). Consolidation and the hippocampal complex revisited: in defense of the multiple-trace model. *Current Opinion in Neurobiology, 8,* 297–300.

Moss, C. (1988). *Elephant memories: thirteen years in the life of an elephant family.* New York: Fawcett Columbine.

Muhlberger, A., Herrmann, M., Wiedeman, G., Ellgring, H., & Pauli, P. (2001). Repeated exposure of flight phobics to flights in virtual reality. *Behavioral Research Therapy, 39,* 1033–1050.

Muller, R. A., Kleinhans, N., & Courchesne, E. (2001). Broca's area and the discrimination of frequency transitions: a functional MRI study. *Brain and Language, 76*(1), 70–76.

Murphy, K. P., Carter, R. J., Lione, L. A., Mangiarini, L., Mahal, A., Bates, G. P., Dunnett, S. B., & Morton, A. J. (2000). Abnormal synaptic plasticity and impaired spatial cognition in mice transgenic for exon 1 of the human Huntington's disease mutation. *Journal of Neuroscience, 20,* 5115–5123.

Myers, C., Ermita, B., Hasselmo, M., & Gluck, M. (1998). Further implications of a computational model of septohippocampal cholinergic modulation in eyeblink conditioning. *Psychobiology, 26,* 1–20.

Myers, C., Shohamy, D., Gluck, M., Grossman, S., Kluger, A., Ferris, S., Golomb, J., Schnirman, G., & Schwartz, R. (2003). Dissociating hippocampal versus basal ganglia contributions to learning and transfer. *Journal of Cognitive Neuroscience, 15*(2), 185–193.

Myers, N., Perris, E., & Speaker, C. (1994). Fifty months of memory: a longitudinal study in early childhood. *Memory, 2,* 383–415.

Nadel, L. (1999). Down syndrome in cognitive neuroscience perspective. In H. Tager-Flusberg (Eds.), *Neurodevelopmental disorders* (pp. 197–221). Cambridge, MA: MIT Press.

Nadel, L. (2003). Down syndrome: a genetic disorder in biobehavioral perspective. *Genes, Brain, and Behavior, 2,* 156–166.

Nadel, L., & Jacobs, W. (1998). Traumatic memory is special. *Current Directions in Psychological Science, 7,* 154–157.

Nadel, L., & Moscovitch, M. (1997). Memory consolidation, retrograde amnesia and the hippocampal complex. *Current Opinion in Neurobiology, 7,* 217–227.

Nadel, L., & Moscovitch, M. (2001). The hippocampal complex and long-term memory revisited. *Trends in Cognitive Science, 5,* 228–230.

Nadel, L., Samsonovich, A., Ryan, L., & Moscovitch, M. (2000). Memory trace theory of human memory: computational, neuroimaging and neuropsychological results. *Hippocampus, 10,* 352–368.

Nader, K. (2003). Memory traces unbound. *Trends in Neurosciences, 26,* 65–72.

Nagell, K., Olguin, R. S., & Tomasello, M. (1993). Processes of social learning in the tool use of chimpanzees (Pan troglodytes) and human children (Homo sapiens). *Journal of Comparative Psychology, 107*(2), 174–186.

Naghdi, N., Majlessi, N., & Bozorgmehr, T. (2005). The effect of intrahippocampal injection of testosterone enanthate (an androgen receptor agonist) and anisomycin (protein synthesis inhibitor) on spatial learning and memory in adult, male rats. *Behavioural Brain Research, 156,* 263–268.

Nargeot, R., Baxter, D., Patterson, G., & Byrne, J. (1999). Dopaminergic synapses mediate neuronal changes in an analogue of operant conditioning. *Journal of Neurophysiology, 81,* 1983–1987.

Nasar, S. (2001). *A beautiful mind.* New York: Simon & Schuster.

National Institutes of Health Consensus Conference. (1985). Electroconvulsive therapy. *Journal of the American Medical Association, 254,* 2103–2108.

National Institutes of Health, National Institute of Deafness and Other Communication Disorders. (1997). Aphasia. NIH Pub No. 97-4257. Retrieved January 25, 2007, from http://www.nidcd.nih.gov/health/voice/ aphasia.htm

Naveh-Benjamin, M. (1991). A comparison of training programs intended for different types of test-anxious students: further support for an information processing model. *Journal of Educational Psychology, 83,* 134–139.

Neisser, U. (1967). *Cognitive psychology.* New York: Appleton-Century-Crofts.

Neisser, U. (1982). Snapshots or benchmarks? In U. Neisser (Ed.), *Memory observed: remembering in natural contexts* (pp. 43–48). San Francisco: Freeman.

Neisser, U., & Harsch, N. (1993). Phantom flashbulbs: false recollections of hearing the news about *Challenger.* In E. Winograd & U. Neisser (Eds.), *Affect and accuracy in recall: studies of "flashbulb" memories* (pp. 9–31). New York: Cambridge University Press.

Nemetz, G. H., Craig, K. D., & Reith, G. (1978). Treatment of sexual dysfunction through symbolic modeling. *Journal for Consulting and Clinical Psychology, 46,* 62–73.

Neufield, P., & Dwyer, J. (2000). *Actual innocence: five days to execution and other dispatches from the wrongly convicted.* New York: Doubleday.

Neuringer, A. (1969). Animals respond for food in the presence of free food. *Science, 166,* 399–401.

Newell, A., & Rosenbaum, P. S. (1981). Mechanism of skill acquisition and the law of practice. In J. R. Anderson (Ed.), *Cognitive skill acquisition* (pp. 1–56). Hillsdale, NJ: Lawrence Erlbaum.

Newell, A., & Simon, H. (1976). Computer science as empirical enquiry: symbols and search. *Communications of the Association for Computing Machinery, 19,* 113–126.

Newell, A., Shaw, J., & Simon, H. (1958). Elements of a theory of human problem solving. *Psychological Review, 65,* 151–166.

Newell, K. M. (1991). Motor skill acquisition. *Annual Review of Psychology, 42,* 213–237.

Newport, E. L. (1990). Maturational constraints on language learning. *Cognitive Science, 14,* 11–28.

Nishitani, N., Avikainen, S., & Hari, R. (2004). Abnormal imitation-related cortical activation sequences in Asperger's syndrome. *Annals of Neurology, 55*(4), 558–562.

Noad, M. J., Cato, D. H., Bryden, M. M., Jenner, M. N., & Jenner, K. C. S. (2000). Cultural revolution in whale songs. *Nature, 408,* 537.

Northcutt, R. G., & Kaas, J. H. (1995). The emergence and evolution of mammalian neocortex. *Trends in Neuroscience, 18,* 373–379.

Nottebohm, F. (1968). Auditory experience and song development in the chaffinch, *Fringilla coelebs. Ibis, 110,* 549–658.

Nowakowski, R., & Hayes, N. (2000). New neurons: extraordinary evidence or extraordinary conclusion? *Science, 288,* 771a.

Nudo, R. J., Milliken, G. W., Jenkins, W. M., & Merzenich, M. M. (1996). Use-dependent alterations of movement representations in primary motor cortex of adult squirrel monkeys. *Journal of Neuroscience, 16,* 785–807.

Nyberg, L., Cabeza, R., & Tulving, E. (1996). PET studies of encoding and retrieval: the HERA model. *Psychological Bulletin and Review, 3,* 135–148.

O'Connor, T., Rutter, M., Beckett, C., Keaveney, L., & Kreppner, J., and the English and Romanian Adoptees Study Team (2000). The effects of global severe privation on cognitive competence: extension and longitudinal follow-up. *Child Development, 71,* 376–390.

O'Doherty, J., Dayan, P., Friston, K., Critchlet, H., & Dolan, R. (2003). Temporal difference models and reward-related learning in the human brain. *Neuron, 28,* 329–337.

O'Kane, G., Kensinger, E., & Corkin, S. (2004). Evidence for semantic learning in profound amnesia: an investigation with patient H.M. *Hippocampus, 14,* 417–425.

O'Keefe, J., & Dostrovsky, J. (1971). The hippocampus as a spatial map: preliminary evidence from unit activity in the freely-moving rat. *Brain Research, 34,* 171–175.

O'Reilly, R., & Rudy, J. (2000). Computational principles of learning in the neocortex and hippocampus. *Hippocampus, 10,* 389–397.

Ohr, P., & Fagen, J. (1991). Conditioning and long-term memory in three-month-old infants with Down syndrome. *American Journal on Mental Retardation, 96,* 151–162.

Ohr, P., & Fagen, J. (1994). Contingency learning in 9-month-old infants with Down syndrome. *American Journal on Mental Retardation, 99,* 74–84.

Okado, Y., & Stark, C. (2003). Neural processing associated with true and false memory retrieval. *Cognitive, Affective, and Behavioral Neuroscience, 3*, 323–334.

Olds, J. (1955). "Reward" from brain stimulation in the rat. *Science, 122*, 878.

Olds, J. (1958). Self-stimulation of the brain. *Science, 127*, 315–324.

Olds, M., & Forbes, J. (1981). The central basis of motivation: intracranial self-stimulation studies. *Annual Review of Psychology, 32*, 523–574.

Oller, D. K., & Eilers, R. E. (1988). The role of audition in infant babbling. *Child Development, 59*(2), 441–449.

Oller, D. K., Eilers, R. E., Bull, D. H., & Carney, A. E. (1985). Prespeech vocalizations of a deaf infant: a comparison with normal metaphonological development. *Journal of Speech and Language Hearing Research, 28*(1), 47–63.

Olney, J., Wozniak, D., & Farber, N. (1997). Excitotoxic neurodegeneration in Alzheimer disease: new hypothesis and new therapeutic strategies. *Archives of Neurology, 54*, 1234–1240.

Olton, D. (1983). Memory functions and the hippocampus. In W. Seifert (Ed.), *Neurobiology of the hippocampus* (pp. 335–373). London: Academic Press.

Ono, K. (1987). Superstitious behavior in humans. *Journal of the Experimental Analysis of Behavior, 47*, 261–271.

Opitz, B., & Friederici, A. D. (2004). Brain correlates of language learning: the neuronal dissociation of rule-based versus similarity-based learning. *Journal of Neuroscience, 24*(39), 8436–8440.

Ottersen, O., & Helm, P. (2002). Neurobiology: how hardwired is the brain? *Nature, 420*, 751–752.

Overman, W., Bachevalier, J., Schuhmann, E., & Ryan, P. (1996). Cognitive gender differences in very young children parallel biologically based cognitive gender differences in monkeys. *Behavioral Neuroscience, 110*, 673–684.

Overmier, J., & Seligman, M. (1967). Effects of inescapable shock upon subsequent escape and avoidance learning. *Journal of Comparative and Physiological Psychology, 63*, 23–33.

Owen, A. M., Evans, A. C., & Petrides, M. (1996). Evidence for a two-stage model of spatial working memory processing within the lateral frontal cortex: a positron emission tomography study. *Cerebral Cortex, 6*(1), 31–38.

Owen, A. M., Roberts, A. C., Hodges, J. R., Summers, B. A., Polkey, C. E., & Robbins, T. W. (1993). Contrasting mechanisms of impaired attentional set-shifting in patients with frontal lobe damage or Parkinson's disease. *Brain, 116*, 1159–1179.

Packard, M. G., Hirsh, R., & White, N. M. (1989). Differential effects of fornix and caudate nucleus lesions on two radial maze tasks: evidence for multiple memory systems. *Journal of Neuroscience, 9*, 1465–1472.

Pakkenberg, B., & Gundersen, H. (1997). Neocortical neuron number in humans: effect of sex and age. *Journal of Comparative Neurology, 384*, 312–320.

Panksepp, J., & Burgdorf, J. (2003). "Laughing" rats and the evolutionary antecedents of human joy? *Physiology and Behavior, 79*, 533–547.

Papez, J. (1937). A proposed mechanism of emotion. *Archives of Neurology and Psychiatry, 38*, 725–744.

Paradis, M., & Goldblum, M. C. (1989). Selective crossed aphasia in a trilingual aphasic patient followed by reciprocal antagonism. *Brain and Language, 36*(1), 62–75.

Paré, D. (2002). Mechanisms of Pavlovian fear conditioning: has the engram been located? *Trends in Neurosciences, 25*, 436–437.

Paré, D. (2003). Role of the basolateral amygdala in memory consolidation. *Progress in Neurobiology, 70*, 409–420.

Park, S., & Holzman, P. S. (1992). Schizophrenics show spatial working memory deficits. *Archives of General Psychiatry, 49*, 975–982.

Park, S., Holzman, P. S., & Goldman-Rakic, P. S. (1992). Spatial working memory deficits in the relatives of schizophrenia patients. *Archives of General Psychiatry, 52*, 821–828.

Parsons, O., & Nixon, S. (1993). Neurobehavioral sequelae of alcoholism. *Neurologic Clinics, 11*, 205–218.

Patel, A. D. (2003). Language, music, syntax and the brain. *Nature Neuroscience, 6*, 674–681.

Patel, A. D., Gibson, E., Ratner, J., Besson, M., & Holcomb, P. J. (1998). Processing syntactic relations in language and music: an event-related potential study. *Journal of Cognitive Neuroscience, 10*(6), 717–733.

Paton, J., & Nottebohm, F. (1984). Neurons generated in the adult brain are recruited into functional circuits. *Science, 225*, 1046–1048.

Pavlov, I. P. (2003). *Conditioned reflexes*. Mineola, NY: Dover Publications.

Pavlov, I. P. (1927). *Conditioned reflexes: an investigation of the physiological activity of the cerebral cortex*. London: Oxford University Press.

Payne, K., & Payne, R. (1985). Large scale changes over 19 years in songs of humpback whales in Bermuda. *Zeitschrift fur Tierpsychologie, 68*, 89–114.

Pearce, J. M., & Bouton, M. E. (2001). Theories of associative learning in animals. *Annual Review of Psychology, 52*, 111–139.

Pearce, J. M., & Hall, G. (1980). A model for Pavlovian learning: variations in the effectiveness of conditioned but not of unconditioned stimuli. *Psychological Review, 87*, 532–552.

Pedreira, M., Romano, A., Tomsic, D., Lozada, M., & Maldonado, H. (1998). Massed and spaced training build up different components of long-term habituation in the crab *Chasmagnathus*. *Animal Learning and Behavior, 26*, 34–45.

Peeke, H. V. S., & Petrinovich, L. (Eds.). (1984). *Habituation, sensitization, and behavior.* Orlando, FL: Academic Press.

Peisner-Feinberg, E., Burchinal, M., & Clifford, R. (2001). The relation of preschool child-care quality to children's cognitive and social developmental trajectories through second grade. *Child Development, 72,* 1534–1553.

Penfield, W., & Boldrey, E. (1937). Somatic motor and sensory representations in cerebral cortex of man as studied by electrical stimulation. *Brain, 60,* 389–443.

Penfield, W., & Rasmussen, T. (1950). *The cerebral cortex of man: a clinical study of the localization of function.* New York: Macmillan.

Pennington, B. F., Moon, J., Edgin, J., Stedron, J., & Nadel, L. (2003). The neuropsychology of Down syndrome: evidence for hippocampal dysfunction. *Child Development, 74,* 75–93.

Pericak-Vance, M., Grubber, J., Bailey, L., Hedges, D., West, S., Santoro, L., Kemmerer, B., Hall, J., Saunders, A., Roses, A., Small, G., Scott, W., Conneally, P., Vance, J., & Haines, J. (2000). Identification of novel genes in late-onset Alzheimer's disease. *Experimental Gerontology, 35,* 1343–1352.

Perret, S. P., Ruiz, B. P., & Mauk, M. D. (1993). Cerebellar cortex lesions disrupt learning-dependent timing of conditioned eyelid responses. *Journal of Neuroscience, 13,* 1708–1718.

Peters, A., Rosene, D., Moss, M., Kemper, T., Abraham, C., Tigges, J., & Albert, M. (1996). Neurobiological bases of age-related cognitive decline in the rhesus monkey. *Journal of Neuropathology and Experimental Neurology, 55,* 861–874.

Petrides, M. (1994). Frontal lobes and working memory: evidence from investigations of the effects on cortical excisions in nonhuman primates. In F. Boller & J. Grafman (Eds.), *Handbook of neuropsychology* (pp. 59–82). Amsterdam: Elsevier.

Petrides, M. (1995). Impairments on nonspatial self-ordered and externally ordered working memory tasks after lesions of the mid-dorsal part of the lateral frontal cortex in the monkey. *Journal of Neuroscience, 15,* 359-375.

Petrides, M. (1996). Specialized systems for the processing of mnemonic information within the primate frontal cortex. *Philosophical Transactions of the Royal Society of London, Series B, 351,* 1451461.

Petrides, M. (2000). Frontal lobes and memory. In F. Boller & J. Grafman (Eds.), *Handbook of neuropsychology* (2nd ed., vol. 2, pp. 67–84). Amsterdam: Elsevier.

Petrides, M., Alivisatos, B., Evans, A. C., & Meyer, E. (1993a, February 1). Dissociation of human mid-dorsolateral from posterior dorsolateral frontal cortex in memory processing. *Proceedings of the National Academy of Sciences USA, 90*(3), 873–877.

Petrides, M., Alivisatos, B., Meyer, E., & Evans, A. C. (1993b, February 1). Functional activation of the human frontal cortex during the performance of verbal working memory tasks. *Proceedings of the National Academy of Sciences USA, 90*(3), 878–882.

Petrides, M., & Milner, B. (1982). Deficits on subject-ordered tasks after frontal- and temporal-lobe lesions in man. *Neuropsychologia, 20,* 249–262.

Phan, K., Wagner, T., Taylor, S., & Liberzon, I. (2002). Functional neuroanatomy of emotion: a meta-analysis of emotion activation studies in PET and fMRI. *NeuroImage, 16,* 331–348.

Phillips, R., & LeDoux, J. (1992). Differential contribution of amygdala and hippocampus to cued and contextual fear conditioning. *Behavioral Neuroscience, 106,* 274–285.

Phillips, S., & Sherwin, B. (1992). Variations in memory function and sex steroid hormone across the menstrual cycle. *Psychoneuroendocrinology, 17,* 497–506.

Piaget, J. (1955). *The child's construction of reality.* London: Routledge.

Piaget, J. (1962). *Play, dreams, and imitation in childhood.* New York: W. W. Norton.

Pilz, K., Veit, R., Braun, C., & Godde, B. (2004). Effects of co-activation on cortical organization and discrimination performance. *Neuroreport, 15,* 2669–2672.

Pinker, S. (1984). *Language learnability and language development.* Cambridge, MA: Harvard University Press.

Pinker, S. (2002*). The blank slate: the modern denial of human nature.* New York: Viking.

Pinsker, H., Kupfermann, I., Castellucci, V., & Kandel, E. (1970). Habituation and dishabituation of the gill-withdrawal reflex in *Aplysia. Science, 167,* 1740–1742.

Piolino, P., Desgranges, B., Benali, K., & Eustache, F. (2002). Episodic and semantic remote autobiographical memory in aging. *Memory, 10,* 239–257.

Pitman, R., Sanders, K., Zusman, R., Healy, A., Cheema, F., Lasko, N., Cahill, L., & Orr, S. (2002). Pilot study of secondary prevention of posttraumatic stress disorder with propranolol. *Biological Psychiatry, 51,* 189–192.

Plaud, J., Gaither, G., Henderson, S., & Devitt, M. (1997). The long-term habituation of sexual arousal in human males: a crossover design. *Psychological Record, 47,* 385–398.

Pohl, P. S., McDowd, J. M., Filion, D. L., Richards, L. G., & Stiers, W. (2001). Implicit learning of a perceptual-motor skill after stroke. *Physical Therapy, 81,* 1780–1789.

Poldrack, R. A. (2000). Imaging brain plasticity: conceptual and methodological issues-A theoretical review. *NeuroImage, 12,* 1–13.

Poldrack, R. A., Clark, J., Pare-Blagoev, E. J., Shohamy, D., Creso-Moyano, J., Myers, C. E., & Gluck, M. A. (2001). Interactive memory systems in the brain. *Nature, 414* (November 29), 546–550.

Poldrack, R. A., & Gabrieli, J. D. (2001). Characterizing the neural mechanisms of skill learning and repetition priming: evidence from mirror reading. *Brain, 124*(Pt. 1), 67–82.

Poldrack, R. A., Prabhakaran, V., Seger, C. A., & Gabrieli, J. D. E. (1999). Striatal activation during acquisition of a cognitive skill. *Neuropsychology, 13,* 564–574.

Poldrack, R. A., Wagner, A. D., Prull, M. W., Desmond, J. E., Glover, G. H., & Gabrieli, J. D. E. (1999). Distinguishing semantic and phonological processing in the left inferior prefrontal cortex. *NeuroImage, 10,* 15–35.

Poo, M. (2001). Neurotrophins as synaptic modulators. *Nature Reviews Neuroscience, 2,* 24–32.

Port, R., & Patterson, M. (1984). Fimbrial lesions and sensory preconditioning. *Behavioral Neuroscience, 98,* 584–589.

Porter, J. (1977). Pseudorca stranding. *Oceans, 4,* 8–14.

Potenza, M., Kosten, T., & Rounsaville, B. (2001). Pathological gambling. *Journal of the American Medical Association, 286,* 141–144.

Power, A., Thal, L., & McGaugh, J. (2002). Lesions of the nucleus basalis magnocellularis induced by 192 IgG-saporin block memory enhancement with posttraining norepinephrine in the basolateral amygdala. *Proceedings of the National Academy of Sciences USA, 99,* 2315–2319.

Prabhakaran, V., Smith, J. A. L., Desmond, J. E., Glover, G. H. and Gabrieli, J. D. E. (1997). Neural substrates of fluid reasoning: An fMRI study of neocortical activation during performance of the Raven's Progressive Matrices Test. *Cognitive Psychology, 33,* 43–63.

Premack, D. (1959). Toward empirical behavior laws: I. Positive reinforcement. *Psychological Review, 66,* 219–233.

Premack, D. (1961). Predicting instrumental performance from the independent rate of contingent response. *Journal of Experimental Psychology, 61,* 163–171.

Premack, D. (1962). Reversibility of the reinforcement relation. *Science, 136,* 255–257.

Premack, D. (1971). On the assessment of language competence in the chimpanzee. In A. M. Schrier & F. Stollnitz (Eds.), *Behavior of nonhuman primates, vol. 4* (pp. 186–228). New York: Academic Press.

Premack, D. (1976). *Intelligence in ape and man.* Hillsdale, NJ: Lawrence Erlbaum.

Premack, D., & Premack, A. J. (1984). *The mind of an ape.* New York: W. W. Norton.

Preston, K., Umbricht, A., & Epstein, D. (2000). Methadone dose increase and abstinence reinforcement for treatment of continued heroin use during methadone maintenance. *Archives of General Psychiatry, 57,* 395–404.

Price, J., & Morris, J. (1999). Tangles and plaques in nondemented aging and 'preclinical' Alzheimer's disease. *Annals of Neurology, 45,* 358–368.

Proteau, L., Marteniuk, R. G., & Levesque, L. (1992). A sensorimotor basis for motor learning: evidence indicating specificity of practice. *Quarterly Journal of Experimental Psychology, 44A,* 557–575.

Pryor, K., Haag, R., & O'Reilly, J. (1969). The creative porpoise: training for novel behavior. *Journal of the Experimental Analysis of Behavior, 12,* 653–661.

Ptito, A., Crane, J., Leonard, G., Amsel, R., & Caramanos, Z. (1995). Visual-spatial localization by patients with frontal-lobe lesions invading or sparing area 46. *Neuroreport, 6*(13), 45–48.

Quillian, M. R. (1967). Word concepts: a theory and simulation of some basic semantic capabilities. *Behavioral Science, 12,* 410–430.

Quirk, G., Likhtik, E., Pelletier, J., & Paré, D. (2003). Stimulation of medial prefrontal cortex decreases the responsiveness of central amygdala output neurons. *Journal of Neuroscience, 23,* 8800–8807.

Radelet, M. (2002). Wrongful convictions of the innocent. *Judicature, 86,* 67–68.

Raine, A., Hulme, C., Chadderton, H., & Bailey, P. (1991). Verbal short-term memory span in speech-disordered children: implications for articulatory coding in short-term memory. *Child Development, 62,* 415–423.

Rakic, P. (2002). Neurogenesis in adult primate neocortex: an evaluation of the evidence. *Nature Reviews Neuroscience, 3,* 65–71.

Ramón y Cajal, S. (1990). *New ideas on the structure of the nervous system in man and vertebrates* (L. Swanson & L. Swanson, Trans.). Cambridge, MA: MIT Press. (Original work, *Les nouvelles idées sur la structure du système nerveux chez l'homme et chez les vertébrés,* published 1894)

Rampon, C., & Tsien, J. Z. (2000). Genetic analysis of learning behavior-induced structural plasticity. *Hippocampus, 10*(5), 605–609.

Rankin, C. H. (2004). Invertebrate learning: what can't a worm learn? *Current Biology, 14,* R617–R618.

Rankin, C. H., & Broster, B. S. (1992). Factors affecting habituation and recovery from habituation in the nematode *Caenorhabditis elegans. Behavioral Neuroscience, 106,* 239–249.

Rapp, P., & Gallagher, M. (1996). Preserved neuron number in the hippocampus of aged rats with spatial learning deficits. *Proceedings of the National Academy of Sciences USA, 93,* 9926–9930.

Rasmussen, T., Schliemann, T., Sorensen, J., Zimmer, J., & West, M. (1996). Memory impaired aged rats: no loss of principal hippocampal and subicular neurons. *Neurobiology of Aging, 17,* 143–147.

Rauscher, F., & Shaw, G. (1998). Key components of the Mozart effect. *Perceptual and Motor Skills, 86,* 835–841.

Rauscher, F., Shaw, G., & Ky, K. (1993). Music and spatial task performance. *Nature, 365,* 611.

Rawson, R., & Tennant, F. (1984). Five-year follow-up of opiate addicts with naltrexone and behavior therapy. *NIDA Research Monograph, 49,* 289–295.

Reber, A. S. (1967). Implicit learning of artificial grammars. *Journal of Verbal Learning and Verbal Behavior, 77,* 317–327.

Recanzone, G. H., Merzenich, M. M., Jenkins, W. M., Grajski, K. A., & Dinse, H. R. (1992). Topographic reorganization of the hand representation in cortical area 3b of owl monkeys trained in a frequency-discrimination task. *Journal of Neurophysiology, 67,* 1031–1056.

Reed, J., & Squire, L. (1998). Retrograde amnesia for facts and events: findings from four new cases. *Journal of Neuroscience, 18,* 3943–3954.

Reisberg, B., Doody, R., Stoffler, A., Schmitt, F., Ferris, S., & Mobius, H. (2006). A 24-week open-label extension study of memantine in moderate to severe Alzheimer disease. *Archives of Neurology, 63,* 49–54.

Reisel, W., & Kopelman, R. (1995). The effects of failure on subsequent group performance in a professional sports setting. *Journal of Psychology: Interdisciplinary and Applied, 129,* 103–113.

Reiss, D., & McCowan, B. (1993). Spontaneous vocal mimicry and production by bottlenose dolphins (Tursiops truncatus): evidence for vocal learning. *Journal of Comparative Psychology, 107*(3), 301–312.

Remington, B., Roberts, P., & Glauthier, S. (1977). The effect of drink familiarity on tolerance to alcohol. *Addictive Behaviors, 22,* 45–53.

Rendell, L., & Whitehead, H. (2001). Culture in whales and dolphins. *Behavioral and Brain Sciences, 24,* 309–382.

Renner, M., & Rosenzweig, M. (1987). *Enriched and impoverished environments: effects on brain and behavior.* New York: Springer-Verlag.

Rescorla, R. A. (1968). Probability of shock in the presence and absence of CS in fear conditioning. *Journal of Comparative & Physiological Psychology, 66*(1), 1–5.

Rescorla, R. A. (1976). Stimulus generalization: some predictions from a model of Pavlovian conditioning. *Journal of Experimental Psychology: Animal Behavior Processes, 2*(1), 88–96.

Rescorla, R. A. (1987). A Pavlovian analysis of goal directed behavior. *American Psychologist, 42,* 119–129.

Rescorla, R. A., & Wagner, A. R. (1972). A theory of Pavlovian conditioning: variations in the effectiveness of reinforcement and non-reinforcement. In A. Black & W. Prokasy, *Classical conditioning II: Current research and theory* (pp. 64–99). New York: Appleton-Century-Crofts.

Ribot, T. (1882). *The diseases of memory.* New York: Appleton-Century-Crofts.

Richards, D. G., Wolz, J. P., & Herman, L. M. (1984). Vocal mimicry of computer-generated sounds and vocal labeling of objects by a bottlenosed dolphin, *Tursiops truncatus. Journal of Comparative Psychology, 98*(1), 10–28.

Rideout, B., Dougherty, S., & Wernert, L. (1998). Effect of music on spatial performance: a test of generality. *Perceptual and Motor Skills, 86,* 512–514.

Rideout, H., & Parker, L. (1996). Morphine enhancement of sucrose palatability: analysis by the taste reactivity test. *Pharmacology, Biochemistry, and Behavior, 53,* 731–734.

Ritvo, E. R., Freeman, B. J., Scheibel, A. B., Duong, T., Robinson, H., Guthrie, D., & Ritvo, A. (1986). Lower Purkinje cell counts in the cerebella of four autistic subjects: initial findings of the UCLA-NSAC Autopsy Research Report. *American Journal of Psychiatry, 143*(7), 862–866.

Ritvo, E. R., & Provence, S. (1953). Form perception and imitation in some autistic children: diagnostic findings and their contextual interpretation. *Psychoanalytic Child Study, 8,* 155–161.

Rizzolatti, G., & Arbib, M. A. (1998). Language within our grasp. *Trends in Neuroscience, 21*(5), 188–194.

Rizzolatti, G., & Craighero, L. (2004). The mirror-neuron system. *Annual Review of Neuroscience, 27,* 169–192.

Rizzolatti, G., Fadiga, L., Matelli, M., Bettinardi, V., Paulesu, E., Perani, D., & Fazio, F. (1996). Localization of grasp representations in humans by PET: 1. Observation versus execution. *Experimental Brain Research, 111*(2), 246–252.

Rizzolatti, G., Fogassi, L., & Gallese, V. (2002). Motor and cognitive functions of the ventral premotor cortex. *Current Opinion in Neurobiology, 12*(2), 149–154.

Robbins, T. (1996). Refining the taxonomy of memory. *Science, 273,* 1353–1354.

Roberts, D. (1941). Imitation and suggestion in animals. *Bulletin of Animal Behaviour, 1,* 11–19.

Roberts, W. (2002). Are animals stuck in time? *Psychological Bulletin, 128,* 473–489.

Roediger, H., & McDermott, K. (1995). Creating false memories: remembering words not presented in lists. *Journal of Experimental Psychology: Learning, Memory, and Cognition, 21,* 803–814.

Rogers, S. J., & Pennington, B. F. (1991). A theoretical approach to the deficits in infantile autism. *Development and Psychopathology, 3,* 137–162.

Roldan, E., Alvarez-Pelaez, R., & Fernandez de Molina, A. (1974). Electrographic study of the amygdaloid defense response. *Physiology and Behavior, 13,* 779–787.

Rolls, E. (1999). *The brain and emotion.* Oxford, England: Oxford University Press.

Romanes, G. J. (1898). *Mental evolution in animals.* New York: Appleton-Century-Crofts.

Romanes, G. J. (1982). *Animal intelligence.* Farnborough, Hants., England: Gregg International, Reprint Edition.

Rose, D. (1996). *A multilevel approach to the study of motor control and learning.* San Francisco: Benjamin Cummings.

Rosenbaum, D. A., Carlson, R. A., & Gilmore, R. O. (2001). Acquisition of intellectual and perceptual-motor skills. *Annual Review of Psychology, 52,* 453–470.

Rosenkranz, J., & Grace, A. (2002). Dopamine-mediated modulation of odour-evoked amygdala potentials during Pavlovian conditioning. *Nature, 417,* 282–287.

Rosenzweig, E. S., & Barnes, C. (2003). Impact of aging on hippocampal function: plasticity, network dynamics, and cognition. *Progress in Neurobiology, 69,* 143–179.

Rosenzweig, E. S., Redish, A. D., McNaughton, B. L., & Barnes, C. A. (2003). Hippocampal map realignment and spatial learning. *Nature Neuroscience, 6,* 609–615.

Rosenzweig, M. (1984). Experience, memory and the brain. *American Psychologist, 39,* 365–376.

Rotenberg, A., Abel, T., Hawkins, R. D., Kandel, E. R., & Muller, R. U. (2000). Parallel instabilities of long-term potentiation, place cells, and learning caused by decreased protein kinase A activity. *Journal of Neuroscience, 20,* 8096–8102.

Rothbaum, B., & Davis, M. (2003). Applying learning principles to the treatment of post-trauma reactions. *Annals of the New York Academy of Sciences, 1008,* 112–121.

Rothi, L., Ochipa, C., & Heilman, K. (1991). A cognitive neuropsychological model of limb praxis. *Cognitive Neuropsychology, 8,* 443–458.

Rotter, J. B. (1954). *Social learning and clinical psychology.* Englewood Cliffs, NJ: Prentice-Hall.

Routtenberg, A., & Lindy, J. (1965). Effects of the availability of rewarding septal and hypothalamic stimulation on bar pressing for food under conditions of deprivation. *Journal of Comparative and Physiological Psychology, 60,* 158–161.

Routtenberg, A., & Malsbury, C. (1969). Brainstem pathways of reward. *Journal of Comparative and Physiological Psychology, 68,* 22–30.

Rovee-Collier, C. (1993). The capacity for long-term memory in infancy. *Current Directions in Psychological Science, 2,* 130–135.

Rovee-Collier, C. (1997). Dissociations in infant memory: rethinking the development of implicit and explicit memory. *Psychological Review, 107,* 467–498.

Rovee-Collier, C. (1999). The development of infant memory. *Current Directions in Psychological Science, 8,* 80–85.

Rowe, J., & Kahn, R. (1998). *Successful aging.* New York: Pantheon.

Roy, N., Cleren, C., Singh, S., Yang, L., Beal, M., & Goldman, S. (2006). Functional engraftment of human ES cell-derived dopaminergic neurons enriched by coculture with telomerase-immortalized midbrain astrocytes. *Nature Medicine, 12,* 1259–1268.

Ruch, F. (1934). The differentiative effects of age upon human learning. *Journal of General Psychology, 11,* 261–286.

Rumbaugh, D. M. (1977). *Language learning by a chimpanzee: the Lana project.* New York: Academic Press.

Rumbaugh, D. M., & Washburn, D. A. (2003). *Intelligence of apes and other rational beings.* New Haven, CT: Yale University Press.

Rumelhart, D., & McClelland, J. (1986). On learning the past tenses of English verbs. In J. McClelland & D. Rumelhart (Eds.) *Parallel distributed processing: explorations in the microstructure of cognition, vol. II: Psychological and biological models* (pp. 216–271). Cambridge, MA: MIT Press.

Rumelhart, D., & McClelland, J. (Eds.). (1986). *Parallel distributed processing: explorations in the microstructure of cognition* (Vols. 1–2). Cambridge, MA: MIT Press.

Rusted, J., Ratner, H., & Sheppard, L. (1995). When all else fails, we can still make tea: a longitudinal look at activities of daily living in an Alzheimer patient. In R. Campbell & M. Conway (Eds.), *Broken memories: case studies in memory impairment* (pp. 396–410). Cambridge, MA: Blackwell.

Rutter, M., & O'Connor, T., and the English and Romanian Adoptees (ERA) Study Team (2004). Are there biological programming effects for psychological development? Findings from a study of Romanian adoptees. *Developmental Psychology, 40,* 81–94.

Rutter, M., and the English and Romanian Adoptees (ERA) study team. (1998). Developmental catch-up, and deficit, following adoption after severe global early privation. *Journal of Child Psychology and Psychiatry, 39,* 465–476.

Ryan, L., Nadel, L., Keil, K., Putnam, K., Schnyer, D., Trouard, T., & Moscovitch, M. (2001). Hippocampal complex and retrieval of recent and very remote autobiographical memories: evidence from functional magnetic resonance imaging in neurologically intact people. *Hippocampus, 11,* 707–714.

Sadato, N., Pascual-Leone, A., Grafman, J., Deiber, M. P., Ibanez, V., & Hallett, M. (1998). Neural networks for Braille reading by the blind. *Brain, 121*(Pt. 7), 1213–1229.

Saffran, J. R., Aslin, R. N., & Newport, E. L. (1996). Statistical learning by 8-month-old infants. *Science, 274*(5294), 1926–1928.

Saffran, J. R., Johnson, E. K., Aslin, R. N., & Newport, E. L. (1999). Statistical learning of tone sequences by human infants and adults. *Cognition, 70*(1), 27–52.

Saffran, J. R., & Thiessen, E. D. (2003). Pattern induction by infant language learners. *Developmental Psychology, 39*(3), 484–494.

Saffran, J. R., & Wilson, D. P. (2003). From syllables to syntax: multilevel statistical learning by 12-month-old infants. *Infancy, 4,* 273–284.

Salamone, J., Arizzi, M., Sandoval, M., Cervone, K., & Aberman, J. (2002). Dopamine antagonists alter response allocation but do not suppress appetite for food: contrasts between the effects of SKF 83566, raclopride, and fenfluramine on a concurrent choice task. *Psychopharmacology, 160,* 371–380.

Salamone, J., Steinpreis, R., McCullough, L., Smith, P., Grebel, D., & Mahan, K. (1991). Haloperidol and nucleus accumbens dopamine depletion suppress lever pressing for food but increase free food consumption in a novel food-choice procedure. *Psychopharmacology, 104,* 515–521.

Salthouse, T. (1984). Effects of age and skill in typing. *Journal of Experimental Psychology: General, 113,* 345–371.

Sapolsky, R. (1996). Why stress is bad for your brain. *Science, 273,* 749–750.

Sapolsky, R. (1998). *Why zebras don't get ulcers.* New York: Freeman.

Saufley, W., Otaka, S., & Bavaresco, J. (1985). Context effects: classroom tests and context independence. *Memory and Cognition, 13,* 522–528.

Savage-Rumbaugh, E. S. (1986). *Ape language: from conditioned response to symbol.* New York: Columbia University Press.

Savage-Rumbaugh, E. S., & Lewin, R. (1994). *Kanzi: the ape at the brink of the human mind.* New York: John Wiley.

Savage-Rumbaugh, E. S., Murphy, J., Sevcik, R. A., Brakke, K. E., Williams, S. L., & Rumbaugh, D. M. (1993). Language comprehension in ape and child. *Monographs of Social Research and Child Development, 58*(3–4), 1–222.

Savage-Rumbaugh, E. S., Rumbaugh, D. M., Smith, S. T., & Lawson, J. (1980). Reference: the linguistic essential. *Science, 210*(4472), 922–925.

Scarmeas, N., & Stern, Y. (2004). Cognitive reserve: Implications for diagnosis and prevention of Alzheimer's disease. *Current Neurology and Neuroscience Reports. 4*(5), 374–380.

Schachter, S., & Singer, J. (1962). Cognitive, social, and physiological determinants of emotional state. *Psychological Review, 69,* 379–399.

Schacter, D. L. (1984). Retrieval without recollection: an experimental analysis of source amnesia. *Journal of Verbal Language and Verbal Behavior, 23,* 593–611.

Schacter, D. L. (1987). Implicit memory: history and current status. *Journal of Experimental Psychology: Learning, Memory, and Cognition, 13,* 501–518.

Schacter, D. L. (1996). *Searching for memory: the brain, the mind and the past.* New York: Basic Books.

Schacter, D. L. (2001). *The seven sins of memory: how the mind forgets and remembers.* New York: Houghton-Mifflin.

Schacter, D. L., & Curran, T. (1995). The cognitive neuroscience of false memories. *Psychiatric Annals, 25,* 726–730.

Schacter, D. L., Curran, T., Reiman, E. M., Chen, K., Bandy, D. J., & Frost, J. T. (1999). Medial temporal lobe activation during episodic encoding and retrieval: a PET study. *Hippocampus, 9,* 575–581.

Schacter, D. L., & Kihlstrom, J. (1989). Functional amnesia. In F. Boller & J. Grafman (Eds.), *Handbook of neuropsychology* (pp. 209–231). New York: Elsevier Science.

Schacter, D. L., Wang, P., Tulving, E., & Freedman, M. (1982). Functional retrograde amnesia: a quantitative case study. *Neuropsychologia, 20,* 523–532.

Schank, R. (1984). *The cognitive computer: on language, learning, and artificial Intelligence.* Reading, MA: Addison-Wesley.

Schauer, F. (2003). *Profiles, probabilities, and stereotypes.* Cambridge, MA: Belknap Press.

Schiltz, C., Bodart, J. M., Michel, C., & Crommelinck, M. (2001). A PET study of human skill learning: changes in brain activity related to learning an orientation discrimination task. *Cortex, 37,* 243–265.

Schlinger, H., & Blakely, E. (1994). The effects of delayed reinforcement and a response-produced auditory stimulus on the acquisition of operant behavior in rats. *Psychological Record, 44,* 391–410.

Schmidt, R. A., & Wulf, G. (1997). Continuous concurrent feedback degrades skill learning: implications for training and simulation. *Human Factors, 39,* 509–525.

Schmidt, R. A., Young, D. E., Swinnen, S., & Shapiro, D. C. (1989). Summary knowledge of results for skill acquisition: support for the guidance hypothesis. *Journal of Experimental Psychology: Learning, Memory and Cognition, 15,* 352–359.

Schmolck, H., Buffalo, E., & Squire, L. (2000). Memory distortions develop over time: recollections of the O. J. Simpson trial verdict after 15 and 32 months. *Psychological Science, 11,* 39–45.

Schneider, D. J. (2004). *The psychology of stereotyping.* New York: Guilford Press.

Schultz, W. (1998). Predictive reward signal of dopamine neurons. *Journal of Neurophysiology, 80,* 1–27.

Schultz, W. (2002). Getting formal with dopamine and reward. *Neuron, 36,* 241–263.

Schultz, W., & Dickinson, A. (2000). Neuronal coding of prediction errors. *Annual Review of Psychology, 23,* 473–500.

Schwartz, B., Colon, M., Sanchez, I., Rodriguez, I., & Evans, S. (2002). Single-trial learning of "what" and "who" information in a gorilla (*Gorilla gorilla*): implications for episodic memory. *Animal Cognition, 5,* 85–90.

Schwartz, B., & Evans, S. (2001). Episodic memory in primates. *American Journal of Primatology, 55,* 71–85.

Schwartz, S., Maquet, P., & Frith, C. (2002). Neural correlates of perceptual learning: a functional MRI study of visual texture discrimination. *Proceedings of the National Academy of Sciences USA, 99,* 17137–17142.

Schweitzer, J. B., Faber, T. L., Grafton, S. T., Tune, L. E., Hoffman, J. M., & Kilts, C. D. (2000). Alterations in the functional anatomy of working memory in adult attention deficit hyperactivity disorder. *American Journal of Psychiatry, 157*(2), 278–280.

Scott, J. (1958). *Animal behavior.* Chicago: University of Chicago Press.

Scott, J. (1962). Critical periods in behavioral development. *Science, 138,* 949–958.

Scoville, W., & Milner, B. (1957). Loss of recent memory after bilateral hippocampal lesions. *Journal of Neurology, Neurosurgery and Psychiatry, 20,* 11–21.

Seager, M. A., Johnson, L. D., Chabot, E. S, Asaka, Y., & Berry, S. D. (2002). Oscillatory brain states and learning: impact of hippocampal theta-contingent training. *Proceedings of the National Academy of Sciences, 99*(3), 1616–1620.

Sears, L. L., Finn, P. R., & Steinmetz, J. E. (1994). Abnormal classical eyeblink conditioning in autism. *Journal of Autism and Development Disorders, 24*(6), 737–751.

Sears, L. L., & Steinmetz, J. E. (1991). Dorsal accessory inferior olive activity diminishes during acquisition of the rabbit classically conditioned eyelid response. *Brain Research, 545,* 114–122.

Sebeok, T. A., & Rosenthal, R. (Eds.). (1981). *The Clever Hans phenomenon: communication with horses, whales, apes, and people.* New York: New York Academy of Sciences.

Sederberg, P. B., Kahana, M. J., Howard, M. W., Donner, E. J., & Madsen, J. R. (2003). Theta and gamma oscillations during encoding predict subsequent recall. *Journal of Neuroscience, 23,* 10809–10814.

Seger, C. A. (1994). Implicit learning. *Psychological Bulletin, 115,* 163–196.

Seidenberg, M. S., & Petitto, L. A. (1987). Communication, symbolic communication, and language: comment on Savage-Rumbaugh, McDonald, Sevcik, Hopkins, and Rupert (1986). *Journal of Experimental Psychology: General, 116,* 279–287.

Seligman, M. (1972). Phobias and preparedness. In M. Seligman & J. Hager (Eds.), *Biological boundaries of learning* (pp. 451–462). New York: Appleton-Century-Crofts.

Seligman, M. (1975). *Helplessness: on depression, development, and death.* San Francisco: Freeman.

Seligman, M., & Maier, S. (1967). Failure to escape traumatic shock. *Journal of Experimental Psychology, 74,* 1–9.

Semenza, C., Sartori, & D'Andrea, J. (2003). He can tell which master craftsman blew a Venetian vase, but he cannot name the pope: a patient with a selective difficulty in naming faces. *Neuroscience Letters, 352,* 73–75.

Senghas, A., & Coppola, M. (2001). Children creating language: how Nicaraguan sign language acquired a spatial grammar. *Psychological Science, 12,* 323–328.

Serres, L. (2001). Morphological changes of the human hippocampal formation from midgestation to early childhood. In C. Nelson & M. Luciana (Eds.), *Handbook of developmental cognitive neuroscience* (pp. 45–58). Cambridge, MA: MIT Press.

Shakow, D. (1930). Hermann Ebbinghaus. *American Journal of Psychology, 42,* 505–518.

Shallice, T. (1988). *From neuropsychology to mental structure.* Cambridge, England: Cambridge University Press.

Shankle, W., Landing, B., Rafii, M., Schiano, A., Chen, J., & Hara, J. (1998). Evidence for a postnatal doubling of neuron number in the developing human cerebral cortex between 15 months and 6 years. *Journal of Theoretical Biology, 191,* 115–140.

Shannon, C. E. (1948). A mathematical theory of communication. *Bell System Technical Journal, 27,* 379–423, 623–656.

Shepard, R. (1987). Towards a universal law of generalization for psychological science. *Science, 237,* 1317–1323.

Sherrington, C. (1906). *The integrative action of the nervous system.* Cambridge, England: Cambridge University Press.

Sherry, D. F., & Galef, B.G., Jr. (1984). Cultural transmission without imitation: milk bottle opening by birds. *Animal Behaviour, 32,* 937–938.

Sherry, D. F., & Galef, B. G., Jr. (1990). Social learning without imitation: more about milk bottle opening by birds. *Animal Behaviour, 40,* 987–989.

Shettleworth, S. J. (1998). *Cognition, evolution, and behavior.* New York: Oxford University Press.

Shimamura, A. P., Jurica, P. J., Mangels, J. A., Gershberg, F. B., & Knight, R. T. (1995). Susceptibility to memory interference effects following frontal lobe damage: findings from tests of paired-associate learning. *Journal of Cognitive Neuroscience, 7,* 144–152.

Shohamy, D., Allen, M. T., & Gluck, M. A. (2000). Dissociating entorhinal and hippocampal involvement in latent inhibition. *Behavioral Neuroscience, 114*(5), 867–874.

Shors, T. J., & Dryver, E. (1994). Effects of stress and long-term potentiation (LTP) on subsequent LTP and the theta burst response in the dentate gyrus. *Brain Research, 666,* 232–238.

Shors, T. J., & Matzel, L. D. (1997). Long-term potentiation: what's learning got to do with it? *Behavioral and Brain Sciences, 20,* 597–614; discussion 614–655.

Sidman, R., & Rakic, P. (1973). Neuronal migration, with special reference to developing human brain: a review. *Brain Research, 62,* 1–35.

Siegel, S. (1983). Classical conditioning, drug tolerance, and drug dependence. In Y. Israel, F. Glaser, H. Kalant, R. Popham, W. Schmidt, & R. Smart (Eds.), *Research advances in alcohol and drug problems. Vol. 7* (pp. 207–246). New York: Plenum Press.

Siegel, S. (2001). Pavlovian conditioning and drug overdose: when tolerance fails. *Addiction Research and Theory, 9*(5), 503–513.

Siegel, S., & Ellsworth, D. W. (1986). Pavlovian conditioning and death from apparent overdose of medically prescribed morphine: a case report. *Bulletin of the Psychonomic Society, 24*, 278–280.

Siegel, S., Hinson, R. E., Krank, M. D., & McCully, J. (1982). Heroin "overdose" death: contribution of drug-associated environmental cues. *Science, 216*(4544), 436–437.

Siegel, S., & Ramos, B. M. C. (2002). Applying laboratory research: drug anticipation and the treatment of drug addiction. *Experimental and Clinical Psychopharmacology, 10*(3), 162–183.

Sigman, M., & Ungerer, J. A. (1984). Attachment behaviors in autistic children. *Journal of Autism and Developmental Disorders, 14*(3), 231–244.

Silverman, I., & Eals, M. (1992). Sex differences in spatial abilities: evolutionary theory and data. In J. Barkow, L. Cosmides, & J. Tooby (Eds.), *The adapted mind: evolutionary psychology and the generation of culture*. New York: Oxford University Press.

Simmons, R. (1924). The relative effectiveness of certain incentives in animal learning. *Comparative Psychology Monographs*, No. 7.

Simon, H. (1977). What computers mean for man and society. *Science, 195*, 1186–1191.

Simon, H., & Gilmartin, K. (1973). A simulation of memory for chess positions. *Cognitive Psychology, 5*, 29–46.

Singh, D. (1970). Preference for bar pressing to obtain reward over freeloading in rats and children. *Journal of Comparative and Physiological Psychology, 73*, 320–327.

Singley, M., & Anderson, J. (1989). *The transfer of cognitive skills*. Cambridge, MA: Harvard University Press.

Sirigu, A., Daprati, E., Ciancia, S., Giraux, P., Nighoghossian, N., Posada, A., & Haggard, P. (2004). Altered awareness of voluntary action after damage to the parietal cortex. *Nature Neuroscience, 7*, 80–84.

Skinner, B. F. (1938). *The behavior of organisms: an experimental analysis*. New York: Appleton-Century-Crofts.

Skinner, B. F. (1945, October). Baby in a box. *Ladies' Home Journal*, pp. 30–31, 135–136, 138.

Skinner, B. F. (1948a). Superstition in the pigeon. *Journal of Experimental Psychology, 38*, 168–172.

Skinner, B. F. (1948b). *Walden Two*. New York: Macmillan.

Skinner, B. F. (1951). How to teach animals. *Scientific American, 185*, 26–29.

Skinner, B. F. (1953). *Science and human behavior*. New York: Free Press.

Skinner, B. F. (1957). *Verbal behavior*. New York: Appleton-Century-Crofts.

Skinner, B. F. (1959). *Cumulative record*. New York: Appleton-Century-Crofts.

Skinner, B. F. (1971). *Beyond Freedom and dignity*. New York: Knopf.

Skinner, B. F. (1979). *The shaping of a behaviorist: part two of an autobiography*. New York: Knopf.

Skinner, D. (2004, March 12). I was not a lab rat. *The Guardian* (Manchester).

Slater, L. (2004) *Opening Skinner's box: great psychological experiments of the twentieth century*. New York: W. W. Norton.

Small, S., Chawla, M., Buonocore, M., Rapp, P., & Barnes, C. (2004). Imaging correlates of brain function in monkeys and rats isolates a hippocampal subregion differentially vulnerable to aging. *Proceedings of the National Academy of Sciences USA, 101*, 7181–7186.

Smith, D., Rapp, P., McKay, H., Roberts, J., & Tuszynski, M. (2004). Memory impairment in aged primates is associated with focal death of cortical neurons and atrophy of subcortical neurons. *Journal of Neuroscience, 24*, 4373–4381.

Smith, E. E., & Jonides, J. (1995). Working memory in humans: neuropsychological evidence. In M. Gazzaniga (Ed.), *The cognitive neurosciences* (pp. 1009–1020). Cambridge, MA: MIT Press.

Smith, E. E., & Jonides, J. (1999). Storage and executive processes in the frontal lobes. *Science, 283*, 1657–1661.

Smith, E. E., & Jonides, J. (2004). Executive control and thought. In L. Squire, *Fundamentals of neuroscience* (pp. 1377–1394). New York: Academic Press.

Smith, I. M., & Bryson, S. E. (1994). Imitation and action in autism: a critical review. *Psychological Bulletin, 116*(2), 259–273.

Smith, I. M., & Bryson, S. E. (1998). Gesture imitation in autism I: Nonsymbolic postures and sequences. *Cognitive Neuropsychology, 15*, 747–770.

Smith, M. (2005). Bilateral hippocampal volume reduction in adults with post-traumatic stress disorder: a meta-analysis of structural MRI studies. *Hippocampus, 15*, 798–807.

Smith, S. M. (1985). Background music and context-dependent memory. *American Journal of Psychology, 98*, 591–603.

Smotherman, W., & Robinson, S. (1992). Habituation in the rat fetus. *Quarterly Journal of Experimental Psychology B, 44*, 215–230.

Sokolov, E. N. (1963). *Perception and the conditioned reflex*. Oxford, England: Pergamon Press.

Solanto, M., Arnsten., A., & Castellanos, F. (2000). *The neuropharmacology of stimulant drugs: implications for ADHD*. New York: Oxford University Press.

Solomon, P., & Groccia-Ellison, M. (1996). Classic conditioning in aged rabbits: delay, trace and long-delay conditioning. *Behavioral Neuroscience, 110*, 427–435.

Solomon, P., & Moore, J. W. (1975). Latent inhibition and stimulus generalization of the classically conditioned nictitating membrane response in rabbits (*Oryctolagus cuniculus*) following dorsal hippocampal ablation. *Journal of Comparative and Physiological Psychology, 89*, 1192–1203.

Solomon, P., Pomerleau, D., Bennett, L., James, J., & Morse, D. (1989). Acquisition of the classically conditioned eyeblink response in humans over the life span. *Psychology and Aging, 4*, 34–41.

Spence, K. W. (1937). The differential response in animals to stimuli varying within a single dimension. *Psychological Review, 44*, 430–444.

Spence, K. W. (1952). Clark Leonard Hull: 1884–1952. *American Journal of Psychology, 65*, 639–646.

Sperling, G. (1960). The information available in brief visual presentations. *Psychological Monographs, 74*, 1–29.

Spiers, H., Burgess, N., Hartley, T., Vargha-Khadem, F., & O'Keefe, J. (2001). Bilateral hippocampal pathology impairs topographical and episodic memory but not visual pattern matching. *Hippocampus, 11*, 715–725.

Squire, L. R. (1989). On the course of forgetting in very long-term memory. *Journal of Experimental Psychology: Learning, Memory, and Cognition, 15*, 241–245.

Squire, L. R. (1992). Memory and the hippocampus: a synthesis from findings with rats, monkeys, and humans. *Psychological Review, 99*, 195–231.

Squire, L. R., & Kandel, E. R. (2000). *Memory: from mind to molecules*. New York: Scientfic American Library.

Squire, L. R., & Knowlton, B. J. (1995). Memory, hippocampus and brain systems. In M. Gazzaniga (Ed.), *The cognitive neurosciences* (pp. 825–837). Cambridge, MA: MIT Press.

Squire, L. R., Knowlton, B., & Musen, G. (1993). The structure and organization of memory. *Annual Review of Psychology, 44*, 453–496.

Squire, L. R., Slater, P., & Chace, P. (1975). Retrograde amnesia: temporal gradient in very long term memory following electroconvulsive therapy. *Science, 1987*, 77–79.

Squire, L. R., Slater, P., & Miller, P. (1981). Retrograde amnesia and bilateral electroconvulsive therapy. *Archives of General Psychiatry, 38*, 89–95.

Squire, L. R., & Zola, S. M. (1998). Episodic memory, semantic memory and amnesia. *Hippocampus, 8*, 205–211.

St George-Hyslop, P. (2000). Genetic factors in the genesis of Alzheimer's disease. *Annals of the New York Academy of Sciences, 924*, 1–7.

Staddon, J. (1995). On responsibility and punishment. *Atlantic Monthly, 275*, 88–94.

Steele, K. (2003). Do rats show a Mozart effect? *Music Perception, 21*, 251–265.

Steele, K., Bass, K., & Crook, M. (1999). The mystery of the Mozart effect—Failure to replicate. *Psychological Science, 10*, 366–369.

Stefanacci, L., Buffalo, E., Schmolck, H., & Squire, L. (2000). Profound amnesia after damage to the medial temporal lobe: a neuroanatomical and neuropsychological profile of patient EP. *Journal of Neuroscience, 20*, 7024–7036.

Steinmetz, J. E., Lavond, D. G., & Thompson, R. F. (1989). Classical conditioning in rabbits using pontine nucleus stimulation as a conditioned stimulus and inferior olive stimulation as an unconditioned stimulus. *Synapse, 3*, 225–233.

Stern Y., Albert, S., Tang, M., & Tsai, W. (1999). Rate of memory decline in AD is related to education and occupation: Cognitive reserve? *Neurology, 53*(9), 1942–1947.

Stiles, J. (1998). The effects of early focal brain injury on lateralization of cognitive function. *Current Directions in Psychological Science, 7*, 21–26.

Stiles, J. (2000). Spatial cognitive development following prenatal or perinatal brain injury. In H. Levin & J. Grafman (Eds.), *Cerebral reorganization of function after brain damage* (pp. 207–217). New York: Oxford University Press.

Stoltz, S., & Lott, D. (1964). Establishment in rats of a persistent response producing a net loss of reinforcement. *Journal of Comparative and Physiological Psychology, 57*, 147–149.

Stone, W. L., Ousley, O. Y., & Littleford, C. D. (1997). Motor imitation in young children with autism: what's the object? *Journal of Abnormal Child Psychology, 25*(6), 475–485.

Stowe, L. A., Paans, A. M., Wijers, A. A., & Zwarts, F. (2004). Activations of "motor" and other non-language structures during sentence comprehension. *Brain and Language, 89*(2), 290–299.

Strack, F., Martin, L., & Stepper, S. (1988). Inhibiting and facilitating conditions of the human smile: a nonobtrusive test of the facial feedback hypothesis. *Journal of Personality and Social Psychology, 54*, 768–777.

Strafella, A. P., & Paus, T. (2000). Modulation of cortical excitability during action observation: a transcranial magnetic stimulation study. *Neuroreport, 11*(10), 2289–2292.

Subkov, A. A., & Zilov, G. N. (1937). The role of conditioned reflex adaptation in the origin of the hyperergic reactions. *Bulletin de Biologie et de Médecine Expérimentale, 4*, 294–296.

Sun, R., Slusarz, P., & Terry, C. (2005). The interaction of the explicit and the implicit in skill learning: a dual-process approach. *Psychological Review, 112*, 159–192.

Swan, G., Reed, T., Jack, L., Miller, B., Markee, T., Wolf, P., DeCarli, C., & Carmelli, D. (1999). Differential genetic influence for components of memory in aging adult twins. *Archives of Neurology, 56*, 1127–1132.

Takahashi, N., & Kawamura, M. (2002). Pure topographical disorientation: the anatomical basis of landmark agnosia. *Cortex, 38*, 717–725.

Takahashi, N., Kawamura, M., Hirayama, K., Shiota, J., & Isono, O. (1995). Prosopagnosia: a clinical and anatomical study of four patients. *Cortex, 31*, 317–329.

Talarico, J., & Rubin, D. (2003). Confidence, not consistency, characterizes flashbulb memories. *Psychological Science, 14*, 455–461.

Tallal, P., Miller, S., Bedi, G., Byma, G., Wang, X., Nagarajan, S., Schreiner, C., Jenkins, W., & Merzenich, M. M. (1996). Language comprehension in language-learning impaired children improved with acoustically modified speech. *Science, 271*, 81–84.

Tallal, P., Stark, R., & Mellits, D. (1985). Identification of language-impaired children on the basis of rapid perception and production skills. *Brain and Language, 25*, 314–322.

Tanaka, J., & Taylor, M. (1991). Object categories and expertise: is the basic level in the eye of the beholder? *Cognitive Psychology, 23*, 457–482.

Taub, E., Uswatte, G., & Elbert, T. (2002). New treatments in neurorehabilitation founded on basic research. *Nature Reviews Neuroscience, 3*, 228–236.

Tayler, C. K., & Saayman, G. S. (1973). Imitative behavior by Indian bottlenose dolphins (*Tursiops aduncus*) in captivity. *Behaviour, 44*, 286–298.

Technau, G. (1984). Fiber number in the mushroom bodies of adult *Drosophilia melanogaster* depends on age, sex and experience. *Journal of Neurogenetics, 1*, 13–26.

Temple, E., Deutsch, G. K., Poldrack, R. A., Miller, S. L., Tallal, P., Merzenich, M. M., & Gabrieli, J. D. (2003). Neural deficits in children with dyslexia ameliorated by behavioral remediation: evidence from functional MRI. *Proceedings of the National Academy of Sciences USA* (March 4), *100*(5), 2860–2865.

Terrace, H. S., Petitto, L. A., Sanders, R. J., & Bever, T. G. (1979). Can an ape create a sentence? *Science, 206* (4421), 891–902.

Teter, B., & Finch, C. (2004). Caliban's heritance and the genetics of neuronal aging. *Trends in Neurosciences, 27*, 627–632.

Thomas, R. (2002). *They cleared the lane: the NBA's black pioneers.* Lincoln, NE: University of Nebraska Press.

Thompson, C., & Cowan, T. (1986). Flashbulb memories: a nicer interpretation of a Neisser recollection. *Cognition, 22*, 199–200.

Thompson, D. (1988). Context and false memory. In G. Davies & D. Thompson (Eds.), *Memory in context: context in memory* (pp. 285–304). Chichester, England: Wiley.

Thompson, R. F. (1962). Role of cerebral cortex in stimulus generalization. *Journal of Comparative and Physiological Psychology, 55*, 279–287.

Thompson, R. F. (1965). The neural basis of stimulus generalization. In D. Mostofsky (Ed.), *Stimulus generalization* (pp. 154–178). Stanford, CA: Stanford University Press.

Thompson, R. F. (1972). Sensory preconditioning. In R. Thompson & J. Voss (Eds.), *Topics in learning and performance* (pp. 105–129). New York: Academic Press.

Thompson, R. F. (1986). The neurobiology of learning and memory. *Science, 233*, 941–947.

Thompson, R. F. (2005). In search of memory traces. *Annual Review of Psychology, 56*, 1–23.

Thompson, R. F., & Krupa, D. J. (1994). Organization of memory traces in the mammalian brain. *Annual Review of Neuroscience, 17*, 519–549.

Thompson, R. F., & Spencer, W. A. (1966). Habituation: a model phenomenon for the study of neuronal substrates of behavior. *Psychological Review, 73*, 16–43.

Thompson-Schill, S. L., D'Esposito, M., Aguirre, G. K., & Farah, M. J. (1997). Role of left inferior prefrontal cortex in retrieval of semantic knowledge: a reevaluation. *Proceedings of the National Academy of Sciences USA, 94*, 14792–14797.

Thorndike, E. L. (1898). Animal intelligence: an experimental study of the associative processes in animals. *Psychological Review Monograph 2*(8).

Thorndike, E. L. (1911). *Animal intelligence.* New York: Macmillan.

Thorndike, E. L. (1923). The variability of an individual in repetitions of the same task. *Journal of Experimental Psychology, 6*, 161–167.

Thorndike, E. L. (1927). The law of effect. *American Journal of Psychology, 39*, 212–222.

Thorndike, E. L. (1932). *The fundamentals of learning.* New York: Teachers College, Columbia University.

Thorndike, E. L. (1949). *Selected writings from a connectionist's psychology.* New York: Appleton-Century-Crofts.

Thorndike, E. L., & Woodworth, R. (1901). The influence of improvement in one mental function upon the efficiency of other functions (I). *Psychological Review, 8*, 247–261.

Thorpe, W. H. (1958). The learning of song patterns by birds with especial reference to the song of the chaffinch, *Fringilla coelebs. Ibis, 100*, 535–570.

Thorpe, W. H. (1963). *Learning and instinct in animals.* Cambridge, MA: Harvard University Press.

Tijsseling, A. G., & Gluck, M. A. (2002). A connectionist approach to processing dimensional interaction. *Connection Science, 14*, 1–48.

Timberlake, W. (1980). A molar equilibrium theory of learned performance. In G. Bower (Ed.), *The psychology of learning and motivation* (pp. 1–58). New York: Academic Press.

Timberlake, W. (1983). Rats' responses to a moving object related to food or water: a behavior-systems analysis. *Animal Learning and Behavior, 11*, 309–320.

Timberlake, W. (1984). Behavior regulation and learned performance: some misapprehensions and disagreements. *Journal of the Experimental Analysis of Behavior, 41*, 355–375.

Timberlake, W., & Allison, J. (1974). Response deprivation: an empirical approach to instrumental performance. *Psychological Review, 81*, 146–164.

Tinbergen, N., & Kruyt, W. (1972). On the orientation of the digger wasp *Philanthus triangulum* Fabr. III. Selective learning of landmarks. In N. Tinbergen (Ed.), *The animal in its world*. Cambridge, MA: Harvard University Press. (Original work published 1938)

Tinklepaugh, O. (1928). An experimental study of representative factors in monkeys. *Journal of Comparative Psychology, 8*, 197–236.

Tolman, E. C. (1932). *Purposive behavior in animals and men.* New York: Appleton-Century-Crofts.

Tolman, E. C. (1948). Cognitive maps in rats and men. *Psychological Review, 55*, 189–208.

Tolman, E. C., & Honzik, C. H. (1930). "Insight" in rats. *University of California Publications in Psychology, 4*, 215–232.

Tomasello, M., Davis-Dasilva, M., Carnak, L., & Bard, K. A. (1987). Observational learning of tool-use by young chimpanzees. *Human Evolution, 2*, 175–183.

Toro, J. M., Trobalon, J. B., & Sebastian-Galles, N. (2005). Effects of backward speech and speaker variability in language discrimination by rats. *Journal of Experimental Psychology: Animal Behavior Processes, 31*, 95–100.

Trachtenberg, J., Chen, B., Knott, G., Feng, G., Sanes, J., Welker, E., & Svoboda, K. (2002). Long-term in vivo imaging of experience-dependent synaptic plasticity in adult cortex. *Nature, 420*, 788–794.

Tranel, D., Damasio, A. R., Damasio, H., & Brandt, J. P. (1994). Sensorimotor skill learning in amnesia: additional evidence for the neural basis of nondeclarative memory. *Learning and Memory, 1*, 165–179.

Travers, J., Akey, L., Chen, S., Rosen, S., Paulson, G., & Travers, S. (1993). Taste preferences in Parkinson's disease patients. *Chemical Senses, 18*, 47–55.

Tremblay, K. L., & Kraus, N. (2002). Auditory training induces asymmetrical changes in cortical neural activity. *Journal of Speech Language and Hearing Research, 45*, 564–572.

Trott, C., Fahn, S., Greene, P., Dillon, S., Winfield, H., Winfield, L., Kao, R., Eidelberg, D., Freed, C., Breeze, R., & Stern, Y. (2003). Cognition following bilateral implants of embryonic dopamine neurons in PD: a double blind study. *Neurology, 60*, 1938–1943.

Tryon, R. (1940). Genetic differences in maze learning in rats. *Yearbook of the National Society for the Study of Education, 39*, 111–119.

Tully, T. (1996). Discovery of genes involved with learning and memory: an experimental synthesis of Hirschian and Benzerian perspectives. *Proceedings of the National Academy of Sciences USA, 93*, 13460–13467.

Tulving, E. (1972). Episodic and semantic memory. In E. Tulving & W. Donaldson (Eds.), *Organization of memory* (pp. 381–403). New York: Academic Press.

Tulving, E. (1983). *Elements of episodic memory.* Oxford, England: Clarendon Press.

Tulving, E. (1985). Memory and consciousness. *Canadian Psychology, 26*, 1–12.

Tulving, E. (1989). Remembering and knowing the past. *American Scientist, 77*, 361–367.

Tulving, E. (2002). Episodic memory: from mind to brain. *Annual Review of Psychology, 53*, 1–25.

Tulving, E., & Markowitsch, H. (1998). Episodic and declarative memory: role of the hippocampus. *Hippocampus, 8*, 198–204.

Turner, A. P., & Martinek, T. J. (1999). An investigation into teaching games for understanding: effects on skill, knowledge, and game play. *Research Quarterly of Exercise and Sport, 70*, 286–296.

Turner, D. C., Robbins, T. W., Clark, L., Aron, A. R., Dowson, J., & Sahakian, B. J. (2003). Relative lack of cognitive effects of methylphenidate in elderly male volunteers. *Psychopharmacology (Berlin), 168*, 455–464.

Turner, R. S., Grafton, S. T., Votaw, J. R., Delong, M. R., & Hoffman, J. M. (1998). Motor subcircuits mediating the control of movement velocity: a PET study. *Journal of Neurophysiology, 80*, 2162–2176.

Ullman, M. T. (2004). Contributions of memory circuits to language: the declarative/procedural model. *Cognition, 92*, 231–270.

Ullman, M. T., Corkin, S, Coppola, M., Hickok, G., Growdon, J. H., Koroshetz, W., & Pinker, S. (1997). A neural dissociation within language: evidence that the mental dictionary is part of declarative memory, and that grammatical rules are processed by the procedural system. *Journal of Cognitive Neuroscience, 9*, 89–299.

Vaegan, T. (1979). Critical period for amblyopia in children. *Transactions of the Ophthalmological Societies of the United Kingdom, 99*, 432–439.

Vaiva, G., Ducrocq, F., Jezequel, K., Averland, B., Levestal, P., Brunet, A., & Marmar, C. (2003). Immediate treatment with propranolol decreases posttraumatic stress two months after trauma. *Biological Psychiatry, 54*, 947–949.

Vale-Martinez, A., Baxter, M. G., & Eichenbaum, H. (2002). Selective lesions of basal forebrain cholinergic neurons produce anterograde and retrograde deficits in a social transmission of food preference task in rats. *European Journal of Neuroscience, 16*(6), 983–998.

van Lehn, K. (1996). Cognitive skill acquisition. *Annual Review of Psychology, 47*, 513–539.

van Rossum, J. H. A. (1990). Schmidt's schema theory: the empirical base of the variability of practice hypothesis. *Human Movement Science, 9*, 387–435.

Vargha-Khadem, F., Gadian, D., Watkins, K., Connelly, A., Van Paesschen, W., & Mishkin, M. (1997). Differential effects of early hippocampal pathology on episodic and semantic memory. *Science, 277*, 376–380.

Vicari, S., Bellucci, S., & Carlesimo, G. (2000). Implicit and explicit memory: a functional dissociation in persons with Down syndrome. *Neuropsychologia, 38*, 240–251.

Volkmann, A. (1858). Über den Einfluss der Übung auf das Erkennen räumlicher Distanzen. *Berichte über die Verhandlungen der Sächsischen Gesellschaft der Wissenschaft zu Leipzig, mathmatische und physische Abtheilung, 10*, 38–69.

Voss, V., & Wiley, J. (1995). Acquiring intellectual skills. *Annual Review of Psychology, 46*, 155–181.

Wade, K., Garry, M., Read, J., & Lindsay, S. (2002). A picture is worth a thousand words. *Psychonomic Bulletin and Review, 9*, 597–603.

Wagner, A. D. (2002). Cognitive control and episodic memory. In L. R. Squire & D. L. Schacter (Eds.), *Neuropsychology of memory* (3rd ed., pp. 174–192). New York: Guilford Press.

Wagner, A. D., Desmond, J. E., Glover, G. H., & Gabrieli, J. D. (1998). Prefrontal cortex and recognition memory. Functional-MRI evidence for context-dependent retrieval processes. *Brain, 121*(Pt. 10), 1985–2002.

Wagner, A. D., Koutstaal, W., Maril, A., Schacter, D. L., & Buckner, R. L. (2000). Task-specific repetition priming in left inferior prefrontal cortex. *Cerebral Cortex, 10*, 1176–1184.

Wagner, A. D., Schacter, D., Rotte, M., Koutstaal, W., Maril, A., Dale, A., Rosen, B., & Buckner, R. (1998). Building memories: remembering and forgetting of verbal experiences as a function of brain activity. *Science, 281*, 1188–1191.

Wagner, A. R. (1969). Stimulus validity and stimulus selection in associative learning. In N. J. Mackintosh & W. K. Honig (Eds.), *Fundamental issues in associative learning* (pp. 90–122). Halifax, Nova Scotia, Canada: Dalhousie University Press.

Wagner, A. R. (1981). SOP: a model of automatic memory processing in animal behavior. In N. E. Spear & R. R. Miller (Eds.), *Information processing in animals: memory mechanisms* (pp. 5–47). Hillsdale, NJ: Laurence Erlbaum.

Waiter, G. D., Williams, J. H., Murray, A. D., Gilchrist, A., Perrett, D. I., & Whiten, A. (2004). A voxel-based investigation of brain structure in male adolescents with autistic spectrum disorder. *Neuroimage, 22*(2), 619–625.

Waldstein, R. S. (1990). Effects of postlingual deafness on speech production: implications for the role of auditory feedback. *Journal of the Acoustical Society of America, 88*(5), 2099–2114.

Waldvogel, S. (1982). The frequency and affective character of childhood memories. In U. Neisser (Ed.), *Memory observed: remembering in natural contexts* (pp. 77–91). San Francisco: Freeman. (Excerpts reprinted from *Psychological Monographs, 62* [291], 1948)

Walker, M. P., Brakefield, T., Hobson, J. A., & Stickgold, R. (2003). Dissociable stages of human memory consolidation and reconsolidation. *Nature, 425*, 616–620.

Walker, M. P., Brakefield, T., Morgan, A., Hobson, J. A., & Stickgold, R. (2002). Practice with sleep makes perfect: sleep-dependent motor skill learning. *Neuron, 35*, 205–211.

Walker, M. P., Brakefield, T., Seidman, J., Morgan, A., Hobson, J. A., & Stickgold, R. (2003). Sleep and the time course of motor skill learning. *Learning and Memory, 10*, 275–284.

Walls, R., Zane, T., & Ellis, T. (1981). Forward and backward chaining, and whole task methods: training assembly tasks in vocational rehabilitation. *Behavior Modification, 5*, 61–74.

Wang, Y., Sereno, J. A., Jongman, A., & Hirsch, J. (2003). fMRI evidence for cortical modification during learning of Mandarin lexical tone. *Journal of Cognitive Neuroscience, 15*(7), 1019–1027.

Warrington, E., & Shallice, T. (1984). Category specific semantic impairments. *Brain, 107*, 829–854.

Waterhouse, L., Fein, D., & Modahl, C. (1996). Neurofunctional mechanisms in autism. *Psychological Review, 103*, 457–489.

Watson, J. B. (1907). Kinaesthetic and organic sensations: their role in the reactions of the white rat to the maze. *Psychological Review, 4*, 211–212.

Watson, J. B. (1913). Psychology as the behaviorist sees it. *Psychological Review, 23*, 158–177.

Watson, J. B. (1922). What cigarettes are you smoking and why? *The J. Walter Thompson News Bulletin, 88*, 1–7.

Watson, J. B. (1924). *Behaviorism.* New York: W. W. Norton.

Watson, J. B., & Rayner, R. (2000). Conditioned emotional reactions. *American Psychologist, 55*, 313–317. (Reprinted from *Journal of Experimental Psychology, 3*, 1–14, 1920)

Wearing, D. (2005). *Forever today: a memoir of love and amnesia.* London: Doubleday UK.

Weber, B., & Depew, D. (Eds.). (2003). *Evolution and learning: the Baldwin effect reconsidered.* Cambridge, MA: MIT Press.

Weeks, D. L., & Kordus, R. N. (1998). Relative frequency of knowledge of performance and motor skill learning. *Research Quarterly for Exercise and Sports, 69*, 224–230.

Weigle, T., & Bauer, P. (2000). Deaf and hearing adults' recollections of childhood and beyond. *Memory, 8*, 293–310.

Weinberger, D. R., Berman, K. F., & Zec, R. F. (1986). *Archives of General Psychiatry, 43*, 114–125.

Weinberger, N. M. (1993). Learning-induced changes of auditory receptive fields. *Current Opinion in Neurobiology, 3,* 570–577.

Weinberger, N. M. (1997). Learning-induced receptive field plasticity in the primary auditory cortex. *Seminars in Neuroscience, 9,* 59–67.

Weinberger, N. M. (2003). The nucleus basalis and memory codes: auditory cortical plasticity and the induction of specific, associative behavioral memory. *Neurobiology of Learning and Memory, 80(3),* 268–284.

Weinberger, N. M. (2004). Specific long-term memory traces in primary auditory cortex. *Nature Reviews Neuroscience, 5(4),* 279–290.

Werker, J. F., & Tees, R. C. (1984). Cross-language speech perception: evidence for perceptual reorganization during the 1st year of life. *Infant Behavior and Development, 7,* 49–63.

Werker, J. F., & Tees, R. C. (1999). Influences on infant speech processing: toward a New Synthesis. *Annual Review of Psychology, 50,* 509–535

Wernicke, C. (1874). *Der aphasiche symptomenkomplex* (Trans. G Eggert). The Hague, The Netherlands: Mouton.

West, M. (1993). Regionally specific loss of neurons in the aging human hippocampus. *Neurobiology of Aging, 14,* 287–293.

Whitehead, A., Perdomo, C., Pratt, R. D., Birks, J., Wilcock, G. K., & Evans, J. G. (2004). Donepezil for the symptomatic treatment of patients with mild to moderate Alzheimer's disease: a meta-analysis of individual patient data from randomised controlled trials. *International Journal of Geriatric Psychiatry, 19,* 624–633.

Whiten, A., & Boesch, C. (2001). The cultures of chimpanzees. *Scientific American, 284(1),* 60–67.

Whiten, A., & Brown, J. (1999). Imitation and the reading of other minds: perspectives from the study of autism, normal children and non-human primates. In S. Braten (Ed.), *Intersubjective communication and emotion in early ontogeny* (pp. 260–280). Cambridge, England: Cambridge University Press.

Whiten, A., Custance, D. M., Gomez, J. C., Teixidor, P., & Bard, K. A. (1996). Imitative learning of artificial fruit processing in children (*Homo sapiens*) and chimpanzees (*Pan troglodytes*). *Journal of Comparative Psychology, 110(1),* 3–14.

Whiten, A., Goodall, J., McGrew, W. C., Nishida, T., Reynolds, V., Sugiyama, Y., Tutin, C. E., Wrangham, R. W., & Boesch, C. (1999). Cultures in chimpanzees. *Nature, 399,* 682–685.

Whiten, A., Horner, V., Litchfield, C. A., & Marshall-Pescini, S. (2004). How do apes ape? *Learning and Behavior, 32(1),* 36–52.

Wichmann, T. (1998). A neuropsychological theory of motor skill learning. *Psychological Review, 105,* 558–584.

Wickelgren, W. (1966). Phonemic similarity and interference in short-term memory for single letters. *Journal of Experimental Psychology, 71,* 396–404.

Wightman, D., & Sistrunk, F. (1987). Part-task training strategies in simulated carrier landing final-approach training. *Human Factors, 29,* 245–254.

Wilbrecht, L., & Nottebohm, F. (2003). Vocal learning in birds and humans. *Mental Retardation and Developmental Disabilities Research Reviews, 9(3),* 135–148.

Williams, A. M., Davids, K., Burwitz, L., & Williams, J. (1992). Perception and action in sport. *Journal of Human Movement Studies, 22,* 147–204.

Williams, J. H., Whiten, A., & Singh, T. (2004). A systematic review of action imitation in autistic spectrum disorder. *Journal of Autism and Developmental Disorders, 34(3),* 285–299.

Williams, J. H., Whiten, A., Suddendorf, T., & Perrett, D. I. (2001). Imitation, mirror neurons and autism. *Neuroscience and Biobehavioral Review, 25,* 287–295.

Williams, L., Phillips, M., Brammer, M., Skerrett, D., Lagopoulos, J., Rennie, C., Bahramali, H., Olivieri, G., David, A., Peduto, A., & Gordon, E. (2001). Arousal dissociates amygdala and hippocampal fear responses: evidence from simultaneous fMRI and skin conductance recording. *NeuroImage, 14,* 1070–1079.

Willingham, D. B. (1999). Implicit motor sequence learning is not purely perceptual. *Memory and Cognition, 27,* 561–572.

Willingham, D. B., & Koroshetz, W. J. (1993). Evidence for dissociable motor skills in Huntington's disease patients. *Psychobiology, 21,* 173–182.

Wilson, B., & Wearing D. (1995). Prisoner of consciousness: a state of just awakening following herpes simplex encephalitis. In R. Campbell & M. Conway (Eds.), *Broken memories: case studies in memory impairments* (pp. 14–30). Cambridge, MA: Blackwell.

Wilson, F. A., Scalaidhe, S. P., & Goldman-Rakic, P. S. (1993). Dissociation of object and spatial processing domains in primate prefrontal cortex. *Science, 260,* 1955–1958.

Wilson, M., & McNaughton, B. L. (1994). Reactivation of hippocampal ensemble memories during sleep. *Science, 265,* 676–679.

Wilson, R., & Bennett, D. (2003). Cognitive activity and the risk of Alzheimer's disease. *Current Directions in Psychological Science, 12,* 87–91.

Wilson, T., & Brown, T. (1997). Reexamination of the effect of Mozart's music on spatial-task performance. *Journal of Psychology, 131,* 365–370.

Winek, C. L., Wahaba, W. W., & Rozin, L. (1999). Heroin fatality due to penile injection. *American Journal of Forensic Medicine and Pathology, 20,* 90–92.

Wingfield, A. (1993). Sentence processing. In J. Gleason & N. Ratner (Eds.), *Psycholinguistics* (pp. 199–235). Fort Worth, TX: Harcourt Brace.

Winocur, G. (1990). Anterograde and retrograde amnesia in rats with dorsal hippocampal or dorsomedial thalamic lesions. *Behavioural Brain Research, 38*(2), 145–154.

Wise, R. (1982). Neuroleptics and operant behavior: the anhedonia hypothesis. *Behavioural Brain Science, 5*, 39–87.

Wise, R. (2002). Brain reward circuitry: insights from unsensed incentives. *Neuron, 36*, 229–240.

Wise, R., Spindler, J., de Wit, H., & Gerberg, G. (1978). Neuroleptic-induced "anhedonia" in rats: pimozide blocks reward quality of food. *Science, 201*, 262–264.

Wixted, J. (2004). The psychology and neuroscience of forgetting. *Annual Review of Psychology, 55*, 235–269.

Wollmer, M., Streffer, J., Lutjohann, D., Tsolaki, M., Iakovidou, V., Hegi, T., Pasch, T., Jung, H., Bergmann, K., Nitsch, R., Hock, C., & Papassotiropoulos, A. (2003). ABCA1 modulates CSF cholesterol levels and influences the age at onset of Alzheimer's disease. *Neurobiology of Aging, 24*, 421–426.

Wood, D. (1989). Social interaction as tutoring. In M. H. Bornstein & J. S. Bruner (Eds.), *Interaction in human development*. Cambridge, MA: Harvard University Press.

Woodruff-Pak, D. S., & Lemieux, S. K. (2001). The cerebellum and associative learning: parallels and contrasts in rabbits and humans. In J. E. Steinmetz, M. A. Gluck, & P. F. Solomon (Eds.), *Model systems of associative learning: a festschrift for Richard F. Thompson* (pp. 271–294). Mahwah, NJ: Lawrence Erlbaum.

Woodruff-Pak, D. S., Logan, C., & Thompson, R. F. (1990). Neurobiological substrates of classical conditioning across the life span. *Annals of the New York Academy of Sciences, 608*, 150–173.

Woodruff-Pak, D. S., & Sheffield, J. (1987). Age differences in Purkinje cells and rate of classical conditioning in young and older rabbits. *Society for Neuroscience Abstracts, 13*, 41.

Woodruff-Pak, D. S., & Thompson, R. F. (1988). Classical conditioning of the eyeblink response in the delay paradigm in adults aged 18–83 years. *Psychology and Aging, 3*, 219–229.

Woolley, C., Weiland, N., McEwen, B., & Schwartzkroin, P. (1997). Estradiol increases the sensitivity of hippocampal CA1 pyramidal cells to NMDA receptor-mediated synaptic input: correlation with spine density. *Journal of Neuroscience, 17*, 1848–1859.

Wulf, G., & Schmidt, R. A. (1997). Variability of practice and implicit motor learning. *Journal of Experimental Psychology: Learning, Memory and Cognition, 23*, 987–1006.

Xiong, J., Rao, S., Gao, J. H., Woldorff, M., & Fox, P. T. (1998). Evaluation of hemispheric dominance for language using functional MRI: a comparison with positron emission tomography. *Human Brain Mapping, 6*, 42–58.

Yerkes, R., & Dodson, J. (1908). The relation of strength of stimulus to rapidity of habit formation. *Journal of Comparative Neurology and Psychology, 18*, 459–482.

Yin, J. C. P., Wallach, J. S., Del Vecchio, M., Wilder, E. L., Zhuo, H., Quinn, W. G., & Tully, T. (1994). Induction of dominant negative CREB transgene specifically blocks long-term memory in *Drosophila*. *Cell, 79*, 49–58.

Youn, G. (2006). Subjective sexual arousal in response to erotica: effects of gender, guided fantasy, erotic stimulus, and duration of exposure. *Archives of Sexual Behavior, 35*, 87–97.

Zadikoff, C., & Lang, A. E. (2005). Apraxia in movement disorders. *Brain, 128*(Pt. 7), 1480–1497.

Zajonc, R. (1980). Feeling and thinking: preferences need no inferences. *American Psychologist, 35*, 151–175.

Zajonc, R. (1984). On the primacy of affect. *American Psychologist, 39*, 117–123.

Zeki, S. (1993). *A vision of the brain*. Oxford, England: Blackwell Scientific Publishing.

Zupanc, G. (2001). A comparative approach towards the understanding of adult neurogenesis. *Brain, Behavior and Evolution, 58*, 246–249.

Wiskott, L., 490
Wittlinger, R., 94
Wixted, J., 116
Woldorff, M., 62
Wolfe, J., 161
Wollmer, M., 496
Wolz, J. P., 431, 512
Wood, D., 428
Woodruff-Pak, D. S., 276, 472, 487
Woodworth, R., 141
Woolley, C., 485
Wrisberg, C. A., 133
Wulf, G., 135, 136

Xiong, J., 62

Yerkes, R., 408
Yin, J. C. P., 283
Youn, G., 209
Young, D. E., 135
Yu, K., 87

Zadikoff, C., 160
Zajonc, R., 385
Zamenhof, L., 512

Zane, T., 300
Zbrozyna, A., 411
Zec, R. F., 197
Zeki, S., 103
Zentall, T. R., 426
Zhao, Z., 107, 404
Zilov, G. N., 252
Zimmer, J., 487
Zola, S. M., 111, 451
Zouzounis, J., 115
Zupanc, G., 489
Zwarts, F., 524
Zwitserlood, P., 521